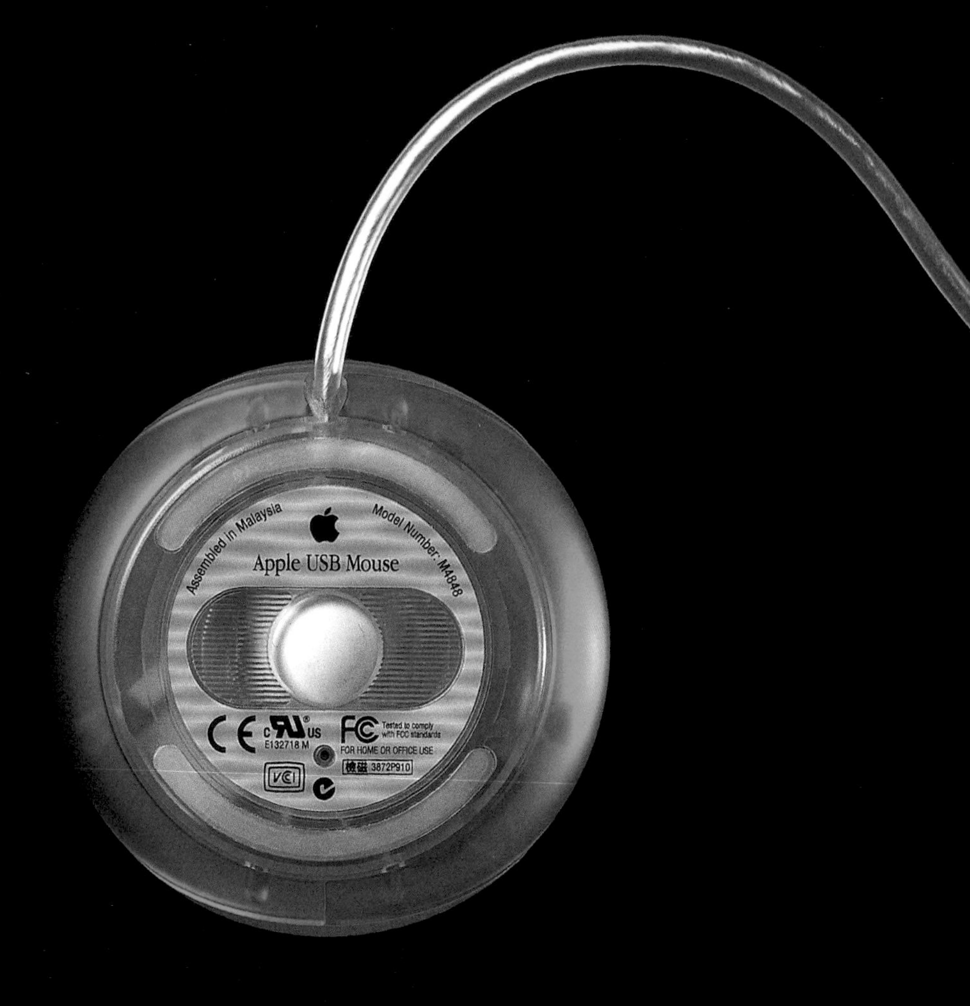
Assembled in Malaysia
Apple USB Mouse
Model Number: M4848
E132718 M
Tested to comply
with FCC standards
FOR HOME OR OFFICE USE
3872P910
VCI

DesignAgencies.Com

*Profiles and portfolios of
twelve innovative and successful
interactive design firms*

Publisher and Creative Director: B. Martin Pedersen

Art Director: Massimo Acanfora
Editor: Chelsey Johnson Associate Editor: Nicole Ray
Production: Dana Shimizu

Published by Graphis Inc.

(opposite) Photograph by Alfredo Parraga

Contents

ISBN: 1-888001-83-6 Printed in Korea by Doosan Dong-A Co., Ltd.

(opposite) Photograph courtesy of Apple Computers, Inc. *(next page)* Detail from Website by Virtual Identity for Algroup; see page 197

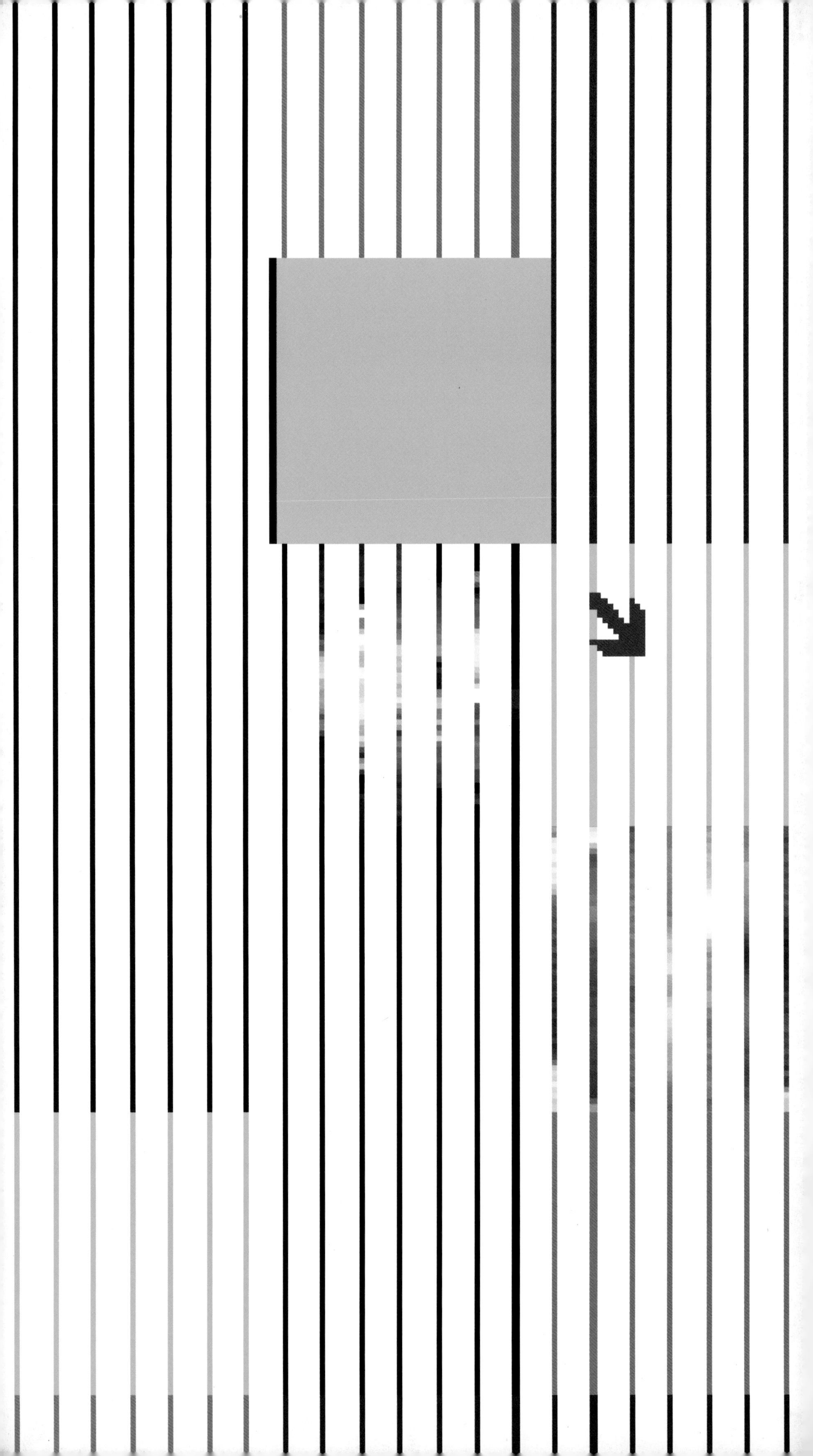

Commentary

Dispatches from the Eyeball Wars

The book you hold in your hands is unusual for Graphis, if for no other reason than that the work on display was submitted at the publisher's request and not, as is usually the case, as a call for entries. DESIGNAGENCIES.COM represents the fourth in a series of books on digital design from Graphis. The first, GRAPHIS NEW MEDIA 1, surveyed a broad range of digital communications; the second, GRAPHIS WEB DESIGN NOW, also by personal invitation, focussed exclusively on the Internet. The third and most recent, GRAPHIS INTERACTIVE DESIGN 1, sampled from the work of a wider array of designers who responded to a public call. Can you detect a pattern here? Yes, it's that numeral 1, which in publishing language implies, of course, there will be a sequel, a number 2. So why then, instead of sequels, has Graphis presented a suite of related books?

The answer is that publishers, like the rest of the human race, aren't necessarily clairvoyant. Way back in 1996, when the first Graphis survey was published, the World Wide Web as we know it had only just begun to come into its own. By the time the second volume was underway, the Internet—surprising even the keenest observers—had materialized as an all-encompassing model for new media. For its third survey, Graphis decided to group new media and Web design together under the rubric of "interactivity." It did so because interactivity appeared to provide an overarching metaphor for what these disparate forms of communication have in common. But more surprises were in store.

What no one seems to have predicted—just as no one seems to have anticipated the Internet's rise to the hegemony it enjoys today—is that what we call interactivity has turned out to be something very problematic indeed. Now that the Internet has been transformed—via its "graphical component" the Web—into a medium of mass communication, cherished concepts of what interactivity means can seem almost quaint. The idea that an audience would passively "interact" with information stored CD-ROM-style by pointing and clicking has given way to the dawning realization that interactivity is, after all, a dynamic. And that's not necessarily the good news.

The Web is a porous medium that demands a new relationship between publisher and audience, in a way that the traditional media of print and broadcasting never have. On one side of the Web are the so-called "content providers"—from corporations to enthusiastic amateurs—and on the other, an intermittently captive but rebellious mass audience that is interested in sex, sports, stocks, and the news and weather, in roughly that order. The same audience that couldn't be less interested in issues of aesthetics or less curious about significant content. An audience to whom a long and leisurely download is only acceptable, it seems, if the payoff is an X-rated photo. An audience which, by its sheer numbers, has the ability—when a celebrity scandal is breaking and millions log on for the latest juicy revelations – to bring the system crashing to its knees.

It's hard to blame designers for throwing up their hands when faced with the Web's newfangled brand of give-and-take. Already frustrated by a medium that is hamstrung with a hopelessly inadequate standardized programming language—the lowly HTML—and hobbled by legacy-style browsers, bottom-line expectations, vaporous profits and truly Darwinian economics, they can be excused for preferring to abandon the Web to programmers and marketers.

As the Web splinters into disproportionate demographics based on highly differentiated audiences, the larger audience is vast and homogenized and, superficially at least, unresponsive, distracted by irrelevant data filtered and diluted from Web content by the dubious information portals offered by popular services. Yet many designers are learning to view these challenges as an opportunity. The smaller, more exclusive audience, relatively tiny in numbers, functions in the design climate of a technically-savvy subculture equipped with powerful machines, high-speed connections and the latest information technology.

But while the Internet evolves into a mass medium whose audience is made up of a few technologically superior haves and many technologically inferior have-nots, the same network is developing with blinding speed into a meeting-ground for trade and commerce—a virtual marketplace. Web customers, meanwhile, have evolved overnight into an increas-

Ken Coupland writes about art, architecture, photography, and interior and graphic design, with a focus on the digital revolution, for an international roster of publications. A contributing editor to GRAPHIS magazine and Graphis Books, he writes as well for EYE, HOW, and WIRED. He has also written and designed several Web-based works of fiction. He wrote and edited GRAPHIS WEB DESIGN NOW 1, and has curated several exhibitions devoted to digital art and design.

(Previous spread)
Detail from website by Virtual Identity for Furnish.net (see page 198)

(Opposite)
Detail from website by BBK Studio for Herman Miller (see page 70)

ingly fickle and demanding audience which, accustomed as it is to the convenience of 800 numbers, credit cards and ATMs, is impatient to purchase, quick to complain and easily turned off. It's a knife that cuts both ways: websites can entice visitors to make purchases and surrender valuable demographic information, but the visitors themselves are the ultimate arbiters of the interaction, ready to desert at a keystroke to another location in cyberspace and firmly in command. Take for example, software that enables viewers to block time-consuming graphics downloads and even—much to the horror of those anticipating vast advertising revenues from the medium—allows them to wipe clean the commercial messages that clutter so much virtual real estate. Imagine tearing all the ads out of a magazine before you read it and you can see that, in the so-called "war for eyeballs," comforting pieties of old-media-style marketing and promotion are crumbling before the ruthless number-crunching of hits and instant feedback that the Internet makes possible. How well a design delivers a commercial message is now easy to calculate and in the process, many of the traditional models of advertising and promotion have been found wanting.

Asked which new models might arise, prognosticators of the Web can sound alarmingly vague. For instance, take interface design, a category which gets paid a good deal of lip service but which still lacks a vocabulary with which to express it. As David Karam of San Francisco-based Post Tool Design notes, to date "... there has been no exploration of interface design to speak of, and by the time people really start to figure it out, the discipline will be a totally different profession."

Confronted by audiences with short attention spans and an alarming freedom of choice, resourceful Web entrepreneurs have responded by resorting to ingenious, even devious countermeasures—witness the piquantly named "circle jerks" that corral visitors to X-rated sites into an endless loop they can only escape by quitting the Web altogether—in an escalating contest of wills.

For more respectable denizens of the Web, the medium's unruly character has shattered some soothing illusions. Corporate websites, in their early iterations as electronic brochures, presented a warm and welcoming facade to the world. Today, however, companies that once established an Internet presence to hold the world comfortably at arm's length are calling on designers to create websites that function as virtual business machines, processing orders and requests, tabulating visitor's identities, preferences and desires, and helping build loyal communities—all within existing technological constraints. As Jeff Zwerner, creative director of Factor Design's San Francisco office, observes, "These database-driven sites are finally turning the Web into a useful tool, as opposed to the 'time sink' of interesting-looking but static content it once was."

As a result, the clientele for website services are becoming increasingly involved with the content and design of their public presence—and demanding results. As if the desktop revolution wasn't wrenching enough, almost overnight the business of graphic design has expanded to include a small battalion of online agencies and support services who operate independently of the graphic design profession—not to mention a vast army made up of online self-publishers. Interface designers, in turn, find themselves less involved with aesthetics and more involved with logistics. Some have become providers of proprietary software, "intelligent engines" that prolong the active life of the product by empowering clients and users to customize and adapt the framework the studios create. As Gong Szeto, creative director of New York City-based io/360 says, "The process begins to resemble software design more than editorial design."

David Peters, an information designer at MetaDesign SF, doesn't think that's necessarily a bad thing. "Designers have been trained to see themselves as form-givers," Peters says, "when in fact design is closer to the diagnostic process we associate with professions like physicians.

"The realistic appraisal of design has evolved from being a profession to the realization that design is a discipline that all professions practice," Peters adds. Does that mean that designers have to become more like engineers, along with all the other things they're supposed to know and do? "It's not so important that designers are multidisciplinary," Peters concludes, "as that the environment we're in is interdisciplinary."

The work that has been selected for inclusion in *DesignAgencies.com* represents the best of this emerging breed. Graphis also asked the featured form-givers to describe themselves, to give you their ideas on designing for the online medium, and to relate that to the thinking behind the interactive products they've de-signed for the Web. To introduce the subject, the people at Factor Design have kindly volunteered a step-by-step elucidation of Web development which addresses the process in practical terms. What follows is some of the most visually compelling work for the Web from design studios worldwide. What follows *that*—in terms of a sequel to this book or some entirely different model—is best left to your crystal ball.

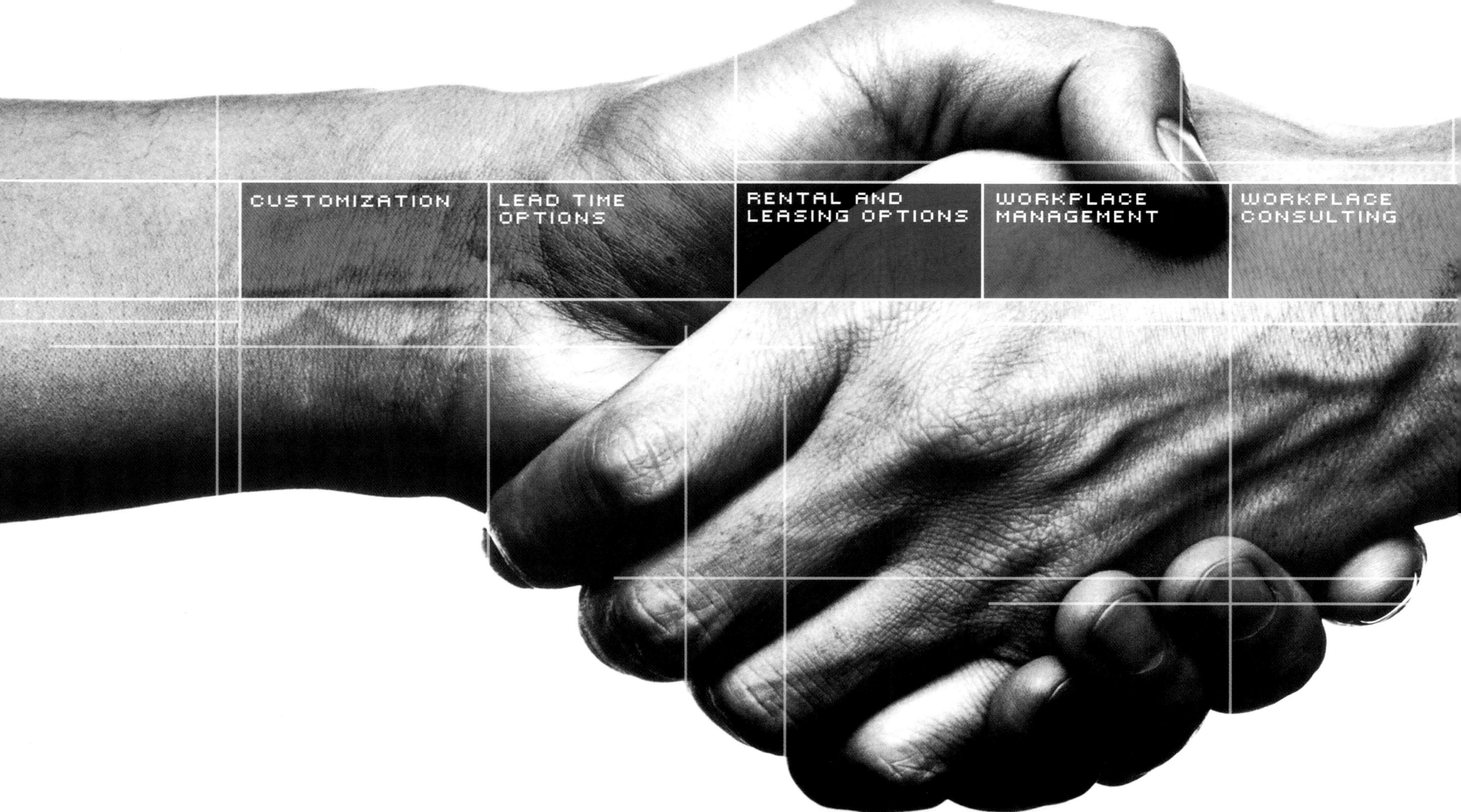
CUSTOMIZATION
LEAD TIME OPTIONS
RENTAL AND LEASING OPTIONS
WORKPLACE MANAGEMENT
WORKPLACE CONSULTING

CONTACT US

NEWS

PROCESS

CORPORATE IDENTITY

PACKAGING

NEW MEDIA

INTRODUCTION

PROJECTS

CASE STUDY

PORTFOLIO

CLIENTS

COLLATERAL

AWARDS

LINKS

TYPEFACES

Factor Design: Our Web Development Process

It should come as no surprise that Web development is a tricky business. The Internet is evolving so rapidly that it's impossible to predict what it holds in store. Small wonder, then, that when new clients approach us to design and produce a website, more often than not they don't have a clear understanding of the scope and scale of what they are asking for. Sometimes you can solicit a bit more information from them—for instance, whether they want to have e-commerce capabilities or a registration process to capture user data and the like—but nine times out of ten the assignment is ... clear blue sky. Yet the same clients will already have fixed a date when they want the site to launch. And, you can be sure, they will want to know how much their website will cost.

Because the clients who approach us need a dollar amount to get approval so we can begin working, once we determine we want to do the project, we begin by outlining how the entire development process will be structured, and the phases within which the work will be completed. At this stage many of those areas can only be outlined. Maybe a timeline can be given, and the deliverables can be defined, but beyond that we cannot commit to a price for those phases of work without first producing a comprehensive site map. The ability to develop this estimate is based on Factor's past experience working on sites of varying complexity and within the aggressive timelines that always accompany work for the Web.

A big part of our job, therefore, involves helping to educate clients in the proper processes and procedures we must follow in order to develop successful websites. The effectiveness and ultimate success of the site hinges on our ability to work very closely with our clients. The process is not for the faint of heart and often requires very difficult and costly decisions to be made at every step to complete our goals.

Thus it is imperative to get our partners on the team to realize how valuable the initial planning and strategy stages are for them and for us. To bring clients around to the concept of having defined roles and responsibilities for the project, detailed schedules and review cycles, Factor has developed a very rigorous and linear process that we follow on every Web-based project we undertake.

Typically at Factor, we begin a Web project by asking for as much specific information about the proposed project as the client can provide. An initial meeting is held to meet the team members and discuss the scope of the site and allow us to hear the specifics of the project firsthand. Sometimes those seemingly unimportant details are essential for the team to begin to understand the site's purpose and on that basis to make recommendations. Depending on what we have found out about the objectives of the client, we can begin to paint a mental picture as well as a written proposal that describes the level of complexity the entire project will sustain.

Factor also pays close attention to the scheduling of the project, listening to clients to understand how far along the path they might already be in terms of developing specific content for the site. All of these details are critical to being able to draft a comprehensive proposal that outlines the phases of the work, a schedule for the work to be completed within, deliverables for each phase, and all estimated fees. Given that this is the first proposal outlining the development process and costs of the site, it is imperative that the Factor team is realistic in establishing ground rules for the project development.

Phase 01: The initial proposal

Based on our past experience, the Factor team is now able to specify all the parameters of the project as outlined in an initial proposal. The individual phases of work and the process need to be defined, and we need to develop a realistic schedule for completing the work, define roles for the team members, and determine estimates for our fees. An element of risk is involved in that—except for an outline for developing detailed user specifications, content assessment, information architecture, site map design and initial design explorations, the remainder of the proposal is written based on educated assumptions. Until the final site map has been developed and approved, Factor has no way of accurately determining a fixed estimate for the production and programming phases of the project. Because of this, it is clearly stated in the proposal that the latter phases mentioned are subject to change, pending completion of the approved site map. At that time, we will produce a second proposal that gives detailed fees for the conclusion of the project phases, specifically production, programming and testing.

Generally, clients understand the financial realities of this process, and if further clarification is necessary we can easily walk them through a case study of past projects, explaining the processes in more detail, or agree to proceed on a time-and-materials basis. Then we obtain approval of the initial proposal.

Phase 02: Developing a user specification

Our first task is understanding the parameters that define the environment we will be designing.

Factor begins the process by having clients complete a brief survey that defines the typical users of the site. We ask questions such as, "What is the primary objective of the site? What platform will the majority of users view the site on? With which browser will they view the site? What is the speed of their Internet connection? What size monitor does the average user own? Do you want users to be able to print the complete Web page?" The answers to these questions allow Factor to gauge several important parameters. First, we develop a consensus with the client as to who their target audience is; second, we determine the technology profile of our baseline user; third, we ascertain the general knowledge base the clients have about their audience, and also the type of medium they will be using to reach them.

Equipped with this information, we target certain strategic areas that need more development and take some additional time to clarify usability issues with the client. Keeping the team focused on the objectives of the site and the messages we want to communicate, and developing the appropriate technology to capture, process, and distribute the information necessary, is something that is constantly reviewed and discussed at every stage. Managing these expectations are critical to the process. It is too often that towards the end of a development project that someone on the team will go home and call up the site under development using AOL and a slow modem connection and begin to panic. We quickly reorient them to the planned objectives and remind them of the approved user specification that profiled our target audience. Corporate professionals using the site primarily at their place of business using Internet Explorer 4.0 on a PC at T-1 connection speeds.

Phase 03: Content assessment

In order to thoroughly understand the communication objectives of the site, the entire team must first engage in some top-level brainstorming. We must define our target demographic and understand what will attract visitors to the website. We have found that initiating the discussion in this way instantly ignites the process and allows us to judge the clarity of the client's strategy. "Do they have a firm understanding of their audience?" is constantly in our thoughts. Often the answer is no. We must then spring into action to facilitate a productive dialog that we will use to categorize the concepts and messages we will need to develop and utilize to communicate our strategy. Once the ideas have been bantered back and forth, with the more successful and innovative solutions rising to the surface, we then begin to assess what action needs to be taken to turn these ideas into tangible text and imagery.

"Where will the content come from?" is the next question. We make a laundry list of tasks, identify team members, line up the appropriate copy writers, and establish a schedule for developing the kernels of content that allow us to develop an information architecture in tandem with the information itself. The key here lies in scheduling the content to be completed after the information architecture has been developed and the design established.

Phase 04: Concept development

Now that raw data and relevant messages are part of our common knowledge, it is time to begin turning them into a coherent and structured concept. We have already acquired new team members for this phase, based on the kind of information that needs to be presented and the audience we expect to reach. The copywriter can now collaborate with us and develop the pesonality and voice the site deserves.

At Factor, we feel you cannot underestimate the importance of the written word where the Web is concerned. Partly this is a practical consideration; given the bandwidth constraints placed upon current mainstream solutions, text is the quickest and cheapest method of developing an effective link with our audience. To that end, we always try to develop a very strong and clear verbal identity in the writing for the site. In reality however, clients usually have difficulty justifying the expenditure of time and money necessary to bring a top-notch writer on board. But if the writing is done well we can keep graphics to a minimum and still maintain a strong overall identity that supports a coherent message.

Phase 05: Information architecture and site map

One advantage of carefully planning how a user will interact with a website is that we are able to strategically structure and place information to maximize its effectiveness. The Factor team begins be developing a rough laundry-list for each page, identifying it by name and content type. Once all of the pages have been itemized, based on the information obtained from the previous two phases of discussions and brainstorming, we are able to develop a matrix of different information types. Using the concepts we have developed in an earlier phase and knowing the information our users will be seeking most frequently, we begin to sort the information in ways that are natural and intuitive. We attempt to minimize the number of different categories, since these individual groupings will ultimately form our navigation. As we remind our clients of the advantages of maintaining a focused vision and voice, it is equally important to maintain a focused and uniform method of navigation.

If the website has too many sections to navigate, users might lose confidence in their intuition about what information is contained within each section. Of course, if the website has too few sections, pertinent information may be placed in too distant a location to be useful. If it takes too many clicks of the mouse to get where they are going, we may frustrate or even lose potential customers or contacts. The key is to create a site in this abstract and paper-based format that is "flat" enough so users can access all of the information with as few clicks of the mouse as possible, while segmenting the content in such a way that users are not overwhelmed with information.

By designing and testing the architecture in paper-based form, Factor is able to effectively determine its extensibility and clarity. At this stage we often pull people into the project who have not been involved in its development and ask them, "If you are on this page, what information would you want access to now?" If we cannot get them to that information within two, or at the most three, mouse-clicks, we need to rethink the navigation and content flow.

Phase 06: Developing the navigation scenario

By rapidly prototyping we can redesign and re-test features relatively quickly and with limited expense. If we had inititated design and programming before this phase was completed, we would have wasted time and exhausted the budget with little to show for it. Most clients can readily grasp the cost efficiencies of such a tactic, but other distinctions may not be as clear. For example, clients often get distracted attempting to visualize how the website will look, rather than focusing on what it will say and how it will function. By establishing expectations up front and clearly describing our working process we can address these issues and, if necessary, remind the clients of the reasons why we are approaching development in this manner.

Once the overall page structure and information flow has been defined, Factor then begins to work collaboratively with the writer to determine how the story will be told. We begin at the homepage, detailing the kinds of information that will be found on that specific page. We then slowly and deliberately work our way through subsequent pages, filling them in with an outline that the writer will expand upon later. The result is a comprehensive overview of the entire site that accurately represents its scale in terms of pages, provides details of the content on every page, diagrams paths of navigation, and most important, provides everyone with a common point of reference to begin delegating development tasks.

Phase 07: Approval of information architecture and navigation

The client then gives written authorization of this new map, reviewing all aspects of content, navigation and architecture required to complete the next phase.

Phase 08: Draft and delivery of the final proposal to the client

At this point in the process we revisit the proposal we delivered to the client in Phase 01. Because we have spent the last few weeks working closely with the client team and have now formulated and received approval of a comprehensive site map, we can use this solid data and page total to generate an accurate proposal of fees and schedules to complete the remainder of the project.

Phase 09: Begin interface and information design

Without proper involvement in the previous phases of work necessary to generate a comprehensive site map and navigation schematic, it is virtually impossible to begin to design how the site will look and function. Without knowing whether we will have, say, six or sixteen navigable content regions available to users at all times, we can waste a lot of time and money. The simple fact is that without knowing what the navigation scheme will be, we are unable to develop a successful design solution to support and clarify its functionality. It is also better to compartmentalize the process in this way so the client can stay focused. If the design phase begins too soon, the client is often unable to concentrate on more important and difficult issues—their strategy and voice.

Factor's usual approach to the design phase is to select and develop four or five unique screens for the site, to explore concepts and design solutions. These screens follow a vertical path through the site, from the home page to the lowest level of information as detailed on the site map. The purpose of this is to design and test how consistent and intuitive the navigation and design will be as the user passes through the levels of information on the site. In much the same way we would approach a printed book or brochure, we always attempt to make it obvious to users that they are moving down through the content. We are trying to establish visual benchmarks our users can call upon to orient themselves within the information of the site. One way to accomplish this is through the use of different-sized elements, so that as they move further down into the content there are fewer graphics, the branding of the site is reduced in scale, and the content becomes more rigid and informational.

Different solutions are then presented to the client. Discussions on typography, color, use of screen real estate, the voice in which we are speaking and overall personality are then discussed. After the presentation a course of action is planned and agreed upon and another phase begins.

Phase 10: Refinement of the final design

Based on decisions made in the first presentation the Factor team continues to evolve, and explore how to strengthen, our overall design solutions. Usually a few rounds of refinement and informal presentations occur, with the client and all team members participating in a discussion of the rationale behind any small tweaks in design and structure. The process allows everyone to put in their two cents and hear the reasons why we chose to pursue or avoid certain recommendations.

Phase 11: Approval of the final design

With the completion of this phase, the result is a

more refined and deliberate solution for which everyone on the team can feel responsibility. The fact that each team member feels a sense of ownership and pride in the final solution means that the design will be better appreciated and allowed to properly evolve, rather than compromised, as it begins to grow.

Once the finishing touches are placed on actual design elements and navigation treatments, the project shifts into higher gear. Until now the programming team have been busy either developing back-end technology for database integration or administration or being semi-active participants in earlier phases, so they will know what they are dealing with when the time rolls around.

Phase 12: Programming and production

The beginning of this phase finds the Factor team once more reviewing site map and architecture. Because everyone involved is able to reference the same information, the design and programming teams develop the strategy for file structures, naming conventions, and compression formats to accurately and efficiently produce and deliver the necessary elements to the programming team with the least confusion and disruption to their process.

The content should also be completed at this time and delivered to the design team. Once Factor has received all content, we review it, divide it into proper file formats and pages, add URL information for missing links, and save it out to the proper folders and naming conventions of the programmers. Graphic elements are simultaneously produced and delivered for each page in a similar manner. The process is painstaking, but now common reference points have all been established and integrated into the site map, sometimes even to the point of including the page name, file name, and browser title description for every page in the site. Now, if a programmer needs to ask too many questions or has to ramp up to understand the site structure, it means we will be less efficient and might introduce errors in the site. Every effort is taken to make this a self-guided process. If the map doesn't answer it, we add the missing information and republish a new version to all team members, in a living document of the process that is easily updated and reprinted. Because in the past, electronic versions have proven too difficult to interact with and mark up, we continue to depend on a tangible hard-copy version.

Once the site begins to take shape and is wired for proper interaction, we release the staging URL for review and testing.

While we want to make the client comfortable that progress is being made, we request that any and all comments, errors, and corrections be noted and shelved until the first programming pass is completed and we can shift our focus away from structural engineering.

Phase 13: User testing and quality assurance

Now we request and assemble all of the remaining comments and begin to address and correct any overlooked or changed information or elements. Bringing in individuals who have not been mired in the development of the site is also important at this phase. The most obvious and the most trivial items will often be instantly recognizable to these new users. We can then discuss and determine if there needs to be any modifications to the content or navigation to improve the performance of the site prior to launch.

Phase 14: Launch of website

Once the finished project has been given the green light, password protection is lifted and the website is available for public consumption. But will anyone see it?

Phase 15: Promotion of web site

Sales and marketing efforts are focused on listing the site with all available search engines, publishing press releases about the launch, and generally building excitement. In some cases brochures, direct mail campaigns, or videos are also produced to help the company spread the word to current or prospective customers of the new site and its features.

Now that the client has established a Web presence, that presence must be nurtured. The beauty of the Web lies in its ability to carry living information. Because websites are only as useful as the information and the products they offer, if a site is launched and then abandoned visitors will quickly be turned away. Factor takes seriously the challenge either to maintain a relationship directly with the client, building and maintaining the site over time or, if capabilities do not exist in-house, to refer the client to outside partners who can simply and cost-effectively continue to publish and maintain the site. As more and more sites becoming living databases of information the update processes will become more critical. Often administrative tools are customized and delivered to clients to allow them a user friendly interface to publish new material, content updates, or corrections to their site on a daily basis without having to go through a design or programming cycle.

The Vans
WARPED TOUR
97

Adjacency

Adjacency, now a division of Sapient Corporation, was founded in 1995 in Madison, Wisconsin by then-students Andrew Sather, Bernie DeChant, Carlo Calica and Anton Prastowo. Grown without any investors or outside capital, Adjacency very quickly established itself as the Internet strategy, design and development firm of choice for highly emotive, premium global brands such as Patagonia, Specialized, Land Rover, TAG Heuer, Rollerblade, Caterpillar, Esprit, Williams-Sonoma, Virgin, the White House and more.

Though it possesses award-winning design and creative capabilities, Adjacency seems to many observers a unique type of business within the Internet services marketplace. The firm rarely partners with other companies or agrees to simply design a brand's Internet presence without strategizing and programming it as well. Adjacency's seamlessly integrated, multi-disciplinary development approach stands out in an industry rife with compartmentalized, throw-it-over-the-wall development methodologies.

Under Sather and DeChant, Adjacency's design approach is based on only a handful of principles. The most fundamental is the conviction that because of the pervasiveness and general availability of the medium, there is no room for the ego-driven, rock star design conceit. Any site, they'd proffer, should be completely and solely brand-appropriate and communicate the visual essence of the brand it's built to represent, not serve as a recognizable commentary or variation on the brand by the designer. With any studio's work separated by only a few clicks and a few seconds, a blatantly recognizable house style can be a dangerous liability.

In March, 1999, Sapient acquired Adjacency for roughly $54 million. The Adjacency brand was retired in June 1999, though the former Adjacency team continues to be an influential and core part of the new Sapient.

Origins
When started: 1995
Parent company, if any: Sapient
Number of employees when founded: 3
Number of employees now: 70
Headquarters: San Francisco

Principals
Andrew Sather, Bernie DeChant, Anton Prastowo, Carlo Calica

Contact
1177 Harrison Street
San Francisco, CA 94103
Tel: 415. 487 4510
Fax: 415. 487 9300
E-mail: e-business@sapient.com
Web: http://www.sapient.com

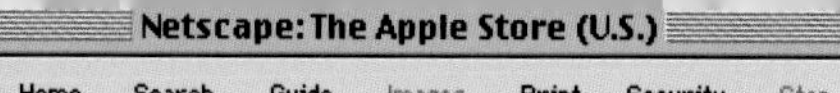

Back Forward Reload Home Search Guide Images Print Security Stop

Netsite: http://store2.apple.com/1-800-795-1000/WebObjects/AppleStore.woa/2471880710740692686148018012314037

Back

iMac

The iMac makes using the internet as easy as using a Macintosh, and that's good. What's even better is that the iMac comes fully loaded with everything you need to get online. Which in turn means that -- perhaps best of all -- you can be up and running for as little as $1,299.

- 233MHz PowerPC G3 processor
- 512K backside level 2 cache
- 32MB, expandable to 128MB SDRAM
- 4GB IDE hard disk drive
- 24x (max) speed CD-ROM drive
- Built-in 15-inch monitor (13.8-inch viewable)

Store Menu **Your Order** **Find** **Help** The Apple Store

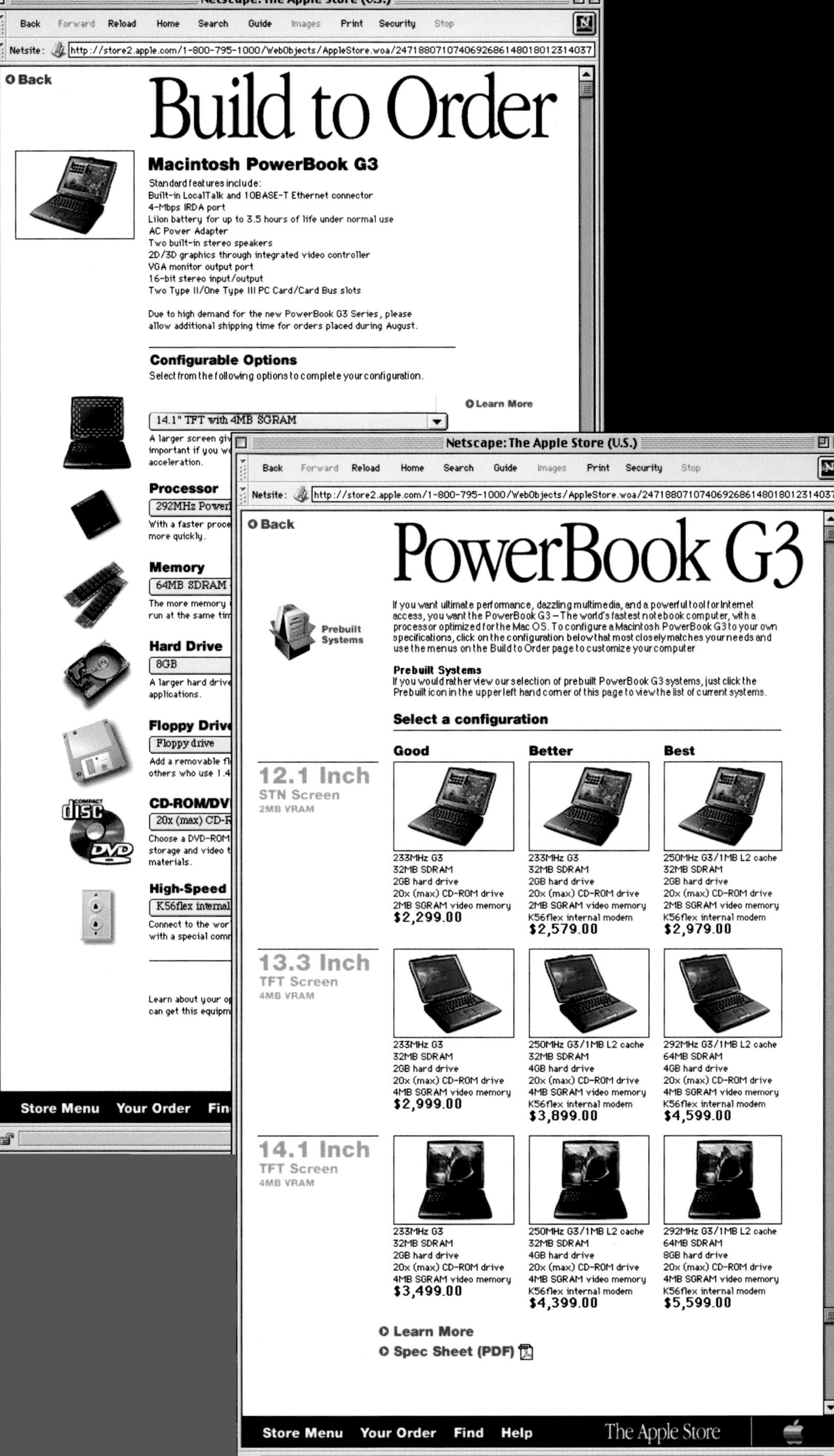

Netscape: The Apple Store (U.S.)
Back Forward Reload Home Search Guide Images Print Security Stop
Netsite: http://store2.apple.com/1-800-795-1000/WebObjects/AppleStore.woa/2471880710740692686148018012314037
Back
Build to Order
Macintosh PowerBook G3
Standard features include:
Built-in LocalTalk and 10BASE-T Ethernet connector
4-Mbps IRDA port
LiIon battery for up to 3.5 hours of life under normal use
AC Power Adapter
Two built-in stereo speakers
2D/3D graphics through integrated video controller
VGA monitor output port
16-bit stereo input/output
Two Type II/One Type III PC Card/Card Bus slots
Due to high demand for the new PowerBook G3 Series, please
allow additional shipping time for orders placed during August.
Configurable Options
Select from the following options to complete your configuration.
Learn More
14.1" TFT with 4MB SGRAM
Processor
292MHz Power
Memory
64MB SDRAM
Hard Drive
8GB
Floppy Drive
Floppy drive
CD-ROM/DV
20x (max) CD-R
High-Speed
K56flex internal
Store Menu Your Order Fin
Netscape: The Apple Store (U.S.)
Back Forward Reload Home Search Guide Images Print Security Stop
Netsite: http://store2.apple.com/1-800-795-1000/WebObjects/AppleStore.woa/2471880710740692686148018012314037
Back
PowerBook G3
Prebuilt Systems
If you want ultimate performance, dazzling multimedia, and a powerful tool for Internet access, you want the PowerBook G3 – The world's fastest notebook computer, with a processor optimized for the Mac OS. To configure a Macintosh PowerBook G3 to your own specifications, click on the configuration below that most closely matches your needs and use the menus on the Build to Order page to customize your computer
Prebuilt Systems
If you would rather view our selection of prebuilt PowerBook G3 systems, just click the Prebuilt icon in the upper left hand corner of this page to view the list of current systems.
Select a configuration
Good
Better
Best
12.1 Inch
STN Screen
2MB VRAM
233MHz G3
32MB SDRAM
2GB hard drive
20x (max) CD-ROM drive
2MB SGRAM video memory
$2,299.00
233MHz G3
32MB SDRAM
2GB hard drive
20x (max) CD-ROM drive
2MB SGRAM video memory
K56flex internal modem
$2,579.00
250MHz G3/1MB L2 cache
32MB SDRAM
2GB hard drive
20x (max) CD-ROM drive
2MB SGRAM video memory
K56flex internal modem
$2,979.00
13.3 Inch
TFT Screen
4MB VRAM
233MHz G3
32MB SDRAM
2GB hard drive
20x (max) CD-ROM drive
4MB SGRAM video memory
$2,999.00
250MHz G3/1MB L2 cache
32MB SDRAM
4GB hard drive
20x (max) CD-ROM drive
4MB SGRAM video memory
K56flex internal modem
$3,899.00
292MHz G3/1MB L2 cache
64MB SDRAM
4GB hard drive
20x (max) CD-ROM drive
4MB SGRAM video memory
K56flex internal modem
$4,599.00
14.1 Inch
TFT Screen
4MB VRAM
233MHz G3
32MB SDRAM
2GB hard drive
20x (max) CD-ROM drive
4MB SGRAM video memory
$3,499.00
250MHz G3/1MB L2 cache
32MB SDRAM
4GB hard drive
20x (max) CD-ROM drive
4MB SGRAM video memory
K56flex internal modem
$4,399.00
292MHz G3/1MB L2 cache
64MB SDRAM
8GB hard drive
20x (max) CD-ROM drive
4MB SGRAM video memory
K56flex internal modem
$5,599.00
Learn More
Spec Sheet (PDF)
Store Menu Your Order Find Help
The Apple Store

Site description

For what the Tag Heuer website lacks in functionality—no e-commerce—it more than compensates with beautiful design and well-organized content. The primary goals of the project: to create the most handsome, appropriate online shrine to the TAG Heuer brand and product line; to define the category by making something no competitor's site can compete with in terms of design, content, or product presentation; and to communicate the spirit and essence of "one of the greatest brands on the planet."

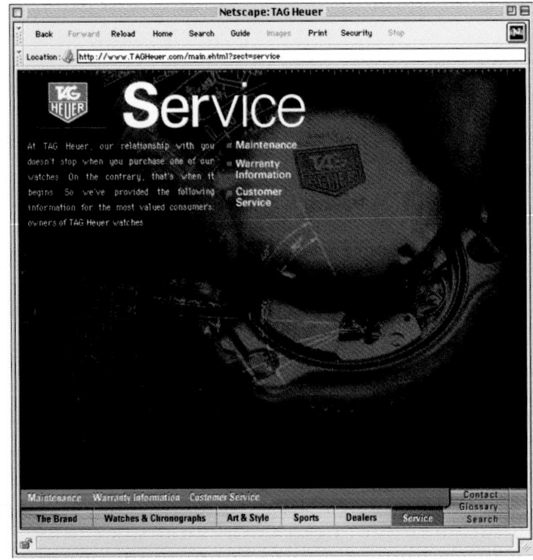

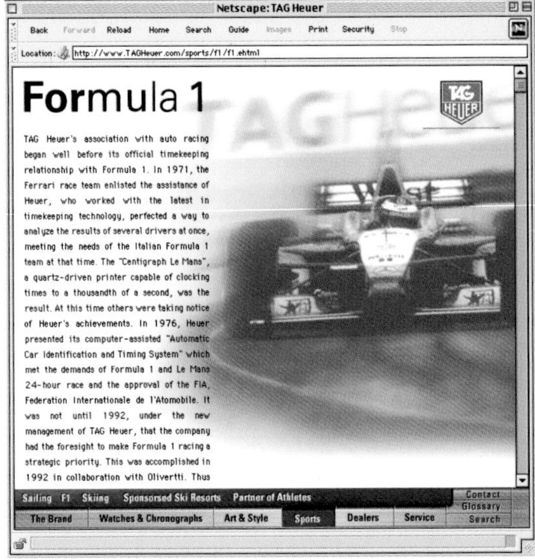

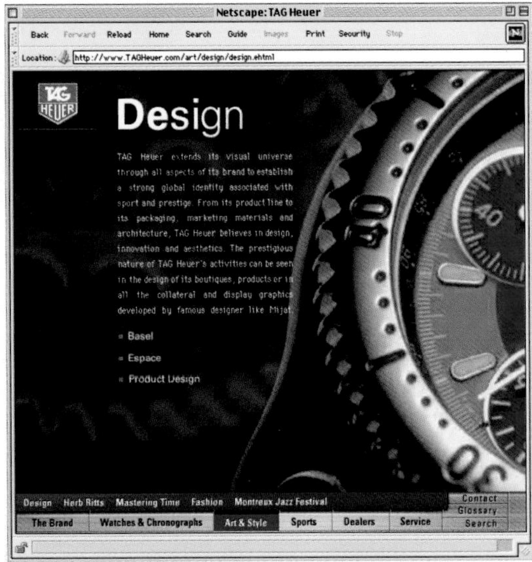

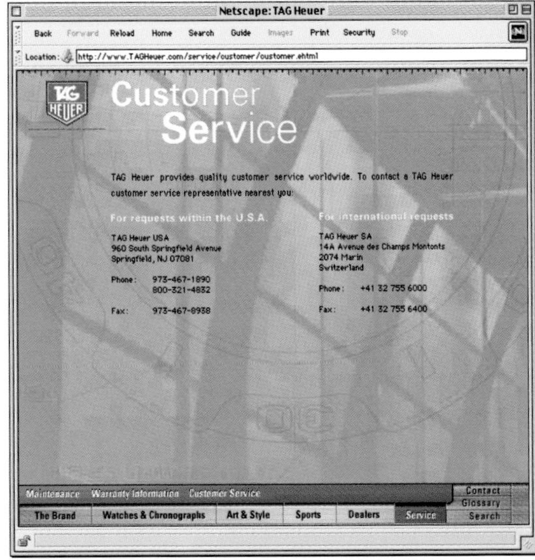

www.TagHeuer.com
Client: Tag Heuer, Inc.
Creative Director: Andrew Sather
Art Directors: Andrew Sather, Bernie DeChant
Designers: Dave Le, Andrew Sather
Programming: Matt Kirchstein, Carlo Calica, Leni Litonjua, Nick Fogler, Jen Wolf

Netscape: TAG Heuer
Back
Forward
Reload
Home
Search
Guide
Images
Print
Security
Stop
Location: http://www.TAGHeuer.com/main.ehtml?sect=art
TAG HEUER
Art&Style
Vision starts inside, in the mind's eye. Everything drawn, built, said, or supported by TAG Heuer is a mirror of the Company's personality. The stronger the identity inside, the more distinctive the image it projects. TAG Heuer supports efforts to produce strong visions of art and style.
Design
Herb Ritts
Mastering Time
Fashion
Montreux Jazz Festival
Design
Herb Ritts
Mastering Time
Fashion
Montreux Jazz Festival
Contact
Glossary
Search
The Brand
Watches & Chronographs
Art & Style
Sports
Dealers
Service

ROLLERBLADE
Racing
Geo Rollerblade Racing Team ®
See the faces behind the blur.
Races and Updates
All the inline racing info you need.
Chat
THE place on the Web for Inline Race discussion.
Featuring Geo
ROLLERBLADE RACING TEAM ®
Bulletin Board
Ask a question, announce a race.
Fast Gear Giveaway
Win the skates, the jersey, and the helmet!
site menu
skate!
contact us

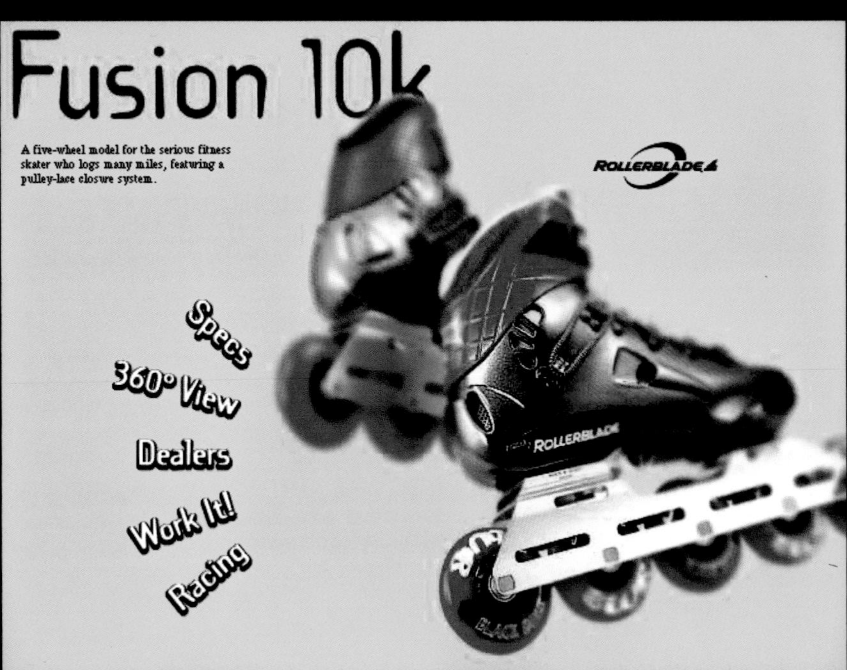
Fusion 10k
A five-wheel model for the serious fitness skater who logs many miles, featuring a pulley-lace closure system.
ROLLERBLADE
Specs
360° View
Dealers
Work It!
Racing

ROLLERBLADE
Skate!
Tarmac ®
Aggressive in-line skating featuring Chris and Matt
The Arena
The where, when, and how of in-line hockey
Racing
Featuring the Geo Rollerblade Racing Team
Kids' Club
Featuring Team Blade Runner
Work It!
Skating for fun and fitness
site menu
contact us

Rollerblade Site
Client: Rollerblade, Inc.
Creative Director: Andrew Sather
Design Director: Bernie DeChant
Designers: Andrew Sather,
Bernie DeChant,
Pascal, Matia Wagabaza
Photographer: Michael Vorhees

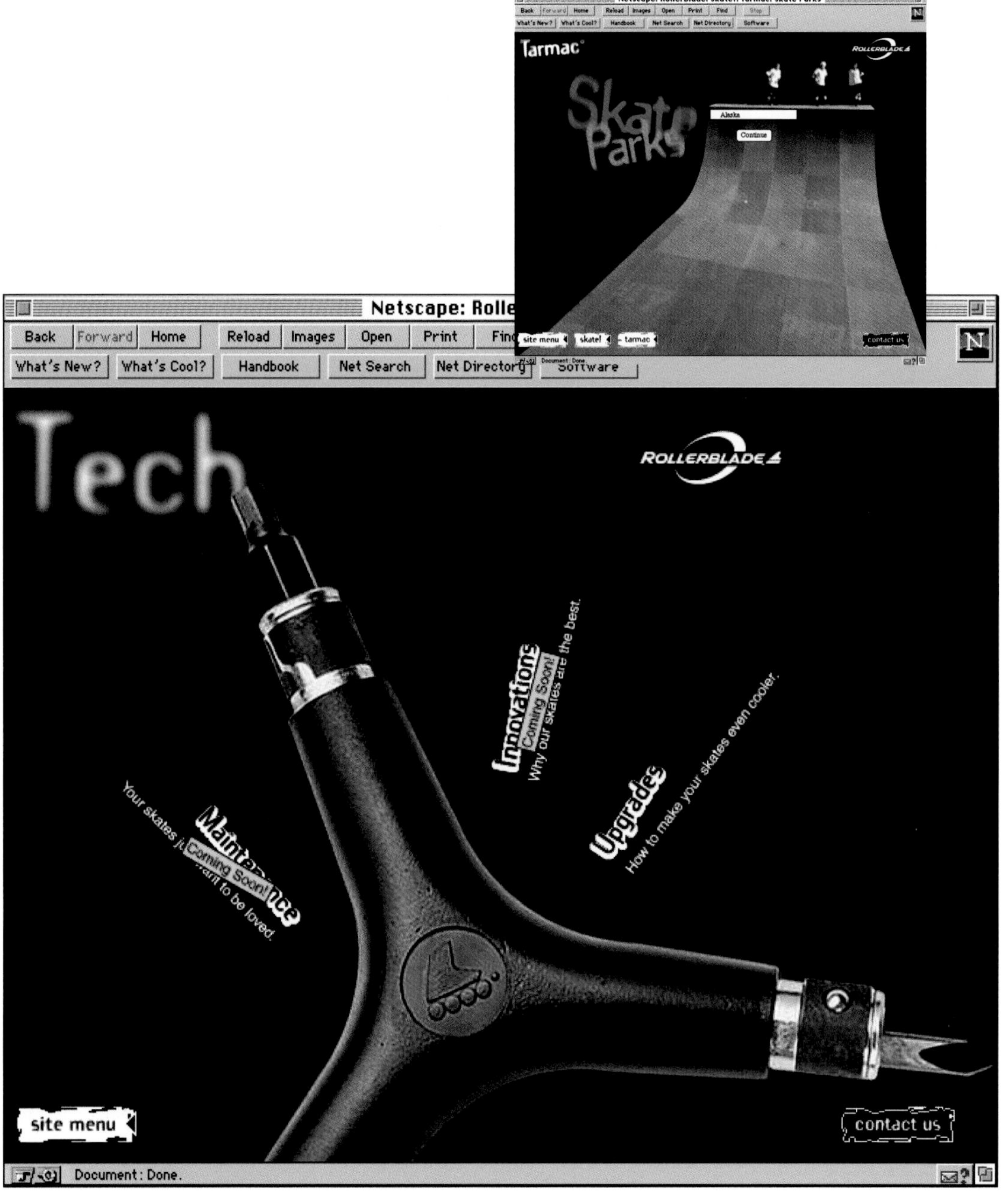

Site description
Rollerblade hired Adjacency to develop a corporate Web presence for them amid a comprehensive brand repositioning. As a result, Adjacency was entrusted with creating a considerable component of Rollerblade's revised global brand identity. The resulting site managed to eclipse competing in-line skating sites on the Web and reinvigorate the company's advertising efforts. The design solution sought to capture the purity and dynamism of the activity of inline skating and attach relevant information and Rollerblade branding devices to images of athletes and products, creating a more epic scale resembling online posters more than traditional Web "pages."

best4x4.landrover.com
Client: Land Rover
Creative Director: Andrew Sather
Design Director:
Bernie DeChant
Designers: Bernie DeChant,
Andrew Sather,
Pascal, Mike Lin
Photographer: Alan Seymour

Project description:
Adjacency and Land Rover have worked together for several years to deliver category-leading branding, marketing and customer service functionality through the North American consumer site. Adjacency effectively visually repositioned the Land Rover brand within the US market when, with the original site design, we gave the brand a much more aggressive, bold off-road aesthetic that their historically patrician look of their older print material. Since that first launch, Land Rover's print efforts have reflected that intitial, Adjacency-led redefinition. In addition, Adjacency's proprietary Outfit Your Land Rover feature was the first Java-based application to deliver real-time product customization functionality to online auto shoppers.

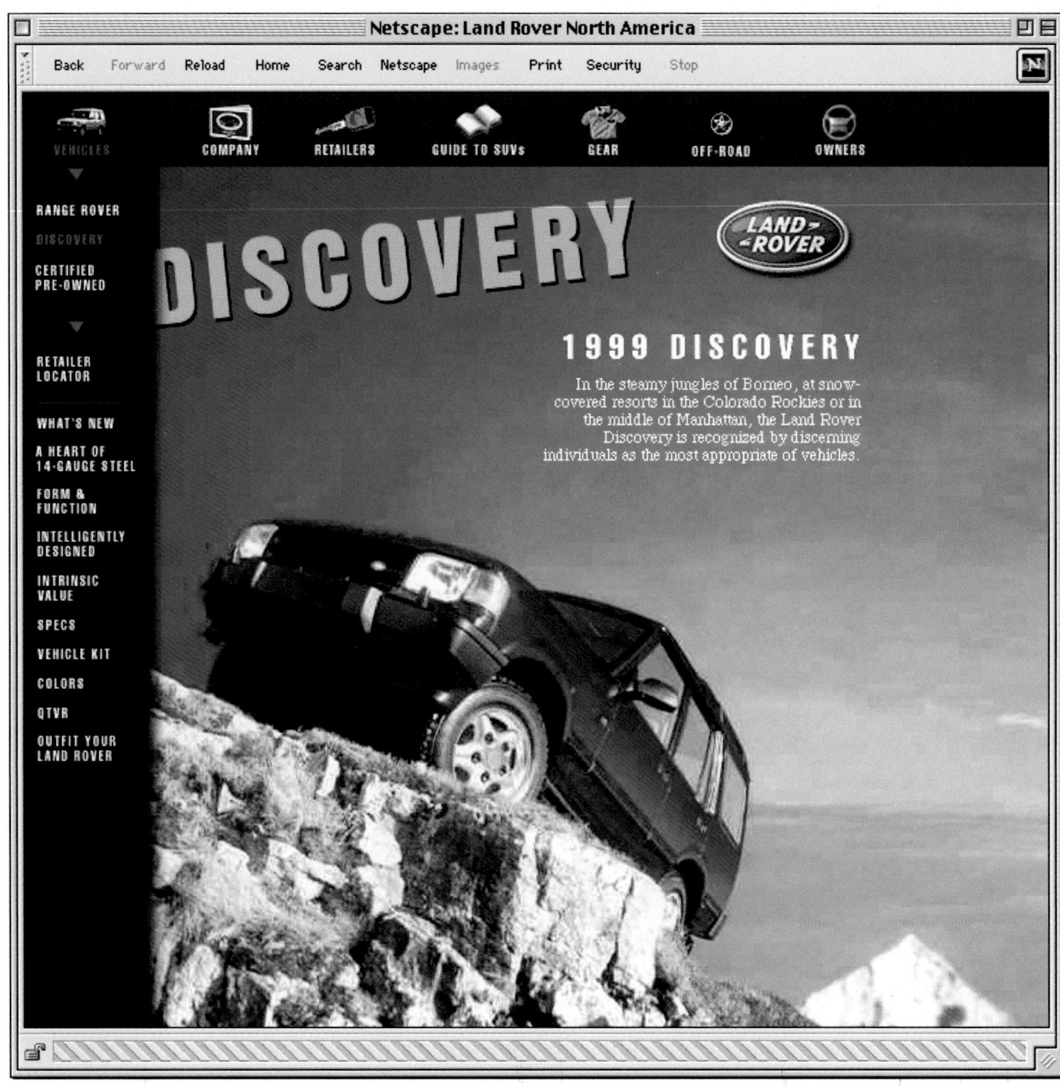

Netscape: Land Rover North America
Back
Forward
Reload
Home
Search
Netscape
Images
Print
Security
Stop
VEHICLES
COMPANY
RETAILERS
GUIDE TO SUVs
GEAR
OFF-ROAD
OWNERS
LAND ROVER
VEHICLES
CERTIFIED PRE-OWNED VEHICLES
RANGE ROVER
DISCOVERY
New! The first 1999 Vehicles have arrived. The Range Rover 4.0, 4.0 S, 4.6 HSE Callaway and Discovery SD are the first vehicles of an extended 1999 model year. Late in the 1998 calender year, the 1999 Range Rover 4.0 SE and 4.6 HSE and new Discovery Series II will be available with new features and refinements.
To request a full-color product brochure, visit our Literature section.
The Defender 90 is no longer available in the United States. Browse the 1997 features and specifications from our Defender Archive.
Land Rover Assured Protection offers extended service plans for newly purchased and Certified Pre-Owned Land Rover vehicles.
Use the Outfit Your Land Rover viewer to choose and accessorize the Land Rover vehicle of your choice.
Netscape: Land Rover North America
Back
Forward
Reload
Home
Search
Netscape
Images
Print
Security
Stop
COMPANY
VEHICLES
RETAILERS
GUIDE TO SUVs
GEAR
OFF-ROAD
OWNERS
LAND ROVER
COMPANY
50TH ANNIVERSARY
EVOLUTION OF A LEGEND
LITERATURE
IN THE NEWS
Land Rover is the premier manufacturer of world-class four-wheel-drive vehicles. This year, Land Rover celebrates its 50th Anniversary and 50 years of dedication to four-wheel drive enthusiasts.
HUE 166
BXC 796L

Netscape: Virgin.Com

THE VIRGIN MEGASTORE ONLINE ENTER NOW

VIRGINMEGA.COM

VIRGIN.COM

The Virgin global e-commerce network. More music, more travel, more of the Virgin experience on-line.

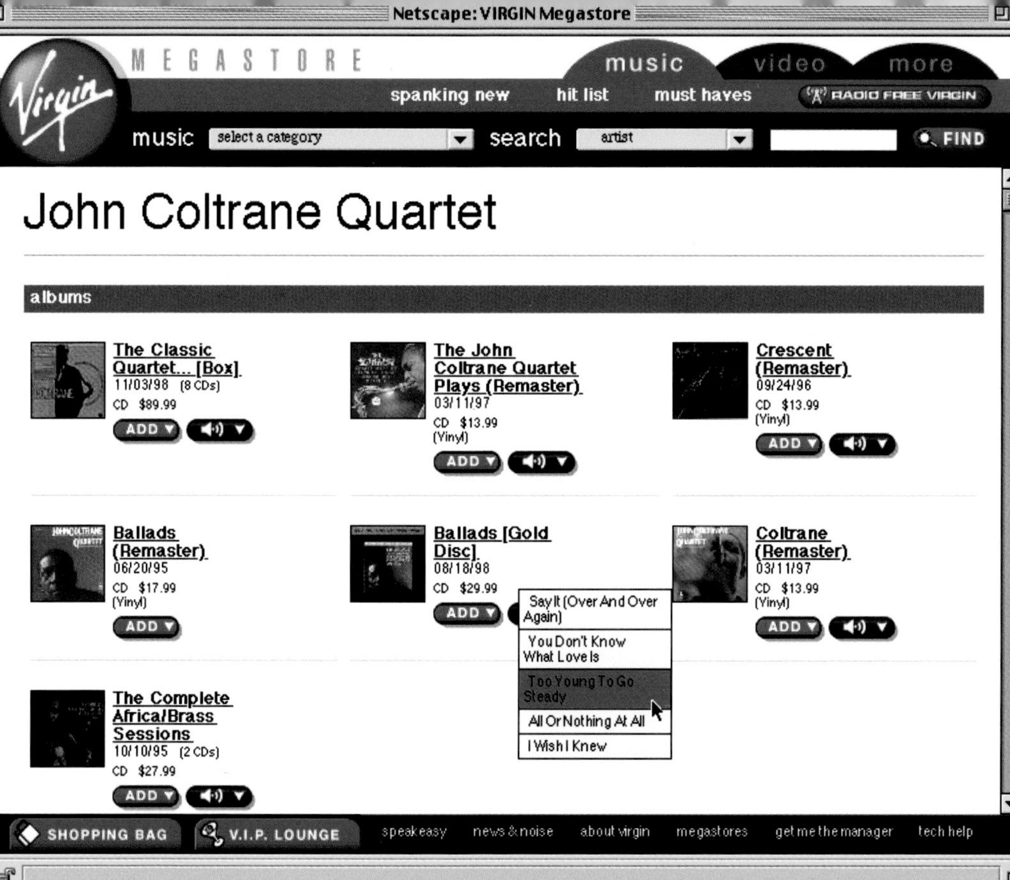
Netscape: VIRGIN Megastore
Virgin
MEGASTORE
music
video
more
spanking new
hit list
must haves
RADIO FREE VIRGIN
music
select a category
search
artist
FIND
John Coltrane Quartet
albums
The Classic Quartet... [Box]
11/03/98 (8 CDs)
CD $89.99
ADD
The John Coltrane Quartet Plays (Remaster)
03/11/97
CD $13.99
(Vinyl)
ADD
Crescent (Remaster)
09/24/96
CD $13.99
(Vinyl)
ADD
Ballads (Remaster)
06/20/95
CD $17.99
(Vinyl)
ADD
Ballads [Gold Disc]
08/18/98
CD $29.99
ADD
Say It (Over And Over Again)
You Don't Know What Love Is
Too Young To Go Steady
All Or Nothing At All
I Wish I Knew
Coltrane (Remaster)
03/11/97
CD $13.99
(Vinyl)
ADD
The Complete Africa/Brass Sessions
10/10/95 (2 CDs)
CD $27.99
ADD
SHOPPING BAG
V.I.P. LOUNGE
speakeasy
news & noise
about virgin
megastores
get me the manager
tech help

Site description

At the time Caterpillar hired Adjacency, Cat.com was visually diverse to the point of being difficult to navigate and potentially dillutive to the brand. Adjacency's assignment was to redesign and redevelop the company's website and develop a system of design and production standards for use around the world. The design distills and communicates the visual essence of the brand and establishes consistency across the Web efforts of the company's various divisions and geographic groups, while still affording them enough flexibility to meet their diverse—and at times, divergent—needs.

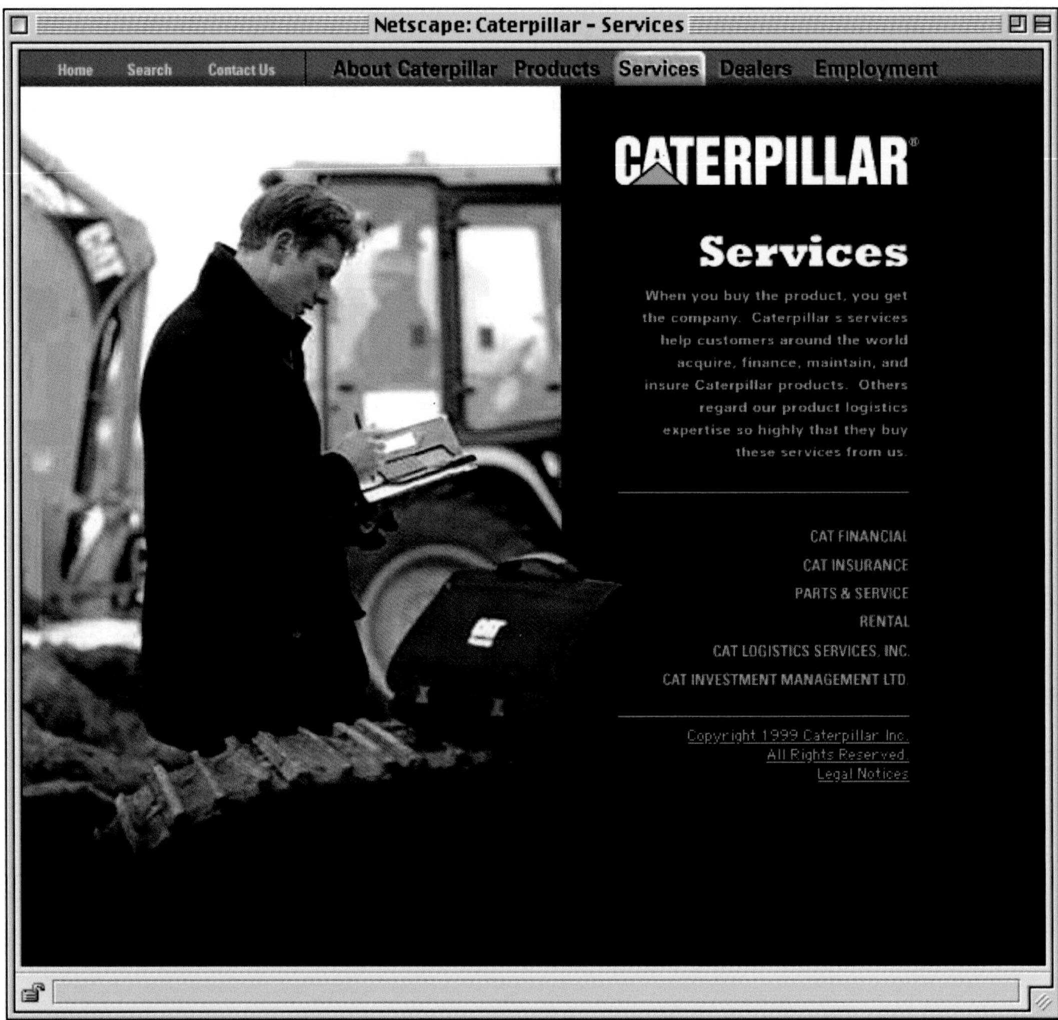

www.cat.com

Client: Caterpillar

Creative Director: Andrew Sather. Design Director: Bernie DeChant

Designers: Dave Le, Bernie DeChant

Netscape: Caterpillar
Home Search Contact Us
About Caterpillar Products Services Dealers Employment
CAT Rental THE STORE
Click on the map to find the Caterpillar dealer nearest you.
NORTH AMERICA
EUROPE
AFRICA
ASIA
OCEANIA
SOUTH AMERICA
AUSTRALIA
Locations
Global Search
Find your Caterpillar dealer by selecting your region.
Select one:
USA & Canada Search
Search for a specific Caterpillar dealer via zip code/postal code or
CITY
San Franc
STATE / PROVI
Select a St
or ZIP CODE
94103
SUBMI
Netscape: Caterpillar
Caterpillar people - employees and dealers - design, manufacture, market, finance and provide support for Cat machines and engines.
And those Cat products help make progress possible around the world.
CATERPILLAR
About Caterpillar
Products
Services
Dealers
Employment
Company Information, News, Sponsorships, Global and Investor Information
Search Global Contact Us
Shortcuts
Select one:
Highlights
Year 2000 Information
Caterpillar's Year 2000 Compliance Information.
The Cat Rental Store
A full range of Caterpillar and other brand-name equipment to meet all of your jobsite needs.
Cat Money Market Account
The Caterpillar Money Market Account can be a great way to put your money to work.
http://www.cat.com/cgi-bin/frameset.pl?nav=about&type=sectionmenu&content=/about/about.html&title=Caterpillar%20-%20About

AGENCY.COM™

Agency.com

AGENCY.COM was founded in 1995. Its first big job: designing a site for the SPORTS ILLUSTRATED swimsuit issue. Since then it has evolved into one of the largest full-service interactive firms in the industry, with twelve offices around the globe, and a client list that spans widely recognized brands including Coca Cola, Gucci, Compaq and British Airways.

"Design" is a term that applies across disciplines at AGENCY.COM. Creative Directors, Art Directors, Information Architects and Copywriters work closely with Strategists, Account Directors, Technologists and HTML Developers to design and implement solutions for clients' businesses online. This fully integrated approach is what distinguishes AGENCY.COM from its competitors.

AGENCY.COM's design ethos? There is no house style. What it takes to "live the brand" for clients such as Gucci and Nike is entirely different from what is involved in repositioning Monsanto as a "life sciences" company. It's the talent and passion of individuals, supported by sound process, that makes it work.

Origins
Founded: 1995
Number of employees
When founded: 2, Now: 800
Headquarters: New York
Location of other offices:
Amsterdam, Avon (CO), Boston, Chicago, Dallas, London, Paris, Portland, San Francisco, Singapore, Woodbridge (NJ)

Principals
Chan Suh (Co-Founder and Chief Executive Officer)
Kyle Shannon (Co-Founder and Chief Creative Officer)
Andy Hobsbawn (Chief Creative Officer, Europe)

Contact
AGENCY.COM
665 Broadway, New York, NY
Tel.: 212. 358 8220
Fax: 212. 358 8255
E-mail: info@agency.com
Web: www.agency.com

MAIN MENU
SPEED
SPIRIT
AMBITION
HARMONY
CONCORDE
SPEED
FLIGHT STATUS
London
New York
PASSENGER COMFORT
FLIGHT SPEED
YOUR SCORE
255
BRITISH AIRWAYS CONCORDE

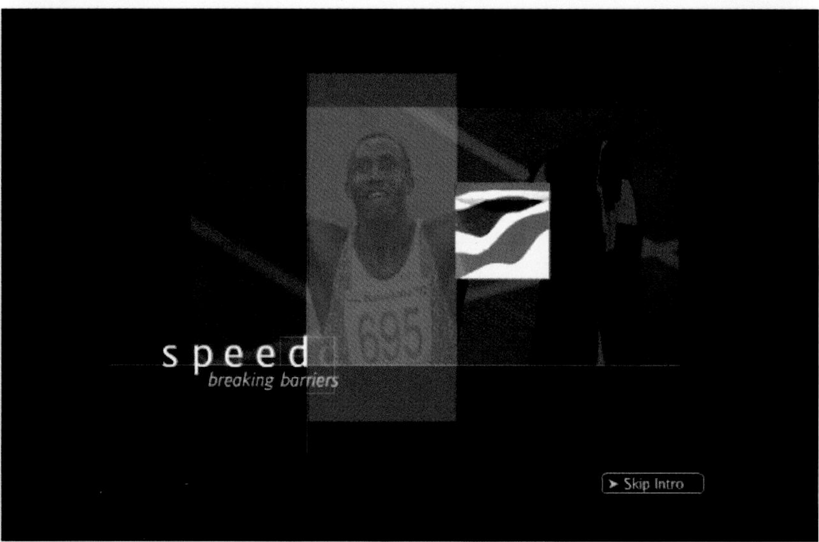
speed
breaking barriers
➤ Skip Intro

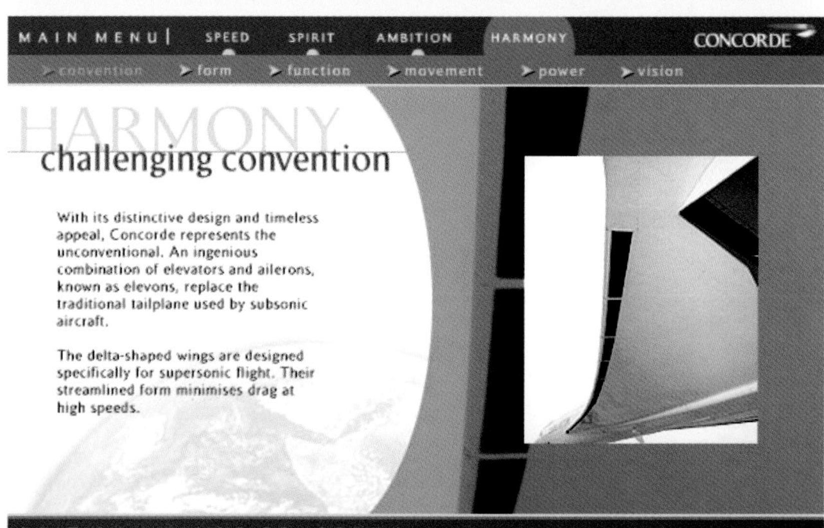
MAIN MENU
SPEED
SPIRIT
AMBITION
HARMONY
CONCORDE
➤ convention
➤ form
➤ function
➤ movement
➤ power
➤ vision
HARMONY
challenging convention
With its distinctive design and timeless appeal, Concorde represents the unconventional. An ingenious combination of elevators and ailerons, known as elevons, replace the traditional tailplane used by subsonic aircraft.
The delta-shaped wings are designed specifically for supersonic flight. Their streamlined form minimises drag at high speeds.
BRITISH AIRWAYS CONCORDE

MAIN MENU | SPEED SPIRIT AMBITION HARMONY CONCORDE

HARMONY

Admire the perfect balance of form and function as you explore Concorde

- challenging convention
- reinventing form
- controlling function
- redefining movement
- generating power
- changing vision

BRITISH AIRWAYS CONCORDE

CONCORDE

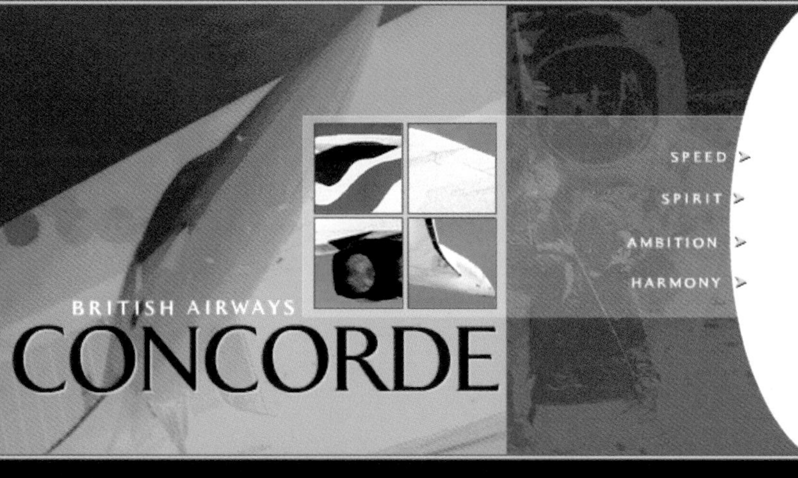

MAIN MENU | SPEED SPIRIT AMBITION HARMONY CONCORDE

convention form function movement power vision

HARMONY

reinventing form

Heat generated during supersonic flight causes the fuselage of Concorde to expand by up to 10 inches.

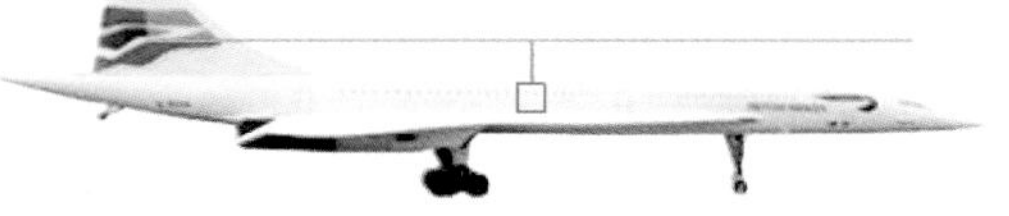

Concorde unifies utility and aesthetics.
Her sleek design was born through her unmatched function.

ROTATE

BRITISH AIRWAYS CONCORDE

www.british-airways.com/ concorde
(preceding spread)
Client: British Airways
Creative Director: Sumin Chou Art Director, Designer: Jean Esquivel. Writers: Elisa Niemack, James Gartside. Site Manager: Nick Cook. Sound Engineers: Alex Heller, Andy Trafford. Shockwave Developer: James McHugh. Flash Developers: John Nack, Min Kyung Chang, Jackie Miao, Nazar Ali Khan, Suzanne Begley. Site Builder: Dheeraj Vasishta. Technical Consultants: Andy Trafford, Ralph Seaman. Graphic Production: Tom Moran, Andy Allman

www.gucci.com
Client: Gucci
Creative Director: Claudia Franzen. Art Direction: Karen Joyce (Gucci), Frankie Winter (Gucci)
Account Director: Marysia Woroniecka

(this page)
Photographer: Mario Testino. Models: Liisa Winkler/IMG Model, New York; Robert Konjic/Select Model Management, London

(opposite)
Photographer: Mario Testino. Models: James Heathcote/MGM Marilyn Men, Paris; Paul Wignall/ Q Model Management, Los Angeles; Hannelore Knuts/Success-Stess, Paris

Site description

The Concorde microsite, a comprehensive resource for information about the Concorde, was designed to provide an immersive online environment for people to share in and contribute to the Concorde experience. British Airways partnered with AGENCY.COM to create the Concorde microsite as part of an integrated marketing program designed to leverage the power of the Concorde brand in raising awareness of the British Airways master brand among a younger audience.

Site description

International luxury goods company Gucci retained AGENCY.COM to carry out strategic and consulting services as a precursor to the creation of a fully developed Web presence. The mandate is to explore and identify the specific business goals, practices and challenges of each division of the company to explore how online technologies can be used to the company's advantage. AGENCY.COM addresses specific operational challenges, communications issues and business opportunities and analyze the needs, interests and concerns of each division. The objective is to develop a strategic plan for online development for Gucci that will embrace the short term requirements of the company while being flexible enough to accommodate both internal growth and technical advances, and keep sight of general trends in interactive media.

Client: Monsanto
Creative Director: Jonathan Glazer
Art Director: PJ Loughran
Designer: Dan Clancy
Site Manager: Allison Strandowitz
Senior Builder: Marcy Mayer

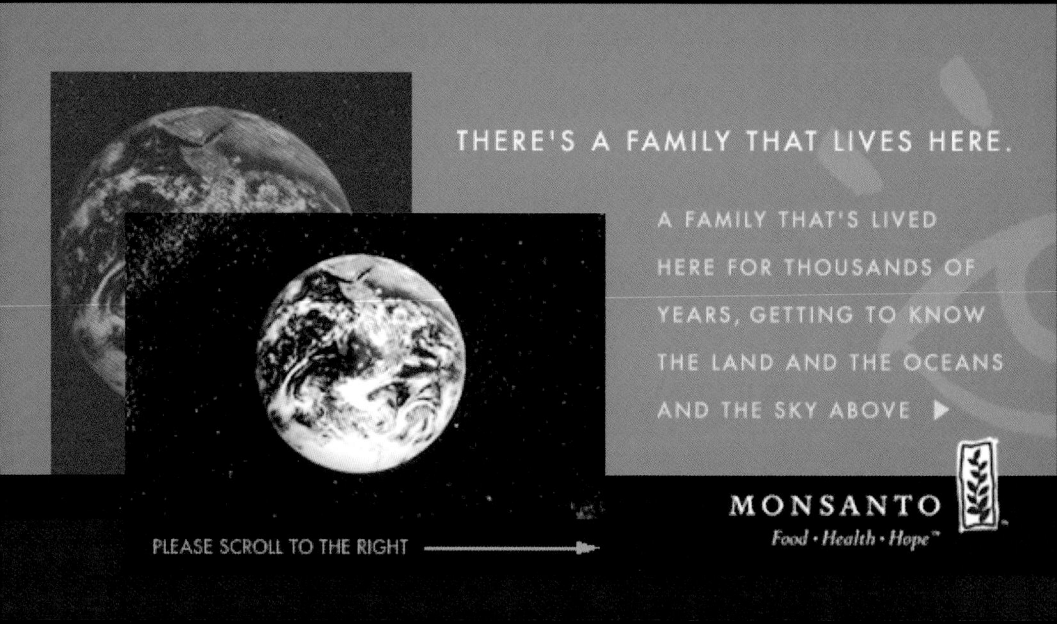

THERE'S A FAMILY THAT LIVES HERE.
A FAMILY THAT'S LIVED HERE FOR THOUSANDS OF YEARS, GETTING TO KNOW THE LAND AND THE OCEANS AND THE SKY ABOVE

Site description

Monsanto is a $9.3 billion, fast-moving, technology-driven company that produces and markets products in the agriculture, nutrition, and health care industries.

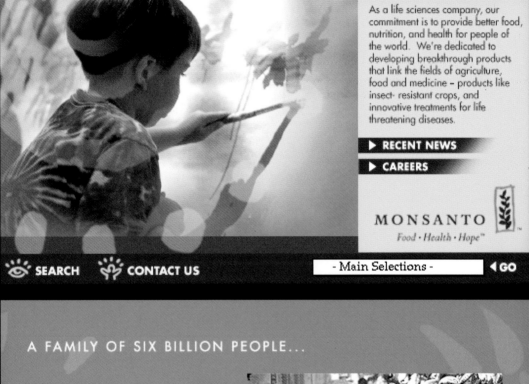

In 1997, Monsanto spun off of its chemical businesses and formed a new life sciences company. Monsanto wanted to use the Internet as the primary medium to communicate the company's new image. They chose AGENCY.COM as their partner, and together, we developed an online venue that reflects their new identity as a global, caring brand.

WELCOME TO MONSANTO
As a life sciences company, our commitment is to provide better food, nutrition, and health for people of the world. We're dedicated to developing breakthrough products that link the fields of agriculture, food and medicine – products like insect- resistant crops, and innovative treatments for life threatening diseases.
RECENT NEWS
CAREERS
MONSANTO
Food · Health · Hope™

SEARCH
CONTACT US
- Main Selections -
GO

A FAMILY OF SIX BILLION PEOPLE...
EACH UNIQUE, YET IDENTICAL TO ALL THOSE WHO HAVE GONE BEFORE

www.desires.com
Client: *Urban Desires*
Creative Director:
PJ Loughran
Editor-in-Chief:
Gabrielle Shannon
Publishers: Kyle Shannon,
Chan Suh

Site description

The stylish brainchild of the New York-based husband-and-wife team Kyle and Gabrielle Shannon, *Urban Desires* was the first magazine of its kind to be published exclusively online. Primarily focusing on literature

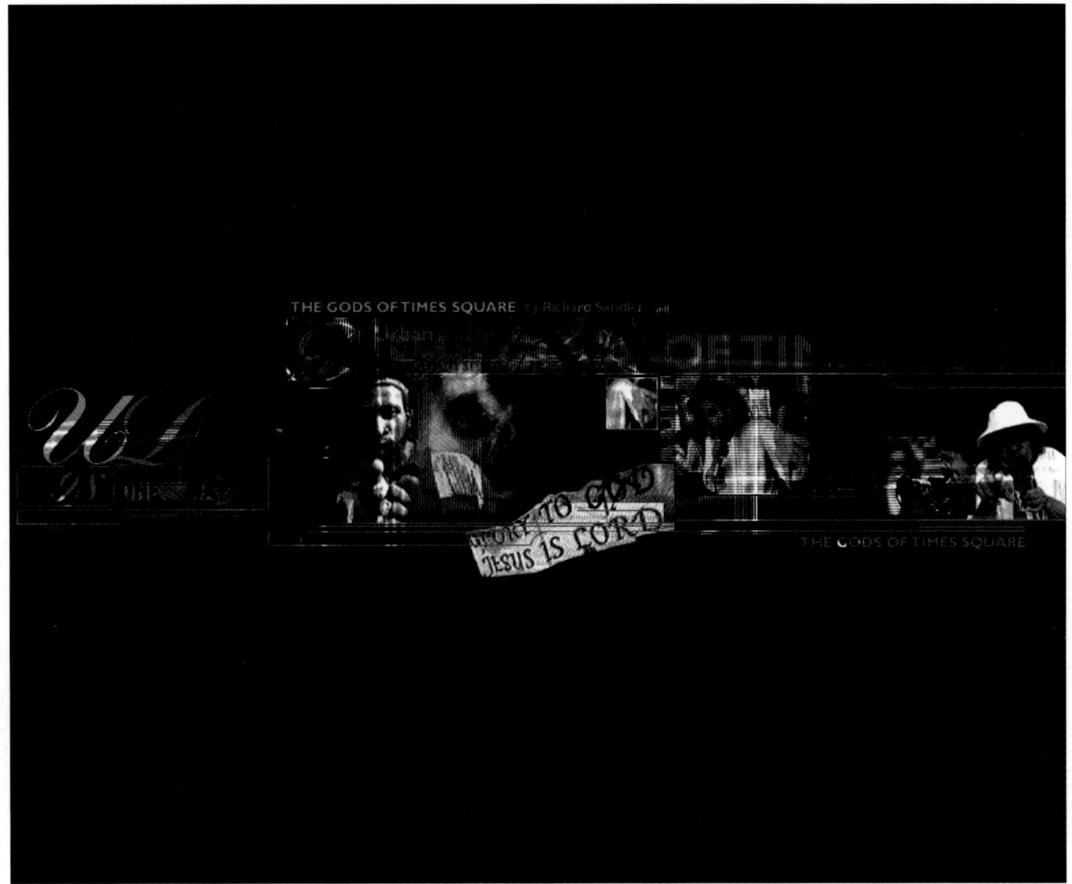

and the arts, *Urban Desires* has a distinctly metropolitan flavor that has been described as a "post-punk hybrid of *Harper's* and *The New York Review of Books*." After four years of critical raves that helped build a loyal and passionate following, *Urban Desires* evolved into a venue for short films, animation, games and experiments in Web specific digital art. Editor Shannon explains, "Our focus still remains on creating the most exciting, intelligent metropolis on the Web."

The Bill Morrison Films: Footprints | The Film of Her
Mailing List | Reviews | Submissions

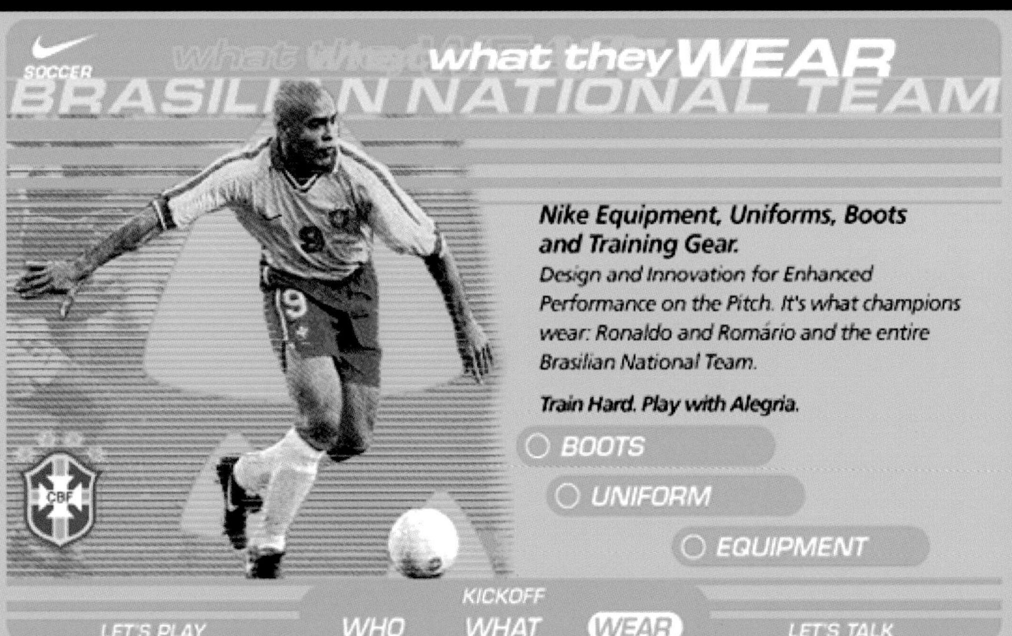
SOCCER
what they WEAR
BRASILIAN NATIONAL TEAM
Nike Equipment, Uniforms, Boots and Training Gear.
Design and Innovation for Enhanced Performance on the Pitch. It's what champions wear: Ronaldo and Romário and the entire Brasilian National Team.
Train Hard. Play with Alegria.
BOOTS
UNIFORM
EQUIPMENT
CBF
KICKOFF
LET'S PLAY
WHO
WHAT
WEAR
LET'S TALK

www.jumpman23.com
(opposite page)
Client: Nike, Inc.
Creative Directors: Deanne Draeger, Andrew Leitch
Art Director: PJ Loughran
Digital Artists: PJ Loughran, Vanessa Pineda, Sabine Roehl
Writer: Jay Zasa
Site Builders: Allison Strandwitz, Richard Kim
Programmers: Alex Lygin
Producers:
Kim Albert, Alex Gadd,

Site description
Nike partnered with AGENCY.COM and Michael Jordan in creating a Web venue to launch the Jordan line of apparel exclusively online. Inspired by the immersive brand experience of Nike Town, the Jumpman site showcases the Jordan line of products in the context of Michael's personal involvement in their design, and his passion for the sport of basketball.

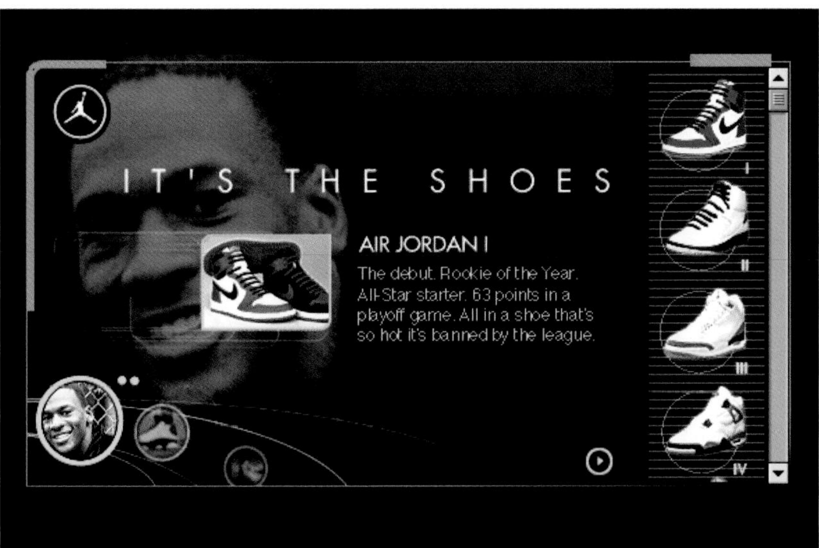

IT'S THE SHOES
AIR JORDAN I
The debut. Rookie of the Year. All-Star starter. 63 points in a playoff game. All in a shoe that's so hot it's banned by the league.
I
II
III
IV

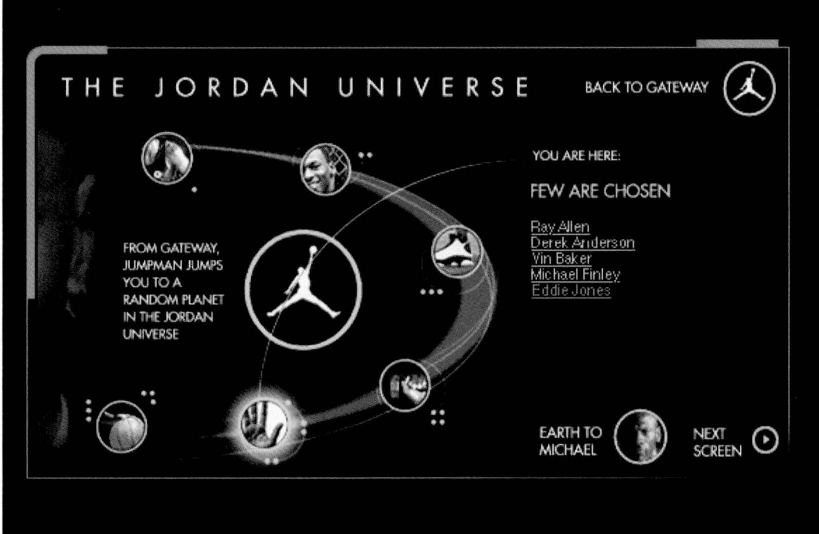

THE JORDAN UNIVERSE
BACK TO GATEWAY
YOU ARE HERE:
FEW ARE CHOSEN
Ray Allen
Derek Anderson
Vin Baker
Michael Finley
Eddie Jones
FROM GATEWAY, JUMPMAN JUMPS YOU TO A RANDOM PLANET IN THE JORDAN UNIVERSE
EARTH TO MICHAEL
NEXT SCREEN

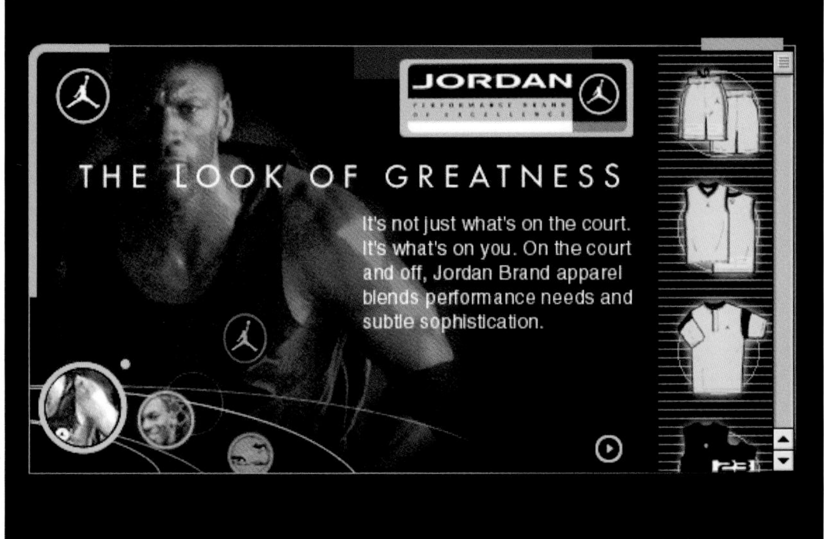

JORDAN
THE LOOK OF GREATNESS
It's not just what's on the court. It's what's on you. On the court and off, Jordan Brand apparel blends performance needs and subtle sophistication.

Site description

When Art + Commerce extended its business operations by launching A+C Anthology, it was clear that online technology would be a critical component in reaching a global client base. By the same token, the artists Art + Commerce represent operate on an ever more borderless stage. AGENCY.COM worked closely with the Art + Commerce project team to produce a website which is a powerful workspace allowing the artists' agents a high level of control over how their artists are represented online. Moreover, it offers professional users tools and services that are designed for the inherently collaborative nature of their work. The Art + Commerce site features portfolios of the latest in photography,

illustration, creative services, hair, makeup and styling by the artists the company represents for assignment. A+C Anthology's fine art photography archive—the most exclusive collection of images available for editorial and commercial licensing—is also available online. Users are able to search for specific images, view recent shoots, and other special online features.

www.artandcommerce.com
Client: Art + Commerce
Creative Director:
Claudia Franzen
Creative Consultant:
Alex Wiederin (a|r media)

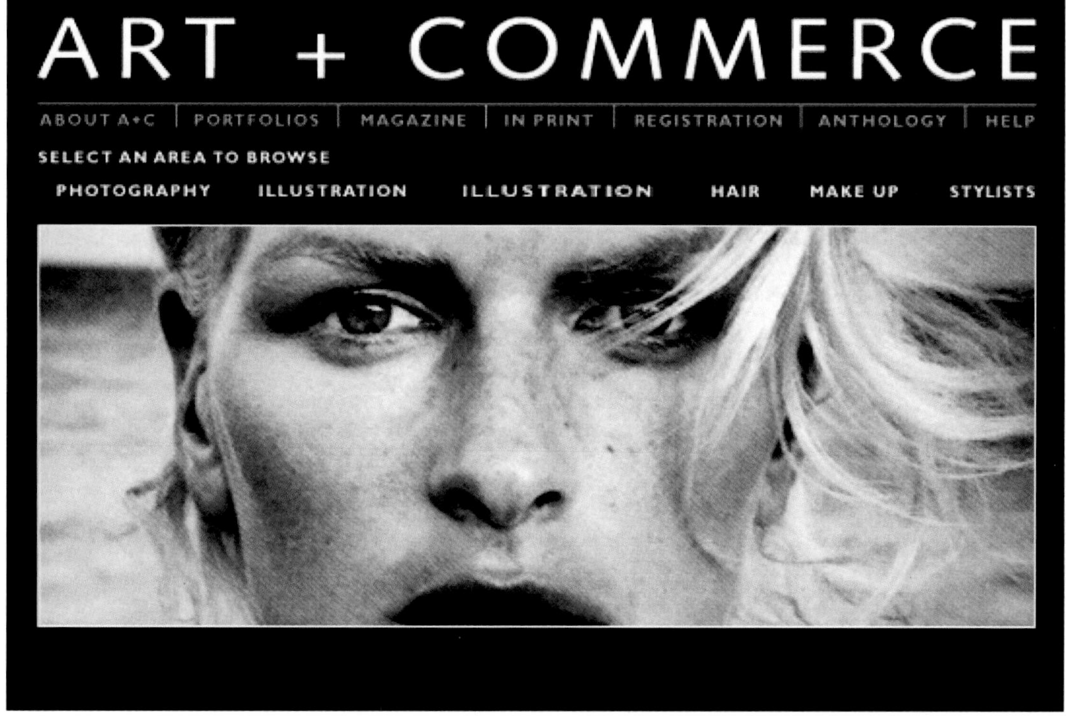

ART TECHNOLOGY GROUP

Art Technology Group

A fusion between a product company and a consulting business, Art Technology Group (ATG) is as comfortable in the world of new media design as it is in the world of Java programming. Our consulting group designs and develops one-of-a-kind websites for Global 1000 companies. Our product group creates core technology—a Web development software suite sold commercially under the Dynamo brand. It's a symbiotic relationship where Dynamo helps us invent for clients and our client work yields critical features that get folded back into Dynamo. This cross-pollination between consulting and product is one of the things that sets us apart. It's also central to our ability to stay ahead of the challenges inherent in designing for a new genre—to continually create experiences that use the fullest potential of the medium.

Understanding that potential is something ATG has been doing for a long time. A full six years ago, we began investigating the design, technology, and communication complexities of networked applications. This intense period of experimentation resulted in projects like the imaging installation developed for Chicago's Museum of Science and Industry (1993) and Oxygen, the virtual office application designed for Chiat/Day (1994). This early work cemented a design and development process that has evolved along with the growth of the Internet and helped us to create a burgeoning portfolio of clients that includes Sony, BMG Music, Eastman Kodak, Herman Miller, and Sun Microsystems.

Design teams at ATG bring a mix of strategic design planning, information design, user research, branding, visual design, user interface design, and prototyping to bear on each project. Multidisciplinary design teams work side by side with engineering teams that plan and implement the code which makes these applications come to life. The close bond between and design and development creates an atmosphere of innovation essential in a fast-moving industry.

Origins
Founded: December 1991
Number of employees
when started: 2
now: 233 and growing;
ATG Design, 19
Headquarters: Cambridge, Massachusetts
Other locations: San Francisco, Chicago, London

Principals
Jeet Singh, CEO/President
Joe Chung, CTO/Chairman

Contact
Art Technology Group
25 First Street, 2nd Floor
Cambridge, MA 02141
Tel.: 617.386 1000
Fax: 617.386 1111
E-mail: info@atg.com
Web: www.atg.com

Folk-o-matic (internal site)
Client: Art Technology Group
Designers: Ted Booth,
Aaron Oppenheimer, Anukam
Edward Opara
Technicians: Aaron Oppenheimer,
Laura Teodosio;
Project Manager: Brenda Sullivan

folk-o-matic (internal site)
Folk-o-matic is an internal tool we developed to support our fast-growing company. A sort of turbo-charged directory, employees throughout ATG can learn about their co-workers by browsing faces and names or personality-rich profiles. Along with learning where someone sits, or when they're likely to be in the office, you can discover their secret weapons and outside interests.

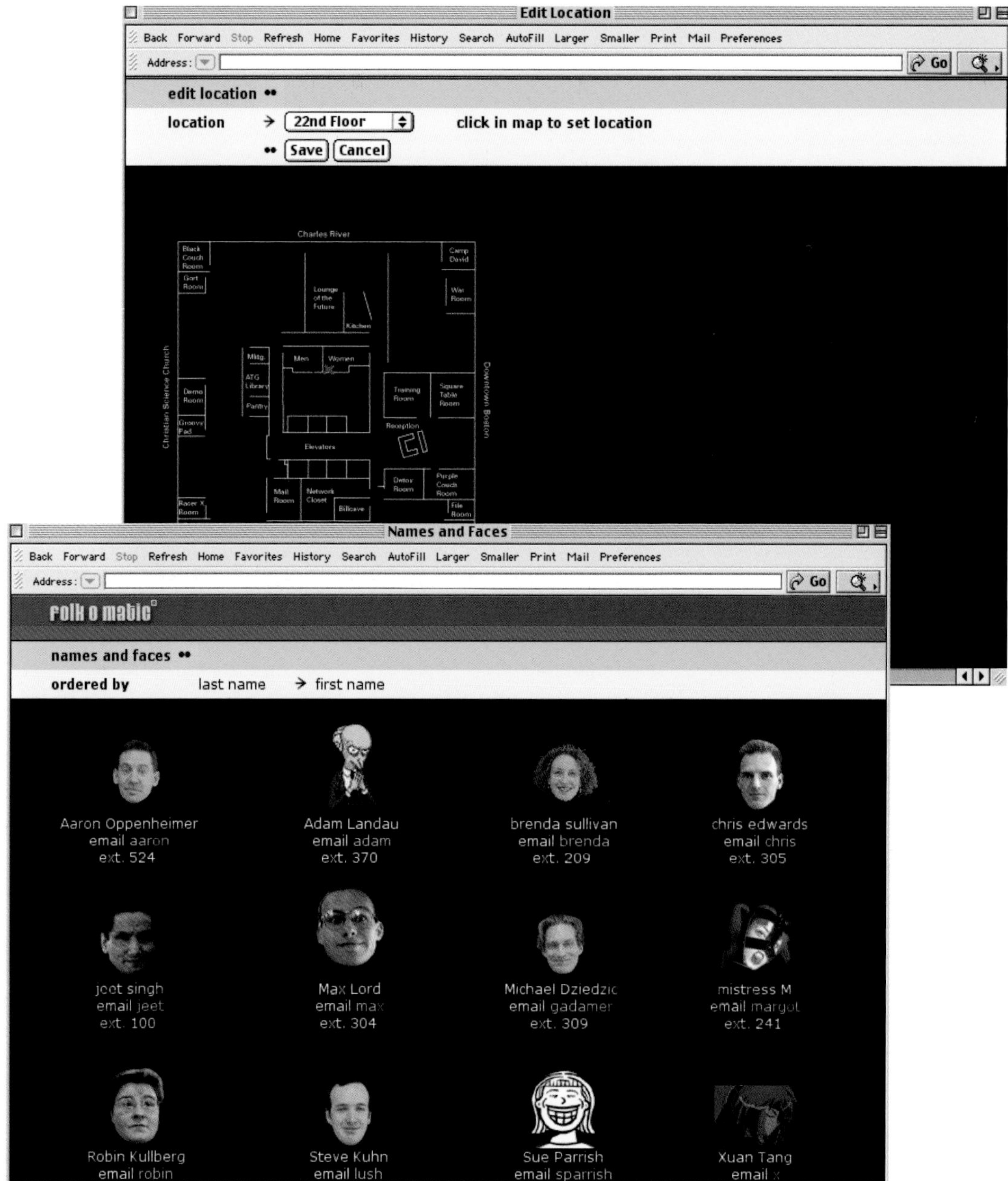

folk o matic

The Folk o matic
is a people finder and communication device
for ATG internal use only.

Everyone creates and maintains their own profiles
so don't blame us for what you find herein.

The idea is to increase interaction between
people who might not otherwise meet each
other.

folk o matic

A Day in the Life of Cyberspace

Back Forward Stop Refresh Home Favorites History Search AutoFill Larger Smaller Print Mail Preferences

Address: Go

The Secret Survey
If you recall the Review in Body, you'll remember the David and Venus that you could click on and travel to appropriate web sites. Well, here's the distribution of clicks on their bodies...

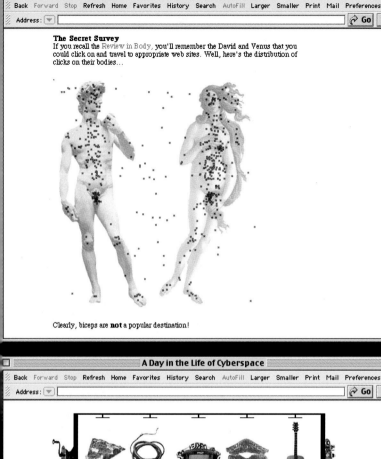

Clearly, biceps are **not** a popular destination!

A Day in the Life of Cyberspace

Back Forward Stop Refresh Home Favorites History Search AutoFill Larger Smaller Print Mail Preferences

Address: Go

Discussion Thread **Submissions**
Day 2: Expression

From the Discussion:

> The whole notion of "ownership" of information has got to change, especially in the creative side of things. The whole point of expressing is to convey and distribute my thoughts. I can't claim ownership of those thoughts once I've sent them out. Digital media brings the thoughts and the product of those thoughts closer and closer together, and in the same way it seems untenable to express strict ownership of the bit stream that represents what I'm trying to say.
>
> Rated 2.9 stars by 57 people

Site description

"10|10, A Day in Cyberspace," was live for ten days in October 1995. This event site was developed to celebrate the 10th anniversary of the MIT Media Lab. A virtual performance, the site contained 10 topics (one every 24 hours) that organized live content submissions from visitors into a dynamic community discussion for all to browse. Day 1: Privacy, Day 2: Expression/Personal Capsule, Day 3: Generations, Day 4: Wealth, Day 5: Faith, Day 6: Body/Visual Survey, Day 7: Place, Day 8: Tongues, Day 9: Environment, Day 10: Review. Other features included personalized homepages, a time capsule and a content rating scale.

BBDP Intranet
Client: BDDP Worldwide/ BDDP North America
Designers: Chris Edwards, Robin Kullberg, Dave Kung, Max Lord, Anukam Edward Opara, George Plesko
Technical: Nathan Abramson, Adrian Banard, Derek Lindner, Eric Negron, Kat Park
Project manager: Dana Goldberg

Site description
Designed for Paris-based BDDP, a global advertising conglomerate, the Disruption Network is an original intranet application that links 81 offices in 42 countries through a virtual information space for networked collaboration and idea-sharing. What sets this site apart from the standard intranet is that there is no canned content. Every piece of information in the system is created by and for BDDP employees.
(*this page*) Disruption central is the nerve center of the network, where flickering advertisements for pieces of content published by BDDP employees draw in readers. The pieces of content, called packets, are organized into six channels, each with its own unique identity.
As packets are authored, read, and evaluated, they bubble up into disruption central. The top of the window holds the functional user interface elements needed to get around the network, to create, to find, and to organize things. The moving "zipper" continually broadcasts messages to the entire network. A user's friends appear in the top window as well, with an "activity meter": an indicator of how active they have been in the system lately.
(*opposite*) Each channel is designed to encourage the publication of a specific kind of content. For example, the think channel is designed for packets that question, examine, or disrupt prevalent modes of thinking. The spy channel is for market and competitor intelligence, and the un-channel is home to anything that refuses to be categorized. A channel gives immediate access to its newest and its most popular packets. Since any user can rate submissions, the best packets are selectively reinforced and find their way to the top of the list.

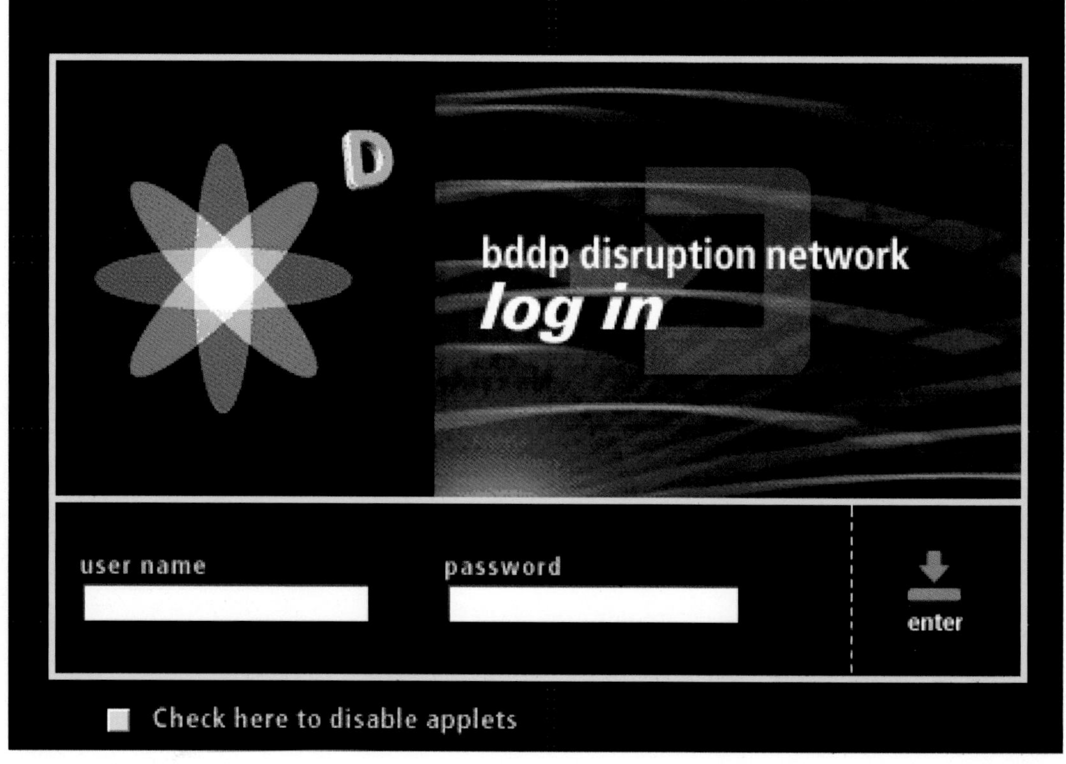

Netscape: BDDP Network
Back
Forward
Reload
Home
Search
Guide
Images
Print
Security
Stop
Netsite:
home
central
search
packets
people
rooms
create
packet
message
room
media
log out
help
...Hey guys, hope that you will disrupt with us soon!!!-Nadege V
edit
homeroom
Robin
Yikes! I'm really busy this week.
messages
your messages
0 new
buddy lists
your buddies logged in:
2
Netscape: BDDP Network
the Virgin room now! 3:45pm EST Deadline LOOMS! - John Greene... No more teletubbies packets please!! - Waitgoiter ...
search packets
create packet
Teletubbies! -c
culture channel
In the Culture Channel you will find:
Netscape: BDDP Network
Virgin Deadline Looms, lets get to work peo
search packets
create a packet
Cigar craze Jef
San Fran boun
un-channel
In the Un-Channel you will find:
humor, diversion, random bits.
top ten
1. Picture of the week
2. Yale Visit
3. Mr. Friendly Wants You!
4. South Park
5. Some Flowers on My Desk
6. Emma
7. My Little Pony Grew Up and Rebelled
newest packets
do you like mickey mouse?
Picture of the week
Yale Visit
Mr. Friendly Wants You!
South Park
Some Flowers on My Desk
Emma

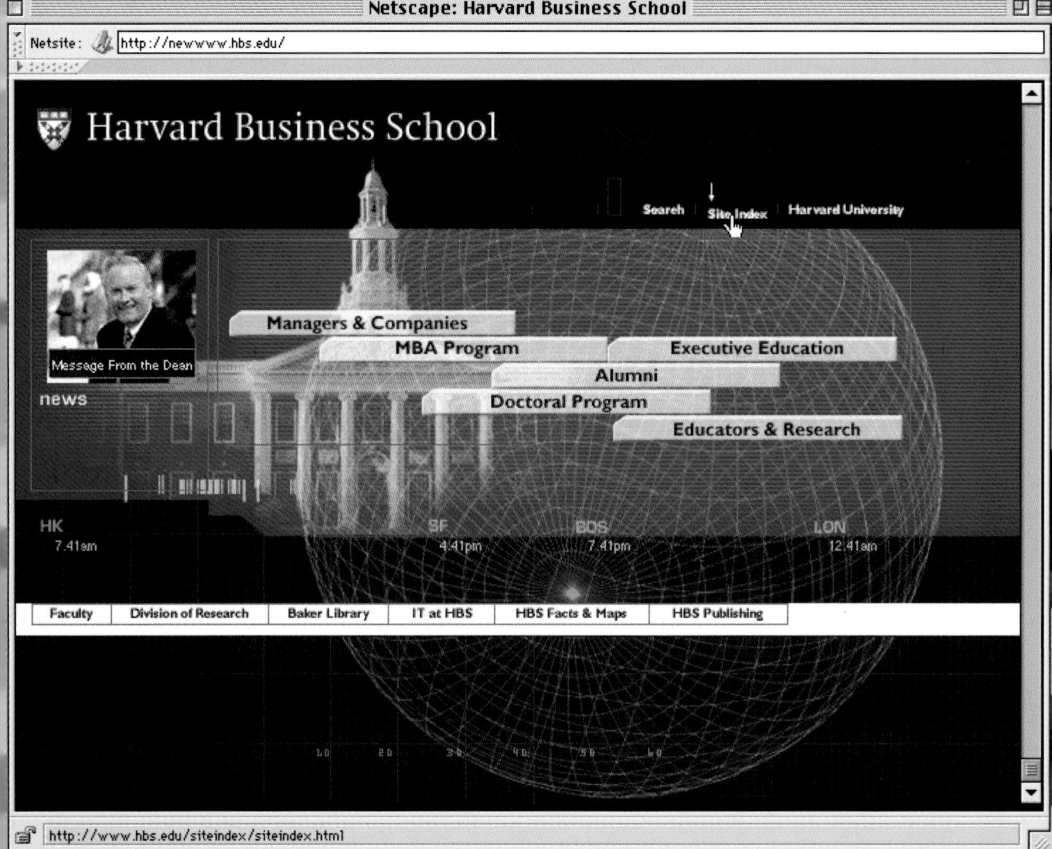

Netscape: Harvard Business School
Netsite: http://newwww.hbs.edu/
Harvard Business School
Search
Site Index
Harvard University
Managers & Companies
MBA Program
Executive Education
Alumni
Doctoral Program
Educators & Research
Message From the Dean
news
HK
7.41am
SF
4.41pm
BOS
7.41pm
LON
12.41am
Faculty
Division of Research
Baker Library
IT at HBS
HBS Facts & Maps
HBS Publishing
http://www.hbs.edu/siteindex/siteindex.html

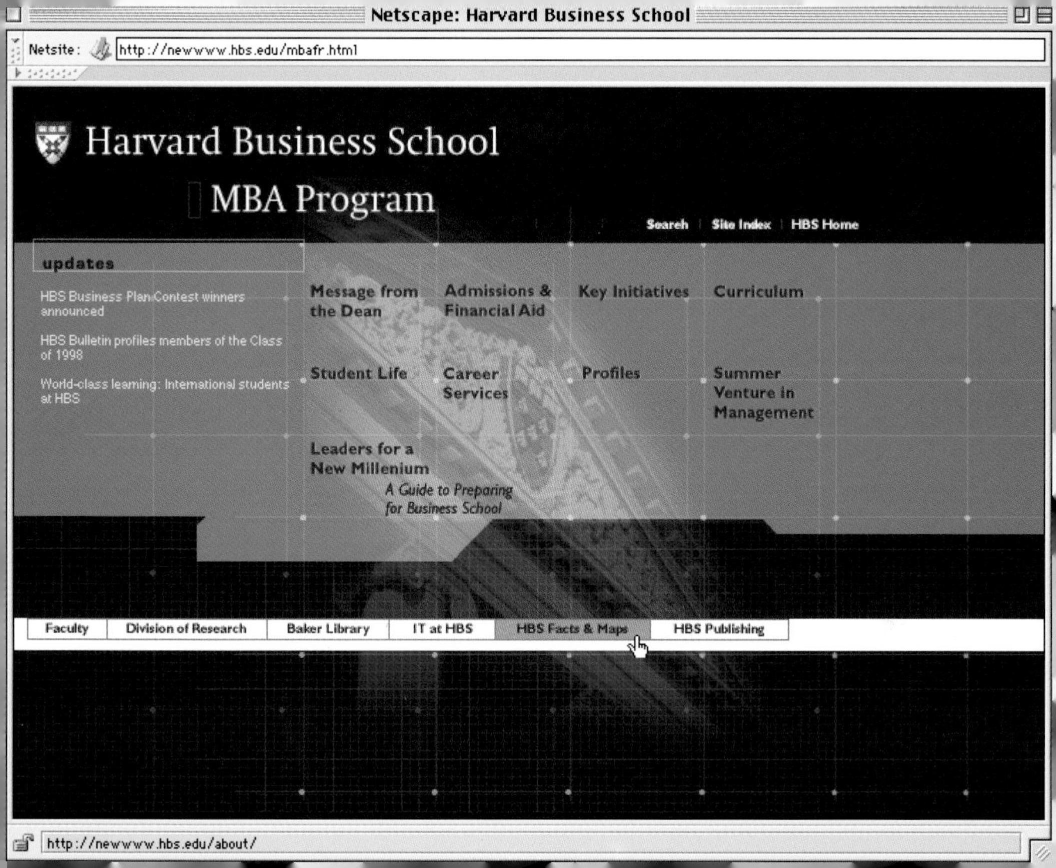

Netscape: Harvard Business School
Netsite: http://newwww.hbs.edu/mbafr.html
Harvard Business School
MBA Program
Search | Site Index | HBS Home
updates
HBS Business Plan Contest winners announced
HBS Bulletin profiles members of the Class of 1998
World-class learning: International students at HBS
Message from the Dean
Admissions & Financial Aid
Key Initiatives
Curriculum
Student Life
Career Services
Profiles
Summer Venture in Management
Leaders for a New Millenium
A Guide to Preparing for Business School
Faculty
Division of Research
Baker Library
IT at HBS
HBS Facts & Maps
HBS Publishing
http://newwww.hbs.edu/about/

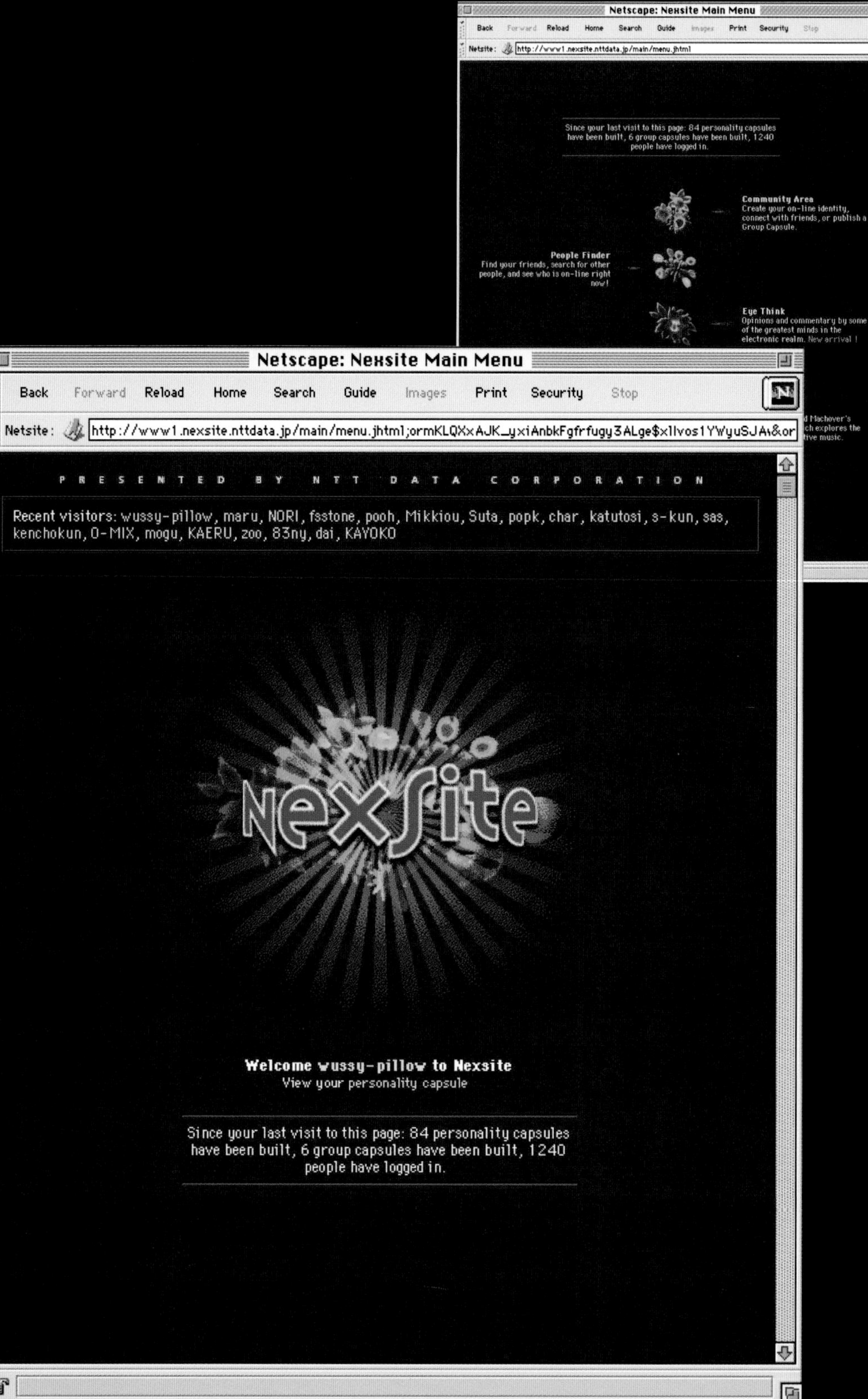

Netscape: Nexsite Main Menu
Back
Forward
Reload
Home
Search
Guide
Images
Print
Security
Stop
Netsite: http://www1.nexsite.nttdata.jp/main/menu.jhtml
Since your last visit to this page: 84 personality capsules have been built, 6 group capsules have been built, 1240 people have logged in.
Community Area
Create your on-line identity, connect with friends, or publish a Group Capsule.
People Finder
Find your friends, search for other people, and see who is on-line right now!
Eye Think
Opinions and commentary by some of the greatest minds in the electronic realm. New arrival !
Netscape: Nexsite Main Menu
Back
Forward
Reload
Home
Search
Guide
Images
Print
Security
Stop
Netsite: http://www1.nexsite.nttdata.jp/main/menu.jhtml;ormKLQXxAJK_yxiAnbkFgfrfugy3ALge$xIlvos1YWyuSJAv&or
PRESENTED BY NTT DATA CORPORATION
Recent visitors: wussy-pillow, maru, NORI, fsstone, pooh, Mikkiou, Suta, popk, char, katutosi, s-kun, sas, kenchokun, O-MIX, mogu, KAERU, zoo, 83ny, dai, KAYOKO
nexsite
Welcome wussy-pillow to Nexsite
View your personality capsule
Since your last visit to this page: 84 personality capsules have been built, 6 group capsules have been built, 1240 people have logged in.

Site description
NTT DATA Corporation, Japan's largest ISP, commissioned Art Technology Group to create an experimental communications and entertainment site for the Internet World Expo in Tokyo. To introduce people to a new range of possibilities in communications and collaboration on the Internet, NTT DATA needed to demonstrate the Web's full potential for people to engage and exchange ideas with others. The goal of the project was to create a self-sustaining community which would grow from a set of tools for community-building and collaborative publishing. Nexsite quickly became a thriving online Web community where users easily exchanged opinions and news through their individual or group capsules.

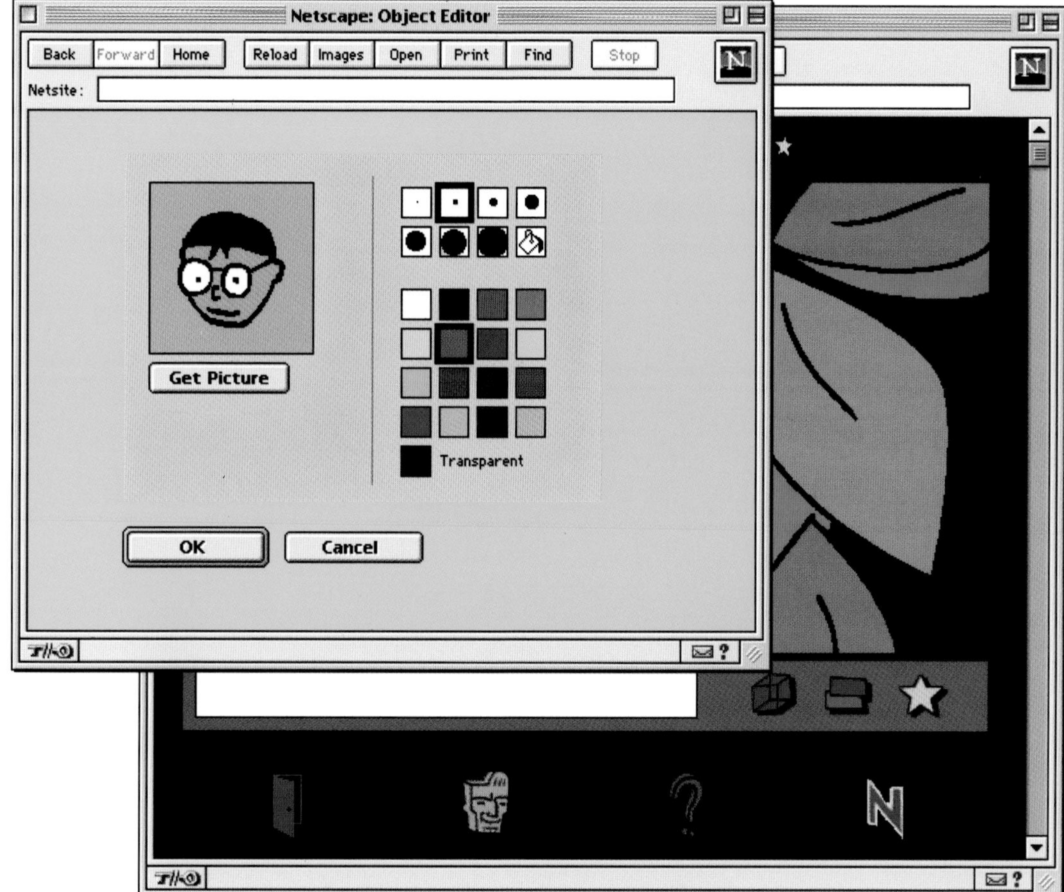

www.nexsite.nttdata.jp
(this and following spread)
Client: NTT DATA
Designers: Michael Dziedzic, Chris Edwards, Margot Howard
Technical team: Nathan Abramson, Geech, Andy Hong, Lizanne Inafuku, Bob Mason, Ellen Walsh
Project manager: Fumi Matsumoto

version 4.0

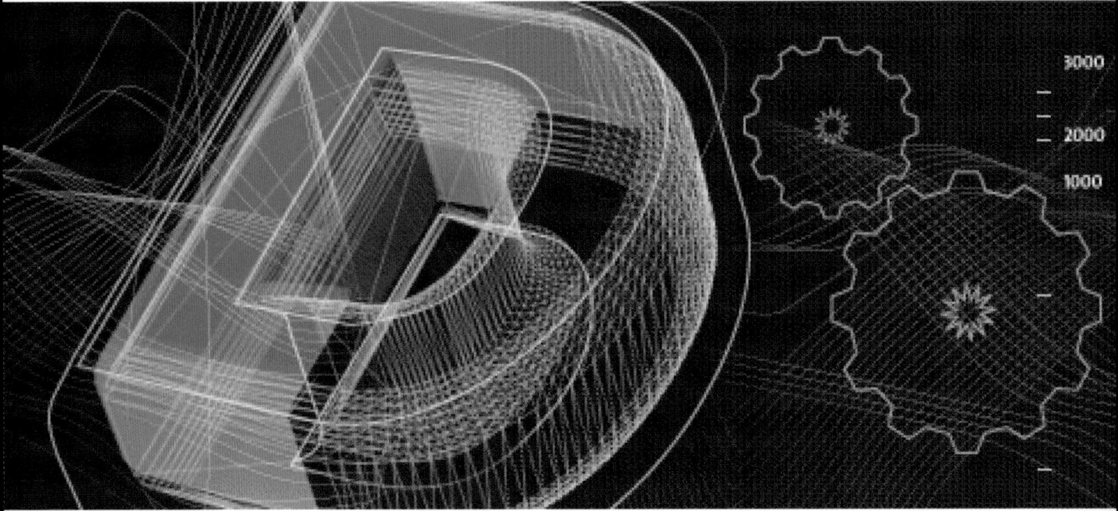

3000

2000

1000

Dynamo Personalization Control Center

Dynamo 4 Web Software
(opposite and this page, bottom)
Client: Art Technology Group
Designers: Doug Follette, Robin Kullberg, Alice Meade, George Plesko. Technical: Nathan Abramson, Stephen Abramson, Joe Berkowitz, Lawrence Byng, Nat Cohen, Peter Eddy, Jim Frost, Dan Guilderson, Craig Johnson, Tareef Kawaf, Michael Keirnan, Matt Landau, Bob Mason, Lew Miller, Sue Parrish, Allan Scott, Tim Walsh, Jeff Vroom
Project manager: Ina Sipser
Documentation: Paul Barrow, Kim Evans, Grant Goodman, Nancy Lee, Amy Sklivas

Site description
Dynamo is the brand for the suite of Web development software we engineer and sell commercially. With it our customers can develop highly personalized Internet applications. Building a complex website necessitates the efforts of disparate groups (developers/designers/business managers) whose different skills, language and culture and technologies must somehow come together to form one seamless web experience.

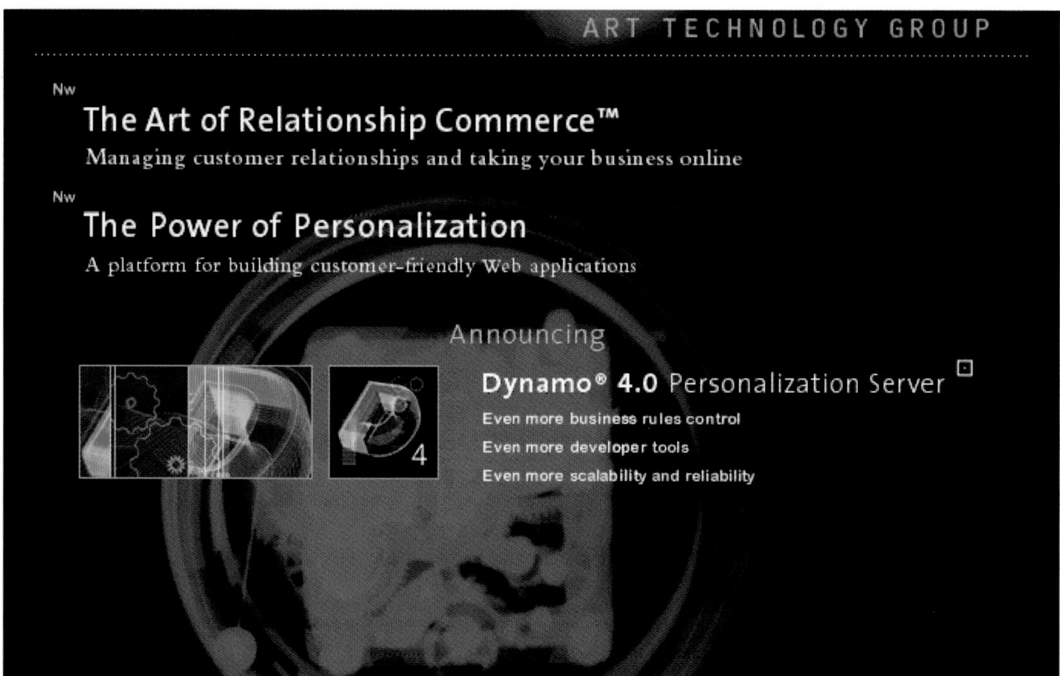

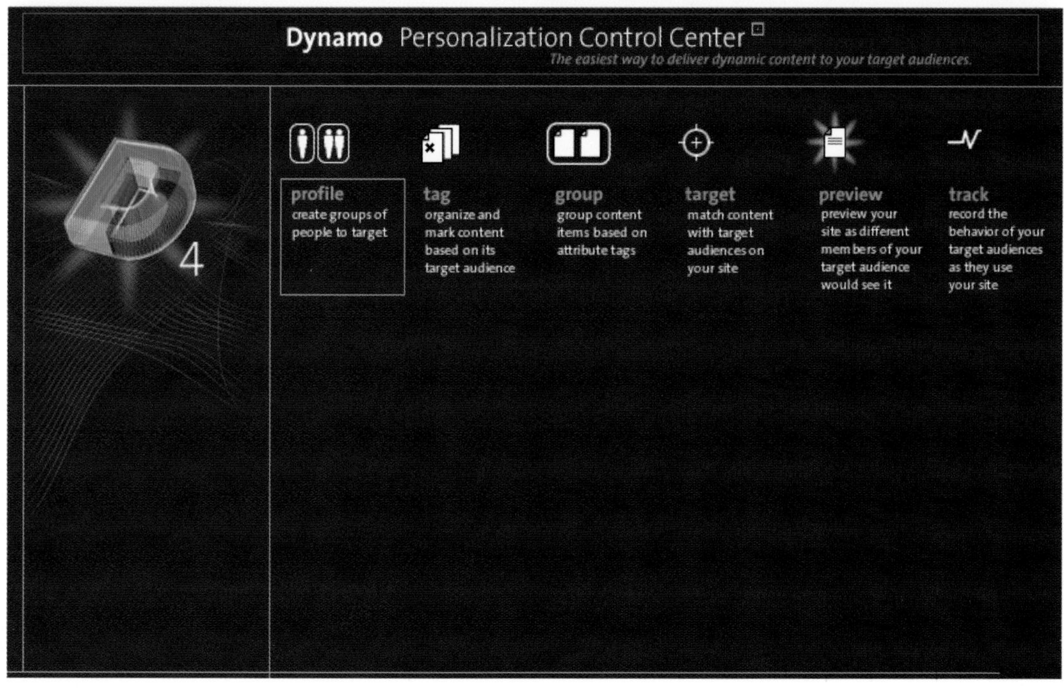

www.atg.com
(this page, top)
Client: Art Technology Group
Designers: Mary Brody, Gregg Foster, Adam Landau, Anukam Edward Opara, Lisa Wist
Technical team: Steven Abramson, Charles Morehead, Janis Stipins
Project managers: Erin Staudt, Dave Steuer

Site description
Our website, www.atg.com, is our primary tool for managing relationships with our customers. We use it to market, distribute and support our products and services. In designing our site, we wanted to communicate ATG's clarity of vision and know-how, our ability to see through the complexity of technology to the fundamental essence of a problem. We did this by combining imagery and typography that "exposes" the internal ethos of Art Technology Group. Luminous x-ray images and textual icons create an immediate sense that one is peering into the inner workings of our company while conveying ATG's unafraid, confident approach. The choice of imagery and typography also denotes a significant differentiation from competitor sites, which tend to be very corporate.

bbkstudio/

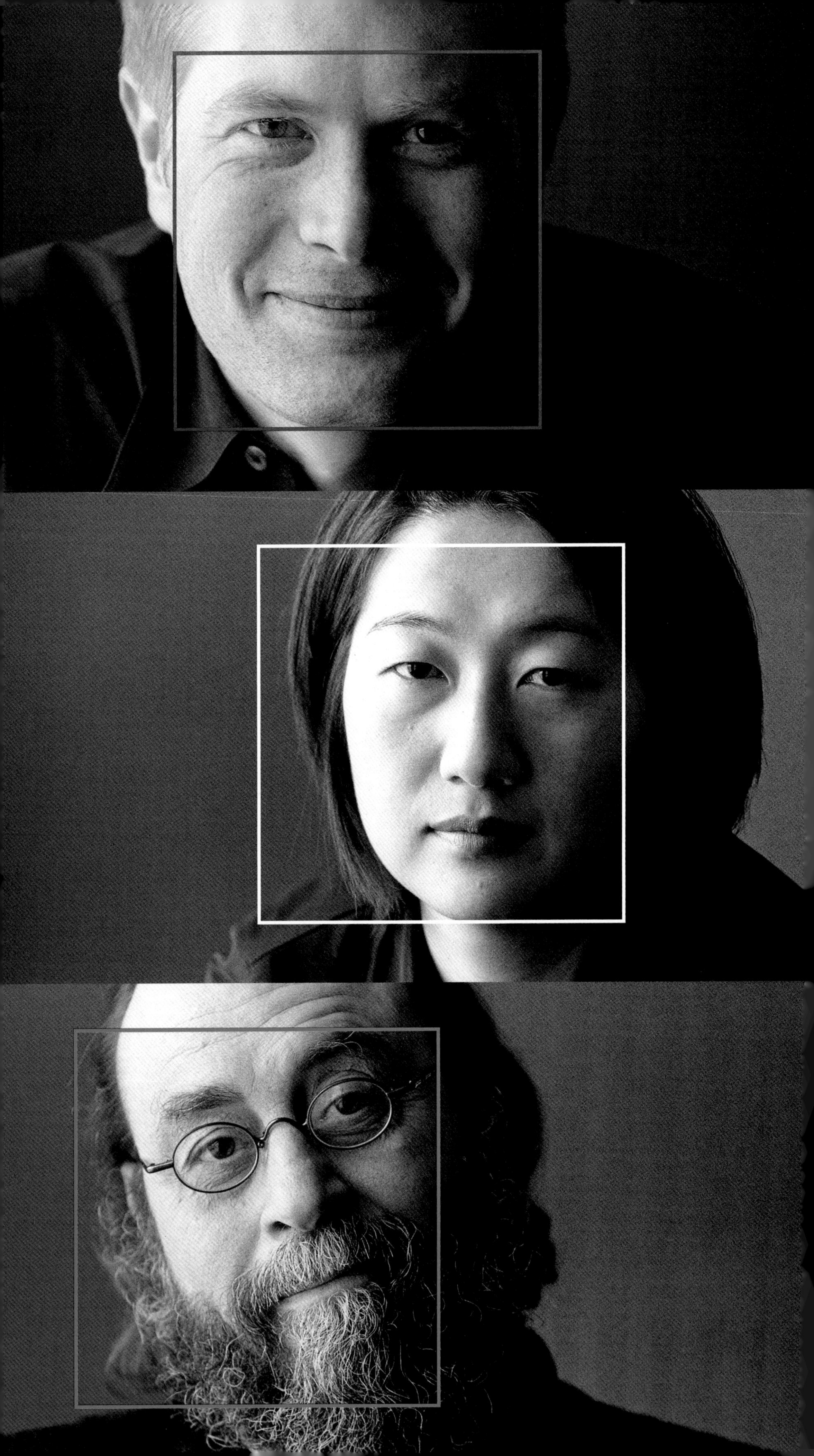

BBK Studio

Design is a way of making sense of things—of a message, of a process, of a dashboard, of one's universe. The good cup of joe, the easily navigated Web site, and the clear tax form all demonstrate that, at its best, design is invisible. It's also powerful. That's the philosophy of BBK Studio, a Grand Rapids, Michigan, firm founded in 1997. The rapidly growing firm is becoming known for its use of graphic design to clarify messages and advance business and culture. BBK believes that the power of design lies in its ability to create emotive and memorable experiences that change the way people think and act. Quite simply, good design shows up on the bottom line.

Partners Michael Barile, Kevin Budelmann, and Yang Kim met at Herman Miller, Inc., which was fertile ground for the formation of their philosophy. Their goal is to produce quality work that helps their clients and their clients' customers make sense of information. Their design sensibility and understanding of business challenges sometimes lead to ask the client to take a step back and look at the problem in a larger context.

That holistic approach to clients' communications needs is becoming increasingly important as clients begin to use interactive design. BBK's entry into interactive design was immediate, the result of the principals' interest in the relationship between the message and technology.

In fact, much of the firm's growth has been in the area of Internet, extranet, and intranet site development for clients who understand that integrating design and technology can help them gain a competitive edge. Those clients include Grand Valley State University, The Greystone Company, Herman Miller, and VMF Capital.

While experiencing growth in new media, the firm's foundation is print design. The principals have more than 30 years of combined experience in print pieces, including annual reports, capabilities brochures, newspaper and magazine ads, and posters. Their work has repeatedly won awards, including all those sponsored by the major design publications.

Currently BBK Studio offers graphic design, interface design, illustration, communications consultation, information architecture, and branding and identity consulting services. The firm intends to continue to seek out interesting work in traditional and new media.

Origins
When started: January 1997
Number of employees when founded: 3
Number of employees now: 13
Headquarters:
Grand Rapids, Michigan

Principals
Michael Barile,
Kevin Budelmann, Yang Kim

Contact
5242 Plainfield Ave NE,
Grand Rapids, MI 49525
Tel: 616. 447 1460
Fax: 616. 447 1461
E-mail: yang@bbkstudio.com
Web: www.bbkstudio.com

BBK Studio site prototype
Client: BBK Studio
Creative Director, Art Director, Designer, Writer: Kevin Budelmann
Photography: Bill Gallery

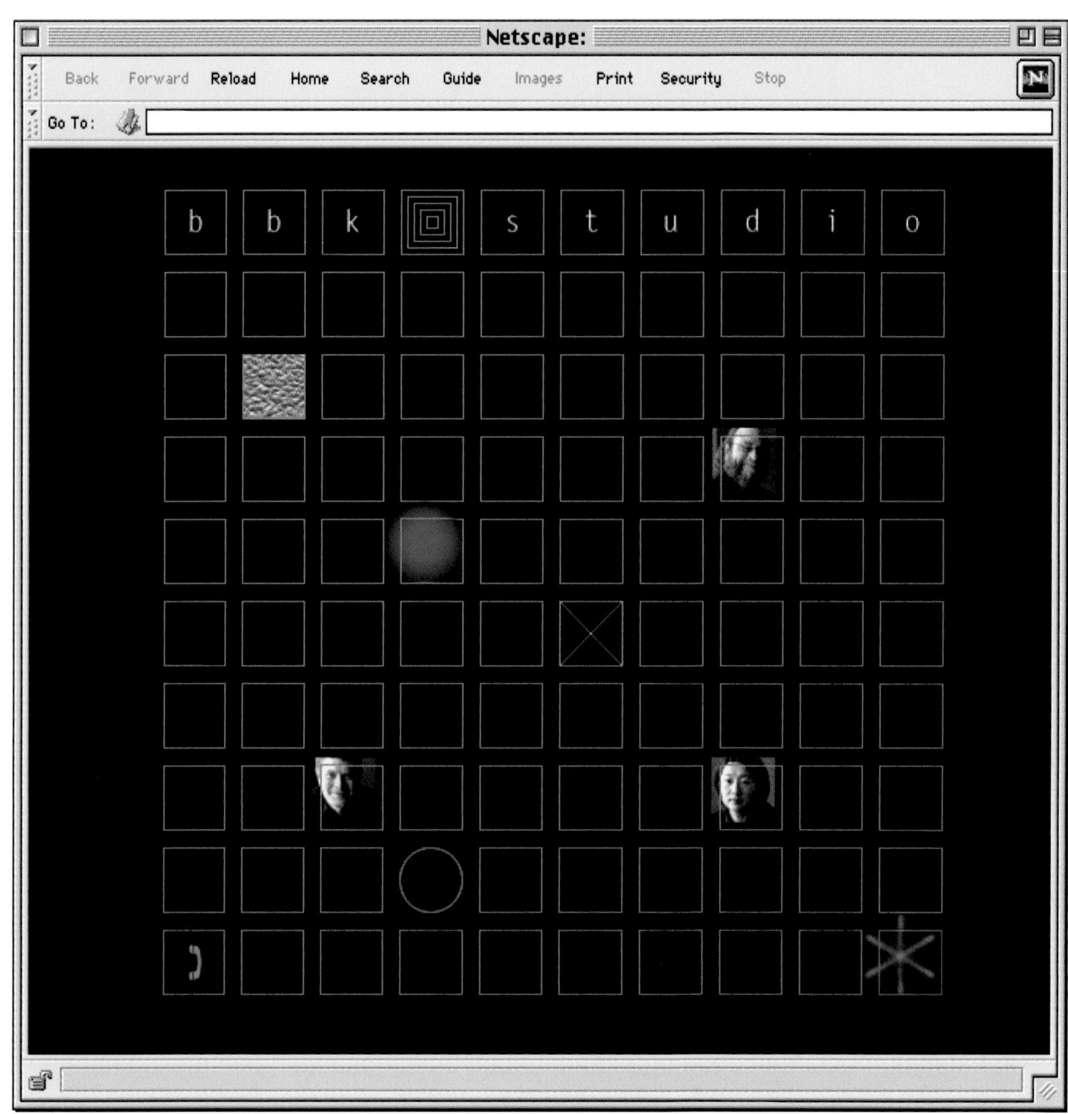

Netscape:
Back
Forward
Reload
Home
Search
Guide
Images
Print
Security
Stop
Go To:
We strongly believes in a collaborative, interdisciplinary approach to solving design problems Our team is our most important asset.
Heather Jensen, Office Manager
Kelly J. Schwartz, Senior Designer
Alison Popp, Designer
Steven Joswick, Junior Designer
Matt Ryzenga, Junior Designer
Leah Weston, New Media Producer
Michael Carnevale, New Media Designer Jeff Sikkema, New Media Developer
Scott Krieger, New Media Developer
Von Neel, New Media Developer
Michael Barile, Principal
Kevin Budelmann, Principal
Yang Kim, Principal

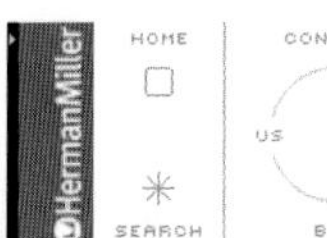

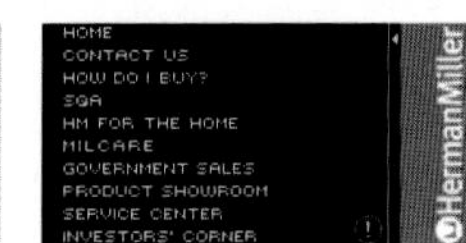

www.hermanmiller.com
Client: Herman Miller
Creative Director, Art Director: Kevin Budelmann
Designers: Kevin Budelmann, Alison Popp, Yang Kim, Steven Joswick, Matt Ryzenga
Editor: Julie Ridl. Producer: Leah Weston. Coding: Scott Kreiger, Jeff Sikkema.

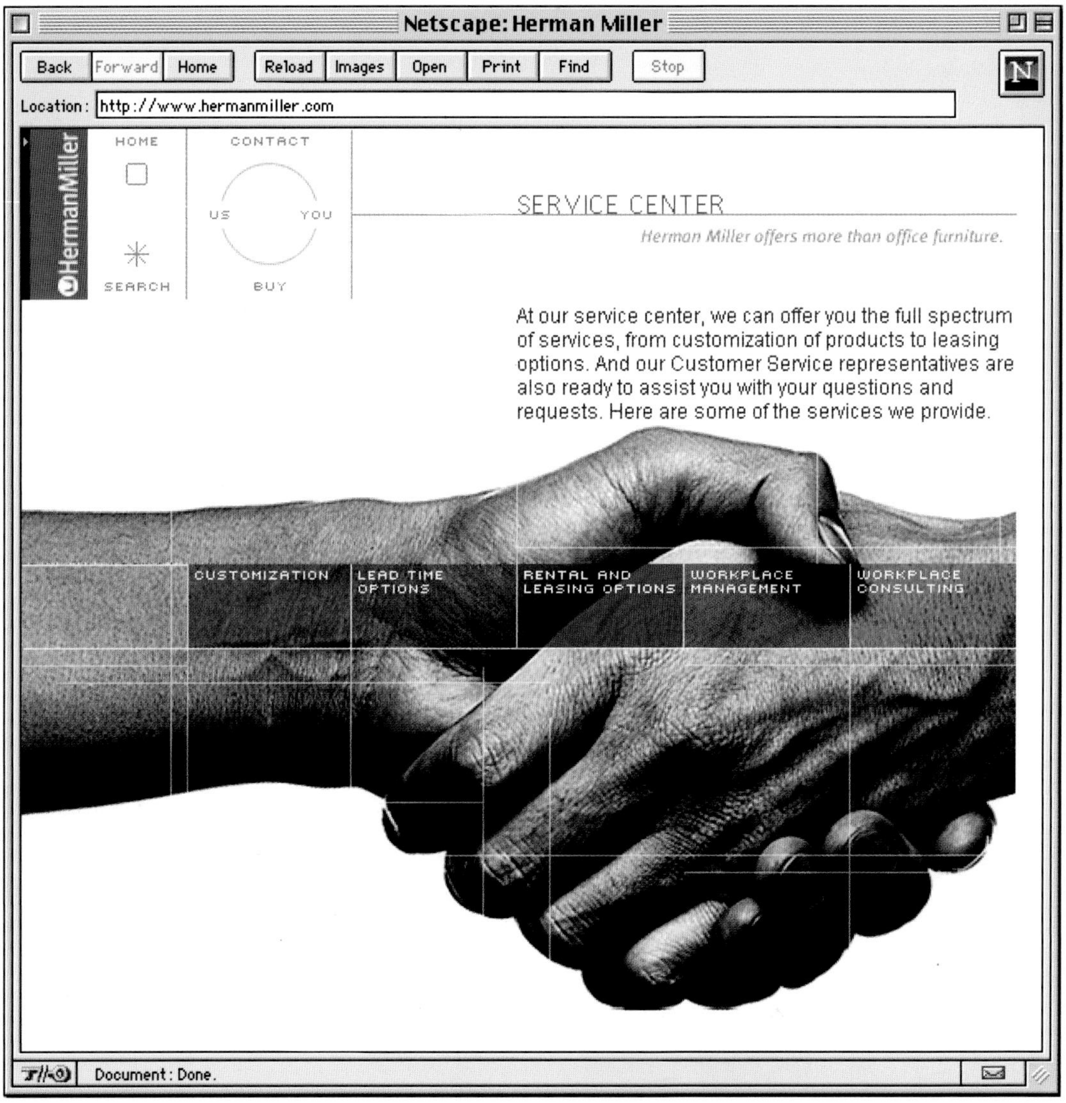

Site description
Herman Miller's Internet site started four years ago as a small, back-room project as a way to establish the furniture company's initial brand presence on the web. Members of BBK Studio have been involved in the website's evolution from the start. During phase two, the site grew to more than 1,500 pages, serving many purposes and providing information about the company's history and philosophy, current products, services, investor relations, product research, and worldwide dealer, retailer, and corporate locations listings. Phase three, shown here, incorporates a new identity, global navigation, and aesthetic. BBK Studio has helped Herman Miller increase the technological and aesthetic sophistication of the site, and paved the way for future site development.

Netscape: Herman Miller
Back
Forward
Home
Reload
Images
Open
Print
Find
Stop
Location: http://www.hermanmiller.com
HermanMiller
HOME
CONTACT
US
YOU
SEARCH
BUY
PRODUCT SHOWROOM
THE DETAILS ARE NOT DETAILS. THEY MAKE THE PRODUCT.
— CHARLES EAMES
CASE STUDIES: PRODUCT APPLICATION
CMF: COLORS, MATERIALS, FINISHES
CALL CENTER APPLICATIONS
GOVERNMENT SALES
CAD PACK SYMBOL LIBRARY
PRODUCT WARRANTY
SEATING
MACHINES FOR SITTING
SYSTEMS
MODULAR FURNITURE
FREESTANDING
FURNITURE THAT MOVES
STORAGE
PUT THINGS AWAY
HOME OFFICE
FURNITURE THAT FITS RIGHT IN
ACCENTS
TOOLS FOR COMFORT AND PERFORMANCE
HEALTHCARE
CLINICAL AND ADMINISTRATIVE FURNITURE
CLASSIC DESIGNS
MODERN FURNITURE ICONS
HermanMillerStore
Don't wait. Buy it online — right now.
Short Cuts
Document: Done.
Netscape: Herman Miller
Back
Forward
Home
Reload
Images
Open
Print
Find
Stop
Location: http://www.hermanmiller.com
HOME
CONTACT US
HOW DO I BUY?
FAQ
HM FOR THE HOME
MILCARE
GOVERNMENT SALES
PRODUCT SHOWROOM
SERVICE CENTER
INVESTORS' CORNER
HermanMiller
ON DESIGN
Back in the 40s, when modern furnit was gaining acceptance, D.J. DePree wrote: "Very often we hear sa esmen stressing the point that Modern furniture is different, as though that were the reason for buying it. Charles Eames says: 'It was never my d ign objective that the furniture be different or novel; only that it be good sit in, good to use, good to look at, and easy for everyone to buy." That is still our design objective today.
Products as art
Throughout t ears of design innovations, the design community has acknowledged Herman Miller's leadership position. Several of Herman Miller's designs are in the permanent collections of major museums, including New York's Museum of Modern Art, the Whitney Museum, and the Smithsonian Ins tion.
The Edsel Ford Design History Center at Henry Ford Museum and Greenfield Village in Dearborn, Michigan, has an extensive collection of Herman Miller furniture, which includes representative product lines and furniture prototypes that exemplify the design history of Herman Miller.
Document: Done.

www.hermanmiller.com/products/freestanding/passage/
(this page)
Client: Herman Miller
Creative Director, Art Director, Designer: Kevin Budelmann
Illustrator: Mark Schlutt
Photographer: Nick Merrick
Editor: Julie Ridl
Writer: Kate Convissor
Coding: Jeff Sikkema, Leah Weston

Site description:
BBK Studio developed this site as part of the promotional launch of Herman Miller's new Passage product line. The site features new photography, product features, and animated illustrations that demonstrate the aesthetics and quality of the furniture, along with detailed descriptions of each piece's dimensions and functions.

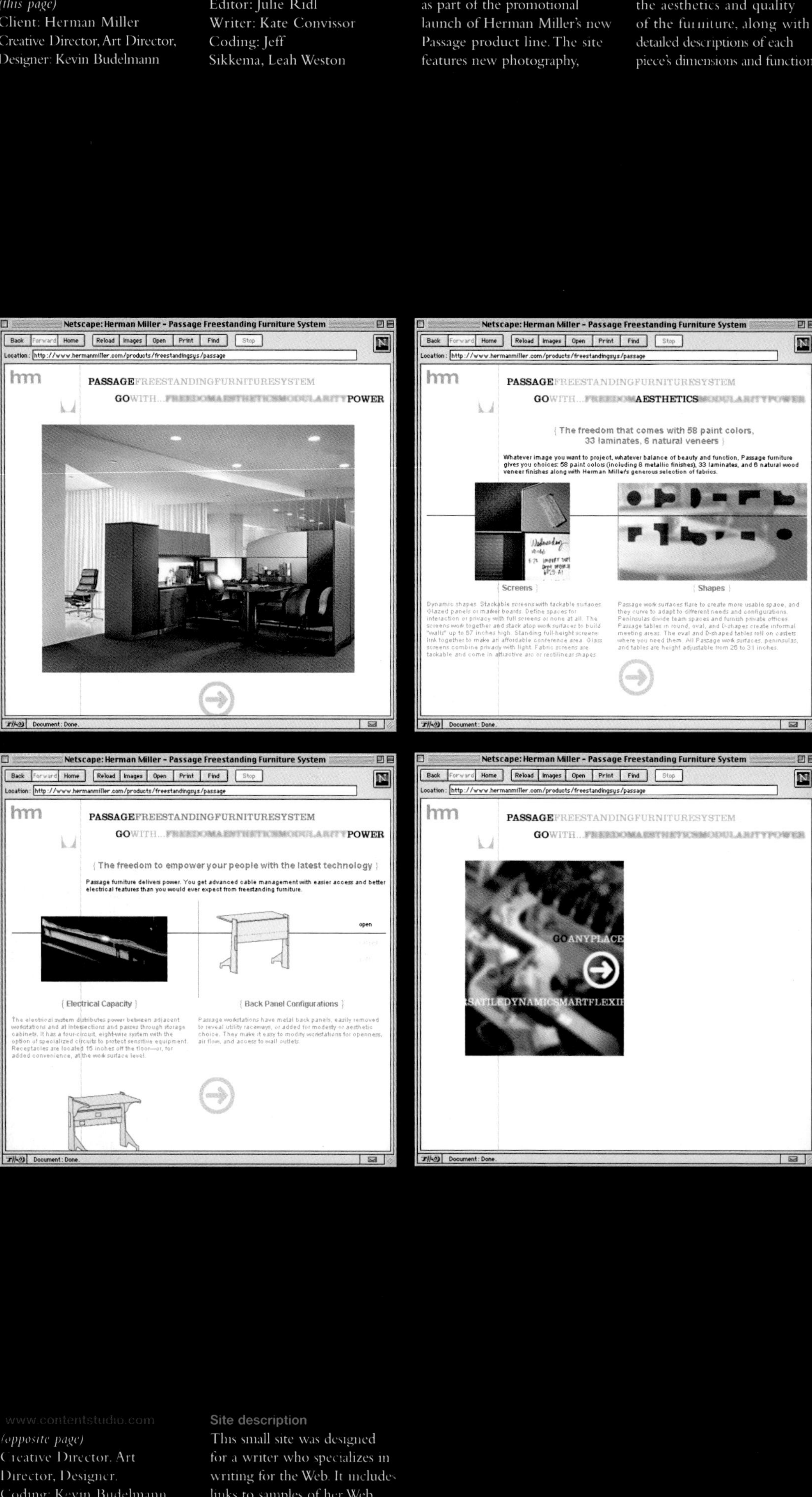

www.contentstudio.com
(opposite page)
Creative Director, Art Director, Designer, Coding: Kevin Budelmann
Writer, Client: Christine MacLean

Site description
This small site was designed for a writer who specializes in writing for the Web. It includes links to samples of her Web writing, as well as several samples for print publications

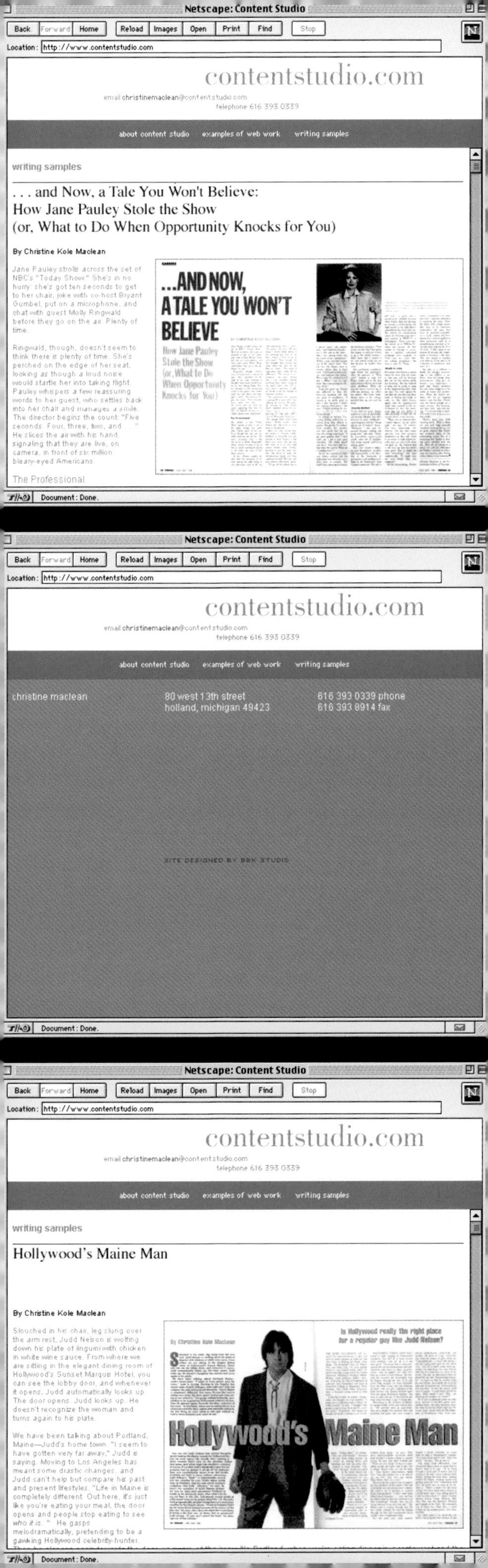

Netscape: Content Studio
Back Forward Home Reload Images Open Print Find Stop
Location: http://www.contentstudio.com
contentstudio.com
email christinemaclean@contentstudio.com
telephone 616 393 0339
about content studio examples of web work writing samples
writing samples
. . . and Now, a Tale You Won't Believe:
How Jane Pauley Stole the Show
(or, What to Do When Opportunity Knocks for You)
By Christine Kole Maclean
Jane Pauley strolls across the set of NBC's "Today Show." She's in no hurry: she's got ten seconds to get to her chair, joke with co-host Bryant Gumbel, put on a microphone, and chat with guest Molly Ringwald before they go on the air. Plenty of time.
Ringwald, though, doesn't seem to think there is plenty of time. She's perched on the edge of her seat, looking as though a loud noise would startle her into taking flight. Pauley whispers a few reassuring words to her guest, who settles back into her chair and manages a smile. The director begins the count: "Five seconds. Four, three, two, and . . ." He slices the air with his hand, signaling that they are live, on camera, in front of six million bleary-eyed Americans.
...AND NOW, A TALE YOU WON'T BELIEVE
How Jane Pauley Stole the Show (or, What to Do When Opportunity Knocks for You)
The Professional
Document: Done.
Netscape: Content Studio
Back Forward Home Reload Images Open Print Find Stop
Location: http://www.contentstudio.com
contentstudio.com
email christinemaclean@contentstudio.com
telephone 616 393 0339
about content studio examples of web work writing samples
christine maclean
80 west 13th street
holland, michigan 49423
616 393 0339 phone
616 393 8914 fax
SITE DESIGNED BY BBK STUDIO
Document: Done.
Netscape: Content Studio
Back Forward Home Reload Images Open Print Find Stop
Location: http://www.contentstudio.com
contentstudio.com
email christinemaclean@contentstudio.com
telephone 616 393 0339
about content studio examples of web work writing samples
writing samples
Hollywood's Maine Man
By Christine Kole Maclean
Slouched in his chair, leg slung over the arm rest, Judd Nelson is wolfing down his plate of linguini with chicken in white wine sauce. From where we are sitting in the elegant dining room of Hollywood's Sunset Marquis Hotel, you can see the lobby door, and whenever it opens, Judd automatically looks up. The door opens. Judd looks up. He doesn't recognize the woman and turns again to his plate.
We have been talking about Portland, Maine—Judd's home town. "I seem to have gotten very far away," Judd is saying. Moving to Los Angeles has meant some drastic changes, and Judd can't help but compare his past and present lifestyles. "Life in Maine is completely different. Out here, it's just like you're eating your meal, the door opens and people stop eating to see who it is." He gasps melodramatically, pretending to be a gawking Hollywood celebrity-hunter.
Is Hollywood really the right place for a regular guy like Judd Nelson?
By Christine Kole Maclean
Hollywood's Maine Man
Document: Done.

Site description

Herman Miller's retailing effort, Herman Miller for the Home, wanted to establish a Web presence that was independent from the parent company. BBK Studio, who developed the division's print collateral and identity, designed this online version of their printed catalog. The site includes information about their classic furniture designs, home office furniture, ergonomic chairs, retailers, product designers, and links to the corporate online store. Its unique horizontal navigation and design suggests a walking tour through a real product showroom or exhibition space.

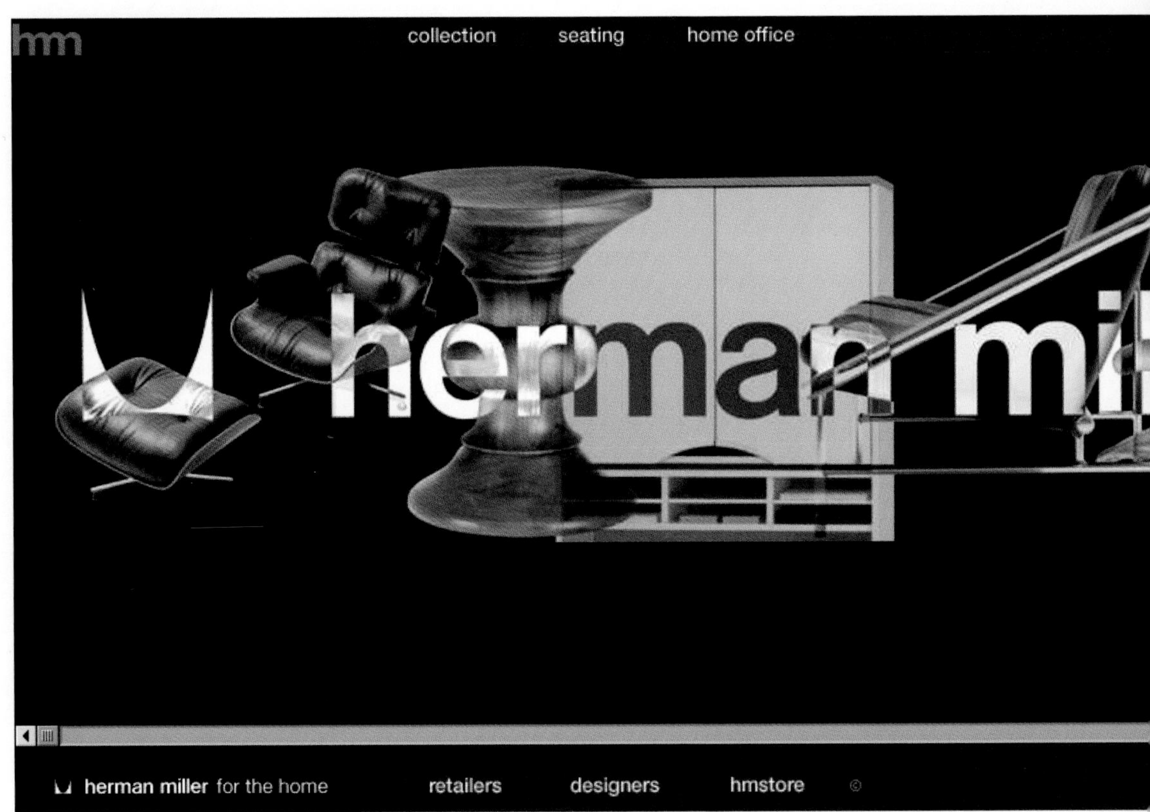

www.hmhome.com
(this and following spread)
Client: Herman Miller
Creative Director, Art Director: Kevin Budelmann
Designers: Kevin Budelmann, Alison Popp
Illustrator: Steven Joswick
Editor: Julie Ridl
Coding: Jeff Sikkema

Netscape: Herman Miller for the Home
Back Forward Reload Home Search Guide Images Print Security Stop
Go To: http://www.hmhome.com/
hm
collection seating home office
We wanted to synthesize the aesthetic elegance of Eames chairs and the comfort of Ergon chairs.
Bill Stumpf
herman miller for the home
retailers designers hmstore

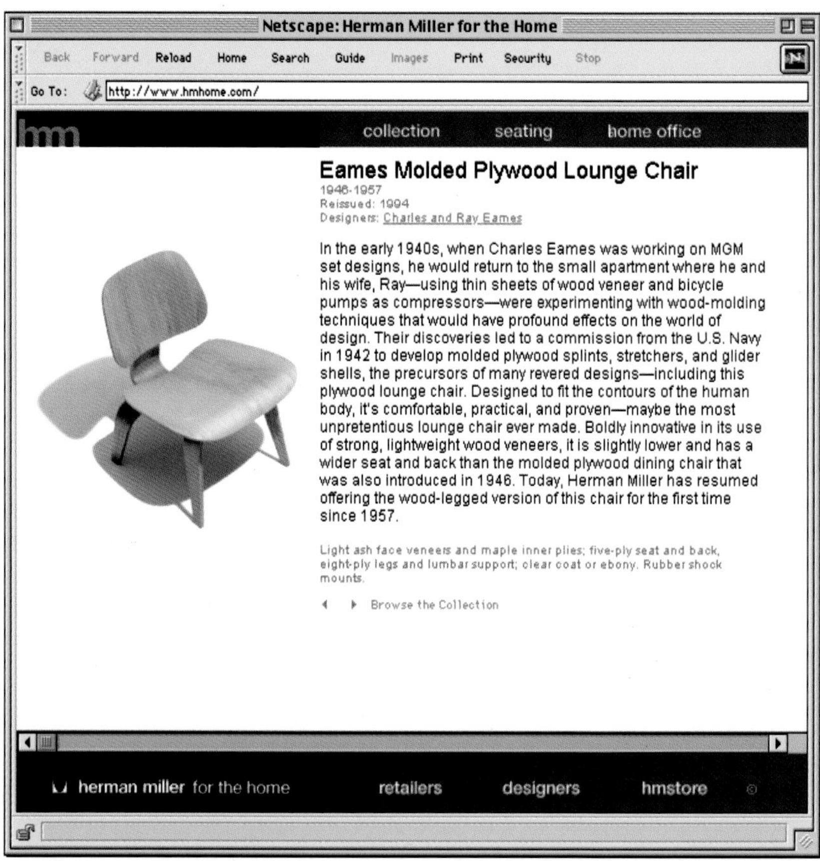
Netscape: Herman Miller for the Home
Back Forward Reload Home Search Guide Images Print Security Stop
Go To: http://www.hmhome.com/
hm
collection seating home office
Eames Molded Plywood Lounge Chair
1946-1957
Reissued: 1994
Designers: Charles and Ray Eames
In the early 1940s, when Charles Eames was working on MGM set designs, he would return to the small apartment where he and his wife, Ray—using thin sheets of wood veneer and bicycle pumps as compressors—were experimenting with wood-molding techniques that would have profound effects on the world of design. Their discoveries led to a commission from the U.S. Navy in 1942 to develop molded plywood splints, stretchers, and glider shells, the precursors of many revered designs—including this plywood lounge chair. Designed to fit the contours of the human body, it's comfortable, practical, and proven—maybe the most unpretentious lounge chair ever made. Boldly innovative in its use of strong, lightweight wood veneers, it is slightly lower and has a wider seat and back than the molded plywood dining chair that was also introduced in 1946. Today, Herman Miller has resumed offering the wood-legged version of this chair for the first time since 1957.
Light ash face veneers and maple inner plies; five-ply seat and back, eight-ply legs and lumbar support; clear coat or ebony. Rubber shock mounts.
Browse the Collection
herman miller for the home
retailers designers hmstore

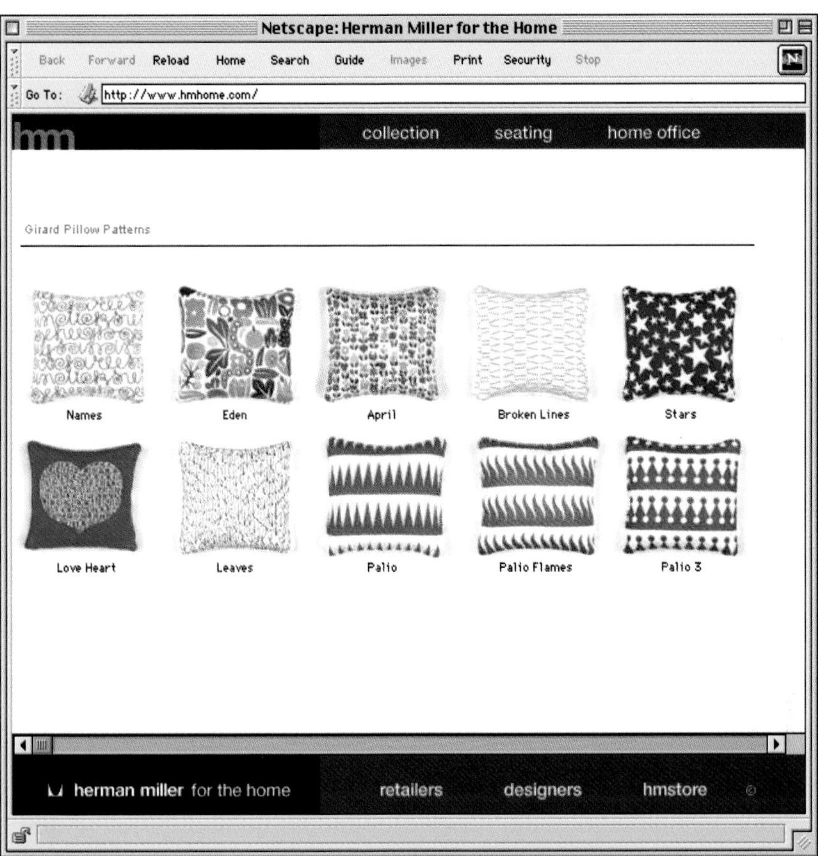
Netscape: Herman Miller for the Home
Back Forward Reload Home Search Guide Images Print Security Stop
Go To: http://www.hmhome.com/
hm
collection seating home office
Girard Pillow Patterns
Names
Eden
April
Broken Lines
Stars
Love Heart
Leaves
Palio
Palio Flames
Palio 3
herman miller for the home
retailers designers hmstore

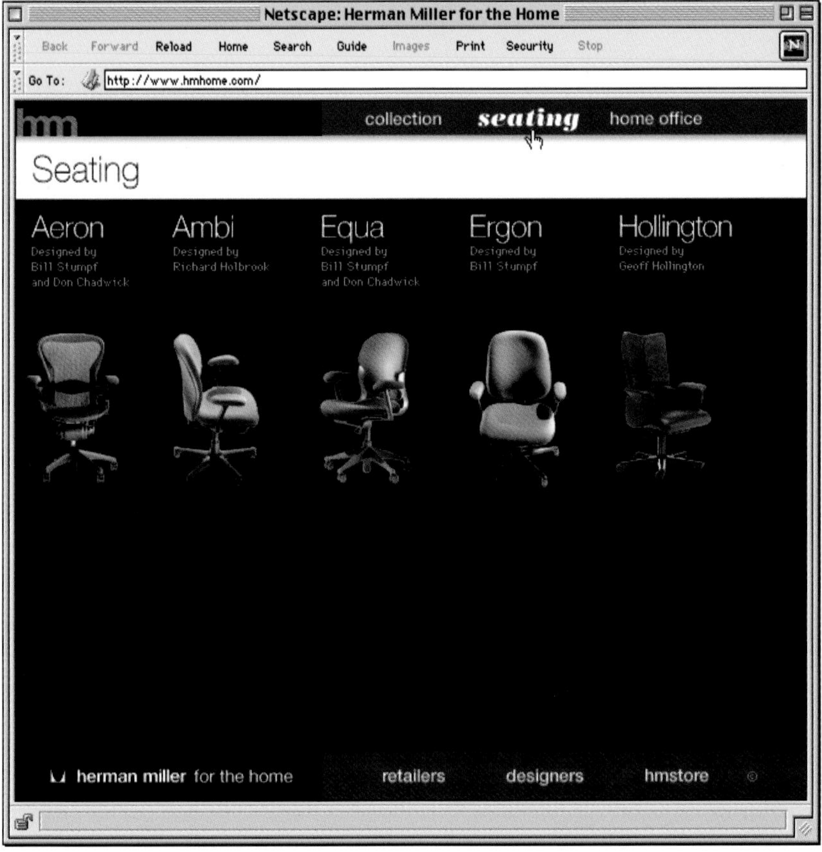
Netscape: Herman Miller for the Home
Back Forward Reload Home Search Guide Images Print Security Stop
Go To: http://www.hmhome.com/
hm
collection seating home office
Seating
Aeron
Designed by
Bill Stumpf
and Don Chadwick
Ambi
Designed by
Richard Holbrook
Equa
Designed by
Bill Stumpf
and Don Chadwick
Ergon
Designed by
Bill Stumpf
Hollington
Designed by
Geoff Hollington
herman miller for the home
retailers designers hmstore

Site description

VMF Capital, formerly AEGON USA Investment Management, is an Iowa-based investment advisor providing portfolio management services for high-net-worth individuals. This site helped launch the new company and identity (also developed by BBK). Since this type of investing is dependent on the character and expertise of the fund managers, we designed the site to highlight the group's personality. Individuals were photographed and interviewed in a personal fashion to make clients feel comfortable and get to know the people of VMF.

www.vmfcapital.com

Client: VMF Capital
Creative Director, Art Director: Kevin Budelmann
Designers: Kevin Budelmann, Alison Popp
Photographer: Bill Gallery
Writer: Christine MacLean
Coding: Jeff Sikkema

Netscape: Herman Miller - NeoCon 98
Back Forward Home Reload Images Open Print Find Stop
Location: http://www.hermanmiller.com/neocon/
hm
NeoCon 1998
Designers' Views
Choices
Designers
Products
Press Room
Show Room
Bill Stumpf
Herman Miller has a long tradition of design excellence. Much of it comes from our unique relationship with the world's foremost designers. Select any designer's photo from the gallery at the top of your screen to learn more about them and the role they've played in NeoCon 98.
Document: Done.
Netscape: Herman Miller - NeoCon 98
Back Forward Home Reload Images Open Print Find Stop
Location: http://www.hermanmiller.com/neocon/
hm
NeoCon 1998
New Products and Capabilities
Choices
Designers
Products
Press Room
Show Room
Acrobat suite
Aeron side chair
Ambi side chair
Aside chair
CLT tables
Colors, Materials, and Finishes (CMF) program
Herman Miller Accents collection
Passage freestanding systems furniture
Puzzle mobile office
Reaction work chair
Preview: Eric Chan design
Preview: Lovegrove and Peart design
Enhancements
Tailored Solutions capability
Document: Done.
Netscape: Herman Miller - NeoCon 98
Back Forward Home Reload Images Open Print Find Stop
Location: http://www.hermanmiller.com/neocon/
hm
NeoCon 1998
Freedom to Choose
Choices
Designers
Products
Press Room
Show Room
Freedom of Expression
Freedom of Choice
Freedom of Movement
Freedom from Worry
Herman Miller Supports Freedom of Movement for feet, legs, arms, wrists, ischial tuberosities, keyboards, monitors, task lighting, computer peripherals, mice, teams, groups, committees, departments, organizations, telecommuters, job-sharers, consultants, nomads, temps, and ideas on screens, disks, whiteboards, and greasy paper napkins.
Freedom of Movement
When it comes to health and productivity in the office workplace, our philosophy is: Keep moving. Study after ergonomic study documents the benefits of movement to people who work in sedentary jobs. Changes in sitting postures improve circulation and reduce discomfort in legs and feet. Moving between sitting and standing at work relieves loading on the spine and reduces disc compression that can lead to back pain. Small adjustments of keyboard height or mouse positioning or monitor placement can help to prevent musculoskeletal injuries, eyestrain, and other discomforts associated with computer work.
Movement is increasingly vital to organizational health as well. Companies need to be agile and responsive to changing business conditions and opportunities. They need physical environments that enable the rapid forming and deployment of cross-functional teams and other collaborative work groups. They need fluid and stimulating workplaces that enhance the flow and exchange of information and ideas.
Herman Miller products embody the ergonomics of motion. We design not for the one ideal posture, the one perfect layout, but for the movement of the human and the organizational body through space and time. We design support for arms, necks, backs, thighs as they shift from one task to another, from sitting to standing, from reclining to reaching. We design
Document: Done.

BRAND A STUDIO

A
B
C

Brand A Studio

In 1997, Brand A opened for business in the heart of San Francisco's financial district. We immediately realized we'd gotten off on the wrong foot. Being way downtown wasn't the right environment for us: we missed the youthful ambience of the city's South of Market district. Our current home in a corner of the loft district that's close to the colorful Mission area is much more a part of who we are.

Brand A strives to maintain our small studio culture while offering the capabilities found at a large full-service agency. We feel we've successfully created a niche for ourselves where we can handle both small projects and large, from brand identity to print communication, through to full-scale execution on the Web.

The designers of Brand A bring to bear on all their projects a combination of training in information design with a background in traditional print media and experience in branding, skill sets that have been honed at some of San Francisco's top agencies. Since the earliest emergence of the Internet as a potent sales and marketing tool, we have viewed interactive and Web design as a critical factor in developing brands.

Now, as we move into this new Internet-driven economy and the Web is becoming a vital consumer touchpoint, we feel that designers need to start thinking about the Web at least as much as they think about any other collateral that finds its way to the consumer. Providing these new tools for businesses is something we take very seriously.

The core staff of four includes Principal and Creative Director Guthrie Dolin, business partner Jennifer Smith, and Matt Carlson and Julie Cristello as key design contributors. Although each individual brings a unique set of design and marketing experience, our common goal is to preserve a high level of quality and attention to detail in the work we do.

At Brand A, we take the view that in the field of graphic design, what we're crafting is communications. We walk the line between creating engaging visuals and purely functional pieces, a process that also lends itself to our aesthetics. Creating beautiful things with real function, and letting the functional aspect of the design become part of that aesthetic, is what we're all about.

On June 1, 1999, Brand A Studio merged with Phoenix Pop Productions, a leading San Francisco Internet services company. The merger is the ideal combination of talent, culture and shared ideology. The Brand A team brings focused branding, traditional design and marketing expertise to bolster and expand the breadth of services currently offered by Phoenix Pop. This extremely synergistic union should prove a powerful combination for consulting with the emerging businesses in our economy.

Origins
Founded: 1997
Number of employees when founded: 1
now: Approximately 50+
Headquarters: San Francisco
Parent company: Phoenix Pop Productions

Principal
Guthrie Dolin

Contact
1211 Folsom Street
San Francisco, CA 94103
Tel.: 415.934 7700
Fax: 415.934 7701
E-mail: gu3@phoenix-pop.com
Web: www.brand-a.com
and www.phoenix-pop.com

Netscape: Freebord - video
CLOSE VIEW BOX

HOME

HOW IT WORKS | WHAT THEY'RE SAYING
WATCH THE RIDE | ABOUT FREEBORD
WHERE TO GET IT | CONTACT FREEBORD

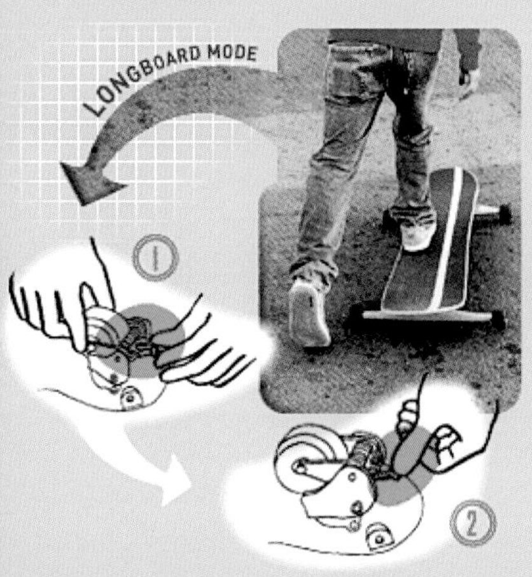

Quick-retract center wheels instantly turn Freebord into a conventional longboard.
For Longboard mode:
(1) While lifting center wheel, use thumb to disengage adjust screw.
(2) Holding adjust screw out of way, release center wheel from hand.
For Freebord mode:
Lift wheel upwards-- adjust screw automatically locks into place.

CRUISE THE FLATS

BREAKTHROUGH DESIGN
RIDE ANY HILL
CRUISE THE FLATS
ADJUSTABLE RIDE

FREEBORD

NO SNOW. COUNTING THE DAYS UNTIL THE SEASON STARTS. YOU DREAMED OF A WAY TO SNOWBOARD YEAR ROUND. WE BUILT IT.

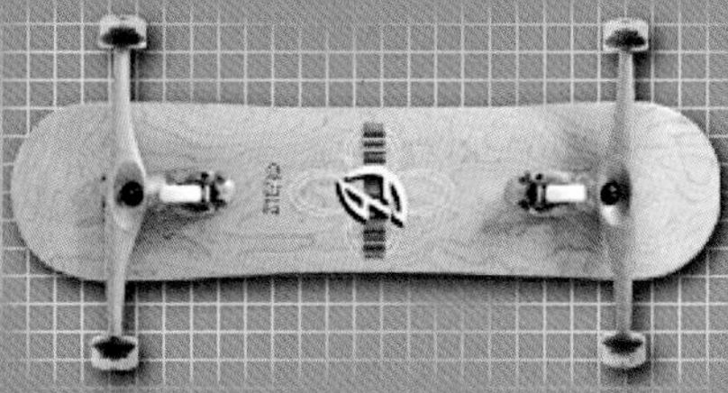

HOW IT WORKS
WATCH THE RIDE
WHAT THEY'RE SAYING
WHERE TO GET IT
ABOUT FREEBORD
CONTACT FREEBORD

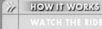

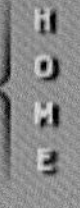

HOW IT WORKS | WHAT THEY'RE SAYING
WATCH THE RIDE | ABOUT FREEBORD
WHERE TO GET IT | CONTACT FREEBORD

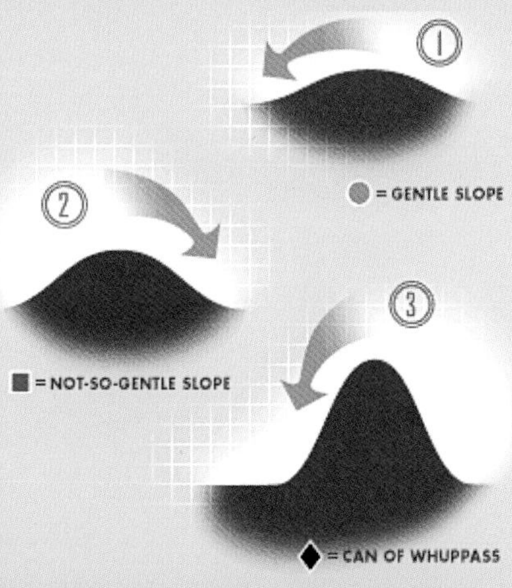

Drop speed just as you would on a snowboard. With practice, you will navigate the steepest of streets:
(1) Gentle speed control: carve your board back and forth across the fall line.
(2) Moderate speed control: rotate your board across the fall line and edge in.
(3) Aggressive speed control: rotate your board across the fall line, grab your downhill edge and lean way back.

RIDE ANY HILL

BREAKTHROUGH DESIGN
RIDE ANY HILL
CRUISE THE FLATS
ADJUSTABLE RIDE

www.nike.com/events/ fun_police
Client: Nike. Creative Director, Illustrator: Guthrie Dolin
Designers: Guthrie Dolin, Mike Maletic
Programming, Development: SF Interactive
Photography: Jan Cook, Shawn Michienzi
Agency: Wieden Kennedy

Site description
Nike wanted to develop a website to support their latest ad campaign, the Fun Police. The spots featured NBA stars, policing to keep basketball fun and serving "Fun Justice" where the spirit of the game had been lost.

THE MISSION PAGE
TIMOTHY HARDAWAY
AKA
TIM BUG
Favorite Cereal: Captain Crunch
Pets and their Names: Dog, Bruno
Coolest Moment of Career: Trade to the Heat
First Memory: Kindergarden nap time
Last album purchased: Wu Tang Clan
What do you sing in the shower: Doris Day songs
Hobbies: Golf and Nintendo
Favorite Video Game: Virtual Fighter 3
Favorite food: Mashed potatos
Favorite thing about the NBA: The Blazer Girls?
GARY PAYTON
TIM HARDAWAY
ALONZO MOURNING
KEVIN GARNETT
BUG
JASON KIDD
TOM GUGLIOTTA
SHAREEF ABDUR-RAHEEM
DAMON STOUDAMIRE
MOSES MALONE
MISSION STATUS
PROFILE
FUN TRIVIA
FUN / NOT FUN

self-contained pop-up website. Content ranges from tips on the latest in cuffing techniques and ironing and washing care to locating the hard-to-find jeans.

www.brand-a.com/hardjeans
Client: Levi Strauss & Co.
Creative Director, Designer: Guthrie Dolin
Programmer: Mike Maletic
Writers: Craig Namba, Guthrie Dolin
Developer: USWeb/CKS
Agency: TBWA Chiat Day

Netscape: HARD JEANS
WASH
WARM
COLD
HOT
Hard jeans' deep indigo color may be preserved by washing at colder temperatures. Dry cleaning is a viable option, although extreme and costly. Avoid using bleach in any form (including detergents containing substitutes) unless you accessorize with headbands and leg warmers.
HARD JEANS
SPECS
SIZE
CUFF
IRON
FOLD
WASH
LOCATE
Netscape: HARD JEANS
FOLDING
Hard jeans are best stored flat. However, if the need arises, several common hardware items may be employed to configure hard jeans for storage and/or transit.
1 2 3 4
NO. 3
ANVIL & HAMMER
An oldie but goodie, just watch those fingers.
HARD JEANS
Netscape: HARD JEANS
LOCATE
SIGHTINGS
(A)
(B)
CAN YOU
TELL THE DIFFERENCE?
Hard jeans (A) are often confused with the elusive Sasquatch (B)
[ANSWER]
AUTHORIZED RETAILERS
HARD JEANS
Netscape: HARD JEANS
CUFFING
There are no strict rules regarding cuffs. With some practice, you will find a cuff size that you are most comfortable with. An iron (not supplied) may be used to secure the cuff.*
* SEE SPECIAL NOTE FOR IRON USERS :)
1 2 3
THE DROPPED-CHANGE-AND-DEAD-LEAF-COLLECTOR
HARD JEANS

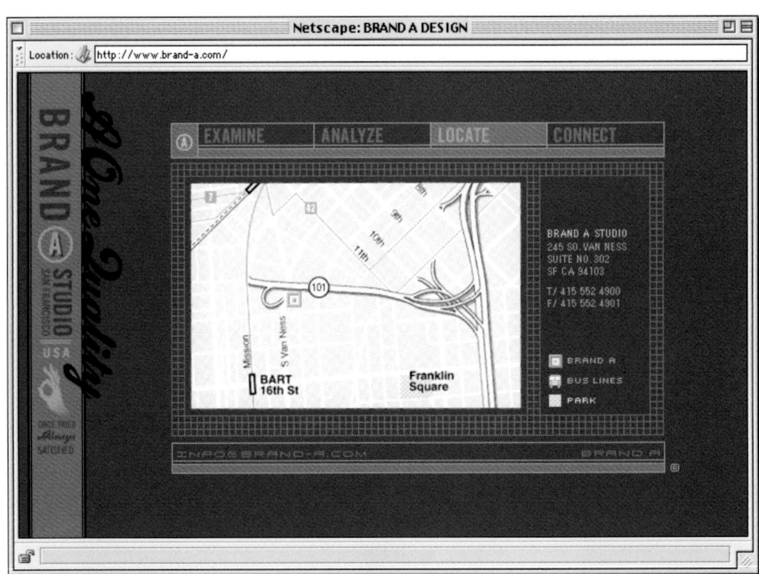
Netscape: BRAND A DESIGN
Location: http://www.brand-a.com/
EXAMINE
ANALYZE
LOCATE
CONNECT
BRAND A STUDIO
245 SO. VAN NESS
SUITE NO. 302
SF CA 94103
T/ 415 552 4900
F/ 415 552 4901
BRAND A
BUS LINES
PARK
Mission
S Van Ness
BART
16th St
Franklin
Square

Netscape: BRAND A DESIGN
Location: http://www.brand-a.com/
MELANCHRONIC
A REMINDER.
THAT THE HAPPIEST OF LIVES ARE ONLY THE SPLENDED WRECKS OF WHAT USED TO BE A FUTURE.

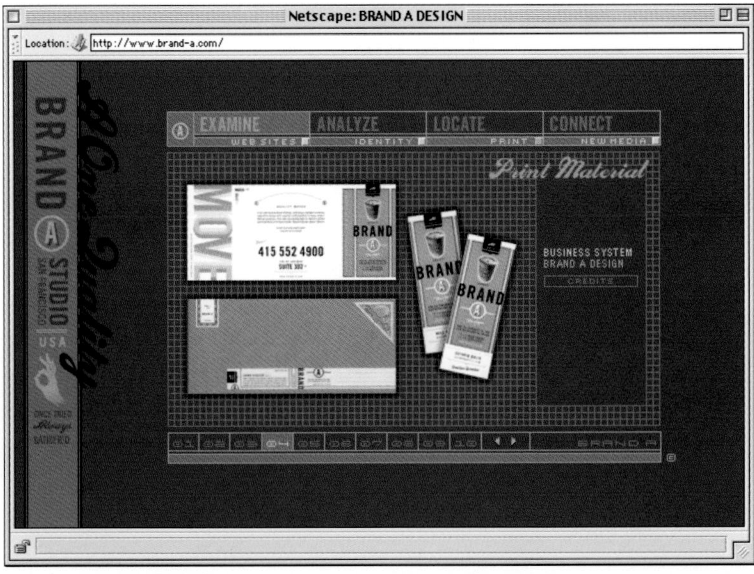
Netscape: BRAND A DESIGN
Location: http://www.brand-a.com/
EXAMINE
ANALYZE
LOCATE
CONNECT
WEB SITES
IDENTITY
PRINT
NEW MEDIA
Print Material
415 552 4900
BUSINESS SYSTEM
BRAND A DESIGN
CREDITS
BRAND A

www.thecontrolgroup.com
(this and next spread)
Client: The Control Group
Creative Director, Designer: Guthrie Dolin
Programmer: Daniel Baldonado
Writers: Robin Petravic, Kurt Dammerma

Site description:
This site for a new industrial design group was designed to serve as a compact yet comprehensive online portfolio that demonstrated and outlined the full capabilities of the company.

In the main site, clicking on images reveals the details of each project; in addition, users can access a detailed breakdown of services provided and profiles of the company's principals.

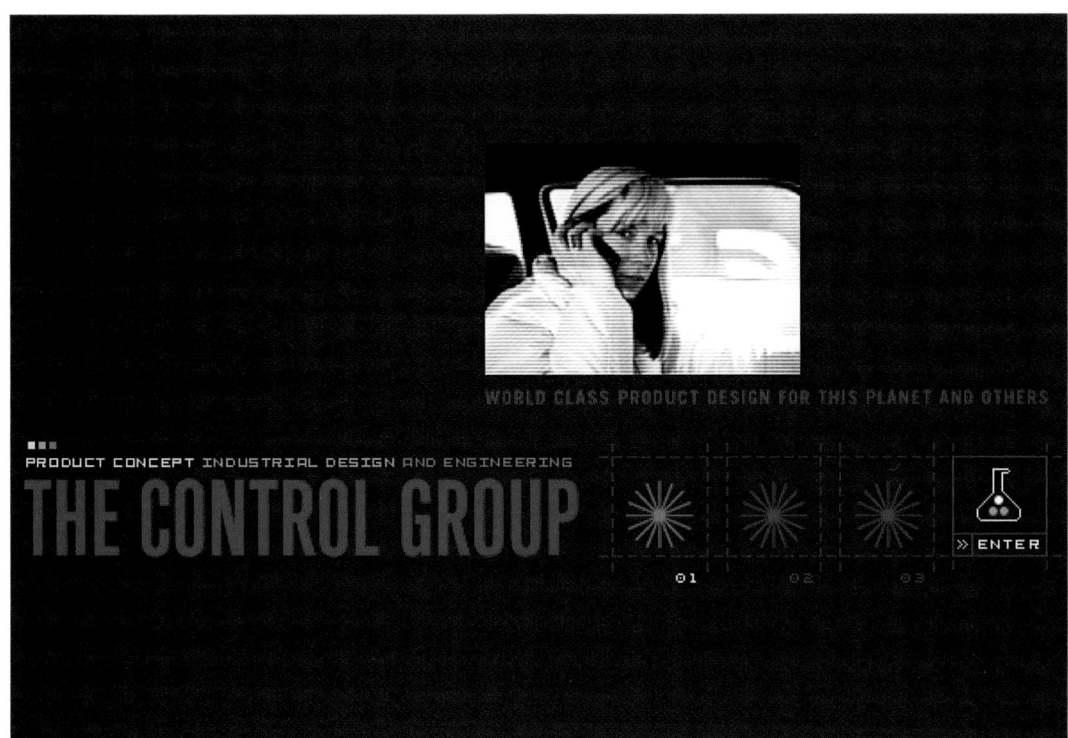

www.brand-a.com
(opposite)
Client: Brand A Studio
Creative Director, Designer, Writer: Guthrie Dolin
Programmer: Mike Maletic

Site description
Our goal was to create a site that represented our creative vision and communicated the depth of our studio's capabilities. The navigation path within the portfolio section "Examine" was designed on two axes: project type and client, allowing the user to view the depth of our experience and complete solutions across multiple paths.

PROJECTS »
SERVICES
IDENTITY

THE CONTROL GROUP
245 SO VAN NESS #304
SAN FRANCISCO CA 94103
415 626 3558

INSTRUCTIONS

no. 00

PARTICULARS
Click on the photos in right hand frame to get project particulars that relate to each image.

PLEASE NOTE
Our company is still new. Many of our projects are still in development and have not yet reached the market. These products are still for our (and our clients) eyes only. Without showing too much, these images (and descriptions) should give a good idea of the product areas we've worked in.

Thank you.

the managment.

» SCROLL ON

01 FLEXIBLE

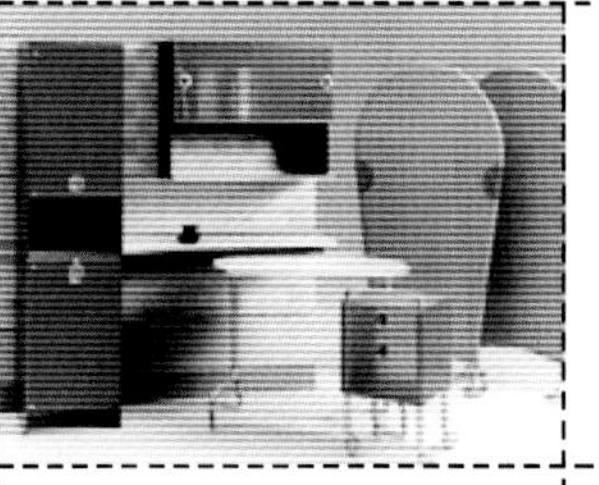

COMFORT 02

PERSPECTIVE 04

03 ENHANCE

05 PERFORMANCE

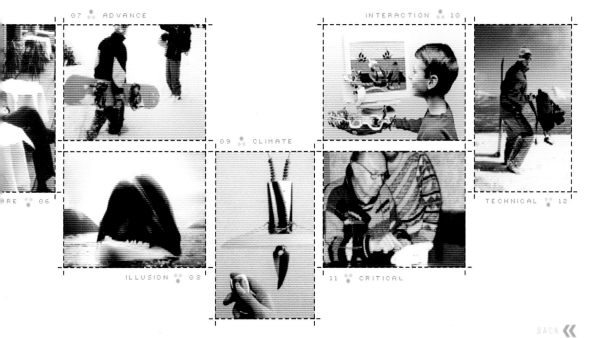

SCROLL ON

07 ADVANCE

INTERACTION 10

RE 06

09 CLIMATE

TECHNICAL 12

ILLUSION 08

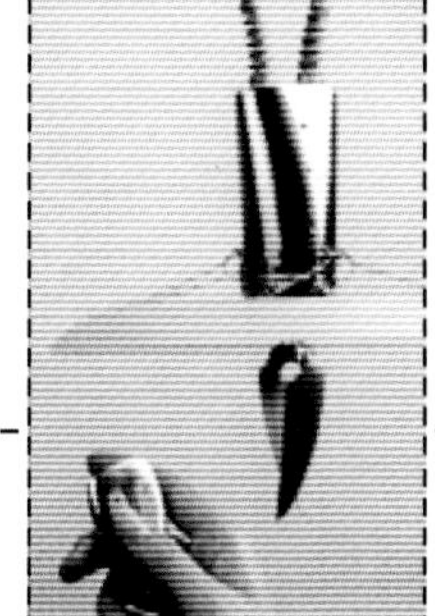

11 CRITICAL

BACK

Netscape: OM RECORDS - MUSIC
Back
Forward
Reload
Home
Search
Guide
Images
Print
Security
Stop
Location:
www.om-records.com
OM HOME
THE MUSIC
ARTISTS
CATALOG
FUTURE
COMPANY
CONTACT
EVENTS
FRIENDS
LOCATION
OM records
SF
FEATURED ARTISTS
V 3.0
NAKED MUSIC NYC
So what's new in the world of OM Records? To compliment the turn in the weather, OM has several new releases for Summer '98 including albums and singles from Terra Deva, Naked Music NYC, and Eighty Mile Beach. Click on these links to get more information on each artist.

OM HOME
THE MUSIC
ARTISTS
CATALOG
FUTURE
COMPANY
CONTACT
EVENTS
FRIENDS
LOCATION
terra deva
terra dëva pulled apart
Many consider San Francisco's prodigious music scene to be one of the most progressive and diverse in the world. Singer, songwriter, and producer Terra Deva - the passionate and sinewy new artist on OM Records - can only strengthen that presumption. Boasting vocal creations that resonate with tremendous soul, backed by an intoxicating soundtrack of hauntingly beautiful drum-and-bass, Terra's debut album "Pulled Apart" can only be described as Future Soul
Terra was born and raised in the San Francisco Bay Area - with brief stays in both Florida and Los Angeles - nurtured in a very musical household. She began singing as a young girl of four while a member of children's theater. At eight years old, Terra picked up the violin and has since blossomed into a singer, songwriter, and producer. It is Terra's diverse history as an artist (she has recorded with artists ranging from Bugs to Charles Webster to Elton John) that has taken her everywhere from the realms of deep house to the world of drum and bass and dubbed out downtempo fuzz.
TERRA DEVA PULLED APART
Boasting vocal creations that resonate with tremendous soul, backed by an intoxicating soundtrack of hauntingly beautiful drum-and-bass.
catalog # OM-009
BUY
LISTEN
return to artists main page

OM HOME
THE MUSIC
ARTISTS
CATALOG
FUTURE
COMPANY
CONTACT
EVENTS
FRIENDS
LOCATION
ALBUMS
SINGLES
MEPHISTO
This exclusive compilation brings you 12 brand new offerings from SF underground label legend, Mephisto. These tunes pour on layers of chunky beats, low fidelity funk, vibey vocals and slippery scratches! (more...)
BUY
LISTEN
CONVERGENCE
Seeking to blow-up the volatile combination of totally-now production talents from the world's foremost underground dance producers, XLR8R and OM have envisioned Convergence . (more...)
BUY
LISTEN
EIGHTY MILE BEACH INCLEMENT WEATHER
Organic, primordial music, influenced by everything from jazz improvisation to the rhythms of modern electronic dance. (more...)
catalog # OM-008OM
BUY

OM HOME
THE MUSIC
ARTISTS
CATALOG
FUTURE
COMPANY
CONTACT
EVENTS
FRIENDS
LOCATION
OMrecords
WORD TO FELLOW CYBERPONIC NET FOOLS
V 3.0
Welcome to the new OM website. Sorry our site has been out of the mix for a while, but we had some critical revamping to do. Version 3.0 has been designed to let you quickly access the info you need about the label, artists, releases, events, and other information of consequence. We hope you enjoy it and feel free to give us a shout if there is anything else you should require.
IN STORES NOW
NAKED MUSIC NYC
terra deva
pulled apart
All audio on the OM website requires the Quicktime plug-in included in most standard browsers.
For the best performance and quality, upgrade to Quicktime 3.0.

Brand Dialogue

Brand Dialogue New York is a full-service interactive agency working within Young & Rubicam, Inc. Our heritage, having grown organically from one of the largest and most prestigious consumer agencies in the world, has placed us ideally within the digital space: Our focus is on completely understanding a customer's desires, needs, and issues as they develop a relationship with a brand online.

We firmly believe that experience with an online product becomes the manifestation of the brand—the experience is the brand. Our approach to design for the Web is synonymous with the approach to any information design task. We take the audience, strategy, technology, and messaging into consideration, and create from there.

We believe that it takes a team to build meaningful design that through collaboration between the client, design, writing, production, technology, media and account groups, great design is born.

Origins
Founded: 1993
Parent company: Young & Rubicam, Inc.
Number of employees when founded: 3; now: 97
Headquarters: New York

Principals
Andreas Panayi, President
Sean Skilling, Creative Director
Gordon Miller, Creative Director
Delia Moran, Design Director

Contact
285 Madison Avenue
New York, NY 10017
Tel.: 212.210.3858
Fax: 212.490.9073
E-mail: delia_moran@yr.com
Web: www.brand-dialogue.com

SCROLL
do you dream in Sony?
RoboCup
COMPETITORS
DREAMERS
Pet Robot
SCROLL
RoboCup
COMPETITORS
DREAMERS
PetRobot

do you dream in Sony?
RoboCup 98

www.YandR.com
Client: Young & Rubicam
Designer: Michele Marx
Design Director: Delia Moran
Creative Director:
Sean Skilling
Production: David Israel

At the helm of Y&R Advertising are some of the most creative, strategic thinkers in the business. Guiding the agency's mission to communicate the brand's essence, these individuals oversee the brilliantly executed advertising that is created by Y&R, advertising that is rooted in strategic insights about the brand and developed for the most effective and efficient media.
At Y&R Advertising, you'll find executives who have held leadership positions at the best agencies in the business, individuals with diverse backgrounds who understand how to maximize the resources of Y&R to create the most dynamic and effective communications for their clients. What's more, they all contribute to the culture which makes Y&R one of the best and most fun places to work in the industry.

About the site:
When one of the largest advertising agencies in the world has a motto that reads, "*Good* is the enemy of *great*," a designer can be sure that putting their portfolio online has a special set of challenges, even for a sister company, as Brand Dialogue was to Y&R. By combining elegant design, excellent writing, innovative technology, and extensive testing, Brand Dialogue was able to satisfy one of their toughest clients.

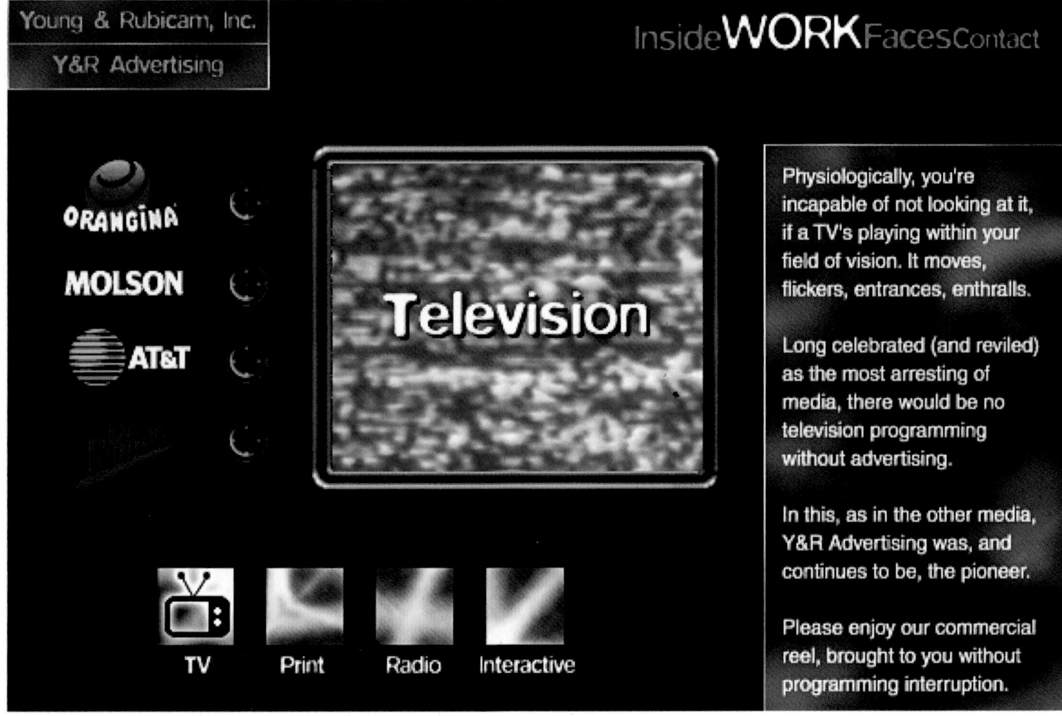

UNITED STATES POSTAL SERVICE®

USING DIRECT MAIL

TERMS OF USE

Fly Like an Eagle.™ 

Tune in crystal clear results!

Nothing tunes in new business like Direct Mail. That's because Direct Mail can effectively reach new prospects and strengthen existing customer loyalty. To learn how, simply select one of the following sections.

Start Now!—learn how to plan, execute & deliver a DM campaign. What You Need—from professional-quality templates to a break-even calculator. Expert Information—valuable advice and tips. Direct Mail Partners—sign up and join our community!

SATELLITE TV
Get better reception!

GO TO USPS.COM | HOME | START NOW! | WHAT YOU NEED | EXPERT INFORMATION | DIRECT MAIL PARTNERS

USING DIRECT MAIL

TERMS OF USE

Fly Like an Eagle.™

Fresh opportunities!

Want to harvest some fresh customers? Then take a look at Direct Mail. Learn how to effectively contact new customers who want (and need) what you're selling. To learn how, simply select one of the following sections:

Start Now!—learn how to plan, execute & deliver a DM campaign. What You Need—from professional-quality templates to a break-even calculator. Expert Information—valuable advice and tips. Direct Mail Partners—sign up and join our community!

Fresh! PRODUCE

GO TO USPS.COM | HOME | START NOW! | WHAT YOU NEED | EXPERT INFORMATION | DIRECT MAIL PARTNERS

Information Desk

/ Home /

- Information Desk
- Getting It There
- Industry Solutions
- A Global View
- Global Links

Calculate Your Cost
International Rate Calculator

Search >>> Help
Go to usps.com Write to us

Select one of the following resources
to help you with your global shipping needs and/or questions

USING DIRECT MAIL

GLOSSARY | CONTACT US | HELP

- Introduction
- Goals & Strategies
- Lists & Databases
- Creative
- Production & Budgets
- Testing
- Mailing

Testing

What sets Direct Mail apart from more "traditional" media is its ability to be "tested." When you test a mailing (whether it be the offer, the list or the "creative," which is the mail package itself), you have a golden opportunity. Because, before you spend your Direct Mail budget, you can determine, in a relatively short time frame, whether your mail piece will be a winner.

Let's say that you've been mailing out postcards to customers from time to time and they've done pretty well for your business.

What would happen if you sent out a brochure instead? With Direct Mail, you can test them both and find out. Do a small sample mailing and send half your customers the postcard and the other half the new brochure. By testing on a small group now, you can avoid costly mistakes later.

In this example, your postcard is the "control." The control refers to the mail piece that's been the most successful for you. If you find that the brochure brings in even greater results, then that becomes the new control, the benchmark against which all your other Direct Mail pieces will be measured.

tip:
25% of a campaign's responses occur in the first week.

GO TO USPS.COM | HOME | START NOW! | WHAT YOU NEED | EXPERT INFORMATION | DIRECT MAIL PARTNERS

Global Links

/ Home /

- Information Desk
- Getting It There
- Industry Solutions
- A Global View
- Global Links

Calculate Your Cost
International Rate Calculator

Search >>> Help
Go to usps.com Write to us

www.uspsglobal.com

- U.S. Government Resources
- International Trade Statistics
- Postal Resources
- International Organizations
- Trade Organizations
- International Chambers of Commerce
- Foreign Embassies and Trade Commissions
- Customs Organizations

U.S. GOVERNMENT RESOURCES

Central Intelligence Agency World Factbook

The World Factbook is prepared by the Central Intelligence Agency for the use of U.S. Government officials, and the style, format, coverage, and content are designed to meet their specific requirements. The Factbook provides economic, demographic, political, geographic and other information for countries around the globe.

International Trade Administration Website

The ITA is a division of the U.S. Department of Commerce and is dedicated to helping U.S. businesses compete in the global marketplace. The site contains country- and industry-specific resource information, trade statistics, links to the U.S. Export Resource Centers and Foreign Commercial Service offices, export and import information and trade

Global Delivery Services

/ Home /

See the World Differently. Fly Like an Eagle.™

Information Desk

Getting It There

Industry Solutions

A Global View

Global Links

Welcome to the United States Postal Service

Take Global Delivery to a New Level

What's New?

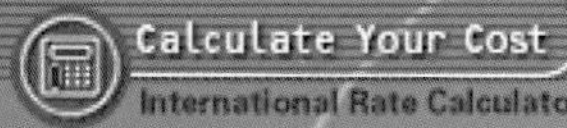

Search .... >>> Help

Go to usps.com ///// Write to us

• Terms of Use

www.drpepper.com/football
(this page)
Creative Director: Sean Skilling
Design Director: Delia Moran
Designer: Paula Wood
Writer: Todd Harrington
Production: Ted Kacandes

Site description
Dr. Pepper's Big 12/SEC college football promotion is a 1970s flashback with the support of 1990s technology. The user is transported back in time to a computer-generated '70s-style recreation room, complete with shag carpeting, wood paneling, Dr. Pepper paraphernalia, college pennants, and hi-fi speakers. From the comfort of a scratchy couch ensconced in red, lime, and yellow plaid, users click the digitally-empowered remote control to choose from a selection of Flash-filled TV channels. The site gives the term "couch potato" a new interactive twist.

www.drpepper.com
(opposite)
Creative Director: Sean Skilling
Design Director: Delia Moran
Designer: Michele Marx
Writer: Todd Harrington
Production: Ted Kacandes
Tech: Duane Grey

Site description
DrPepper.com begins at the core of the Dr. Pepper Chill Factory. Animated with refreshing visuals and sounds that fizz, flop, twist, and pop in perfect unison, it's Flash technology at its frostiest.

THIS IS
THE TASTE!
Dr Pepper
chill factory
COOL PROMOS
FROSTY FACTS
PEPPER PICKINS
PEPPER PASSPORT
CHILL OUT
OFF ON
SOUND OFF

Dr Pepper
chill factory
WELCOME

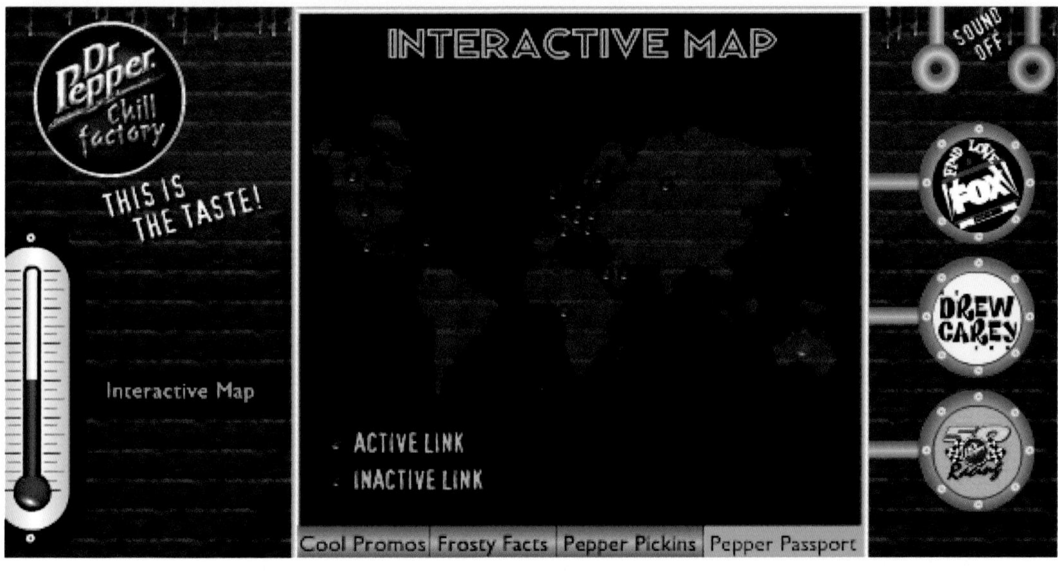
Dr Pepper
chill factory
THIS IS
THE TASTE!
Interactive Map
INTERACTIVE MAP
ACTIVE LINK
INACTIVE LINK
Cool Promos
Frosty Facts
Pepper Pickins
Pepper Passport
SOUND OFF
DREW CAREY

NeuroCentral

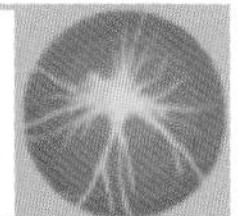

AMERICAN EPILEPSY SOCIETY

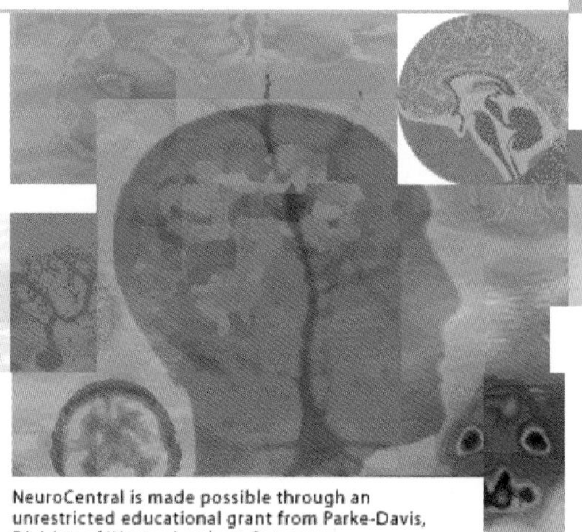

NeuroCentral is made possible through an unrestricted educational grant from Parke-Davis, Division of Warner Lambert Company.

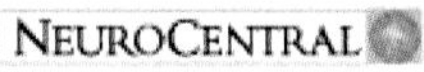

Member Sign-in

About NeuroCentral

Register Now

What's New

Member Sign-in

Welcome to NeuroCentral

Welcome to NeuroCentral, the official educational site of the American Epilepsy Society for the exchange of research, treatment, and management data concerning seizure disorders. This site is made possible through an unrestricted educational grant from Parke-Davis, Division of Warner-Lambert Company.

For those of you already familiar with NeuroCentral, you've probably noticed a change in the site's design. We've adjusted the site's navigation, but we still have all of your favorite features.

In addition, we have enhanced our Bulletin Board system to more easily enable physicians to build their very own community.

Enter your password and get connected to the most current resources available in the area of neurology and seizure disorders.

If you're an AES member and currently access AESnet.org, you can use your current username and password to enter the site.

For first-time visitors, we suggest browsing our Visitor's Guide to learn more about what NeuroCentral has to offer.

Duffy Design

Our mission is to use interactive technology to create, build, and nurture profitable relationships between consumers and a short list of enlightened brands. Started in 1984 by Joe Duffy and the partners of Fallon McElligott advertising, Duffy Design became a key element in an integrated marketing communications approach that focused on surrounding the brand 360 degrees. "The more we erased the lines between marketing communications disciplines," said Duffy, "the more we realized that a brand's singular voice is best conveyed when a commitment to design is a core value. Our design philosophy is grounded in that reality."

As design entered the world of new media, so did Duffy Design, becoming Duffy Design and Interactive and offering yet another strategic opportunity to surround the brand and deliver a direct experience to the consumer. "The interactive work we do relates directly to the overall branding strategy. Each component of this strategy expresses the appropriate brand message, using the appropriate technology for the audience to whom we are talking."

This valuable consumer insight is made possible through a partnership with the award-winning expertise of Fallon's account planning—"a partnership that enables us to understand exactly how and why consumers connect with a brand online." This understanding is then harnessed to create design for new media that reinforces the unique personality of each brand.

Origins
Founded: 1984
Parent company: Fallon McElligott
Number of employees when founded: 6
Number of employees now: 75
Headquarters: Minneapolis
Other locations: New York

Principal
Joe Duffy, CEO

Contact
Shari Troje, Duffy Design
901 Marquette Ave.
Suite 3000
Minneapolis, MN 55402
Tel.: 612. 321 2333
Fax: 612. 321 2334
E-mail: shari.troje@duffy.com
Web: www.duffy.com

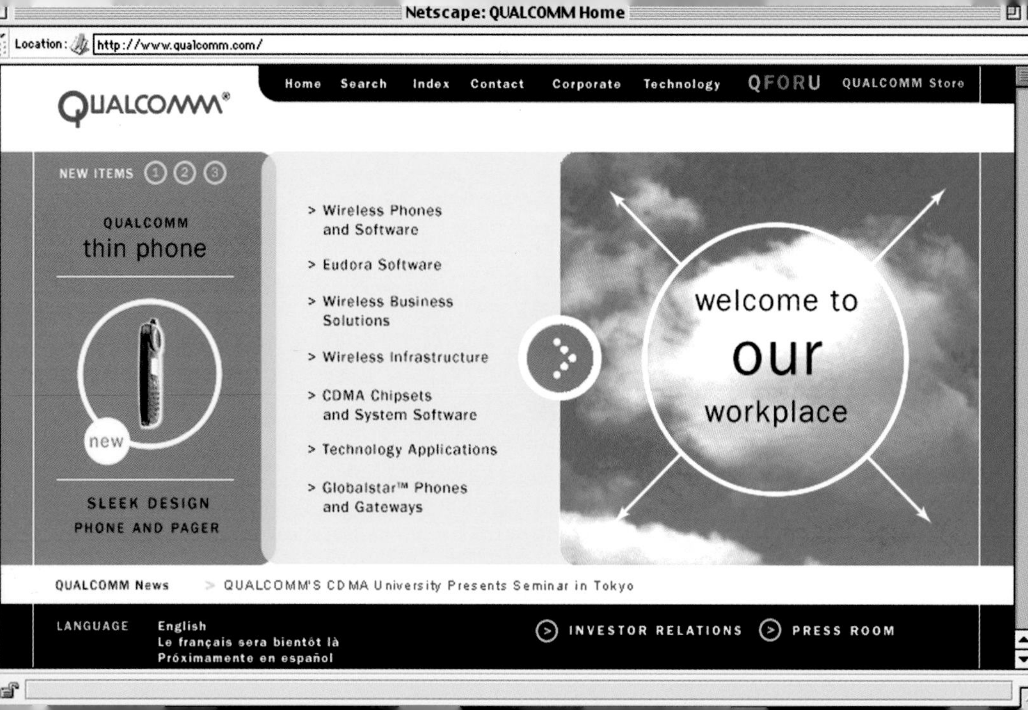
Netscape: QUALCOMM Home
Location: http://www.qualcomm.com/
QUALCOMM®
Home
Search
Index
Contact
Corporate
Technology
QFORU
QUALCOMM Store
NEW ITEMS 1 2 3
QUALCOMM
thin phone
new
SLEEK DESIGN
PHONE AND PAGER
> Wireless Phones and Software
> Eudora Software
> Wireless Business Solutions
> Wireless Infrastructure
> CDMA Chipsets and System Software
> Technology Applications
> Globalstar™ Phones and Gateways
welcome to
our
workplace
QUALCOMM News
> QUALCOMM'S CDMA University Presents Seminar in Tokyo
LANGUAGE
English
Le français sera bientôt là
Próximamente en español
INVESTOR RELATIONS
PRESS ROOM

Netscape: QUALCOMM Phone Finder

Location: http://www.qualcomm.com/

QUALCOMM®

Home Search Index Contact Corporate Technology QFORU QUALCOMM Store

Wireless Phones

BACK TO PHONES

- Sleek Style
- Colors
- Small Size & Weight
- Roaming
- Talk and Standby Time
- E-mail, Data Access & Computer Connectivity

CHOOSE A FEATURE

To find the QUALCOMM phone(s) most likely to make you a happy caller, click on a feature important to you.

phone

finder

Compare all phones

LANGUAGE English
Français · Coming Soon
Español · Coming Soon
Português · Coming Soon

SUGGESTED LINKS
- This is a suggested link.
- This is another suggested link.
- This is a link to the QUALCOMM Store.

Site Requirements © Copyright 1999 QUALCOMM Incorporated

Netscape: home

Location: http://www.qualcomm.com/

QUALCOMM®

Home Search Index Contact Corporate Technology QFORU QUALCOMM Store

Wireless Phones

BACK TO PHONES

- Features/Benefits
- Get a Closer Look
- Interactive Demo
- Accessories
- Models: pdQ 800/pdQ 1900
- pdQ In the News
- Support
- Developer Zone
- pdQsuite
- Click here if you are viewing this page from your pdQ smartphone
- Phone Finder and Comparison
- About CDMA Digital Phones
- Where to Buy
- Owner's Club

pdQ™ Smartphone

CONNECTED

Meet the web browsing, Palm Computing® Platform, e-mailing, wireless phone.

BUY NOW

PALM

Netscape: QUALCOMM Wireless Phones

Location: http://www.qualcomm.com/

QUALCOMM®

Home Search Index Contact Corporate Technology QFORU QUALCOMM Store

Wireless Phones

- The pdQ smartphone
- The Q phone
- The QUALCOMM thin phone
- QCP-820/QCP-1920/QCP-2700
- Fixed Wireless Products
- Accessories
- Data Products
- pdQsuite Software
- Phone Finder and Comparison
- About CDMA Digital Phones
- Where to Buy
- Owners Club

ULTRA THIN

FEATURES

PHONE AND PAGER
DUAL MODE
CDMA DIGITAL

The new pdQ™ smartphone

come in and think some

FUN ADS, BRAINTEASERS, AND MORE ARE COMING.

check back soon

LANGUAGE English
Français · Coming Soon
Español · Coming Soon
Português · Coming Soon

SUGGESTED LINKS
- This is a suggested link.
- This is another suggested link.
- This is a link to the QUALCOMM Store.

Site Requirements © Copyright 1999 QUALCOMM Incorporated

http://wip.fallon.com/qualcomm/mini_site/wireless/pdq_smartphone/pdq_smartphone.html

116,117 **Duffy Design**

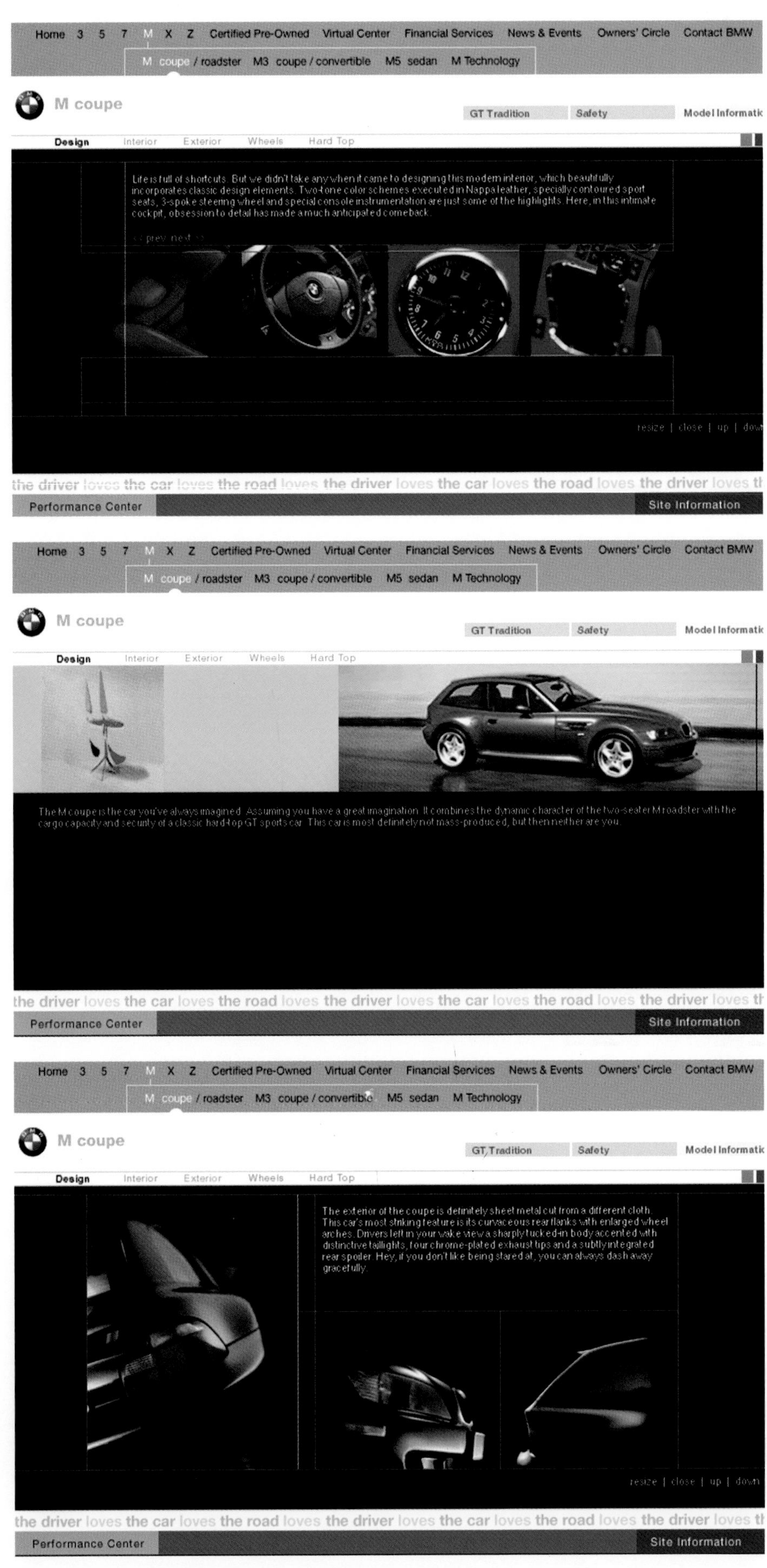

Home 3 5 7 M X Z Certified Pre-Owned Virtual Center Financial Services News & Events Owners' Circle Contact BMW
M coupe / roadster M3 coupe / convertible M5 sedan M Technology
M coupe
GT Tradition
Safety
Model Informati
Design Interior Exterior Wheels Hard Top
Life is full of shortcuts. But we didn't take any when it came to designing this modern interior, which beautifully incorporates classic design elements. Two-tone color schemes executed in Nappa leather, specially contoured sport seats, 3-spoke steering wheel and special console instrumentation are just some of the highlights. Here, in this intimate cockpit, obsession to detail has made a much anticipated comeback.
prev next
resize | close | up | dow
the driver loves the car loves the road loves the driver loves the car loves the road loves the driver loves th
Performance Center
Site Information
Home 3 5 7 M X Z Certified Pre-Owned Virtual Center Financial Services News & Events Owners' Circle Contact BMW
M coupe / roadster M3 coupe / convertible M5 sedan M Technology
M coupe
GT Tradition
Safety
Model Informati
Design Interior Exterior Wheels Hard Top
The M coupe is the car you've always imagined. Assuming you have a great imagination. It combines the dynamic character of the two-seater M roadster with the cargo capacity and security of a classic hard-top GT sports car. This car is most definitely not mass-produced, but then neither are you.
the driver loves the car loves the road loves the driver loves the car loves the road loves the driver loves th
Performance Center
Site Information
Home 3 5 7 M X Z Certified Pre-Owned Virtual Center Financial Services News & Events Owners' Circle Contact BMW
M coupe / roadster M3 coupe / convertible M5 sedan M Technology
M coupe
GT Tradition
Safety
Model Informati
Design Interior Exterior Wheels Hard Top
The exterior of the coupe is definitely sheet metal cut from a different cloth. This car's most striking feature is its curvaceous rear flanks with enlarged wheel arches. Drivers left in your wake view a sharply tucked-in body accented with distinctive taillights, four chrome-plated exhaust tips and a subtly integrated rear spoiler. Hey, if you don't like being stared at, you can always dash away gracefully.
resize | close | up | down
the driver loves the car loves the road loves the driver loves the car loves the road loves the driver loves th
Performance Center
Site Information

Client: BMW of North America, Inc.
Creative Director: Joe Duffy
Design Director: Dan Olson
Art Director: Kevin Flatt
Designers: Kevin Flatt, Jason Strong, Paul Bastyr
Writers: Chuck Carlson, Deborah Dachis Gold, Riley Kane, Tom Rosen, Russ Stark, Andrew Ault
Photographer: Mark LaFavor
Sandau, Leslie Fandich
Programmers: Heather Gowdy, John Keller, Karen Donahue, Bob Carlson, Ben Garcia, Dave Thompson

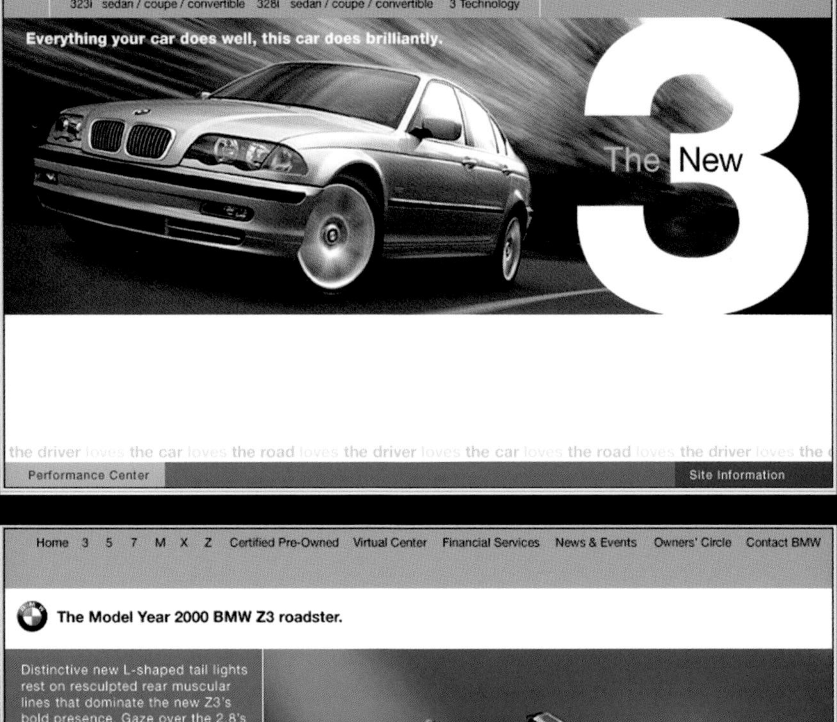

Site description
BMW of North America represents one of our first integrated clients, involving advertising, print and interactive design, Web hosting, and public relations. Befitting BMW cars, bmwusa.com is a technologically advanced site. The Build Your BMW feature allows customers to configure a BMW, price it, save it for future recall and editing, explore financing, apply for credit online, and transmit their saved selections to their preferred BMW center.

The Products We Share

The Community We Make

Netscape: Purina Dogs

Netsite: http://www.purina.com/

HOME NEWS DOGS CATS PRODUCTS COMMUNITY ADVICE PLAY SEARCH

Dogs

- Breed Categories
- Breeders & Champions
- Breed Selector
- Weight Management
- Training and Behavior
- Health and Grooming
- Puppies
  - Puppy Care Kit
- Questions and Answers
- Organizations
- Join Our Community

More Purina Sites

PURINA CHAMPIONS
VETERINARY CENTER
THE PURINA STORE

Purina®

The Dogs We Love

No other animal has the capacity to give so much and demand so little in return. Dogs give us unyielding, unconditional love and devotion for their entire lifetime. Like a true friend, they always seem to be there when you need them most.

Dogs forgive and forget. They have no shame. When they are home alone, they don't pretend to be busy. They wait. They will beg and drool and rest a heavy head on your knee or in your lap if it means a pat on the head or some extra food. Dogs learn to understand our language and see no reason why they can't sleep in our beds. Some of us let them.

For this and for all the in-your-face kind of love they give us, this section is devoted to The Dogs We Love.

The Cats We Love

The Advice We Want

Client: Purina
Creative Director: Joe Duffy
Design Director,
Art Director: Dan Olson
Designers: Dan Olson,
Nhan Nguyen, Nathan Hinz

Writer: Deborah Dachis Gold
Animators: Mark Sandau,
Leslie Fandrich
Programmers: Margaret Bossen,
Kore Peterson, Matt Jannusch,
Colin Schaub, Brad Olson

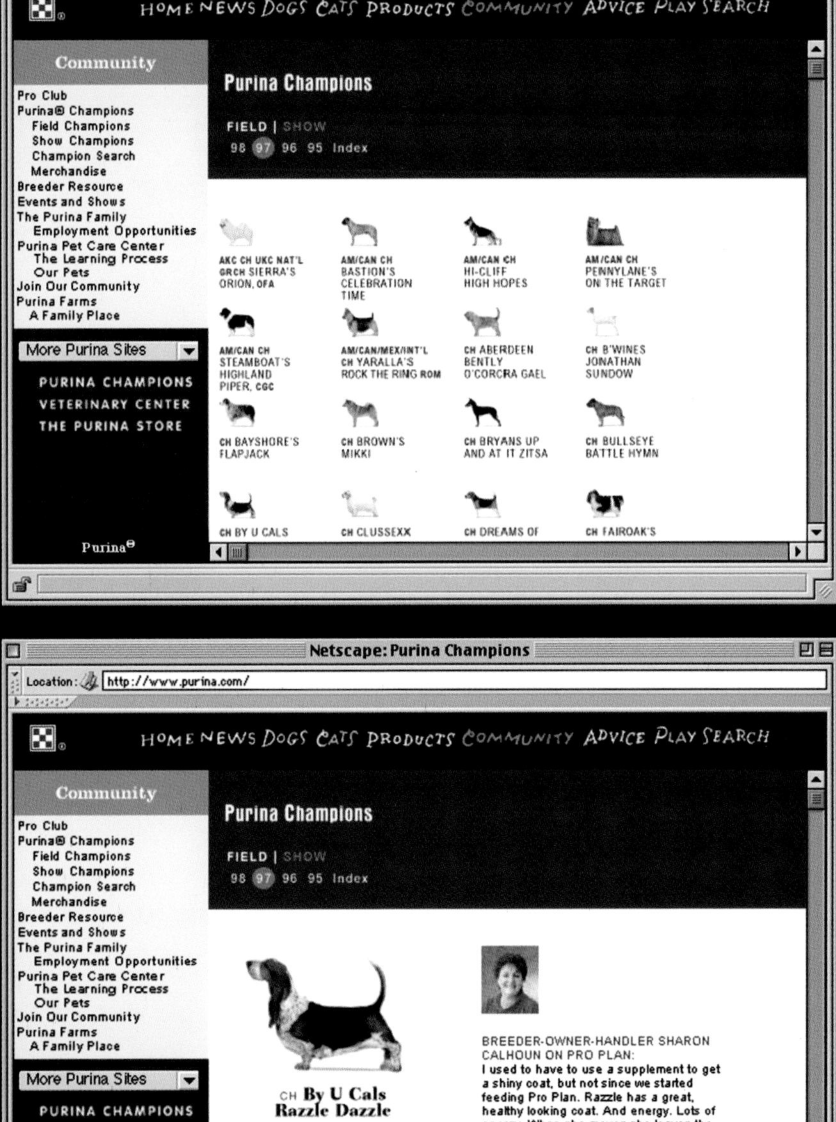

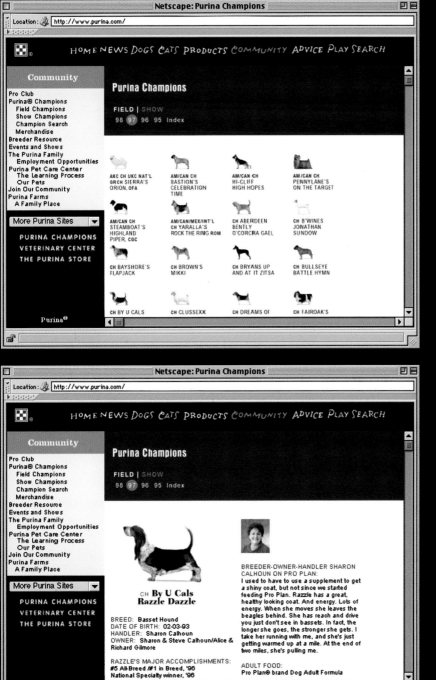

Site description

The Purina website was designed to create an online community by and about pet lovers that establishes Purina as an authority on pet in caring for the pets people love. The copy, design, illustrations and animation work together to create a warmth and understanding of the emotions

Nikon
PRONEA S

Nikon
PRONEA S

DESIGN
COMPACT
ADVANCED
PHOTO SYSTEM
SLR

SINGLE LENS REFLEX

Drag your mouse over the camera to see the dynamic flash action of the Pronea S. (Apple's **QuickTime 3** plug-in needed.)

You see it clearly in the big, bright viewfinder. It's in a pool of blinding sunlight, with dark shadows all around it. Not to worry - the

Netscape: BMW Motorcycles

Location: http://www.bmwusacycles.com/

The Machine

R1100S

Specifications
Equipment & Options
Color Selector
Gallery
Accolades
MSRP

Printable format (PDF)
Brochure Request
Product Questions
Motorcycle Retailer
Accessories
Ownership Support

Mandarin Orange

Night Black

Bright Red

Motorcycles

Financial Services   Contact BMW   Site Information

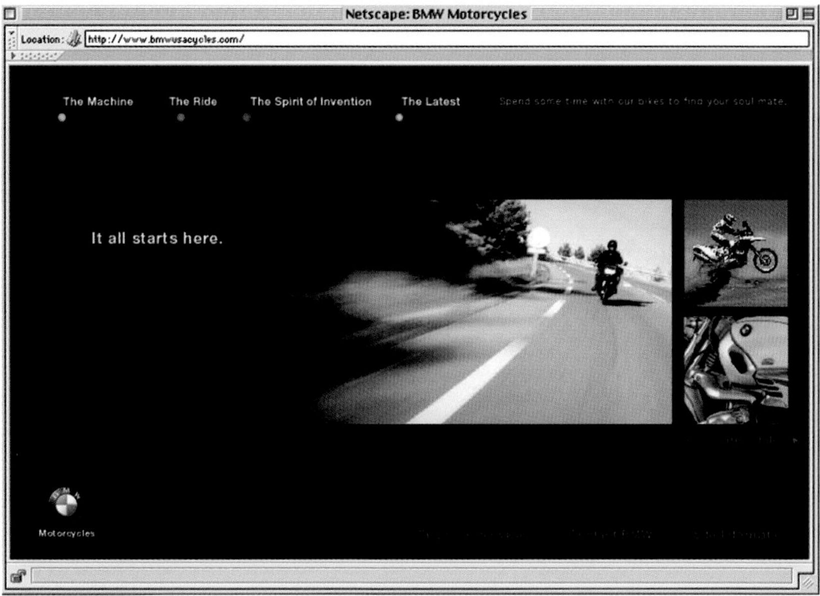
Netscape: BMW Motorcycles
Location: http://www.bmwusacycles.com/
The Machine
The Ride
The Spirit of Invention
The Latest
Spend some time with our bikes to find your soul mate.
It all starts here.
Motorcycles

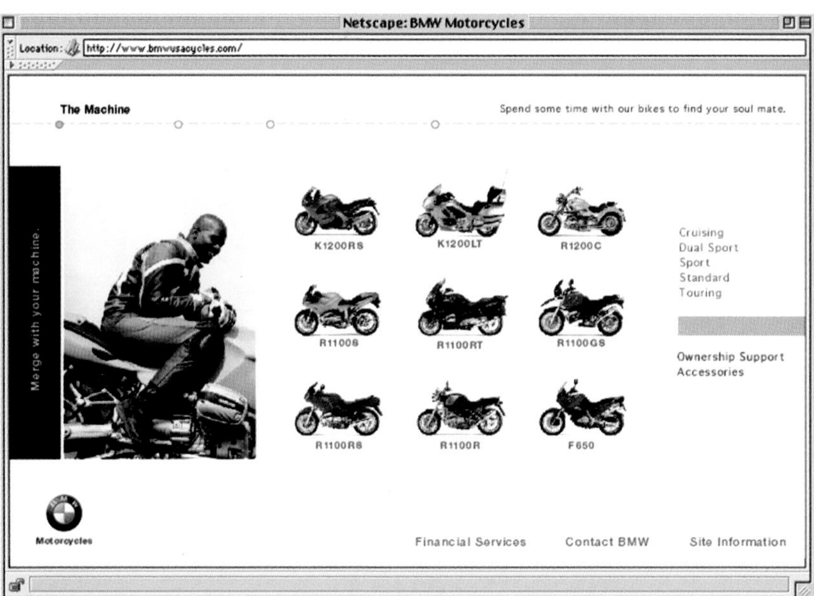
Netscape: BMW Motorcycles
Location: http://www.bmwusacycles.com/
The Machine
Spend some time with our bikes to find your soul mate.
Merge with your machine.
K1200RS
K1200LT
R1200C
R1100S
R1100RT
R1100GS
R1100RS
R1100R
F650
Cruising
Dual Sport
Sport
Standard
Touring
Ownership Support
Accessories
Motorcycles
Financial Services
Contact BMW
Site Information

Netscape: BMW Motorcycles
Location: http://www.bmwusacycles.com/
The Ride
Prepare yourself and your bike for the next adventure.
Remember to send us a postcard.
Great Rides
Maintenance Tips
Riding Tips
Motorcycle Organizations
Weather Channel
MapQuest
Assessories
Motorcycles

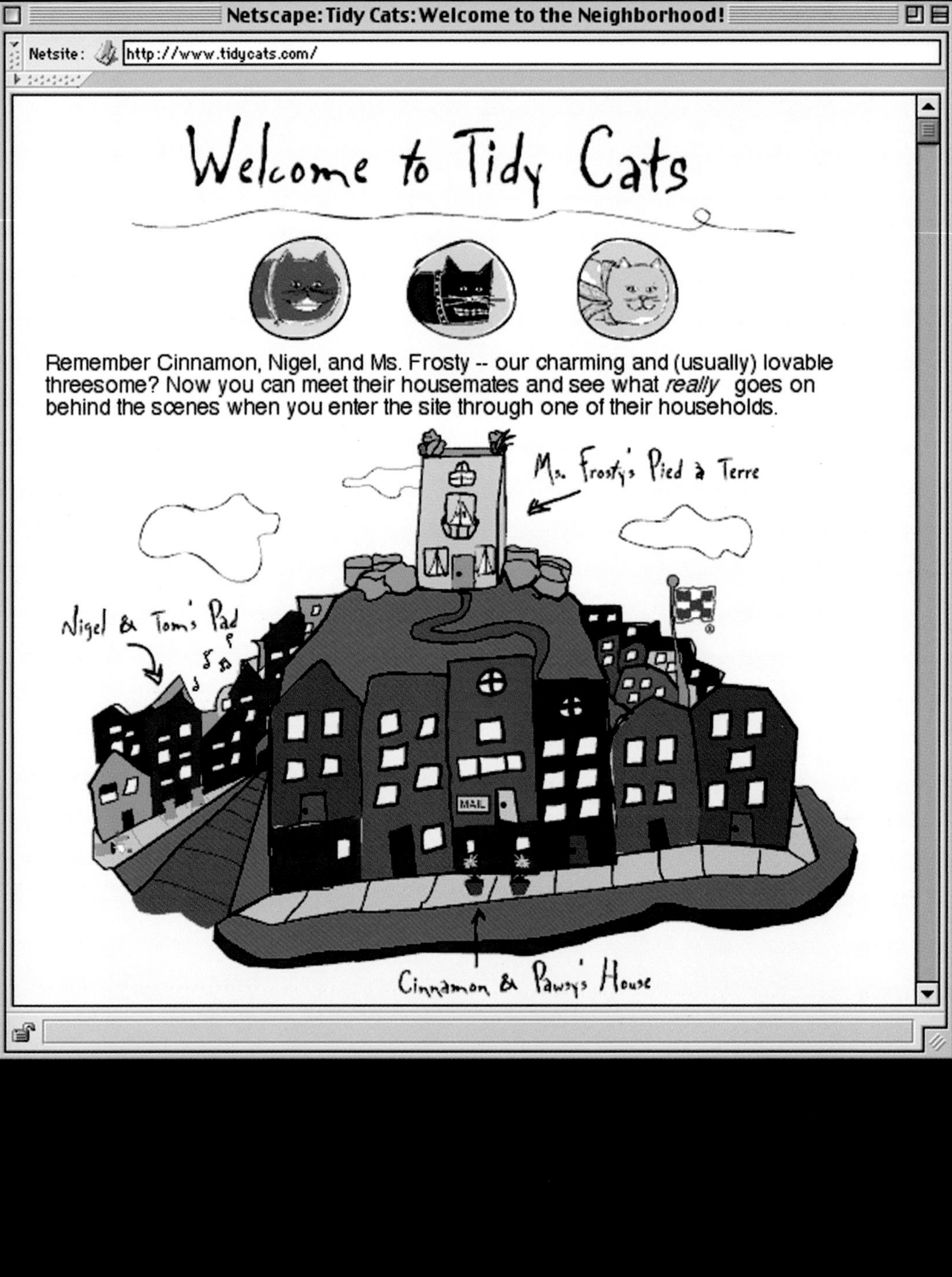
Netscape: Tidy Cats: Welcome to the Neighborhood!
Netsite:
http://www.tidycats.com/
Welcome to Tidy Cats
Remember Cinnamon, Nigel, and Ms. Frosty -- our charming and (usually) lovable threesome? Now you can meet their housemates and see what *really* goes on behind the scenes when you enter the site through one of their households.
Ms. Frosty's Pied à Terre
Nigel & Tom's Pad
MAIL
Cinnamon & Pawsy's House

www.tidycats.com
(this page)
Client: Tidy Cats
Creative Director: Joe Duffy
Design Director: Dan Olson
Art Director: Kobe Suvongse
Designers: Kobe Suvongse, Genevieve Gorder
Illustrators: Genevieve Gorder, Lourdes Banez
Writer: Deborah Dachis Gold
Animator: Mark Sandau
Programmers: Margaret Bossen, Joe Corbett

Site description

The newly designed Tidy Cats site reflects a shift in the brand's positioning to a high-performance formula created for multiple-cat households. The illustrative design and quirky storyline featuring original cat characters endear visitors to the brand and help them find everything they need to know about caring for their cats, from nutrition and health to body language and personality.

Netscape: Meow Mix Home Page
Location: http://www.meowmix.com/
FREE Calendar!
What should we do, Mop?
I don't know, Tango. You decide tonight.
MEOW MIX
NEW!
TANGO & MOP
FuN!
CAT A LOG
purina.com
tidycats.com
catchow.com
guest book
tango
MEOW MIX

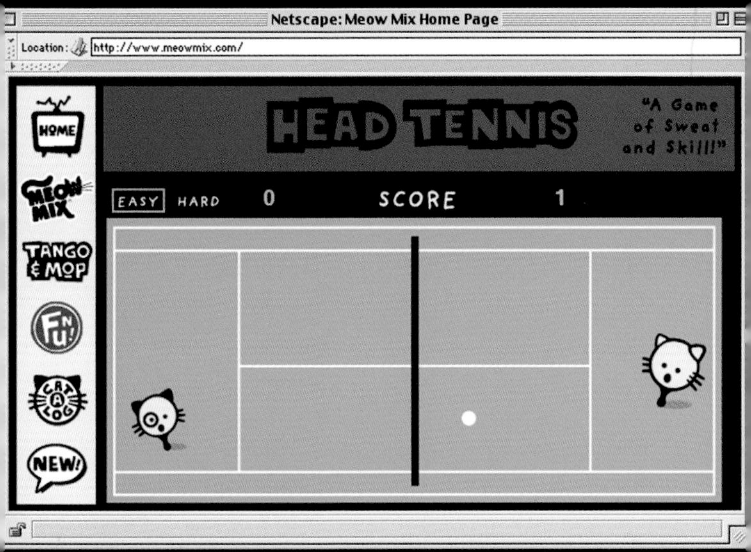

Netscape: Meow Mix Home Page
Location: http://www.meowmix.com/
HOME
MEOW MIX
TANGO & MOP
FuN!
CAT A LOG
NEW!
HEAD TENNIS
"A Game of Sweat and Skill!"
EASY HARD 0 SCORE 1

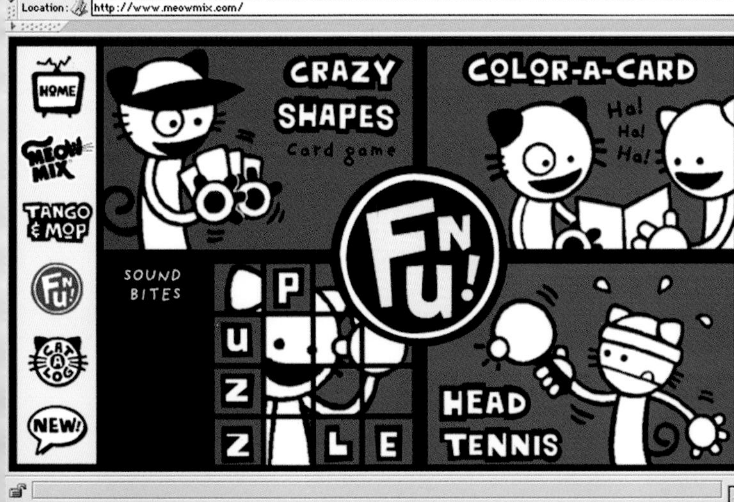

e-media-c

e-media-c is the new media division of Grafik Marketing Communications, Ltd., a full service marketing communications firm formed in 1979 and located in the Washington, DC area. Numbering more than 25 seasoned professionals, including designers, writers, production and new media experts, Grafik provides marketing strategy, creative and production services for diverse clients across the ever-widening spectrum of communications, including digital media.

e-media-c was launched in 1997 when many of Grafik's clients asked for help in translating their brand and message to the digital world. Working under the direction of Eric Goetz, director of new media, and in concert with Grafik's extensive resources, which are spearheaded by Judy Kirpich, e-media-c specializes in the design and integration of identity and message without regard to technology platforms or medium. Rapid success comes not from harnessing our clients to work with technology, but in shaping the complexity and confusion of technology to work on behalf of our clients.

e-media-c always begins from the user's perspective in applying the principles of branding to the void of the Web. No matter what technology is needed—e-shopping, e-locator, e-chat, or e-mail—all are virtual until the user finds them, chooses to interact, and ultimately is receptive to the brand and the message.

e-media-c has helped extend the brand and message of such clients as the National Human Genome Research Institute, the Museum of Jewish Heritage, IBM, and the Fannie Mae Foundation. Our firm's philosophy is based on collaboration, client service and problem solving. Every project is assigned a team string in concept development, marketing, design, production and technical integration. Within the team, ideas are developed, discussed, critiqued and refined. Our portfolio of work demonstrates that great ideas come out of collaboration with clients, designers, programmers, writers, illustrators and photographers. Grafik's work has been recognized as among the best in the business, earning more than 300 awards, coverage in GRAPHIS, COMMUNICATION ARTS, PRINT, and HOW, and publication in more than 25 books.

Origins
Founded: 1997
Parent company: Grafik Communications
Number of employees: 10
Headquarters: Alexandria, VA (Washington, DC Metro Area)

Principals
Eric Goetz, Judy Kirpich

Contact
e-media c
1199 N. Fairfax St., Suite 700
Alexandria, VA 22314
Tel.: 703. 683 0511
Fax: 703. 683 3740
E-mail: info@e-media-c.com
Web: www.e-media-c.com, www.grafik.com

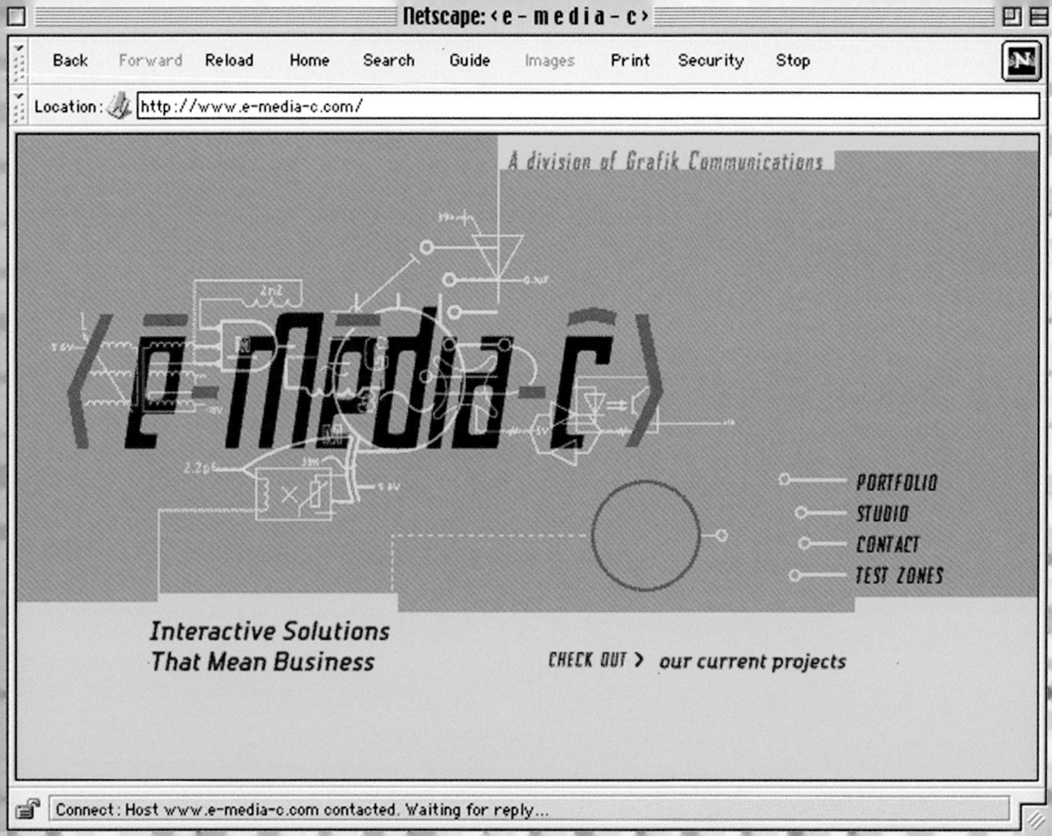
Netscape: ‹e-media-c›
Back
Forward
Reload
Home
Search
Guide
Images
Print
Security
Stop
Location: http://www.e-media-c.com/
A division of Grafik Communications
‹e-media-c›
PORTFOLIO
STUDIO
CONTACT
TEST ZONES
Interactive Solutions
That Mean Business
CHECK OUT › our current projects
Connect: Host www.e-media-c.com contacted. Waiting for reply...

e features and technology. s a division of Grafik arketing Communications, media-c has produced many ebsites as part of larger rporate programs. In those

include details and images of the collateral system developed for an entire campaign. We include a secure testing area so clients can review and "beta-test" a site while we

And, to keep our clients informed, we added a chart of 216 "Internet-safe" colors and a comparison of image quality based on file size and format.

(this and following spread)
Art Director: Eric Goetz
Designers:
Eric Goetz, Jonathan Amen
Production:
Eric Goetz, Joel Fisher

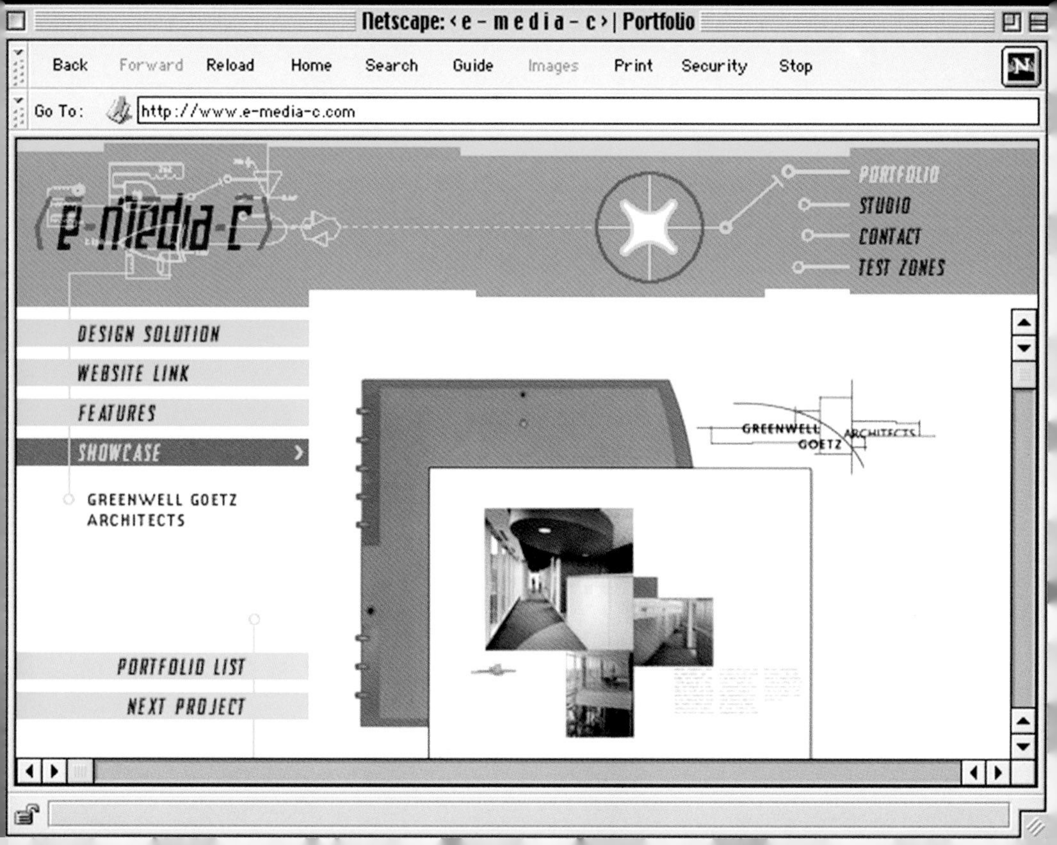

Netscape: <e-media-c> | Portfolio

Back Forward Reload Home Search Guide Images Print Security Stop

Go To: http://www.e-media-c.com

(e-media-c)

PORTFOLIO
STUDIO
CONTACT
TEST ZONES

DESIGN SOLUTION
WEBSITE LINK
FEATURES
SHOWCASE

GREENWELL GOETZ
ARCHITECTS

PORTFOLIO LIST
NEXT PROJECT

GREENWELL GOETZ ARCHITECTS

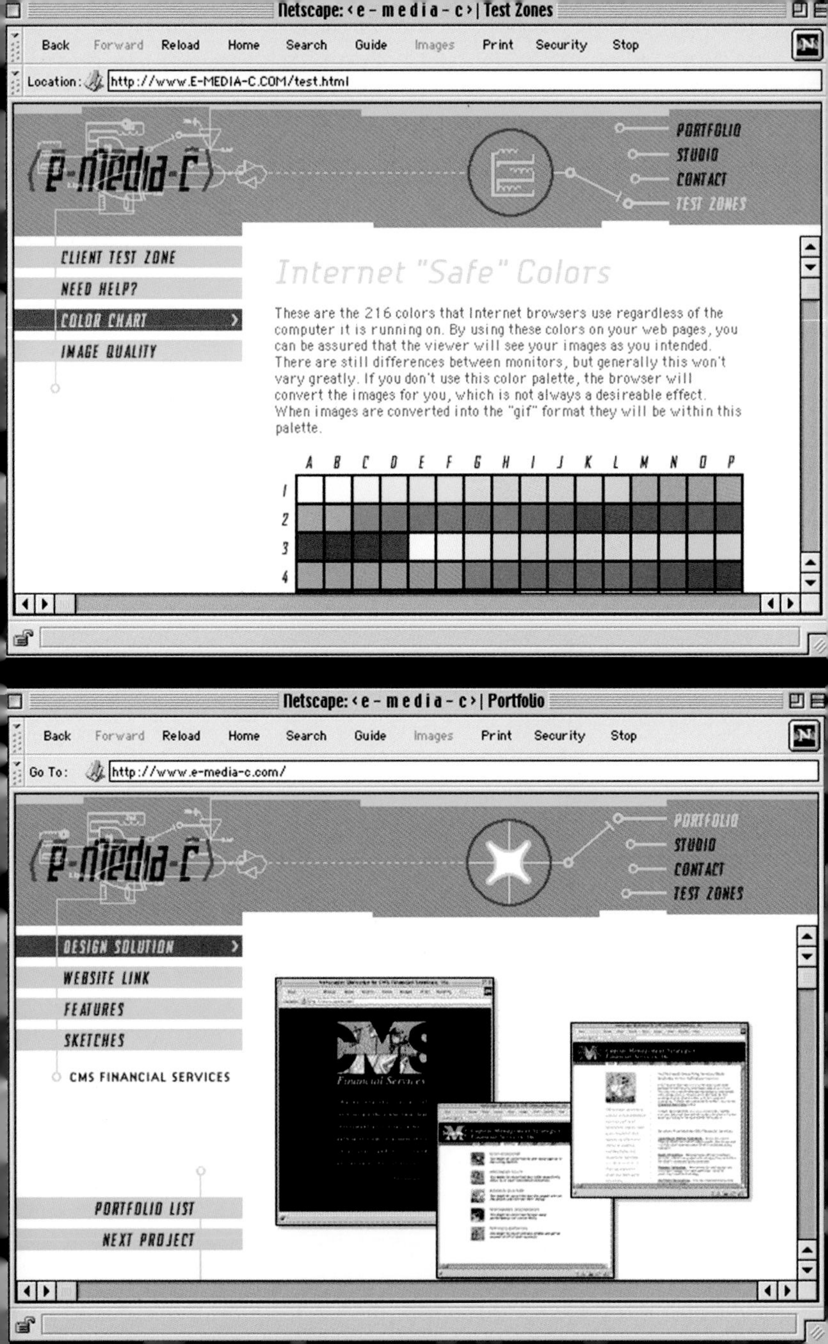

Netscape: < e - m e d i a - c >| Test Zones
Back Forward Reload Home Search Guide Images Print Security Stop
Location: http://www.E-MEDIA-C.COM/test.html
PORTFOLIO
STUDIO
CONTACT
TEST ZONES
CLIENT TEST ZONE
NEED HELP?
COLOR CHART
IMAGE QUALITY
Internet "Safe" Colors
These are the 216 colors that Internet browsers use regardless of the computer it is running on. By using these colors on your web pages, you can be assured that the viewer will see your images as you intended. There are still differences between monitors, but generally this won't vary greatly. If you don't use this color palette, the browser will convert the images for you, which is not always a desireable effect. When images are converted into the "gif" format they will be within this palette.
A B C D E F G H I J K L M N O P
1
2
3
4
Netscape: < e - m e d i a - c >| Portfolio
Back Forward Reload Home Search Guide Images Print Security Stop
Go To: http://www.e-media-c.com/
PORTFOLIO
STUDIO
CONTACT
TEST ZONES
DESIGN SOLUTION
WEBSITE LINK
FEATURES
SKETCHES
CMS FINANCIAL SERVICES
PORTFOLIO LIST
NEXT PROJECT

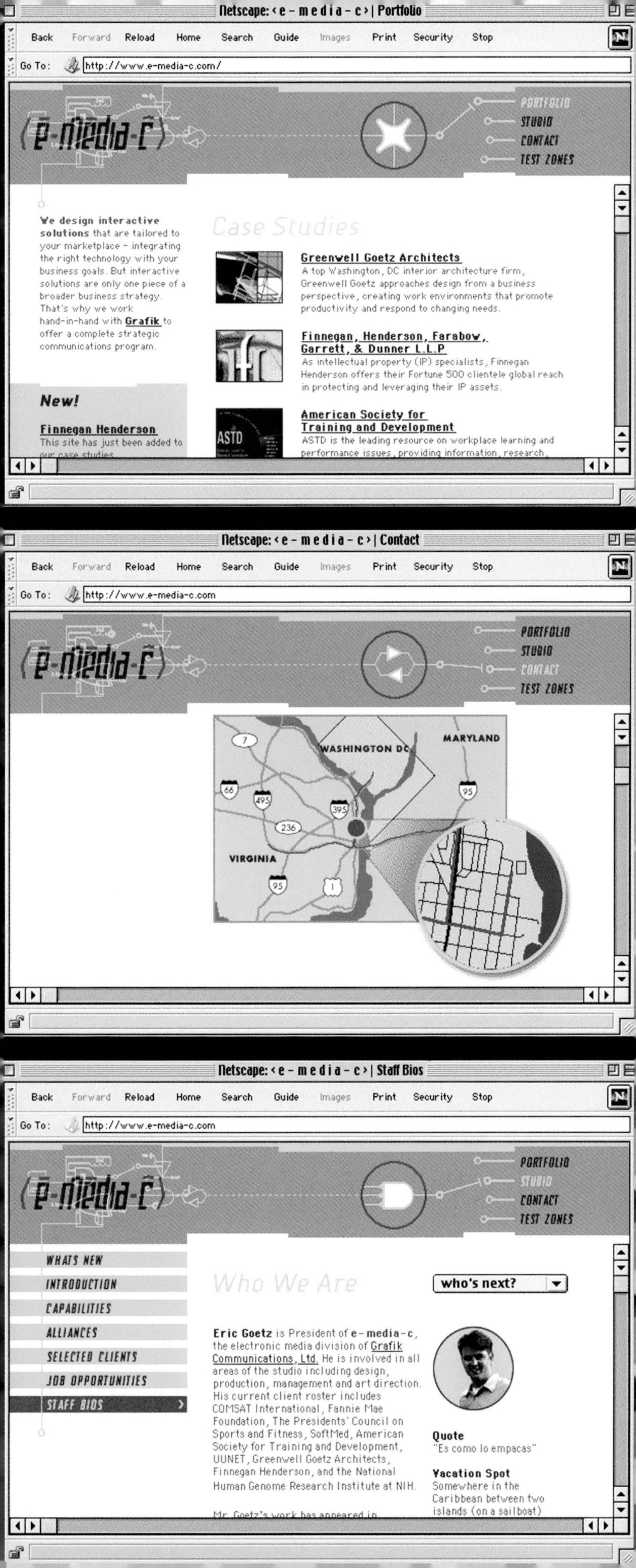
Netscape: < e - m e d i a - c > | Portfolio
Back Forward Reload Home Search Guide Images Print Security Stop
Go To: http://www.e-media-c.com/
PORTFOLIO
STUDIO
CONTACT
TEST ZONES
We design interactive solutions that are tailored to your marketplace - integrating the right technology with your business goals. But interactive solutions are only one piece of a broader business strategy. That's why we work hand-in-hand with Grafik to offer a complete strategic communications program.
New!
Finnegan Henderson
This site has just been added to our case studies
Case Studies
Greenwell Goetz Architects
A top Washington, DC interior architecture firm, Greenwell Goetz approaches design from a business perspective, creating work environments that promote productivity and respond to changing needs.
Finnegan, Henderson, Farabow, Garrett, & Dunner L.L.P
As intellectual property (IP) specialists, Finnegan Henderson offers their Fortune 500 clientele global reach in protecting and leveraging their IP assets.
American Society for Training and Development
ASTD is the leading resource on workplace learning and performance issues, providing information, research,
Netscape: < e - m e d i a - c > | Contact
Go To: http://www.e-media-c.com
WASHINGTON DC
MARYLAND
VIRGINIA
Netscape: < e - m e d i a - c > | Staff Bios
WHATS NEW
INTRODUCTION
CAPABILITIES
ALLIANCES
SELECTED CLIENTS
JOB OPPORTUNITIES
STAFF BIOS
Who We Are
who's next?
Eric Goetz is President of e-media-c, the electronic media division of Grafik Communications, Ltd. He is involved in all areas of the studio including design, production, management and art direction. His current client roster includes COMSAT International, Fannie Mae Foundation, The Presidents' Council on Sports and Fitness, SoftMed, American Society for Training and Development, UUNET, Greenwell Goetz Architects, Finnegan Henderson, and the National Human Genome Research Institute at NIH.
Mr. Goetz's work has appeared in
Quote
"Es como lo empacas"
Vacation Spot
Somewhere in the Caribbean between two islands (on a sailboat)

Site description

Rockwater is a combination youth center / coffeehouse / cyber-cafe "where artistry meets conviction." It offers young people in Wausau, Wisconsin not only a place to hang out, but a multimedia experience. The center's technology combines audio / video production capabilities with computers and Internet access to deliver far beyond anything currently offered to this audience. To appeal to the high school market, the Rockwater site has a unique, edgy feel, with a different format for each section and highly focused content.

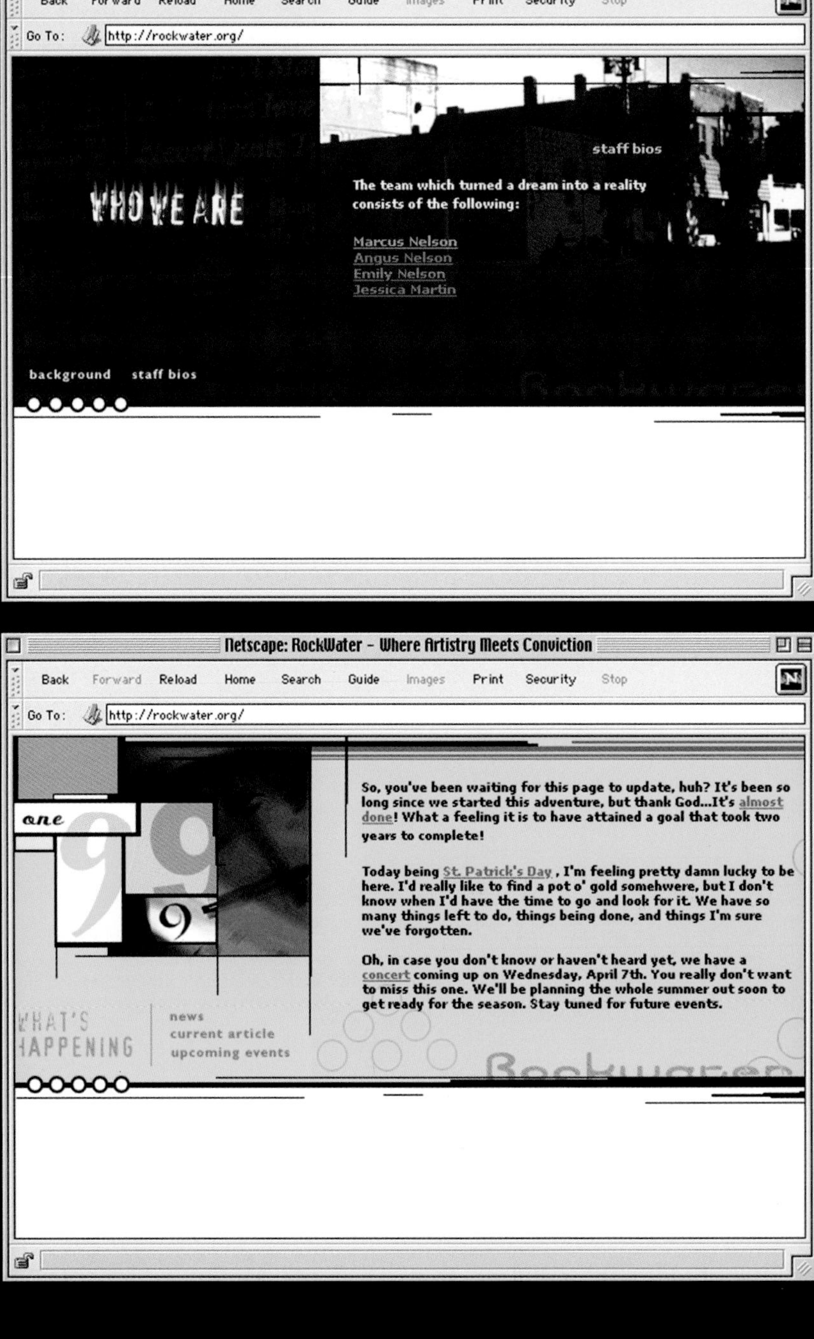

Client: Rockwater
Art Director: Eric Goetz
Designer: Joel Fisher
Production: Joel Fisher

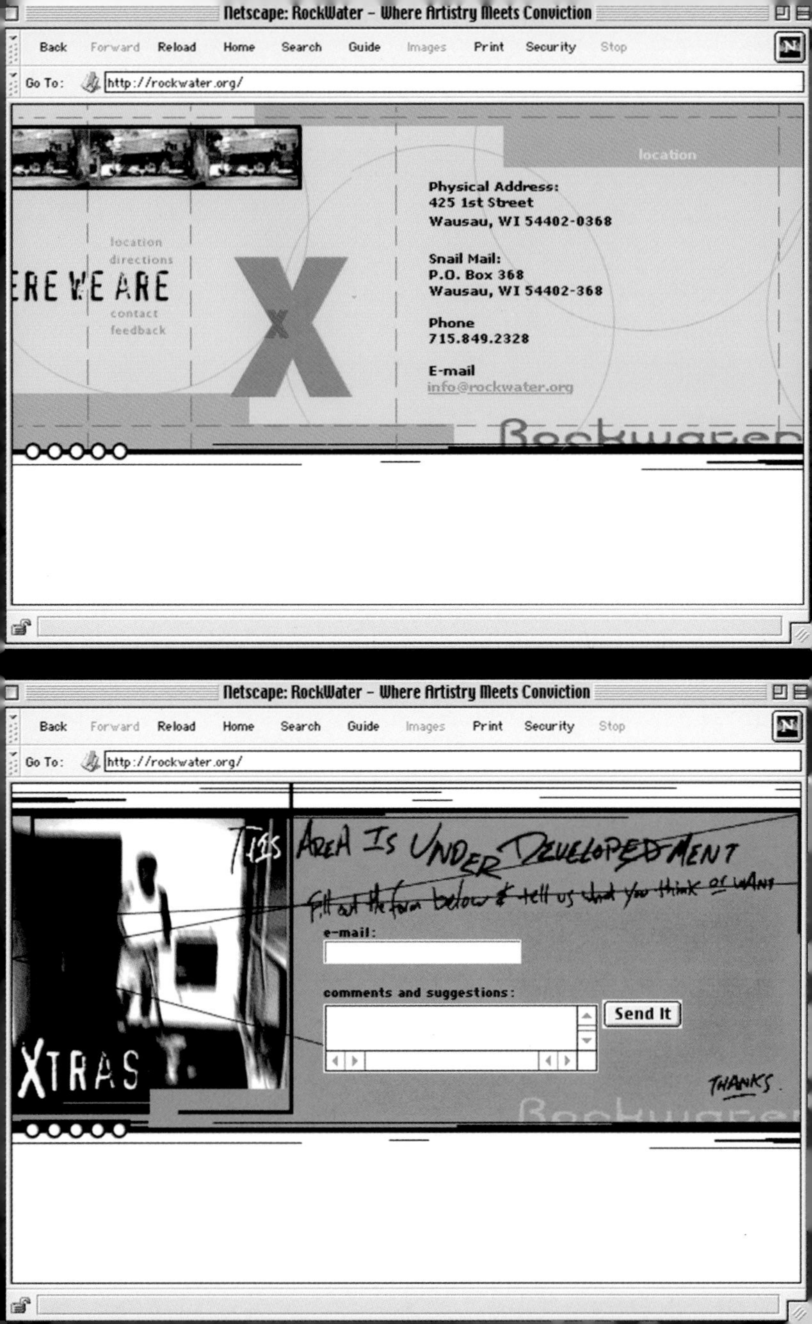
Netscape: RockWater – Where Artistry Meets Conviction
Back
Forward
Reload
Home
Search
Guide
Images
Print
Security
Stop
Go To:
http://rockwater.org/
location
location
directions
ERE WE ARE
contact
feedback
Physical Address:
425 1st Street
Wausau, WI 54402-0368
Snail Mail:
P.O. Box 368
Wausau, WI 54402-368
Phone
715.849.2328
E-mail
info@rockwater.org
Netscape: RockWater – Where Artistry Meets Conviction
Back
Forward
Reload
Home
Search
Guide
Images
Print
Security
Stop
Go To:
http://rockwater.org/
THIS AREA IS UNDER DEVELOPED MENT
Fill out the form below & tell us what you think or want
e-mail:
comments and suggestions:
Send It
XTRAS
THANKS

Netscape: Fannie Mae Foundation
Back Forward Reload Home Search Guide Images Print Security Stop
Go To: http://www.fanniemaefoundation.org/
FannieMae FOUNDATION
Home-Buyer Information
ICE CREAM
Home-Buying Fairs
Opening The Door To A Home Of Your Own
Choosing The Mortgage That's Right For You
Who We Are
Home-Buyer Information
News
Grantmaking and Community Initiatives
Housing Research
Innovative Partnerships
What's New
Site Map
Home-Buying Fairs
Get More Information Than You Ever Hoped To Receive About Buying A Home.
How long have you wanted your own home but you just didn't know how to get it? Come to the FREE Fannie Mae Foundation Home-Buying Fair where mortgage lenders, credit experts, real estate professionals, and members of community housing groups will answer all of your home-buying questions. For more information, please call 1-888-752-7170. You may not walk out with an actual house, but you'll finally know how to go about buying one. Besides, the house wouldn't fit in your trunk anyway.
Attend Our Workshops!
At the Fannie Mae Foundation Home-Buying Fairs, panel sessions such as the
Netscape: Fannie Mae Foundation
Back Forward Reload Home Search Guide Images Print Security Stop
Go To: http://www.fanniemaefoundation.org/
FannieMae FOUNDATION
The Fannie Mae Foundation transforms communities through innovative partnerships and initiatives that revitalize neighborhoods and create affordable homeownership and housing opportunities across America.
Find out more about us
Netscape: Fannie Mae Foundation
Back Forward Reload Home Search Guide Images Print Security Stop
Go To: http://www.fanniemaefoundation.org/
FannieMae FOUNDATION
Welcome to the Fannie Mae Foundation
WHO WE ARE
HOME-BUYER INFORMATION
INNOVATIVE PARTNERSHIPS
NEWS
GRANTMAKING AND COMMUNITY INITIATIVES
HOUSING RESEARCH
CHOOSE FROM ABOVE
[Story on photo]
Site Map
What's New?
The Fannie Mae Foundation's Web site has a new look! We have redesigned our site to be easier to use and provide even more helpful information about the Foundation's many programs.
Want to buy a home of your own? The Fannie Mae Foundation offers free information about how to get on the path

opposite page)
Client: Fannie Mae Foundation
Art Director: Eric Goetz
Designers: Eric Goetz
Production: Eric Goetz, Joel Fisher
Photography: Various
from Fannie Mae Foundation

Providing funding for affordable housing to millions of lower- and middle-income Americans, the Fannie Mae Foundation transforms communities through innovative partnerships and initiatives that

of navigation and a "human face" were key attributes that our client wanted, since the site would frequently be accessed from public libraries and/or by users who might not be Internet savvy. As with any pub-

also a key factor . Users come to the site for quick information, not entertainment, and we had to assume potential users would not have the biggest, and fastest computers. This clearly drove design elements.

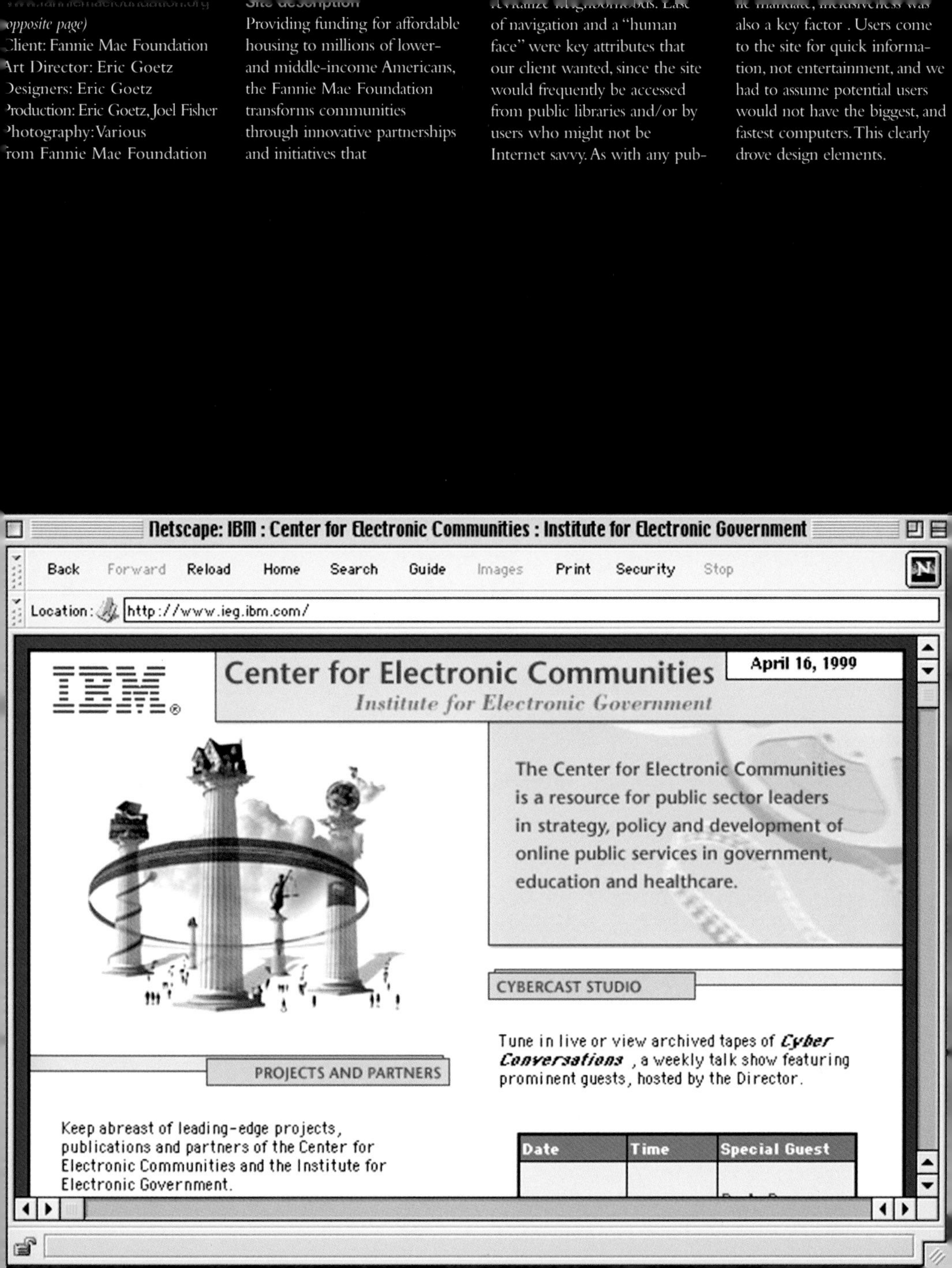

www.gga.com
(this spread)
Client: Greenwell Goetz Architects
Art Director: Eric Goetz
Designers: Eric Goetz, Jonathan Amen
Production: Eric Goetz
Photography: Thomas Arledge

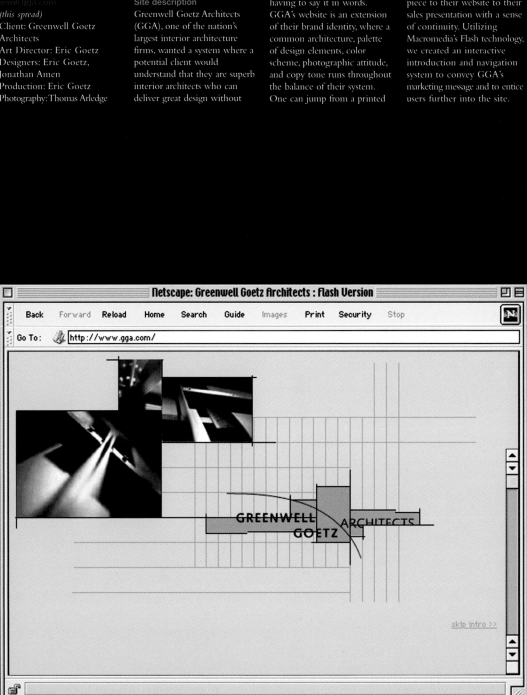

Site description
Greenwell Goetz Architects (GGA), one of the nation's largest interior architecture firms, wanted a system where a potential client would understand that they are superb interior architects who can deliver great design without having to say it in words. GGA's website is an extension of their brand identity, where a common architecture, palette of design elements, color scheme, photographic attitude, and copy tone runs throughout the balance of their system. One can jump from a printed piece to their website to their sales presentation with a sense of continuity. Utilizing Macromedia's Flash technology, we created an interactive introduction and navigation system to convey GGA's marketing message and to entice users further into the site.

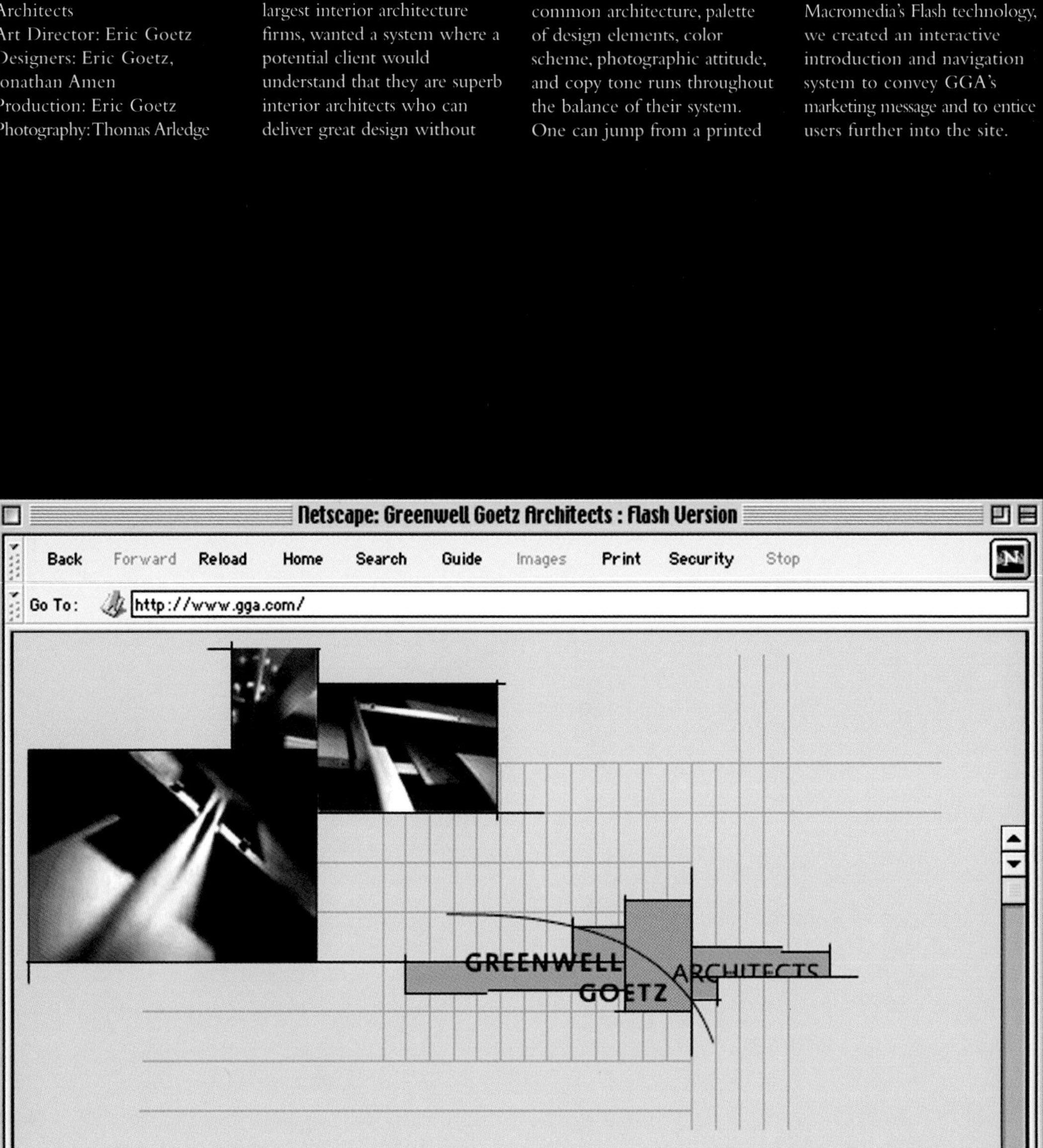

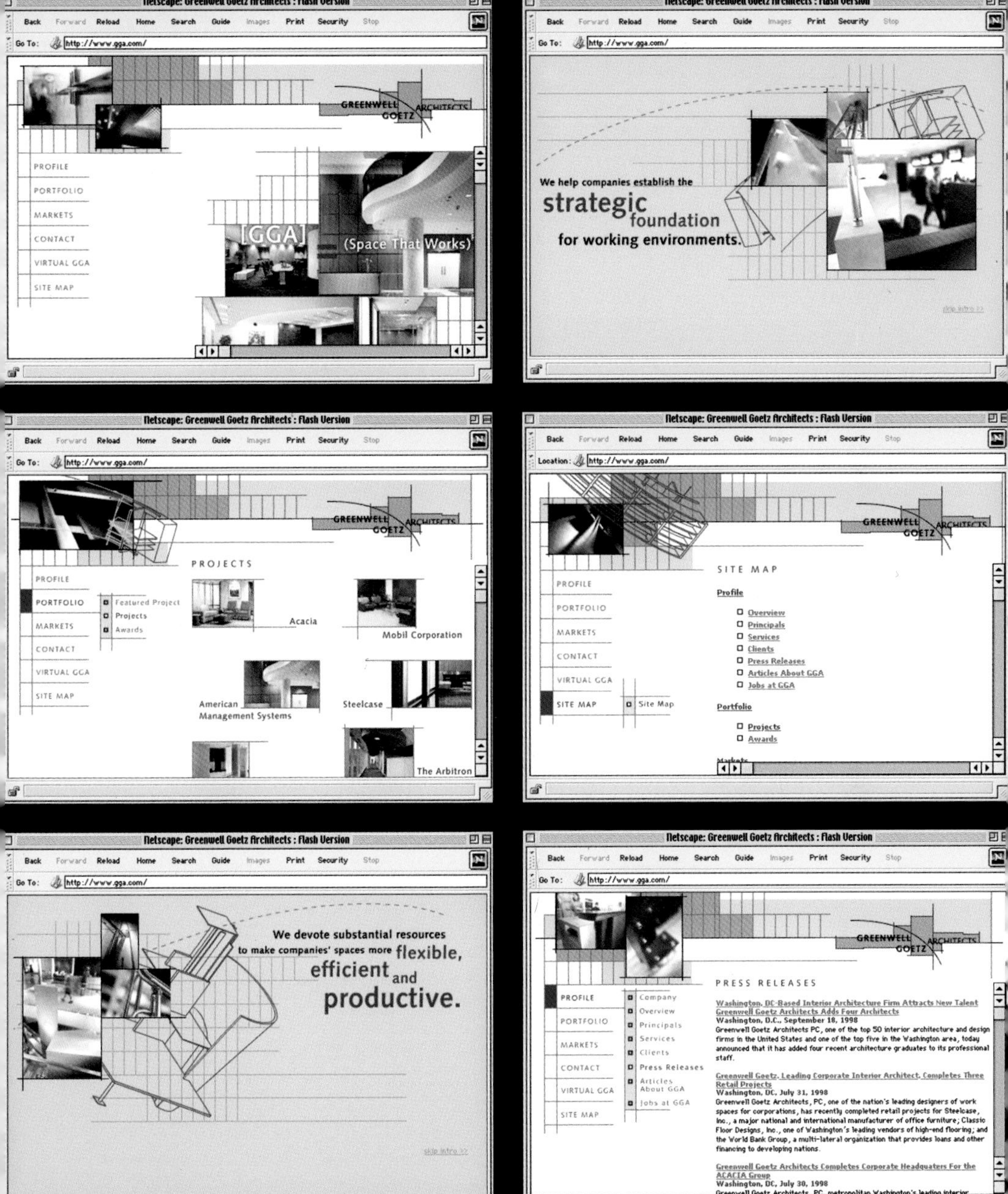

Netscape: Greenwell Goetz Architects : Flash Version
Back Forward Reload Home Search Guide Images Print Security Stop
Go To: http://www.gga.com/
GREENWELL GOETZ ARCHITECTS
PROFILE
PORTFOLIO
MARKETS
CONTACT
VIRTUAL GGA
SITE MAP
[GGA]
(Space That Works)
Netscape: Greenwell Goetz Architects : Flash Version
Go To: http://www.gga.com/
We help companies establish the
strategic
foundation
for working environments.
Netscape: Greenwell Goetz Architects : Flash Version
Go To: http://www.gga.com/
GREENWELL GOETZ ARCHITECTS
PROJECTS
PROFILE
PORTFOLIO
Featured Project
Projects
Awards
MARKETS
CONTACT
VIRTUAL GGA
SITE MAP
Acacia
Mobil Corporation
American Management Systems
Steelcase
The Arbitron
Netscape: Greenwell Goetz Architects : Flash Version
Location: http://www.gga.com/
GREENWELL GOETZ ARCHITECTS
SITE MAP
PROFILE
PORTFOLIO
MARKETS
CONTACT
VIRTUAL GGA
SITE MAP
Site Map
Profile
Overview
Principals
Services
Clients
Press Releases
Articles About GGA
Jobs at GGA
Portfolio
Projects
Awards
Netscape: Greenwell Goetz Architects : Flash Version
Go To: http://www.gga.com/
We devote substantial resources
to make companies' spaces more flexible,
efficient and
productive.
Netscape: Greenwell Goetz Architects : Flash Version
Go To: http://www.gga.com/
GREENWELL GOETZ ARCHITECTS
PRESS RELEASES
PROFILE
PORTFOLIO
MARKETS
CONTACT
VIRTUAL GGA
SITE MAP
Company
Overview
Principals
Services
Clients
Press Releases
Articles About GGA
Jobs at GGA
Washington, DC-Based Interior Architecture Firm Attracts New Talent
Greenwell Goetz Architects Adds Four Architects
Washington, D.C., September 18, 1998
Greenwell Goetz Architects PC, one of the top 50 interior architecture and design firms in the United States and one of the top five in the Washington area, today announced that it has added four recent architecture graduates to its professional staff.
Greenwell Goetz, Leading Corporate Interior Architect, Completes Three Retail Projects
Washington, DC, July 31, 1998
Greenwell Goetz Architects, PC, one of the nation's leading designers of work spaces for corporations, has recently completed retail projects for Steelcase, Inc., a major national and international manufacturer of office furniture; Classic Floor Designs, Inc., one of Washington's leading vendors of high-end flooring; and the World Bank Group, a multi-lateral organization that provides loans and other financing to developing nations.
Greenwell Goetz Architects Completes Corporate Headquaters For the ACACIA Group
Washington, DC, July 30, 1998

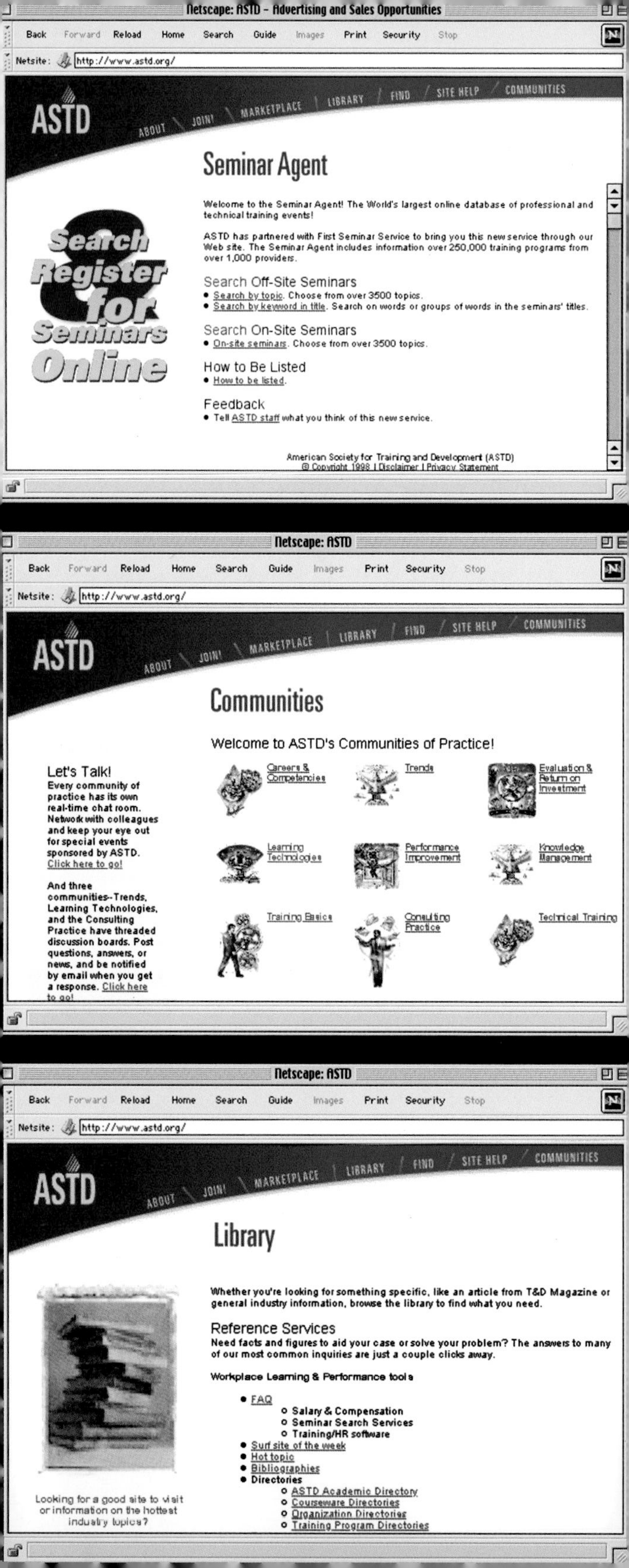

Netscape: ASTD – Advertising and Sales Opportunities
Back Forward Reload Home Search Guide Images Print Security Stop
Netsite: http://www.astd.org/
ASTD
ABOUT JOIN! MARKETPLACE LIBRARY FIND SITE HELP COMMUNITIES
Search & Register for Seminars Online
Seminar Agent
Welcome to the Seminar Agent! The World's largest online database of professional and technical training events!
ASTD has partnered with First Seminar Service to bring you this new service through our Web site. The Seminar Agent includes information over 250,000 training programs from over 1,000 providers.
Search Off-Site Seminars
Search by topic. Choose from over 3500 topics.
Search by keyword in title. Search on words or groups of words in the seminars' titles.
Search On-Site Seminars
On-site seminars. Choose from over 3500 topics.
How to Be Listed
How to be listed.
Feedback
Tell ASTD staff what you think of this new service.
American Society for Training and Development (ASTD)
© Copyright 1998 | Disclaimer | Privacy Statement
Netscape: ASTD
Back Forward Reload Home Search Guide Images Print Security Stop
Netsite: http://www.astd.org/
ASTD
ABOUT JOIN! MARKETPLACE LIBRARY FIND SITE HELP COMMUNITIES
Communities
Welcome to ASTD's Communities of Practice!
Let's Talk!
Every community of practice has its own real-time chat room. Network with colleagues and keep your eye out for special events sponsored by ASTD. Click here to go!
And three communities–Trends, Learning Technologies, and the Consulting Practice have threaded discussion boards. Post questions, answers, or news, and be notified by email when you get a response. Click here to go!
Careers & Competencies
Trends
Evaluation & Return on Investment
Learning Technologies
Performance Improvement
Knowledge Management
Training Basics
Consulting Practice
Technical Training
Netscape: ASTD
Back Forward Reload Home Search Guide Images Print Security Stop
Netsite: http://www.astd.org/
ASTD
ABOUT JOIN! MARKETPLACE LIBRARY FIND SITE HELP COMMUNITIES
Library
Whether you're looking for something specific, like an article from T&D Magazine or general industry information, browse the library to find what you need.
Reference Services
Need facts and figures to aid your case or solve your problem? The answers to many of our most common inquiries are just a couple clicks away.
Workplace Learning & Performance tools
FAQ
Salary & Compensation
Seminar Search Services
Training/HR software
Surf site of the week
Hot topic
Bibliographies
Directories
ASTD Academic Directory
Courseware Directories
Organization Directories
Training Program Directories
Looking for a good site to visit or information on the hottest industry topics?

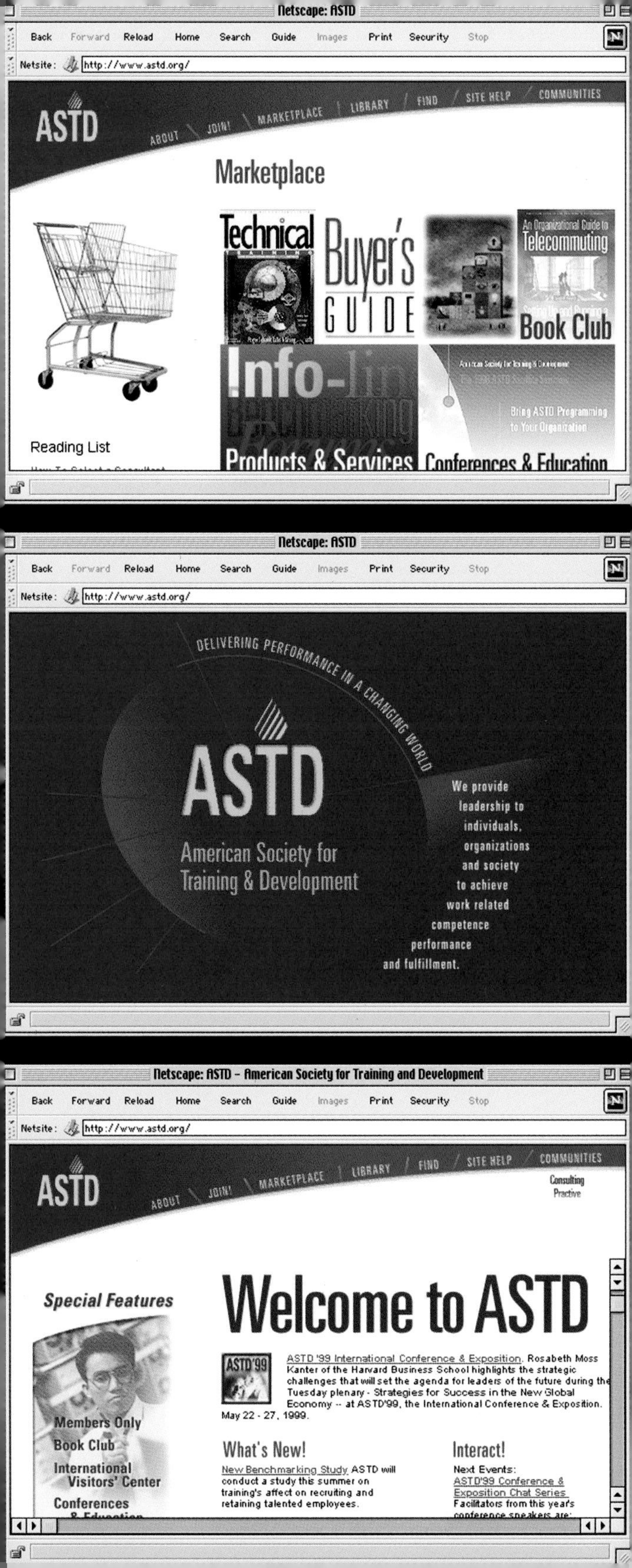

Netscape: ASTD
Back Forward Reload Home Search Guide Images Print Security Stop
Netsite: http://www.astd.org/
ASTD
ABOUT JOIN! MARKETPLACE LIBRARY FIND SITE HELP COMMUNITIES
Marketplace
Technical Training
Buyer's Guide
An Organizational Guide to Telecommuting
Book Club
Info-line
Benchmarking
Products & Services
Bring ASTD Programming to Your Organization
Conferences & Education
Reading List
Netscape: ASTD
Back Forward Reload Home Search Guide Images Print Security Stop
Netsite: http://www.astd.org/
DELIVERING PERFORMANCE IN A CHANGING WORLD
ASTD
American Society for Training & Development
We provide leadership to individuals, organizations and society to achieve work related competence performance and fulfillment.
Netscape: ASTD – American Society for Training and Development
Back Forward Reload Home Search Guide Images Print Security Stop
Netsite: http://www.astd.org/
ASTD
ABOUT JOIN! MARKETPLACE LIBRARY FIND SITE HELP COMMUNITIES
Consulting Practice
Special Features
Welcome to ASTD
ASTD'99
ASTD '99 International Conference & Exposition. Rosabeth Moss Kanter of the Harvard Business School highlights the strategic challenges that will set the agenda for leaders of the future during the Tuesday plenary - Strategies for Success in the New Global Economy -- at ASTD'99, the International Conference & Exposition. May 22 - 27, 1999.
Members Only
Book Club
International Visitors' Center
Conferences
What's New!
New Benchmarking Study. ASTD will conduct a study this summer on training's affect on recruiting and retaining talented employees.
Interact!
Next Events:
ASTD'99 Conference & Exposition Chat Series
Facilitators from this year's

FACTOR

Factor Design

Factor Design is a five-year-old design firm with offices in Hamburg, Germany and San Francisco, California. Purposely straddling the worlds of traditional print media and interactive environments, Factor strives to educate clients, enhancing their understanding of the various opportunities available on the Web. By strategically exploiting those opportunities, we are able to provide useful and appropriate information swiftly and memorably. By developing strong collaborative relationships with our clients, Factor often develops not only the final design solutions but is also integral in defining the overall marketing strategy of a given product or project. Keeping one eye on the road ahead while solving the immediate challenge has been what clients expect when asking Factor to join their teams.

The work of the studio and its members has been widely published and recognized by The American Center for Design 100 Show, Type Directors Club, and GRAPHIS, COMMUNICATION ARTS and PRINT magazines, among others. Current and former clients include Adobe Systems, Apple Computer, Elemental Software, Microsoft/WebTV, MTV Germany, Roemerturm Feinstpapier, Wieden and Kennedy Amsterdam, and WR Hambrecht and Company.

The ultimate value of the Web today is defined by a website's ability to intelligently capture information, process it, swiftly make connections between the entirety of stored information, and then deliver the appropriate data back to the user. These database-driven sites are finally turning the Web into a useful tool versus the 'time sink' of interesting-looking but static content it once was, finally making the Web approachable and useful without being cute.

Due to the inherent complexities of this technology and, likewise, the amount of information that can potentially be displayed on any given page, the underlying navigation structures and content hierarchies must be equally developed and clearly defined. The entire site structure must be intelligently architected to accommodate the many variables offered to the user. The age of 600 x 400 pixel GIFs laboriously downloaded to the screen to present a glamorous but static page are dead. Living content must now enter stage left at the Web design beauty pageant.

Consumers have become very savvy and expect sophisticated content retrieval and delivery. Intuitive navigation and instant access to the content of a robust site with one or two clicks of the mouse is not only expected, in most cases it is demanded. This slow evolution of information access and retrieval as it pertains to websites has presented a number of interesting challenges to the design community and is seldom challenged or explored because, after all, it takes hours and hours of hard work, work that is never seen by the user of a site, and work that is definitely not discussed or included in the beauty contests staged by design magazines and award annuals.

Origins
Founded: Hamburg office: May 1993; San Francisco office: October 1996
Number of employees when founded: 2, now: 21
Headquarters: Hamburg
Location of other offices: San Francisco

Principals
Johannes Erler, Thomas Leifer, Uwe Melichar, Andreas Ribowski Olaf Stein, Jeff Zwerner

Contact
Factor Design, Inc.; Jeff Zwerner
461 Second Street, Suite 202
San Francisco, CA 94107,
Tel.: 415. 896 6051
Fax: 415. 896 6053
E-mail: info@factordesign.com
Web: http://www.factordesign.com

Contact Germany
Factor Design AG; Thomas Leifer
Schulterblatt 58
20357 Hamburg, Germany
Tel: 49. 40. 43 2571-0
Fax: 49. 40. 43 2571-99
E-mail: mail@factordesign.com
Web: http://www.factordesign.com

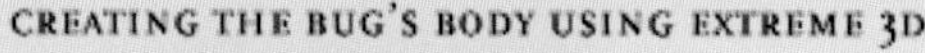

JIM **LUDTKE** PART TWO

AND **THE BUG**

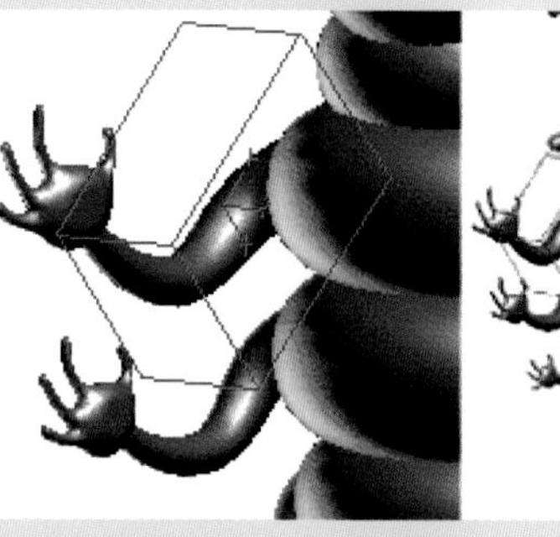

Here you see the finished model of the Bug in Extreme 3D's Smooth Shaded Mode. The Bug's hands are simple Metaform objects that were duplicated, resized and placed at the end of each of his six arms.

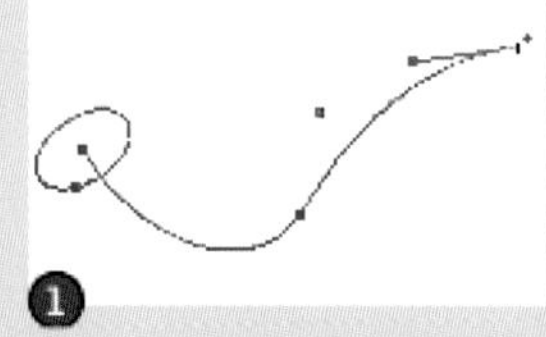

The Bug's arms are made of **Swept objects**. I first draw a spline (seen in blue) that I want to be the basic path of his arm. The points that define the spline have bezier handles that can be

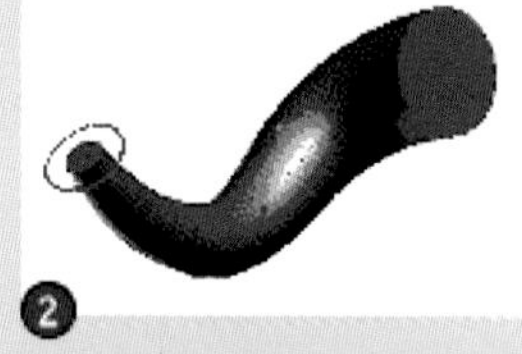

When I have the line where I think I want it, I click on the **Sweep Tool**, then the circle, and finally the line I want it to sweep along. In the **Info Window** I can define the

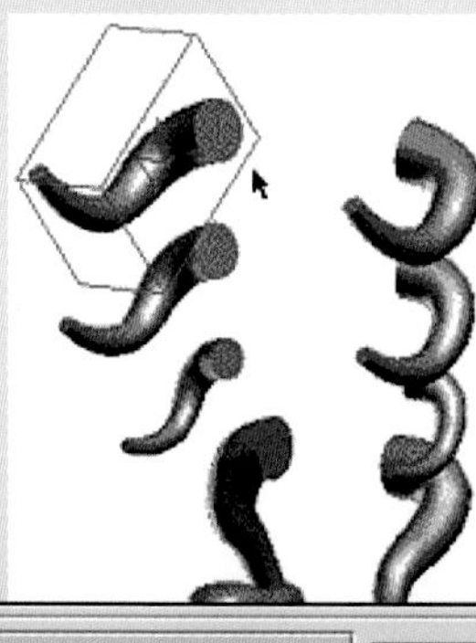

Site description

This site for Apple Computer, AppleMasters program was conceived at a point in Apple's history that saw its market share drop to all-time lows. Famous Mac loyalists came out of the woodwork and rallied to support the Macintosh platform. The Apple Masters program and website were developed in an effort to communicate that although Apple had only a 3% market share, it was used by the top 3% of nearly every profession.

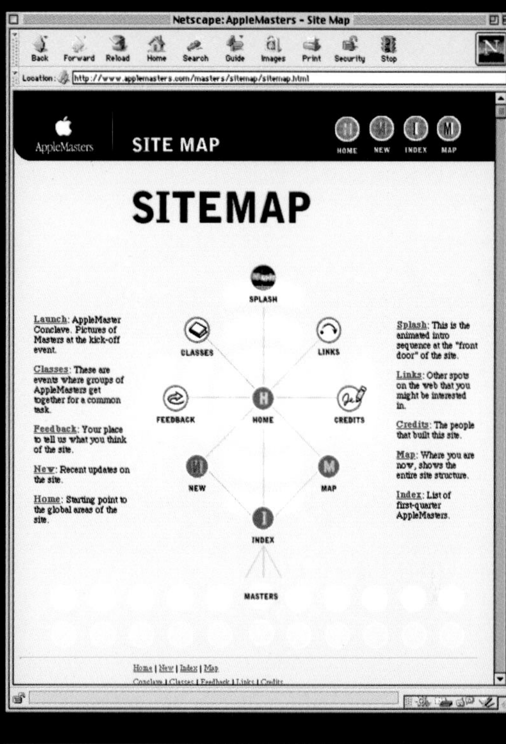

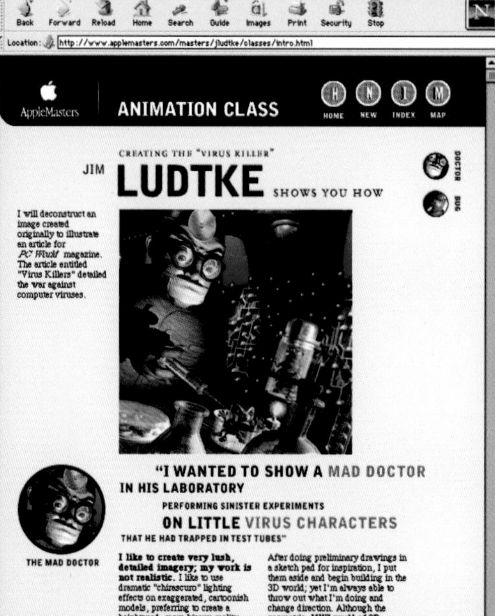

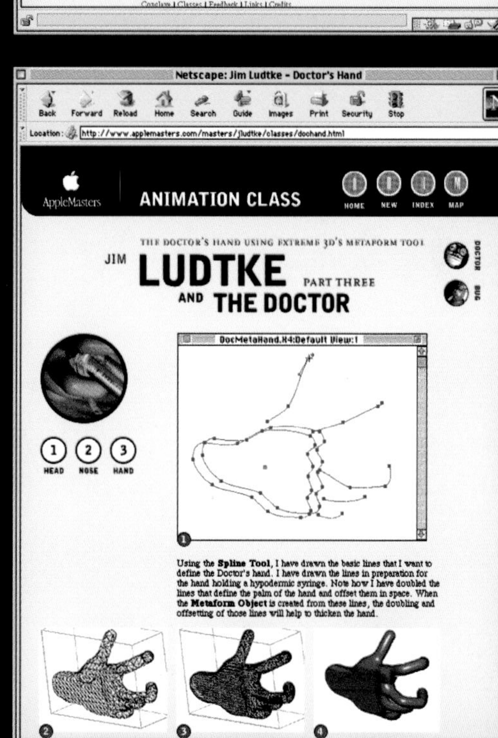

Site description

This site architecture map represents the information architecture developed for the Apple Imaging website, also developed by Factor Design. Each and every Factor Web project begins with a rigorous and thorough architecture development cycle to establish the information flow and navigation scenario we will use to communicate our core messages.

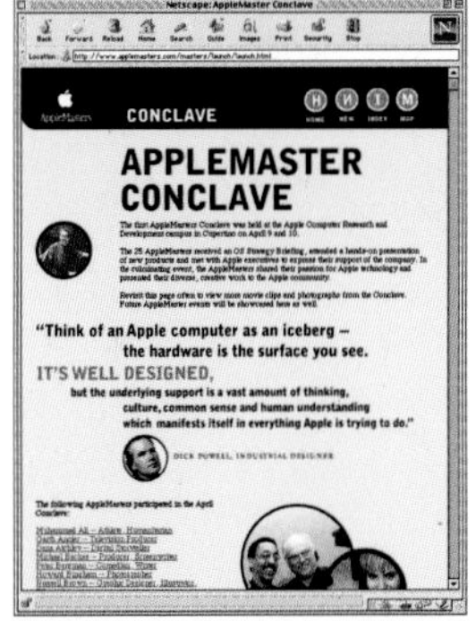

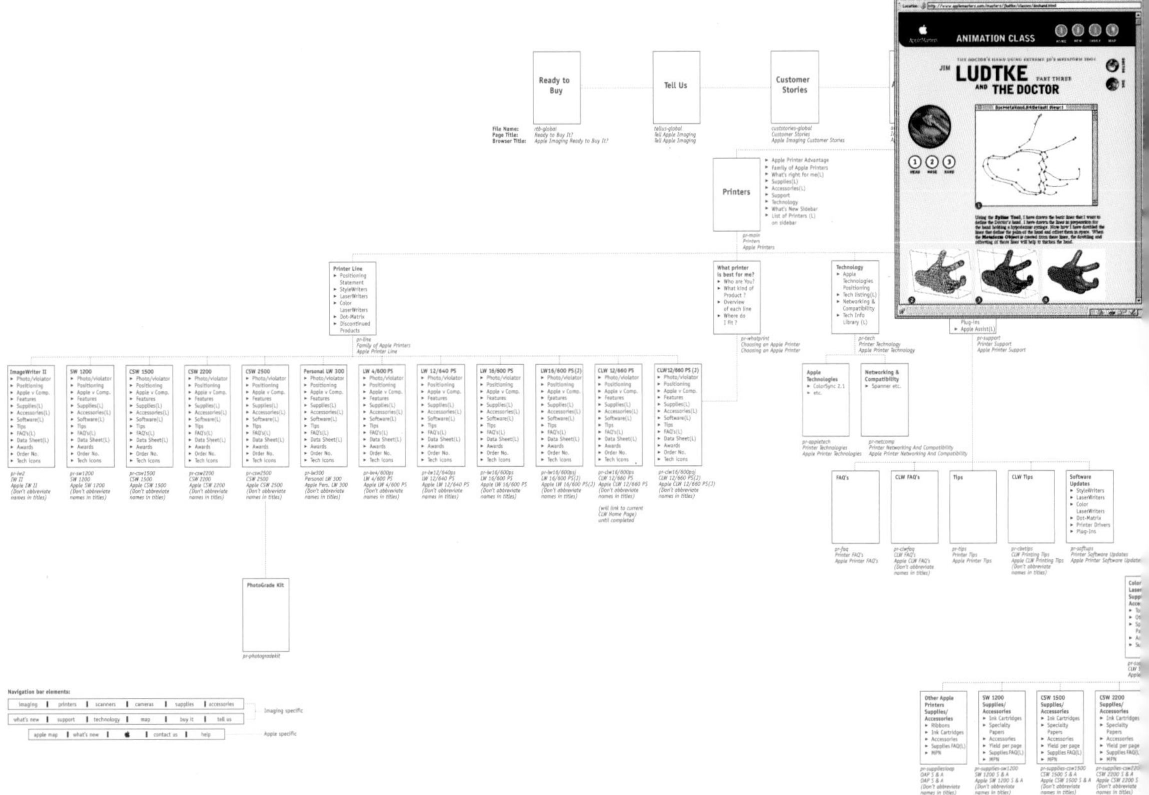

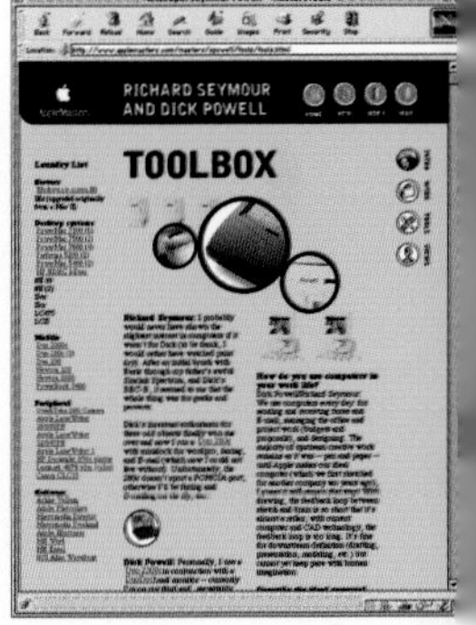

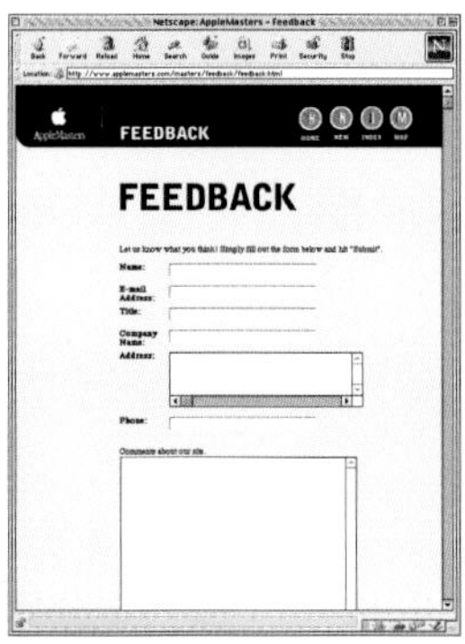
FEEDBACK
FEEDBACK

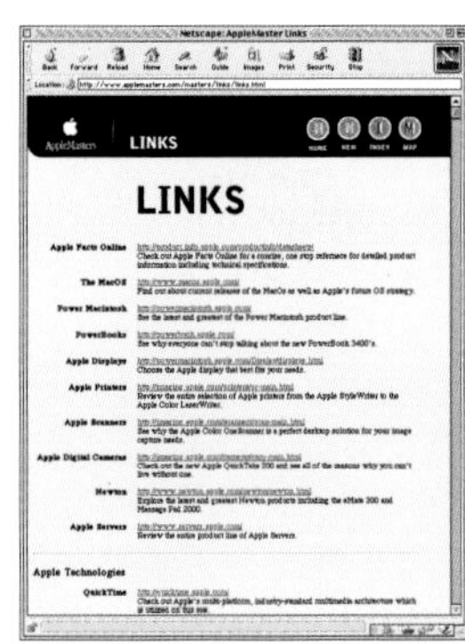
LINKS
LINKS

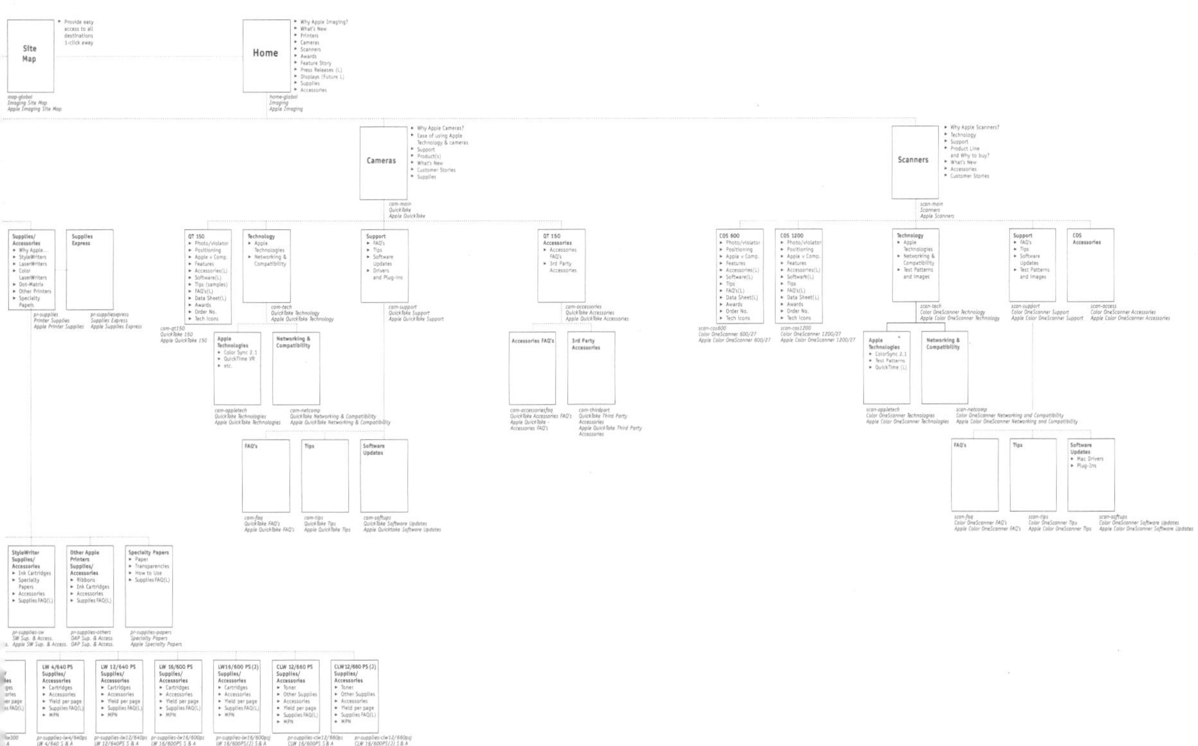
Site Map
Home
Cameras
Scanners

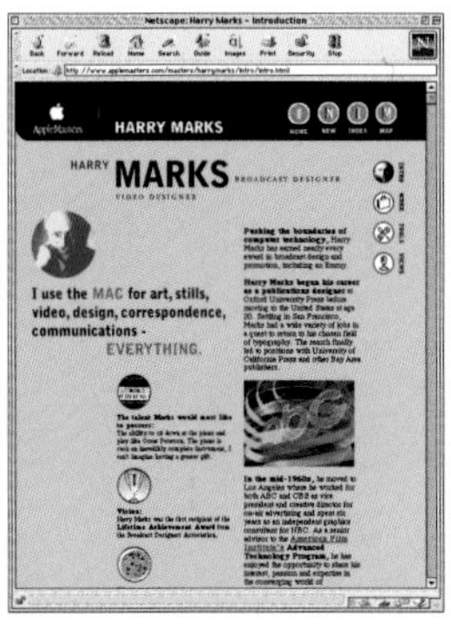
HARRY MARKS
MARKS
I use the MAC for art, stills, video, design, correspondence, communications - EVERYTHING.

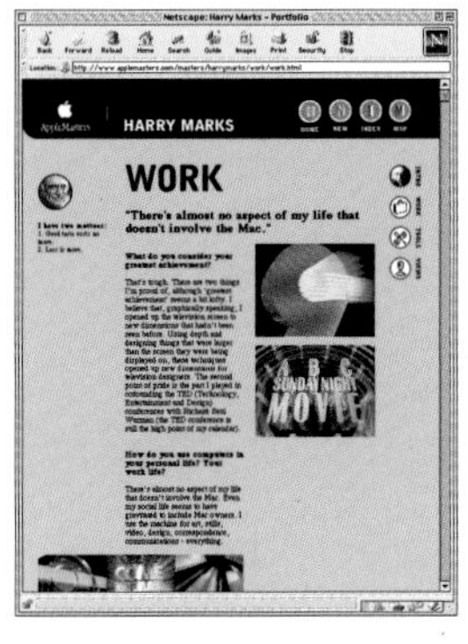
HARRY MARKS
WORK

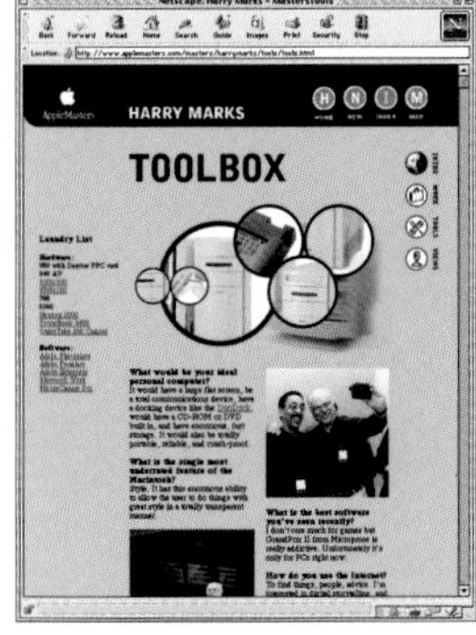
HARRY MARKS
TOOLBOX

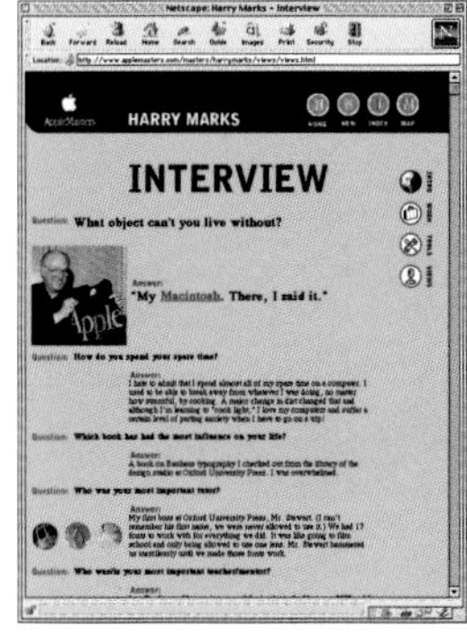
HARRY MARKS
INTERVIEW

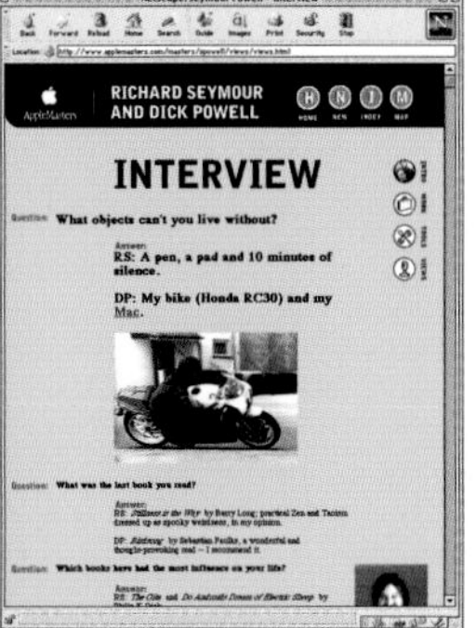
RICHARD SEYMOUR AND DICK POWELL
INTERVIEW

BELL GOTHIC

FF SCALA

"THE MAC WAS THE FIRST
machine to cross the machine/human gulf.
IT ACTUALLY COMMUNICATED
ON A HUMAN LEVEL."

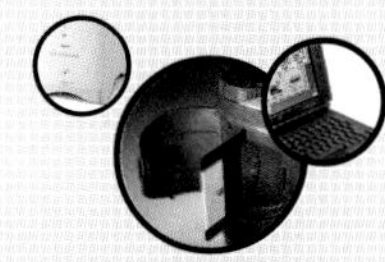

DR. MAE JEMISON

DR.MAE JEMISON

EDUCATOR

ASTRONAUT

"I believe at the heart of science are the words, 'I think, I wonder, and I understand.'"

Examining the use of existing and novel approaches to store collected power in the form of potential energy.

NASA:
It was September, 1992 when as a science mission specialist on the space

Mae Jemison earned a chemical engineering degree from Stanford followed by an M.D. from Cornell. After over two years as a Peace Corps doctor in Africa and two years in private practice in Los Angeles, she was accepted in NASA's training program in 1987 (one of 15 chosen from nearly 2,000 applicants). Dr. Mae Jemison was the first African American woman to enter space.

She left NASA in 1993 and founded The Jemison Group, Inc., a private company that focuses on projects that integrate social science issues into the design development and implementation of technologies. Current projects include a satellite-based telecommun-

TYPE DESIGNER

DIRECTOR

PRODUCT DESIGNERS

BROADCAST DESIGNER

ACTRESS

AppleMasters

APPLEMASTER NO.

42 PRODUCT DESIGNERS

CLICK HERE TO VISIT THE APPLEMASTERS WEB SITE

APPLEMASTER NO.

SIR CHRIS BONINGTON

13 MOUNTAINEER

MY LOVE AFFAIR WITH THE MAC

CLICK HERE TO SEE THE APPLEMASTERS

Apple Promotional Banners
(opposite page)
Client: Apple Computer
Creative Director: Jeff Zwerner
Designers: Andrea Herstowki, Jeff Zwerner

Project description
These advertising banners from the Apple.com homepage were developed to promote various individuals associated with the AppleMasters program website.

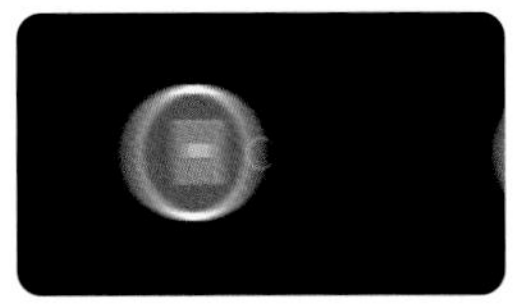

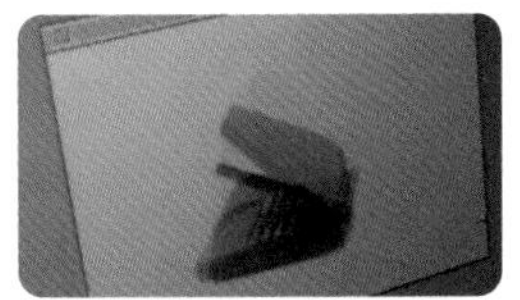
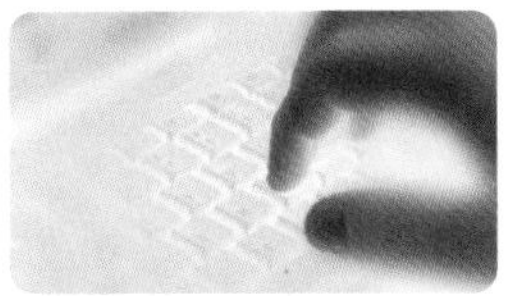

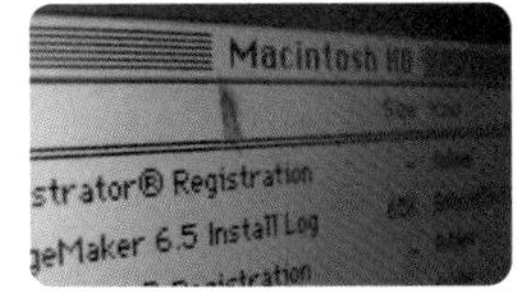

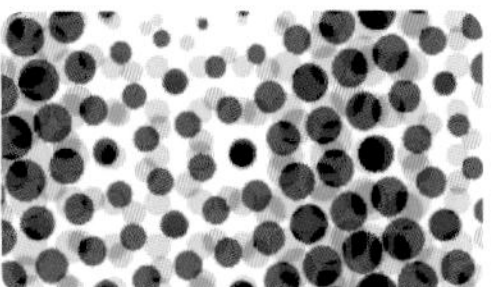

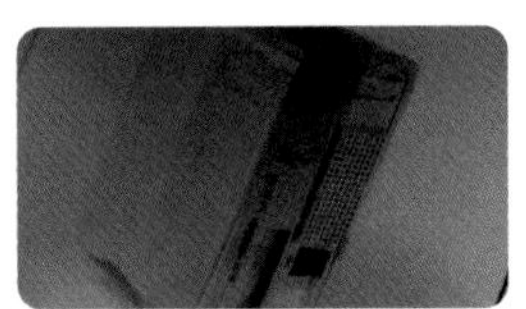
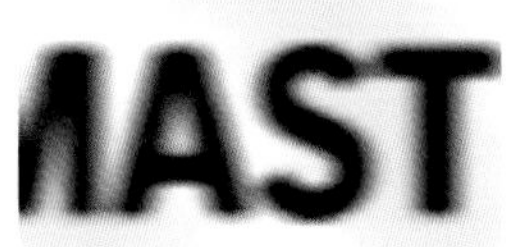
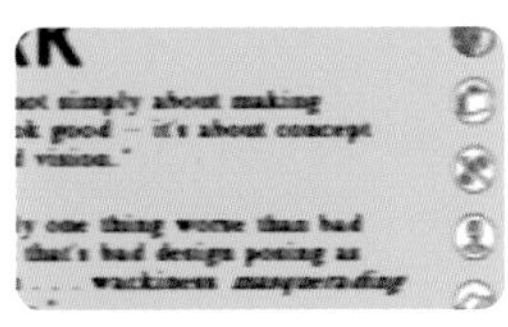
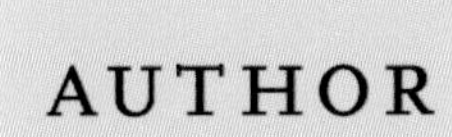

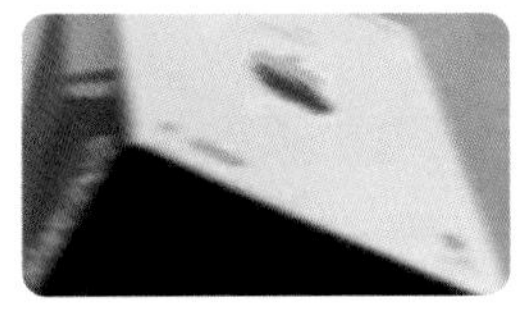
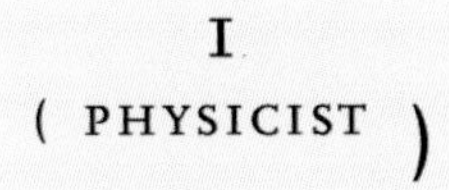

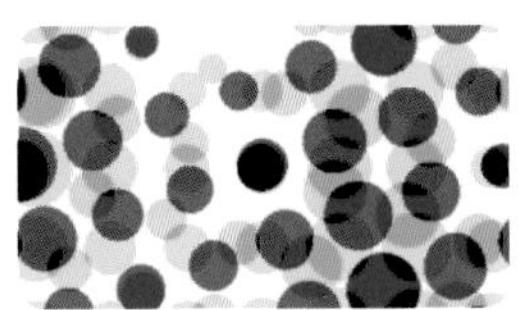

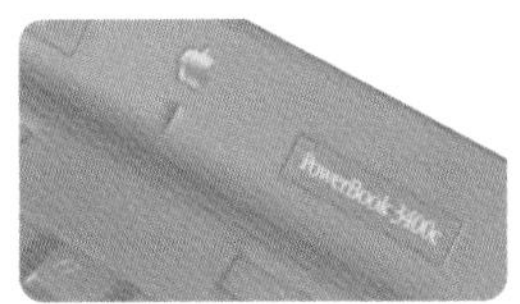

AppleMasters launch video
(this page)
Client: Apple Computer
Creative Directors, Designers: Jeff Zwerner, Joshua Distler

Project description
These are stills from a one-minute launch video designed to introduce the Apple Masters program website.

http://www.factordesign.com
Client: Factor Design
Creative Director: Jeff Zwerner
Designers: Andrea Herstowki, Jeff Zwerner
Photographers: Frank Stöckel, Steven Underwood
Writers: Hannah S. Fricke, Peter Chase, Jeff Zwerner
Programmer: Ryan Dee, Metagraphics

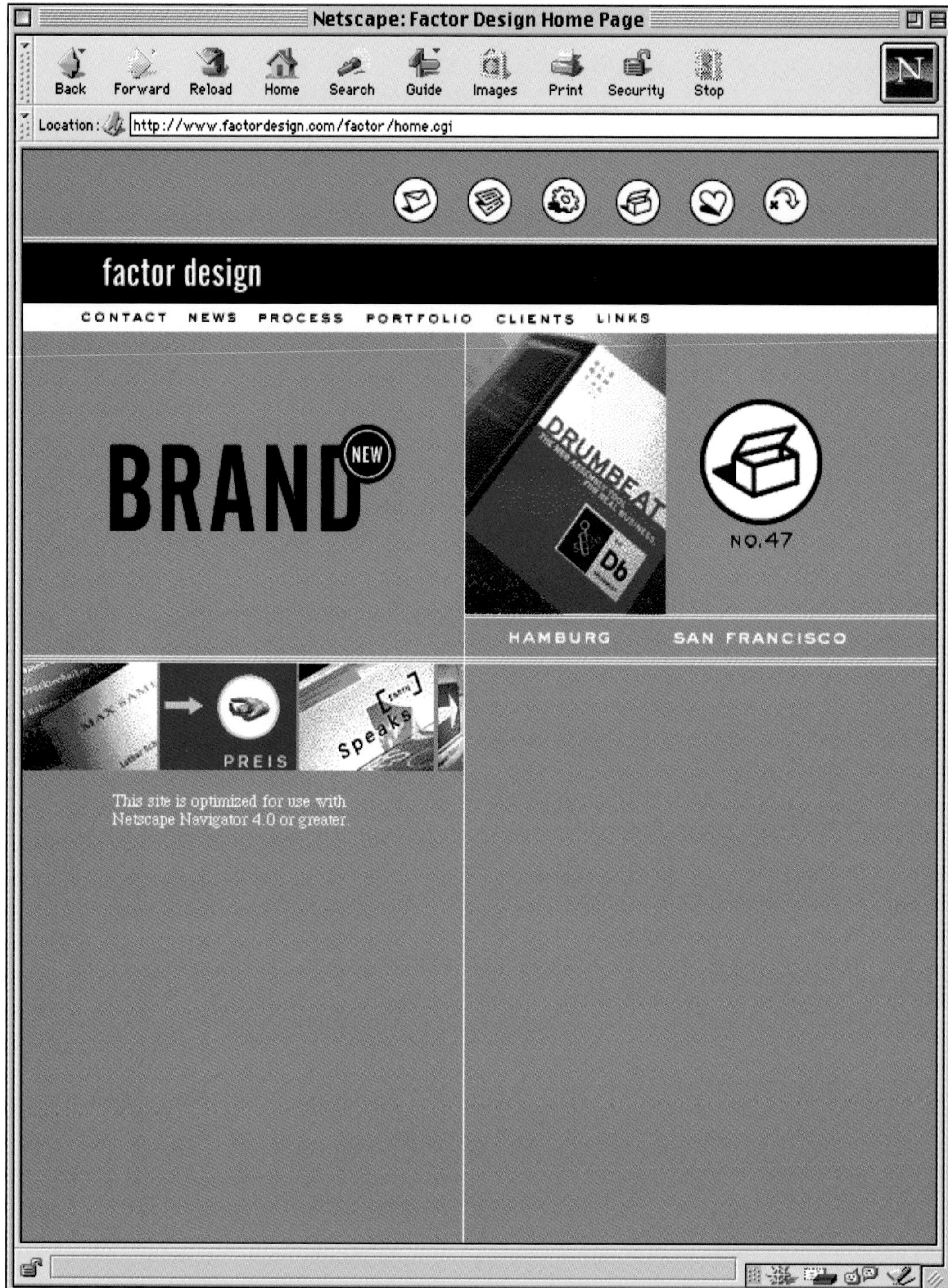

Site description

The Factor Design website was developed to provide potential clients with an overview of the agency's capabilities and philosophy. The site content and design was developed to serve both the San Francisco and Hamburg offices of Factor Design equally well, with all content written and produced in German and English. To save visitors time and effort, the languages appear side by side instead of separately.

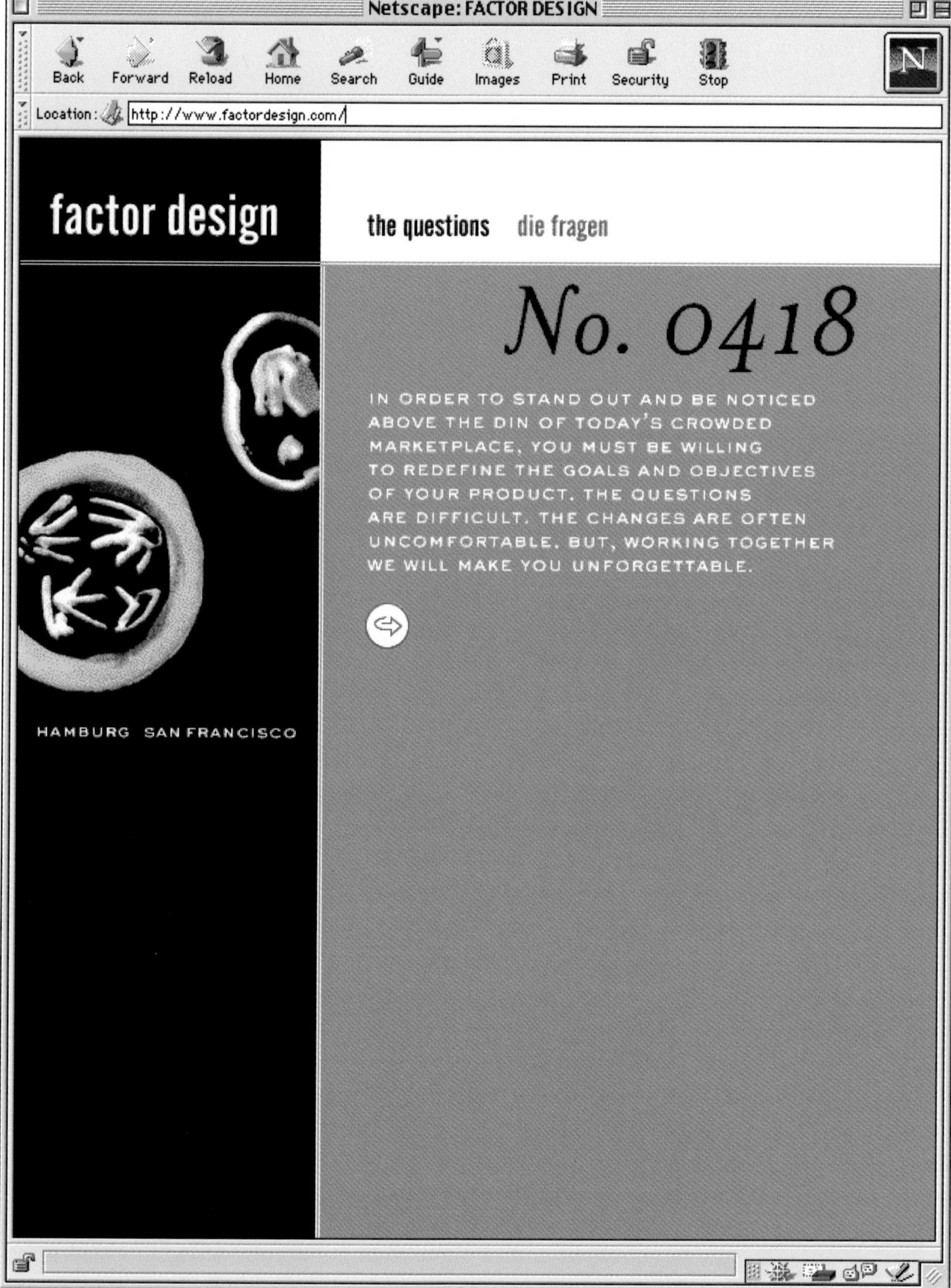

Edit View Go Help

Netscape: Octavo: Digi

site: http://www.octavo.com/

CHARTER PARTNERS COLLECTION

Octavo

Discover for yourself th
Octavo Editions! Buy
items, the world's firs

COMING SOON:

GALILEO GALILEI
SIDEREUS NUNCIUS

WILLIAM HARVEY
DE MOTU CORDIS

JOSEPH SMITH
THE BOOK OF MORMON

WILLIAM MORRIS
KELMSCOTT CHAUCER

Site description

The design of the Octavo website was a wonderful challenge. A newly formed start-up with limited resources needed a site that would not only represent their distinctive product but be flexible enough to grow with their business. Using the typeface HTF Felltypes by Jonathan Hoefler, we were able to bring a subtle sense of the hand-craft to the Web identity surrounding Octavo and the rare books they work with. The site is always evolving.

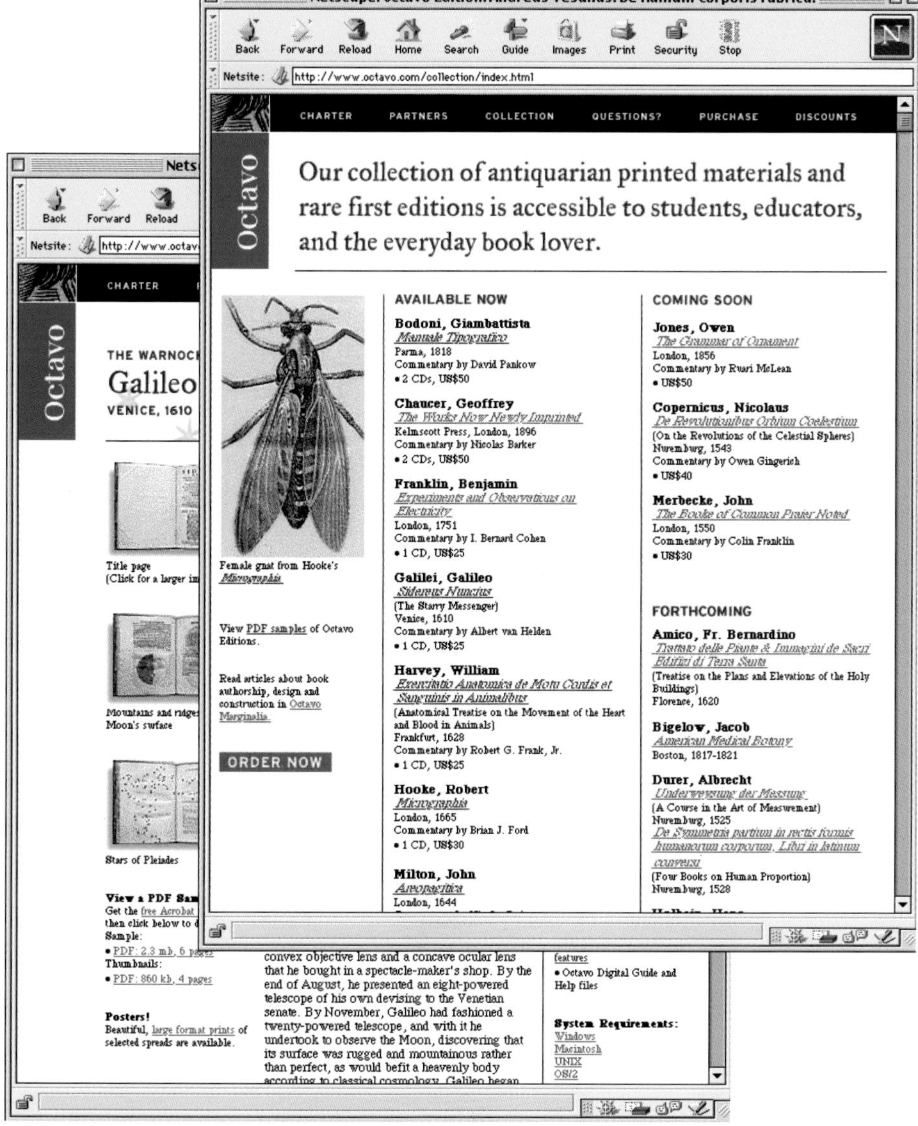

www.octavo.com

Client: Octavo Corporation
Creative Director: Jeff Zwerner
Designers: Andrea Herstowki, Jeff Zwerner
Writers:
E.M. Ginger, Jocelyn Bergen
Programmers:
Jocelyn Bergen, Metagraphics

nuforia

Nuforia

Nuforia's approach to interactive design is to mix technical performance with reason and emotion. Our design solutions are both useful and playful, sophisticated and simple, complex and intuitive. Whether we are working online or in print, our goal remains the same: to create memorable media experiences that are inviting, engaging and establish connections with their audiences.

Nuforia is a result of the 1999 merger between Belk Mignogna Associates, the New York-based communications design firm, and Net Explorer, Inc., the professional Internet services firm with ofices in Atlanta, Boston, Chicago, Houston, Irvine and New York. BMA developed the projects featured here prior to the merger.

When Howard Belk and Steve Mignogna co-founded BMA in 1988, it was a traditional graphic design studio producing mostly annual reports. In 1996 they added a third partner, Wendy Blattner, to strengthen the firm's offering in branding and print communications. In 1995 Hans Neubert joined as BMA's fourth partner and developed its interactive design group. The firm has embraced the medium to push its limits and explore new ways of helping companies establish and maintain robust interactive relationships with their customers. The merger with Net Explorer has expanded the scale and scope of these opportunities.

Nuforia is a leading provider of integrated e-business and strategic branding solutions with an international cast of strategists, designers, engineers and developers. Our mission is to help clients increase their presence, potential and profitability through technology, strategy and design. Nuforia works with corporate clients ranging from Fortune 500 companies to e-commerce pioneers.

Origins
Founded: 1999
Number of employees when founded: 200, now: 208
Headquarters: New York
Other offices: Atlanta, Boston, Chicago, Houston, Irvine (CA)

Principals
Bill Bingham, Howard Belk
Jay Williams, Mark Schulz
Stephen Mignogna
Richard Kalman, Joe Neely
Kurt Franke, Wendy Blattner
Hans Neubert

Contact
Nuforia
373 Park Ave. South, 7th floor
New York, NY 10016
Tel.: 212. 684 7060
Fax: 212. 684 7074
E-mail: info@nuforia.com
Web: www.nuforia.com

nonstøck.2 CD-ROM catalog
Client: nonstøck, Inc.
Creative Director: Hans Neubert
Designer: Hans Neubert,
Jutta Kirchgeorg
Photographers: Various stock
Animators: Jutta

Kirchgeorg, Bryan Yee.
Lingo Programming: Bryan Yee
Database Programming:
Matt Anacleto
Executive Producer:
Alberta Jarane
Music: Jarryd Lowder

Editorial Directors: Jerry
Tavin, Janou Pakter
Photo Editors: Susan
Christenson, Deborah Dalton
Producer: Rupert Rogers
Production Coordinator:
Maryann Camilleri

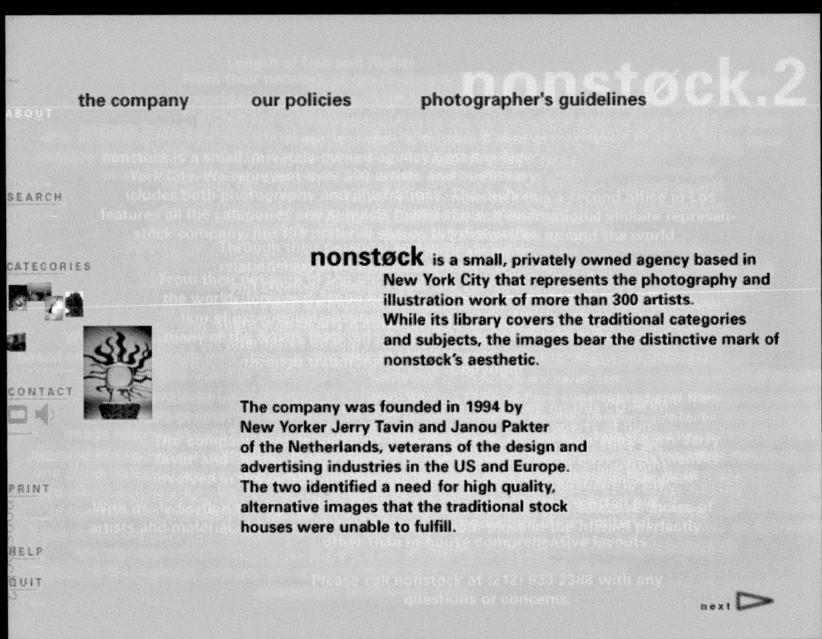

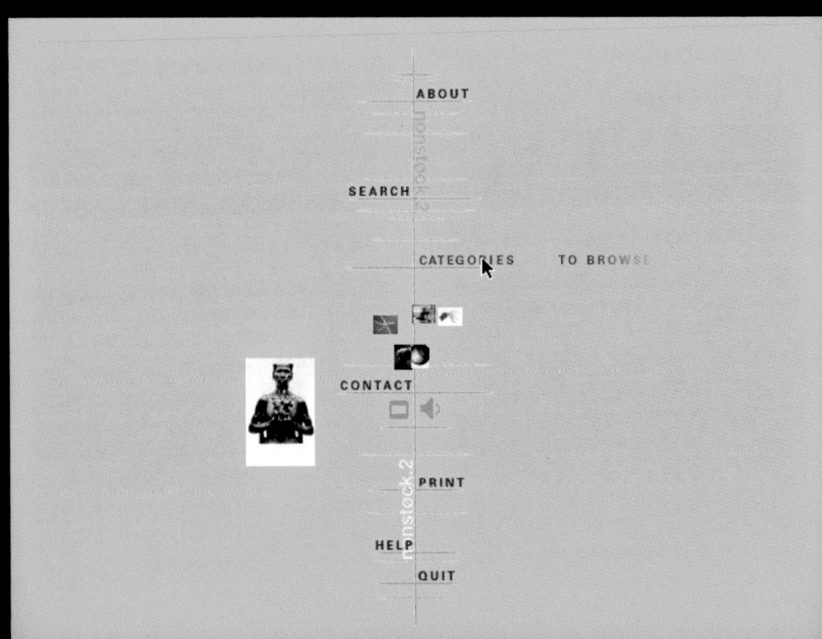

Site description

Nonstock is an international stock image company specializing in high-end photography and illustration. BMA was asked to create nonstock's first interactive catalogue, *nonstock.2*, which has since been distributed in 18 countries. BMA's approach was to create a useful search tool that is easy to use, but entertaining and thought-provoking at the same time. The resulting CD-ROM works like an application or a virtual desktop, where the experience of the search takes into consideration the way creative people think and play, striking a perfect balance between useful tool and playful toy.

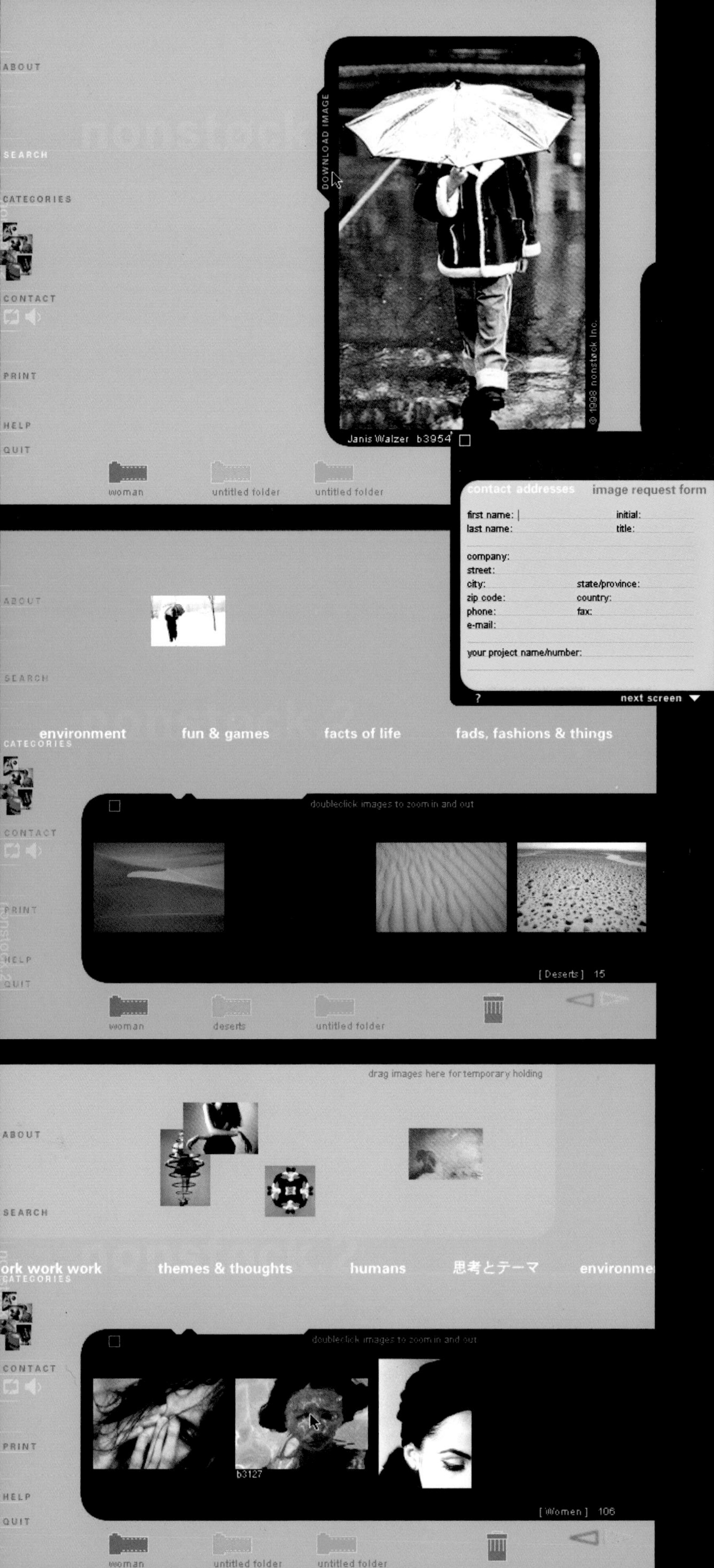
ABOUT
SEARCH
CATEGORIES
CONTACT
PRINT
HELP
QUIT
DOWNLOAD IMAGE
© 1998 nonstock Inc.
Janis Walzer b3954
woman
untitled folder
untitled folder
contact addresses
image request form
first name:
initial:
last name:
title:
company:
street:
city:
state/province:
zip code:
country:
phone:
fax:
e-mail:
your project name/number:
?
next screen
environment
fun & games
facts of life
fads, fashions & things
doubleclick images to zoom in and out
[Deserts] 15
woman
deserts
untitled folder
drag images here for temporary holding
ork work work
themes & thoughts
humans
思考とテーマ
environme
doubleclick images to zoom in and out
b3127
[Women] 106
woman
untitled folder
untitled folder

Site description

Sony asked BMA to transform its corporate website into a "portal" to its product lines. The assignment required that we 1) present a unified picture of a company with very diverse operating units; 2) develop appealing creative support for one of the world's strongest international brands; and 3) build consensus within an organization notorious for being driven by strong, independent personalities.

The redesign is elegant, contemporary, and easy to use—everything consumers expect from a Sony product. BMA constructed a site information architecture consistent with customers' knowledge of Sony; simplified the interface and streamlined main navigation and layout; and created a frequently changing main visual where each operating unit promotes its properties.

www.sony.com
Client: Sony Corporation of America
Creative Director: Hans Neubert
Art Director: Arturo Aranda
Designer: Ninja von Oertzen
Illustrators: Various
Photographers: Various
Programmer: Adam Coti
Producer: Jennifer Marks

Netscape:
Back Forward Reload Home Search Guide Images Print Security Stop
Location: http://www.sony.com
SONY
Sony online USA
May 27, 1998
Music
Movies & TV Shows
Electronics
PlayStation
Play Online Games Now!
VAIO 505
Online Shop
Quick Link
Search or Keyword
Go

Netscape:
Back Forward Reload Home Search Guide Images Print Security Stop
Location: http://www.sony.com
SONY
Sony Online, USA
June 16, 1998
Music
Movies & TV Shows
Electronics
PlayStation
Play Online Games Now!
VAIO 505
Online Shop
Quick Link
Search or Keyword
Go
Sony Online World

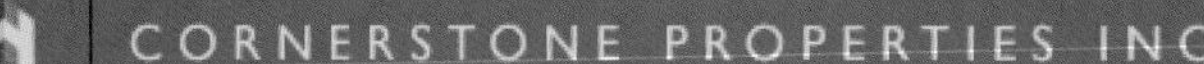

Last Price: $15.62
52 Week High: 19.81
52 Week Low: 13.25

>>DEUTSCHE VERSION

Cornerstone Properties Inc. Concludes $1.81 Billion Merger With William Wilson & Associates

erstone Properties seeks to maximize total return to its shareholders over an extended period of time by creating

PORTFOLIO

ABOUT CORNERSTONE PORTFOLIO NEWS INVESTOR RELATIONS

search contact

seattle
minneapolis
boston
san francisco
chicago
new york city
denver
washington, d.c.
los angeles
charlotte
atlanta

New York City
Regarded as the commercial and cultural center of the world, the New York City economy is firing on all cylinders, led by the bull market on Wall Street, explosive growth in the financial services sector, the emergence of the "new media" industry, dramatic decreases in the crime rate and record levels of tourism.

Properties

imize total return to its shareholders over an extended period of time by creating a diversified, national office build

PORTFOLIO

ABOUT CORNERSTONE PORTFOLIO NEWS INVESTOR RELATIONS

search contact

Maps by Microsoft Expedia Maps
www.expediamaps.com

Regarded as the commercial and cultural center of the world, the New York City economy is firing on all cylinders, led by the bull market on Wall Street, explosive growth in the financial services sector, the emergence of the "new media" industry, dramatic decreases in the crime rate and record levels of tourism.

Cornerstone Properties owns two assets in Midtown Manhattan totaling 378,000 square feet. The combined occupancy rate for the two properties is 99.5%. The Midtown office submarket includes 183 million square feet of Class A office space, and is the largest submarket in the nation. Midtown Manhattan is comprised of 12 distinct submarkets, with Cornerstone's assets located in the Park/Lexington and Madison Avenue submarkets. As of third quarter 1998, the entire Midtown Class A market posted an occupancy rate of approximately 97%, with the Park/Lexington and Madison Avenue submarkets recording occupancy

nts who share our vision and embrace our long-term goals.

www.dowjones.com/annual/index.html
Client: Dow Jones & Company
Creative director: Hans Neubert
Art directors: Hans Neubert, Craig Williamson
Designer: Thai Nguyen
Writers: Dick Toefel, Nancy Garfinkel
Photographers: Various stock
Programmer: Margaret Savage
Producer: D'Este Hanson

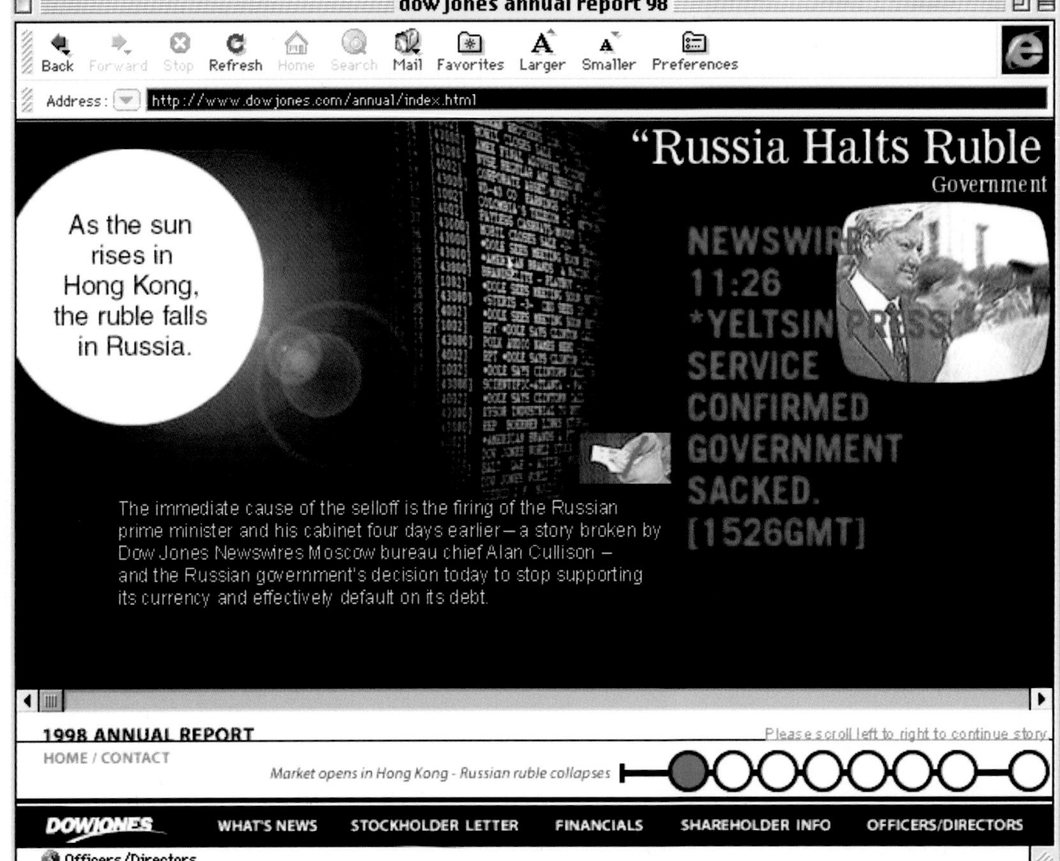

Site description

The site captures a day in a life of news during the market crash on August 27, 1998. The site and annual report tell the story, bringing to bear the company's services and capabilities in delivering 24-hour quality business news around the world. The coverage for the story won Dow Jones two Pulitzer prizes in 1999.

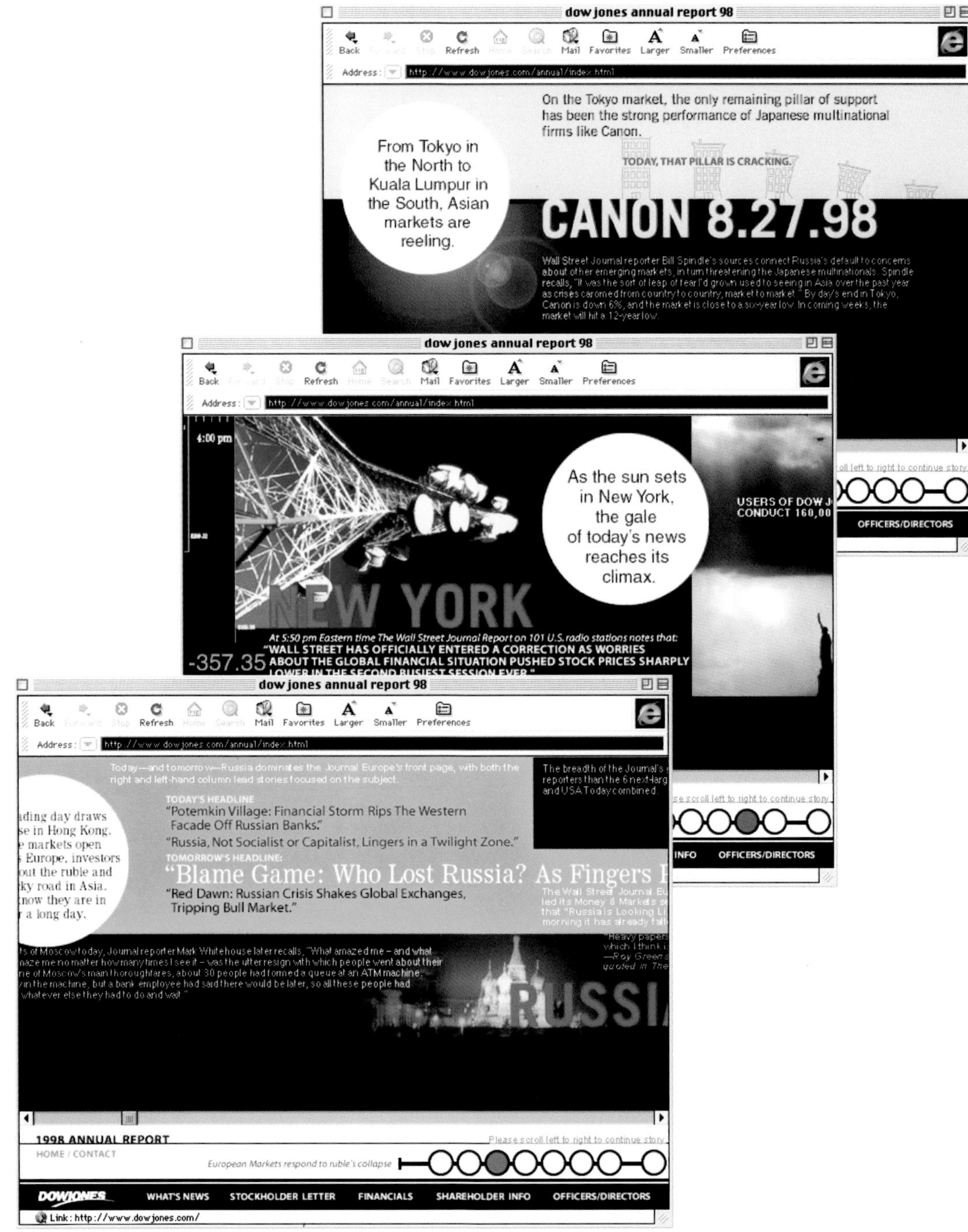

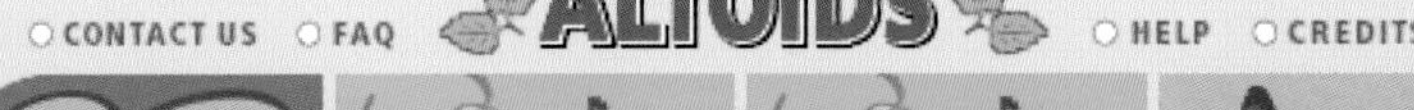

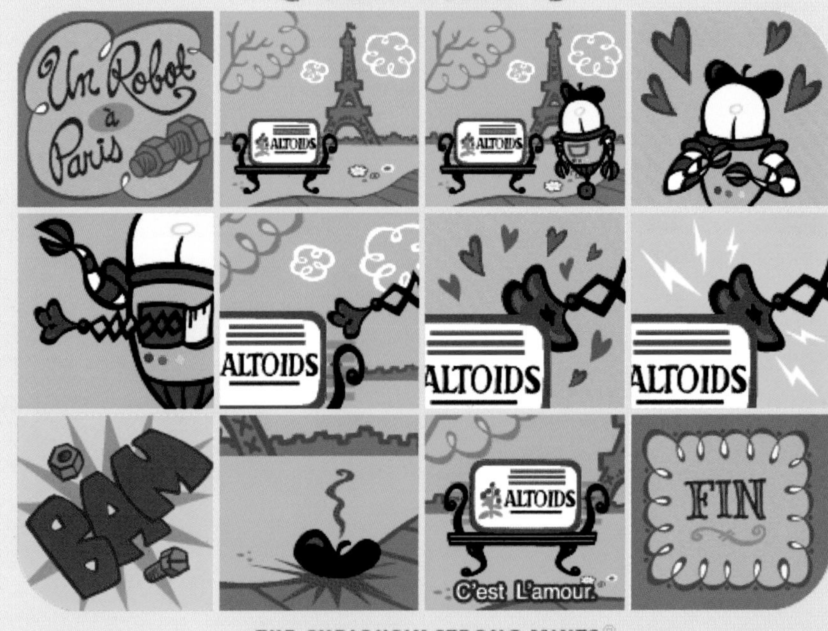

www.altoids.com
Client: Callard & Bowser-Suchard, Inc.
Creative Director: Hans Neubert
Art Director: Laurel Janensch
Designers: Ninja von Oertzen, Thai Nguyen, David DeCheser, Andreas Zeischegg
Illustrators: Sam Ashley, George Bates, Paul Kim, Takeshi Murata, Karl Ackermann, Susan Crawford, Aaron Meshon, Jeffrey Fohl, Matt Owens, Mark Napier
Writers: Jeff Greenspan, Sam Kaufman, Peter Mattei, Brint Banta
Programmers: Adam Coti, Matt Fanuele, Chris Carter, Margaret Savage
Executive Producer: Esteban Gonzalez
Producer: Louise Zonis
Sound: Chris Burke

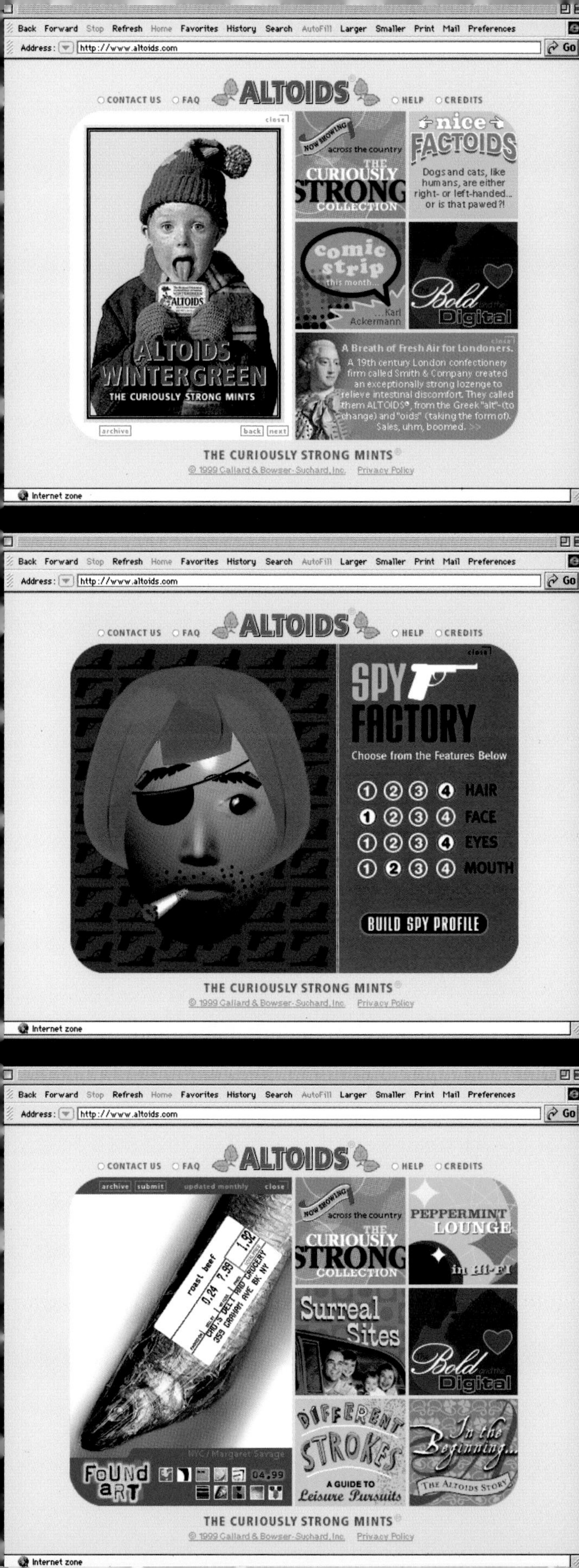
Back Forward Stop Refresh Home Favorites History Search AutoFill Larger Smaller Print Mail Preferences
Address: http://www.altoids.com
CONTACT US
FAQ
ALTOIDS
HELP
CREDITS
ALTOIDS WINTERGREEN
THE CURIOUSLY STRONG MINTS
archive
back
next
NOW SHOWING across the country
THE CURIOUSLY STRONG COLLECTION
nice FACTOIDS
Dogs and cats, like humans, are either right- or left-handed... or is that pawed?!
comic strip
this month...
...Karl Ackermann
The Bold and the Digital
A Breath of Fresh Air for Londoners.
A 19th century London confectionery firm called Smith & Company created an exceptionally strong lozenge to relieve intestinal discomfort. They called them ALTOIDS®, from the Greek "alt"-(to change) and "oids" (taking the form of). Sales, uhm, boomed.
THE CURIOUSLY STRONG MINTS
© 1999 Callard & Bowser-Suchard, Inc.
Privacy Policy
Internet zone
SPY FACTORY
Choose from the Features Below
HAIR
FACE
EYES
MOUTH
BUILD SPY PROFILE
archive
submit
updated monthly
close
roast beef
FOUND ART
PEPPERMINT LOUNGE in HI-FI
Surreal Sites
DIFFERENT STROKES
A GUIDE TO Leisure Pursuits
In the Beginning...
THE ALTOIDS STORY

Children's Scholarship Fund

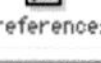

Back Forward Stop Refresh Home Search Mail Favorites Larger Smaller Preferences

Address: www.scholarshipfund.org/

Children's Scholarship Fund

about csf
community
press room
application
contact us

Learn more about the Children's Scholarship Fund.

- national board of advisors
- our founders
- faq
- quotes
- timeline

about csf

The Children's Scholarship Fund was created to expand educational opportunity for low-income families. Our founders, Ted Forstmann and John Walton, have underwritten CSF with $100 million and have raised matching funds around the country to award 40,000 scholarships. By awarding up to 75% of a child's private or parochial school's tuition, CSF gives disadvantaged families more choice in their child's education.

The diversity of the National Board of Advisors is just one indication of the Children's Scholarship Fund's broad support around the country. Throughout the United States thousands of community, political, and business leaders have joined together to support CSF and help offer low-income families new opportunity.

On April 21, 1999, using a computer drawing, CSF will award at least

Internet zone

helping disadvantaged families afford a private education. The site allowes applicants to fill out an online application and provides CSF a forum to

website to the public on the Oprah Winfrey Show; the day the show aired, the site received more than 800 applications in one day.

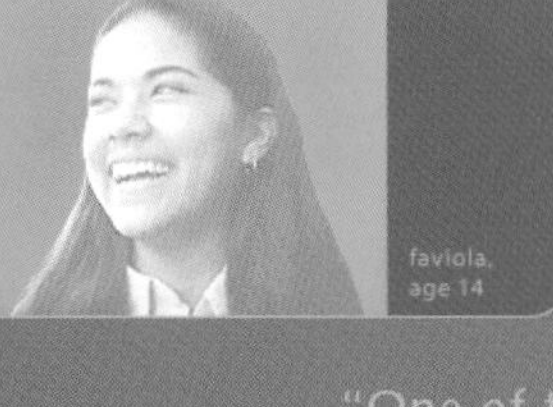

USWeb/CKS

USWeb/CKS

USWeb/CKS is an Internet professional services firm that works with companies to define strategies and implement innovative ways to build their businesses by combining the expertise of strategy, Internet technology, and marketing communications.

We create market leadership for our clients by delivering time-to-value. Time-to-value is the time it takes to realize value from a business initiative, whether the value is expanded sales, efficient supply chain management or productive employees.

We create winning strategies, redefine work processes and build systems that make our clients more profitable, bring them closer to their customers and help their employees work better, faster and more efficiently.

With 3,000 clients (47 of whom are Fortune 100) and a combined total of 39,549 years of Internet experience, we are transforming businesses for the digital economy.

Origins

Founded: December 1995
Reborn: November 1998
Headquarters: San Francisco
Employees: 3,000
Other locations: 61 offices in 22 states and ten countries

Principals

Tom Suiter, Andy Dreyfus
Robert Wong , Mark Frankel
Jill Savini, Mark Silber

Contact

USWeb/CKS
410 Townsend Street
San Francisco CA 94107
Tel.: 415. 369 6700
Fax: 415. 905 1649
E-mail: info@uswebcks.com
Web: www.uswebcks.com

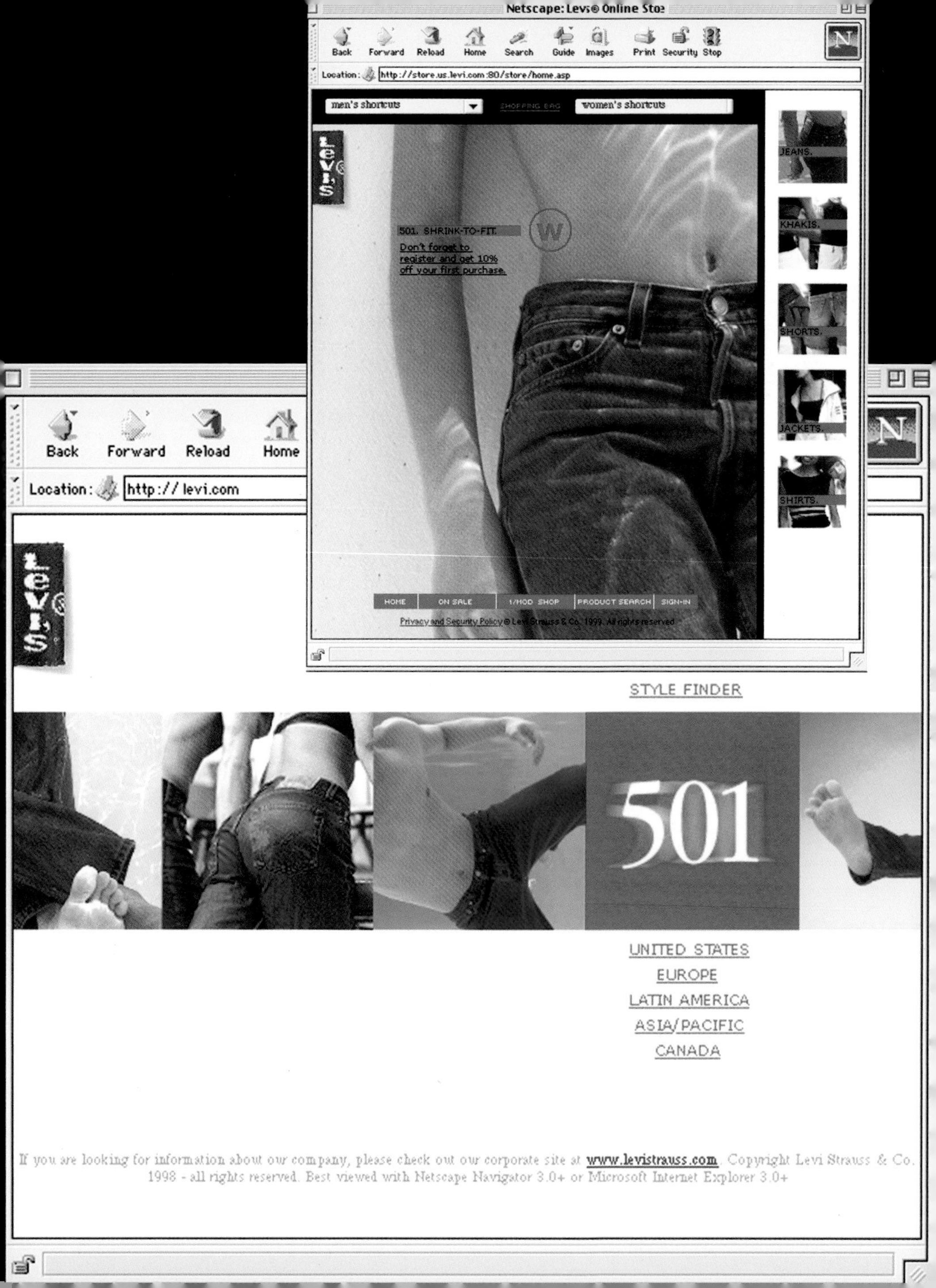

Netscape: Levi's® Online Sto

Back Forward Reload Home Search Guide Images Print Security Stop

Location: http://store.us.levi.com:80/store/home.asp

men's shortcuts | SHOPPING BAG | women's shortcuts

Levi's

501. SHRINK-TO-FIT.

Don't forget to register and get 10% off your first purchase.

JEANS.

KHAKIS.

SHORTS.

JACKETS.

SHIRTS.

HOME | ON SALE | 1/MOD SHOP | PRODUCT SEARCH | SIGN-IN

Privacy and Security Policy

Back Forward Reload Home

Location: http:// levi.com

Levi's

STYLE FINDER

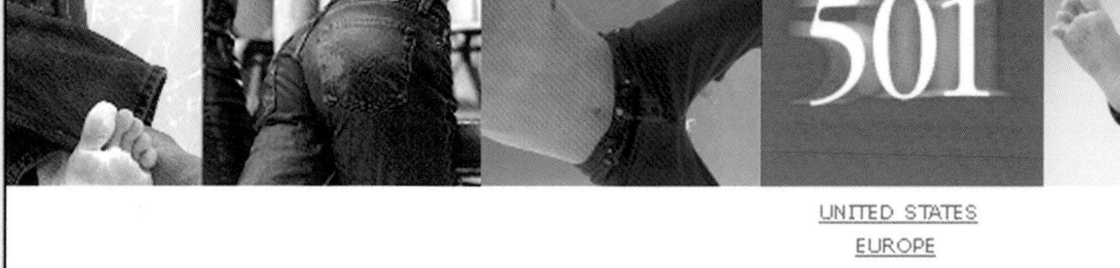

UNITED STATES

EUROPE

LATIN AMERICA

ASIA/PACIFIC

CANADA

If you are looking for information about our company, please check out our corporate site at **www.levistrauss.com**. Best viewed with Netscape Navigator 3.0+ or Microsoft Internet Explorer 3.0+

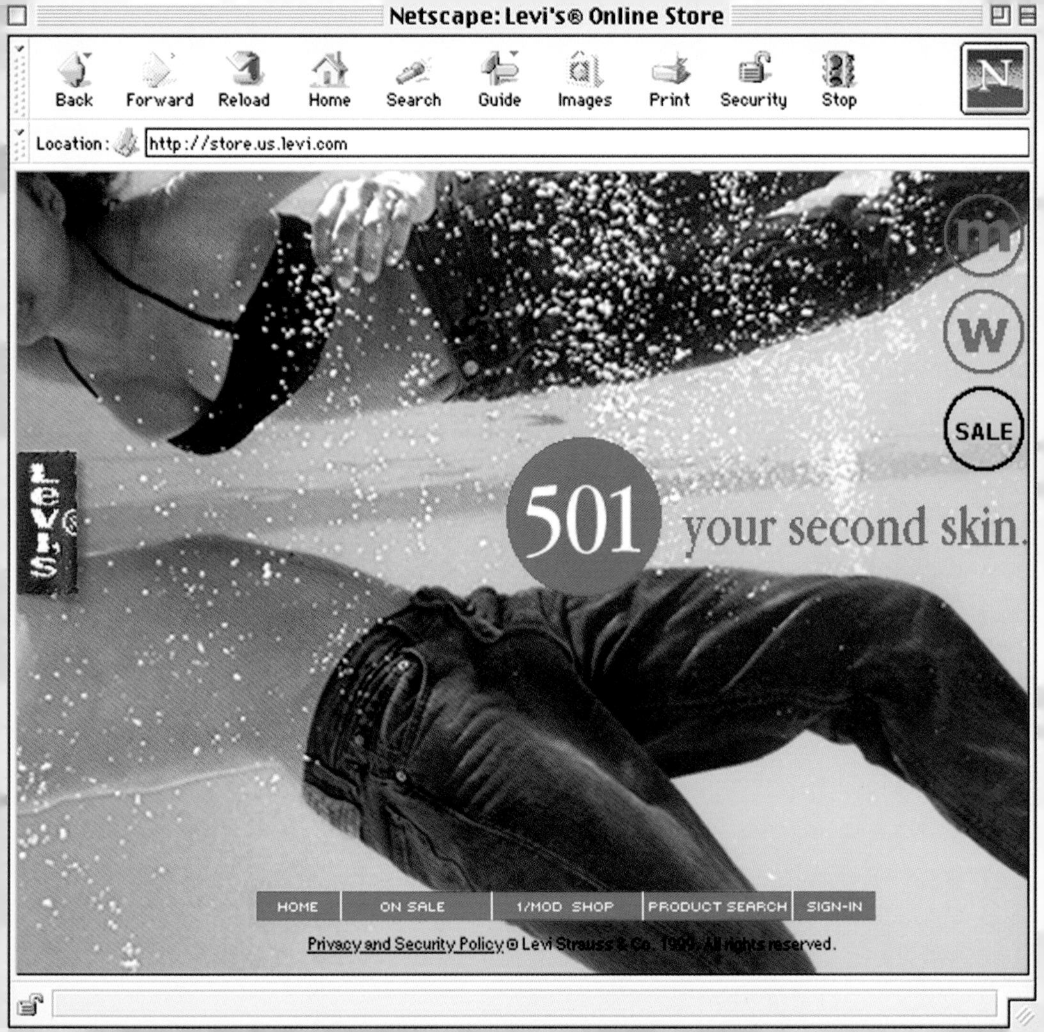
Netscape: Levi's® Online Store
Back
Forward
Reload
Home
Search
Guide
Images
Print
Security
Stop
Location:
http://store.us.levi.com
Levi's
SALE
501
your second skin.
HOME
ON SALE
1/MOD SHOP
PRODUCT SEARCH
SIGN-IN
Privacy and Security Policy

Site description

USWeb/CKS created E-photo.com, a resource for amateur photographers and a source for photo processing couponing and promotions. E-Photo also gives customers the opportunity to view their photos online, request enlargements, send photos through the mail to family and friends and order merchandise with their pictures on it. There also randomly placed numbers peppered throughout the site that link to one of the 100 reasons to take photographs.

www.e-photo.com

Client: Eckerd Drug
Creative Director: Robert Wong
Art Director: Kurt Thesing
Designer: Mike Reger
Writer: Mike Harms
Producer: Patrick Fitzgerald
Programmer: Bernd Jaehnigen

Netscape: Eckerd
Back Forward Reload Home Search Guide Images Print Security Stop
Netsite: http://www.e-photo.com/HTML/photoshoot/index.html
e photo
ECKERD
photoshoot
digital image center
ECKERD in - store services
photoshoot
tips from the pros
picture perfect websites
ask e-photographer
tips from the pros
Get expert advice on taking great shots.
picture perfect websites
Links to other great Web sites.
ask e-photographer
Coming Soon! Professional photographers answer your question.
Netscape: Eckerd
Back Forward Reload Home Search Guide Images Print Security Stop
Netsite: http://www.e-photo.com/HTML/center/index.html
e photo
ECKERD
photoshoot
digital image center
ECKERD in - store services
digital image center
customer viewing
view your pictures online!
Picture Yourself on the Internet
The next time you drop off your film for processing at select Eckerd locations, you can have your pictures displayed on the Internet at the same time! A password gives you complete control over who views them. It's the easiest way to see your photos and share them with family and friends everywhere. Click here for more information.

Netscape: Timberland
Back
Forward
Reload
Home
Search
Netscape
Images
Print
Security
Stop
Location: http://www.timberland.com/index.asp?tab=boot&id=3
What's Related
Communicate • International • Site Map • Search • Home
BOOT
THE TIMBERLAND COMPANY
Inside Timberland | Jobs | History
BRAND
TIMBERLAND® PRODUCTS
Footwear | Apparel | Accessories
BELIEF
SOCIAL ENTERPRISE
What We Believe | Pull On Your Boots
HISTORY
CLICK ON SELECTION
TIMELINE
YEAR: '52 '55 '65 '73 '80 '83 '86 '88 '89 '91 '92 '94 '96 '97 '98
1952 Founder Nathan Swartz buys 50% interest in Abington Shoe Company.
1955 Nathan Swartz buys remaining 50% interest in Abington Shoe Company. Son Sidney joins his father in building the family shoe business.
1965 Timberland's injection molding technology results in legendary waterproof leather boots.
1973 Abington Shoe Company markets first rugged waterproof leather boot under the Timberland® brand name.
1980 Timberland® footwear is launched in Italy, its first foray into the international market.
1983 Timberland begins field-testing products in the Iditarod® sled dog race.
1986 The first Timberland® store opens in Newport, Rhode Island.

www.timberland.com
Creative Director: Oscar Reza
Art Director: Oscar Reza
Writer: Martin Agency
Photographer: Martin Agency
Producer: Josh Hurwitz
Programmer: Glenn Eastman

Back Forward Reload Home Search

Location: http://www.timberland.com/

BOOT
THE TIMBERLAND COMPANY
Inside Timberland | Jobs | History

Timberland

OF SOMEONE GREAT, we think they've got something we don't. We are trained to think that only a tiny percentage of us have the stuff it takes to be a hero. Not many of us will cure any diseases or slay any dragons, but every single one of us, EVERY SINGLE ONE OF US, is called to be a king, a queen, a hero in our ordinary lives. We don't build statues to worship the exceptional life, we build them to remind ourselves what is POSSIBLE IN OUR OWN.

< MORE >

DOCKERS® KHAKIS
THE DEFINITIVE AMERICAN KHAKI

ORDER THESE SPECIAL KHAKIS HERE!

FIND OUT WHAT'S PLAYING.

- Men's Store
- Women's Store
- Dockers® K-1 Khakis
- Hot Deals
- Membership/Promotions
- Customer Service
- Store Finder
- Site Map

Browser Information

Terms & Conditions

DOCKERS® HOME | Men's Store

(fits & fabrics) [FIT COMPARISON | GLOSSARY OF TERMS | COLOR PALETTE]

Choose a different fit from each pull-down menu and then click "compare" to view them side by side.

5-Pocket Fit ◄ COMPARE ► Classic Fit

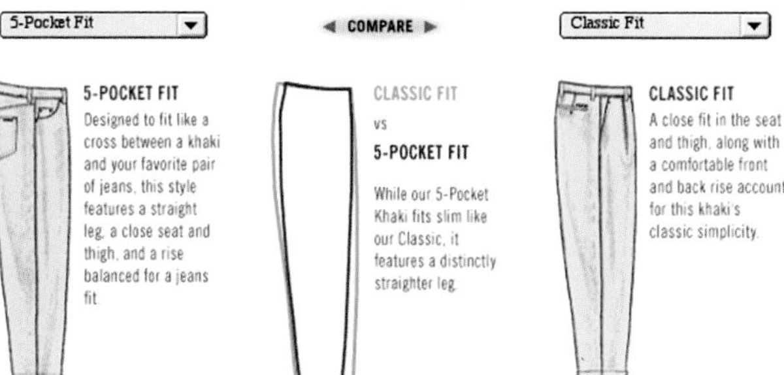

5-POCKET FIT
Designed to fit like a cross between a khaki and your favorite pair of jeans, this style features a straight leg, a close seat and thigh, and a rise balanced for a jeans fit.

CLASSIC FIT
vs
5-POCKET FIT
While our 5-Pocket Khaki fits slim like our Classic, it features a distinctly straighter leg.

CLASSIC FIT
A close fit in the seat and thigh, along with a comfortable front and back rise account for this khaki's classic simplicity.

DOCKERS® KHAKIS | Men's Store

what's in store
- Khakis
- Shirts
- Shorts
- Accessories
- Golf
- Dockers® K-1 Khakis
- Find a Favorite

lifestyle
Make yourself comfortable whether you're dressing casual, sport, buttoned-up, or just putting around.

changing room
Mix and match some of our most popular colors and styles.

Currently only 4.0 and up browsers compatible.

hot deals
Special springtime savings, and all the latest promotions.

fits & fabrics
Fit Comparison, Glossary of Terms and Color Palette.

www.dockers.com
Client: Levi Strauss & Co.
Creative Director: Mark Frankel
Art Directors: Tim Kain, Hollimarie O'Carroll
Designers: Joey Wu, Mark Insalaco
Writer: Mary Jeanne Deery
Digital Artists: Joey Wu, Mark Insalaco
Photographers: David Martinez, Richard Rethemeyer
Producers: AnneLise Staal, Charl Morkel
Programmer: Judi Hengeveld

Site description
USWeb/CKS created an online store that is the only place to shop and buy from the entire line of Dockers offerings. The site provides shoppers with an "online guide to effortless style," a style finder, and fit calculators with which shoppers can "try on" different styles, shirts and pants in the online changing room. They can even e-mail their choices to friends.

www.ibm.com
Client: IBM
Creative Directors: Jill Savini, Robert Wong
Art Director: Jonathan Hudson
Information Architecture. Tony Hahn
Writer: Tom Elia
Digital Artist: Almer Perez
Producer: Maura Brady
Programmer: Brian Pang

Site description
USWeb/CKS created an online store that is the only place to shop from the entire line of Dockers offerings. The site provides an "online guide to effortless style," a style finder, and fit calculators with which shoppers can "try on" different styles of shirts and pants in the online changing room.

Netscape: Audi Splash Screen 2
Back
Forward
Reload
Home
Search
Guide
Images
Print
Security
Stop
Netsite:
http://www.audiusa.com/splash2.htm
your parents will actually
think you listened to all
those lectures on family
values

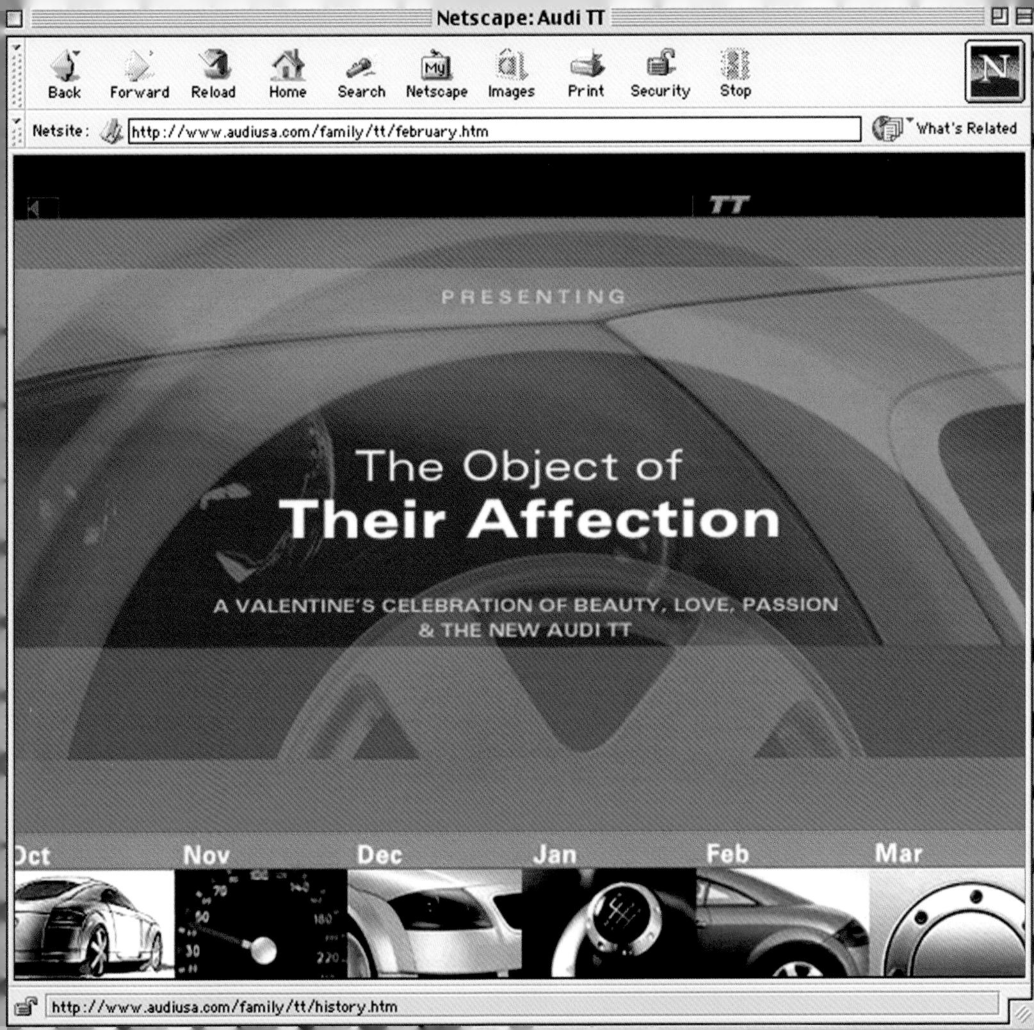

Netscape: Audi TT
Back
Forward
Reload
Home
Search
Netscape
Images
Print
Security
Stop
Netsite:
http://www.audiusa.com/family/tt/february.htm
What's Related
TT
PRESENTING
The Object of
Their Affection
A VALENTINE'S CELEBRATION OF BEAUTY, LOVE, PASSION
& THE NEW AUDI TT
Oct
Nov
Dec
Jan
Feb
Mar
http://www.audiusa.com/family/tt/history.htm

www.audi.com
(this and previous spread)
Creative Director: Robert Wong
Art Directors: Jeffrey Martin, Kurt Thesing, Hien Im
Writers: Tom Elia, Tom Keener, Keith Byrne
Photographer: Claudio Vasquez
Producer: Michael Capecci
Programmer: Network Publishing

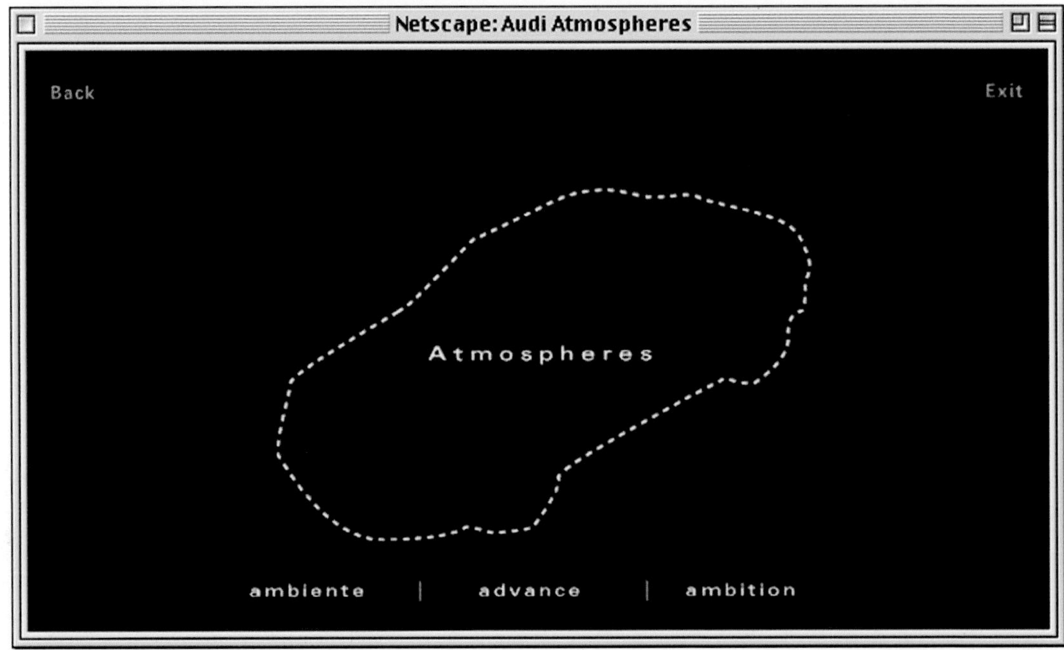

Site description
USWeb/CKS designed a site that communicates the attributes of the Audi brand experience. This site includes a special microsite for the new TT coupe, a "Create Your Audi" configurator, and an experimental multimedia area on the "Audi Experience"—which includes the use of Flash, RealVideo, and Shockwave.

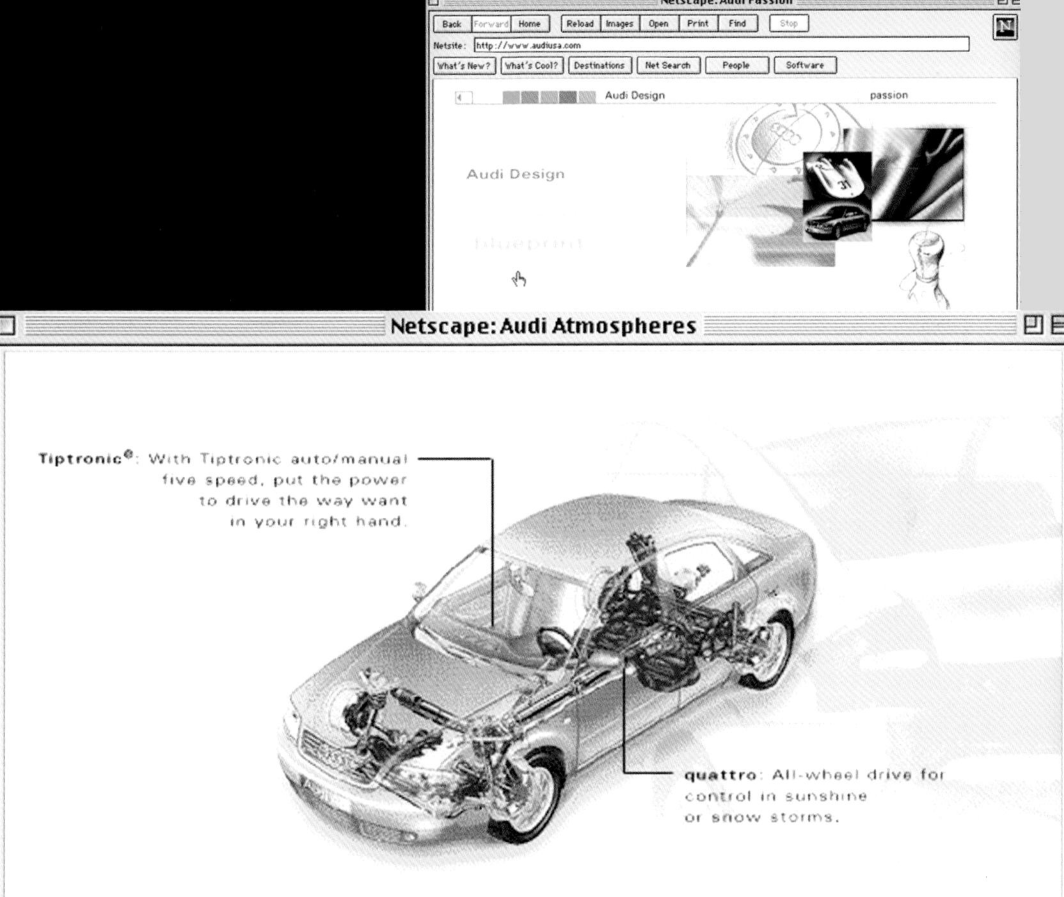
Netscape: Audi Passion
Back
Forward
Home
Reload
Images
Open
Print
Find
Stop
Netsite:
http://www.audiusa.com
What's New?
What's Cool?
Destinations
Net Search
People
Software
Audi Design
passion
Audi Design
blueprint
Netscape: Audi Atmospheres
Tiptronic®: With Tiptronic auto/manual
five speed, put the power
to drive the way want
in your right hand.
quattro: All-wheel drive for
control in sunshine
or snow storms.
Forward

www.vitra.com
www.algroup.ch
www.vitra.com
www.algroup.ch
staff.co.at
virtual
identity
virtual
.com
.com
museum.com
www.furnish.net

Virtual Identity

In developing more efficient business and communications applications that are at once functional and aesthetic, we face a classic design challenge. These applications provide a platform for defining or creating new services, products and brands. They shape an organization and its vision. They become an integral part of its corporate culture. They create an identity that is virtual yet ubiquitous.

Successful digital communication requires comprehensive and interdisciplinary approaches to solve its complex challenges. We develop interfaces to dissolve borders which, to date, have seemed unsurpassable. Design communicates this permutation—it is an essential part of the transformational process. Virtual Identity is one of the leading digital communications companies in Germany. By combining design, technical, and consulting expertise, we develop innovative and holistic solutions for a wide range of international clients. Founded in 1995 by Roland Fesenmayr, Ralf Heller and Uschi Hilpert, Virtual Identity now employs 60 people.

Origins
When started: 1995
Number of employees: 60
Headquarters:
Freiburg, Germany
Other location: Berlin

Principals
Roland Fesenmayr
Ralf Heller, Uschi Hilpert

Contact
Virtual Identity
Gerberau 5, 79098 Freiburg,
Germany
Tel.: (49) 761. 207 5800
Fax: (49) 761. 207 5801
E-mail: info@virtual-identity.com
Web: www.virtual-identity.com

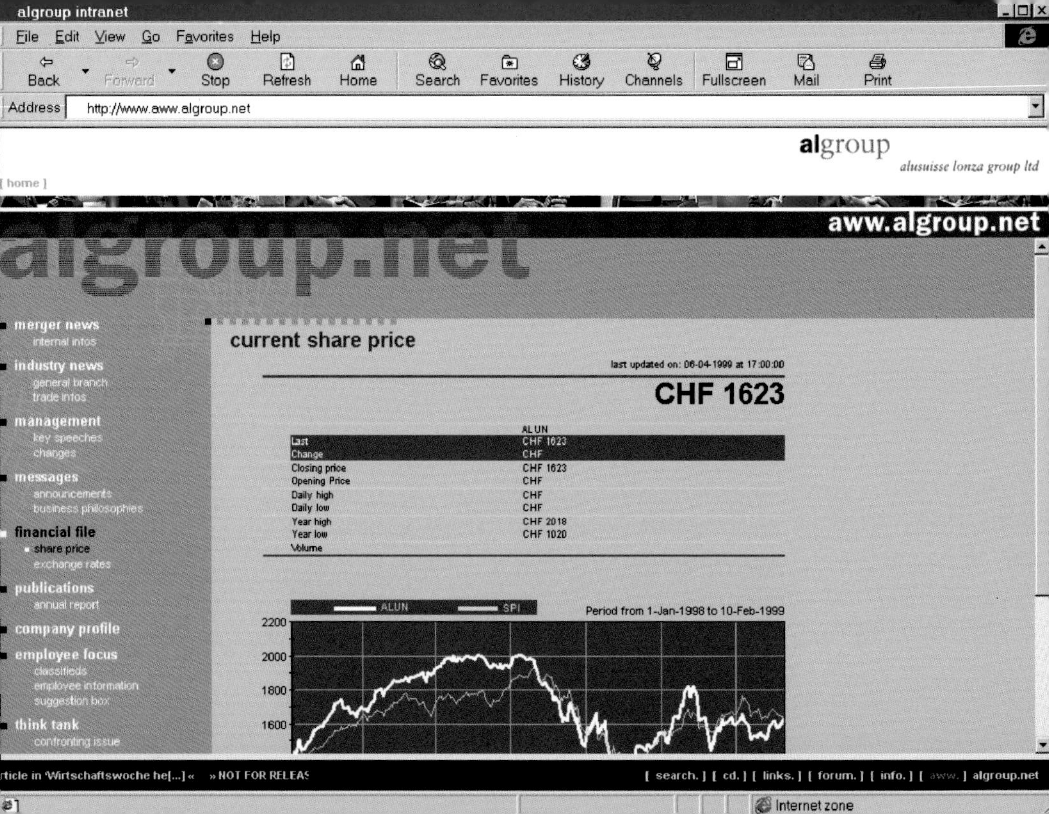

algroup intranet
File Edit View Go Favorites Help
Back Forward Stop Refresh Home Search Favorites History Channels Fullscreen Mail Print
Address http://www.aww.algroup.net
algroup
alusuisse lonza group ltd
[home]
aww.algroup.net
algroup.net
merger news
internal infos
industry news
general branch
trade infos
management
key speeches
changes
messages
announcements
business philosophies
financial file
share price
exchange rates
publications
annual report
company profile
employee focus
classifieds
employee information
suggestion box
think tank
confronting issue
current share price
last updated on: 06-04-1999 at 17:00:00
CHF 1623
ALUN
Last CHF 1623
Change CHF
Closing price CHF 1623
Opening Price CHF
Daily high CHF
Daily low CHF
Year high CHF 2018
Year low CHF 1020
Volume
ALUN SPI
Period from 1-Jan-1998 to 10-Feb-1999
2200
2000
1800
1600
rticle in 'Wirtschaftswoche he[...] « » NOT FOR RELEAS
[search.] [cd.] [links.] [forum.] [info.] [aww.] algroup.net
Internet zone

algroup product explorer
info
4 | 20 - time: 0' 16"
Product:
Injection Molded Packaging Solutions
Business:
algroup wheaton pharmaceutical and
algroup product explorer
info
7 | 20 - time: 1' 34"
EXPECO
algroup product explorer
info
14 | 20 - time: 1' 28"
EXPECO
Product:
Alucobond® Aluminium Composite
Business:
algroup alusuisse primary materials and
fabricated products
Aesthetic building materials for displays and
facades
Around the world leading architects are

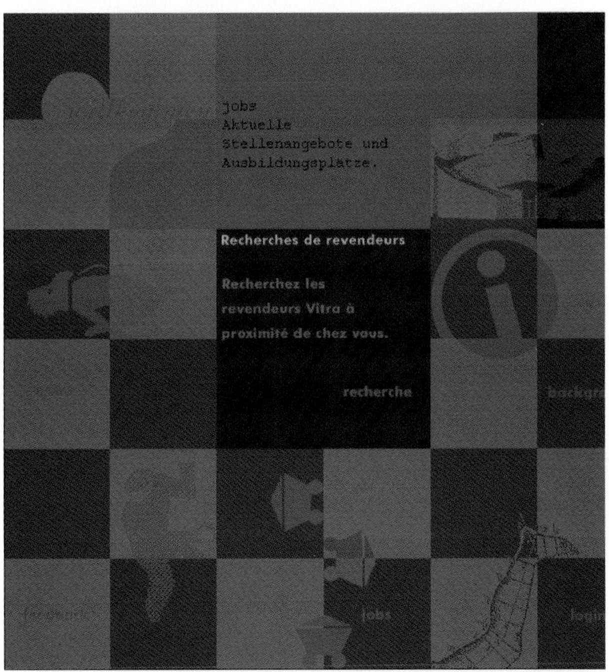
jobs
Aktuelle
Stellenangebote und
Ausbildungsplätze.
Recherches de revendeurs
Recherchez les
revendeurs Vitra à
proximité de chez vous.
recherche
jobs

welcome to furnish.net
Land wählen

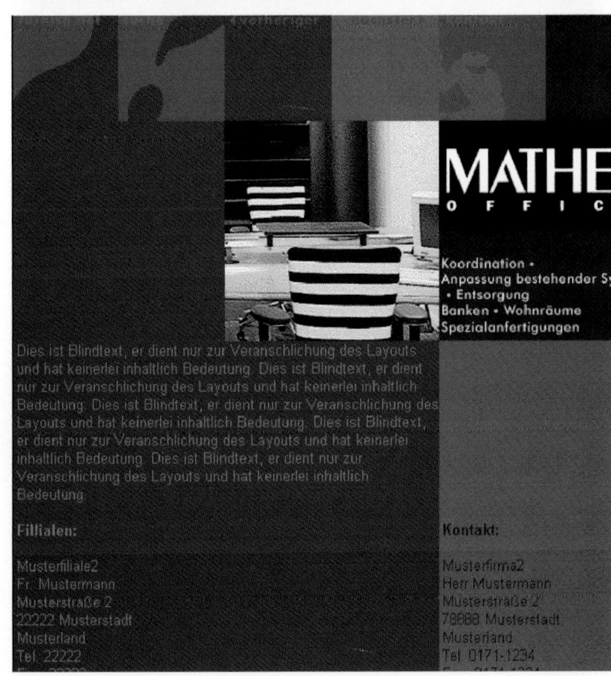
MATHE
Koordination •
Anpassung bestehender Sy
• Entsorgung
Banken • Wohnräume
Spezialanfertigungen
Dies ist Blindtext, er dient nur zur Veranschlichung des Layouts und hat keinerlei inhaltlich Bedeutung. Dies ist Blindtext, er dient nur zur Veranschlichung des Layouts und hat keinerlei inhaltlich Bedeutung. Dies ist Blindtext, er dient nur zur Veranschlichung des Layouts und hat keinerlei inhaltlich Bedeutung. Dies ist Blindtext, er dient nur zur Veranschlichung des Layouts und hat keinerlei inhaltlich Bedeutung. Dies ist Blindtext, er dient nur zur Veranschlichung des Layouts und hat keinerlei inhaltlich Bedeutung.
Fillialen:
Musterfiliale2
Fr. Mustermann
Musterstraße 2
22222 Musterstadt
Musterland
Tel. 22222
Kontakt:
Musterfirma2
Herr Mustermann
Musterstraße 2
78888 Musterstadt
Musterland
Tel. 0171-1234

www.furnish.net
(opposite page)
Client: Vitra
Designers: Nhan Nguyen, Uli Weidner

Site description
As the online network of furniture retailers associated with Vitra, this site offers dealers the opportunity to create and maintain up-to-date Web profiles for themselves both effectively and cost-efficiently. The design recalls a printer's letter case.

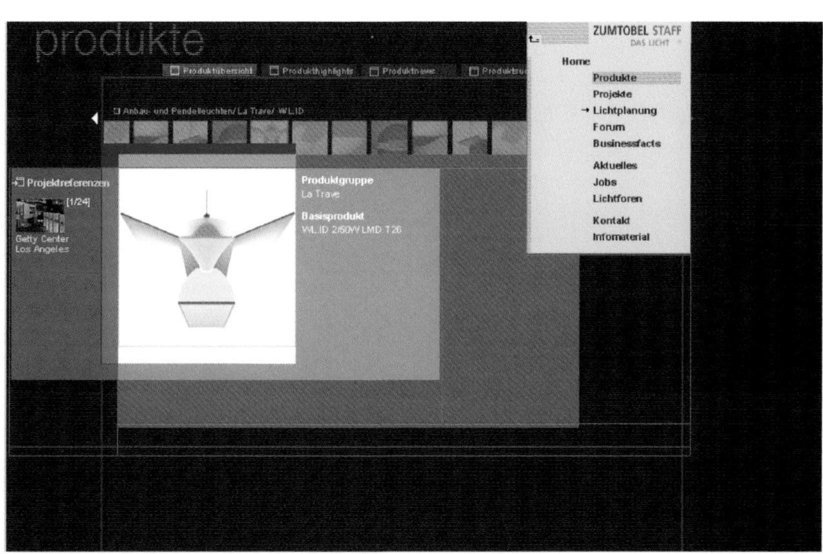

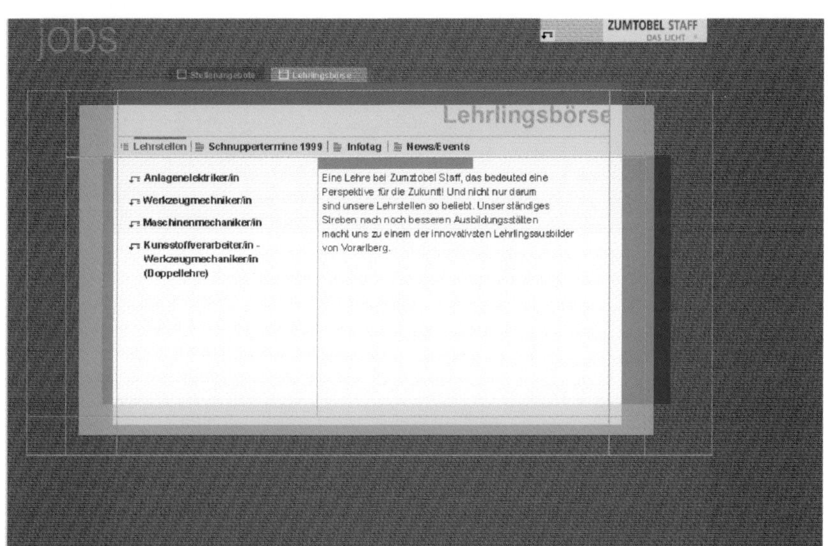

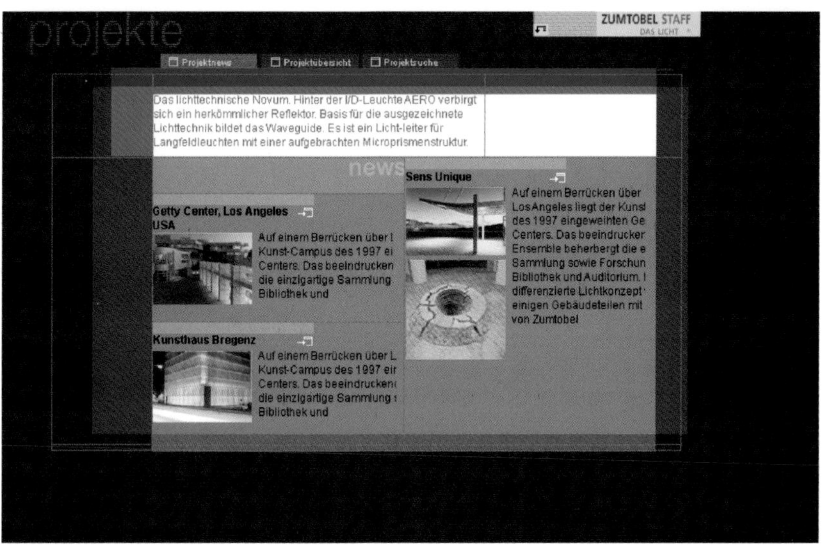

www.zumtobelstaff.co.at.
(this page)
Client: Zumtobel Staff
Designers: Oliver Habboub, Uli Weidner

Site description
Virtual Identity designed this website for Zumtobel Staff, a lighting design company with several locations across Europe. Users can view the catalog, browse product information, and view recent projects carried out with Zumtobel products.

Site description

The Web-ROM was developed as an integral part of the publications prepared for Novartis' 1998 AGM. Rather than focusing on finance and management information, the objective was to examine the then-new concept of a life sciences company. Presenting a comprehensive picture of the areas of activity of the company, the Web-ROM explores how Novartis products affect the individual in everyday life. The user requires a standard browser, an Internet connection and the attached CD-ROM. The CD-ROM contains bandwidth-intensive media such as sounds, videos, animations, and photographic images. Only the texts are dynamically accessible from the website. In this way Novartis can offer the most up-to-date information combined with a broad diversity of media types.

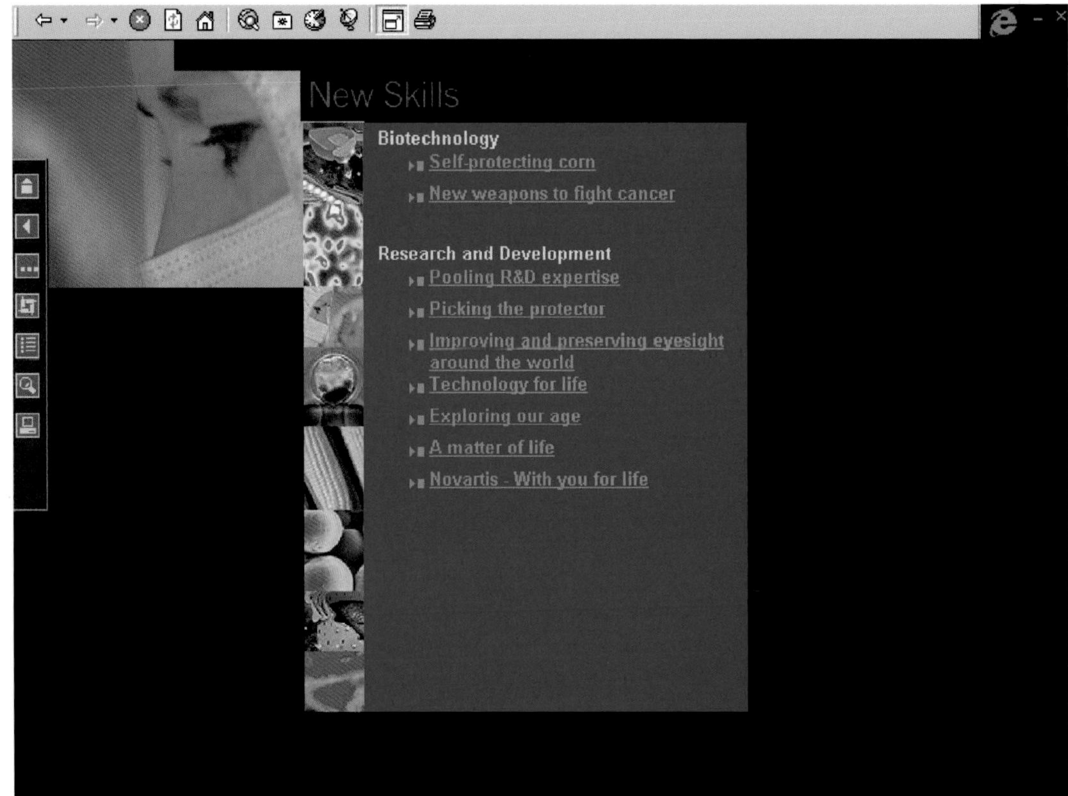

web-rom.novartis.com
Client: Novartis
Designers: Sonja Schäfer, Uli Weidner

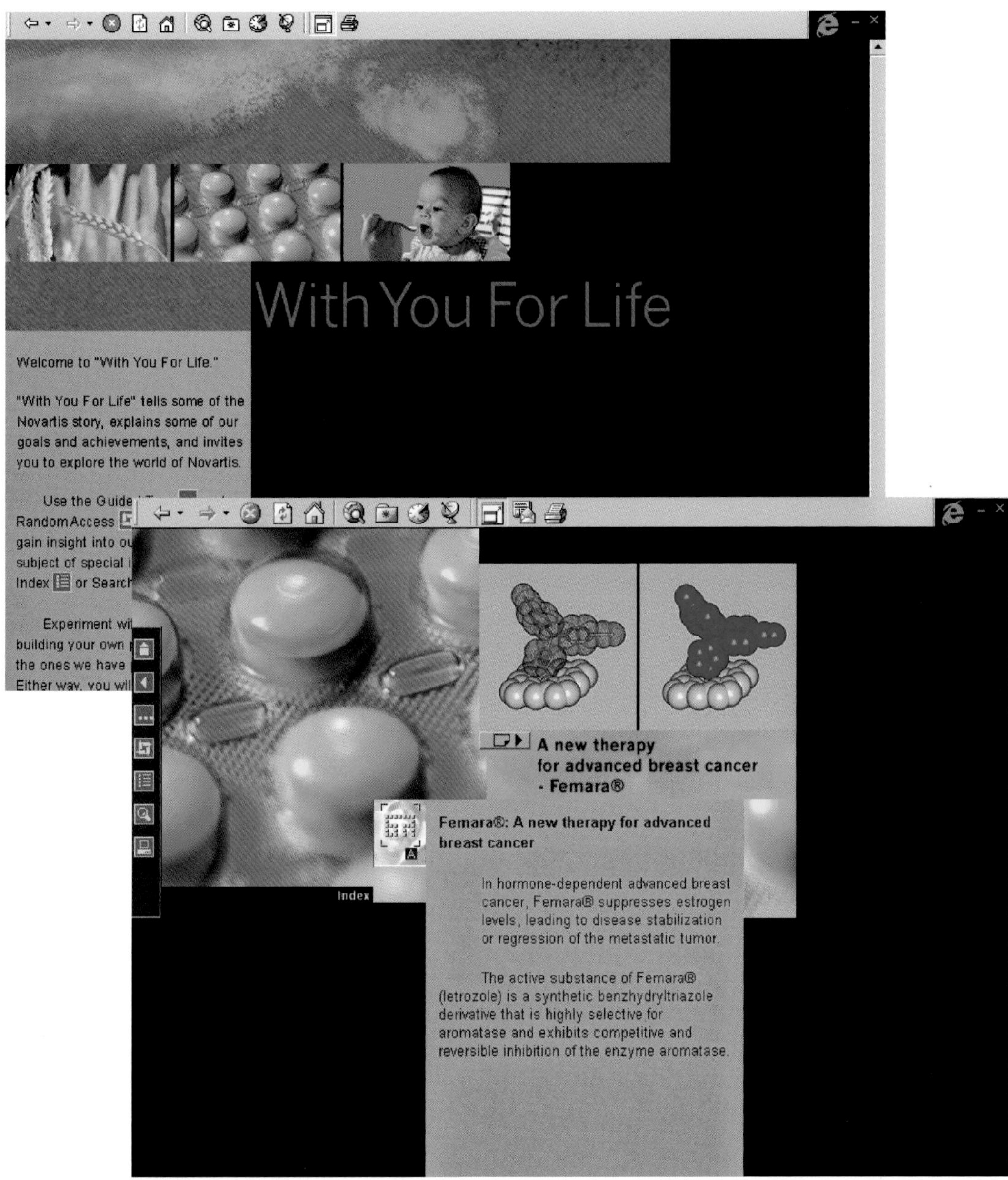
With You For Life
Welcome to "With You For Life."
"With You For Life" tells some of the Novartis story, explains some of our goals and achievements, and invites you to explore the world of Novartis.
A new therapy for advanced breast cancer - Femara®
Femara®: A new therapy for advanced breast cancer
In hormone-dependent advanced breast cancer, Femara® suppresses estrogen levels, leading to disease stabilization or regression of the metastatic tumor.
The active substance of Femara® (letrozole) is a synthetic benzhydryltriazole derivative that is highly selective for aromatase and exhibits competitive and reversible inhibition of the enzyme aromatase.
Index

he Vitra Marketing Information ystem (VMIS) is a key omponent of Vitra's overall gital media strategy. he VMIS offers full portfolio formation and equips sales

to communicate Vitra's unique system, project and solution-based approaches. Enhanced by PentiumÆ III technologies, the VMIS makes it possible to develop visually compelling

that combine technical and design information with photographic images, Flash animations, realistic 3D imaging and real and virtual situational references.

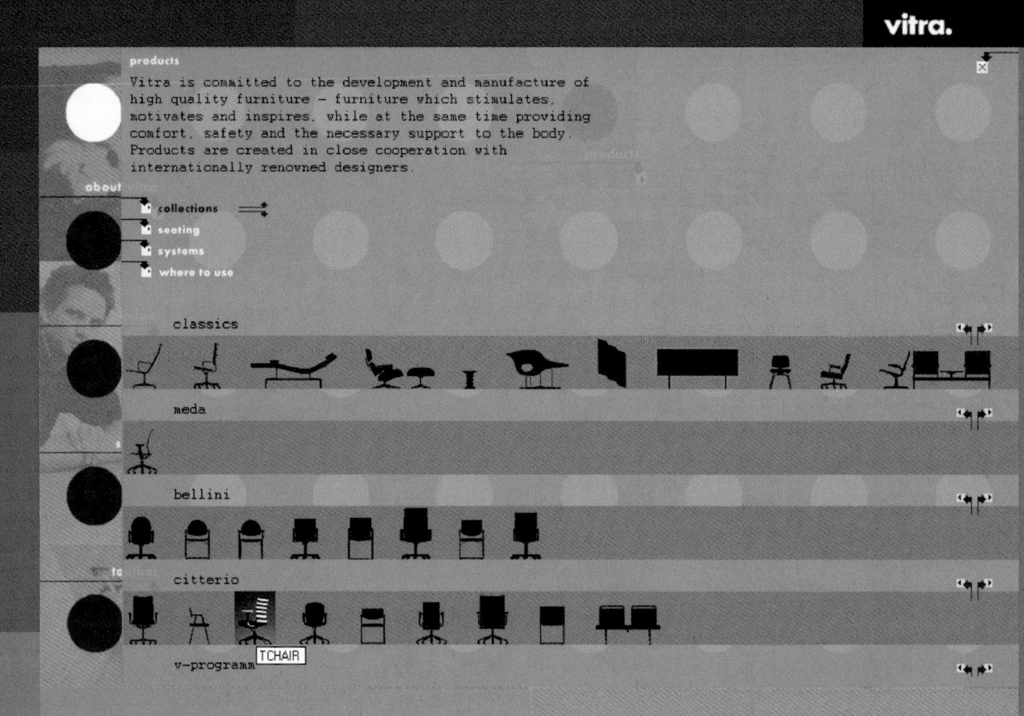
vitra.
products
Vitra is committed to the development and manufacture of high quality furniture – furniture which stimulates, motivates and inspires, while at the same time providing comfort, safety and the necessary support to the body. Products are created in close cooperation with internationally renowned designers.
about
collections
seating
systems
where to use
classics
meda
bellini
citterio
TCHAIR
v-programm

The slim, movable backrest of the AC1 is connected to the seat by means of the armrests. In this way, the position of the seat surface changes when the position of the backrest changes.

vitra.
T-Chair
Antonio Citterio
Glen Olivier Löw
work
wait
Type of feets: Aluminium(polished)
Type of rolls: soft
Type of armrests: Armsupports(I)
Material of Armsupports: green
Material: azzurro

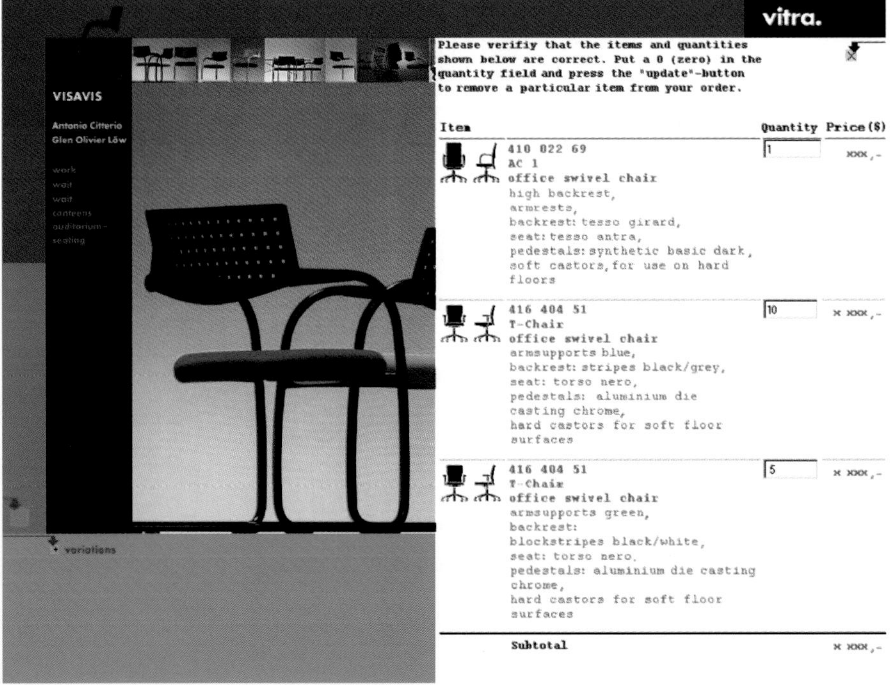
vitra.
VISAVIS
Antonio Citterio
Glen Olivier Löw
work
wait
wait
canteens
auditorium -
seating
variations
Please verifiy that the items and quantities shown below are correct. Put a 0 (zero) in the quantity field and press the "update"-button to remove a particular item from your order.
Item
Quantity
Price ($)
410 022 69
AC 1
office swivel chair
high backrest,
armrests,
backrest: tesso girard,
seat: tesso antra,
pedestals: synthetic basic dark,
soft castors, for use on hard floors
1
xxx,-
416 404 51
T-Chair
office swivel chair
armsupports blue,
backrest: stripes black/grey,
seat: torso nero,
pedestals: aluminium die casting chrome,
hard castors for soft floor surfaces
10
x xxx,-
416 404 51
T-Chair
office swivel chair
armsupports green,
backrest:
blockstripes black/white,
seat: torso nero,
pedestals: aluminium die casting chrome,
hard castors for soft floor surfaces
5
x xxx,-
Subtotal
x xxx,-

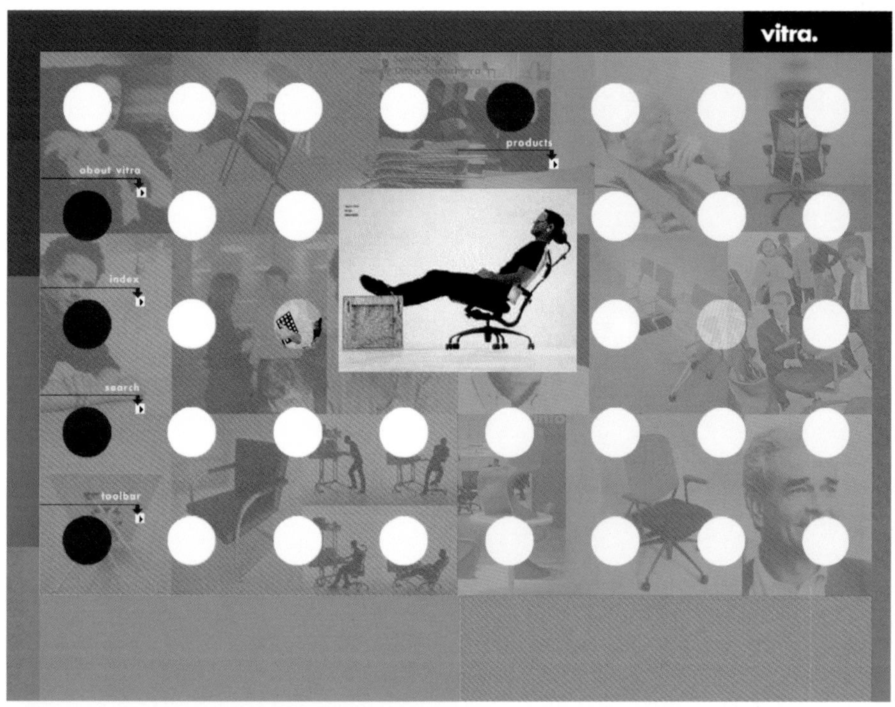
vitra.
products
about vitra
index
search
toolbar

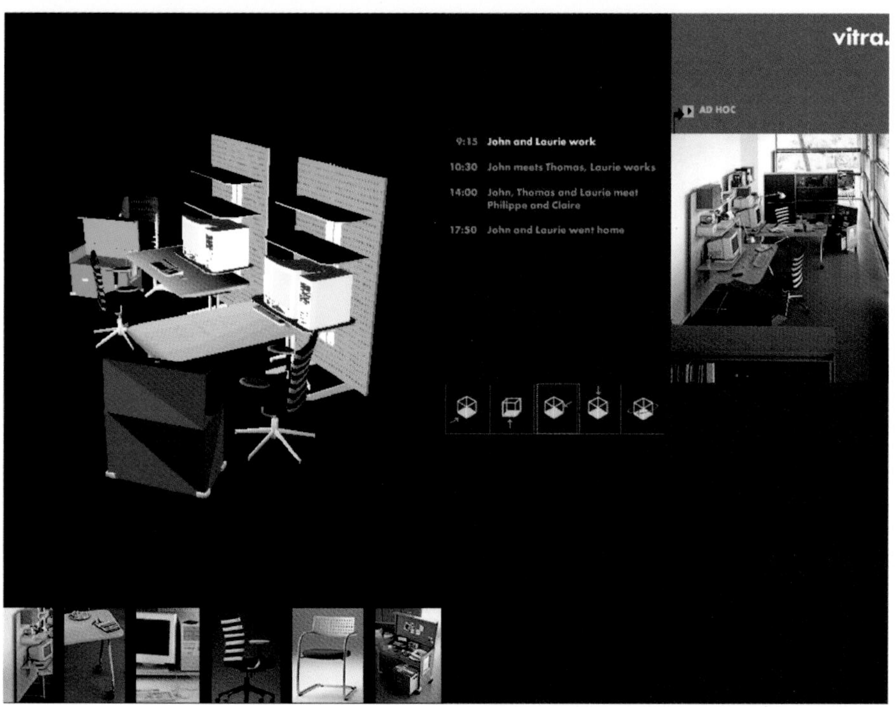
vitra.
AD HOC
9:15 John and Laurie work
10:30 John meets Thomas, Laurie works
14:00 John, Thomas and Laurie meet Philippe and Claire
17:50 John and Laurie went home

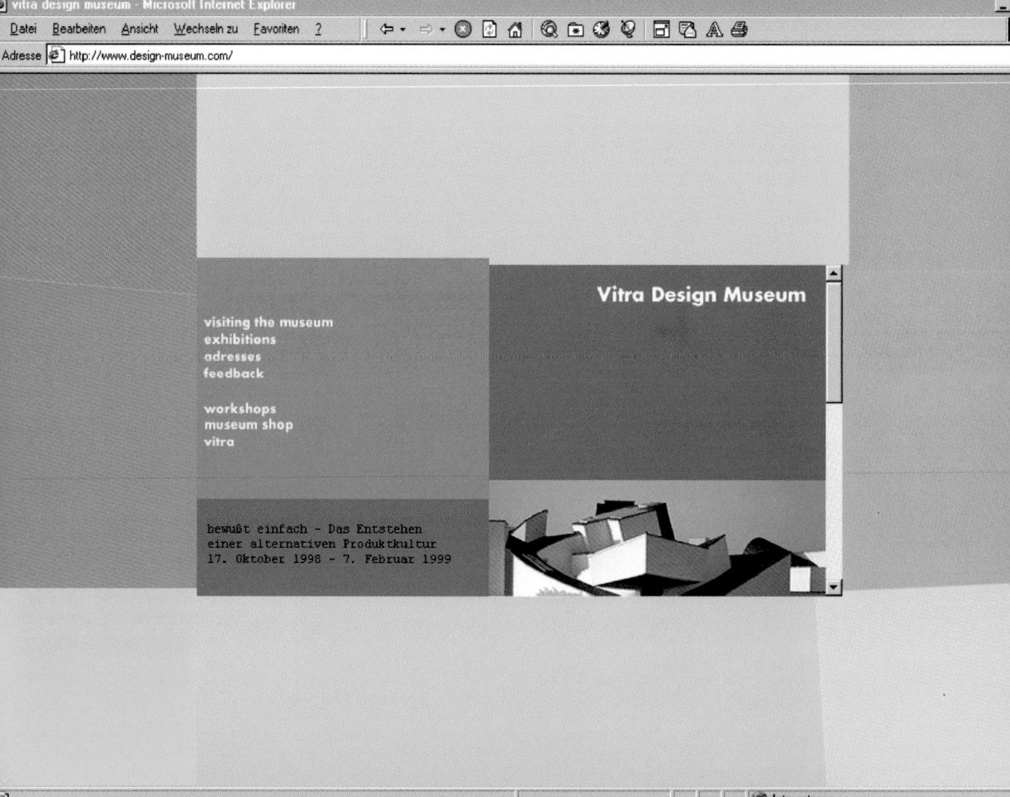
vitra design museum - Microsoft Internet Explorer
Datei Bearbeiten Ansicht Wechseln zu Favoriten ?
Adresse http://www.design-museum.com/
Vitra Design Museum
visiting the museum
exhibitions
adresses
feedback
workshops
museum shop
vitra
bewußt einfach - Das Entstehen
einer alternativen Produktkultur
17. Oktober 1998 - 7. Februar 1999
Internetzone

www.design-museum.com
Client: Vitra Design Museum
Designers:
Sonja Schäfer, Uli Weidner

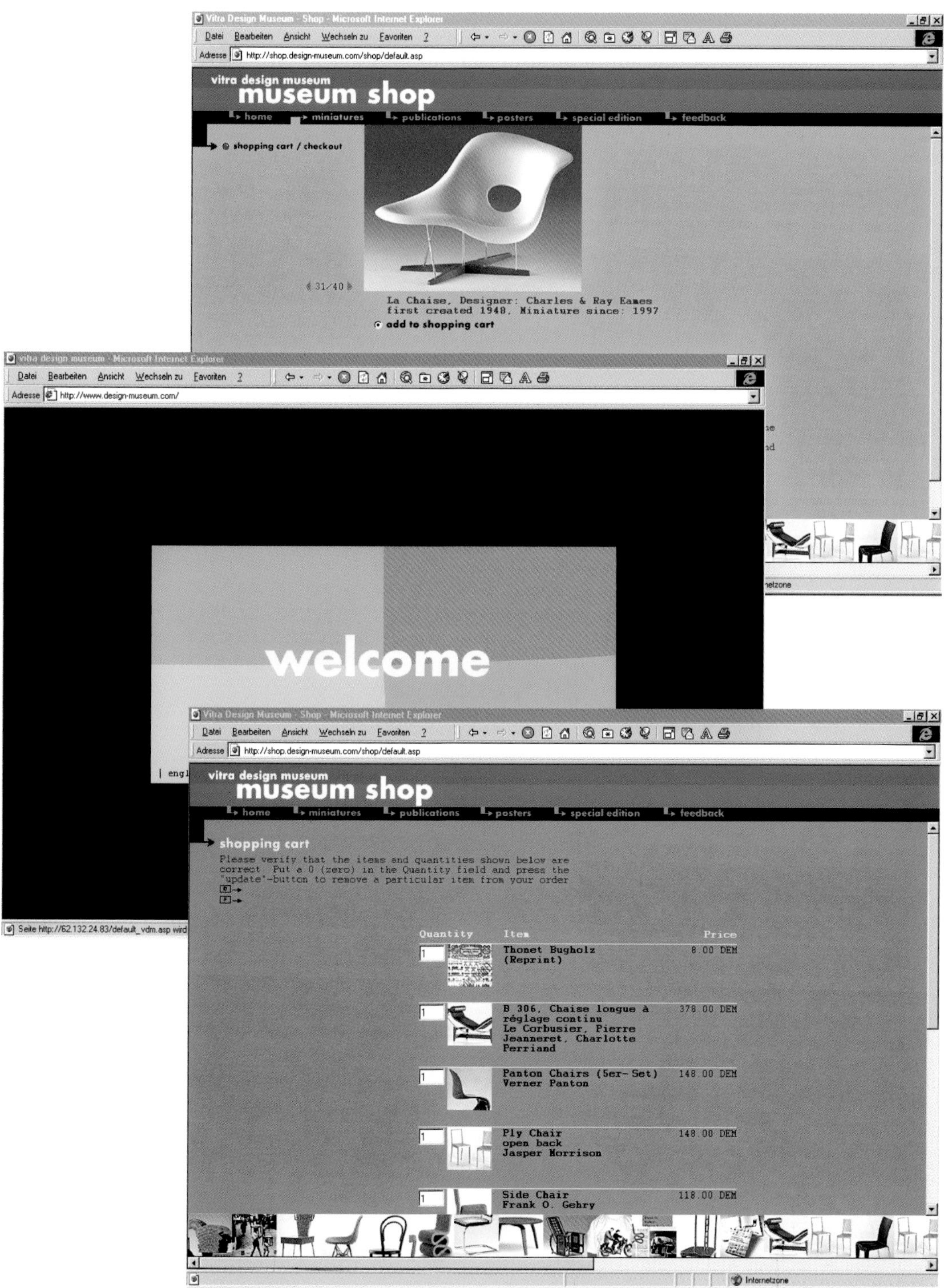

Site description
This site encompasses the spirit and activities of the Vitra Design Museum, with a style that reflects the deconstructivism of Frank O. Gehry's spectacular architecture.
In addition to the archive and information on current exhibitions, the site also features a virtual Museum Shop, where, catalogues, posters, and the Vitra's line of miniature designer chairs may be ordered online.

Technology

SOFTWARE

3D Studio Max
Adobe After Effects
Adobe Dimensions
Adobe Go Live
Adobe Illustrator
Adobe Image Ready
Adobe Photoshop
Adobe Premiere
Adobe Screen Ready
Allaire Homesite
Anarchie Pro
BB Edit
Compaq Desktop Pro
Cyber Studio
Debabelizer
Gif Builder
Gifwizard.Com
Image Ready
Macromedia
Director
Macromedia
Dream Weaver
Macromedia
Fireworks
Macromedia Flash
Microsoft Office
Microsoft
Visual Source Safe
Quark XPress
Quicktime
Sound Forge
Sun JDK
Windows NT 4.0
450 Mhz

HARDWARE

Agfa Scanners
Apple Power
Macintosh
Apple Macintosh G3
Apple Macintosh
G3 Power Book
Compaq servers
Cisco 2500 Routers
for Internet
Cisco 2500 Router
Frame Relay
Pentium II

Creative Directors Art Directors Designers

Clients

Design Firms

Graphis321

TANAKA / BIG BANG / MC DEAN / LINS / LEVINE / WATSON / TANG

Ikko Tanaka
Big Bang
Craig McDean
Rico Lins
David Levine
Albert Watson
David Tang

Advertising Annual 2000

GRAPHIS
Photo Annual 2000

GRAPHIS
New Talent Design Annual 1999

"One of the great achievements in a professional's career is to have their work reproduced in Graphis. The greater achievement is to do it as a student."

Order Form

We're introducing a great way to reward Graphis magazine readers: If you subscribe to Graphis, you'll qualify for a 40% discount on our books. If you subscribe and place a Standing Order, you'll get a 50% discount on our books. A Standing Order means we'll reserve your selected Graphis Annual or Series title(s) at press, and ship it to you at 50% discount. With a Standing Order for Design Annual 1999, for example, you'll receive this title at half off, and each coming year, we'll send you the newest Design Annual at this low price—an ideal way for the professional to keep informed, year after year. In addition to the titles here, we carry books in all communication disciplines, so call if there's another title we can get for you. Thank you for supporting Graphis.

Book title	Order No.	Retail	40% off Discount	Standing Order 50% off	Quantity	Totals
Advertising Annual 1999	1500	☐ $70.00	☐ $42.00	☐ $35.00		
Annual Reports 6 (s)	1550	☐ $70.00	☐ $42.00	☐ $35.00		
Apple Design	1259	☐ $45.00	☐ $27.00	N/A		
Black & White Blues	4710	☐ $40.00	☐ $24.00	N/A		
Book Design 2 (s)	1453	☐ $70.00	☐ $42.00	☐ $35.00		
Brochures 3 (s)	1496	☐ $70.00	☐ $42.00	☐ $35.00		
Corporate Identity 3 (s)	1437	☐ $70.00	☐ $42.00	☐ $35.00		
Digital Photo 1 (s)	1593	☐ $70.00	☐ $42.00	☐ $35.00		
Ferenc Berko	1445	☐ $60.00	☐ $36.00	N/A		
Information Architects	1380	☐ $35.00	☐ $21.00	N/A		
Interactive Design 1 (s)	1631	☐ $70.00	☐ $42.00	☐ $35.00		
Letterhead 4 (s)	1577	☐ $70.00	☐ $42.00	☐ $35.00		
Logo Design 4 (s)	1585	☐ $60.00	☐ $36.00	☐ $30.00		
New Talent Design Annual 1999	1607	☐ $60.00	☐ $36.00	☐ $30.00		
Nudes 1	212	☐ $50.00	☐ $30.00	N/A		
Photo Annual 1998	1461	☐ $70.00	☐ $42.00	☐ $35.00		
Pool Light	1470	☐ $70.00	☐ $42.00	N/A		
Poster Annual 1999	1623	☐ $70.00	☐ $42.00	☐ $35.00		
Product Design 2 (s)	1330	☐ $70.00	☐ $42.00	☐ $35.00		
Promotion Design 1 (s)	1615	☐ $70.00	☐ $42.00	☐ $35.00		
T-Shirt Design 2 (s)	1402	☐ $60.00	☐ $36.00	☐ $30.00		
Typography 2	1267	☐ $70.00	☐ $42.00	☐ $35.00		
Walter Iooss	1569	☐ $60.00	☐ $36.00	N/A		
World Trademarks	1070	☐ $250.00	☐ $150.00	N/A		
Shipping & handling per book, US $7.00, Canada $15.00, International $20.00.						
New York State shipments add 8.25% tax.						
Standing Orders I understand I am committing to the selected annuals and/or series and will be automatically charged for each new volume in forthcoming years, at 50% off. I must call and cancel my order when I am no longer interested in purchasing the book. (To honor your Standing Order discount you must sign below.) Signature / Date						
Graphis magazine	☐ One year subscription		USA $90	Canada $125	Int'l $125	
	☐ Two year subscription		USA $165	Canada $235	Int'l $235	
	☐ One year student*		USA $65	Canada $90	Int'l $90	
	☐ Single or Back Issues (per)		USA $24	Canada $28	Int'l $28	

*All students must mail a copy of student ID along with the order form.

(s)= series (published every 2-4 years)

Name	☐ American Express ☐ Visa ☐ Mastercard ☐ Check
Company	
Address	Card #
City State Zip	Expiration
Daytime phone	Card holder's signature

Send this order form (or copy) and make check payable to Graphis Inc. For even faster turn-around service, or if you have any questions about subscribing, contact us at the following numbers: in the US (800) 209. 4234; outside the US (212) 532. 9387 ext. 242 or 240; fax (212) 696. 4242. Mailing address: Graphis, 141 Lexington Avenue, New York, New York 10016-8193. Order Graphis on the Web from anywhere in the world: <www.graphis.com>.

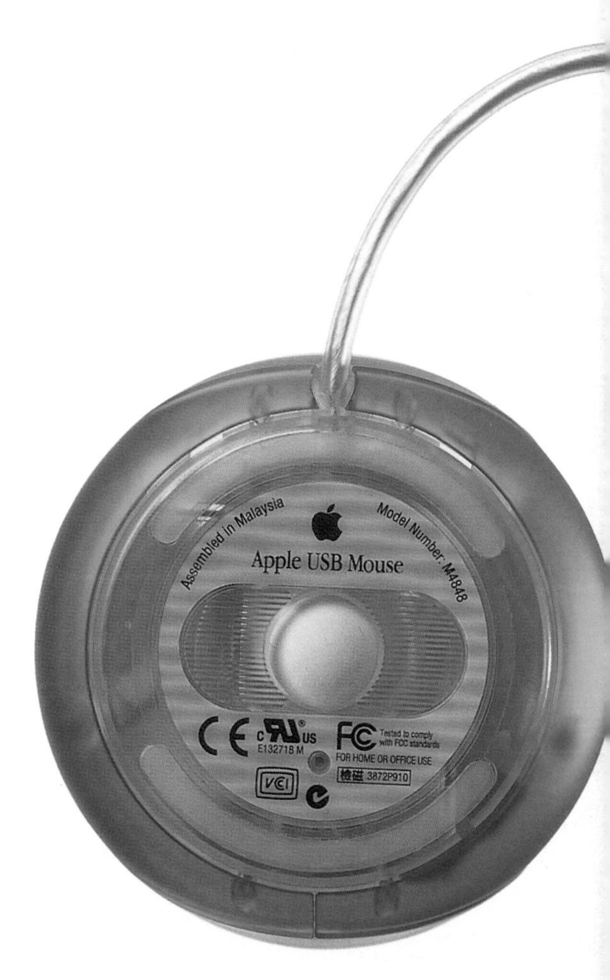
Assembled in Malaysia
Apple USB Mouse
Model Number: M4848
E132718 M
Tested to comply
with FCC standards
FOR HOME OR OFFICE USE
檢磁 3872P910

JUNIOR CERTIFICATE – SECOND AND THIRD YEAR

MATHS IN ACTION 3

Higher Level

Project Maths Strands 1–5

Glen Brennan, Mary Daly and Jackie Kaye

educate.ie 

PUBLISHED BY:
Educate.ie
Walsh Educational Books Ltd
Castleisland, Co. Kerry, Ireland
www.educate.ie

EDITOR
Ciara McNee

DESIGN AND DIAGRAMS
Compuscript

COVER
Kieran O'Donoghue

PRINTED AND BOUND BY:
Walsh Colour Print, Castleisland

ISBN: 978-1-909376-98-4

ACKNOWLEDGEMENTS
The publisher and authors would like to thank the following for permission to reproduce images:
© The British Library Board, Add. 23387, f.28; Mind Candy Ltd; Glow Images Inc; Alamy Images Limited; Dreamstime LLC; Shutterstock, Inc. (including BigstockPhoto.com); Wikicommons (public domain); Getty Images

Contents

Introduction

Maths in Action 3 is a new textbook that covers the Higher Level Junior Certificate Project Maths curriculum. Written by teachers from Project Maths Pilot schools, all material is up to date with latest syllabus requirements and has been extensively class tested.

This book guides second and third year maths students through their syllabus, using methods that will prepare them for their Junior Certificate exam and for the application of maths in real-life scenarios.

Key features of this book include:

- **Revision** of material covered in first year
- **Learning Outcomes** show content is in line with syllabus requirements
- **Key Words** at the start of each chapter help with literacy
- **Language** is simple and accessible
- **Examples** are clear and concise
- **Questions** are well graded and in line with the syllabus
- **Activities** link to the new approach
- End-of-chapter **'Challenges'** show how maths can be fun!
- **Self-Check Tests** encourage independent learning and assessment of learning
- **Knowledge Checklists** aid revision

Digital Features

For the Student:

- **FREE eBook with** each textbook purchase – see your personal code at the back of this book!
- **Extra resources** on www.educateplus.ie

For the Teacher:

- **Extra resources** on www.educateplus.ie
- **Teacher's Resource Book** with lesson plans and additional questions, activities and content

Good luck!

Glen Brennan
Mary Daly
Jackie Kaye
March 2014

NUMBERS AND INDICES

LEARNING OUTCOMES

In this chapter you will learn:

✓ **About the sets of rational and irrational numbers**

✓ **About the set of real numbers**

✓ **How to use the rules of indices**

✓ **How to add, subtract and multiply numbers in the form $a \pm \sqrt{b}$ where $a \in \mathbb{Q}$, $b \in \mathbb{Q}^+$**

✓ **How to express non-zero positive rational numbers in approximate form $a \times 10^n$, where $n \in \mathbb{Z}$ and $1 \leq a < 10$**

KEY WORDS

- **Indices**
- **Irrational numbers**
- **Rational numbers**
- **Reciprocals**
- **Standard form**
- **Surds**

1

INTRODUCTION

Maths in Action 1 introduced you to different sets of numbers, such as **natural numbers, integers** and **real numbers.** You also learned about using **powers,** or **indices,** to raise a number to a power.

In this chapter, you will learn about the difference between the sets of **rational** and **irrational** numbers. You will also learn about the rules of indices and how to apply them to numbers and variables.

First year revision

1. Paul states that 3 and 10 are natural numbers but that –1 and $\frac{3}{5}$ are not natural numbers. Do you agree with Paul? Explain your answer fully.
2. Copy the following number line and mark all the natural numbers with a dot.

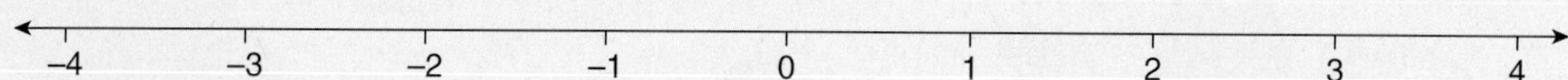

3. Ann states that –1, 5, 4 and –11 are integers but that 3.65 and $\frac{4}{9}$ are not integers. Do you agree with Ann? Explain your answer fully.
4. Copy the following number line and mark all the integers with a dot.

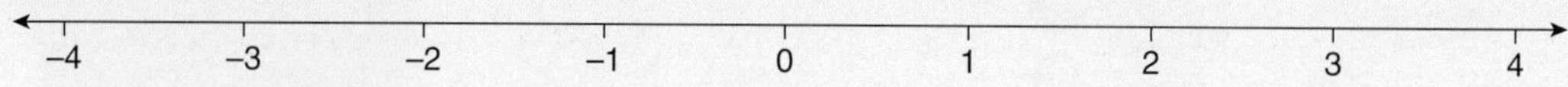

5. What are real numbers?
6. Copy the following number line and mark all the real numbers on it.

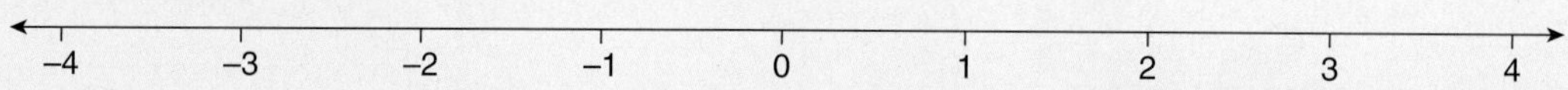

7. Copy the following Venn diagram and place the letters $\mathbb{N}$, $\mathbb{Z}$ and $\mathbb{R}$ in the correct positions.

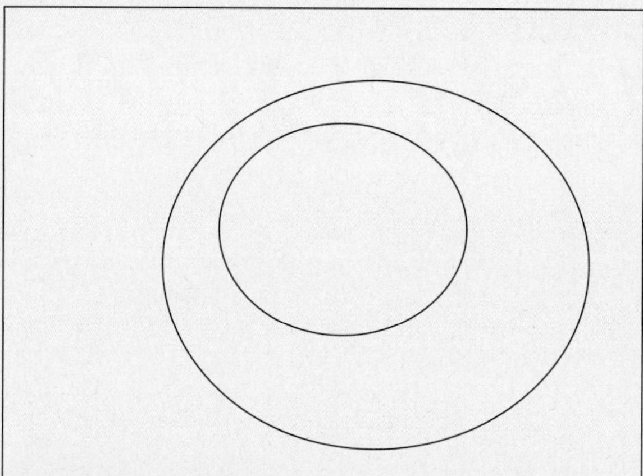

8. Match each number set with its correct symbol and description.

Symbol
$\mathbb{N}$
$\mathbb{R}$
$\mathbb{Z}$

Number set
Integers
Natural numbers
Real numbers

Description
Whole positive numbers greater than zero
Whole numbers, positive and negative
Whole numbers, fractions and decimals, both positive and negative

9. Write the reciprocal of each of the following fractions:

(a) $\frac{2}{5}$ (c) $\frac{5}{4}$ (e) $1\frac{7}{10}$ (g) $-\frac{7}{4}$

(b) $\frac{3}{8}$ (d) $2\frac{3}{4}$ (f) $-\frac{3}{4}$ (h) $-1\frac{1}{2}$

Section 1.1: Number sets

Student Activity 1A

1. Draw a number line from −7 to +7 inclusive. From your number line, write down the elements of the set:
   (a) A = {integers from −7 to 7 inclusive}
   (b) B = {natural numbers from −7 to 7 inclusive}
   (c) Which of the following statements is true? Give a reason for each answer.
   (i) A = B (ii) $A \subset B$ (iii) $B \subset A$
2. Which of the following statements is true?
   (a) Integers are a subset of natural numbers.
   (b) Natural numbers are a subset of integers.
3. Write two examples for each of the following statements (if possible).
   (a) A number which is a natural number and an integer
   (b) A number which is a natural number but is not an integer
   (c) A number which is not a natural number but is a real number
   (d) A number which is an integer but is not a natural number

NUMBER SETS EXPLAINED

In mathematics, it is important to understand that numbers are all part of a common set.

From the Venn diagram, you can see which sets of numbers are subsets of other sets of numbers. For example, natural numbers are a subset of integers.

It is also important to remember the meaning and symbol for each number set.

Symbol	Number set	Description
ℕ	Natural numbers	Whole positive numbers greater than zero
ℤ	Integers	Whole numbers, positive and negative
ℝ	Real numbers	Whole numbers, fractions and decimals, both positive and negative

EXAMPLE 1

For each number, identify all the number sets of which it is an element.

(a) 5 (b) 2.1 (c) −4

Solution

(a) $5 \in \mathbb{N}, \mathbb{Z}$ and $\mathbb{R}$ (b) $2.1 \in \mathbb{R}$ (c) $-4 \in \mathbb{Z}$ and $\mathbb{R}$

Exercise 1.1

1. Identify the sets, ($\mathbb{N}$, $\mathbb{Z}$ and $\mathbb{R}$) of which each number is an element:
   (a) 6 (b) −9 (c) 3.7 (d) $\frac{1}{2}$ (e) −5.45 (f) 7 (g) $\frac{1}{7}$
2. A = {natural numbers from 0 to 10 inclusive} and B = {squares of the first ten natural numbers}.
   (a) List the elements of set A and of set B.
   (b) Draw a Venn diagram to represent sets A and B.
3. G = {$x|x$ is an integer from −3 to 6 inclusive} and H = {$x|x$ is a natural number less than 7}.
   (a) List the elements of set G.
   (b) List the elements of set H.
   (c) Find $G \cap H$.
   (d) Find $G \cup H$.
   (e) Find G'.
   (f) Find H'.
4. D = {$x|x$ is a factor of 8} and M = {$x|x$ is a factor of 12}.
   (a) List the elements of D.
   (b) List the elements of M.
   (c) Draw a Venn diagram to show the sets D and M.
   (d) Find $D \cap M$.
   (e) Find $D \cup M$.
   (f) By examining your Venn diagram, find the highest common factor of 8 and 12.

Section 1.2: Rational and irrational numbers

The set of real numbers contains all the numbers we use on the Junior Certificate course. Real numbers can be divided into two subsets called **rational numbers** and **irrational numbers.**

Rational numbers ($\mathbb{Q}$) are numbers which can be written in the form $\frac{a}{b}$, where ***a*** and ***b*** are integers and ***b*** is not zero.

Rational numbers can terminate (end) after a certain number of digits, or they can **recur.** A **recurring** number repeats a digit or group of digits.

$\frac{3}{4}$ is an example of a rational number.

- It is written in the form $\frac{a}{b}$.
- It can be written as 0.75, which has terminated.

$\frac{1}{3}$ is also an example of a rational number as it can be written as $0.3333333333\dot{3}$. The dot over the final 3 indicates that the number repeats forever. Your calculator may show this as $0.\dot{3}$.

We use the symbol $\mathbb{Q}$ to represent the set of rational numbers.

Irrational numbers ($\mathbb{R}\backslash\mathbb{Q}$) are numbers which **cannot** be written in the form $\frac{a}{b}$, where ***a*** and ***b*** are integers and ***b*** is not equal to zero.

Irrational numbers are real numbers which **cannot** be represented as terminating or as repeating decimals.

$\sqrt{2}$ is an example of an irrational number. $\sqrt{2}$ written as a decimal is 1.41421362... It neither terminates nor begins a repeating pattern. This shows that it is **irrational.**

Irrational numbers are real numbers which are not rational.

There is no definitive symbol for the set of irrational numbers. We can use $\mathbb{R}\backslash\mathbb{Q}$ – meaning the set of real numbers less the set of rational numbers.

Hippasus was a student of **Pythagoras.** Hippasus discovered irrational numbers when trying to represent the square root of 2 as a fraction. Pythagoras could not accept the existence of irrational numbers and had Hippasus thrown into the sea and drowned!

EXAMPLE 2

Use your calculator to identify which of the following numbers are rational and which are irrational. Explain your answers.

(a) $\frac{2}{5}$ (b) $\sqrt{3}$ (c) $\frac{2}{3}$ (d) $\sqrt{6.25}$ (e) $\sqrt{5}$

Solution

(a) $\frac{2}{5}$ As this is a fraction containing two integers, it is a rational number.

(b) $\sqrt{3} = 1.7320508...$ It does not terminate or repeat, so it is an irrational number.

(c) $\frac{2}{3} = 0.\dot{6}$ It is a recurring number, so it is a rational number.

(d) $\sqrt{6.25} = 2.5$ It has terminated, so it is a rational number.

(e) $\sqrt{5} = 2.23606797...$ It does not terminate or repeat, so it is an irrational number.

Exercise 1.2

State whether the following numbers belong to the set of rational numbers $\{\mathbb{Q}\}$ or to the set of irrational numbers $\{\mathbb{R}\backslash\mathbb{Q}\}$. Explain your answers.

1. $\frac{6}{10}$
2. $\sqrt{27.04}$
3. $\frac{33}{99}$
4. $\sqrt{11}$
5. $\frac{-5}{50}$
6. $\sqrt{30}$
7. $\sqrt{2} - 1$
8. $\sqrt{36.69}$
9. $\frac{25}{1000}$
10. $\sqrt{27}$
11. $\sqrt{26}$
12. $\frac{7}{35}$
13. $\sqrt{3} + 1$
14. $\sqrt{37}$
15. $\sqrt{37.21}$
16. $\frac{25}{125}$
17. $\sqrt{7} + 2$
18. $\frac{33}{126}$

19. Using your calculator, write each of the following fractions as a recurring decimal:

(a) $\frac{2}{3}$ (b) $\frac{4}{7}$ (c) $\frac{1}{6}$ (d) $\frac{9}{11}$ (e) $\frac{5}{7}$ (f) $\frac{8}{13}$ (g) $\frac{5}{6}$ (h) $\frac{1}{11}$ (i) $\frac{17}{21}$ (j) $\frac{13}{37}$

20. State if each of the following is true or false:

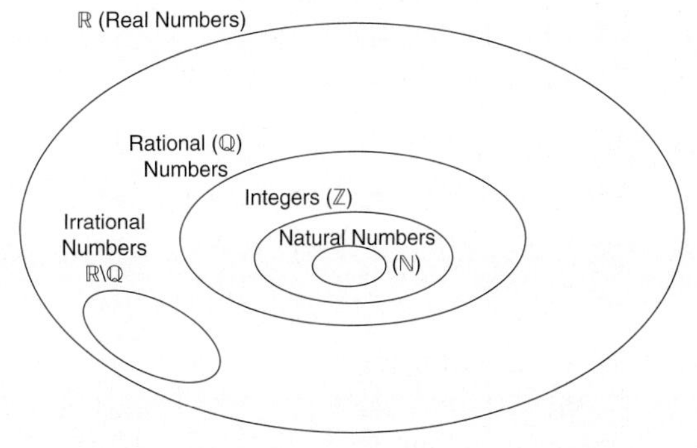

(a) $\mathbb{N} \subset \mathbb{Z}$ (b) $\mathbb{R} \subset \mathbb{N}$ (c) $\mathbb{Z} \subset \mathbb{Q}$ (d) $\mathbb{Q} \subset \mathbb{Z}$

(e) $\mathbb{Q} \subset \mathbb{R}$ (f) $\mathbb{N} \subset \mathbb{Q}$ (g) $\mathbb{Q} \subset \mathbb{N}$ (h) $\mathbb{Z} \subset \mathbb{Z}$

(i) $\mathbb{Z} \subset \mathbb{N}$ (j) $\mathbb{R} \subset \mathbb{Z}$ (k) $\mathbb{N} \subset \mathbb{R}$ (l) $\mathbb{R}\backslash\mathbb{Q} \subset \mathbb{R}$

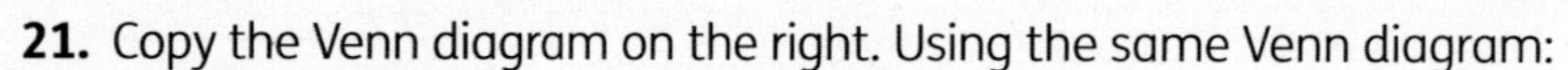

21. Copy the Venn diagram on the right. Using the same Venn diagram:
    (a) Draw a region $\mathbb{Q}$ (where $\mathbb{Q} \subset \mathbb{R}$).
    (b) Draw a region $\mathbb{Z}$ (where $\mathbb{Z} \subset \mathbb{Q}$).
    (c) Draw a region $\mathbb{N}$ (where $\mathbb{N} \subset \mathbb{Z}$).
    (d) Place each of the following ten elements in their correct regions: $1, -3, 0.54, \frac{1}{3}, \sqrt{7}, -5.4, 13.45, -\frac{1}{4}, -\sqrt{42}, 16$.

22. Which of the numbers in the following list are irrational?
    (a) $\sqrt{3}$ (b) $\frac{1}{3}$ (c) 0 (d) $\frac{22}{7}$ (e) $\sqrt{36}$ (f) $\sqrt{56.25}$

23. Which of the following numbers are not irrational?
    (a) $\sqrt{2} + \sqrt{7}$
    (b) $\sqrt{2 + 7}$
    (c) $\sqrt{2} + 7$
    (d) $2 + \sqrt{7}$
    (e) $\sqrt{6 \times 2}$
    (f) $\sqrt{6 + 2}$
    (g) $\sqrt{6 - 2}$
    (h) $\sqrt{6 \div 2}$

24. Pi, which has the symbol π, is a famous irrational number. People have calculated pi to over a quadrillion (1,000,000,000,000,000, which is one thousand million million) decimals without finding a pattern. The first set of digits look like this:
    $\pi = 3.14159265358979323846264338327 95...$
    (a) Suggest why 3.14 is the popular approximation of pi.
    (b) Research the importance of pi in mathematics. You can use history books, the internet or any other source of information.

Section 1.3: Indices rule 1

Student Activity 1B

1. Answer the following questions:
   (a) Calculate $2^2 = ? \times ? =$
   (b) Calculate $2^3 = ? \times ? \times ? =$
   (c) Calculate $2^5 = ? \times ? \times ? \times ? \times ? =$
   (d) Calculate $2^2 \times 2^3 = ? \times ? \times ? \times ? \times ? =$
   (e) Can you see a relationship between the powers in (c) and (d)?
2. Answer the following questions:
   (a) Calculate $3^2 = ? \times ? =$
   (b) Calculate $3^4 = ? \times ? \times ? \times ? =$
   (c) Calculate $3^6 = ? \times ? \times ? \times ? \times ? \times ? =$
   (d) Calculate $3^2 \times 3^4 = ? \times ? \times ? \times ? \times ? \times ? =$
   (e) Can you see a relationship between the powers in (c) and (d)?
3. Using the information you have learned in the previous questions, can you find the number to replace the question mark in each of the following?
   (a) $2^3 \times 2^4 = 2^?$
   (b) $3^4 \times 3^3 = 3^?$
   (c) $4^2 \times 4^5 = 4^?$
   (d) $5^3 \times 5^2 = 5^?$
   (e) $6^3 \times 6^2 = 6^?$

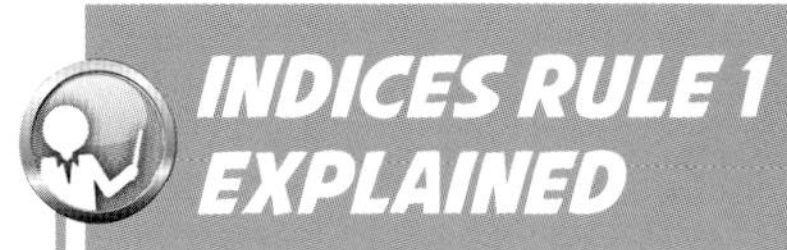

INDICES RULE 1 EXPLAINED

In *Maths in Action 1*, you learned about raising a number to a power. Powers are also called **indices** or **exponents.**

Number of base → $\mathbf{3^4}$ ← Power or index (exponent)

It is often necessary to multiply numbers that are raised to powers.

Rule 1

When multiplying numbers of the same base, **add** the indices.

$$a^p \times a^q = a^{p+q}$$

In order to apply this rule, the **base** number must be the same. For example, in $2^3 \times 2^4$, 2 is the base number. This rule cannot be applied to $4^3 \times 3^3$ as the base numbers are not the same.

EXAMPLE 3

Simplify each of the following:

(a) $2^2 \times 2^3$ (c) $5^3 \times 5^4$

(b) $3^3 \times 3^9$ (d) $6^3 \times 6^7$

Solution

(a) $2^2 \times 2^3 = 2^5$ (c) $5^3 \times 5^4 = 5^7$

(b) $3^3 \times 3^9 = 3^{12}$ (d) $6^3 \times 6^7 = 6^{10}$

Exercise 1.3

Simplify each of the following:

1. $4^3 \times 4^5$	**5.** $9^2 \times 9^4$	**9.** $5^2 \times 5^9 \times 5^{10}$	**13.** $p^4 \times p^{12}$
2. $3^6 \times 3^7$	**6.** $10^4 \times 10^5$	**10.** $3^3 \times 3^8 \times 3^7$	**14.** $c^6 \times c^8$
3. $5^6 \times 5^4$	**7.** $2^8 \times 2^{11} \times 2^3$	**11.** $a^2 \times a^3$	**15.** $t^3 \times t^7$
4. $8^3 \times 8^8$	**8.** $6^4 \times 6^6 \times 6^{10}$	**12.** $m^6 \times m^4$	**16.** $p^3 \times p^2 \times p$

Section 1.4: Indices rule 2

Student Activity 1C

1. Answer each of the following:
   (a) Calculate $3^5 = ? \times ? \times ? \times ? \times ? =$
   (b) Calculate $3^2 = ? \times ? =$
   (c) Calculate $3^3 = ? \times ? \times ? =$
   (d) Calculate $\frac{3^5}{3^2} = \frac{? \times ? \times ? \times ? \times ?}{? \times ?} = ? \times ? \times ? = 3^? =$
   (e) Can you see a relationship between the powers in (c) and (d)?

2. Answer each of the following questions:
   (a) Calculate $2^2 = ? \times ? =$
   (b) Calculate $2^6 = ? \times ? \times ? \times ? \times ? \times ? =$
   (c) Calculate $2^4 = ? \times ? \times ? \times ? =$
   (d) Calculate $\frac{2^6}{2^2} = \frac{? \times ? \times ? \times ? \times ? \times ?}{? \times ?} = ? \times ? \times ? \times ? = 2^? =$
   (e) Can you see a relationship between the powers in (c) and (d)?

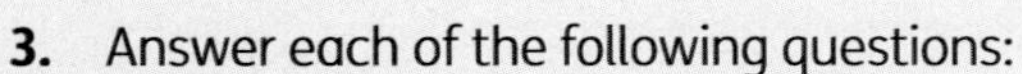

3. Answer each of the following questions:
   (a) Calculate $2^7 = ? \times ? \times ? \times ? \times ? \times ? \times ? =$
   (b) Calculate $2^4 = ? \times ? \times ? \times ? =$
   (c) Calculate $2^3 = ? \times ? \times ? =$
   (d) Calculate $\frac{2^7}{2^4} = \frac{? \times ? \times ? \times ? \times ? \times ? \times ?}{? \times ? \times ? \times ?} = ? \times ? \times ? = 2^? =$
   (e) Can you see a relationship between the powers in (c) and (d)?

INDICES RULE 2 EXPLAINED

In Student Activity 1C, you investigated the division of numbers containing indices.

Rule 2

When dividing numbers of the same base, **subtract** the indices:

$$\frac{a^p}{a^q} = a^{p-q}$$

Again when dividing numbers with indices, the **base** numbers must be the same.

EXAMPLE 4

Simplify each of the following:

(a) $\frac{2^5}{2^2}$

(b) $\frac{3^7}{3^3}$

(c) $\frac{7^5}{7^3}$

(d) $\frac{8^9}{8^7}$

(e) Write $\frac{3^4 \times 3^5}{3^3 \times 3^4}$ in the form of 3^n.

Solution

(a) $\frac{2^5}{2^2}$

Method 1: Expanding the powers

$\frac{2^5}{2^2} = \frac{\cancel{2 \times 2} \times 2 \times 2 \times 2}{\cancel{2 \times 2}}$

$= 2 \times 2 \times 2 = 2^3 = 8$

Method 2: Using rule 2

$\frac{2^5}{2^2} = 2^{5-2} = 2^3 = 8$

(b) $\frac{3^7}{3^3}$

Method 1: Expanding the powers

$\frac{3^7}{3^3} = \frac{\cancel{3 \times 3 \times 3} \times 3 \times 3 \times 3 \times 3}{\cancel{3 \times 3 \times 3}}$

$= 3 \times 3 \times 3 \times 3 = 3^4 = 81$

Method 2: Using rule 2

$\frac{3^7}{3^3} = 3^{7-3} = 3^4$

(c) $\frac{7^5}{7^3} = 7^{5-3} = 7^2 = 49$

(d) $\frac{8^9}{8^7} = 8^{9-7} = 8^2 = 64$

(e) $\frac{3^4 \times 3^5}{3^3 \times 3^4}$

Method 1: Expanding the powers

$\frac{3^4 \times 3^5}{3^3 \times 3^4} = \frac{\cancel{3 \times 3 \times 3 \times 3 \times 3 \times 3 \times 3} \times 3 \times 3}{\cancel{3 \times 3 \times 3 \times 3 \times 3 \times 3 \times 3}}$

$= 3 \times 3 = 3^2 = 9$

Method 2: Using the rules

$\frac{3^4 \times 3^5}{3^3 \times 3^4} = \frac{3^9}{3^7}$ **Add the powers using rule 1**

$\frac{3^9}{3^7} = 3^{9-7} = 3^2$ **Subtract the powers using rule 2**

Exercise 1.4

Simplify each of the following, leaving your answer in index form:

1. $\frac{5^7}{5^3} = 5^?$
2. $\frac{2^3}{2^2} = 2^?$
3. $\frac{3^5}{3^2} = 3^?$
4. $\frac{7^5}{7^3} = 7^?$
5. $\frac{6^8}{6^5} = 6^?$
6. $\frac{8^4}{8^3} = 8^?$
7. $\frac{5^8}{5^5} = 5^?$
8. $\frac{4^7}{4^4} = 4^?$
9. $\frac{7^8}{7^3}$
10. $\frac{9^7}{9^4}$
11. $\frac{3^9}{3^4}$
12. $\frac{2^8}{2^6}$
13. $\frac{4^9 \times 4^3}{4^7 \times 4^2}$
14. $\frac{2^3 \times 2^5}{2^4 \times 2^3}$

15. $\frac{3^2 \times 3^6}{3^3 \times 3^2}$	**17.** $\frac{7^4 \times 7^3}{7^2 \times 7^2}$	**19.** $\frac{a^2 \times a^4}{a^3 \times a^2}$	**21.** $\frac{v^7 \times v^4 \times v^8}{v^5 \times v^4}$	**23.** $\frac{q^5 \times q^{11} \times q}{q^9 \times q^3}$
16. $\frac{5^5 \times 5^5}{5^4 \times 5^2}$	**18.** $\frac{9^8 \times 9^3}{9^6 \times 9^4}$	**20.** $\frac{w^5 \times w^6}{w^6 \times w^3}$	**22.** $\frac{y^9 \times y^3 \times y^5}{y^6 \times y^4}$	**24.** $\frac{p^7 \times p^3 \times p^5}{p^5 \times p^5 \times p^5}$

Section 1.5: Indices rule 3

Student Activity 1D

1. Answer each of the following questions:
   (a) Calculate $(2^2)^3 = 2^? \times 2^? \times 2^? = ? \times ? \times ? \times ? \times ? \times ? = 2^? =$
   (b) Use your calculator to evaluate 2^6.
   (c) Can you see a relationship between the powers in (a) and (b)?
2. Answer each of the following questions:
   (a) Calculate $(3^2)^4 = 3^? \times 3^? \times 3^? \times 3^? = ? \times ? \times ? \times ? \times ? \times ? \times ? \times ? = 3^? =$
   (b) Calculate 3^8.
   (c) Can you see a relationship between the powers in (a) and (b)?

INDICES RULE 3 EXPLAINED

In Student Activity 1D, you began raising a power by a power.

Rule 3

When raising the index of a number to an index, **multiply** the indices:

$$(a^p)^q = a^{pq}$$

EXAMPLE 5

Simplify each of the following:

(a) $(3^2)^3$ (b) $(2^4)^5$ (c) $(3abf)^3$

Solution

(a) $(3^2)^3 = 3^6$

Method 1: Expanding the powers

$(3^2)^3 = 3^2 \times 3^2 \times 3^2 = 3 \times 3 \times 3 \times 3 \times 3 \times 3$
$= 3^6 = 729$

Method 2: Using Rule 3

$(3^2)^3 = 3^{2 \times 3} = 3^6 = 729$

(b) $(2^4)^5 = 2^{20}$

Method 1: Expanding the powers

$(2^4)^5 = 2^4 \times 2^4 \times 2^4 \times 2^4 \times 2^4$
$= 2 \times 2 \times 2 \times 2 \times 2 \times 2 \times 2 \times 2 \times 2 \times 2$
$\times 2 \times 2 \times 2 \times 2 \times 2 \times 2 \times 2 \times 2 \times 2 \times 2$
$= 2^{20} = 1{,}048{,}576$

Method 2: Using Rule 3

$(2^4)^5 = 2^{4 \times 5} = 2^{20} = 1{,}048{,}576$

(c) $(3abf)^3$

Method 1: Expanding the powers

$(3abf)^3 = 3abf \times 3abf \times 3abf = 27a^3b^3f^3$

Method 2: Using Rule 3

$(3abf)^3 = (3^1a^1b^1f^1)^3 = 3^{1 \times 3}a^{1 \times 3}b^{1 \times 3}f^{1 \times 3} = 27a^3b^3f^3$

1

MATHS IN ACTION 3

Exercise 1.5

Simplify each of the following:

1. $(3^2)^5 = 3^?$
2. $(2^4)^5 = 2^?$
3. $(4^2)^4 = 4^?$
4. $(7^2)^3 = 7^?$
5. $(2^5)^5 = 2^?$
6. $(9^2)^3 = 9^?$
7. $(6^8)^3 = 6^?$
8. $(4^5)^2 = 4^?$
9. $(3^3)^3 = 3^?$
10. $(8^2)^5 = 8^?$
11. $(a^5)^3$
12. $(h^3)^4$
13. $(n^4)^4$
14. $(x^2)^8$
15. $(y^9)^8$
16. $(ab)^2 = a^{\square} \times b^{\square}$
17. $(xy)^4 = x^{\square} \times y^{\square}$
18. $(ac)^3 = a^{\square} \times c^{\square}$
19. $(zw)^4 = z^{\square} \times w^{\square}$
20. $(uv)^7 = u^{\square} \times v^{\square}$
21. $(2bc)^3$
22. $(2a^2x)^5$
23. $(5xy^2)^4$
24. $(12a^3b)^2$
25. $(2z^2w^3)^4$

Section 1.6: Indices rule 4

Student Activity 1E

1. Answer the following questions:
   (a) What do you call $\sqrt{\ }$ in maths?
   (b) Use your calculator to find $\sqrt{25}$.
   (c) Type $25^{\frac{1}{2}}$ into your calculator as follows:
      (i) 25
      (ii) The $x^{\square}$ key
      (iii) Type $\frac{1}{2}$ using the fraction key. (Alternatively type 0·5.)
      (iv) Press =.
      (v) Compare your answers from parts (b) and (c). What do you notice?
2. Repeat Question 1 using the number 36.

INDICES RULE 4 EXPLAINED

In Student Activity 1E, you raised a number to a power of one-half.

Rule 4

Raising a number to a power of one-half is the same as finding the square root of the number:

$$a^{\frac{1}{2}} = \sqrt{a}$$

EXAMPLE 6

Calculate the value of each of the following:

(a) $4^{\frac{1}{2}}$

(b) $64^{\frac{1}{2}}$

(c) $100^{\frac{1}{2}}$

Solution

(a) $4^{\frac{1}{2}} = \sqrt{4} = 2$

(b) $64^{\frac{1}{2}} = \sqrt{64} = 8$

(c) $100^{\frac{1}{2}} = \sqrt{100} = 10$

Exercise 1.6

Find the value of each of the following:

1. $81^{\frac{1}{2}}$
2. $25^{\frac{1}{2}}$
3. $625^{\frac{1}{2}}$
4. $900^{\frac{1}{2}}$
5. $8{,}100^{\frac{1}{2}}$
6. $400^{\frac{1}{2}}$
7. $169^{\frac{1}{2}}$
8. $225^{\frac{1}{2}}$
9. $289^{\frac{1}{2}}$
10. $1{,}089^{\frac{1}{2}}$

Section 1.7: Indices rule 5

Student Activity 1F

1. Use your calculator to answer each of the following:
   (a) Calculate $\sqrt[3]{8}$.
   (b) Calculate $8^{\frac{1}{3}}$.
   (c) What did you notice about your answers for (a) and (b)?
2. Use your calculator to answer each of the following:
   (a) Calculate $\sqrt[3]{125}$.
   (b) Calculate $125^{\frac{1}{3}}$.
   (c) What did you notice about your answers for (a) and (b)?
3. Use your calculator to answer each of the following:
   (a) Calculate $\sqrt[4]{16}$.
   (b) Calculate $16^{\frac{1}{4}}$.
   (c) What did you notice about your answers for (a) and (b)?

INDICES RULE 5 EXPLAINED

In Student Activity 1F, you investigated one of the rules for dealing with indices which are fractions.

For example, raising a number to a power of one-third is the same as finding the cube root of the number.

We can write this mathematically as:

Rule 5

$a^{\frac{1}{p}} = \sqrt[p]{a}$, where $p \in \mathbb{Z}, p \neq 0, a > 0$

EXAMPLE 7

Calculate each of the following:

(a) $64^{\frac{1}{3}}$ (b) $81^{\frac{1}{4}}$ (c) $32^{\frac{1}{5}}$

Solution

(a) $64^{\frac{1}{3}} = \sqrt[3]{64} = 4$ (b) $81^{\frac{1}{4}} = \sqrt[4]{81} = 3$ (c) $32^{\frac{1}{5}} = \sqrt[5]{32} = 2$

Exercise 1.7

Calculate each of the following:

1. $\sqrt[3]{1,000}$
2. $\sqrt[3]{216}$
3. $\sqrt[3]{512}$
4. $625^{\frac{1}{4}}$
5. $216^{\frac{1}{3}}$
6. $512^{\frac{1}{3}}$
7. $1,296^{\frac{1}{4}}$
8. $10,000^{\frac{1}{4}}$
9. $2,401^{\frac{1}{4}}$
10. $16^{\frac{1}{4}}$
11. $1,331^{\frac{1}{3}}$
12. $39.0625^{\frac{1}{4}}$
13. $4,096^{\frac{1}{4}}$
14. $2.197^{\frac{1}{3}}$
15. $15,625^{\frac{1}{6}}$
16. $\left(\frac{1}{8}\right)^{\frac{1}{3}}$
17. $729^{\frac{1}{3}}$
18. $1,728^{\frac{1}{3}}$
19. $1^{\frac{1}{4}}$
20. $28,561^{\frac{1}{4}}$

Section 1.8: Indices rule 6

Student Activity 1G

1. Use your calculator to calculate each of the following:
   (a) $9^{\frac{3}{2}}$
   (b) $\left(9^{\frac{1}{2}}\right)^3$
   (c) $(\sqrt{9})^3$
   (d) What do you notice about each of your answers above?

2. Use your calculator to calculate each of the following:
   (a) $25^{\frac{3}{2}}$
   (b) $\left(25^{\frac{1}{2}}\right)^3$
   (c) $(\sqrt{25})^3$
   (d) What do you notice about each of your answers above?

INDICES RULE 6 EXPLAINED

In Student Activity 1G, you investigated another rule for dealing with indices which are fractions.

We can write this mathematically as:

Rule 6

$a^{\frac{p}{q}} = (\sqrt[q]{a})^p$, where $p, q \in \mathbb{Z}, q \neq 0, a > 0$

EXAMPLE 8

Calculate each of the following:

(a) $16^{\frac{3}{4}}$ (b) $64^{\frac{2}{3}}$ (c) $81^{\frac{3}{4}}$ (d) $\left(\frac{4}{9}\right)^{\frac{1}{2}}$

Solution

(a) $16^{\frac{3}{4}} = \left(16^{\frac{1}{4}}\right)^3$ **Split the fraction**

$= (\sqrt[4]{16})^3$ **A power of $\frac{1}{4}$ means the fourth root of the number, i.e. what number multiplied by itself 4 times gives 16?**

$= (2)^3 = 8$

(b) $64^{\frac{2}{3}} = \left(64^{\frac{1}{3}}\right)^2$ **Split the fraction**

$= (\sqrt[3]{64})^2$ **A power of $\frac{1}{3}$ means the cube root of the number, i.e. what number multiplied by itself 3 times gives 64?**

$= 4^2 = 16$

(c) $81^{\frac{3}{4}} = \left(81^{\frac{1}{4}}\right)^3$ **Split the fraction**

$= (\sqrt[4]{81})^3$ **A power of $\frac{1}{4}$ means the fourth root of the number, i.e. what number multiplied by itself 4 times gives 81?**

$= 3^3 = 27$

(d) $\left(\frac{4}{9}\right)^{\frac{1}{2}}$ **Apply the power to both the numerator and denominator**

$= \frac{4^{\frac{1}{2}}}{9^{\frac{1}{2}}}$ **A power of $\frac{1}{2}$ means the square root of each number**

$= \frac{\sqrt{4}}{\sqrt{9}} = \frac{2}{3}$

Exercise 1.8

Rewrite the following and fill in the boxes:

1. $16^{\frac{3}{4}} = \left(16^{\frac{\square}{\square}}\right)^{\square} = \left(\sqrt[\square]{16}\right)^{\square} = ?$
2. $25^{\frac{3}{2}} = \left(25^{\frac{\square}{\square}}\right)^{\square} = \left(\sqrt{25}\right)^{\square} = ?$
3. $27^{\frac{2}{3}} = \left(27^{\frac{\square}{\square}}\right)^{\square} = \left(\sqrt[\square]{27}\right)^{\square} = ?$
4. $64^{\frac{2}{3}} = \left(64^{\frac{\square}{\square}}\right)^{\square} = \left(\sqrt[\square]{64}\right)^{\square} = ?$
5. $729^{\frac{2}{3}} = \left(729^{\frac{\square}{\square}}\right)^{\square} = \left(\sqrt[\square]{729}\right)^{\square} = ?$
6. $81^{\frac{3}{4}} = \left(81^{\frac{\square}{\square}}\right)^{\square} = \left(\sqrt[\square]{81}\right)^{\square} = ?$
7. $625^{\frac{2}{4}} = \left(625^{\frac{\square}{\square}}\right)^{\square} = \left(\sqrt[\square]{625}\right)^{\square} = ?$
8. $1{,}000^{\frac{2}{3}} = \left(1{,}000^{\frac{\square}{\square}}\right)^{\square} = \left(\sqrt[\square]{1{,}000}\right)^{\square} = ?$

Calculate each of the following:

9. $10{,}000^{\frac{3}{4}}$
10. $9^{\frac{5}{2}}$
11. $8^{\frac{4}{3}}$
12. $32^{\frac{3}{5}}$
13. $16^{\frac{5}{4}}$
14. $27^{\frac{4}{3}}$
15. $\left(2\frac{1}{4}\right)^{1\frac{1}{2}}$
16. $4^{\frac{3}{2}}$
17. $\left(25^{\frac{5}{2}}\right)^{2}$
18. $\left(1{,}000^{\frac{2}{3}}\right)^{2}$
19. $\left(125^{\frac{1}{3}}\right)^{3}$
20. $\left(8^{\frac{2}{3}}\right)^{3}$
21. $\left(\frac{8}{27}\right)^{\frac{2}{3}}$
22. $\left(\frac{25}{81}\right)^{\frac{1}{2}}$
23. $\left(\frac{27}{64}\right)^{\frac{2}{3}}$
24. $\left(\frac{8}{125}\right)^{\frac{2}{3}}$
25. $\left(\frac{16}{81}\right)^{\frac{1}{4}}$

Section 1.9: Indices rule 7

Student Activity 1H

Use your calculator to calculate each of the following:

(a) 5^{-2} and $\frac{1}{5^2}$

(b) 4^{-2} and $\frac{1}{4^2}$

(c) 3^{-3} and $\frac{1}{3^3}$

(d) 7^{-2} and $\frac{1}{7^2}$

(e) 10^{-3} and $\frac{1}{10^3}$

(f) What relationship can you see between the powers in your answers above?

INDICES RULE 7 EXPLAINED

In Student Activity 1H, you discovered how to handle negative indices.

Rule 7

Indices can be changed into fractions or moved out of the denominator by changing the sign on the indices:

$$a^{-p} = \frac{1}{a^p}$$

EXAMPLE 9

Evaluate the following:

(a) 5^{-2}

(b) 7^{-3}

(c) $\frac{1}{3^{-2}}$

(d) Write the following in index form: $\frac{1}{27}$

Solution

(a) $5^{-2} = \frac{1}{5^2} = \frac{1}{25}$

(b) $7^{-3} = \frac{1}{7^3} = \frac{1}{343}$

(c) $\frac{1}{3^{-2}} = 3^2 = 9$

(d) $\frac{1}{27} = \frac{1}{3^3} = 3^{-3}$

Exercise 1.9

Evaluate each of the following:

1. 2^{-2} **5.** 6^{-3} **9.** $\frac{1}{10^{-4}}$

2. 3^{-3} **6.** $\frac{1}{4^{-2}}$ **10.** $\frac{1}{6^{-2}}$

3. 7^{-2} **7.** $\frac{1}{5^{-3}}$

4. 9^{-3} **8.** $\frac{1}{2^{-5}}$

Write each of the following in index form:

11. $\frac{1}{64}$ **15.** $\frac{1}{900}$ **19.** $\frac{1}{125}$

12. $\frac{1}{100}$ **16.** $\frac{1}{9}$ **20.** $\frac{1}{32}$

13. $\frac{1}{36}$ **17.** $\frac{1}{4}$

14. $\frac{1}{81}$ **18.** $\frac{1}{2,500}$

Section 1.10: Indices rule 8

Student Activity 1I

1. Calculate each of the following:

(a) $(5 \times 3)^2$ and $5^2 \times 3^2$

(b) $(2 \times 4)^2$ and $2^2 \times 4^2$

(c) $(3 \times 4)^2$ and $3^2 \times 4^2$

(d) $(6 \times 2)^2$ and $6^2 \times 2^2$

(e) What do you notice about each of your answers?

2. Calculate each of the following:

(a) $\left(\frac{2}{3}\right)^2$ and $\frac{2^2}{3^2}$

(b) $\left(\frac{3}{4}\right)^2$ and $\frac{3^2}{4^2}$

(c) $\left(\frac{1}{5}\right)^3$ and $\frac{1^3}{5^3}$

(d) $\left(\frac{5}{6}\right)^2$ and $\frac{5^2}{6^2}$

(e) What did you notice about each of the answers above?

INDICES RULE 8 EXPLAINED

Student Activity 1I shows the **distributive property** of indices.

Rule 8

- A power on the outside of a bracket can be distributed on each number inside the bracket:

$$(ab)^p = a^p b^p$$

- If an index is applied to a fraction, it can be distributed to the numerator and denominator separately:

$$\left(\frac{a}{b}\right)^p = \frac{a^p}{b^p}$$

EXAMPLE 10

Evaluate each of the following:

(a) $(3 \times 2)^3$

(b) $(5 \times 3)^2$

(c) $\left(\frac{3}{4}\right)^2$

(d) $\left(\frac{2}{7}\right)^3$

Solution

(a) $(3 \times 2)^3 = 3^3 \times 2^3 = 27 \times 8 = 216$

(b) $(5 \times 3)^2 = 5^2 \times 3^2 = 25 \times 9 = 225$

(c) $\left(\frac{3}{4}\right)^2 = \frac{3^2}{4^2} = \frac{9}{16}$

(d) $\left(\frac{2}{7}\right)^3 = \frac{2^3}{7^3} = \frac{8}{343}$

Exercise 1.10

Evaluate each of the following:

1. $(3 \times 2)^2 = 3^\square \times 2^\square = ?$

2. $(4 \times 3)^2 = 4^\square \times 3^\square = ?$

3. $(5 \times 3)^2 = 5^\square \times 3^\square = ?$

4. $(6 \times 2)^2 = 6^\square \times 2^\square = ?$

5. $(3 \times 3)^2 = 3^\square \times 3^\square = ?$

6. $(2 \times 2)^3 = 2^\square \times 2^\square = ?$

7. $(5 \times 6)^2 = 5^\square \times 6^\square = ?$

8. $\left(\frac{2}{3}\right)^4 = \frac{2^\square}{3^\square} = \frac{\square}{\square}$

9. $\left(\frac{3}{5}\right)^3 = \frac{3^\square}{5^\square} = \frac{\square}{\square}$

10. $\left(\frac{4}{7}\right)^2 = \frac{4^\square}{7^\square} = \frac{\square}{\square}$

11. $\left(\frac{5}{6}\right)^3 = \frac{5^\square}{6^\square} = \frac{\square}{\square}$

Section 1.11: Indices rule 9

Student Activity 1J

(a) 5^0

(b) 100^0

(c) 7^0

(d) 15^0

(e) 23^0

(f) What observation can you make about each of your answers?

INDICES RULE 9 EXPLAINED

In Student Activity 1J, you examined the effect of raising any number to the power of zero.

Rule 9

Any number or variable raised to a power of zero equals 1:

$$a^0 = 1$$

This can also be shown using all of the previous rules.

For example, $\frac{6^2}{6^2} = \frac{36}{36} = 1$ or $\frac{6^2}{6^2} = 6^{2-2} = 6^0 = 1$.

Note

All the rules for indices can be found on page 21 of the *Formulae and Tables*.

Indices rules

- Rule 1: $a^p \times a^q = a^{p+q}$
- Rule 2: $\frac{a^p}{a^q} = a^{p-q}$
- Rule 3: $(a^p)^q = a^{pq}$
- Rule 5: $a^{\frac{1}{p}} = \sqrt[p]{a}$
- Rule 6: $a^{\frac{p}{q}} = \sqrt[q]{a^p} = (\sqrt[q]{a})^p$
- Rule 7: $a^{-p} = \frac{1}{a^p}$
- Rule 8: $(ab)^p = a^p b^p$; $\left(\frac{a}{b}\right)^p = \frac{a^p}{b^p}$
- Rule 9: $a^0 = 1$

You do **not** have to learn off the rules, but you **must** know how to use them in questions. You must also be able to combine the rules in questions.

EXAMPLE 11

Without using a calculator, simplify each of the following:

(a) Write as a power of 2:
$\frac{2^7 \times 2^5}{2^4 \times 2^5}$

(b) Write as a power of 3:
$\frac{3^4 \times 3^5}{3^3 \times 3^4}$

(c) Simplify $\frac{x^7 \times \sqrt[4]{x} \times x^4}{x^6 \times \sqrt[3]{x}}$.

(d) Express $\frac{25 \times 5^3}{5^4 \times \sqrt[4]{625}}$ in the form 5^n.

Solution

(a) $\frac{2^7 \times 2^5}{2^4 \times 2^5} = \frac{2^{12}}{2^9} = 2^{12-9} = 2^3$

(b) $\frac{3^4 \times 3^5}{3^3 \times 3^4} = \frac{3^9}{3^7} = 3^{9-7} = 3^2$

(c) $\frac{x^7 \times \sqrt[4]{x} \times x^4}{x^6 \times \sqrt[3]{x}}$

$\frac{x^7 \times x^{\frac{1}{4}} \times x^4}{x^6 \times x^{\frac{1}{3}}}$ **Add the indices**

$= \frac{x^{11\frac{1}{4}}}{x^{6\frac{1}{3}}}$ **Subtract the indices**

$= x^{4\frac{11}{12}}$

(d) $\frac{25 \times 5^3}{5^4 \times \sqrt[4]{625}} = \frac{5^2 \times 5^3}{5^4 \times 5}$ **Writing all numbers as powers of 5**

$\frac{5^2 \times 5^3}{5^4 \times 5} = \frac{5 \times 5 \times 5 \times 5 \times 5}{5 \times 5 \times 5 \times 5 \times 5} = 1$

Exercise 1.11

Simplify each of the following without using a calculator:

1. $\frac{2^4 \times 2^8}{2^3 \times 2^2}$
2. $\frac{4^3 \times 4^9}{4^7}$
3. $\frac{5^2 \times 5^7}{5^3 \times 5^4}$
4. $\frac{3^9 \times 3^5}{3^4 \times 3^7}$
5. $\frac{7^7 \times 7^7}{7^3 \times 7^6}$
6. $\frac{g^6 \times \sqrt{g^6} \times \sqrt[3]{g^5}}{g^2 \times g^{\frac{3}{2}}}$
7. $\frac{x^3 \times \sqrt{x} \times x^2}{x^4 \times x}$
8. $\frac{c^{\frac{3}{5}} \times c^{\frac{1}{4}} \times \sqrt[3]{c}}{c^2 \times c^{\frac{1}{3}}}$
9. $\frac{\sqrt{p} \times p^{10}}{p^3 \times p^{\frac{1}{3}}}$

10. Express each of the following in the form 3^n:
(a) 9 (b) 81 (c) 243 (d) 2,187 (e) $\frac{9 \times 81 \times 243}{2,187}$

11. Express each of the following in the form 5^n:
(a) 625 (b) 3,125 (c) 15,625 (d) 78,125 (e) $\frac{625 \times 25 \times 78,125}{3,125 \times 125 \times 15,625}$

12. Express $\dfrac{\sqrt{5} \times 78{,}125}{25 \times 5^{\frac{7}{2}}}$ in the form 5^n.

13. Simplify $\dfrac{\sqrt[3]{27} \times 3}{9^{\frac{1}{2}} \times 3^4}$ in the form 3^n, where $n \in \mathbb{Z}$.

14. Simplify $\dfrac{125^{\frac{1}{3}} \times 5^2}{5^3 \times 25^{\frac{5}{2}}}$ in the form 5^n, where $n \in \mathbb{Z}$.

15. Simplify $\dfrac{2^5 \times 8^{\frac{2}{3}}}{64^{\frac{1}{2}} \times 4^2}$ in the form 2^n, where $n \in \mathbb{N}$.

16. Solve for x: $2^x = \dfrac{2^3 \times \sqrt{128}}{8 \times \sqrt{32}}$

17. Solve for x: $9^{x+1} = \dfrac{27 \times \sqrt{81}}{243 \times (\sqrt{27})^3}$

Section 1.12: Surds and numbers in the form $a \pm \sqrt{b}$

Student Activity 1K

1. Use your calculator to find the value of each of the following:
   (a) $\sqrt{3} \times \sqrt{3}$
   (b) $\sqrt{2} \times \sqrt{2}$
   (c) $\sqrt{5} \times \sqrt{5}$
   (d) $\sqrt{8} \times \sqrt{8}$
   (e) What did you notice about your answers to the questions above?
2. Use your calculator to find the value of each of the following:
   (a) $\sqrt{3} \times \sqrt{10}$
   (b) $\sqrt{7} \times \sqrt{3}$
   (c) $\sqrt{7} \times \sqrt{2}$
   (d) $\sqrt{5} \times \sqrt{2}$
   (e) What did you notice about your answers to the questions above?
3. Simplify each of the following:
   (a) $x + x = ?$
   (b) $2y + y = ?$
   (c) $4z + 3z = ?$
   (d) $1\sqrt{2} + 1\sqrt{2} = ?\sqrt{2}$
   (e) $4\sqrt{3} + 5\sqrt{3} = ?\sqrt{3}$
   (f) $2\sqrt{7} + 7\sqrt{7} = ?\sqrt{7}$

SIMPLIFYING SURDS EXPLAINED

A **surd** is a number that contains a root such as a square root. For example, $5\sqrt{3}$ is a surd.

Surds can be added or subtracted in the same way that x's and y's are added or subtracted when simplifying expressions.

We will look at surds in the form $\boldsymbol{a} \pm \sqrt{\boldsymbol{b}}$, where $\boldsymbol{b} \in \mathbb{Q}^+$. This means that the number inside the surd will always be a positive rational number.

Most calculators can simplify surds. However, in the Junior Certificate exam it is often necessary to show your workings.

Multiplying surds

When multiplying surds, multiply the numbers inside the surds.

$\sqrt{3} \times \sqrt{5} = \sqrt{15}$

We can use this to break down a surd:

$\sqrt{44} = \sqrt{4}\sqrt{11} = 2\sqrt{11}$

EXAMPLE 12

(a) Simplify $3 + \sqrt{5} - 7 - 2\sqrt{5} + 6 + 9\sqrt{5}$.

(b) Simplify $\sqrt{200} - \sqrt{50} - \sqrt{18}$.

Solution

(a) $3 + \sqrt{5} - 7 - 2\sqrt{5} + 6 + 9\sqrt{5}$

$= (3 + 6 - 7) + (\sqrt{5} - 2\sqrt{5} + 9\sqrt{5})$

$= 2 + 8\sqrt{5}$

(b) $\sqrt{200} - \sqrt{50} - \sqrt{18}$

$= \sqrt{100}\sqrt{2} - \sqrt{25}\sqrt{2} - \sqrt{9}\sqrt{2}$ **Break down each surd**

$= 10\sqrt{2} - 5\sqrt{2} - 3\sqrt{2}$ **Simplify each surd**

$= 2\sqrt{2}$

Exercise 1.12

Simplify each of the following without using a calculator:

1. $8\sqrt{2} - 3\sqrt{2}$
2. $9\sqrt{11} - 4\sqrt{11}$
3. $11\sqrt{3} - 4\sqrt{3}$
4. $4\sqrt{7} + 2\sqrt{7}$
5. $10\sqrt{8} - 5\sqrt{8}$
6. $4\sqrt{5} + 9\sqrt{5}$
7. $9\sqrt{2} - 3\sqrt{2}$
8. $15\sqrt{7} + 5\sqrt{7}$
9. $21\sqrt{13} - 15\sqrt{13}$
10. $6\sqrt{21} + 9\sqrt{21}$
11. $4 - \sqrt{2} + 10 + 3\sqrt{2} + 11 + 4\sqrt{2}$
12. $7 + \sqrt{3} - 5 + 8\sqrt{3} + 2 + 9\sqrt{3}$
13. $6\sqrt{11} - 5 - 5\sqrt{11} + 3\sqrt{11} - 8 + 10$
14. $9 - 4\sqrt{3} + 4 + 4\sqrt{3} - 13$
15. $\sqrt{7} - 12 + 10 - 4\sqrt{7} + 13 + 6\sqrt{7}$
16. $4\sqrt{2} + 2\sqrt{2} - 3 - 2 + 15 - 3\sqrt{2}$
17. $12 - 4\sqrt{3} + 7\sqrt{3} - 8 + 2\sqrt{3}$
18. $9\sqrt{7} - 13 + 5\sqrt{7} + 12 - 10\sqrt{7} + 5$
19. $4\sqrt{3} - \sqrt{2} + 1 + 3\sqrt{2} + 11 + 4\sqrt{3}$
20. $\sqrt{5} - \sqrt{2} + 6\sqrt{5} + 3\sqrt{5} + 7\sqrt{2} + 4\sqrt{2}$
21. $\sqrt{18} + \sqrt{2}$
22. $\sqrt{200} - \sqrt{8}$
23. $\sqrt{128} + \sqrt{72}$
24. $\sqrt{27} + \sqrt{12} + \sqrt{3}$
25. $\sqrt{72} - \sqrt{8} + \sqrt{2}$
26. $\sqrt{12} + \sqrt{48} - \sqrt{75}$
27. $\sqrt{99} - \sqrt{44} + \sqrt{11} - \sqrt{33}$
28. $2\sqrt{18} - 4\sqrt{2} + \sqrt{2}$
29. If $\sqrt{75} - \sqrt{48} + \sqrt{27} = k\sqrt{3}$, find the value of k.
30. If $\sqrt{72} + \sqrt{50} - \sqrt{128} = k\sqrt{2}$, find the value of k.
31. Express $\sqrt{108} - \sqrt{175} + \sqrt{27} - \sqrt{343}$ in the form $p\sqrt{3} + q\sqrt{7}$, where $p, q \in \mathbb{Z}$.
32. Express $\sqrt{48} + \sqrt{32} - \sqrt{12} - \sqrt{72}$ in the form $a\sqrt{2} + b\sqrt{3}$, where $a, b \in \mathbb{Z}$.
33. Express $\sqrt{18} + \sqrt{45} + \sqrt{20} - \sqrt{50}$ in the form $-a\sqrt{a} + b\sqrt{b}$, where $a, b \in \mathbb{N}$.

Section 1.13: Multiplying numbers in the form $a \pm \sqrt{b}$

It is also possible to multiply numbers that contain surds. To do this, you can either use multiplication grids (you used these in Maths in Action 1 to multiply large numbers) or expand the brackets.

EXAMPLE 13

(a) Simplify $(6 + \sqrt{4})(3 - \sqrt{4})$.

(b) Show that $(3 + \sqrt{3})(3 - \sqrt{3})$ simplifies to a constant.

(c) Simplify $\frac{\sqrt{288}}{\sqrt{32}}$.

Solution

(a) Simplify $(6 + \sqrt{4})(3 - \sqrt{4})$.

Method 1: Using a multiplication grid

When using a multiplication grid, multiply the length and width of each box:

	6	$\sqrt{4}$
3	18	$3\sqrt{4}$
$-\sqrt{4}$	$-6\sqrt{4}$	-4

Simplify like terms:

$18 - 6\sqrt{4} + 3\sqrt{4} - 4$

$= 18 - 3\sqrt{4} - 4$

$= 14 - 3\sqrt{4}$

Method 2: Splitting the brackets

$(6 + \sqrt{4})(3 - \sqrt{4})$

$= 6(3 - \sqrt{4}) + \sqrt{4}(3 - \sqrt{4})$ **Split the first bracket**

$= 18 - 6\sqrt{4} + 3\sqrt{4} - 4$ **Multiply out the brackets**

$= 14 - 3\sqrt{4}$ **Simplify the expression**

(b) Show that $(3 + \sqrt{3})(3 - \sqrt{3})$ simplifies to a constant.

When using a multiplication grid, multiply the length and width of each box:

	3	$\sqrt{3}$
3	9	$3\sqrt{3}$
$-\sqrt{3}$	$-3\sqrt{3}$	-3

Simplify like terms:

$= 9 - 3\sqrt{3} + 3\sqrt{3} - 3$

$= 9 - 3$

$= 6$

(c) $\frac{\sqrt{288}}{\sqrt{32}} = \frac{\sqrt{144}\sqrt{2}}{\sqrt{16}\sqrt{2}} = \frac{12\sqrt{2}}{4\sqrt{2}} = \frac{12}{4} = 3$

Exercise 1.13

Simplify each of the following using a multiplication grid:

1. $(4 + \sqrt{3})(2 + \sqrt{3})$
2. $(5 - \sqrt{2})(3 + \sqrt{2})$
3. $(6 + \sqrt{7})(4 - \sqrt{7})$
4. $(2 - \sqrt{3})(5 - \sqrt{3})$
5. $(3 + \sqrt{11})(3 + \sqrt{11})$

Simplify each of the following by splitting the brackets:

6. $(5 + \sqrt{5})(5 + \sqrt{5})$
7. $(7 + \sqrt{3})(10 - \sqrt{3})$
8. $(2 + \sqrt{5})(8 - \sqrt{5})$
9. $(9 - \sqrt{13})(3 - \sqrt{13})$
10. $(6 - \sqrt{7})(3 - \sqrt{7})$

Show that each of the following simplifies to a constant:

11. $(5 + \sqrt{13})(5 - \sqrt{13})$
12. $(1 + \sqrt{2})(1 - \sqrt{2})$
13. $(2 + \sqrt{3})(2 - \sqrt{3})$
14. $(4 + \sqrt{5})(4 - \sqrt{5})$
15. $(1 + \sqrt{7})(1 - \sqrt{7})$

Simplify each of the following:

16. $4(1 + \sqrt{3}) - \sqrt{3}(2 + \sqrt{3})$
17. $8(1 + \sqrt{5}) - \sqrt{5}(2 + \sqrt{5})$
18. $\sqrt{5}(4 + 2\sqrt{5}) - 3(2 + \sqrt{5})$
19. $\sqrt{7}(2 + 3\sqrt{7}) - 3(4 - \sqrt{7})$
20. $(3\sqrt{2} + 2\sqrt{3})(3\sqrt{2} - 2\sqrt{3})$
21. $(7\sqrt{5} + 5\sqrt{2})(7\sqrt{5} - 3\sqrt{2})$
22. $(\sqrt{11} + \sqrt{3})(\sqrt{11} - \sqrt{3})$
23. $(\sqrt{13} + \sqrt{11})(\sqrt{13} - \sqrt{11})$
24. $(\sqrt{3} - 7)^2$
25. $(\sqrt{5} + 8)^2$
26. $(5\sqrt{7} + 4\sqrt{3})^2$
27. $(4\sqrt{2} - 3\sqrt{5})^2$
28. $(3 + \sqrt{5})^2 + (3 - \sqrt{5})^2$
29. $(\sqrt{3} + \sqrt{7})^2 + (\sqrt{3} - \sqrt{7})^2$
30. Find the value of p, where $p \in \mathbb{N}$ and $p = (3 + \sqrt{5})^2 + (3 - \sqrt{5})^2$.

Simplify each of the following:

31. $\frac{\sqrt{100}}{\sqrt{25}}$ **33.** $\frac{\sqrt{81}}{\sqrt{36}}$ **35.** $\frac{\sqrt{5}}{\sqrt{20}}$ **37.** $\frac{12\sqrt{2}}{\sqrt{50}}$

32. $\frac{\sqrt{36}}{\sqrt{16}}$ **34.** $\frac{\sqrt{20}}{\sqrt{45}}$ **36.** $\frac{8}{\sqrt{18}}$ **38.** $\frac{\sqrt{12}}{\sqrt{27}}$

39. Find the value of k if $\left(\frac{5}{2}+\frac{\sqrt{3}}{2}\right)\left(\frac{5}{2}-\frac{\sqrt{3}}{2}\right)=k$, where $k \in \mathbb{R}$.

40. Find the value of m if $\left(\frac{9}{5}+\frac{\sqrt{7}}{5}\right)\left(\frac{9}{5}-\frac{\sqrt{7}}{5}\right)=m$, where $m \in \mathbb{R}$.

Section 1.14: Numbers in standard form

Student Activity 1L

1. The Sun has a mass of 1,988,000,000,000,000,000,000,000,000,000 kg. Scientists write this very long number as 1.988×10^{30} kg. How do you think they might have got this number?
2. Scientists write the number 0.0000000013 as 1.3×10^{-9}. How do you think they might have got this number?
3. In pairs, suggest an easier way of reading and writing the following numbers:
   (a) 7,000,000,000
   (b) 5,600,000,000
   (c) 0.00000005
   (d) 0.000000714

NUMBERS IN STANDARD FORM EXPLAINED

Scientist and mathematicians often have to deal with very large or very small numbers. For example, the diameter of a nucleus of an atom is about 0.00000000000001 metres, which is very small indeed! With so many digits involved, it would be quite easy to make an error when writing down the number.

To reduce the chance of making an error, we write very large or very small numbers using **standard form.** This is also known as **index notation** or **exponential notation.** It was previously known as **scientific notation.**

When changing to standard form, you must write the number in two parts:

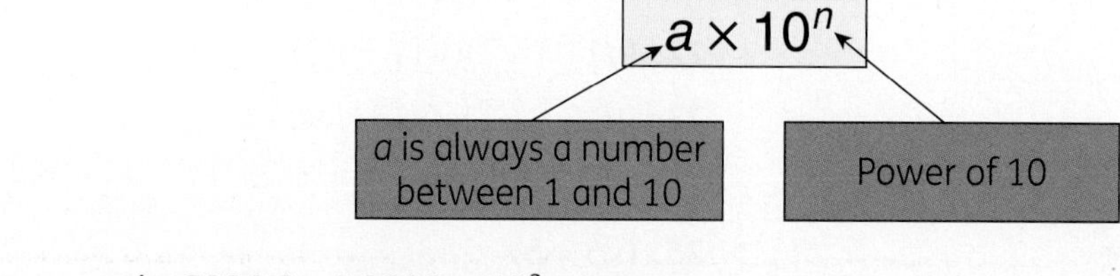

For example, $5326.6 = 5.3266 \times 10^3$

Digits — Power of 10

$5326.6 = 5.3266 \times 1{,}000$ and $1{,}000 = 10^3$

Writing a number in this form reduces the chance of leaving out a zero, which would change the number by a lot. If you won €10,000,000 in a lottery and the person writing the cheque missed out a zero, you would only get €1,000,000 (though this is still a lot of money)!

To figure out what the power of 10 should be, think 'How many places do I move the decimal point?'

- ⟵ If the number is 10 or greater, the decimal point has to move to the left, and the power of 10 will be positive.
- ⟶ If the number is smaller than 1, the decimal point has to move to the right, so the power of 10 will be negative.

After putting the number in standard form, check that:

- The 'digits' part is between 1 and 10 (it can be 1, but never 10).
- The 'power' part shows exactly how many places to move the decimal point.

Remember:

- Moving the decimal point to the left gives a positive power.
- Moving the decimal point to the right gives a negative power.

EXAMPLE 14

(a) Express (i) 300,000 and (ii) 0.00043 in the form $a \times 10^n$, where $1 \leq a < 10$ and $n \in \mathbb{Z}$.

(b) Calculate $2.3 \times 10^4 + 1.6 \times 10^6$ and give your answer in the form $a \times 10^n$, where $1 \leq a < 10$ and $n \in \mathbb{N}$.

Solution

(a) (i) The number needs to be between 1 and 10.

300,000.00 **Move the decimal point**

$= 3.0 \times 10^5$ **The power is the number of times you move the decimal point**

(ii) The number needs to be between 1 and 10.

0.00043

$= 4.3 \times 10^{-4}$ **The power is negative as the original number was less than 1**

(b) $2.3 \times 10^4 = 23{,}000$ **On your calculator, type 2.3 followed by × 10x button and the 4**

$1.6 \times 10^6 = 1{,}600{,}000$ **On your calculator, type 1.6 followed by × 10x button and the 6**

$23{,}000 + 1{,}600{,}000 = 1{,}623{,}000$

$= 1.623 \times 10^6$

Exercise 1.14

Write each of the following in the form $a \times 10^n$, where $1 \leq a < 10$ and $n \in \mathbb{Z}$:

1. 4,500,000	**6.** 37,000,000	**11.** 1,090,000	**16.** 0.000015
2. 2,130,000	**7.** 54,100,000	**12.** 409,000	**17.** 0.0078
3. 6,780,000	**8.** 21,000	**13.** 0.000034	**18.** 0.00000067
4. 687	**9.** 3,100	**14.** 0.0098	**19.** 0.000057
5. 1,420	**10.** 450	**15.** 0.0056	**20.** 0.0096

Calculate each of the following and give your answer in the form $a \times 10^n$, where $1 \leq a < 10$ and $n \in \mathbb{Z}$:

21. $1.7 \times 10^5 + 1.8 \times 10^7$

22. $5.76 \times 10^4 + 1.68 \times 10^3$

23. $3.4 \times 10^4 + 5.66 \times 10^5$

24. $6.9 \times 10^2 + 4.3 \times 10^3$

25. $6.1 \times 10^7 + 2.45 \times 10^6$

26. $5.8 \times 10^4 + 1.6 \times 10^3$

27. $2.31 \times 10^4 + 4.23 \times 10^5$

28. $3.3 \times 10^4 + 2.4 \times 10^3$

29. $5.4 \times 10^4 - 1.6 \times 10^3$

Use your calculator to evaluate each of the following and give your answer in the form $a \times 10^n$, where $1 \leq a < 10$ and $n \in \mathbb{Z}$:

30. $(2.5 \times 10^6) - (5.2 \times 10^4)$

31. $(7.5 \times 10^3) \times (5.7 \times 10^2)$

32. $(1.44 \times 10^{-2}) - (5.4 \times 10^{-3})$

33. $(3.48 \times 10^{-4}) - (5.4 \times 10^{-5})$

34. $(8.4 \times 10^7) \div (3.5 \times 10^3)$

35. $(1.35 \times 10^7) \div (2.5 \times 10^4)$

36. $(2.53 \times 10^3)^2$

37. $(1.78 \times 10^{-2})^2$

38. $(1.25 \times 10^{-3})^2$

39. $(2.89 \times 10^{-4})^{\frac{1}{2}}$

40. $\dfrac{(4 \times 10^3)^3}{8 \times 10^{-3}}$

41. $\dfrac{\sqrt{2.89 \times 10^4}}{2 \times 10^{-2}}$

42. $\dfrac{\sqrt{6.4 \times 10^3}}{0.2 \times 10^2}$

43. $\dfrac{(2.4 \times 10^4) \times (1.5 \times 10^2)}{1.2 \times 10^3}$

44. $\dfrac{(2.45 \times 10^5) - (1.8 \times 10^4)}{2.27 \times 10^2}$

45. $\dfrac{(3.2 \times 10^5) + (8.5 \times 10^4)}{0.125 \times 10^3}$

---

46. The speed of light in a vacuum is 299,792,458 m/s. Write this speed in the form $a \times 10^n$, where $1 \leq a < 10$ and $n \in \mathbb{Z}$.

47. The mass of an electron is 0.000000000000000000000000000000910938 kg. Write the mass in standard form.

48. The mass of the moon is 73,000,000,000,000,000,000,000 kg. Write the mass in standard form.

49. The charge on an electron in 1.6×10^{-19} coulombs. How many electrons are in a charge of 2 coulombs? Write your answer in the form $a \times 10^n$, where $1 \leq a < 10$ and $n \in \mathbb{Z}$.

50. Photocopy paper is sold in packs of 500 sheets. Each pack is 41 mm thick. What is the thickness of one sheet of paper in metres written in standard form?

51. The average mass of a grain of salt is 0.3 mg. How many grains are in a 1 kg bag of salt? Give your answer in the form $a \times 10^n$, where $1 \leq a < 10$ and $n \in \mathbb{Z}$.

52. One nanometre (nm) is one-billionth, or 1×10^{-9}, of a metre. How many nanometres are in 5.3 metres? Give your answer in the form $a \times 10^n$, where $1 \leq a < 10$ and $n \in \mathbb{Z}$.

53. The average bacteria cell has a mass of 0.02×10^{-9} g. How many bacteria are in a 500 g mass. Give your answer in the form $a \times 10^n$, where $1 \leq a < 10$ and $n \in \mathbb{Z}$.

CHAPTER 1 SELF-CHECK TEST

Write each of the following in index notation:

1. $2^4 \times 2^6$

2. $3^4 \times 3^6$

3. $7^8 \times 7^2$

4. $5^4 \times 5^3$

5. $9^3 \times 9^4$

6. $6^3 \times 6^5$

7. $8^2 \times 8^5$

8. $a^4 \times a^5$

9. $x^7 \times x^8$

10. $v^9 \times v^4$

11. $\dfrac{3^5}{3^3}$

12. $\dfrac{4^7}{4^5}$

13. $\dfrac{5^9}{5^6}$

14. $\dfrac{9^7}{9^4}$

15. $\frac{2^8}{2^6}$

16. $\frac{a^6}{a^4}$

17. $\frac{x^5}{x^4}$

18. $\frac{w^7}{w^3}$

19. $\frac{t^4}{t^2}$

20. $\frac{2^3 \times 2^7}{2^4 \times 2^3}$

21. $\frac{3^9 \times 3^8}{3^6 \times 3^4}$

22. $\frac{5^4 \times 5^6}{5^7}$

23. $\frac{a^6 \times a^7}{a^3 \times a^2}$

24. $\frac{u^9 \times u^3}{u^6 \times u^6}$

25. $\frac{w^3 \times w^5}{w^2 \times w^4}$

26. Solve for x:
$4x = \frac{16 \times \sqrt{32}}{128 \times 256}$

27. Write each of the following in fraction form:

(a) 2^{-3} (d) 5^{-3} (g) b^{-5} (j) v^{-9}
(b) 3^{-2} (e) 3^{-5} (h) a^{-2} (k) s^{-1}
(c) 4^{-3} (f) 4^{-2} (i) t^{-3} (l) h^{-6}

28. Without using a calculator, evaluate each of the following:

(a) $25^{\frac{3}{2}}$ (c) $125^{\frac{2}{3}}$ (e) $81^{\frac{5}{4}}$ (g) $27^{\frac{2}{3}}$ (i) $625^{\frac{2}{4}}$
(b) $64^{\frac{2}{3}}$ (d) $10{,}000^{\frac{3}{4}}$ (f) $36^{\frac{3}{2}}$ (h) $216^{\frac{2}{3}}$ (j) $225^{\frac{1}{2}}$

29. Find the reciprocal of each of the following numbers:

(a) 6^3 (c) 2^{-4} (e) $(-3)^5$ (g) $5^2 + 6^2$ (i) $2^2 - 2^{-2}$
(b) 3^4 (d) 5^{-2} (f) $(-2)^{-5}$ (h) $(-10)^0$ (j) $(100^3)^0$

30. Simplify each of the following:

(a) $\sqrt{7} - 12 + 10 - 4\sqrt{7} + 13 + 6\sqrt{7}$
(b) $4\sqrt{2} + 2\sqrt{2} - 3 - 2 + 15 - 3\sqrt{2}$
(c) $12 - 4\sqrt{3} + 7\sqrt{3} - 8 + 2\sqrt{3}$
(d) $\sqrt{32} + \sqrt{2} + \sqrt{8}$
(e) $\sqrt{20} + \sqrt{45} + \sqrt{80}$
(f) $\sqrt{72} + \sqrt{12} - \sqrt{48}$
(g) $\sqrt{20} - \sqrt{5} + \sqrt{45}$

31. If $\sqrt{405} + \sqrt{20} - \sqrt{80} - \sqrt{45} = k\sqrt{5}$, find the value of k.

32. Express $\sqrt{12} + \sqrt{48} - \sqrt{8} + \sqrt{72}$ in the form $a\sqrt{2} + b\sqrt{3}$, where $a, b \in \mathbb{N}$.

33. Express $\sqrt{125} + \sqrt{175} - \sqrt{80} - \sqrt{7}$ in the form $a\sqrt{5} + b\sqrt{7}$, where $a, b \in \mathbb{N}$.

34. Simplify $(\sqrt{5} - 3\sqrt{2})(4\sqrt{2} - 2\sqrt{5})$ without the use of a calculator. Express your answer in the form $a\sqrt{10} + b$, where $a, b \in \mathbb{Z}$.

35. Simplify $\left(\sqrt{14} + \frac{1}{\sqrt{14}}\right)\left(\sqrt{14} - \frac{1}{\sqrt{14}}\right)$, without the use of a calculator. Express your answer in the form $\frac{a}{b}$, where $a, b \in \mathbb{N}$.

36. Simplify $\sqrt{2}(3\sqrt{6} - 3\sqrt{2}) - \sqrt{5}(2\sqrt{15} - 3\sqrt{5})$, without the use of a calculator. Express your answer in the form $a\sqrt{3} + b$, where $a, b \in \mathbb{Z}$.

37. Simplify $\sqrt{3}(\sqrt{2} + \sqrt{3}) - \sqrt{6}(2 - \sqrt{24})$ without the use of a calculator. Express your answer in the form $a\sqrt{6} + b$, where $a, b \in \mathbb{Z}$.

38. (a) Simplify $(625)^{\frac{3}{4}}$. (b) Simplify $(64)^{\frac{2}{3}}$.

39. When written as an ordinary number, 7.085×10^{-14} is equivalent to which of the following?

(a) 0.000000000007085
(b) 0.0000000000007085
(c) 0.00000000000007085
(d) 0.000000000000007085

40. Write 3.56×10^{11} as an ordinary number.

41. Write 2.345×10^{-5} as an ordinary number.

42. Given that 1 billion is a thousand million, find the sum of €3.6 billion and €700 million. Give your answer in the form $a \times 10^n$, where $1 \leq a < 10$ and $n \in \mathbb{N}$.

43. Using a calculator, or otherwise, multiply $7.8 \times 450,000$. Then express your answer in the form $a \times 10^n$, where $1 \leq a < 10$ and $n \in \mathbb{N}$.

44. In 1981, the population of Peru was approximately 1.8×10^7. By 1988, the population had increased by 2.5 million. What was the approximate population of Peru in 1988? Express your answer in the form $a \times 10^n$, where $n \in \mathbb{Z}$ and $1 \leq a < 10$.

45. The surface area of the Earth is approximately 5.2×10^{14} m^2. Around 70% of the Earth's surface is covered in water. Express the area of the Earth covered by water in the form $a \times 10^n$, where $n \in \mathbb{N}$ and $1 \leq a < 10$.

46. A tiny space inside a computer chip has been measured to be 0.00000256 m wide, 0.00000014 m long and 0.000275 m high.

Convert the width, length and height into standard form.

47. The table below shows the values when 2 is raised to certain powers.

(a) Copy and complete the table.

Power of 2	Expanded power of 2	Answer
2^1	2	2
2^2	2×2	4
2^3	$2 \times 2 \times 2$	8
2^4		
2^5		
2^6		
2^7		
2^8		
2^9		

(b) Maria wins a prize in a lottery and is given two options.

Option A: €1,000 cash today

or

Option B: Take €2 today, €4 tomorrow, €8 the next day, and doubling every day for 9 days.

€2 + €4 + €8 + € + ...

Which option should Maria choose if she wants to get the most prize money? Explain your answer.

48. The columns in the table below represent the following sets of numbers: natural numbers ($\mathbb{N}$), integers ($\mathbb{Z}$), rational numbers ($\mathbb{Q}$), irrational numbers ($\mathbb{R}\backslash\mathbb{Q}$) and real numbers ($\mathbb{R}$).

(a) Complete the table by writing 'Yes' or 'No' to indicate whether or not a number is an element of each set.

Set / Number	$\mathbb{N}$	$\mathbb{Z}$	$\mathbb{Q}$	$\mathbb{R}\backslash\mathbb{Q}$	$\mathbb{R}$
$\sqrt{5}$					
8					Yes
-4					
$3\frac{1}{2}$					
$\frac{3\pi}{4}$					

(b) In the case of $\sqrt{5}$, explain why or why not it is an element of the set of irrational numbers ($\mathbb{R}\backslash\mathbb{Q}$).

(c) Use the properties of surds to show that $\sqrt{98} - \sqrt{18} + \sqrt{2}$ simplifies to $5\sqrt{2}$.

49. Using your ruler, draw the following rectangles. All measurements are in centimetres.

Rectangle	Length	Width
A	2	1
B	3	2
C	4	3
D	5	4

(a) On each rectangle, draw a diagonal and measure its length.

(b) The length of the diagonal of which rectangle is not irrational?

CHAPTER 1 KNOWLEDGE CHECKLIST

After completing this chapter, I now:

- **Am able to distinguish between rational and irrational numbers**
- **Am able to use the rules of indices**
- **Am able to express numbers in the form $a \times 10^n$, where $n \in \mathbb{N}$**
- **Am able to add, subtract and multiply numbers in the form $a \pm \sqrt{b}$, where $a \in \mathbb{Q}$, $b \in \mathbb{Q}^+$**
- **Am able to express non-zero positive rational numbers in approximate form $a \times 10^n$, where $n \in \mathbb{Z}$ and $1 \leq a < 10$**

Challenge

Many years ago when Violet was a little girl, she used to spend hours in her room working on various strange projects and making notes she'd never show to anyone else.
One evening as I was passing her room I noticed that she'd fallen asleep with her bedside light on. I went in to turn it off and spotted a sheet on her desk filled with numbers. The series began 1, 1, 2, 3, 5, 8, 13, 21, 34 and continued for some way. The last number she'd written before falling asleep was 317811. I looked down at the Rautillus Shell she used as a paperweight and smiled.
Had Violet stayed awake a little longer, what would have been the next number in the series?

ALGEBRAIC EXPRESSIONS

KEY WORDS

- Coefficient
- Constant
- Expression
- Like terms
- Term
- Variable

LEARNING OUTCOMES

In this chapter you will learn:

- ✓ The language used in algebra
- ✓ How to simplify expressions by adding and subtracting like terms
- ✓ How to multiply variables together by working with indices
- ✓ How to multiply out (or expand) expressions
- ✓ How to multiply expressions which contain more than one term
- ✓ How to add, subtract and multiply algebraic fractions

INTRODUCTION

Algebraic expressions can be used in almost all parts of life to give a mathematical meaning to relationships. Some of these relationships can be found in the most unusual places.

In 1920, an astronomer named Harlow Shapley showed that the walking speed of ants increased as the air temperature increased. Shapley could predict the air temperature to within 1 °C, by measuring the walking speed of an ant.

The relationship is governed by the rule:

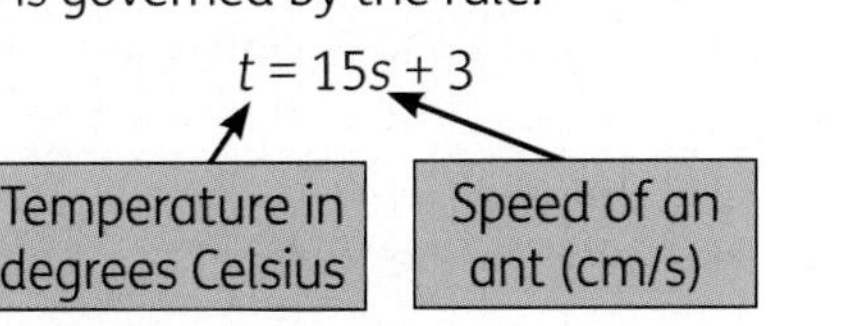

First year revision

Identify the **variables, coefficients** and **terms** in each of the following:

1. $5x$
2. $-2p$
3. $x^2 + 2y$
4. $3w + 5t - 6z$
5. $-4s - 6t + 3z$

If $w = 1$, $x = 2$, $y = 3$ and $z = 6$, evaluate each of the following:

6. $w + x + y$
7. $x + 8y + 5w + 2z$
8. $2x + 3w^2 + 5$
9. $x(2z - 3w)$
10. $wxy + 8yz^2$
11. $2x + 3wz$
12. $2(3x + w) - 2z$
13. $3(z + 2) - 10$
14. $\frac{8w + wz}{2x + 6y}$
15. $\frac{5x + zy}{x - 4y}$

Given $x = -3\frac{1}{2}$, evaluate each of the following:

16. $3x^2 + 9x - 7$
17. $-2x^2 - 7x + 13$
18. $x^3 + 5x^2 - 6x + 22$
19. $x^3 - 4x^2 - 5x - 3$
20. $x^3 - 6x^2 + 4x - 16$

Section 2.1: Simplifying expressions

Student Activity 2A

1. Jack has 6 blue marbles and 4 green discs. Jill has 6 blue marbles and 7 green discs.
   (a) Choose a suitable variable (letter) to use instead of the underlined words.
   (b) Rewrite the given information using the letters you have chosen.
   (c) How many blue marbles have Jack and Jill in total? Explain your answer.
   (d) How many green discs have Jack and Jill in total? Explain your answer.
2. James has 6 shirts and 4 jumpers. Keith has 4 shirts and 3 jumpers.
   (a) How many shirts and jumpers have Keith and James in total?
   (b) Choose a suitable variable to represent shirts and a suitable variable to represent jumpers.
   (c) Using the variables you have chosen, write an expression to show how you would add the numbers of shirts and jumpers.
   (d) Why is it not possible to say that James and Keith have 17 shirts or 17 jumpers?
3. Tom, Dick and Harry are aged $(y - 5)$, $(y + 3)$ and (y) years respectively.
   (a) Who is the oldest? Explain your answer.
   (b) Who is the youngest? Explain your answer.

SIMPLIFYING EXPRESSIONS EXPLAINED

Before beginning working with expressions, it is very important to revise and understand the terms or words used in algebra.

You have met some of these already in *Maths in Action 1*.

Word	Meaning
Variable	Any letter whose value can change. Examples: x, y, z, a
Constant	The value of a constant cannot change. Examples: 5, −1, 10
Term	A term can be a number, a variable or a variable with a number attached to it. Examples: $5x$, $6y$, $3a$, $2b$, y, 7
Coefficient	A coefficient is the number attached to a letter in a term. Examples: in $5x$, 5 is the coefficient; in $-3w$, −3 is the coefficient
Expression	An expression is a list of terms separated by mathematical operations. Example: $4a + 2x + 3z$
Equation	An equation is a statement showing the equality of two mathematical expressions. Both expressions are separated to the left and right by an equals sign. Example: $3x - 5 = 2x + 1$.

You should always think of terms in algebra as **objects in the real world.** In Student Activity 2A, you examined how to add and subtract **like** or **similar terms.** Only **similar terms** can be added or subtracted together.

Remember!

Simplifying an expression means putting like terms together.

As with objects in the real world, we cannot add or subtract unlike objects. For example, if you had 1 bar of chocolate and 1 packet of crisps and someone gave you another bar of chocolate and another packet of crisps you would have 2 bars of chocolate and 2 packets of crisps. You cannot say you have four of a particular item as they are different items.

EXAMPLE 1

Simplify the following expressions:

(a) $2x + 3 + 6x + 7$ (b) $2a + 3b - 2 + 2b - a + 9$ (c) $4xyz + 2 + 5yzx + 6$

Solution

(a) $2x + 3 + 6x + 7$

$= 2x + 6x + 3 + 7$ **Add x-terms together and add the constants together**

$= 8x + 10$

(b) $2a + 3b - 2 + 2b - a + 9$

$= 2a - a + 3b + 2b - 2 + 9$ **Add/subtract like terms**

$= 1a + 5b + 7$

(c) Before beginning this question, check that all terms have their variables in alphabetical order. This will help when you are looking for **like terms.**

$4xyz + 2 + 5yzx + 6$

$= 4xyz + 5xyz + 2 + 6$

$= 9xyz + 8$

Exercise 2.1

1. Lisa is n years old. Eileen is three years younger than Lisa. Express Eileen's age in terms of n.
2. Eamonn is x years old. His father is twice as old. Express Eamonn's father's age in terms of x.
3. Michael has t cattle. Patrick has triple Michael's amount of cattle. Express Patrick's number of cattle in terms of t.
4. Laura has €r in her bank account. Claire has half that amount of money in her account. Express Claire's amount of money in terms of r.
5. Team A's score is x points. Team B's score is double that less three. Express Team B's number of points in terms of x.
6. The attendance at a football match is b. The attendance at the previous match was six less. Express the previous match's attendance in terms of b.
7. The temperature in an oven is x degrees. It should be double that amount plus five degrees. Express the correct temperature in terms of x.
8. Ita has $2z + 5$ sheep. That is a threefold increase in the amount she had last year. Express the amount of sheep she had last year in terms of z.
9. A restaurant had $3y + 7$ customers this week. Last week, they had 17 fewer customers. Express last week's amount of customers in terms of y.
10. The temperature on Monday is $(5x - 1)$ °C. On Tuesday the temperature was 7 °C colder. But by Wednesday, the temperature was double Tuesday's temperature. Express Wednesday's temperature in terms of x.

Simplify each of the following algebraic expressions:

11. $3n - 2 + 2n + 6$
12. $4b + 1 + 3b - 4$
13. $w + 3 + 2w - 7$
14. $13r - 6 + 3r + 6$
15. $9q - 9 + 14 - 4q$
16. $7 - 3k + 4 - 8k$
17. $8 - 3t - 12 + 7t$
18. $2d + 4d - 3 - 6d + 7$
19. $2y + 5x - 3y + 2x$
20. $3w + 2r - 7w + 2r + 8$
21. $5x + 3y + 3 - 2x + 4y + 7$
22. $2a + 6b + 7a + 4b$
23. $-4t + 3s + 7 + 8t - 5s - 10$
24. $2x^2 + 4x + 6 - 3x^2 + 5x + 12$
25. $12ab + 3 - 9ba + 4 - 3ab$
26. $2x^2 + 3x + 2 + 6x + 1 - 4x^2$
27. $2a^2b + 6ab + 8a^2b + 9 - 7ab$
28. $1 - 2x + 8x^2 + 3 + 2x - 6x^2$
29. $6xyz + 2 - 3zxy - 9 + 2yxz$
30. $4t^2s - 3 + 7ts - 2ts - 3t^2s + 8t^3m$
31. $2xyz + 5y^3x^2 + 3xzy - 4pm - 5x^2y^3 - 12mp$
32. $3cxd - 5cdy + 14x^2 - 9dxc + 2dyc - 11x^2$
33. $6a^3b + 2dcm - 3ba^2 + 2 + 2cdm$
34. $6 - 2x^2wz - 3px + 5 - 2zx^2w + 1 + 5xp - 2$
35. $(3x + 5y + 8) + (4x + 9y - 7)$
36. $(2w^2 - 6w + 8) + (7w^2 + 4w + 5)$
37. $(7x^2 + 5x - 7) - (6x^2 + 7x + 16)$
38. $(5x^2 + 7x - 7) + (6x^2 - 6x - 6)$
39. $(17v^2 - v + 18) - (-23v^2 + 15v - 19)$
40. $(6m^2 + 34m - 17) + (17m^2 + 12m - 25)$

Simplify and evaluate each of the following algebraic expressions:

41. $(2x + 3y - 5) + (6x - 4y + 10)$ given $x = 2$ and $y = 3$
42. $(6x - 5y + 12) - (9x + 7y + 6)$ given $x = 7$ and $y = 5$
43. $(15p - 13q - 47) + (3p - 8q - 17)$ given $p = -2$ and $q = 4$
44. $(4x - 6y - 9) + (-2x + 7y - 3)$ given $x = \frac{3}{4}$ and $y = \frac{1}{2}$
45. $(7f - g - 11) - (5f - 2g - 12)$ given $f = 3\frac{2}{3}$ and $g = 1\frac{1}{4}$

46. $(5x - y + 4) + (-3x + 4y + 1)$ given $x = -2\frac{4}{5}$ and $y = 4\frac{1}{4}$
47. $(4x + 3y + 1) + (-2x - 9y - 5)$ given $x = -3\frac{1}{2}$ and $y = -1\frac{1}{3}$
48. $(3x^2 - 8x + 2) + (6x^2 + x + 9)$ given $x = 4$
49. $(2t^2 + 7t + 4) - (6t^2 - 2t + 1)$ given $t = 5$
50. $(s^2 + 4s + 3) + (2s^2 + 5s - 5)$ given $s = -3$
51. $(3x^2 + 7x + 1) - (3x^2 - 7x - 1)$ given $x = -1$
52. $(4w^2 - w + 8) + (3w^2 - w + 2)$ given $w = \frac{1}{2}$
53. $(2y^2 + y - 5) - (2y^2 - 5y + 3)$ given $y = \frac{2}{3}$
54. $(3x^2 + 6x - 4) + (-8x^2 + 8x + 5)$ given $x = -\frac{1}{3}$
55. Jack, Jill and Jemma spent €t, €$(t + 2)$ and €$2t$ in the shop respectively. Who spent the most amount of money? Explain your answer.
56. Ciara, Glen, Jackie and Mary watch television for t minutes, $(t + 5)$ minutes, $\frac{t}{2}$ minutes and $(t + 4)$ minutes per day respectively. Who watches the least amount of television? Explain your answer.
57. The heights of three people were recorded as y, $y - 1$ and $y + 1$ metres respectively. Rank the heights from smallest to tallest. Explain your answer.

Section 2.2: Expressions with brackets

Student Activity 2B

1. Diarmuid has started working in a restaurant. In his first week, he was trained to become a waiter. His first lesson was laying a table.
   For a 2-course meal, **each** place-setting needs a knife, a fork, a spoon and a glass.
   (a) Choose a suitable variable to represent each item listed above.
   (b) Write an expression to show how many utensils Diarmuid will need if he is to set the table for 4 people.
   (c) Write an expression to show how many utensils Diarmuid will need if he is to set the table for 5 people.
   (d) Write an expression to show how many utensils Diarmuid will need if he is to set the table for 6 people.
   (e) Can you write down a general rule to show how Diarmuid can work out how many utensils he will need based on the number of people at the table?
2. All dogs have 4 paws, 2 eyes and 1 tail.
   (a) Choose a suitable variable to represent each part of the dog mentioned above.
   (b) Describe how you would determine the number of paws, eyes and tails for any number of dogs (such as, for 10 dogs).
   (c) Write an expression to allow you to quickly work out the number of paws, tails and eyes for any number of dogs.
   (d) Pauline has 6 dogs and Justin has 8 dogs. Use your expression to work out the number of eyes, paws and tails for all of these dogs.

EXPRESSIONS WITH BRACKETS EXPLAINED

In Student Activity 2B, you examined expressions that contained brackets. It is often necessary to expand or multiply out brackets in order to simplify an expression.

For example, most cars have 4 wheels ($4w$) and 1 steering wheel ($1s$). We could write that for any number of cars (n) the number of wheels and steering wheels is:

Total = $n(4w + 1s)$

Total = $4nw + 1ns$

Distributive law

When multiplying an expression in brackets, all the terms inside the brackets **must** be multiplied by the number or term outside the bracket. This follows the distributive law.

When multiplying or expanding brackets:

- If a minus sign is outside the bracket, change the sign of each term inside the bracket.
- If a plus sign or no sign is outside the bracket, do not change the sign of any term inside the bracket.

EXAMPLE 2

(a) Simplify the following expression:
$5(t + 2)$

(b) Simplify the following expression:
$2(2s + 1) + 3(2s - 2)$

(c) Simplify the following expression:
$y - 3(4y - 2) - (-3y + 6) + 14$

(d) Simplify the following expression:
$2x^2 + 3x + 7(x^2 + x - 1)$

Solution

(a) $5(t + 2)$
$= 5t + 10$

(b) $2(2s + 1) + 3(2s - 2)$
$= 4s + 2 + 6s - 6$
$= 10s - 4$

(c) $y - 3(4y - 2) - (-3y + 6) + 14$
$= y - 12y + 6 + 3y - 6 + 14$
$= -8y + 14$

(d) $2x^2 + 3x + 7(x^2 + x - 1)$ **Multiply out the bracket**
$= 2x^2 + 3x + 7x^2 + 7x - 7$
$= 9x^2 + 10x - 7$ **Add like terms**

Exercise 2.2

Simplify each of the following expressions:

1. $3(a - b) + 4(2a - b)$
2. $(2a - 3b) + 2(4a - 2b)$
3. $4(2b - 3a) + 3(3a - b)$
4. $a + 3(3b + a) - 2b$
5. $10a - 4(a + 2b)$
6. $4(10a + 3b) - 3(9a + 4b)$
7. $3(2p^2 + q) + 3(q - 4p^2)$
8. $2(p + 2q) + 2(p - 2q)$
9. $3(2x - 3y^2) - 5(2x - 4y^2)$
10. $3a^3 - 4b + 4(2b - 5a^3)$
11. $4(2a - 3b) + 3(a - 2b)$
12. $6(c - d) - c + d$

13. $3w - 1 + 2(4w + z)$
14. $5a - 3(2a - 6b)$
15. $7x - 2(3x - 2) - 3(2x + 1) + 8$
16. $5(2a - 3c) + 16 - 4c$
17. $3 + 4(2x - 3y) + 4x + 17 - 3y$
18. $2(t + s) + 5s + 7(s - 3t) + 10$
19. $3(x^2 + 2x + 5) - 6x + 5(2x - 2)$
20. $3(x + y) - 4(2x - 3y) + 10$
21. $5a + 4(2a - 4) - 3 + 2(1 - a)$
22. $5(2w - 2) - w(3) + 2 - w + 7$
23. $7(p + 2q) - 3(p - 2q) + 5p$
24. $5(6x - y) + 4(x + y - 2)$
25. $3x - 4(2 + 3x) + 7 - 2(x + 3)$
26. $2 + 3(2a + 3b) - 4(a - b) + 5$
27. $1 - (1 - 5x) + 8 - 5(2 - 3x) + 5$
28. $y^2x + 3(xy - x^2y) + 2(2 + 2y^2x)$
29. $3xy + 2(8yx - 2) - 5 + 6xy - 3x$
30. $-2(-3 - 2q) - 5 + 4(3p + 2)$
31. $-3(3x + 5y + 8) + 5(4x + 9y - 7)$
32. $7(6x - 7y - 11) - 3(8x - 6y - 11)$
33. $8(-4x - 6y - 8) + 4(6x + 5y + 7)$
34. $-3(-5x + 6y + 23) - 4(6x - 7y - 12)$
35. $-4(2v^2 - 6v + 8) + 5(7v^2 + 4v + 5) - 5$
36. $8(7x^2 + 5x - 7) - 2(6x^2 + 7x + 16) - 4x(5x^2 + 3)$
37. $-7(5f^2 + 7f - 7) + 6(6f^2 - 6f - 6) + (-5f + 6f + 3)$
38. $2(17x^2 - x + 18) - 3(-23x^2 + 15x - 19) - 2(2x + x - 1)$
39. $-(6c^2 + 34c - 17) + 10c(17c^2 + 12c - 25) + 6c(2c^2 - 6c + 8)$
40. $4(23b^2 - 14b - 15) - 11b(14b^2 + 23b - 17) - 5b(7b^2 + 4b + 5)$

Simplify and evaluate each of the following algebraic expressions:

41. $2(x + 4y - 3) + 3(2x + 5y - 5)$ given $x = -2$ and $y = 4$
42. $5(3h + y + 6) - 2(5h - 7y + 10)$ given $h = 1$ and $y = 3$
43. $8(2e^2 - 5e + 6)$ given $e = 5$
44. $3(5k^2 + 7k - 1)$ given $k = -3$
45. $7(2x^2 - x - 1)$ given $x = 10$
46. $5r(6r^2 + 2)$ given $x = 2$
47. $8x(4x^2 - 3)$ given $x = -1$
48. $4g(3g^2 + 4)$ given $g = \frac{1}{2}$
49. $10x(8x^2 - 5)$ given $x = -\frac{3}{4}$
50. $7y(10y^2 + 4y)$ given $y = -1\frac{2}{3}$
51. Investigate if $ax(bx^2 + c) = a(bx^2 + c) + x(bx^2 + c)$.
52. Investigate if $5(2n^2 + 3n + 4) = 5(2n^2) + 5(3n) + 5(4)$.

Section 2.3: Expressions and indices

Student Activity 2C

1. Write the following in index notation:
   (a) $2^3 \times 2^5 = 2^?$
   (b) $3^4 \times 3^2 = 3^?$
   (c) $5^6 \times 5^6 = 5^?$
   (d) $x^2 \times x^3 = x^?$
   (e) $a^3 \times a^5 = a^?$
2. In Chapter 1, you learned the rules for indices. Copy and complete the following rule:
   $a^p \times a^q = a^?$

EXPRESSIONS AND INDICES EXPLAINED

In Chapter 1, you met terms such as x^2 and y^3. These terms contain powers or indices.

When multiplying similar terms:
$$a^p \times a^q = a^{p+q}$$

When multiplying terms, it is useful to use the **SNL** (**S**igns first, **N**umbers next, **L**etters last) rule.

EXAMPLE 3

(a) Simplify the following expression:
$(4t)(-2t)$

(b) Simplify the following expression:
$(-3xy)(x)(-2x^3y)$

(c) Simplify the following expression:
$(4pq)(-2p)(3q)(2p^2q^3)$

Solution

(a) Signs
$(+)(-) = -$
Numbers
$(4)(2) = 8$
Letters
$(t)(t) = t^2$
$= -8t^2$

(b) Signs
$(-)(+)(-) = +$
Numbers
$(3)(1)(2) = 6$
Letters
$(x)(x)(x^3)(y)(y) = x^5y^2$
$= 6x^5y^2$

(c) $(4)(-2)(3)(2)(p)(p)(p^2)(q)(q)(q^3)$
$= -48p^4q^5$

Exercise 2.3

Simplify each of the following:

1. $(2x)(3x)$
2. $(2d)(3d)(-d)$
3. $(-e)(5e)(3e)$
4. $(-2f)(2f)(-4f)$
5. $(5x)(-x)(2x^2)$
6. $(3y^3)(-2y)(y^2)$
7. $(-a)(3a)(2a^3)$
8. $(-4y)(2y)(3y^3)$
9. $(4x)(3x)(-x)(-2x)$
10. $(3w)(2w)(-4w)(3w)$
11. $(-3xy)(4x)$
12. $(2rs)(-3r)(2s)$
13. $(rt)(-rt)(3r^2t^3)$
14. $(2x^3)(3xy)(2y^3)$
15. $(-3x^3)(2x^4y^2)(y^2)$
16. $(ab^2)(3a^3)(2a^2)$
17. $(3pq)(-3qp^2)(-2)$
18. $(-3)(3x^3y^2)(-4xy^2)$
19. $(-2cd)(2d)(3c)$
20. $(-3abc)(3a)(4cb)$
21. $(-2ab)(3abc)(4b^3c)$
22. $(2xy)(-6x^3y^2)(-y^2)$
23. $(4rt)(3sr^2)(-rs^3)$
24. $(3y^3)(-2xy)(4x^3y^2)$
25. $(3x)(x^2y^3)(-4xy)(2y)$
26. $(4abc)(3abc)(-a^2b^3)$
27. $(-5ab)(bc)(-3bc^2)$
28. $(3z)(-4xy)(2yz)(-5xz)$
29. $(2qr)(-4pq)(-3p^3q^2r)$
30. $(3bc)(a^3c)(3a^3b)$

Section 2.4: Multiplying expressions

Student Activity 2D

1. Simplify each of the following:
   (a) $x(x + 1)$
   (b) $-2s(3s + 2)$
   (c) $a(a - 3)$
   (d) $2ab(-2ab + b)$
   (e) $x(x + 3) + 2(x + 3)$
2. Discuss in pairs how you can multiply the following two expressions: $(x + 2)(x + 3)$. (Hint: Remember all of the rules in the last two sections.)

MULTIPLYING EXPRESSIONS EXPLAINED

In the previous sections, you have studied how to multiply an expression by a single term or variable. However, you will often need to multiply an expression by another expression, and both expressions may have more than one term.

There are a number of different methods of doing this. The following example shows two different methods.

Remember!

Every term in the first bracket must be multiplied with every term in the second bracket. Any terms not inside a bracket remain unchanged.

EXAMPLE 4

Simplify the following: $(d + 1)(d + 4)$

Solution

Method 1: Splitting the brackets

$(d + 1)(d + 4)$ **Split the first bracket**

$d(d + 4) + 1(d + 4)$ **Multiply the brackets**

$= d^2 + 4d + 1d + 4$ **Add or subtract like terms**

$= d^2 + 5d + 4$

Method 2: Using a multiplication table

$(d + 1)(d + 4)$

Draw a multiplication table. Each term along the side will be multiplied by each term along the top.

	d	**+1**
d	d^2	$+1d$
+4	$+4d$	$+4$

Write out the resulting terms:

$d^2 + 1d + 4d + 4$ **Simplify the expression**

$= d^2 + 5d + 4$

EXAMPLE 5

Simplify the following: $(r - 2)(r + 2)(r + 3)$

Solution

Method 1: Splitting the brackets

Take the first two brackets:

$(r - 2)(r + 2)$ **Split the first bracket**

$r(r + 2) - 2(r + 2)$ **Multiply the brackets**

$= r^2 + 2r - 2r - 4$ **Add or subtract like terms**

$= r^2 - 4$

Now multiply this answer by the third bracket:

$(r^2 - 4)(r + 3)$ **Split the first bracket**

$r^2(r + 3) - 4(r + 3)$ **Multiply the brackets**

$= r^3 + 3r^2 - 4r - 12$ **Add or subtract like terms**

Method 2: Using a multiplication table

$(r - 2)(r + 2)$

Draw a multiplication table. Each term along the side will be multiplied against each term along the top.

	r	**−2**
r	r^2	$-2r$
+2	$+2r$	-4

Write out the resulting terms:

$= r^2 + 2r - 2r - 4$ **Add or subtract like terms**

$= r^2 - 4$

Now multiply this answer by the third bracket, using a second grid.

$(r^2 - 4)(r + 3)$

	r^2	**−4**
r	r^3	$-4r$
+3	$+3r^2$	-12

Write out the resulting terms:

$= r^3 + 3r^2 - 4r - 12$ **Add or subtract like terms**

EXAMPLE 6

Simplify the following: $(4sd + 3h)(2sd^2 - hd - 1)$

Solution

Method 1: Splitting the brackets

Take the first two brackets:

$(4sd + 3h)(2sd^2 - hd - 1)$ **Split the first bracket**

$4sd(2sd^2 - hd - 1) + 3h(2sd^2 - hd - 1)$ **Multiply the brackets as before**

$= 8s^2d^3 - 4shd^2 - 4sd + 6shd^2 - 3h^2d - 3h$ **Add or subtract like terms**

$= 8s^2d^3 + 2shd^2 - 4sd - 3h^2d - 3h$

Method 2: Using a multiplication table

	$2sd^2$	$-hd$	-1
$4sd$	$8s^2d^3$	$-4shd^2$	$-4sd$
$+3h$	$+6shd^2$	$-3dh^2$	$-3h$

$= 8s^2d^3 - 4shd^2 - 4sd + 6shd^2 - 3h^2d - 3h$ **Add or subtract like terms**

$= 8s^2d^3 + 2shd^2 - 4sd - 3h^2d - 3h$

Exercise 2.4

Simplify each of the following:

1. $(a + 3)(a + 1)$
2. $(b + 2)(b + 3)$
3. $(x + 4)(x + 5)$
4. $(c + 3)(c + 2)$
5. $(e + 4)(3 - e)$
6. $(y + 4)(y + 3)$
7. $(x + 5)(x + 6)$
8. $(x - 1)(x + 2)$
9. $(w + 3)(w - 5)$
10. $(2t - 3)(t - 4)$
11. $(5k - 1)(k + 5)$
12. $(c + 2)(6c - 2)$
13. $(4d + 5)(5d - 5)$
14. $(-2d + 1)(3d + 1)$
15. $(x + 2)(3x - 2)$
16. $(2y - 3)(y + 2) + y^2$
17. $(5 - x)(x + 1) - 10$
18. $(3 - 2x)(x + 1) - 5$
19. $(y - 3)(6 - 2y) - 8$
20. $(x + 1)(x^2 + 2x - 1)$
21. $(1 - x^2)(x - 3) + 5x$
22. $(x - 1)(2x^2 + 2)$
23. $(2x^2 + x - 3)(x + 1)$
24. $(3 - x)(3x + 2)$
25. $(4x + 2)(4 - 2x)$
26. $(x + 3)^2$
27. $(x - 4)^2$
28. $(2a + 2)^2$
29. $(2x - 5)^2$
30. $(2x + 1y)^2$
31. $(x - 6y)^2$
32. $(x - y)(x + y)$
33. $(x - y)(x - y)$
34. $(t - p)(t - p)$
35. $(y - x)(x - y)$
36. $(p - g)(p - g)$
37. $(k - 6)(k - 8)$
38. $(x - 1)(x + 2)(x + 1)$
39. $7 - [4 + (w - 1)^2]$
40. $(3r + 2)(2r - 1) + 3(r + 3) + 4(1 - 2r)$
41. $3(2 + x) + 3[1 - 2(x - 3)]$
42. $7 + 6(3a - 35 - 2a + 37)$
43. $(x - 2)(x - 1) + 2(3x - 1) + x(x + 4x)$
44. $5 + [3(x - 2) - (2 - 4x)]$
45. $1 - [3 - 2(2a - 1) + 3a - 6a + 9]$
46. $3c[c - 2c(3 + 4c) + 2c(2 - 5c) + 6(3 - 2c)]$
47. $(3x + 7)(5x^2 + 6x - 7)$
48. $(-6x + 4)(9x^2 - 5x - 3)$
49. $(5g - 8)(4g^2 - 5g - 10)$
50. $(-2u - 2)(5 - 4u - 5u^2)$
51. $(10 - 8p)(6 - 11p + 4p^2)$
52. $(3 - 3e + 7e^2)(1 - 5e)$
53. $(3ax + 7a)(5ax^2 + 6ax - 7)$
54. $(9hx + 5h)(3hx^2 - hx - 1)$
55. $(8x - 4y)(5x^2 - 4xy - 3y)$
56. Investigate if $(x - y)(x + y) = x^2 - y^2$.
57. Investigate if $(x - y)(x - y) = x^2 - 2xy + y^2$.
58. By letting $x = 0$, investigate if $(5x - 1)(-x^2 + 7x - 10) =$ $-x^2(5x - 1) + 7x(5x - 1) - 10(5x - 1)$
59. By letting $x = -2$ and $y = 3$, investigate if $x^3 - y^3 = (x - y)(x^2 + xy + y^2)$.
60. By letting $x = \frac{2}{3}$ and $y = \frac{1}{2}$, investigate if $x^3 + y^3 = (x + y)(x^2 - xy + y^2)$.

Section 2.5: Adding and subtracting algebraic fractions

Student Activity 2E

1. Paul buys two 12-inch pizzas and eats $\frac{1}{3}$ of the cheese pizza and $\frac{1}{6}$ of the pepperoni pizza. How much pizza did Paul eat in total?

2. Keith has $\frac{4}{7}$ of a bar of chocolate left. He gives $\frac{1}{3}$ of it to his friend Seán. Using the letter **'b'** to represent the bar of chocolate, write an expression to show how much of the bar Keith has left.

ADDING AND SUBTRACTING ALGEBRAIC FRACTIONS EXPLAINED

You must be able to add and subtract fractions without using a calculator, as you cannot use a calculator for algebraic fractions.

- **Step 1:** Place the numerator (the top part) of each fraction in brackets.
- **Step 2:** Find the lowest common multiple (LCM) for the denominators (the bottom part) of the fractions.
- **Step 3:** Divide the LCM by the denominator and multiply the numerator by the answer.
- **Step 4:** Simplify the numerator and the denominator of the fraction into its simplest form.

EXAMPLE 7

Express each of the following as a single fraction:

(a) $\frac{x+2}{3}+\frac{2x-3}{2}$ (c) $\frac{5}{2x+1}+\frac{4}{5x-3}$

(b) $\frac{x+1}{2}+\frac{x+4}{4}-\frac{x}{3}$ (d) $\frac{-3}{x+2}-\frac{4}{x+3}$

Solution

(a) $\frac{(x+2)}{3}+\frac{(2x-3)}{2}$ **Place the top in brackets**

LCM of 3 and 2 is 6, so rewrite both fractions as:

$$=\frac{2(x+2)}{6}+\frac{3(2x-3)}{6}$$

$$=\frac{2(x+2)+3(2x-3)}{6}$$

$$=\frac{2x+4+6x-9}{6}$$

$$=\frac{8x-5}{6}$$

(b) $\frac{(x+1)}{2}+\frac{(x+4)}{4}-\frac{(x)}{3}$ **Place the top in brackets**

LCM of 2, 4 and 3 is 12, so rewrite both fractions as:

$$=\frac{6(x+1)}{12}+\frac{3(x+4)}{12}-\frac{4(x)}{12}$$

$$=\frac{6(x+1)+3(x+4)-4(x)}{12}$$

$$=\frac{6x+6+3x+12-4x}{12}$$

$$=\frac{5x+18}{12}$$

(c) LCM of $(2x+1)$ and $(5x-3)$ is the product of $(2x+1)(5x-3)$.

$$=\frac{5(5x-3)}{(2x+1)(5x-3)}+\frac{4(2x+1)}{(2x+1)(5x-3)}$$

$$=\frac{5(5x-3)+4(2x+1)}{(2x+1)(5x-3)}$$

$= \frac{25x - 15 + 8x + 4}{2x(5x - 3) + 1(5x - 3)}$

$= \frac{25x + 8x - 15 + 4}{10x^2 - 6x + 5x - 3}$

$= \frac{33x - 11}{10x^2 - x - 3}$

(d) $\frac{-3}{x + 2} - \frac{4}{x + 3}$

LCM of $(x + 2)$ and $(x + 3)$ is $(x + 2)(x + 3)$.

$= \frac{-3(x + 3)}{(x + 2)(x + 3)} - \frac{4(x + 2)}{(x + 2)(x + 3)}$

$= \frac{-3(x + 3) - 4(x + 2)}{(x + 2)(x + 3)}$

$= \frac{-3x - 9 - 4x - 8}{x(x + 3) + 2(x + 3)}$

$= \frac{-7x - 17}{x^2 + 3x + 2x + 6}$

$= \frac{-7x - 17}{x^2 + 5x + 6}$

Exercise 2.5

Simplify each of the following, writing your answer as a single fraction:

1. $\frac{3}{2} + \frac{4}{3}$ **2.** $\frac{5}{2} - \frac{7}{3}$ **3.** $\frac{2}{3} + \frac{4}{7}$ **4.** $\frac{x}{2} - \frac{x}{3}$ **5.** $\frac{x}{2} + \frac{2x}{3}$

6. $\frac{x}{3} - \frac{x}{7}$ **7.** $\frac{x+1}{2} + \frac{x+2}{5}$ **8.** $\frac{x+3}{3} + \frac{x-7}{-2}$ **9.** $\frac{x+1}{4} + \frac{x-3}{3}$ **10.** $\frac{2x+1}{-4} + \frac{x-2}{-6}$

11. $\frac{x-3}{3} + \frac{4x+6}{6}$ **12.** $\frac{2x-2}{3} + \frac{x+4}{2}$ **13.** $\frac{2x-1}{3} + \frac{2x-4}{2}$ **14.** $\frac{2x}{5} + \frac{3x+1}{4}$

15. $\frac{3x+1}{4} + \frac{x+2}{7}$ **16.** $\frac{2x+1}{-3} - \frac{x-1}{2}$ **17.** $\frac{2x+4}{4} - \frac{x+1}{7}$ **18.** $\frac{3x-1}{2} - \frac{x+2}{5}$

19. $\frac{x-4}{3} - \frac{2x+4}{4}$ **20.** $\frac{2x+5}{-2} - \frac{4x-3}{3}$ **21.** $\frac{3x+3}{5} - \frac{x+3}{3}$ **22.** $\frac{x+2}{3} + \frac{2x+1}{4} - \frac{x+3}{2}$

23. $\frac{3-2x}{-2} - \frac{x+1}{-5} + \frac{2x+7}{-10}$ **24.** $\frac{3x-5}{3} + \frac{4-3x}{6} - \frac{4x+9}{2}$ **25.** $\frac{x+2}{-21} + \frac{3x-1}{3} - \frac{x+4}{7}$

26. $\frac{2x+7}{5} - \frac{x+9}{15} + \frac{2x-10}{-3}$ **27.** $\frac{x-7}{3} + \frac{2x-8}{2} - \frac{2x-4}{4}$ **28.** $\frac{3p+7}{-6} + \frac{p-3}{2} + \frac{2p+2}{-3}$

29. $\frac{6h-5}{10} - \frac{3h+1}{5} + \frac{h+7}{2}$ **30.** $\frac{4y+3}{-3} + \frac{5-2y}{-2} - \frac{y+4}{4}$ **31.** $\frac{2}{x-2} + \frac{4}{x+5}$

32. $\frac{5}{3x+5} + \frac{7}{x-2}$ **33.** $\frac{-3}{x+8} + \frac{2}{x-3}$ **34.** $\frac{7}{x+2} - \frac{4}{x+1}$ **35.** $\frac{8}{x+4} - \frac{2}{x-3}$

36. $\frac{3}{x+5} - \frac{6}{x+2}$ **37.** $\frac{10}{x+7} - \frac{6}{x-3}$ **38.** $\frac{1}{2x+1} + \frac{2}{x-1}$ **39.** $\frac{4}{2x-1} + \frac{2}{x+1}$

40. $\frac{6}{3x+2} + \frac{5}{x-6}$ **41.** $\frac{2}{x+7} + \frac{4}{4x-2}$ **42.** $\frac{3}{2x-1} + \frac{3}{x-2}$ **43.** $\frac{-4}{6x-5} + \frac{3}{2x+5}$

44. $\frac{-7}{6x+1} + \frac{5}{2x+2}$ **45.** $\frac{-3}{3x+1} + \frac{-2}{5x-2}$ **46.** $\frac{-5}{2-4x} - \frac{-1}{3-6x}$ **47.** $\frac{-2}{5-x} - \frac{-7}{3-2x}$

48. (a) Express $\frac{3}{3x+1} + \frac{2}{4x-2}$ as a single fraction.

(b) Verify your answer to part (a) by substituting $x = 4$ into $\frac{3}{3x+1} + \frac{2}{4x-2}$ and into your answer to part (a).

49. (a) Express $\frac{5x-3}{4} - \frac{x+2}{5}$ as a single fraction.

(b) Verify your answer to part (a) by substituting $x = -2$ into $\frac{5x-3}{4} - \frac{x+2}{5}$ and into your answer to part (a).

50. (a) Express $\frac{11}{3-4x} + \frac{7}{3x+8}$ as a single fraction.

(b) Verify your answer to part (a) by substituting $x = -1$ into $\frac{11}{3-4x} + \frac{7}{3x+8}$ and into your answer to part (a).

Section 2.6: Multiplying algebraic fractions

Student Activity 2F

1. Paul won $\frac{1}{3}$ of $\frac{3}{4}$ of a sum of money. What fraction of the money did he win?

2. Síle gave away $\frac{2}{7}$ of $\frac{1}{5}$ of her clothes to charity. What fraction of her clothes did she give away?

3. Calculate each of the following:
   (a) $\frac{3}{12} \times \frac{2}{4}$ (b) $\frac{3}{12}x \times \frac{2}{4}x$ (c) $\frac{3x}{12} \times \frac{2x}{4}$
4. Calculate each of the following:
   (a) $\frac{4}{9} \times \frac{1}{3}$ (b) $\frac{4}{9}x \times \frac{1}{3}x$ (c) $\frac{4x}{9} \times \frac{1x}{3}$

MULTIPLYING ALGEBRAIC FRACTIONS EXPLAINED

You have already learned how to add and subtract algebraic fractions. It is also important to know how to multiply fractions without using a calculator, as you cannot use a calculator to multiply algebraic fractions.

- **Step 1:** Place the numerator of each fraction in brackets and multiply.
- **Step 2:** Place the denominator of each fraction in brackets and multiply.

In Chapter 3, you will examine how it is sometimes possible to simplify the resulting fraction.

EXAMPLE 8

(a) Express the following as a single fraction:
$\frac{x}{2} \times \frac{x}{3}$

(b) Express the following as a single fraction and find its value if $x = 5$ and $y = 3$:
$\frac{x+2}{3} \times \frac{y}{7}$

(c) Express the following as a single fraction and find its value if $x = 1$.
$\frac{x+1}{2} \times \frac{x+4}{4} \times \frac{x}{3}$

Solution

(a) $\frac{x}{2} \times \frac{x}{3}$

$= \frac{(x)(x)}{(2)(3)} = \frac{x^2}{6}$

(b) $\frac{x+2}{3} \times \frac{y}{7}$

$= \frac{(x+2)(y)}{(3)(7)}$

$= \frac{x(y)+2(y)}{21}$

$= \frac{xy+2y}{21}$

Letting $x = 5$ and $y = 3$, and substituting into the answer, we get $\frac{(5)(3)+2(3)}{21} = \frac{15+6}{21} = \frac{21}{21} = 1$

(c) $\frac{x+1}{2} \times \frac{x+4}{4} \times \frac{x}{3}$

$= \frac{(x+1)(x+4)(x)}{(2)(4)(3)}$

$= \frac{[x(x+4)+1(x+4)](x)}{24}$

$= \frac{[x^2+4x+1x+4](x)}{24}$

$= \frac{(x^2+5x+4)(x)}{24}$

$= \frac{x^3+5x^2+4x}{24}$

Letting $x = 1$, we get:

$\frac{(1)^3+5(1)^2+4(1)}{24} = \frac{1+5+4}{24} = \frac{10}{24} = \frac{5}{12}$

Exercise 2.6

Simplify each of the following, writing the answer as a single fraction:

1. $\frac{3}{2} \times \frac{4}{3}$
2. $\frac{5}{2} \times \frac{7}{3}$
3. $\frac{2}{3} \times \frac{4}{7}$
4. $\frac{x}{2} \times \frac{x}{3}$
5. $\frac{x}{2} \times \frac{2x}{3}$
6. $\frac{x}{3} \times \frac{x}{7}$
7. $\frac{x+1}{2} \times \frac{x+2}{5}$
8. $\frac{x+3}{3} \times \frac{x-7}{2}$
9. $\frac{x+1}{4} \times \frac{x-3}{3}$
10. $\frac{2x+1}{4} \times \frac{x-2}{6}$
11. $\frac{x-3}{3} \times \frac{4x+6}{6}$
12. $\frac{2x-2}{3} \times \frac{x+4}{2}$
13. $\frac{2x-1}{3} \times \frac{2x-4}{2}$
14. $\frac{2x}{5} \times \frac{3x+1}{4}$
15. $\frac{3x+1}{4} \times \frac{x+2}{7}$
16. $\frac{2x+1}{3} \times \frac{x-1}{2}$
17. $\frac{2x+4}{4} \times \frac{x+1}{7}$
18. $\frac{3x-1}{2} \times \frac{x+2}{5}$
19. $\frac{y-4}{3} \times \frac{2y+4}{4}$
20. $\frac{2x+5}{2} \times \frac{4x-3}{3}$
21. $\frac{3x+3}{5} \times \frac{x+3}{3}$
22. $\frac{x+2}{3} \times \frac{2x+1}{4} \times \frac{x}{2}$
23. $\frac{3-2x}{2} \times \frac{x+1}{5} \times \frac{2x}{10}$
24. $\frac{3p-5}{3} \times \frac{4-3p}{6} \times \frac{4p}{2}$

Express each of the following as a single fraction and find its value if $x = 1$, $p = 2$, $h = 3$ and $y = 4$:

25. $\frac{x+2}{21} \times \frac{3x-1}{3} \times \frac{x+4}{7}$
26. $\frac{2x+7}{5} \times \frac{x+9}{15} \times \frac{2x-10}{3}$
27. $\frac{x-7}{3} \times \frac{2x-8}{2} \times \frac{2x-4}{4}$
28. $\frac{3p+7}{6} \times \frac{p-3}{2} \times \frac{2p+2}{3}$
29. $\frac{6h-5}{10} \times \frac{3h+1}{5} \times \frac{h+7}{2}$
30. $\frac{4y+3}{3} \times \frac{5-2y}{2} \times \frac{y+4}{4}$

CHAPTER 2 SELF-CHECK TEST

Evaluate each of the following expressions:

1. $3n + 1 + (12n + 9)$ when $n = 2$
2. $(3n - 2) + (5n - 6)$ when $n = 5$
3. $(5n - 11) - (2 - n)$ when $n = -3$
4. $(3a + b - 2) + a + 9$ when $a = -4$ and $b = 3$
5. $5p - q - 2 + (p - q + 7)$ when $p = 2\frac{1}{2}$ and $q = 1\frac{1}{2}$
6. $(a^2 - b + 8) - (a - b^2 - 7)$ when $a = 4$ and $b = -3$
7. $16 + (3x + y - 5)^3 - (y - 2x)$ when $x = 1$ and $y = 0$

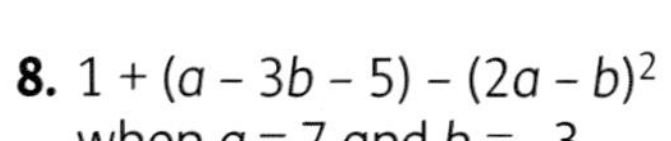

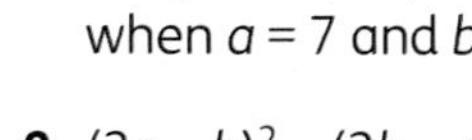

8. $1 + (a - 3b - 5) - (2a - b)^2$ when $a = 7$ and $b = -3$

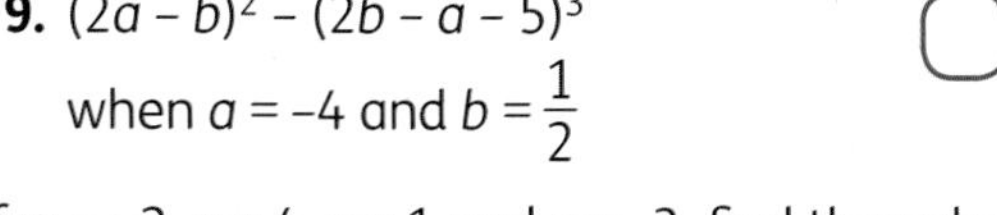

9. $(2a - b)^2 - (2b - a - 5)^3$ when $a = -4$ and $b = \frac{1}{2}$

If $w = -2$, $x = 4$, $y = 1$ and $z = -3$, find the value of each of the following:

10. $x^2 + 2x + 2y$
11. $y^2 + z^2 - x^3$
12. $(x + y)(w + x)$
13. $\frac{w+y+z}{2(x+y)}$
14. $\frac{x^2+z^2}{6y+2}$
15. $\frac{4z+5y}{z+3w+2x}$
16. $x^3 + 2y - z$
17. $\frac{2w+5x}{2z}$
18. $\frac{3w}{x} + \frac{4x}{z}$
19. $\frac{2w-4x}{5y+8z}$
20. $\frac{6xy+2xz}{wy-5wx}$

Simplify each of the following:

21. $5p - 7q + 8 - 2p - 3q$
22. $7n - 3m - 5m - 6n$
23. $3(2n - 5) + 2(3n - 6)$
24. $5(1 - 2n^2) - 5(n^2 - 10n - 3)$
25. $3(a^2 - 2a + 1) + 5(2 - a + 4a^2)$
26. $7 - 2(1 - 3x + y) - (4x + 8y - 8)$

27. Use the multiplication tables to simplify the following expressions:

(a) $(2x + y)(5x + 3y)$

	$5x$	$+3y$
$2x$		
$+y$		$3y^2$

(b) $(ab + b^2)(a^2 + b)$

	a^2	$+b$
ab		
$+b^2$		

(c) $(2a + 5b + 7)(3a + 5a^2)$

	$3a$	$+5a^2$
$2a$		
$+5b$		
$+7$		

(d) $(3x + 5y)(x^2 + x^3)$

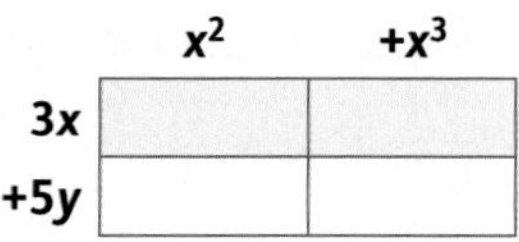

	x^2	$+x^3$
$3x$		
$+5y$		

28. Simplify each of the following:

(a) $(2x^3)(-3x^2)$

(b) $(2x^3)^2$

(c) $(3xy)(2x^2y^3)$

(d) $(2x)(3yz)(-4xyz^2)$

(e) $(acb)(bca)(c^2ab)$

29. Simplify each of the following:

(a) $(-x^2 + 3x - 6)(2 - 2x)$

(b) $(3 - 3x - 4x^2)(2 + 4x)$

(c) $(9x^2 - 3x)(4x^2 - 5x + 6)$

(d) $(7x^2 + 2)(-1 - 5x + 9x^2)$

(e) $6[3 - 6(5x - 8)(1 - 3x)]$

(f) $(3 - 4x)^2 - (7 - 4x)^2$

30. Simplify each of the following, writing your answer as a single fraction:

(a) $\frac{x}{4} + \frac{2x}{3}$

(b) $\frac{2x+3}{2} + \frac{x-2}{3}$

(c) $\frac{3-8x}{-5} + \frac{6x+3}{4}$

(d) $\frac{11x+7}{11} + \frac{5-8x}{5}$

(e) $\frac{-4}{7-2x} + \frac{3}{2x-3}$

(f) $\frac{4}{3x-1} - \frac{2}{3x+1}$

(g) $\frac{-2}{4-3x} - \frac{5}{6-2x}$

(h) $\frac{2x-1}{2} - \frac{x-1}{3} + \frac{x+4}{4}$

(i) $\frac{x}{5} - \frac{2x+1}{15} - \frac{x}{3}$

(j) $\frac{3}{4} + \frac{3}{2x-1} - \frac{6}{x+2}$

(k) $\frac{4}{7x-9} \times \frac{2}{4x-1}$

(l) $\frac{6}{2x-1} \times \frac{-9}{x+1}$

(m) $\frac{7x+5}{3} \times \frac{2x-3}{5}$

(n) $\frac{4x-7}{10} \times \frac{-3x-3}{6}$

31. Simplify and then evaluate each of the following algebraic expressions:

(a) $(-x^2 - 9x + 1) - (x^2 + x + 1)$ given $x = -\frac{3}{5}$

(b) $(2x^2 + x - 3) + (-4x^2 - 5x + 10)$ given $x = 2\frac{1}{2}$

(c) $(3x^2 + 7x + 2) - (-x^2 - 5x + 1)$ given $x = -1\frac{1}{5}$

(d) $(14x - 6y - 19) - (-6x + 7y - 11)$ given $x = -1$ and $y = -5$

(e) $(6x - 7y + 22) + (-13x + 14y - 6)$ given $x = -4$ and $y = -4$

(f) $(x - 5y + 7) - (-6x + 4y - 8)$ given $x = \frac{1}{2}$ and $y = \frac{4}{5}$

32. Given that $x = 2a + 1$ and $y = 2ax - 4a^2$, express y in terms of a.

33. Given that $x = 2t - 1$ and $y = \frac{2}{3}t + 2$, express $3x - y + 2$ in terms of t, in its simplest form.

CHAPTER 2 KNOWLEDGE CHECKLIST

After completing this chapter, I now:

- Am able to identify and explain terms associated with algebra
- Am able to simplify expressions by adding and subtracting like terms
- Am able to multiply variables together by working with indices
- Am able to expand (or multiply) expressions in brackets
- Am able to expand (or multiply) expressions containing more than one term
- Am able to add, subtract and multiply algebraic fractions

Challenge

While waiting for an acquaintance at Fenlon's, one of the better games coffee houses on Van den Huyghes Street, I noticed that some fool had damaged the chessboard on my table by removing the bottom left and top right corner squares. As I picked up some black and white dominoes as a replacement, I became intrigued - with the chessboard only having 62 squares instead of 64, would it be possible to arrange the dominoes in such a way that they would match the pattern of the entire board?

CHAPTER

3

FACTORS

KEY WORDS

- Coefficient
- Difference
- Grouping
- Highest common factor
- Perfect square
- Quadratic
- Trinomial

LEARNING OUTCOMES

In this chapter you will learn:

- ✓ How to factorise expressions by finding the highest common factor and by grouping
- ✓ How to factorise quadratic trinomials
- ✓ How to factorise the difference of two perfect squares
- ✓ To simplify algebraic fractions by factorising

INTRODUCTION

3

FACTORS

In first year, you learned how to find the factors of natural numbers. You also learned how to find the highest common factor for a group of natural numbers.

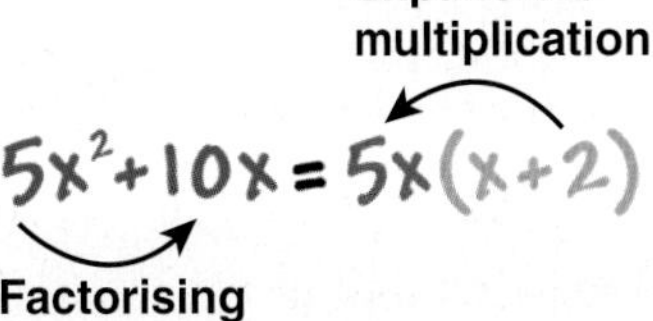

Factors are a very important part of algebra. They are used to predict the shapes of graphs and to solve many equations.

In Chapter 2, you learned how to expand or multiply out brackets. Factorising is the **inverse** (opposite) operation of expanding brackets.

In this chapter, we will examine four types of factorisation.

- **Type 1:** taking out the highest common factor
- **Type 2:** factorising by grouping terms
- **Type 3:** factorising quadratic trinomials
- **Type 4:** factorising the difference of two perfect squares

First year revision

1. Explain in your own words what you understand by the term **factor.**
2. List all the factors of:
   (a) 12
   (b) 6
   (c) What is the HCF of 12 and 6?
   (d) Display the factors on a Venn diagram.
3. How many factors have each of the following numbers?
   (a) 3
   (b) 5
   (c) 7
   (d) What do we call any number with this amount of factors?

Section 3.1: Factorising using the highest common factor

Student Activity 3A

1. Write out the factor pairs of 12 and 20 and find the highest common factor.
2. Write out the factor pairs of 28 and 35 and find the highest common factor.
3. (a) Write out the factor pairs of 8.
   (b) Write out the factor pairs of $8x$.
4. (a) Write out the factor pairs of 11.
   (b) Write out the factor pairs of $11x$.
5. (a) Write out the factor pairs of $6x$ and of 8.
   (b) Identify the highest common factor in both lists.
   (c) Copy and complete the following, replacing the ■ with the correct value:
   $6x + 8 = ■(3x + 4)$
6. (a) What are the factor pairs of $4x^2$?
   (b) What are the factor pairs of $10x$?
   (c) Copy and complete the following, replacing the ■ with the correct value:
   $4x^2 + 10x = ■(2x + 5)$
   (d) Multiply out the bracket in (c) to check your solution.

FACTORISING USING THE HIGHEST COMMON FACTOR EXPLAINED

In Student Activity 3A, you began identifying the **highest common factor** (HCF) for numbers and for algebraic terms.

You also saw that the HCF can be placed as a multiplier of the remaining factors in a bracket.

We recall that $\boldsymbol{a^2}$ means **'a times a'** and is sometimes written as ($\boldsymbol{a}$)($\boldsymbol{a}$) or $\boldsymbol{a}$. $\boldsymbol{a}$ (when we want to show it in its factor form).

Similarly, $\boldsymbol{a^3}$ means **$(a)(a)(a)$** *or* **$(a)(a^2)$** (when we want to show it in its factor form).

When trying to find the highest common factor, use **SNL** (Signs first, then Numbers, then Letters) rule.

First check if the terms have signs in common. Then check if they have numbers in common and finally check if they have variables (letters) in common.

When factorising using the HCF:

- **Step 1:** Find the HCF.
- **Step 2:** Place the HCF in front of the brackets.
- **Step 3:** Divide the HCF into each term and place the answer inside the brackets.

EXAMPLE 1

Simplify: $\dfrac{8x^2}{4x}$

Solution

$\dfrac{8x^2}{4x}$

SNL

Signs: $\dfrac{+}{+} = +$

Numbers: $\dfrac{8}{4} = 2$

Letters: $\dfrac{x^2}{x} = \dfrac{(x)(x)}{x} = x$

$\therefore \dfrac{8x^2}{4x} = +2x$

EXAMPLE 2

Simplify: $\dfrac{-15xy^2}{3xy}$

Solution

$\dfrac{-15xy^2}{3xy}$

SNL

Signs: $\dfrac{-}{+} = -$

Numbers: $\dfrac{15}{3} = 5$

Letters: $\dfrac{xy^2}{xy} = \dfrac{(x)(y)(y)}{(x)(y)} = y$

$\therefore \dfrac{-15xy^2}{3xy} = -5y$

EXAMPLE 3

Factorise each of the following expressions:

(a) $4x + 2$ (c) $5y^2 + 20$

(b) $3a + 15$ (d) $6x^2 - 12x$

Solution

(a) Check SNL: both terms are positive so '+' is common.

Checking the numbers, 2 is the highest factor of 2 and 4.

Checking the letters, only one term contains a letter so no common letter exists.

HCF = **2**

$\therefore 4x + 2 = 2(2x + 1)$

(b) HCF = **3**

$\therefore 3a + 15 = 3(a + 5)$

(c) Examine the factor pairs of both terms:

$5y^2 = (5y)(1y)$ **or** $(5)(1y^2)$ **or** $(5y^2)(1)$.

$20 = (1)(20)$ **or** $(2)(10)$ **or** $(5)(4)$

HCF = **5**

$\therefore 5y^2 + 20 = 5(y^2 + 4)$

(d) Examine the factor pairs of both terms:

$6x^2 = (6x)(1x)$ **or** $(3x)(2x)$ **or** $(6)(1x^2)$ **or** $(1)(6x^2)$

$12x = (12)(1x)$ **or** $(2)(6x)$ **or** $(3)(4x)$ **or** $(12x)(1)$ **or** $(2x)(6)$ **or** $(3x)(4)$

HCF = **6x**

$\therefore 6x^2 - 12x = 6x(x - 2)$

Exercise 3.1

Replace the shapes in each of the following with the highest common factor:

1. $ap + bp =$ ●$(a + b)$
2. $sr - 3st =$ ■$(r - 3t)$
3. $3m - 12n =$ ●$(m - 4n)$
4. $2ay - 4by =$ ●$(a - 2b)$
5. $x + 7xy =$ ♦$(1 + 7y)$
6. $2w + 8a =$ ☺$(w + 4a)$
7. $5pq - 3p =$ ●$(5q - 3)$
8. $4x - 16xy =$ ●$(1 - 4y)$
9. $3rs + 15rt =$ ♦$(s + 5t)$
10. $5z^2 + 7wz =$ ☺$(5z + 7w)$

Factorise each of the following expressions:

11. $5a + 5b = 5$ (□ + □)
12. $3g - 9m = 3$ (□ − □)
13. $4x^2 - 6y = 2$ (□ − □)
14. $2p^2 + 8p + 6 = 2$ (□ + □ + □)
15. $5pq + 10pt = 5p$ (□ + □)
16. $8mn + 7pn = n$ (□ + □)
17. $3x^2 - 3x = 3x$ (□ − □)
18. $5a^2b + 15ab^2 - 10ab = 5ab$ (□ + □ − □)
19. $7p^2q^3 - 14p^2q^2 - 21pq = 7pq$ (□ − □ − □)
20. $xy + xz - x = x$ (□ + □ − □)
21. $5a + 15b$
22. $14p - 21q$
23. $12c + 14d$
24. $pq - 3q$
25. $17c + ac$
26. $x - ax$
27. $14 - 4q$
28. $13p - ap$
29. $10p^2 + 30p$
30. $a^2 + abc$
31. $5xy + 20xy^2$
32. $abc + bcd$
33. $\frac{1}{2}e - \frac{1}{2}f$
34. $3xy^2 + 9y + 6y^2$
35. $15g^3 - 25g + 5g^2$
36. $3a + ab$
37. $3ts - 6tp$
38. $7x^2 + 14$
39. $g^2 - 8g$
40. $mp^2 + mp$
41. $8ab^2 + 4a^2b$
42. $3g^2 + 15gm$
43. $5m^2 + m$
44. $5m^2 - 5$
45. $xy + 3xy^2 - 2x^2y$
46. $bd + bc + b$
47. $4t^2p - 7pg + 6pn + 2p^2j$
48. $14a^2x^2 - 28a^3x + 21ax^3$
49. $10x^5 + 5x^4 - x^3$
50. $27y^5 + 9y - 3y^2$

Section 3.2: Factorising by grouping terms

Student Activity 3B

1. (a) Write out the factor pairs for each of the following terms: $4x^2$, $16xy$, $3y^2$ and $9wy$.
   (b) Is it possible to factorise $4x^2 + 9wy$? Explain your answer.
   (c) Is it possible to factorise $3y^2 + 16xy$? Explain your answer.
   (d) Working in pairs, discuss how you could factorise $4x^2 + 16xy + 3y^2 + 9wy$.
2. (a) Multiply the following expression: $(x + 2)(y + 3)$
   (b) Factorise the following expression:
   $xy + 2y + 3x + 6 =$ ♦$(x + 2) +$ ●$(x + 2) = (x + 2)($♦ + ●$)$

FACTORISING BY GROUPING TERMS EXPLAINED

In Student Activity 3B, you were presented with a slightly more difficult method of factorisation. You had an expression of more than two terms where certain terms had common factors and certain terms did not.

To factorise these expressions, you must first group terms into pairs that have common factors.

$ax + bx + ay + by$ **Group terms**

The first two terms have an ***x*** in common and the third and fourth terms have a ***y*** in common. Once grouped, you can use the HCF to factorise each group of terms.

$= x(a + b) + y(a + b)$ **HCF**

$= (x + y)(a + b)$

When factorising by grouping terms:

- **Step 1:** Group the terms with a common factor into pairs.
- **Step 2:** Place the HCF in front of the brackets of each pair.
- **Step 3:** Divide the HCF into each term and place the answer inside the brackets.
- **Step 4:** Ensure that both brackets contain the same terms.
- **Step 5:** Put the HCFs in one bracket and the common term in the other bracket.

EXAMPLE 4

Factorise fully each of the following expressions:

(a) $rt - 4t + 2r - 8$ (b) $6 + 3x + cx + 2c$ (c) $cd - 3c - ad + 3a$

Solution

(a) $rt - 4t + 2r - 8$

$= t(r - 4) + 2(r - 4)$

$= (t + 2)(r - 4)$

You can check your solution by expanding the brackets:

$(t + 2)(r - 4)$

$= t(r - 4) + 2(r - 4)$

$= tr - 4t + 2r - 8$

(b) $6 + 3x + cx + 2c$ **Group terms**

$= 3(2 + x) + c(x + 2)$ **HCF**

$= 3(x + 2) + c(x + 2)$ **Note that $x + 2 = 2 + x$ as addition is commutative**

$= (3 + c)(x + 2)$

You can check your solution by expanding the brackets:

$3(x + 2) + c(x + 2)$

$= 3x + 6 + cx + 2c$

$= 6 + 3x + cx + 2c$

(c) $cd - 3c - ad + 3a$

Method 1

$cd - 3c - ad + 3a$ **Group terms**

$= c(d - 3) + a(-d + 3)$ **Signs in brackets are not the same**

$= c(d - 3) - a(d - 3)$ **Factorise by placing a minus sign outside the second bracket**

$= (c - a)(d - 3)$

Method 2

We can also factorise by reordering the terms.

$cd - ad - 3c + 3a$ **Rearrange and group terms**

$= d(c - a) - 3(c - a)$ **Signs in brackets are the same**

$= (d - 3)(c - a)$

You can check your solution by expanding the brackets:

$d(c - a) - 3(c - a)$

$= cd - ad - 3c + 3a$

Exercise 3.2

Replace the shapes in each of the following with the correct term:

1. $4x + 8 =$ ●$(x + 2)$
2. $3y - 15 =$ ◇$(y - 5)$
3. $6x + 9 =$ □$(2x + 3)$
4. $5x^2 + 20x =$ ☺$(x + 4)$
5. $4ab + 18b^2 =$ ◇$(2a + 9b)$
6. $12xy + 20x^2y =$ ○$(3 + 5x)$
7. $8a^2b^3 - 14a^3b =$ ◆$(4b^2 - 7a)$
8. $7xyz + 35xy^2 =$ ■$(z + 5y)$
9. $xy + 3y + 2x + 6$
   = ◇(● + 3) + ○(● + 3)
   = (◇ + ○)(● + 3)
10. $ab + cb + ad + cd$
    = ■(○ + c) + ●(○ + c)
    = (■ + ●)(○ + c)
11. $wy + xy + wz + xz$
    = ☺(○ + x) + ◆(○ + x)
    = (☺ + ◆)(○ + x)

Factorise fully each of the following and check your solution:

12. $ac + ad + bd + bc$
13. $ax + 2x + az + 2z$
14. $ax + 2ay + bx + 2by$
15. $3y - xz + 3z - xy$
16. $ar + br + 3a + 3b$
17. $st + 2t + 3s + 6$
18. $yz - 2y + 4z - 8$
19. $ad - 3g - ag + 3d$
20. $rw - st - rt + sw$

Replace the shapes in each of the following with the correct term:

21. $bm - 3m + 3n - bn$
    = ☺(○ − 3) + ◆(3 − b)
    = ☺(○ − 3) − ◆(−3 + b)
    = (☺ − ◆)(○ − 3)
22. $2a + cx - 2c - ax$.
    = □ ($a - c$)+ ◆($c - a$)
    = □($a - c$) − ◆($a - c$)
    = (□ − ◆)($a - c$)
23. $3t - 6 + 2s - ts$
    = ■(t − 2) + ◆(2 − t)
    = ■(t − 2) − ◆(t − 2)
    = (■ − ◆)(t − 2)

Factorise fully each of the following:

24. $bx - 3y + by - 3x$
25. $np - nr + mp - mr$
26. $yz + 2y - 4z - 8$
27. $pb - 4p - qb + 4q$
28 $2a + 3cx - 2c - 3ax$
29. $ad - 3g + ag - 3d$
30. $as - at + bt - bs$
31. $ab - a^2 + bd - ad$
32. $4pr + 3q - 6p - 2qr$
33. $a^2 - dw + ad - aw$
34. $w^2 - 2aw + 3bw - 6ab$
35. $by - 2xy - b^2 + 2bx$
36. $x^2 - cx - bx + bc$
37. $15ps + 3p^2 - 5ts - tp$
38. $m^2 - 2m - nm + 2n$
39. $3at + bs - as - 3bt$
40. $c^2 - 4s + 2c - 2cs$
41. $am - bm - bn + an$
42. $12df - 20dg - 10cg - 6cf$
43. $14cm - 12dh + 6ch - 28dm$
44. $20bk - 40eh - 50ek + 16bh$
45. $15hl - 30hm - 35lj + 70jm$
46. $6dg + 5cf + 2cd + 15fg$
47. $21cm + 5n - 15cn - 7m$
48. $p^2st - 28mn - 7mpt + 4nps$
49. $14a^2b^2 - 35a^2bg + 25a^2cg - 10a^2bc$
50. $6pst^2 - 8gp^2t - 36g^2ps + 27gs^2t$

Remove the brackets and re-arrange before factorising each of the following:

51. $3g^2 - h(g + f) + 3fg$
52. $b(10a - c) - 5ac + 2b^2$
53. $b^2 - b(2d + 2) + 4d$
54. $-4p(3m - n) - mn + 3m^2$
55. $t^2 + 2s - t(-1 - 2s)$
56. $7m(m + 3p) - mn - 3pn$
57. $xy + z^2 - z(x + y)$
58. $-2kh + j^2 - j(-h + 2k)$
59. $-x(3 + y) + x^2 + 3y$
60. $pt(12h^2 + pt) - 2hpt(p + 3t)$

Section 3.3: Factorising quadratic trinomials 1

Student Activity 3C

1. What do the letters 'tri' imply? (Hint: **tri**athlon, **tri**dent, **tri**angle, **tri**plets.)
2. (a) Factorise fully $n^2 + 3n + 4n + 12$.
   (b) Based on your answer to (a), can you find the factors of $n^2 + 7n + 12 = $ (■ + 3)(■ + 4)?
3. (a) Factorise fully $x^2 + 2x + 4x + 8$.
   (b) Based on your answer to (a), can you find the factors of $x^2 + 6x + 8 = $ (■ + ◆)(■ + 4)?
4. (a) Factorise fully $x^2 + 3x + 5x + 15$.
   (b) Based on your answer to (a), can you find the factors of $x^2 + 8x + 15 = $ (■ + ◆)(■ + ●)?

FACTORISING QUADRATIC TRINOMIALS 1 EXPLAINED

In Student Activity 3C, you began to examine the factors of a **quadratic trinomial.**
A quadratic trinomial has a highest power of **2** (for example, $\mathbf{x^2}$) and it contains **three** terms.

A **tri**nomial contains 3 terms just as a triathlon contains 3 sports.

For the moment, we will consider a general quadratic expression $\mathbf{1x^2 + bx + c}$, where $b, c \in \mathbb{Z}$.

When factorising a quadratic trinomial, use the following rules:

Rule 1

If the sign on the constant is positive, $x^2 \pm bx + c$:

- You need a pair of factors of **c** that will **add or subtract** to give b.
- Both brackets will contain the sign of b.

When factorising, $x^2 + bx + c$ **Note: *b* has a + sign**

$= (x + \text{number})(x + \text{number})$

These numbers:
multiplied together = $+c$
added together = $+b$

As in the previous section, you can check your answer by multiplying out the brackets and comparing the quadratic expressions.

When factorising, $x^2 - bx + c$ **Note: *b* has a – sign**

$= (x - \text{number})(x - \text{number})$

These numbers:
multiplied together = $+c$
added together = $-b$

Rule 2

If the sign on the constant is negative, $x^2 \pm bx - c$:

- You need a pair of factors of c that will **subtract** to give b.
- One bracket will contain a + and the other bracket a –.
- You will need to check the signs are in the correct bracket. To do this, multiply the two outer terms together and the two inner terms together and add/subtract the answers to get b.

When factorising, $x^2 + bx - c$

$= (x + \text{number})(x - \text{number})$ **Note: c has a – and b has a +**

or

$(x - \text{number})(x + \text{number})$

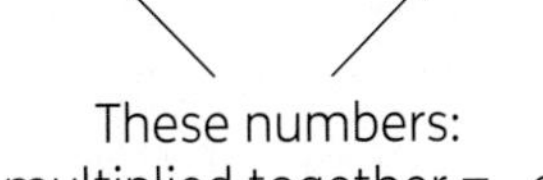

These numbers:
multiplied together = $-c$
added together = $+b$

When factorising, $x^2 - bx - c$

$= (x + \text{number})(x - \text{number})$ **Note: c has a – and b has a –**

or

$(x - \text{number})(x + \text{number})$

These numbers:
multiplied together = $-c$
added together = $-b$

EXAMPLE 5

Factorise $x^2 + 8x + 12$.

Solution

Method 1

$x^2 + 8x + 12$

The sign on the constant, 12, is +. Factor pairs of 12 are 1×12, 2×6, 3×4.

We need a pair of factors that **add** to give +8. These are +6 and +2.

$x^2 + 6x + 2x + 12$

$= x(x + 6) + 2(x + 6)$

$= (x + 2)(x + 6)$

Method 2

$x^2 + 8x + 12$

$x \quad + \quad 2$

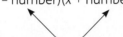

$x \quad + \quad 6$

$= (x + 2)(x + 6)$

Since $+2x$
$+6x$
$+8x$

Factor pairs of 12
= 1 × 12
= 2 × 6
= 3 × 4
Since 2 + 6 = 8

You can check your solution by multiplying the brackets:

$(x + 2)(x + 6)$

$= (x + 6) + 2(x + 6)$

$= x^2 + 6x + 2x + 12$

$= x^2 + 8x + 12$

EXAMPLE 6

Factorise $x^2 - 9x + 20$.

Solution

Method 1

$x^2 - 9x + 20$

The sign on the constant is +. Factors pairs of 20 are 1×20, 2×10, 4×5.

We need a pair of factors that **add** to give −9. These are −4 and −5.

$x^2 - 5x - 4x + 20$

$= x(x - 5) - 4(x - 5)$

$= (x - 4)(x - 5)$

Method 2

$x^2 - 9x + 20$

$x \quad - \quad 5$

$x \quad - \quad 4$

$= (x - 5)(x - 4)$

Since

$-5x$

$-4x$

$-9x$

Factor pairs of 20

= 1 × 20

= 2 × 10

= 4 × 5

Since −4 − 5 = −9

EXAMPLE 7

Factorise $x^2 + 5x - 6$.

Solution

Method 1

$x^2 + 5x - 6$

The sign on the constant is −. Factor pairs of 6 are 1×6, 2×3.

We need a pair of factors that **subtract** to give +5. These are −1 and +6.

$x^2 - 1x + 6x - 6$

$= x(x - 1) + 6(x - 1)$

$= (x + 6)(x - 1)$

Method 2

Factorise $x^2 + 5x - 6$

$x \quad + \quad 6$

$x \quad - \quad 1$

$= (x + 6)(x - 1)$

Since

$+6x$

$-1x$

$+5x$

Factor pairs of 6

= 1 × 6

= 2 × 3

Since −1 + 6 = +5

EXAMPLE 8

Factorise $x^2 - 4x - 21$.

Solution

Method 1

$x^2 - 4x - 21$

The sign on the constant is −. Factor pairs of 21 are 1×21, 3×7.

We need a pair of factors that **subtract** to give −4. These are +3 and −7.

$x^2 - 7x + 3x - 21$

$= x(x - 7) + 3(x - 7)$

$= (x + 3)(x - 7)$

Method 2

$x^2 - 4x - 21$

$x \quad - \quad 7$

$x \quad + \quad 3$

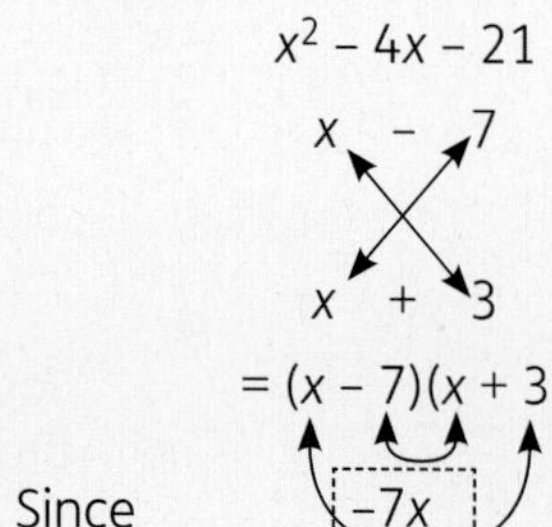

$= (x - 7)(x + 3)$

Since

$-7x$

$+3x$

$-4x$

Factor pairs of 21

= 1 × 21

= 3 × 7

Since −7 + 3 = −4

Exercise 3.3

Fill in the missing factor for each of the following:

1. $n^2 + 4n + 3 = (n + 1)(n + ●)$
2. $n^2 + 5n + 6 = (n + 2)(n + ▲)$
3. $n^2 + 6n + 9 = (n + 3)(● + ♦)$
4. $n^2 + 11n + 18 = (n + 9)(■ + ☺)$
5. $n^2 + 10n + 25 = (n + 5)(■ + ●)$
6. $n^2 + 4n - 12 = (n - 2)(n + ♦)$
7. $x^2 + 7x - 8 = (x + 8)(● - ♦)$
8. $x^2 - 11x + 24 = (x - 3)(♦ - ■)$
9. $x^2 - 14x + 49 = (x - 7)(☺ - ■)$
10. $a^2 - 11a - 12 = (a + 1)(♦ - ●)$

11. The linear factors in the box can be multiplied to give the quadratics shown. Choose the correct pair which multiply to make each of the following quadratic expressions. (Each factor can only be used once.)

$(a + 3)$ $(a + 5)$ $(a + 7)$ $(a - 1)$ $(a - 3)$
$(a + 4)$ $(a + 6)$ $(a - 2)$ $(a - 5)$ $(a + 8)$

(a) $a^2 + 7a + 12$
(b) $a^2 + 13a + 40$
(c) $a^2 + 6a - 7$
(d) $a^2 + 4a - 12$
(e) $a^2 - 8a + 15$

Factorise each of the following quadratic trinomials and check your solution:

12. $x^2 + 4x + 3$
13. $x^2 + 3x + 2$
14. $x^2 + 5x + 4$
15. $x^2 + 5x + 6$
16. $x^2 + 7x + 12$
17. $x^2 + 7x + 10$
18. $x^2 + 11x + 28$
19. $x^2 + 13x + 36$
20. $x^2 + 11x + 10$
21. $x^2 - 5x + 6$
22. $x^2 - 8x + 7$
23. $x^2 - 6x + 8$
24. $x^2 - 10x + 25$
25. $x^2 - 10x + 24$
26. $x^2 - 11x + 28$
27. $x^2 + x - 6$
28. $x^2 - 2x - 24$
29. $x^2 + 3x - 4$
30. $x^2 + 2x - 15$
31. $x^2 - 2x - 8$
32. $x^2 - 4x - 12$
33. $x^2 + 3x - 18$
34. $x^2 - 3x - 40$
35. $x^2 - 2x - 63$
36. $x^2 + 4x - 60$
37. $x^2 - 6x - 40$
38. $x^2 + x - 56$
39. $x^2 - 4x - 96$
40. $x^2 - 7x - 44$
41. $p^2 + 11p + 18$
42. $l^2 - 5l - 24$
43. $w^2 - 2w - 3$
44. $b^2 - 10b + 21$
45. $a^2 + 17a + 30$
46. $j^2 - 4j - 5$
47. $t^2 + 9t - 22$
48. $d^2 - 3d + 2$
49. $e^2 - 2e - 15$
50. $c^2 + 8c + 12$

Section 3.4: Factorising quadratic trinomials 2

You have already factorised quadratic trinomials of the form $x^2 + bx + c$ where $b, c \in \mathbb{Z}$.
For Higher Level, you must now learn how to factorise quadratic trinomials of the form $ax^2 + bx + c$, where $a \in \mathbb{N}$ and $b, c \in \mathbb{Z}$.

When factorising a quadratic of this type:

- **Step 1:** Write out the pairs of factors of a (the coefficient of x^2).
- **Step 2:** Write out the pairs of factors of the constant c.
- **Step 3:** Use the pairs of factors from a and c which multiplied together **add** or **subtract** to give b (depending on the quadratic expression).

or

When factorising a quadratic of this type:

- Multiply the pairs of factors of $a \times c$ which **add** or **subtract** to give b (depending on the quadratic expression).

EXAMPLE 9

Factorise:

$2x^2 + 7x + 3$

Solution

$2x^2 + 7x + 3$

Method 1

$2x^2 + 7x + 3$

Write out the factors of *a* and *c*

2, 1　　3, 1

Use pairs of factors from *a* and *c*, which when multiplied **add** or **subtract** to give *b*.

$(2)(1) + (3)(1) \neq 7$

$(2)(3) + (1)(1) = 6 + 1 = 7$

$= 2x^2 + 6x + 1x + 3$

$= 2x(x + 3) + 1(x + 3)$

$= (2x + 1)(x + 3)$

Method 2

Factors of $2x^2 = (2x)(x)$

$2x^2 + 7x + 3$ **Factors of 3 = 1 × 3**

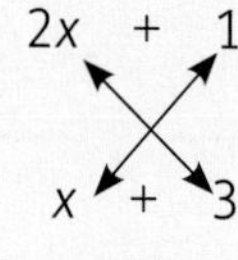

$= (2x + 1)(x + 3)$

Since

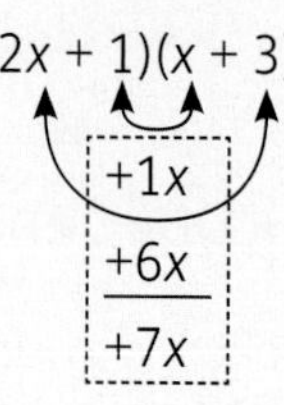

middle term

EXAMPLE 10

Factorise:

$3x^2 + 10x - 8$

Solution

Method 1

$3x^2 + 10x - 8$

3, 1　　8, 1
　　　　4, 2

$(3)(1) \pm (1)(8) \neq 10$

$(3)(8) \pm (1)(1) \neq 10$

$(3)(4) \pm (2)(1) = 12 \pm 2 = 10$ or 14

As we are looking for 10, we can use 12 and 2:

$= 3x^2 + 12x - 2x - 8$

$= 3x(x + 4) - 2(x + 4)$

$= (3x - 2)(x + 4)$

Method 2

Factors of $3x^2 = (3x)(x)$

$3x^2 + 10x - 8$

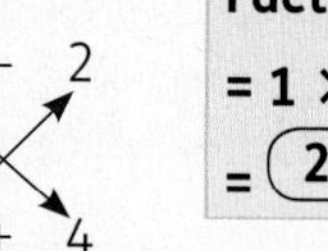

Factors of 8

= 1 × 8

= 2 × 4

$= (3x - 2)(x + 4)$

Since

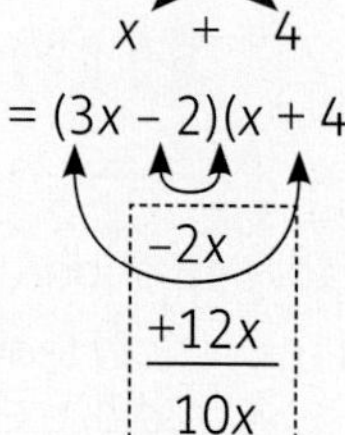

middle term

Exercise 3.4

Factorise each of the following:

1. $2x^2 - 5x - 3$

2. $2x^2 - 4x - 16$

3. $3x^2 + 8x - 3$

4. $5x^2 + 14x - 24$

5. $3x^2 + 11x + 6$

6. $2x^2 - 4x - 6$

7. $7x^2 - 30x + 8$

8. $3x^2 + 7x - 6$

9. $5x^2 - 22x + 21$

10. $3x^2 - 8x + 4$

11. $2x^2 + 11x + 14$

12. $7x^2 - 23x + 6$

13. $11x^2 - 31x - 6$

14. $7x^2 - 28x + 21$

15. $3x^2 - 5x - 50$

16. $13x^2 + 90x - 7$
17. $13x^2 + 7x - 20$
18. $7x^2 + 40x + 25$
19. $3x^2 - 3x - 18$
20. $5x^2 + 28x - 49$
21. $3x^2 + 26x - 9$
22. $5x^2 - 22x + 8$
23. $2x^2 + 10x + 12$
24. $7x^2 - 17x + 6$
25. $3x^2 + 11x + 8$
26. $6x^2 + 17x + 12$
27. $12x^2 + 2x - 2$
28. $10x^2 + 22x + 4$
29. $21x^2 - 36x + 15$
30. $4c^2 + 13c + 3$
31. $3d^2 - d - 2$
32. $5e^2 + 9e - 2$
33. $2f^2 + 7f + 6$
34. $11g^2 - 19g - 6$
35. $3h^2 + 11h + 6$
36. $5j^2 - 7j - 6$
37. $6k^2 - k - 2$
38. $2l^2 + 11l + 14$
39. $6m^2 - 13m + 2$

Section 3.5: Factorising the difference of two perfect squares

Student Activity 3D

1. What is the difference between 7 and 11?
   (a) Explain how you arrived at your answer.
   (b) What does the word **difference** mean in mathematics?
   (c) What is a squared number? Give an example of a squared number.
2. Calculate the value of:
   (a) 10^2
   (b) 7^2
   (c) $10^2 - 7^2$
   (d) $(10 - 7)(10 + 7)$
   (e) In one sentence, can you explain the relationship between the answers in parts (c) and (d)?
3. (a) Simplify $(a - b)(a + b)$.
   (b) Based on your answer to part (a), find the missing terms for (♥ + ●)(♥ − ●) to give $a^2 - b^2$.
4. (a) Simplify $(x - y)(x + y)$.
   (b) Based on your answer to part (a), find the missing terms for $(x +$ ♦$)(x -$ ♦$)$ to give $x^2 - y^2$.

FACTORISING THE DIFFERENCE OF TWO SQUARES EXPLAINED

In Student Activity 3D, you factorised the difference of two squares. If you examine each of the previous questions, you should notice that each term in the expression is a **perfect square.**

When factorising a quadratic of this type:

- **Step 1:** Write each term as a square number, using brackets.
- **Step 2:** Use the rule $\boldsymbol{a^2 - b^2 = (a + b)(a - b)}$.

EXAMPLE 11

Factorise each of the following expressions:

(a) $x^2 - r^2$ (d) $25d^2 - 36$

(b) $p^2 - q^2$ (e) $3x^2 - 3y^2$

(c) $16 - a^2$

Solution

(a) $x^2 - r^2$

$(x)^2 - (r)^2$ **Squares in brackets**

$(x + r)(x - r)$ **Use rule**

(b) $p^2 - q^2$

$(p)^2 - (q)^2$ **Squares in brackets**

$(p + q)(p - q)$ **Use rule**

(c) $16 - a^2$

$(4)^2 - (a)^2$ **Squares in brackets**

$(4 + a)(4 - a)$ **Use rule**

(d) $25d^2 - 36$

$(5d)^2 - (6)^2$ **Squares in brackets**

$(5d + 6)(5d - 6)$ **Use rule**

(e) $3x^2 - 3y^2$

$= 3(x^2 - y^2)$ **HCF = 3**

$= 3(x - y)(x + y)$ **Difference of 2 squares**

Exercise 3.5

Fill in each of the missing terms:

1. a^2 = (■)^2

2. x^2 = (♦)^2

3. 1 = (■)^2

4. $4x^2$ = (♥)^2

5. 16 = (●)^2

6. $25y^2$ = (♦)^2

Factorise each of the following:

7. $r^2 - t^2$

8. $s^2 - w^2$

9. $a^2 - y^2$

10. $x^2 - h^2$

11. $k^2 - v^2$

12. $m^2 - n^2$

13. $d^2 - b^2$

14. $e^2 - c^2$

15. $x^2 - 25$

16. $y^2 - 1$

17. $t^2 - 100$

18. $a^2 - 64$

19. $w^2 - 121$

20. $r^2 - 81$

21. $144 - g^2$

22. $49 - m^2$

23. $169 - a^2$

24. $4x^2 - 16y^2$

25. $81a^2 - 36d^2$

26. $25c^2 - 64s^2$

The following expressions have three factors. First, take out a common factor and then factorise what remains inside the brackets.

27. $s^2 - t^2$

28. $121y^2 - 49x^2$

29. $100p^2 - q^2$

30. $5s^2 - 5t^2$

31. $2w^2 - 2r^2$

32. $7d^2 - 7b^2$

33. $11q^2 - 11p^2$

34. $13x^2 - 13v^2$

35. $15y^2 - 15t^2$

36. $3 - 3b^2$

37. $9pu^2 - 9p$

38. $14g^2 - 14$

39. $4c^2g^4e - 25c^2d^2e$

40. $9t - 64w^6t$

41. $196cp^4 - 49c$

42. $12pq^2 - 75p^3$

43. $8xyz^2 - 2xyw^2$

44. $98de^2 - 50d^3$

Remove the brackets and simplify each of the following:

45. $(2a + 1)^2 - (a + 3)^2$

46. $(4c - 2)^2 - (c + 1)^2$

47. $(5h + 3)^2 - (2h - 1)^2$

48. $(3x + 7)^2 - (5x - 2)^2$

49. $(m + 3d)^2 - (3m + d)^2$

Section 3.6: Simplifying algebraic fractions using factors

Student Activity 3E

1. Evaluate each of the following:

(a) $\frac{5}{5}$ (b) $\frac{8}{8}$ (c) $\frac{-2}{-2}$ (d) $\frac{-1}{-1}$ (e) $\frac{x}{x}$ (f) $\frac{3x}{3x}$ (g) $\frac{x + 2}{x + 2}$ (h) $\frac{-5x}{-5x}$ (i) $\frac{x^2}{x^2}$ (j) $\frac{x^2 + 2}{x^2 + 2}$

2. Factorise each of the following:
   (a) $3x + 6$
   (b) $4x + 8$
   (c) Using your answers for parts (a) and (b), factorise fully the following fraction:
   $\frac{3x+6}{4x+8}$
   (d) Can you simplify the fraction in part (c)?

SIMPLIFYING ALGEBRAIC FRACTIONS USING FACTORS EXPLAINED

In Student Activity 3E, you examined how to factorise algebraic fractions. An algebraic fraction is where the numerator and/or the denominator are both made up of algebraic expressions.

If the top expression is identical to the bottom expression, the fraction is equal to 1, since the denominator divides into the numerator exactly once. For example:

$$\frac{x+2}{x+2} = \frac{4-7x}{4-7x} = \frac{x^2+18x-3}{x^2+18x-3} = \frac{-3x}{-3x} = 1$$

When working with algebraic fractions, always factorise the numerator and denominator fully. Any common factors can then be divided into each other. This will always leave an equivalent fraction in its simplest form.

EXAMPLE 12

(a) Simplify $\frac{9x+27}{3x+3}$.   (b) Simplify $\frac{x^2+7x+12}{x^2+5x+6}$.

Solution

(a) $\frac{9x+27}{3x+9}$

$= \frac{9(x+3)}{3(x+3)}$ **Factorise the denominator and the numerator by getting the HCF**

$= \frac{9\cancel{(x+3)}}{3\cancel{(x+3)}} = \frac{9}{3} = 3$

(b) $\frac{x^2+7x+12}{x^2+5x+6}$ **Factorise both the denominator and the numerator**

$= \frac{\cancel{(x+3)}(x+4)}{\cancel{(x+3)}(x+2)}$

$= \frac{(x+4)}{(x+2)}$

Exercise 3.6

Simply each of the following:

1. $\frac{5x+20}{x+4}$
2. $\frac{14-7x}{2-x}$
3. $\frac{3x+15}{2x+10}$
4. $\frac{8x+16}{9x+18}$
5. $\frac{6x+24}{x+4}$
6. $\frac{21-3x}{x-7}$
7. $\frac{ac+bd+ad+bc}{a+b}$
8. $\frac{sp-qt+pt-sq}{sq+tq+sp+tp}$
9. $\frac{4x-x^2}{x-4}$
10. $\frac{7x-14x^2}{2x-1}$
11. $\frac{x^2-2x-15}{x^2+8x+15}$
12. $\frac{6+x-x^2}{x^2+4x+4}$
13. $\frac{x^2-4x-21}{x^2-9}$
14. $\frac{7x-x^2-12}{x^2-4x+3}$
15. $\frac{10x+3x^2-x^3}{x^2+2x}$
16. $\frac{x^2+5x}{2x+10}$
17. $\frac{2x^2+5x+3}{x^2+5x+4}$
18. $\frac{3x^2-8x+4}{x^2-9x+14}$
19. $\frac{2+3x-2x^2}{2x^2-x-1}$
20. $\frac{6-x-2x^2}{3x^2+7x+2}$

CHAPTER 3 SELF-CHECK TEST

Factorise each of the following:

1. $ab + ac = ☺(b + c)$
2. $ab - b = b(a + ▲)$
3. $a^3 - a = a(■ - 1)$
4. $pq^2 + pq$
5. $10pq - 15pr$
6. $20cd + 30d$
7. $x^2 + x^3$
8. $5pq - 10p$
9. $5x^3 + 10x$
10. $8x^4 - 4x^3$
11. $2pq - 4p + 3q - 6$
12. $ac - 2bd - ad + 2bc$
13. $rs + 3rt + 2ps + 6pt$
14. $ax + bx + ay + by$
15. $2x^2 + 2xw - 2xz - 2wz$
16. $6pr + 3ps - 8r^2 - 4rs$
17. $2wx - 2wy - 3xz + 3yz$
18. $x^2 + 8x + 16$
19. $x^2 + 13x + 30$
20. $x^2 - 6x + 8$
21. $x^2 + 4x - 45$
22. $x^2 - 18x + 77$
23. $x^2 - 17x + 72$
24. $x^2 + 12x + 36$
25. $x^2 + 17x - 60$
26. $6x^2 - 15x - 18$
27. $10x^2 - 8x - 2$
28. $20x^2 - 19x + 3$
29. $21x^2 + 32x - 5$
30. $6x^2 + 7x - 3$
31. Match the following quadratic trinomials with factors from the list. (Note: each factor can only be used once.)

   $(a + 6)$ $(a + 2)$ $(a + 8)$ $(a + 5)$
   $(a + 3)$ $(a + 10)$ $(a + 1)$ $(a + 4)$

   (a) $a^2 + 4a + 3$ (c) $a^2 + 10a + 24$
   (b) $a^2 + 13a + 40$ (d) $a^2 + 12a + 20$

32. Match the following quadratic trinomials with factors from the list. (Hint: factors can be used more than once.)

   $(n + 7)$ $(n + 4)$ $(n - 1)$ $(n + 3)$
   $(n - 3)$ $(n - 6)$ $(n + 5)$ $(n - 2)$

   (a) $n^2 + 7n + 12$ (f) $n^2 - 3n - 18$
   (b) $n^2 - 2n + 1$ (g) $n^2 + 3n - 10$
   (c) $n^2 - 8n + 12$ (h) $n^2 + 2n - 3$
   (d) $n^2 + 6n - 7$ (i) $n^2 + 8n + 16$
   (e) $n^2 - 9n + 18$ (j) $n^2 - 12n + 36$

Factorise each of the following (hint: difference of two perfect squares):

33. $x^2 - a^2$
34. $d^2 - 25b^2$
35. $w^2 - r^2$
36. $9w^2 - 16y^2$
37. $c^2 - 1$

Factorise each of the following:

38. $x^2 - 12x + 11$
39. $6ab + 12ab^2$
40. $18x^4 + 27x$
41. $5x^2y - 10xy^2$
42. $8x^3y^2z - 10xyz^2$
43. $2tx + 3sx - 4ty - 6sy$
44. $2a^2b + 6a^2$
45. $12w^2 - 20wt^2$

46. $10x^2 - 14x + 4$

47. $6x^2 + 22x - 8$

48. $7m^2 - 63g^2$

49. $x^2 + 10x - 39$

50. $bx - 12a + 4b - 3ax$

51. $35x^2 - 22x - 24$

52. $36y^2 - 16v^2$

53. $27w^4 - 3h^2$

54. $20ts^2 - 80tp^2$

55. $8vw^3 - 2v^3w$

56. $50 - 98a^2$

57. $3fg^2 - 42fg + 72f$

Simplify each of the following fractions:

58. $\dfrac{5x + 25}{3x + 15}$

59. $\dfrac{2x + 19}{6x + 57}$

60. $\dfrac{x^2 + 3x}{2x^2 + 6x}$

61. $\dfrac{7x - x^2}{49 - 7x}$

62. $\dfrac{x^2 + 13x + 36}{x^2 + 4x}$

63. $\dfrac{x^2 + 6x - 27}{9x + x^2}$

64. $\dfrac{x^2 - x - 20}{x^2 + 2x - 35}$

65. $\dfrac{5x^2 - 3x - 2}{2x^2 + x - 3}$

66. $\dfrac{6 - 3x - 3x^2}{7x^2 + 15x + 2}$

67. $\dfrac{17x - 15 - 4x^2}{-4x + 5 - x^2}$

CHAPTER 3 KNOWLEDGE CHECKLIST

After completing this chapter, I now:

- Am able to factorise expressions using the highest common factor
- Am able to factorise by grouping terms
- Am able to recognise and factorise quadratic trinomials
- Am able to recognise and factorise the difference of two perfect squares
- Am able to simplify algebraic fractions by factorising

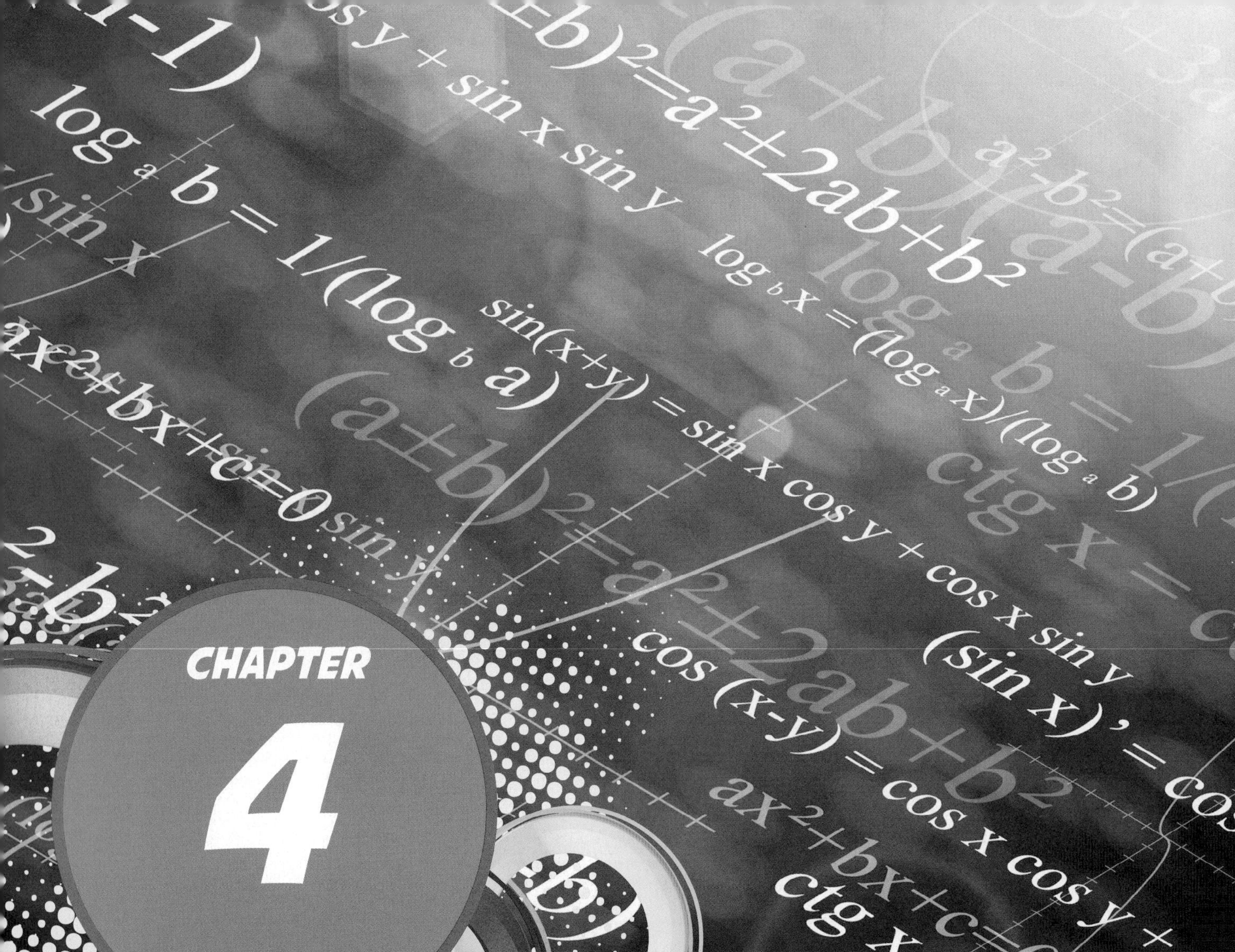

CHAPTER 4

LINEAR EQUATIONS

KEY WORDS

- Balanced equation
- Equation
- Expression
- Linear

LEARNING OUTCOMES

In this chapter you will learn:

- ✓ How to balance an equation
- ✓ How to solve linear equations
- ✓ How to solve equations involving algebraic fractions
- ✓ How to solve problems involving linear equations

INTRODUCTION

The picture shows the title-page of a book translated into Latin from Greek in 1621 AD. The original was written in Greek by Diophantus of Alexandria.

Diophantus was born in 210 AD and died in 290 AD. He is often referred to as the Father of Algebra. Diophantus wrote equations, such as $x + y = 15$, and was interested in discovering how many pairs of numbers (an x-value and a corresponding y-value) could be substituted into any equation.

In this chapter, you will learn to solve equations like Diophantus did many years ago.

DIOPHANTI
ALEXANDRINI
ARITHMETICORVM
LIBRI SEX,
ET DE NVMERIS MVLTANGVLIS
LIBER VNVS.
Nunc primùm Græcè & Latinè editi, atque absolutissimis Commentariis illustrati.
AVCTORE CLAVDIO GASPARE BACHETO MEZIRIACO SEBVSIANO, V.C.

LVTETIAE PARISIORVM,
Sumptibus SEBASTIANI CRAMOISY, via Iacobæa, sub Ciconiis.
M. DC. XXI.
CVM PRIVILEGIO REGIS.

Section 4.1: Balanced equations

Student Activity 4A

Work in pairs to carry out the following activity.

1. The tins of beans on this balance all weigh the same. Find the weight of one tin.

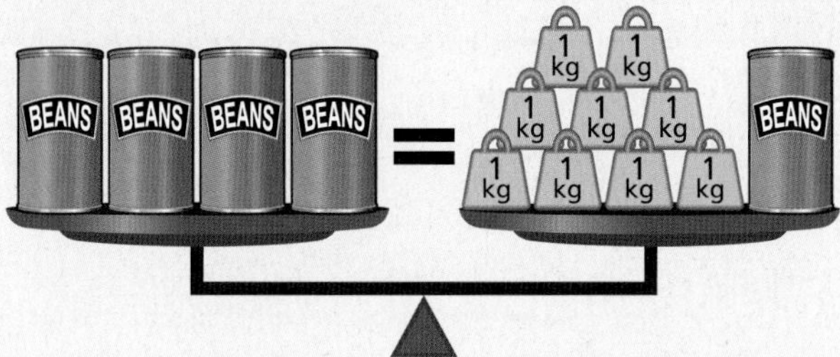

2. Study the picture.

(a) In your own words, describe what items are on both sides of the equation.

Using the letter ***b*** to represent each bag of flour and **1** to represent each kg:

(b) Write an expression for the items on the left-hand side.

(c) Write an expression for the items on the right-hand side.

(d) Find the weight of one bag of flour.

BALANCED EQUATIONS EXPLAINED

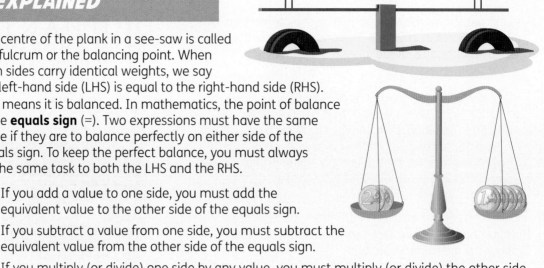

The centre of the plank in a see-saw is called the fulcrum or the balancing point. When both sides carry identical weights, we say the left-hand side (LHS) is equal to the right-hand side (RHS). This means it is balanced. In mathematics, the point of balance is the **equals sign** (=). Two expressions must have the same value if they are to balance perfectly on either side of the equals sign. To keep the perfect balance, you must always do the same task to both the LHS and the RHS.

- If you add a value to one side, you must add the equivalent value to the other side of the equals sign.
- If you subtract a value from one side, you must subtract the equivalent value from the other side of the equals sign.
- If you multiply (or divide) one side by any value, you must multiply (or divide) the other side of the equals sign by the exact same value.

In Chapter 2, you learned that the word **'equation'** means that two algebraic expressions are equal to each other. In the following example:

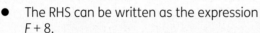

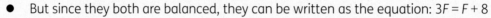

- The LHS can be written as the expression $3F$.
- The RHS can be written as the expression $F + 8$.
- But since they both are balanced, they can be written as the equation: $3F = F + 8$

By ensuring we keep an equation balanced, we can solve any algebraic equation. The following example will help you to understand the process for balancing equations.

EXAMPLE 1

Calculate the weight of a single cat, assuming each cat is identical.

Solution

$C + C + C$ *or* $3C$	**Write the LHS as an expression**
$C + 10$	**Write the RHS as an expression**
$3C = C + 10$	**Write a balanced equation where LHS = RHS**
$3C - C = C + 10 - C$	**Remove a cat from each side**
$2C = 10$	**Simplify both sides of the equation**

If two cats weigh 10 kg, we can divide across by 2 to get the weight of one cat:

$$\frac{2C}{2} = \frac{10}{2}$$

$$C = 5$$

A cat weighs 5 kg.

It is important that we check that our answer is correct.

On the LHS of the puzzle, we had $5 + 5 + 5 = 15$.

On the RHS of the puzzle, we had $5 + 10 = 15$.

Both sides balance so $C = 5$ is correct.

Exercise 4.1

Solve each of the balancing puzzles below.

1. 

2.

3. 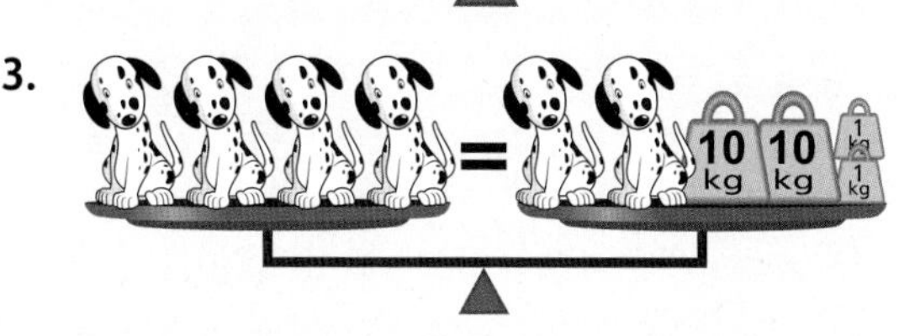

4. 5. 6. 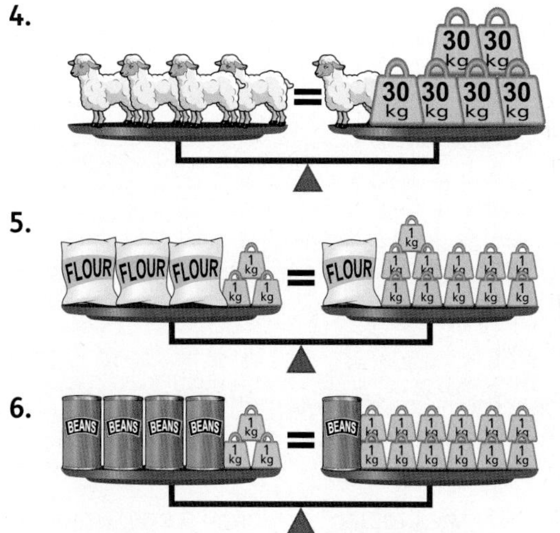

7.

Section 4.2: Linear equations

Student Activity 4B

1. Jane thinks of a number, and adds 5 to it. If the answer is 15, what number did Jane think of? Explain how you arrived at your answer.
2. Paul thinks of a number. He multiplies it by three and adds four. The number he arrives at is 25.
   (a) What number did Paul think of? Explain your answer fully.
   (b) How can you show that your answer is correct?
3. A number is multiplied by 4, and 6 is added to the result.
   (a) Write an expression to represent this information.
   (b) What was the value of the original number if the answer arrived at is 46? Explain your answer.
   (c) How can you show that your answer is correct?

LINEAR EQUATIONS EXPLAINED

In Section 4.1, you learned how to balance and solve picture equations. In algebra, an equation must always be balanced when we are solving it.

An equation is an algebraic expression equal to another expression. For example, $3x + 2 = 11$.

When solving an equation, use the following rules:

- **Add** the same number or variable to both sides of an equation.
- **Subtract** the same number or variable from both sides of an equation.
- **Multiply** both sides of an equation by the same number.
- **Divide** both sides of an equation by the same number.

You can perform any mathematical operation on an equation as long as the equation is kept balanced.

When you are asked to solve an equation in algebra, your final answer will always be in the form: a **letter** = a **number.**

For example, $x = 5$ or $a = -2$ or $t = 3\frac{1}{2}$.

EXAMPLE 2

Solve the following equation: $x - 21 = -5$

Solution

First say the problem in words: some number minus 21 gives an answer of −5.

$x - 21 = -5$	**Add 21 to both sides**
$x - 21 + 21 = -5 + 21$	**The equation is still balanced**
$x = 16$	**The equation is solved**

Check your solution:

$16 - 21 = -5$	
$-5 = -5$	**True, so the solution is correct**

EXAMPLE 3

Solve the following equation: $x + 14 = -20$

Solution

First say the problem in words: some number plus 14 gives an answer of −20.

$x + 14 = -20$	**Subtract 14 from both sides**
$x + 14 - 14 = -20 - 14$	**The equation is still balanced**
$x = -34$	**The equation is solved**

Check your solution:

$-34 + 14 = -20$	
$-20 = -20$	**True, so the solution is correct**

EXAMPLE 4

Solve the following equation: $\frac{x}{4} = 7$

Solution

First say the problem in words: some number divided by 4 gives an answer of 7.

$\frac{x}{4} = \frac{7}{1}$	**Multiply both sides by 4, to remove the denominators**
$\frac{(x)4}{4} = \frac{7(4)}{1}$	**The equation is still balanced**
$x = 28$	**The equation is solved**

Check your solution:

$\frac{28}{4} = 7.$	
$7 = 7$	**True, so the solution is correct**

EXAMPLE 5

Solve the following equation: $7x = -21$

Solution

First say the problem in words: some number multiplied by 7 gives an answer of −21.

$7x = -21$	**Divide both sides by 7**
$\frac{7x}{7} = \frac{-21}{7}$	**The equation is still balanced**
$x = -3$	**The equation is solved**

Check your solution:

$7(-3) = -21$	
$-21 = -21$	**True, so the solution is correct**

EXAMPLE 6

Solve the following equation:
$5x + 7 = 37$

Solution

First say the problem in words: 5 times some number plus 7 gives an answer of 37.

$5x + 7 = 37$

$5x + 7 - \mathbf{7} = 37 - \mathbf{7}$ **Subtract 7 from both sides**

$5x = 30$

$\frac{5x}{\mathbf{5}} = \frac{30}{\mathbf{5}}$ **Divide both sides by 5**

$x = 6$

Check your solution:

$5(6) + 7 = 37$

$30 + 7 = 37$

$37 = 37$ **True, so solution is correct**

EXAMPLE 7

Solve the following equation: $\frac{x}{3} - 9 = 4$

Solution

First say the problem in words: 9 is subtracted from one-third of a number to give an answer of 4.

$\frac{x}{3} - 9 = 4$

$\frac{x}{3} - 9 \mathbf{+ 9} = 4 \mathbf{+ 9}$ **Add 9 to both sides**

$\frac{x}{3} = 13$ **Multiply both sides by 3, to remove the denominator**

$\frac{x(\mathbf{3})}{3} = 13(\mathbf{3})$ **Tidy up the equation**

$x = 39$

Check your solution:

$\frac{39}{3} - 9 = 4$

$13 - 9 = 4$

$4 = 4$ **True, so solution is correct**

EXAMPLE 8

Solve the following equation: $8n - 3 = 2n + 21$

Solution

Say the problem in words:

- LHS: 8 times a number minus 3
- RHS: 2 times a number plus 21
- Both calculations give the same answer.

$8n - 3 = 2n + 21$

$8n - 3 \mathbf{- 2n} = 2n + 21 \mathbf{- 2n}$ **Subtract 2*n* from both sides of the equation**

$6n - 3 = 21$ **Tidy up**

$6n - 3 \mathbf{+ 3} = + 21 \mathbf{+ 3}$ **Add 3 to both sides of the equation**

$6n = 24$

$\frac{6n}{\mathbf{6}} = \frac{24}{\mathbf{6}}$ **Divide both sides by 6**

$n = 4$

Check your solution:

$8(4) - 3 = 2(4) + 21$

$32 - 3 = 8 + 21$

$29 = 29$ **True, so solution is correct**

EXAMPLE 9

Solve the following equation: $2(x - 2) = 3(x + 2)$

Solution

Say the problem in words:

- LHS: Subtract two from a number and then double the answer.
- RHS: Add two to a number and then triple the answer.
- Both calculations give the same answer.

$2(x-2) = 3(x+2)$ **Remove the brackets first**

$2x - 4 = 3x + 6$ **Multiply out the brackets**

$2x - 4 \mathbf{- 3x} = 3x \mathbf{- 3x} + 6$ **Subtract 3x from both sides**

$-1x - 4 = 6$

$-1x - 4 \mathbf{+ 4} = +6 \mathbf{+ 4}$ **Add 4 to both sides**

$-1x = 10$ **Multiply both sides by −1 to make x positive**

$x = -10$

Check your solution:

$2(-10 - 2) = 3(-10 + 2)$

$2(-12) = 3(-8)$

$-24 = -24$ **True, so solution is correct**

EXAMPLE 10

Paul thinks of a number and adds 4 to it. Niamh takes the same starting number and multiplies it by 3. If they both arrive at the same answer, what number did they both think of?

Solution

Call the number x:

Paul: $\mathbf{x + 4}$

Niamh: $\mathbf{3x}$

As they are both equal, we can form an equation:

$x + 4 = 3x$

$x + 4 \mathbf{- 3x} = 3x \mathbf{- 3x}$

$-2x + 4 \mathbf{- 4} = 0 \mathbf{- 4}$

$-2x = -4$

$\frac{-2x}{\mathbf{-2}} = \frac{-4}{\mathbf{-2}}$

$x = 2$

Check your answer:

Paul: $2 + 4 = 6$

Niamh: $3(2) = 6$

Exercise 4.2

1. Write the following sentences as mathematical expressions:
   (a) Three times a number plus six
   (b) Double a number minus five
   (c) Seventeen added to a number
   (d) Eighteen subtracted from four times a number
   (e) Eleven times a number plus fourteen
   (f) Add fourteen to a number and multiply the answer by eleven
   (g) Subtract ten from five times a number.
2. Write the following mathematical expressions in words:
   (a) $x - 4$
   (b) $2x + 5$
   (c) $4(d - 8)$
   (d) $5(4 - s) + 10$
   (e) $-1(g + 9)$
   (f) $3 + \left(\frac{u}{3} + 8\right)$
3. Write the following word problems as equations and, hence, find the number:
   (a) A number added to twelve gives an answer of fourteen.
   (b) A number added to minus seven gives an answer of twenty.
   (c) A number minus four gives an answer of six.

(d) A number subtracted from seventeen gives an answer of three.
(e) A number multiplied by five gives an answer of ten.
(f) A number multiplied by minus seven gives an answer of thirty-five.
(g) A number divided by five gives an answer of seven.
(h) A number divided by eleven gives an answer of minus four.
(i) A number doubled gives an answer of thirty-six.
(j) A number halved gives an answer of twenty-three.
(k) A number multiplied by one-third gives an answer of nine.
(l) A number tripled gives an answer of thirty-three.

4. Write the following equations as word problems and, hence, find the value of the letter:

(a)	$x + 8 = 14$	(f)	$14 = f - 8$
(b)	$a + 6 = 12$	(g)	$2d = 20$
(c)	$7 + c = 11$	(h)	$5g = -30$
(d)	$x - 5 = 16$	(i)	$\frac{x}{3} = 10$
(e)	$b - 11 = -5$	(j)	$\frac{h}{6} = -4$

5. Solve each of the following equations and verify your answers:

(a)	$x - 6 = -5$	(i)	$x + 10 = -11$
(b)	$4w = 24$	(j)	$-t - 13 = -13$
(c)	$11 = 4 + c$	(k)	$5 - s = -17$
(d)	$3 = 3 - k$	(l)	$-3 - x = 6$
(e)	$p + 19 = 29$	(m)	$-7 - f = -9$
(f)	$x - 7 = -21$	(n)	$-9 + e = 10$
(g)	$3 - q = 4$	(o)	$r - 15 = 15$
(h)	$12 - y = 24$	(p)	$f - 8 = -2$

6. Solve each of the following equations and verify your answers:

(a)	$5x = 100$	(k)	$11x = -121$
(b)	$7a = 35$	(l)	$-6k = -36$
(c)	$6x = 72$	(m)	$-12x = 72$
(d)	$-7b = -14$	(n)	$-5p = -45$
(e)	$6c = -18$	(o)	$-13z = -39$
(f)	$-21 = -3p$	(p)	$-14t = 56$
(g)	$-5x = 25$	(q)	$-20e = -120$
(h)	$-7f = 49$	(r)	$19a = -57$
(i)	$8x = -24$	(s)	$-3h = 153$
(j)	$5g = -35$	(t)	$-8k = 64$

7. Solve each of the following equations and verify your answers:

(a)	$4a + 9 = 21$	(k)	$4y + 3 = -15 + y$
(b)	$5a - 8 = 27$	(l)	$2x + 25 = -75$
(c)	$4a - 5 = 7$	(m)	$5x + 14 = 24$
(d)	$3x + 19 = 31$	(n)	$2y - 10 = -50$
(e)	$2x + 30 = 50$	(o)	$10 - 2a = 6$
(f)	$8a + 40 = 0$	(p)	$22 = 1 - 7a$
(g)	$7x - 10 = 74$	(q)	$17 - 3a = 20$
(h)	$4x + 10 = 90$	(r)	$3x + 10 = -35$
(i)	$5x + 15 = 75$	(s)	$50 - 2x = -34$
(j)	$2x + 7 = 13$	(t)	$-16 - 7x = -65$

8. Solve each of the following equations and verify your answers:

(a) $4n + 3 = 3n + 10$
(b) $11n + 22 = 8n + 55$
(c) $10n + 17 = n + 80$
(d) $2 + 12n = 6n + 44$
(e) $22n - 43 = n + 20$
(f) $4x + 3 = -x + 13$
(g) $4(10 - a) = 24$
(h) $5(a - 3) = 2(6 - 2a)$
(i) $6(8 - a) = 3(2a - 4)$
(j) $5(10 - 3a) = 4(2a + 1)$
(k) $2(c - 3) = c + 1$
(l) $3(n - 2) = n$
(m) $3(x + 6) = 2(x - 2)$
(n) $3(4a + 10) + 5(2a + 12) = 2$
(o) $2(2a + 4) - 3(a - 1) = 14$
(p) $2(2n + 2) + 3(n - 1) = 15$
(q) $4(3n + 7) + 3(5 - 2n) = 25$
(r) $3(2x - 1) + 4(3x - 4) - 1 = 5(3x - 1)$
(s) $2(3n + 2) - 2(2n - 1) = 8$
(t) $4(p - 4) = 2(2p - 11) - 2p + 8$

9. In a certain school in the Midlands, there are 150 students in third year. There are 10 more boys than there are girls in that year. How many girls are there and how many boys?

10. The other two angles in a right-angled triangle are $(4x - 25)°$ and $(x + 15)°$. Find the value of x.

11. Sam thinks of a number. He doubles this number, and then subtracts it from 100. His answer is 1 more than the number he first thought of. What number did he first think of?

12. Courtney is 2 years older than her brother, Robert. The sum of their ages is 30. How old is each of them?

13. A garden has four sides of length 7, $7 + 2a$, $3a$ and $5a - 4$. If 200 m of wire is needed to fence in the garden, calculate the value of a.

14. A triangle has the following angles: $(a + 40)°$, $(a - 20)°$ and $(2a)°$.

(a) Find the value of a.

(b) Check your solutions.

15. Aíne's mother is 24 years older than Aíne. In 6 years' time, Aíne's mother will be exactly four times as old as Aíne.

(a) Let y be Aíne's age now. Write an expression for Aíne's age in 6 years' time.

(b) Write an expression for Aíne's mother's age in 6 years' time.

(c) Hence, form an equation and solve it to find the value of y.

16. Clare thinks of a number. She first adds 4 to the number and then multiplies the result by 3. Mike thinks of the same starting number. He multiplies it by 5 and then subtracts 2. They both end up with the same answer. What number did they both think of?

17. John has some DVDs. Siobhán has 8 fewer than John. Let x stand for the number of DVDs that John has.

(a) Write an expression for the number of DVDs that Siobhán has.

(b) Write an expression in terms of x for the number of DVDs they have altogether.

(c) If they have 100 DVDs in total, use your expression from part (b) to write an equation in x.

(d) Solve the equation and calculate how many DVDs each owns.

18. An apple costs €a and an orange costs €0.20 more than an apple.

(a) Write down an expression for the cost of an orange.

(b) Write down an expression for the total cost of 2 apples and 1 orange.

(c) If the total cost of 2 apples and 1 orange is €4, use your expression from part (b) to form an equation in a.

(d) Solve the equation to find the cost of one apple.

Section 4.3: Linear equations involving fractions

Student Activity 4C

Paul thinks of a number and divides it by 7.

(a) If the answer is 4, what was the original number? Explain your answer.

(b) Write an equation to represent the information. (Hint: $\frac{?}{?} = ?$)

LINEAR EQUATIONS INVOLVING FRACTIONS EXPLAINED

In algebra, you will often meet problems that involve working with algebraic fractions. To solve these, use the following steps:

- **Step 1:** Insert brackets around each numerator.
- **Step 2:** Multiply each numerator by the LCM of all the denominators.
- **Step 3:** Simplify the fractions.
- **Step 4:** Multiply out any remaining brackets and simplify.

When finished, verify your answer by substituting the value into the starting equation. If correct, the LHS will be equal to the RHS.

EXAMPLE 11

Solve the following equation: $\frac{x+3}{4} = x - 6$

Solution

LCM of the denominators is 4.

$$\frac{x+3}{4} = \frac{x-6}{1}$$

$$\frac{\mathbf{4}(x+3)}{4} = \mathbf{4}(x-6)$$ **Multiply each side by 4 to remove the fraction**

$$x + 3 = 4x - 24$$

$$x + 3 \mathbf{- 4x} = 4x - 24 \mathbf{- 4x}$$ **Subtract 4*x* from both sides**

$$-3x + 3 = -24$$ **Simplify**

$$-3x + 3 \mathbf{- 3} = -24 \mathbf{- 3}$$ **Subtract 3 from both sides**

$$-3x = -27$$

$$\frac{-3x}{\mathbf{-3}} = \frac{-27}{\mathbf{-3}}$$ **Divide both sides by −3**

$$x = 9$$

Check your solution:

$$\frac{9+3}{4} = 9 - 6$$

$$\frac{12}{4} = 3$$

$$3 = 3$$ **True, so solution is correct**

EXAMPLE 12

Solve the following equation: $\frac{a+4}{5} = \frac{2a-8}{2}$

Solution

$$\frac{a+4}{5} = \frac{2a-8}{2}$$

LCM of the denominators is (5)(2).

$$\frac{\mathbf{(5)(2)}(a+4)}{5} = \frac{\mathbf{(5)(2)}(2a-8)}{2}$$ **Multiply across by (5)(2) and simplify the fractions**

$$\mathbf{2}(a+4) = \mathbf{5}(2a-8)$$ **Multiply the brackets**

$$2a + 8 = 10a - 40$$

$$2a - 10a = -40 - 8$$ **Letters on one side, numbers on the other side**

$$-8a = -48$$ **Tidy up**

$$\frac{-8a}{-8} = \frac{-48}{-8}$$ **Divide both sides by −8**

$$a = 6$$

Check your solution: $\frac{6+4}{5} = \frac{2(6)-8}{2}$

$$\frac{10}{5} = \frac{12-8}{2}$$

$$2 = \frac{4}{2}$$

$$= 2$$ **True, so solution is correct**

EXAMPLE 13

Solve the following equation: $\frac{1}{5}(4a+3) - \frac{1}{2}(3a-1) = \frac{1}{3}(-10a+27)$

Solution

$$\frac{1}{5}(4a+3) - \frac{1}{2}(3a-1) = \frac{1}{3}(-10a+27)$$ **Write each term as a fraction**

$$\frac{(4a+3)}{5} - \frac{(3a-1)}{2} = \frac{(-10a+27)}{3}$$

$$30\left(\frac{(4a+3)}{5}\right) - 30\left(\frac{(3a-1)}{2}\right) = 30\left(\frac{(-10a+27)}{3}\right)$$ **LCM for the denominators is 30**

$$6(4a+3) - 15(3a-1) = 10(-10a+27)$$

$$24a + 18 - 45a + 15 = -100a + 270$$

$$-21a + 33 = -100a + 270$$

$$-21a + 100a = -33 + 270$$

$$79a = 237$$

$$a = 3$$

Check your solution:

$$\frac{1}{5}(4(3)+3) - \frac{1}{2}(3(3)-1) = \frac{1}{3}(-10(3)+27)$$

$$\frac{1}{5}(12+3) - \frac{1}{2}(9-1) = \frac{1}{3}(-30+27)$$

$$\frac{1}{5}(15) - \frac{1}{2}(8) = \frac{1}{3}(-3)$$

$$3 - 4 = -1$$

$$-1 = -1$$ **True, so solution is correct**

Exercise 4.3

Solve each of the following equations:

1. $\frac{a+1}{2} = a - 2$
2. $\frac{a+2}{3} = a - 4$
3. $\frac{x+1}{3} = 4$
4. $\frac{x-3}{2} = 5$
5. $\frac{2x+17}{7} = 1$
6. $2 = \frac{3x-2}{5}$
7. $6 = \frac{x}{3}$
8. $12 = \frac{2x}{5}$
9. $\frac{5x+7}{4} = 2$
10. $14 = 6 + \frac{4x}{5}$
11. $7 = 3 - \frac{2x}{3}$
12. $11 = 5 - \frac{3x}{4}$
13. $\frac{x}{3} + 2 = 7$
14. $3 + \frac{2x}{5} = 11$
15. $5 - \frac{x}{2} = 2$
16. $10 - \frac{x}{6} = 8$
17. $12 = \frac{3x}{2} - 3$
18. $\frac{1}{3}(x) + 4 = 7$
19. $\frac{4x+1}{3} = 7$
20. $1\frac{1}{2} = \frac{1+x}{2}$
21. $\frac{12-x}{2} = 1$
22. $\frac{2x+1}{3} = \frac{1+x}{2}$
23. $\frac{2x+1}{3} + \frac{x-4}{2} = \frac{2}{3}$
24. $\frac{n-2}{4} + \frac{2n-7}{3} = \frac{5}{6}$
25. $\frac{12-11x}{6} + \frac{3x-5}{4} = 4$
26. $\frac{n-2}{3} + \frac{2n+3}{6} = \frac{5}{2}$
27. $\frac{2x+1}{3} + \frac{3x-1}{2} = 8\frac{1}{2}$
28. $\frac{x-1}{5} + \frac{x+1}{6} = 4$
29. $\frac{a+1}{3} + \frac{a-2}{4} = a - 6$
30. $\frac{3x+1}{5} - \frac{1}{2} = \frac{3}{2}$
31. $\frac{5-x}{3} - \frac{x-1}{4} = \frac{1}{6}$
32. $\frac{1-2x}{3} - \frac{1}{4} = \frac{1}{12}$
33. $\frac{1}{2}(3x+1) = \frac{1}{3}(5x+3)$
34. $\frac{(3x-1)}{4} + \frac{(8x+3)}{5} = \frac{(7x+1)}{3}$
35. $\frac{1}{5}(4n+1) = \frac{1}{8}(7n-2)$

CHAPTER 4 SELF-CHECK TEST

1. Write the following sentences as mathematical expressions:
(a) Three times a number plus ten
(b) Double a number minus six
(c) Seventeen added to five times a number
(d) Eight subtracted from ten times a number
(e) Six times a number plus fourteen
(f) A number is added to fourteen and the answer is multiplied by three

2. Write the following mathematical expressions as sentences:
(a) $x - 9$
(b) $3x + 1$
(c) $2(x - 5)$
(d) $3(7 - x) + 8$
(e) $-2(x + 4)$
(f) $2 + \left(\frac{x}{3} + 1\right)$

Solve each of the following equations. Remember to verify your answers.

3. $2a + 5 = 5a - 16$

4. $3(x + 4) - 2(x + 3) = 0$

5. $4(x - 1) = 5(2x + 4)$

6. $40 - a = 27$

7. $11 = 3a + 5$

8. $b + 12 = 4b$

9. $3b + 7 = 7b - 3$

10. $12 + 12n = 3n + 66$

11. $8n + 1 = 2n + 49$

12. $11n + 13 = 3n + 7$

13. $11n - 3 = 3n + 37$

14. $10(a + 3) = 18(4 - a)$

15. $4(10 - a) = 3(11 - a)$

16. $6(12 - 2a) = 8(a + 2)$

17. $3(2 - a) = 8(a - 2)$

18. $3(2x + 5) - 3(x - 1) = 6(4x - 4)$

19. $5(2x + 7) = 9(x - 2)$

20. $7(2b - 5) = 4b + 15$

21. $9(1 + a) = 4(11 - 4a)$

22. $5(n + 7) - 3(2n + 1) = 35$

23. $6(5 - x) - 2(3x - 1) = 2$

24. $6(a + 2) = 12(5 - 3a)$

25. $4(x - 5) = 3(x - 4)$

26. $3(1 + 2b) = 4(2 - b)$

27. $4(2 + d) = 5 - 2d$

28. $4(a + 1) = 5$

29. $\frac{5 + n}{2} = 1$

30. $\frac{n}{2} + 5 = 2$

31. $5 = \frac{5 + 2x}{3}$

32. $\frac{3x + 12}{4} = 6$

33. $\frac{1 - x}{4} = \frac{2 - 2x}{3}$

34. $\frac{2x + 1}{3} = \frac{1}{2}$

35. $4\frac{1}{2} = \frac{9 + 3x}{6}$

36. $\frac{7 + x}{2} = \frac{1 + x}{5}$

37. $\frac{x + 1}{2} - \frac{1}{3} = \frac{5}{3}$

38. $\frac{x + 1}{2} + \frac{x - 1}{4} = 4$

39. $\frac{3x}{4} = \frac{4x - 1}{5}$

40. $\frac{5x + 3}{4} - \frac{x}{2} = 6$

41. $\frac{2x + 6}{4} = \frac{x}{5}$

42. Seamus is w years old. Seamus' father is 30 years older than him.
(a) Write an expression for Seamus' father's age.

In 5 years' time, Seamus' father will be exactly 5 times as old as Seamus.

(b) Write an expression for Seamus' age in 5 years' time.
(c) Write an expression for Seamus' father's age in 5 years' time.
(d) Use the above information to form an equation to calculate Seamus' age.

43. Patrick's father is 30 years older than Patrick. In four years' time, Patrick's father will be exactly 3 times as old as Patrick.

(a) Using x to represent Patrick's present age, write an expression for his father's current age.

(b) Write an expression for Patrick's father's age in 4 years' time.

(c) Write an expression for Patrick's age in 4 years' time.

(d) Write an equation in x and solve for Patrick's present age.

44. In a triangle the three angles are the following sizes: $(2a)°$, $(a + 40)°$ and $(a - 20)°$. Write an equation to find the value of a.

45. Ciarán is twice as old as Bríd. 30 years ago, Ciarán was 12 times as old as Bríd. How old are they now?

46. In a triangle the three angles are the following sizes: $x°$, $(2x - 60)°$, and $(120 - x)°$. Find the value of x.

47. Conor spent €y on a book. He then spent €$(4y + 6)$ *on* a football jersey. In total, he spent €61.

(a) Write an equation in terms of y to represent this information.

(b) Solve your equation to find the value of y.

48. The temperature on Sunday is $x°$. The temperature rose by 3° each day for the next two days. The temperature then dropped by 4° each day for the next three days. Derive an expression in x for the temperature on the fifth day (Friday).

49. Lea drove from Town A to Town B, a distance of x km. She then drove from Town B to Town C, a distance of $(2x + 2)$ km. The total distance she drove was 56 km. Find the value of x, correct to the nearest kilometre.

50. Shane is x years old. Eileen is three years younger than Shane.

(a) Find Eileen's age in terms of x.

(b) If the sum of Shane's age and Eileen's age is 47, write an equation in terms of x to represent this information.

(c) Solve the equation that you formed in part (b) above for x.

(d) When Eileen is $2x + 5$ years old, find the sum of Shane's age and Eileen's age.

CHAPTER 4 KNOWLEDGE CHECKLIST

After completing this chapter, I now:

- Know how to balance a linear equation
- Know how to solve linear equations
- Know how to solve linear equations involving algebraic fractions
- Know how to solve problems involving linear equations

Challenge

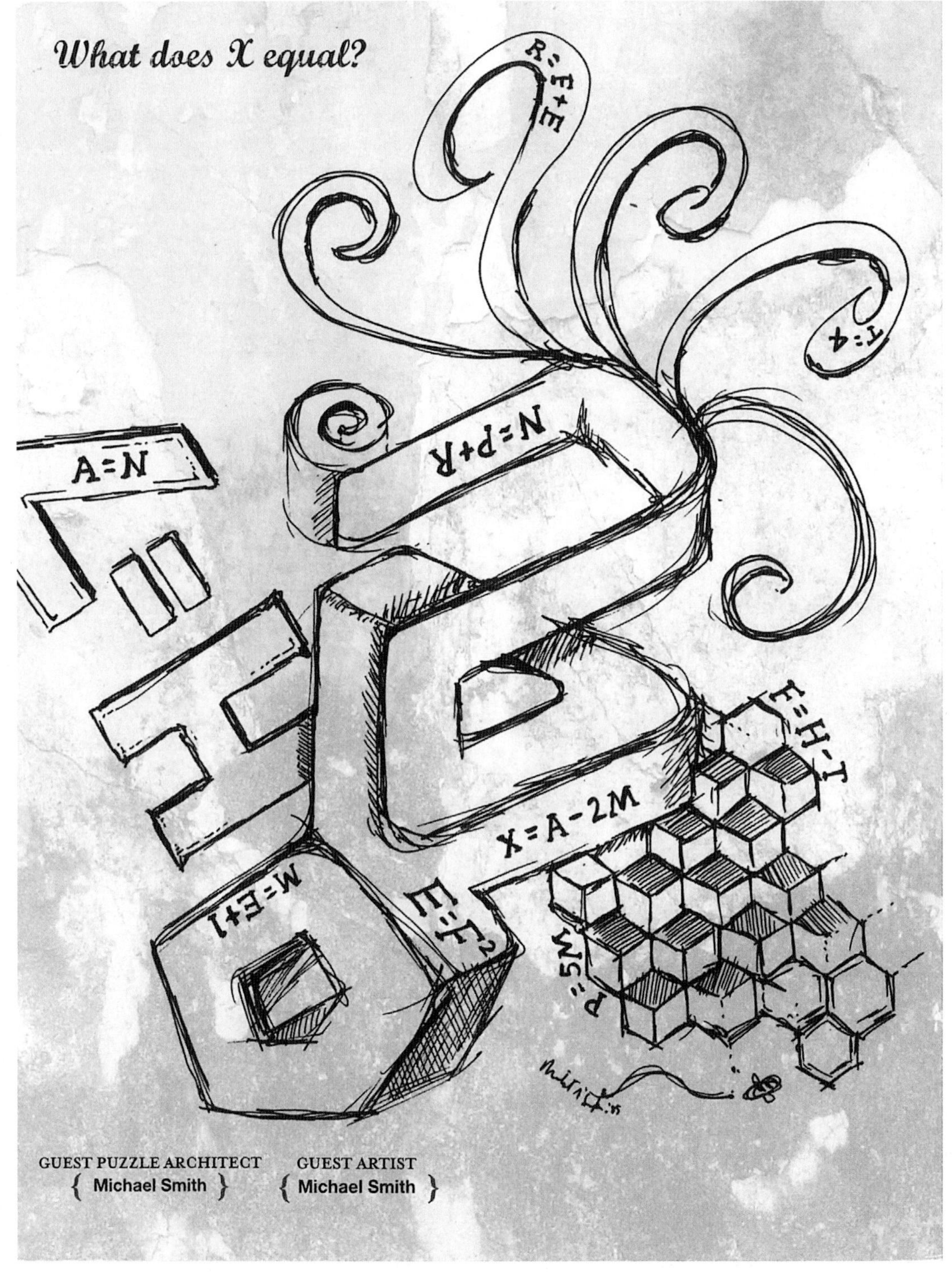
What does X equal?
R=E+E
T=4
N=P+R
A=N
E=H-T
X=A-2M
M=E+1
$E=F^2$
P=5M
GUEST PUZZLE ARCHITECT
{ Michael Smith }
GUEST ARTIST
{ Michael Smith }

LINEAR RELATIONSHIPS AND FUNCTIONS

KEY WORDS

- Codomain
- Common difference
- Domain
- Function
- General term
- Input
- Linear pattern
- Mapping
- Output
- Point of intersection
- Range
- *x*-intercept
- *y*-intercept

LEARNING OUTCOMES

In this chapter you will learn:

- ✓ To identify a pattern
- ✓ To identify, name and draw linear patterns
- ✓ To describe a linear pattern using a general formula
- ✓ To understand the terms associated with graphs and functions such as domain, codomain, range and *y*-intercept
- ✓ To use function notation and to interpret linear graphs
- ✓ To find solutions to problems of the form $f(x) = g(x)$ and to interpret these results
- ✓ To apply all the above to real-life situations

INTRODUCTION

The world is full of interesting patterns and designs that we see every day. From patterns on a shell to the complex camouflage of certain animals, patterns play a very important role in the world.

Many patterns and designs can be modelled using mathematical sequences. In this chapter, you will begin to examine some of these patterns around us.

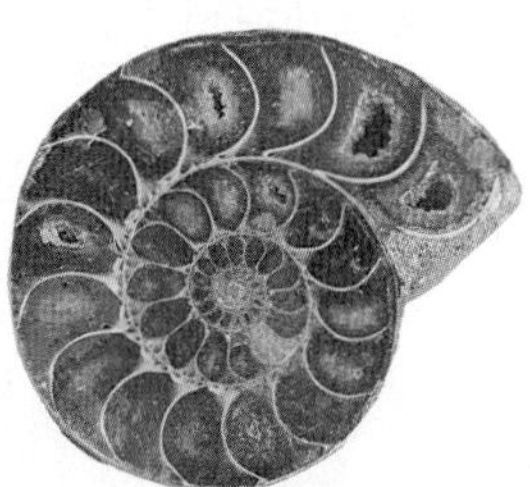

Section 5.1: Patterns

Student Activity 5A

1. Síle is making friendship bracelets for her friends using different coloured beads.

She decides to make a unique bracelet for each of her friends. Examine the bracelets shown and predict the colour of the next three beads in each bracelet.

(a) ●●●●●●●???

(b) ●●●●●●●●???

(c) ●●○●●●○●●???

(d) ●●●●●●●???

(e) ●○●●●●○●●???

2. Paul and Shay are playing a game by forming a pattern using letters. Examine the patterns and predict the next three letters in each pattern.
   (a) A, C, E, G, I, A, C, E, ?, ?, ?
   (b) B, B, C, D, D, B, B, C, ?, ?, ?
   (c) X, X, X, Y, X, X, X, Y, ?, ?, ?
   (d) S, S, T, V, P, S, S, T, V, ?, ?, ?
   (e) H, A, P, P, Y, H, A, P, ?, ?, ?

3. (a) Explain in your own words what a pattern is.
   (b) Can you identify three patterns around you?
   (c) Explain why patterns are useful.

4. A repeating pattern is made up of the following shapes:

If the pattern continued, what shape would:
   (a) The 10th shape be?
   (b) The 36th shape be?
   (c) The 70th shape be?
   (d) The 6,000th shape be?
   (e) Explain in words how you calculated each of the answers.

5. (a) Determine the next three values in the following number sequences.
   (b) Explain what rule you used to determine your answers.
      (i) 11, 11, 9, 9, 7, 7, 5, ?, ?, ?
      (ii) 31, 28, 25, 22, 19, 16, 13, ?, ?, ?
      (iii) −2, −2, −5, −5, −8, −8, −11, −11, ?, ?, ?
      (iv) 50, 65, 80, 95, 110, 125, 140, ?, ?, ?
      (v) 2, 36, 70, 104, 138, 172, 206, ?, ?, ?

PATTERNS EXPLAINED

A pattern is a set of numbers, letters, colours, objects or images that repeat at various intervals. A pattern obeys some mathematical rule to create a predictable sequence. Every day, we are surrounded by patterns in nature and in designs such as wallpaper and clothes.

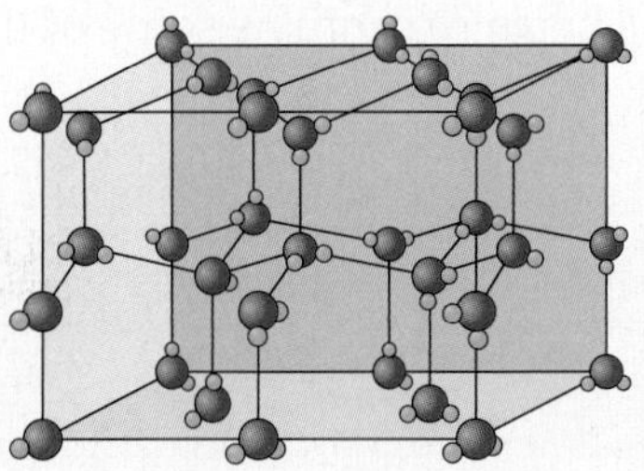

To understand any pattern, we need to carefully study the sequence. Starting at the beginning, we must determine if the pattern is increasing or decreasing by some numerical value or whether the pattern is repeating itself at regular intervals.

For example, if we study the following sequence of numbers we will notice an obvious pattern: 1, 3, 5, 7, 9, ...

The numbers are increasing in value by two each time.

Some patterns can be more complex:

5, 2, 7, 4, 9, 6, 11, 8, 13, ...

This numerical pattern first decreases by 3 and then increases by 5. The pattern repeats in this way. So, if we want to find the next two terms, we subtract 3 to get the next term and then add 5 to find the term after that:

5, 2, 7, 4, 9, 6, 11, 8, 13, **minus three, add 5.**

This gives: 5, 2, 7, 4, 9, 6, 11, 8, 13, **10, 15.**

To understand any **repeating pattern,** we need to carefully study the sequence. Starting at the beginning, we must determine where the pattern block starts and identify where the pattern repeats itself. Examine the following sequence of letters:

A, B, C, D, E, A, B, C, D, E, A, B, C, D, E, A, B, C, D, E, ...

Notice that it consists of blocks:

A, B, C, D, E,	A, B, C, D, E,	**A, B, C, D, E,**	**A, B, C, D, E**
Block 1	Block 2	**Block 3**	**Block 4**

The letters in this sequence repeat after every block of 5 letters. Each letter in a block can be called a **term,** which follows its own particular pattern. The first letter or term in each block is always an **A,** the second term is the letter **B,** the third term is **C** which is followed by the letter **D** and finally the block always ends with the letter **E.**

Once we have identified the pattern in the sequence, we can identify any later term without having to list or draw out the pattern.

x=y EXAMPLE 1

(a) In the following number sequence:

$-66, -32, 2, 36, 70, 104, 138, 172, 206, ?, ?, ?$

(i) Determine the next three values.

(ii) Explain what rule you used to determine your answers.

Solution

(a) (i) $-66, -32, 2, 36, 70, 104, 138, 172, 206, 240, 274, 308$

(ii) Each term in the sequence is increasing by 34.

(b) Study the following pattern:

A, B, C, D, E, F, A, B, C, D, E, F, A, B, C, D, E, F, A, B, C, D, E, F, ...

If the pattern continued, what letter would:

(i) Term 21 be? (ii) Term 25 be? (iii) Term 518 be?

Solution

(b) The pattern is made up of the following blocks of 6 terms:

A, B, C, D, E, F **A, B, C, D, E, F** **A, B, C, D, E, F** **A, B, C, D, E, F**

Block 1 **Block 2** **Block 3** **Block 4**

Each block of terms can be put in the following table:

Term	1	2	3	4	5	6
Letter	A	B	C	D	E	F

(i) To determine what letter would be the 21st term, we do the following:

$21 \div 6 = 3$, with a remainder of 3.

This means 21 consists of 3 repeating blocks and 3 extra letters. The remainder of 3 corresponds with the letter C.

(ii) To determine what letter would be the 25th term, we do the following:

$25 \div 6 = 4$, with a remainder of 1. This means 25 consists of 4 repeating blocks and 1 extra letter. The remainder of one corresponds with the letter A.

(iii) Therefore, we find the 518th as follows:

$518 \div 6 = 86$, with a remainder of 2. This means 518 consists of 86 repeating blocks and 2 extra letters. The remainder of two corresponds with the letter B.

EXAMPLE 2

If the pattern continued, what colour would each of the following blocks be?

(a) The 19th block (b) The 39th block (c) The 270th block (d) The 6,000th block

Solution

The pattern is made up of the following blocks of 9 terms, which can be put in the following table:

Term	1	2	3	4	5	6	7	8	9
Colour	Red	Red	Yellow	Green	Green	Yellow	Blue	Blue	Yellow

(a) What colour would the 19th term be?

$19 \div 9 = 2$, with a remainder of one. This means 19 consists of 2 repeating blocks and 1 extra colour. The remainder of one corresponds with the colour red.

(b) What colour would the 39th term be?

$39 \div 9 = 4$, with a remainder of three. This means 39 consists of 4 repeating blocks and 3 extra colours. The remainder of three corresponds with the colour yellow.

(c) What colour would the 270th term be?

$270 \div 9 = 30$, with a remainder of zero. This means 270 consists of 30 repeating blocks and 0 extra colours. The remainder of zero corresponds with the ninth colour yellow, since it has an entire block.

(d) What colour would the 6,000th term be?

$6{,}000 \div 9 = 666$, with a remainder of six. This means 6,000 consists of 666 repeating blocks and 6 extra colours. The remainder of six corresponds with the sixth colour yellow.

Exercise 5.1

1. Complete the following patterns:
   (a)
   (b)
   (c)
   (d)
   (e)
   (f)
   (g)
   (h)
   (i)

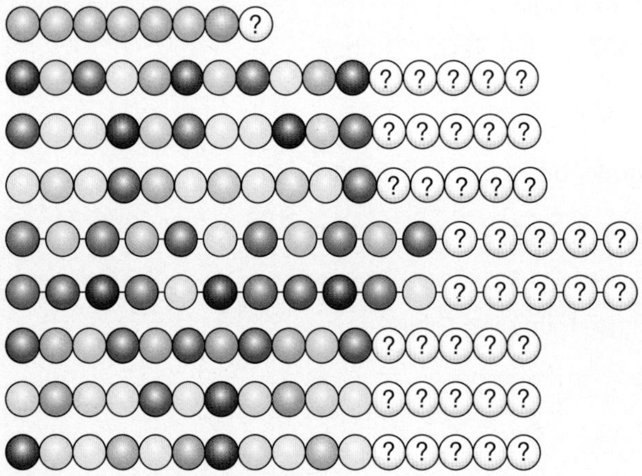

2. Complete the following patterns:
   (a)
   (b)
   (c)
   (d)
   (e)

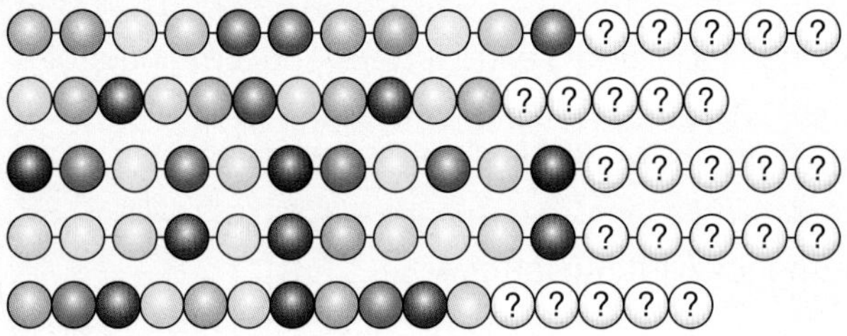

3. (a) Complete the following patterns.
   What image would be in the:
   (b) 19th box?
   (c) 45th box?
   (d) 100th box?
   (i)
   (ii)
   (iii)
   (iv)
   (v)
   (vi)
   (vii)
   (viii)
   (ix)
   (x)

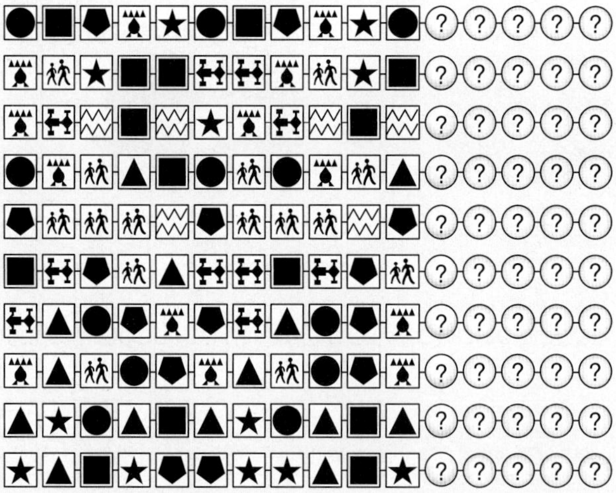

4. (a) Complete the following patterns.
   What number would be in:
   (b) the 50th box?
   (c) the 120th box?
   (d) the 999th box?

(i)	8	7	1	7	5	8	7	1	7	5	8	?	?	?	?	?	?
(ii)	0	7	6	6	6	0	7	6	6	6	0	?	?	?	?	?	?
(iii)	8	0	2	2	2	0	8	0	2	2	2	?	?	?	?	?	?
(iv)	8	8	8	8	8	8	8	8	8	8	8	?	?	?	?	?	?

(v)	6	3	1	8	7	7	6	3	1	8	7	?	?	?	?	?
(vi)	3	6	2	2	4	5	6	3	6	2	2	?	?	?	?	?
(vii)	1	7	3	0	8	8	4	1	7	3	0	?	?	?	?	?
(viii)	8	1	1	1	6	0	8	1	1	1	6	?	?	?	?	?

5. Complete the next three patterns:

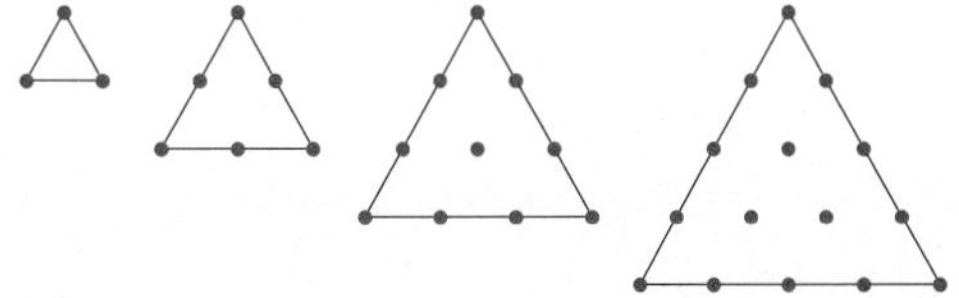

6. In the following number sequences:

(a) Determine the next three values.

(b) Explain what rule you used to determine your answers.

(i) 8, 8, 11, 14, 14, 17, 20, 20, 23, ?, ?, ?

(ii) 7, 10, 13, 16, 19, 22, 25, 28, 31, ?, ?, ?

(iii) 20, 35, 50, 65, 80, 95, 110, 125, 140, ?, ?, ?

(iv) −7, −7, −5, −3, −3, −1, 1, 1, 3, ?, ?, ?

(v) 33, 31, 29, 27, 25, 23, 21, 19, 17, ?, ?, ?

(vi) 10, 10, 7, 4, 4, 1, −2, −2, −5, ?, ?, ?

(vii) 11, 12, 13, 14, 15, 16, 17, 18, 19, ?, ?, ?

(viii) 6, 8, 10, 12, 14, 16, 18, 20, 22, ?, ?, ?

(ix) −3, −3, −2, −1, −1, 0, 1, 1, 2, ?, ?, ?

(x) 3, 2, 1, 0, −1, −2, −3, −4, −5, ?, ?, ?

(xi) 85945, 17189, 17195, 3439, 3445, 689, 695, 139, 145, ?, ?, ?

(xii) 2, 7, 8, 13, 14, 19, 20, 25, 26, ?, ?, ?

(xiii) 9, 45, 38, 190, 183, 915, 908, 4540, 4533, ?, ?, ?

(xiv) 9, 10, 11, 12, 13, 14, 15, 16, 17, ?, ?, ?

(xv) 7, 21, 14, 42, 35, 105, 98, 294, 287, ?, ?, ?

(xvi) 195, 180, 165, 150, 135, 120, 105, 90, 75, ?, ?, ?

(xvii) 25, 23, 21, 19, 17, 15, 13, 11, 9, ?, ?, ?

(xviii) 37, 34, 31, 28, 25, 22, 19, 16, 13, ?, ?, ?

(xix) 13, 13, 11, 11, 9, 9, 7, 7, 5, ?, ?, ?

(xx) −2, 10, 1, 13, 4, 16, 7, 19, 10, ?, ?, ?

Section 5.2: Linear number patterns

Student Activity 5B

1. Examine each of the following patterns and predict the next three numbers in each.

(a) −13, −8, −3, 2, 7, 12, ?, ?, ?

(b) 12, 5, −2, −9, −16, ?, ?, ?

(c) 91, 79, 67, 55, 43, ?, ?, ?

(d) 13.5, 25.7, 37.9, 50.1, ?, ?, ?

(e) 78.3, 62.6, 46.9, 31.2, ?, ?, ?

2. Julia earns €2.00 an hour for her first hour of work; €4.00 for her second hour; €6.00 for her third hour and so on. How much money will she earn for her tenth hour of work?

3. Ciarán is constantly improving in his maths tests. On his first test he scored 52%, on the next three tests he scored 55%, 58% and 61%. If he keeps improving at the same rate, how many more tests must he take before he will score 100%.

LINEAR NUMBER PATTERNS EXPLAINED

A sequence is a set of numbers that follow a pattern. We call each number in any sequence a **term.** The starting number of any pattern is called the first term, written as T_1. The next number is the second term (T_2), which is followed by the third term (T_3) and so on. In Student Activity 5B, we examined a special type of sequence called a **linear pattern.**

A **linear pattern** is a sequence of numbers that increases or decreases by the same value.

A linear pattern is found by adding or subtracting the same value from one term to the next. We call this value the **'first change'** or the **'common difference'.** It is represented by the letter ***d***. The common difference is sometimes called the **first difference.**

The following is an increasing linear pattern: 1, 4, 7, 10, 13, 16, 19, ...

Looking carefully, you can see that each term is found by adding 3 to the previous term. This is the common difference between any term and the previous term.

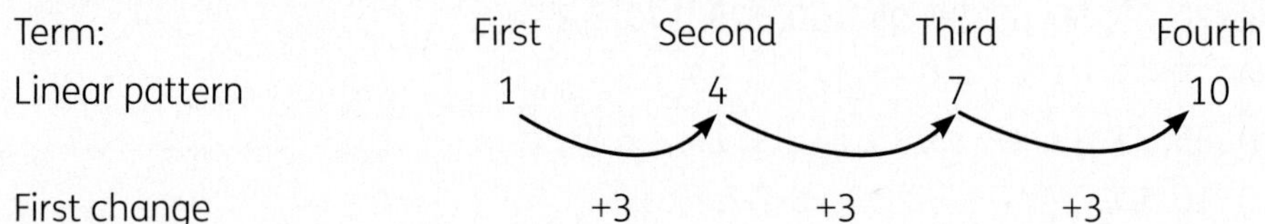

Term:	First	Second	Third	Fourth
Linear pattern	1	4	7	10
First change	+3	+3	+3	

The following is a decreasing linear pattern: 70, 62, 54, 46, 38, ...

This time, to find each term, we subtract 8. This is the common difference from the previous term.

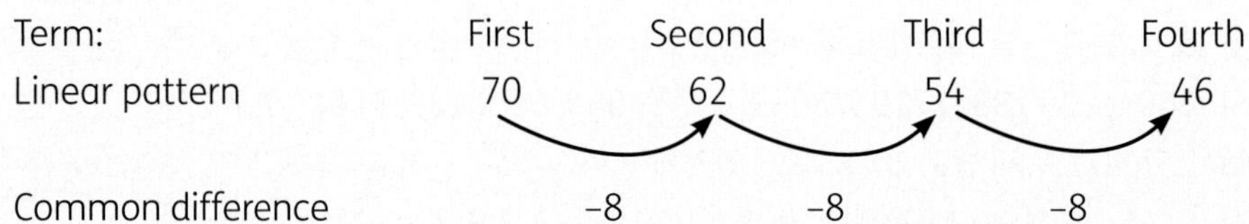

Term:	First	Second	Third	Fourth
Linear pattern	70	62	54	46
Common difference	−8	−8	−8	

When describing a sequence, it is normal practice to use T_n to represent any term in the sequence.

Common difference or first change = $T_2 - T_1$

EXAMPLE 3

(a) Investigate whether the following are linear patterns:

(i) 2, 4, 8, 16, 32, 64, ...

(ii) 0.7, −2.8, −6.3, −9.8, −13.3, ...

(iii) $\frac{1}{2}, 1\frac{1}{3}, 2\frac{1}{6}, 3, 3\frac{5}{6}, 4\frac{2}{3}, \ldots$

Solution

(a) (i) 2, 4, 8, 16, 32, 64, ... is not a linear pattern since there is no common difference.

(ii) 0.7, −2.8, −6.3, −9.8, −13.3, ... is a linear pattern since the common difference is −3.5.

(iii) $\frac{1}{2}, 1\frac{1}{3}, 2\frac{1}{6}, 3, 3\frac{5}{6}, 4\frac{2}{3}, \ldots$ is a linear pattern since the common difference is $\frac{5}{6}$.

(b) Write down (i) the first four terms in the following pattern and (ii) evaluate the common difference when given the following general term: $T_n = 5n - 7$.

Solution

(b) (i) The first four terms in the following pattern are found by substituting $n = 1, 2, 3$ and 4 into the general term.

$T_n = 5n - 7$

$T_1 = 5(1) - 7 = -2$

$T_2 = 5(2) - 7 = 3$

$T_3 = 5(3) - 7 = 8$

$T_4 = 5(4) - 7 = 13$

The first four terms in the pattern are −2, 3, 8, 13

(ii) The common difference is $T_2 - T_1 = 3 - (-2) = 5$

Exercise 5.2

1. Investigate whether the following are linear patterns. Give reasons for your answers.

(a) 1, 1, 2, 3, 5, 8, 13, 21, ...
(b) 22, 45, 68, 91, 114, ...
(c) 17, 27, 38, 50, ...
(d) 67, 45, 24, 4, ...
(e) 89, 92, 95, 98, ...
(f) 61, 48, 35, 22, ...
(g) 73.5, 67.7, 61.9, 56.1, ...
(h) 34.7, 29.1, 23.5, 17.9, ...
(i) 15.9, 3.7, −7.8, −18.6, −28.7, ...
(j) −35, −47, −59, −71, −83, ...

2. For each of the following linear patterns:

(a) Identify the first term.
(b) Find the first change.
(c) Write the next three terms in the sequence.

(i) 11, 22, 33, 44, 55, ...
(ii) 4, 9, 14, 19, 24, ...
(iii) 19, 12, 5, −2, −9, ...
(iv) 63, 57, 51, 45, 39, ...
(v) 51, 38, 25, 12, −1, ...
(vi) 27, 42, 57, 72, 87, ...
(vii) 112, 175, 238, 301, 364, ...
(viii) −71, −93, −115, −137, −159, ...
(ix) −56, −34, −12, 10, 32, ...
(x) 18, −11, −40, −69, −98, ...

3. Fill in the missing terms in the following linear patterns:

(a)

1st term	2nd term	3rd term	4th term	5th term	6th term
−18	−60				

(b)

1st term	2nd term	3rd term	4th term	5th term	6th term
		34	51		

(c)

1st term	2nd term	3rd term	4th term	5th term	6th term
	17		43		

(d)

1st term	2nd term	3rd term	4th term	5th term	6th term
		84			3

(e)

1st term	2nd term	3rd term	4th term	5th term	6th term
11					51

4. For each of the following, find the first five terms of each of the linear patterns if:
(a) The first term is 3 and the common difference is 6.
(b) The first term is 9 and the common difference is 20.
(c) The first term is −6 and the common difference is 9.
(d) The first term is −13 and the common difference is 14.
(e) The first term is 56 and the common difference is −7.
(f) The first term is 24 and the common difference is −11.
(g) The first term is −29 and the common difference is −23.
(h) The first term is −16 and the common difference is −6.
(i) The first term is 22 and the common difference is −110.
(j) The first term is −51 and the common difference is −8.

5. Write down the first four terms in the following patterns and find the common difference:
(a) $T_n = 4n - 3$
(b) $T_n = 3n + 1$
(c) $T_n = 4n - 9$
(d) $T_n = 2n - 1$
(e) $T_n = 5n - 3$
(f) $T_n = 2(3 - n)$
(g) $T_n = 2 - 4n$
(h) $T_n = 4n + 3$
(i) $T_n = 3n + 2$
(j) $T_n = 5n - 2$

6. The following are the first three terms in a linear pattern. Find the value of x.
(a) $-x - 2, 11, 4x$
(b) $3x, 2x, 3 - x$
(c) $2x - 1, 2x + 1, 3x$
(d) $x + 3, 15, x + 1$
(e) $3x - 5, 3x, 5x + 5$
(f) $2x + 1, 4x - 3, 4x + 1$

7. Colm has been making patterns with some different-sized T-shapes.

(a) Can you draw the next two patterns?
(b) Explain how you found the patterns.

8. Aoife has been making tiling patterns. Aoife's 1st, 3rd and 6th patterns are shown below.

(a) Copy and complete the following table:

Number of red tiles	1	2	3	4	5	6	7	8
Number of blue tiles	8							

(b) If there were 20 red tiles, how many blue tiles will be required?
(c) If there were 50 blue tiles, how many red tiles will be required?
(d) Describe in words how the pattern is growing.

9. Michelle is constantly improving in her science tests. On her first test, she scored 50 marks, on her second she scored 53 marks and her third she scored 56 marks. If her marks continue to increase in this linear pattern, how many marks will she get in her 11th test?

10. Aidan recorded the different times commercials were shown on the television shopping channel. Different commercials were shown at 7:23, 7:38, 7:53 and 8:08.
(a) Can you predict when the next four commercials will be shown?
(b) Explain the reasons for your answers.

Section 5.3: Finding the general term of a linear sequence

Student Activity 5C

Study the following sequence of blocks:

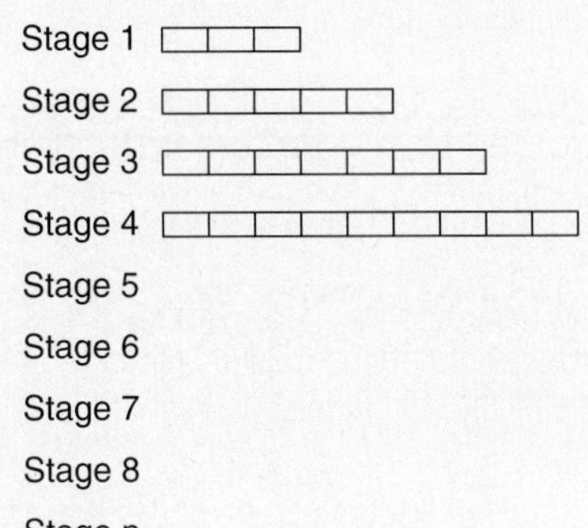

(a) On graph paper, construct the next sequences of blocks.

(b) Can you describe in words the growth pattern of the blocks?

(c) Can you write in words a formula to describe the linear growth pattern of the blocks?

(d) Copy the following graph and plot a point to show the number of blocks used in each pattern:

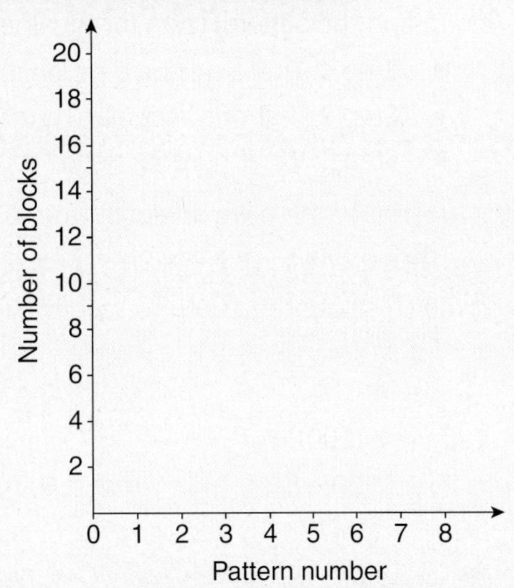

(e) What pattern is formed when the dots are joined using a straight edge?

(f) Using letters, try to write a formula to find the number of blocks in any pattern. Clearly explain what each letter stands for.

FINDING THE GENERAL TERM OF A LINEAR SEQUENCE EXPLAINED

In Student Activity 5C, you examined a pattern that grew in a linear fashion. By plotting the pattern on graph paper, we can clearly see it forms a line. Every linear pattern is based on a general algebraic expression.

To find the general rule for any term in a linear pattern:

- **Step 1:** Find the value of *d*, the common difference in the sequence.
- **Step 2:** Part of the general term is the 'difference times *n*' where *n* is the term number we are looking for.
- **Step 3:** Finally determine what number needs to be added (or subtracted) to the 'difference times *n*' to get the first term.

$$T_n = (d)(n) \pm \text{some number}$$

EXAMPLE 4

Examine the following linear pattern and then answer the questions:

3, 12, 21, 30, 39, ...

(a) Find the common difference *d*.

(b) Find the general term for the linear sequence.

(c) Calculate the 100th term in the linear pattern.

Solution

(a)

Term	First	Second	Third	Fourth	Fifth
Linear pattern	3	12	21	30	39
First change		+9	+9	+9	+9

The first difference or the value of d is +9.

(b) To find the general term for the linear sequence, follow the relevant steps:

- Step 1: The common difference in the sequence is +9.
- Step 2: Part of the general term is $9n$.
- Step 3: What number needs to be added or subtracted to $T_n = 9n$ to get the first term?

$T_1 = 9(1) = 9$, so we must subtract 6 to get the first term of 3.

The general term is $T_n = 9n - 6$

(c) To calculate the 100th term in the linear sequence, just substitute 100 in for n in the general term.

$T_n = 9n - 6$

$T_{100} = 9(100) - 6$

$T_{100} = 900 - 6$

$T_{100} = 894$

EXAMPLE 5

Find the general term for the following linear sequence: 90, 79, 68, 57, 46, ...

Solution

- Step 1: The common difference in the sequence is −11.
- Step 2: Part of the general term is $-11n$.
- Step 3: What number needs to be added to or subtracted from $T_n = -11n$ to get the first term?

$T_1 = -11(1) = -11$, so we must add 101 to get the first term of 90.

The general term is $T_n = -11n + 101$ or $T_n = 101 - 11n$.

EXAMPLE 6

The *nth* term of a sequence is given by $T_n = 5n - 7$. Which term of the sequence is equal to 58?

Solution

Let $T_n = 58$

$5n - 7 = 58$

$5n = 58 + 7$

$5n = 65$

$n = \frac{65}{5}$

$n = 13$

Therefore 58 is the 13th term of the sequence.

Exercise 5.3

1. For each of the following linear patterns:

(a) Identify the first term.

(b) Find the first change.

(c) Write as an algebraic expression the formula for the general term.

(d) Hence, evaluate the 21st term in the sequence.

(i) 5, 10, 15, 20, 25, 30, ...

(ii) 2, 4, 6, 8, 10, 12, ...

(iii) 1, 3, 5, 7, 9, 11, 13, ...

(iv) 100, 90, 80, 70, 60, ...

(v) 88, 77, 66, 55, 44, 33, ...

(vi) 55, 41, 27, 13, −1, −15, ...

(vii) 95, 70, 45, 20, −5, −30, ...

(viii) 14, 26, 38, 50, 62, 74, ...

(ix) −27, −42, −57, −72, −87, ...

(x) −33, −7, 19, 45, 71, ...

(xi) 75, 57, 39, 21, 3, −15, ...

(xii) 3.7, 9.9, 16.1, 22.3, 28.5, ...

(xiii) −108, −117.9, −127.8, −137.7, ...

(xiv) $\frac{1}{2}, 1\frac{1}{4}, 2, 2\frac{3}{4}, 3\frac{1}{2}, 4\frac{1}{4}, \ldots$

(xv) $\frac{42}{5}, \frac{36}{5}, \frac{30}{5}, 4\frac{4}{5}, 3\frac{3}{5}, \ldots$

2. Examine the following linear pattern and then answer the questions: 55, 26, −3, −32, ...

(a) Find the first term in the sequence.

(b) Find the first change *d*.

(c) Write down the next three terms in the sequence.

(d) Describe the sequence in your own words.

(e) Use the information above to complete the following table:

1st term	2nd term	3rd term	4th term	5th term	6th term	7th term	8th term	9th term	10th term	11th term	12th term
55	26	−3	−32								

(f) Find the general term for the linear sequence.

(g) Calculate the 23rd term in the linear pattern.

3. Examine the following linear pattern and then answer the questions: 73, 92, 111, 130, ...

(a) Find the first term in the sequence.

(b) Find the first change *d*.

(c) Write down the next three terms in the sequence.

(d) Describe the sequence in your own words.

(e) Use the information above to complete the following table:

1st term	2nd term	3rd term	4th term	5th term	6th term	7th term	8th term	9th term	10th term	11th term	12th term
73	92	111	130								

(f) Find the general term for the linear sequence.

(g) Calculate the 47th term in the linear pattern.

4. Examine the following linear pattern and then answer the questions: 67, 41.5, 16, −9.5, ...

(a) Find the first term in the sequence.

(b) Find the first change *d*.

(c) Write down the next three terms in the sequence.

(d) Describe the sequence in your own words.

(e) Use the information above to complete the following table:

1st term	2nd term	3rd term	4th term	5th term	6th term	7th term	8th term	9th term	10th term	11th term	12th term
67	41.5	16	−9.5								

(f) Find the general term for the linear sequence.

(g) Calculate the 100th term in the linear pattern.

5. The nth term of a sequence is given by $T_n = 3n - 5$. Which term of the sequence is 19?

6. The nth term of a sequence is given by $T_n = 17n + 15$. Which term of the sequence is 202?

7. The nth term of a sequence is given by $T_n = 13 - 4n$. Which term of the sequence is −59?

8. The nth term of a sequence is given by $T_n = 5 + 7n$. Which term of the sequence is 166?

9. The nth term of a sequence is given by $T_n = 6n + 18$. Which term of the sequence is 330?

10. While waiting in a restaurant, Laura starts making the following three patterns using toothpicks:

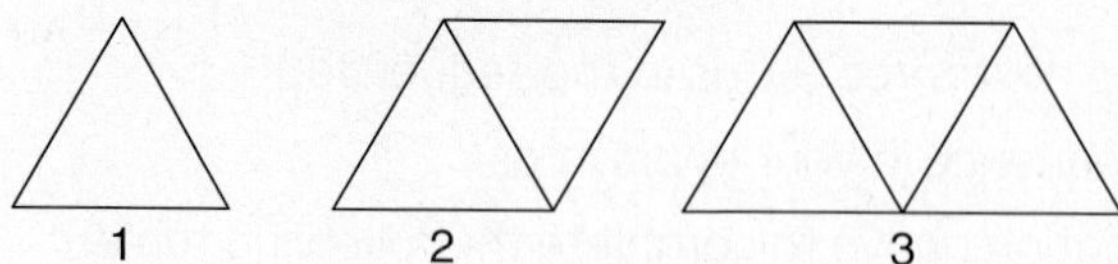

(a) Determine how many toothpicks are needed to make the 4th, 5th and 6th shapes in the pattern.

(b) Fill the following table to show how the pattern grows:

Triangles	1	2	3	4	5	6
Toothpicks	3	5				

(c) Explain in words how the above pattern works.

(d) Can you write a general term to predict the number of toothpicks needed for any pattern?

11. Patrick makes €3.00 an hour for his first hour of work, €6.00 for his second and €9.00 for his third.

(a) Write a general term for the amount of money Patrick earns in n hours.

(b) Calculate how much money he earned after seven hours of work.

12. Ita is constantly improving her score at the same rate in a video game she plays. She scored 23 points in her first attempt, 25 points in her second and 27 points in her third and so on.

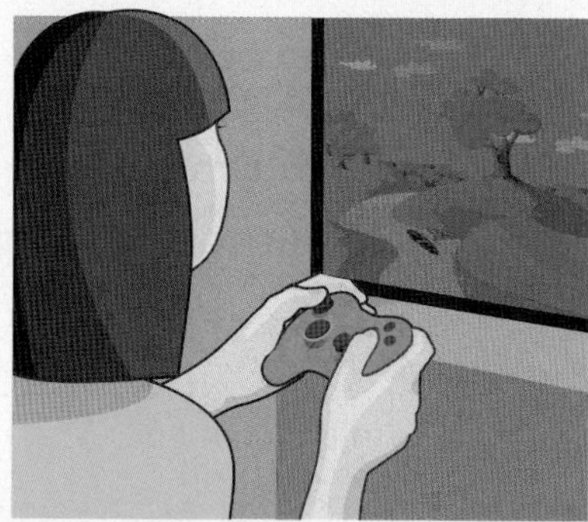

(a) Write a general term for the amount of points she scored in the nth game.

(b) How many points will she have scored in her tenth game?

(c) If she must score 65 points to progress to the next level, how many games must she play to do so?

13. All the sequences we studied in this section are called 'linear patterns'. What do you think the word 'linear' means?

Section 5.4: The function machine

Student Activity 5D

1. Copy each diagram and fill in the missing numbers.

(a) 25 → ×5 → ? → −10 → ?

(b)

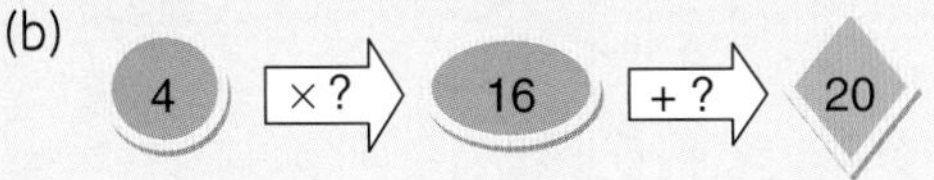

(c)

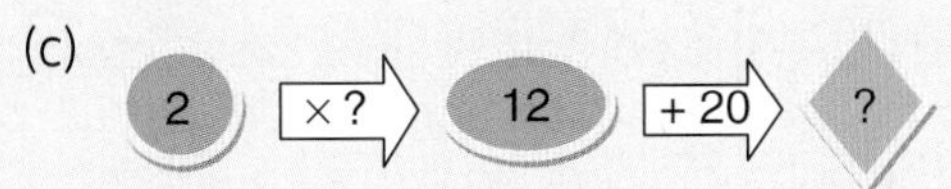

(d)

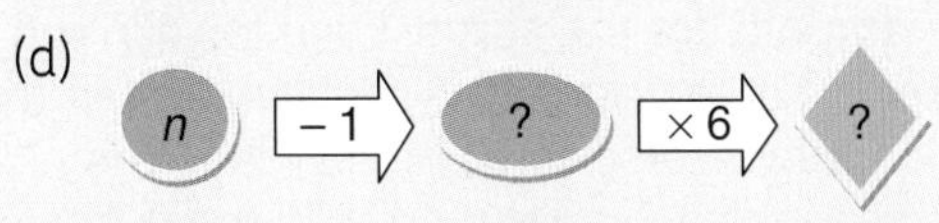

(e)

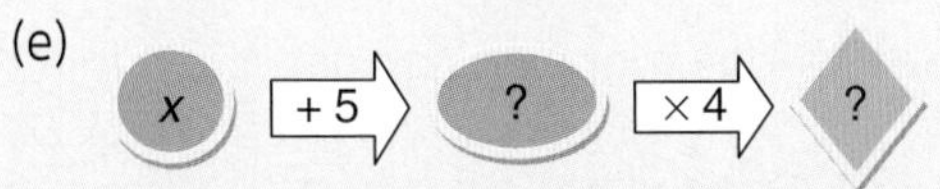

(f)

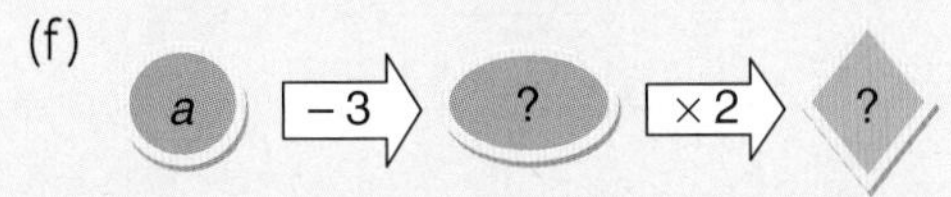

2. Seán and Mary are playing a numbers game. Seán tells Mary that he will think of a number, multiply it by 3 and will then subtract 1 from the answer. Given the following numbers, Mary must find the number. Can you help her?

(a) 2 (d) 0

(b) 3 (e) −8

(c) 12 (f) $\frac{1}{2}$

3. Mary then tells Seán that she will think of a number, multiply it by 2 and will then subtract 10 from the answer. Given the following answers, Seán must find the number Mary thought of originally. Can you help him?

(a) 10 (d) 74

(b) 90 (e) −10

(c) 38

THE FUNCTION MACHINE EXPLAINED

In mathematics, we often compare functions to **'number machines'**. As in a real machine, functions require raw material to work with. In mathematics, numbers are the raw material. A function takes a number, called its **input,** and performs a mathematical operation on it. The operations depend on the function in question.

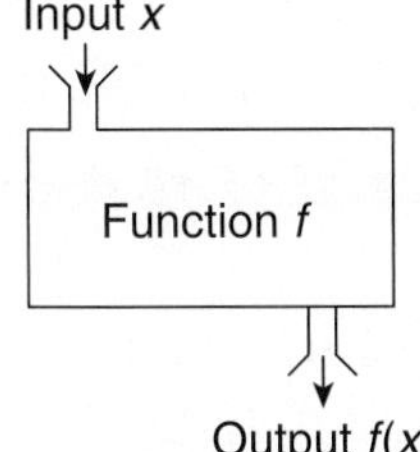

Once complete, the function gives us an end product. We call this end product the **output** or **range** of the function.

- All inputs to the machine belong to the set of inputs called the **domain.**
- All of the outputs from the function belong to the set of outputs called the **range.**
- All possible outputs are called the **codomain** of the function.

We often use notation rather than a sentence to write a function. There are many ways to write a function:

$f(x) =$

$f: x \rightarrow$

$y =$

The letter f can be replaced by any letter. The letters g and h are often used.

When performing a function, we are simply using a mathematical rule. Suppose we have a function f, which takes an input x. The function doubles the input and then adds one to the answer.

We could write this in a mathematical form as follows:

$f : x \rightarrow 2x + 1$
The function f maps all inputs x onto the result from this.

The x is just a place-holder. It is there to show us where the input goes and what happens to it. It can be any value! For example:

Input x	Function $2x + 1$	Output y
1	2(1) + 1	3
2	2(2) + 1	5
3	2(3) + 1	7
4	2(4) + 1	9

Every input of a function can have only **one** output. In mathematics, we say that each input is mapped to one output only.
A **mapping** diagram can be used to represent the function above.

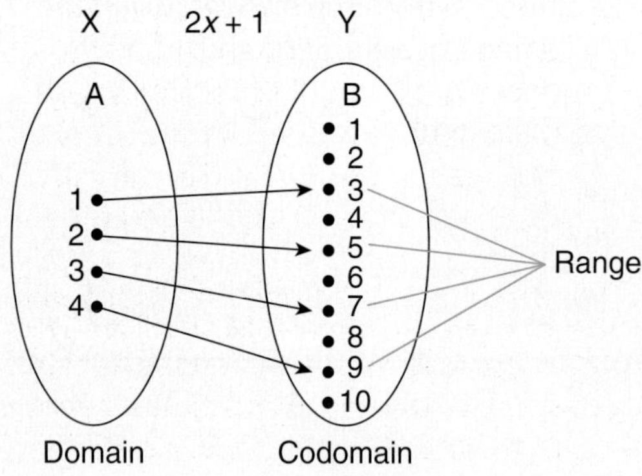

- In this example, the **domain** is {1, 2, 3, 4}.
- The **range** is {3, 5, 7, 9}.
- The **codomain** is {1, 2, 3, 4, 5, 6, 7, 8, 9, 10}.

We normally write our answers as an ordered pair, or a **couple,** in the form of (x-value, y-value) or (input, output).

The couples for the above example are: {(1, 3), (2, 5), (3, 7), (4, 9)}.

A function can be defined as follows:

A **function** is a relation in which no two couples have the same first component and which works for every possible input value.

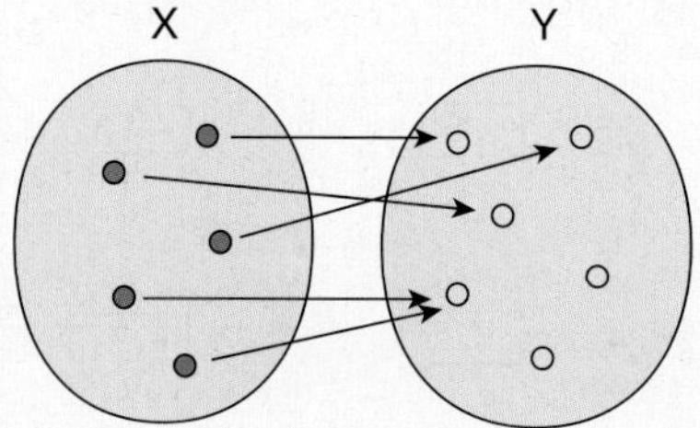

Therefore, the domain is all of the possible inputs to the function and the range is all of the outputs used. No two elements in the domain are the same. Each term in the domain corresponds to a specific term in the range. However, a term in the range may correspond to multiple terms in the domain.

A one-to-one mapping can occur in a function.

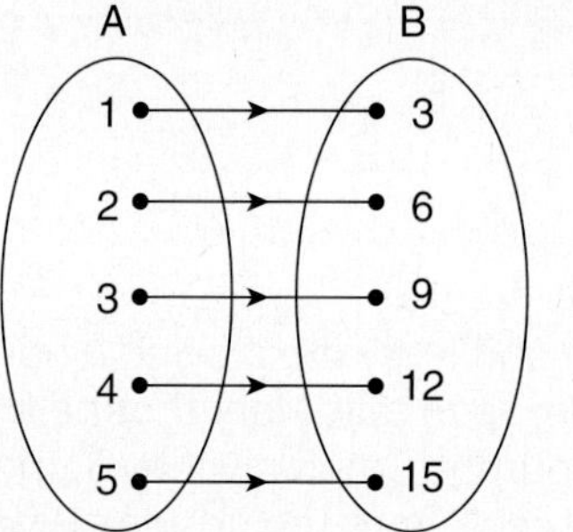

Likewise many inputs can be mapped to one specific output.

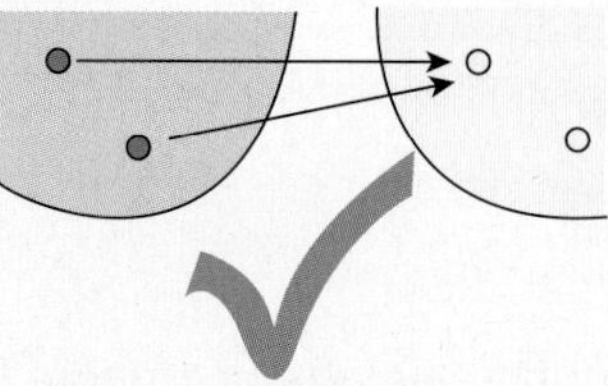

However, one input cannot be mapped onto many possible outputs.

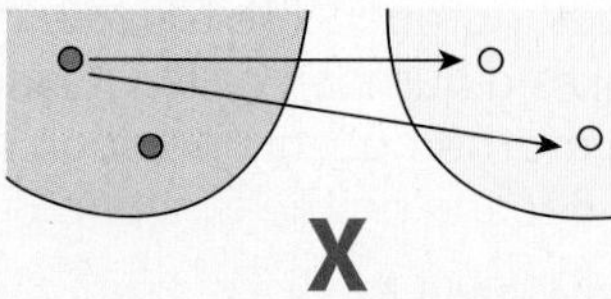

EXAMPLE 7

(a) Investigate whether the following sets of couples are functions. Give reasons for your answers.

(i) {(1, 5) (2, 6) (3, 7) (4, 8) (5, 9)}

(ii) {(−2, 8) (0, 10) (2, 12) (7, 17) (10, 20)}

(iii) {(−2, 4) (−2, 1) (−3, 0) (−4, −6) (−5, 8)}

(iv) {(11, 8) (11, 4) (12, −1) (12, −3) (12, −5)}

Solution

(a) (i) {(1, 5) (2, 6) (3, 7) (4, 8) (5, 9)} is a function since all the highlighted first or x-components are different.

(ii) {(−2, 8) (0, 10) (2, 12) (7, 17) (10, 20)} is a function since all the highlighted first or x-components are different.

(iii) {(−2, 4) (−2, 1) (−3, 0) (−4, −6) (−5, 8)} is not a function since all the highlighted x-components are not different. In a function, −2 cannot be mapped to both 4 and 1.

(iv) {(11, 8) (11, 4) (12, −1) (12, −3) (12, −5)} is not a function since the highlighted x-components of 11 and 12 repeat in the couples. 11 cannot be mapped to both 8 and 4 in a function. Neither can 12 be mapped to −1, −3 and −5 in a function.

(b) State whether each of the following mapping diagrams represents a function. Explain your answer.

(i) Domain Codomain

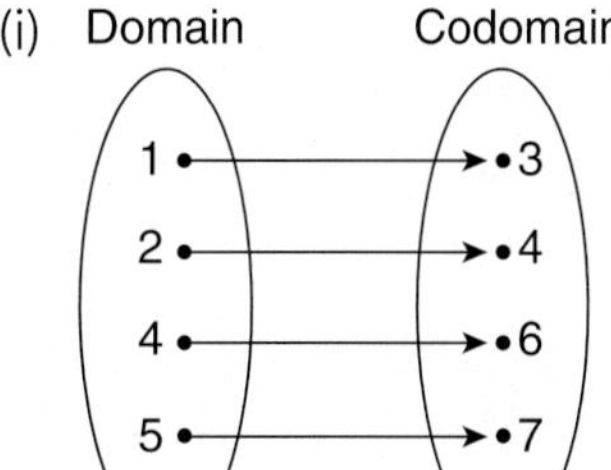

(ii) Domain Codomain

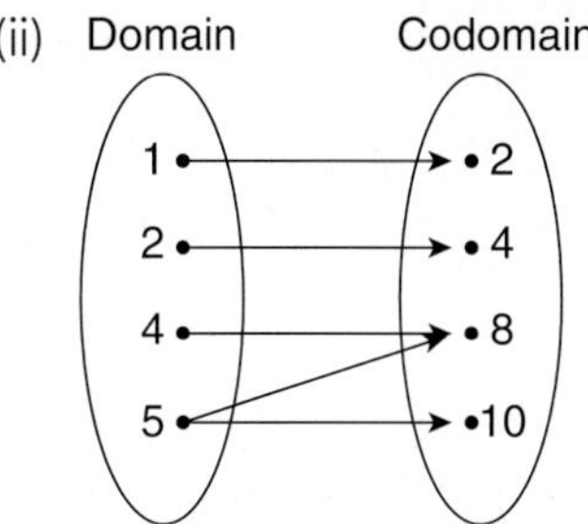

Solution

(b) (i) This mapping diagram represents a function as each element in the domain is mapped onto only one element in the range. In the set of couples {(1, 3), (2, 4), (4, 6), (5, 7)}, each first component is different.

(ii) This mapping diagram does not represent a function as each element in the domain is not mapped to only one element in the range. The number 5 is mapped onto both 8 and 10.

In the set of couples {(1, 2), (2, 4), (4, 8), (5, 8), (5, 10)}, first components are repeated.

EXAMPLE 8

(a) A function g is defined as $g: x \to 3x - 2$. Find:

(i) $g(1)$ (iii) $g\left(\frac{2}{3}\right)$

(ii) $g(-2)$ (iv) $g(k)$

Solution

(a) (i) $g(1) = 3(1) - 2 = 3 - 2 = 1$

(ii) $g(-2) = 3(-2) - 2$
$= -6 - 2$
$= -8$

(iii) $g\left(\frac{2}{3}\right) = 3\left(\frac{2}{3}\right) - 2 = 2 - 2$
$= 0$

(iv) $g(k) = 3(k) - 2$
$= 3k - 2$

(b) Given that $y = 5x - 2$, complete the table below, showing all your workings:

x	1	2	3	4
y				

Solution

(b) Turn the table sideways and add an extra column for your workings.

x	$5x - 2$	y
1	5(1) − 2	3
2	5(2) − 2	8
3	5(3) − 2	13
4	5(4) − 2	18

So the answer is (1, 3), (2, 8), (3, 13), (4, 18).

(c) A function f is defined as $f: x \to 2x + 5$. Given that $f(t) = 13$, find the value of t.

Solution

(c) $f(t) = 2(t) + 5$

$= 2t + 5$

We are given $f(t) = 13$.

$\therefore 2t + 5 = 13$

$2t = 13 - 5$

$2t = 8$

$t = 4$

Exercise 5.4

1. Write the outputs for each of the following inputs if a function adds 21 to an input:

(a) 0 (b) −4 (c) 10 (d) −11 (e) 8

2. Write the outputs for each of the following inputs if a function subtracts 3 from an input:

(a) 9 (b) −8 (c) 7 (d) 0 (e) −33

3. Write the outputs for each of the following inputs if a function multiplies any input by 3:

(a) −7 (b) 8 (c) 0 (d) 23 (e) $17\frac{1}{3}$

4. Write the range for the following inputs if a function divides an input by 5:

(a) −25 (b) 75 (c) 3 (d) 55 (e) −120

5. List the couples of a function which triples the following inputs and adds 8 to the result:

(a) −7 (b) 0 (c) 9 (d) 23 (e) −71

6. List the couples of a function which divides the following inputs by 3 and adds 5 to the result:

(a) −90 (b) 27 (c) 159 (d) −39 (e) 180

7. List the couples of a function which divides the following inputs by 4 and subtracts 6 from the result:

(a) −8 (b) −44 (c) 0 (d) −820 (e) 2,412

8. Given that $y = 5x - 2$, complete the following table. Show all your workings.

x	−1	0	1	2	3	4
y						

9. Given that $y = 8 - 6x$, complete the following table. Show all your workings.

x	−6	−3	0	3	6	9
y						

10. A function g is defined as $g: x \to 3x - 1$. Find:

(a) $g(1)$ (b) $g(3)$ (c) $g(5)$ (d) $g(7)$ (e) $g(9)$

11. A function f is defined as $f: x \to 4x - 5$. Find:

(a) $f(0)$ (b) $f(-1)$ (c) $f(-2)$ (d) $f(-3)$ (e) $f(-4)$

12. A function h is defined as $h: x \to 2x - 4$. Find:

(a) $h(3)$ (b) $h(7)$ (c) $h(-3)$ (d) $h(-5)$ (e) $h(4)$

13. A function k is defined as $k: x \to 4x$. Find:

(a) $k(0)$ (b) $k(3)$ (c) $k(-2)$ (d) $k(5)$ (e) $k(-4)$

14. For each of the following mapping diagrams, list the elements in:

(a) The domain

(b) The range

(c) The codomain

(d) The coupled pairs

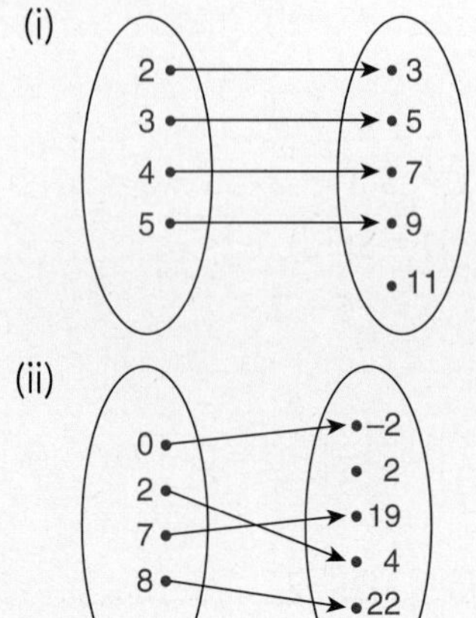

(iii)

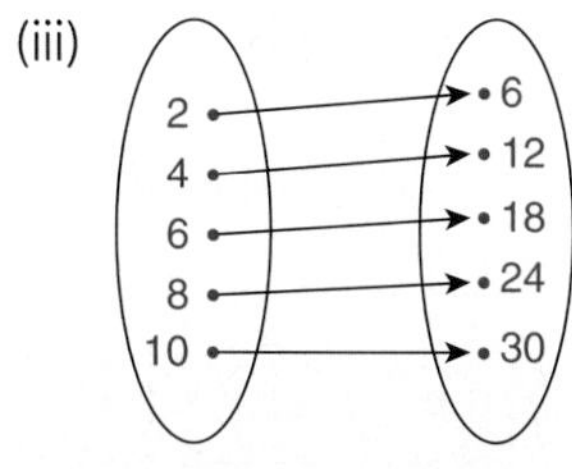

(iv)

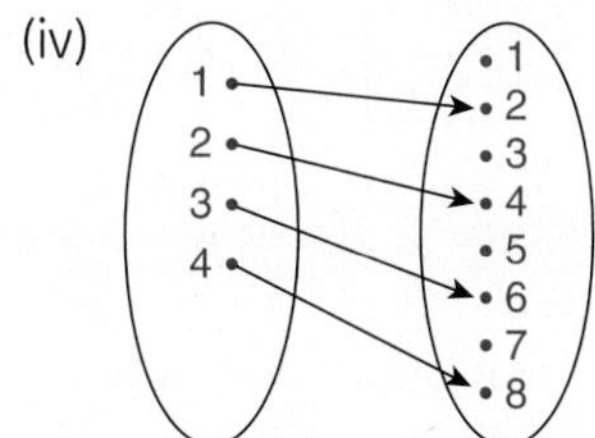

(v)

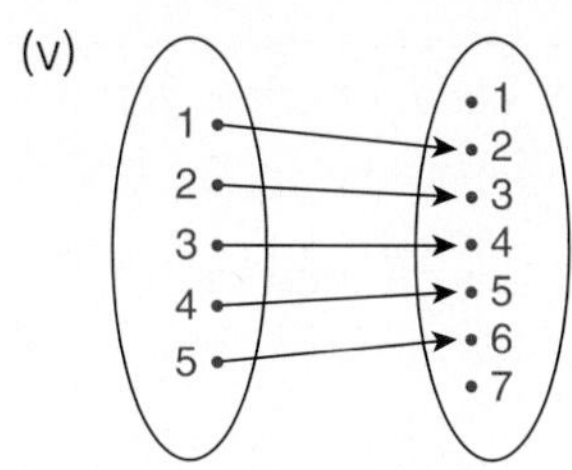

15. In your own words, explain what a function is.

16. In your own words, explain what a non-function is.

17. For each of the following mapping diagrams, state whether it represents a function. Give reasons for your answers.

(a)

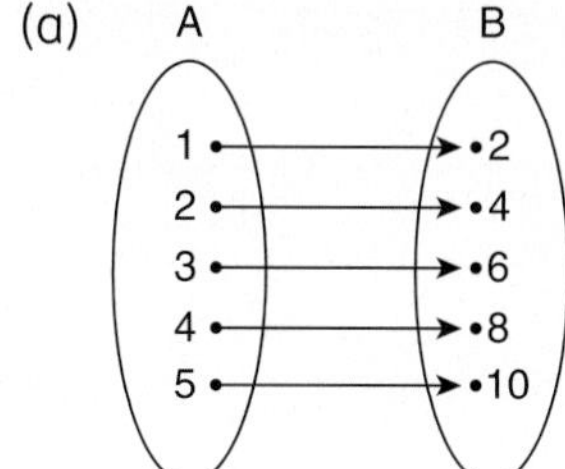

(b)

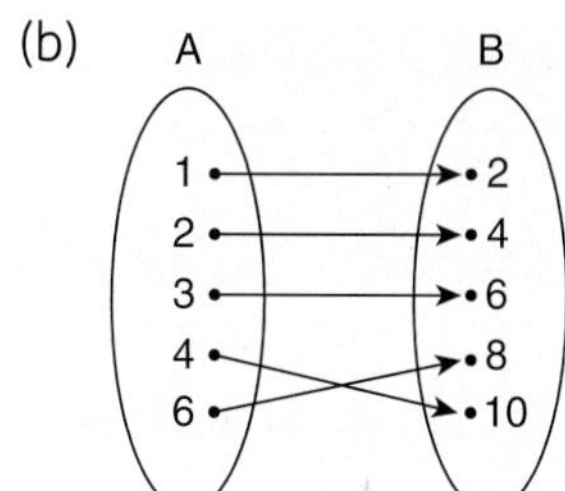

(c)

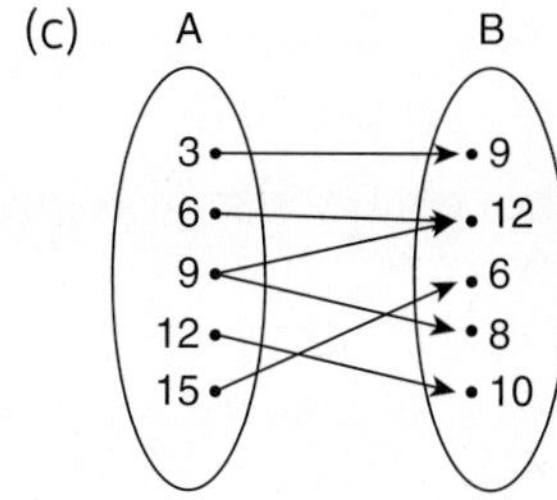

(d)

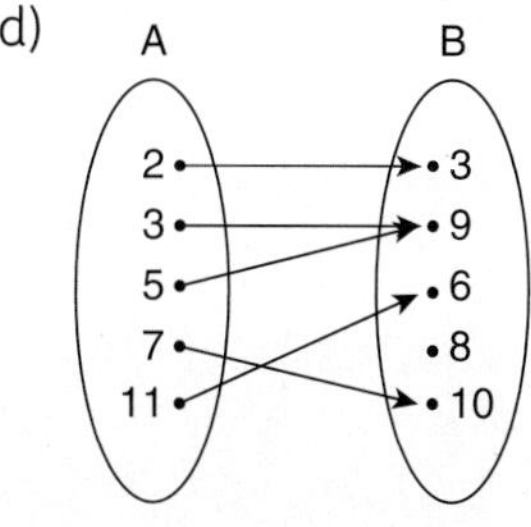

(e)

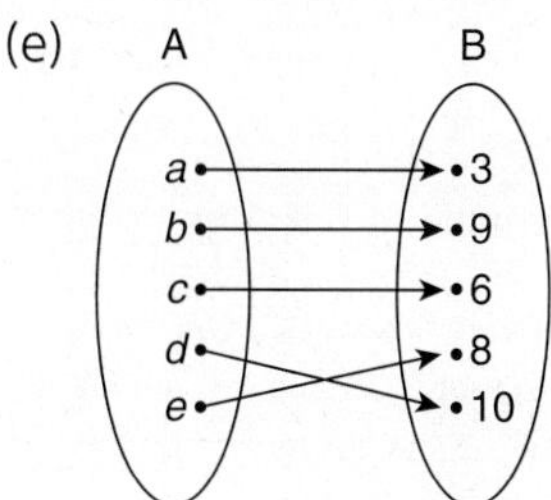

(f)

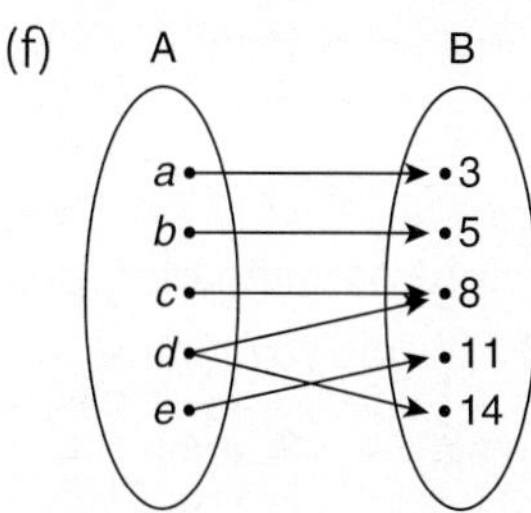

18. A function multiplies any input it is given by 2 and adds 1 to the result.

(a) Copy and complete the following mapping diagam:

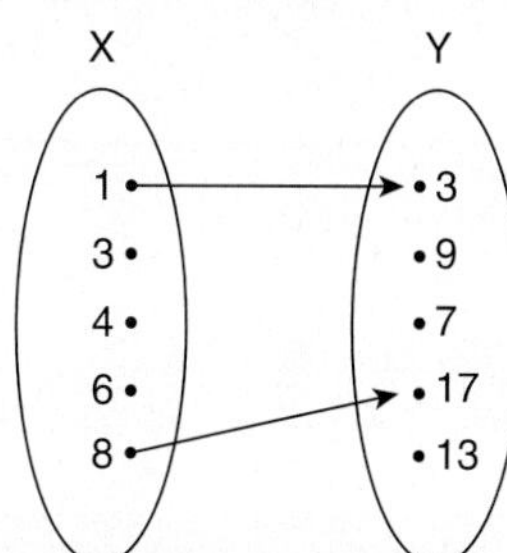

(b) List all of the couples.

19. A function divides any domain it is given by 3.

(a) Copy and complete the following mapping diagam:

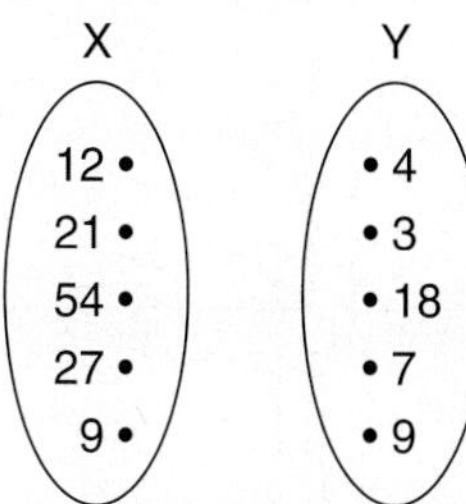

(b) List the codomain values.

(c) List the values of the range.

(d) List the set of couples that satisfy the function.

20. $f: x \to -3x + 2$ is a function. If $f(k) = 7$, find the value of k.

21. $f: x \to 2x + 7$ is a function. If $f(t) = 13$, find the value of t.

22. $f: x \to -4x - 5$ is a function. If $f(k) = -25$, find the value of k.

23. A function f is defined as $f: x \to 3x - 3$. Copy the following mapping diagram and find the missing numbers w, x and y:

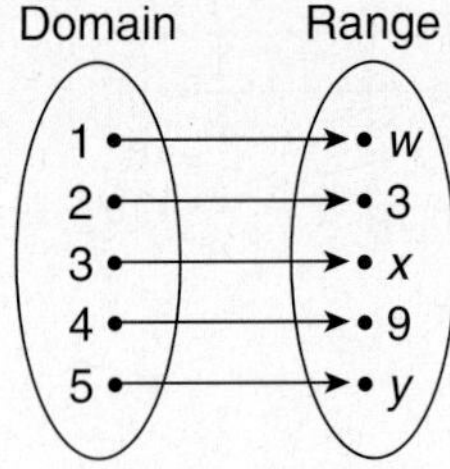

24. A function f is defined as $f: x \to -2x + 5$. Copy the following mapping diagram and find the missing numbers r, s and t:

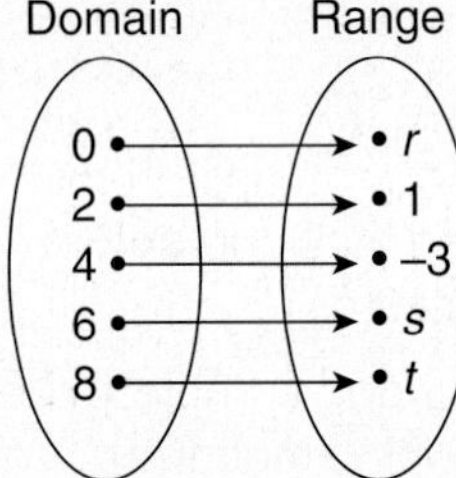

25. A function f is defined as $f: x \to 4x - 8$. Copy the following mapping diagram and find the missing numbers w, x and y:

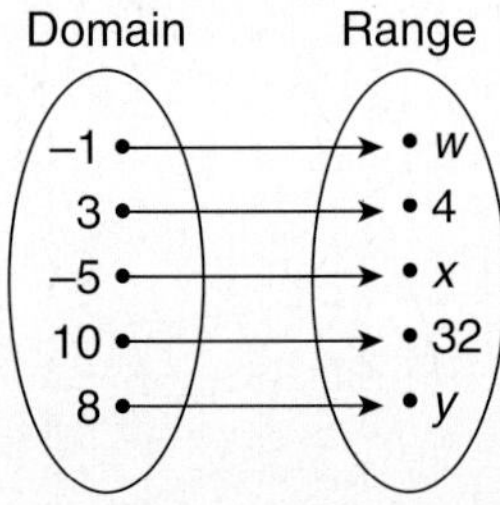

26. $f: x \to 4x - 7$ is a function. If $f(s) = -3$, find the value of s.

27. $f: x \to 3x + 1$ is a function. If $f(k) = 34$, find the value of k.

28. $f: x \to 5x + 2$ is a function. If $f(t) = 37$, find the value of t.

29. $f: x = 3 - 2x$ is a function. If $f(h - 2) = 21$, find the value of h.

Section 5.5: Linear graphs

Student Activity 5E

(a) Copy the following Cartesian plane:

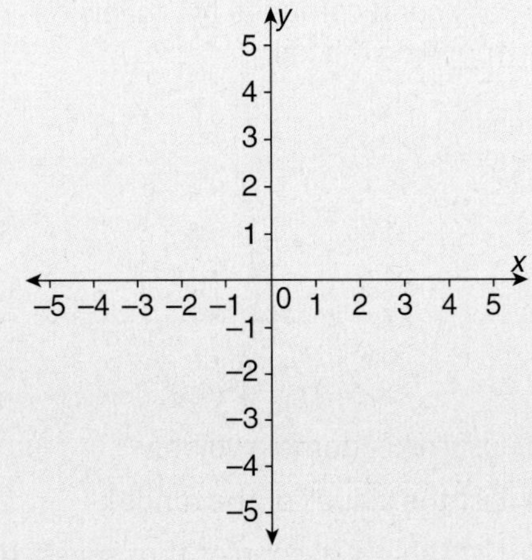

(b) Plot each of the following series of points and join the points with a ruler.

(i) (−5, 4) (−2, 4) (0, 4) (2, 4) (4, 4)

(ii) (3, 4) (3, 1) (3, 0) (3, −2) (3, −5)

(iii) (−5, −5) (−3, −3) (0, 0) (2, 2) (4, 4)

(iv) (−5, 4) (−3, 2) (−1, 0) (0, −1) (3, −4)

(c) Describe what each series of points forms.

LINEAR GRAPHS EXPLAINED

Functions can be used in mathematics to draw graphs. The input into the function f is the **x-coordinate** and output is the $f(x)$ value. This $f(x)$ value is more commonly known as the ***y*-coordinate** of the point that satisfies the function. Therefore, we can write any couple belonging to a function as a point on the Cartesian plane:

$$(\text{input, output}) = (x, f(x)) = (x, y)$$

These points plotted and joined together produce a graph. The graph shows us how certain mathematical patterns behave.

> A **linear function** is a sequence of numbers that increases or decreases by the same value to form a straight line when graphed.

To plot any linear function, all we need is a minimum of two points. These two points indicate the direction the line is taking. A **non-linear function** does not form a straight line when graphed.

To draw a linear function:

- **Step 1:** Find at least two points that satisfy the function.
- **Step 2:** On graph paper, draw a horizontal (x-axis) and a vertical (y-axis) line.
- **Step 3:** On these axes, insert an appropriate scale and clearly label what each axis represents.
- **Step 4:** Draw the graph of the function by plotting at least two points and drawing a line through the points using a straight edge.

When we are working with a new function or a linear word problem, it is useful to know as much as we can about the function before we graph it. Important points to note are:

- The output when the input of the function is zero
- The first change or common difference, d
- Any other special behaviours of the function

The point where the graph crosses the x-axis is called the **x-intercept.** Its coordinate is always (real number, 0). The point where the graph crosses the y-axis is called the **y-intercept.** Its coordinate is always (0, real number).

EXAMPLE 9

Draw the graph of the function $f(x) = 5x$ in the domain $-2 \le x \le 3$.

Solution

Input x	Function $5x$	Output y
−2	5(−2)	−10
−1	5(−1)	−5
0	5(0)	0
1	5(1)	5
2	5(2)	10
3	5(3)	15

So the points on the graph are: (−2, −10), (−1, −5), (0, 0), (1, 5), (2, 10), (3, 15).

Note that the x-values go from −2 to 3 and the corresponding y-values go from −10 to 15. So, this should be the scale on the graph.

Plotting the points and joining them together, we get the following graph:

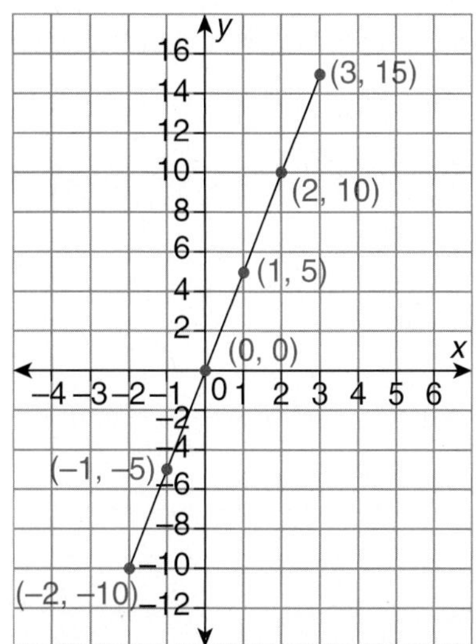

EXAMPLE 10

Draw the graph of the function $f:x \rightarrow 2x + 1$ in the domain $-3 \leq x \leq 3$.

Solution

Input x	Funcion $2x + 1$	Output y
−3	2(−3) + 1	−5
−2	2(−2) + 1	−3
−1	2(−1) + 1	−1
0	2(0) + 1	1
1	2(1) + 1	3
2	2(2) + 1	5
3	2(3) + 1	7

The points on the graph are: (−3, −5), (−2, −3), (−1, −1), (0, 1), (1, 3), (2, 5), (3, 7). Plotting the points and joining them together, we get the following graph:

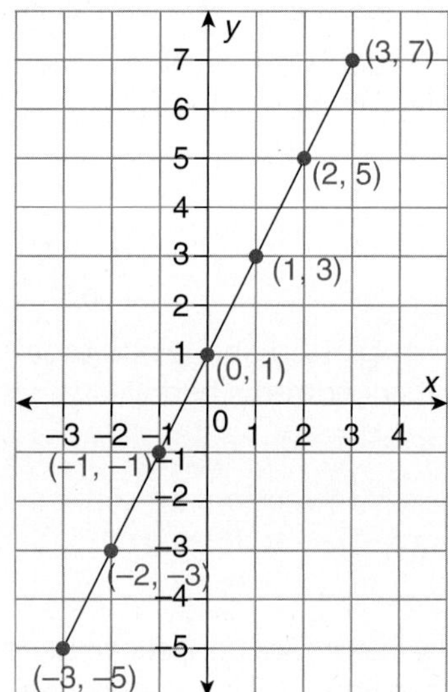

EXAMPLE 11

(a) Graph $f(x) = 5 - \frac{2}{3}x$ by plotting points.

Solution

(a) In general, we evaluate the function for two or more inputs to find at least two points on the graph. Try to select input values that will work nicely into the equation. For this equation, multiples of 3 work nicely due to the $\frac{2}{3}$ in the equation. Using $x = 0$ to get the intercept at the y-axis, evaluate $f(x)$ at $x = 0$, 3 and 6.

x	$5 - \frac{2}{3}x$	y
0	$5 - \frac{2}{3}(0)$	5
3	$5 - \frac{2}{3}(3)$	3
6	$5 - \frac{2}{3}(6)$	1

The points on the graph are: (0, 5), (3, 3), (6, 1). Plotting the points and joining them together, we get the following graph:

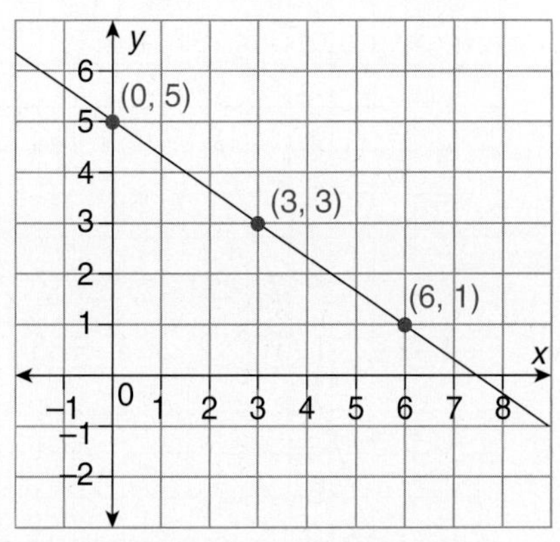

(b) Explain why it is a linear function.

Solution

(b) This graph is a linear function because, when all the points in the function are joined together, they form a straight line.

(c) Using your graph, evaluate where the graph cuts the y-axis.

Solution

(c) From the diagram we can see the graph cuts the y-axis at the point (0, 5).

(d) Use your graph to evaluate $f(1.5)$ and verify your answer algebraically.

Solution

(d) Using a ruler, draw a vertical line from 1.5 on the x-axis until you meet the graph. Mark the intersection point.

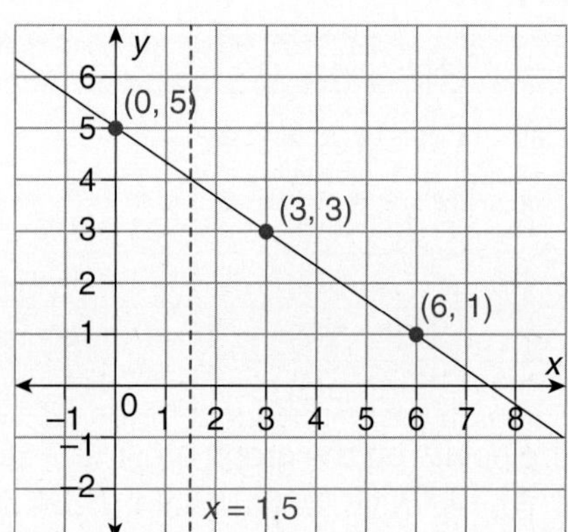

Using a ruler, draw a horizontal line to intersect the y-axis. Read off the y-value.

We can see graphically that $f(1.5) = 4$ by the green dotted line in the diagram.

To evaluate $f(1.5)$ algebraically, substitute the value 1.5 in for x in the function:

$f(x) = 5 - \frac{2}{3}x$

$f(1.5) = 5 - \frac{2}{3}(1.5)$

$f(1.5) = 4$

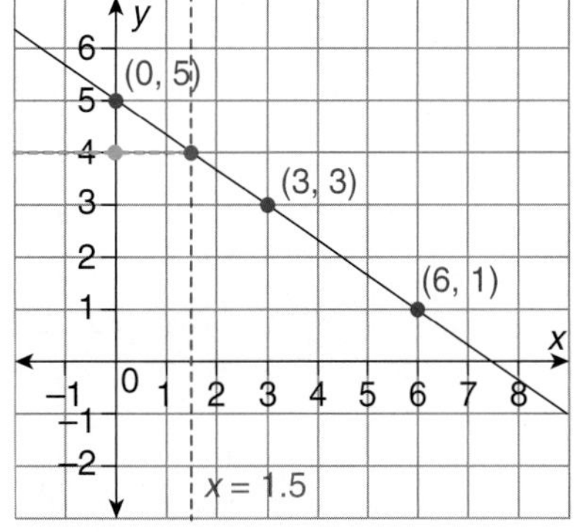

(e) Use your graph to evaluate for what value of x is $f(x) = 1.5$.

Solution

(e) To evaluate graphically the value of x for which $f(x) = 1.5$, go to 1. 5 on the y-axis and draw a horizontal line across till you hit the graph. Mark the intersection point.

Using a ruler, draw a vertical line to intersect the x-axis and read off the x-value.

Therefore $f(x) = 1.5$ when x is approximately 5.3 by the orange dotted line in the diagram on the right.

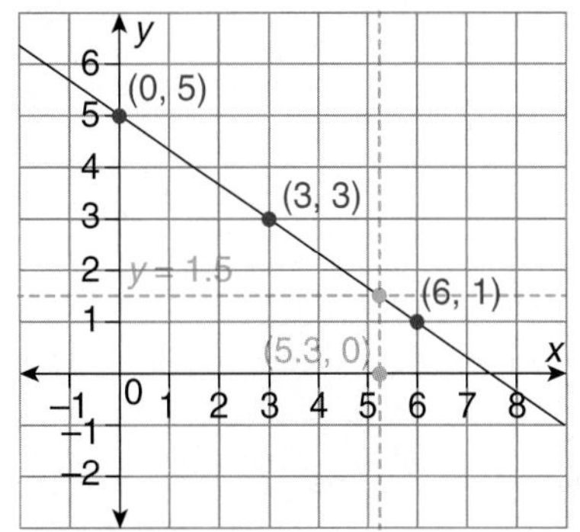

(f) Evaluate algebraically the value of x for which $f(x) = 1.5$.

Solution

(f) To evaluate the more accurate answer algebraically, let the function equal 1.5:

$f(x) = 1.5$

$5 - \frac{2}{3}x = 1.5$

$-\frac{2}{3}x = 1.5 - 5$

$-\frac{2}{3}x = -3.5$

$x = -3.5 \div -\frac{2}{3}$

$x = 5.25$

EXAMPLE 12

A shrub bought in a garden centre measures 5 cm in height. The shrub grows at a rate of 1 cm per month.

(a) Write down a function to represent the growth of the shrub.

(b) Draw a graph to show the growth of the shrub over four months.

(c) Using your graph, find how many months it will take the shrub to grow to exactly 11 cm.

Solution

(a) The shrub starts at 5 cm. For every month, x, it grows 1 cm so our function is:

Height of shrub = $5 + 1x$

(b) First create a suitable table:

Month	0	1	2	3	4
Height of shrub	5	6	7	8	9

Once we have a minimum of two points, we can graph the function using the points (0, 5), (1, 6), (2, 7), (3, 8) and (4, 9).

(c) If a line is drawn from 11 cm on the y-axis across to the graph and dropped down to the months on the x-axis, we can see that it takes 6 months for the shrub to reach a height of 11 cm.

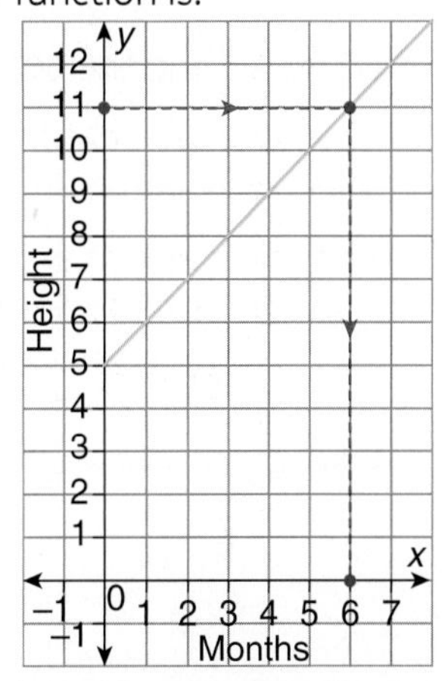

Exercise 5.5

1. Complete the following for (i) to (vi):
   (a) By substituting 1, 2, 3, 4 and 5 into each variable, find the first 5 terms in the sequence.
   (b) List each of the couples and draw the pattern on a Cartesian plane.

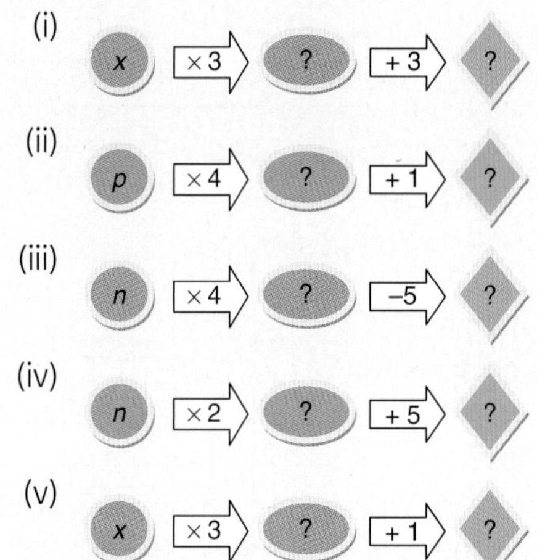

2. Draw the graph of the function $f:x \rightarrow 2x$ in the domain $-3 \leq x \leq 5$.
3. Draw the graph of the function $g:x \rightarrow 3x$ in the domain $-1 \leq x \leq 3$.
4. Draw the graph of the function $h:x \rightarrow x$ in the domain $-4 \leq x \leq 4$.
5. Draw the graph of the function $g:x \rightarrow -2x$ in the domain $-3 \leq x \leq 3$.
6. Draw the graph of the function $f:x \rightarrow -3x$ in the domain $-2 \leq x \leq 3$.
7. Draw the graph of the function $h:x \rightarrow 4x$ in the domain $-1 \leq x \leq 2$.
8. Draw the graph of the function $f:x \rightarrow -5x$ in the domain $-2 \leq x \leq 3$.
9. Draw the graph of the function $g:x \rightarrow 3x - 5$ in the domain $0 \leq x \leq 5$.
10. Draw the graph of the function $g:x \rightarrow -2x + 2$ in the domain $-2 \leq x \leq 3$.
11. Draw the graph of the function $h:x \rightarrow -x - 1$ in the domain $-3 \leq x \leq 4$.
12. Draw the graph of the function $f:x \rightarrow 7 - 2x$ in the domain $-3 \leq x \leq 5$.
13. Draw the graph of the function $f:x \rightarrow -x + 3$ in the domain $-3 \leq x \leq 4$.
14. Draw the graph of the function $f:x \rightarrow 4x - 7$ in the domain $-1 \leq x \leq 3$.
    (a) The function $f(x)$ cuts the y-axis at the point P. Mark the point P on your graph.
    (b) Write the coordinates of the point P.
15. Draw the graph of the function $h:x \rightarrow -5x + 12$ in the domain $0 \leq x \leq 4$.
    (a) The function $h(x)$ cuts the y-axis at the point W. Mark the point W on your graph.
    (b) Write the coordinates of the point W.
16. Draw the graph of the function $g:x \rightarrow -2x + 1$ in the domain $-3 \leq x \leq 4$.
    (a) The function $g(x)$ cuts the y-axis at the point S. Mark the point S on your graph.
    (b) Write the coordinates of the point S.
    (c) Examine the equations of the function and the corresponding point where it cuts the y-axis for Questions 14 to 16. Write a sentence explaining how the y-intercept is calculated.
17. An electrician has an initial callout charge of €25 and then charges €30 per hour.
    (a) Draw a graph to show the electrician's cost against time for the first six hours of work.
    (b) After how many hours will the electrician's cost be €175?
    (c) How much would the electrician charge for 8 hours' work?

18. A sunflower seed is planted. After 1 week a shoot of 1.5 cm appears and it increases in height by 1.5 cm every week.
    (a) Draw a graph to show the height of the sunflower against time for the first five weeks.
    (b) After how many weeks will the sunflower be 24 cm?
    (c) What will be the height of the sunflower after 6 weeks?

19. A water storage tank holds 150 litres of water. A small leak in the tank results in a 2 litre loss of water each day.

(a) Draw a graph to show the volume of water in the tank against time.

(b) After how many days will the tank be empty?

(c) What will the volume of water be in the tank after 36 days?

(d) After how many days will the volume of water in the tank have halved?

20. John watches a caterpillar climbing up a vertical post. When he first notices the caterpillar, it is 15 cm from the ground. John measures the height of the caterpillar from the ground every hour and finds it climbs 10 cm each hour.

(a) Draw a graph to show the height of the caterpillar against time.

(b) After how many hours will the caterpillar be 85 cm off the ground?

(c) What will the height of the caterpillar be after 4 hours?

21. The ground clearance for a trailer is 90 cm. For every tonne that the trailer holds, its ground clearance decreases by 4 cm.

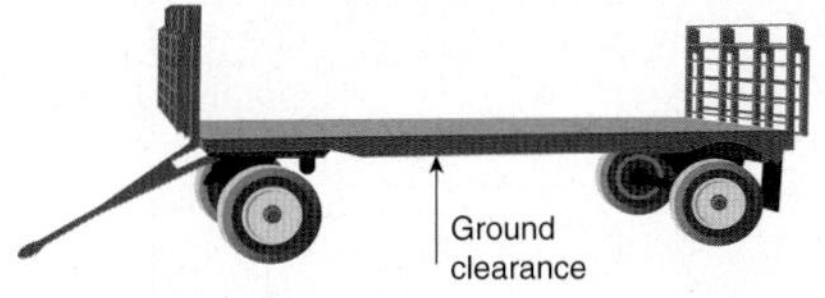

(a) Draw a graph to show the ground clearance of the trailer against its load.

(b) What will the clearance of the trailer be after 6 tonnes have been loaded?

(c) What will the clearance of the trailer be after 10 tonnes have been loaded?

(d) How many tonnes of material are on the trailer if the clearance is 74 cm?

22. Jane buys a candle of height 80 cm. She records that after burning the candle for 1 hour its height decreases by 5 cm.

(a) Draw a suitable graph to show the decrease in the height of the candle over time.

(b) What will be the height of the candle after burning for 8 hours?

(c) After how many hours will the candle have burned away completely?

23. The air pressure in a tyre decreases at a steady rate of 2 kPa per day due to a slow puncture. The initial pressure in the tyre was 36 kPa.

(a) Draw a graph to show the pressure of the tyre against time.

(b) What will be the pressure after 6 days?

(c) After how many days will the pressure be 0 kPa?

24. Scientists have discovered that a linear pattern exists between the number of cricket chirps per minute and the temperature in degrees Fahrenheit. They have come up with an equation relating cricket chirps to temperature. At 50 °F the number of chirps is 40, and at 80 °F the number of chirps is 160. Those values have been entered in the table below.

(a) Complete the table to show the temperature when the number of cricket chirps is:

Chirps	40	50	60	70	80	90	100	110	120	130	140	150	160
Temp in °F	50												80

(b) Calculate the first change or common difference.

(c) Represent the above information on a suitable graph.

(d) Using your graph, what is the temperature when the crickets first start chirping?

(e) Evaluate at what temperature there will be 200 chirps.

(f) Laura suggests that the previous answer may not necessarily be true. Suggest a reason for Laura's statement.

Section 5.6: Intersecting linear graphs

Student Activity 5F

1. Explain the word 'intersection'. Give an example of where you have met the word before.
2. (a) Draw the graph of the function $g: x \to 2x + 1$ in the domain $0 \leq x \leq 8$.
   (b) On the same graph, draw the function $h: x \to 6 - 3x$ in the domain $0 \leq x \leq 8$.
   (c) Find the coordinates of the point where the functions $g(x)$ and $h(x)$ intersect.
   (d) Will both graphs intersect at another point? Explain your answer.
3. After knee surgery, Denis' personal trainer tells him to return to his jogging programme slowly. She suggests jogging for 12 minutes each day for the first week. Each week after that, she suggests that Denis increase that time by 6 minutes.
   (a) Represent Denis' jogging times over the first 10 weeks on a suitable graph.

   Meanwhile Denis' sister Karen starts jogging for 8 minutes each day in the first week. Each week after that, she increases her jogging time by a further 8 minutes.

   (b) Represent Karen jogging times over the first 10 weeks on the same graph as Denis.
   (c) By studying both Denis' and Karen's graphs, find the point of intersection.
   (d) Explain what the point of intersection means with respect to Denis' and Karen's jogging programmes.

INTERSECTING LINEAR GRAPHS EXPLAINED

Sometimes when two different linear patterns are drawn on one graph, they cross or intersect each other. The point where the two graphs meet is called the **point of intersection.**

This is the only x and y value common to both functions. In the diagram, $f(x) = g(x)$ at the point (1, 5). The two functions will not meet again on the Cartesian plane.

In Chapter 12 Coordinate geometry, we will examine how to find the point of intersection algebraically.

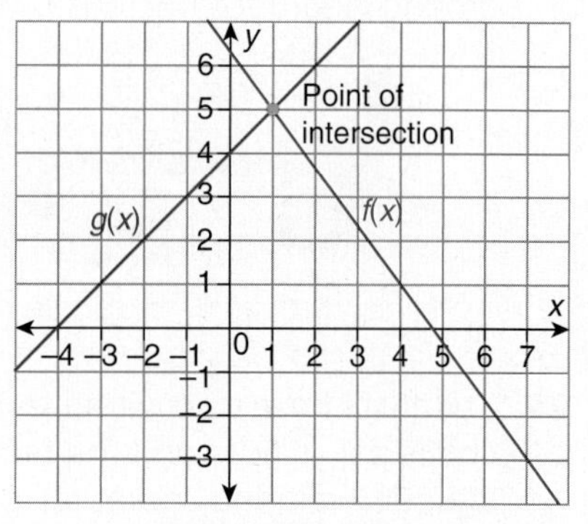

EXAMPLE 13

Graph the functions $f(x) = 3x + 1$ and $g(x) = 2x + 3$ in the domain $-4 \leq x \leq 4$. Hence, find the point of intersection.

Solution

First we must determine the points on the functions $f(x)$ and $g(x)$.

The points on $f(x)$ are:

(−4, −11), (−3, −8), (−2, −5), (−1, −2), (0, 1), (1, 4), (2, 7), (3, 10), (4, 13).

x	$3x + 1$	y
−4	3(−4) + 1	−11
−3	3(−3) + 1	−8
−2	3(−2) + 1	−5
−1	3(−1) + 1	−2
0	3(0) + 1	1
1	3(1) + 1	4
2	3(2) + 1	7
3	3(3) + 1	10
4	3(4) + 1	13

x	$2x + 3$	y
−4	2(−4) + 3	−5
−3	2(−3) + 3	−3
−2	2(−2) + 3	−1
−1	2(−1) + 3	1
0	2(0) + 3	3
1	2(1) + 3	5
2	2(2) + 3	7
3	2(3) + 3	9
4	2(4) + 3	11

The points on $g(x)$ are:

(−4, −5), (−3, −3), (−2, −1), (−1, 1), (0, 3), (1, 5), (2, 7), (3, 9), (4, 11).

Next we graph the two functions $f(x)$ and $g(x)$ on the same diagram:

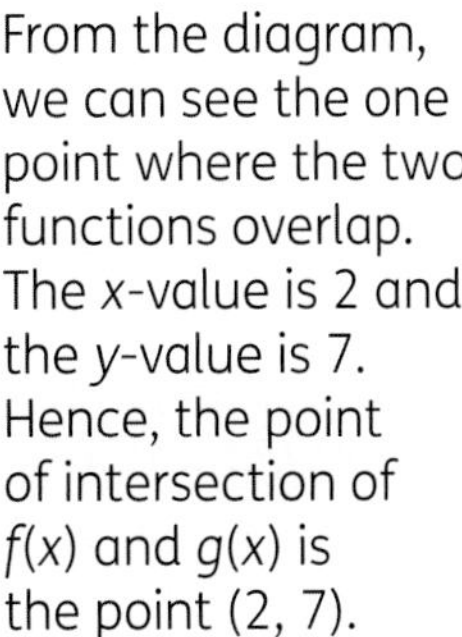

From the diagram, we can see the one point where the two functions overlap. The x-value is 2 and the y-value is 7. Hence, the point of intersection of $f(x)$ and $g(x)$ is the point (2, 7).

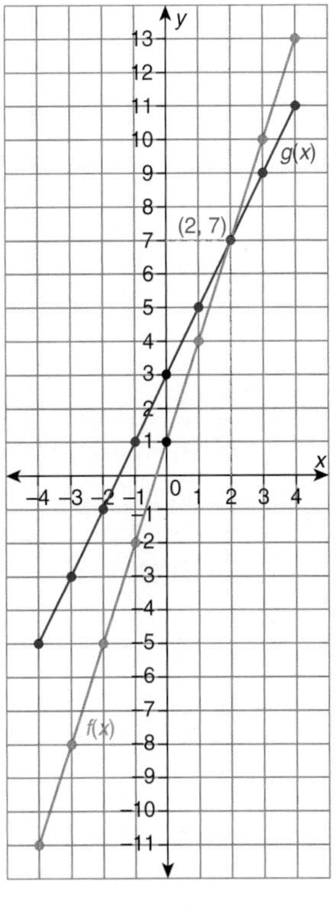

EXAMPLE 14

A gardener plants an ash and a beech sapling in his glasshouse.

When the ash sapling was planted it was exactly 12 cm tall. It grows at a rate of 8 cm per month. The beech sapling was 24 cm tall when planted. It grows at a slower rate of 5 cm per month.

(a) Write down two equations to represent the growth rates of the ash and beech saplings.

(b) Represent the two growth rates on the same graph.

(c) After how many months will both saplings be the same height?

Solution

(a) To quickly calculate the linear functions showing the different rates of growth, first study the information given as clues in the question. A general formula would be:

Present height = Starting height + (Amount grown × Number of months).

Therefore, the equation representing the growth rates of the ash sapling is $y = 12 + 8x$.

The equation representing the growth rates of the beech sapling is $y = 24 + 5x$.

(b) First we need to determine at least two points on both the ash plant's and beech plant's functions.

Week	Ash plant's height	Beech plant's height
0	12 cm (starting height)	24 cm (starting height)
1	20 cm	29 cm
2	28 cm	34 cm

Three points on the function showing the ash plant's growth are (0, 12), (1, 20) and (2, 28). Plot these points and extend the line. This shows the ash tree's growth rate over the next few months.

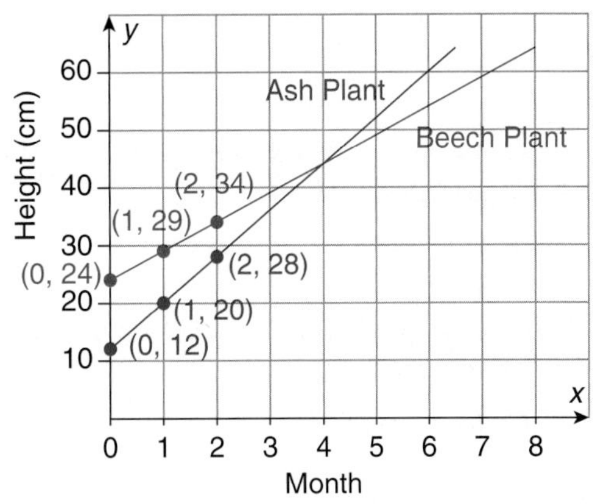

Three points on the function showing the beech plant's growth are (0, 24), (1, 29) and (2, 34). Plot these three points on the same graph and extend the line. This shows the beech tree's growth rate over the next few months.

Note that the x-axis represents Time in months and the y-axis represents the Height in centimetres.

(c) By studying the graph, we can see the point of intersection of both growth functions is (4, 44). This means that after 4 months both trees will be 44 cm in height.

Exercise 5.6

1. The diagram shows the two functions: $y = 2x$ and $y = -2x + 8$. Find the point of intersection.

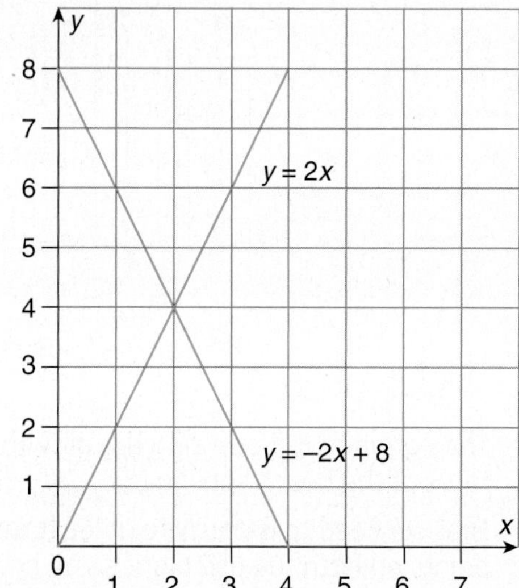

2. Using the same scale and axes, draw each of the following graphs. Hence, find the point of intersection between the two lines.

(a) $g{:}x \to x + 1$ and $f{:}x \to 7 - x$ in the domain $-5 \le x \le 5$

(b) $h{:}x \to x + 4$ and $k{:}x \to -6x + 18$ in the domain $-1 \le x \le 6$

(c) $m{:}x \to -1 - 2x$ and $n{:}x \to 4 - 3x$ in the domain $1 \le x \le 7$

(d) $p{:}x \to x - 2$ and $q{:}x \to 3x$ in the domain $-5 \le x \le 2$

(e) $c{:}x \to 5x - 10$ and $k{:}x \to 2 - 3x$ in the domain $-4 \le x \le 2$

(f) $f{:}x \to 4x + 3$ and $h{:}x \to -2 - x$ in the domain $-5 \le x \le 2$

(g) $p{:}x \to 8 - 2x$ and $b{:}x \to 3x$ in the domain $-2 \le x \le 6$

(h) $w{:}x \to 2x$ and $n{:}x \to 4x + 8$ in the domain $-7 \le x \le -1$

(i) $t{:}x \to 1 - x$ and $r{:}x \to 2x - 5$ in the domain $4 \le x \le 9$

(j) $n{:}x \to 3x - 5$ and $q{:}x \to 2x - 3$ in the domain $0 \le x \le 5$

3. Using the same scale and axes, draw each of the following graphs:

$g{:}x \to x + 2$ and $f{:}x \to 2x + 6$ in the domain $-5 \le x \le 1$.

From your graph write down:

(a) The point of intersection of the two lines

(b) The point A, where $f(x)$ cuts the y-axis

(c) The point B, where $g(x)$ cuts the y-axis

4. Using the same scale and axes, draw each of the following graphs:

$g{:}x \to 3x + 2$ and $f{:}x \to -x + 6$ in the domain $-2 \le x \le 2$.

From your graph write down:

(a) The point of intersection of the two lines

(b) The point A, where $f(x)$ cuts the y-axis

(c) The point B, where $g(x)$ cuts the y-axis.

5. Using the same scale and axes, draw each of the following graphs:

$g{:}x \to -2x - 1$ and $f{:}x \to 3x$ in the domain $-3 \le x \le 1$.

From your graph write down:

(a) The point of intersection of the two lines

(b) The point A, where $f(x)$ cuts the y-axis

(c) The point B, where $g(x)$ cuts the y-axis

6. Two tomato plants are planted in a glasshouse.

When tomato plant A was planted it was exactly 5 cm tall and grows at a rate of 3 cm per day. Tomato plant B was 11 cm tall when planted and grows at a slower rate of 2 cm per day.

(a) Write down two functions to represent the growth rates of the two tomato plants.

(b) Represent the two growth rates on the same suitably labelled graph.

(c) After how many days will both plants be equal in height?

(d) What is their height on that day?

7. Weather balloons are released at different stations located at Cork and Dublin Airports.

The Cork weather balloon is released 25 m above sea level and climbs at a rate of 17 m per minute. The Dublin weather balloon is released 40 m above sea level and climbs at a rate of 12 m per minute.

(a) Write down two functions to represent the rates at which both balloons rise up into the atmosphere.

(b) Represent the two balloons' changes in height on the same graph.

(c) After how many minutes will both balloons be an equal height above sea level?

(d) What is the balloons' height at that time?

(e) A third balloon is released at Knock Airport 45 m above sea level and rises at a rate of 20 m per minute. After how many minutes will all three balloons be at the same height? Explain your answers.

8. During frosty weather, a woman fills two saucepans of hot water to thaw out her frozen water pipes. The first saucepan of water has a temperature of 67 °C but cools at a rate of 4 °C every minute on the kitchen worktop. The second saucepan contains the same volume of water and has a temperature of 89 °C. When left outside, this saucepan's water cools at a quicker rate of 9 °C every minute.

(a) Represent the changes in temperature for both saucepans on the same graph.

(b) Which saucepan will be the first to cool to a temperature of 0 °C? Explain your answer.

(c) After how many minutes will both saucepans' contents be the same temperature?

(d) What was the temperature of the water at this point?

9. A restaurant has two boilers which store hot water. The stainless steel boiler contains water at a temperature of 74 °C but cools by 3 °C every minute when turned off. The copper boiler's water is 87 °C but cools by 5 °C every minute when turned off.

(a) Plot both sets of information on a single graph.

(b) After how many minutes will both boilers be at the same temperature?

10. Two competing oil companies are drilling for oil. The Norwegian company has already drilled 300 m beneath sea level and can drill at a constant rate of 25 m per day. Their rival Scottish company is only starting to drill but it can drill at a constant rate of 45 m per day.

(a) Write down two equations to represent the depths drilled by both companies.

(b) Using these two equations, represent the drilling progress of both companies on the same graph.

(c) Hence, find the point of intersection between the two lines.

(d) After how many days will both companies have drilled to the same depth?

(e) It takes the Norwegian company 18 days to strike oil. Use your graph to calculate how many metres beneath sea level the Norwegians must drill before striking oil.

CHAPTER 5 SELF-CHECK TEST

1. The following are the first three terms in a linear pattern. Find the value of x.
   (a) $x - 2, 2x + 1, x + 14$
   (b) $x - 2, 3x + 1, 6x$
   (c) $5x - 1, 1, x + 1$
   (d) $5x + 5, 3x - 4, 2x - 7$
   (e) $2x, 3x + 5, 5x + 2$

2. Write down the first four terms in the following patterns and evaluate the common difference when given the following general terms:
   (a) $T_n = 5n + 3$
   (b) $T_n = 3n + 2$
   (c) $T_n = 10 - 7n$
   (d) $T_n = 4 - 2n$
   (e) $T_n = 4n$

3. A function f is defined as $f: x \rightarrow 2x + 2$. Find:
   (a) $f(0)$
   (b) $f(1)$
   (c) $f(2)$
   (d) $f(3)$
   (e) $f(4)$

4. A function f is defined as $f: x \rightarrow -2x - 3$. Find:
   (a) $f(0)$
   (b) $f(2)$
   (c) $f(4)$
   (d) $f(6)$
   (e) $f(8)$

5. A function f is defined as $f: x \rightarrow 17 - 2x$. Find:
   (a) $f(0)$
   (b) $f(3)$
   (c) $f(-1)$
   (d) $f(-3)$
   (e) $f(5)$

6. A function f is defined as $g: x \rightarrow 3x - 6$. Find:
   (a) $g\left(\frac{1}{3}\right)$
   (b) $g\left(\frac{5}{6}\right)$
   (c) $g(t)$
   (d) $g(2k)$
   (e) $g(-k)$

7. $f: x \rightarrow 5x + 4$ is a function. If the domain of f is {0, 1, 2, 3}, find the range.

8. $f: x \rightarrow -6x - 3$ is a function. If the domain of f is {3, −4, 5, −6}, find the range.

9. $f: x \rightarrow 3x$ is a function. If the domain of f is {0, 1, 4, 7, 10}, find the range.

10. $f: x \rightarrow 7 - 8x$ is a function. If the domain of f is {3, −4, 5, −6}, find the range.

11. A function f is defined as $f: x \rightarrow -x$. Copy the following mapping diagram and find the missing numbers represented by w, x and y.

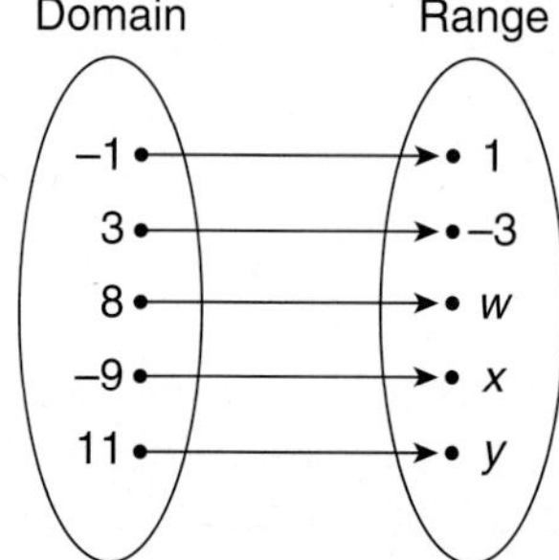

12. A function f is defined as $f: x \rightarrow 5x - 10$. Copy the following mapping diagram and find the missing numbers represented by w, x and y.

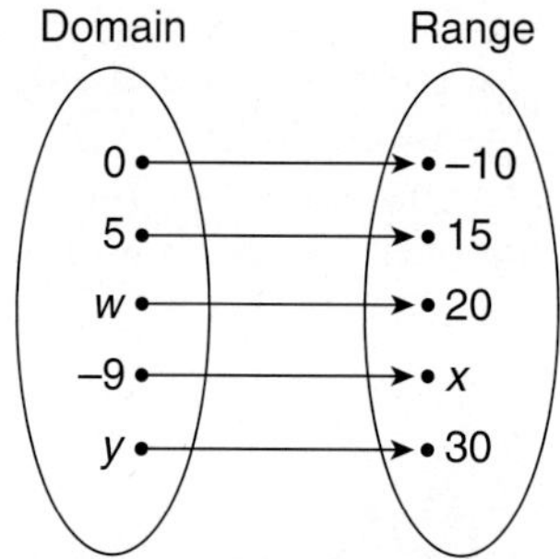

13. Examine the following linear pattern and then answer the questions:
   3, 12, 21, 30, 39, ...
   (a) Find the first term in the sequence.
   (b) Find the common difference, d.
   (c) Write down the next three terms in the sequence.
   (d) Describe the sequence in your own words.
   (e) Use the information above to complete the following table.

1st term	2nd term	3rd term	4th term	5th term	6th term	7th term	8th term	9th term	10th term	11th term	12th term
3	12	21	30	39							

   (f) Find the general term for the linear sequence.
   (g) Calculate the 72nd term in the linear pattern.

14. Patrick makes €12.00 an hour for his first hour of work, €17.00 for his second and €22.00 for his third.

(a) Write a general formula for the amount of money Patrick earns for n hours.

(b) Calculate how much money he earned after his fifth hour of work.

15. Eddie has drawn the following set of shapes:

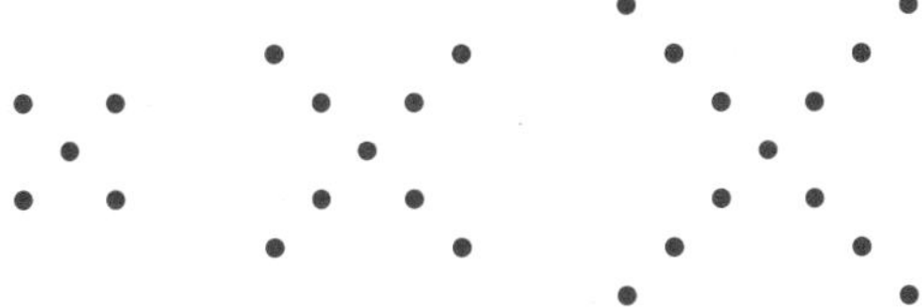

(a) Describe the growth of the pattern.

(b) What is changing in the pattern?

(c) Copy and complete the table to show the growth of the pattern.

Pattern	1	2	3	4	5	6
Number of dots						

(d) By putting the pattern number on the x-axis and the number of dots on the y-axis, plot the pattern on a Cartesian plane.

(e) How many dots would be in the 20th pattern? Explain your answer fully.

16. Ciarán has been experimenting with a tiling pattern. The first three patterns are shown here:

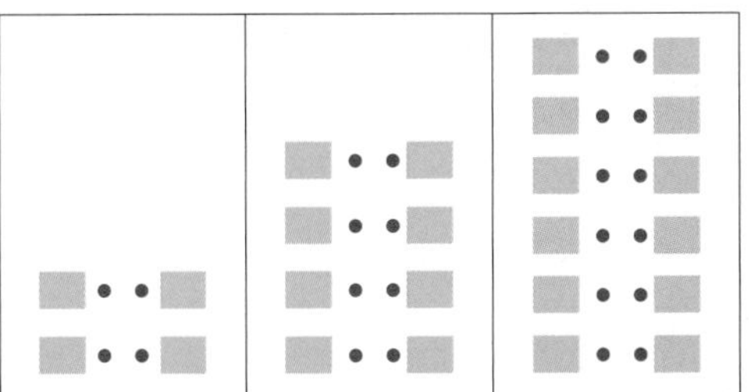

(a) Copy and complete the following table:

Number of ●	2	4	6	?	?	?
Number of ■		8				

(b) Describe how the pattern is growing.

(c) Plot the pattern on a Cartesian plane.

17. Emily has made some different patterns. These are the first three shapes in Emily's set:

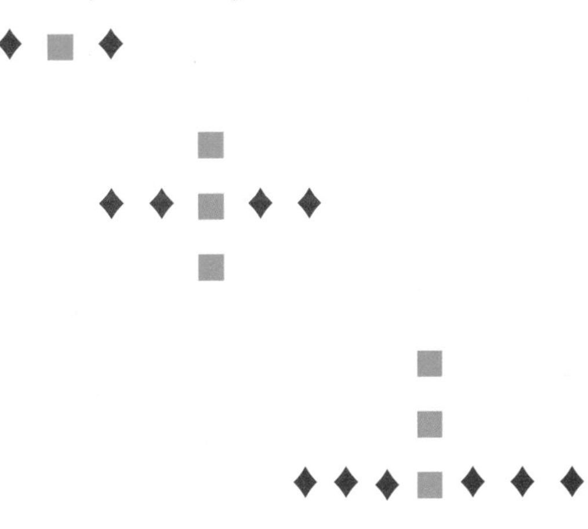

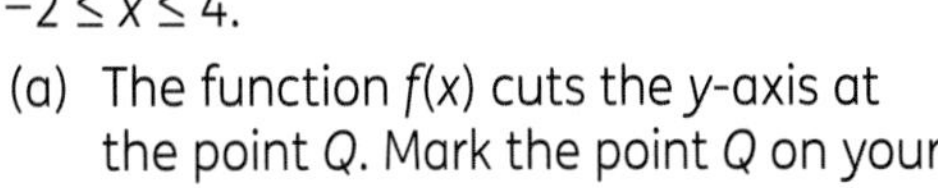

(a) Plot the pattern on a Cartesian plane.

(b) How many reds are needed if 13 greens are used?

18. Draw graphs of the following linear functions:

(a) $f{:}x \rightarrow 6x$ in the domain $-1 \leq x \leq 3$

(b) $g{:}x \rightarrow 10x$ in the domain $0 \leq x \leq 5$

(c) $h{:}x \rightarrow -4x$ in the domain $-1 \leq x \leq 3$

(d) $j{:}x \rightarrow 2x + 1$ in the domain $-2 \leq x \leq 5$

(e) $k{:}x \rightarrow x - 3$ in the domain $-3 \leq x \leq 4$

19. Draw the graph of the function $f{:}x \rightarrow 4 - 2x$ in the domain $-2 \leq x \leq 4$.

(a) The function $f(x)$ cuts the y-axis at the point Q. Mark the point Q on your graph.

(b) Write down the coordinates of the point Q.

20. Draw the graph of the function $g{:}x \rightarrow 3x - 9$ in the domain $0 \leq x \leq 4$.

(a) The function $g(x)$ cuts the y-axis at the point F. Mark the point F on your graph.

(b) Write down the coordinates of the point F.

21. Complete the table by matching each of the following functions to a suitable diagram and appropriate sentence.

Function	$f{:}x \to 2x$	$f{:}x \to -3x$	$f{:}x \to -x$	$f{:}x \to x$
Graph				
Sentence				

Graphs

A.
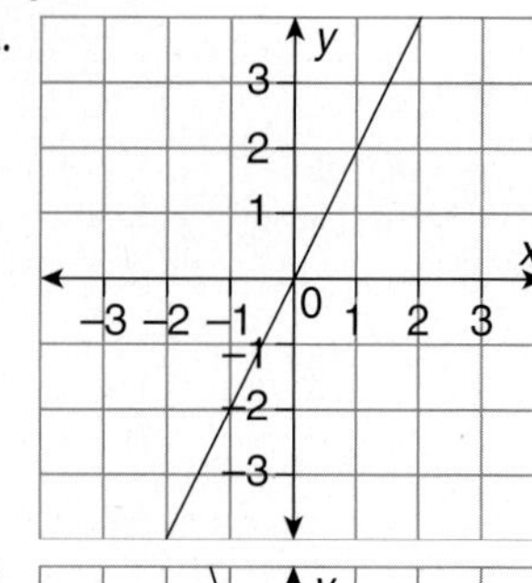

C.
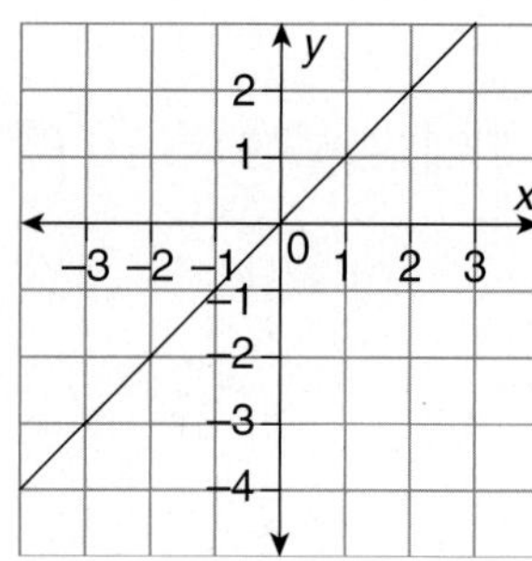

B.
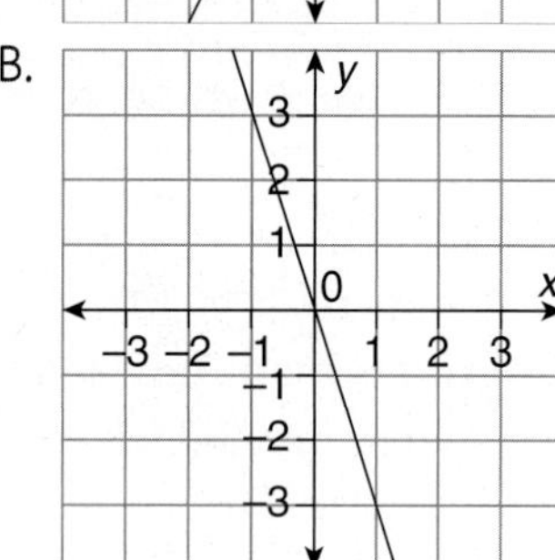

D.
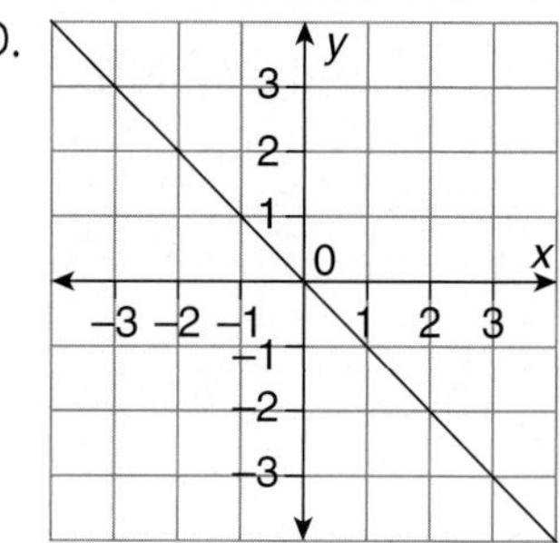

Sentences

(a) This is a decreasing function, where the y-intercept is 0 and the line passes through the point (2, −6).

(b) The domain and range in this function are identical values.

(c) The output has the opposite sign to the input in this function.

(d) In each coordinate of this function the x-value is half the y-value.

22. Explain why this relationship is not a function.

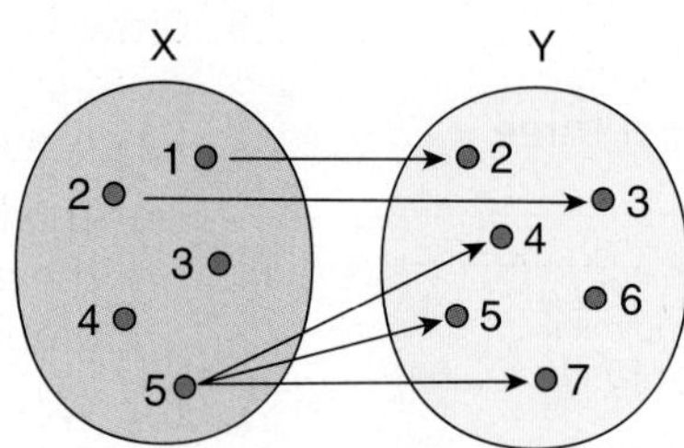

23. (a) Which of the following tables could represent a linear function? Give reasons for your answers.

(b) For each that could be linear, find a general term for the linear pattern.

(i)

x	g(x)
0	5
5	-10
10	-25
15	-40

(ii)

x	h(x)
0	5
5	30
10	105
15	230

(iii)

x	f(x)
0	5
5	20
10	45
15	70

(iv)

x	k(x)
5	13
10	28
20	58
25	73

(v)

x	t(x)
0	6
2	-19
3	-44
4	-69

(vi)

x	s(x)
2	13
4	23
8	43
10	53

(vii)

x	p(x)
2	-4
4	16
6	36
8	56

(viii)

x	m(x)
0	6
2	31
6	106
8	231

24. There is a stack of logs in the backyard. There are 15 logs in the first layer, 14 in the second, 13 in the third, 12 in the fourth, and so on with the last layer having exactly three logs.

(a) How many logs in total are in the stack?

(b) Write a general term to show this is a linear pattern.

25. Into her piggy bank, Catherine dropped €1.00 on 1 May, €1.75 on 2 May, €2.50 on 3 May and so on until the last day of May.

(a) How much did Catherine place in her piggy bank on 19 May?

(b) How much did she deposit in her piggy bank on 30 May?

26. A tube well is bored 800 m deep. The first metre costs €250 and the cost per metre increases by €50 for every subsequent metre.

(a) Find the cost of boring the 750th metre.

(b) Find the total cost for the entire job.

27. A theatre has 60 seats in the first row, 68 seats in the second row, 76 seats in the third row and so on in the same increasing pattern.

(a) If the theatre has 20 rows of seats, how many seats are in the 20th row of the theatre?

(b) How many seats are in the 13th row?

(c) For a concert, the first 4 rows were sold at a cost of €24.99 per seat. Calculate how much money the theatre made.

28. Maura has 55 blocks. She decides to stack up all the blocks so that each row has one less block than the row below. She wants to end up with just 1 block on top. How many should she put in the bottom row?

29. Brendan deposited €20,000 and will earn €1,750 interest for every year that his money stays in the account.

(a) How much money will he have in his account by the end of the eighth year?

(b) Meanwhile his wife Margaret saves €500 each month. If her money earns no interest at all, how much money will she have in her account by the end of the eighth year?

30. A house worth €350,000 when purchased was worth €335,000 after the first year and €320,000 after the second year.

(a) Write a formula for the sequence, explaining all notation used.

(b) If this trend continues, what will the value of the house be after 6 years?

(c) Represent the above information on a suitable graph.

31. The sum of the interior angles of a triangle is 180°, of a quadrilateral is 360° and of a pentagon is 540°. Assuming this pattern continues, find the sum of the interior angles of a dodecagon. (Hint: it has 12 sides.)

32. Paula decides to open a savings account in her local credit union. She saves €10 a week.

(a) Copy and complete the following table:

Week	1	2	3	4	5	6	7
Total savings (€)							

(b) How much will Paula have saved in week 5?

(c) Copy the following Cartesian plane and plot the points to show the growth of Paula's savings each week.

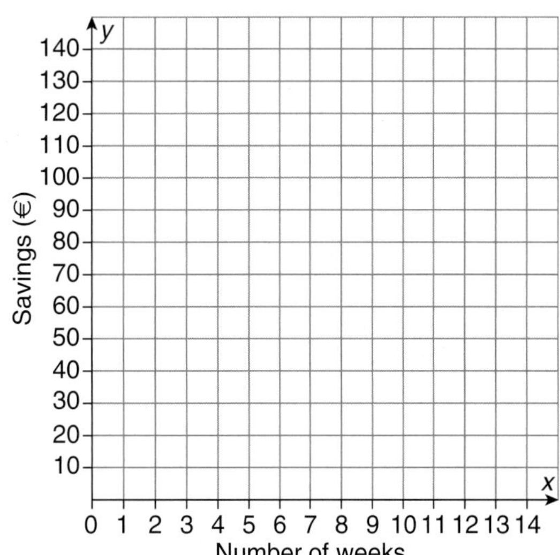

(d) Using a straight edge, join the points on your plane. What have they formed?

(e) Explain how you can use the graph to find the amount of savings Paula has at any time.

(f) How much will Paula have saved after 12 weeks?

(g) Paula's friend Nigel opens an account four weeks later but saves €15 a week. Copy and complete the following table:

Week	4	5	6	7	8	9	10
Total savings (€)							

(h) On the Cartesian plane drawn for Paula's account, plot the points to show the growth of Nigel's savings each week.

(i) After how many weeks will Nigel have the same amount saved as Paula?

CHAPTER 5 KNOWLEDGE CHECKLIST

After completing this chapter, I now:

- Am able to identify a pattern ☐
- Am able to identify, name and draw linear patterns ☐
- Am able to describe a linear pattern using a general formula ☐
- Understand the terms associated with graphs and functions such as domain, codomain, range and y-intercept ☐
- Am able to use function notation and to interpret linear graphs ☐
- Am able to find solutions to problems of the form $f(x) = g(x)$ and to interpret these results ☐
- Am able to apply all the above to real-life situations ☐

Challenge

A magic square is a square grid containing numbers. Each column and row add to give the same value.

Can you work out what each of these symbols stand for, so that the square becomes a magic square?

♥	1	♦
3	5	7
♣	9	♠

STATISTICS 1

LEARNING OUTCOMES

In this chapter you will learn:

- ✓ About types of data
- ✓ About the data handling cycle
- ✓ How to select a sample to ensure it is truly representative of the population
- ✓ That numerical data can be divided into continuous and discrete data
- ✓ That categorical data can be divided into nominal or ordinal data
- ✓ How to identify an outlier in a set of data
- ✓ To calculate the mean
- ✓ To identify the mode
- ✓ To order or rank data and numbers
- ✓ To identify the median
- ✓ To find the range for a set of numerical data
- ✓ To construct and read data from frequency tables and grouped frequency tables
- ✓ To calculate the mean from a grouped frequency table
- ✓ Which measure of central tendency to use

KEY WORDS

- Ascending
- Biased
- Categorical data
- Continuous data
- Descending
- Discrete data
- Extreme values
- Frequency table
- Grouped frequency table
- Mean
- Measures of central tendency
- Measures of spread
- Median
- Mode
- Nominal data
- Numerical data
- Ordinal data
- Outlier
- Range
- Reliability
- Sampling
- Unbiased

INTRODUCTION

In *Maths in Action 1*, you examined some of the basic principles of statistics.

You looked at how and why statisticians gather statistics. You also learned how to display the different types of data collected.

We will now look at statistics in more detail.

Some staggering statistics!

- A baby blue whale gains about 90 kg a day. The blue whale is the largest animal on earth. An adult blue whale can be 30.5 m long and weigh up to 150 tonnes. That's as large as a Boeing jet! A blue whale's heart is as large as a small car. Fifty people could stand on its tongue. Its spout shoots up at least 10 m when it surfaces for air.

- Over 3.2 million students are victims of bullying in the US each year. Around 160,000 teens skip school every day because of bullying. 56 per cent of students have seen some type of bullying at school. 1 in 10 students leaves school because of repeated bullying.
- Abraham Lincoln was elected to the US Congress in 1846. John F. Kennedy was elected to Congress in 1946. Abraham Lincoln was elected US president in 1860. John F. Kennedy was elected president in 1960. Both were shot in the back of the head in the presence of their wives on a Friday. Both were succeeded by men named Johnson, who came from the southern states of the US. Andrew Johnson, who succeeded Lincoln, was born in 1808. Lyndon Johnson, who succeeded Kennedy, was born in 1908. Lincoln was shot in the Ford Theatre. Kennedy was shot in a Lincoln, made by Ford. Lincoln was shot in a theatre and his assassin ran and hid in a warehouse. Kennedy was shot from a warehouse and his assassin ran and hid in a theatre. The killers, Booth and Oswald, were both assassinated before their trials.

First year revision

1. Explain the following terms:

(a) Census
(b) Population
(c) Sample
(d) Primary data
(e) Secondary data
(f) Numerical data
(g) Categorical data
(h) Continuous data
(i) Discrete data

2. Copy the following table and place each quantity or measurement in the appropriate column:

Continuous data	Discrete data
Example: The number of waves in the sea	Example: The number of people at a match on a certain day

(a) The speed of a car
(b) The number of matches in a new matchbox
(c) The air temperature of the air outside at midday today

(d) The temperature of water in a boiling kettle

(e) The population of the Republic of Ireland at midnight tonight

(f) The height of Mount Everest

(g) The distance from the Earth to the Moon

(h) The amount of water people use when they take a shower

(i) The number of pages in a book

(j) The cost of a holiday

(k) The number of words on a page of a newspaper

3. 30 people were asked which film they had watched when they were leaving the cinema. Examine the results below:

Saw, Blind Side, New Moon, Robin Hood, Avatar, Robin Hood, Avatar, Avatar, Avatar, Avatar, Blind Side, Blind Side, Saw, Avatar, Blind Side, Saw, Saw, Avatar, Robin Hood, Robin Hood, Robin Hood, Saw, Avatar, Robin Hood, Saw, Avatar, Robin Hood, Saw, Avatar, Avatar

Copy and complete the following table:

Film	Tally	No. of People
Avatar		
Saw		
Robin Hood		
Blind Side		
New Moon		

(a) Which film was the least popular among the 30 viewers?

(b) Which was the most popular film among the 30 viewers?

(c) The answers were given as the people left the cinema. What film did the 20th person see?

(d) Copy and complete the following frequency table:

Film	Avatar	Saw	Robin Hood	Blind Side	New Moon
No. of people					

(e) Suggest different ways this information could have been collected.

(f) Suggest three possible **unbiased** questions that could have been asked in this survey.

(g) Give an example of a biased question for the above survey?

Section 6.1: Data types

DATA TYPES EXPLAINED

In *Maths in Action 1*, you looked at different types of data. Data is either **numerical** or **categorical.**

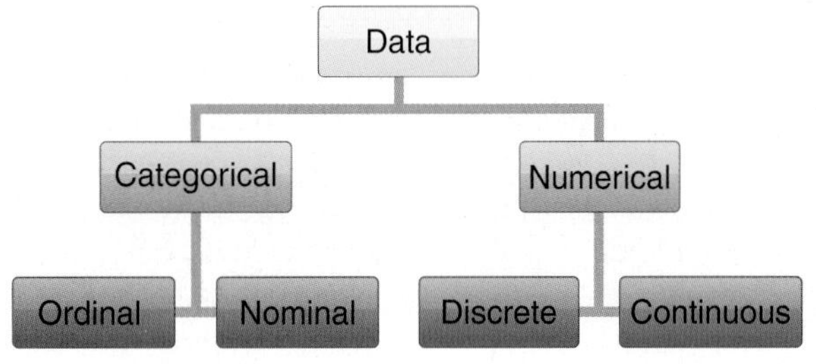

Numerical data

Numerical data can be divided into two types: **discrete** or **continuous.**

Numerical data that is **discrete** can be counted. Examples include:

- The number of Smarties in a packet
- The number of eggs laid by a hen
- The number of children in a family

Numerical data that is continuous can be measured on a scale but may not have an exact value. Examples include:

- The height of a mountain
- The temperature of an atom bomb
- The age of a fossil

Numerical data is also known as **quantitative data.**

Categorical data

Categorical data can be divided into two types: **nominal** and **ordinal.**

Nominal data is information in words that cannot be put in order. Examples include:

- The names of your friends
- The colour of a person's eyes
- The counties in Connacht

Ordinal data ranks or orders the data. Examples include:

- First, second, third
- Fastest, slowest
- Small, medium, large, extra large

Categorical data is 'describing' data. It cannot be counted. It is also known as **qualitative data.**

Exercise 6.1

1. A doctor keeps detailed records of her patients. For each of her patients, she fills in a 'Patient Record' card. John Doe's card is shown below:

Patient record		
Name: John Doe		D.O.B: 04/12/1990
Address: Green Street, Enniscorthy, Co. Wexford	Weight (kg): 130	Height (m): 1.7
	Blood Type: O	Next of Kin: Jane Doe
Allergies: Penicillin	Phone: 087 999 3333	Occupation: Tax Inspector

For each of the categories in this 'Patient Record' card, state whether the data is numerical data (discrete or continuous) or categorical data (nominal or ordinal).

2. The following table shows the breakfast cereals Paddy ate over a number of months:

Cereal	Preference	Calories/100 g	Sodium (mg) per serving
Frosted Flakes	4th	110	290
Fruity Pebbles	2nd	110	200
Rice Bubbles	1st	100	135
Puffy Wheat Flakes	5rd	70	10
Choco Flakes	3th	140	290

(a) For each piece of data, state whether it is numerical data (discrete or continuous) or categorical data (nominal or ordinal).
(b) List two pieces of data that Paddy might use on a spreadsheet in future years.

3. The following table gives some details of tall sailing ships. For each piece of data, state whether it is numerical or categorical. Also state if it is nominal, ordinal, discrete or continuous data.

Boat name	Flag	Built	Length
Antigua	Holland	1956	48.158 m
Asgard II*	Ireland	1981	31.670 m
Belem	France	1896	50.902 m
Anna Christina	Norway	1889	33.045 m
Amerigo Vespucci	Italy	1931	100.584 m
HMS Bounty	USA.	1960	51.511 m

Asgard II was the successor to *Asgard*, which was owned and captained by Erskine Childers. *Asgard* was a wedding present to him from his father-in-law. *Asgard II* sank in French waters in the Bay of Biscay in September 2008.

4. There are four horses in a field. Use one of the words to complete these sentences.

Discrete **Numerical** **Continuous** **Categorical**

(a) The colour of the horses is ___________ data.

(b) The number of horses in the field is ___________ numerical data.

(c) The total number of legs in the field is ___________ numerical data.

(d) The weight of each horse is ___________ data.

Section 6.2: The data handling cycle

Statisticians use the data handling cycle to help plan surveys and experiments. The cycle is a structured plan to collect, analyse, arrange, examine and explain the results of the data gathered.

The data handling cycle has four main stages:

1. **Ask a question:** The statistician writes suitable questions to get the data needed.
2. **Collect data:** The statistician decides from whom to collect the data and how it will be collected.
3. **Analyse the data:** Once collected, the data will be studied, analysed, arranged into tables and graphed to make the information easier to understand.
4. **Interpret the results:** The data is then examined for the answers to the questions asked. This shows how important it is to ask suitable and unbiased questions at the beginning of the data handling cycle.

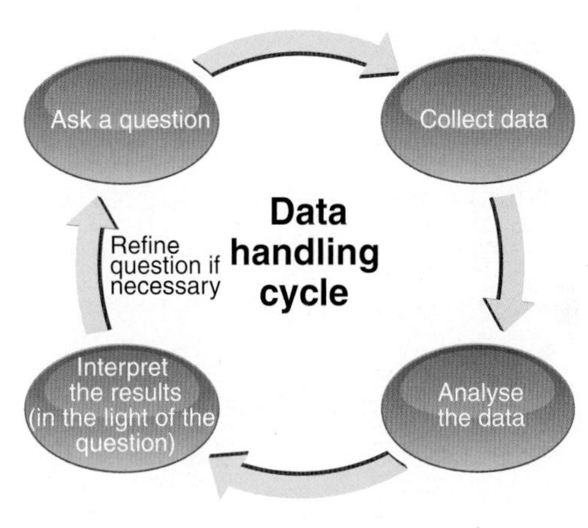

Section 6.3 Sampling and the reliability of data

Student Activity 6A

Working in pairs, discuss each of the following scenarios.

1. Ann wants to survey people on the attitudes to religion in Ireland. She decides to carry out a survey outside her local church after mass on Sunday. When completed, Ann's results show that everyone in Ireland has a very positive attitude towards religion. Is Ann's claim valid? Explain your answer fully.
2. A marketing company in Galway decides to carry out a phone survey about internet packages and internet usage countrywide. They phone 100 houses between 5 p.m. and 7 p.m. each evening for a week. If the phone is answered, they ask each person a number of questions about their internet package and daily usage.
   (a) Can you think of two disadvantages of carrying out the survey in this manner?
   (b) Will the company be able to determine internet usage and packages countrywide? Explain your answer.
   (c) Give an example of how you could improve this survey.

SAMPLING AND THE RELIABILITY OF DATA EXPLAINED

Sampling

In *Maths in Action 1*, you learned the difference between a **population** and a **sample.**

Collecting information from an entire **population** means asking everyone who could be asked. For example, data could be collected from a whole school, or from everyone who lives in Co. Wexford. Data collected from a population is called **census data.**

Collecting information from a **sample** means only a part of the population will be surveyed. The sample information may then be used to make conclusions about the whole population. For example, 30 first year students could be surveyed and the information could be taken as representing the opinions of the whole year. Data collected from a sample is called **sample data.**

You also looked at the process of choosing an **unbiased** sample for a survey. If an incorrect sample is chosen, the results of any survey or experiment will be **biased.**

Bias is anything that distorts the truth.

Bias may result from many factors such as:

- Failure to correctly identify the population
- Choosing a sample that is not representative of the population
- Failure of some people to respond to a survey
- Ambiguous or vague questions, like 'Are you tall?'
- People being careless when filling in a questionnaire and making errors
- People being dishonest when answering certain questions
- Asking leading questions that suggest a particular answer, such as 'Do you agree that Liverpool FC are the greatest football team in the world?'

Designing a survey

Designing a survey correctly is an important part of the process. When designing a survey keep the following points in mind:

1. **Provide an introduction so the respondent understands the purpose of the survey.** For example: This is a short survey to collect data about teenager's hobbies. This information will be used to help us decide whether we need more clubs in our school. Please answer the questions below.
2. **Avoid questions that are too personal or may cause embarrassment.** For example: How well educated are you? How old are you? A more appropriate way of asking the previous question is: Which age category do you fall into? Please tick.

   Under-16, 16–18, 18–21, 21–30, 30–40, Over-40.
3. **Ensure the questions are relevant to your survey.** For example, if you are carrying out a survey about music, there is no point asking questions about sport or food.
4. **Keep the questions brief and use simple language.** This encourages people to complete the survey. Record the answers clearly. For example: How often do you go to the cinema? Please tick.

   Never, Once a month, Twice a month, At least three times a month
5. **Ask for only one response at a time.** For example: What is your favourite colour?
6. **Use simple questions at the start and progress to more difficult questions later in the survey.** For example: Which type of film do you prefer? Please tick. Fantasy, Romance, Thriller, Horror, Comedy, None of the above.
7. **Allow for every possible answer.** How old are you? Please tick. Under-10, 11–35, 35+

   This question does not allow a response from those who are aged 10.

8. **Avoid vague questions.** For example: How often do you take part in physical exercise? Please tick. Sometimes, Always, Never.

   This question could instead be asked as follows: How many hours do you spend exercising each week? Please tick. Less than 2, 2–6, 6+

9. **Avoid leading questions, which are questions that suggest a particular answer.** For example: Do you think that statistics is:

   (a) A very interesting subject? (c) Quite an interesting subject?

   (b) An interesting subject?

   This question does not allow for the person to answer that they do not like statistics.

10. **Avoid open-ended questions, which are questions that have no specific answer.** This type of question allows the respondent to give an essay-style answer. For example: What is your opinion of this school?

11. **Always carry out a pilot study.** Before using a questionnaire, it is essential to know that it works. There may be questions that need to be rewritten or new questions that need to be added. Use a small group of people as a pilot study to perfect the questions before carrying out the real study.

Misleading statistics

Statistics can often be intentionally misused or misrepresented to the public. The results of a statistical investigation can be affected in a number of ways. You examined these in your first year course. They can be summarised as follows:

1. **Sources:** It is important to note where all collected information has come from and who generated it. It is common practice for companies to carry out their own research, which makes their product appear to be the best on offer.

2. **Misleading graphics:** Graphical representation of statistics can often be distorted in order to mislead the public.

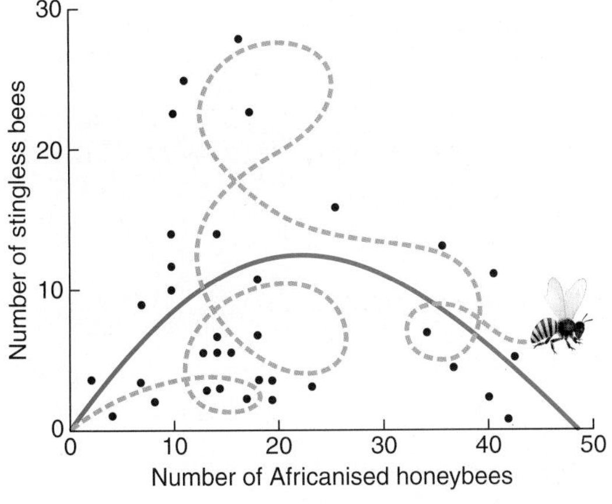

3. **Misleading figures:** Many advertisements contain figures that are distorted or not truly representative of the population. Again it is important to note where the figures are coming from.

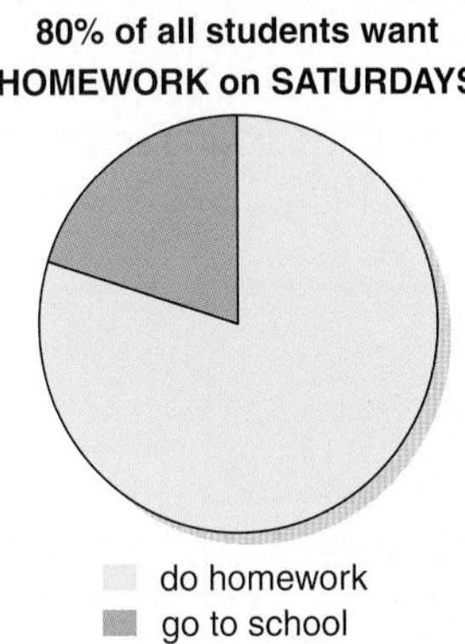

4. **Unfair or biased samples:** As we have seen, it is very important to choose a fair and large sample when carrying out a survey, to ensure the results are representative. This makes sure any sample is a fair representation of the entire population. For example, a national newspaper reported on feelings towards the Irish government but only asked people who were openly opposed to the government:

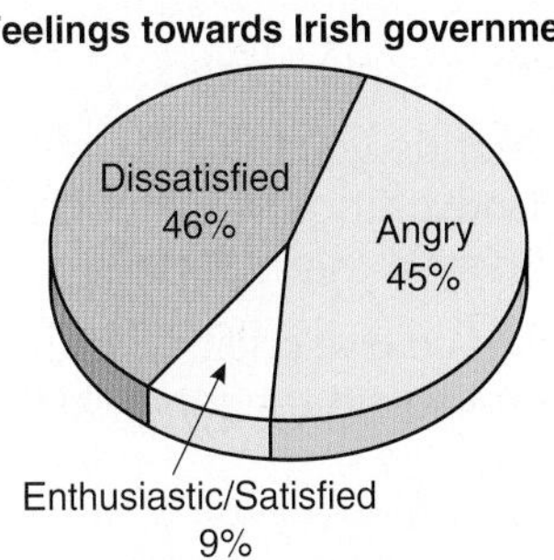

5. **Misleading comparisons:** 'The cost of living now is 4 times higher than in the 1970s.' This is an unfair comparison since society has developed into a better educated and more skilled workforce rewarded with higher wages. Another example is a sports journalist complaining about the increase in the cost of tickets to games.

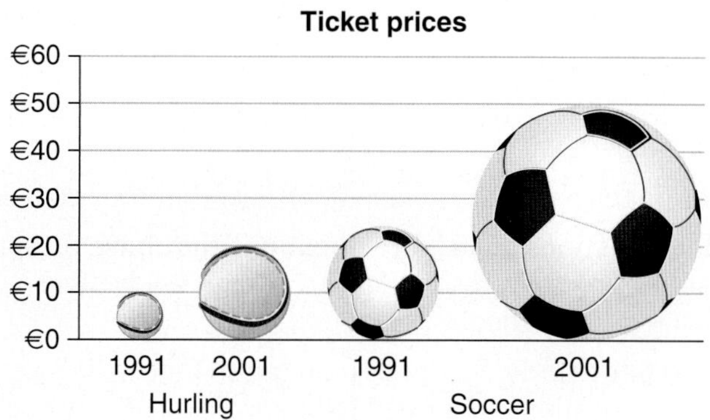

6. **Outliers in data:** Sometimes we may encounter a value in the data which is not consistent with the rest of the data. Such a value is called an **outlier.**

   In a survey, an outlier might be caused by the surveyor recording an incorrect answer or by a person providing incorrect data. For example, ten students wrote their heights to the nearest cm as follows: 150, 147, 139, 156, 160, 155, **1153**, 153, 152, 152.

   From this set of data, you can see that 1153 is an outlier as nobody could be that tall. This incorrect data can affect the analysis and interpretation of the data. According to these figures, the average height of these ten students is 252 cm! We can easily see this is incorrect. If we omit the outlier from our calculations, we get an average height of 152 cm which is accurate and more likely.

   Outliers can also occur naturally in statistics. For example, if a survey was carried out in a factory on the wages of employees, the managing director's salary would be far higher than the other workers'. In this case the managing director's salary might seem to be an outlier. This shows how important it is to carefully examine all data in terms of its context. Statisticians must identify outliers and decide if they should omit them from the data collected.

Exercise 6.2

1. A supermarket is carrying out a survey about the shopping habits of people in its locality. They decide to carry out a postal survey of all houses in the locality.

   (a) Is this a fair sample for this survey? Explain your answer.
   (b) What do you think is the main disadvantage of carrying out the survey in this manner?
   (c) Can you give one advantage of carrying out the survey in this manner?

2. A newspaper reporter is carrying out a survey on the price of properties nationwide. She visits 40 different real estate offices in Co. Dublin. She records the prices of the houses in each of the areas and then calculates the average national house price.

   (a) Did the reporter choose a fair sample for this survey? Explain your answer.
   (b) Suggest how the reporter could improve this survey?

3. Carry out a face-to-face survey in your locality on any topic of interest. Before carrying out the survey you need to:
   (a) Design a questionnaire with ten questions. (Remember to keep the questions short and relevant to the topic.)
   (b) Pick a location you think would be suitable for the survey. Explain your choice.
   (c) List any problems you think you might encounter while carrying out the survey.
   (d) Discuss with your teacher the sample you would hope to use.
4. Your school has been asked to take part in a European survey comparing second year groups around Europe. Your class is the only class in Ireland taking part in the survey. You must answer questions based on pastimes, favourite subjects, family size and so on.
   Working in pairs, make lists of ways in which your maths class:
   (a) Is typical and representative of all Irish second year students
   (b) Is not typical or truly representative of all Irish second year students
   Can you suggest how this survey could be carried out quickly and with a better sample?

Section 6.4: Measures of central tendency

Statisticians are often concerned with finding the **average** for a set of figures, such as the average temperature or average rainfall.

Average power of new registered cars in Germany

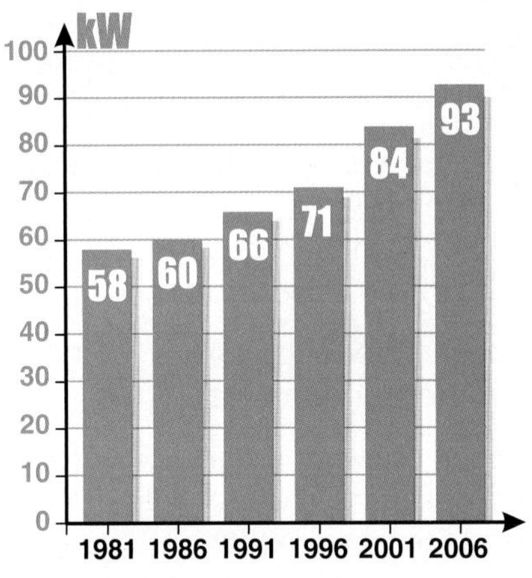

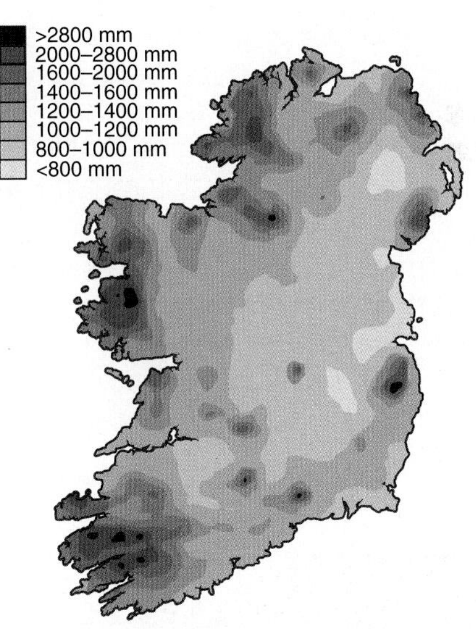

Average rainfall in Ireland

In the following sections, you will look at three specific **measures of central tendency** called the **mean, mode and median.**

Section 6.5: The mean

Student Activity 6B

1. Read each of the following statements. Discuss each statement in pairs.
   - You might consider yourself as having **average** sporting ability.
   - Some people might consider themselves as being **average** at art or a musical skill.

   (a) Can you identify any problems with the use of the word **'average'** in these statements?
   (b) What do you understand by the word **'average'**? Compare your answers with others in your class.
2. How would you calculate the average value for the following set of figures?
   (a) The average age of the students in your class
   (b) Your average grade in all subjects at school

THE MEAN EXPLAINED

The word 'average' can be used in many contexts and so its meaning can be uncertain and unclear. In statistics, we often deal with the **mean** instead of **average.** The mean can be found using the following formula:

$$\bar{x} = \frac{\text{The total of the numbers added together}}{\text{The number of numbers}}$$

We use $\bar{x}$ as the symbol for **mean.** It takes account of all the values in the data set.

EXAMPLE 1

(a) Find the mean of 1, 2, 3, 4 and 5.

(b) The mean of 6 numbers is 5. If five of the numbers are 2, 3, 5, 8 and 9, find the value of the sixth number.

Solution

(a) $\bar{x} = \frac{1+2+3+4+5}{5} = \frac{15}{5} = 3$

(b) $6 \times 5 = 30$ **Find the sum of the numbers**

$2 + 3 + 5 + 8 + 9 = 27$ **Find the sum of the numbers we are given**

$30 - 27 = 3$ **The missing number must be 3**

Exercise 6.3

For each of the following sets of values, calculate the mean:

1. 1, 2, 3, 4, 5, 9
2. 17.3, 8.9, 31.7, 15.4, 25.2
3. 2.8, 1.4, 1.6, 2.9, 3.1, 0.2
4. €3.46, €2.85, €0.92, €1.48, €4.76, €0.57
5. 3 min 15 sec, 2 min 40 sec, 3 min 28 sec, 2 min 18 sec, 3 min 54 sec
6. 1.85 kg, 2.04 kg, 886 g, 1.051 kg, 978 g
7. 2.16 m, 3.5 m, 14 m, 89 cm, 665 mm, 1.906 m
8. 17 hr 45 min; 21 hr 30 min; 16 hr 20 min; 19 hr 50 min; 20 hr 15 min
9. 10.2, 19.5, 28.7, 17.6, 6.9
10. 10, 21.9, 35.8, 11.4, 2.5, 39.0
11. The mean of five numbers is 6. Find the sum of the five numbers.
12. The mean of seven numbers is 3. Find the sum of the seven numbers.
13. The mean of ten numbers is 2. Find the sum of the ten numbers.
14. The mean of three numbers is 10. Find the sum of the three numbers.
15. The mean of four numbers is 8. Find the sum of the four numbers.
16. The mean of five numbers is 8. If four of the numbers are 2, 6, 7 and 13, find the value of the fifth number.
17. The mean of four numbers is 7. If three of the numbers are 3, 7 and 9, find the value of the fourth number.
18. The mean of eight numbers is 6. If seven of the numbers are 2, 3, 4, 5, 9, 11 and 13, find the value of the eighth number.
19. The mean of nine numbers is 8. If eight of the numbers are 2, 4, 6, 8, 10, 12, 14 and 15, find the value of the ninth number.
20. The mean of six numbers is 7. If five of the numbers are 1, 5, 7, 8 and 11, find the value of the sixth number.
21. The mean of four numbers is 5. When a fifth number is added, the mean is 7. Find the value of the fifth number.
22. The mean of five numbers is 7. When a sixth number is added, the mean is 10. Find the value of the sixth number.

23. The mean of nine numbers is 5. When a tenth number is added, the mean is 7. Find the value of the tenth number.

24. The mean of seven numbers is 5. When an eighth number is added, the mean is 7. Find the value of the eighth number.

25. The mean of three numbers is 5. When a fourth number is added, the mean is 7. Find the value of the fourth number.

26. The mean of four numbers is 21. Two of the numbers are 14 and 24. The other two numbers have an equal value. Find the value of each of the missing numbers.

27. The mean of five numbers is 37. Three of the numbers are 19, 41 and 51. The other two numbers have an equal value. Find the value of each of the missing numbers.

28. The mean of five numbers is 52. Two of the numbers are 60 and 65. The other three numbers have an equal value. Find the value of each of the missing numbers.

29. The mean of five numbers is 11. When one of the numbers is removed, the mean is increased by 2. Find the value of the removed number.

30. The mean of seven numbers is 32. When two identical numbers are removed, the mean is increased by 8. Find the value of one of the removed numbers.

31. The mean of seven numbers is 18. When two of the numbers are removed, the mean is decreased by 2. Find the value of the sum of the removed numbers.

32. The mean price of four cakes is €5.60. The price of two cakes is €7.17 and €3.99. The other two cakes are the same price. Find the price of one of the other cakes.

33. The mean price of five bunches of grapes is €2.79. The first two bunches cost €1.68 and €2.94. The three other bunches cost the same price. Calculate the price of one of these bunches.

34. The mean price of six bags of animal feed is €6.75. If two bags of dairy nuts cost €6 each, calculate the mean price of each of the remaining bags of sheep nuts purchased.

35. Six people have a meal in a restaurant. The mean cost of the meal per person was €24.58.
   (a) What is the total cost of the bill if a service charge of 25% of the bill is then added on?
   (b) What is the mean cost per customer, correct to the nearest euro?

36. A basketball player scores an average of 6 points per game in her last six games. How many points must she score:
   (a) In her next match to increase her mean score to 8 points per game?
   (b) In her next match to increase her mean score to 10 points per game?
   (c) How many more scoreless matches must she play to reduce her mean to 3 points per game?

Section 6.6: The mode

Student Activity 6C

Follow the instructions:

1. Write down which football team in the Premiership you support. If you do not support a team, write 'none'.
2. When all your classmates have finished, hold up your answer for all to see.
3. By looking around, can you write down the most popular team in the class?
4. Why do you think that team is the most popular?

THE MODE EXPLAINED

In statistics, we often use the number that occurs **most often** as a more representative number. This is the most frequent answer.

The word **'mode'** comes from the French, **'mode'**, which means fashion.

The **mode** is the most frequent or popular answer.

EXAMPLE 2

Identify the mode in the following data.
2, 3, 3, 2, 5, 1, 6, 7, 8, 3

Solution

2, 3, 3, 2, 5, 1, 6, 7, 8, 3
3 appears most often in the list
So the mode = 3

Exercise 6.4

1. Write down the mode for each of the following lists of numbers. If you cannot identify a mode, explain why.

   (a) 1, 4, 2, 5, 3, 2, 2
   (b) 2, 12, 34, 12, 1, 1, 5, 5, 1
   (c) 5, 7, 8, 9, 10, 2, 3, 2, 3
   (d) 1, 1, 1, 3, 3, 3, 3, 4, 4, 5, 1, 1, 4
   (e) 53, 57, 58, 54, 61, 66, 54, 60
   (f) 28, 26, 22, 32, 35, 33, 22, 36
   (g) 106, 101, 105, 113, 106, 102

2. Twenty students were asked what their favourite food was. The results were recorded in the following frequency table:

Food	Pizza	Chips	Steak	Fish	Lasagne
No. of students	8	3	3	2	4

   (a) What was the most popular or modal food choice?
   (b) What was the least popular food?
   (c) Is the data numerical or categorical?

3. Thirty pedestrians were asked to name their favourite pastime.
   The results were recorded in the table.

Pastime	Reading	Walking	Watching TV	Playing computer games	Going to the cinema
No. of pedestrians	10	7	4	6	3

   (a) What was the most popular or modal pastime?
   (b) What was the least favourite pastime?
   (c) Is the data numerical or categorical?

4. One hundred students were asked how they travelled to school each day. The results were recorded in the table.

Mode of transport	Bus	Car	Walking	Cycling
No. of students	67	17	9	7

   (a) What was the most popular or modal method of transport?
   (b) What was the least popular method of transport?
   (c) Is the data numerical or categorical?

5. A number of people were asked which tourist attraction in the world they would most like to visit. The results were recorded in the table:

Attraction	Great Wall of China	Eiffel Tower	Niagara Falls	Grand Canyon	Great Barrier Reef
No. of people	42	27	33	51	47

(a) How many people were surveyed?
(b) What was the most popular or modal tourist attraction?
(c) What was the least favourite tourist attraction?
(d) Is the data numerical or categorical?

6. A group of second year boys was asked what their favourite sport was. The table shows how they voted.

Sport	Number of boys
Hurling	9
Rugby	7
Football	6
Golf	8
Swimming	3

(a) How many people took part in the survey?
(b) What is the most popular or modal sport in this survey?
(c) What is the least popular sport?
(d) Is the data numerical or categorical?
(e) Would the mean be a useful statistic in this survey? Explain your answer.

7. A group of second year students was asked what make of car they hoped to buy when they started working. The table shows their responses.

Make of car	Frequency
Audi	8
BMW	9
Ford	3
Honda	2
Kia	1
Opel	4
Peugeot	4
Suzuki	7
Volvo	6

(a) What is the modal make of car in this survey?
(b) What make of car is the least popular in this survey?
(c) Is the data numerical or categorical?

8. The bar chart shows the weekly number of sales of DVDs in a small shop in Dúnbeg.

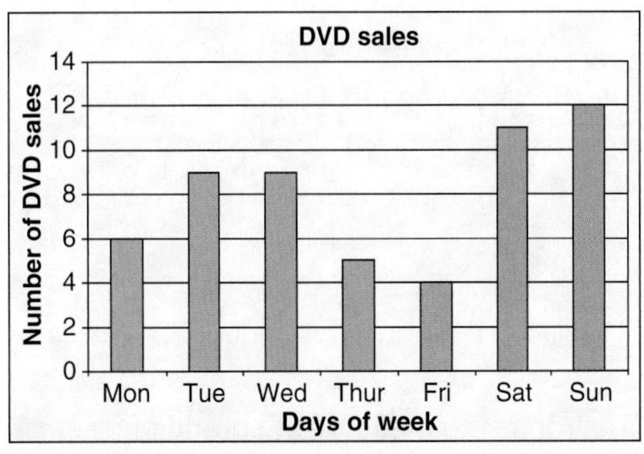

(a) On how many days in the week were more than 6 DVDs sold?
(b) What is the modal number sold that week?
(c) On which day were the most DVDs sold?
(d) In three sentences, describe the sales of DVDs in this shop over the week.

9. The bar graph shows the types of fish Stephen caught when he went fishing in a lake near Athlone.

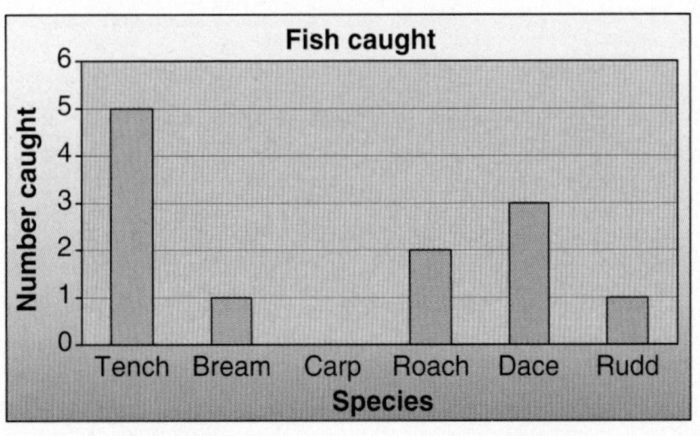

(a) What is the modal species caught by Stephen?
(b) What species of fish in this list did he fail to catch?
(c) Is the mean number of the species caught a useful statistic in your opinion? Explain your answer.

10. A group of customers in a DVD rental outlet were asked which type of movie they preferred. The results are shown in the bar chart.

(a) How many customers were surveyed?

(b) What was the modal type of film?

(c) What was the least popular film type?

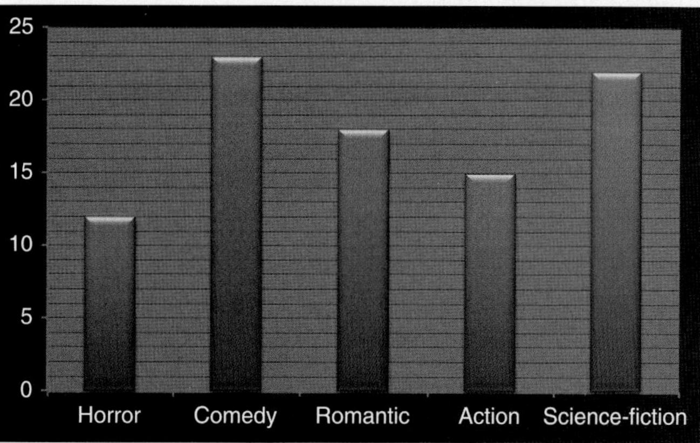

11. Find the value of x when given the mode of the following lists of numbers:

(a) 3, 4, x, 2, 1, 3, 2 (Mode is 2)

(b) 7, 5, 5, 6, 3, x, 7 (Mode is 5)

(c) 10, x , 12, 11, 10, 13, 11 (Mode is 11)

(d) 13, 11, 13, 11, 11, x, 13 (Mode is 13)

(e) 15, 14, x, 3, 7, 11, 12 (Mode is 15)

(f) 18, 8, 14, 18, 7, x, 14 (Mode is 18)

(g) x, 17, 19, 17, 19, 17, 19 (Mode is 19)

(h) 21, 19, 19, x, 21, 19, 21 (Mode is 21)

12. Write down any five numbers so that the mode is 7 and the mean is 4.

13. Write down any five numbers so that the mode is 10, the mean is 9 and four of the numbers are identical.

14. Write down any six numbers so that the mean is 4 and the mode is 5.

15. Write down three numbers so that the mean is 5 and the mode is 6.

Section 6.7: Ordering data

When Olympic athletes compete, they are **ordered** according to how they finish. So gold goes to the athlete in 1st place, silver goes to the 2nd placed athlete and bronze is awarded to the 3rd placed athlete. We assume that there are no 'ties' when the medals are awarded.

- Sometimes, we order data starting with the smallest number, for example, 2, 3, 6, 9, 13. This is called **ascending** order.
- Sometimes we order data starting with the largest number, for example, 13, 9, 6, 3, 2. This is called **descending** order.

Ordering is an important part of statistics. Once data has been ordered, statisticians can find the **range.**

The **range** is the difference between the highest and lowest values in the ordered table or list.

Range = The largest value – The smallest value

The range is a **measure of spread** of a set of data.

EXAMPLE 3

Study the following students' heights:

1.2 m, 1 m, 1.3 m, 0.8 m, 0.85 m, 1.25 m

(a) Arrange the data in ascending order.

(b) Find the range of the students' heights.

Solution

(a) Order the data starting with the smallest:
0.8 m, 0.85 m, 1 m, 1.2 m, 1.25 m, 1.3 m

(b) The range of the data is the largest value minus the smallest value:
1.3 m - 0.8 m = 0.5 m

Exercise 6.5

For Questions 1–7, order each list of numbers and find:

(a) The mode of the data set (if any)

(b) The mean of the data set

(c) The range of the data

1. 1, 5, 3, 4, 2, 7, 8, 4, 9, 4
2. 0.34, 2.6, 1.9, 0.57, 1.2, 4.3, 2.1, 1.2
3. 1, 5, 2, 6, 3, 2, 2
4. 2, 12, 38, 14, 2, 2, 5, 5, 1
5. 5, 8, 8, 7, 19, 3, 3, 2, 3
6. 2.04 kg, 886 g, 1.051 kg, 978 g, 850 g, 249 g
7. 25 m, 10 m, 45 m, 12 m, 10 m, 89 m, 47 m, 55 m, 10 m, 17 m, 105 m
8. Eight students entered a long throw competition. The distances thrown were recorded as follows: 37 m, 45 m, 29 m, 47 m, 51 m, 44 m, 53 m and 59 m.
   (a) Rank these distances in descending order.
   (b) What is the range of the distances thrown?
9. A group of students decided to host a competition to see who could stand on one leg for the longest. The times they achieved were recorded as follows: 1 min 50 sec, 2 min 10 sec, 1 min 46 sec, 2 min 9 sec and 3 min 1 sec.

   Rank the competitors' times from first to last.
10. In a 400 m sprint race, six athletes finished in the following times: 1 min 12 sec; 1 min 17 sec; 1 min 22 sec; 1 min 11 sec; 1 min 13 sec; and 1 min 19 sec.

    Rank these times by listing them in ascending order and state the finishing place for each time.
11. Can you suggest three examples in everyday life where data is arranged in:
    (a) Ascending order?
    (b) Descending order?
12. Write down five numbers in ascending order so that the mode is 7 and the mean is 6.

Section 6.8: The median

Student Activity 6D

Follow the instructions:

1. Select seven students.
2. Line up seven students against the wall in any order.
3. Ask the students to reorganise themselves, standing according to their heights from shortest to tallest.
4. Write down the name of the person you think will be in the centre when they have finished. Were you correct?
5. If you arranged them from tallest to smallest, would the middle person change? Explain your answer.
6. You have just found the student with the **median** height for the group. Can you explain in your own words what you understand by the word 'median'?
7. If another student joins the first 7 students, who is in the middle now?

THE MEDIAN EXPLAINED

In Student Activity 6D, you discovered another measure of central tendency. The middle value of an ordered list is called the **median.**

> The **median** is the middle ranked value in an ordered set of values.

- If there is an odd number of values, the median is the middle value of a **ranked** or **ordered** list.
- If there is an even number of values, the median is the **mean** of the two central values.

EXAMPLE 4

(a) The number of jelly beans in five packets of sweets is 31, 33, 40, 35 and 37. Find the median number of sweets per packet.

Solution

(a) First arrange in ascending order: 31, 33, 35, 37, 40.

Identify the middle number: 31, 33, <u>35</u>, 37, 40.

The median number of sweets per packet is 35.

(b) The number of points scored by a hurling team in six matches is recorded as follows: 17, 15, 22, 13, 14 and 28. Find the median number of points scored per match.

Solution

(b) First arrange in ascending order: 13, 14, 15, 17, 22, 28

Identify the middle numbers: 13, 14, <u>15</u>, <u>17</u>, 22, 28.

Calculate the mean of the two middle numbers: $\frac{15+17}{2} = \frac{32}{2} = 16$

The median number of points scored per match is 16.

(c) For the following set of data: 4, 5, 3, 8, 8, 7, 3, 2, 4, 3, 9, 3, 5, 6, 7, 3,

find: (i) The mean (ii) The mode (iii) The median (iv) The range

Solution

(c) (i) The mean or $\overline{x} = \frac{4+5+3+8+8+7+3+2+4+3+9+3+5+6+7+3}{16}$

$\overline{x} = \frac{80}{16} = 5$

(ii) Mode is the most frequent number = 3.

(iii) In order to find the median we must first arrange the list in ascending order:

2, 3, 3, 3, 3, 3, 4, 4, 5, 5, 6, 7, 7, 8, 8, 9

Median = mean of 8th and 9th value

Median = $\frac{4+5}{2} = 4.5$

(iv) The range is the biggest value minus the smallest value = 9 – 2 = 7

Exercise 6.6

1. Order the following lists of numbers from smallest to largest. From your ordered sets of numbers, write down the median for each list.

(a) 135, 209, 78, 160, 47, 78, 98

(b) 10, 13, 12, 10, 19, 7, 15, 16, 11

(c) €13.50, €10.85, €0.95, €10.80, €8.45

(d) 5, 2, 6, 7, 8, 4, 3, 5, 6, 7, 7, 3

(e) 74%, 51%, 88%, 0.5%, 50%

(f) 125 cm, 1.45 m, 89.5 cm, 1 m, 0.595 m, 1.05 m

2. Sally recorded the number of occupants of the first 20 cars going down her street one morning as follows:

2, 2, 1, 3, 5, 1, 1, 1, 2, 1, 2, 1, 1, 5, 2, 1, 1, 4, 2, 2

(a) Rewrite these numbers and order (or rank) them in ascending order.

(b) What is the median number of occupants per car?

(c) What is the modal number of occupants per car?

(d) Calculate the mean number of occupants per car.

(e) Write a sentence suggesting which of these three averages (the **mean, median** and **mode**) might be most meaningful, and which might be the least useful or meaningful.

3. A group of fifteen students playing the game 'This is the age I would most like to be' stated their *ideal* age as follows:

18, 18, 21, 23, 24, 150, 45, 35, 21, 18, 12, 25, 30, 25, 30

Find:

(a) The mean of these ages

(b) The modal age given

(c) The median of the ages

(d) Write down the range in the ages given.

(e) Is there any answer in the list you might disregard? Explain your answer.

4. Bríd visited a number of shops one Saturday afternoon to compare the prices on a standard size sliced pan of white bread.

The following prices were recorded by Bríd:

€1.28, €1.35, €1.00, €0.99, €0.79, €1.18, €1.04, €1.39, €0.69, €3.99

(a) Rank these prices from the smallest to the largest.

(b) What is the median price? (Hint: what do think you should do with the outlier?)

(c) What is the mean price of a sliced pan?

(d) What is the modal price of a sliced pan?

(e) You have to help Bríd to write a short paragraph for her local newspaper on the cost of living in her town. Write the paragraph explaining the figures found by Bríd and the calculations you have carried out.

5. Twelve second year boys listed their shoe sizes:

6, 8, 5, 7, 9, 8, 8, 11, 6, 8, 7, 7

Find:

(a) The mean shoe size, correct to 1 decimal place

(b) The modal size

(c) The median shoe size

(d) The range of shoe sizes

(e) Which of these four measurements might be useful to a shoe retailer? Give reasons for your answer.

(f) Which of these four statistics would probably be of no use? Give a reason for your answer.

6. The number of goals scored in a season by the Hoops was recorded as follows:

0, 2, 2, 5, 6, 2, 3, 1, 0, 0, 0, 1, 1, 2, 4, 0, 1, 1, 1, 1, 1, 2, 3, 1, 5

Find:

(a) The mean number of goals scored per match

(b) The modal number of goals scored

(c) The median number of goals scored

(d) The range of the number of goals scored

(e) Which of the four statistical measurements above might be the most useful to the team manager? Give reasons for your answer.

(f) Which of these four statistical measurements would be of no use to the manager? Give a reason for your answer.

7. Write down five numbers so that the mode is 3, the mean is 9 and the median is 7.

8. Write down five numbers so that the mode is 11, the mean is 10 and the median is 11.

9. Write down six numbers so that the mode is 6, the mean is 6 and the median is 6.

10. In this data set, the mode is 8:

3, 2, 7, 12, x, 6, 8, 9, 11

(a) Find the value of x.

(b) What is the median of the set?

(c) What is the mean of the set?

(d) What is the range?

11. A chess player recorded the time in minutes between each move in a game:

2, 1, 3, 4, 2, 3, 1, 4, 3, 1, 1, 2, 3, 2, 2, 3, 2, 4, 2, 2, 3, 1, 4, 1, 2.

Find:

(a) The mean length of time to complete a move

(b) The modal length of time to complete a move

(c) The median length of time to complete a move

(d) The range of times to complete a move

12. The height of 20 students was recorded as follows:

1 m, 1.2 m, 1.3 m, 0.90 m, 1.3 m, 1 m, 1 m, 1.1 m, 1.05 m, 1.2 m, 1.2 m, 1 m, 1 m, 1.2 m, 1.15 m, 1.05 m, 0.95 m, 1.05 m, 1 m, 1.2 m

Find:

(a) The mean height of the students
(b) The modal height of the students
(c) The median height of the students
(d) The range in the heights of the students

13. A shopkeeper recorded how much each customer spent in his shop over an hour one afternoon as follows:

€1.50, €4, €2.57, €10.50, €0.90, €3.50, €4, €1.35, €4, €3.43, €4, €5.25, €4.35, €1.98, €4, €4, €2.42, €1.60, €4, €2.65

Find:

(a) The mean amount of money spent
(b) The modal amount of money spent
(c) Calculate the median amount of money spent.
(d) Find the range of the money spent in the shop.
(e) Which of the above calculations might be most useful to the shopkeeper? Explain your answer.

14. The following information shows the price per litre of petrol in a number of filling stations in Co. Kildare in November 2013.

Station	Road	Area	Price (c)
Top	Dublin Road	Kildare Town	130.9
Applegreen	Caragh	Naas	132.8
Maxol	Dublin Road	Kildare Town	132.9
Maxol	Celbridge Road	Clane	132.9
Esso	The Woods	Clane	132.9
Esso	Naas Dual Carriageway Eastbound	Kill	133.9
Esso	Naas Dual Carriageway Westbound	Kill	133.9
Fraser Oil	Nicholstown Road	Kilcullen	133.9
Tougher	Main Street	Horsepasstown	133.9

Find:

(a) The mean price per litre of petrol in the Kildare area
(b) The modal price per litre of petrol
(c) The median price per litre of petrol
(d) What is the cheapest price for petrol?
(e) What is the range of prices for petrol in the area?
(f) Which of these statistics would be most useful to motorists in the Kildare area? Explain your answer.

Section 6.9: Frequency tables and grouped frequency tables

Student Activity 6E

1. What do you understand by the word **'frequency'**?

2. A GAA player recorded the ages of all his clubmates in his local GAA club. Examine the results below and answer the questions that follow.

14, 13, 14, 15, 13
14, 13, 12, 13, 15
12, 14, 13, 16, 15
13, 14, 14, 16, 16
15, 13, 14, 14, 15

(a) Copy the following table. Use tally counts to record the number of clubmates of each age. (The first one has been done for you.)

Age	Tally of clubmates
12	| |
13	
14	
15	
16	

(b) What age occurred most frequently?

(c) Calculate the mean age for the clubmates from the list above.

(d) Copy and complete the following table:

Age	12	13	14	15	16
No. of clubmates	2				

(e) Copy and complete the following calculation:

$$\frac{(12 \times 2) + (13 \times ?) + (14 \times ?) + (15 \times ?) + (16 \times ?) + (17 \times ?)}{\text{Total number of clubmates}}$$

(f) What do you notice about the answers in part (c) and (e) above?

FREQUENCY TABLES AND GROUPED FREQUENCY TABLES EXPLAINED

The word **'frequency'** means 'how often something occurs'. So a frequency table is a way of recording how often something occurs in table form.

There are two types of tables:

1. **A frequency table:** This type of table is used to record single data values.
2. **A grouped frequency table:** This type of table is used to record data that is best examined in groups.

Frequency tables make it easy to find measures of central tendency and measures of spread.

In a frequency table, it is normal practice to put the **variable** we are studying on the top row and its related frequency on the bottom row beneath it.

Variable	x_1	x_2	x_3	x_4
Frequency	f_1	f_2	f_3	f_4

To calculate the mean of a frequency table, use the following:

$$\text{Mean } (\bar{x}) = \frac{\text{The sum of each number multiplied by its frequency}}{\text{The sum of the frequencies}}$$

It can also be written as a formula: $\bar{x} = \dfrac{\sum fx}{\sum f}$

where:

- f represents the frequency.
- x represents the variable.
- $\sum$ is a Greek letter called **sigma.** It means **'add together'.**

A grouped frequency table studies the data in groups such as age.

Ages	0–10	10–20	20–30	30–40	40–50
No. of people	7	8	10	8	7

(Note: 0–10 means greater than or equal to 0 but less than 10.)

For example, seven people are aged between 40 and 50 years and the modal age group is 20–30 years.

EXAMPLE 5

The following frequency table shows the marks out of 5 achieved by 20 students in a class test.

Mark	0	1	2	3	4	5
No. of students	1	3	6	7	2	1

(a) Calculate the mean mark in the class.

(b) What is the modal mark in the class?

(c) If a score of 2 or higher is needed to pass, what percentage of students passed the test?

Solution

(a) Mean mark $= \bar{x} = \dfrac{(0 \times 1) + (1 \times 3) + (2 \times 6) + (3 \times 7) + (4 \times 2) + (5 \times 1)}{1 + 3 + 6 + 7 + 2 + 1}$

$$\bar{x} = \frac{0 + 3 + 12 + 21 + 8 + 5}{20}$$

$$\bar{x} = \frac{49}{20}$$

$$\bar{x} = 2.45$$

(b) Modal mark = 3 since seven students scored this mark, which has the highest frequency.

(c) People who scored 2 or more: 6 + 7 + 2 + 1 = 16

$\frac{16}{20} \times 100 = 80\%$

Grouped frequency tables are used to study information that is best looked at in groups due to the variety, range or quantity of the data. For example, in a census a question might ask how many people living in a household lie in certain age bands, such as 0–10 years. This makes it easier for statisticians to study the **demographics** in our country.

We use the **mid-interval value** for each group to help determine the overall mean. The mid-interval value is the mean of each group and is determined as follows:

$$\text{Mid-interval value} = \frac{\text{Upper interval value} + \text{Lower interval value}}{2}$$

This allows for the fact that some figures will be above the mean and some below the mean. Once you have calculated the mid-interval values for each group, you can then calculate the mean as before.

EXAMPLE 6

The following grouped frequency table shows the time spent on mobile phones by a group of students on a particular morning.

No. of mins	0–4	4–8	8–12	12–16
Frequency	3	5	6	11

(Note: 0–4 means greater than or equal to 0 but less than 4 mins.)

(a) Calculate the number of students in the group.

(b) What is the modal class interval for the time spent?

(c) Calculate the mean number of minutes spent by each student.

Solution

(a) 3 + 5 + 6 + 11 = 25 students

(b) Modal group is 12–16 minutes, which occurs 11 times.

(c) Before calculating the mean, calculate the mid-interval value for each group.

Group	Mid-interval value
0-4	$\frac{0+4}{2} = 2$
4-8	$\frac{4+8}{2} = \frac{12}{2} = 6$
8-12	$\frac{8+12}{2} = \frac{20}{2} = 10$
12-16	$\frac{12+16}{2} = \frac{28}{2} = 14$

$$\bar{x} = \frac{(2 \times 3) + (6 \times 5) + (10 \times 6) + (14 \times 11)}{3 + 5 + 6 + 11} = \frac{6 + 30 + 60 + 154}{25} = \frac{250}{25} = 10$$

Therefore, each person spent 10 minutes on average.

EXAMPLE 7

The following grouped table shows the length of time taken by a number of students to complete a puzzle. Given that the mean ($\overline{x}$) is 21.2 minutes, calculate the value of x.

Time (minutes)	0–8	8–16	16–24	24–32	32–40
No. of students	2	3	x	6	2

(Note: 0–8 means greater than or equal to 0 but less than 8 minutes.)

Solution

Calculate the mid-interval values for each group.

Group	Mid-interval value
0–8	$\frac{0+8}{2} = 4$
8–16	$\frac{8+16}{2} = 12$
16–24	$\frac{16+24}{2} = 20$
24–32	$\frac{24+32}{2} = 28$
32–40	$\frac{32+40}{2} = 36$

Calculate the mean x:

$$\overline{x} = \frac{(2)(4) + (3)(12) + (x)(20) + (6)(28) + (2)(36)}{2 + 3 + x + 6 + 2}$$

$$\frac{8 + 36 + 20x + 168 + 72}{13 + x} = 21.2$$

$$\frac{20x + 284}{13 + x} = 21.2$$

$$20x + 284 = (21.2)(13 + x) \quad \textbf{Cross-multiply}$$

$$20x + 284 = 275.6 + 21.2x$$

$$284 - 275.6 = 21.2x - 20x$$

$$8.4 = 1.2x$$

$$x = \frac{8.4}{1.2} = 7$$

Exercise 6.7

1. Paul recorded the number of goals his football team scored in 25 matches throughout the season.

0, 0, 2, 3, 4, 1, 1, 3, 5, 1, 1, 3, 2, 1, 1, 1, 6, 3, 2, 3, 2, 3, 1, 1, 0

(a) Copy and complete the frequency table.

No. of goals	0	1	2	3	4	5	6
No. of matches							

(b) What number of goals did the team score most frequently?

(c) In how many matches did the team score no goals?

(d) In how many matches did the team score 3 or more goals?

(e) How many goals did the team score in the 13th match?

(f) Use your frequency table to complete the following calculation:

$$\text{Mean} = \frac{(0 \times 3) + (1 \times ?) + (2 \times ?) + (3 \times ?) + (4 \times ?) + (5 \times ?) + (6 \times ?)}{\text{Total number of matches}}$$

2. The colours of 40 cars in a car park were recorded as follows:

Red	White	Blue	Black	Silver	Red	Blue	White
Silver	Silver	Blue	Red	Red	Orange	White	Red
Silver	Black	Black	Silver	Black	Silver	Red	White
Silver	Blue	Black	Blue	Silver	Silver	Blue	White
Silver	Blue	Silver	Black	Silver	Red	Silver	Blue

(a) Copy and complete the following tally table:

Colour	Tally
Red	
White	
Black	
Blue	
Silver	
Orange	

(b) Copy and complete the following frequency table.

Colour	Red	Black	Blue	Silver	Orange	White
Frequency						

(c) What was the modal colour?

(d) Is the data numerical or categorical?

(e) Explain why you cannot calculate the mean, median or range of the car colours.

3. A group of students sat a mathematics exam. The table shows the number of correct answers given.

No. of correct answers	9	10	11	12	13	14	15
No. of students	1	2	5	9	5	2	1

(a) How many students sat the exam?

(b) What was the modal score?

(c) What was the lowest score in the class?

(d) What was the highest score in the class?

(e) What was the range of scores?

(f) Calculate the mean mark for the class.

4. The following frequency table shows the number of computer games owned by a group of teenagers.

No. of games	3	4	5	6	7	8
No. of people	2	1	2	3	5	2

(a) How many teenagers took part in the survey?

(b) What is the mean number of games owned by these teenagers?

(c) What is the most popular number of games owned?

5. This table shows the body temperature in °C to the nearest 0.1° of a group of students during a science class.

Body temp. (°C)	36.7	36.8	36.9	37.0	37.1	37.2
No. of students	2	4	k	3	1	0

(a) What is the difference between the highest temperature and the lowest temperature?

(b) Calculate the value of k given the mean temperature was 36.875 °C.

(c) What was the modal body temperature?

6. Sarah carried out a survey of the ages of all the members of her local GAA club. She recorded the following results:

13, 12, 14, 18, 11, 12, 13, 17, 18, 19, 13, 16, 16, 17, 17, 24, 24, 14, 14, 12, 13, 16, 15, 10, 11, 10, 11, 20, 21, 13, 12, 14, 15, 24, 14, 17, 23, 21, 7, 9, 6, 9, 6, 7, 8, 8, 8, 8, 8, 9

(a) Copy and complete the following grouped frequency table:

Ages	0–5	5–10	10–15	15–20	20–25
No. people					

(Note: 0–5 means greater than or equal to 0 but less than 5 years.)

(b) What was the modal age group?

7. Siobhán asked her class how many hours they spent watching television over the weekend. She decided to group the times into class intervals of 4 hours.

No. of hours	0–4	4–8	8–12	12–16	16–20
No. of students	2	7	11	5	5

(Note 0–4 means 0 or more but less than 4 hours.)

(a) How many people are in the class?

(b) What is the modal amount of time spent watching television?

(c) What percentage of students watched television for 12 hours or more?

(d) What is the maximum number of students who spent at least 14 hours watching television?

(e) What is the minimum number of students who spent at least 14 hours watching television?

(f) How long did the median person spend watching television?

8. A survey was carried out to see how long it took a group of students to travel from home to school on a certain morning.

Time in minutes	0–5	5–10	10–15	15–20	20–25
No. of students	3	7	11	5	4

(Note 0–5 means 0 or more but less than 5 mins.)

(a) How many students are in the class?

(b) What is the modal amount of time spent travelling to school?

(c) What percentage of students spent 10 minutes or more travelling to school?

(d) What is the maximum number of students who spent at least 14 minutes travelling to school?

(e) What is the minimum number of students who spent at least 14 minutes travelling to school?

(f) In which time interval does the median person lie?

(g) What was the mean time spent travelling to school?

9. At a Garda speed-check on a road in Co. Laois, the speeds of a number of cars were recorded in a grouped frequency table:

Speed in km/h	20–30	30–40	40–50	50–60	60–70
No. of cars	0	12	48	25	15

(Note: 20–30 means greater than or equal to 20 but less than 30 km/h.)

(a) How many cars passed the speed-check?

(b) What is the modal speed of the cars?

(c) The speed limit on this road is 50 km/h. What percentage of cars should have received a speeding ticket?

(d) What is the maximum number of cars that were travelling at 41 km/h?

(e) What is the minimum number of cars that were travelling at 41 km/h?

(f) In which time interval does the median car lie?

(g) What was the mean speed?

10. The following grouped frequency table shows the amount of money spent by students in a shop at lunchtime. Study the table and answer the questions that follow.

Amount spent in €	0–2	2–4	4–6	6–8	8–10
No. of students	2	4	7	5	2

(Note: 0–2 means €0 or more but less than €2.)

(a) How many students took part in the survey?

(b) What is the modal amount of money spent?

(c) How many people spent between €6 and €8?

(d) Do you think that these people all spent €6 or all spent €8? Explain your answer.

(e) Is it possible that some of these people spent €7?

(f) For each group, write down the figure you think could be used as an average. Explain your choice.

(g) What is the maximum number of people that could have spent at least €5?

(h) What is the minimum number of people that could have spent at least €5?

11. The following frequency table shows the number of children in 40 families:

No. of children	0	1	2	3	4	5
Frequency	0	4	12	15	8	1

(a) Calculate the mean number of children per family.

(b) What is the modal number of children?

(c) What percentage of families has more than three children?

12. The table shows the number of skittles knocked down per ball in a bowling alley on a certain day.

No. of skittles	0	1	2	3	4	5	6	7	8	9	10
Frequency	6	3	1	7	8	3	2	3	0	1	1

(a) Calculate the mean number of skittles knocked down per ball.

(b) What is the modal number knocked down?

(c) Calculate the range in the scores of skittles knocked down per ball.

(d) What percentage of people scored less than three?

(e) What percentage of people scored at least seven?

(f) What is the median score?

13. The time in minutes spent exercising daily by a group of students is shown in the following grouped frequency table:

Time (minutes)	0–20	20–40	40–60	60–80	80–100
No. of students	2	5	8	6	4

(Note: 0–20 means greater than or equal to 0 but less than 20 minutes.)

(a) How many students were surveyed?

(b) What is the modal amount of time spent exercising?

(c) Taking mid-interval values, estimate the mean amount of time spent exercising by each student.

(d) In which time interval does the median person lie?

(e) What percentage of students spends between 20 to 40 minutes exercising?

(f) What is the maximum number of students that could have spent at least 65 minutes exercising?

(g) What is the minimum number of students that could have spent at least 65 minutes exercising?

14. The amount of money spent on petrol per month by a number of families is shown in the following grouped frequency table:

Money spent in €	€0–60	€60–120	€120–180	€180–240	€240–300
No. of families	18	35	21	16	10

(Note: 0–60 means greater than or equal to €0 but less than €60.)

(a) How many families were surveyed?

(b) What is the modal amount of money spent on petrol?

(c) Taking mid-interval values, calculate the mean amount of money spent on petrol.

(d) In which interval does the median amount lie?

(e) What percentage of families spends between €120 and €180 on petrol?

(f) What is the maximum number of families that could have spent at least €150?

(g) What is the minimum number of students that could have spent at least €150?

15. The number of hours a group of people spent at a local cinema in one month was recorded in the following grouped frequency table:

No. of hours	0–2	2–4	4–6	6–8
No. of people	12	9	6	3

(Note: 0–2 means greater than or equal to 0 but less than 2 hours.)

(a) How many people were surveyed?

(b) Taking mid-interval values, calculate the mean number of hours spent at the cinema.

16. The length of time to the nearest minute taken by 20 students to complete an obstacle course was recorded as follows:

2, 4, 6, 1, 8, 9, 1, 3, 5, 6, 7, 3, 2, 1, 4, 5, 3, 6, 3, 8

(a) Copy and complete the following grouped frequency distribution table.

Time in minutes	0–2	2–4	4–6	6–8	8–10
No. of students					

(Note: 0–2 means greater than or equal to 0 but less than 2 minutes.)

(b) What was the modal time to complete the obstacle course?

(c) Taking mid-interval values, calculate the mean time taken to complete the obstacle course.

(d) In which time interval does the median person lie?

17. The following grouped frequency table shows the amount of money that a certain number of people spent on phone credit in a month. The mean amount is €51.

Amount of money in €	€0–20	€20–40	€40–60	€60–80	€80–100
No. of people	4	6	18	x	4

(Note: 0–20 means greater than or equal to €0 but less than €20.)

(a) Calculate the value of x.

(b) What was the modal amount of money spent on phone credit?

18. The following grouped frequency table shows the amount of time spent by a group of students on a particular maths problem:

No. of minutes	0–4	4–8	8–12	12–16	16–20
No. of students	1	3	5	6	x

(Note: 0–4 means greater than or equal to 0 but less than 4 mins.)

Given that the mean is 12.2:

(a) Calculate the value of x.

(b) What was the modal time interval spent on the maths problem?

19. The following table shows the length of time a group of students were capable of running without stopping:

Time (minutes)	5–15	15–25	25–35	35–45
No. of students	x	5	7	4

(Note: 5–15 means greater than or equal to 5 but less than 15 minutes.)

The mean time spent running for the group was 25.5 minutes. Calculate:

(a) The value of x

(b) How many students were in the group

(c) The modal length of time spent running by the group

20. The following grouped frequency table shows the heights of saplings in a wooded area:

Height (cm)	0–6	6–12	12–18	18–24	24–30
No. of saplings	2	4	7	x	4

(Note: 0–6 means greater than or equal to 0 but less than 6 cm.)

The mean height of the saplings was 15.9 cm.

(a) Calculate the value of x.

(b) What is the modal class interval for the height of the saplings?

Section 6.10: Which measure of central tendency to use?

It is important to understand that each measure of central tendency has advantages and disadvantages. There are also limits as to when each can be used.

The following table summarises each measure:

Measure of central tendency	When to use	Disadvantages	Advantages
Mean	Can only be used for numerical data	Is distorted by outliers or extreme values	Uses every value in the data set Can be used for further statistical analysis
Median	Used to find the middle number in a set of data Can only be used for numerical data	Requires ordering of values in ascending order	Easy to identify Not affected by outliers or extreme values Not of use for further statistical analysis
Mode	Used to find the most common piece of data Can be used for numerical or categorical data	A unique mode may not exist	Easy to identify Not affected by outliers or extreme values Not of use for further statistical analysis

EXAMPLE 8

Eight stamp collectors hold a competition to see who can collect the rarest stamps over a month. The number collected by each is shown below:

8 9 10 15 15 21 25 97

(a) What is the median number of stamps collected?

(b) Calculate the mean number of stamps collected.

(c) Which of these two measures of central tendency is best suited to describe the data set? Explain your answer.

Solution

(a) $\frac{15 + 15}{2} = \frac{30}{2} = 15$ stamps

(b) Mean = 25 stamps

(c) The median is a better measure. The mean is distorted by the one collector who collected 97 stamps. Six of the eight collectors are below the mean.

Exercise 6.8

1. Ten part-time workers in a car wash are paid according to the number of cars washed one Saturday afternoon as follows:

€30 €29 €5 €40 €37 €90 €30 €31 €32 €30

(a) Write down the median wage earned.

(b) What is the modal wage earned?

(c) Calculate the mean wage earned.

(d) Which measure or measures of central tendency are unsuitable to use with this set of data? Explain your answer fully.

2. The eye colour of 15 students in a class was recorded. Which measure of central tendency could be used with this set of data? Explain your answer fully.
3. The type of doughnuts sold at a deli counter were recorded over a lunch hour:

Type	Plain	Jam	Chocolate	Iced
Number	6	12	2	5

(a) What is the modal type of doughnut sold?
(b) Can you write down the median number of doughnuts sold? Explain your answer fully.
(c) Can the mean be used for this set of data? Explain your answer fully.

4. Ten students were asked to name their favourite type of music. The results were recorded as follows:

Pop	Rock	Dance	Pop	Pop
Pop	Dance	Rock	Pop	Dance

(a) State, explaining your choice fully, which measure of central tendency can be used for this data.
(b) Is it possible to calculate the mean for this data set? Explain your answer fully.

CHAPTER 6 SELF-CHECK TEST

1. Calculate the mean of each of the following:
(a) 2, 3, 0, 0, 6, 6, 8, 0, 1, 4
(b) 0.3 , 5.4, 5.3, 2.3, 4.2
(c) $1\frac{1}{2}, 1\frac{1}{2}, 5\frac{7}{12}, \frac{2}{3}, 2\frac{3}{4}$
(d) −4, −2, −1, 3, 1, −3, 6
(e) $3x + 1, 2x + 1, 2x + 3, x - 5$
(f) $4x - 3, x + 12, 7x + 6, 7 - x, 4x + 3$

2. In the following grouped frequency table, the percentage mean mark using mid-interval values is 4.

Percentage marks	2–4	4–6	6–8
No. of students	3	y	3

(Note: 2–4 means 2 or more but less than 4 per cent.)
Calculate the value of y.

3. The mean of the following frequency distribution table is $1\frac{1}{2}$.

x	0	1	2	3	4
Frequency	6	2	a	4	1

(a) Calculate the value of a.
(b) Calculate the mode.

4. The mean age in a group of 6 pupils is ten years and nine months. When a new pupil joins the group, the average age drops to ten years and three months. Calculate, in years and months, the age of the new pupil.

5. An internet service provider is carrying out a survey about the internet usage habits of its customers. They are unsure what type of survey to carry out.

(a) Choose two different types of survey that the company could use.
(b) List two advantages and two disadvantages for the survey types you have chosen.
(c) List three pieces of categorical data that the company might collect.
(d) List three pieces of numerical data that the company might collect.

6. Jack is considering opening a launderette and dry cleaning shop in his locality. He decides to carry out a survey in the local area.

(a) What type of survey should he carry out?
(b) Give two advantages of carrying out this type of survey.
(c) Give two disadvantages of carrying out this type of survey.
(d) Design six questions he could ask potential customers.
(e) List three pieces of categorical data that he might collect.
(f) List three pieces of numerical data that he might collect.

7. A mobile telephone company has decided to carry out a phone survey of its customers. It called 100 customers in Belfast between 2 a.m. and 5 a.m. from Monday until Friday.

(a) Can you identify three flaws with how this survey was carried out?
(b) For each of the reasons, offer a solution.
(c) List three pieces of categorical data that the company might collect.
(d) List three pieces of numerical data that the company might collect.

8. The time spent by a group of children watching television each day was recorded in the following grouped frequency table:

Time in minutes	0–20	20–40	40–60	60–80	80–100
No. of children	4	6	9	11	10

(Note: 0–20 means greater than or equal to 0 but less than 20 minutes.)
(a) How many children were surveyed?
(b) What is the modal amount of time spent watching television?
(c) Taking mid-interval values, calculate the mean time spent watching television.
(d) In which interval does the median person lie?

9. The ages of all the members of a GAA club were recorded in a grouped frequency table as follows:

Age in years	0–10	10–20	20–30	30–40	40–50
No. of members	30	25	35	30	10

(Note: 0–10 means greater than or equal to 0 but less than 10 years.)
(a) How many members are in the club?
(b) What is the modal age group in the club?
(c) Taking mid-interval values, calculate the mean age of the members.
(d) Calculate the minimum number of people who could be aged over 25.

10. The percentage marks out of 100 in a class test were recorded in a grouped frequency table as follows:

Percentage marks	0–20	20–40	40–60	60–80	80–100
No. of students	1	3	9	5	2

(Note: 0–20 means greater than or equal to 0 but less than 20 per cent.)
(a) How many students were in the class?
(b) What is the modal score in the test?
(c) Taking mid-interval values, calculate the mean percentage test score for the class.
(d) Calculate the maximum number of people who scored over 55% in their test.

11. A gardener recorded the height in centimetres of a number of sunflowers in her greenhouse after two weeks of growing. She recorded the results in the following grouped frequency table:

Height (cm)	0–10	10–20	20–30	30–40	40–50
No. of plants	3	7	14	21	15

(Note: 0–10 means greater than or equal to 0 but less than 10 cm.)

(a) How many sunflower plants were growing?

(b) Taking mid-interval values, calculate the mean height of the plants.

(c) What is the modal height of the plants?

(d) In a paragraph, describe the results obtained from the gathered data.

12. The salaries of 10 workers in a small company are as follows:

€25,000	€28,000	€35,000	€110,000	€27,000
€26,000	€25,000	€30,000	€32,000	€25,000

(a) Calculate the mean salary of the workers.

(b) Write down the modal salary.

(c) Write down the median salary.

(d) Which measure is unsuitable to use for this set of data? Explain your answer fully.

(e) If you needed to use the mean as the measure of central tendency, what alterations might you make to the data set? Explain your answer fully.

CHAPTER 6 KNOWLEDGE CHECKLIST

After completing this chapter, I now:

- Know about data types
- Know about the data handling cycle
- Know how to select a sample to ensure it is truly representative of the population
- Know that numerical data can be divided into continuous and discrete data
- Know that categorical data can be divided into nominal or ordinal data
- Know how to identify an outlier in a set of data
- Am able to calculate the mean
- Am able to identify the mode
- Know how to order or rank data and numbers
- Know how to identify the median
- Am able find the range for a set of numerical data
- Can construct and read data from frequency tables and grouped frequency tables
- Am able to calculate the mean from a grouped frequency table
- Know which measure of central tendency to use

CONSTRUCTIONS

LEARNING OUTCOMES

In this chapter you will learn:

- ✓ **How to construct an angle of a given number of degrees with a given ray as one arm**
- ✓ **How to construct a triangle, given the lengths of three sides (SSS)**
- ✓ **How to construct a triangle, given two sides and the included angle (SAS)**
- ✓ **How to construct a triangle, given two angles and the included side (ASA)**
- ✓ **How to construct a right-angled triangle, given the length of the hypotenuse and one other side (RHS)**
- ✓ **How to construct a right-angled triangle, given one side and one of the acute angles**
- ✓ **How to construct a rectangle, given the lengths of the sides**
- ✓ **How to construct a line perpendicular to a given line *l*, passing through a given point not on *l***
- ✓ **How to divide a line segment into any number of equal parts, without measuring it**

KEY WORDS

- Construct
- Hypotenuse
- Parallel
- Perpendicular
- Quadrilateral
- Ray
- Rectangle
- Right-angled triangle

INTRODUCTION

For this chapter, you will need the following equipment:
Compass, Ruler, Set Squares, Protractor

In *Maths in Action 1*, you studied six constructions. This chapter covers the rest of the constructions on the Junior Certificate course.

In each section, a specific example is given. The method in each construction can be used for different measurements.

First year revision

1. Examine the diagram below and name each of the angles using three-letter notations.

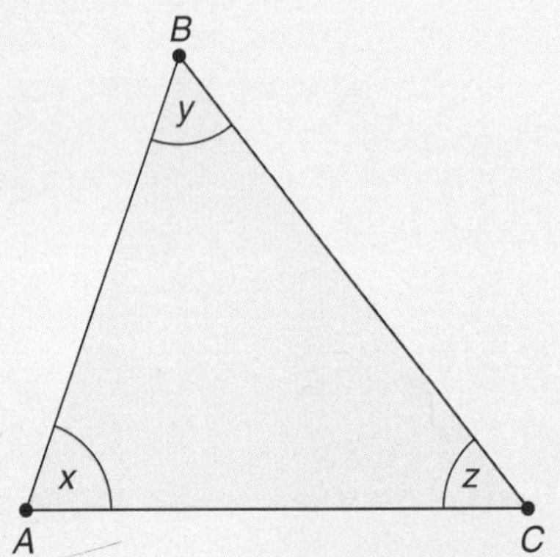

2. Explain each of the following terms:

(a) Ray

(b) Line segment

(c) Plane

(d) Line

(e) Vertex

3. For each piece of equipment shown, state its name and use.

(a)

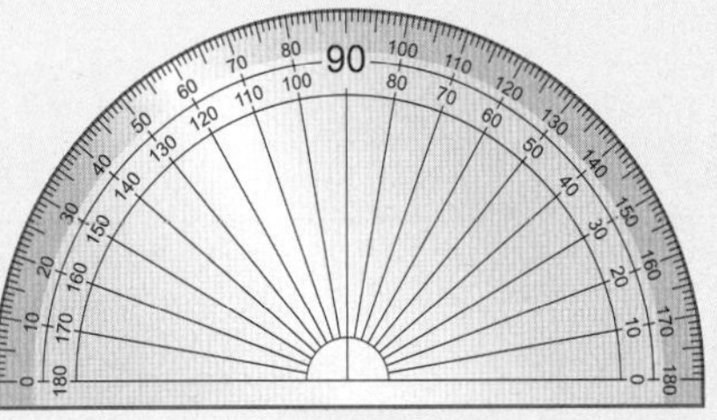

(b)

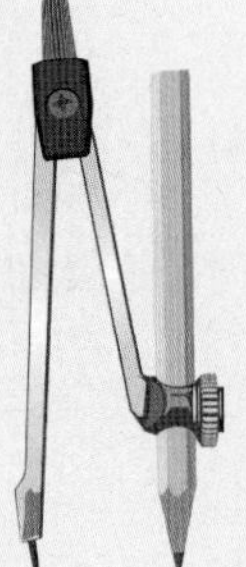

(c)

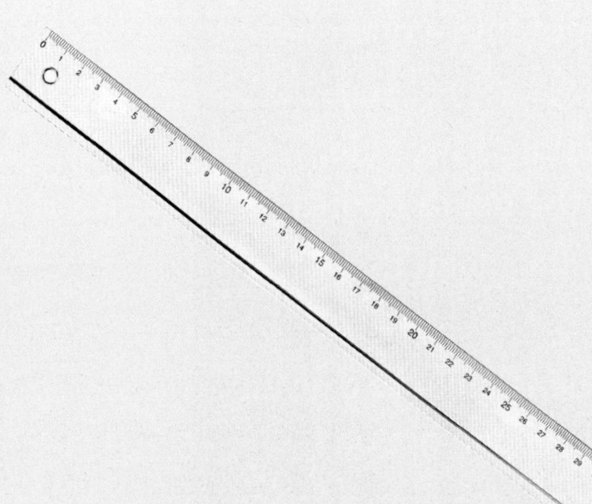

(d)

Section 7.1: Construct an angle of a given number of degrees with a given ray as one arm

Student Activity 7A

Construct an angle of 60° on the ray [*AB*.

1. Draw a long ray [*AB* in your copy.

2. Mark a point *C* on the ray.

3. Place the centre of your protractor on the point *C* and mark the point *D* by reading the required angle (in this case 60°) from your protractor.

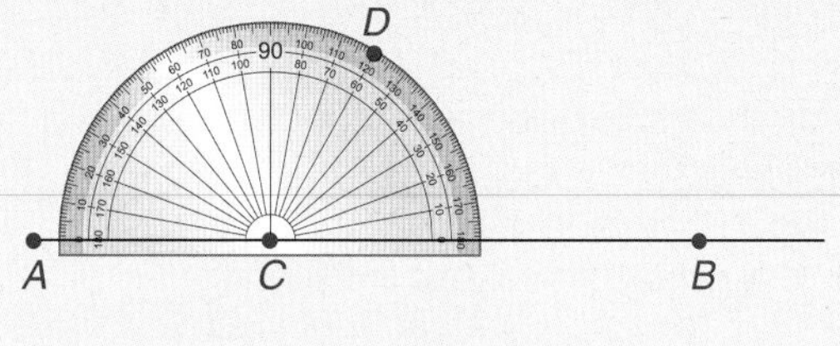

4. Remove the protractor and join C to D.

5. Write in the required angle size of 60°.

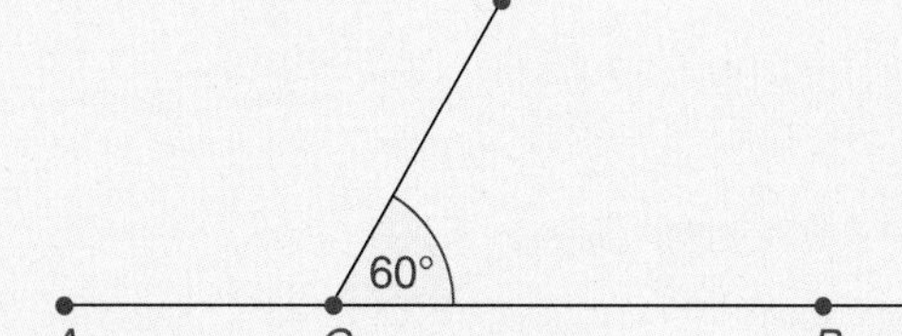

The construction method in Student Activity 7A can be used to draw an angle of any size. Use your protractor to accurately measure the required angle.

Before constructing the given angle, draw a sketch so you have a clear picture of the angle you expect to draw. Always clearly label the angle after completing the construction.

If you are asked to construct an angle of 70°, make sure it is the acute angle you label and not the obtuse angle.

$|\angle ABC| = 70°$ and $|\angle CBD| = 110°$. As the angle required is 70°, you must clearly label $|\angle ABC|$.

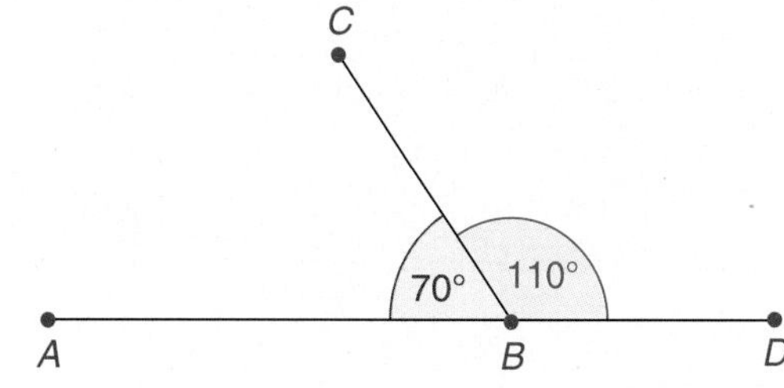

Exercise 7.1

1. Construct an angle of 40° on a ray [*BC*.
2. Construct an angle of 25° on a ray [*AB*.
3. Construct an angle of 120° on a ray [*DE*.
4. Construct an angle of 85° on a ray [*XY*.
5. Construct an angle of 37° on a ray [*YZ*.
6. Construct an angle of 145° on a ray [*FG*.
7. Construct an angle of 175° on a ray [*JK*.
8. Construct an angle of 55° on a ray [*MN*.
9. Construct an angle of 43° on a ray [*PQ*.
10. Construct an angle of 15° on a ray [*RS*.
11. Construct $|\angle ABC| = 200°$ on a ray *AB*].
12. Construct $|\angle DEF| = 240°$ on a ray *DE*].
13. Construct $|\angle GHI| = 265°$ on a ray *GH*].
14. Construct $|\angle JKL| = 300°$ on a ray *JK*].
15. Construct $|\angle MNO| = 210°$ on a ray *MN*].
16. Construct $|\angle ABC| = 80°$ on a ray [*AB*.

Section 7.2: Construct a triangle, given the lengths of three sides (SSS)

Student Activity 7B

Draw triangle *ABC* where |*AB*| = 6 cm, |*AC*| = 5 cm and |*BC*| = 4 cm.

1. Always draw a rough sketch and insert the given information. This acts as an aid to the actual construction.

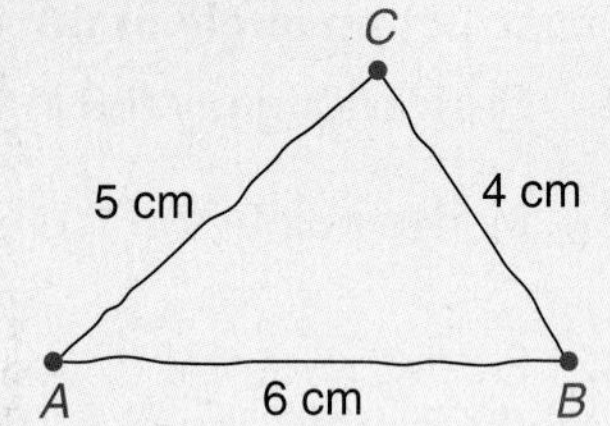

2. Construct a 6 cm line segment and mark the endpoints *A* and *B* using your ruler. This is the longest side of the triangle and it will always act as the base of the triangle.

A 6 cm B

3. Set your compass to 5 cm and draw an arc from the point *A*.

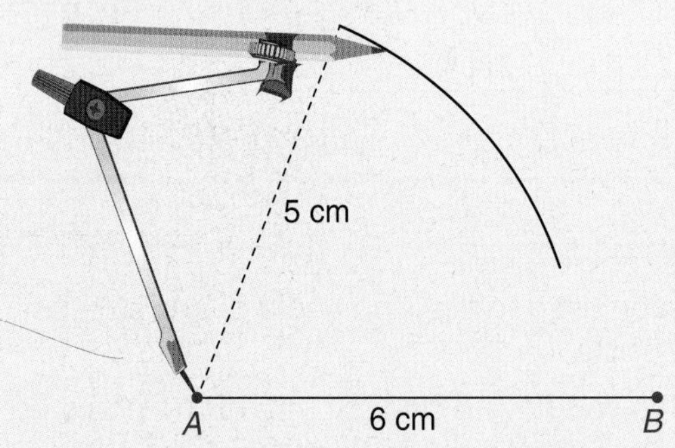

4. Set your compass to 4 cm and draw an arc from the point *B*, until it overlaps the previous arc.

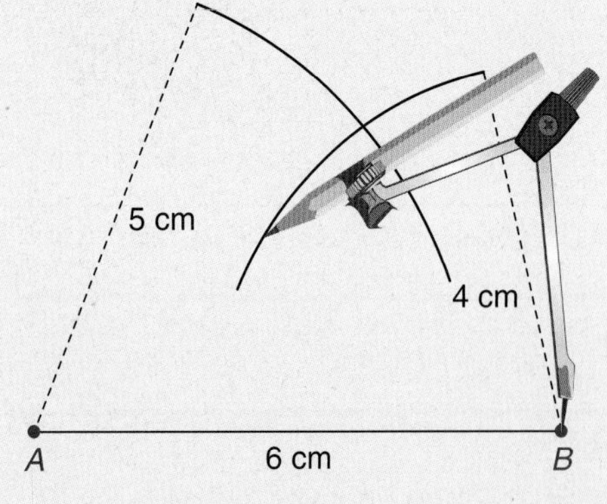

5. Mark the intersection point of the two arcs as *C*.

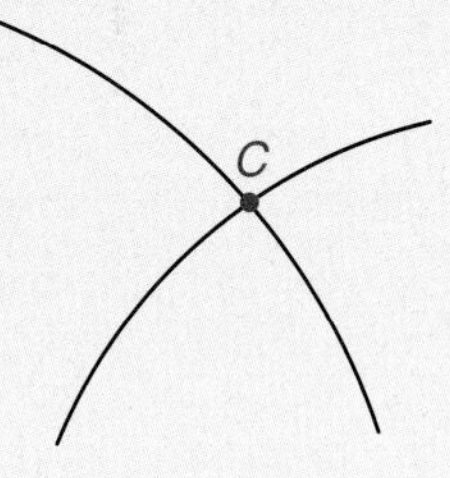

A 6 cm B

6. Join points *A* to *C* and *C* to *B* to complete the triangle *ABC*. Using a ruler, check and insert the required measurements of the three sides, |*AB*|, |*AC*| and |*BC*|.

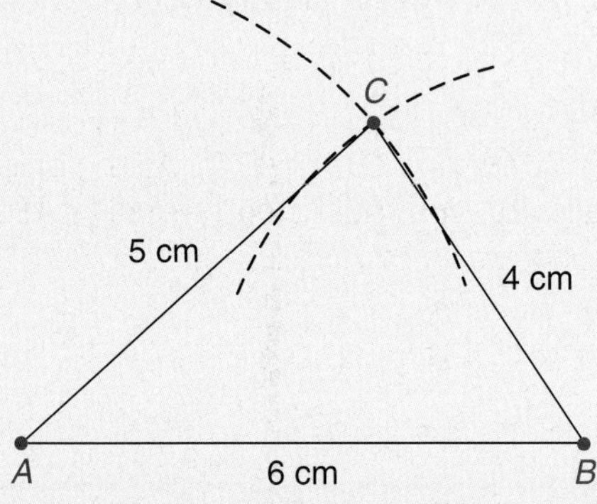

7. Make sure to label your triangle clearly.

The construction method in Student Activity 7B can be used to draw any triangle where you are given the lengths of the three sides. This is often referred to as **S**ide, **S**ide, **S**ide **(SSS)** as we know all three sides of the triangle.

When you have finished your construction, always check the lengths of the sides using your ruler, label the vertices and insert all of the relevant measurements.

Exercise 7.2

1. Construct a triangle ABC with sides $|AB| = 4$ cm, $|BC| = 3$ cm and $|AC| = 5$ cm.
2. Construct a triangle XYZ with sides $|XY| = 7$ cm, $|YZ| = 6$ cm and $|XZ| = 8$ cm.
3. Construct a triangle DEF with sides $|DE| = 4$ cm, $|DF| = 9$ cm and $|EF| = 11$ cm.
4. Construct a triangle RST with sides $|RS| = 9$ cm, $|RT| = 8$ cm and $|ST| = 4$ cm.
5. Construct a triangle ABC with sides $|AB| = 7$ cm, $|BC| = 7$ cm and $|AC| = 7$ cm.

Construct each of the following triangles. The dimensions given are in centimetres. For each construction, name the **type** of triangle you have constructed.

6.

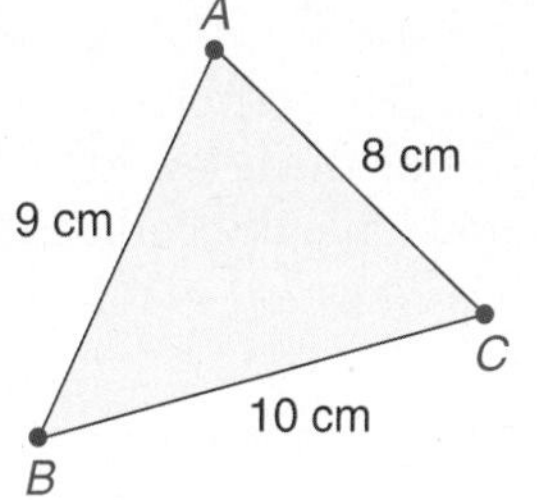

7.

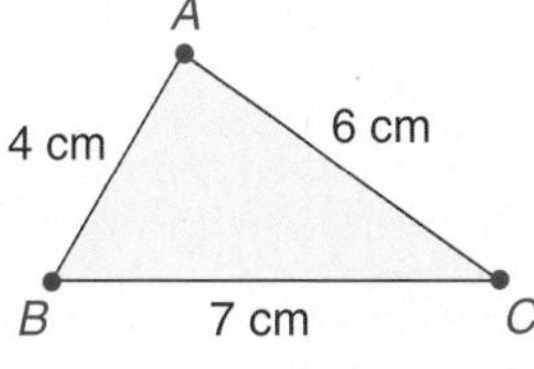

8.

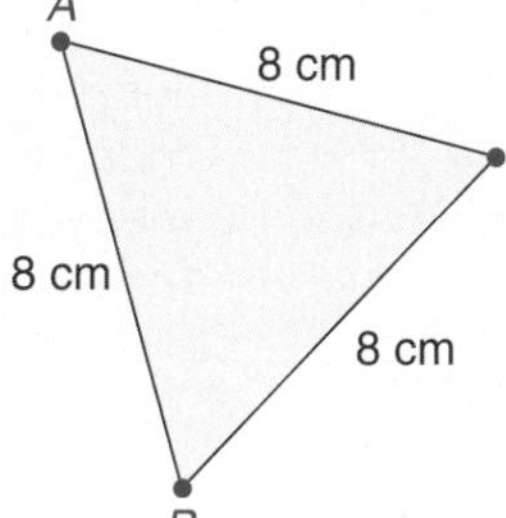

9.

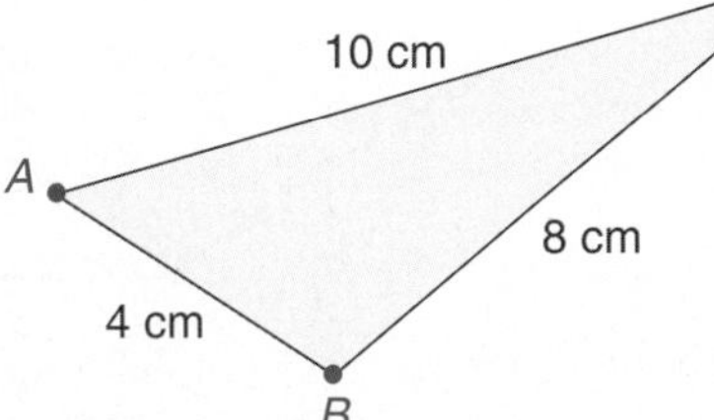

10.

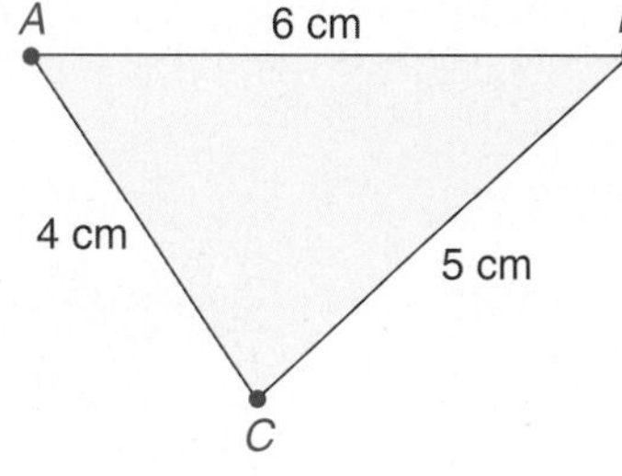

11.

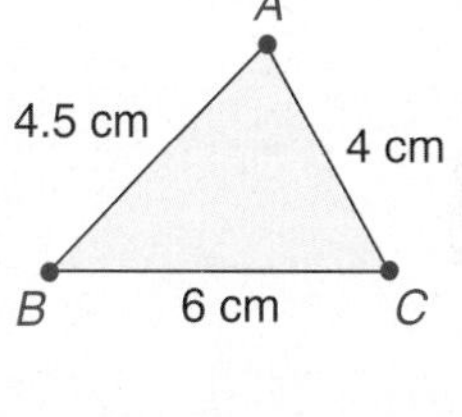

Section 7.3: Construct a triangle, given two sides and an included angle (SAS)

Student Activity 7C

Draw triangle ABC where $|AB| = 5$ cm, $|BC| = 4$ cm and $|\angle ABC| = 70°$.

1. Always draw a rough sketch and insert the given information. This acts as an aid to the actual construction. Let the longest side given be the base of the triangle.

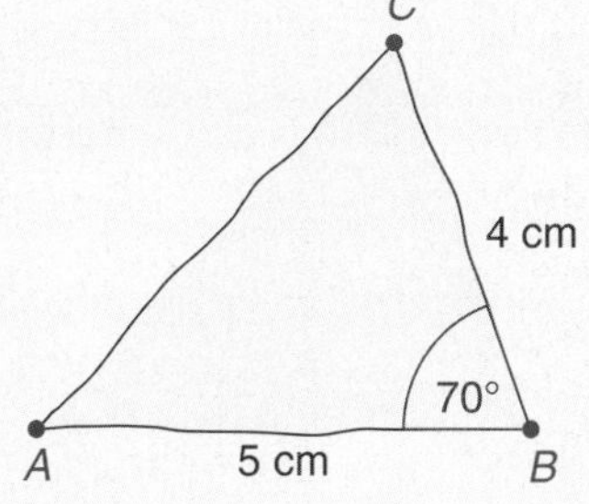

2. Draw a 5 cm line segment and mark the endpoints A and B.

A 5 cm B

3. With the centre of your protractor on B, measure an angle of 70°.

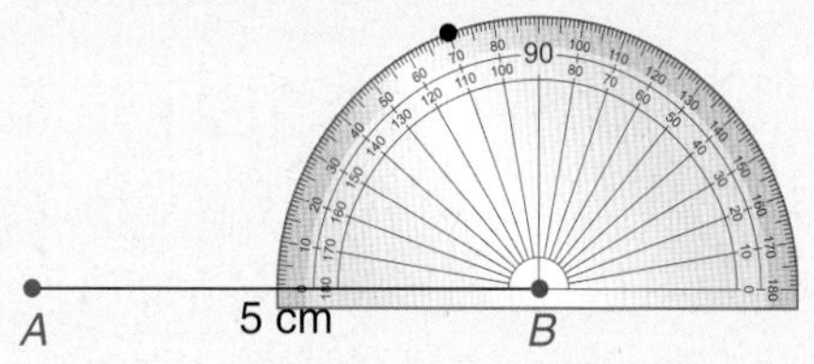

4. Draw a ray from *B* at an angle of 70°.

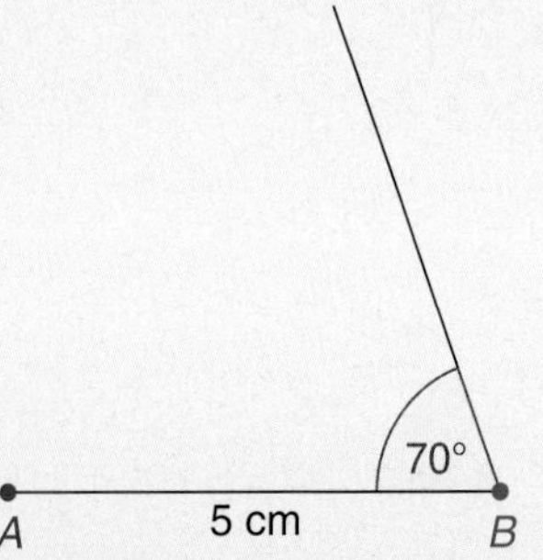

5. Set your compass to 4 cm and draw an arc from centre *B* to intersect the ray at a 70° angle.

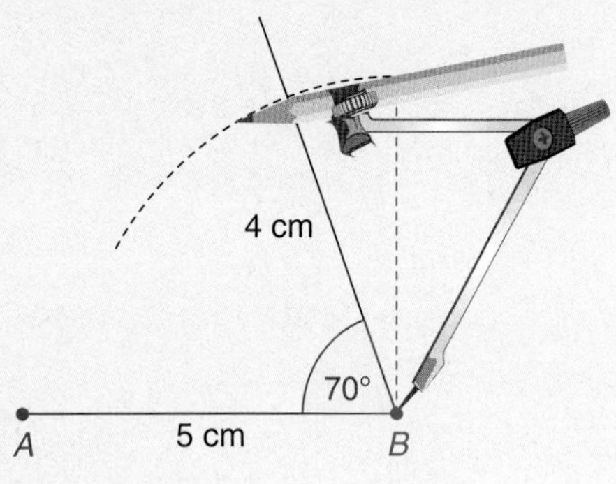

6. Mark the intersection of the arc and the ray as *C*.

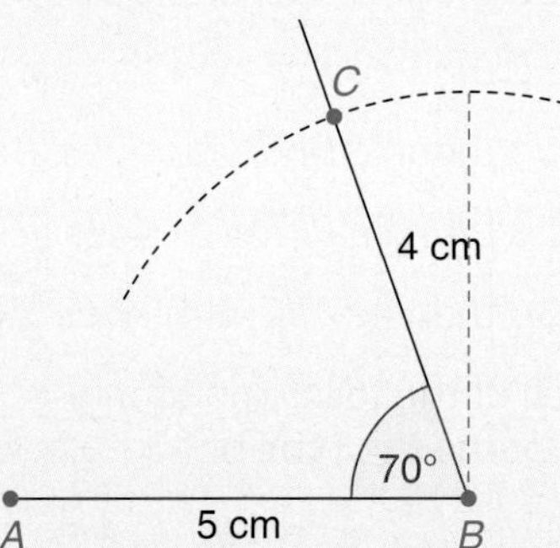

7. Join *C* to *A* and *C* to *B* to complete the triangle *ABC*. Insert all the relevant measurements and label the vertices of the triangle.

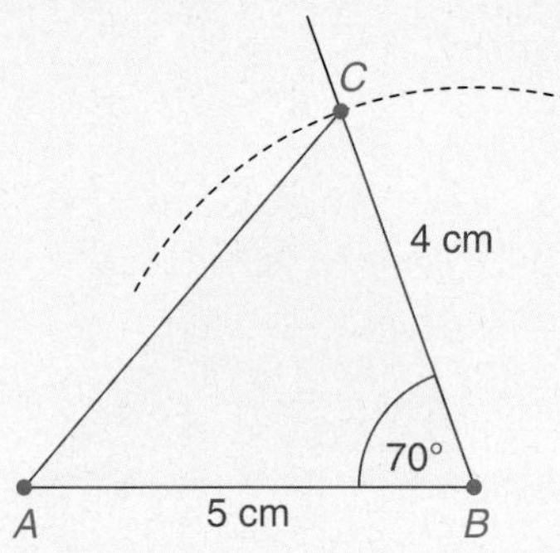

The construction method used in Student Activity 7C can be used to draw any triangle where you are given the lengths of two sides and the included angle. This is often referred to as **S**ide, **A**ngle, **S**ide **(SAS)** as we know two sides of the triangle and the angle in between them. When you have finished your construction, insert all the relevant measurements and label the vertices of the triangle.

Exercise 7.3

Construct each of the following triangles. For each construction, name the **type** of triangle you have constructed.

1.

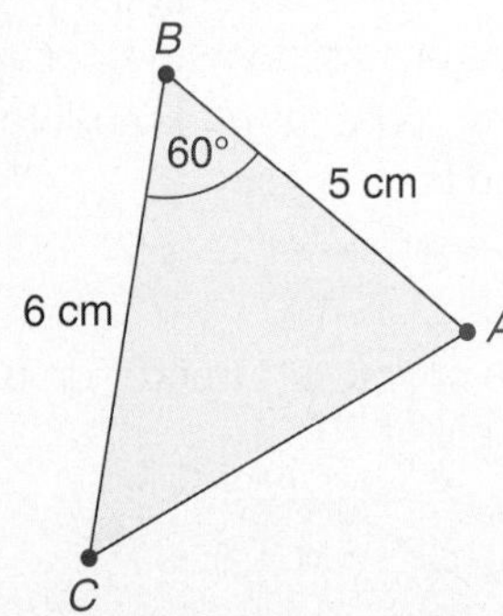

2.

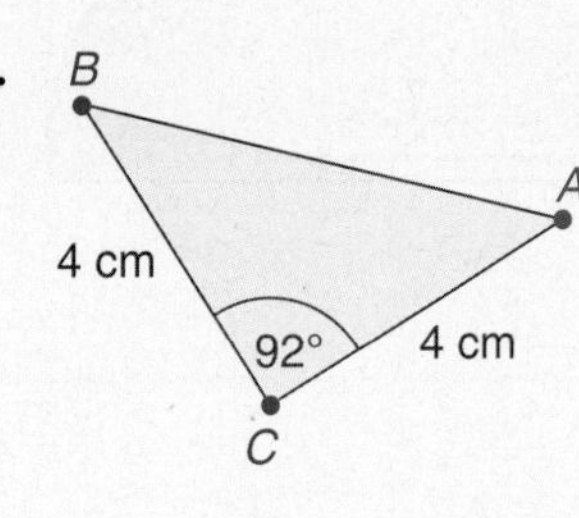

3.

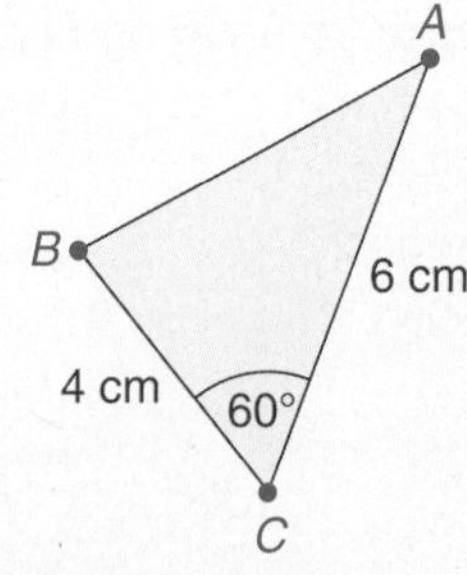

4.

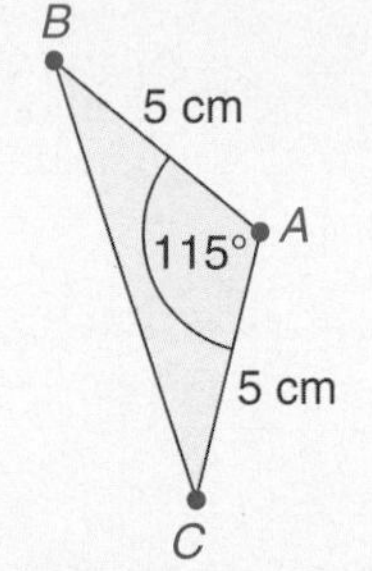

5.

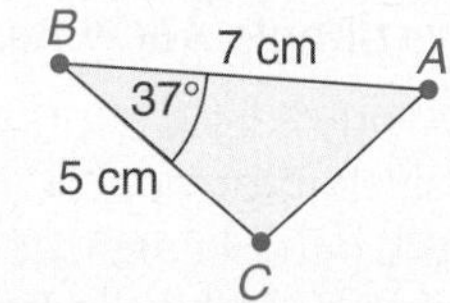

6.

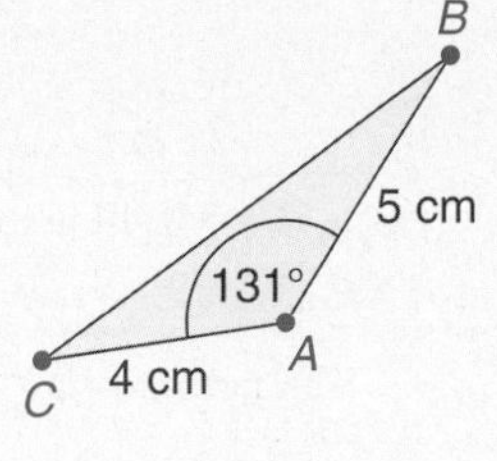

7.
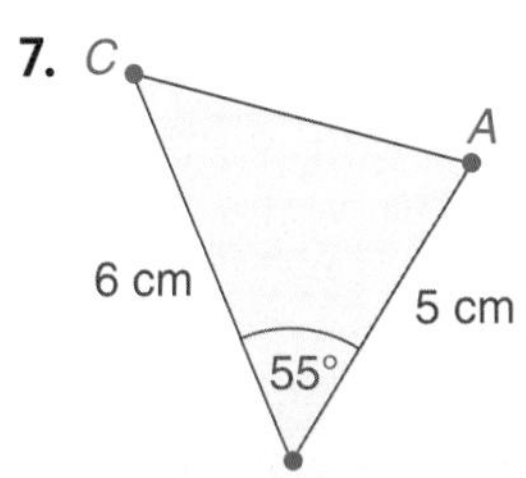

9.
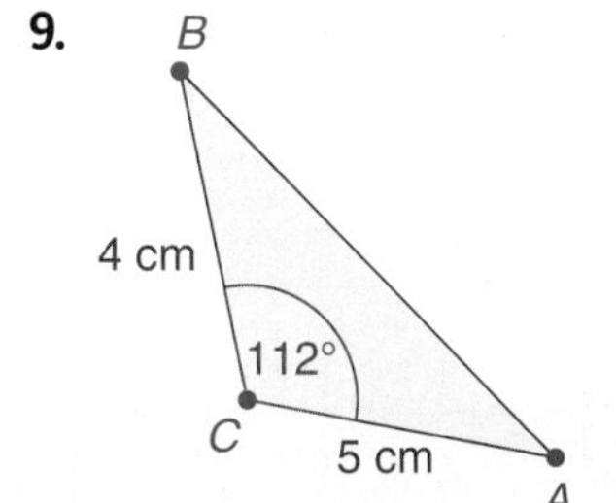

8.
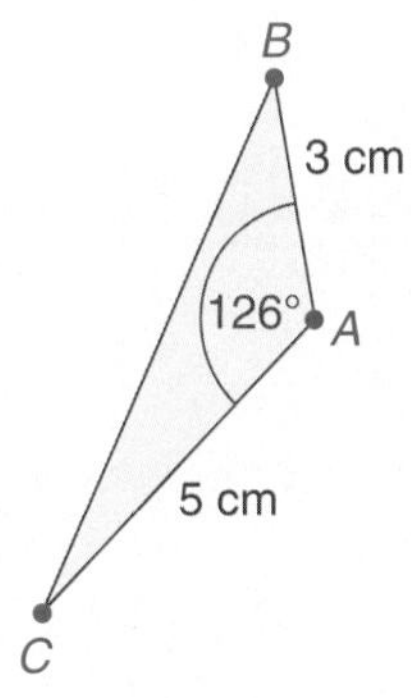

10.
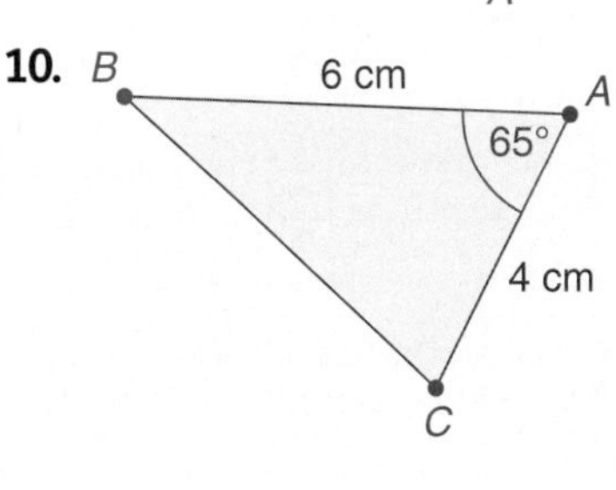

11. Construct a triangle ABC, where $|\angle ABC| = 65°$, $|AB| = 7$ cm and $|BC| = 6$ cm.
12. Construct a triangle DEF, where $|\angle DFE| = 45°$, $|DF| = 9$ cm and $|EF| = 6$ cm.
13. Construct a triangle GHI, where $|\angle HGI| = 65°$, $|GH| = 7.2$ cm and $|GI| = 8.5$ cm.
14. Construct a triangle JKL, where $|\angle LJK| = 50°$, $|LJ| = 35$ mm and $|KJ| = 60$ mm.
15. Construct a triangle MNP, where $|\angle MNP| = 60°$, $|PN| = 50$ mm and $|MN| = 75$ mm.
16. Construct a triangle XYZ, where $|\angle XYZ| = 60°$, $|XY| = 4$ cm and $|YZ| = 4$ cm.

Section 7.4: Construct a triangle, given two angles and the included side (ASA)

Student Activity 7D

Construct triangle ABC where $|AB| = 7$ cm, $|\angle BAC| = 50°$ and $|\angle ABC| = 70°$.

1. Always draw a rough sketch and insert the given information. This acts as an aid to the actual construction. Let the longest side be the base of the triangle.

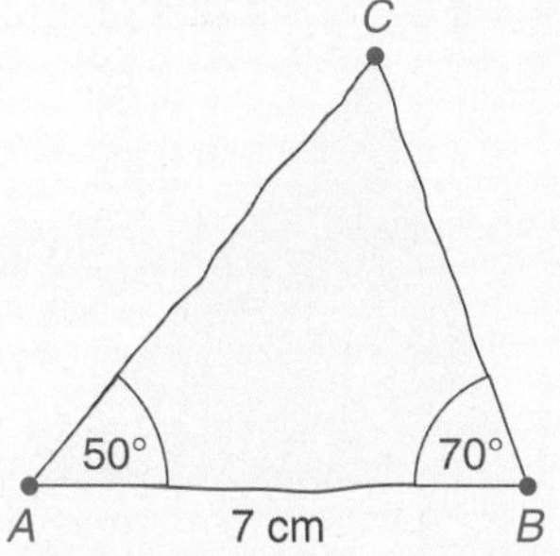

2. Draw a 7 cm line segment and mark endpoints A and B.

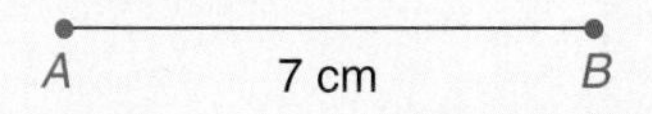

3. With your protractor centre on the point B, measure an angle of 70° and draw a ray through the point B.

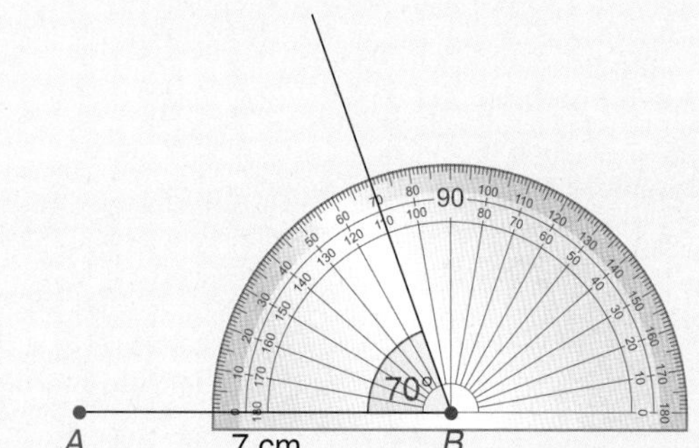

4. With your protractor centre on *A*, measure an angle of 50° and draw a ray through *A*.

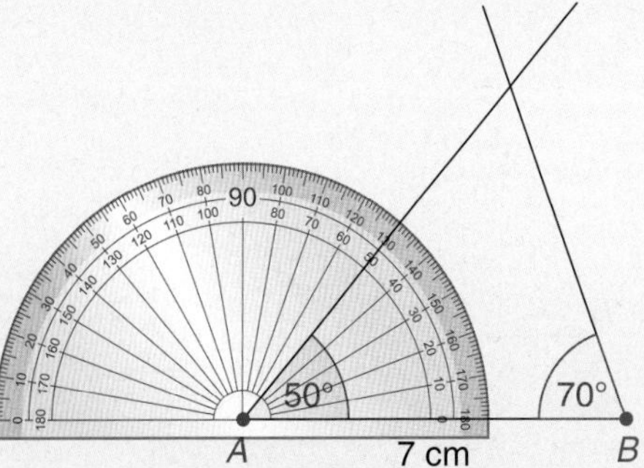

5. Mark the intersection point of the two rays as *C*.

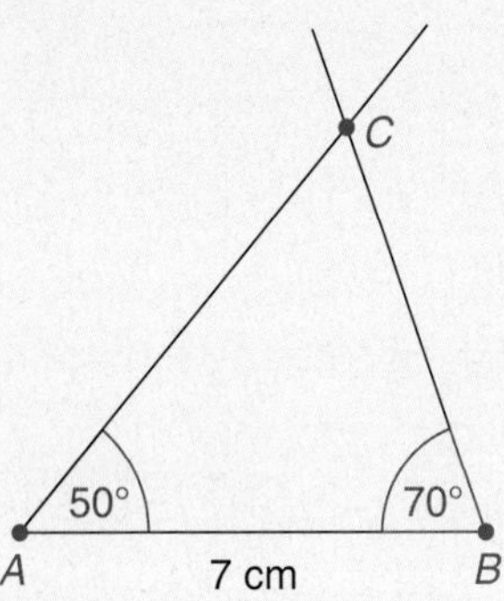

6. Complete the triangle *ABC*, inserting the relevant labels and measurements.

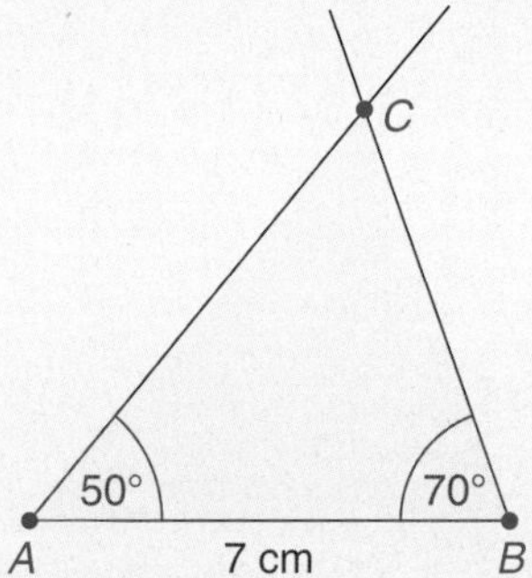

The construction method in Student Activity 7D can be used to draw any triangle where you are given the size of two angles and the included side. This is often referred to as **A**ngle, **S**ide, **A**ngle **(ASA)** as we know two angles and one side of the triangle. The triangle is easier to construct if we make the given side the base of the triangle.

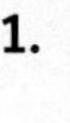

Exercise 7.4

Construct each of the following triangles. For each construction, name the **type** of triangle you have constructed.

1.

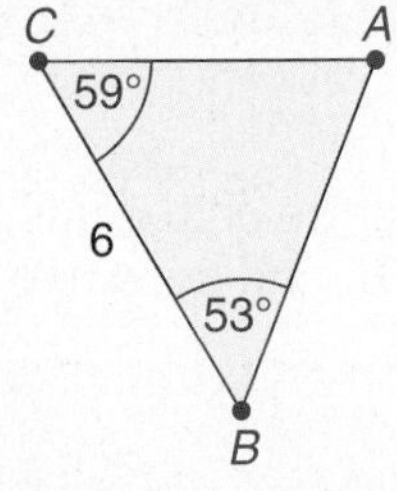

2.

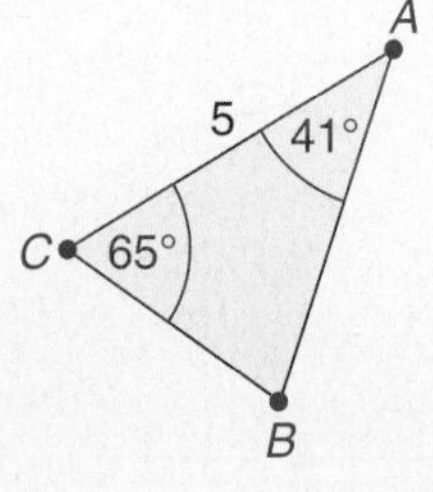

3.

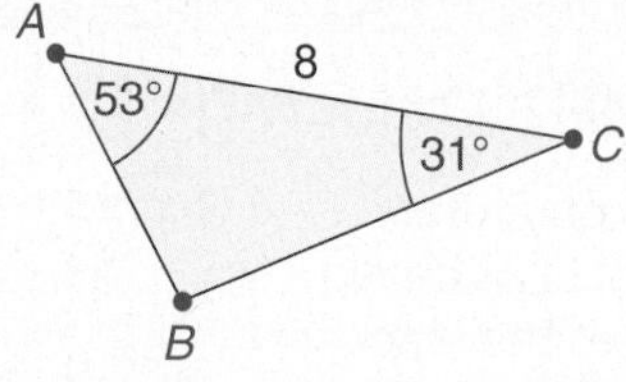

4.

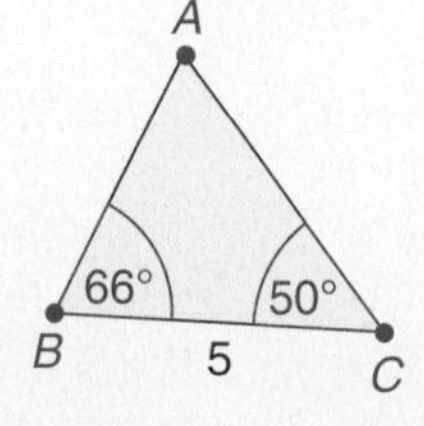

5.

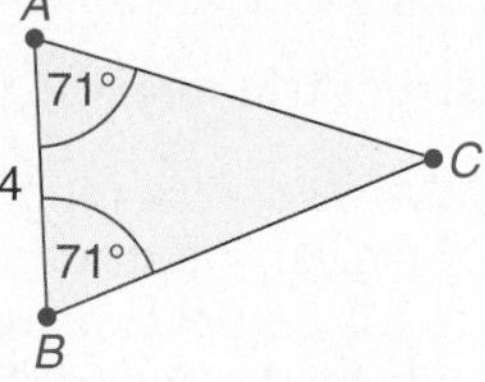

6.

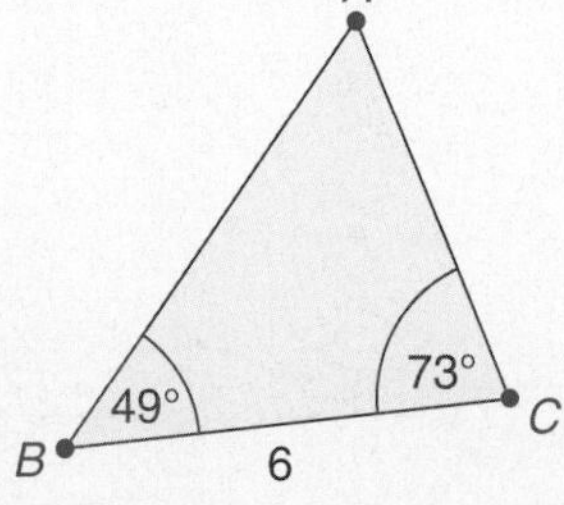

7. Construct the triangle *ABC*, where $|AB| = 75$ mm, $|\angle ABC| = 50°$ and $|\angle BAC| = 65°$.

8. Construct the triangle *DEF*, where $|EF| = 65$ mm, $|\angle FED| = 35°$ and $|\angle DFE| = 55°$.

9. Construct the triangle *XYZ*, where $|YX| = 8.5$ cm, $|\angle ZYX| = 48°$ and $|\angle ZXY| = 96°$.

10. Construct the triangle *PQR*, where $|PQ| = 5$ cm, $|\angle PQR| = 70°$ and $|\angle QPR| = 70°$.

Section 7.5: Construct a right-angled triangle, given the length of the hypotenuse and one other side (RHS)

Student Activity 7E

Draw a right-angled triangle *ABC*, where |*AB*| = 4 cm, |*AC*| = 5 cm and |∠*ABC*| = 90°.

1. Always draw a rough sketch and insert the given information. This acts as an aid to the actual construction. Let the right angle rest on the baseline.

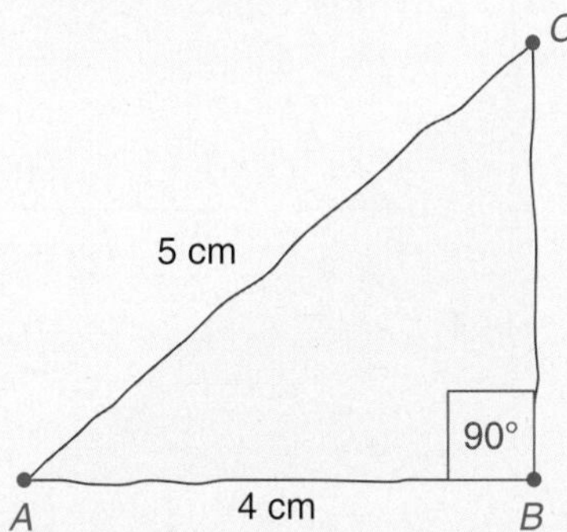

2. Draw a 4 cm line segment and mark the endpoints *A* and *B*.

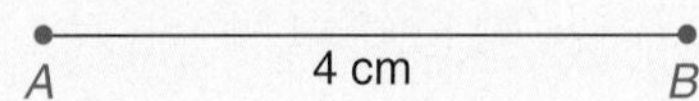

3. With your protractor centre on *B*, measure an angle of 90° and draw a ray through *B*.

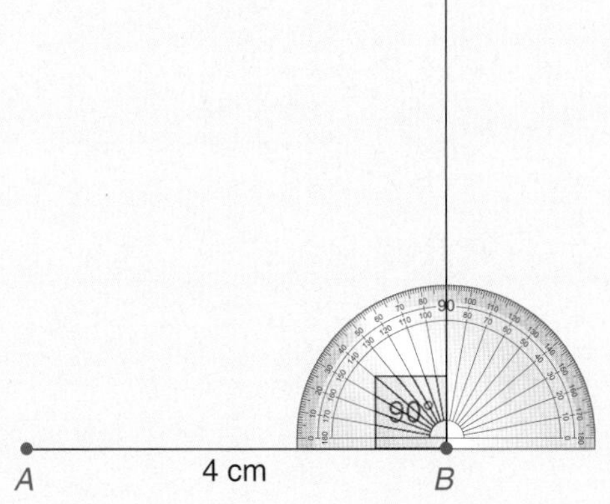

4. Set your compass to 5 cm and draw an arc from the point *A*.

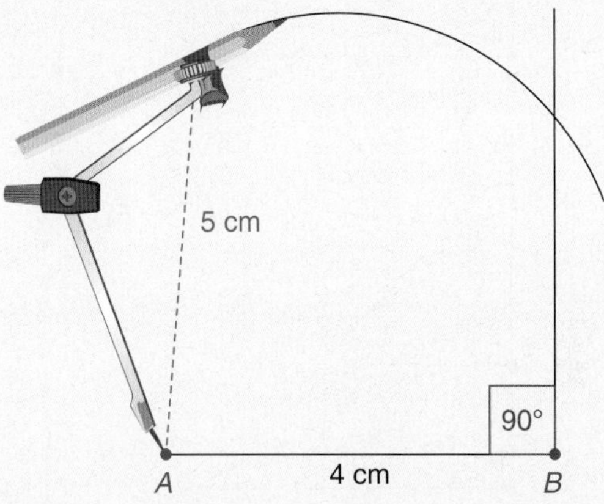

5. Mark the intersection point of the arc and the vertical line as point *C*.

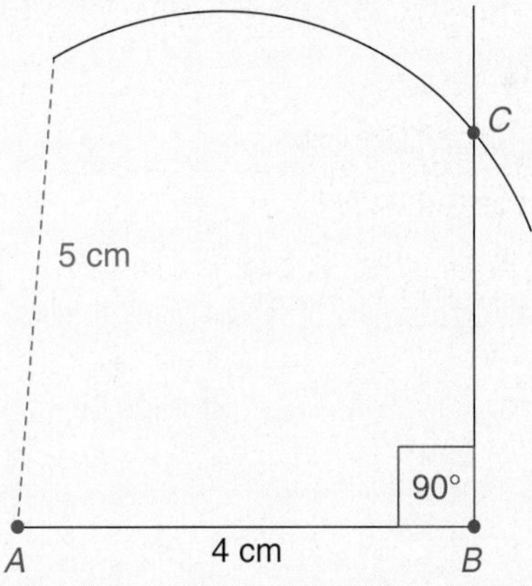

6. Draw triangle *ABC*, inserting the relevant labels and measurements.

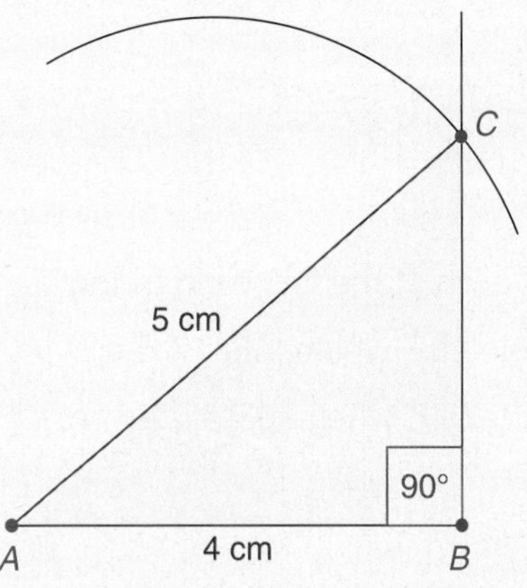

The construction method in Student Activity 7E can be used to draw any right-angled triangle, where you are given the length of the hypotenuse and one other side. This is often referred to as **R**ight angle, **H**ypotenuse, **S**ide **(RHS)**. Remember the hypotenuse is the side directly opposite the right angle.

Exercise 7.5

Construct each of the following triangles. All dimensions are in centimetres.

1.

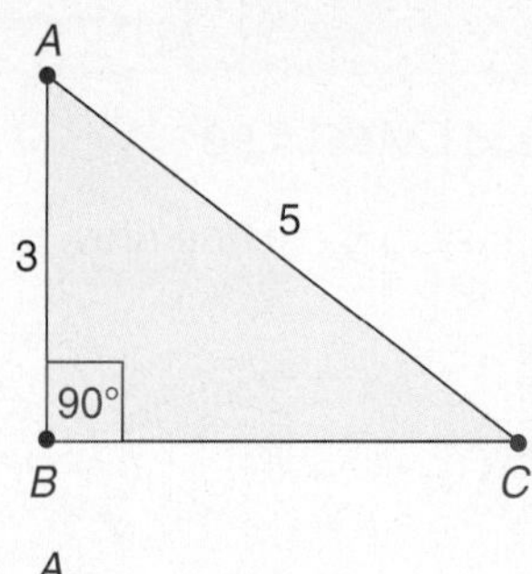

2.

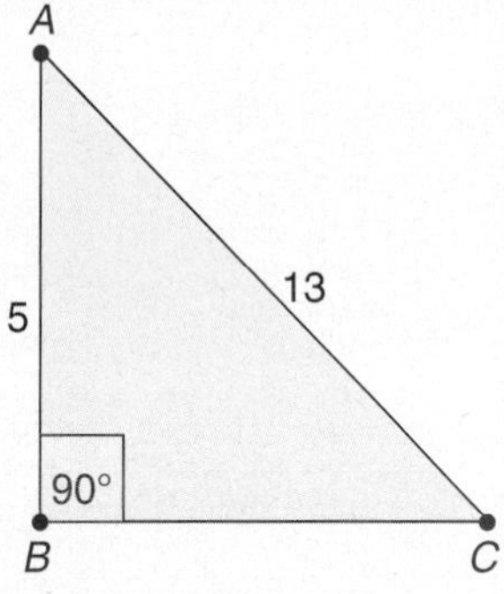

3.

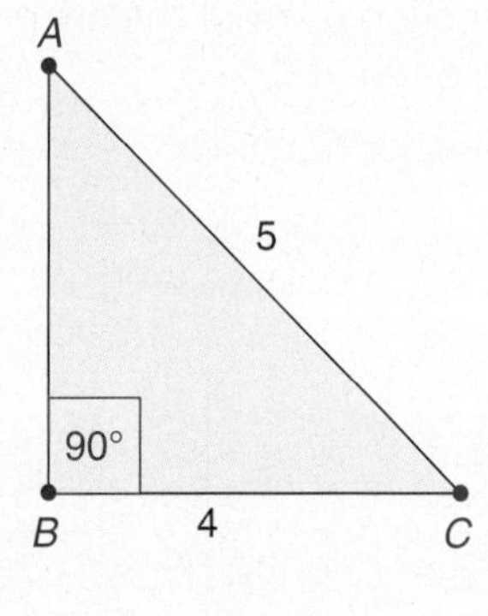

4.

A
13
90°
C
12
B

5.

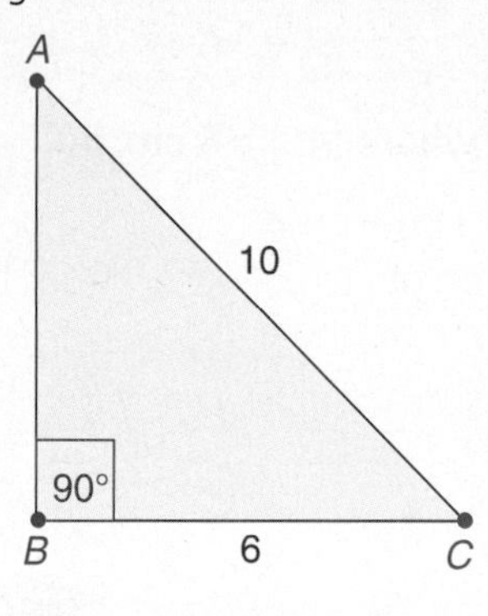

6.

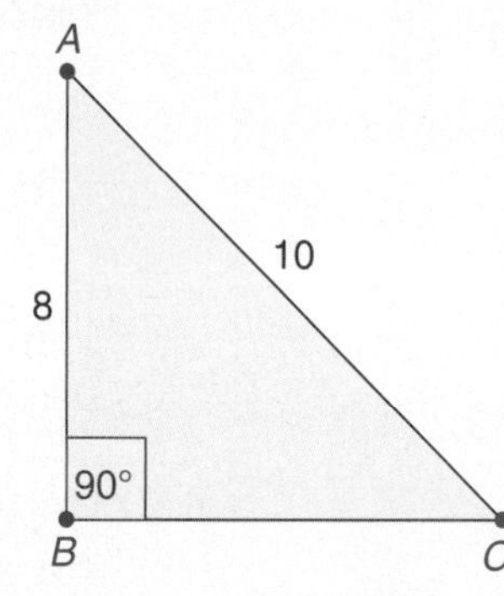

7.

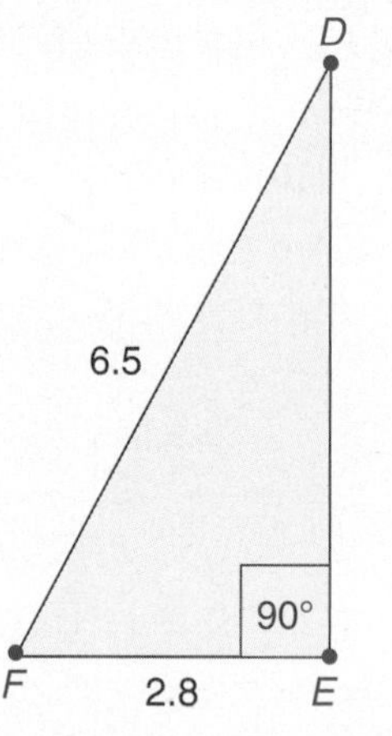

8.

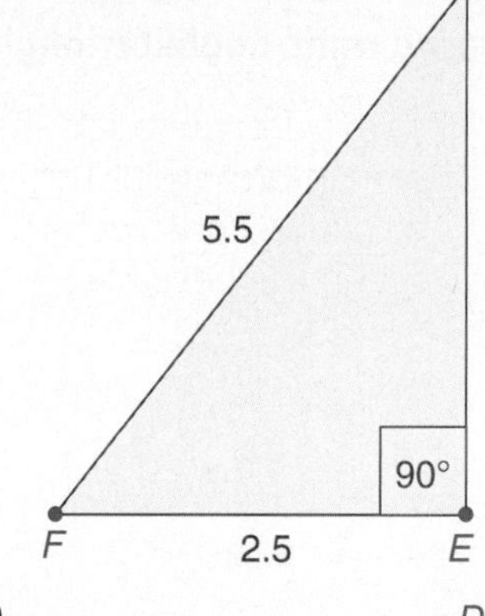

9.

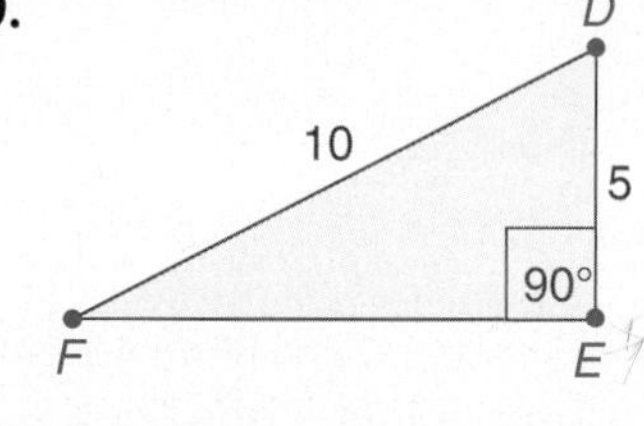

10.

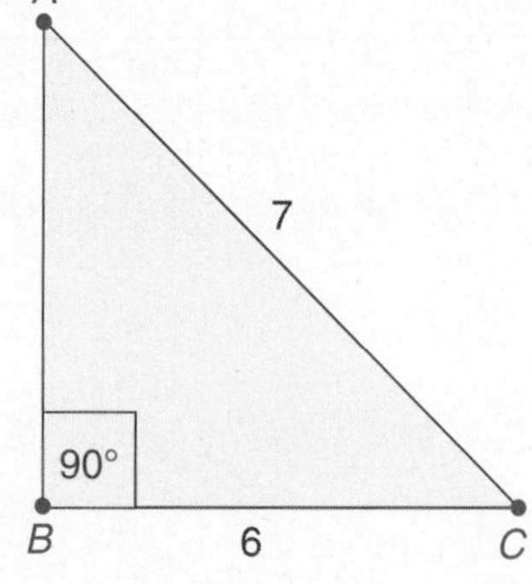

Construct each of the following triangles:

11. Triangle *ABC*, where $|AB| = 6.5$ cm, $|AC| = 8$ cm and $|\angle BAC| = 90°$

12. Triangle *DEF*, where $|DE| = 72$ mm, $|DF| = 66$ mm and $|\angle DEF| = 90°$

13. Triangle *GHI*, where $|GH| = 6.7$ cm, $|GI| = 9.6$ cm and $|\angle GHI| = 90°$

14. Triangle *KJL*, where $|JK| = 68$ mm, $|JL| = 96$ mm and $|\angle JKL| = 90°$

15. Triangle *MNP*, where $|MN| = 10$ cm, $|MP| = 12$ cm and $|\angle MNP| = 90°$

Section 7.6: Construct a right-angled triangle, given one side and one of the acute angles

Student Activity 7F

Draw a right-angled triangle *ABC* where |*AB*| = 5 cm and |∠*BAC*| = 40° and |∠*ABC*| = 90°.

1. Make a rough sketch of the triangle and insert the given information. Identify the missing angle and use it in the construction if necessary. Let the right angle rest on the baseline of the triangle.

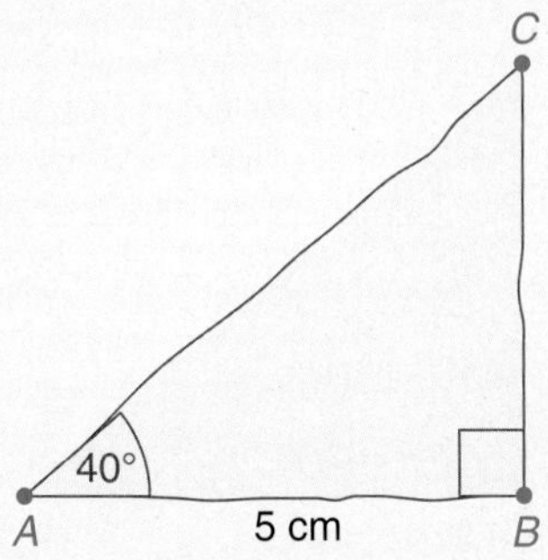

2. Draw a 5 cm line segment and mark the endpoints *A* and *B*.

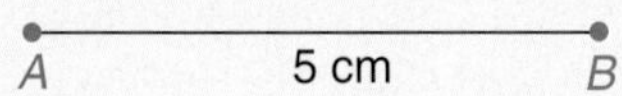

3. With your protractor on *A*, measure an angle of 40° and draw a ray through *A*.

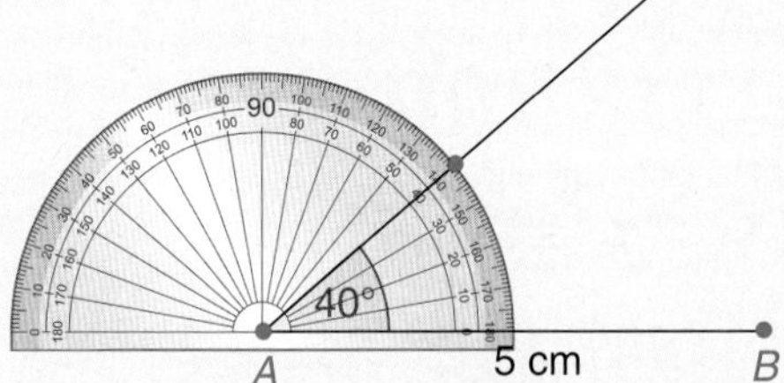

4. Using your protractor, draw a right angle at *B*.

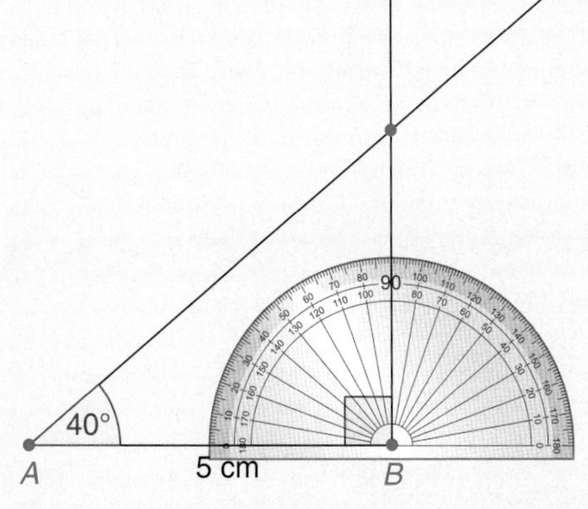

5. Mark the intersection point of the two rays as *C*.

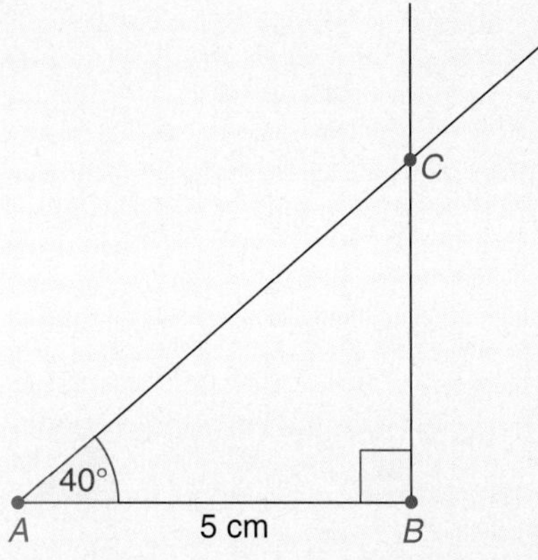

6. Draw the triangle *ABC*, inserting all labels.

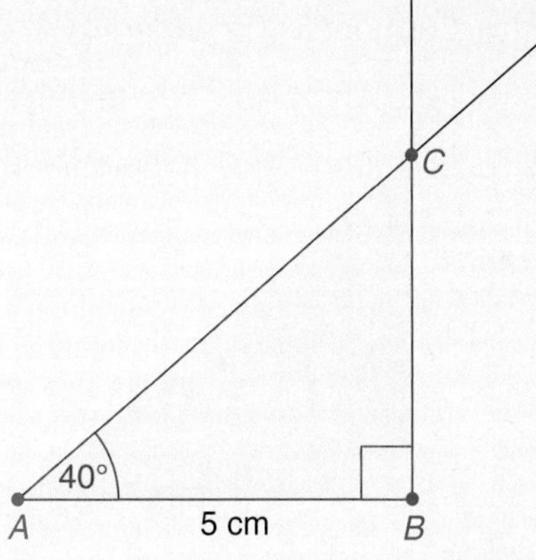

Exercise 7.6

Construct each of the following triangles. All dimensions are in centimetres.

1. 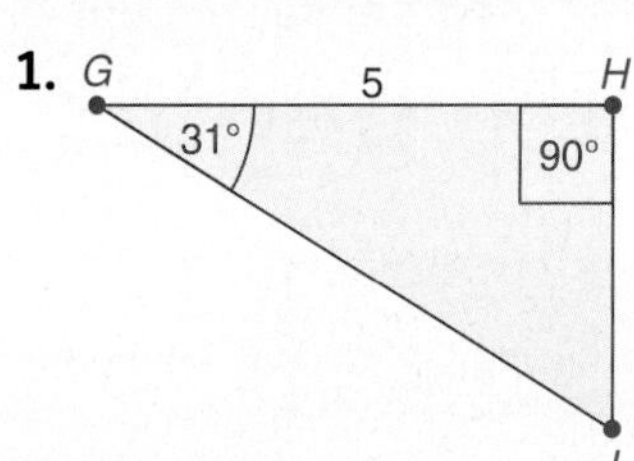

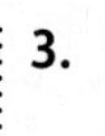

3. 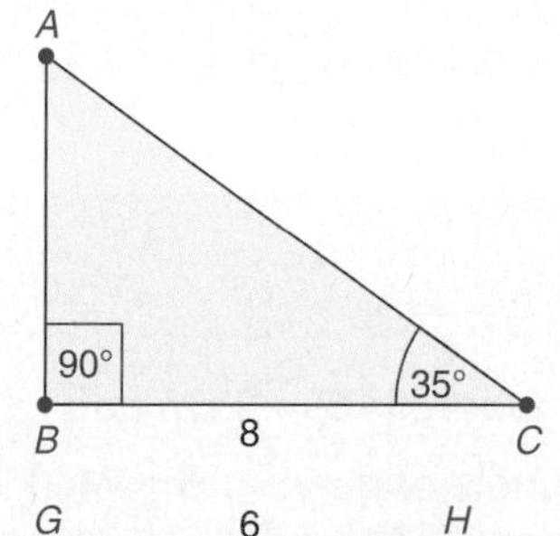

5. 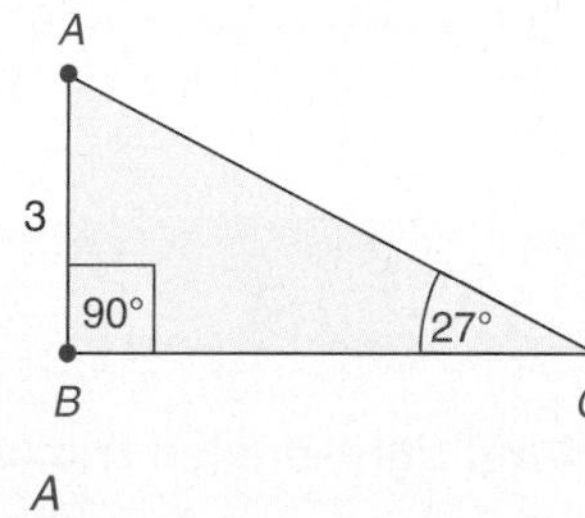

2. 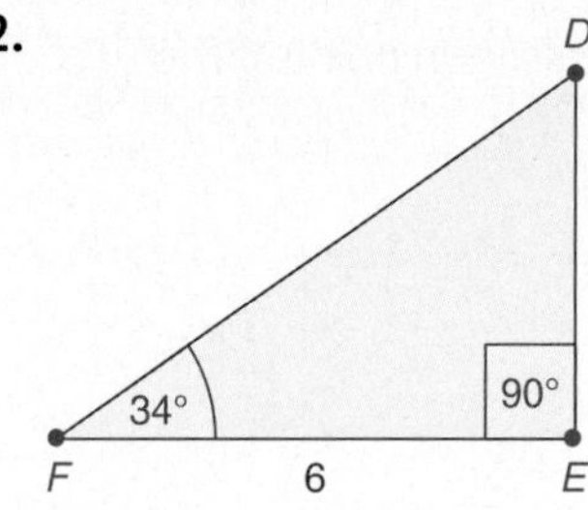

4. 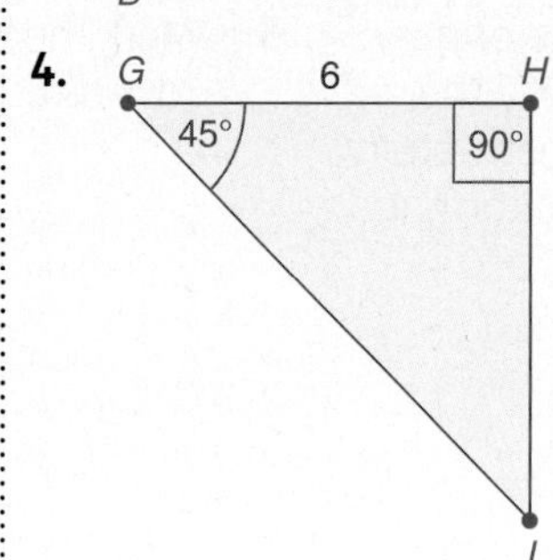

6. 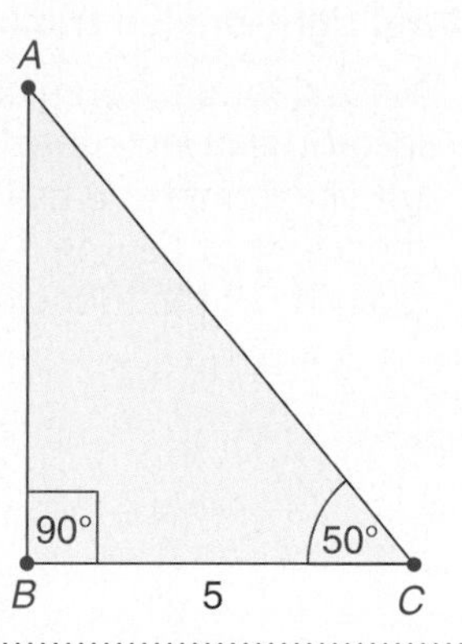

7. Construct a triangle XYZ, where $|XY| = 8$ cm, $|\angle XYZ| = 90°$ and $|\angle XZY| = 50°$.
8. Construct a triangle GHI, where $|HI| = 10$ cm, $|\angle IHG| = 55°$ and $|\angle GIH| = 90°$.
9. Construct a triangle JKL, where $|JK| = 12$ cm, $|\angle JKL| = 90°$ and $|\angle LJK| = 60°$.
10. Construct a triangle STR, where $|ST| = 11$ cm, $|\angle RST| = 35°$ and $|\angle STR| = 90°$.
11. Construct a triangle XYZ, where $|XY| = 7$ cm, $|\angle XZY| = 90°$ and $|\angle XYZ| = 80°$.
12. Construct a triangle ABC, where $|AC| = 5$ cm, $|\angle ABC| = 90°$ and $|\angle ACB| = 25°$.
13. Construct a triangle MNP, where $|MP| = 7.5$ cm, $|\angle MNP| = 90°$ and $|\angle MPN| = 60°$.
14. Construct a triangle DEF, where $|DF| = 8$ cm, $|\angle FDE| = 35°$ and $|\angle EFD| = 90°$.

Section 7.7: Construct a rectangle, given the lengths of the sides

Student Activity 7G

Draw a rectangle *ABCD* with |*AB*| = 7 cm and |*BC*| = 5 cm.

1. Draw a rough sketch of the rectangle and insert the given information.

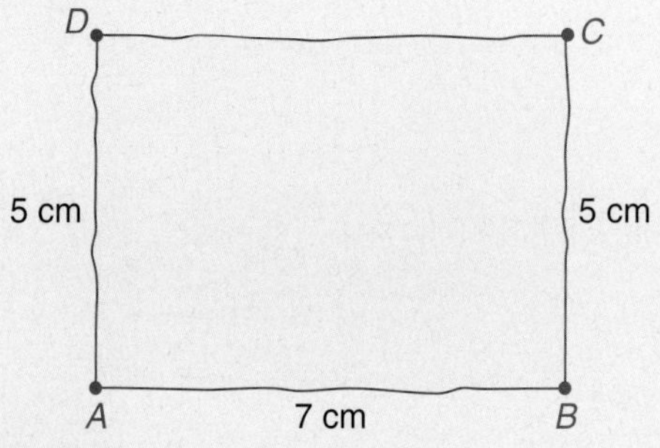

2. Draw a 7 cm line segment and mark the endpoints as *A* and *B*.

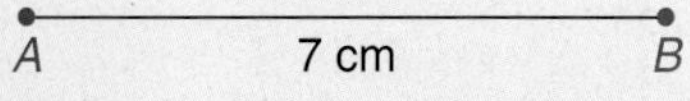

3. With your protractor centre on the point *A*, measure an angle of 90° and draw a ray from the point *A*.

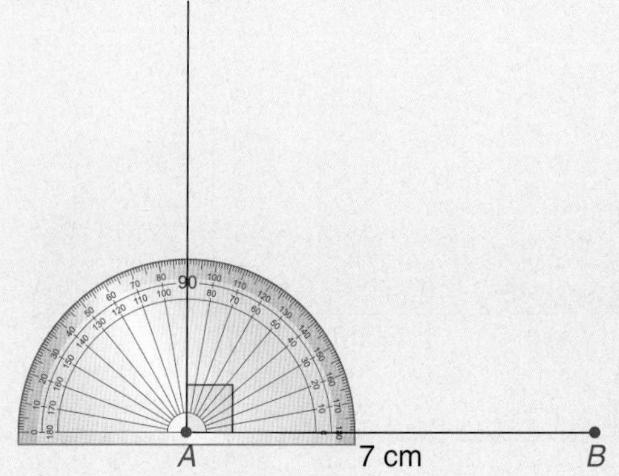

4. With your protractor centre on the point B, measure an angle of 90° and draw a ray from the point B.

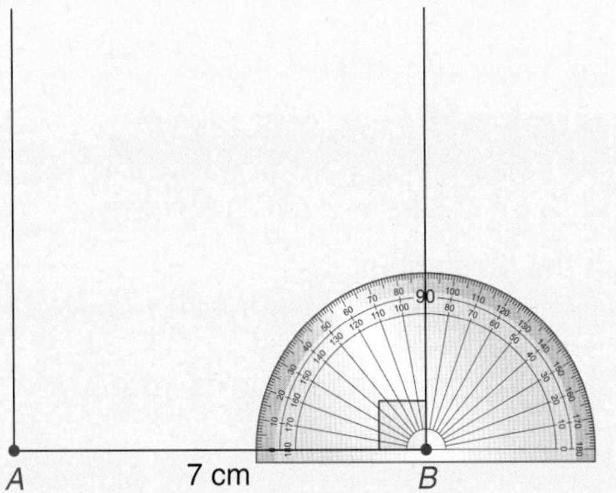

5. Use your ruler to measure 5 cm on each ray from A and from B.

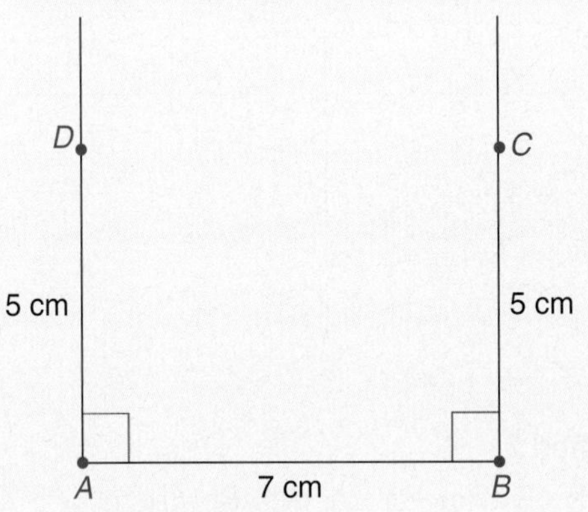

Mark the points C and D (note that C is above B and D is above A).

6. Join C to D to form the required rectangle, $ABCD$. Label all measurements.

Note

The points $ABCD$ go in a clockwise or an anticlockwise direction about the shape.

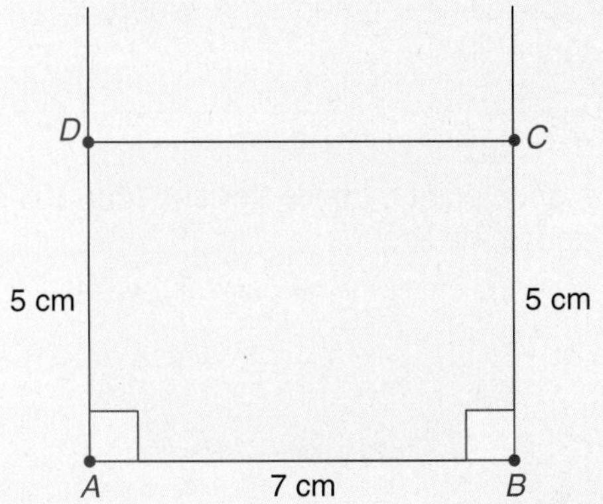

Exercise 7.7

Construct each of the following rectangles. All dimensions are in centimetres.

1. 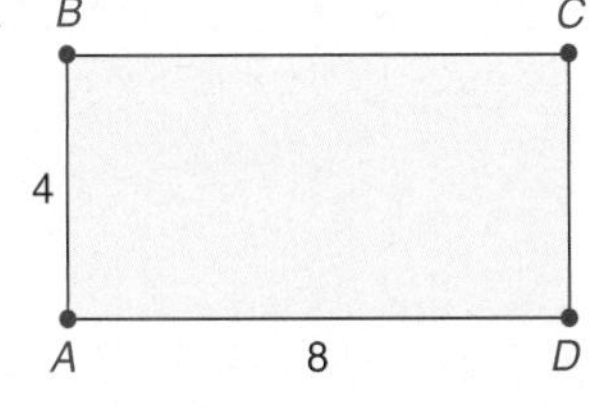

2. 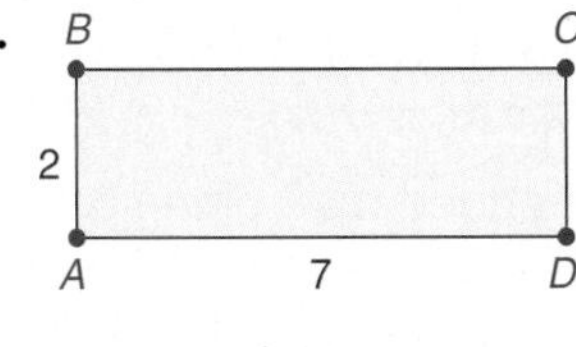

3. 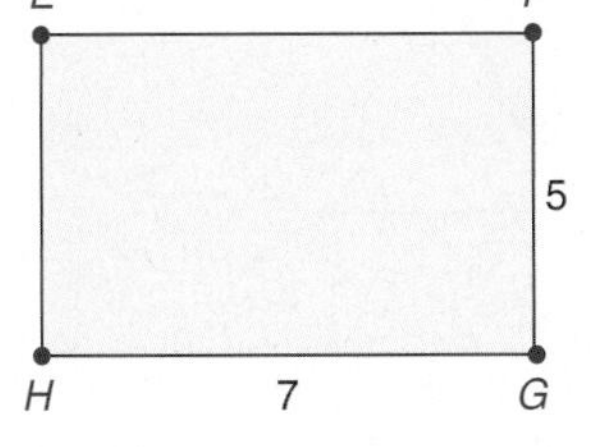

4. 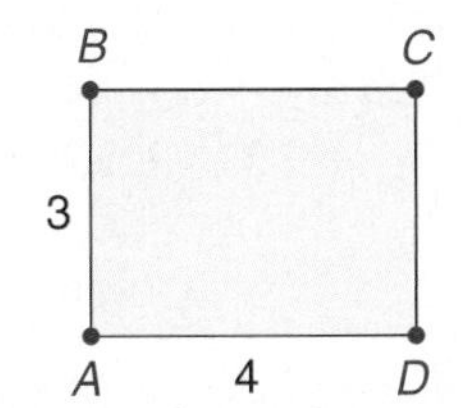

5. 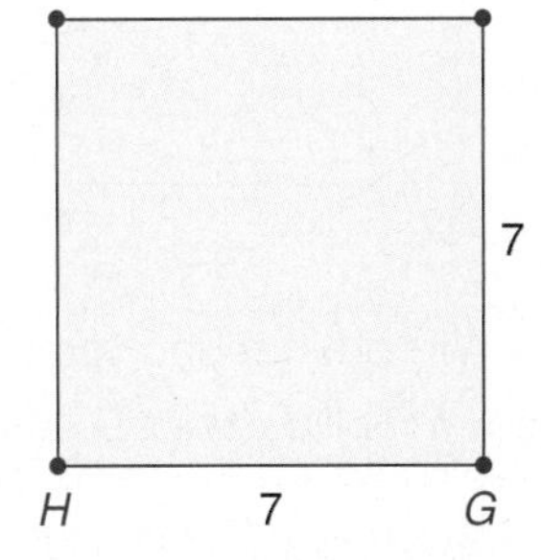

6. 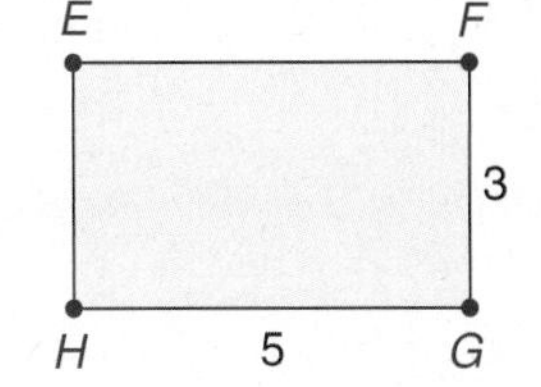

Construct the following quadrilaterals:

7. The square $ABCD$, where $|AB| = 7.5$ cm
8. The square $EFGH$, where $|EF| = 80$ mm
9. The rectangle $IJKL$, such that $|IJ| = 3$ cm and $|JK| = 6$ cm
10. The rectangle $MNPQ$, such that $|MN| = 65$ mm and $|NP| = 45$ mm

Section 7.8: Construct a line perpendicular to a given line *l*, passing through a given point not on *l*

Student Activity 7H

Construct a perpendicular line to the line *l* through the given point *C*.

Method 1

1. Draw a line segment [*AB*], where |*AB*| = 10 cm.

A 10 cm B

2. Mark a point *C* above this line (about 5 cm above the line).

C

A 10 cm B

3. Centre your compass on the point *C* and draw an arc intersecting the line segment [*AB*]. Mark the two intersection points as *X* and *Y*.

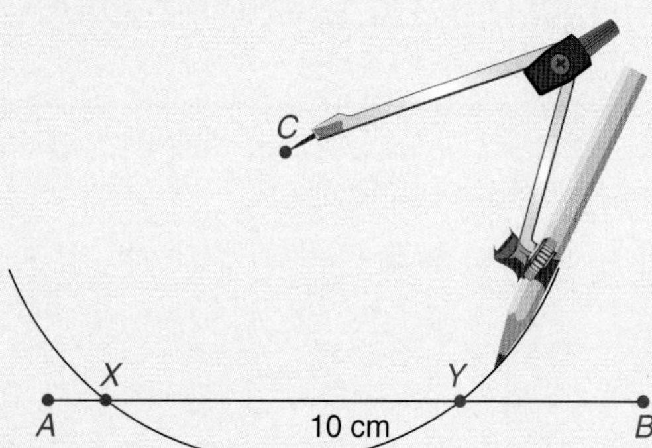

4. Without altering your compass length, centre it in turn on the two intersection points *X* and *Y* and draw two intersecting arcs below the line segment [*AB*]. Mark the intersection points of the arcs as *Z*.

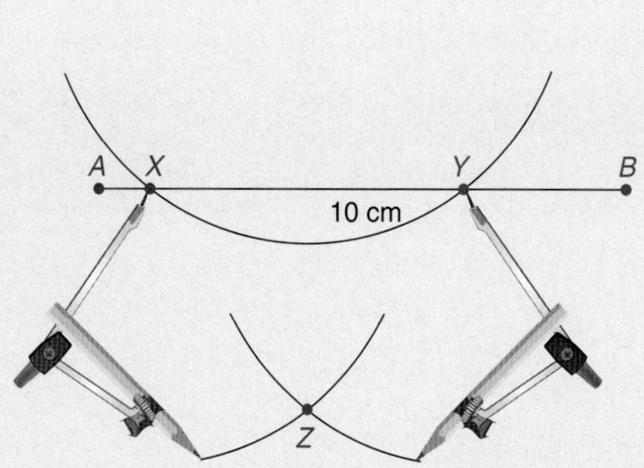

5. Using a straight edge, join *C* to *Z*.

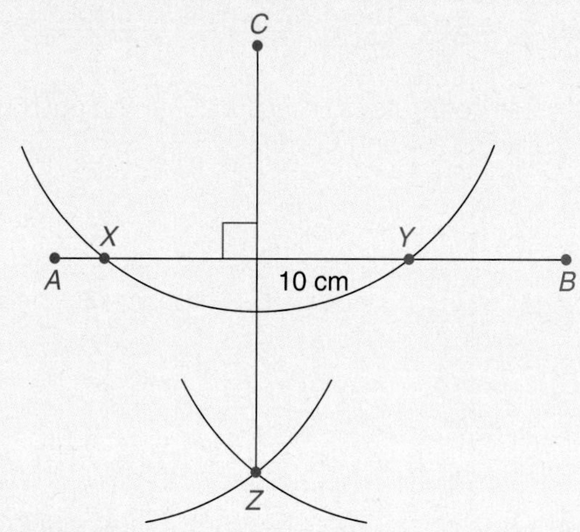

Method 2

1. Draw a line segment [*AB*], where |*AB*| = 10 cm.

A 10 cm B

2. Mark a point *C* above this line (about 5 cm above the line).

C

A 10 cm B

3. Place a straight-edged ruler along the line [*AB*] and place the set square on the ruler.

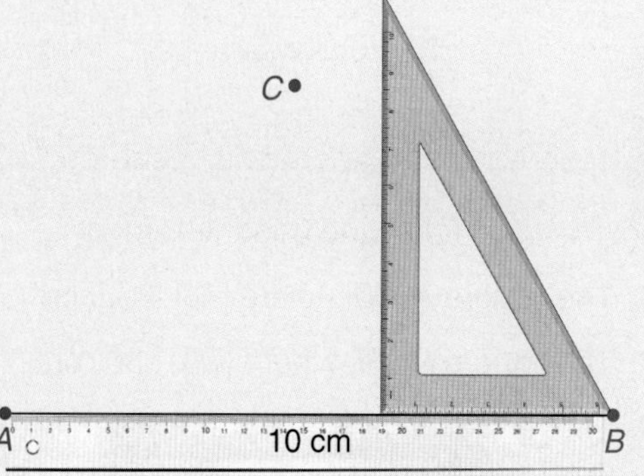

4. Move the set square along the ruler until it reaches the point C.

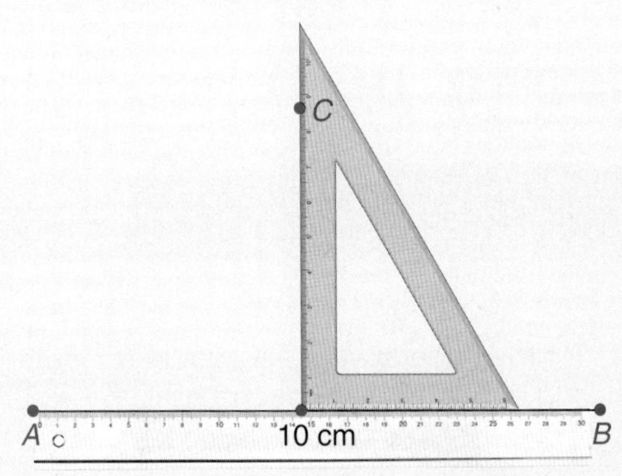

5. Draw a line through the point C. This line is perpendicular to the line l.

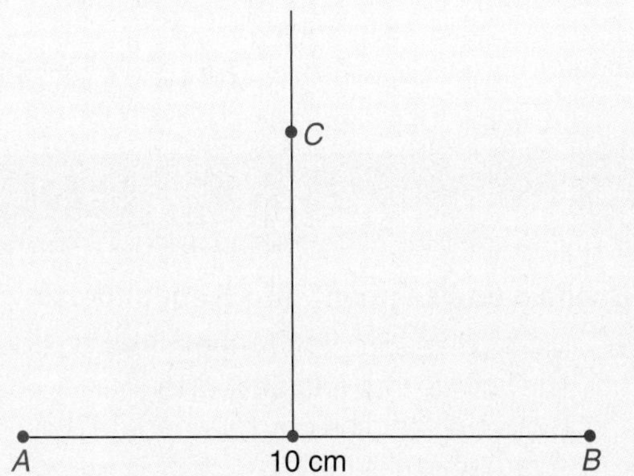

The construction in Student Activity 7H has two methods. If you are asked to use a compass, you must use Method 1. It is necessary to be able to carry out both methods.

Exercise 7.8

Construct each of the following. All measurements are in centimetres.

1. 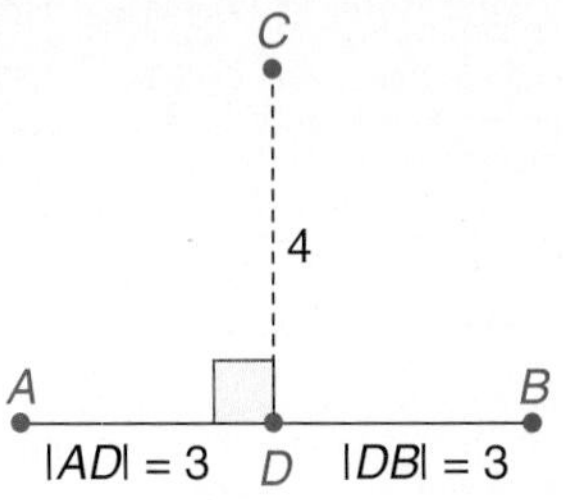

2. 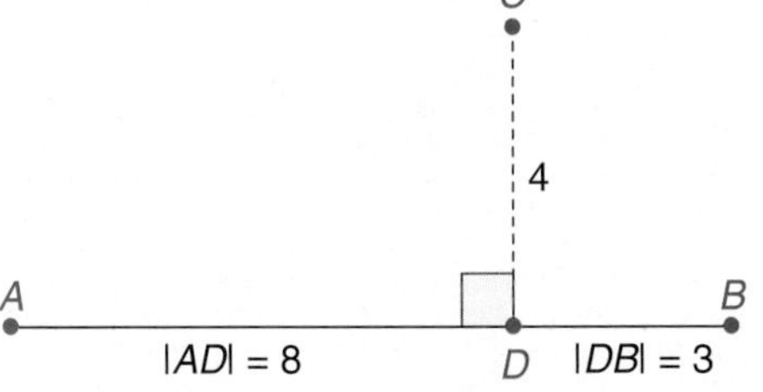

3. 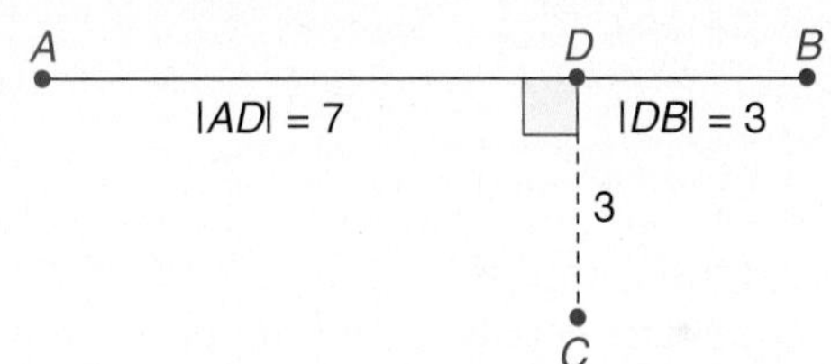

4. 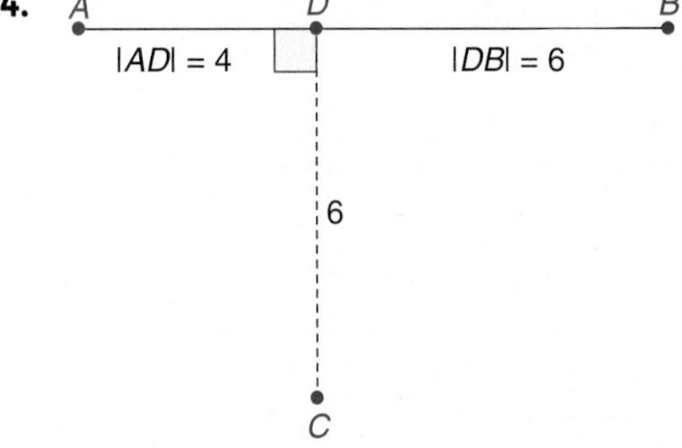

5. Draw a line segment $[XY]$ where $|XY| = 9$ cm. Draw a point Z, where Z is 3 cm above the line segment $[XY]$. Construct a line through Z perpendicular to $[XY]$.

6. Draw a line segment $[AB]$ where $|AB| = 12$ cm. Draw a point C, where C is 4 cm above the line segment $[AB]$. Construct a line through C perpendicular to $[AB]$.

7. Draw a line segment $[ST]$ where $|ST| = 10$ cm. Draw a point Q, where Q is 5 cm below the line segment $[ST]$. Construct a line through Q perpendicular to $[ST]$.

Section 7.9: Divide a line segment into any number of equal segments, without measuring it

Student Activity 7I

Divide a line segment into 5 equal parts.

1. Draw a line segment [AB] that we shall divide into ***n* equal parts** (where ***n*** could be any number). In this case, we shall let ***n*** = 5.

A B

2. From point *A*, draw a ray at an acute angle to the line segment [*AB*], which is roughly the same length as [*AB*]. The exact length is not important.

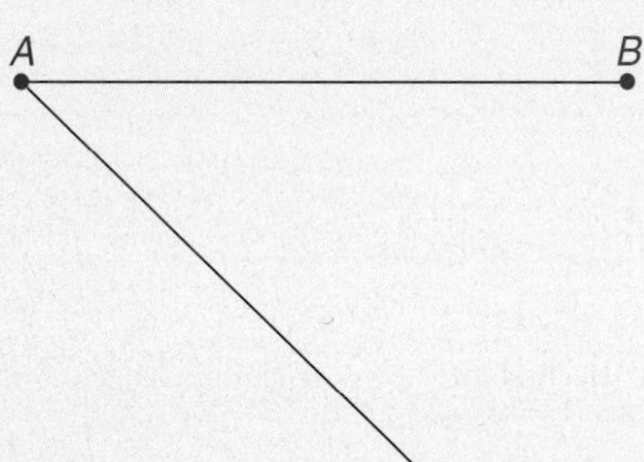

3. Set the compass on *A*, and mark off 5 equal arcs on the ray by stepping the compass along the ray.

   Label the 5th point on the ray marked by the arc as *C*.

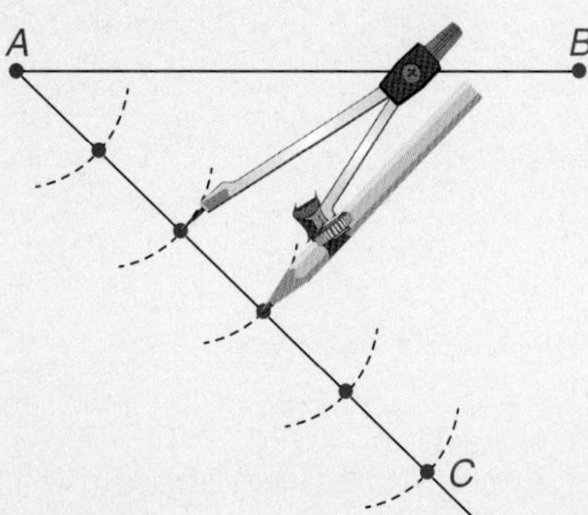

4. Using your ruler join *B* to *C*.

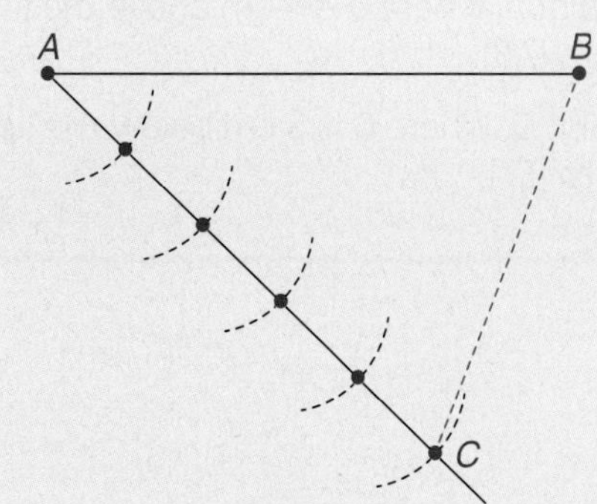

5. Set the edge of your set square on [*BC*] and put your ruler underneath it.

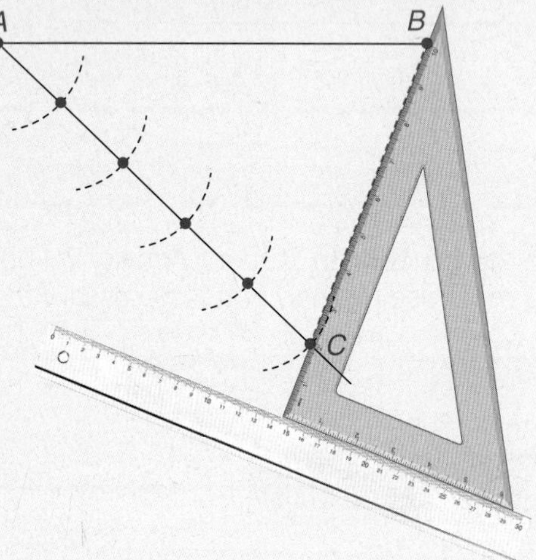

6. Slide your set square along the ruler until you reach the next point on the ray and draw a line back to [*AB*]. This line should be parallel to *BC*.

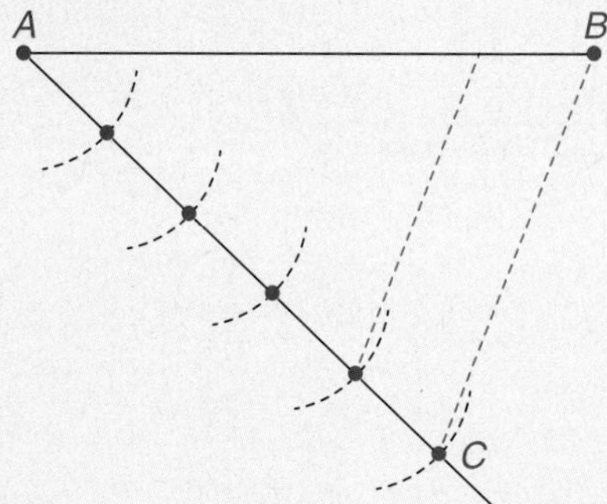

7. Repeat step 6 for each remaining point. Your new points should divide [*AB*] into 5 equal parts.

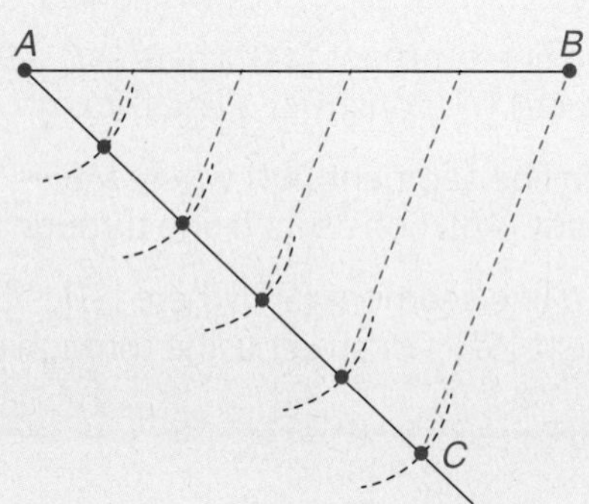

In *Maths in Action 1*, you learned to divide a line segment into 3 equal parts. For the Higher Level Course, you must be able to divide a line segment into any number of equal parts.

This construction method used in Student Activity 7I can be used for any number of equal parts.

Exercise 7.9

1. Draw a line segment, where $|AB| = 6$ cm. Divide the line segment into 3 equal parts.
2. Draw a line segment, where $|CD| = 8$ cm. Divide the line segment into 4 equal parts.
3. Draw a line segment, where $|XY| = 5$ cm. Divide the line segment into 3 equal parts.
4. Draw a line segment, where $|ST| = 10$ cm. Divide the line segment into 4 equal parts.
5. Draw a line segment, where $|GH| = 7$ cm. Divide the line segment into 5 equal parts.
6. Draw a line segment, where $|UV| = 12$ cm. Divide the line segment into 3 equal parts.
7. Draw a line segment, where $|AB| = 6$ cm. Divide the line segment into 5 equal parts.
8. Draw a line segment, where $|CD| = 8$ cm. Divide the line segment into 5 equal parts.
9. Draw a line segment, where $|XY| = 5$ cm. Divide the line segment into 4 equal parts.
10. Draw a line segment, where $|ST| = 10$ cm. Divide the line segment into 5 equal parts.

CHAPTER 7 SELF-CHECK TEST

Construct each of the following triangles. All dimensions are in centimetres. Show all construction lines clearly.

1.

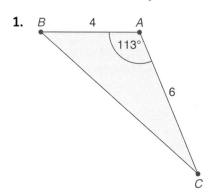

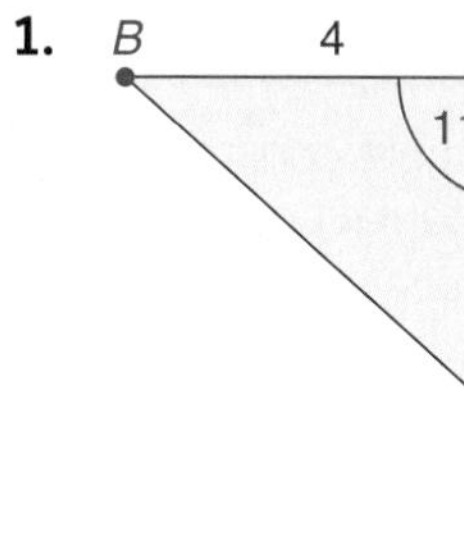

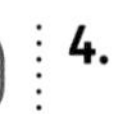

2.

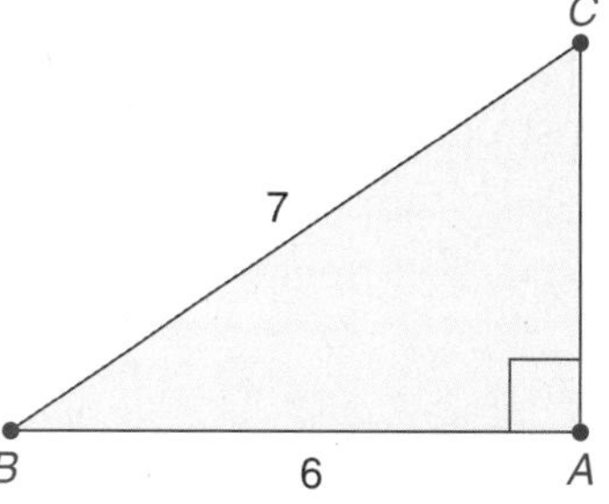

3.

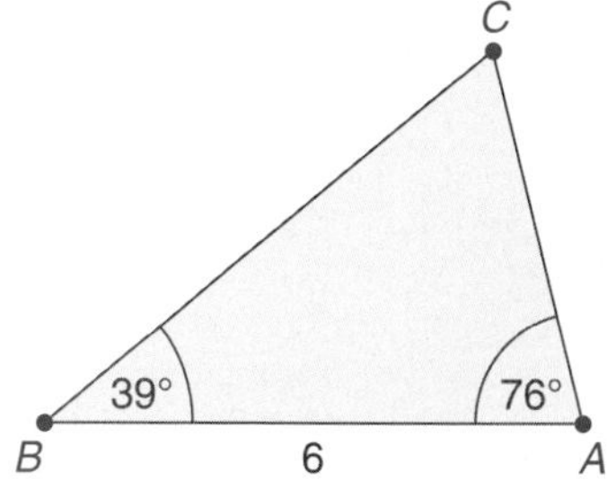

4.

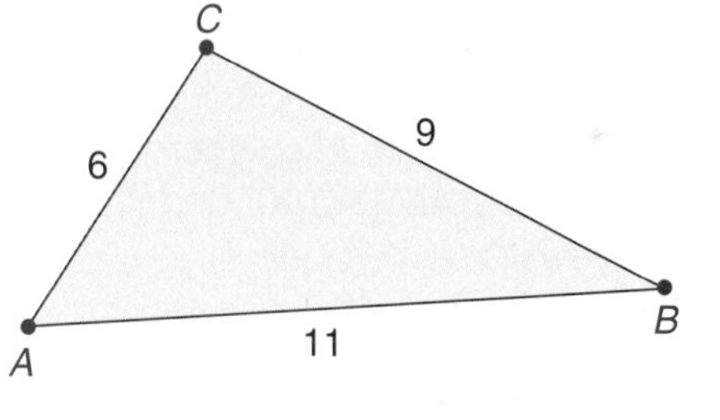

5.

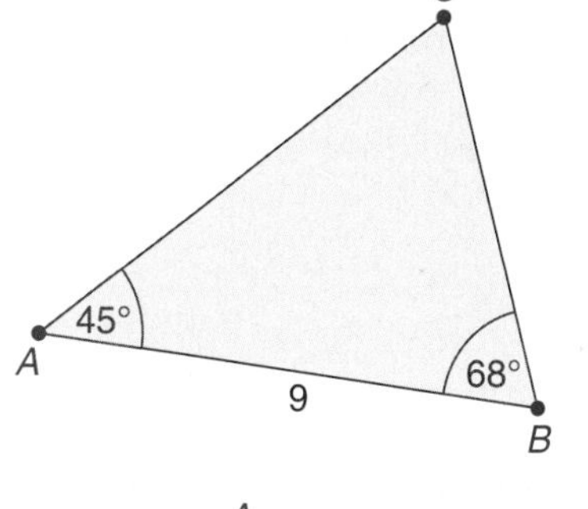

6.

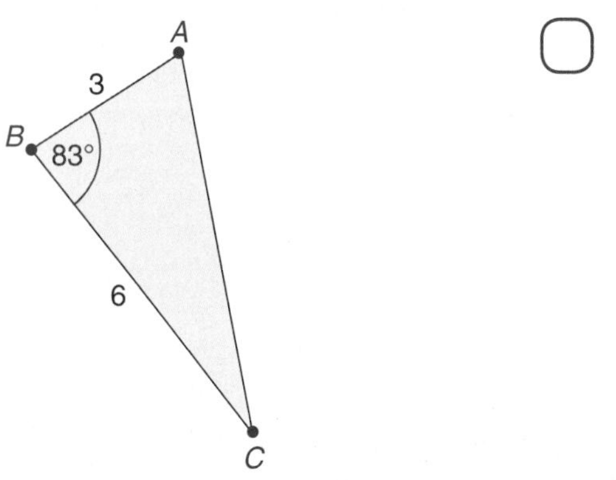

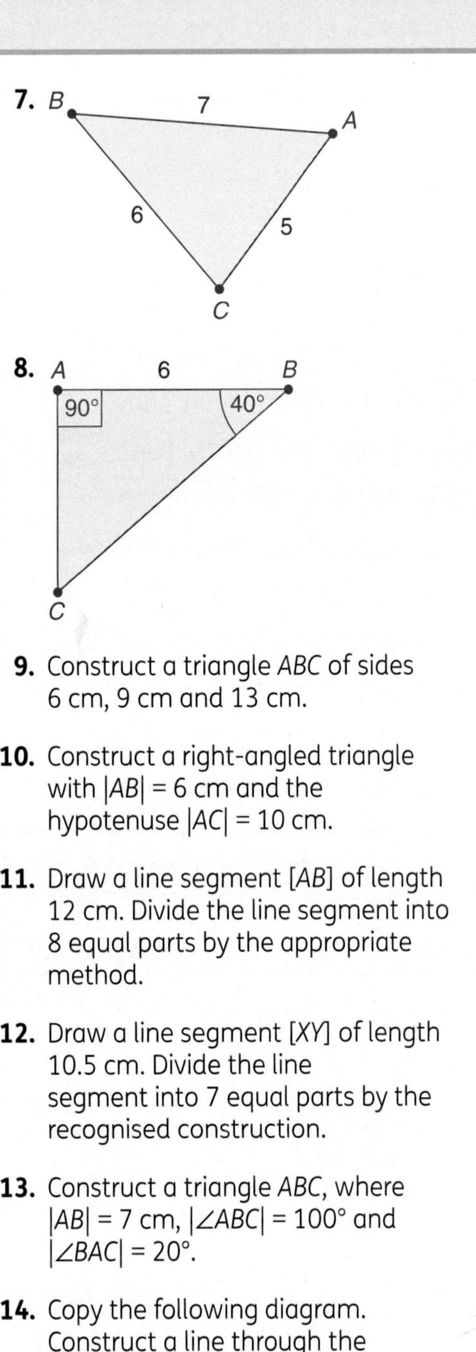

9. Construct a triangle ABC of sides 6 cm, 9 cm and 13 cm.

10. Construct a right-angled triangle with $|AB| = 6$ cm and the hypotenuse $|AC| = 10$ cm.

11. Draw a line segment $[AB]$ of length 12 cm. Divide the line segment into 8 equal parts by the appropriate method.

12. Draw a line segment $[XY]$ of length 10.5 cm. Divide the line segment into 7 equal parts by the recognised construction.

13. Construct a triangle ABC, where $|AB| = 7$ cm, $|\angle ABC| = 100°$ and $|\angle BAC| = 20°$.

14. Copy the following diagram. Construct a line through the point C perpendicular to the line segment $[AB]$.

C

A B

15. Construct a right-angled triangle ABC, where $|AB| = 5$ cm and $|\angle BAC| = 40°$ and $|\angle ABC| = 90°$.

16. Paul wants to divide his bar of chocolate equally among 4 friends. Measure the length of the bar and show by means of a suitable construction how Paul could divide the bar equally.

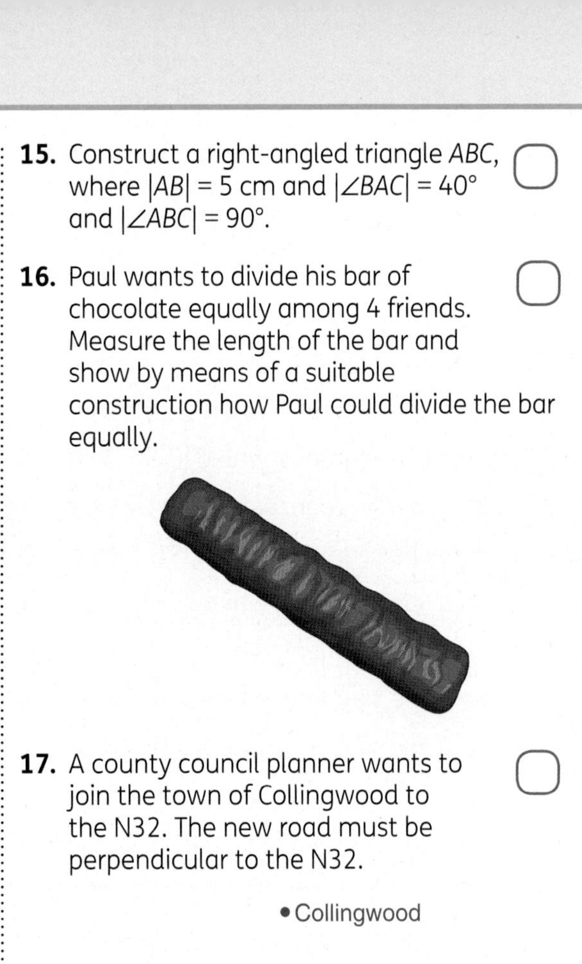

17. A county council planner wants to join the town of Collingwood to the N32. The new road must be perpendicular to the N32.

• Collingwood

Show by means of a suitable construction how the planner can construct a plan for the road.

18. A gardener is designing a triangular flower-bed with sides 6 m, 8 m and 10 m. Using a scale of 1 cm:1 m, construct a plan of the flower-bed.

The gardener then decides to put two identical flower-beds beside each other so that they form a rectangle. Construct the rectangle using a suitable construction.

CHAPTER 7 KNOWLEDGE CHECKLIST

After completing this chapter, I now:

- Am able to construct an angle of a given number of degrees with a given ray as one arm
- Am able to construct a triangle, given the lengths of three sides
- Am able to construct a triangle, given two sides and the included angle
- Am able to construct a triangle, given two angles and the included side
- Am able to construct a right-angled triangle, given the length of the hypotenuse and one other side
- Am able to construct a right-angled triangle, given one side and one of the acute angles
- Am able to construct a rectangle, given the lengths of the sides
- Am able to construct a line perpendicular to a given line l, through a given point not on l
- Am able to divide a line segment into any number of equal parts, without measuring it

Challenge

Can you find your way through the maze moving vertically, horizontally or diagonally, following the colours correctly to find the hidden image?

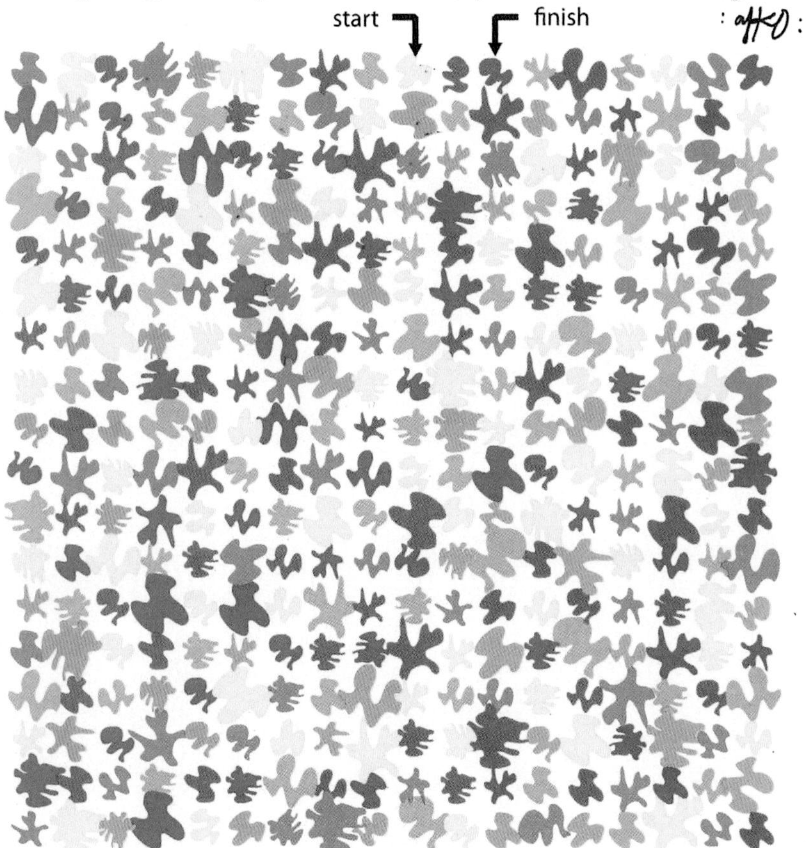

GEOMETRY 1

KEY WORDS

- Congruent
- Corollary
- Corresponding
- Diagonal
- Equiangular
- Polygon
- Proportion
- Similar
- Theorem

LEARNING OUTCOMES

In this chapter you will learn:

- ✓ **That if two triangles are similar, then their sides are in proportion**
- ✓ **The terms equiangular and congruent**
- ✓ **To compare triangles and decide whether they are congruent**
- ✓ **About the conditions necessary for congruency in polygons**

INTRODUCTION

Many jobs require people to work with scaled models. This allows the design to be examined and improved before the full-size item is made. It would be very expensive if, halfway through building a skyscraper, you realised the design was wrong!

These pictures show the Herodian Temple in Jerusalem, which was built around 51 BC. The picture on the right is a 1:50 scale model of the temple.

8

GEOMETRY 1

Section 8.1: Similar triangles

Student Activity 8A

1. Felix the cat has lost her kittens. They have a similar footprint to their mother. Can you help her?

Felix's paw print

A B C D E

2. The infamous Dr Evil and Mini-Me, from the film *Austin Powers*, are considered to be similar in many ways.
   (a) Suggest ways in which they are similar.
   (b) Explain how similar does not mean identical.

3. Laura says, 'My dog Nero and my puppy Hercules are similar but not identical.' With reference to the photograph, explain what she means.

4. Examine the triangles and answer the questions which follow.
   (a) Using your protractor, measure the angles in both triangles. (Remember to use the correct notation when writing down each angle: $|\angle ABC| = ?$
   (b) What do you notice about the angles in these triangles?
   (c) Examine the triangles. Write down the sides that **correspond** between one triangle and the other triangle.
   (d) For each pair of corresponding sides, express their lengths as a proper fraction $\left(\text{for example } \frac{5}{9}\right)$.
   (e) Express each fraction as a decimal number, correct to two decimal places. What do you notice about your answers?

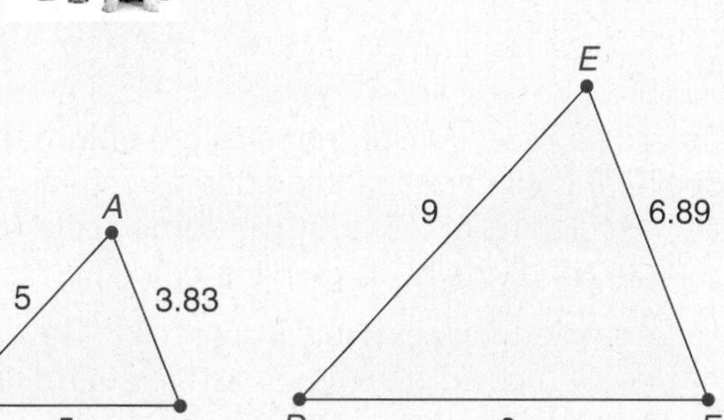

5. For each of the following pairs of triangles (a) measure the angles, (b) state the sides that correspond and (c) write the three side ratios, correct to one decimal place.

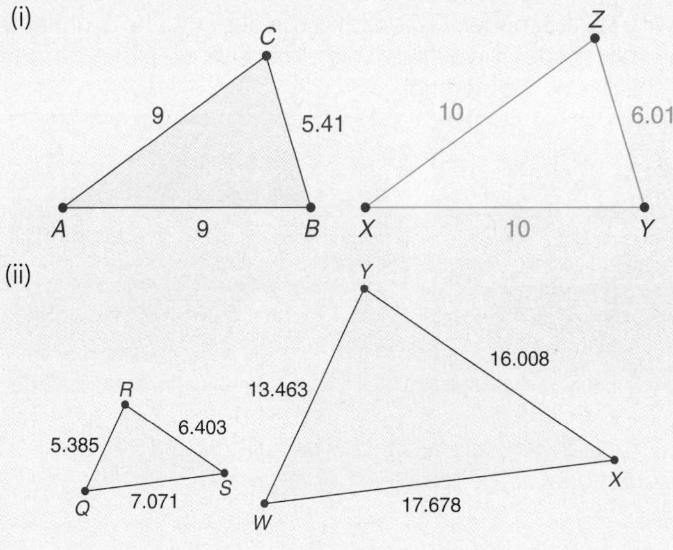

SIMILAR TRIANGLES EXPLAINED

In Student Activity 8A, you began looking at similar shapes. In geometry, two polygons are similar when one is a replica, or a scale model, of the other. Triangles are similar if matching angles remain the same size.

Triangles in which all three angles are equal are called **equiangular triangles.**

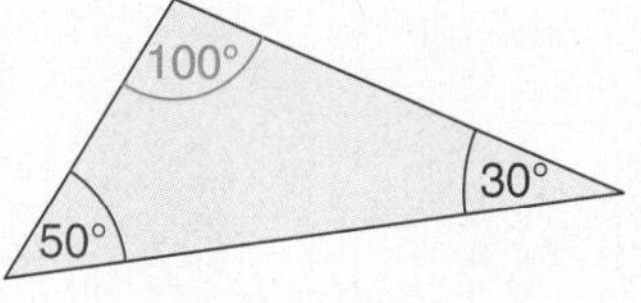

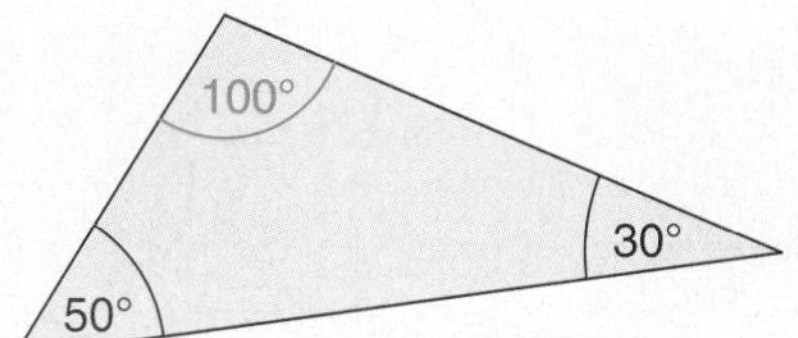

To check whether shapes are similar, we might need to turn or flip them around and mark equal angles with the same number of arcs or symbols. All of the following triangles are similar:

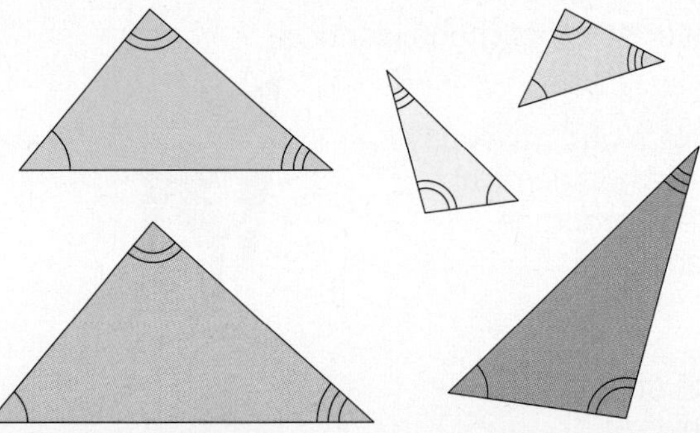

As you can see, similar triangles are **enlargements** or **reductions** of each other. Triangles are similar if their corresponding angles are equal and the lengths of their corresponding sides have been scaled up or down by the same **scale factor.** To calculate the missing sides, we either multiply or divide by the scale factor.

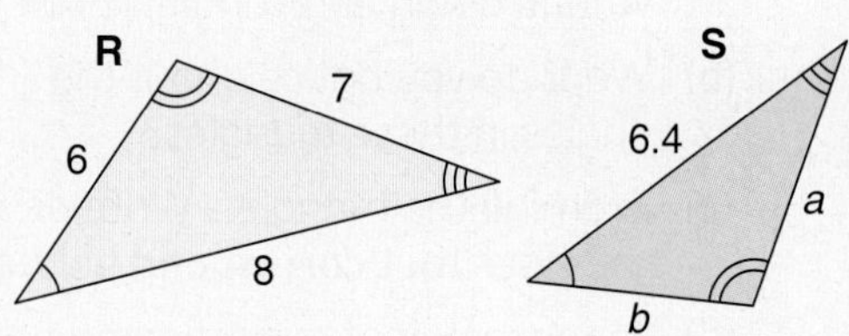

For example, triangles **R** and **S** are similar. The equal angles are marked with the same numbers of arcs.

- The lengths **7 in R** and ***a* in S** are corresponding (they face the angle marked with one arc).
- The lengths **8 in R** and **6.4 in S** are corresponding (they face the angle marked with two arcs).
- The lengths **6 in R** and ***b* in S** are corresponding (they face the angle marked with three arcs).

This leads to Theorem 13 on the Junior Certificate course, which states:

Theorem 13

If two triangles are similar, then their sides are proportional, in order.

The converse of this theorem is also true. It states:

Converse

If the sides of two triangles are proportional (in order), then the two triangles are similar.

Examining two similar triangles, we can form an equation using the ratios:

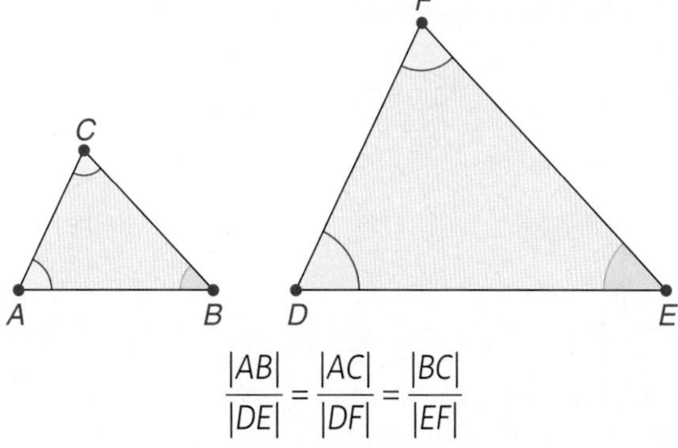

$$\frac{|AB|}{|DE|} = \frac{|AC|}{|DF|} = \frac{|BC|}{|EF|}$$

We can use similar triangles to find the length of the missing sides in scaled diagrams. The symbol for similarity is |||. If two triangles *ABC* and *DEF* are similar we can write:

$$\Delta ABC \;|||\; \Delta DEF$$

There are four conditions for similarity:

1. If the lengths of corresponding (matching) sides are in proportion
2. If two pairs of matching angles are equal (as the third angle must also be equal)
3. If the lengths of two sides are in proportion and the included angles are equal
4. In a right-angled triangle, if the length of the hypotenuse and another side are in proportion

EXAMPLE 1

(a) The triangle on the left is a scaled model of the triangle on the right. Find the scale factor.

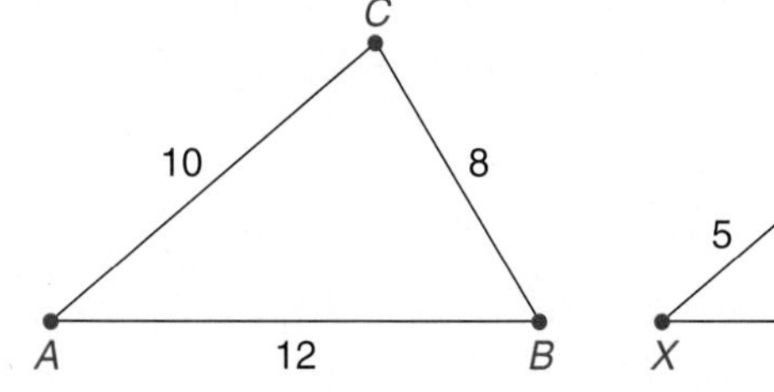

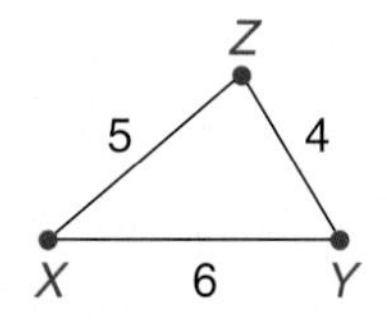

Solution

(a) The scale factor is $\frac{10}{5}$ or $\frac{12}{6}$ or $\frac{8}{4} = 2$.

Therefore, the triangle on the left is enlarged by a scale factor of 2. Or alternatively, the triangle on the right is enlarged by a scale factor of $\frac{1}{2}$.

(b) Find the length of the side marked x in the triangle below.

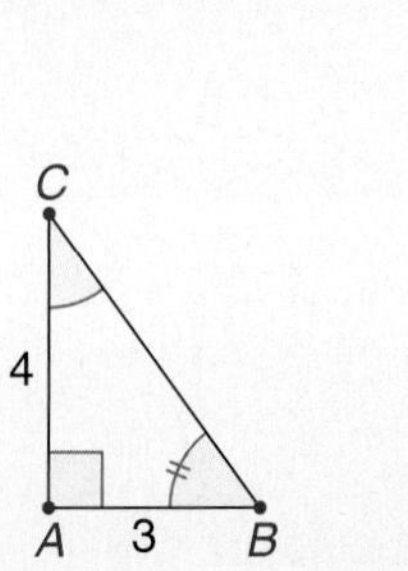

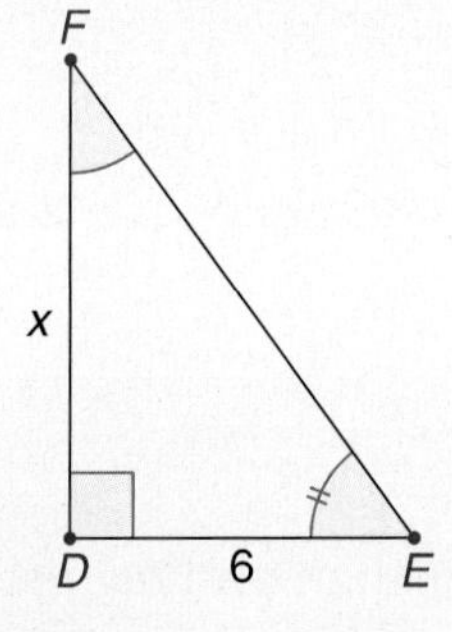

Solution

(b) From our earlier investigation we know that:

$$\frac{|AC|}{|DF|} = \frac{|AB|}{|DE|}$$

$$\frac{4}{x} = \frac{3}{6}$$

$$3x = 24$$

$$x = 8 \text{ units}$$

$$\therefore |DF| = 8 \text{ units}$$

Exercise 8.1

1. Which triangle is **not** similar to the other three?

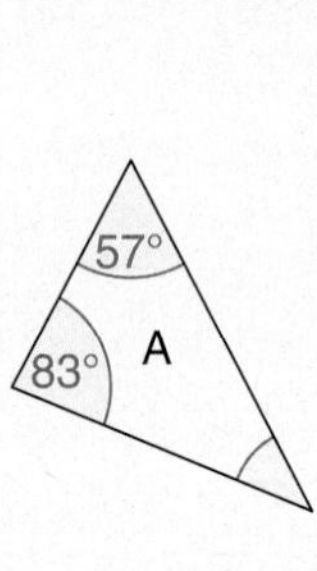

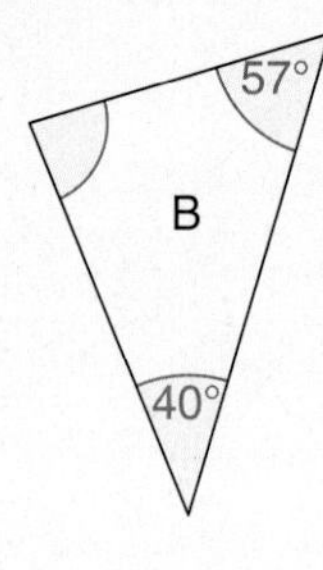

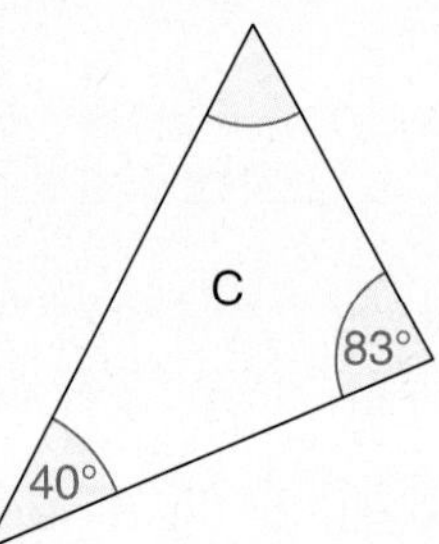

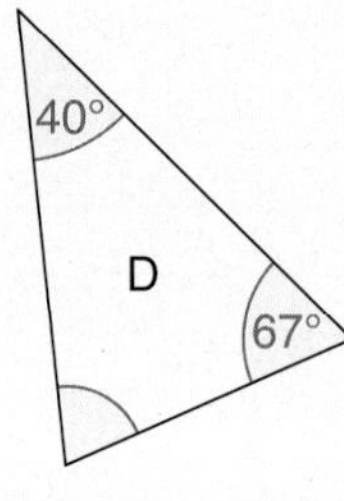

2. Identify the pairs of corresponding sides in each of the following similar triangles:

(a)

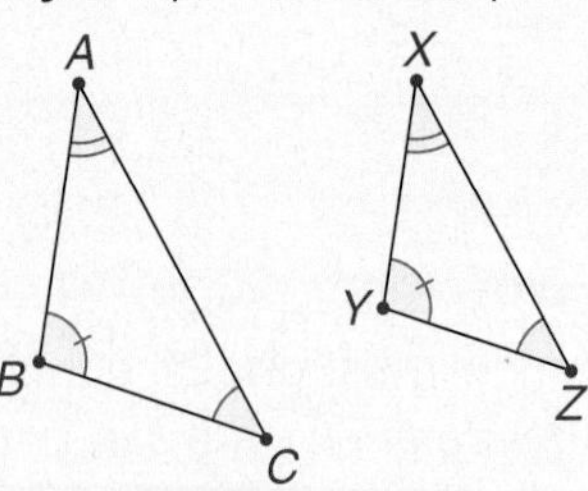

(d)

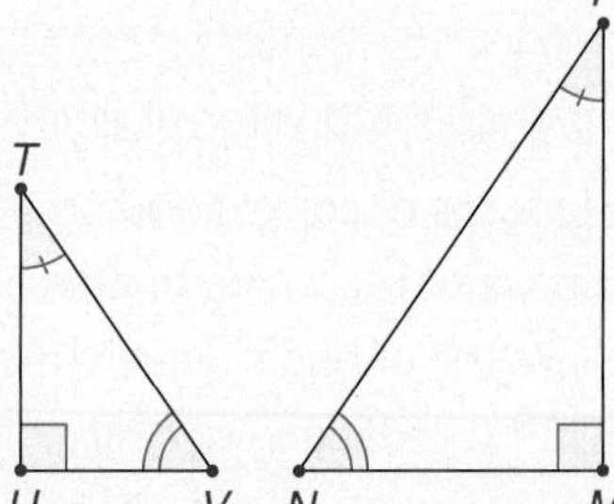

(b)

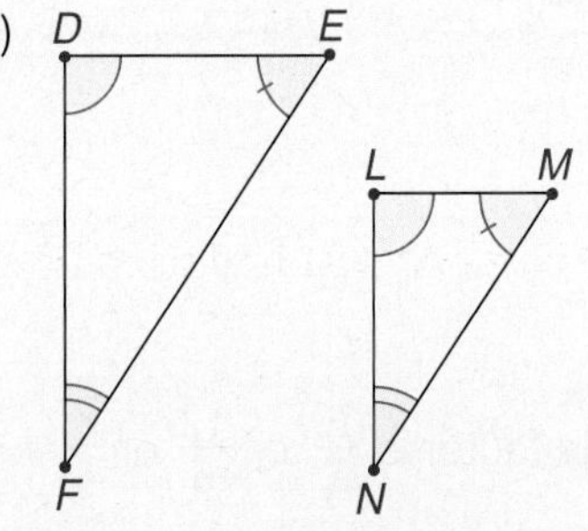

(e)

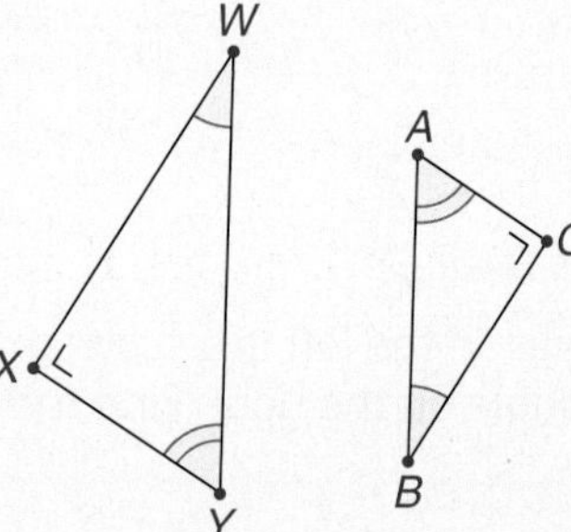

(c)

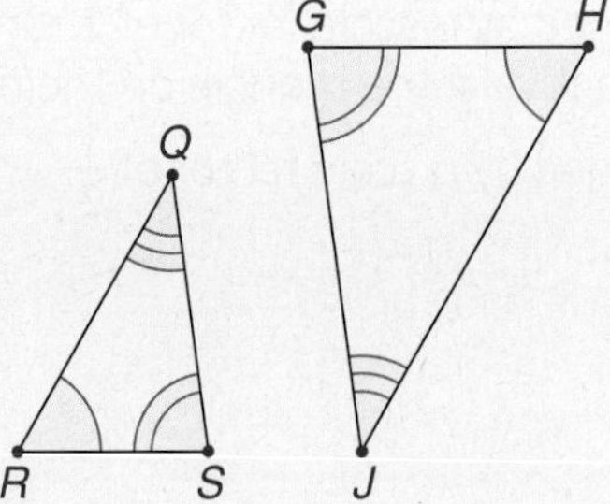

(f)

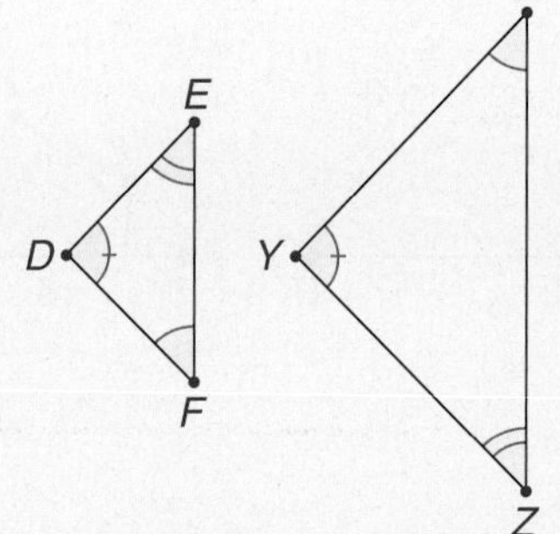

3. Find the length of the side marked x in each of the following pairs of similar triangles:

(a)

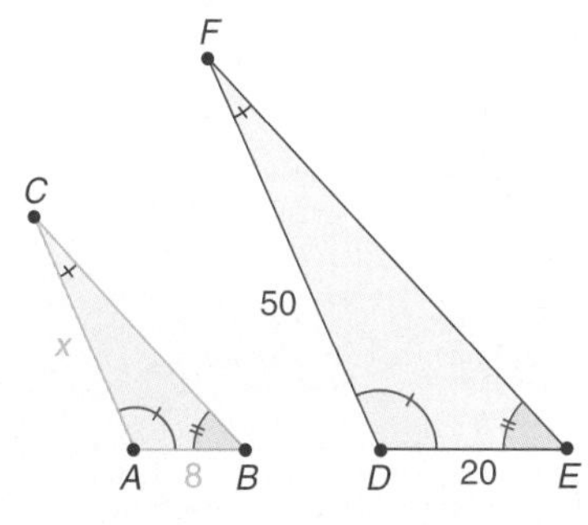

(b)

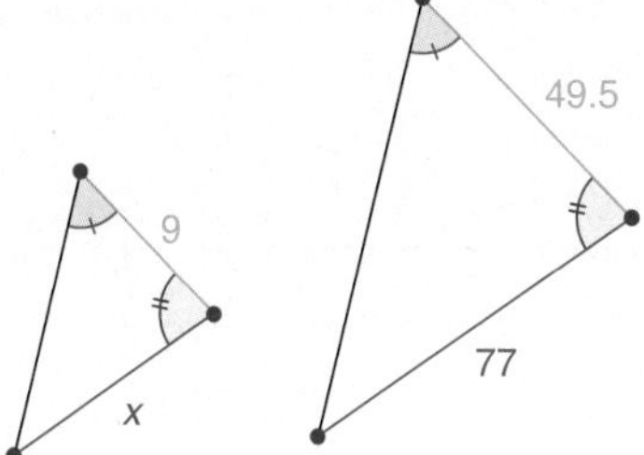

(c)

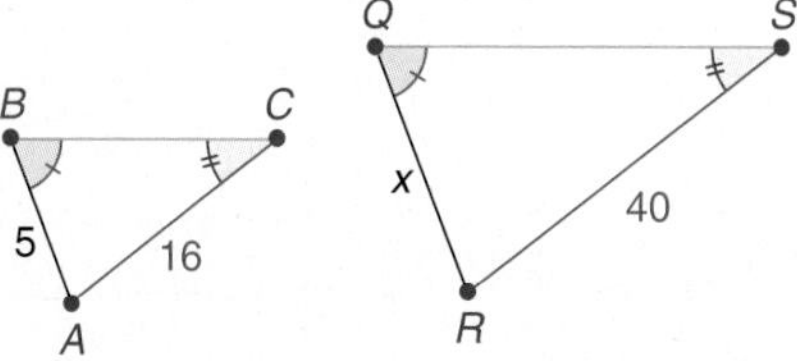

(d)

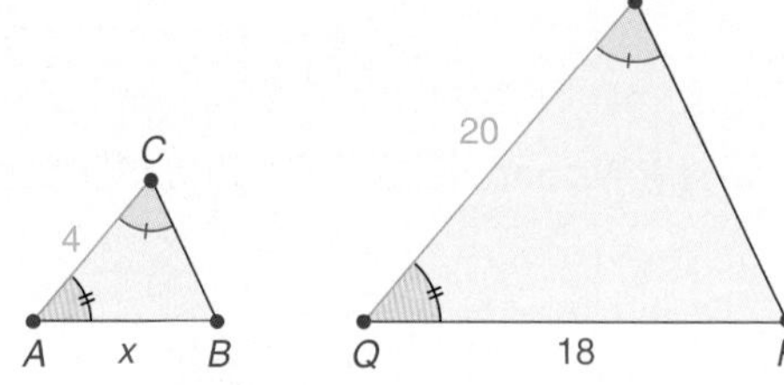

(e)

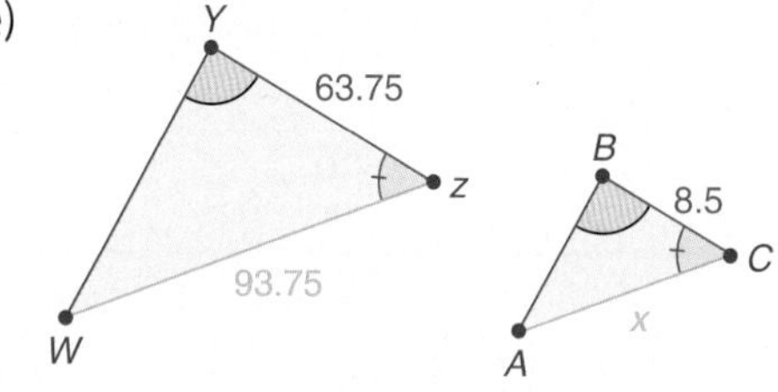

(f)

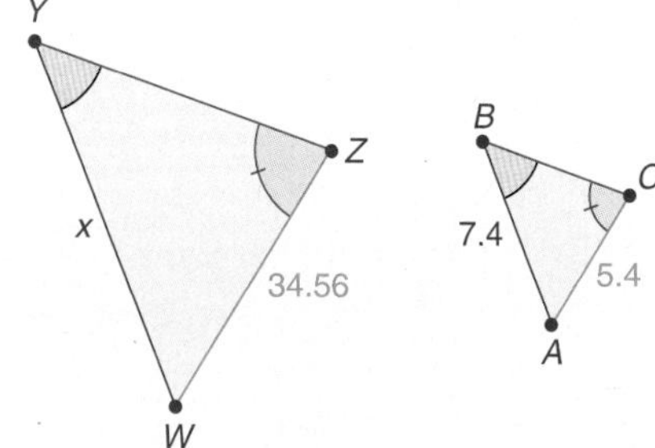

(g)

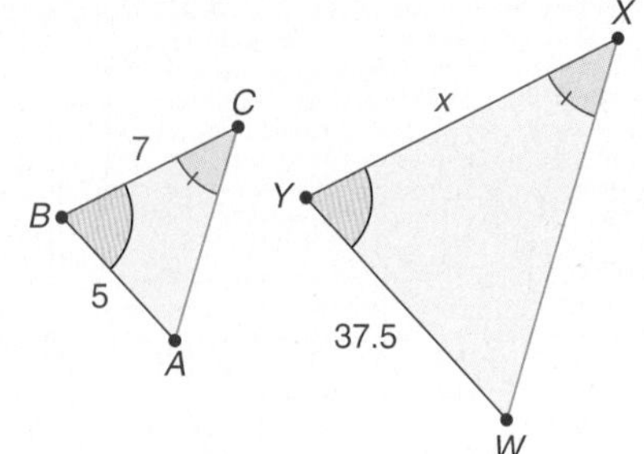

(h)

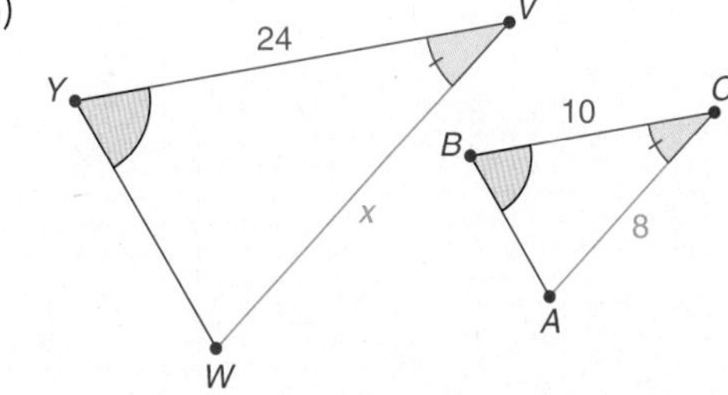

(i)

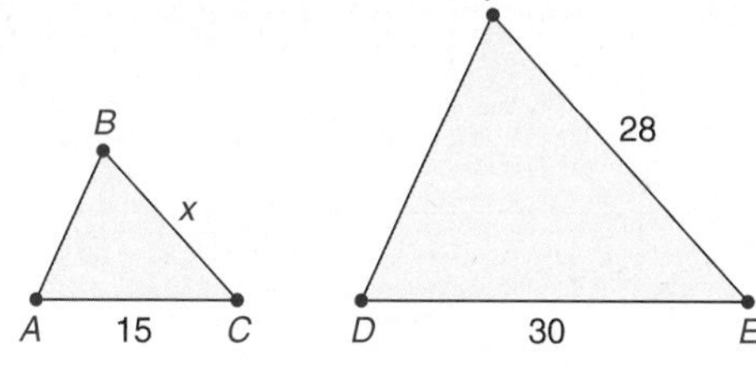

(j)

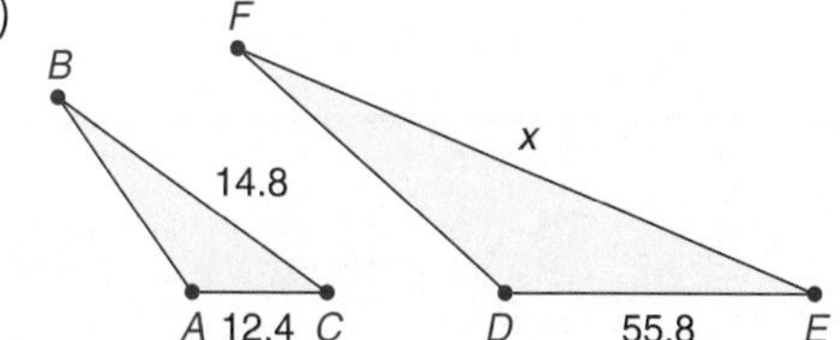

4. In each of the following pairs of similar triangles, find (i) the length of the missing sides and (ii) the scale factor.

(a)

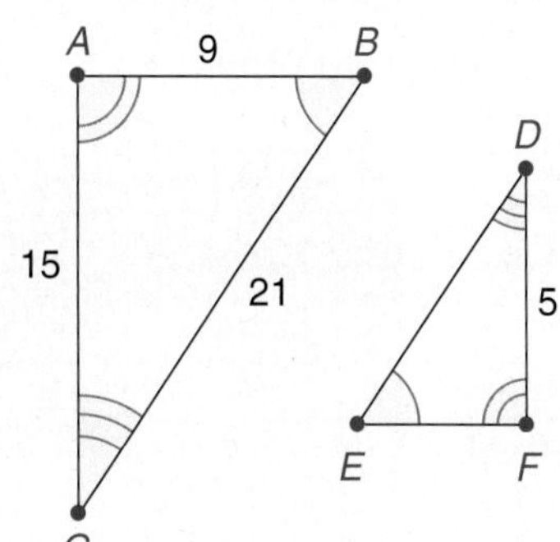

(b)

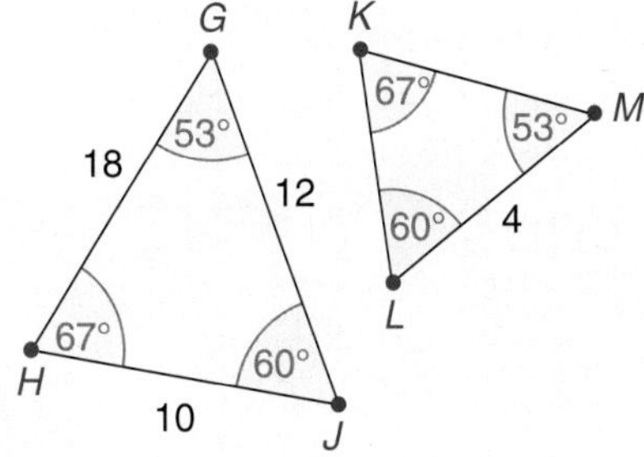

(c)

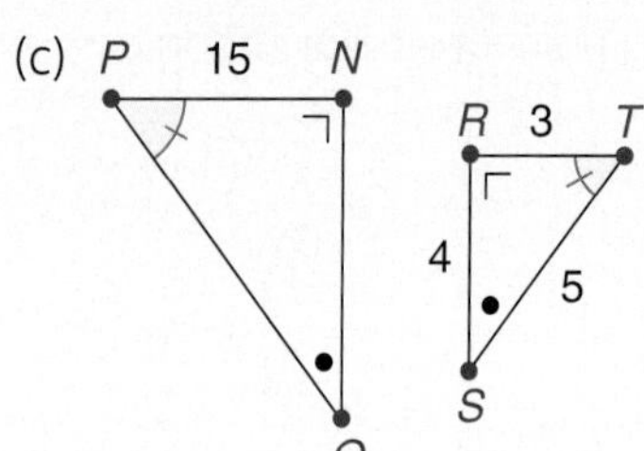

(d)

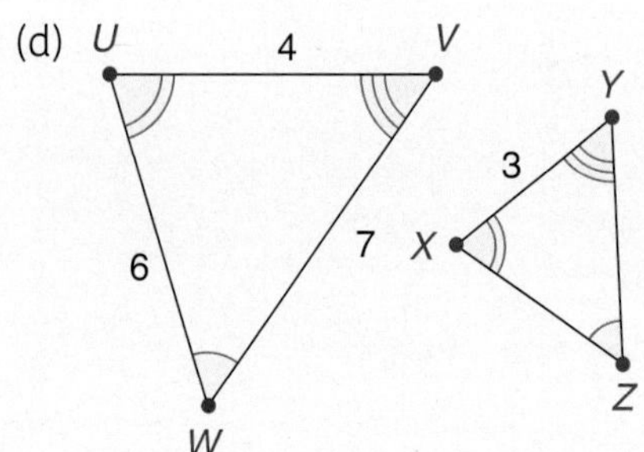

(e)

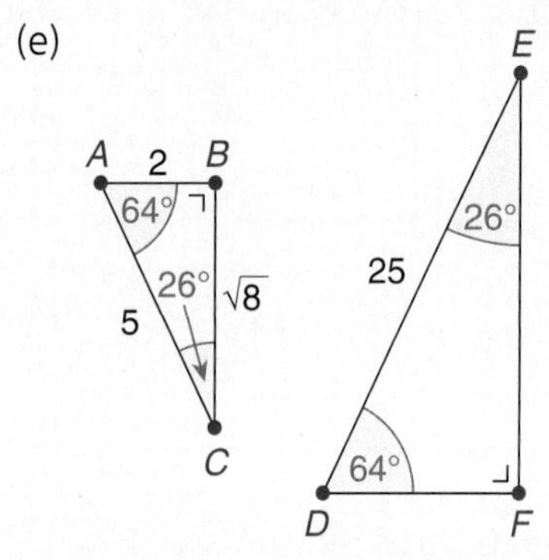

(f)

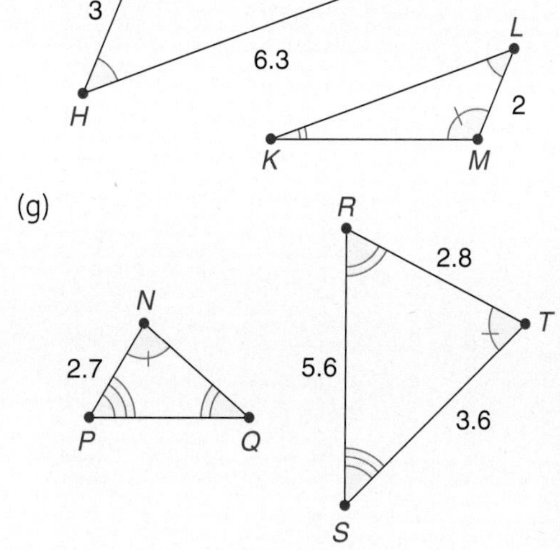

(g)

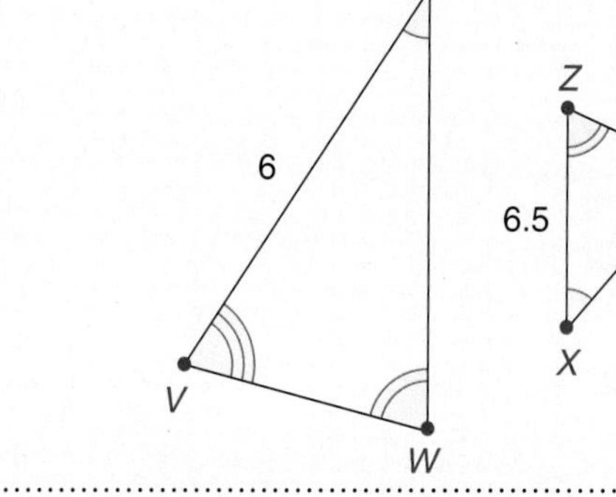

(h)

U

6

V

W

Z

5

Y

6.5

3.6

X

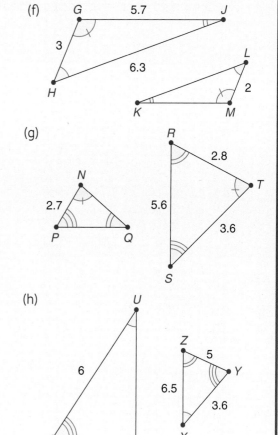

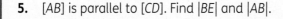

5. $[AB]$ is parallel to $[CD]$. Find $|BE|$ and $|AB|$.

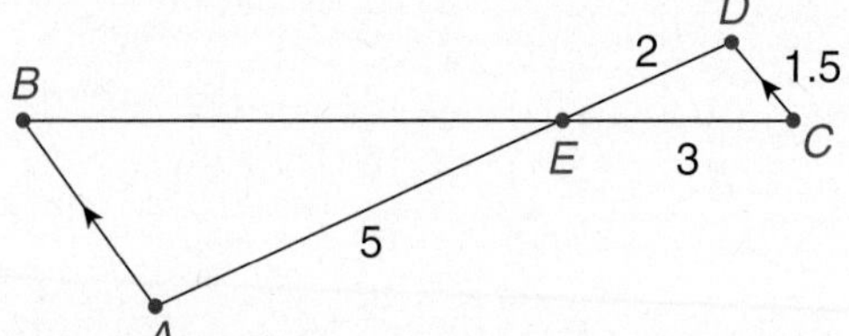

6. $[BC]$ is parallel to $[DE]$. Find $|BC|$ and $|CE|$.

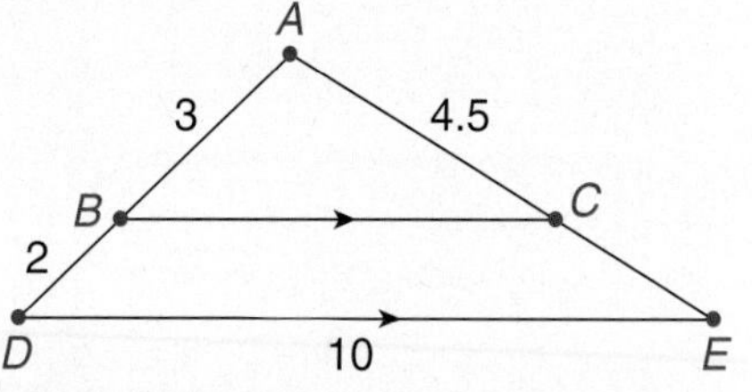

Section 8.2: Congruent triangles

Student Activity 8B

1. Examine the following photographs and record what they have in common.

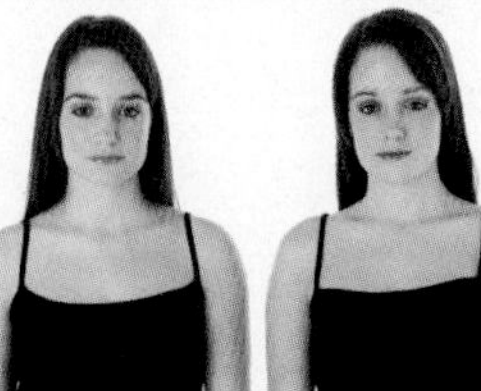

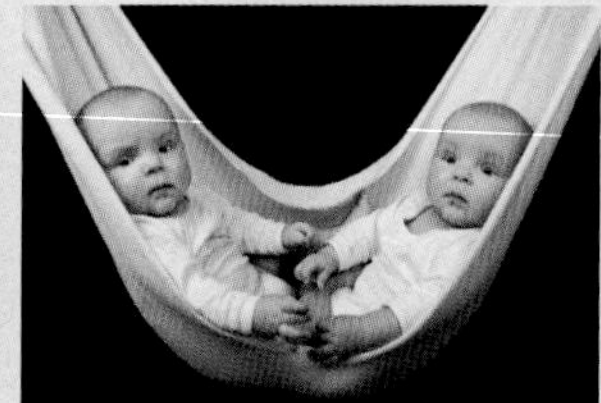

2. Dolly the sheep was born in Edinburgh in Scotland on 5 July 1996. Dolly was the first clone produced from a cell taken from an adult mammal, to produce a whole healthy individual.

Dolly was expected to live for around 12 years, but she lived to be only six years. Some have speculated that a contributing factor to Dolly's death was that she could have been born with a genetic age of six years, the same age as the sheep from which she was cloned.

(a) Explain in your own words, what you think the word 'clone' means.

(b) Suggest mathematical words that have a similar meaning to cloning.

3. Give three reasons why each pair of triangles is identical.

(a)

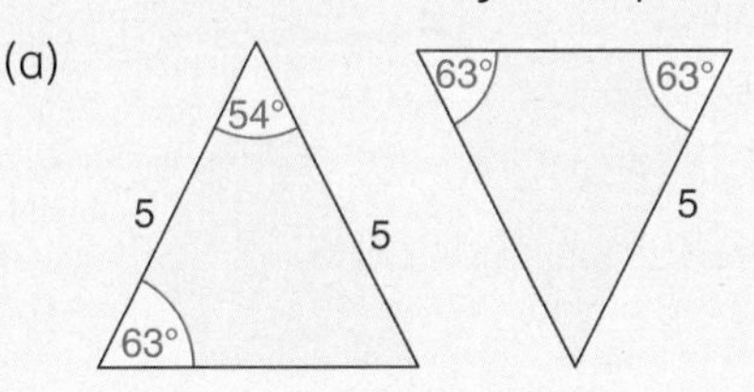

(b)

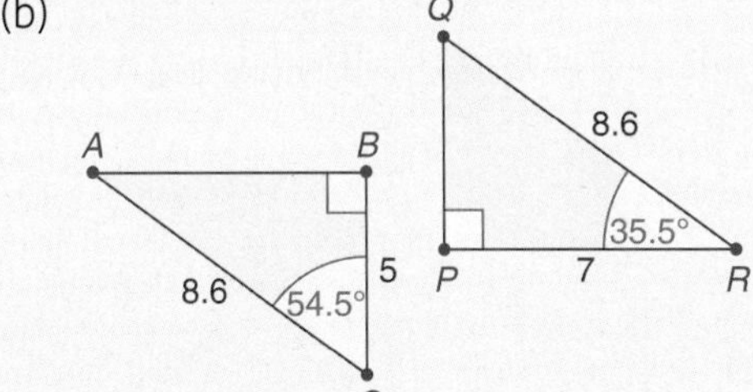

(c)

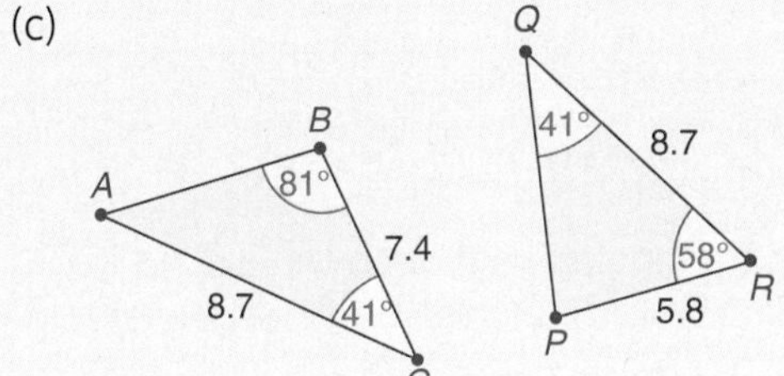

(d)

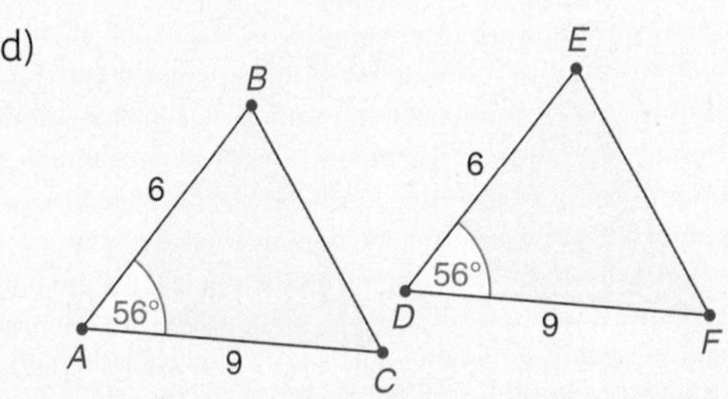

(e)

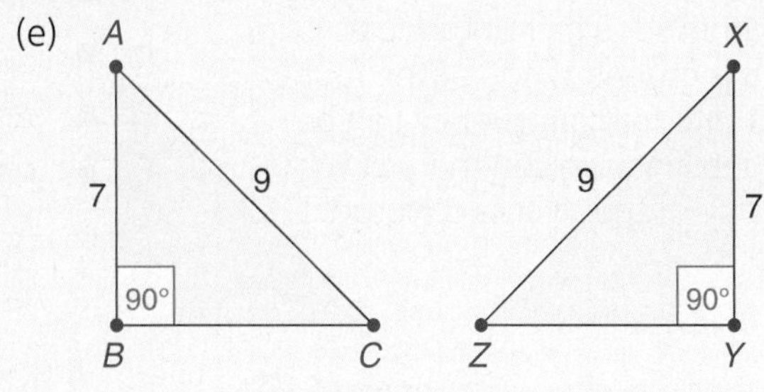

(f)

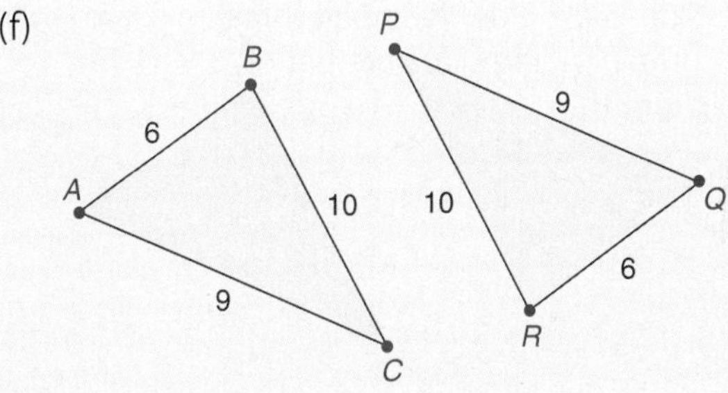

(g)

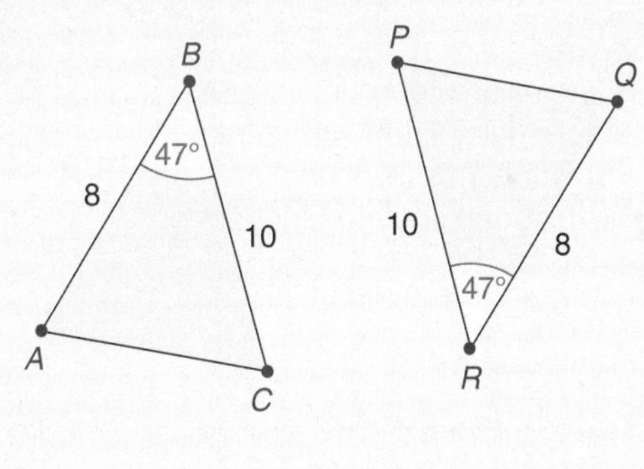

CONGRUENT TRIANGLES EXPLAINED

Congruent means that two shapes are geometrically identical. Look at the pictures of the buses below. They are congruent because they are identical.

> **Congruent** means that two shapes are geometrically identical.

Polygons such as triangles are congruent or identical when they have the same number of sides and all corresponding sides and interior angles are the same measure. Congruent polygons will also have the same area, perimeter and exterior angles.

One way to think about congruency in triangles is to imagine they are made of cardboard. They are congruent if you can slide them around or flip them over so they exactly fit over each other. The symbol for congruency is **'≡'.**

Any triangle is defined by six measurements: its three sides and its three angles. You do not need to know all of these measurements to show whether a pair of triangles is congruent. If one of the four **tests for congruency** can be satisfied, we can then say a pair of triangles is congruent.

Axiom 4

The four sets of conditions for congruent triangles:

- Side Side Side (**SSS**)
- Side Angle Side (**SAS**)
- Angle Side Angle (**ASA**)
- Right angle Hypotenuse Side (**RHS**)

Case 1

Triangles are congruent by **SSS** (**S**ide, **S**ide, **S**ide) when all three corresponding sides are equal in length.

Lengths of 3 sides in one triangle = Lengths of 3 sides in the other triangle

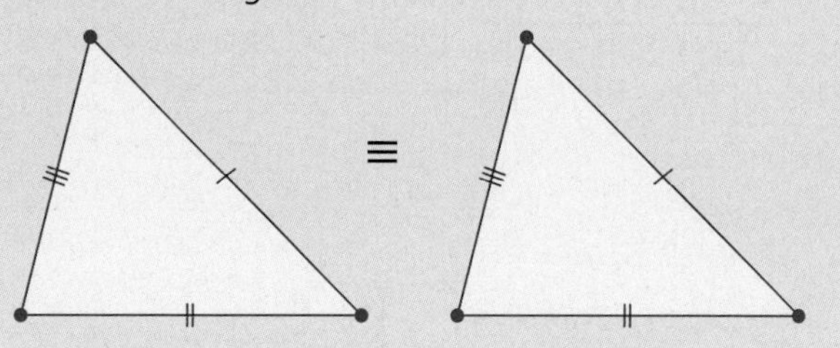

Case 2

Triangles are congruent by **SAS** (**S**ide, **A**ngle, **S**ide) when a pair of corresponding sides and the included angle are equal.

2 sides and the angle in between the 2 sides in one triangle = 2 sides and the angle in between the 2 sides in the other triangle

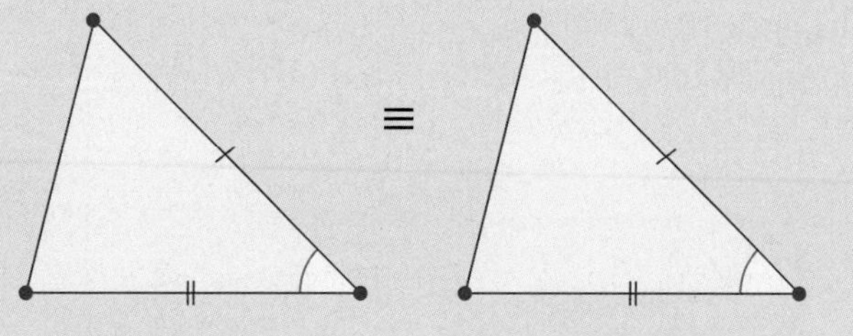

Case 3

Triangles are congruent by **ASA** (**A**ngle, **S**ide, **A**ngle) when a pair of corresponding angles and the included side are equal.

2 angles and the included side in one triangle = 2 angles and the included side in the other triangle

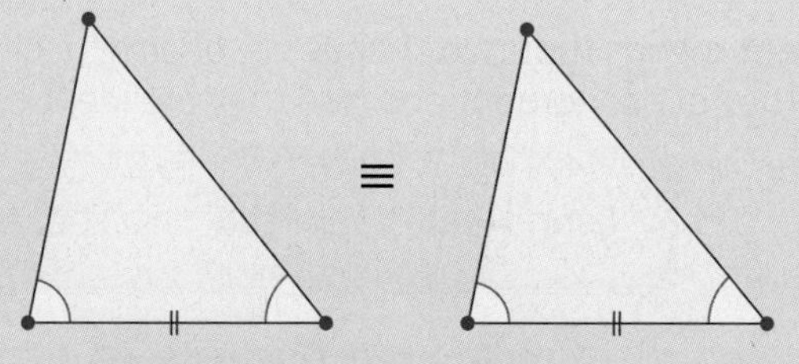

Case 4

Triangles are congruent by **RHS** (**R**ight angle, **H**ypotenuse, **S**ide) where the two triangles are right-angled and the hypotenuse and one other side are equal.

A right angle, the hypotenuse and another side in one right-angled triangle = A right angle, the hypotenuse and another side in the other right-angled triangle

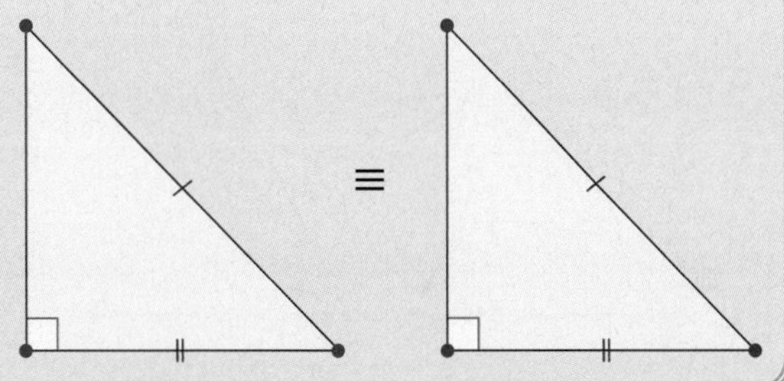

Another way to think of this is to ask if it is possible to construct a unique triangle given what you know. For example, if you were given the lengths of two sides and the included angle (SAS), there is only one possible triangle you could draw. If you drew two of them, they would be the same shape and size – the definition of congruent!

A **corollary** is a result that is proven as part of another statement or proof.

Corollary 1

A diagonal divides a parallelogram into two congruent triangles.

The following example shows how we can use congruent triangles to prove corollary 1.

EXAMPLE 2

Show that the diagonal of the parallelogram *ABCD* bisects the area.

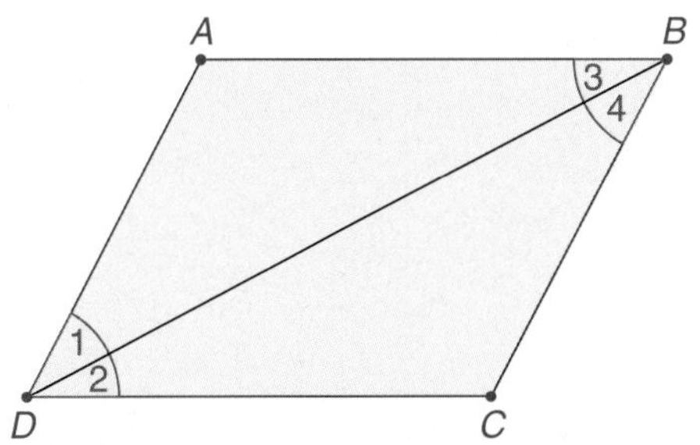

Solution

Consider the two triangles:

ΔABD		ΔBCD	
$\lvert\angle 1\rvert$	=	$\lvert\angle 4\rvert$	**Alternate angles**
$\lvert BD\rvert$	=	$\lvert BD\rvert$	**Common side**
$\lvert\angle 3\rvert$	=	$\lvert\angle 2\rvert$	**Alternate angles**

$\therefore \Delta ABD \equiv \Delta BCD$ **By ASA**

$\therefore$ Area ΔABD = Area ΔBCD

Exercise 8.2

1. State the condition for congruency that is satisfied for each of the pairs of triangles shown.

(a)

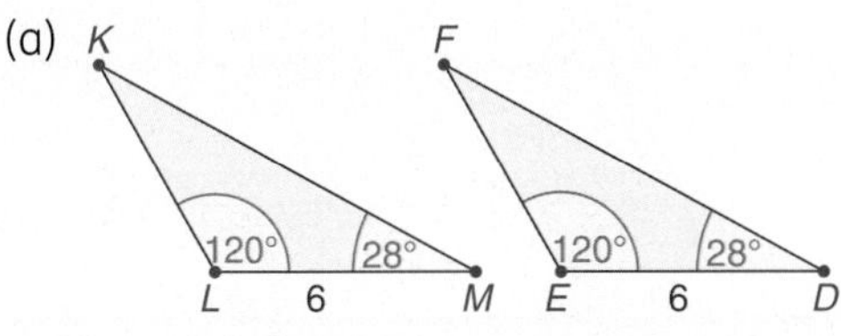

(b)

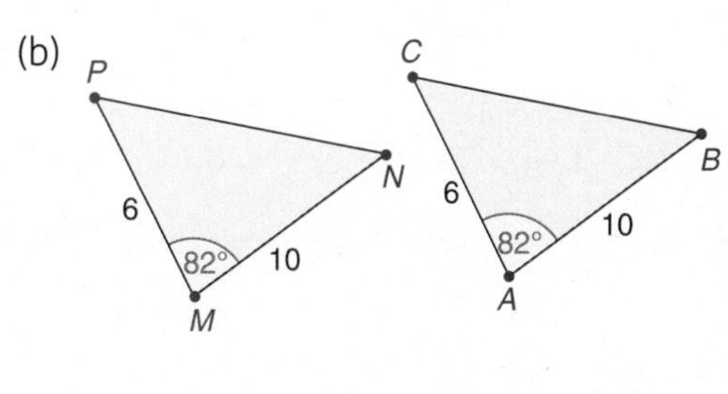

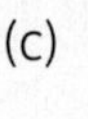
(c)
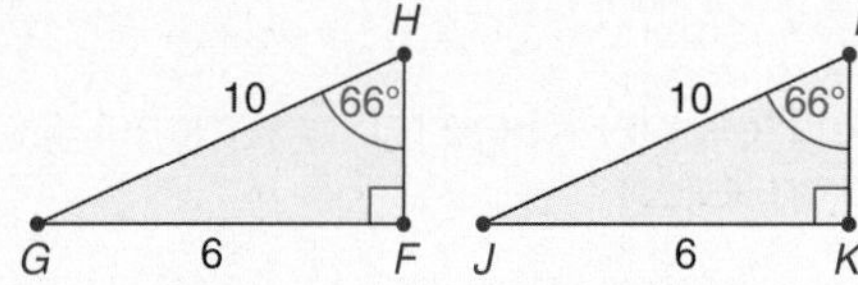

(d)
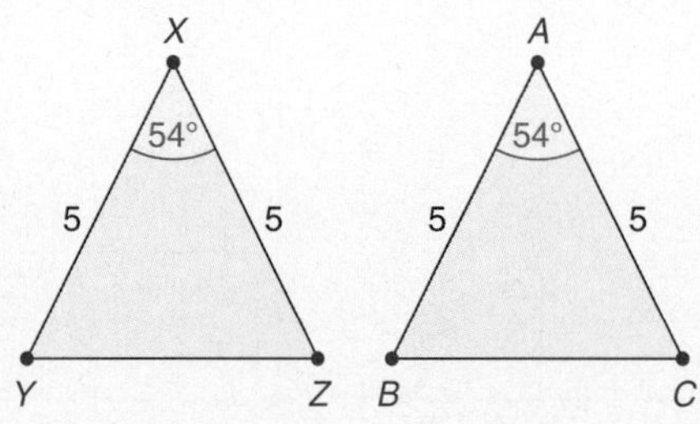

(e)
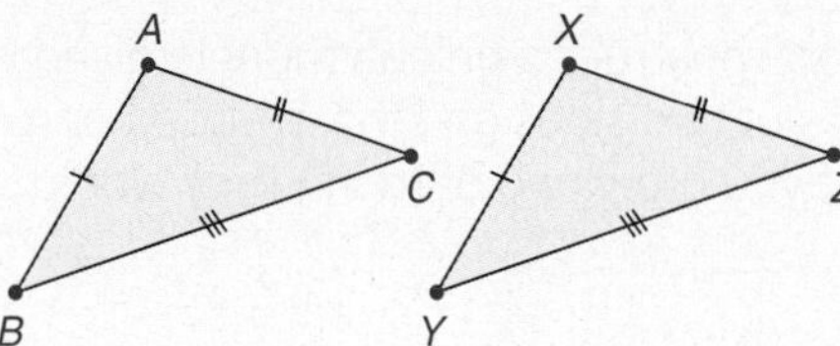

(f)
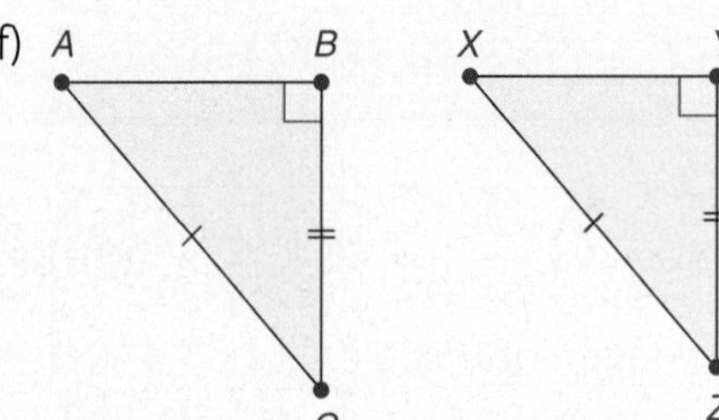

(g)
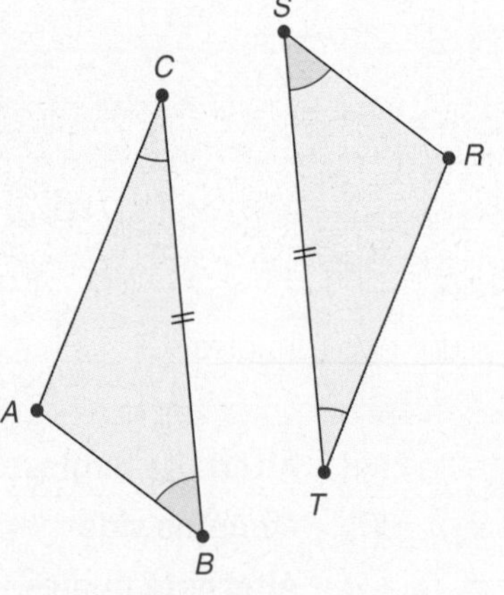

(h)
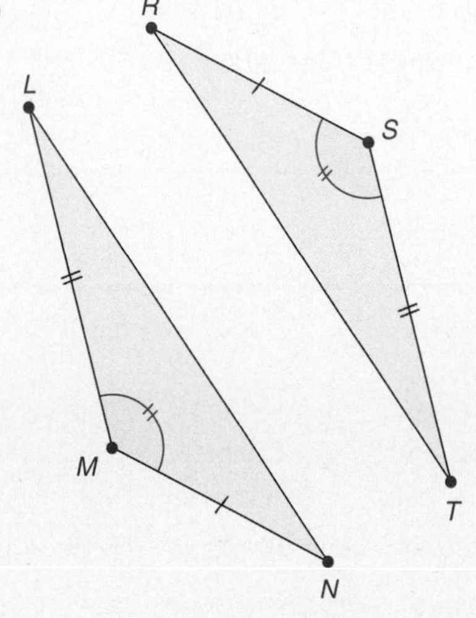

(i)
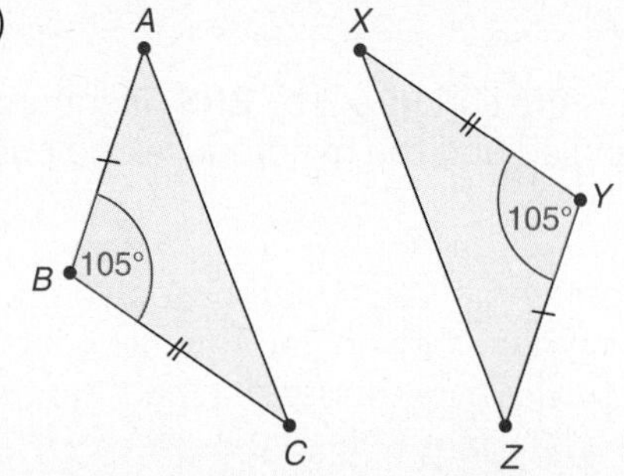

(j)
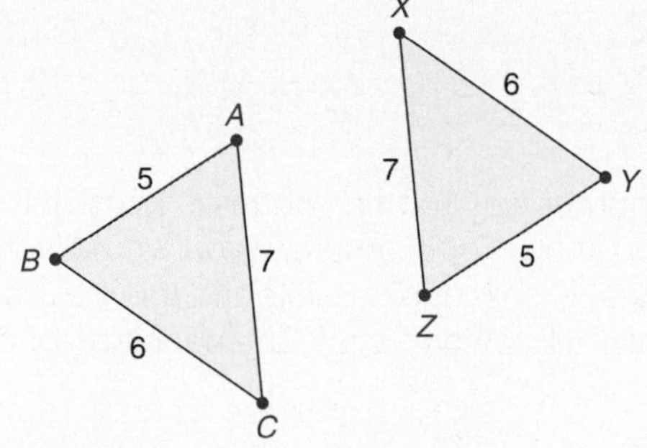

2. In the diagram, $|AC| = |CE|$ and $|BC| = |CD|$. Show that $\Delta ABC \equiv \Delta EDC$.

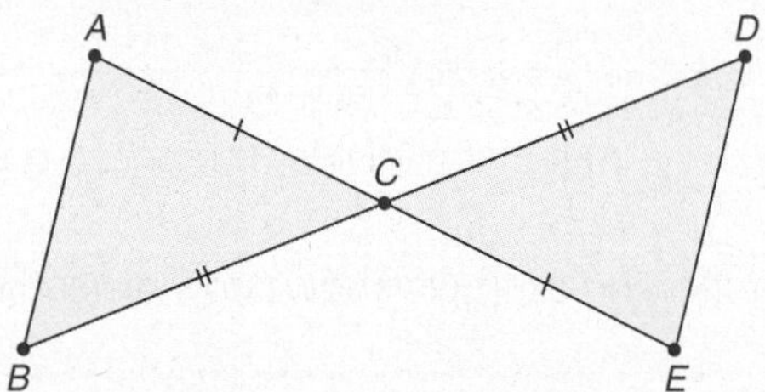

3. In the diagram, $|AC| = |AD|$ and $|BC| = |BD|$. Show that $\Delta ABC \equiv \Delta ABD$.

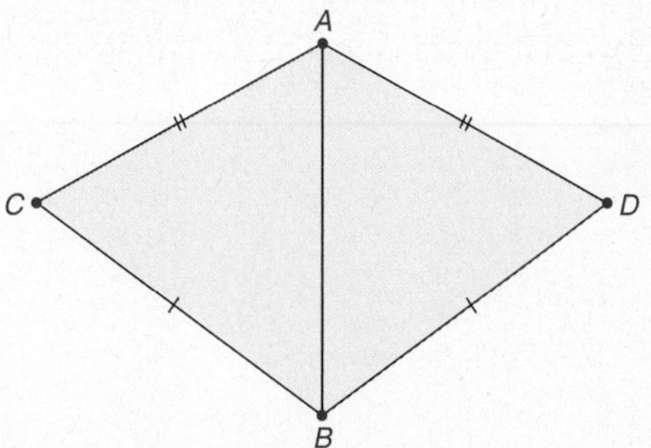

4. In the diagram, $|BC| = |CD|$ and $|\angle BCA| = 90°$. Show that $\Delta ABC \equiv \Delta ADC$.

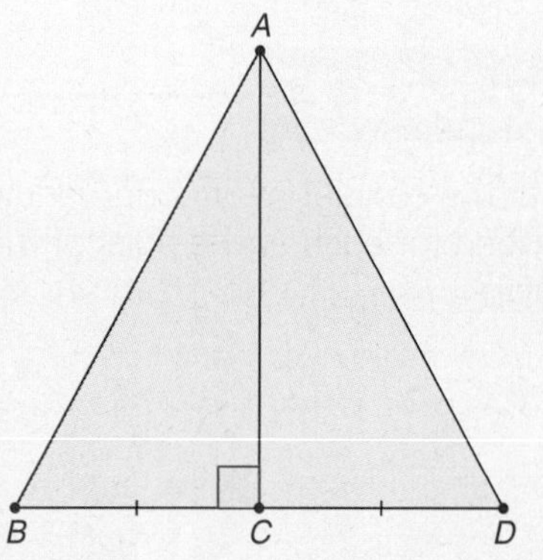

5. The line l bisects $|\angle FCD|$ and $|CF| = |CD|$. Show that $\Delta CDE \equiv \Delta CFE$.

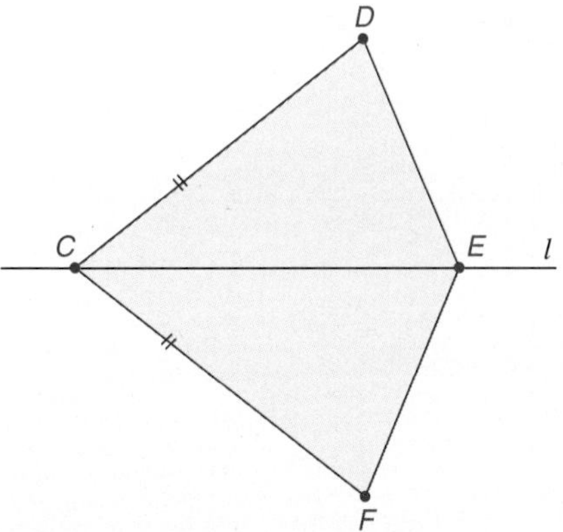

6. $ABCD$ is a parallelogram as shown with diagonal $[DB]$. Show that $\Delta ABE \equiv \Delta CDF$.

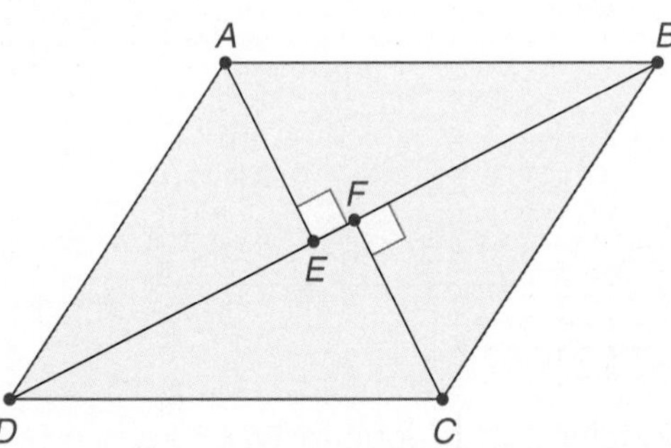

7. Show that $\Delta ABC \equiv \Delta DBC$.

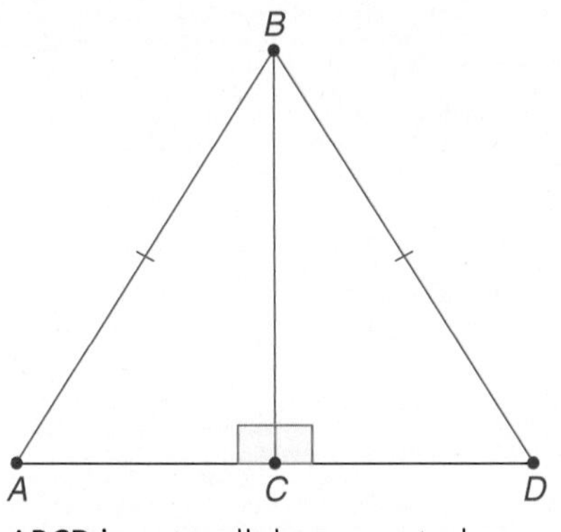

8. $ABCD$ is a parallelogram as shown with $[AC]$ as diagonal.

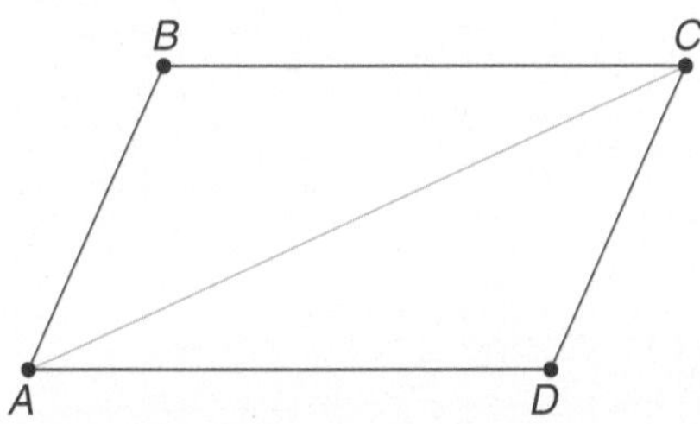

(a) $[AC]$ breaks the parallelogram $ABCD$ into what two shapes?

(b) Show that $\Delta ABC \equiv \Delta CDA$.

9. Show that $\Delta EOD \equiv \Delta FOG$.

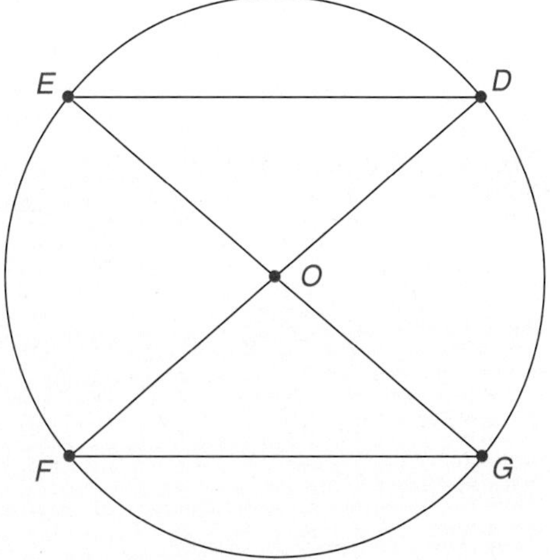

10. In the parallelogram $PQRS$, A and B are on the diagonal $[QS]$ and $|\angle QPA| = |\angle SRB|$. Show that $|PA| = |BR|$.

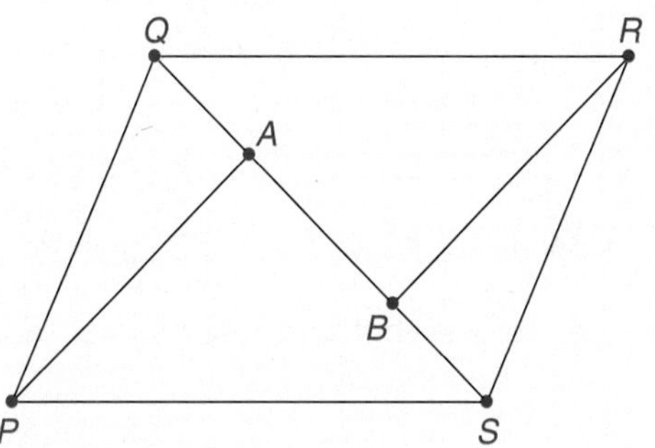

11. A circle with centre O is shown below. $[AC]$ and $[BD]$ are two chords. $[BC]$ and $[AD]$ intersect at the point F.
Show that $|AC| = |BD|$. (Hint: first use congruent triangles.)

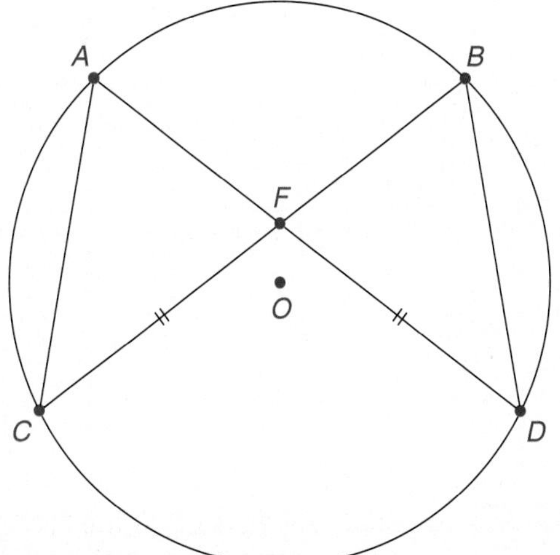

CHAPTER 8 SELF-CHECK TEST

1. Explain the terms 'similar' and 'dissimilar', giving real-life examples.

2. Which picture shows similarity and which picture shows a non-similar figure? Clearly explain your reasons.

A

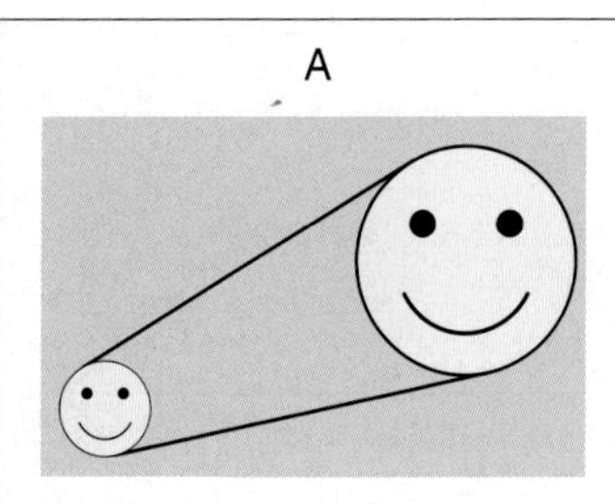

B

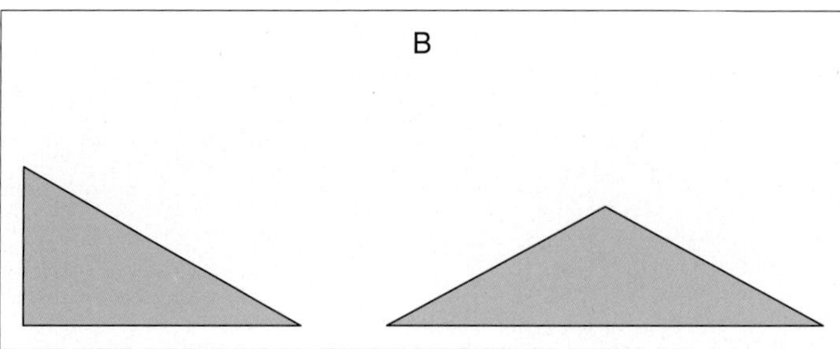

3. Which image is similar to the original triangle?

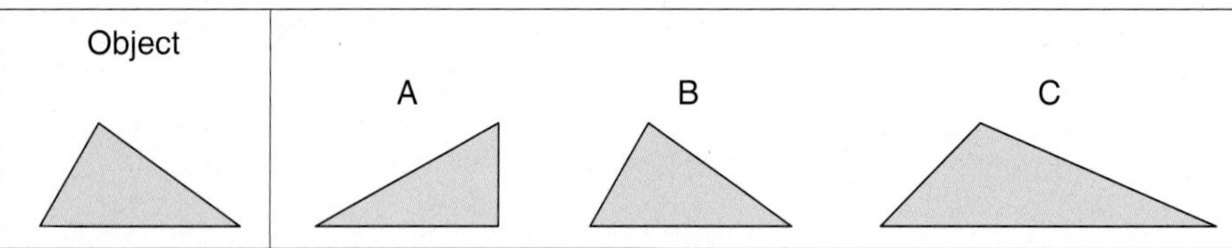

4. How do we know if two triangles are similar or proportional?

5. Determine whether these pairs of triangles are similar. Justify your answer.

(a)

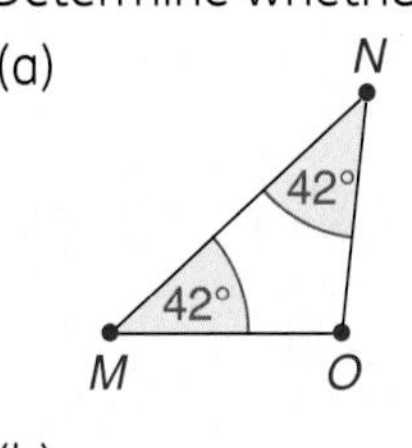

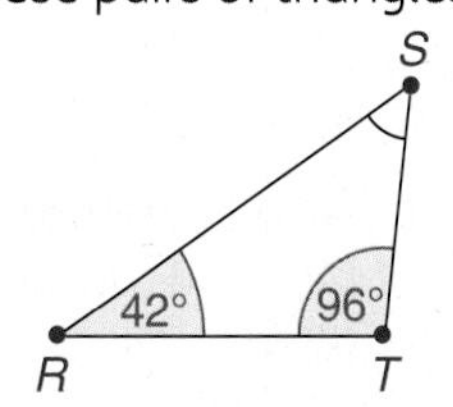

(b)

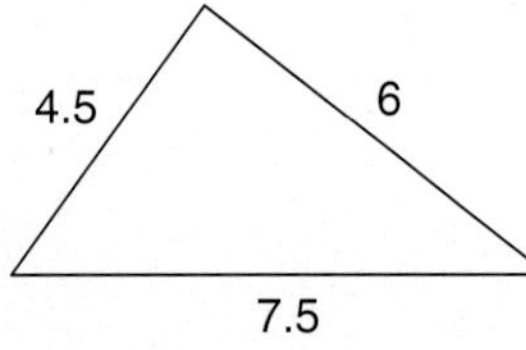

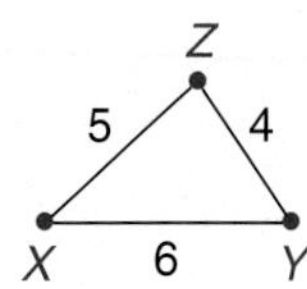

(c)

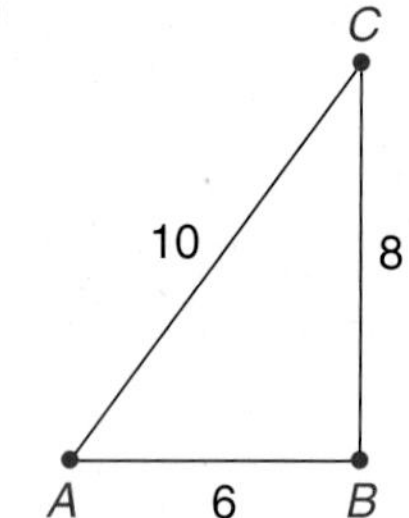

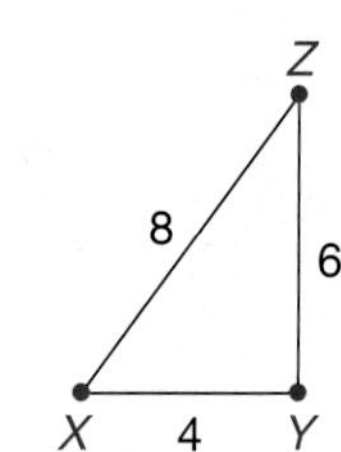

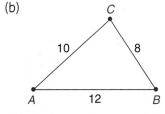

6. Find the value of x, given that the two triangles are similar.

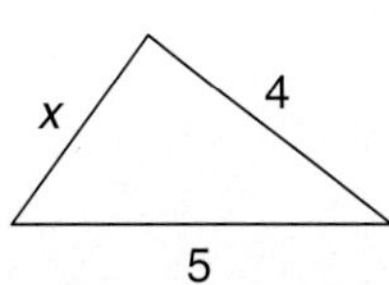

4.5 6 7.5 — x 4 5

7. By comparing the pairs of similar triangles below, find the missing sides or angles. Give a reason for each decision.

(a)

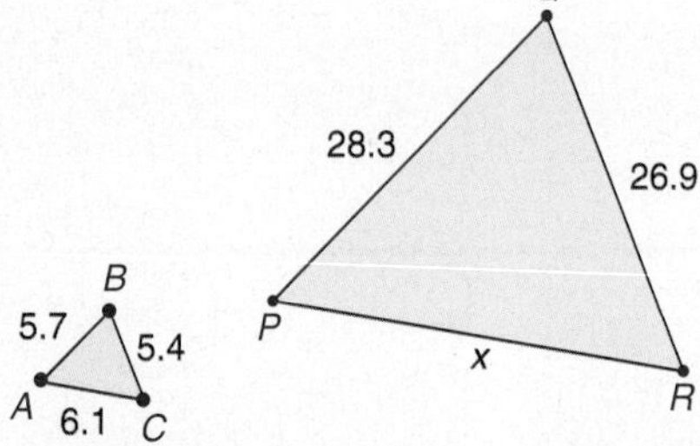

(b)

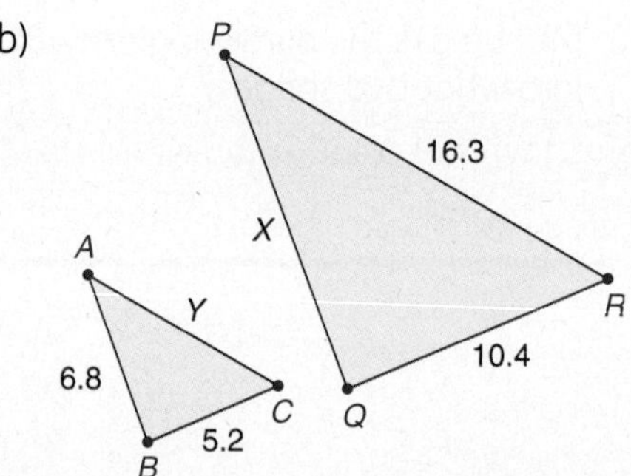

(c)

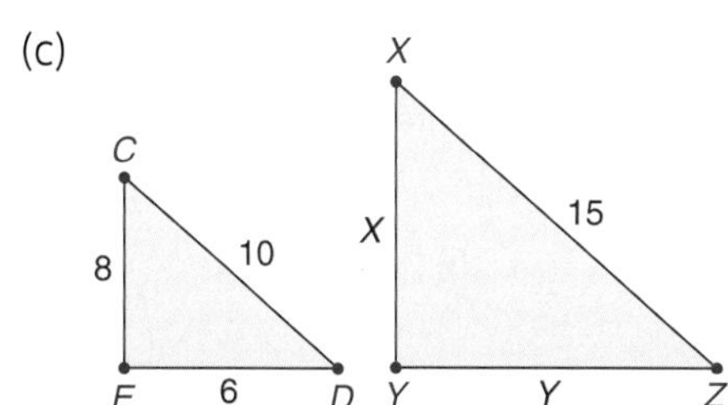

(d)

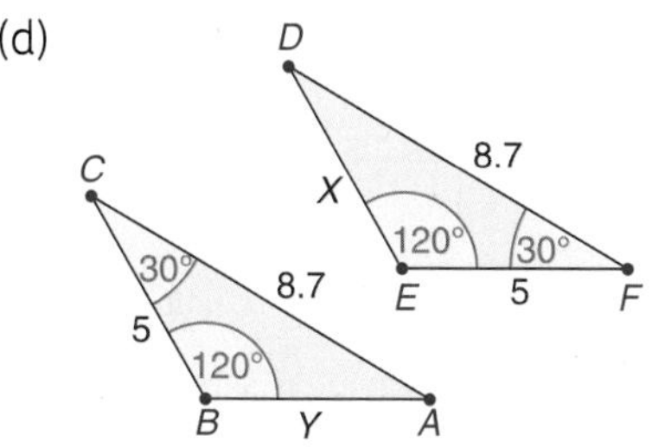

8. In the two similar triangles, find the value of c and d.

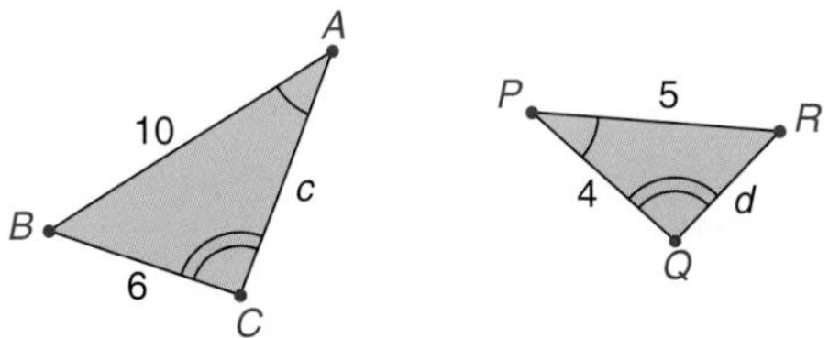

9. Explain why having all three corresponding angles equal (**AAA**) is not enough to show congruency but enough to show two triangles are similar.

10. Using your knowledge of similar triangles, calculate the height of the tree.

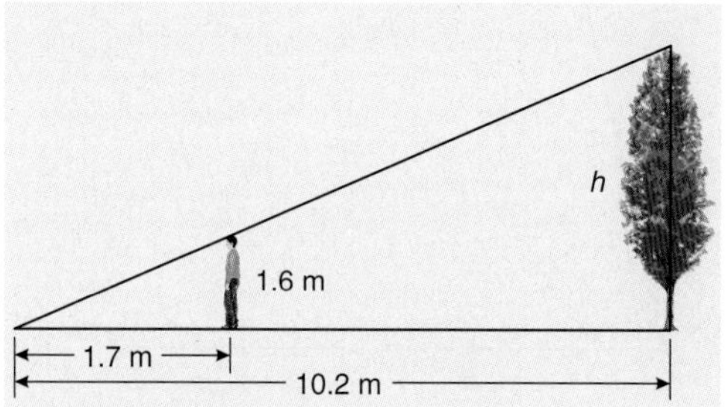

11. The triangle ABC is similar to the triangle ADE. DE is parallel to BC. Calculate the length of BC.

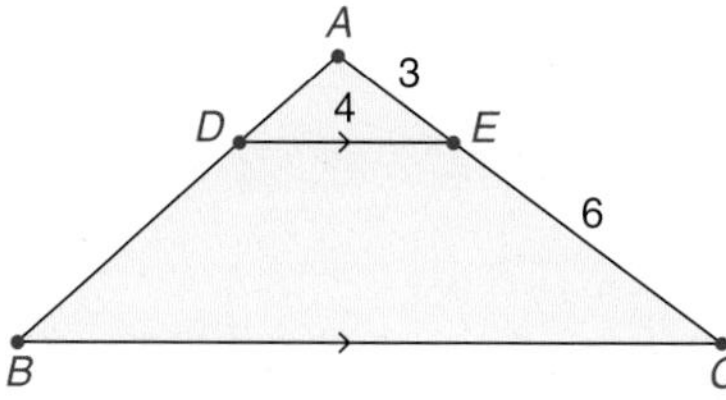

12. AB and DE are parallel to each other.

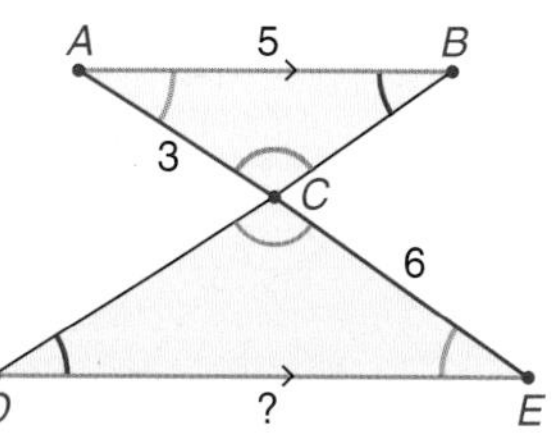

(a) Show that the triangle ABC is similar to the triangle CDE.

(b) Calculate $|DE|$.

13. Draw a rectangle $ABCD$ with sides of length 10 cm and width 8 cm. Now draw two similar rectangles of scale factor 2 and scale factor $\frac{1}{2}$. Clearly show all of your measurements.

14. Draw the similar rectangles $ABCD$ of length 16 cm and width 12 cm and $EFGH$ of length 12 cm and width 9 cm. Then calculate the scale factor.

15. State the type of congruence for each pair of triangles shown.

(a)

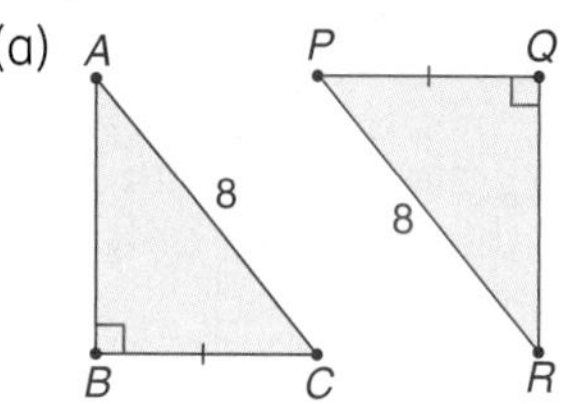

(b)

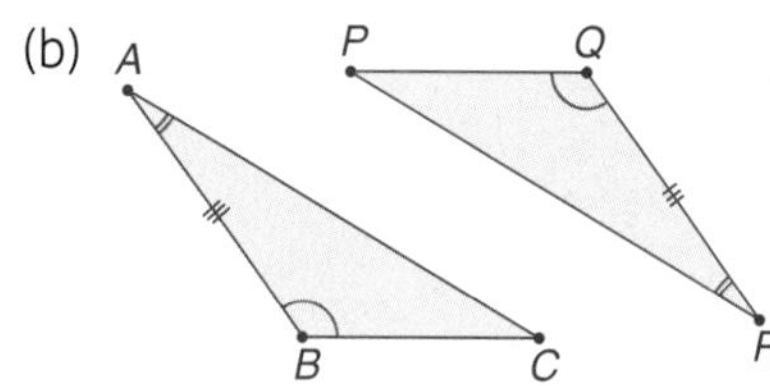

(c)

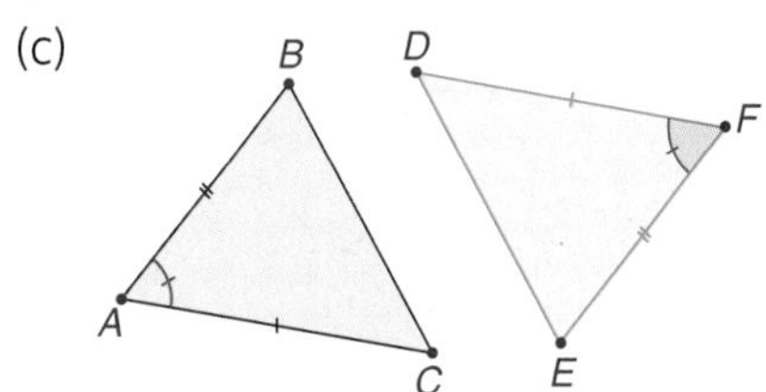

(d)

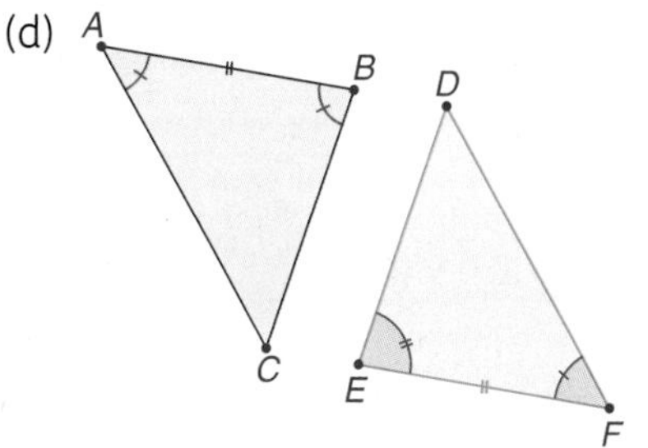

(e)

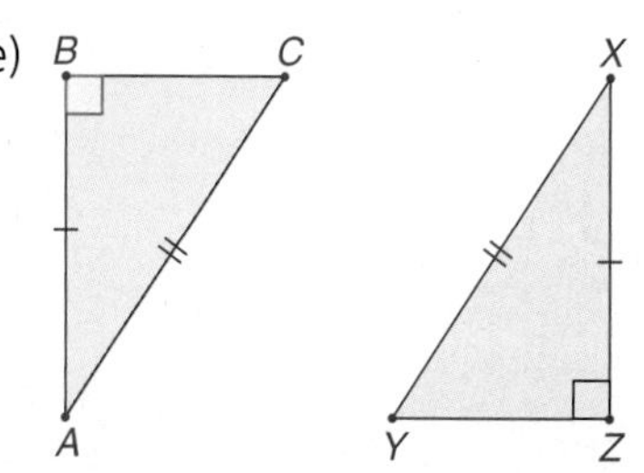

16. Use congruent triangles to show that the diagonal bisects the area of the square.

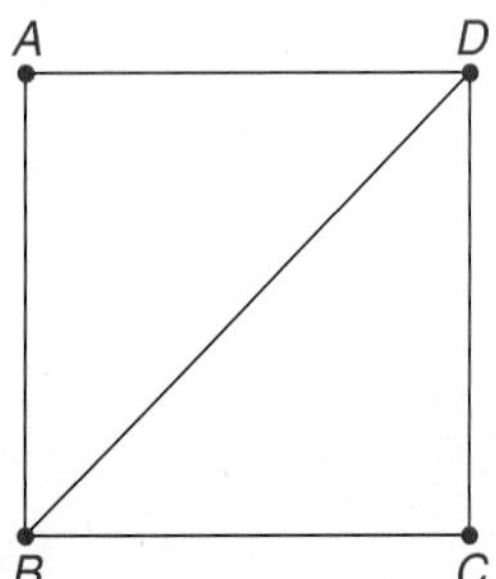

17. Show that the triangles ABC and ADC are congruent.

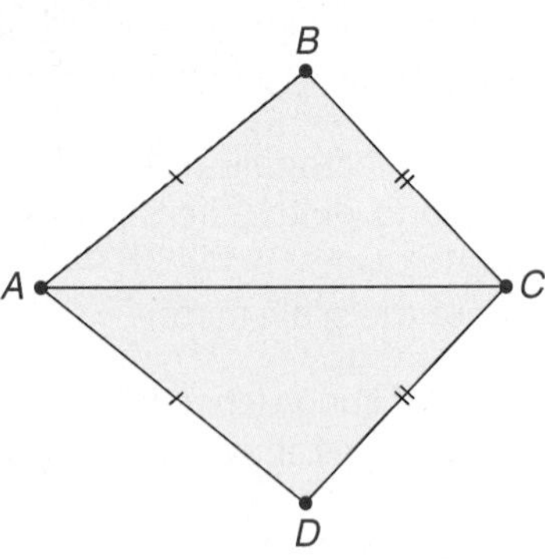

18. Given that $WXYZ$ is a parallelogram with diagonals that intersect at the point A, show that $|XA| = |AZ|$.

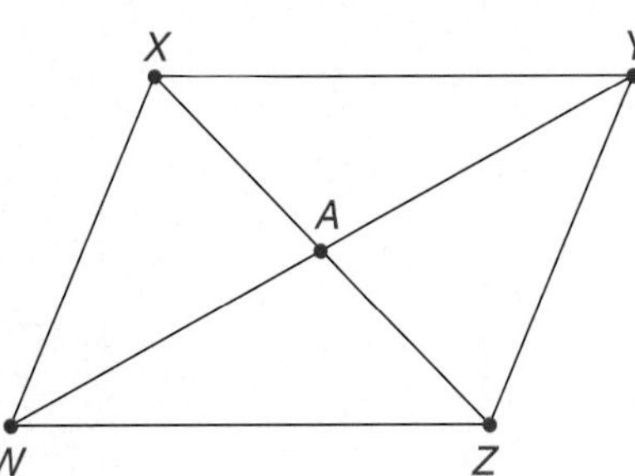

19. In the triangle ABC, $[BD]$ is the perpendicular bisector of $[AC]$. Show that if E is any point on $[BD]$, then $|AE| = |EC|$.

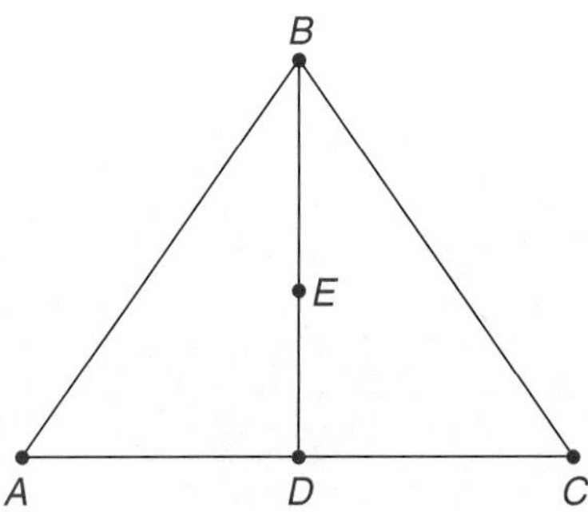

20. $ABCD$ is a parallelogram with F as the midpoint of $[CD]$. Show that $|BC| = |DE|$.

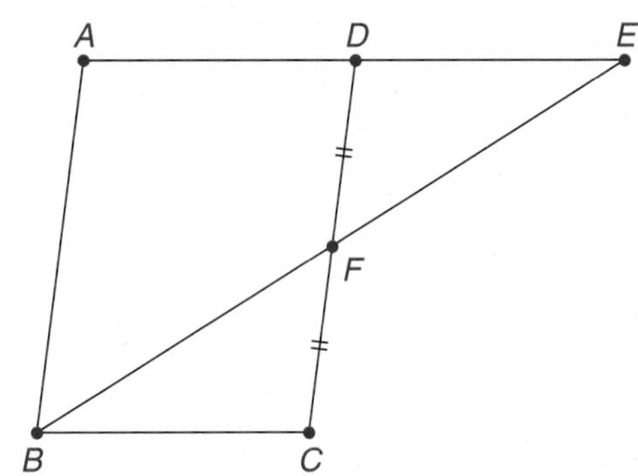

21. $ABCD$ is a parallelogram as shown. Show that $|BE| = |DF|$.

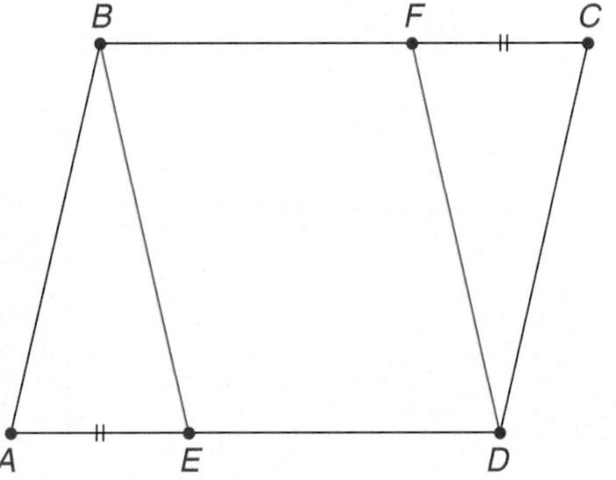

CHAPTER 8 KNOWLEDGE CHECKLIST

After completing this chapter, I now:

- **Know that if two triangles are similar, then their sides are in proportion**
- **Understand the terms equiangular and congruent**
- **Know how to compare triangles and decide whether they are congruent**
- **Know about the conditions necessary for congruency in polygons**

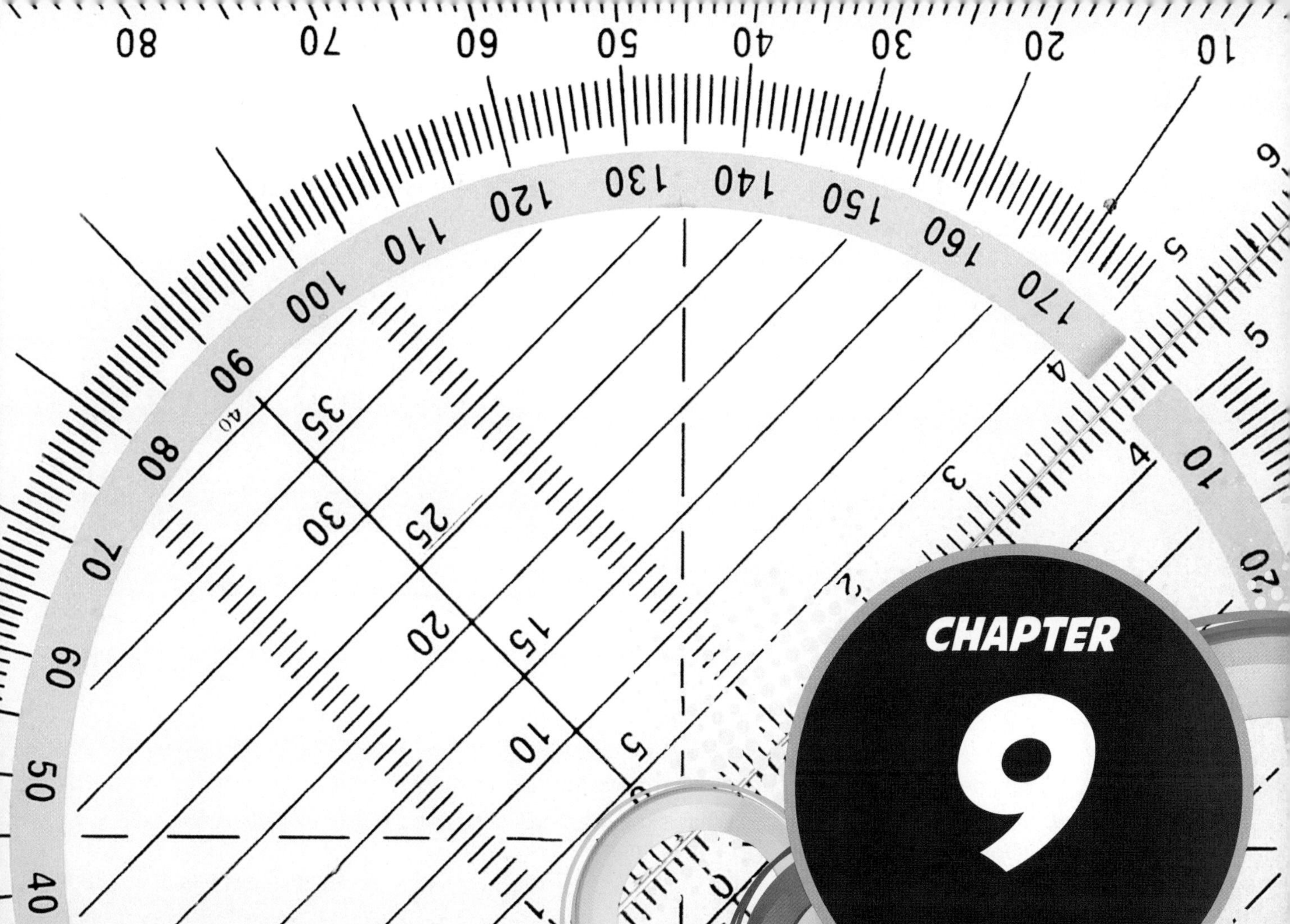

GEOMETRY 2

LEARNING OUTCOMES

In this chapter you will learn:

- ✓ **The meaning of the term transversal**
- ✓ **That a transversal line makes equal alternate angles and corresponding angles on parallel lines**
- ✓ **That, if three parallel lines cut off equal segments on some transversal line, they will cut off equal segments on any other transversal**
- ✓ **That, if a line is drawn across a triangle, parallel to one side of the triangle, it will cut the other two sides in the same ratio**

KEY WORDS

- **Alternate**
- **Converse**
- **Corresponding**
- **Parallel**
- **Proportional**
- **Ratio**
- **Similar**
- **Theorem**
- **Transversal**

INTRODUCTION

In *Maths in Action 1*, you studied parallel lines. You examined how parallel lines never meet, just like the train tracks shown in the image.

First year revision

1. What do you understand by the term 'parallel lines'? Identify two sets of parallel lines in your classroom. Give reasons for your answers.
2. Use suitable mathematical notation to state that line *m* is parallel to line *n*.
3. What do you understand by the term 'perpendicular lines'? Identify two sets of perpendicular lines in your classroom. Give reasons for your answers.
4. Explain the following terms. What is the the smallest size and largest size each angle can be? Draw an example of each type of angle.

   (a) Acute angle (b) Right angle (c) Obtuse angle (d) Reflex angle
5. Explain the following terms:

   (a) Ordinary angle (c) Full angle (e) Complementary angles

   (b) Straight angle (d) Complete revolution (f) Supplementary angles

6. Without using a protractor, calculate the missing angles in the following diagrams:

   (a) X°, 45°, 56°

   (b) 36.87°, X°, 45°, W°, 32.44°

   (c) X°, 52°

7. (a) What are vertically opposite angles?

   (b) Find each of the missing angles. Give reasons for your answers.

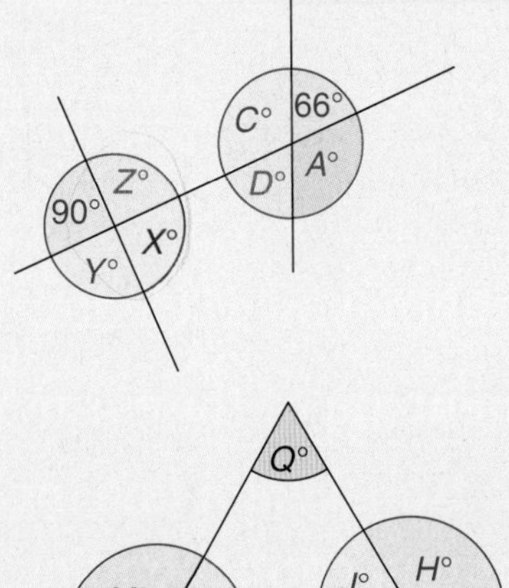

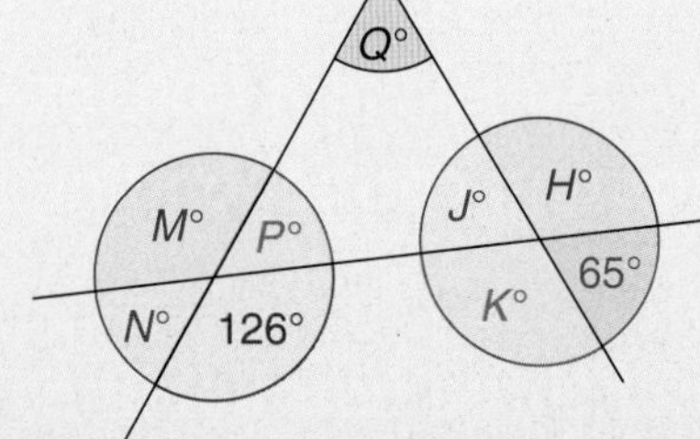

8. (a) What is a transversal?

   (b) What are corresponding angles? Explain your answer and draw a suitable diagram.

   (c) What are alternate angles? Explain your answer and draw a suitable diagram.

9. Find the missing angles and explain how you found your answer (for example, vertically opposite, corresponding, alternate or straight angles).

(a)

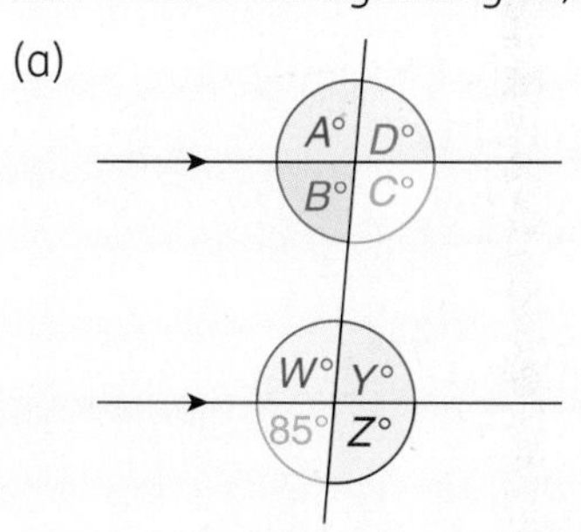

(b)

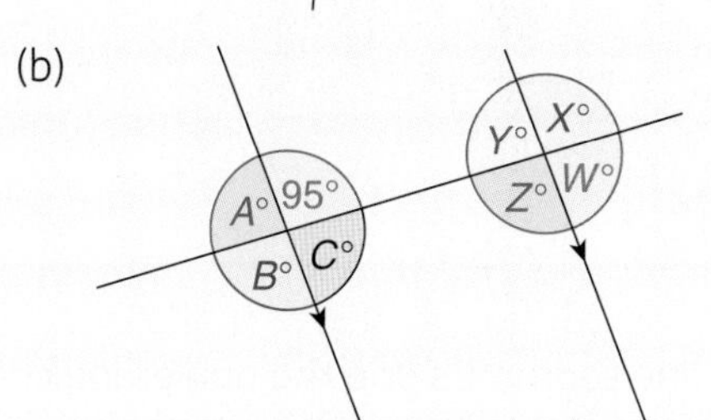

10. Examine both diagrams. State, giving reasons, which has:

(a) Vertically opposite angles

(b) Alternate angles

(c) Corresponding angles

(i)

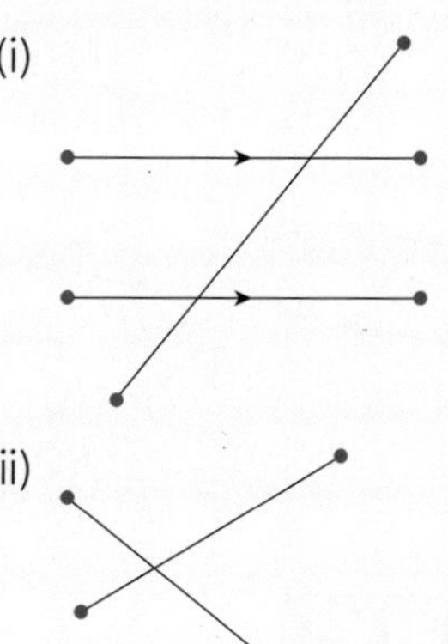

(ii)

Section 9.1: Transversal lines

Student Activity 9A

(a) Draw three horizontal parallel lines, each the same distance apart.

(b) Draw a slanted line that crosses all three parallel lines at an acute angle.

(c) Mark the intersection points of the lines.

(d) Use your ruler to measure and record the distances between the points.

(e) What do you notice?

(f) Measure the angles in your diagram. Record which angles are equal in measure and explain why they are equal.

TRANSVERSAL LINES EXPLAINED

In geometry, a **transversal** is a line that passes through at least two other lines in the same plane at different points.

A **transversal** is a line that passes through at least two other lines in the same plane at different points.

When the lines are parallel, the transversal forms **alternate** and **corresponding** angles. The parallel lines also cut a transversal into segments of equal length.

In the diagram on the right, we see three parallel lines, a, b and c, the same distance apart. The lines m and n are transversals. The transversal m cuts the three parallel lines at X, Y and Z. So, we can say $|XY| = |YZ|$. Likewise, the transversal n cuts the parallel lines at the points R, S and T. Therefore, $|RS| = |ST|$.

This leads to another theorem on our course.

Theorem 11

If three parallel lines cut off equal segments on some transversal line, then they will cut off equal segments on any other transversal.

EXAMPLE 1

Find the size of the missing angles and the length of the line segments [AB] and [PN] in the following diagram. The parallel lines are equidistance (the same distance) apart.

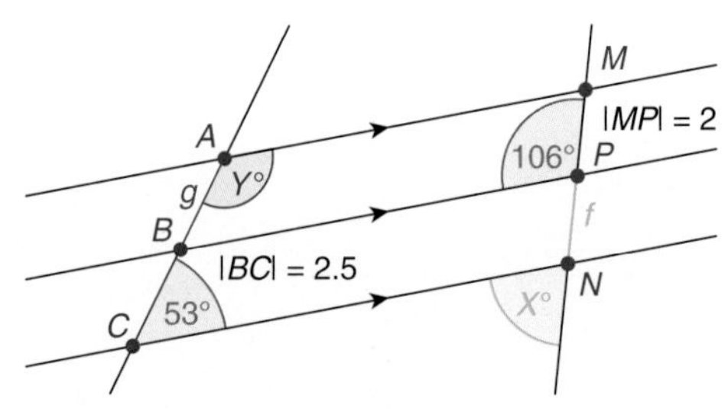

Solution

$|BC| = |AB| = 2.5$

$\therefore g = 2.5$ units

$|\angle Y| = 180° - 53° = 127°$

$|MP| = |PN| = 2$

$\therefore f = 2$ units

$|\angle X| = 180° - 106° = 74°$

Exercise 9.1

For each of the diagrams below, write the lengths of the line segments and the angles indicated. Each set of parallel lines is equidistant from each other.

1.

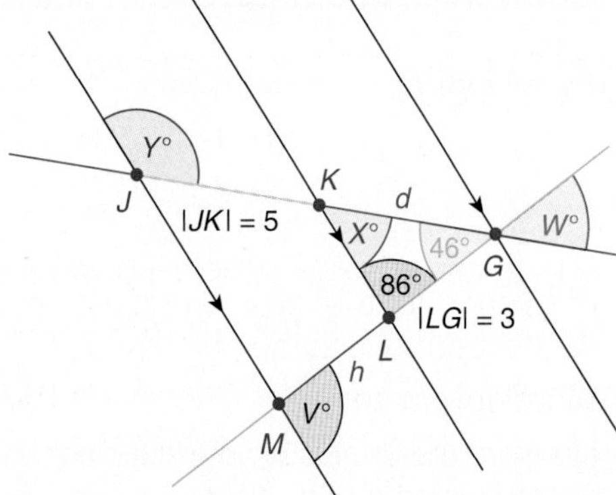

2.

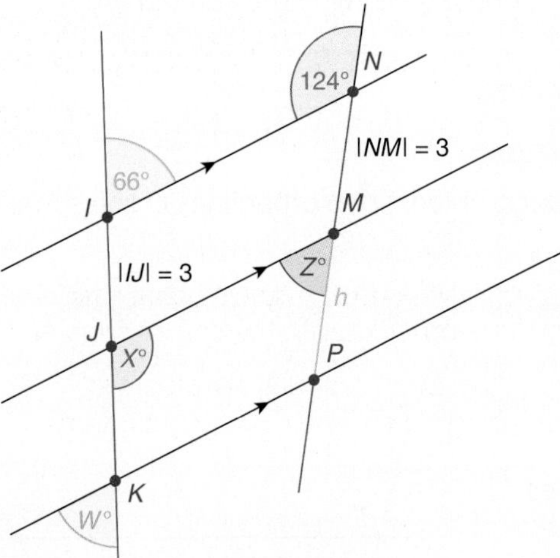

3.

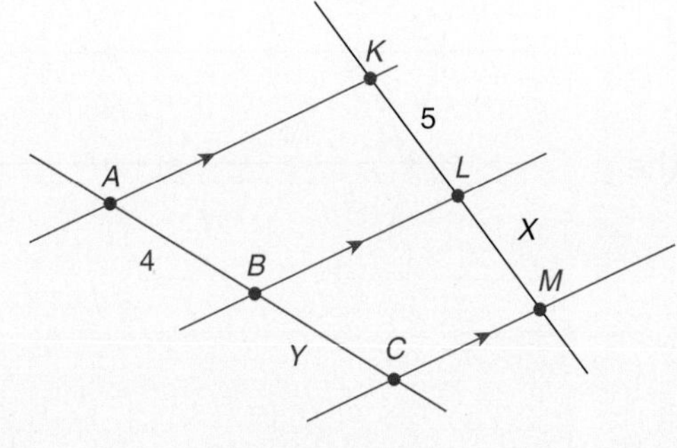

4.

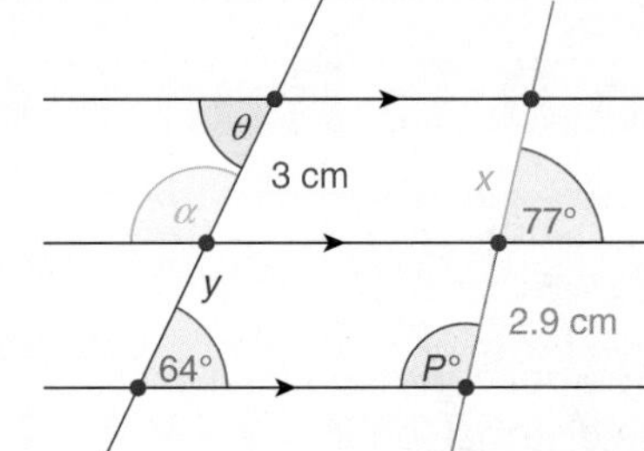

5.

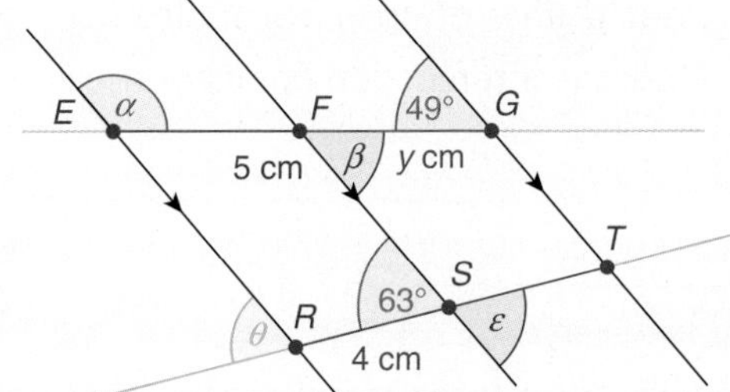

6.

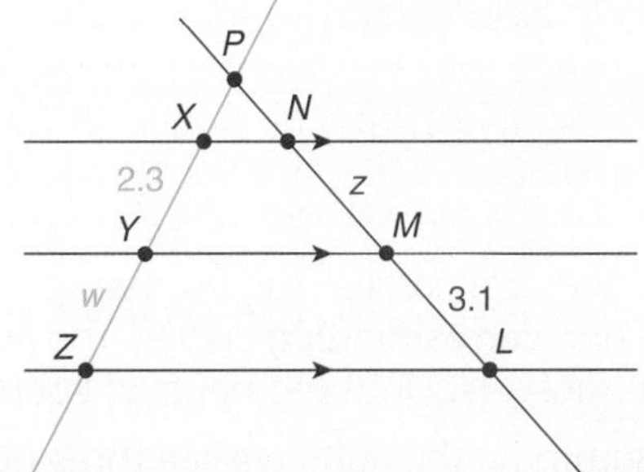

7.

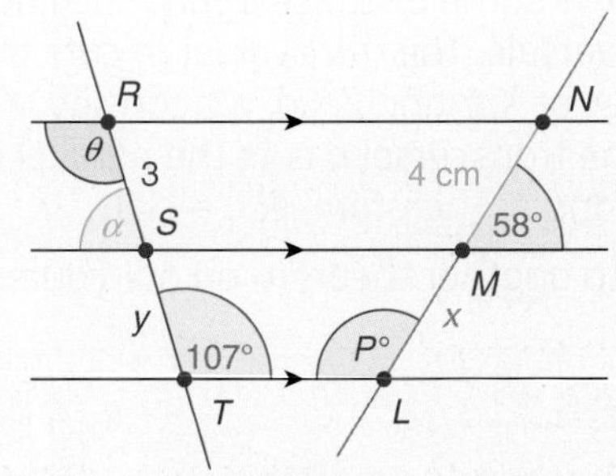

8.

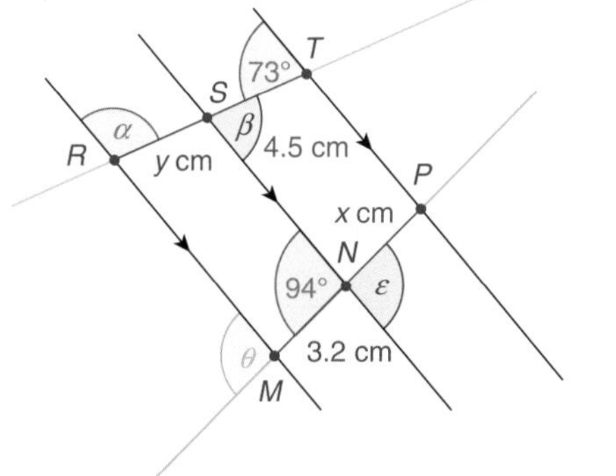

9.

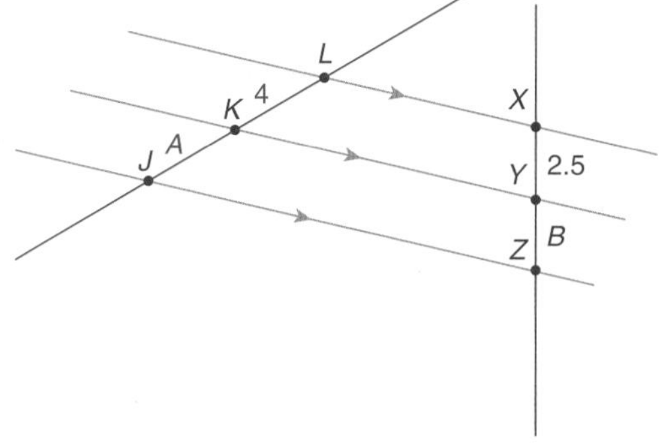

10.

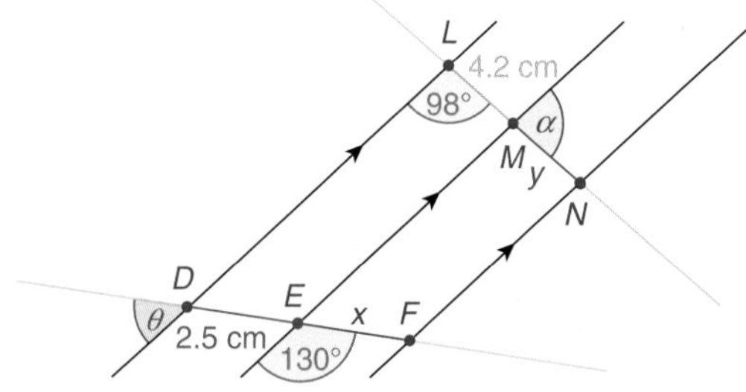

11.

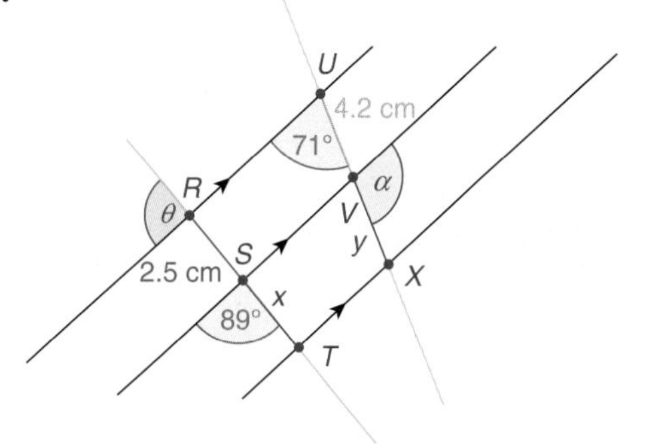

Section 9.2: Parallel lines and triangles

Student Activity 9B

1. Copy the diagram and answer the questions that follow. All dimensions are in centimetres.

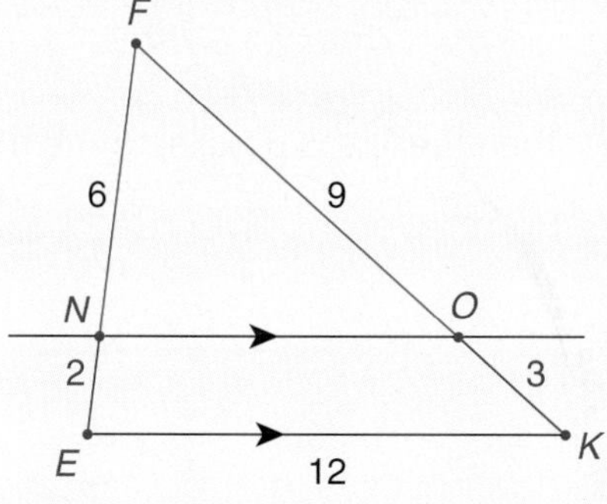

(a) Copy and complete the following table:

$\|FN\|$ =	$\|FO\|$ =	$\|FE\|$ =
$\|NE\|$ =	$\|OK\|$ =	$\|FK\|$ =

(b) Write the following fractions in their simplest form:

$\frac{|NE|}{|FN|} = \frac{|OK|}{|FO|} =$

(c) Do you notice anything about your answers?

(d) Write the following fractions in their simplest form:

$\frac{|FN|}{|FE|} = \frac{|FO|}{|FK|} =$

(e) What do you notice about your answers?

(f) Write the following fractions in their simplest form:

$\frac{|FN|}{|FE|} = \frac{|FO|}{|FK|} =$

(g) What do you notice about your answers?

2. From what you have just learned, evaluate x in the following diagram:

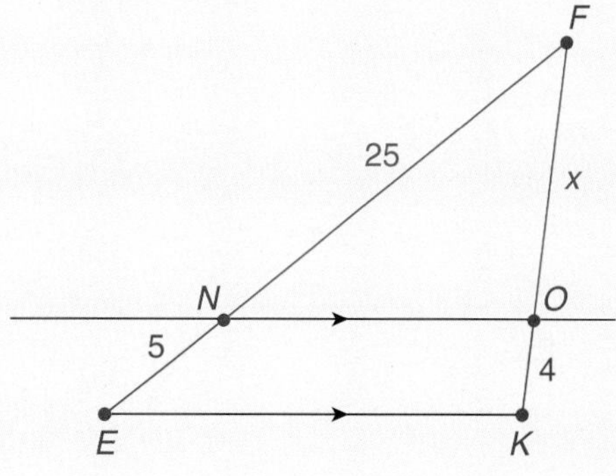

PARALLEL LINES AND TRIANGLES EXPLAINED

In Student Activity 9B, you worked on two triangles: the small triangle *FNO* and a similar but larger triangle *FEK*. These two triangles are **similar** since the shapes are the same and the angles are identical. You also discovered that the corresponding lengths of the sides are in the same ratio. In other words, the lengths of the sides are **proportional.**

$$\frac{\text{Left side of small triangle}}{\text{Left side of big triangle}} = \frac{\text{Right side of small triangle}}{\text{Right side of big triangle}} = \frac{\text{Bottom of small triangle}}{\text{Bottom of big triangle}}$$

These fractions can also be inverted (turned upside-down) and still hold true. This is another theorem on your course.

Theorem 12

Let *ABC* be a triangle. If a line *l* is parallel to *BC* and cuts [*AB*] in the ratio $s:t$, then it also cuts [*AC*] in the same ratio.

For the triangle on the right, it can be shown that:

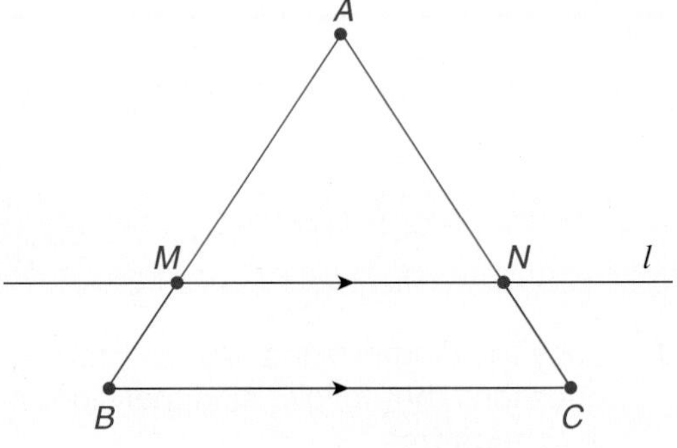

1. $\frac{|BM|}{|AM|} = \frac{|CN|}{|AN|}$ or $\frac{|AM|}{|BM|} = \frac{|AN|}{|CN|}$
2. $\frac{|BM|}{|AB|} = \frac{|CN|}{|AC|}$ or $\frac{|AB|}{|BM|} = \frac{|AC|}{|CN|}$
3. $\frac{|AM|}{|AB|} = \frac{|AN|}{|AC|} = \frac{|MN|}{|BC|}$ or $\frac{|AB|}{|AM|} = \frac{|AC|}{|AN|} = \frac{|BC|}{|MN|}$

The **converse** of the theorem is also true.

Converse

If a line cuts two sides of a triangle in the same ratio, then the line is parallel to the third side of that triangle.

EXAMPLE 2

(a) Find the value of z in the given triangle.

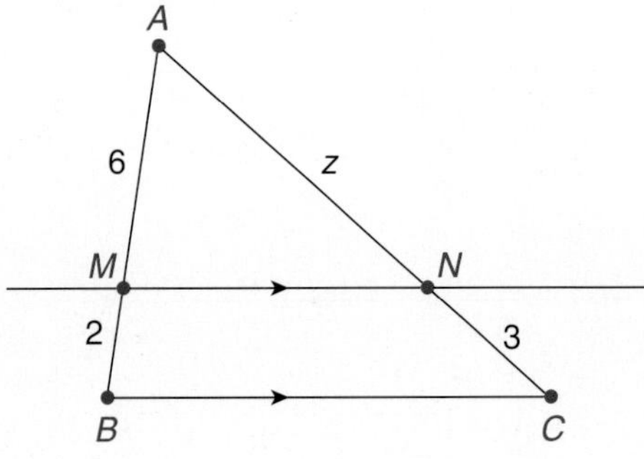

Solution

(a) $\frac{|BM|}{|AM|} = \frac{|CN|}{|AN|}$

$z = |AN|$ **From the diagram**

$\frac{2}{6} = \frac{3}{z}$ **Cross-multiply**

$2z = 18$

$z = 18 \div 2 = 9$

$\therefore |AN| = 9$ units

(b) Find $|CN|$ in the diagram below.

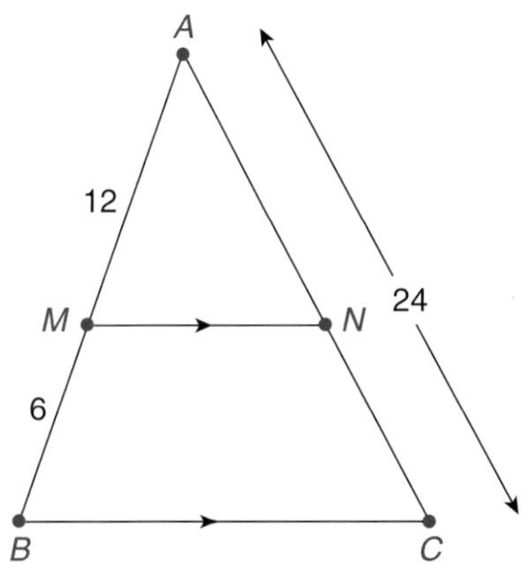

Solution

(b) $\frac{|CN|}{|AC|} = \frac{|BM|}{|AB|}$

$\frac{|CN|}{24} = \frac{6}{18}$ **Cross-multiply**

$18|CN| = (6)(24)$

$18|CN| = 144$

$|CN| = 144 \div 18$

$|CN| = 8$ units

Exercise 9.2

Find the value of y in each of the following diagrams. All dimensions are in centimetres.

1.

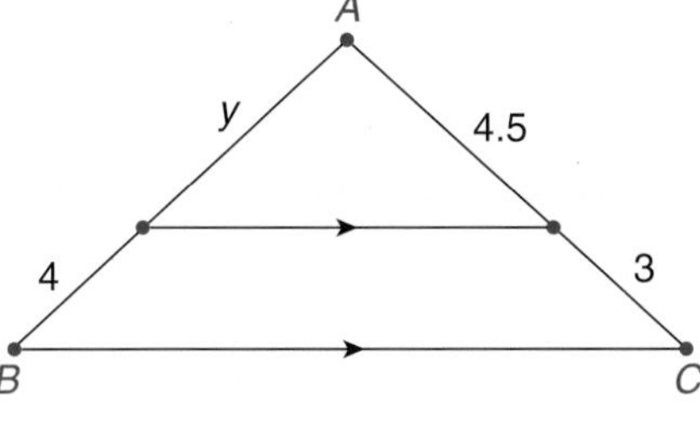

2.

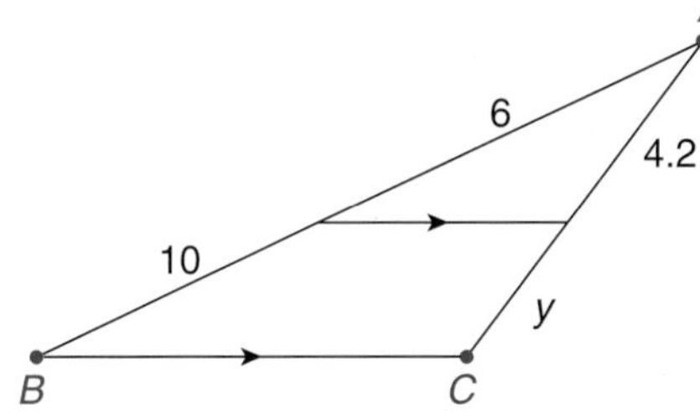

3.

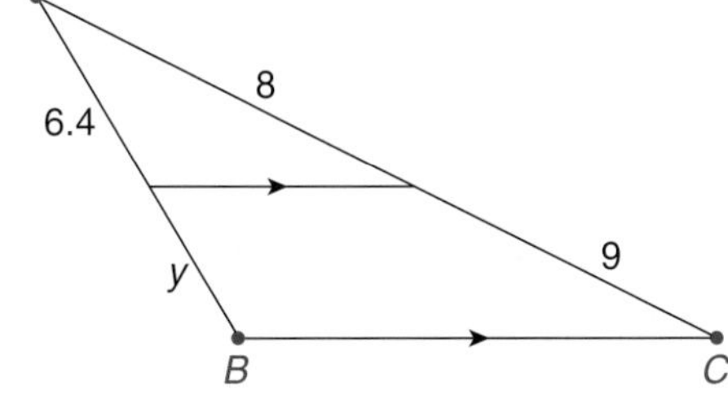

4.

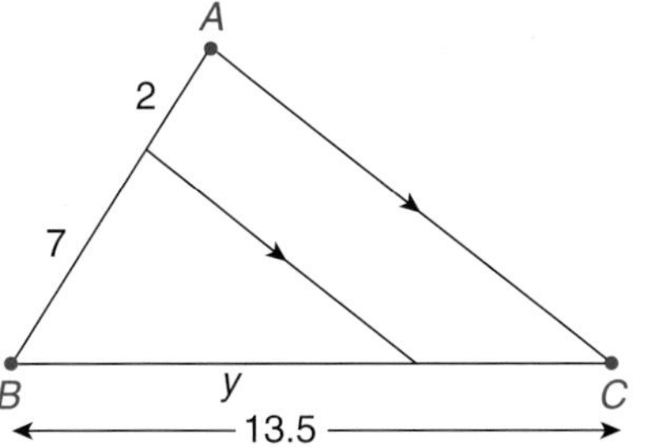

5.

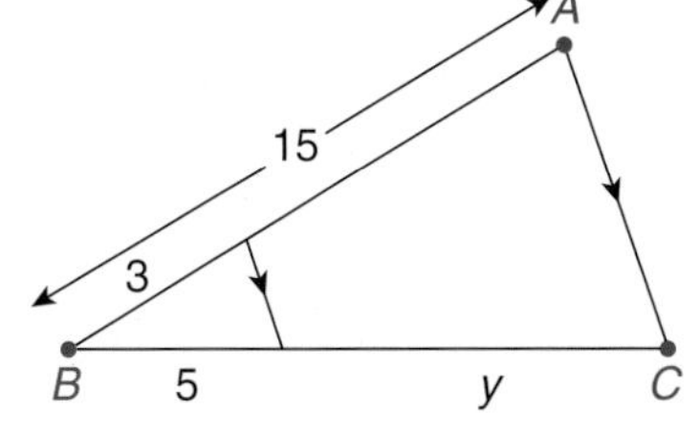

6.

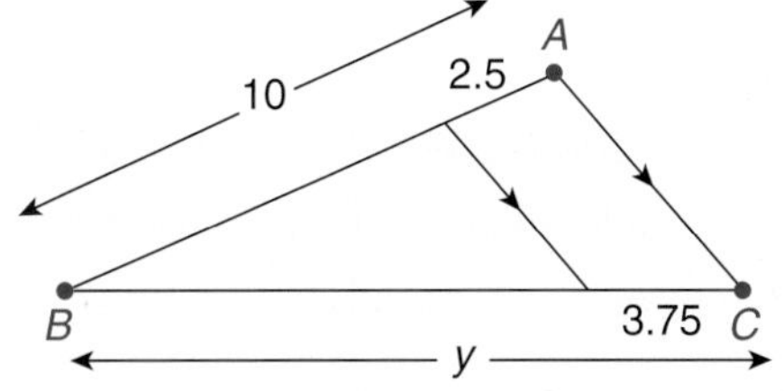

7. In the following diagram, $QR \parallel BC$ and $|AQ| : |QB| = 4 : 6$.

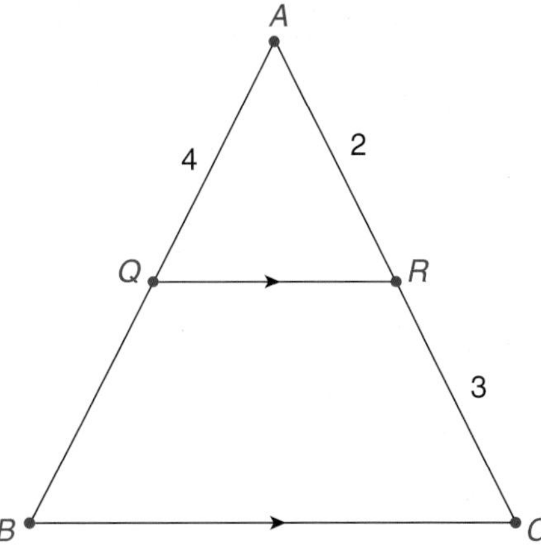

Find the following ratios:

(a) $|AR| : |RC|$

(b) $|AQ| : |AB|$

(c) $|QB| : |AB|$

(d) $|QR| : |BC|$

8. Using ratios, investigate whether $DE \parallel AC$.

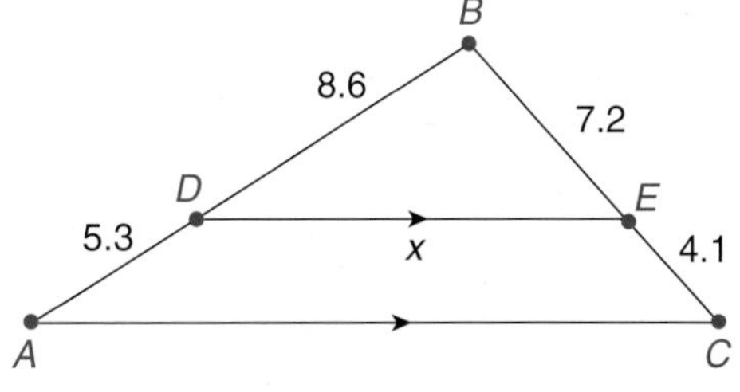

9. In the diagram, $AB \parallel DE$, $|AB| = 9.4$, $|BC| = 14$, $|CE| = 8.5$ and $|CD| = 7.3$.

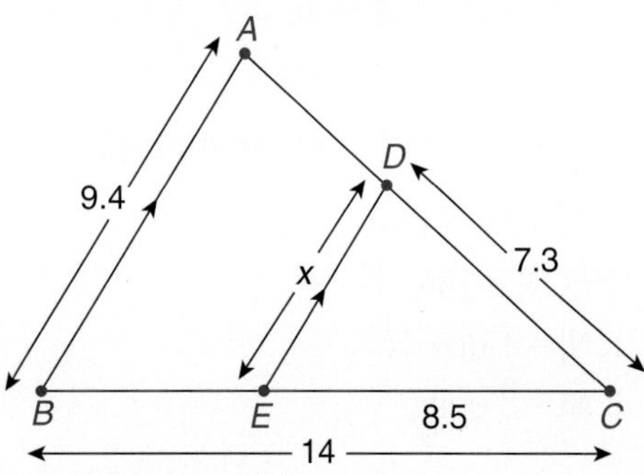

(a) Find the value of x correct to one decimal place.

(b) Find $|AC|$ correct to the nearest whole number.

(c) Hence, find $|AD|$ correct to one decimal place.

(d) Find $|BE|$.

10. In the diagram, $AB \parallel DE$, $|AB| = 7.6$, $|AC| = 11.6$, $|CB| = 8.5$ and $|AD| = 4.5$.

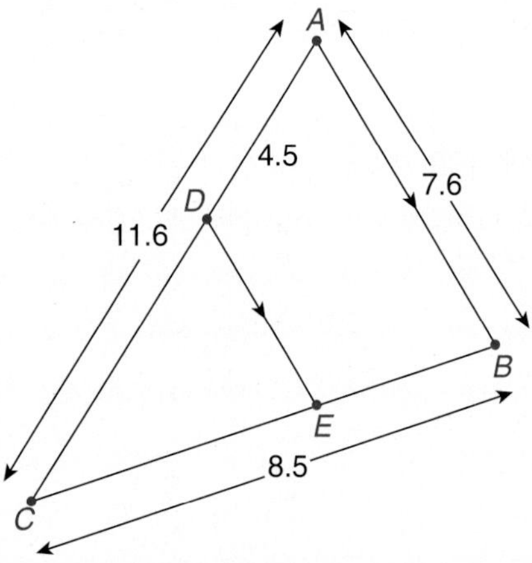

(a) Find $|BE|$ correct to one decimal place.

(b) Find $|CE|$ correct to one decimal place.

(c) Find $|ED|$ correct to one decimal place.

(d) Find $|CD|$ correct to one decimal place.

11. In the ΔXYZ, $PQ \parallel YZ$, $|XP| = 3$, $|XQ| = 4$, $|PQ| = 10$ and $|YZ| = 25$.

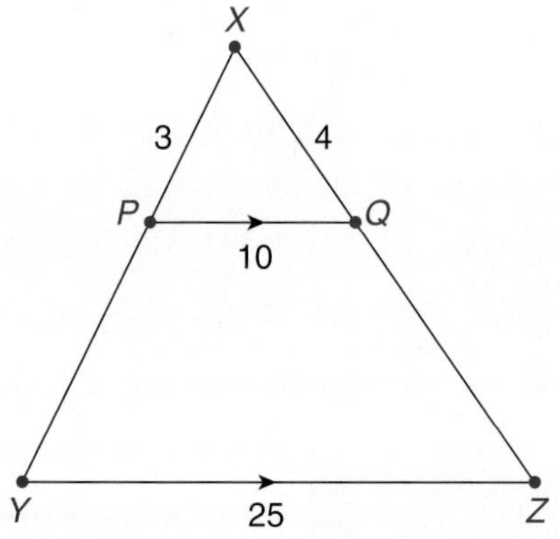

Find:

(a) $|XY|$

(b) $|XZ|$

(c) $|PY|$

12. In the ΔABC, $AC \parallel DE$. $|AD| = 6$, $|DB| = 16$ and $|EB| = 20$.

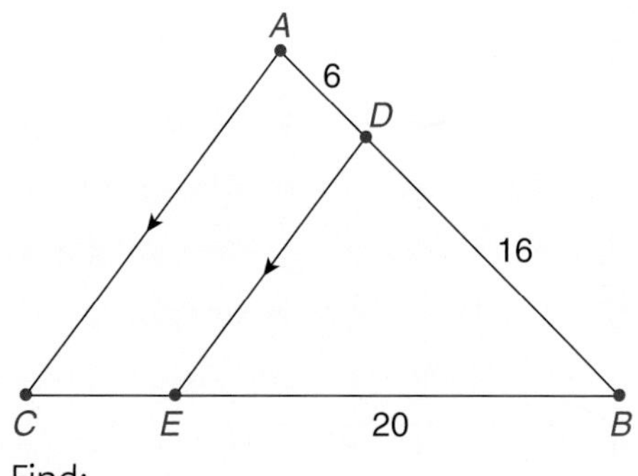

Find:

(a) $|CE|$

(b) $|CB|$

(c) If $|DE| = 12$, find $|AC|$.

CHAPTER 9 SELF-CHECK TEST

1. Calculate each of the following angles. State the reasons for each answer and clearly show all workings .

(a)

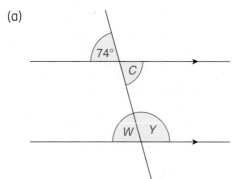

74°
C
W
Y

(b)

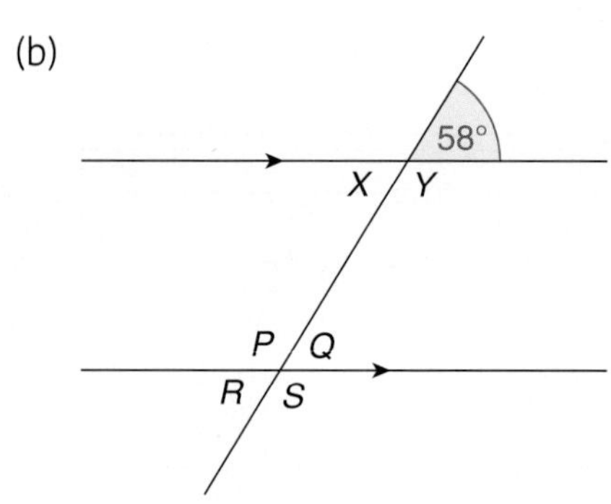

(c)

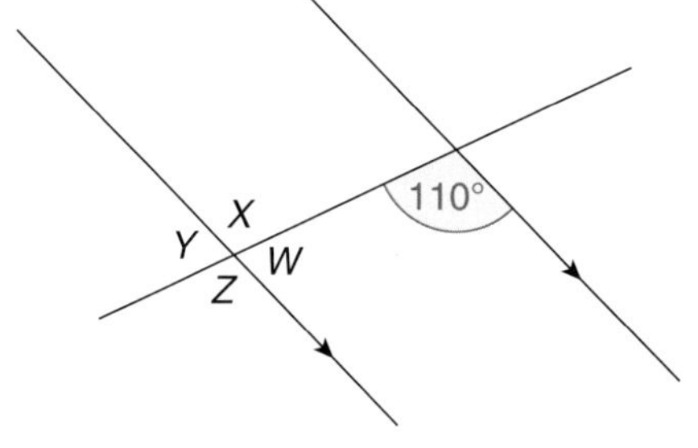

(d)

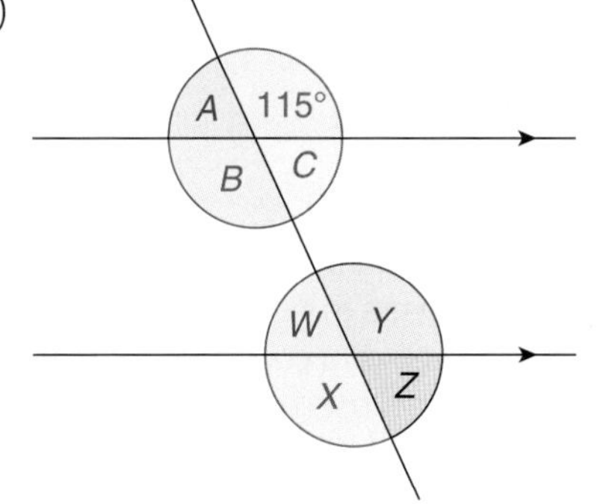

(e)

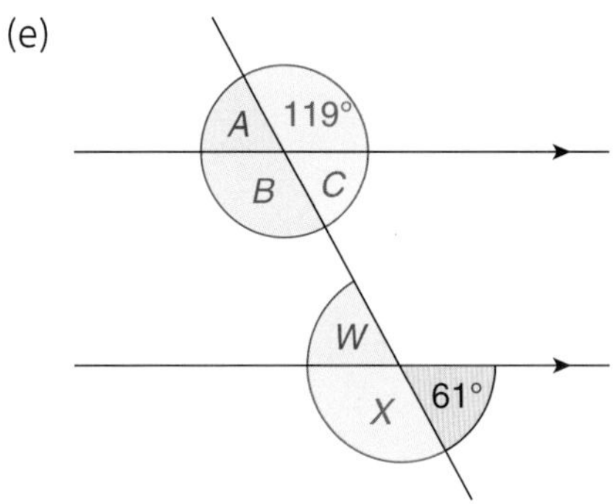

(f)

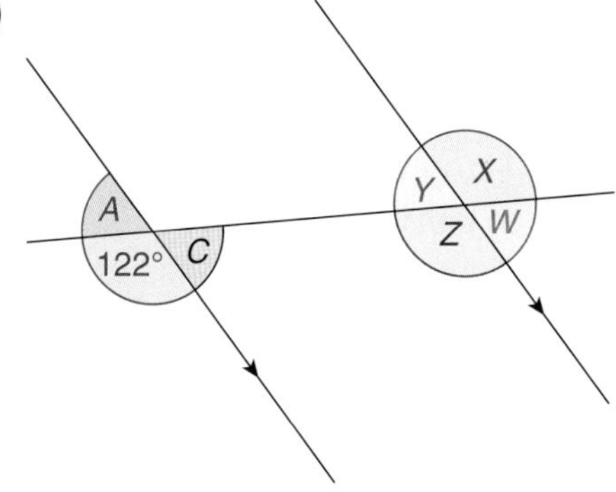

2. Find the value of y in each of the following:

(a) If $|AC| + |DF| = 130$ cm

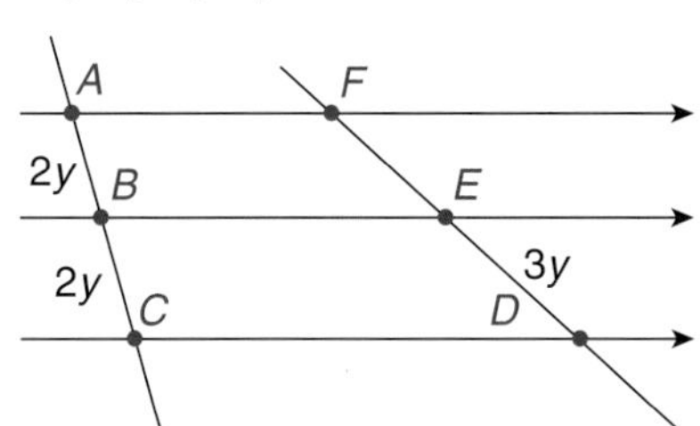

(b) If $|AC| + |DF| = 180$ m

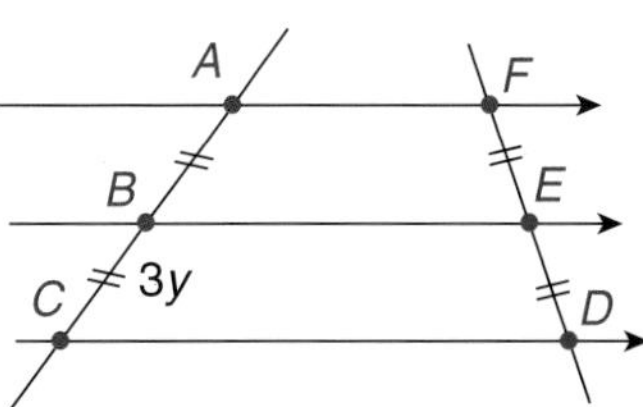

(c) If $|AC| + |DF| = 210$ m

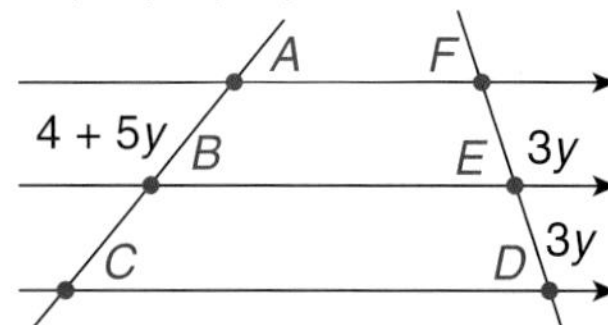

(d) If $|AD| + |EA| = 330$ m

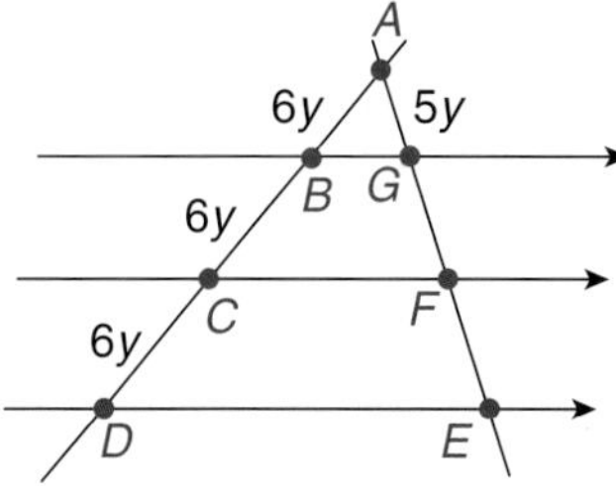

(e) If $|AC| + |AD| = 72$ m

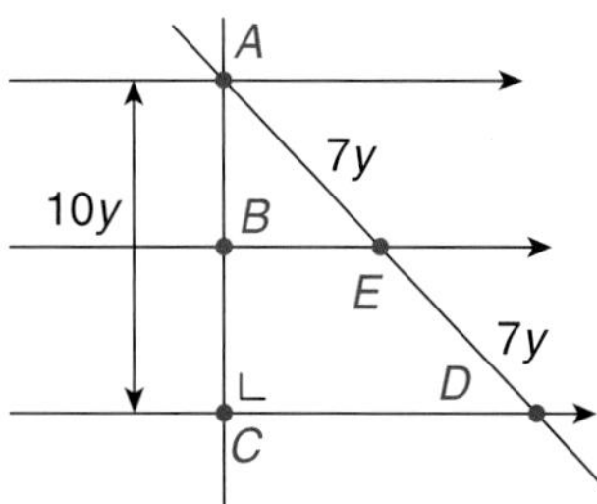

3. In the diagram, $|AD| = 18$ cm and $|GF| = 9$ cm. Four parallel lines x, y, z, and w are drawn perpendicular to $[AD]$.

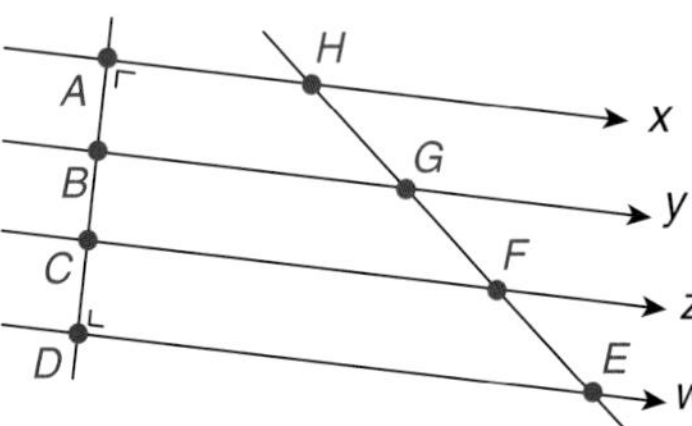

Calculate:

(a) $|AB|$ (b) $|GH|$

(c) $|EF|$ (d) $|EH|$

4. In each of the diagrams, the lines cut each transversal into segments of equal length. Calculate the value of a and b in each diagram.

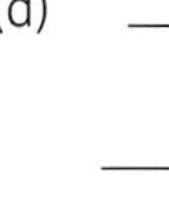

(a)

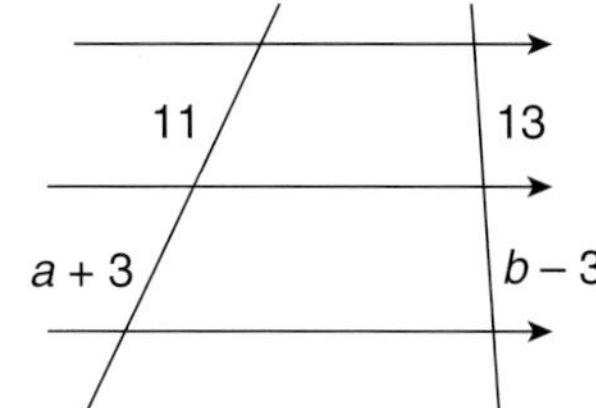

(b)

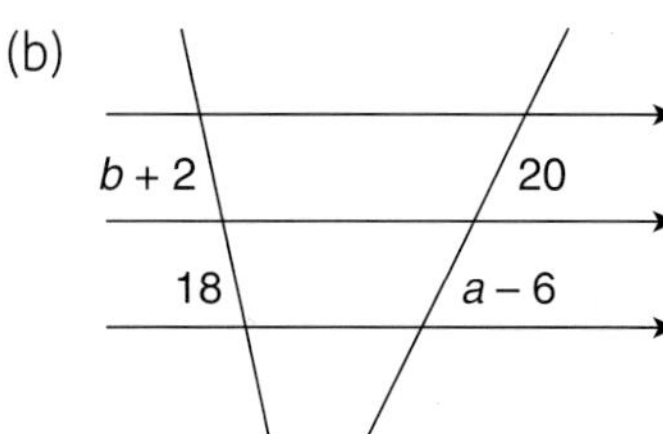

(c)

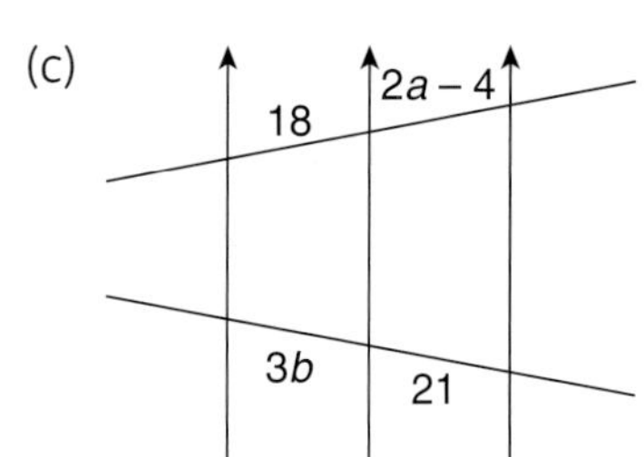

5. For each of the following, investigate whether $BE \parallel CD$:

(a)

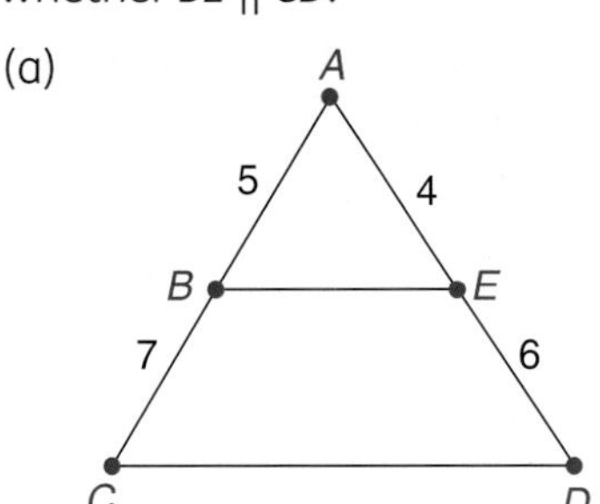

(b)

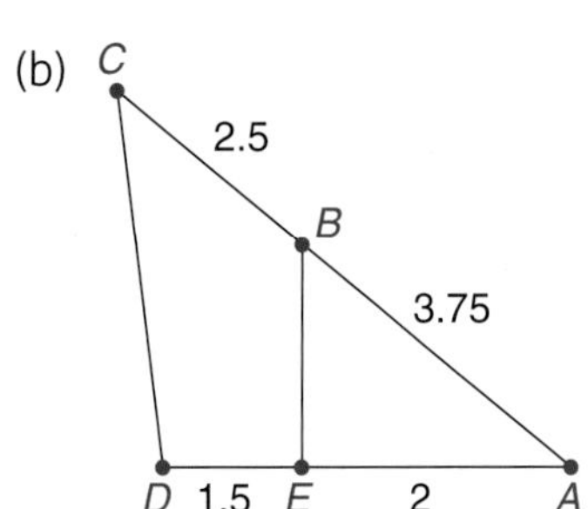

(c)

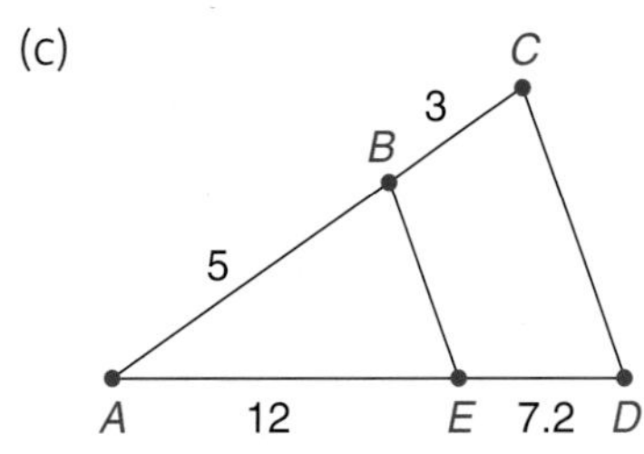

(d)

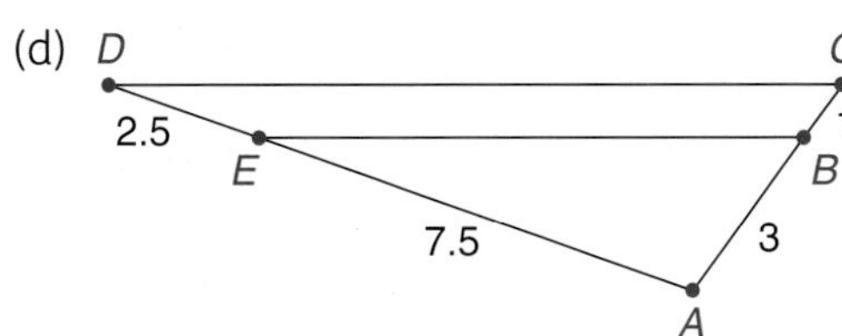

6. In the given diagram, $|AE| = 12$ cm, $|ED| = 15$ cm, $|AB| = 16$ cm and $|BE| = 10$ cm.

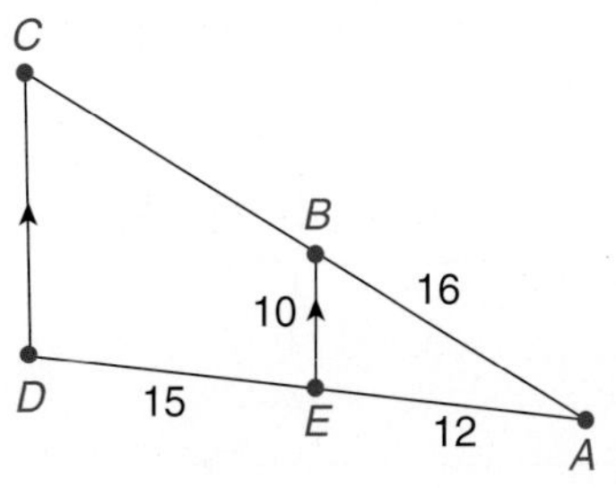

(a) Find $|BC|$. (b) Find $|CD|$.

7. In the given diagram, $|XR| = 30$ mm, $|RS| = 24$ mm, $|SZ| = 15$ mm and $|YZ| = 54$ mm.

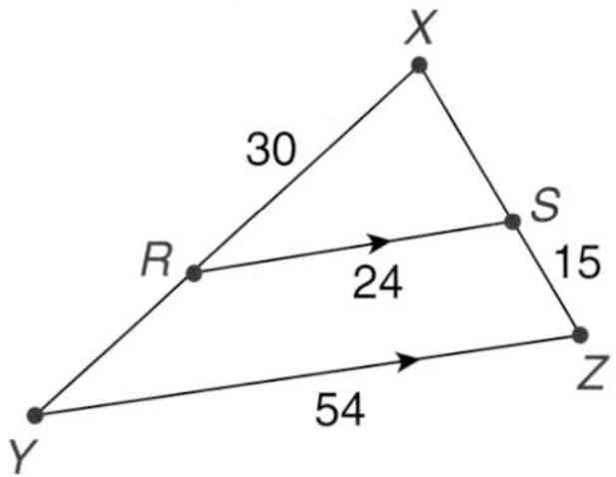

Find the value of:

(a) $|RY|$ (b) $|XS|$

8. In the given diagram, we can see the scaffolding used to hold up a large plasma screen at a concert. Some of the lengths of steel used are recorded as follows: $|NO| = 10.2$ m, $|MQ| = 22.5$ m and $|QP| = |NP| = 7.5$ m.

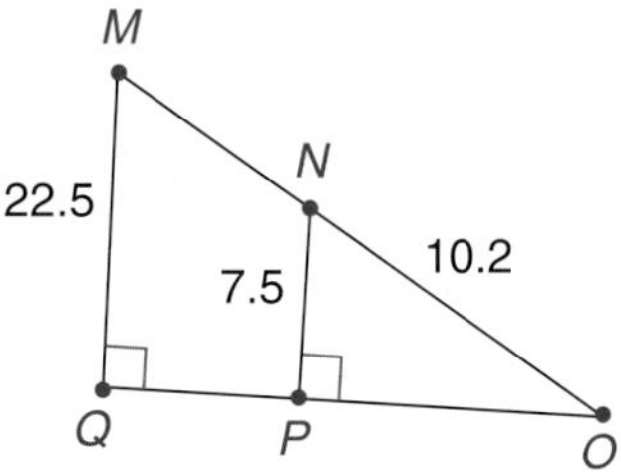

Calculate:

(a) $|MN|$

(b) $|OP|$

(c) The total length of scaffolding used

9. A man who is 162 cm tall casts a shadow of 486 cm. Find the height of the beech tree if its shadow is 21.3 m in length.

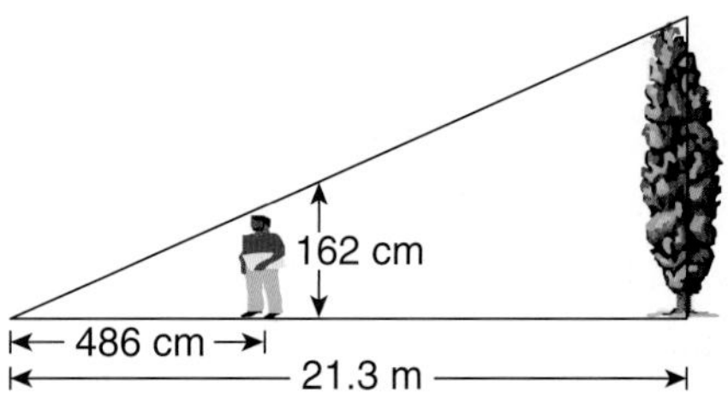

10. A building casts a shadow of length 40 m. A nearby garden shed of height 2.3 m casts a shadow of length 1.84 m.

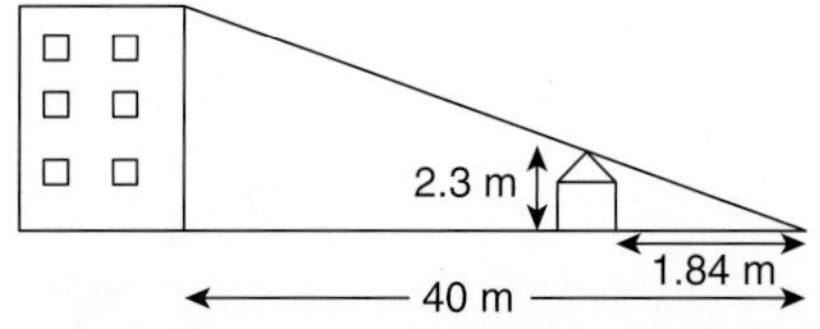

(a) Describe in words how you might calculate the height of the building.

(b) Using the method described, calculate how tall the building is.

11. A group of teenagers measure the height of their dog as 30 cm. They record that the dog casts a shadow of 42 cm. In turn, each teenager gets their shadow to coincide on the ground with the dog's shadow.

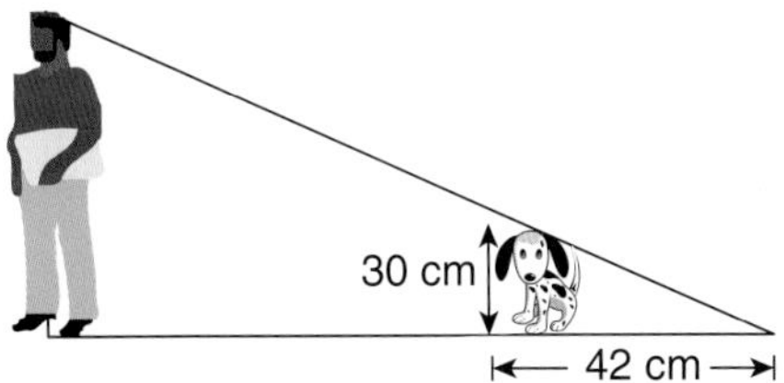

Calculate each teenager's height if:

(a) Joe's shadow is 155.4 cm in length

(b) Antonio's shadow is 172.2 cm in length

(c) Fran's shadow is 165.2 cm in length

(d) Julianne's shadow is 175 cm in length

12. A designer made the following logo for a company but forgot to include some essential measurements. All we know is that $BC \parallel DE \parallel FG$, and that $|AB| = 3$ cm, $|BD| = 4$ cm, $|DF| = 5$ cm, $|AC| = 4$ cm and $|BC| = 5$ cm.

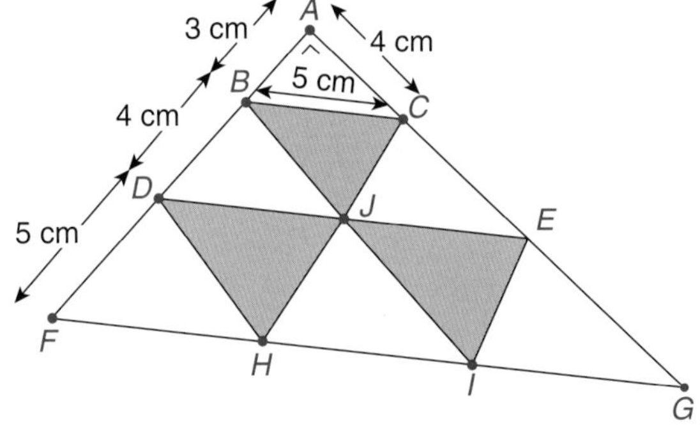

(a) Explain how the company can calculate the lengths of [AG] and [FG].

Using this information described in part (a), find:

(b) $|AG|$ (c) $|CE|$ (d) $|FG|$

13. A surveyor wants to calculate the distance across a lake. The lake is surrounded by woods. Three paths have been constructed to provide access to the lake from the road, [AC], as shown in the diagram.

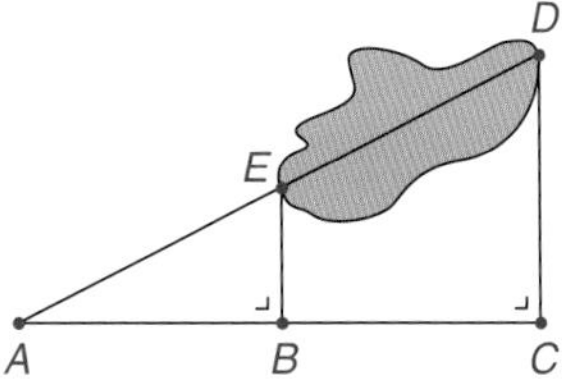

The lengths of the paths from the road to the lake are as follows:

$|AE| = 160$ m, $|BE| = 120$ m and $|CD| = 480$ m.

(a) Explain how these measurements can be used to find $|ED|$, the distance across the lake.

(b) Calculate $|ED|$, the distance across the lake.

14. A group of students were trying to find the distance between two trees on opposite sides of a river using pegs, a measuring tape and a long piece of string. They align the pegs in a particular way, take several measurements and sketch the diagram. On the diagram, *A* and *B* are trees, and C, *D* and *E* are the pegs.

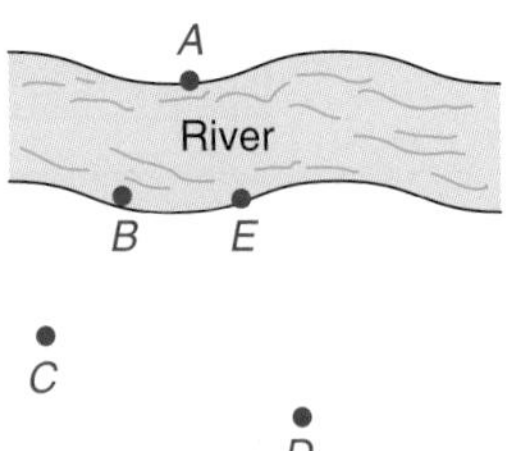

The measurements recorded are $|BE| = 48$ m, $|BC| = 52$ m and $|CD| = 128$ m.

(a) In what way must the pegs and the trees be aligned if the students are to use these measurements to calculate $|AB|$?

(b) Calculate the distance between the trees.

(c) Another group of students repeats the activity. They have a similar diagram but different measurements. Their measurements are $|BE| = 42$ m and $|BC| = 10$ m. Based on the value of $|AB|$ that the first group got, what measurement will this second group have for $|CD|$?

(d) Suggest how the group of students might have ensured that $|BE|$ was parallel to $|CD|$.

9

MATHS IN ACTION 3

15. Complete the word search.

PARALLEL
PERPENDICULAR
TRANSVERSAL
ACUTE
OBTUSE
THEOREM
CONVERSE
RATIO
PROPORTION
SIMILAR
TRIANGLE

P	A	R	A	L	L	E	L	S	R	V	B	X	C	P
X	W	H	A	G	X	O	T	Y	O	U	E	Y	R	E
U	T	X	S	J	L	B	M	D	N	P	Q	O	I	R
V	D	T	B	D	C	T	X	E	S	Y	P	Z	A	P
E	G	R	D	H	I	U	P	Z	R	O	I	A	O	E
S	O	A	B	Q	Y	S	S	P	R	O	M	B	C	N
R	I	N	I	R	M	E	N	T	H	K	E	F	J	D
E	M	S	R	A	H	V	I	B	O	U	M	H	X	I
V	U	V	T	L	K	O	E	N	J	F	M	Y	T	C
N	J	E	Q	I	N	T	R	I	A	N	G	L	E	U
O	R	R	A	M	Q	W	C	A	F	T	P	K	O	L
C	Z	S	X	I	S	T	H	R	A	T	I	O	N	A
E	K	A	K	S	M	G	B	P	G	Y	U	N	O	R
G	I	L	Z	P	R	O	P	O	R	T	I	O	N	V
H	A	C	U	T	E	M	R	Q	Y	U	Z	A	N	A

CHAPTER 9 KNOWLEDGE CHECKLIST

After completing this chapter, I now:

- Understand the meaning of the term transversal
- Know that a transversal line makes equal corresponding angles and equal alternate angles on parallel lines
- Know that, if three parallel lines cut off equal segments on a transversal, they will cut off equal segments on any other transversal
- Know that, if a line is drawn across a triangle, parallel to one side of a triangle, it will cut the other two sides in the same ratio

CHAPTER 10

TRIGONOMETRY 1

LEARNING OUTCOMES

In this chapter you will learn:

✓ **About the theorem of Pythagoras and its converse**

✓ **To identify the hypotenuse of a right-angled triangle**

✓ **To solve problems involving right-angled triangles**

KEY WORDS

- **Adjacent side**
- **Hypotenuse**
- **Opposite side**
- **Pythagoras**
- **Right-angled triangle**

INTRODUCTION

Pythagoras of Samos was born in Greece around 569 BC. He is often described as the first 'pure' mathematician. He studied mathematics in Egypt, Babylon (an ancient city situated in what is now Iraq) and Italy. In 520 BC, Pythagoras returned to Samos and set up a famous school called The Semicircle where his many followers lived and worked.

Pythagoras was a very important figure in the development of mathematics. However, we know relatively little about his mathematical achievements. The Semicircle society had strict religious and scientific beliefs. They also followed a code of secrecy. Many other Greek mathematicians wrote books, which we still have today. But we have none of Pythagoras' writings. As a result, Pythagoras remains a mysterious figure to this day.

We will now look at a branch of mathematics which deals with triangles. The word 'trigonometry' comes from the Greek words 'trigōnon', meaning triangle, and 'metron', meaning to measure.

Section 10.1: Right-angled triangles

Student Activity 10A

1. Examine the right-angled triangle and answer the questions that follow.
   (a) How many small boxes do you think should be in the large square?
   (b) Explain why you have picked that number of boxes.
   (c) Which side is **opposite** the right angle in the triangle? Can you say anything about this side compared to the other two sides?
   (d) If you add up the number of boxes on the two smaller sides what total do you get? Do you notice anything about this?
2. Examine the right-angled triangle and answer the questions that follow.
   (a) How many small boxes could be drawn on each side of the triangle?
   (b) Which side is **opposite** the right angle?
   (c) What do you notice about the measurement of this side?
   (d) What will the number of boxes on the smaller sides add up to?
3. Rewrite the following sentences and fill in the gaps.
   (a) In a right-angled triangle, the side opposite the right angle is always the l _ _ _ _ _ _ side.
   (b) In a right-angled triangle, the s _ _ _ _ _ of the length of the longest side is equal in value to the s _ _ of the squares of the lengths of the other t _ _ sides.

RIGHT-ANGLED TRIANGLES EXPLAINED

Pythagoras discovered an amazing fact about triangles: if a triangle has a right angle (90°) and you make a square on each of the three sides, then the biggest square has the same area as the other two squares added together!

For example:

$(3)^2 + (4)^2 = (5)^2$

$9 + 16 = 25$

This is called the theorem of Pythagoras and can be written in one short equation:

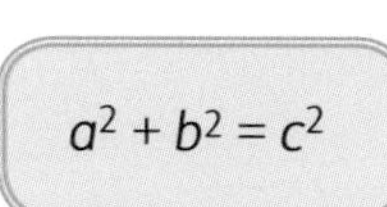

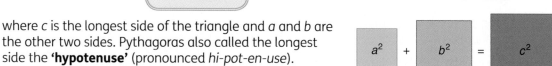

where c is the longest side of the triangle and a and b are the other two sides. Pythagoras also called the longest side the **'hypotenuse'** (pronounced *hi-pot-en-use*).

a^2 + 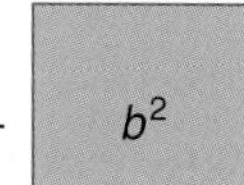

= 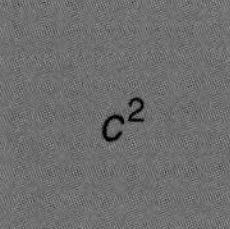

Pythagoras proved that:

Theorem of Pythagoras

In a right-angled triangle, the square of the hypotenuse is equal to the sum of the squares of the other two sides.

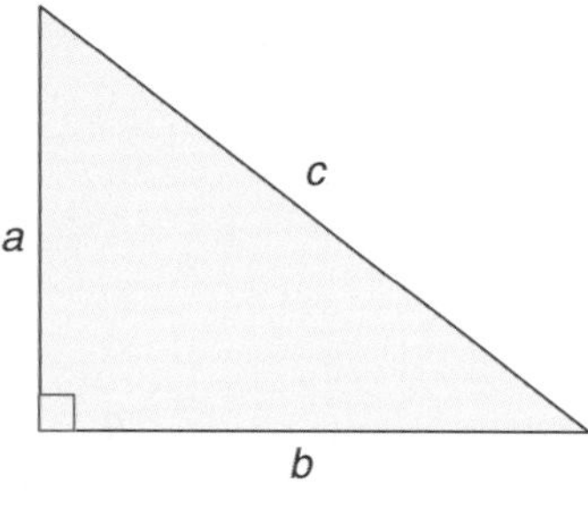

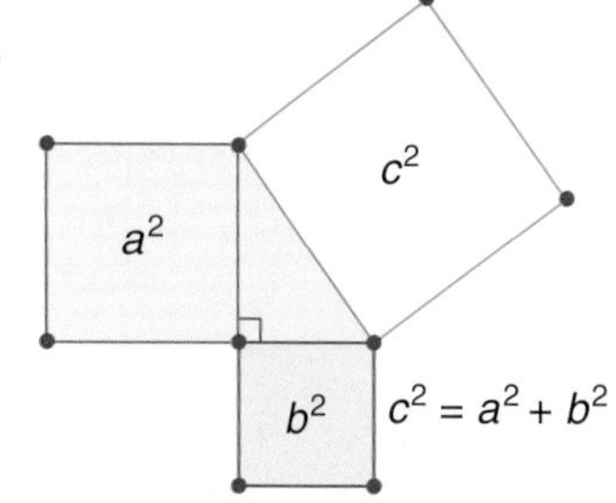

The converse of the theorem of Pythagoras is also true:

Converse

If the square of the length of the longest side of a triangle is equal to the sum of the squares of the lengths of the other two sides, then the triangle is a right-angled triangle.

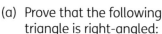

EXAMPLE 1

(a) Prove that the following triangle is right-angled:

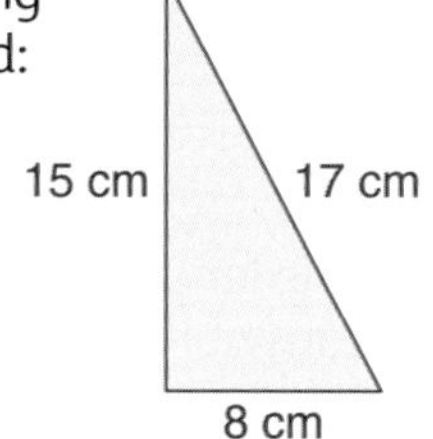

(b) Find the length of the hypotenuse in the right-angled triangle shown.

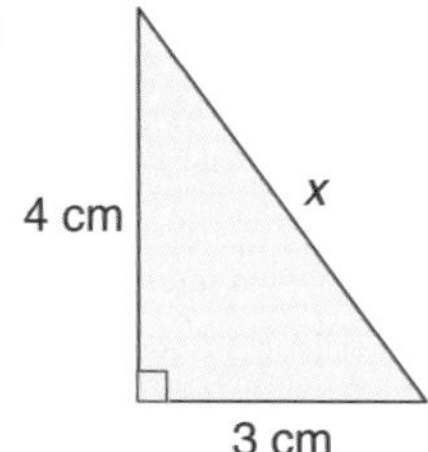

(c) Find the length of the side marked a in the right-angled triangle shown.

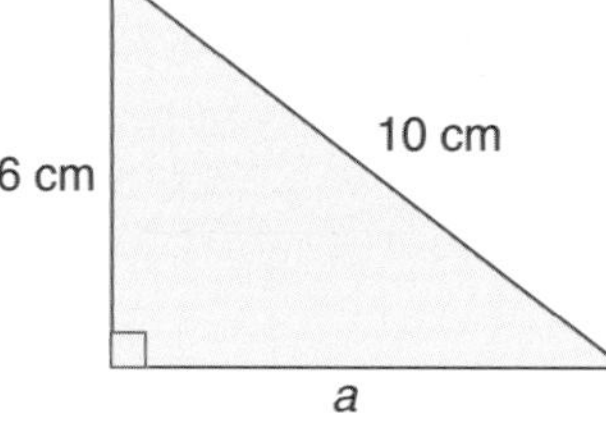

Solution

(a) Hypotenuse (longest side) = 17

$(17)^2 = (15)^2 + (8)^2$

$289 = 225 + 64$

$289 = 289$

$\therefore$ The triangle is right-angled.

(b) x is the longest side as it is opposite the right angle, so it is the hypotenuse.

$(x)^2 = (4)^2 + (3)^2$

$x^2 = 16 + 9$

$x^2 = 25$

$x = \sqrt{25}$

$\therefore x = 5$ cm

(c) 10 is the longest side as it is opposite the right angle, so it is the hypotenuse.

$(10)^2 = a^2 + (6)^2$

$100 = a^2 + 36$

$100 - 36 = a^2$

$64 = a^2$

$\sqrt{64} = a$

$\therefore a = 8$ cm

Exercise 10.1

1. In your own words, explain what a hypotenuse is. Does every triangle have one?
2. What type of triangle does the theorem of Pythagoras only work for?
3. What does the theorem of Pythagoras state?
4. State the converse of the theorem of Pythagoras.
5. Investigate whether the following triangles are right-angled. All measurements are in cm.

(a)

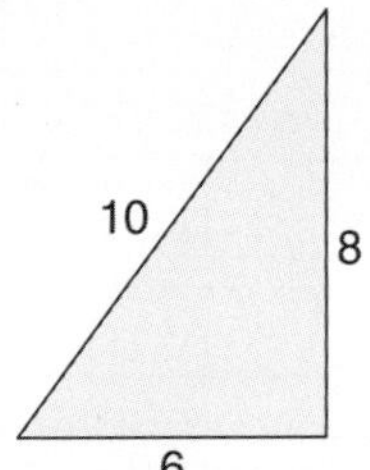

(b)

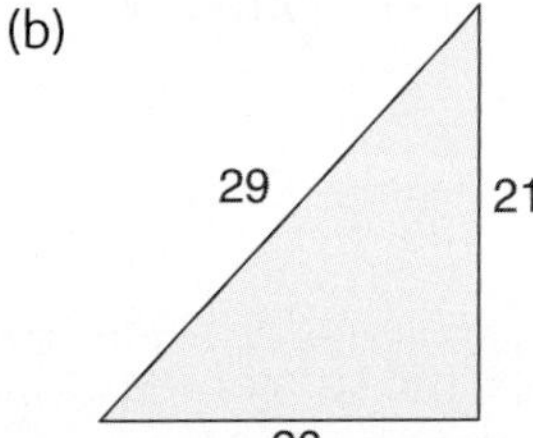

(c)

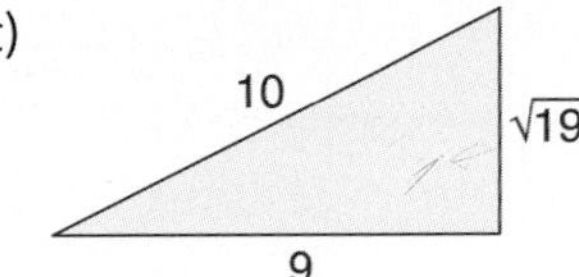

(d)

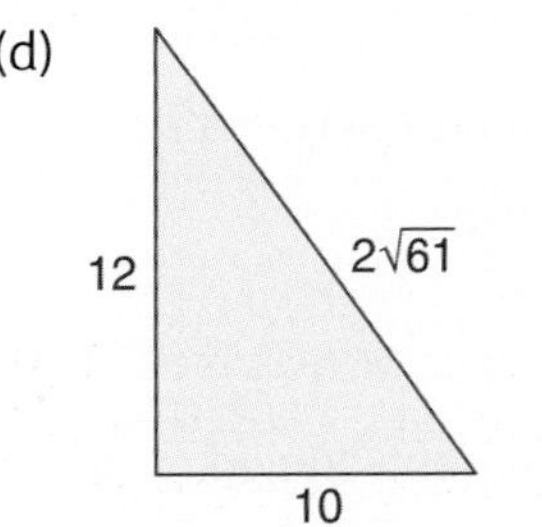

(e)

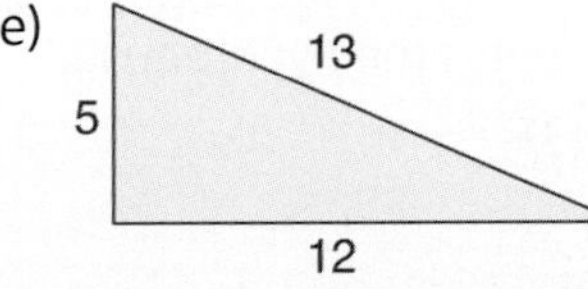

Find the length of the missing side in each of the following right-angled triangles. All dimensions are in centimetres.

6.

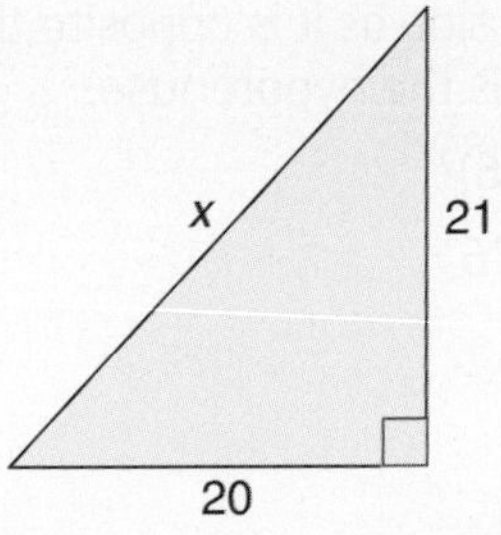

7.

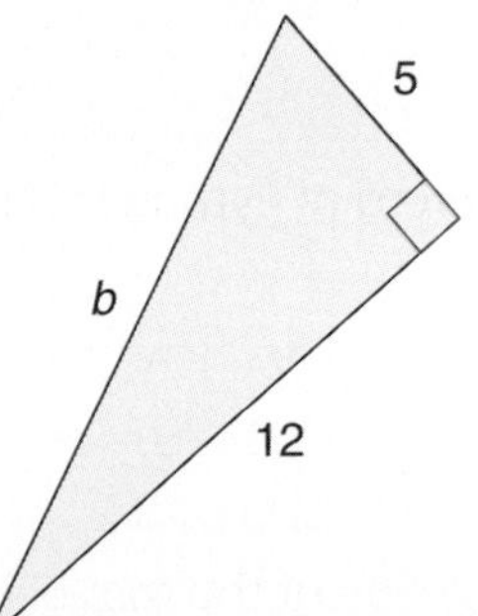

8.

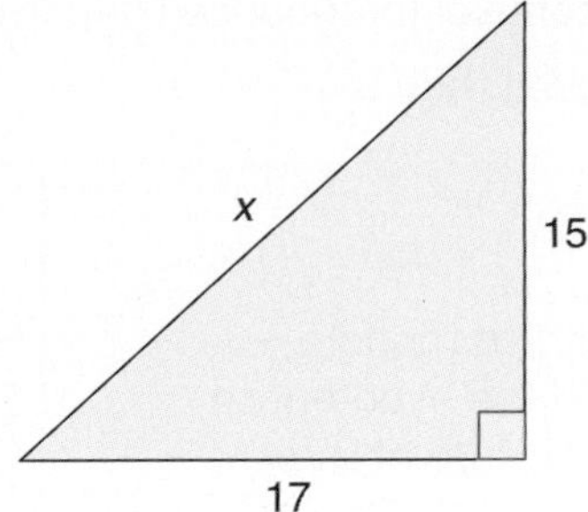

9.

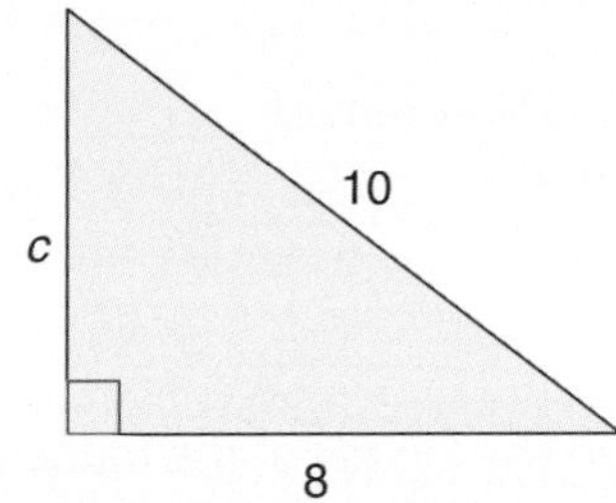

10.

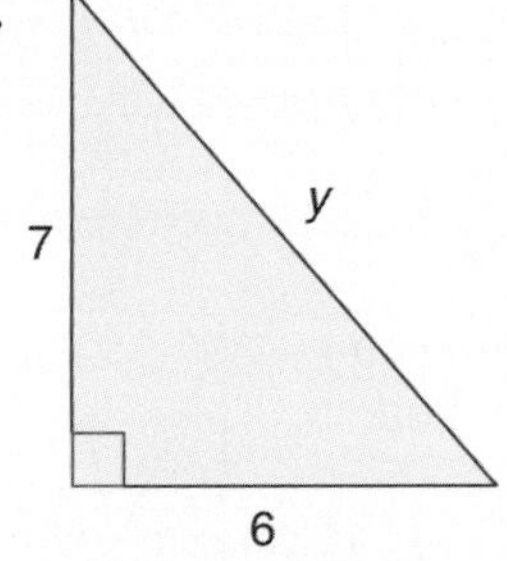

Find the length of each missing side, giving your answer in surd form, where necessary:

11.

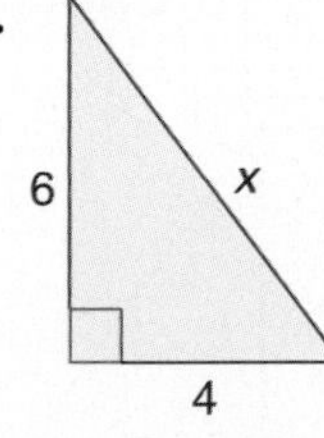

13.

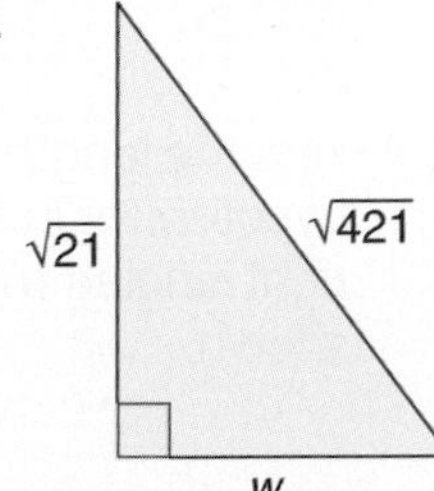

12.

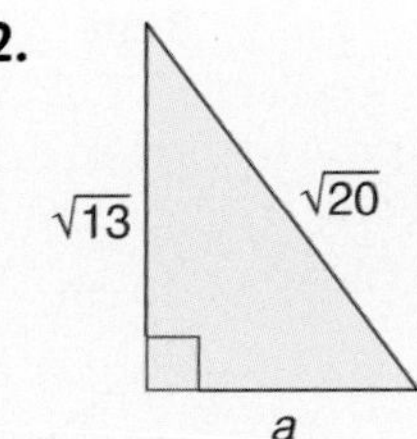

14.

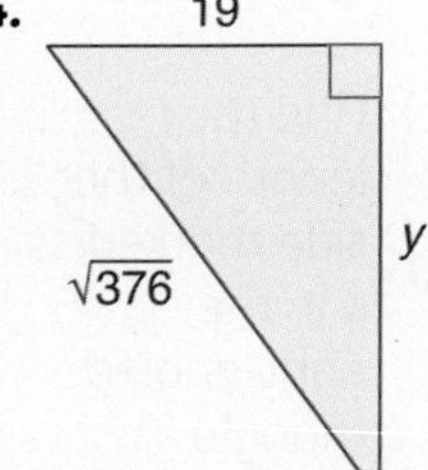

15. Use the theorem of Pythagoras to investigate which of the following are right-angled triangles:

(a)

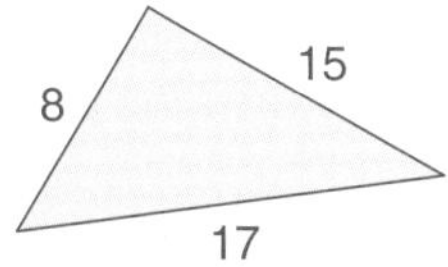

(b)

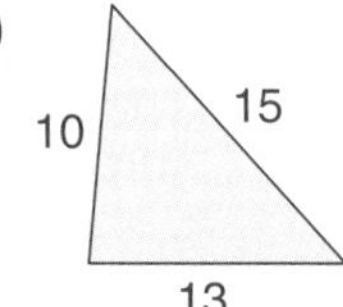

(c)

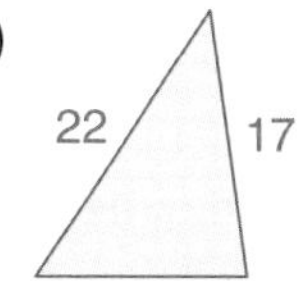

(d)

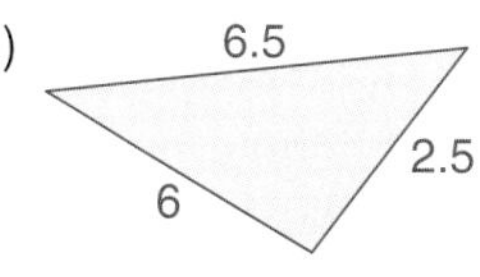

16. A Pythagorean triple is a set of three whole numbers (a, b and c) that satisfies the theorem of Pythagoras.

(a) Identify whether the following are Pythagorean triples, giving a reason for your answer:

(i) 3, 4, 5
(ii) 7, 24, 25
(iii) 5, 12, 13
(iv) 11, 27, 35
(v) 6, 8, 10
(vi) 4, 13, 29
(vii) 14, 7, 34
(viii) 300, 400, 500
(ix) 10, 24, 26
(x) 6, 13, 21

(b) If each number in a Pythagorean triple is multiplied by the same whole number, are the resulting numbers also a Pythagorean triple? Explain your answer.

Section 10.2: Solving problems using the theorem of Pythagoras

What Pythagoras proved is a cornerstone of mathematics. It is so interesting to mathematicians that there are more than 400 different proofs of the theorem! We will examine one of these proofs in Chapter 29.

The Babylonians understood Pythagoras' idea 1,000 years before Pythagoras proved it. We will now examine some real-life situations in which the theorem of Pythagoras is useful.

EXAMPLE 2

(a) A builder wants to use corrugated iron sheets 3 metres long to build a shed roof. The height of the gable above point D is 1.5 metres. What length are the horizontal rafters?

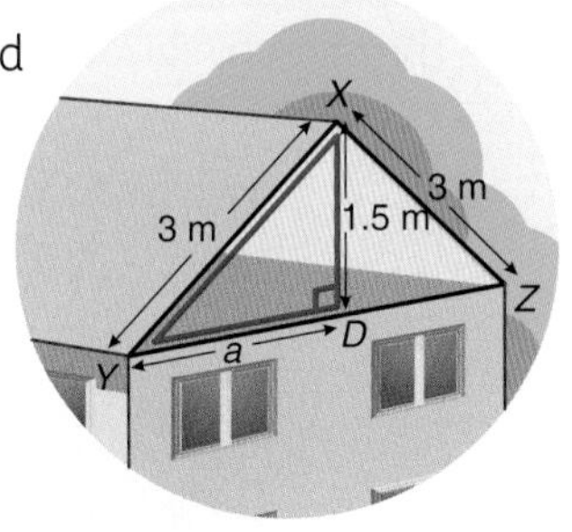

Note

A gable is the triangular portion of a wall between the edges of a sloping roof.

Solution

(a) XYZ is an isosceles triangle and the point D is the halfway point or midpoint of $[YZ]$. The builder needs to calculate $|YD|$ first.

Let $|YD| = a$ metres

$a^2 + (1.5)^2 = (3)^2$

$a^2 = c^2 - b^2$

$a^2 = (3)^2 - (1.5)^2$

$a^2 = 9 - 2.25$

$a^2 = 6.75$

$a = \sqrt{6.75}$

$a = 2.6$ m, correct to 2 decimal places

The length of the rafter $= 2 \times 2.6$ m

$= 5.2$ m

(b) The joint of a bridge is in equilibrium due to three forces acting on it. The force in one girder is 5 MN. The force from the bridge support is 12 MN. Calculate the force exerted by the second girder *F*.

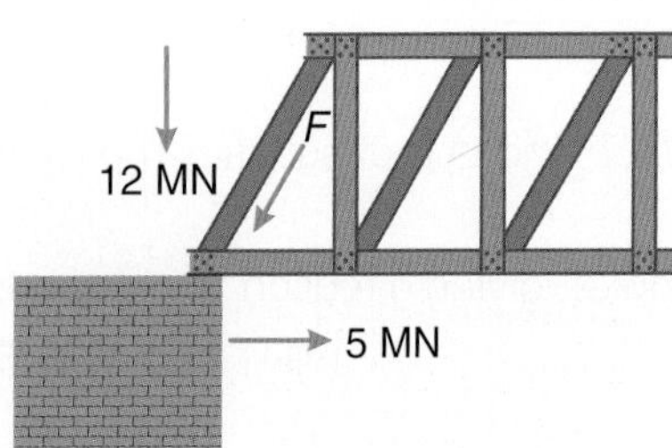

Note

MN means meganewton.

Solution

(b) The force exerted by the second girder *F* can be calculated by drawing a triangle of forces:

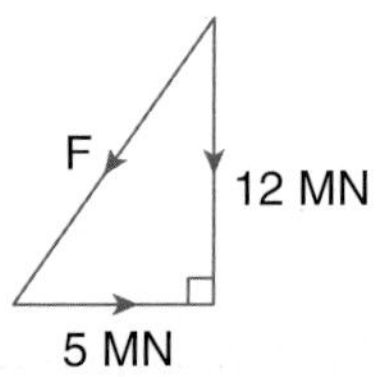

$F^2 = (12)^2 + (5)^2$

$F^2 = 144 + 25$

$F^2 = 169$

$F = \sqrt{169}$

$F = 13$ MN

The force on the second girder is 13 MN.

Exercise 10.2

1. Paul is designing a vegetable bed for his garden. He decides to make the bed in the shape of a right-angled triangle. Calculate the length of timber Paul needs to complete his bed.

15 m, 17 m, *x*

2. Mary is making a picture frame for a painting. How long is the diagonal in the picture?

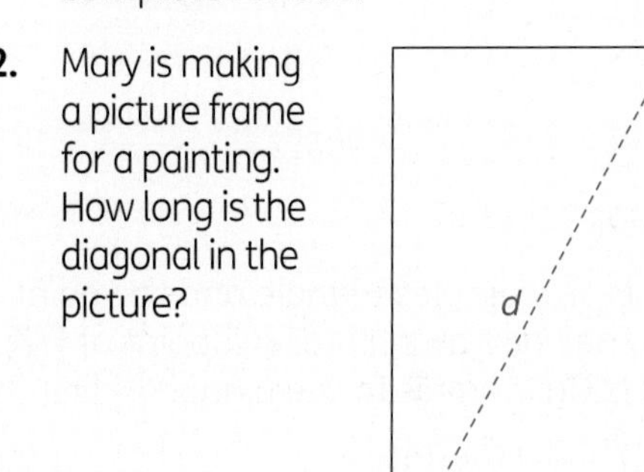

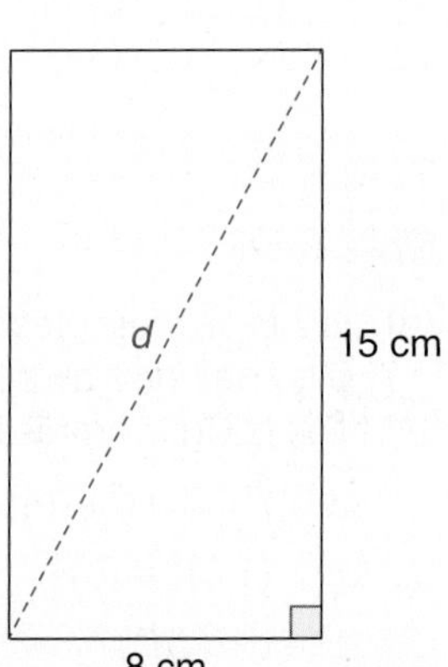

3. A ladder leans against a building as shown. How far from the building is the foot of the ladder?

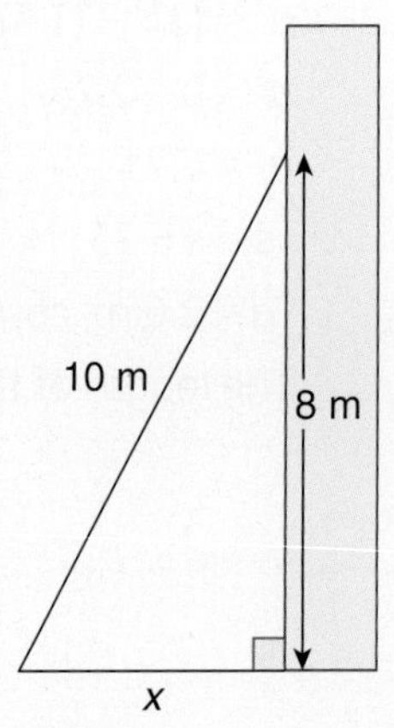

4. A carpenter is making a gate for a house as shown. How long will the diagonal piece of timber need to be?

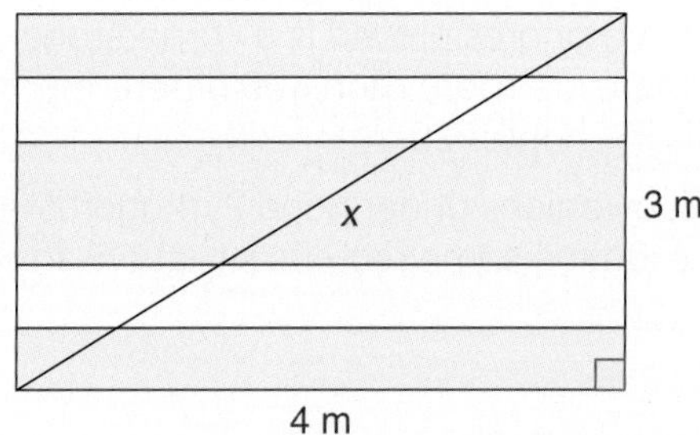

5. A television screen is 120 cm diagonally from corner to corner. If the screen is 100 cm wide, calculate *b*, the height of the screen, correct to the nearest cm.

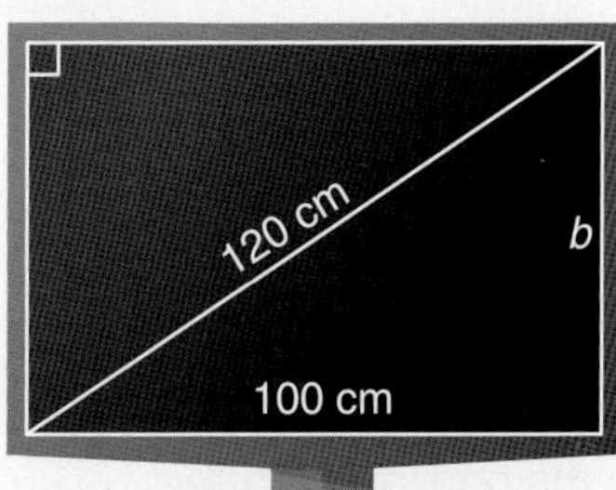

6. A carpenter is making a roof for a house as shown. Calculate the perpendicular height of the roof.

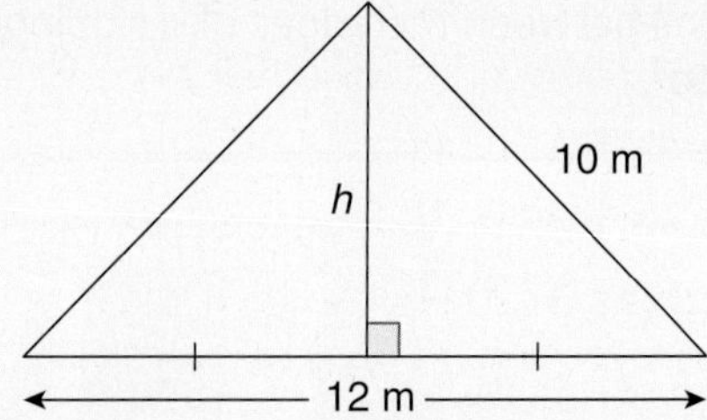

7. A vertical mast on a boat is 7 m high and is tied to the back of the boat by 10 m of rope as shown. Calculate the distance from the back of the boat to the bottom of the mast, correct to the nearest cm.

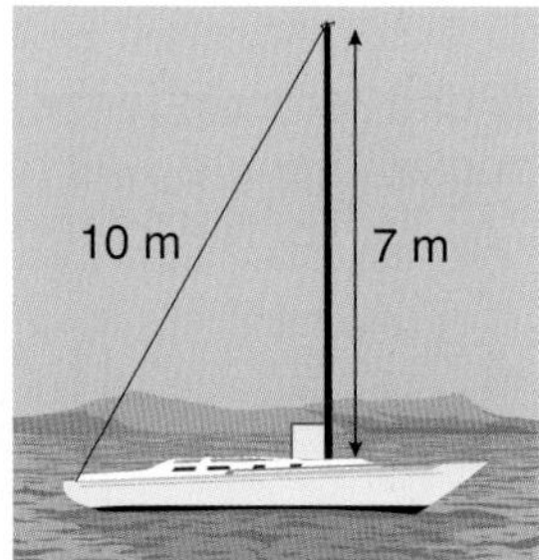

8. A typical iPod Touch has a width of 58.6 mm and slant height of 136.607 mm. Calculate its perpendicular height, correct to one decimal place.

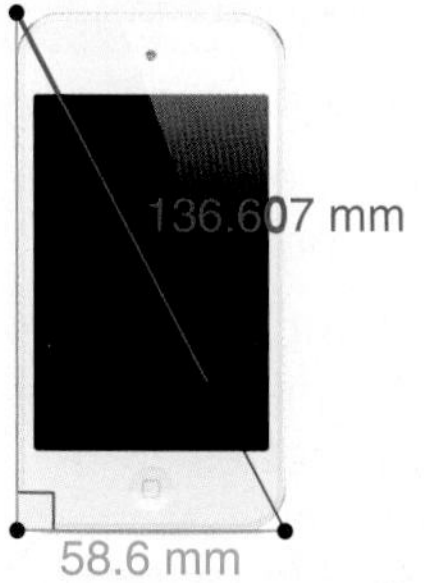

9. A book 250 mm in height leans against the edge of a bookcase at an angle. The foot of the book is 160 mm from the bottom of the shelf. Calculate the perpendicular height of the shelf, correct to the nearest mm.

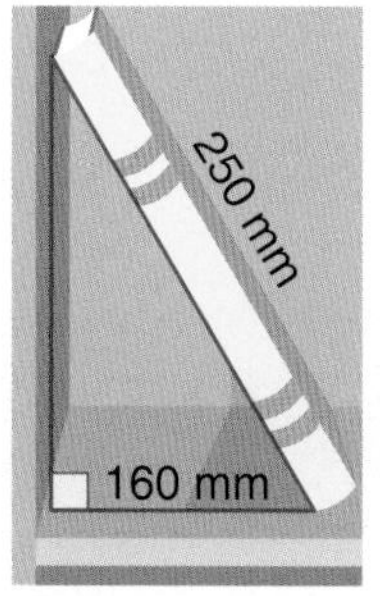

10. Turlough Hill in County Wicklow is Ireland's only pumped storage hydroelectric power station. Its perpendicular height is 681 m, and the generator is located at the foot of the mountain 640 m from the centre. Find the length of the slanted edge where the water flows down, correct to the nearest metre.

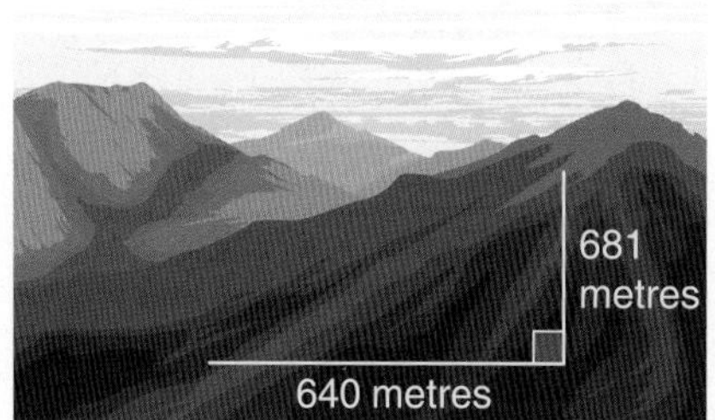

CHAPTER 10 SELF-CHECK TEST

1. Explain what the theorem of Pythagoras states.

2. What is the diagonal distance across a square of the following side lengths? Draw a rough sketch of each square. Give your answers in surd form where necessary.

(a) 1 m
(b) 2 cm
(c) 4 m
(d) 5 cm
(e) 8 mm
(f) 11 km
(g) $\sqrt{7}$ m
(h) $\sqrt{10}$ km
(i) $2\sqrt{3}$ cm
(j) $7\sqrt{5}$ mm

3. What is the length of the diagonal of each rectangle? Give your answers in surd form where necessary.

(a) length 3 cm and width 2 cm
(b) length 17 cm and width 8 cm
(c) length 2 m and width 13 cm
(d) length 6 m and width 99 cm
(e) length $\sqrt{5}$ m and width $\sqrt{2}$ m
(f) length $\sqrt{7}$ m and width $\sqrt{3}$ m
(g) length $4\sqrt{2}$ m and width $5\sqrt{3}$ m
(h) length $6\sqrt{5}$ cm and width $7\sqrt{10}$ m
(i) length $11\sqrt{2}$ mm and width $9\sqrt{13}$ mm
(j) length $0.75\sqrt{6}$ km and width $0.4\sqrt{2}$ km

4. Given the lengths of the three sides of the following triangles, investigate which of the triangles have a right angle:

(a) 8, 15, 16
(b) 10, 24, 26
(c) 17, 21, 29
(d) $\sqrt{3}, \sqrt{5}, \sqrt{8}$
(e) $2\sqrt{7}, 5\sqrt{2}, \sqrt{8}$

5. Which one of the following triangles is **not** a right-angled triangle?

(a)

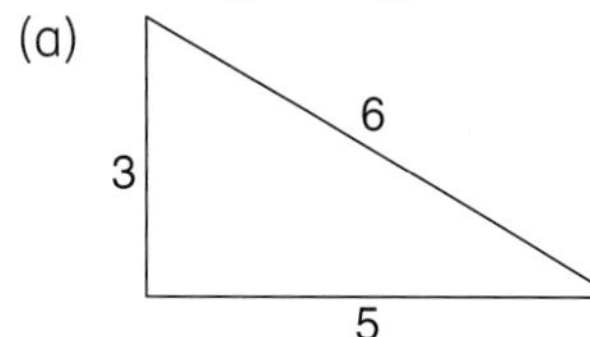

(b)

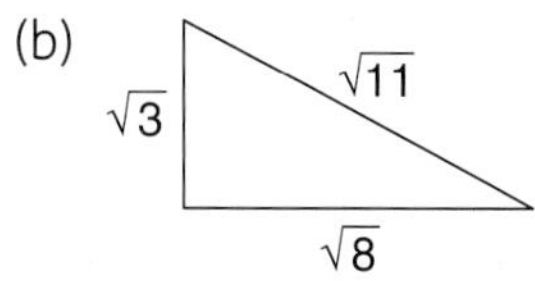

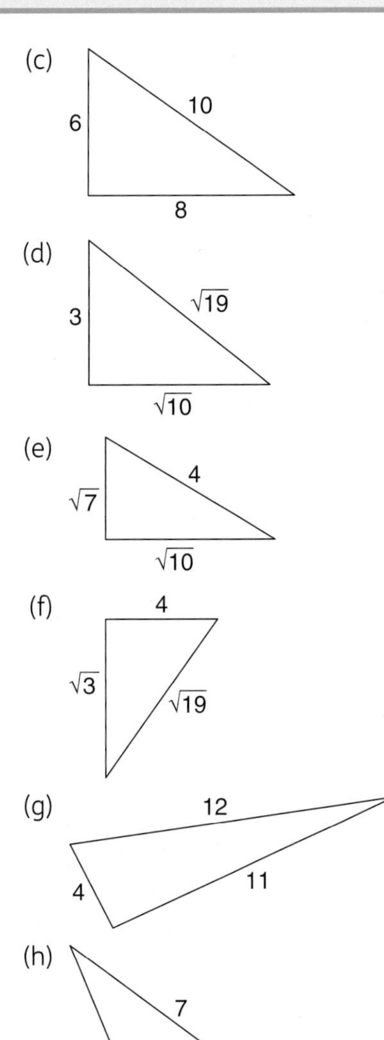

6. A Pythagorean triple is a set of three whole numbers that satisfy the equation $a^2 + b^2 = c^2$. The numbers 20, 21 and 29 make up a Pythagorean triple. Check whether the following numbers can be the measures of the sides of a right-angled triangle.

(a) 8, 15 and 17
(b) 2, 9 and 11
(c) 15, 20 and 25
(d) 20, 48 and 52
(e) 39, 80 and 89
(f) 60, 63 and 87

7. Find the value of x in the following right-angled triangles:
   (a) Sides x and $(x + 3)$ and hypotenuse $3\sqrt{5}$
   (b) Sides x and $(2x - 1)$ and hypotenuse $(2x + 1)$

8. The sail of a keelboat forms a right-angled triangle. Find the base length of each of the following sails if:

   (a) The slant height is $20\sqrt{3}$ metres and its perpendicular height is $10\sqrt{3}$ metres
   (b) The slant height is $34\sqrt{5}$ metres and its perpendicular height is $30\sqrt{5}$ metres

9. A ramp runs from the back of a trailer to a road. The length of the ramp is 3.7 metres and the horizontal distance from the bottom of the ramp to the base of the trailer is 1.2 metres. Calculate the perpendicular height from the road to the top of the ramp.

10. (a) Fireman Bob has a 5.2 m long ladder. Safety instructions for all ladders tell him that he should put the base at least 1.5 m away from the base of whatever he is using the ladder to climb. How tall is the tallest building that Bob can climb using his ladder, correct to the nearest cm?
    (b) An 8 m ladder stands on horizontal ground and reaches 6.8 m up a vertical wall. How far is the foot of the ladder from the base of the wall, correct to two decimal places?
    (c) Is the position of this ladder obeying Bob's safety laws? Explain your answer.

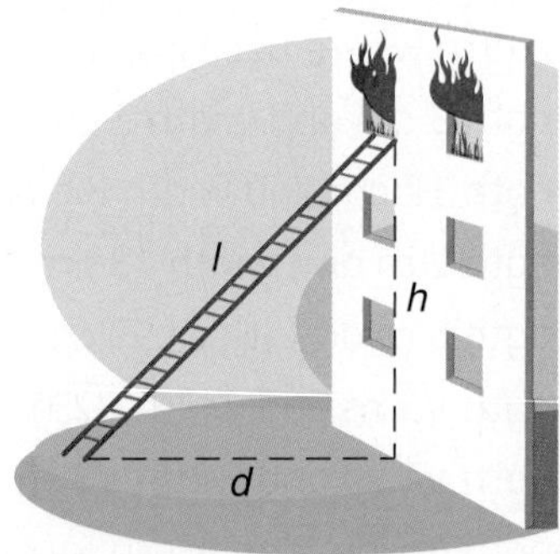

11. (a) A rectangular field is 125 m long and the length of one diagonal of the field is 145 m. What is the width of the field?

(b) Another rectangular field is 225 m long and the length of one diagonal of the field is 250 m. What is the width of the field?

12. The diagram shows a kite *ABCD*. The diagonals cut at right angles and intersect at *O*. What is the length of the diagonal *AC*?

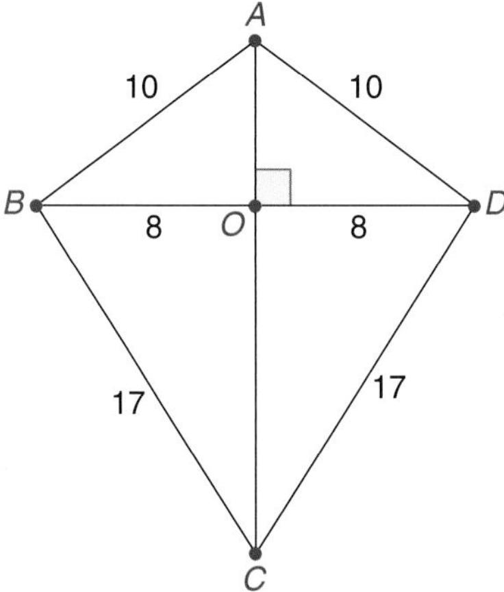

13. Town B is 15 km north of town C and 20 km east of town A. What is the shortest distance between the two towns A and C?

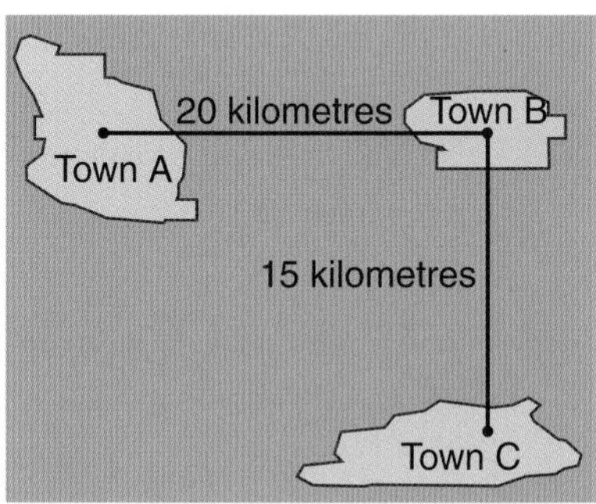

14. What is the length of the side marked *x*?

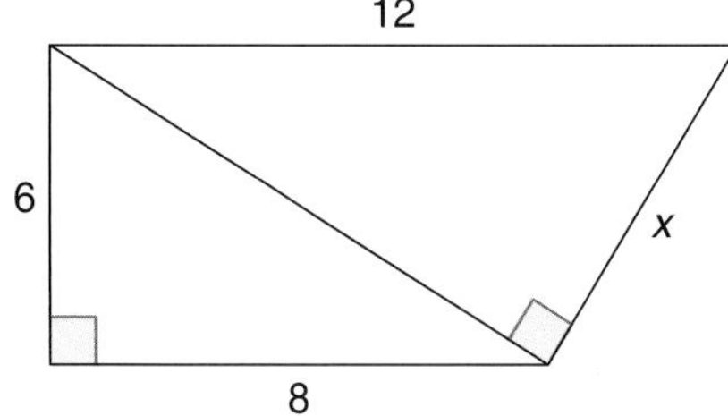

15. A tent is supported by a rope tied to a stake, as shown in the diagram. What is the length of the rope, correct to the nearest cm?

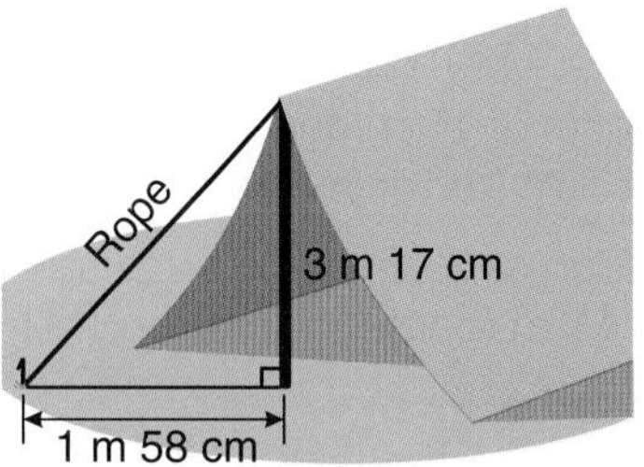

16. The great pyramid at Giza in Egypt is 146 m high and has a base width of 219 m. Calculate the length of the slanted edge, correct to the nearest metre.

17. A bridge is 386 m in length. A cable connected to the middle of the bridge is exactly 225 m in length. Calculate, correct to the nearest m, the height of the tower to which the cable is connected.

18. The Boston Red Sox baseball stadium has a field approximately 198 m wide and 217 m long.

(a) Calculate the total perimeter of the field.

(b) Calculate the length of the diagonal of the field, correct to the nearest m.

(c) During a training session, a baseball player must jog 20 full laps of the field. How many times would the player have to run diagonally to complete the equivalent distance?

19. The diagram on the right shows a drawing of a roof. Assume the roof is an isosceles triangle, making a right angle at the apex (top point). Calculate the missing measurement given in brackets. Give your answer correct to the nearest cm, given:

(a) Roof span of 15 m and perpendicular height 3 m (rafter line)

(b) Roof span of 19.8 m and each rafter line is 11 m (perpendicular height)

(c) Roof span of 13 m 42 cm and perpendicular height 6.5 m (rafter line)

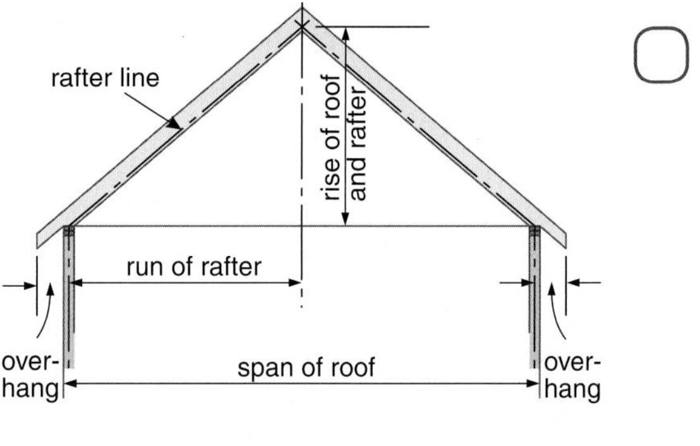

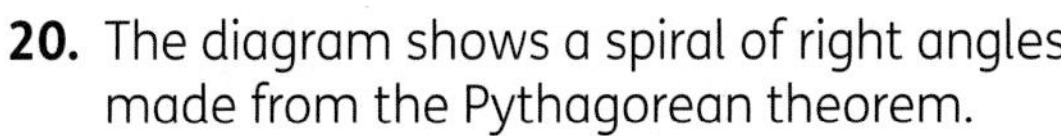

20. The diagram shows a spiral of right angles made from the Pythagorean theorem.

(a) Use the theorem of Pythagoras to find the value of a in surd form.

(b) Find the value of f in surd form.

(c) Continue on the pattern for the next ten triangles, leaving your answer in surd form. Describe the pattern in words and in table form.

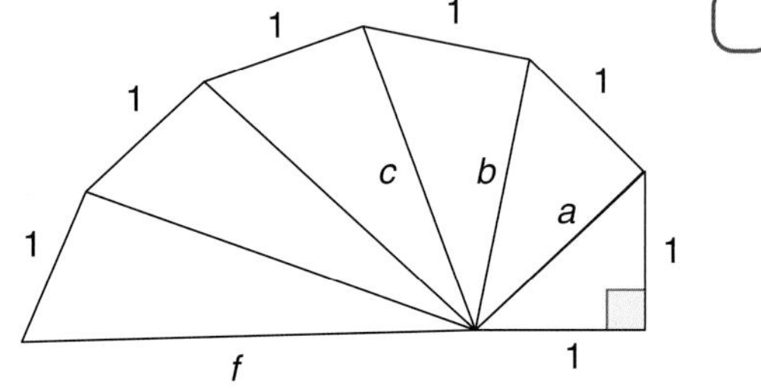

(d) Now using an A4 page, a set square, a ruler and a compass, construct the first 15 triangles of this famous pattern using the exact measurements calculated earlier.

(e) Explain why this construction that goes on to infinity is better known as the Pythagorean snail.

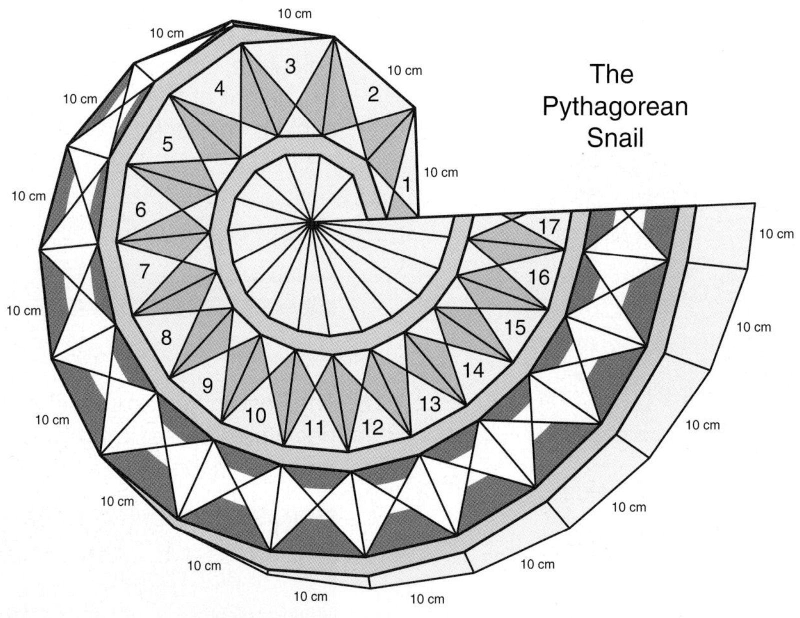

CHAPTER 10 KNOWLEDGE CHECKLIST

After completing this chapter I now:

- **Know about the theorem of Pythagoras and its converse**
- **Am able to identify the hypotenuse in a right-angled triangle**
- **Am able to solve problems involving right-angled triangles**

Challenge

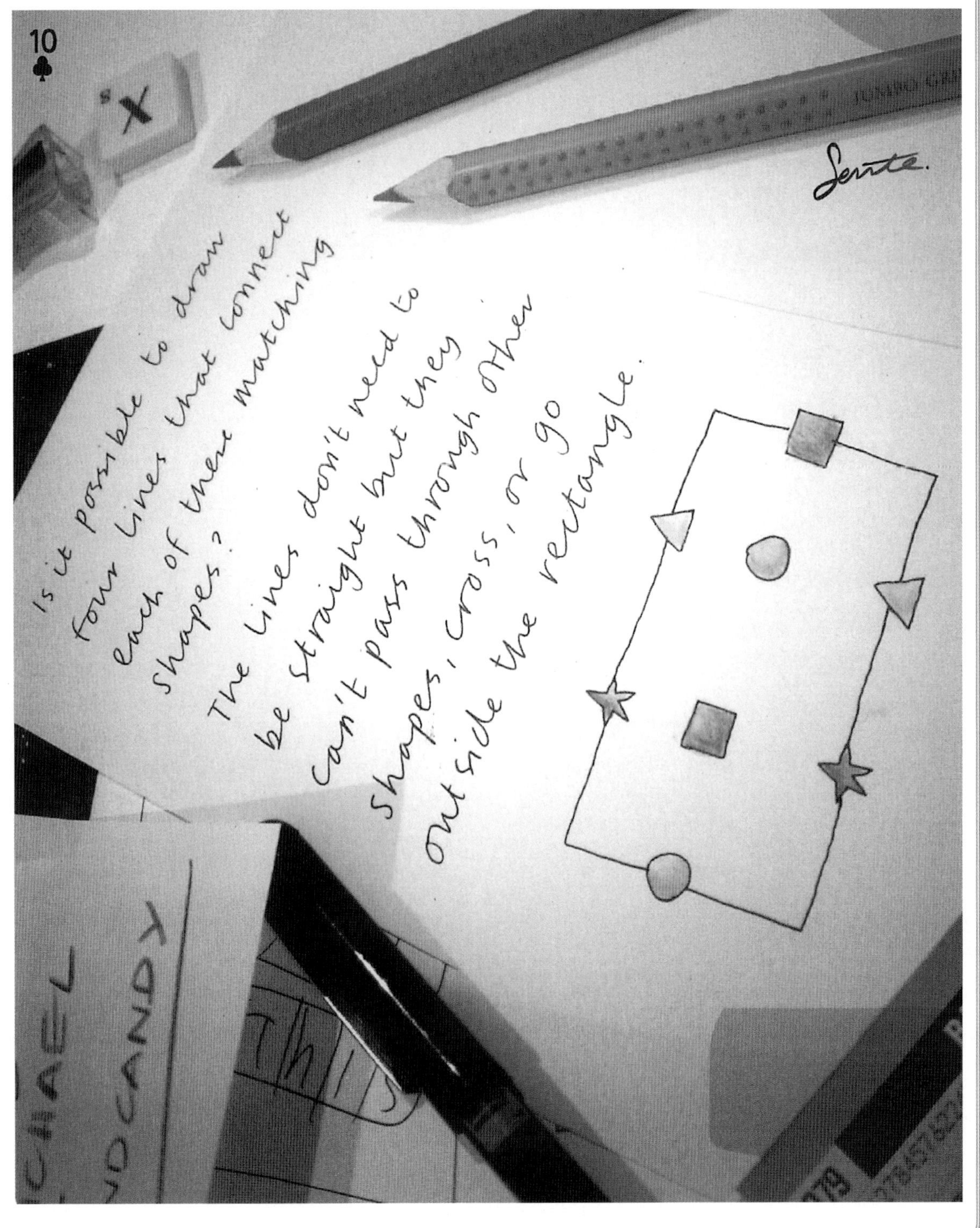
10 ♣
Is it possible to draw
four lines that connect
each of these matching
shapes?
The lines don't need to
be straight but they
can't pass through other
shapes, cross, or go
outside the rectangle.
Sente.

APPLIED ARITHMETIC 1

KEY WORDS

- Compound interest
- Cost price
- Depreciation
- Discount
- Foreign exchange
- Interest
- Loss
- Mark-up
- Percentage
- Principal
- Profit
- Profit margin
- Sale
- Selling price
- Standing charge
- VAT

LEARNING OUTCOMES

In this chapter you will learn:

- ✓ To calculate a quantity from a given percentage
- ✓ To calculate profit and loss as a percentage of cost price
- ✓ To calculate discounts and percentage discounts
- ✓ To apply percentages to mobile phone bills, meter readings and bills containing VAT and standing charges
- ✓ To carry out currency transactions
- ✓ To calculate percentage rates
- ✓ To calculate compound interest and depreciation
- ✓ To calculate percentage mark-up and percentage profit margins
- ✓ To calculate profit and loss as a percentage of sale price

INTRODUCTION

In *Maths in Action 1*, you learned how to change between fractions, decimals and percentages. You also learned how to find a percentage of a number.

In this chapter, you will learn how to apply this knowledge in real-life situations. Whether it is the amount paid for an item bought in a sale or the tax on a person's wages, percentages are used all the time.

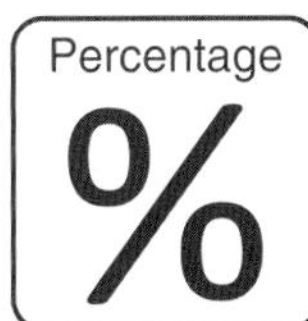

First year revision

1. Explain how to change a fraction to a percentage.
2. Change each of the following fractions to (i) a decimal and (ii) a percentage:

(a) $\frac{1}{2}$ (b) $\frac{1}{4}$ (c) $\frac{4}{10}$ (d) $\frac{1}{5}$ (e) $\frac{1}{20}$

(f) $\frac{1}{50}$ (g) $\frac{4}{5}$ (h) $\frac{21}{25}$ (i) $\frac{2}{10}$ (j) $\frac{1}{100}$

(k) $\frac{1}{40}$ (l) $\frac{1}{3}$ (m) $\frac{12}{20}$ (n) $\frac{4}{5}$ (o) $\frac{3}{8}$

(p) $\frac{19}{25}$ (q) $\frac{6}{9}$ (r) $\frac{10}{12}$ (s) $\frac{50}{100}$ (t) $\frac{9}{15}$

3. Divide €150 in the ratio of 2:3.
4. Cement and sand are mixed in the ratio 5:11. If 45 kg of cement is used in a mix, how much sand is needed?
5. Four men can build a wall in 12 days. If all men worked at the same rate, how long would it take:

(a) 1 man? (b) 6 men? (c) 2 men?

Section 11.1: Calculating a quantity from a given percentage

Student Activity 11A

1. $\frac{3}{4}$ of a number is 27.
   (a) Find $\frac{1}{4}$ of the number.
   (b) Find the whole number $\left(\text{i.e. } \frac{4}{4}\right)$.
   (c) Express $\frac{3}{4}$ as a percentage.
   (d) If 75% of a number is 27, how would you find 1% of the number?
   (e) Explain how you would find the full number (i.e. 100%).

2. $\frac{4}{10}$ of a number is 520.
   (a) Find $\frac{1}{10}$ of the number.
   (b) Find the whole number $\left(\text{i.e. } \frac{10}{10}\right)$.
   (c) Express $\frac{4}{10}$ as a percentage.
   (d) If 75% of a number is 520, how would you find 1% of the number?
   (e) Explain how you would find the full number (i.e. 100%).

CALCULATING A QUANTITY FROM A GIVEN PERCENTAGE EXPLAINED

In *Maths in Action 1*, you learned how to calculate a certain percentage of a given number.

- Always let the starting amount equal 100%.
- Divide the starting amount by 100 to calculate 1%.
- Then multiply by the percentage required.

This can be summarised using the following formula:

$$\text{Percentage of a number} = \frac{\text{Number}}{100} \times \%\text{ required}$$

If you are told a certain value equals a percentage of the whole value:

- Divide by the percentage to calculate 1%.
- Next multiply your answer by 100 and this gives you the missing value.

This can be summarised using the following formula:

$$\text{Missing value} = \frac{\text{Number given}}{\%\text{ given}} \times 100$$

EXAMPLE 1

(a) Calculate 17.5% of €3,000.

(b) If 56% of a number is 448, find the number.

Solution

(a) **Method 1**

100% = 3,000

$1\% = \frac{3{,}000}{100} = 30$

17.5% = 30 × 17.5 = €525

Method 2: Using your calculator

On a Casio calculator, type:

3,000 × 17.5 to get €525

Hit the 'Shift' button followed by the '%' button

On a Sharp calculator, type:

3,000 × 17.5 to get €525

Hit the '2ndF' button followed by the '%' button

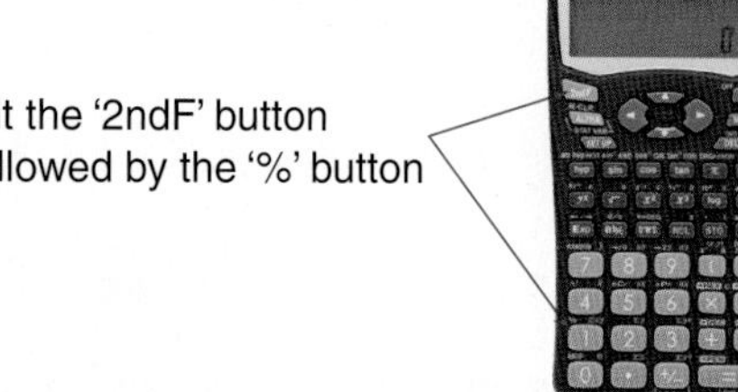

(b) **Method 1**

56% = 448

$1\% = \frac{448}{56} = 8$

100% = 8 × 100 = 800

Method 2: Using your calculator

$\frac{448}{56}\% = 800$

Exercise 11.1

1. $\frac{13}{100}$ of a number is 182.

(a) Find $\frac{1}{100}$ of the number.

(b) Find the whole number $\left(\text{i.e. } \frac{100}{100}\right)$.

(c) Express $\frac{13}{100}$ as a percentage.

2. 26% of a number is 312.
   (a) Find 1% the number.
   (b) Find the whole number.
3. If 14% of a number is 126, find the number.
4. If 27% of a number is 162, find the number.
5. If 45% of a number is 405, find the number.
6. If 3% of a number is 366, find the number.
7. If 92% of a number is 1,104, find the number.
8. If 78% of a number is 1,053, find the number.
9. If 22.5% of a number is 585, find the number.
10. If 51.7% of a number is 258.5, find the number.
11. If 21% of a number is 1,785, find the number.
12. If 13.5% of a number is 783, find the number.
13. A restaurant adds a service charge of 10% to all bills. If the service charge was €12.75, how much was the total bill?
14. A builder adds 13.5% tax to his bill for work on a house. If the tax came to €1,687.50, how much was the builder's total invoice.
15. A bank charges a 2% commission on all money transactions. If the bank charge was €23.50, how much money was involved in the transaction?
16. 7% interest is applied to a short-term personal loan. If the interest totals €392 over the life of the loan, how much money was borrowed?
17. An internet site charges a 2.5% charge on all credit card transactions. If the charge for a certain transaction was €30, what was the value of the transaction?
18. A tax of 21% is added to the price of a television. If the tax amounted to €113.40, calculate the selling price of the television.
19. A charge of 15% is added to a bill in a restaurant. If the charge amounted to €33.75, calculate the total bill including the charge.
20. An electrician charges 13.5% tax on his work. If the tax for a particular job amounts to €101.25, calculate the total price of the job.
21. An online store charges 5% for all credit card transactions. If the charge on a certain transaction is €13.70, calculate the total price of the transaction, including the charge.
22. A tax of 21% is added to the price of a mobile phone bill. If the tax amounts to €47.04, calculate the total price of the bill, including the tax.

Section 11.2: Profit and loss as a percentage of the cost price

Student Activity 11B

1. What do you understand by the term 'profit'?
2. What do you understand by the term 'loss'?
3. What do you understand by the term 'cost price'?
4. What do you understand by the term 'selling price'?
5. Study the table, which shows the cost price and selling price for a number of items.
   (a) State whether each item was sold at a profit or at a loss.
   (b) Calculate the profit or the loss for each item.
   (c) Create a fraction for each using either the formula $\frac{\text{Profit}}{\text{Cost price}}$ or $\frac{\text{Loss}}{\text{Cost price}}$.
   (d) Change each fraction to a percentage.

Cost price	Selling price
(i) €50	€60
(ii) €100	€147.50
(iii) €230	€190
(iv) €190	€210
(v) €200	€200.10
(vi) €199	€198.99
(vii) €55	€45

PROFIT AND LOSS AS A PERCENTAGE OF THE COST PRICE EXPLAINED

A **profit** is made when something is sold for more than it cost to buy or produce.
A **loss** is made when something is sold for less than it cost to buy or produce.

Any **profit** or **loss** can be expressed as a percentage of the **cost price.**

$$\text{Percentage profit on cost price} = \frac{\text{Profit}}{\text{Cost price}} \times \frac{100}{1}$$

$$\text{Percentage loss on cost price} = \frac{\text{Loss}}{\text{Cost price}} \times \frac{100}{1}$$

EXAMPLE 2

(a) A hardware store buys a lawnmower for €150 and sells it for €240. Calculate:

(i) The amount of profit the store made

(ii) The percentage profit on the cost price

Solution

(a) (i) Profit = €240 − €150

Profit = €90

(ii) $\% \text{ Profit on the cost price} = \frac{90}{150} \times \frac{100}{1}$

% Profit on the cost price = 60%

(b) A phone shop is having a clearance sale of old phones. It sells one phone for €119.99. The phone originally cost the shop €150.

(i) Is the shop making a profit or a loss? Explain your answer.

(ii) Calculate the amount of profit or loss.

(iii) Express this profit or loss as a percentage of the cost price, correct to the nearest whole number.

Solution

(b) (i) The shop is making a loss as it is selling the phone for less than it paid for it.

(ii) Loss = €150 − €119.99

Loss = €30.01

(iii) $\% \text{ Loss} = \frac{30.01}{150} \times \frac{100}{1}$

% Loss = 20.006%

% Loss = 20% **Correct to the nearest whole number**

(c) A computer game was sold for a 20% profit on the cost price. If the profit was €5, what was the original price of the game?

Solution

(c) 20% = €5

1% = 5 ÷ 20

100% = 5 ÷ 20 × 100

100% = 25

Cost price = €25

Exercise 11.2

1. Calculate the percentage profit or loss for each of the following, correct to the nearest whole number:

Cost price	Selling price
(a) €25	€30
(b) €55	€65
(c) €42	€35
(d) €20	€22
(e) €10	€8
(f) €15	€25
(g) €125	€150
(h) €20.50	€29.99
(i) €9.45	€19.95
(j) €27.85	€22.50

2. A clothes shop purchases jeans at a cost of €12 a pair. The jeans sell for €49.99. Calculate the percentage profit on the cost price.
3. A car dealer bought a used car for €4,500. If he sold it for €3,900 12 months later, what was his percentage loss?
4. An item was sold online for a profit of 20% on the cost price. If the profit was €24, what was the original cost of the item?
5. A coat was sold for a loss of 15% on the cost price. If the loss was €14.40, what was the original cost of the coat?
6. A racehorse was sold for a profit of 18.5% on the cost price. If the profit was €629, how much did the horse cost originally?
7. A restored motorbike was sold for a profit of 45% on the cost price. If the profit was €420, what was the original cost of the motorbike?
8. A car was sold at a loss of 43% on the cost price. If the car was sold for €11,970, calculate the cost price of the car.
9. A house was sold for a loss of 24.5% on the cost price. If the loss was €78,400, what was the original cost of the house?
10. A piece of land was sold for a profit of 18.7% on the cost price. If the profit made was €23,936, calculate the cost price of the piece of land.

Section 11.3: Profit and loss as a percentage of the selling price

Student Activity 11C

1. Paul bought a car at a cost of €1,200. Two years later he sold it at a loss of 25%.
   (a) Calculate 25% of €1,200.
   (b) Should the selling price be more or less than €1,200? Explain your answer.
   (c) Calculate the selling price and explain how you got your answer.
2. Siobhán bought a painting for €3,000. Several years later, she sold it for a profit of 10%.
   (a) Find 10% of €3,000.
   (b) Should the selling price be more or less than €3,000? Explain your answer.
   (c) Calculate the selling price and explain how you got your answer.

PROFIT AND LOSS AS A PERCENTAGE OF THE SELLING PRICE EXPLAINED

All retail businesses need to be able to calculate the selling price of the items they sell. This enables them to sell items at a high enough price to cover their costs and to make a profit.

EXAMPLE 3

(a) An electrical wholesaler buys DVD players at a cost of €58 per unit. She sells them later at a profit of 39%. Calculate the selling price, correct to the nearest euro.

(b) A new car was purchased for €25,000. Two years later, it is sold for €15,000. Calculate:

(i) The loss

(ii) The loss as a percentage of the selling price

Solution

(a) Profit $= \frac{39}{100} \times 58$

Profit = €22.62

Selling price = €58 + €22.62

Selling price = €80.62

Selling price = €81 **Correct to the nearest euro**

(b) (i) Loss = €25,000 − €15,000

Loss = €10,000

(ii) % Loss on the selling price $= \frac{10{,}000}{25{,}000} \times 100$

% Loss on the selling price = 40%

Exercise 11.3

Calculate the selling price for each of the following items:

1. Cost price = €100, Profit = 23%
2. Cost price = €57, Profit = 19%
3. Cost price = €325, Profit = 18.5%
4. Cost price = €34, Profit = 7.5%
5. Cost price = €90, Profit = 30%
6. Cost price = €250, Loss = 20%
7. Cost price = €85, Loss = 23%
8. Cost price = €460, Loss = 35%
9. Cost price = €1,250, Loss = 12.5%
10. Cost price = €4,670, Profit = 20%
11. Cost price = €357, Loss = 21%
12. Cost price = €489, Profit = 22.5%
13. Cost price = €1,790, Profit = 19%
14. Cost price = €10,980, Loss = 15%
15. Cost price = €9,870, Profit = 17.5%
16. A shopkeeper bought an item for €19 and wants to sell it for a profit of 41%. What price should the item be sold for?
17. A house was bought for €350,000 and was sold two years later for a loss of 36.5%. Calculate the selling price of the house.
18. An antique painting was originally bought for €52,500 and was later sold at an auction for a profit of 26%. Calculate the price of the painting at the auction.
19. Five acres of land originally purchased for €267,000 was later sold at a loss of 23%. How much was the land sold for?
20. A greyhound was bought for €540. After winning two races, the greyhound was sold for a profit of 39.5%. How much was the greyhound sold for?
21. An item is bought for €100 and resold for €98. Calculate the loss as a percentage of the selling price.
22. A farmer purchased land at a cost of €250,000. The land was later sold to a property developer for €340,000. Calculate the profit as a percentage of the selling price.
23. A computer game was purchased for €59.99 and resold online for €25.99. Calculate the loss as a percentage of the selling price, correct to one decimal place.
24. An antique table was bought for €135. After being restored, it was sold at an auction for €375. Calculate the profit as a percentage of the selling price.

Section 11.4: Calculating discounts and percentage discounts

Student Activity 11D

1. During the Christmas sales, a shop manager decides to offer a discount of 10% on all items.
   (a) A shirt costs €100 before the sale. Find 10% of the cost of the shirt.
   (b) After applying the discount, find the sale price of the shirt.
2. A holiday company offers a 15% discount on all holidays during the month of May. A family purchased a holiday at a total cost of €1,275.
   (a) Calculate 15% of the cost of the holiday.
   (b) How much will the holiday cost after the discount has been applied?
3. A shop offers €5 off all products for one day only.
   (a) If a game cost €50, how much will it be sold for on this day?
   (b) What percentage discount did the shop offer on the game?

CALCULATING DISCOUNTS AND PERCENTAGE DISCOUNTS EXPLAINED

A **discount** is a reduction in the price of an item or a service. A discount reduces the price of something.

Retail businesses often use discounts during sales to encourage customers to buy a product and as a way of selling older stock. As shoppers, it is important to be able to calculate both the discount in actual money and as a percentage.

$$\text{Percentage discount} = \frac{\text{Discount offered}}{\text{Sale price}} \times 100$$

Sometimes an item loses its value for other reasons, such as **depreciation.** Cars can lose around 20% of their value within the first year. Depreciation is calculated in the same way as a discount.

Depreciation is a decrease in value.

EXAMPLE 4

(a) A car dealer offers a 5% discount on all new cars for one week. If a certain car normally costs €22,500, how much will it cost after the discount is applied?

Solution

(a) **Method 1**

Find 1% of the cost: $\frac{22{,}500}{100}$ = €225

Therefore, 5% of the cost: €225 × 5 = €1,125

Sale price = €22,500 − €1,125

Cost price − Discount

Sale price = €21,375

Method 2

If the dealer is offering a discount of 5%, it means she is selling the car for 95% of the cost price.

Find 1% of the cost: $\frac{22{,}500}{100}$ = €225

Therefore, 95% of the cost:
€225 × 95 = €21,375

(b) A phone shop offers a €12 discount on all phones for one day. If a phone normally costs €192, what percentage discount is the store offering? What will be the sale price of the phone?

Solution

(b) Percentage discount: $\frac{12}{192} \times 100 = 6.25\%$

Sale price = 192 – 12 = €180

Exercise 11.4

1. Calculate the discount and the percentage discount for each of the following, correct to one decimal place:

Original selling price	Discounted price
(a) €150	€135
(b) €120	€107
(c) €95	€82
(d) €55	€49
(e) €39.99	€29.99
(f) €199.95	€179.95
(g) €999.99	€900
(h) €1500	€1,375
(i) €47.50	€40
(j) €19.99	€15

2. An electrical wholesaler offers a 12.5% discount on all items during a bank holiday weekend. Calculate the discounted price for each of the following items:

(a) A washing machine with a price of €350

(b) A microwave with a price of €190

(c) A DVD player with a price of €450

(d) An LCD television with a price of €990

(e) An electric oven with a price of €685

3. A store offers a €5 discount on all products during a sale. Calculate the percentage discount for each of the following items:

(a) A computer game priced at €60

(b) A CD priced at €19.99

(c) A phone priced at €126

(d) A pack of blank DVDs priced at €24

(e) A boxset of DVDs priced at €55

(f) A digital camera priced at €240

(g) A games console priced at €199.99

4. A machine costs €18,000 to purchase new.

(a) If it depreciated in value by 22% in the first year, find its value at the end of the first year.

(b) In the second year, the machine depreciated by a further 15%. What is its value at the end of the second year?

5. A new car depreciates by 10% the moment it is driven from a car dealership. For the next three years, it depreciates at a rate of 12% per annum. After the three years, it depreciates by 8% per annum.

Per annum means per year.

(a) If Michael purchases a new car for €28,000, how much will it be worth after 5 years? Give your answer correct to the nearest euro.

(b) If Donna buys a six-year-old car for €6,000, how much did the car cost when it was originally bought?

6. A farmer purchases a new tractor at a cost of €25,000. It depreciates at 9% per annum. Calculate the value of the tractor after 3 years.

7. A new yacht costing €150,000 depreciates in value by 11.5% per annum. Calculate the value of the yacht after 3 years.

8. A house was purchased for €250,000. During the boom years, it rose in value by 12% per annum for 3 years. When the recession hit, its value fell by 8.9% per annum for 4 years. Calculate the value of the house after 7 years, correct to the nearest euro.

9. A motorbike costs €18,550 and depreciates at 6% per annum. Calculate the value of the motorbike after 3 years.

Section 11.5: Value added tax (VAT) and other charges

Student Activity 11E

1. What is VAT?
2. What do the terms 'inclusive' and 'exclusive' mean?
3. If an item is priced at €121 **inclusive** of VAT, would the selling price of the item be less than or more than €121? Explain your answer.
4. If an item is priced at €121 **exclusive** of VAT, would the cost price of the item be less than or more than €121? Explain your answer.
5. The price of a phone in a shop is €100 **exclusive** of VAT at 10%.
   (a) Calculate the amount of VAT to be added to the price of the phone.
   (b) Calculate the selling price of the phone.

VALUE ADDED TAX (VAT) AND OTHER CHARGES EXPLAINED

Value added tax (VAT) is a tax charged by the government. It is often included in the price of goods a customer buys. It is added to anything from a bar of chocolate to a car. Self-employed people such as builders and carpenters add VAT to their bill. The rate of VAT varies from year to year and is different in each country.

VAT is always charged on the original cost figure. In 2014 in Ireland, the VAT rate for most goods was 23%, while the VAT for services was 13.5%.

Other charges can also appear on bills. Standing charges are charged by companies such as phone companies for supplying fixed lines to a house. Tradesmen such as electricians often charge a call-out charge.

EXAMPLE 5

(a) A car is priced at €19,000 exclusive of VAT at 21%. Calculate the selling price of the car.

(b) A television is priced at €60.50 inclusive of VAT at 21%. Calculate the price of the television exclusive of VAT.

Solution

(a) Amount of VAT: $19{,}000 \div 100 \times 21 = €3{,}990$

Selling price = €19,000 + €3,990 = €22,990

(b) **Note:** VAT is already included so the total selling percentage is 121%.

121% = €60.50

1% = €60.50 ÷ 121 = 0.5

100% = $0.5 \times 100 = 50$

Price exclusive of VAT = €50

In the following exercise you will use many different VAT rates to practise calculating VAT.

Exercise 11.5

1. Calculate the amount of VAT and total price of each of the following:

Price	VAT rate
(a) €30	21%
(b) €120	13.5%
(c) €840	12%
(d) €147	11%
(e) €250	26%
(f) €24	13.5%
(g) €25	21%
(h) €9	14%
(i) €79	19%
(j) €1300	17.5%

2. Each of the following prices is inclusive of VAT. Calculate their prices without VAT.

Price	VAT rate
(a) €181.50	21%
(b) €227	13.5%
(c) €365.94	14%
(d) €192.50	10%
(e) €111.60	24%
(f) €52.65	17%
(g) €2832	18%
(h) €1,7948.70	15.5%
(i) €4,923.50	14.5%
(j) €193.05	17%

3. Copy and complete the following electricity bill:

Present reading	11,450
Previous reading	10,250
Number of units used	______
Cost @ 8.5c per unit	€______
VAT @ 13.5%	€______
Total price	**€______**

4. A carpenter supplies a quote of €2,300 for a job. Calculate the total price if VAT at 13.5% must also be charged.

5. A mobile phone bill comes to €110 exclusive of VAT at 21%. Calculate the total bill.

6. A restaurant places a 12% VAT charge on all of their bills. Calculate the total bill if the price for a group's meal exclusive of VAT amounts to €165.

7. A garage charges €249.70 inclusive of VAT at 13.5% for a full service. Calculate:
   (a) The amount of VAT
   (b) The price without VAT

8. VAT at 15% is included in a hotel bill at €228.85. Calculate the price without VAT.

9. A mobile phone package costing €40 per month includes 100 free text messages and 40 minutes of free calls to any network. In a particular month, a person sends 140 text messages and spends 50 minutes talking on the phone. Calculate:
   (a) The cost of the extra text messages at 10c per text
   (b) The cost of calls at 20 cent per minute
   (c) The total cost of the phone bill for the month
   (d) The price if VAT at 14% is added to the bill

10. A car is sold at a price of €34,200 inclusive of VAT at 20%. Calculate the price of the car without VAT.

11. A Blu-ray player costs €320 exclusive of VAT at 22.5%. Calculate the selling price of the Blu-ray player.

12. An item is priced at €275 including VAT at 10%. Calculate the price of the item without VAT.

13. A €20 mobile top-up charge includes VAT charged at 20%. Calculate the price of the top-up without VAT.

14. A coat is priced at €179.08 inclusive of VAT at 21%.
    (a) Calculate the price without VAT.
    (b) The VAT rate is increased to 24%. Calculate the new selling price inclusive of VAT.

15. A television is priced at €255 exclusive of VAT at 20%. Calculate:
    (a) The amount of VAT on the television
    (b) The total price of the television
    (c) If the VAT rate was increased to 25%, by how much would the price of the television increase?

16. Laura receives a phone bill. It reads as follows:
    Standing charge of €22
    Texts 223 @ 10c per text
    Landline calls 53 @ 42c per minute
    Other network calls 68 @ 18c per call
    (a) Calculate Laura's bill.
    (b) VAT at 13.5% is then applied to the total amount. How much must Laura pay in total to the nearest cent?

17. An electrician charges a fixed call-out charge of €30. He then charges €40 per hour. If he works in a house for 3.5 hours, calculate:
    (a) His total charge
    (b) The total bill if VAT at 13.5% is added on

Section 11.6: Currency transactions

When you go on holiday in countries that do not use the euro, you must change your currency. This is known as **foreign exchange.** You can do this at the Bureau de Change in your local bank or post office. The bank usually charges a small commission for each transaction, as a payment for this service.

It is important to understand what the currency exchange rates mean. For example, €1 = STG£0.89 means that for every euro you give a bank, they will give you back 89 pence sterling.

Every foreign exchange board has two columns called 'We Buy' and 'We Sell'. These contain the different rates. The 'We Buy' column gives the exchange rate for tourists coming into Ireland, who want to exchange their currency for euro. The 'We Sell' column gives the exchange rate for people who need a different currency to spend abroad.

When changing from one currency to another, you will either multiply or divide by the exchange rate. A useful tip is to keep the currency you are looking for on the right-hand side in your calculations.

The rules are simple to follow:

1. When changing from € to another currency, multiply by the exchange rate.
2. When changing from another currency to €, divide by the exchange rate.

EXAMPLE 6

(a) A man wants to change €200 into sterling. If the exchange rate is €1 = STG£0.87, how much sterling will the man receive?

(b) On returning to Ireland from a foreign holiday, a person wants to change US$468 back to euro. If the exchange rate offered on the day is €1 = US$1.20, how much in euro will the person receive?

(c) Jill wants to change €700 into dollars when the exchange rate is €1 = US$1.15. The bank charges a 2% commission fee on the transaction. How much in dollars will Jill receive?

Solution

(a) If €1 = STG £0.87

Then €200 × 0.87

= STG£174

(b) $1.20 = €1

Then $468 ÷ 1.20

= €390

(c) €700 × 1.15 = US$805

Commission = 805 ÷ 100 × 2 = US$16.10

$805 − $16.10 = US$788.90

Exercise 11.6

1. Match each currency with its country:

Currency
US$
Yen
Euro
Baht
Rand
NZ$
Peso
Dong

Country
Thailand
New Zealand
Vietnam
USA
Japan
Cuba
South Africa
Latvia

2. A tourist wants to change currency when the exchange rate is €1 = STG£0.79. How much will the tourist get if she changes:

(a) €260 to sterling?

(b) €500 to sterling?

(c) STG£592.50 to euro?

(d) STG£948 to euro?

(e) If the bank charges 5% commission on each transaction, how much will the tourist receive for each of the transactions?

3. A bank offers the following exchange rates:

€1= US$1.30, €1 = STG£0.81, €1 = ¥25,200 (Japanese yen).
Convert each of the following:

(a) €510 to yen

(b) €300 to US$

(c) US$975 to euro

(d) ¥15,120,000 to euro

(e) ¥15,120,000 to US$

(f) STG£340.20 to euro

(g) STG£340.20 to yen

(h) US$325 to sterling

(i) STG£263.25 to yen

(j) ¥11,340,000 to US$

4. A businessman is travelling from Ireland to England and then on to Thailand. He wants to change €250 to sterling and €500 to baht (the Thai currency). The exchange rate offered is €1 = STG£0.87 = 42 baht. The bank charges 5% on each transaction. How much will the businessman receive in each currency?

5. A family are travelling to South Africa for a safari. The exchange rate offered is €1 = 2.4 rand (the South African currency). The bank charges a 2.5% charge on all transactions.

(a) If the family change €3,500 how much in rand will they receive?

(b) On arriving in South Africa, they see the exchange rate offered by a bank is €1 = 2.6 rand with a charge of 3.5%. Would the family have got better value if they changed their money in South Africa? Explain your answer.

6. (a) A car in England sells for STG£16,198 and the same car in Ireland sells for €18,999. If €1 = STG£0.89 in which country is the car cheaper and by how much?

(b) An Irish person decides to import the car. If the import tax on the car is 22% of the cost price, is the car still cheaper? What is the price difference?

7. Jane wants to convert €320 to sterling for a shopping trip to Belfast. The exchange rate is €1 = STG£0.85.

(a) If the bank charges a fee of 1.5% for the transaction, how much will Jane receive?

(b) On arriving in Belfast, a local bank is offering an exchange rate of €1 = STG£0.90. The charge on the transaction is 2%. Should Jane have waited to change her currency in Belfast? Explain your answer.

8. A flight to Australia from London is priced at STG £1,087.50 when the exchange rate is €1 = STG£0.87. Calculate the price of the flight in euro.

9. A hotel bill in London reads as follows:

- A room for 5 days at £90 sterling per day
- 10 breakfasts at £5.99 each
- 10 dinners at £18.50 each
- A service charge of $12\frac{1}{2}$%

Calculate the total cost in euro to the nearest cent if the exchange rate is €1 = £0.89.

10. A watch in New York costs US$299 and the same watch in London costs £220. Given the exchange rates €1 = STG£0.87 and €1 = US$1.27, calculate where the watch is cheaper.

Section 11.7: Calculating percentage rates

Student Activity 11F

1. Express each of the following as a fraction, as a decimal and as a percentage:
   (a) 250 out of 750
   (b) 4 out of 100
   (c) 3.5 out of 50
   (d) 120 out of 2400
   (e) 18 out of 720
2. Write each of the following percentages as decimals:
   (a) 5%
   (b) 12%
   (c) 13.5%
   (d) 11%
   (e) 3%
3. Write each of the following as a decimal:
   (a) 1 + 14%
   (b) 1 + 5%
   (c) 1 + 65%
   (d) 1 + 2.5%
   (e) 1 + 0.5%
4. Interest of €200 was charged on a loan of €4,000.
   (a) Express the interest as a fraction of the loan.
   (b) Change the interest to a percentage of the loan.
5. A charge of €75 was added to a bill of €900. Express the charge as a percentage of the original bill.
6. VAT at €60 was added to a bill of €480. Express the VAT as a percentage of the original bill.

CALCULATING PERCENTAGE RATES EXPLAINED

It is often necessary to be able to calculate an increase or a decrease in the price of an item as a percentage of the original price. To calculate the percentage rate, do the following:

$$\text{Percentage rate} = \frac{\text{Increase or decrease in price}}{\text{Original price}}$$

EXAMPLE 7

VAT at €252 is added to a bill of €1,200. Calculate the rate of VAT.

Solution

$\frac{252}{1,200} \times 100 = 21\%$

Exercise 11.7

1. A service charge of €5 is added to a bill of €110. Calculate the percentage rate of the charge.
2. A bill of €220 amounts to €266.20 after VAT is added to the bill. Calculate the rate of VAT.
3. A savings account of €10,200 amounts to €10,404 after one year. Calculate the interest rate on the account.
4. When VAT is added to a mobile phone bill of €82, the total bill amounts to €99.22. Calculate the rate of VAT as a percentage.

5. (a) An electricity bill of €220 amounts to €264 after VAT is applied. Calculate the rate of VAT.
   (b) The VAT rate is increased by 2% after a government budget. Calculate the total bill with the new VAT rate.
6. A DVD player is priced at €175 exclusive of VAT. If the total price of the DVD player is €218.75, calculate the VAT rate.
7. A TV service provider is offering all sports channels and movie channels for a combined total of €65 per month. The price when VAT is applied is €78.65. Calculate the rate of VAT on the bill.
8. An internet company charges €30 for wireless broadband per month.
   (a) If the bill inclusive of VAT amounts to €37.20, calculate the VAT rate applied to the bill.
   (b) If the VAT rate is increased by 4%, how much would the total bill amount to?

Section 11.8: Compound interest and depreciation

Student Activity 11G

1. A person puts €1,000 into a saving account for one year and receives 2.5% interest.
   (a) How much is in the bank at the end of the first year?
   (b) The person decides to reinvest **all of the money** for a second year at 2% interest. How much is in the bank account at the end of the second year?
   (c) All the money is reinvested for a third year at 2% interest. How much is in the bank at the end of the third year?
   (d) How much interest in total did the person earn over the three years?
2. An investor places €5,000 into a bonus account for four years at an interest rate of 3% per annum.
   (a) How much is in the account at the end of the first year?
   (b) How much is in the account at the end of the second year?
   (c) How much is in the account at the end of the third year?
   (d) How much is in the account at the end of the fourth year?
   (e) How much interest did the investor earn over the four years?
3. A car loses 20% of its value after the first year.
   (a) Calculate the value of a car after one year if it originally cost €25,000.
   (b) Calculate the value of the car after two years.

COMPOUND INTEREST AND DEPRECIATION EXPLAINED

Every day, people borrow from or invest in financial institutions, such as banks or credit unions.

Any money borrowed must be paid back over a certain period of time. It will include an additional payment called **interest.** This is a charge for using the bank's or credit union's money. It is always given as a percentage.

For example, an interest rate of 5% means the customer must pay back an extra €5 for every €100 borrowed. So the greater the interest rate being charged, the more expensive the loan. Some credit cards have an interest rate as high as 21%!

To make sure they have enough money to lend, banks encourage savers to save money with them. The banks pay the savers an interest rate.

The most common form of interest is **compound interest.** This is calculated on the whole investment each year and not just the amount of the original investment, which is called the **principal.**

Compound interest is paid on the principal and on any interest earned.

The **principal** is the original amount invested or borrowed.

To calculate compound interest, you can use either of the following methods:

Method 1

Calculate the interest for each year and add it to the principal for that year.

Method 2

Use the formula found on page 30 of the *Formulae and Tables*. This formula is generally used when the interest rate does not change from year to year.

$F = P(1 + i)^t$

where:

F = Final value

P = Principal amount

t = Time in years

i = Interest rate (in decimal form)

Note

If the rate is 15%, then $(1 + i) = 1.15$.

If the rate is 5%, then $(1 + i) = 1.05$.

If the rate is $5\frac{1}{2}$%, then $(1 + i) = 1.055$.

When the value of an item decreases, it is said to depreciate. As you have already learned, when a new car is purchased, its value falls as soon as it leaves the car dealership. After this, its value falls by a certain amount each year.

To calculate the amount of depreciation, you can use either of the following methods:

Method 1

Calculate the depreciation for each year and subtract it from the principal for that year.

Method 2

Use the formula found on page 30 of the *Formulae and Tables*. This formula is generally used if the rate of depreciation does not change from year to year.

$F = P(1 - i)^t$

where:

F = Final value

P = Principal amount

t = Time in years

i = Interest rate (in decimal form)

EXAMPLE 8

€8,000 is invested for two years at 5% interest. Calculate the amount of interest earned over the two years.

Solution

Method 1

Year 1: Principal = €8,000

$\frac{8,000}{100} \times 5 = 400$

Final amount = 8,000 + 400 = €8,400

Year 2: Principal = €8,400

$\frac{8,400}{100} \times 5 = 420$

Final amount = 8,400 + 420 = €8,820

Interest earned = 8,820 – 8,000 = €820

Method 2

The interest rate does not change over the two years so we can use the formula:

Where $P = 8,000$; $i = \frac{5}{100}$ or 0.05 and $t = 2$:

$F = P(1 + i)^t$

$F = 8,000(1 + 0.05)^2$

$F = 8,000(1.05)^2$

$F = €8,820$

Interest earned = 8,820 – 8,000 = €820

EXAMPLE 9

€20,000 is invested for three years at 4% in the first year, 2.5% interest in the second year and 2% interest in the third year. Calculate the amount of interest earned over the three years.

Solution

Year 1: Principal = €20,000

$\frac{20,000}{100} \times 4 = 800$

Final amount = 20,000 + 800 = €20,800

Year 2: Principal = €20,800

$\frac{20,800}{100} \times 2.5 = 520$

Final amount = 20,800 + 520 = €21,320

Year 3: Principal = €21,320

$\frac{21,320}{100} \times 2 = 426.40$

Final amount = 21,320 + 426.40 = €21,746.40

Interest earned = 21,746.40 – 20,000 = €1,746.40

EXAMPLE 10

€5,000 in invested at 3% compound interest for two years. The full amount is reinvested for a third year at a rate of r% and amounts to €5,410.59. Calculate the value of r, the rate for the third year.

Solution

Years 1 and 2:

$F = P(1 + r)^t$

$F = 5,000(1 + 0.03)^2$

$F = 5,000(1.03)^2$

$F = €5,304.50$

Year 3:

Interest = 5,410.59 – 5,304.50

Interest = €106.09

$\% \text{ Rate} = \frac{\text{Interest}}{\text{Year starting amount}} \times 100$

$= \frac{106.09}{5,304.50} \times 100$

$= 2\%$

x=y EXAMPLE 11

€10,000 is borrowed for 3 years at 5% compound interest. €1,500 is repaid at the end of the first year and at the end of the second year. How much must be repaid at the end of the third year to clear the loan, correct to the nearest euro?

Solution

Year 1:

€10,000 × 5% = €500

€10,000 + €500 = €10,500 **Outstanding loan**

€10,500 − €1,500 = €9,000 **Loan less the repayment**

Year 2:

€9,000 × 5% = €450

€9,000 + €450 = €9,450 **Outstanding loan**

€9,450 − €1,500 = €7,950 **Loan less the repayment**

Year 3:

€7,950 × 5% = €397.50

€7,950 + €397.50 = €8,347.50 **Outstanding loan to be repaid**

x=y EXAMPLE 12

A tractor is purchased for €84,000. It depreciates at a rate of 9.5% in the first year and 5% every year after that. Calculate the value of the tractor after 3 years.

Solution

Year 1:

€84,000 × 9.5% = €7,980

€84,000 − €7,980 = €76,020

Year 2:

€76,020 × 5% = €3,801

€76,020 − €3,801 = €72,219

Year 3

€72,219 × 5% = €3,610.95

€72,219 − €3,610.95 = €68,608.05

x=y EXAMPLE 13

What sum of money invested for 3 years at 5% compound interest will amount to €11,576.25 after the three years?

Solution

$F = P(1 + r)^t$

$F = €11{,}576.25, \quad P = ?, \quad r = 0.05, \quad t = 3$

$11{,}576.25 = P(1 + 0.05)^3$

$11{,}576.25 = P(1.05)^3$

$\frac{11{,}576.25}{(1.05)^3} = P$

$P = €10{,}000$

Exercise 11.8

1. Calculate the interest earned on €2,500 invested at 5% compound interest for two years.
2. An investment of €9,000 is made for 3 years at 3% compound interest. Calculate the amount of the investment at the end of the 3 years.
3. An investment of €15,000 is made for 3 years at a rate of 2% per annum.
   (a) Calculate the amount of the investment at the end of the 3 years.
   (b) Calculate the total interest earned during the 3 years.
4. €6,000 is invested at 4% compound interest for two years. Calculate the interest earned.
5. A person places €25,000 in a savings account at 3% compound interest for 3 years.
   (a) Calculate the final amount in the account after 3 years.
   (b) Calculate the total interest earned over the 3 years.
6. How much will €30,000 amount to after two years at 3% compound interest?
7. A bank offers a special interest rate of 4% for investments over €50,000 and under €250,000 that are untouched for 3 years. How much would a person earn if they invested €130,000?
8. An investor places €75,000 in a ten-year savings bond at 5% for the first three years, 5.5% for the following three years and 6% for the final four years.
   (a) How much interest will the investor earn?
   (b) Alternatively the investor could have put her money into a special savings scheme. The scheme guarantees 5.7% compound interest per annum if the money is invested for ten years. How much interest will the investor earn in this saving scheme?
9. Calculate the final amount and the interest earned for each of the following:

Principal amount	Year 1 % rate	Year 2 % rate	Year 3 % rate
(a) €10,000	2%	3%	9%
(b) €5,000	5%	5%	5%
(c) €20,000	6%	6%	4%
(d) €10,000	4%	3%	4%
(e) €10,000	4%	4%	3%
(f) €35,000	5%	7%	10%
(g) €90,000	8%	8%	8%
(h) €25,000	2%	2.5%	3.5%
(i) €50,000	1.5%	2%	3.6%
(j) €150,000	0.8%	1.6%	2.5%

10. Mark bought a car for €16,500 six years ago. Assuming it depreciates at the compound rate of 13% per annum, calculate its present value correct to the nearest euro.
11. A printing press has a present value of €26,386.60. Assuming a rate of depreciation of 12% per annum over the past five years, calculate its original value correct to the nearest euro.
12. €12,000 was invested for three years at compound interest. Interest was applied at a rate of 4% for the first year and 3% for the second year. If the total amount at the end of third year was €13,497.12, calculate the interest rate for the third year.
13. Eva invested €1,000 at 15% per annum for the first year and 12% per annum for the second year. At the end of the second year, she withdrew a certain amount. During the third year the rate was 10%. At the end of the third year her investment was 55% of the original amount. How much did she withdraw at the end of the second year?
14. James invested €32,000 at 11% per annum compound interest. At the end of the first year, he withdrew a certain amount. During the second year, the rate of interest decreased to 10% per annum. At the end of the second year, the investment was worth 66% of the original amount. How much did James withdraw at the end of the first year?
15. Ita invested €3,000 at 10% per annum compound interest. At the end of each of the first two years, she withdrew equal amounts. At the end of the third year, her investment was $71\frac{1}{2}$ % of the original sum. What was the value of each of the equal withdrawals?

16. Aidan invested €3,000 for three years. At the end of the first year, he invested another €2,000 in the account. But at the end of the second year Aidan withdrew €4,000. If the rate of interest for the first year was 14%, for the second year 15% and the third year 11%, find correct to the nearest euro, the value of the investment at the end of the third year.

17. Laura invested €1,000 to be withdrawn in two equal instalments. The first instalment was to be withdrawn at the end of the second year and the other to be withdrawn at the end of the third year. If the investment earned 15% in the first year, 12% in the second year and 10% in the third year, find the amount of each instalment withdrawn, correct to the nearest euro.

18. €12,000 is borrowed at a rate of 4% compound interest per annum. €4,000 is repaid at the end of the first year and €3,500 is repaid at the end of the second year. How much is outstanding on the loan at the end of the third year?

19. A loan of €11,000 is borrowed at compound interest over three years. The interest rate is 6.5%, 5% and 4.5 over the three years respectively. At the end of year one, €2,500 is repaid. At the end of year two, half the outstanding amount is repaid. How much must be repaid at the end of the third year to pay off the loan.

20. A sum of money was invested for 2 years. The interest rate for the first year was 5% and for the second year was 3%. The investment was worth €21,630 after two years. What was the original sum of money invested?

21. John invested €25,000 in a bank. The rate of interest for the first year was 3%. At the beginning of the second year John doubled the value of the investment. The rate of interest for the second year was 2.5%.
    (a) Calculate the value of the investment at the end of the second year.
    (b) At the beginning of the third year John withdrew €11,000 from the account. If at the end of the third year the investment was worth €43,459, calculate the interest rate for the third year.

22. A car depreciates by 12% per annum. If the car is worth €34,073.60 after 3 years, what was the original cost of the car?

23. A truck depreciates by 15% per annum.
    (a) Calculate the value of a €165,000 truck after 4 years.
    (b) If a truck is worth €122,825 after 3 years, how much did it cost brand new?

24. A house is purchased for €285,000. It depreciates at a rate of 3% in the first year. It increases in value by 5% in year 2 and depreciates by 1% in year 3.
    (a) Calculate the value of the house after 3 years, correct to the nearest euro.
    (b) If the house was sold after 3 years, calculate the profit as a percentage of the cost price.

Section 11.9: Calculating percentage mark-ups and percentage profit margins

Student Activity 11H

1. A shop owner buys an item for €150. The item is sold at a **mark-up** of 23%.
    (a) What do you think the term in bold means?
    (b) Why do you think the shop owner would place a mark-up on the item?
    (c) Find 23% of €150.
    (d) Calculate the selling price of the item.

2. A boutique buys dresses for €35 each. The shop owner places a mark-up of 70% on the dresses.
   (a) Find 70% of €35.
   (b) Calculate the selling price of the dresses.
3. An electrical store sells a certain brand of washing machine for €400. The cost to the store was €250.
   (a) Calculate the profit on the sale of the washing machine.
   (b) Calculate the percentage profit on the cost price.
   (c) Calculate the percentage profit on the selling price.

CALCULATING MARK-UPS AND PROFIT MARGINS EXPLAINED

Mark-ups and **profit margins** are a very important part of any business. Business owners need to be able to calculate their income so that they can budget for expenses such as electricity and heating bills, insurance costs and staff wages.

Percentage mark-up is calculated as a percentage of the **cost price:**

$$\text{Percentage mark-up} = \frac{\text{Profit}}{\text{Cost price}} \times 100$$

Percentage profit margin is calculated as a percentage of the **selling price:**

$$\text{Percentage profit margin} = \frac{\text{Profit}}{\text{Selling price}} \times 100$$

EXAMPLE 14

An item costing €75 is sold for €120. Calculate:

(a) The percentage mark-up on the item

(b) The percentage profit margin on the item

Solution

(a) Profit = 120 – 75 = €45

$$\text{Percentage mark-up} = \frac{\text{Profit}}{\text{Cost price}} \times 100$$

$$\text{Percentage mark-up} = \frac{45}{75} \times 100$$

Percentage mark-up = 60%

(b) $$\text{Percentage margin} = \frac{\text{Profit}}{\text{Selling price}} \times 100$$

$$\text{Percentage margin} = \frac{45}{120} \times 100$$

Percentage margin = 37.5%

EXAMPLE 15

An item was sold for €246 at a percentage profit margin of 20%. Calculate:

(a) The cost price of the item to the store

(b) The profit on the item

(c) The percentage mark-up on the item

Solution

(a) 120% = €246

1% = 246 ÷ 120 = 2.05

100% = 2.05 × 100 = €205 = Cost price

(b) Profit = 246 – 205 = €41

(c) $$\text{Percentage mark-up} = \frac{\text{Profit}}{\text{Cost price}} \times 100$$

$$\text{Percentage mark-up} = \frac{41}{205} \times 100 = 20\%$$

Exercise 11.9

1. A newsagent sells a bottle of soft drink for €1.50 at a profit of €0.75.
   (a) Calculate the profit in money on the sale of the soft drink.
   (b) Calculate the percentage profit on the cost price.
   (c) Calculate the percentage profit on the selling price.
2. A car was bought for €18,500 and sold for €15,725 one year later.
   (a) Calculate the loss on the sale of the car.
   (b) Express the loss as a fraction of the selling price, correct to one decimal place.
   (c) Change the fraction to a percentage.
3. A house was bought for €235,000 and sold one year later for €258,500.
   (a) Calculate the profit in money on the sale of the house.
   (b) Express the profit as a fraction of the selling price.
   (c) Express the fraction as a percentage.
4. Calculate the percentage mark-up and percentage profit margin on each of the following:

Cost price	Selling price
(a) €55	€66
(b) €90	€135
(c) €40	€90
(d) €9	€15
(e) €120	€195
(f) €236	€323.32
(g) €149	€216.05
(h) €378	€515.97
(i) €684	€1005.48
(j) €521	€698.14

5. A mobile phone shop sells a certain make of phone for a profit of €90. If the cost price to the shop is €70, calculate:
   (a) The selling price
   (b) The percentage mark-up on the phone
   (c) The percentage profit margin on the phone
6. A DVD player is sold for €237.50 at a margin of 25%. Calculate:
   (a) The price before the margin is added
   (b) The selling price of a television if the cost to the retailer was €133
7. A car was sold for €22,500 at a profit margin of 17%. Calculate:
   (a) The cost price of the car
   (b) The profit made on the sale
   (c) The percentage mark-up on the car, correct to the nearest per cent
8. A house was sold for €258,300 at a percentage profit margin of 23%. Calculate:
   (a) The cost price of the house
   (b) The profit made on the sale
   (c) The percentage mark-up on the house, correct to the nearest per cent
9. A racehorse that cost €23,600 was later sold for €57,900. Calculate:
   (a) The profit made on the sale of the horse, correct to one decimal place
   (b) The percentage mark-up, correct to one decimal place
   (c) The percentage profit margin on the sale, correct to the nearest per cent
10. An online music store sells albums to download for €16.99. If the cost of the album to the store is €9.99, calculate:
    (a) The profit made on the sale of an album
    (b) The percentage mark-up on the album, correct to the nearest per cent
    (c) The percentage profit margin on the album, correct to the nearest per cent

    During a sale, the price of the album is dropped to €12.99. Calculate:
    (d) The profit made on the sale of the album during the sale
    (e) The percentage mark-up on the album during the sale, correct to the nearest per cent
    (f) The percentage profit margin on the album during the sale, correct to the nearest per cent
11. A toy shop sells a certain games console for €280. The cost of the console to the shop was €200. Calculate:
    (a) The profit made on the sale of the console
    (b) The percentage mark-up on the console, correct to the nearest per cent
    (c) The percentage profit margin on the console, correct to the nearest per cent

    If the price of the console is reduced by 10% in the run-up to Christmas, calculate:
    (d) The profit made after the reduction, correct to the nearest euro
    (e) The percentage mark-up after the reduction, correct to the nearest per cent
    (f) The percentage profit margin after the reduction, correct to the nearest per cent

12. Paul bought a watch for €180. Six months later he sold the watch for €150. Calculate the percentage loss on:
    (a) The cost price
    (b) The selling price
13. Michelle sold her mobile phone to her friend for €25 less than she paid for it. If Michelle paid €200, calculate:
    (a) The percentage loss on the cost price
    (b) The percentage loss on the selling price, correct to one decimal place
14. An old car was bought for €1,858.50. After some refurbishment, the car was resold for €2,950. Calculate the profit as a percentage of the selling price of the car.
15. A clothes shop purchases jeans at €23 per pair. If the retail price of the jeans is €78 calculate:
    (a) The profit as a percentage of the cost price, correct to the nearest per cent
    (b) The profit as a percentage of the retail price, correct to the nearest per cent

CHAPTER 11 SELF-CHECK TEST

Calculate each of the following:

1. 10% of 135
2. 12.5% of 240
3. 25% of 400
4. 50% of 590
5. 75% of 2,500
6. 18% of 500
7. $33\frac{1}{3}$% of €330
8. 63% of 940
9. 13% of 39
10. 47% of 1,240
11. 87% of 300
12. 37.5% of 800

Express the first quantity as a percentage of the second quantity:

13. 12, 30
14. 7, 28
15. 6, 60
16. 5, 30
17. 4, 8
18. 200, 1,200
19. 12, 144
20. An item bought for €35 is sold for €40. Calculate the profit as a percentage of the cost price, correct to one decimal place.
21. Paul bought an old motorbike for €350 and restored it. He later sold it for a profit of €250. Calculate:
    (a) The selling price of the bike
    (b) The percentage profit of the cost price, correct to the nearest per cent
22. In a sale, an electrical retailer reduces a DVD player priced at €150 by 15%. Calculate the sale price of the DVD player.
23. A car is sold for €21,500 plus VAT at 15%. Calculate the selling price of the car.
24. A restaurant bill of €134.40 includes a service charge of 12%. Calculate the cost of the bill excluding the service charge.
25. A washing machine is priced at €181.50 inclusive of VAT at 21%. Calculate the price exclusive of VAT.

26. €2,500 is invested at 3% compound interest for 3 years. Calculate the amount of the investment at the end of the three years.

27. €4,000 is invested for 4 years at compound interest. If the rate is 5% for the first two years, 4% for the third year and 2% for the fourth year, calculate the interest earned on the investment at the end of the 4 years.

28. A tourist changes US$250 to euro when the exchange rate is €1 = $1.20. Calculate how much the tourist receives, correct to the nearest euro.

29. A bank charges a 2% commission on each foreign exchange transaction. The exchange rates are €1 = US$1.20, €1=STG£0.85 and €1 = ¥21,000. Calculate how much a tourist will receive after commission is deducted on each of the following transactions:

(a) €1,500 is changed to yen.

(b) STG£1,870 is converted euro.

(c) US$900 is converted to yen.

30. A retailer sells an item for €350. The cost of the item to the shop was €200. Calculate:

(a) The profit made on the sale of the item

(b) The percentage mark-up on the item, correct to the nearest per cent

(c) The percentage profit margin on the item, correct to the nearest per cent

31. An old house was bought for €124,000. After some refurbishment, the house was resold for €152,520. Calculate the profit as a percentage of the selling price of the house, correct to the nearest per cent.

32. A mobile phone shop purchases a certain model of phone for €45.50. The phone retails at €110. Calculate:

(a) The profit as a percentage of the selling price, correct to the nearest per cent

(b) The profit as a percentage of the cost price, correct to the nearest per cent

A number of phones remain unsold and the shop places a discount of €21 on the selling price.

(c) Calculate the profit as a percentage of the discounted selling price, correct to the nearest per cent

33. An electrical retailer sells outdoor heaters for €57. If the cost price to the retailer is €33, Calculate:

(a) The profit on the sale of a heater

(b) The profit as a percentage of the cost price, correct to the nearest per cent

(c) The profit as a percentage of the selling price, correct to the nearest per cent

34. A tractor depreciates in value by 15% per annum.

(a) If a tractor is bought for €45,200, find its value at the end of the third year.

(b) By how much did it depreciate?

(c) If another tractor has a value if €31,934.50 after three years, find the value it was bought for.

35. Any new car depreciates by 10% the moment it is driven from the car dealership. For the next three years, it depreciates at a rate of 15% per annum. Then for each year after that, it depreciates by 10% per annum.

(a) If Seán purchases a new car for €31,000, how much will it be worth after 5 years? Give your answer correct to the nearest euro.

(b) If Laura buys a six-year-old car for €5,000, how much did the car cost when it was originally bought brand new?

36. Laura invested €1,200 to be withdrawn in two equal instalments. The first instalment was to be withdrawn at the end of the second year and the other to be withdrawn at the end of the third year. If the investment earned 12% in the first year, 10% in the second year and 8% in the third year, find the amount of each instalment withdrawn, correct to the nearest euro.

CHAPTER 11 KNOWLEDGE CHECKLIST

After completing this chapter, I now:

- Know how to calculate a quantity from a given percentage
- Know how to calculate profit and loss as a percentage of cost price
- Know how to calculate profit and loss as a percentage of selling price
- Know how to calculate discounts and percentage discounts
- Know how to apply percentages to mobile phone bills, VAT and meter readings
- Know how to perform currency transactions
- Know how to calculate percentage rates
- Know how to calculate compound interest and depreciation
- Know how to calculate percentage mark-up and percentage profit margin

Challenge

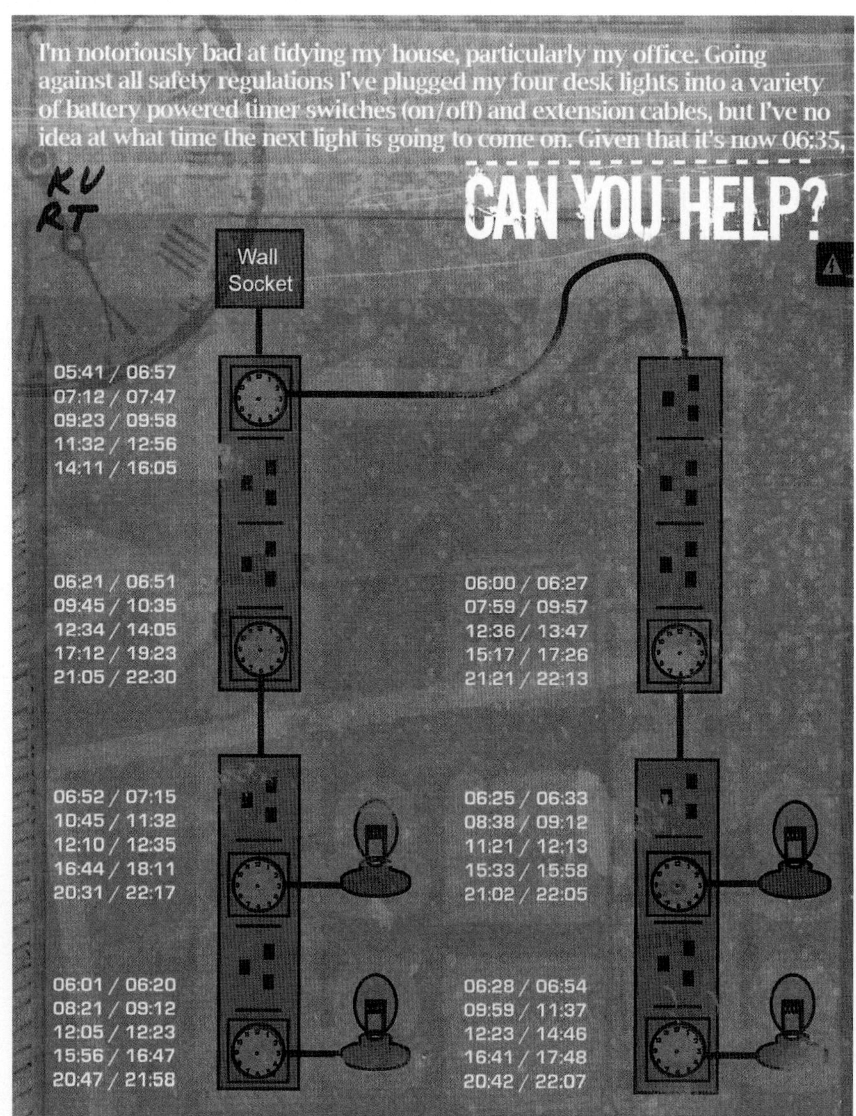

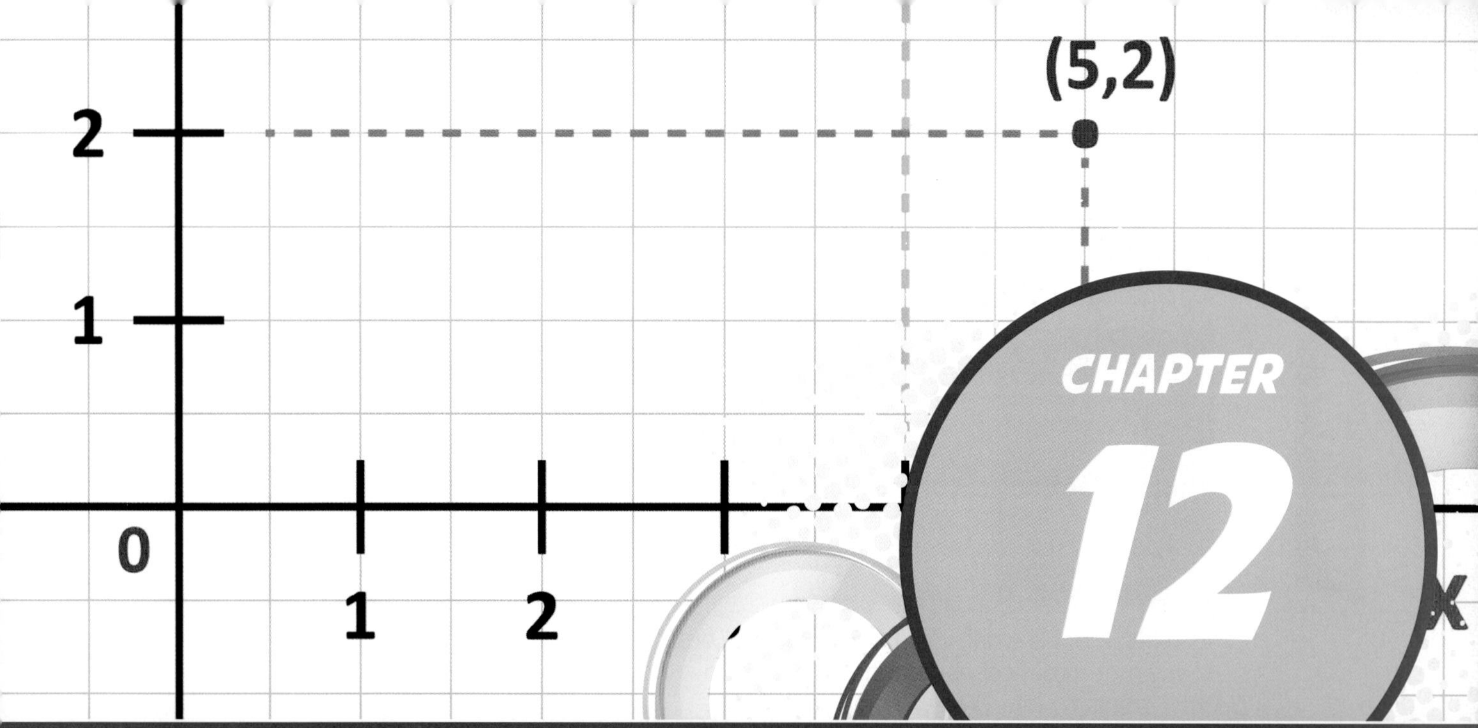

COORDINATE GEOMETRY

LEARNING OUTCOMES

In this chapter you will learn:

- ✓ To find the distance between two points (length of a line segment)
- ✓ To find the midpoint of a line segment
- ✓ To find the slope of a line
- ✓ That parallel lines have equal slopes
- ✓ That the product of two perpendicular slopes is –1
- ✓ To find and understand the equation of a line
- ✓ To translate a point
- ✓ To graph a line
- ✓ To find the slope of a parallel or a perpendicular line to a given line
- ✓ To verify that a point lies on a given line
- ✓ To find the intersection point of two lines graphically
- ✓ To solve simultaneous linear equations
- ✓ To find the intersection point of a line and both the *x*- and *y*-axes
- ✓ To find the symmetry of a point

KEY WORDS

- Axiom
- Collinear
- Cartesian plane
- Intersection
- Midpoint
- Parallel
- Perpendicular
- Point
- Simultaneous linear equations
- Slope
- Translation
- *x*-intercept
- *y*-intercept

12

MATHS IN ACTION 3

INTRODUCTION

In *Maths in Action 1*, you learned that René Descartes invented the Cartesian plane for plotting points.

As a result of his work, it is possible to carry out many mathematical operations on points on the Cartesian plane. You will now explore these ideas.

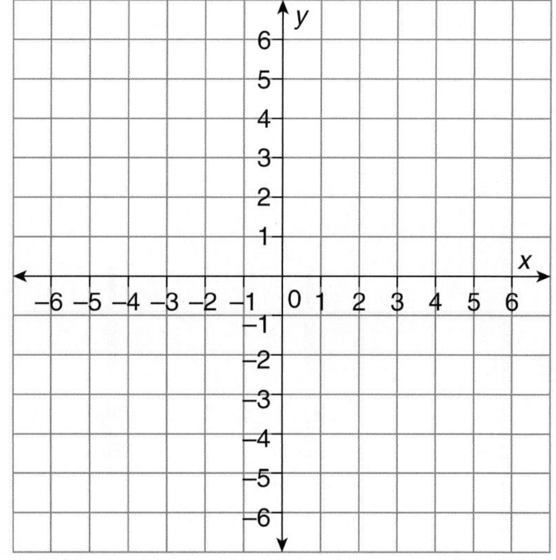

First year revision

1. Plot the following points on a coordinate diagram:

(a) $A(3, -2)$	(d) $D(-4, -4)$	(g) $G(-5, -3)$	(j) $J(3, -1)$	(m) $M(0, -4)$
(b) $B(2, 0)$	(e) $E(0, -2)$	(h) $H(5, 2)$	(k) $K(-3, 1)$	(n) $N(4, -2)$
(c) $C(-1, 2)$	(f) $F(0, 4)$	(i) $I(4, 2)$	(l) $L(1, 1)$	(o) $P(2, -1)$

2. Indicate the y-axis and the x-axis on your diagram.
3. Use the points above to make a coded message. Ask your classmates to solve the code.
4. How many points do you need to draw a line segment?

Section 12.1: The distance between two points

Student Activity 12A

Study the diagram and answer the following questions:

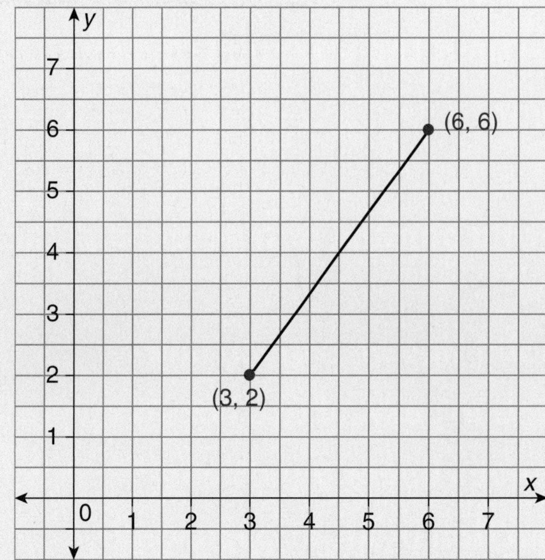

1. What is the horizontal distance between the two points? Show how you found your answer.
2. What is the vertical distance between the two points? Show how you found your answer.
3. Draw a long horizontal line through the lower point. Draw a long vertical line through the higher point. What shape have you formed?
4. Can you now remember what name is given to the slanting side in the shape?
5. Calculate the length of the slanting side using the theorem of Pythagoras.
6. In your own words, write a simple explanation of how you found the distance between the two points.

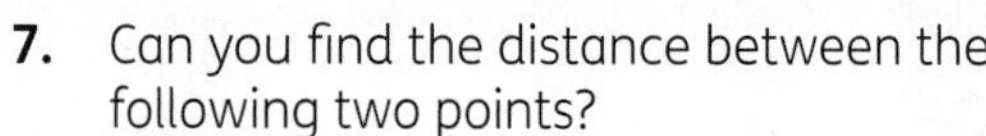

7. Can you find the distance between the following two points?

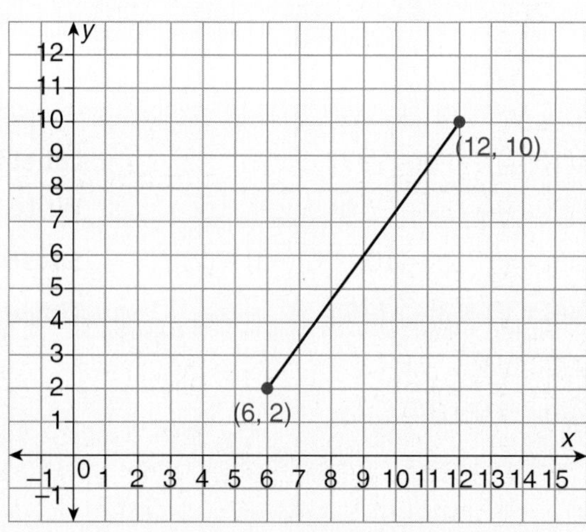

THE DISTANCE BETWEEN TWO POINTS EXPLAINED

In the following diagram, we use two general points $A(x_1, y_1)$ and $B(x_2, y_2)$ as shown:

1. The horizontal distance is found by subtracting x_1 from x_2: $(x_2 - x_1)$
2. The vertical distance is found by subtracting y_1 from y_2: $(y_2 - y_1)$
3. Using the theorem of Pythagoras, we get:

$$|AB|^2 = (x_2 - x_1)^2 + (y_2 - y_1)^2$$

This gives us our formula for the distance between two points **or** the length of the line segment $[AB]$:

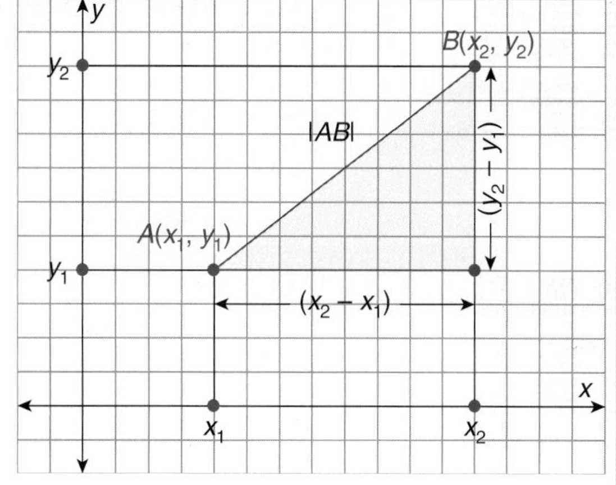

$$|AB| = \sqrt{(x_2 - x_1)^2 + (y_2 - y_1)^2}$$

This formula can be found on page 18 of the *Formulae and Tables*.

Note

Straight line brackets called the modulus are used to indicate distance or length. They are also a reminder that the answer must always be positive. For example, it is impossible to run −5 km!

Collinear points are on the same line.

In *Maths in Action 1*, you met a number of axioms. An axiom is a statement that we accept without any proof. One axiom deals with the distance between two **collinear** points.

Axiom 2 (ruler axiom)

The distance between points has the following properties:

- The distance $|AB|$ is never negative.
- $|AB| = |BA|$ A ← 10 cm → B
- If C lies on AB, between A and B, then $|AB| = |AC| + |CB|$
- Given any ray from A and given any real number $k \geq 0$, there is a unique point B on the ray whose distance from A is k.

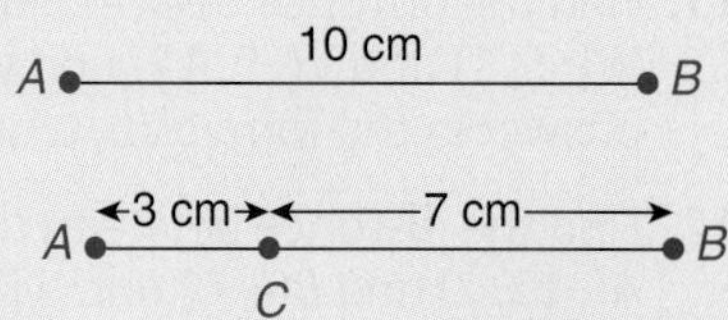

EXAMPLE 1

Given the points $A(10, 2)$ and $B(-2, -3)$, find $|AB|$.

Solution

$\quad x_1\, y_1 \qquad\quad x_2\ \ y_2$

$A(10, 2) \qquad B(-2, -3)$ — **Label the points (x_1, y_1) and (x_2, y_2) as shown**

$|AB| = \sqrt{(x_2 - x_1)^2 + (y_2 - y_1)^2}$ — **Write down the formula**

$|AB| = \sqrt{((-2) - (10))^2 + ((-3) - (2))^2}$ — **Substitute in the values using brackets**

$|AB| = \sqrt{(-12)^2 + (-5)^2}$ — **Tidy up**

$|AB| = \sqrt{169}$

$|AB| = 13$ units

EXAMPLE 2

Given the points $X(7, 3)$ and $Y(-2, -5)$, find the length of the line segment $[XY]$ in surd form.

Solution

$\quad x_1\, y_1 \qquad\quad x_2\ \ y_2$

$X(7, 3) \qquad Y(-2, -5)$ — **Label the points (x_1, y_1) and (x_2, y_2) as shown**

$|XY| = \sqrt{(x_2 - x_1)^2 + (y_2 - y_1)^2}$ — **Write down the formula**

$|XY| = \sqrt{((-2) -(7))^2 + ((-5) - (3))^2}$ — **Substitute in the values using brackets**

$|XY| = \sqrt{145}$ units

Exercise 12.1

Find the distance between each of the following pairs of points:

1. $A(0, 0), B(3, 4)$
2. $X(2, 5), Y(8, -3)$
3. $C(4, 5), D(5, 5)$
4. $S(3, 2), T(-1, -2)$
5. $A(-3, -5), B(-1, 4)$
6. $X(-2, 5), Y(-1, -6)$
7. $X(-9, -3), Y(4, 7)$
8. $S(0, -6), T(-8, 0)$
9. $X(-5, 8), Y(3, -3)$
10. Find the distance between the points $X(9, 5)$ and $Y(3, 1)$ and write your answer in the form $a\sqrt{b}$, where $a, b \in \mathbb{N}$.
11. Find the distance between the points $W(-6, 1)$ and $V(-9, 10)$ and write your answer in the form $a\sqrt{b}$, where $a, b \in \mathbb{N}$.
12. Find the distance between the points $A(-12, 2)$ and $B(4, 0)$ and write your answer in the form $a\sqrt{b}$, where $a, b \in \mathbb{N}$.
13. Find the length of the line segment $[XY]$ in surd form, if $X(8, -1)$ and $Y(3, -5)$.
14. Find the length of the line segment $[AB]$ if $A(3, 3)$ and $B(-2, -2)$, giving your answer correct to one decimal place.
15. $A(3, -2)$, $B(4, -2)$ and $C(10, 1)$ are three points.
    (a) Investigate whether $|AC| = |AB| + |BC|$. What does this result tell us about the three points?
    (b) Investigate whether $|AC| = |CA|$. What does this result tell you about the length of a line segment?
16. $P(1, 1)$, $Q(4, -1)$ and $R(7, -3)$ are three points.
    (a) Investigate whether $|PR| = |PQ| + |QR|$. What does this result tell us about the three points?
    (b) Investigate whether $|PQ| = |QP|$. What does this result tell you about the length of a line segment?

17. $D(3, 5)$, $E(6, 3)$ and $F(11, -1)$ are three points. Investigate whether $|DF| = |DE| + |EF|$. What does this result tell us about the three points?

18. Mary's car is running low on petrol and she is trying to decide which petrol station is nearer to her. Can you help her decide which one to go to?

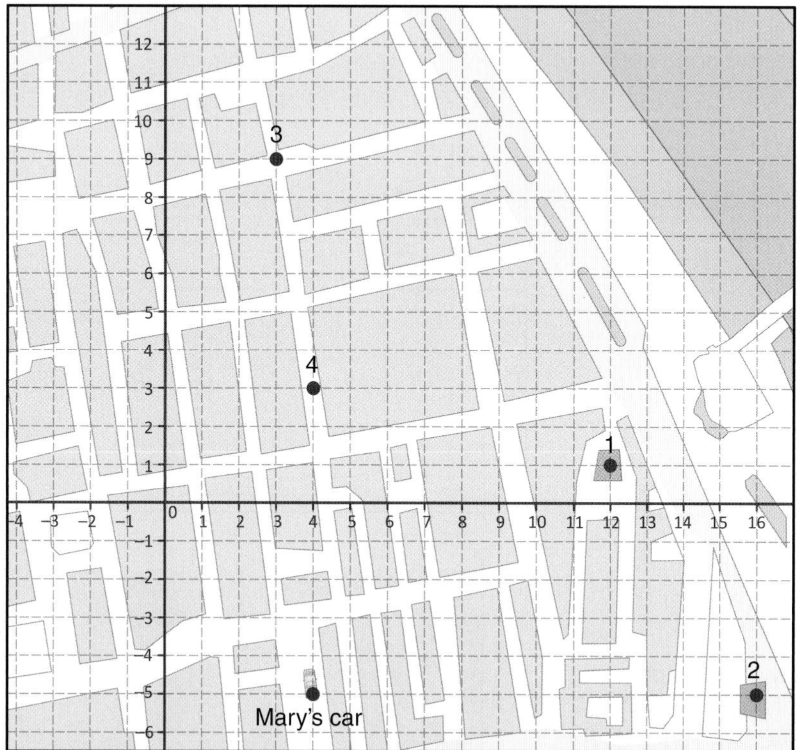

19. *A* ship is at point *X* as shown. The captain is calculating the distance to the port shown. Calculate the distance in surd form.

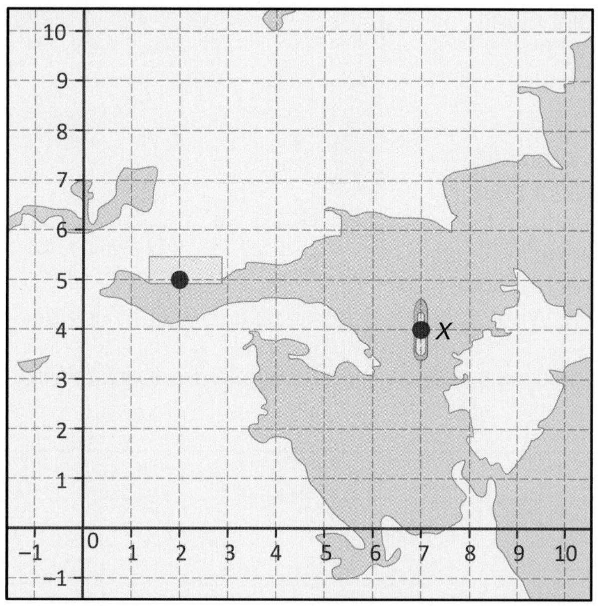

20. Seán draws a triangle using the points $A(8, 6)$, $B(5, 10)$ and $C(4, 9)$. Investigate whether the triangle is isosceles.

21. The points $X(4, 2)$, $Y(10, 2)$ and $Z(4, 10)$ are the vertices of a triangle. By finding the lengths of all three sides, show that the triangle is a right-angled triangle.

22. Plot the points $A(-2, 1)$, $B(2, -3)$, $C(6, 3)$ and $D(2, 7)$ on a Cartesian plane. Investigate whether *ABCD* is parallelogram.

23. Identify the type of triangle formed by the points $A(0, 0)$, $B(-5, 3)$ and $C(4, 6)$.

24. Verify that the points $P(4, -5)$, $Q(7, -5)$, $R(7, -2)$ and $S(4, -2)$ form a rhombus.

25. Examine the coordinate diagram of a town. Find the distances between each of the following buildings. Leave your answer in surd form where necessary.

(a) The cinema and Paul's house

(b) The GAA pitch and the shop

(c) The DVD store and the pizzeria

(d) Arcadia and the shopping centre

(e) Paul's house and the GAA pitch

(f) The church and the butcher's

(g) The school and the church

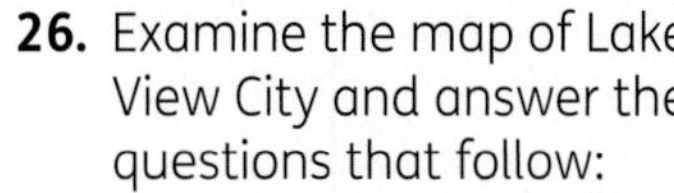

26. Examine the map of Lake View City and answer the questions that follow:

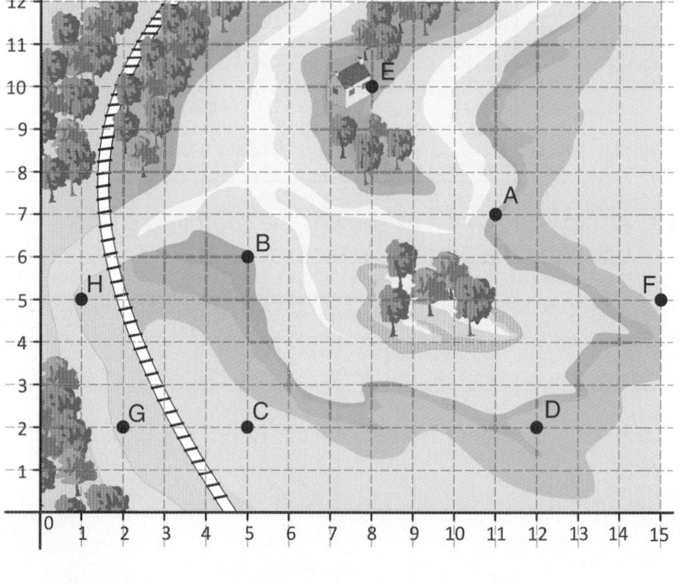

(a) Jane swims from point A to point B daily. How far does she swim each day?

(b) The harbour master lives on the island at the point E. He must travel by boat to the shore via point A and moors his boat at the point B. How far must he row?

(c) Jack, who loves running, lives in the house at point F. His run takes him from his home to point H via points D, C and G. He then runs home again. What distance does he run, correct to one decimal place?

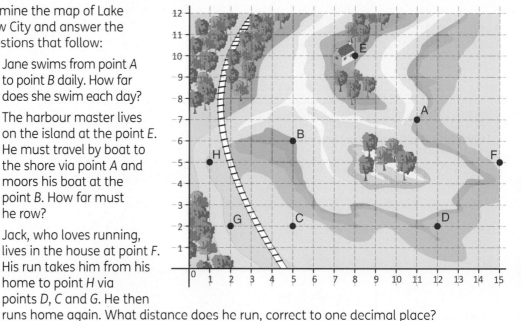

27. Paul views a map and sees a castle which he would like to visit. What is the distance from Paul to the castle?

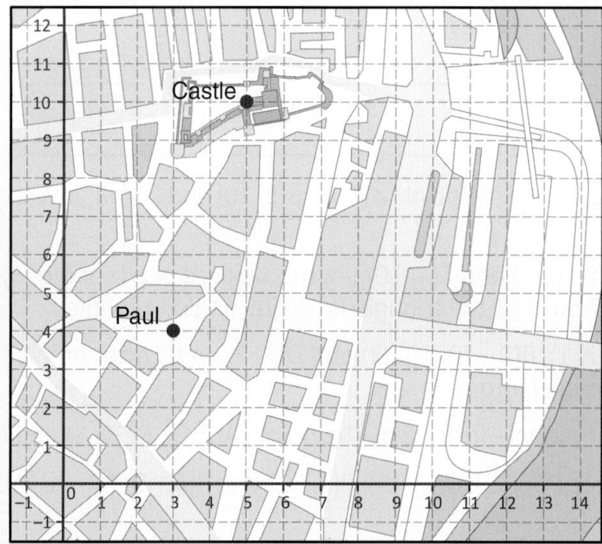

28. Orion was a giant huntsman in Greek mythology. Zeus placed Orion among the stars as the constellation of Orion.

The following graph shows some of the stars in the constellation.

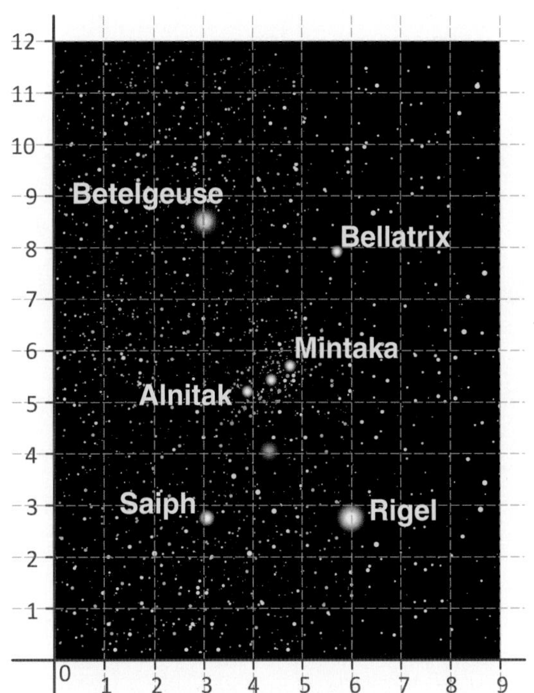

By choosing appropriate coordinates for each star, find the distance between:

(a) Betelgeuse and Bellatrix

(b) Alnitak and Mintaka

(c) Saiph and Rigel

(d) The distance to each star from Earth is measured in light years. A light year is the distance light travels in one year: 9,458,000,000,000 km. Express the distance to each of the following stars from Earth in standard form, given that:

(i) Betelgeuse is 427 light years away.

(ii) Bellatrix is 243 light years away.

Section 12.2: The midpoint of a line segment

Student Activity 12B

Study the following diagram and answer the questions:

1. What is the horizontal distance between the two points? Show how you found your answer.
2. What is the vertical distance between the two points? Show how you found your answer.
3. Can you find the midpoint of both the horizontal and the vertical lines? Indicate them on your diagram.
4. Draw a straight line horizontally and vertically through both midpoints on your diagram. Mark the point where they intersect. What do you notice?

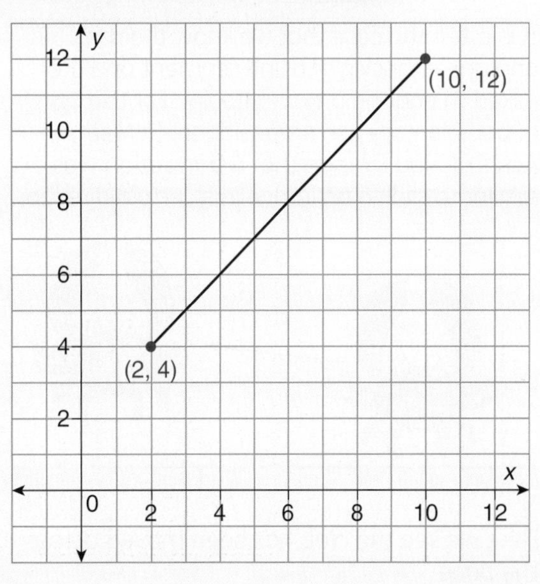

5. Can you find the midpoint of the following two points?

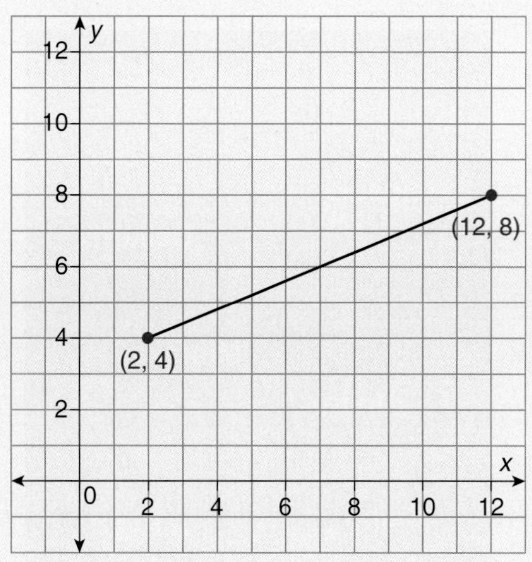

6. Find the image of the point A under central symmetry in the point B as shown.

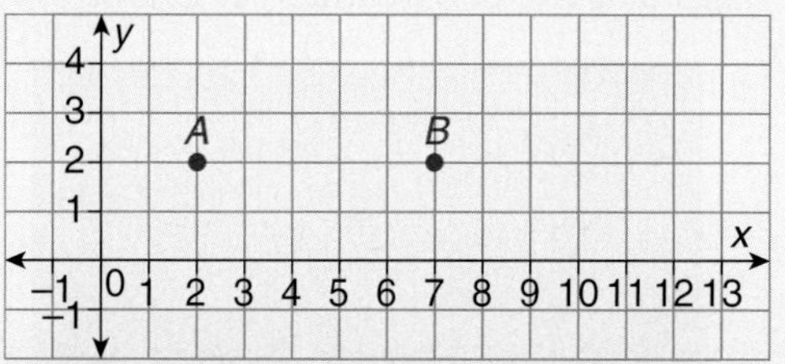

Explain how you arrived at your answer.

7. Find the image of the point A under central symmetry in the point B as shown.

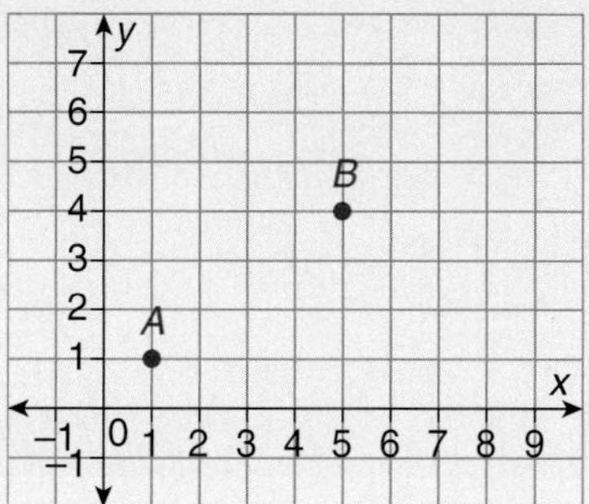

Explain how you arrived at your answer.

THE MIDPOINT OF A LINE SEGMENT EXPLAINED

In *Maths in Actions 1*, you learned how to bisect a line segment using a compass and a straight edge. In coordinate geometry, you need to be able to find the midpoint between two points mathematically.

We use the **midpoint formula** for a line segment:

Midpoint of a line segment

$$= \left(\frac{x_1 + x_2}{2}, \frac{y_1 + y_2}{2}\right)$$

This formula can be found on page 18 of the *Formulae and Tables*.

It is often the case that we know the midpoint and one endpoint of a line segment and are asked to find the other endpoint. For this type of question, we use a translation. In *Maths in Action 1*, you learned that a translation was similar to sliding an image in a certain direction.

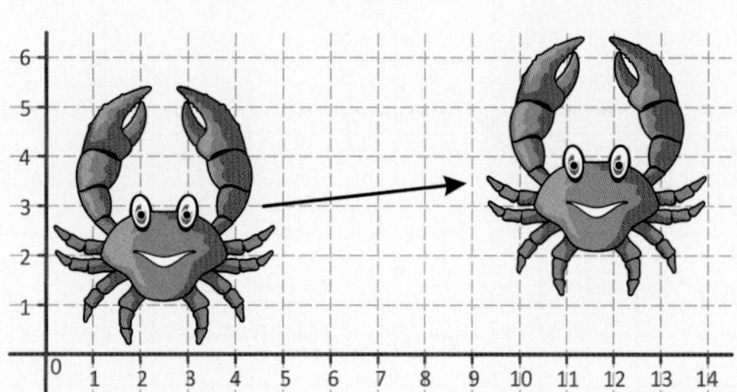

Here we see the crab has been moved across the page.

A translation can also be carried out on a point. Here the point $F(2, 3)$ is moved four units to the right and two units up to $F'(6, 5)$.

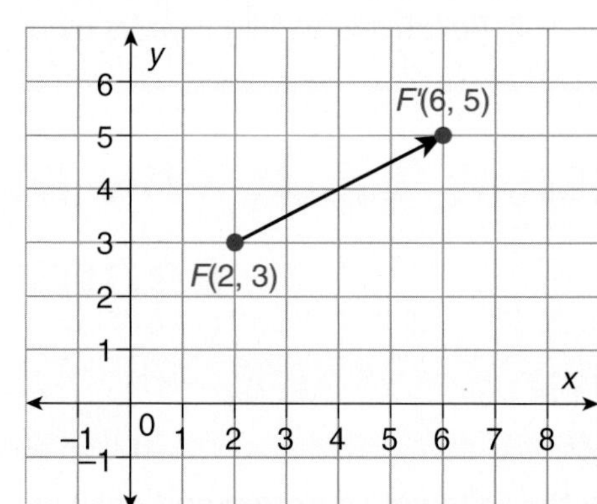

The midpoint of a line segment is the point of central symmetry for the line segment. Every point on a line segment has an image under central symmetry in the midpoint, where $|AB| = |AC| + |CB|$.

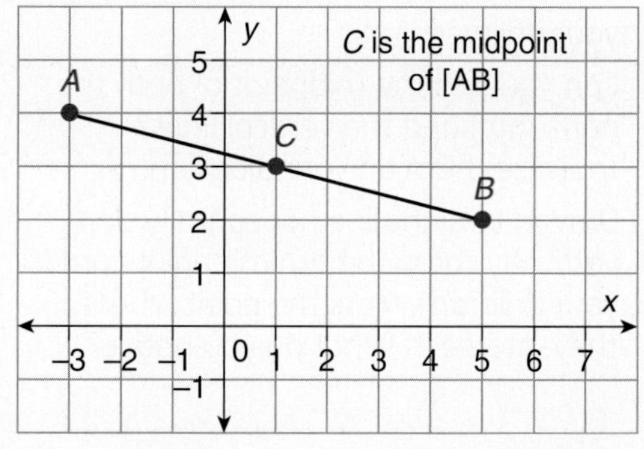

EXAMPLE 3

Given the points $A(10, 2)$ and $B(-2, 4)$, find the midpoint of $[AB]$.

Solution

$\begin{matrix} x_1\ y_1 & & x_2\ y_2 \\ A(10, 2), & & B(-2, 4) \end{matrix}$ **Label the points (x_1, y_1) and (x_2, y_2) as shown**

$\left(\frac{x_1 + x_2}{2}, \frac{y_1 + y_2}{2}\right)$ **Write down the formula**

$\left(\frac{10 + (-2)}{2}, \frac{2 + 4}{2}\right)$ **Substitute in the values using brackets**

$\left(\frac{8}{2}, \frac{6}{2}\right)$ **Use your calculator to evaluate the answer**

$(4, 3)$ is the midpoint of $[AB]$.

EXAMPLE 4

The point $N(3, 4)$ is the midpoint of the line segment $[PQ]$. If the coordinates of P are $(6, 2)$, find the coordinates of Q.

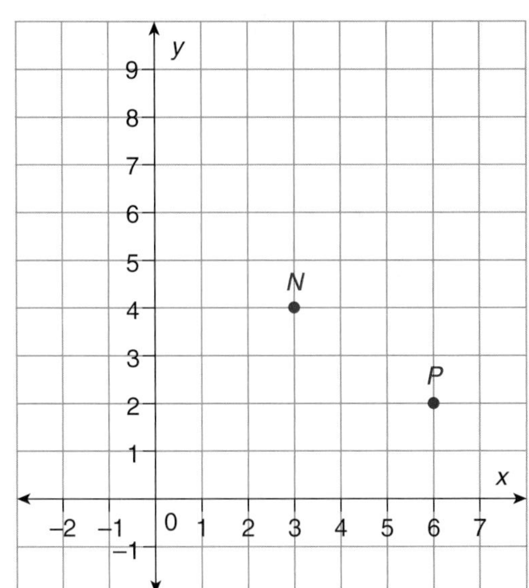

Solution

For this type of question, we use a **translation.**

Go from $P \rightarrow N \rightarrow Q$ as that is the order of the points on the line segment.

$P(6, 2)$ $N(3, 4)$ $Q(?, ?)$

To translate P to N, we must subtract 3 from the x value and add 2 to the y value.

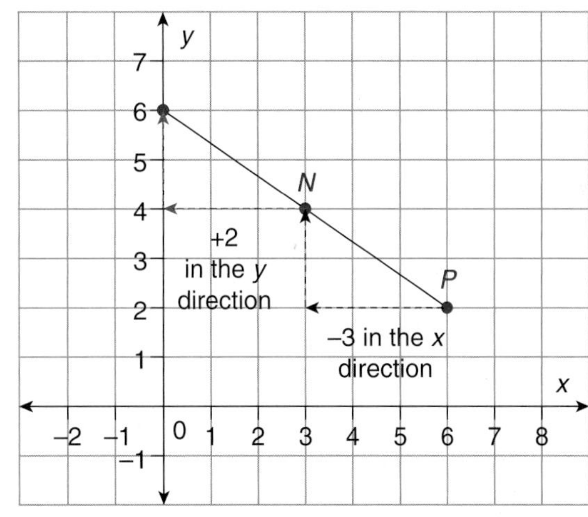

Now, carry out the same translation from N to find Q:

$Q(3 - 3, 4 + 2) = Q(0, 6)$

Exercise 12.2

Find the midpoint of the each of the following pairs of points:

1. $A(2, 5), B(4, 3)$

2. $A(4, 6), B(0, 8)$

3. $X(3, 7), Y(5, 3)$

4. $S(5, -3), T(-2, -5)$

5. $X(8, 10), Y(-4, 7)$

6. $X(7, 9), Y(3, 7)$

7. $X(-2, 4), Y(-7, -4)$

8. $A(4, 6), B(-1, -3)$

9. $X(3, -4), Y(4, -3)$

10. Team Fitness are planning to run from town $A(2, 4)$ to town $B(4, 8)$. They plan to stop for a break at the halfway point of the journey. Using the midpoint formula, calculate where they should stop.

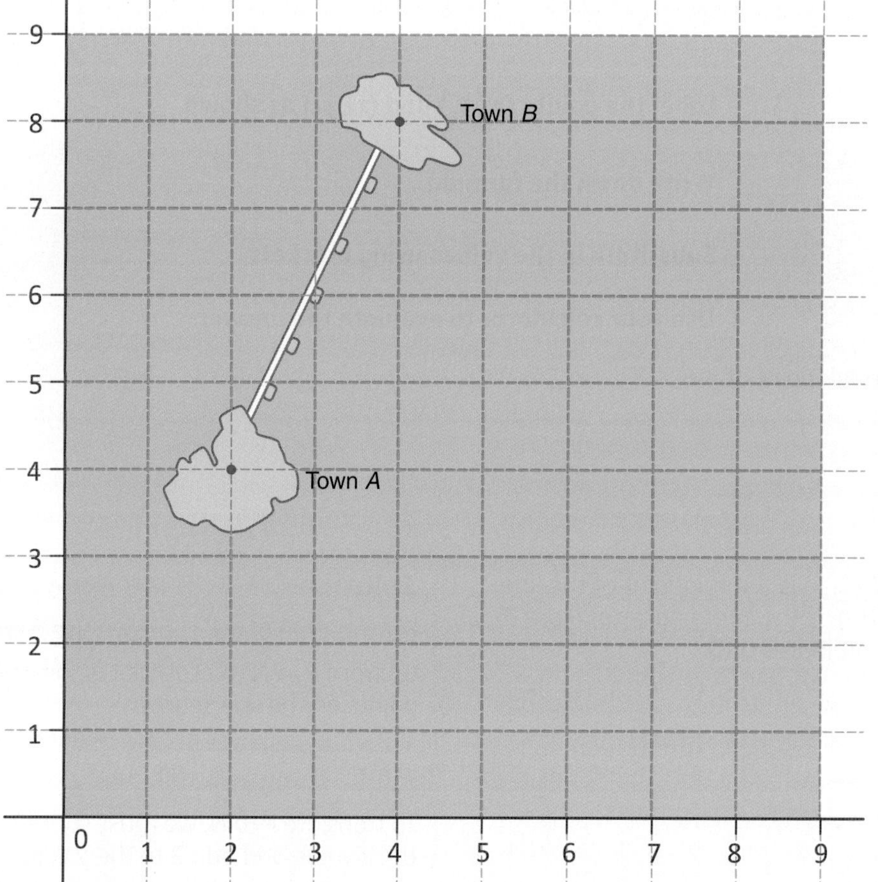

11. A triangle has vertices at points $A(4, -5)$, $B(12, 1)$ and $C(18, 9)$. Find:

(a) Find the midpoint of $[AB]$.

(b) Find the midpoint of $[AC]$.

(c) Find the midpoint of $[BC]$.

12. Show, using a coordinate diagram, that the midpoint of the line segment joining $A(5, 4)$ and $B(7, -4)$ is on the x-axis.

13. Show by calculation that the midpoint of the line segment joining $A(-5, 10)$ and $B(5, -4)$ is on the y-axis.

14. The point $Q(5, 2)$ is the midpoint of the line segment $[PR]$. If the coordinates of R are $(7, 5)$, find the coordinates of P.

15. The point $S(4, 0)$ is the midpoint of the line segment $[RT]$. If the coordinates of T are $(5, -2)$, find the coordinates of R.

16. The point $D(-2, 1)$ is the midpoint of the line segment $[CE]$. If the coordinates of C are $(-5, 3)$, find the coordinates of the point E.

17. The points $P(2, 6)$, $Q(2, -2)$, $R(13, -2)$ and $S(13, 6)$ form a quadrilateral.

(a) Plot the points on a coordinate plane.

(b) Find the point M, the midpoint of the line segment $[PR]$.

(c) Find the point M, the midpoint of the line segment $[QS]$.

(d) What do you notice about your answers in parts (b) and (c)?

(e) Verify that $|PM| = |MR|$.

(f) Verify that $|QM| = |MS|$.

(g) What do you notice about your answers in parts (e) and (f)? What does this tell us about the diagonals of a parallelogram?

18. Examine the map of Australia below and answer the questions that follow:

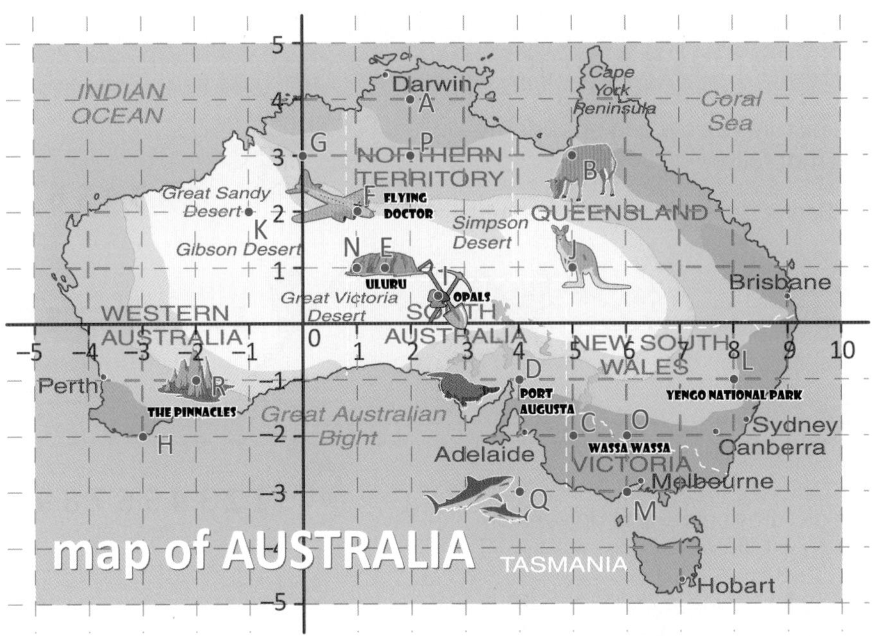

(a) A medical shipment is being transported from Port Augusta (D) to the Flying Doctor Station (F). What landmark will the driver pass halfway through her journey?

(b) A tourist is travelling from the Northern Territory (P) to Yengo National Park (L). What animal will they encounter at the halfway point in their journey?

(c) A nature enthusiast wants to see Great White Sharks (Q). If he travels from Yengo National Park (L), what is the midpoint of his journey?

19.

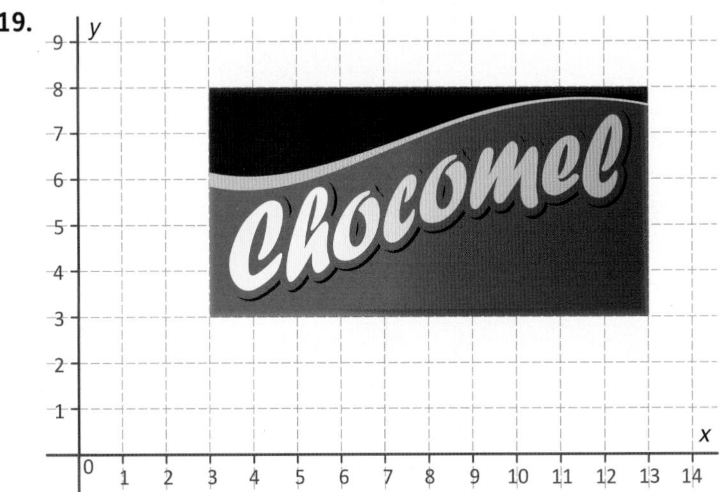

(a) Find the midpoint of the longer side of the chocolate bar shown.

(b) Using a suitable geometrical construction, construct the perpendicular bisector of the longer sides of the bar.

20. A triangle has vertices $F(2, 3)$, $G(2, 11)$ and $H(10, 3)$.

(a) Show the triangle on a coordinate plane.

(b) Find the coordinates of the point W, the midpoint of $[FG]$.

(c) Find the coordinates of the point X, the midpoint of $[FH]$.

(d) Find the coordinates of the point Y, the midpoint of $[GH]$.

(e) Find the midpoints of the line segments joining each midpoint to its opposite vertex.

(f) What do you notice about your answers in part (e)?

Section 12.3: The slope of a line

Student Activity 12C

1. Study the pictures below and answer the questions that follow:

Flat (horizontal)	Gentle slope	Steeper	Steepest

   Which road would the cyclist find it hardest to cycle up? Explain your answer.

2. Study the pictures below and answer the questions that follow:

   (a) On which road would the cyclist be fastest coming down? Explain your answer.

   (b) On which slope would the cyclist be slowest? Explain your answer.

3. Can you think of words used to describe how steep a hill or road is?

4. Have you heard the word **'slope'** before? What do you understand it to mean?

5. For each line shown, assign a value to its steepness using a scale from 1 to 9 (9 being the steepest).

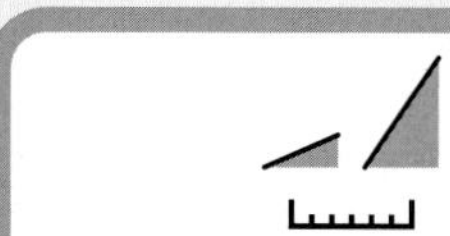

Steepness scale

1 2 3 4 5 6 7 8 9

1 2 3 4 5 6 7 8 9

1 2 3 4 5 6 7 8 9

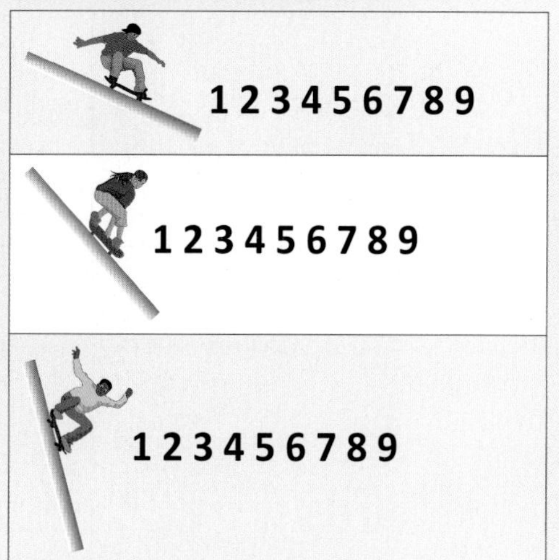

6. Study the line below and answer the questions that follow:

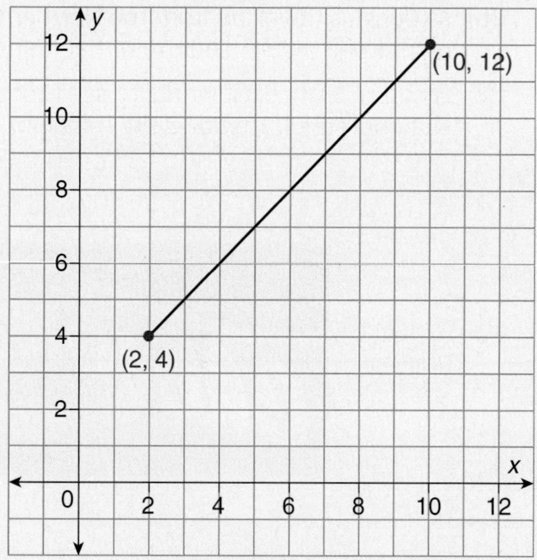

   (a) Do you think this line has a positive or a negative slope?

   (b) Copy the diagram above.

   (c) What is the horizontal distance (run) between the two points? Show how you found your answer.

   (d) What is the vertical distance (rise) between the two points? Show how you found your answer.

   (e) Put the vertical distance over the horizontal distance as a fraction.

THE SLOPE OF A LINE EXPLAINED

We examine every line from left to right as we would read a sentence in English.

Look at the following lines:

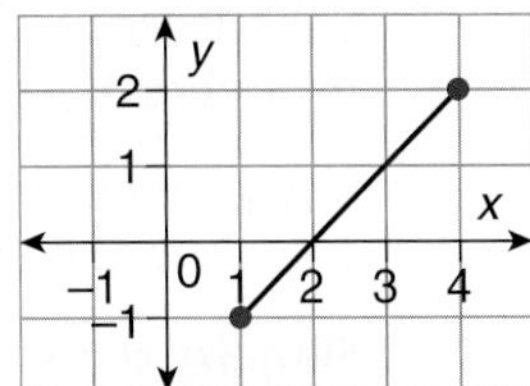

- As you can see, this line is rising from left to right. We say that this has a **positive slope.**

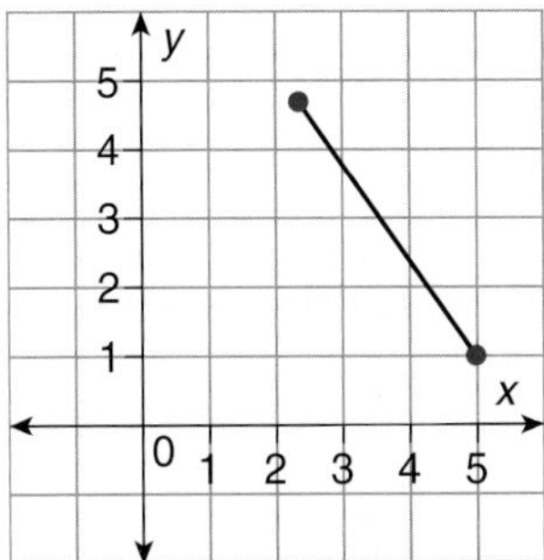

- This line is falling from left to right. We say that this has a **negative slope.**

The letter ***m*** is used to denote the slope of a line.

In other words we say:

$$\text{Slope or } m = \frac{\text{Vertical change}}{\text{Horizontal change}} \text{ or } \frac{\text{Rise}}{\text{Run}}$$

If we examine our general points again, we can use them to write another formula:

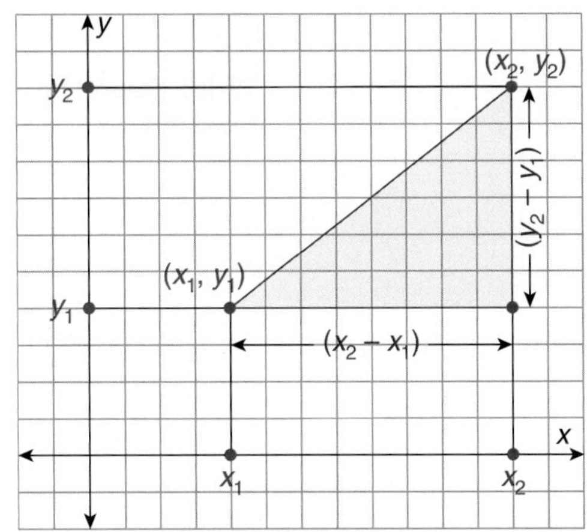

Rise = $y_2 - y_1$ and Run = $x_2 - x_1$

The formula becomes:

$$\text{Slope of a line: } m = \frac{y_2 - y_1}{x_2 - x_1}$$

This formula can be found on page 18 of the *Formulae and Tables.*

Remember to put a – sign in front of the slope if it is negative (falling from left to right).

EXAMPLE 5

Examine the lines shown in the diagram and write down the slope of each line.

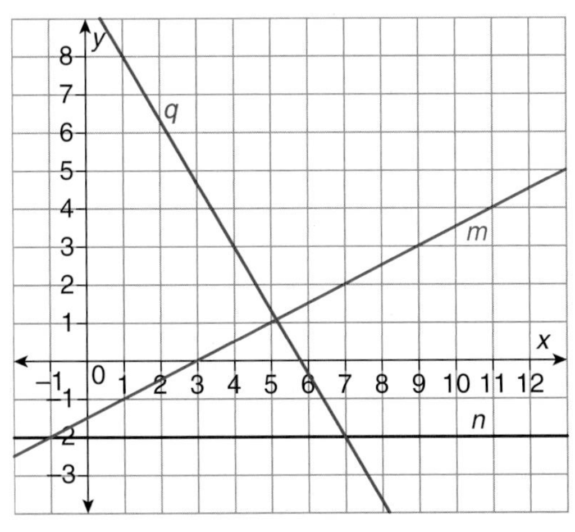

Solution

Mark two points on each line as shown.

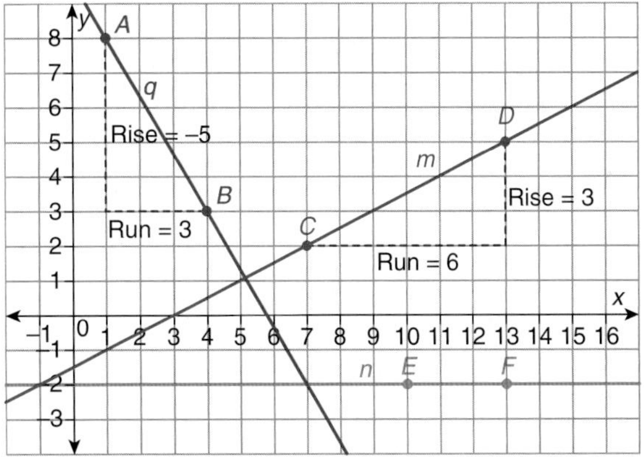

Line *q* using the points *A* and *B*

$$m = \frac{\text{Rise}}{\text{Run}} = \frac{-5}{3} = -\frac{5}{3}$$

Line *m* using the points *C* and *D*

$$m = \frac{\text{Rise}}{\text{Run}} = \frac{3}{6} = \frac{1}{2}$$

Line *n* using the points *E* and *F*:

$$m = \frac{\text{Rise}}{\text{Run}} = \frac{0}{3} = 0$$

EXAMPLE 6

Given the points $A(10, 2)$ and $B(-2, 4)$, find the slope of $[AB]$.

Solution

$x_1\ y_1 \qquad x_2\ y_2$

$A(10, 2)$, $B(-2, 4)$ **Label the points (x_1, y_1) and (x_2, y_2) as shown**

$m = \frac{y_2 - y_1}{x_2 - x_1}$ **Write down the formula**

$m = \frac{(4) - (2)}{(-2) - (10)}$ **Substitute in the values using brackets**

$m = \frac{2}{-12}$ **Use your calculator to calculate the value**

$m = -\frac{1}{6}$ **Simplify the fraction**

EXAMPLE 7

If the slope of the line joining the points $(1, 3)$ and $(3, k)$ is $\frac{3}{2}$, find the value of k.

Solution

$x_1\ y_1 \qquad x_2\ y_2$

$(1, 3)$, $(3, k)$ **Label the points (x_1, y_1) and (x_2, y_2) as shown**

$m = \frac{y_2 - y_1}{x_2 - x_1}$ **Write down the formula**

$\frac{k - 3}{3 - 1} = \frac{3}{2}$ **Substitute values into the formula**

$\frac{k - 3}{2} = \frac{3}{2}$

$k - 3 = 3$ **Multiply both sides by 2**

$k = 3 + 3$

$k = 6$

Exercise 12.3

Calculate the slope of each of the following lines:

1. 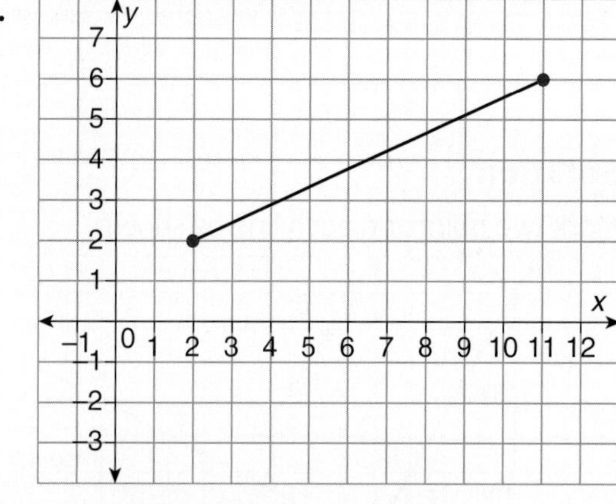

2. 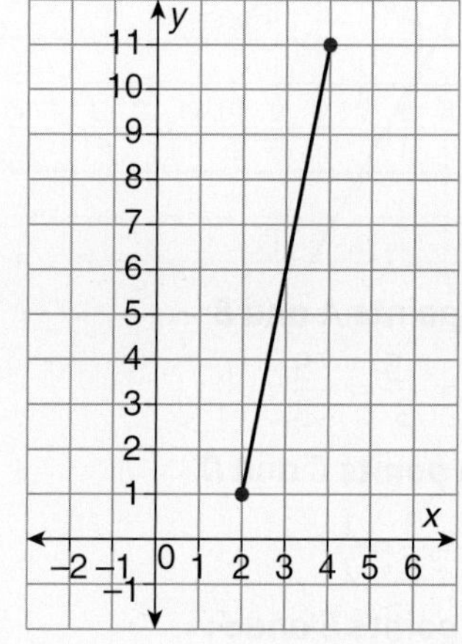

3. 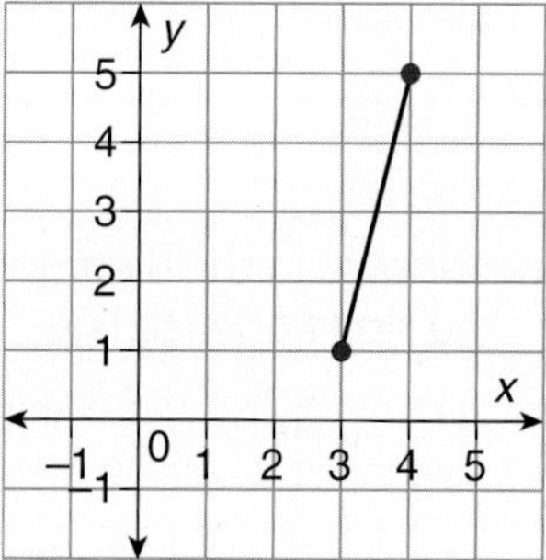

4. 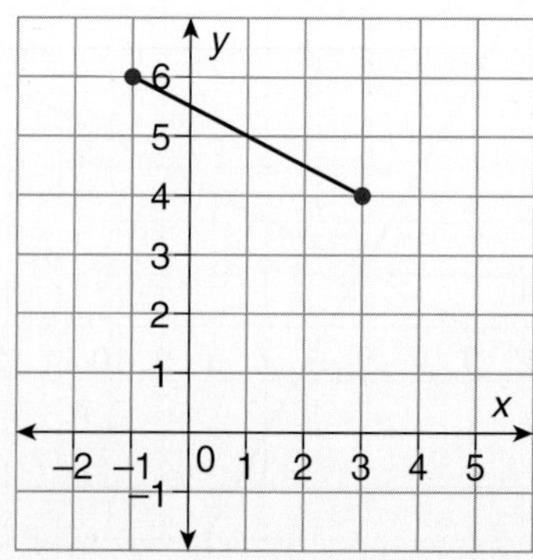

5.

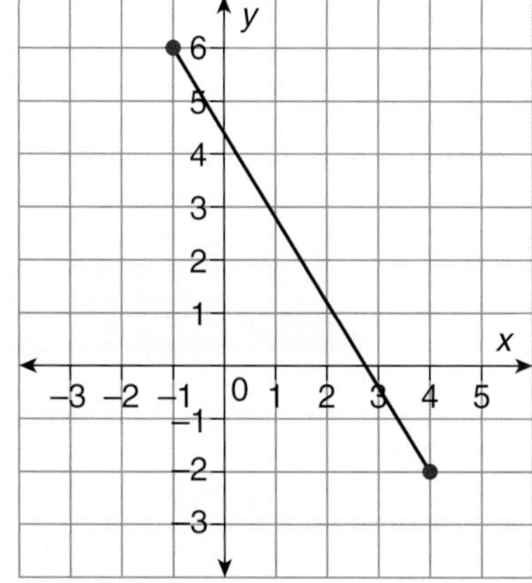

6.

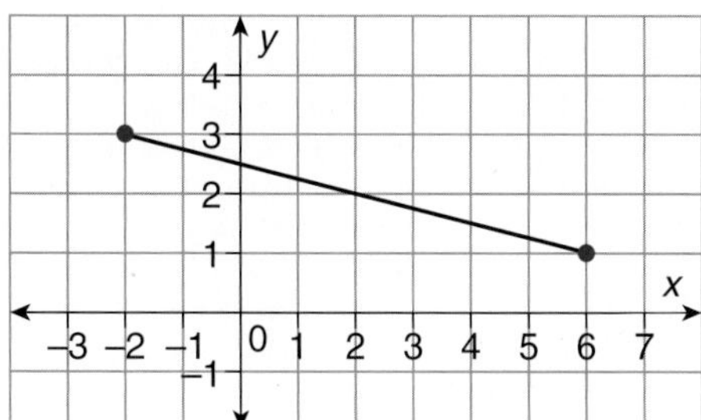

7.

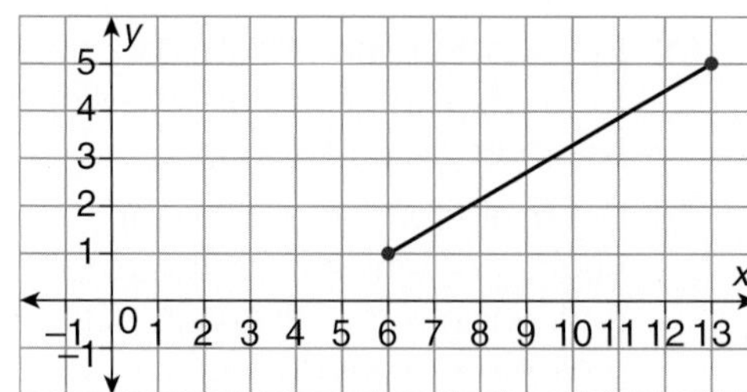

8.

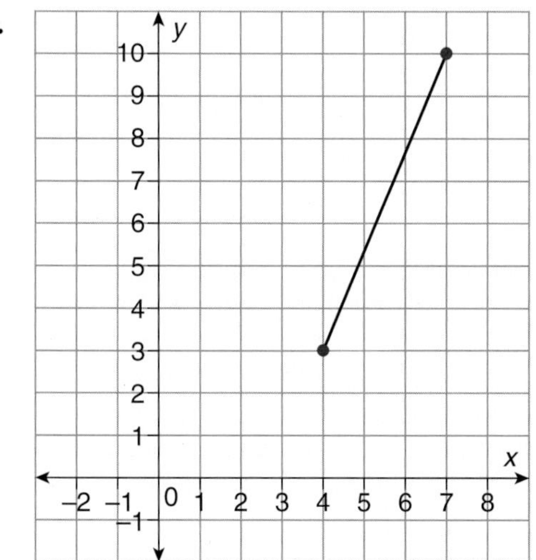

Find the slope of the line that contains the following points:

9. $A(4, 2)$, $B(6, 8)$

10. $X(3, 7)$, $Y(7, 15)$

11. $R(6, 2)$, $S(4,8)$

12. $C(-2, -4)$, $P(0, 0)$

13. $P(3, -5)$, $Q(-1, 3)$

14. $X(-4, 3)$, $Y(3, -4)$

15. $M(2, -7)$, $N(-3, -2)$

16. $A(-3, -6)$, $B(2, 1)$

17. $X(-4, 7)$, $Y(0, -5)$

18. Examine the lines in the picture below. Match each line to a slope listed in the table.

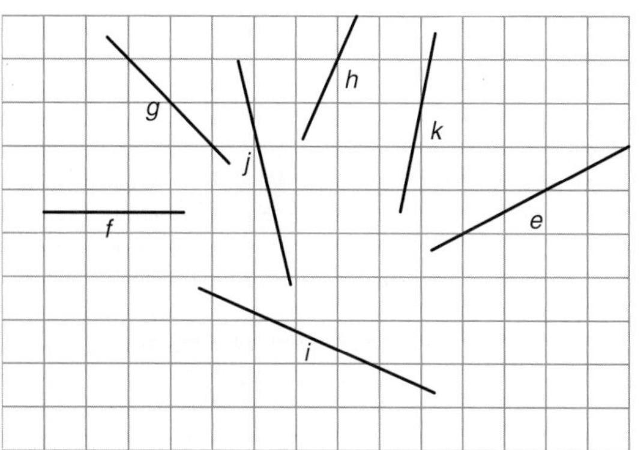

Slope = –1	Slope = 2	Slope = $-\frac{2}{5}$	Slope = 0.5
Slope = 0	Slope = –4		Slope = 7

19. Find the slopes of [AB] and [BC] in each of the following:

(a)

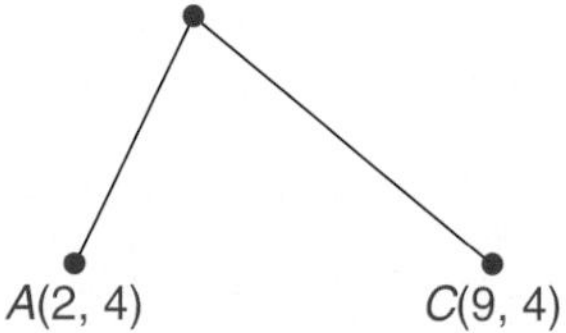

(b)

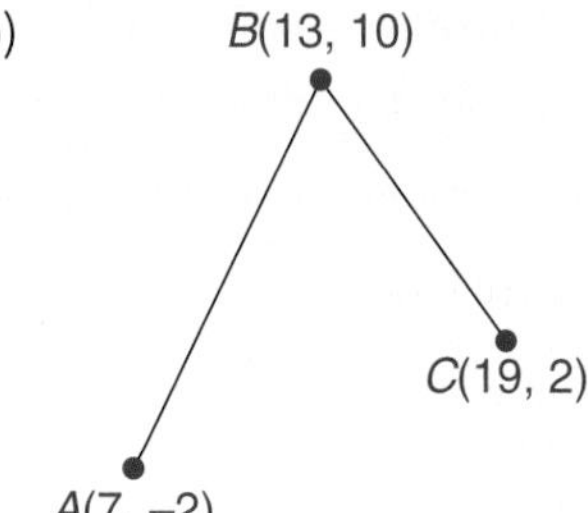

(c)

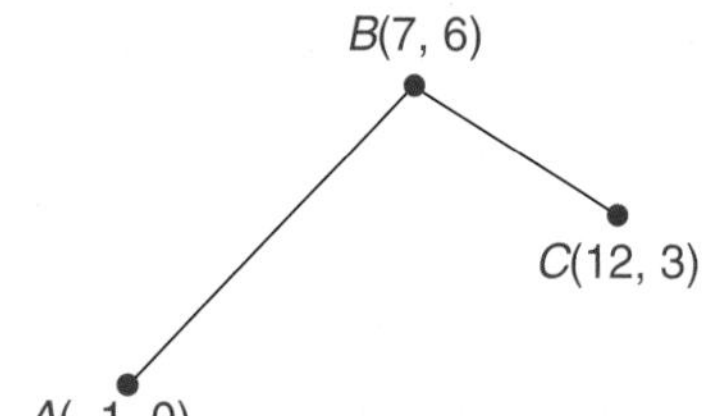

(d)

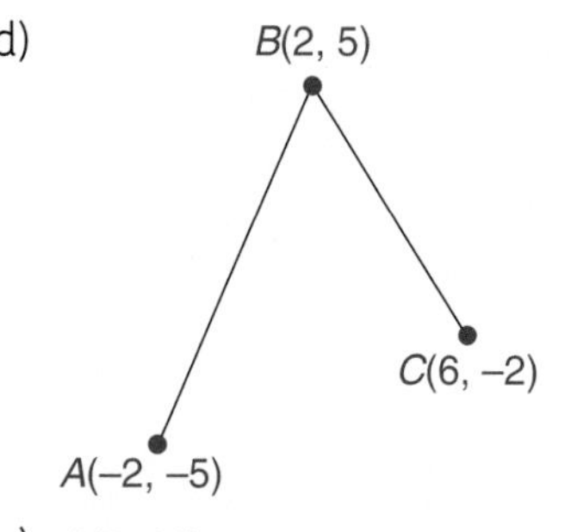

(e) (f)

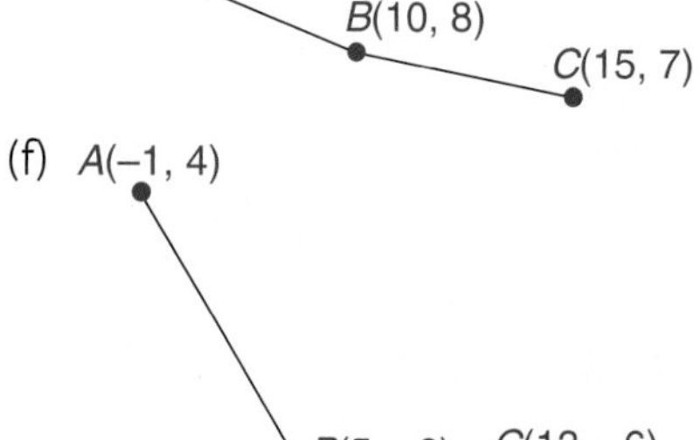

20. Three hills lie between the towns *A*, *B* and *C*, where *A* is (4, –5), *B* is (12, 1) and *C* is (18, 9).

(a) Find the slope of [*AB*].

(b) Find the slope of [*AC*].

(c) Find the slope of [*BC*].

21. A metal cable holds a flag pole in place as shown. Calculate the slope of the cable.

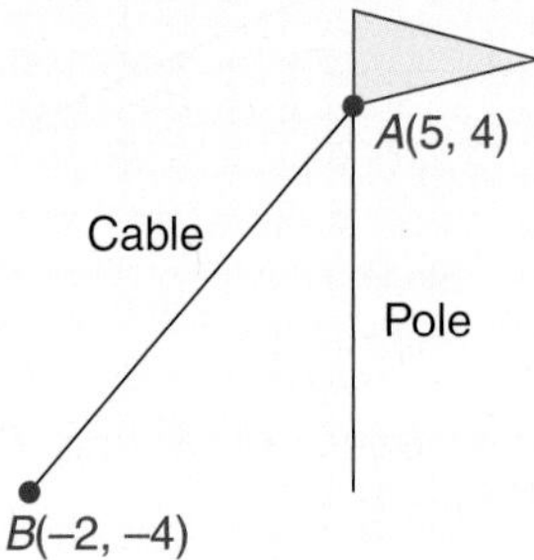

22. If the slope of the line joining (−2, 1) and (−4, *h*) is −2, find the value of *h*.

23. If the slope of the line joining (*t*, 7) and (−7, 4) is $-\frac{1}{11}$, find the value of *t*.

24. If the slope of the line joining (5, 8) and (−4, *k*) is $-\frac{2}{9}$, find the value of *k*.

25. If the slope of the line joining (10, 6) and (*s*, −2) is $\frac{4}{7}$, find the value of *s*.

26. Find the slope of the roof of the dog house shown.

27. A map of the Hakuba Goryu Ski Resort in Japan is shown below:

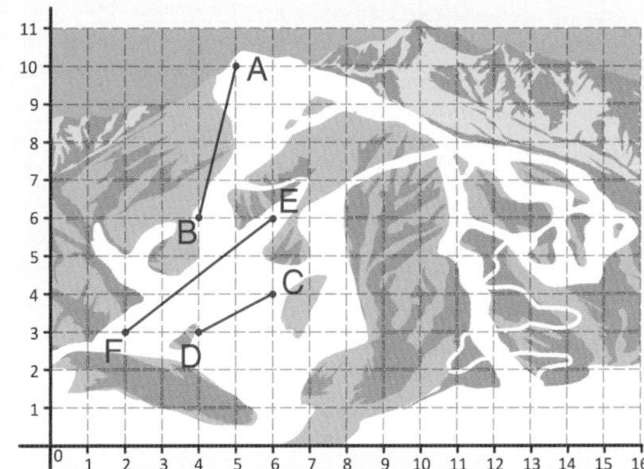

(a) By choosing appropriate coordinates for each point, calculate the slopes of the three ski paths shown.

(b) Determine which slope is for Beginners, which is for Intermediate and which is for Advanced skiers. Give reasons for your answers.

Section 12.4: Parallel and perpendicular slopes

Student Activity 12D

1. Study the diagram and answer the following questions:

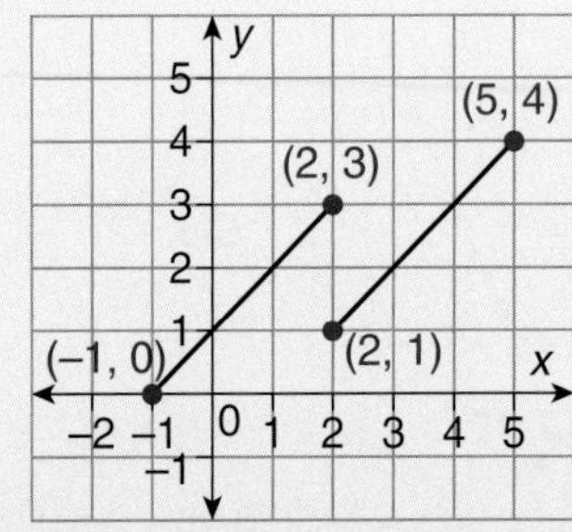

(a) Can you make any observation about these lines?

(b) Find the slopes of both of these lines.

(c) What do you notice about the slopes of these lines?

2. Find the slopes of the line marked *k* in the diagram below. What do the arrows on the lines indicate? What do you think is the slope of the line marked *p*? Explain your answer.

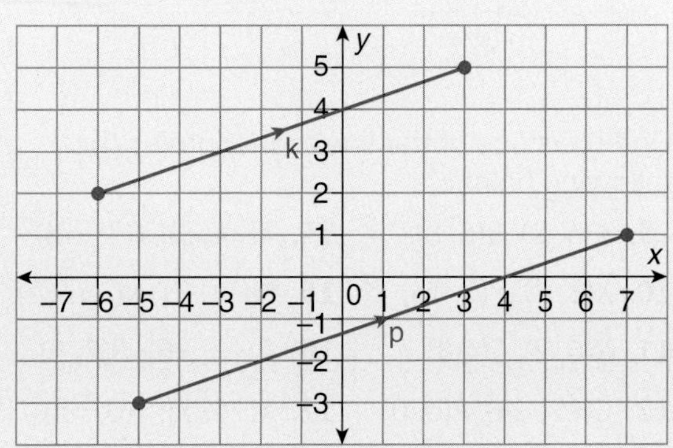

3. Copy and complete the following sentence:

P______l lines have e___l s_____.

4. Study the diagram and answer the following questions:

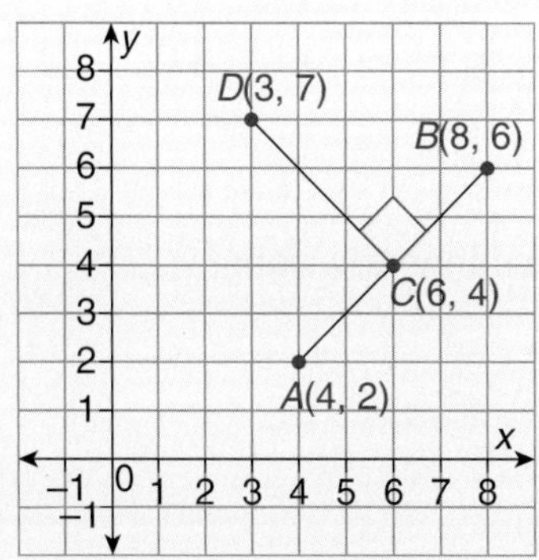

(a) What observation can you make about the lines above?
(b) Find the slope of [AB].
(c) Find the slope of [CD].
(d) Can you make any observation about the slopes you have found?
(e) Multiply the slopes you have found.

5. If the slope of a line k is $\frac{5}{2}$, can you work out what you think the slope of any line perpendicular to k will be? Explain your answer.

6. Examine the lines below and answer the questions that follow.

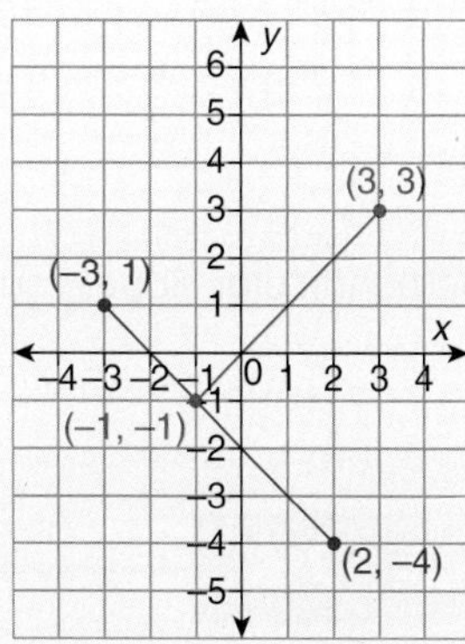

(a) Are these lines parallel or perpendicular?
(b) Find the slopes of both lines.
(c) Can you make any observation about the two slopes?
(d) What number will you get if you multiply the two slopes?

7. Copy and complete the following sentence:
If two lines are perpendicular, their slopes will m _ _ _ _ _ _ _ to give minus _.

PARALLEL AND PERPENDICULAR LINES EXPLAINED

In Student Activity 12D, you examined slopes of lines that are parallel or perpendicular to each other.

Parallel lines run side by side but never meet or intersect. Parallel lines have the same slope. Since they have the same slope, we say $\mathbf{m_1 = m_2}$ (the slope of the first line is equal to the slope of the second line).

> If two lines have slopes m_1 and m_2 respectively, they are parallel if and only if $m_1 = m_2$.

If two lines are **perpendicular,** the lines intersect at one point only and at right angles to each other. The slope of one line is the negative inverted slope of the other line:

- If $m_1 = \frac{3}{4}$, then the perpendicular slope is $\perp m_1 = -\frac{4}{3}$.
- If $m_1 = 4$, then the perpendicular slope is $\perp m_1 = -\frac{1}{4}$

> If two lines have slopes m_1 and m_2 respectively, they are perpendicular if and only if $m_1 \times m_2 = -1$.

EXAMPLE 8

The line l contains the points (2, 3) and (5, 8).
The line k contains the points (5, 6) and (8, 11).
Investigate whether the lines are parallel.

Solution

Slope of $l = \frac{y_2 - y_1}{x_2 - x_1} = \frac{8 - 3}{5 - 2} = \frac{5}{3}$

Slope of $k = \frac{y_2 - y_1}{x_2 - x_1} = \frac{11 - 6}{8 - 5} = \frac{5}{3}$

Slope of l = Slope of k

$\therefore$ The lines are parallel

EXAMPLE 9

Write down the slope that is perpendicular to each of the following slopes:

(a) $\frac{2}{3}$ (b) $-\frac{4}{3}$ (c) 2 (d) $\frac{5}{3}$

Solution

To find the perpendicular slope, you invert the fraction and change the sign:

(a) $-\frac{3}{2}$ (b) $\frac{3}{4}$ (c) $-\frac{1}{2}$ (d) $-\frac{3}{5}$

Exercise 12.4

Find the slopes of the lines that contain the following pairs of points and state whether or not the lines are parallel.

1. The line l contains the points (0, 3) and (4, 0). The line k contains the points (1, 9) and (5, 6).
2. The line m contains the points (9, −2) and (7, −6). The line n contains the points (6, 0) and (5, −2).
3. The line b contains the points (−5, 10) and (−8, 3). The line d contains the points (0, 8) and (−3, 1).
4. The line l contains the points (4, 2) and (6, 11). The line k contains the points (−1, −4) and (3, 5).
5. The line s contains the points (3, −2) and (0, −3). The line t contains the points (−9, 0) and (3, −4).
6. The line l contains the points (2, 1) and (4, 3). The line k contains the points (5, 7) and (6, 9).
7. The line m contains the points (−1, 6) and (6, 3). The line n contains the points (−13, −7) and (−6, −10).
8. The line p contains the points (−1, 4) and (2, 2). The line q contains the points (2, −3) and (5, −7).

9. Investigate whether the following pairs of lines are parallel:

(a)

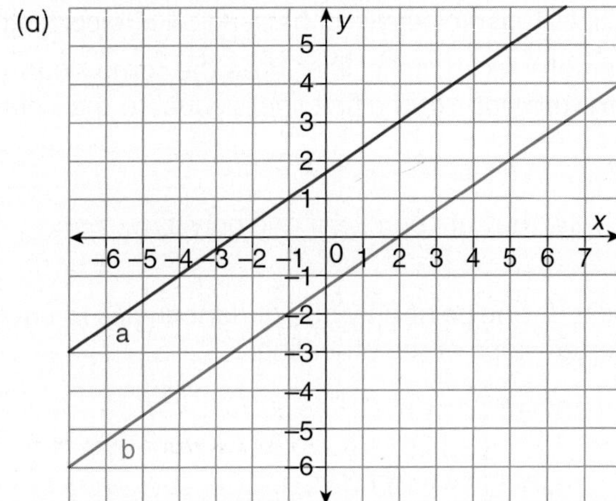

(c)

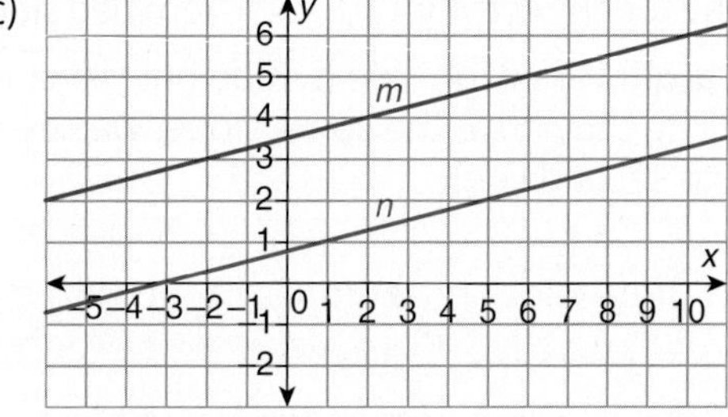

(b)

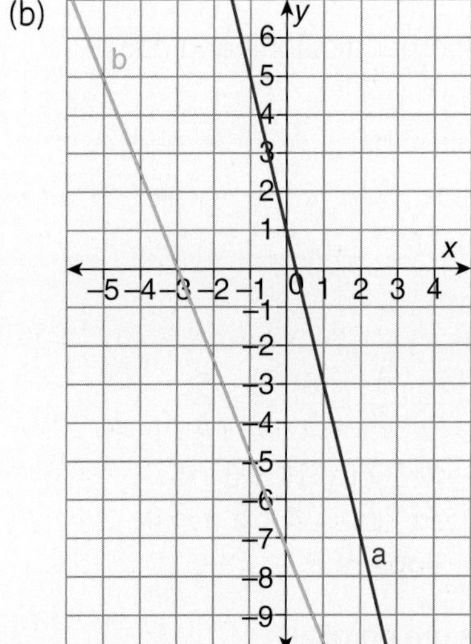

(d)

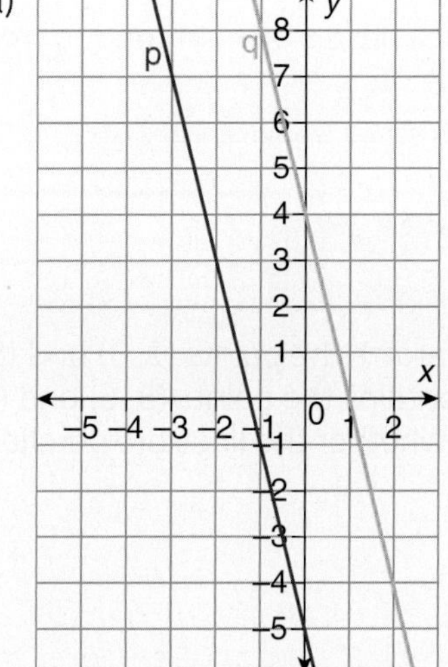

10. John's house and Peter's house are on two roads as shown in the diagram. Are the roads parallel? Explain your answer.

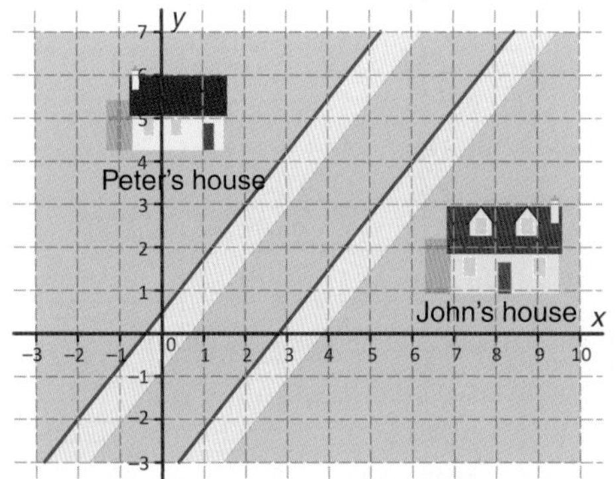

11. Plot the points $X(-1, 5)$, $Y(2, 12)$, $W(-2,-4)$, $Z(1, 3)$ on a coordinate diagram.

(a) Find the slope of $[XY]$.

(b) Find the slope of $[WZ]$.

(c) Verify that $[XY] \parallel [WZ]$.

12. Two birds are flying on two different routes as shown. Are their flight-paths parallel? Explain your answer.

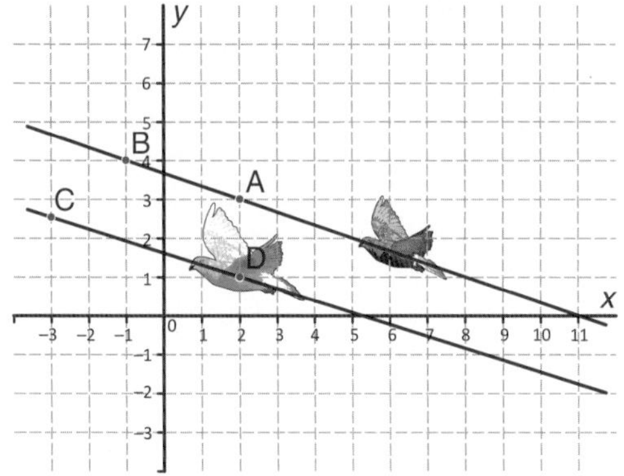

13. Write down the perpendicular slope of each of the following slopes:

(a) $\frac{4}{3}$	(f) $-\frac{2}{3}$	(k) $\frac{1}{9}$
(b) $\frac{3}{2}$	(g) 2	(l) $\frac{1}{13}$
(c) $\frac{5}{7}$	(h) −3	(m) $-\frac{4}{13}$
(d) $-\frac{4}{9}$	(i) 4	(n) $\frac{11}{3}$
(e) $-\frac{5}{11}$	(j) $\frac{1}{7}$	(o) $-1\frac{3}{7}$

14. $A(1, 2)$, $B(3, 5)$, $C(7, 5)$, $D(10, 3)$ are four points. Show that $AB \perp CD$.

15. The line M has a slope of $\frac{4}{7}$. Find the slope of the line L if $M \perp L$.

16. The points $A(2, 1)$, $B(3, 6)$ and $C(5, 1)$ are the vertices of a triangle. Investigate whether ΔABC is right-angled.

17. The points $A(5, 1)$, $B(7, 5)$ and $C(3, 7)$ are the vertices of a triangle. Investigate whether ΔABC is a right-angled triangle.

18. The points $X(-2, 5)$, $Y(1, 4)$ and $Z(2, -1)$ are the vertices of a triangle. Investigate whether ΔXYZ contains a right angle.

19. A builder is trying to discover whether an old wall is perpendicular to the ground, as shown. Can you help him?

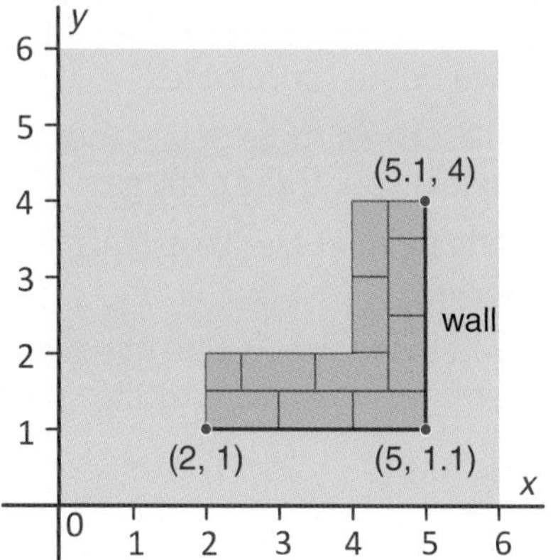

20. A carpenter is making a table as shown. Will the table stand upright when finished?

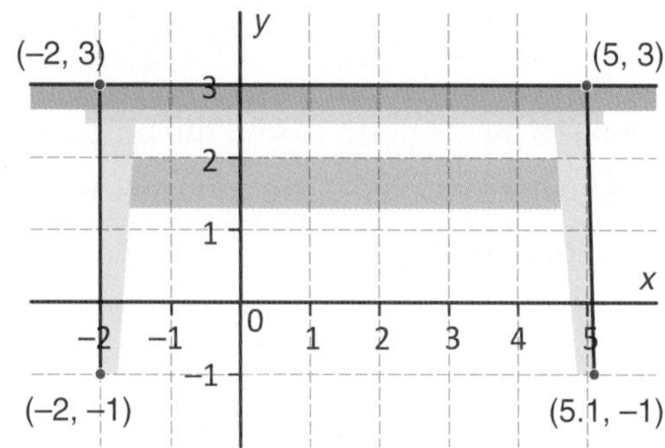

21. The points $W(3, 5)$, $X(10, 5)$, $Y(10, -2)$ and $Z(3, -2)$ form a quadrilateral. Verify that the quadrilateral is a parallelogram.

22. The points $A(1, -3)$, $B(4, 3)$, $C(10, 3)$ and $D(8, -3)$ form a quadrilateral. Investigate whether $ABDC$ is a parallelogram.

23. The points $G(-3, 9)$, $H(-3, 5)$, $I(1, 5)$ and $J(1, 9)$ form a quadrilateral.

(a) Investigate whether the quadrilateral is a rhombus.

(b) Using slopes, verify that the quadrilateral is a square.

(c) Verify that the diagonals of the square are perpendicular to each other.

24. On a coordinate plane, plot four points that form a rectangle.

(a) Using slopes, verify that the opposite sides are parallel.

(b) Using slopes, verify that the adjoined sides are perpendicular to each other.

(c) Investigate whether the diagonals of the rectangle are perpendicular.

Section 12.5: The equation of a line 1

Student Activity 12E

Study the following diagram and answer the questions.

(a) Examine the x and y values of each point. Can you see any pattern using the numbers for each point? (Hint: check the sum and difference of the coordinates.)

(b) Can you list three more points that will follow this rule? Explain your three choices.

(c) Would the point (12, 2) lie on this line? Explain your answer.

(d) If you add the x and y value of each point along the given line, what is the total in each case?

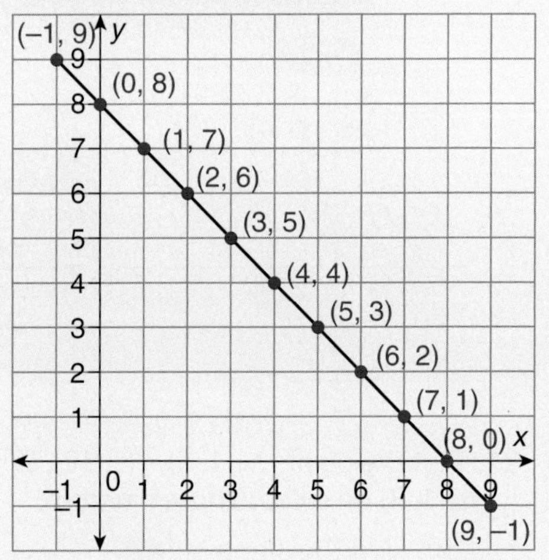

THE EQUATION OF A LINE 1 EXPLAINED

In Student Activity 12E, you looked at the **equation of a line.** Every point on a line follows the same rule. '$x + y = 8$' was the equation of the line because the x and y value always add to give a total of 8.

We often encounter problems where the pattern is more complicated to find or there might not be enough points given to find the pattern.

To solve these problems, we can use the formula to find the equation of any line.

We will need **either:**

1. Two points on the line (which we use to calculate the slope)

or

2. One point and the slope of the line

We use the following formula when we know a point on the line and its slope:

> **Equation of a line**
>
> $y - y_1 = m(x - x_1)$, where m is the slope of the line. (x_1, y_1) is a point on the line.

This formula can be found on page 18 of the *Formulae and Tables*.

EXAMPLE 10

Find the equation of the line shown.

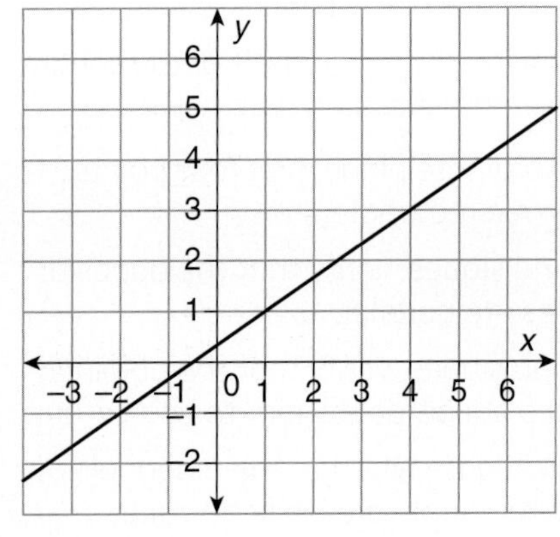

Solution

Find a point and the slope of the line from the graph.

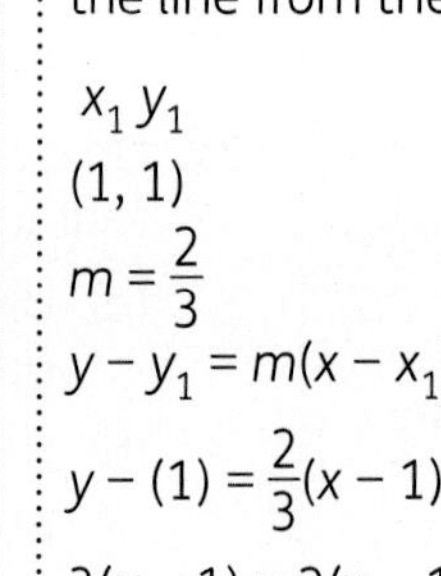

$x_1\ y_1$

$(1, 1)$

$m = \frac{2}{3}$

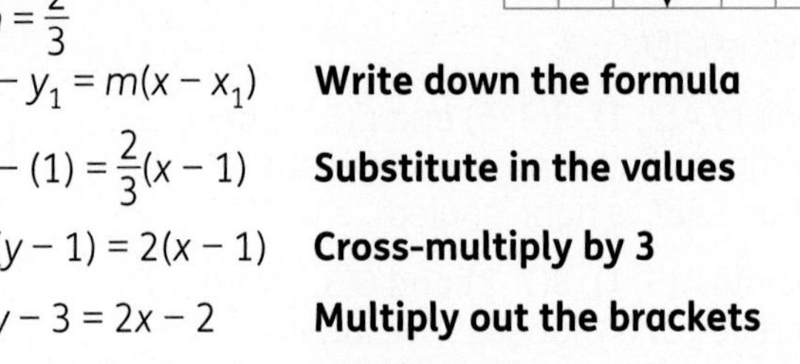

$y - y_1 = m(x - x_1)$	**Write down the formula**
$y - (1) = \frac{2}{3}(x - 1)$	**Substitute in the values**
$3(y - 1) = 2(x - 1)$	**Cross-multiply by 3**
$3y - 3 = 2x - 2$	**Multiply out the brackets**
$2x - 3y + 1 = 0$	**Bring all the terms to one side**

EXAMPLE 11

Find the equation of the line that contains the points $A(-4, 0)$ and $B(-2, 4)$.

Solution

$\begin{matrix} x_1 & y_1 \end{matrix} \quad \begin{matrix} x_2 & y_2 \end{matrix}$

$A(-4, 0)$ $B(-2, 4)$

First, we need to calculate the slope of the line:

$m = \dfrac{y_2 - y_1}{x_2 - x_1}$

$m = \dfrac{4 - 0}{-2 - (-4)}$

$m = \dfrac{4}{2}$

$m = 2$

Now use the formula for the equation of a line:

$y - y_1 = m(x - x_1)$

$y - 0 = 2(x + 4)$

$y = 2x + 8$

or

$2x - y = -8$

Every point on this line will follow the rule expressed by this equation.

EXAMPLE 12

Find the equation of the line that contains the point $D(2, 3)$ and has a slope of $-\frac{2}{3}$.

Solution

$\begin{matrix} x_1 & y_1 \end{matrix}$

$D(2, 3)$

As we have the slope already, we can use the equation formula:

$y - y_1 = m(x - x_1)$

$y - 3 = -\frac{2}{3}(x - 2)$

$3(y - 3) = -2(x - 2)$

$3y - 9 = -2x + 4$

or

$2x + 3y = 13$

Exercise 12.5

Find the equation of each of the following lines:

1. 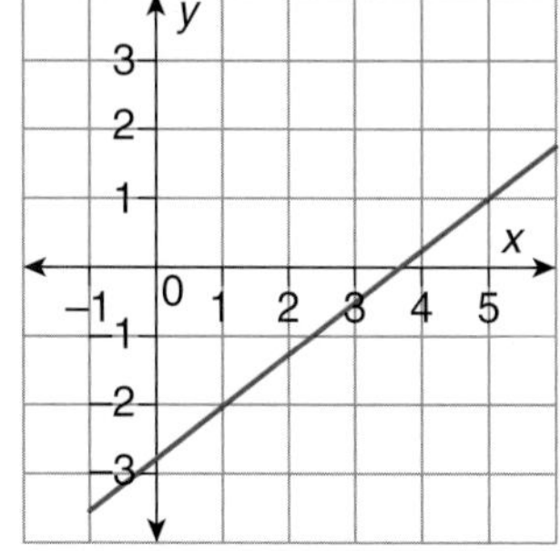

2. 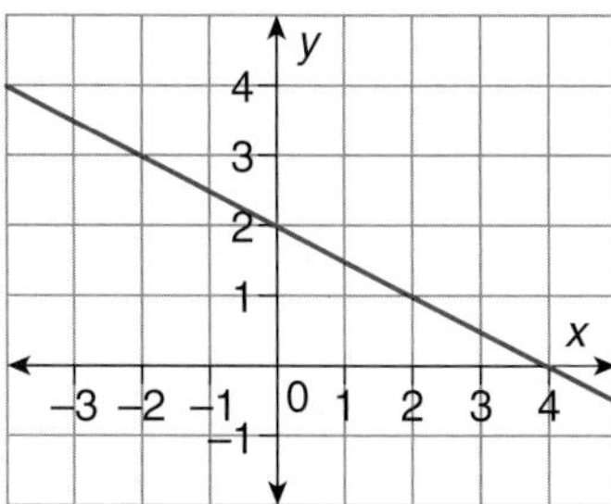

3. 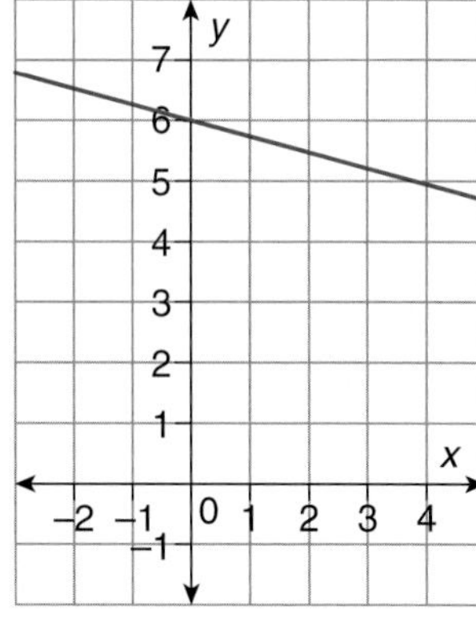

4. 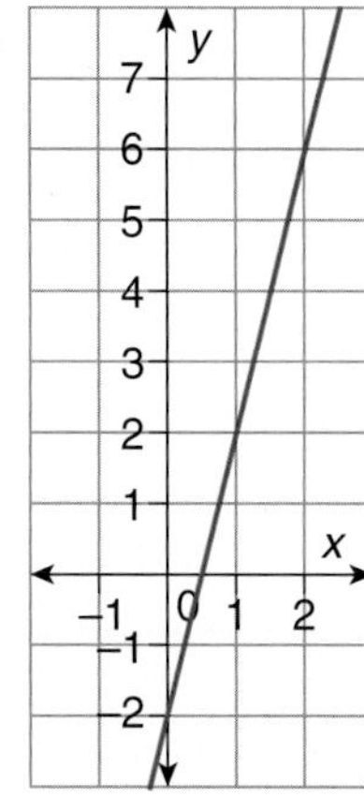

5. 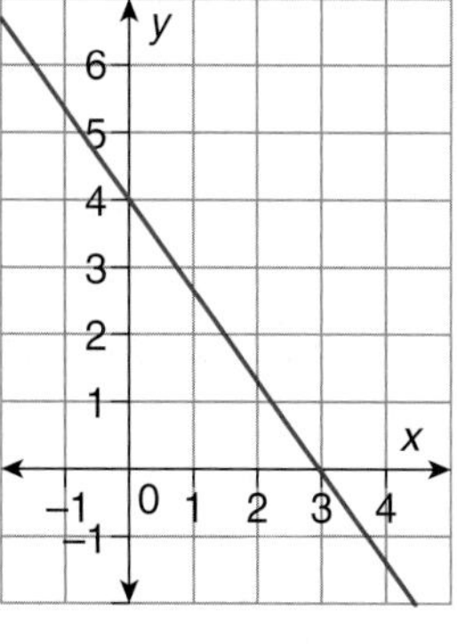

6. 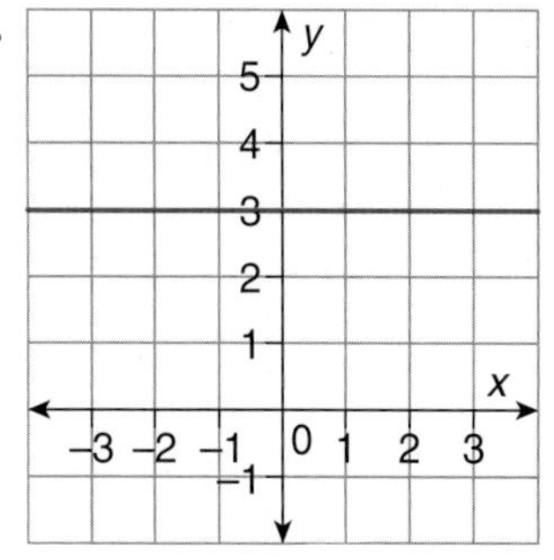

Find the equations of the lines containing the following pairs of points:

7. (2, 4) and $B(4, 8)$

8. $E(-1, 0)$ and $F(7, 6)$

9. $H(5, 10)$ and $J(7, 8)$

10. $P(5, -1)$ and $Q(-3, 0)$

11. $U(0, 2)$ and $V(-3, 3)$

12. $R(1, -4)$ and $S(-2, 6)$

13. $M(-1, -3)$ and $N(2, 1)$

14. $A(-4, -1)$ and $C(1, 1)$

15. $X(-1, -2)$ and $Y(-3, 4)$

16. Given the points $A(4, -5)$, $B(12, 1)$ and $C(18, 9)$, find:

(a) The equation of [AB]

(b) The equation of [AC]

(c) The equation of [BC]

17. Find the equation of the following lines, given a point and the slope:

(a) $A(2, 2)$, $m = 4$

(b) $D(-3, 1)$, $m = 2$

(c) $Q(4, -1)$, $m = -1$

(d) $H(0, 4)$, $m = -2$

(e) $T(1, 0)$, $m = \frac{3}{7}$

(f) $M(-3, 2)$, $m = -\frac{4}{7}$

(g) $S(2, 1)$, $m = \frac{3}{4}$

(h) $P(2, -3)$, $m = -\frac{3}{5}$

18. A line passes through the points $A(3, 5)$ and $B(6, 5)$.

(a) Find the equation of the line.

(b) Show the line on a coordinate plane.

(c) Write down the point where the line intersects the y-axis. What do you notice about this point and the equation of the line?

19. A line passes through the points $P(-2, 1)$ and $Q(1, 1)$.

(a) Find the equation of the line.

(b) Show the line on a coordinate plane.

(c) Write down the point where the line intersects the y-axis. What do you notice about this point and the equation of the line?

20. Write down the equations of each of the following lines:

(a)

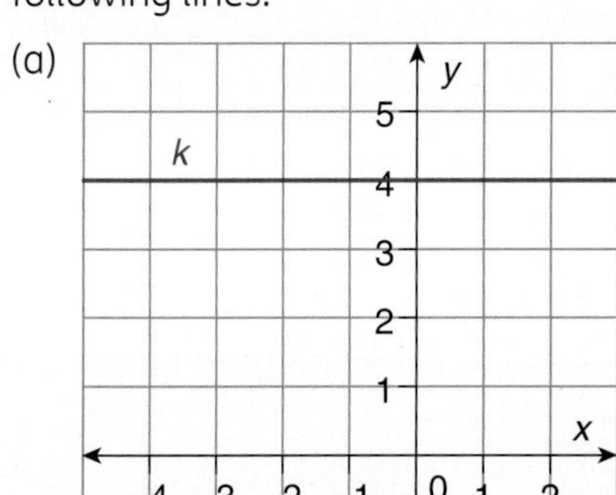

(b)

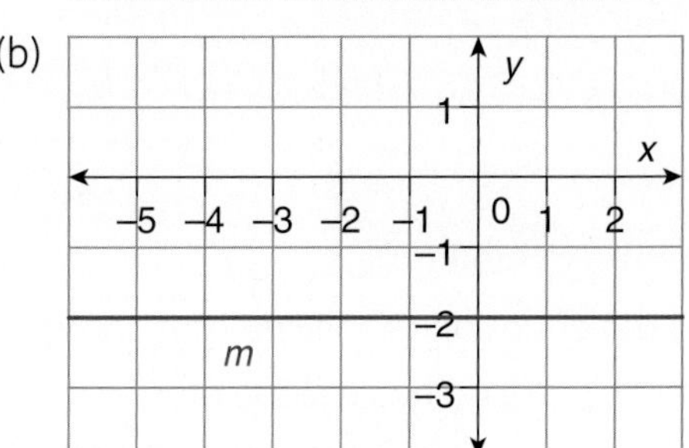

(c)

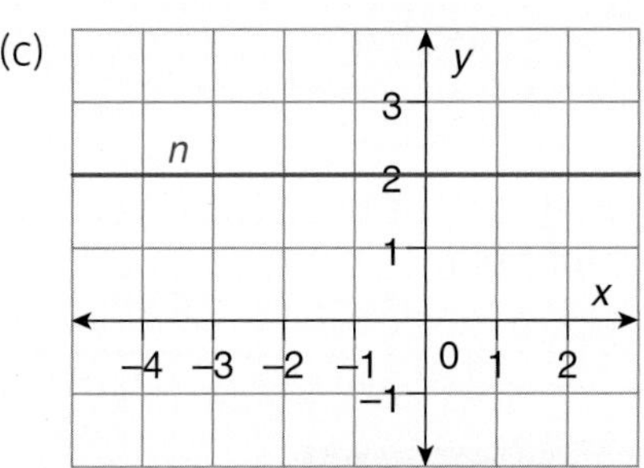

(d)

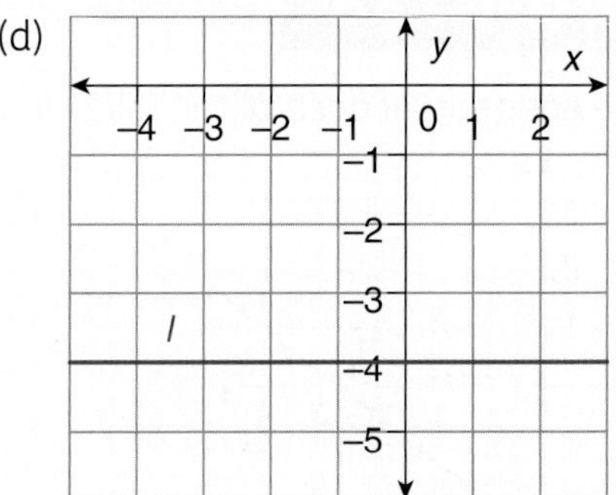

(e)

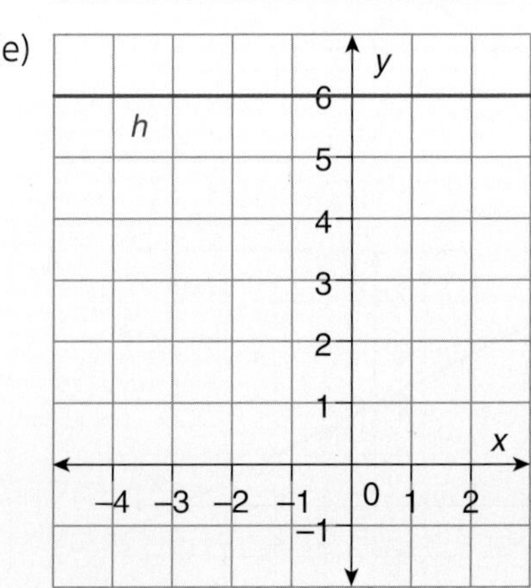

21. Write down the equations of each of the following lines:

(a)

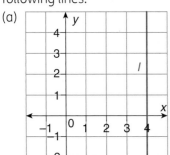

(b)

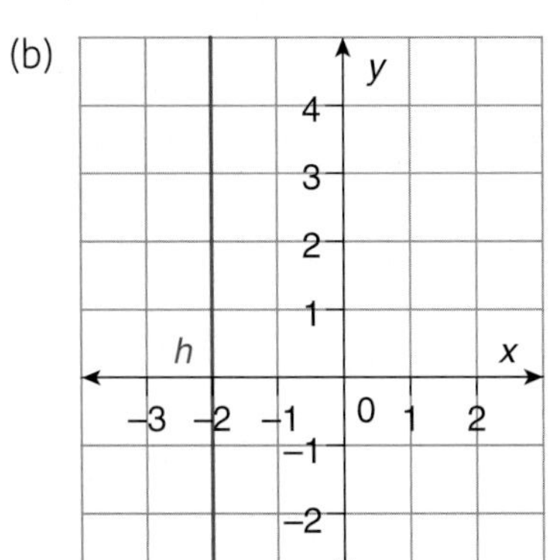

(c)

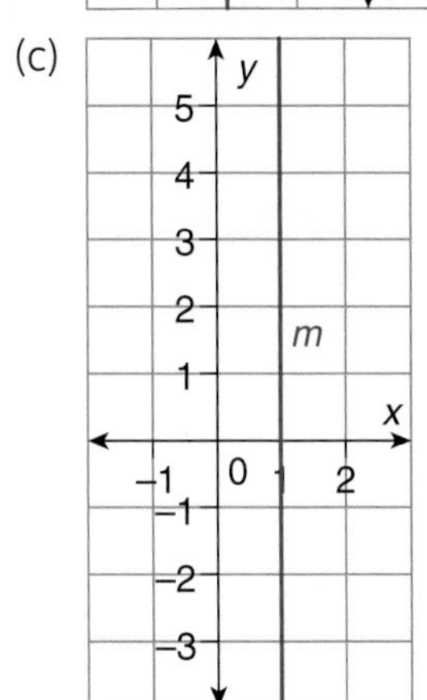

(d)

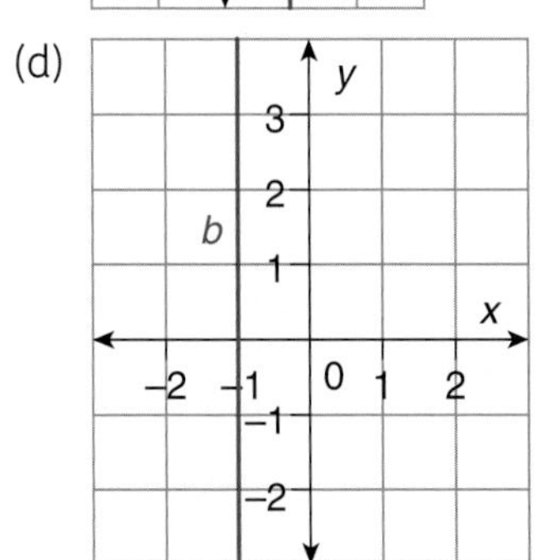

(e)

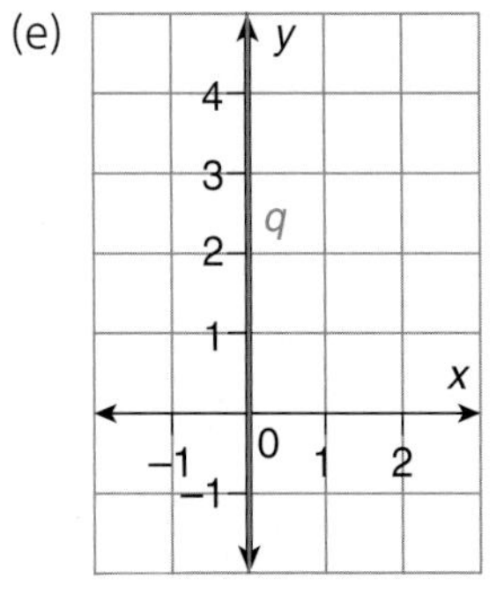

22. Investigate whether the lines m: $3x + 2y = 7$ and n: $3x + 2y = 5$ are parallel or perpendicular.

23. Plot the lines s: $2x - y = 4$ and t: $4x - 2y = 8$ on a coordinate plane. What do you notice about the lines?

24. Aeroplanes must set a course in the form of the equation of a line to fly between airports.

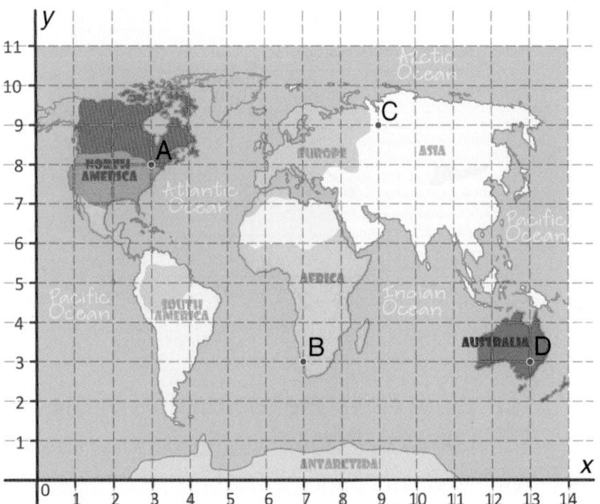

Find the equation that must be programmed into the plane's computer to fly from:

(a) Airport A to airport C

(b) Airport D to airport B

(c) Airport B to airport C

(d) Use an atlas to identify the cities that the points A, B, C and D could represent.

25. A torpedo is fired from a submarine to hit a battleship as shown. Find the equation of the line the torpedo must travel to hit the ship.

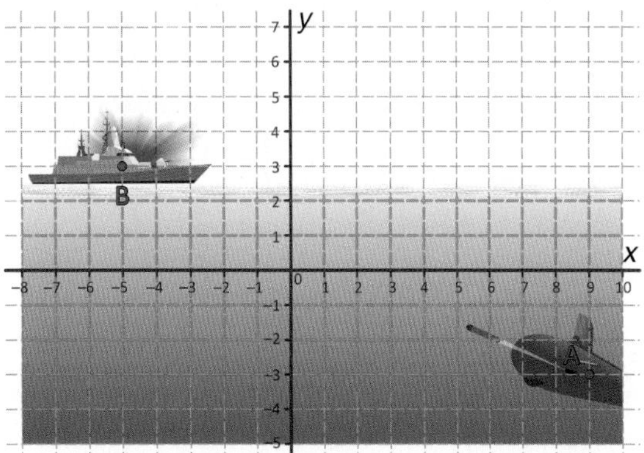

Section 12.6: The equation of a line 2

Student Activity 12F

1. Study the following diagram and answer the questions:

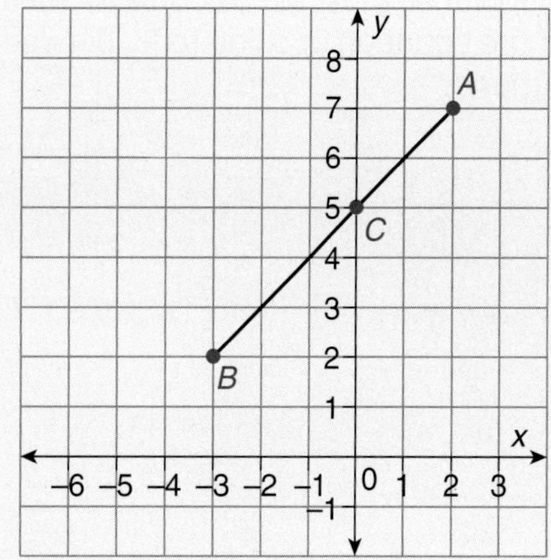

   (a) Write down the coordinates of the points A, B and C.
   (b) Find the slope of $[AB]$.
   (c) Find the equation of $[AB]$.
   (d) The equation of the line in this diagram can also be rewritten as $y = 1x + 5$. By referring to the diagram and your previous answers, explain in your own words any similarities.

2. Examine the line:

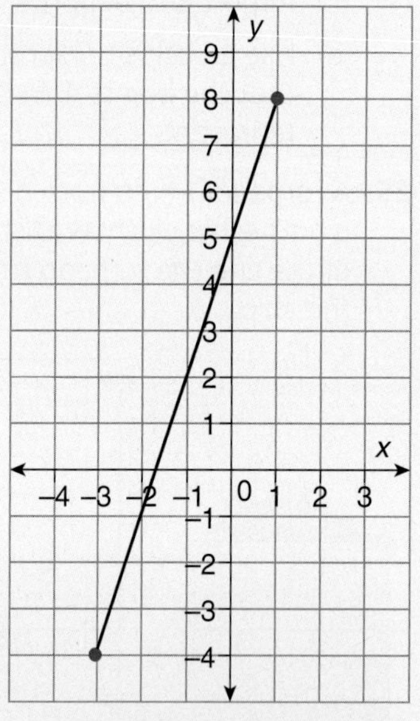

   (a) Write down the slope of the line.
   (b) Write down the point where the line crosses the y-axis.
   (c) The equation of the line is $y = 3x + 5$. Using your answers in part (a) and (b), can you explain how they relate to the equation of the line given.

3. Examine each of the lines below:
   (a) Calculate the slope of each line.
   (b) Try to fill in the missing parts of the equation for each question part: $y = (\text{slope})x + c$

(i)

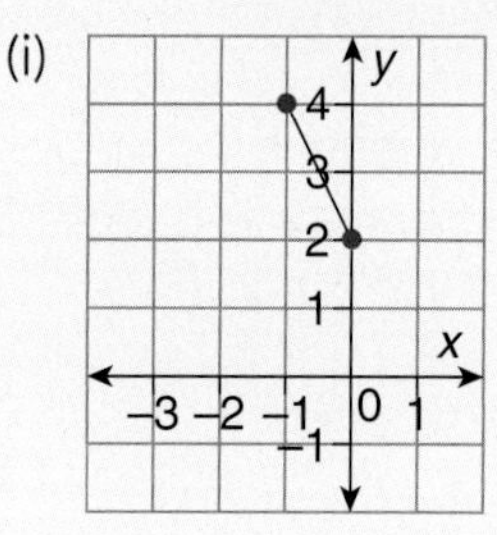

(ii)

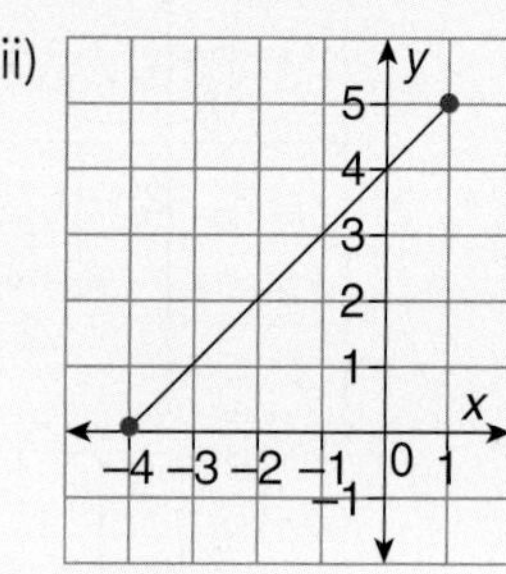

(iii)

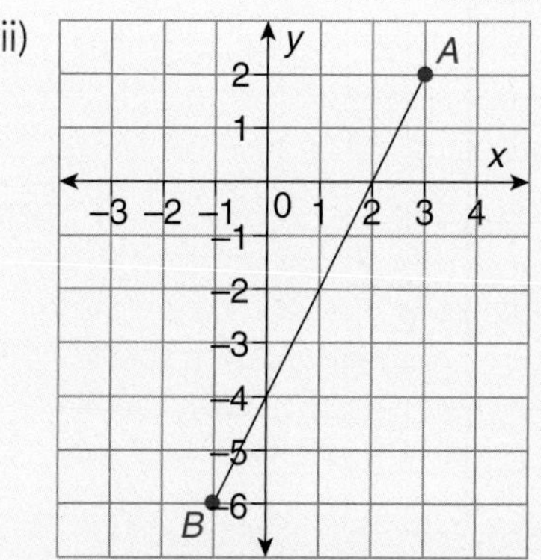

(iv)

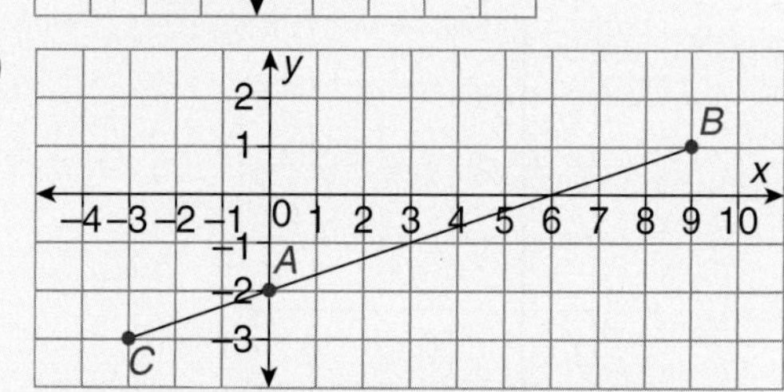

   (c) What do you notice about the missing parts in the answers?

THE EQUATION OF A LINE 2 EXPLAINED

In Section 12.5, you learned how to find the equation of a line using the formula. However, you will often encounter questions where we are given the equation of a line and you have to find the slope or important points on the line.

It is often helpful to write the equation of a line in the form:

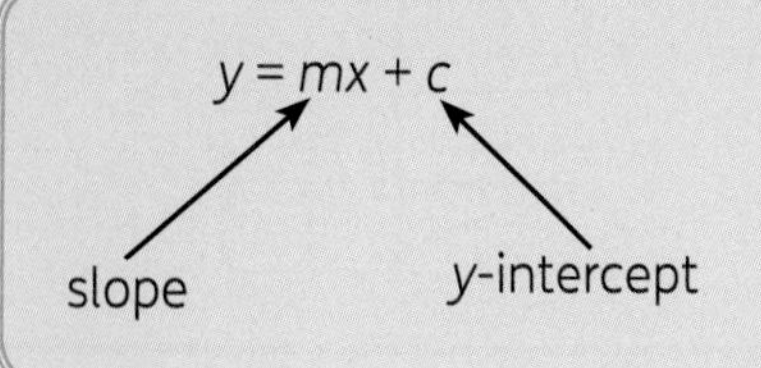

To do this, you must first make ***y*** the subject of the formula. By writing the equation of the line in this form, it is possible to quickly sketch the line by finding the slope (m) and the y-intercept $(0, c)$.

EXAMPLE 13

Find the slope of the line L: $4x - 2y + 6 = 0$ and the point where it crosses the y-axis. Draw the line using this information.

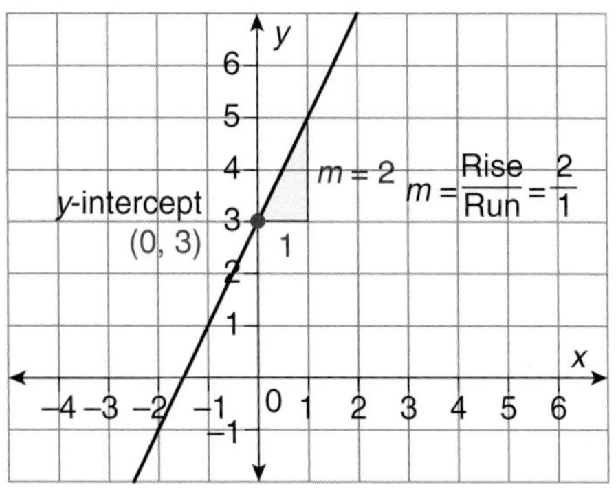

Solution

$4x - 2y + 6 = 0$

$-2y = -4x - 6$

$2y = 4x + 6$

$y = \frac{4}{2}x + \frac{6}{2}$

$y = 2x + 3$ **In the form $y = mx + c$**

$\therefore$ Slope $(m) = 2$ y-intercept $= (0, 3)$

Exercise 12.6

Find the slope and y-intercept of each of the following lines and write down the equation of the line in the form $y = mx + c$:

1. 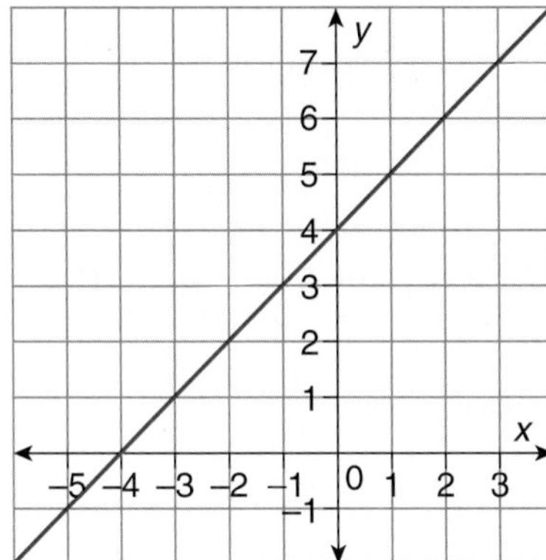

2. 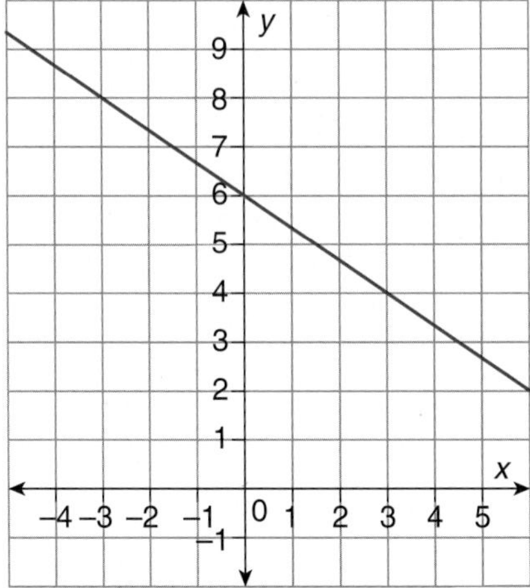

3. 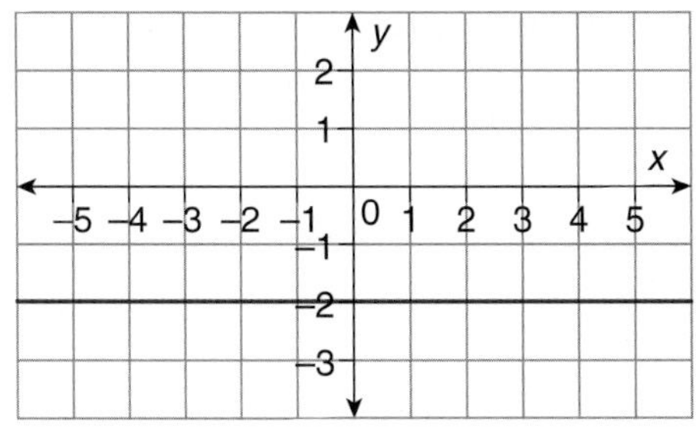

4. 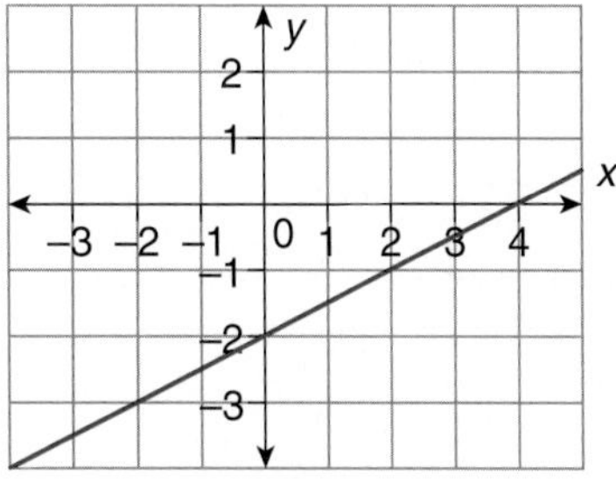

5. 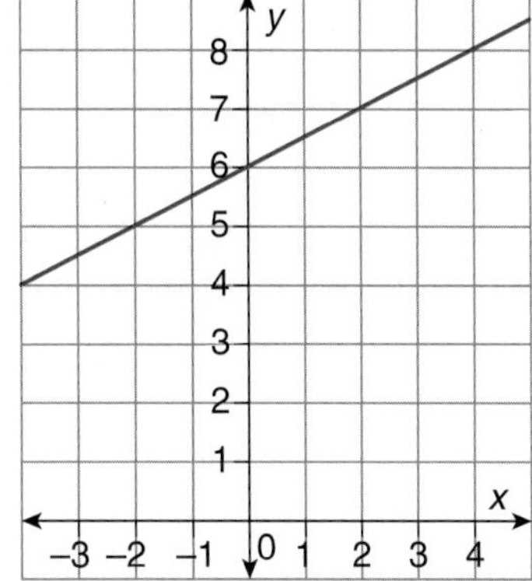

6. 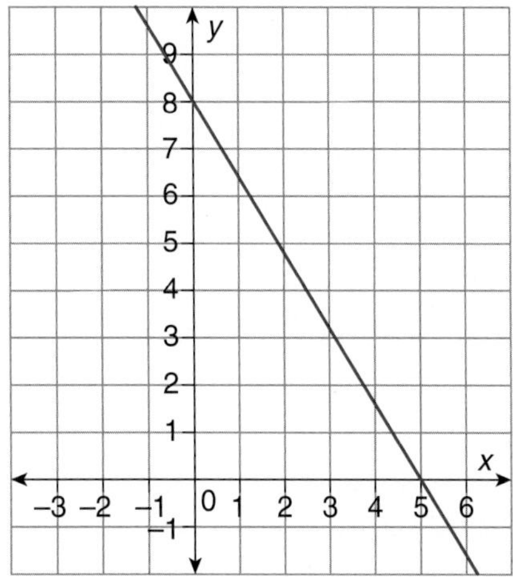

7.

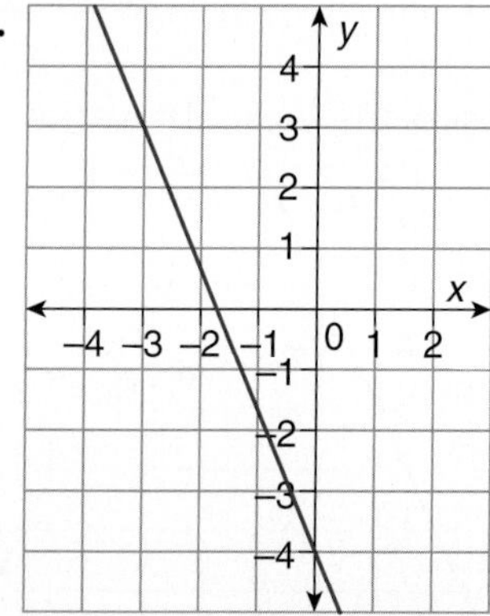

8.

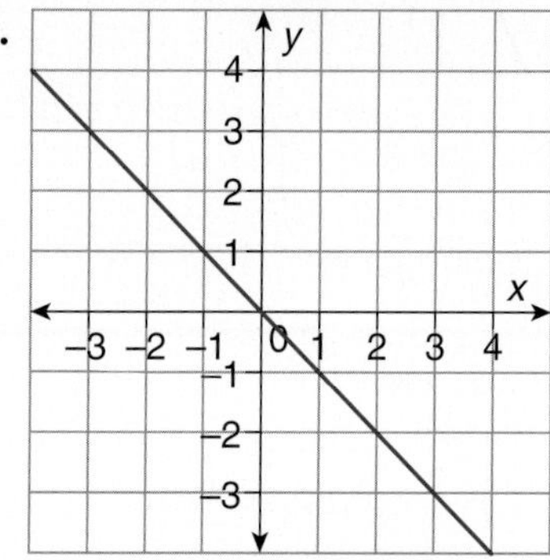

9.

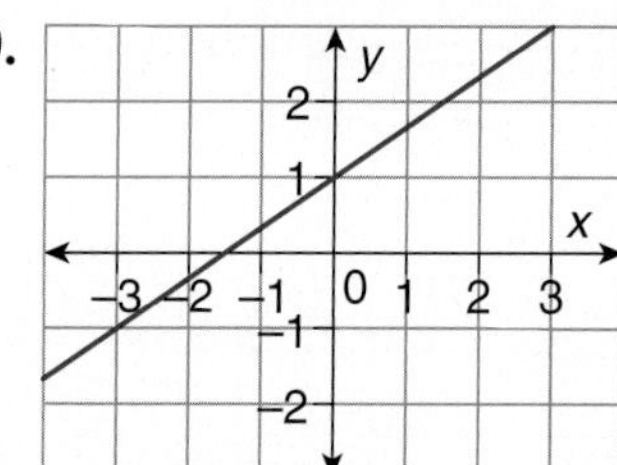

10.

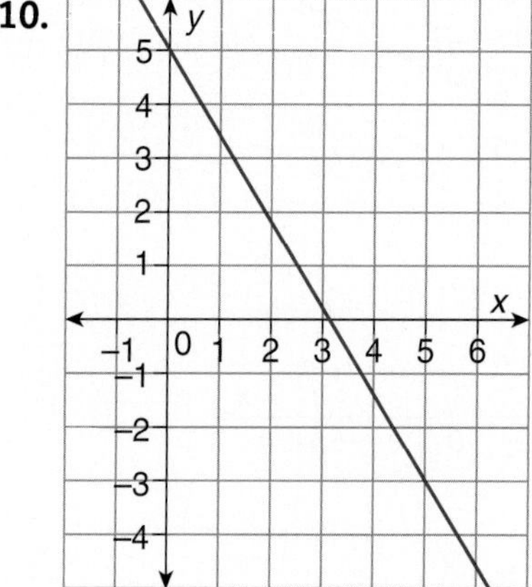

Write the following lines in the form $y = mx + c$ and draw the line on a coordinate plane:

11. $2x - 3y - 15 = 0$

12. $x + 2y = 0$

13. $5x + 2y = 8$

14. $-3x + y = 12$

15. $-5x + 2y - 7 = 0$

16. $12 - 5y + 7x = 0$

17. $3y - 2x = 7$

18. $x + 12y = 24$

19. $y + 5x - 9 = 0$

20. $x - 3y = 8$

21. Find the equation of each of the following lines given the slope and y-intercept of each line:

(a) $(0, 2)$, $m = 3$

(b) $(0, -1)$, $m = -4$

(c) $(0, 5)$, $m = \frac{2}{3}$

(d) $(0, -3)$, $m = -\frac{3}{5}$

(e) $(0, 4)$, $m = 2.5$

22. A missile is fired to intercept a moving target. The missile's path follows the line $-x + y = -1$ while the target follows the path $x + 5y = 25$.

(a) Write both lines in the form $y = mx + c$.

(b) Graph both lines on a coordinate plane.

(c) Write down the point where the missile will intercept the target.

23. A ship's engine has failed at sea and it sends a distress signal. It is drifting in the currents along the path $x + 2y = 8$. A rescue ship sets out to help the distressed ship along the path $-2x + 3y = -9$.

(a) Write both lines in the form $y = mx + c$.

(b) Graph both lines on a coordinate plane.

(c) Write down the point where the rescue ship will intercept the distressed ship.

24. A fishing boat travels along the path $x - 4y = -8$. Its air spotter has marked a school of herring swimming along the path $-3x - 2y = 10$.

(a) Write both lines in the form $y = mx + c$.

(b) Graph both lines on a coordinate plane.

(c) Write down the point where the fishing boat will intercept the school of herring.

Section 12.7: The equation of a line 3

Student Activity 12G

Study the line shown and answer the questions that follow:

(a) Write down the coordinates of the points A and B.

(b) Find the slope of the line.

(c) Find the equation of the line in the form $ax + by + c = 0$.

(d) Find the equation of the line in the form $y = mx + c$.

(e) Can you see any relationship between the different forms of the equations of the line? Explain your answer fully.

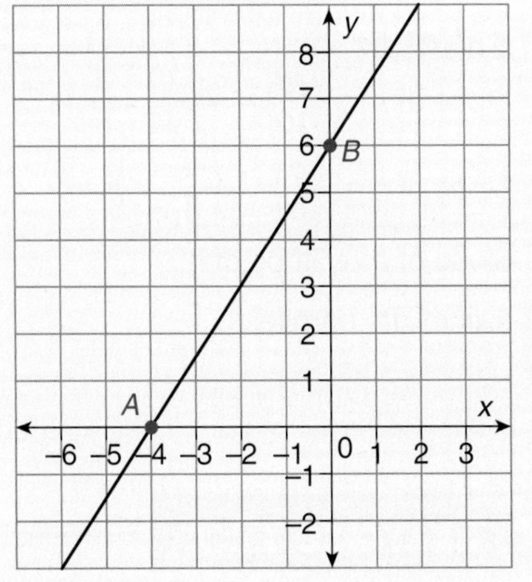

THE EQUATION OF A LINE 3 EXPLAINED

You are often given the equation of a line in the form $ax + by + c = 0$. From this, you can easily find both the slope and the y-intercept of the line.

Given the equation of a line is $ax + by + c = 0$, its:

$$\text{Slope} = -\left(\frac{x\text{-coefficient}}{y\text{-coefficient}}\right)$$

$$y\text{-intercept} = -\left(\frac{\text{constant}}{y\text{-coefficient}}\right)$$

Or if we take the general equation of any line as $ax + by + c = 0$, we can also say that:

$$\text{Slope} = -\left(\frac{a}{b}\right) \quad \text{and} \quad y\text{-intercept} = -\left(\frac{c}{b}\right)$$

EXAMPLE 14

Find the slope of the line L: $4x - 2y + 6 = 0$ and the point where it crosses the y-axis.

Solution

$4x - 2y + 6 = 0$

$\text{Slope} = -\left(\frac{x\text{-coefficient}}{y\text{-coefficient}}\right)$

$\text{Slope} = -\left(\frac{4}{-2}\right)$

Slope $(m) = 2$

$y\text{-intercept} = -\left(\frac{\text{constant}}{y\text{-coefficient}}\right)$

$y\text{-intercept} = -\left(\frac{6}{-2}\right)$

y-intercept $= 3$

y-intercept $= (0, 3)$

EXAMPLE 15

Investigate whether the lines m: $3x - 4y = 20$ and n: $-6x + 8y = 13$ are parallel.

Solution

Slope of $m = -\left(\frac{a}{b}\right) = -\left(\frac{3}{-4}\right) = \frac{3}{4}$

Slope of $n = -\left(\frac{a}{b}\right) = -\left(\frac{-6}{8}\right) = \frac{6}{8} = \frac{3}{4}$

Slope of m = Slope of n

$\therefore$ lines are parallel.

EXAMPLE 16

Investigate whether the lines l: $3x + 2y = 6$ and m: $2x - 3y = -7$ are perpendicular.

Solution

Slope of $l = -\left(\frac{3}{2}\right) = -\frac{3}{2}$

Slope of $m = -\left(\frac{2}{-3}\right) = \frac{2}{3}$

Multiply the two slopes:

$-\frac{3}{2} \times \frac{2}{3} = -1$

$\therefore$ lines are perpendicular.

Exercise 12.7

For each of the following lines:

(a) Find the slope and the point where the line crosses the y-axis,

(b) Write each line in the form $y = mx + c$ to check your answer.

1. $3x - 6y + 30 = 0$

2. $5x - 2y = 8$

3. $3x + 4y = 0$

4. $-4x - 3y = 12$

5. $2x - 3y - 18 = 0$

6. $-x + 2y - 8 = 0$

7. $5y - 2x = 15$

8. $5x + 5y + 20 = 0$

9. $3x + 7y = 5$

10. Investigate whether the following pairs of lines are perpendicular or parallel:

(a) $3x - 2y = 12$ and $2x + 3y = 7$

(b) $4x - 7y = 9$ and $7x + 4y = 20$

(c) $11x - 3y = 33$ and $3x + 11y = -28$

(d) $-3x - 2y = 0$ and $4x - 6y = 11$

(e) $7x - y = 14$ and $x + 7y = -21$

(f) The lines m: $3x - 2y = 8$ and n: $-3x + 2y = 0$

(g) The lines k: $5x - 3y = 2$ and l: $5x + 3y = 2$

(h) The lines b: $7x - 3y = 15$ and a: $3x - 7y = -3$

Section 12.8: Finding the equations of lines that are parallel and perpendicular to a given line

Student Activity 12H

1. Examine the lines and answer the questions that follow:

(a) Write down the coordinates of the points A, B, C and D.

(b) Find the slope of the line l.

(c) Find the slope of the line m.

(d) What do you notice about the slopes?

(e) What shape do the points A, B, D and C form? Use the slopes and length of the sides to verify your answer.

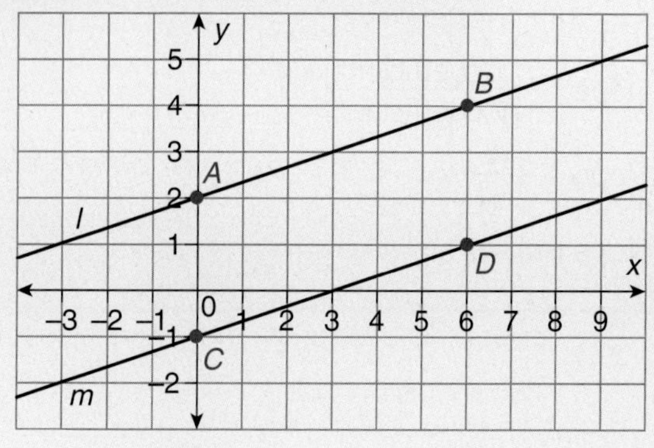

(f) What can you deduce about the slopes of parallel lines?

(g) What will be the slope of any line parallel to the lines l or m?

2. Examine the lines and answer the questions that follow:

(a) Write down the coordinates of the points A, B, E and F.

(b) Find the slope of $[AB]$.

(c) Find the slope of $[BF]$.

(d) What do you notice about the slopes?

(e) Find the slope of $[AE]$.

(f) Find the slope of $[EF]$.

(g) What do you notice about the slopes?

(h) What shape do the points A, B, F and E form? Use the slopes and length of the sides to verify your answer.

(i) What can you deduce about the slopes of perpendicular lines?

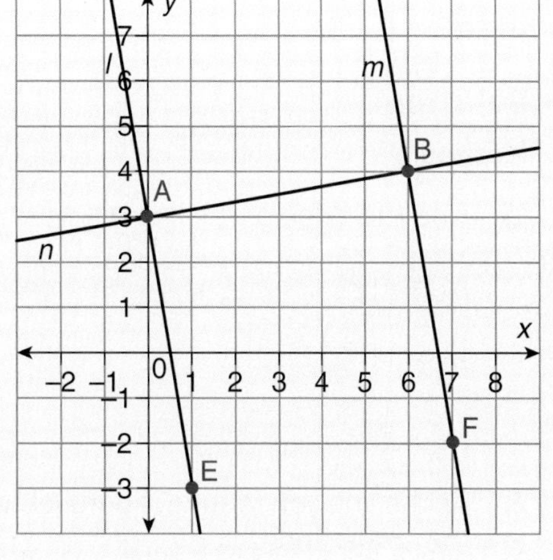

FINDING THE EQUATIONS OF PARALLEL AND PERPENDICULAR LINES TO A GIVEN LINE EXPLAINED

Many lines and shapes such as parallelograms, squares, triangles and rectangles contain parallel and perpendicular lines.

Examine the following lines:

- These lines are all parallel, running side by side but never intersecting.
- The slopes of each of these lines is $-\frac{2}{5}$.
- All of the equations are of the format $2x + 5y \pm$ *any number* $= 0$.
- Hence, we can write an infinite number of other line equations parallel to these by keeping the same x- and y-coefficients and changing the constant or c value.

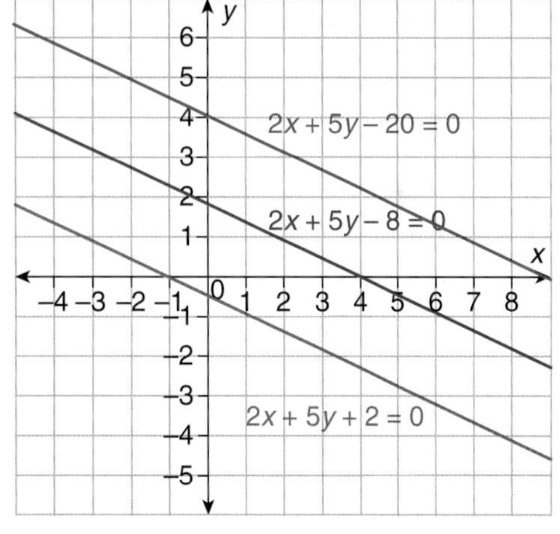

Now examine the perpendicular lines in the diagram on the bottom right:

- Here we notice that the x- and y-coefficients have swapped around and one value also changed its sign.
- Hence, any equation of the form $ax + by + c = 0$ has a perpendicular line of equation $bx - ay + c = 0$ or $-bx + ay + c = 0$.

An alternative method of finding the equation of a line parallel or perpendicular to a given line, given a point on the required line and the equation of another line is:

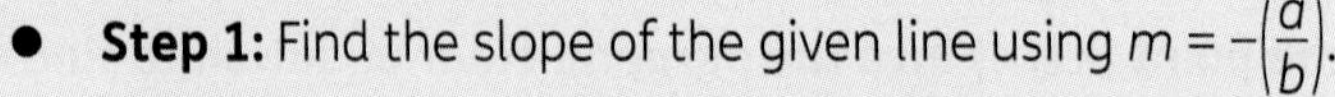

- **Step 1:** Find the slope of the given line using $m = -\left(\frac{a}{b}\right)$.
- **Step 2:** (a) If the required line is parallel, we use this slope. (b) If the required line is perpendicular, invert the slope and change its sign. Remember if two lines are perpendicular $m_1 \times m_2 = -1$.
- **Step 3:** Use the slope and any point in the formula for the equation of a line $y - y_1 = m(x - x_1)$.

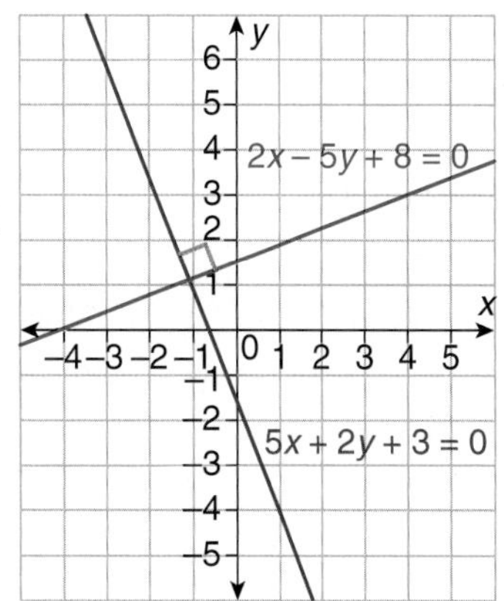

EXAMPLE 17

Find the equation of the line that is parallel to the line n: $3x - 2y + 1 = 0$ and passes through the point (4, 3).

Solution

Method 1

1. Find the slope of the line n:

$$m_n = -\left(\frac{a}{b}\right)$$
$$m_n = -\left(\frac{3}{-2}\right)$$
$$m_n = \frac{3}{2}$$

2. As the line you require is parallel to n, use the same slope.

$$y - y_1 = m(x - x_1)$$
$$y - (3) = \frac{3}{2}(x - (4))$$
$$2(y - 3) = 3(x - 4)$$
$$2y - 6 = 3x - 12$$
$$-3x + 2y - 6 + 12 = 0$$
$$-3x + 2y + 6 = 0$$
$$3x - 2y - 6 = 0$$

Method 2

Since the line is parallel it must have the equation $3x - 2y + ? = 0$. Substitute in the point (4, 3) to find the value of c.

$$3x - 2y - c = 0$$
$$3(4) - 2(3) - c = 0$$
$$12 - 6 - c = 0$$
$$-6 = c$$

Hence, the equation is $3x - 2y - 6 = 0$.

EXAMPLE 18

Find the equation of the line that is perpendicular to the line l: $2x - 5y + 6 = 0$ and passes through the point (−1, 4).

Solution

Method 1

1. Find the slope of the line l. As the line you require is perpendicular to l, invert its slope and change the sign.

$$m_1 = -\left(\frac{2}{-5}\right)$$

$m_1 = \frac{2}{5} \quad \therefore m_\perp = -\frac{5}{2}$ **m_1 invert and change sign**

2. $y - y_1 = m(x - x_1)$

$$y - (4) = -\frac{5}{2}(x - (-1))$$
$$2(y - 4) = -5(x + 1)$$
$$2y - 8 = -5x - 5$$
$$5x + 2y - 8 + 5 = 0$$
$$5x + 2y - 3 = 0$$

Method 2

$2x - 5y + 6 = 0$	**The equation of the line**
$5x + 2y + c = 0$	**The equation of the perpendicular line**
$5(-1) + 2(4) + c = 0$	**Substitute the point (−1, 4) into the perpendicular equation to find c**
$-5 + 8 + c = 0$	
$c = -3$	
$5x + 2y - 3 = 0$	**Complete the equation**

Exercise 12.8

1. Given the equation of the line l: $3x - 4y + 12 = 0$, find:
   (a) The slope of l
   (b) The slope of any line parallel to l
   (c) The equation of the line that is parallel to l and which passes through the point $(1,-1)$
   (d) Write the equation of both lines in the form $y = mx + c$. What is the difference between the equations?
2. Given the equation of the line m: $2x - 7y - 3 = 0$, find:
   (a) The slope of m
   (b) The slope of any line perpendicular to m
   (c) The equation of the line that is parallel to the line m and which passes through the point $(2, 3)$
3. The line k is perpendicular to the line l: $3x + 2y - 12 = 0$ and passes through the point $(5, 4)$. Find the equation of the line k.
4. The line m is parallel to the line n: $-2x + 3y + 9 = 0$ and passes through the origin. Find the equation of the line m.
5. The line p is parallel to the line l: $-2x - 2y + 14 = 0$ and passes through the point $(2, 4)$. Find the equation of the line p.
6. The line k is perpendicular to the line $3x + 3y - 12 = 0$ and passes through the point $(2, 6)$. Find the equation of the line k.
7. A line m passing through the point $(2, 0)$ is perpendicular to the line $4x - 3y + 13 = 0$. Find the equation of the line m.
8. A line passing through the point $(4, 7)$ is perpendicular to a line whose slope is $\frac{3}{4}$. Find the equation of the line.
9. A line passing through the point $(3, 5)$ is parallel to a line whose slope is $-\frac{2}{3}$. Find the equation of the line.
10. Find the equation of the line that passes through the point $(4, 0)$ and is perpendicular to the line n: $-3x + 4y = -12$.
11. Find the equation of the line that passes through the point $(-2, 0)$ and is parallel to the line k: $4x + 3y = 16$.
12. Find the equation of the line l, which passes through the point $(2, -2)$ and is parallel to the line $-2x + 5y = 11$.
13. Find the equation of the line that passes through the point $(3, 4)$ and is perpendicular to the line $5x + 6y = 30$.
14. The line h passes through the point $(3, -2)$ and is parallel to the line k: $3x - 5y = 36$. Find the equation of the line h.
15. The line m passes through the point $(-1, 2)$ and is perpendicular to the line n: $-2x + 3y = -12$. Find the equation of the line m.
16. Find the equation of the line that passes through the point $(6, 2)$ and is parallel to the line $x - 5y = 14$.
17. Find the equation of the line that passes through the point $(5, 5)$ and is perpendicular to the line $4x - 3y = 23$.
18. The line l passes through the point $(9, 5)$ and is parallel to the line k: $x - 6y = 14$. Find the equation of the line l.
19. The line m passes through the point $(7, -2)$ and is perpendicular to the line n: $-2x + 3y = -16$. Find the equation of the line m.
20. The line d passes through the point $(6, -4)$ and is parallel to the line b: $-x - 2y = 0$. Find the equation of the line d.
21. A carpenter is designing a picture frame on a computer package. She starts with the outline given and wants to be sure the frame is rectangular.

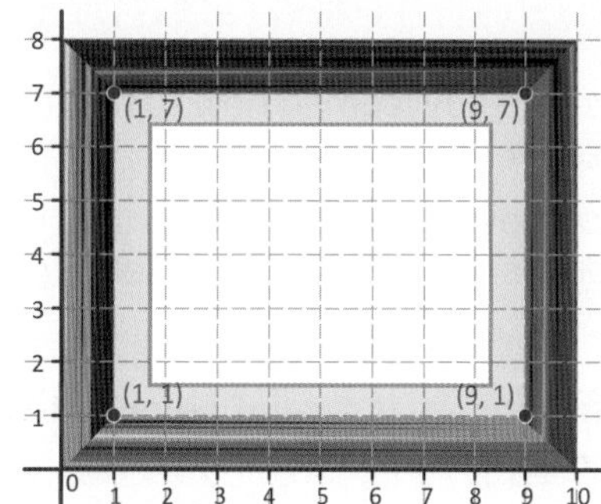

Using slopes, show that the frame is rectangular.

22. A builder is planning an extension to a house. Show that the roof beam is not perpendicular to the wall.

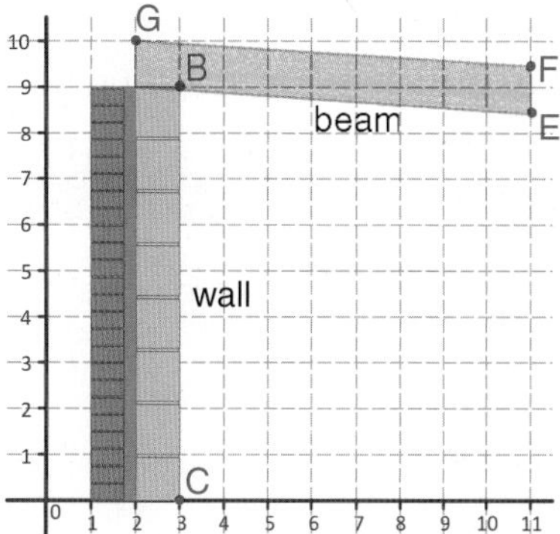

23. Show that the points $W(5, -3)$, $X(8, -3)$, $Y(8, 0)$ and $Z(5, 0)$ form the vertices of a square.

12

MATHS IN ACTION 3

Section 12.9: To verify that a point lies on a given line

Student Activity 12I

1. Study the diagram and answer the following questions:

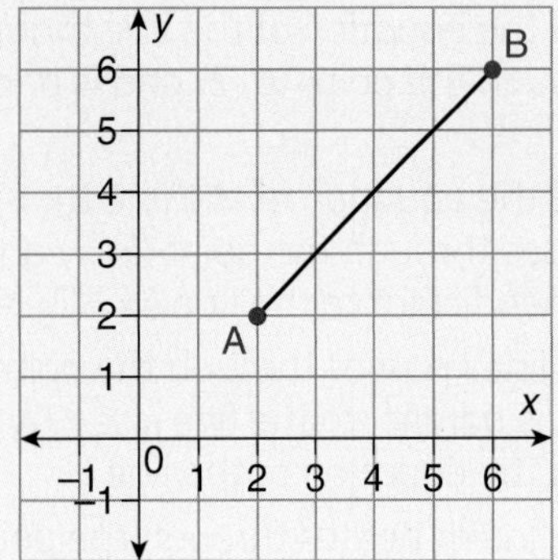

(a) Write down the coordinates of *A* and *B*.

(b) Find the slope of [*AB*].

(c) Find the equation of the line joining *A* and *B*.

(d) Can you write down three more points which are on this line?

(e) Can you use the equation of the line to verify that the points you wrote down are on the line?

(f) Is the point (–25, 25) on this line? Explain your answer.

(g) Is the point (11, 12) on this line? Explain your answer.

2. Write down three points that lie on the line $p: x + y = 5$.

(a) Explain why you chose the three points.

(b) Would the point (3, 4) lie on the line *p*? Explain your answer fully.

3. Explain how you could test whether or not a point lies on a line.

TO VERIFY THAT A POINT BELONGS TO A GIVEN LINE EXPLAINED

You have already learned how to find the equation of a line using the formulae $y - y_1 = m(x - x_1)$ or $y = mx + c$.

Once you have the equation of a line, you can use it to show whether a point is on that line or whether it is an element of the set of points on the line.

To investigate if a point belongs to a given line:

- **Step 1:** Substitute in the *x* and *y* values of the point into the given equation.
- **Step 2:** If the right-hand side = left-hand side, the point is an element of the line.

EXAMPLE 19

Show that the point $A(-4, 10)$ is on the line $k: 2x - y = -18$.

Solution

Substitute the values into the equation of the line:

$2(-4) - (10) = -18$

$-8 - 10 = -18$

$-18 = -18$

$0 = 0$

$\therefore$ The point is on the line as LHS = RHS.

EXAMPLE 20

The point $(3, t)$ is on the line $m: 2x + 3y - 9 = 0$. Find the value of t.

Solution

$2(3) + 3(t) - 9 = 0$

$6 + 3t - 9 = 0$

$3t - 3 = 0$

$3t = 3$

$t = 1$

Investigate whether the point $T(4, -2)$ is on the line k: $3x + 2y = 15$.

Solution

Substitute in the values for x and y into the equation of the line: $3(4) + 2(-2) = 15$

$12 - 4 = 15$

$8 \neq 15$

$\therefore$ Point is not on the line.

Exercise 12.9

1. Show that the point $Q(-6, -2)$ is on the line $5x - 15y = 0$.
2. Show that the point $(4, 2)$ is on the line $x + 5y = 14$.
3. Investigate whether the point $F(7, -6)$ is on the line n: $4x + 4y - 3 = 0$.
4. Investigate whether the point $A(2, -4)$ is on the line m: $5x + y - 6 = 0$.
5. If the point $(t, -2)$ is on the line l: $2x - 3y = 10$, find the value of t.
6. The point (k, k) is on the line $x + y = 10$. Find the value of k.
7. The point $(s, 3s)$ is on the line $x + 4y = 26$. Find the value of s.
8. The point $(-2k, -k)$ is on the line $3x - 2y = 4$. Find the value of k.
9. The point $(5, 6s)$ is on the line $-5x + 4y = -49$. Find the value of s.
10. The point $(-g, -7g)$ is on the line $5x - 2y = -18$. Find the value of g.

Section 12.10: Graphing lines

Student Activity 12J

1. Can you remember how many points you need to draw a line?
2. Study the following diagrams and write down the coordinates of the points that are indicated:

(a)

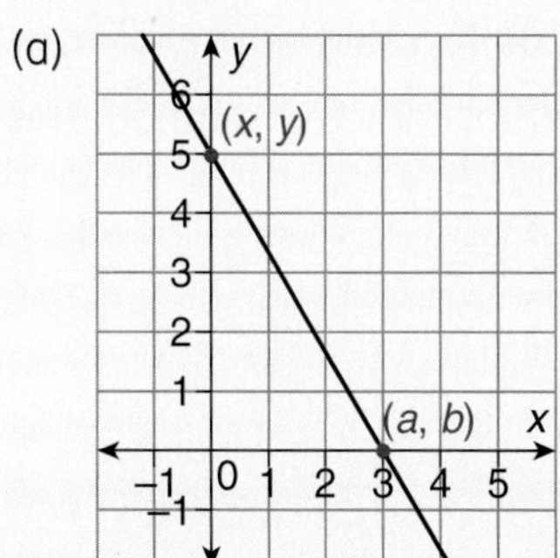

(b)

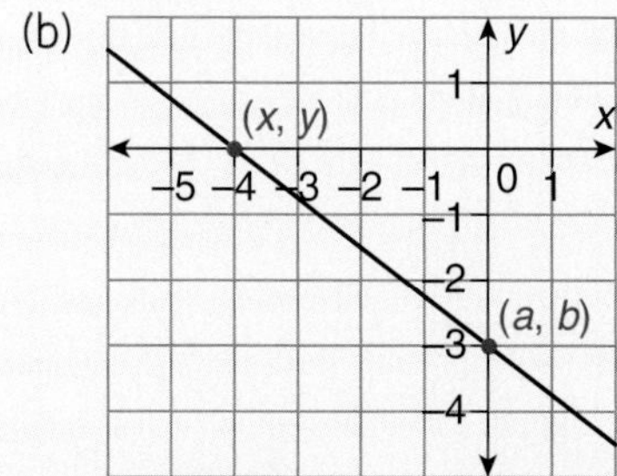

(c)

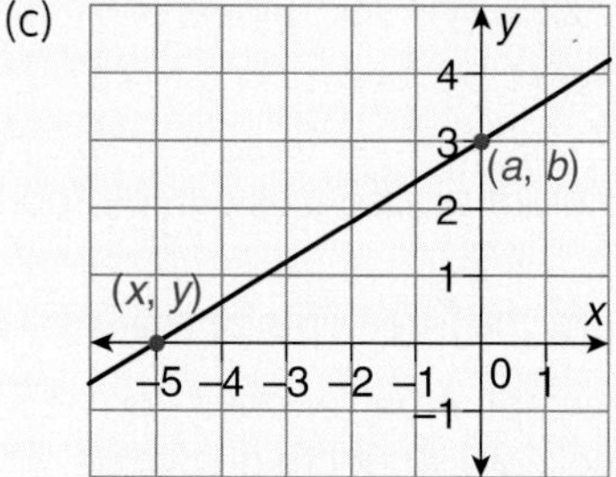

(d)

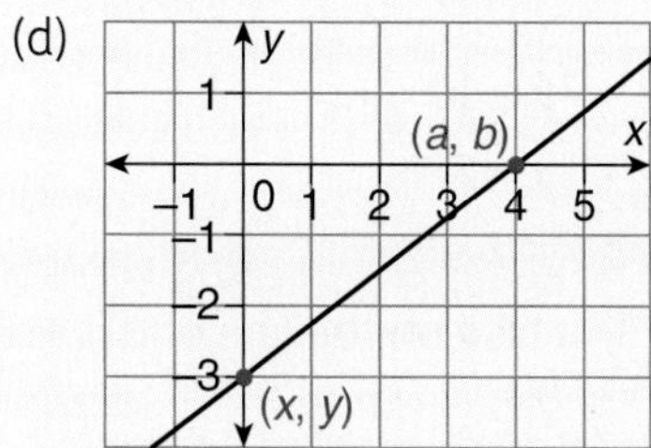

(e) Have you noticed any common fact about all the points on the x-axis?

(f) Have you noticed any common fact about all the points on the y-axis?

GRAPHING LINES EXPLAINED

You have already learned an axiom that stated that only one line can be drawn through any two given points. When drawing a line, it is often easier to find the x- and y-intercepts.

From Student Activity 12J, we can conclude that:

- Every point on the x-axis is of the form $(x, 0)$.
- Every point on the y-axis is of the form $(0, y)$.

In order to graph any line:

- **Step 1:** Let $x = 0$ and find y, to get the point $(0, y)$. This point is also called the y-intercept.
- **Step 2:** Let $y = 0$ and find x, to get the point $(x, 0)$. This point is also called the x-intercept.
- **Step 3:** Plot both of these points on a coordinate diagram.
- **Step 4:** Draw a line through these points.

EXAMPLE 22

Find the points where the line k: $2x + 3y - 12 = 0$ intersects the x- and y-axes.

Solution

On the x-axis, $y = 0$.

$$2x + 3(0) = 12$$
$$2x = 12$$
$$x = 6$$
$$\therefore (6, 0)$$

On the y-axis, $x = 0$.

$$2(0) + 3y = 12$$
$$3y = 12$$
$$y = 4$$
$$\therefore (0, 4)$$

EXAMPLE 23

Plot the line $-2x + 7y = 19$.

Solution

Sometimes a point on the axis can be too difficult to plot.

In this example, the intercepts of the axis will be $\left(0, \frac{19}{7}\right)$ and $(-9.5, 0)$. It would be very difficult to plot the y-intercept. A better point can be found on the line using a trial and error method. This involves letting x or y equal to any value.

Try $x = 1$:

$$-2(1) + 7y = 19$$
$$\Rightarrow 7y = 19 + 2$$
$$\therefore y = 3$$

The point $(1, 3)$ is also on the line and is easier to plot.

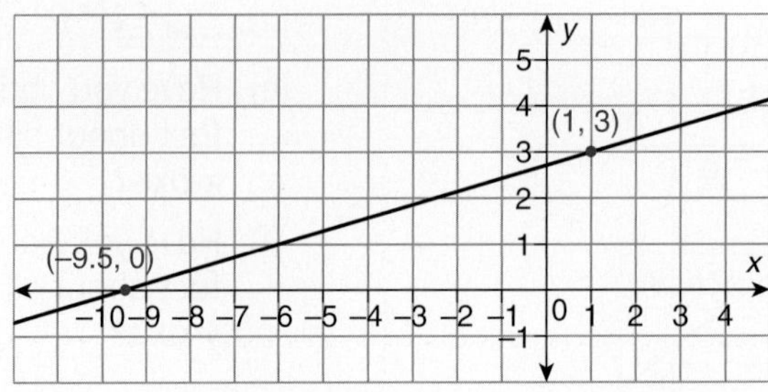

Exercise 12.10

Write down the coordinates where each line crosses the x- and y-axes:

1.

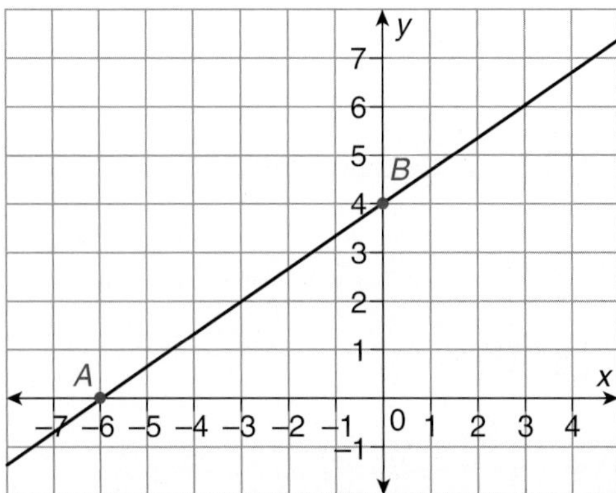

2.

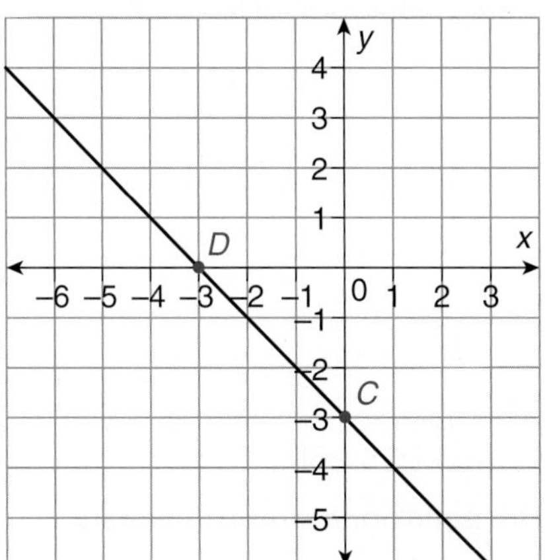

3.

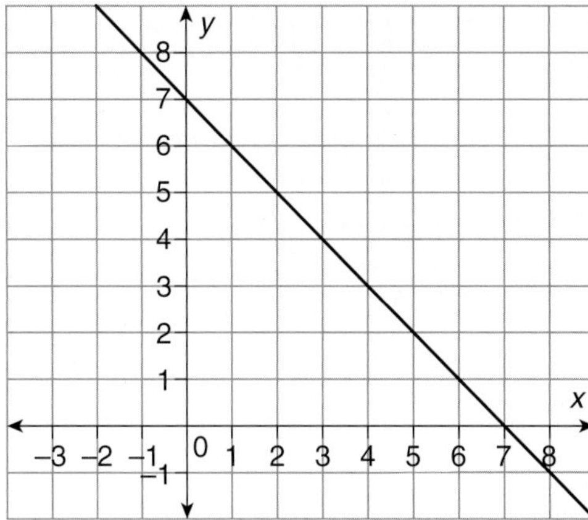

4.

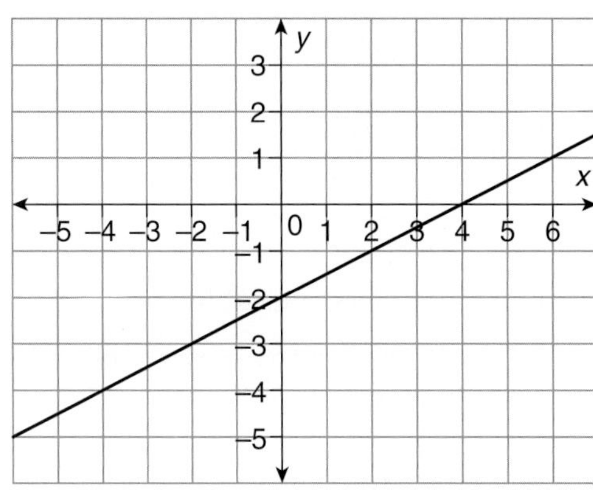

5.

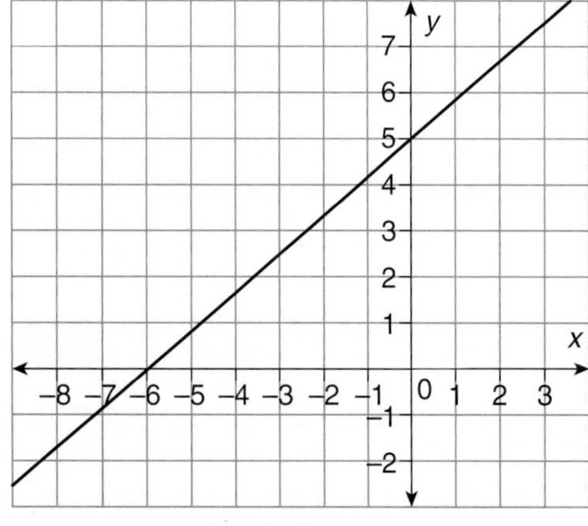

6.

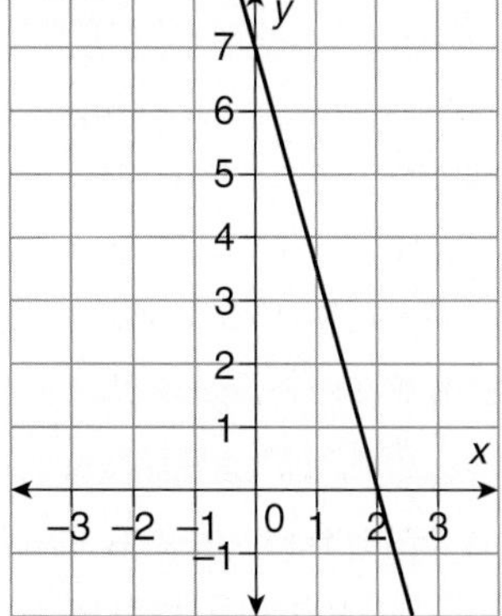

7.

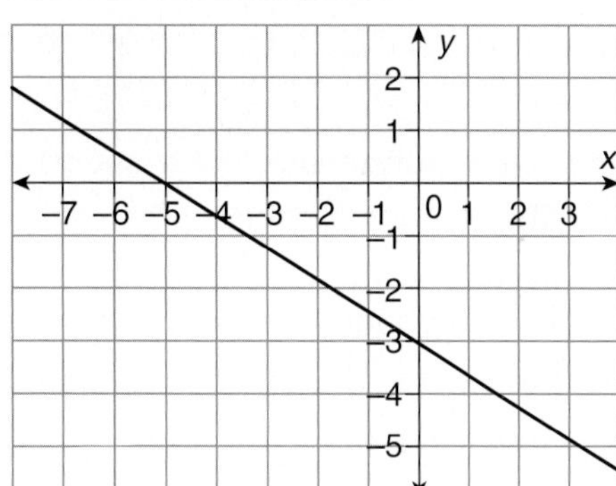

8.

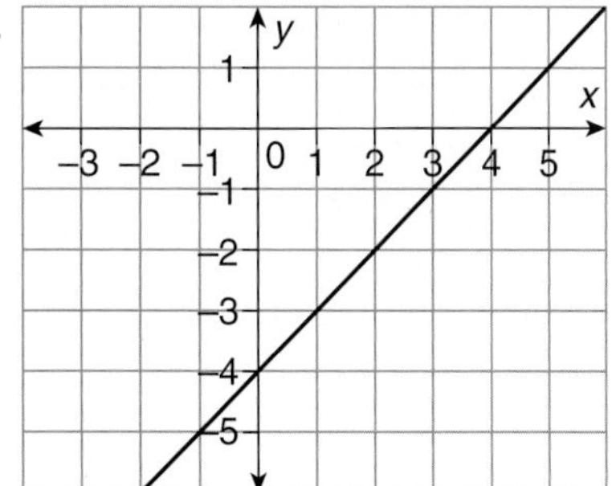

9. Find the points where each of the following lines cross the x- and y-axes:

(a) $4x + 2y = 12$

(b) $3x - 2y - 6 = 0$

(c) $-5x + 2y - 10 = 0$

(d) $6x - 3y + 12 = 0$

(e) $2x + 5y - 10 = 0$

(f) $7x + 2y = 14$

Plot the following lines and state for each line whether it has a positive or negative slope:

10. $4x + 2y = 12$

11. $3x - 2y - 6 = 0$

12. $-5x + 2y - 10 = 0$

13. $6x - 3y + 12 = 0$

14. $x + y = -5$

15. $x = 4$

16. $x = -2$

17. $y = 3$

18. $y = -1$

19. $3x - 5 = 18$

20. $-2x + 3y = 16$

21. $x - 8y = -27$

Section 12.11: The intersection point of two lines

Student Activity 12K

Plot the following lines and write down their point of intersection from your graph:

$l: x + y - 5 = 0$ and $k: x - y - 1 = 0$

THE INTERSECTION POINT OF TWO LINES EXPLAINED

You can find the point of intersection of two lines by graphing the lines. Sometimes the intersection point is not easy to read as it may contain an irrational number.

You can also find the intersection of two lines by **solving the equations simultaneously.**

To solve simultaneous linear equations:

- **Step 1:** Choose either of the variables to work with.
- **Step 2:** Using multiplication, get the coefficients of one variable equal in value in both equations and with opposite signs.
- **Step 3:** Add the equations (your chosen variable will cancel at this point).
- **Step 4:** Substitute the value of the first variable into either of the original equations to solve for the second variable.

EXAMPLE 24

Solve the following simultaneous equations:

$x - y = 5$

$x + y = 7$

Solution

1. Work with the y's as they already have equal coefficients with opposite signs:

   $x - y = 5$

   $x + y = 7$

2. Add the equations:

   $x - y = 5$

   $x + y = 7$

   $2x = 12$

   $x = 6$ **First variable**

3. Substitute back into either equation to get the second variable:

   $(6) - y = 5$

   $-y = 5 - 6$

   $-y = -1$

   $y = 1$

Point of intersection of the two lines is (6, 1).

EXAMPLE 25

Solve the following simultaneous equations:

$3a + 2b = 21$

$5a - b = 22$

Solution

1. Work with the b's as they have opposite signs.
2. Multiply the bottom equation by 2 (the coefficient of b in the first equation) and the top equation by 1 (the coefficient of b in the second equation).

   $3a + 2b = 21$

   $10a - 2b = 44$

3. Add the equations:

$$\begin{aligned} 3a + 2b &= 21 \\ 10a - 2b &= 44 \\ \hline 13a &= 65 \\ a &= 5 \quad \textbf{First variable} \end{aligned}$$

4. Substitute the value back into either equation to find the second variable:

$$\begin{aligned} 3(5) + 2b &= 21 \\ 15 + 2b &= 21 \\ 2b &= 21 - 15 \\ 2b &= 6 \\ b &= 3 \end{aligned}$$

The point of intersection is (5, 3).

EXAMPLE 26

A drinks machine takes €1 and €2 coins only. When it was last restocked and the cash was taken out, there were 30 coins, and their value was €48. Using simultaneous equations, find the number of each type of coin present.

Solution

Let x be the number of €1 coins and y be the number of €2 coins:

$x + y = 30$ **The number of coins**

$1x + 2y = 48$ **The value of the coins**

$x + y = 30$

$-2x - 2y = -60$ **Multiply by −2**

Add the equations:

$$\begin{aligned} 1x + 2y &= 48 \\ -2x - 2y &= -60 \\ \hline -x &= -12 \\ \therefore x &= 12 \end{aligned}$$

Solve for the second variable:

$$\begin{aligned} 1(12) + 2y &= 48 \\ 12 + 2y &= 48 \\ 2y &= 48 - 12 \\ 2y &= 36 \\ y &= 18 \end{aligned}$$

The machine contained 12 €1 coins and 18 €2 coins.

Exercise 12.11

Plot each pair of lines and find their points of intersection. Solve the simultaneous equations to verify your answers.

1. $2x - y = -8$, $x + y = 2$
2. $6x - 3y = 18$, $x + y = 3$
3. $x + 2y = 7$, $3x - 2y = 5$
4. $-3x + 2y = 0$, $3x + 2y = 24$
5. $x + y = 11$, $-3x + 4y = -12$
6. $2x + 3y = -9$, $y = x - 8$
7. $3x - 2y = 1$, $-3x + y = 2$
8. $3x - y = 12$, $2x + y = 3$
9. $4x + 3y = 14$, $4x + 4y = 17$
10. $5x + 2y = 30$, $6x + 2y = 34$
11. $9x + 2y = 23$, $-2x + y = -8$
12. $x + 7y = 24$, $x + 3y = 12$
13. $4x + 2y = 12$, $3y + 2y = 10$
14. $x + 5y = 29$, $y = x - 5$
15. $3x + 2y = 13$, $-x - 2y = -7$

16. Solve each of the following pairs of simultaneous equations graphically. Verify your answer algebraically.
   (a) $x + y = 14$
   $x - y = 6$
   (b) $3x + y = 9$
   $3x + 4y = 0$
   (c) $2x + y = 4$
   $2x - y = 2$
   (d) $2x + y = 9$
   $2x - y = 7$
   (e) $4x + 3y = 27$
   $2x - 6y = 6$

17. Five 'standard' sheets of A4 paper and two 'superior' sheets weigh 51 grams. Five 'standard' sheets and three 'superior' sheets weigh 59 grams. By forming a pair of equations, find the weight of a 'standard' sheet and the weight of a 'superior' sheet of paper.

18. A certain fraction can be rewritten in its lowest terms as $\frac{1}{2}$. The sum of its numerator and its denominator is 45 and the difference between the numerator and its denominator is 15. What is the fraction?

19. Róisín decided to buy some flowering shrubs for her garden. She discovered that 12 abelia shrubs and 15 camellia shrubs would cost her €369, but 15 abelia shrubs and 12 camellia shrubs would cost her €360. What is the cost of each type of shrub?

20. On a special offer deal from Iarnród Éireann, five adult tickets and three children's tickets cost €120. On the same journey four adult tickets and five children's tickets cost €122. Calculate the cost of an adult ticket and the cost of a child ticket.

21. A certain number of geese were grazing in a field with some sheep. Altogether there were 21 heads and a total of 54 legs. Write two equations and, hence, calculate the number of sheep and the number of geese.

22. The sum of two numbers is 81. The difference between these two numbers is 9. What are the two numbers?

Section 12.12: Symmetry of a point

Student Activity 12L

1. Examine the following image:

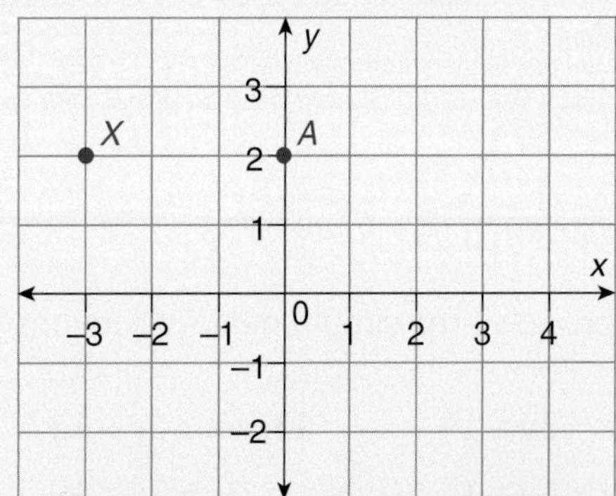

   (a) Find the image of the point X by reflecting it through the point A.
   (b) Describe the change in the coordinates of the point X under this transformation.

2. Examine the following image:

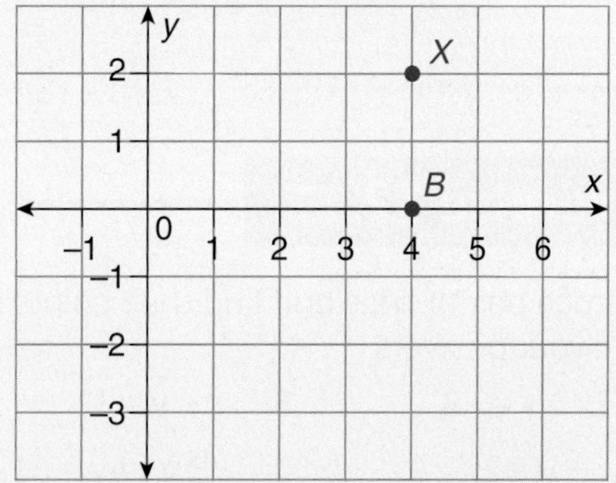

   (a) Find the image of the point X by reflecting it through the point B.
   (b) Describe the change in the coordinates of the point X under this transformation.

3. Examine the following image:

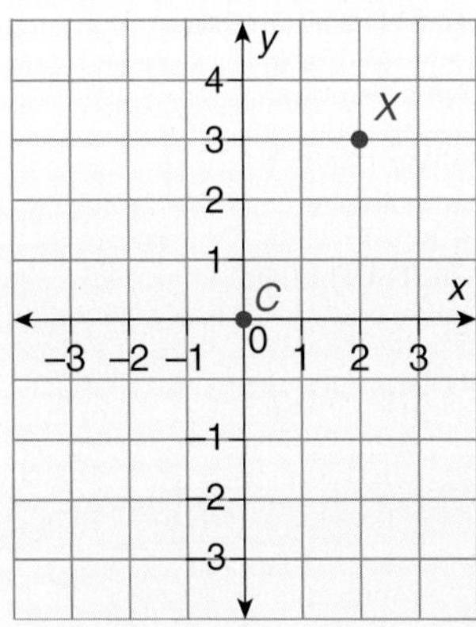

(a) Find the image of the point X by reflecting it through the point C.

(b) Describe the change in the coordinates of the point X under this transformation.

4. The points $ABCD$ form a rectangle. The diagonals of the rectangle intersect at the point E.

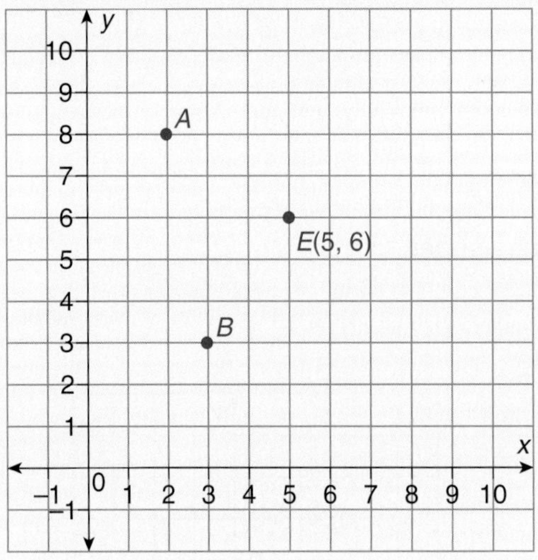

(a) Use transformations to find the coordinates of the points C and D.

(b) Calculate $|AC|$.

(c) Calculate $|AE|$.

(d) What do you notice about your answers to (b) and (c)?

(e) Calculate $|BD|$.

(f) Calculate $|BE|$.

(g) What do you notice about your answers to (e) and (f)?

SYMMETRY OF A POINT EXPLAINED

In Student Activity 12L, you found the image of a number of points by reflecting them through another point. You also saw that the point of reflection is the midpoint of the original point and its image.

In Questions 1 and 2 in the activity, the points were lying on the y- and x-axes respectively. These transformations are also called **symmetries in the axis.** Mathematically, we can write these as:

1. S_x: symmetry in the x-axis

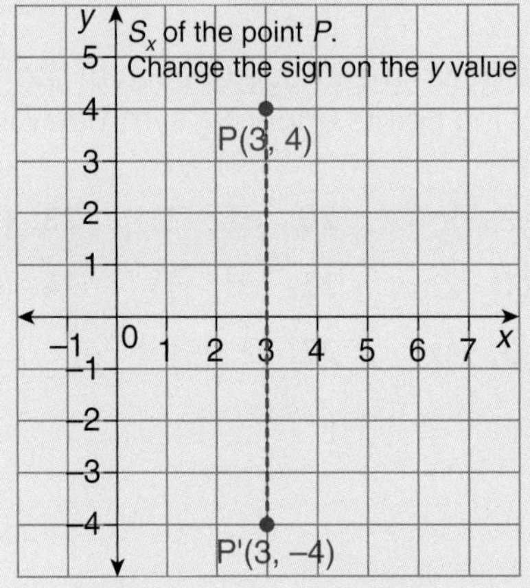

2. S_y: symmetry in the y-axis

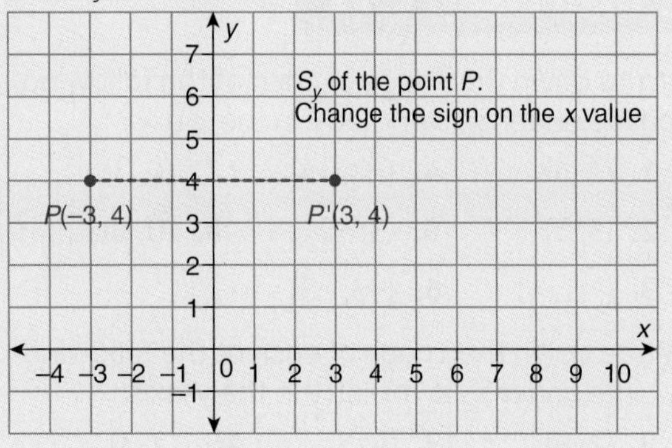

3. S_o: central symmetry through the origin

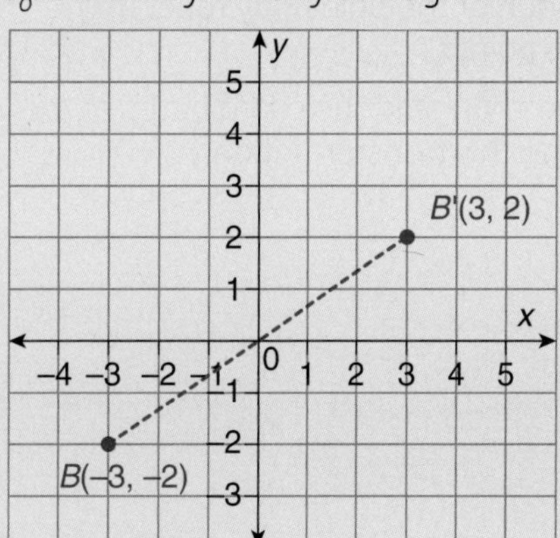

Each of these symmetries follows a simple rule:

1. S_x: change the sign on the y-coordinate.
2. S_y: change the sign on the x-coordinate.
3. S_o: change the sign on both coordinates.

EXAMPLE 27

Plot the point $A(2, 3)$ on a graph paper. Show its image under:

(a) S_x (b) S_y (c) S_o

Solution

(a) S_x **Change the sign on the y-coordinate**

$(2, 3) \rightarrow (2, -3)$

(b) S_y **Change the sign on the x-coordinate**

$(2, 3) \rightarrow (-2, 3)$

(c) S_o **Change both signs**

$(2, 3) \rightarrow (-2, -3)$

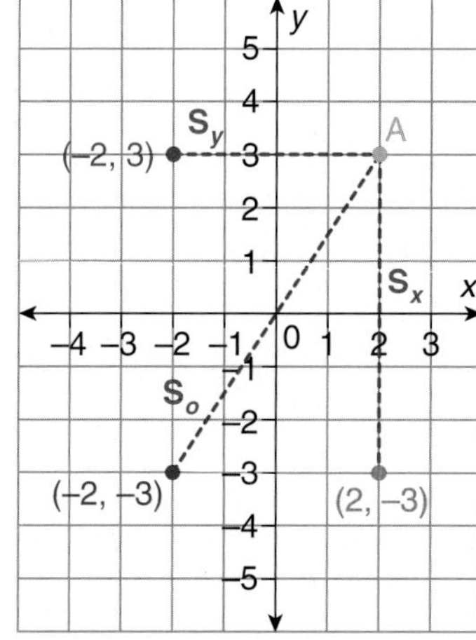

Exercise 12.12

Write down the image of each of the following points under S_x, symmetry in the x-axis:

1. (2, 4) **4.** (−2, −3) **7.** (0, 3)

2. (3, 5) **5.** (3, −2) **8.** (0, 0)

3. (− 1, 4) **6.** (−3, −5)

Write down the image of each of the following points under S_y, symmetry in the y-axis:

9. (2, 9) **12.** (4, 5) **15.** (1, 3)

10. (3, 0) **13.** (0, −3) **16.** (−1, −2)

11. (0, 4) **14.** (−3, 0)

Write down the image of each of the following points under S_o, symmetry in the origin:

17. (2, 3) **20.** (−6, −1) **23.** (3, −1)

18. (1, −2) **21.** (−1, −1) **24.** (0, −5)

19. (5, −4) **22.** (2, −9)

CHAPTER 12 SELF-CHECK TEST

For Questions 1–8, find the following for each pair of points:

(a) Length of [AB]
(b) Midpoint of AB
(c) Slope of AB
(d) Equation of the line AB in the form $y = mx + c$
(e) Sketch each line.

1. $A(6, 4)$ and $B(3, 8)$

2. $A(5, 6)$ and $B(5, 0)$

3. $A(-4, 12)$ and $B(-4, 5)$

4. $A(2, 6)$ and $B(5, 8)$

5. $A(-4, 7)$ and $B(-5, -8)$

6. $A(-3, 6)$ and $B(5, -4)$

7. $A(-1, 4)$ and $B(3, -8)$

8. $A(5, -10)$ and $B(4, -17)$

9. Examine the line m in the diagram and find:

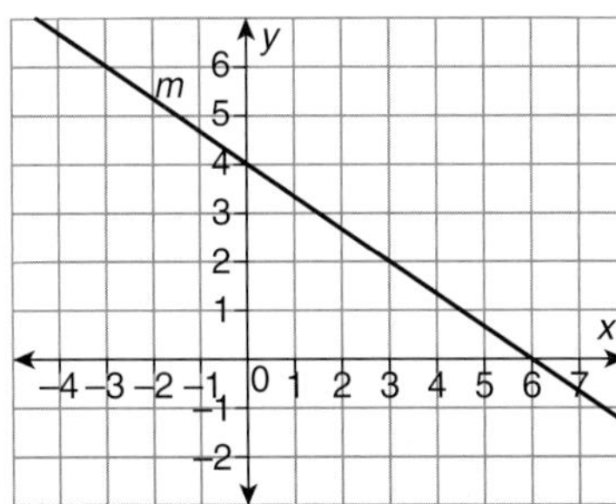

(a) The point where the line crosses the x-axis
(b) The point where the line crosses the y-axis
(c) The slope of the line
(d) The equation of the line

10. The lines l and k are shown in the diagram:

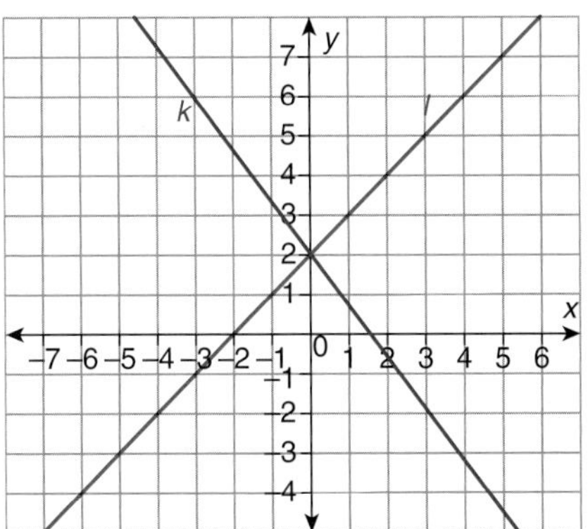

(a) Find the equation of the line l.
(b) Find the equation of the line k.
(c) From the diagram write down the point of intersection of the two lines.
(d) Verify your answer by solving the equations simultaneously.

11. The diagram shows the lines k and n.

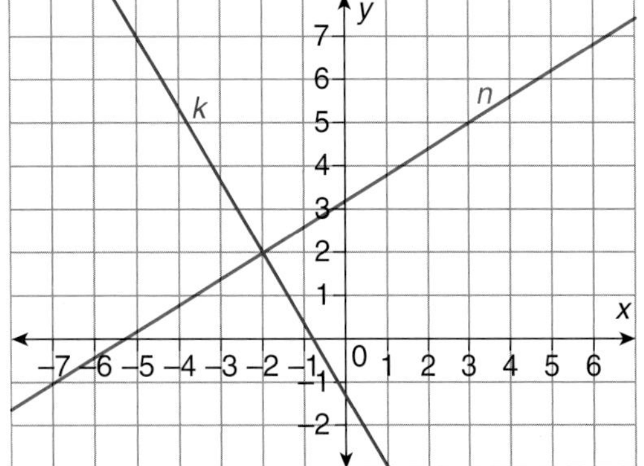

Find:

(a) The slope of the line k
(b) The slope of the line n
(c) Using the slopes, investigate whether the lines are perpendicular.

12. Graph each of the following lines on graph paper:

(a) $3x - 5y = -15$
(b) $-3x + 4y = -12$
(c) $x + 4y = 8$
(d) $7x + y = 7$
(e) $-7x + 4y = -40$
(f) $-2x + 3y = -26$

13. The line l is perpendicular to the line k: $-2x + y = -11$ and passes through the point $(2, 4)$. Find the equation of the line l.

14. Solve each of the pairs of simultaneous equations:

(a) $3p + 8q = 79$
$3p + 2q = 31$

(b) $3a + 2b = 10$
$4a - 2b = 18$

(c) $3m + 2n = 13$
$4m - 2n = -6$

(d) $5h + 2k = 19$
$6h - k = 16$

(e) $10m - 4n = 18$
$11m + 4n = 24$

(f) $7x - 6y = 9$
$6x + 4y = 26$

15. Study the line m shown in the diagram:

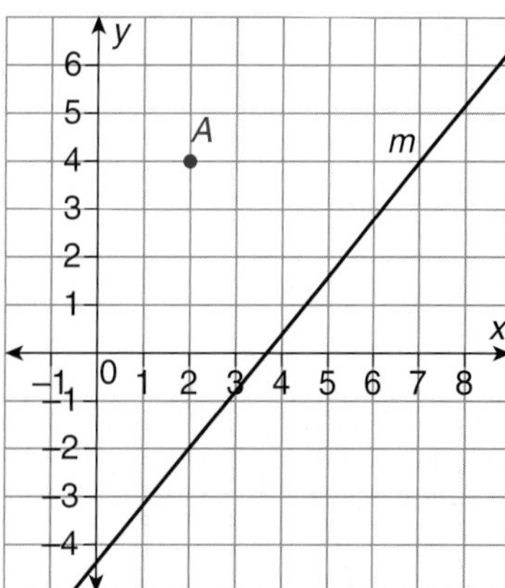

(a) Find the equation of the line m.

(b) Find the equation of the line perpendicular to m and which passes through the point A as indicated.

(c) Find the equation of the line parallel to m and which passes through the point A as indicated.

16. Investigate using slopes whether the lines shown are parallel:

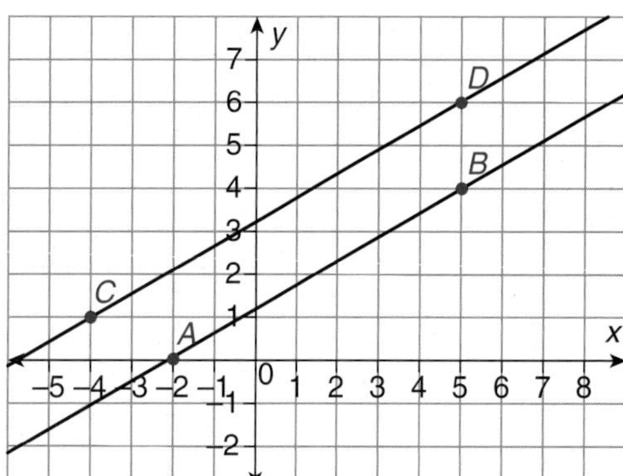

17. Investigate whether the lines shown are perpendicular.

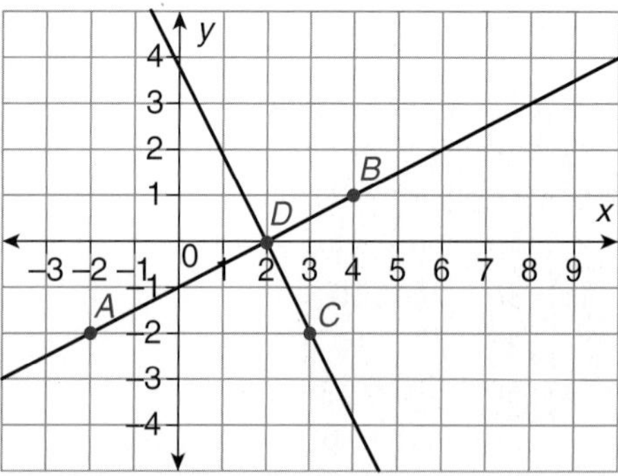

18. Investigate what type of quadrilateral is formed by the points $A(-1, 5)$, $B(1, -2)$, $C(8, -2)$ and $D(6, 5)$.

19. Two jets are flying on paths given by the equations $-x + 3y = 11$ and $7x + 2y = 84$. Use an algebraic method to find whether the jets are on a collision path.

20. A swimmer in distress is being pulled out to sea by strong currents on the path $-2x + 5y = 10$.
A lifeguard starts to swim to the swimmer along the path $4x - y = 16$.

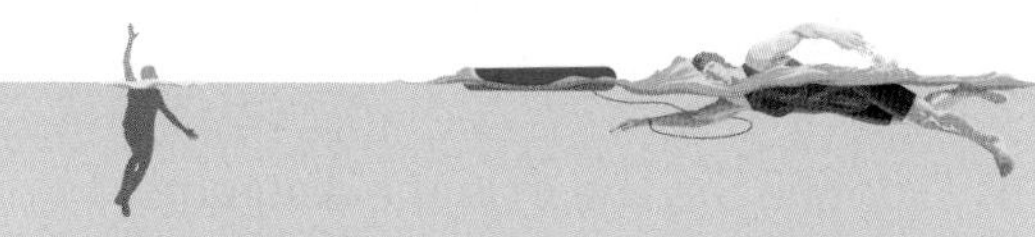

Find the point where the lifeguard will reach the swimmer.

21. A comet is travelling along the path $x + 2y = 3$. A second comet is travelling along the path $3x - y = -12$.

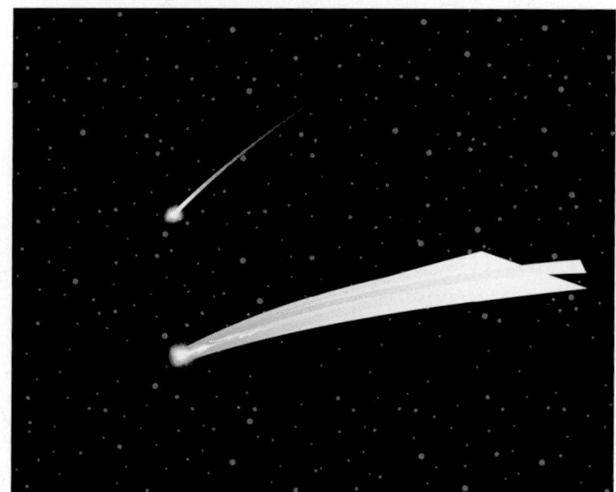

Find where the comets will collide.

CHAPTER 12 KNOWLEDGE CHECKLIST

After completing this chapter, I now:

- Know how to find the distance between two points (length of a line segment)
- Know how to find the midpoint of a line segment
- Know how to find the slope of a line
- Know that parallel lines have equal slopes
- Know that if two lines are perpendicular, the product of their slopes is −1
- Know how to find the equation of a line
- Know how to translate a point
- Know how to plot a line
- Know how to find the slope of a parallel or a perpendicular line to a given line
- Know how to verify that a point lies on a given line
- Know how to find the intersection point of two lines graphically
- Know how to solve simultaneous linear equations
- Know how to find the points where a line intersects the *x*- and *y*-axes
- Understand symmetry of a point

Challenge

Two bottles of water are stored in coolers. One is stored at 30 °F and the second is stored at 40 °F. After 3 hours both are taken out of their respective coolers and a steel ball is dropped into each bottle. Which steel ball reaches the bottom of the bottle first?

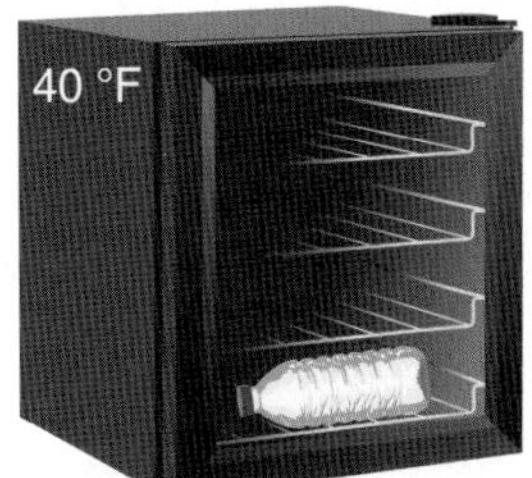

PERIMETER, AREA AND NETS

KEY WORDS

- Area
- Circumference
- Cone
- Cube
- Cuboid
- Cylinder
- Dimension
- Hemisphere
- Net
- Parallelogram
- Perimeter
- Perpendicular height
- Pi
- Prism
- Scale
- Sphere
- Scale model
- Surface area

LEARNING OUTCOMES

In this chapter you will learn:

- ✓ How to calculate the perimeter of a shape
- ✓ How to calculate the areas of squares, rectangles, triangles, parallelograms, circles, semicircles and sectors
- ✓ How to calculate the circumference of a circle
- ✓ How to draw and interpret scaled models
- ✓ How to investigate the nets of rectangular solids to find their surface areas
- ✓ How to investigate the nets of prisms, cylinders, cones, cubes and cuboids
- ✓ How to calculate surface areas for prisms, cylinders, cones, cubes and cuboids
- ✓ How to calculate curved surface areas for cylinders, cones and spheres

INTRODUCTION

As far back as the 23rd century BC, people of the ancient city of Babylonia were trying to find methods of calculating areas and measuring boundaries of land.

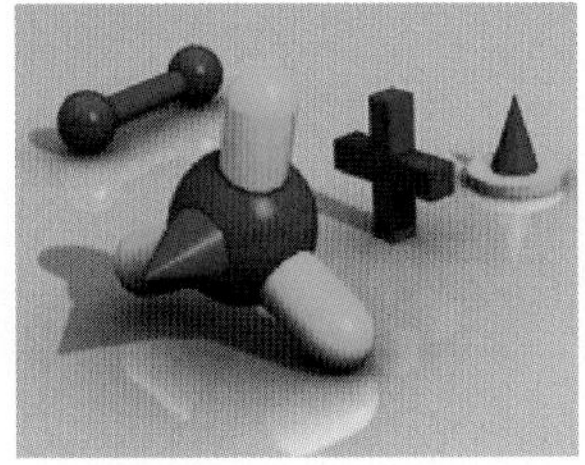

In this chapter, you will examine the results of centuries of mathematical investigations to calculate perimeters and areas of different shapes.

Varignon's Theorem was first published in 1732. It states that a parallelogram is formed when the midpoints of the sides of a quadrilateral are joined in order. Also, the area of the parallelogram is half the area of the quadrilateral and the perimeter is equal to the sum of the diagonals of the original quadrilateral.

Section 13.1: Perimeter

Student Activity 13A

1. A farmer is fencing a field as shown. How much wire will she have to buy to completely enclose the field?

   19 m

   10 m

2. How much skirting board is needed to go around the room shown?

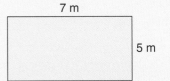

   7 m

   5 m

3. How much rope is needed to enclose the following triangle?

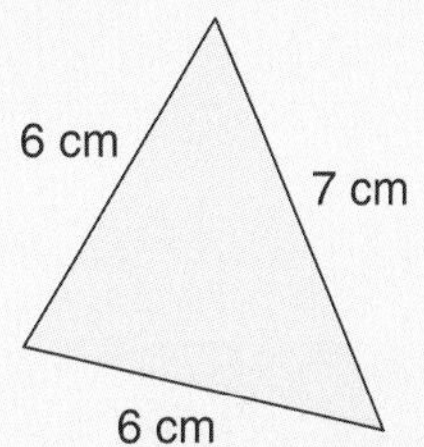

4. Can you explain in your own words how you would find the perimeter of a shape?
5. A rectangular vegetable patch will be enclosed by a wire fence of 20 metres in order to keep rabbits out.

   List all of the possible widths and lengths of the rectangle.

PERIMETER EXPLAINED

If you look at a map or an aerial photograph showing an area of land, you will notice that fields are not always regular in shape. Surveyors must be able to measure the boundary of the fields. The perimeter of a shape is the total length of its boundary.

Since perimeter is a measure of all the lengths around the edges added together, the answer is given in units (for example, mm, cm, m or km). Remember to always convert all measurements to the same unit before starting.

You need to know these conversion scales:

10 millimetres (mm) = 1 centimetre (cm)
100 centimetres (cm) = 1 metre (m)
1,000 metres (m) = 1 kilometre (km)

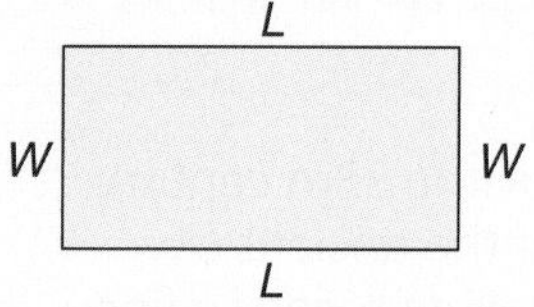

Perimeter of a rectangle
$= L + W + L + W = 2L + 2W$ or $2(L + W)$

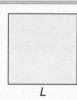

Perimeter of a square $= L + L + L + L = 4L$

EXAMPLE 1

Find the perimeter of the following shape:

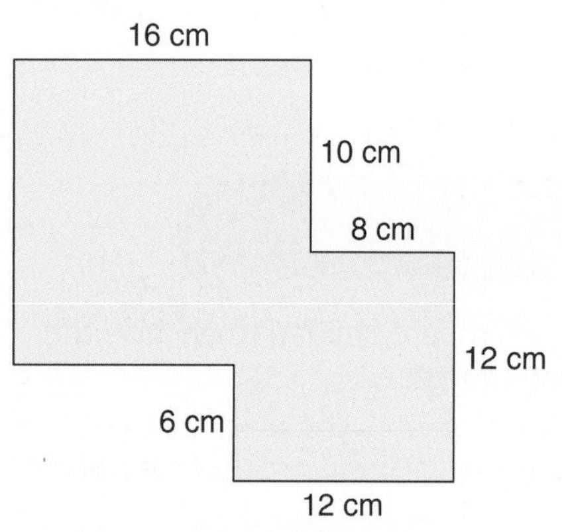

Solution

First, we need to find all the missing measurements of the shape.

The total vertical length = 10 + 12 = 22 cm.
So the missing length is 22 – 6 = 16 cm.

The total horizontal width = 16 + 8 = 24 cm.
So the missing width is 24 – 12 = 12 cm.

Total perimeter:

16 + 10 + 8 + 12 + 12 + 6 + 12 + 16 = 92 cm

Exercise 13.1

Find the perimeter of each of the following shapes:

1.

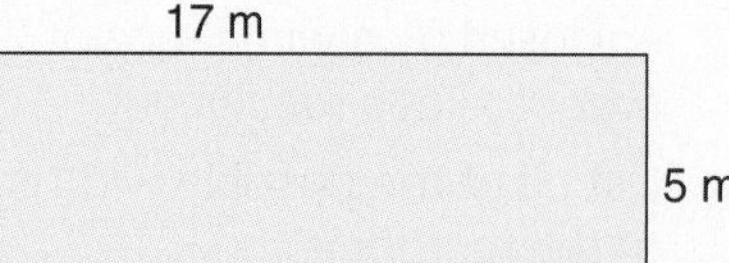

2.

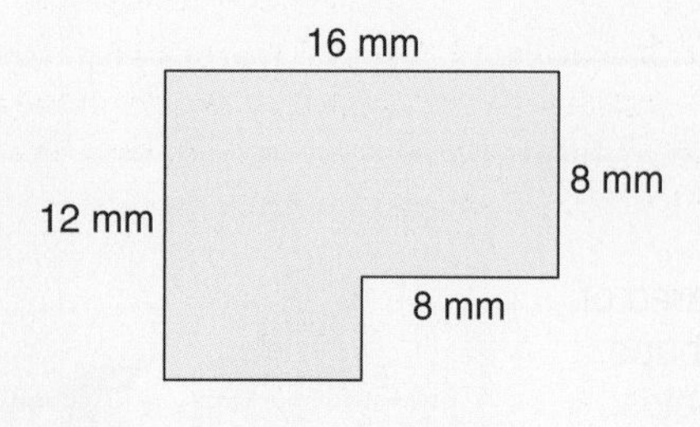

3.

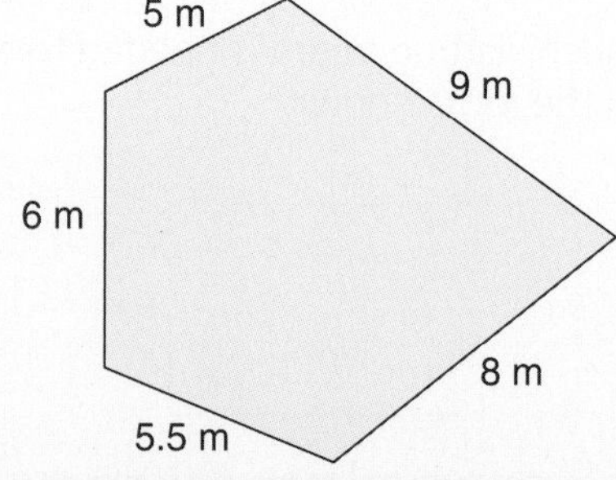

4.

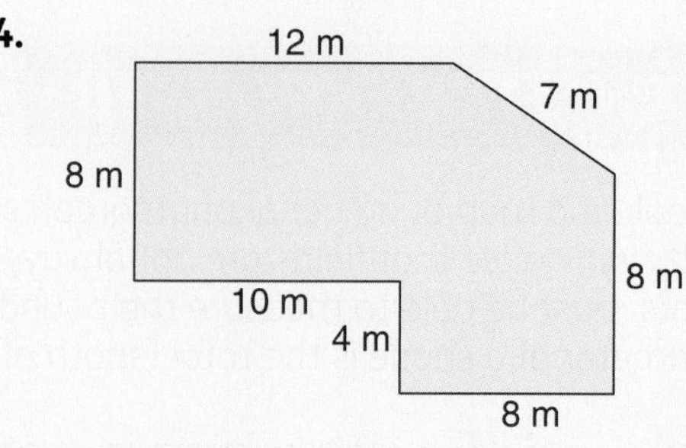

5.

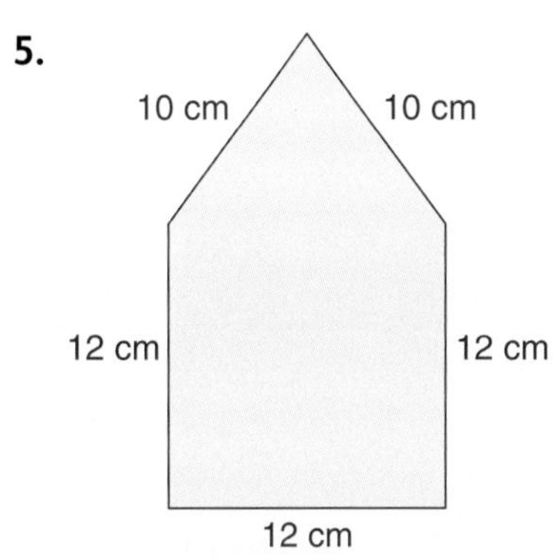

6.

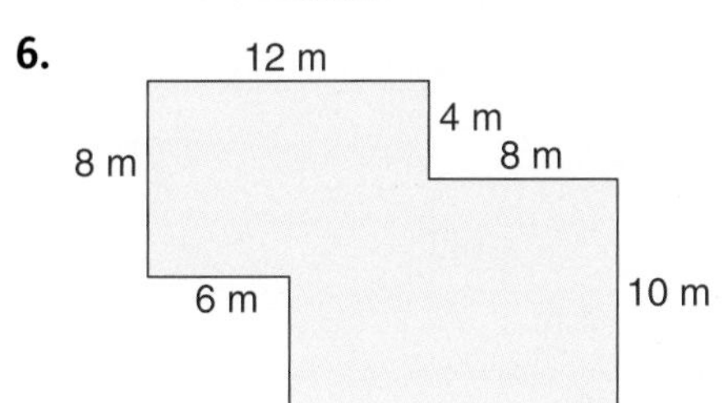

7.

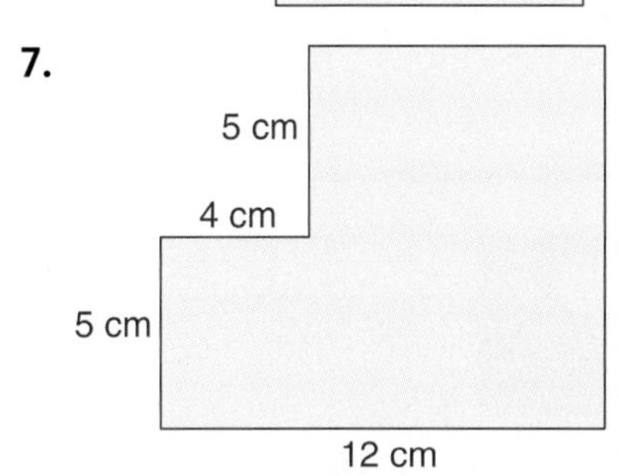

8.

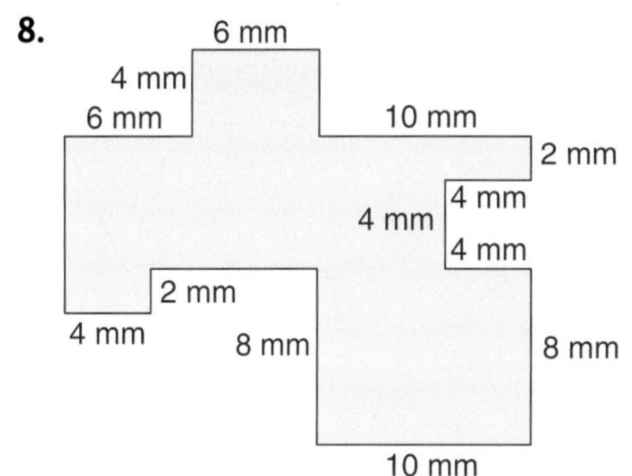

9.

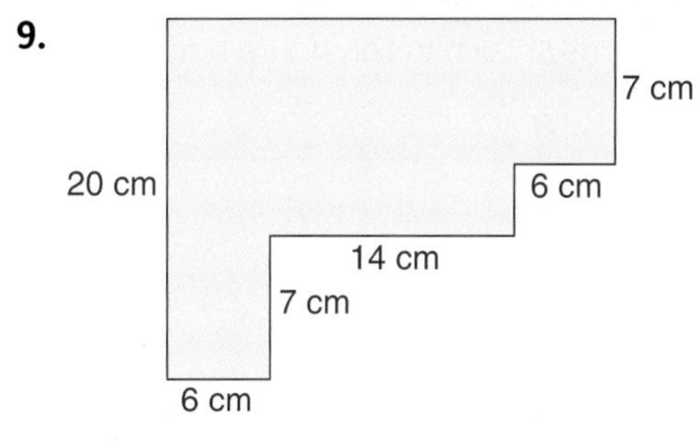

10.

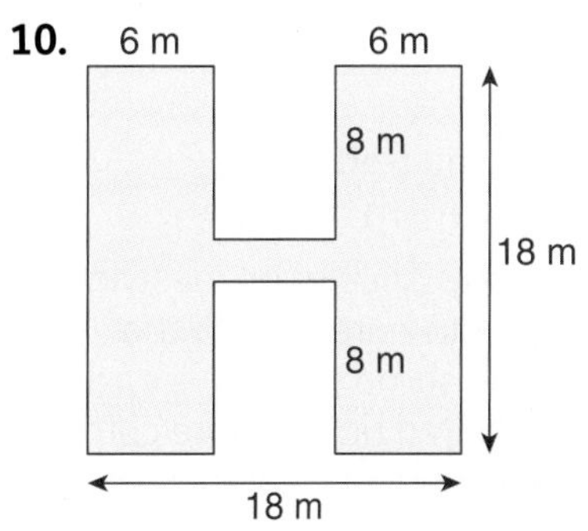

11.

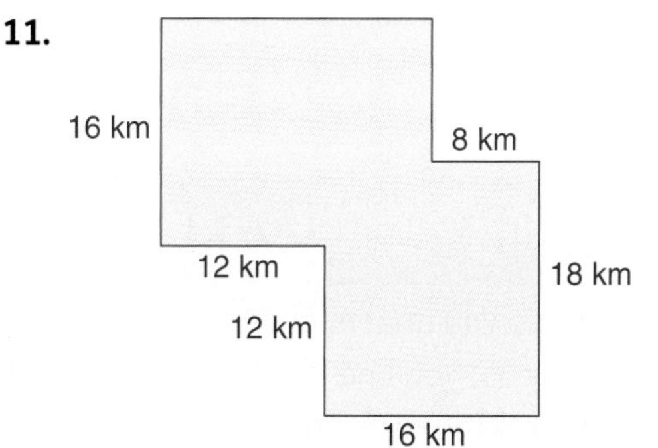

12. A 3 m long piece of wire is bent to form a rectangle. One side of the rectangle is 45 cm. Calculate the length of the longer side of the rectangle.

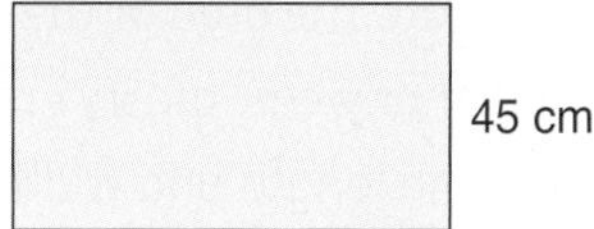

13. If the perimeter of a square is 48 cm, calculate the length of one side.

14. If the perimeter of a square is 58 m, calculate the length of one side.

15. If the perimeter of a square is 40 cm, calculate the length of the diagonal.

16. Find the length of a rectangle if the width is 14.2 cm and the perimeter is 108 cm.

17. The perimeter of a rectangle is 350 m. Calculate its dimensions if the sides are in the ratio of 4:1.

18. The perimeter of a rectangle is 284 m. Calculate its dimensions if the sides are in the ratio of 1:3.

19. The perimeter of a rectangle is 108 cm. Calculate the value of x if the length is $(3x + 5)$ and the width is $(7x - 1)$.

20. Calculate the length of a side in an equilateral triangle whose perimeter is 171 cm.

21. The side lengths of a triangle are $(x + 3)$, x and $(2x - 5)$. Find the value of x if the perimeter of the triangle is 90 m. What type of triangle is it?

22. A farmer must make a rectangular pen to enclose his sheep in a grazing paddock. He has 100 m of wire. What whole number dimensions could the pen have? What dimensions would you recommend to him not to use and why?

Section 13.2: Area of squares, rectangles and parallelograms

Student Activity 13B

1. What do you understand the word 'area' to mean?
2. How would you find the area of a rectangle or a square?
3. Complete the following:
   To calculate the area of a rectangular shape you m _ _ _ _ _ _ _ its l _ _ _ _ _ by its w _ _ _ _. The units for area are called s _ _ _ _ _ units.
4. (a) How many centimetres in 1 metre?
   (b) Calculate the area of the square shown in m^2.
   (c) Calculate the area of the square in cm^2.
   (d) How many cm^2 are in 1 m^2?

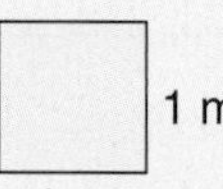

5. Measure the length and width of your desk.
   (a) Calculate the perimeter of your desk.
   (b) Calculate the area of your desk.

AREA OF SQUARES, RECTANGLES AND PARALLELOGRAMS EXPLAINED

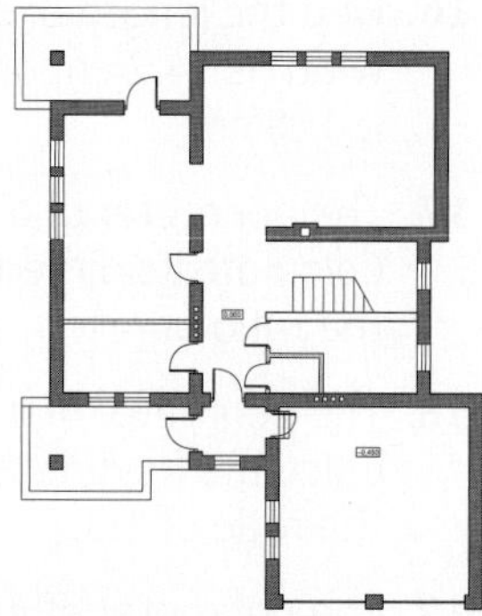

The area of a shape is the amount of space inside its boundary. For a square or rectangular 2D shape, the area is given by:

Area of a rectangle = Length × Width

A **parallelogram** is a four-sided shape formed by two pairs of parallel lines.

In a parallelogram, opposite sides are equal in length and opposite angles are equal in measure. To find the area of a parallelogram, use the formula:

Area of a parallelogram = Base × Perpendicular height

The base and height of a parallelogram must be perpendicular. A dotted line is drawn to represent the perpendicular height.

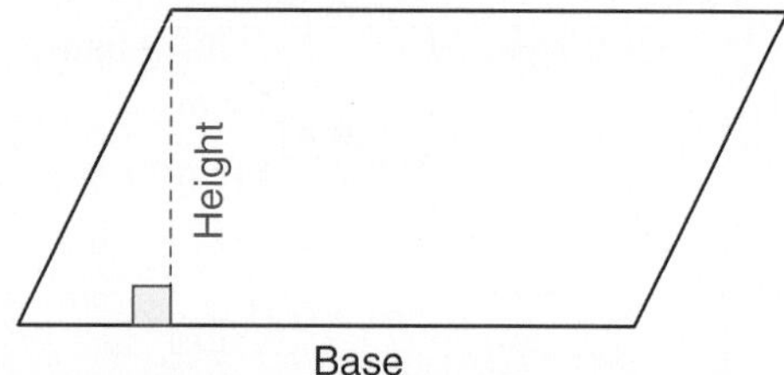

Note that you can cut a triangle from one end and paste it onto the other end to form a rectangle as shown in the figure below.

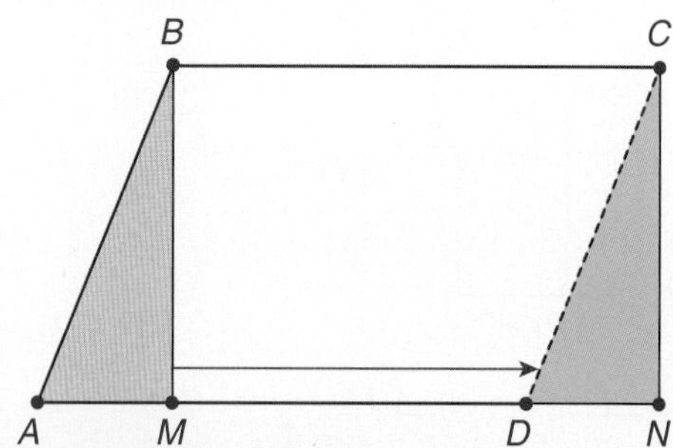

Area is measured in **squared units** (for example, mm^2, cm^2, m^2 and km^2).

When carrying out any calculation involving perimeter or area, make sure that all the dimensions are in the same units. It is easier to change to the required units before carrying out the calculations.

In science, when different elements are put together, it creates a compound. Likewise in maths, many smaller shapes put together make a **compound shape.**

To find the area of a compound shape:

- **Step 1:** Divide the shape up into smaller parts and label each part.
- **Step 2:** Fill in any required missing measurements.
- **Step 3:** Calculate the area of each part.
- **Step 4:** Add all areas to find the total area.

EXAMPLE 2

Find the area of the following parallelogram:

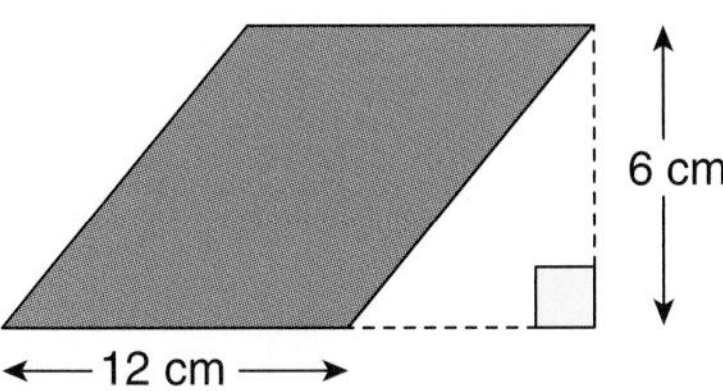

Solution

Area of a parallelogram

= Base × Perpendicular height

= 12 cm × 6 cm

= 72 cm^2

EXAMPLE 3

Find the area of the shaded part of the diagram below.

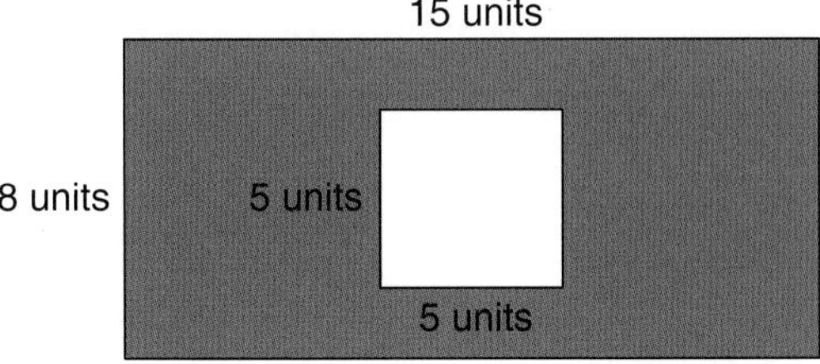

Solution

Shaded area = Area of large rectangle – Area of the inside square

= (8 × 15) – (5 × 5)

= 120 – 25

= 95 $units^2$

EXAMPLE 4

Find the area of the following compound shape.

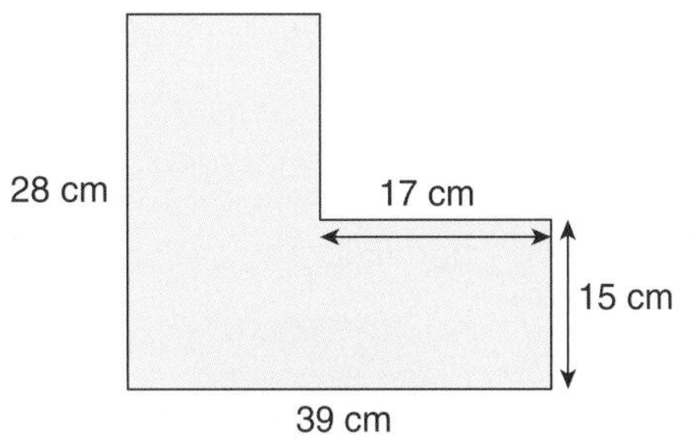

Solution

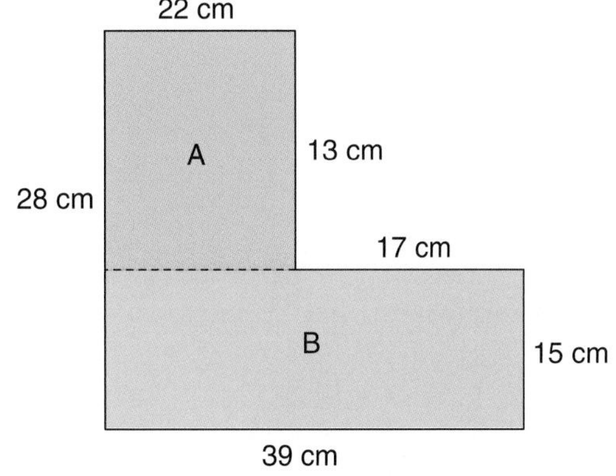

Total area =

Area of rectangle A + Area of rectangle B

= (13 × 22) + (39 × 15)

= 286 + 585

= 871 cm^2

Exercise 13.2

1. A field has dimensions 30 m × 50 m.
   (a) Draw a rough sketch of the field.
   (b) Calculate the perimeter of the field.
   (c) Calculate the area of the field.

2. A dining room measures 6 m × 6 m.
   (a) Draw a sketch of the dining room.
   (b) Calculate the perimeter of the dining room.
   (c) Calculate the area of the dining room.

3. Calculate the perimeter and surface area of each sheet of timber with the following dimensions:

(a) 4 m × 6 m	(f) 20 mm × 1 m
(b) 40 cm × 30 cm	(g) 5 m × 6 m
(c) 10 mm × 20 cm	(h) 20 cm × 30 cm
(d) 15 mm × 20 mm	(i) 3.0 m × 3.2 m
(e) 20 cm × 2 m	(j) 20.5 m × 25.5 m

4. Calculate the area of each of the following parallelograms:

(a)

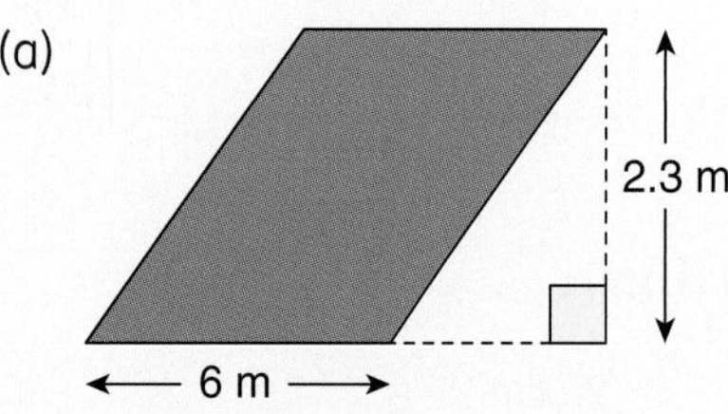

(b)

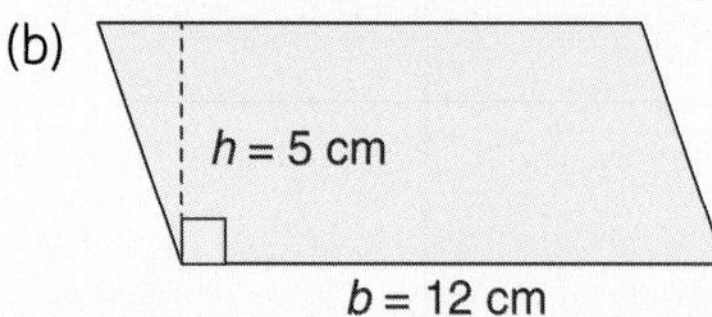

(c)

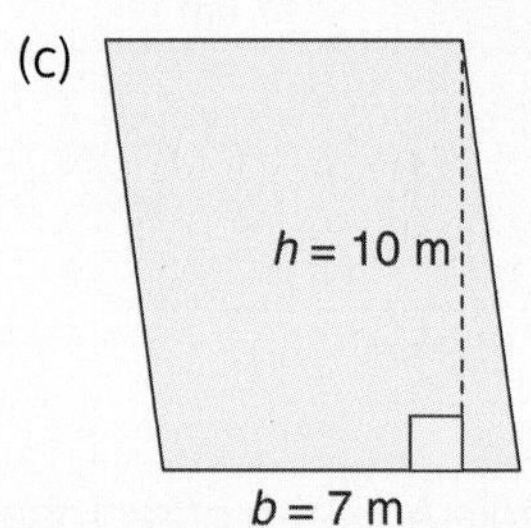

(d)

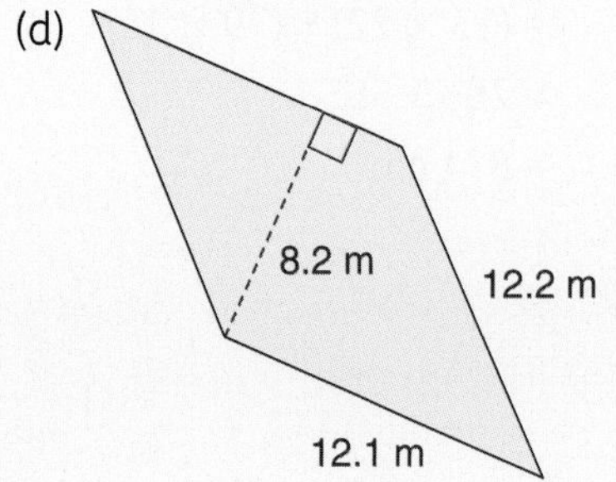

(e)

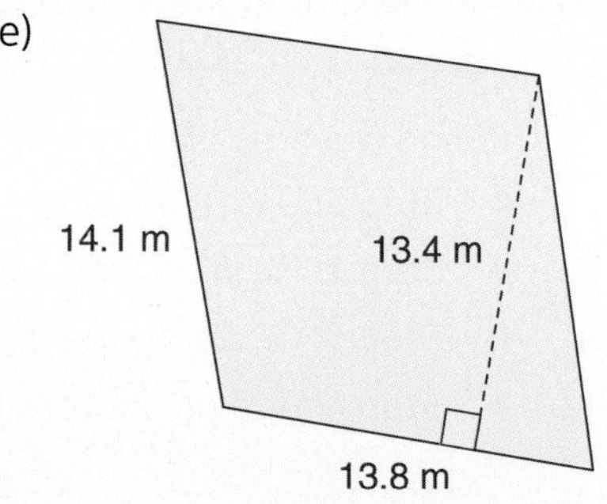

(f)

20 mm

13 mm

12 mm

(g)

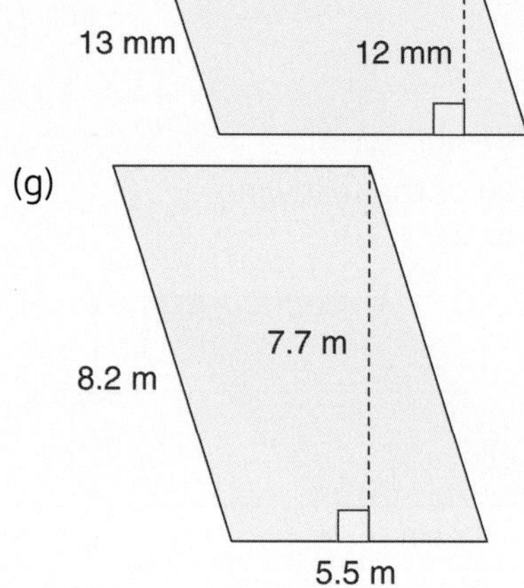

(h)

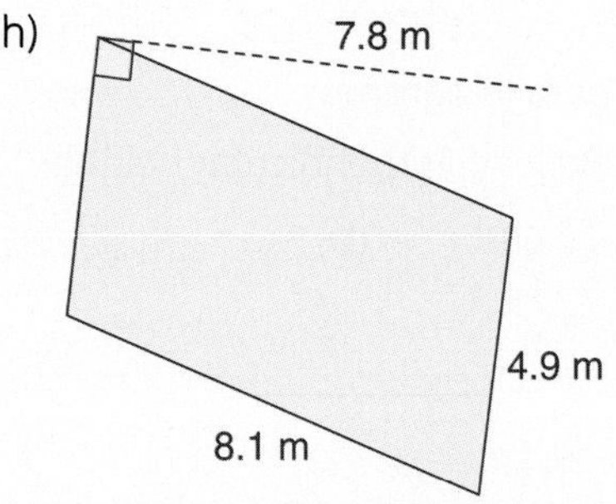

5. Calculate the (i) area and (ii) the perimeter of each of the following shapes:

(a)

16 mm

9 mm

20 mm

7 mm

4 mm

6 mm

14 mm

(b)

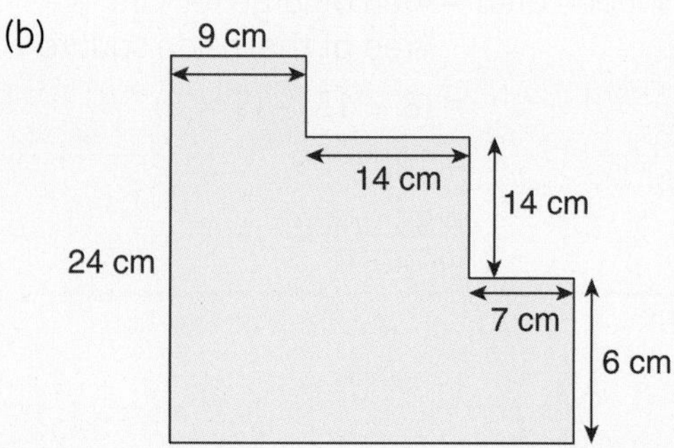

(c)

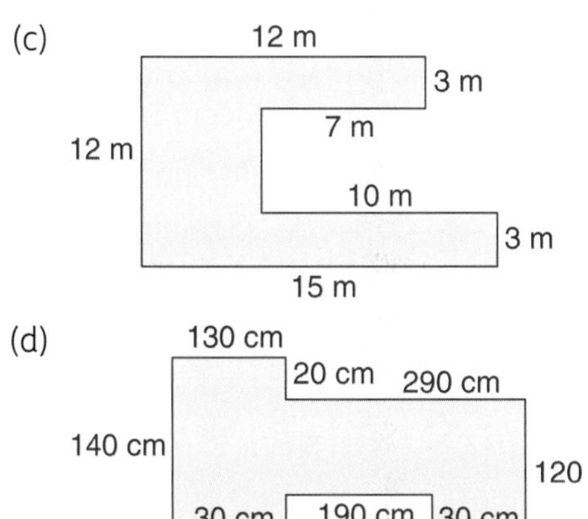

(d)

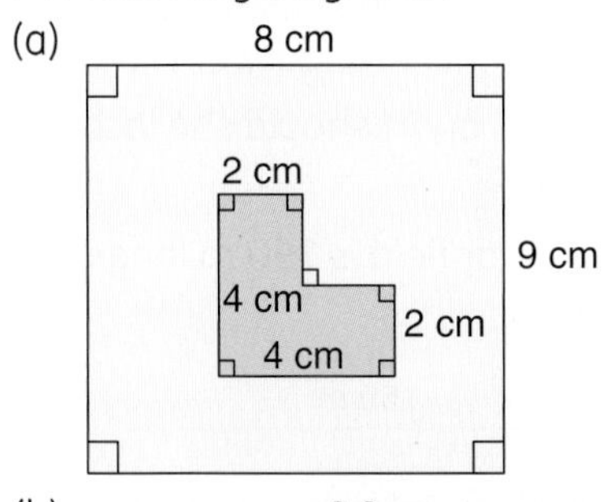

6. Calculate the coloured areas in each of the following diagrams:

(a)

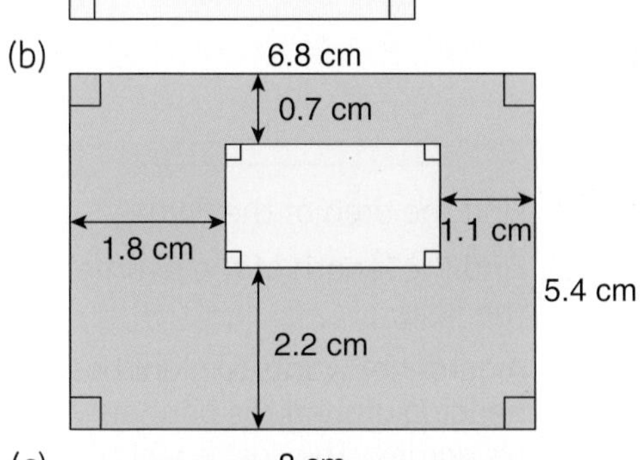

(b)

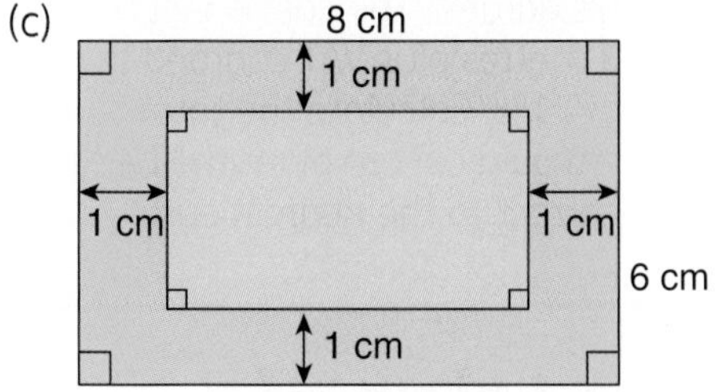

(c)

8 cm
1 cm
1 cm
1 cm
6 cm
1 cm

7. The area of a parallelogram is 24 square centimetres. It has a base of 4 centimetres. Find the perpendicular height.

8. A landscaper is spreading grass seed on the lawn shown.

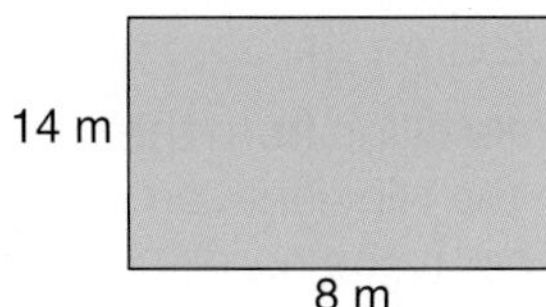

Calculate:

(a) The amount of wire needed to enclose the lawn

(b) The area of the lawn

(c) If a bag of lawn seed covers 32 m², how many bags will be needed to seed the lawn?

9. A tiler is tiling the floor shown with square tiles. Each tile measures 20 cm × 20 cm.

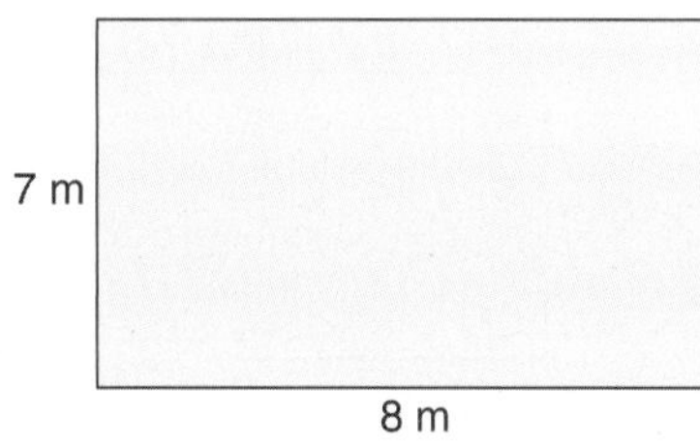

(a) What is the area of each tile in m²?

(b) What is the area of the floor shown?

(c) How many tiles will be required to cover the floor?

10. The dimensions of a sitting room are shown.

(a) Calculate the area of the sitting room.

(b) Floor boards are sold in packs. Each pack covers 5 m². How many packs will be needed to floor the sitting room?

(c) If the floor boards cost €15.99 per pack, what is the total cost of flooring the sitting room?

(d) A carpet costing €3.75 per m² could be bought instead. Which is the cheaper option and how much would the shopper save?

11. A farmer is spraying his crops in the two adjoining fields shown.

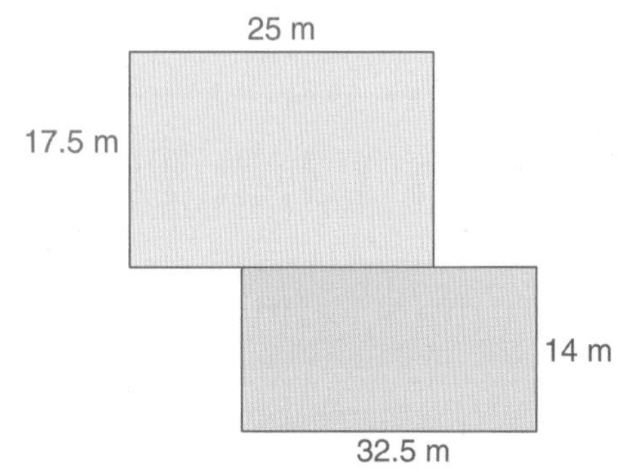

(a) Calculate the total area of the two fields.

(b) If each pack of spray covers 85 m², how many packs will be needed to spray the two fields?

(c) If the cost of a pack is €31, how much will all the packs of spray cost the farmer?

12. A family wants to lay paving stones on the area shown.

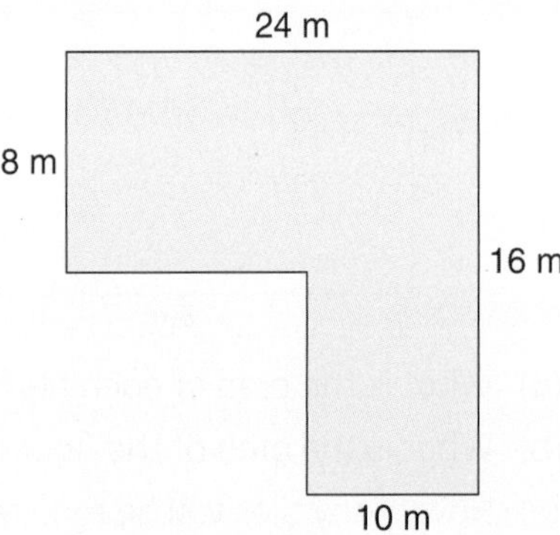

(a) Calculate the area.

(b) A paving stone has dimensions 50 cm x 50 cm. Calculate the area of each paving stone.

(c) How many paving stones will be required to cover the area?

(d) If the paving stones cost 75c each, what will be the total cost of the paving stones?

(e) An alternative paving stone with dimensions 40 cm × 40 cm costs just 50c each. Investigate which is the cheaper option, explaining your answer.

13. The perimeter of a rectangular playing field is 440 m. The length of the shorter side is 85 m.

(a) Find the length of the longer side.

(b) Find the area of the playing field.

(c) The field is resurfaced at a cost of €185 for every 10 square metres. Find the cost of resurfacing the field.

14. The diagram shows a fish pond in a garden.

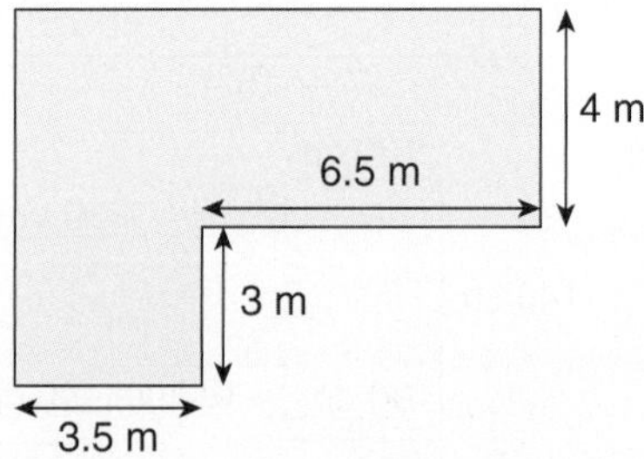

(a) Calculate the area of the pond.

(b) The owner wants to install 8 lights, each at an equal distance apart, around the boundary of the pond.

How far apart should she locate the lights?

15. A rectangular field is 150 m long and 90 m wide.

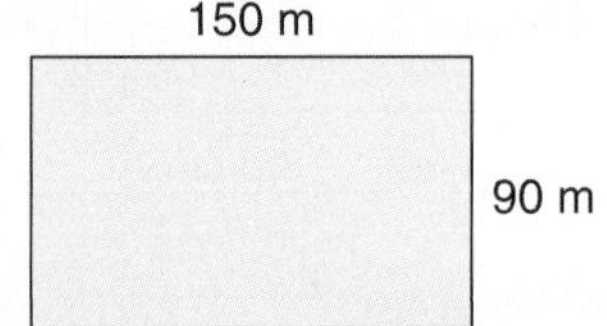

(a) Find the area of the field.

(b) Find the length of the perimeter of the field.

(c) A gardener wants to plant beech hedging around the boundary edge of his garden. The cost is €21.99 for every 3 metres plus VAT charged at a rate of 21%. Calculate the total amount it would cost to plant the hedging, correct to the nearest euro.

Section 13.3: The area of a triangle

Student Activity 13C

1. Draw a rectangle with width 4 cm and length 5 cm.

(a) Calculate the area of the rectangle.

(b) Draw a line from the bottom left corner to the top right corner of the rectangle. What name is given to this line?

(c) What two shapes have you formed?

(d) Calculate the area of each of the shapes. Is there a relationship between the area of the two shapes and the area of the rectangle? Explain your answer.

2. Draw a square of side 4 cm.

(a) Calculate the area of the square.

(b) Draw a line from the bottom left corner to the top right corner of the square. What is the name given to this line?

(c) What two shapes have you formed?

(d) Calculate the area of each of the shapes. Is there a relationship between the area of the two shapes and the area of the square? Explain your answer.

3. Copy and complete the following sentence:
   A diagonal of a rectangle or a square divides the rectangle or square into two t _ _ _ _ _ _ _ _ of equal a _ _ _.
4. Copy and complete the following sentence:
   The area of a triangle can be found by dividing the area of a rectangle or of a square by t _ _.
5. What do you think is the formula for calculating the area of a triangle?

THE AREA OF A TRIANGLE EXPLAINED

In Student Activity 13C, you discovered that all rectangles are made up of two triangles. This allows us to calculate the area of a triangle.

If the area of a rectangle is given by:

Area of a rectangle = Length × Width

Then the area of a triangle is given by:

Area of a triangle = $\frac{1}{2}$ × Length × Width

In maths, we use the terms height and base when dealing with triangles.

The height of any triangle always refers to its perpendicular height. The width is called the base of the triangle.

The **perpendicular height** is the distance from the base of the triangle to the highest point.

Using the correct terms, we can say that the area of a triangle is given by:

Area of a triangle = $\frac{1}{2}$ × Base × Perpendicular height

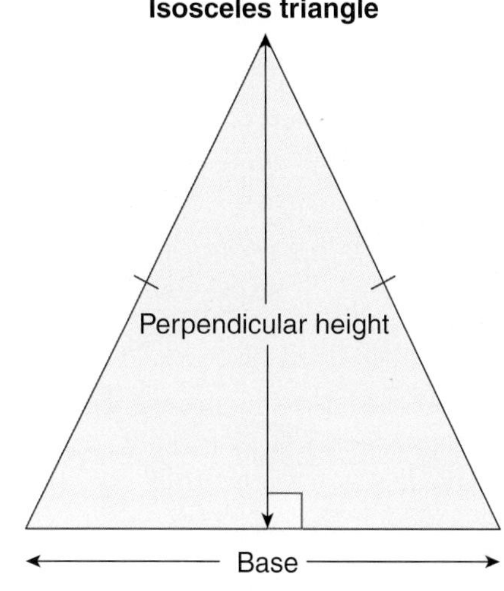

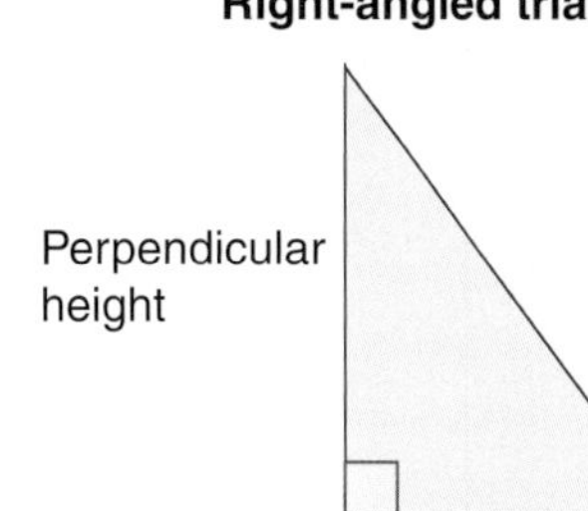

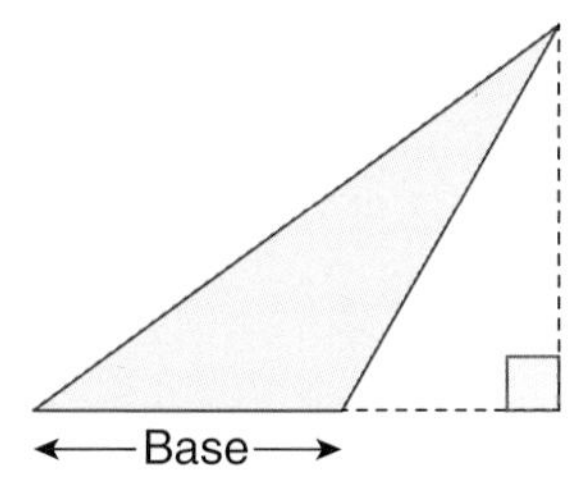

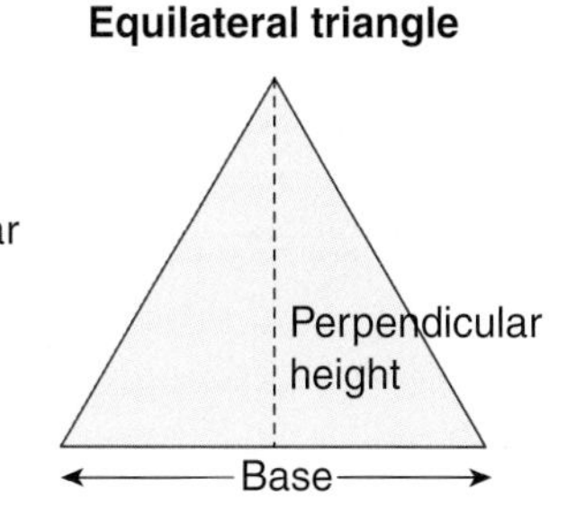

EXAMPLE 5

Find the area of the following triangle:

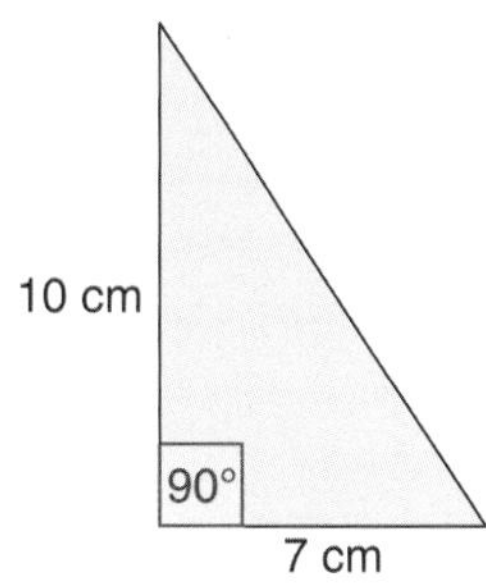

Solution

Area = $\frac{1}{2}$ × Base × ⊥ Height

Area = $\frac{1}{2} \times 7 \times 10$

Area = 35 cm^2

EXAMPLE 6

The area of the following triangle is 100 cm². Find the length of the base of the triangle.

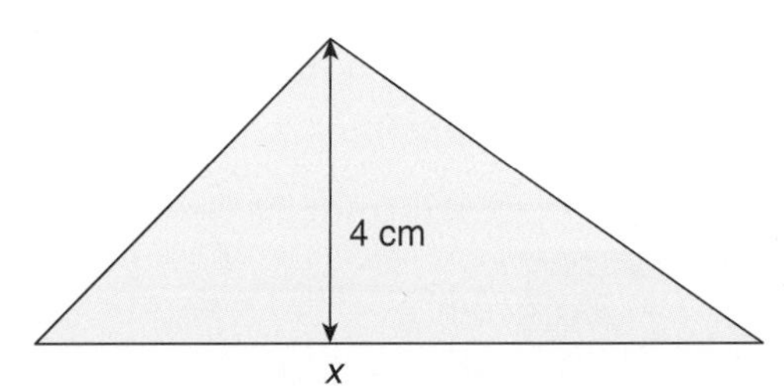

Solution

Area = $\frac{1}{2}$ × Base × ⊥ Height

$100 = \frac{1}{2}(x)(4)$

$100 = 2(x)$

$50 = x$

Base = 50 cm

Exercise 13.3

1. Estimate the area of these shapes, given each square on the grid equals 1 cm².

(a)

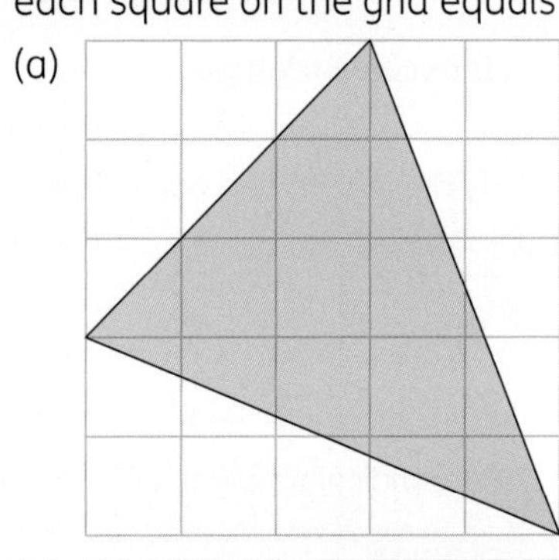

(b)

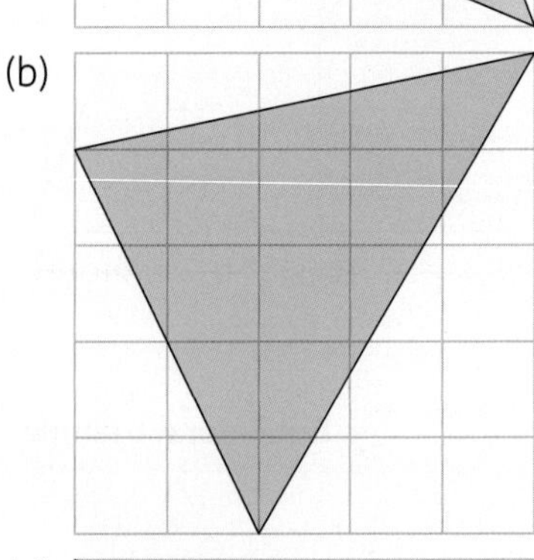

(c)

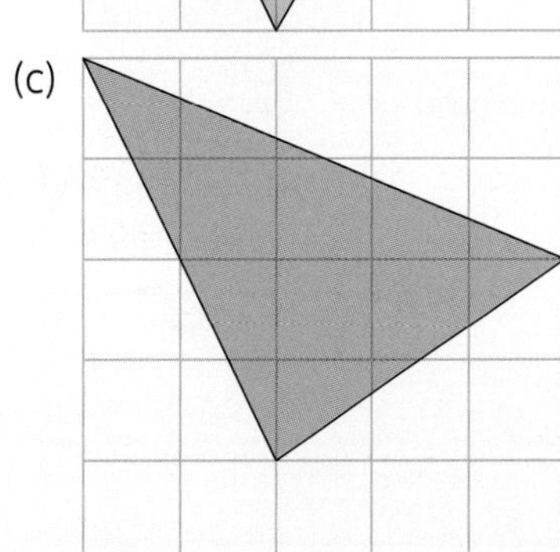

2. Calculate the area of each of the following triangles:

(a)

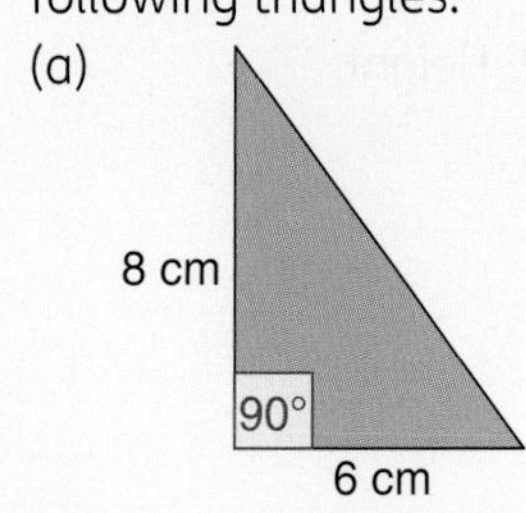

(b)

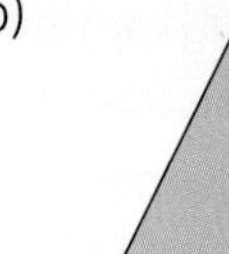
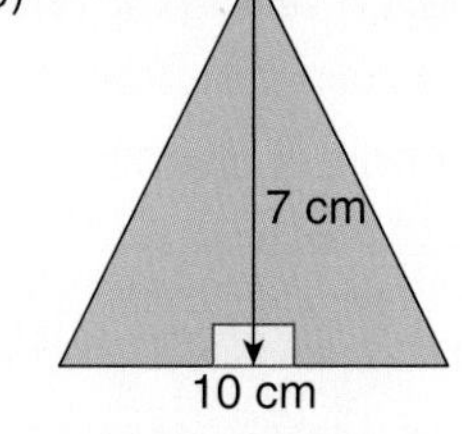

(c)

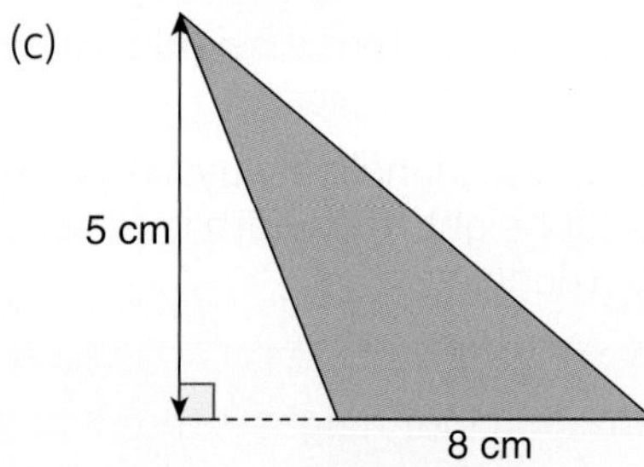

(d)

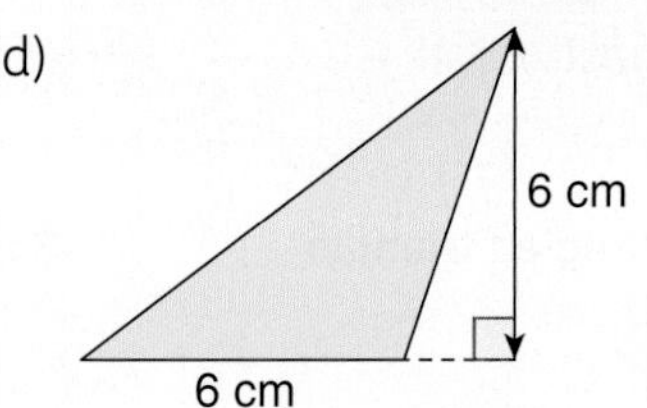

(e)

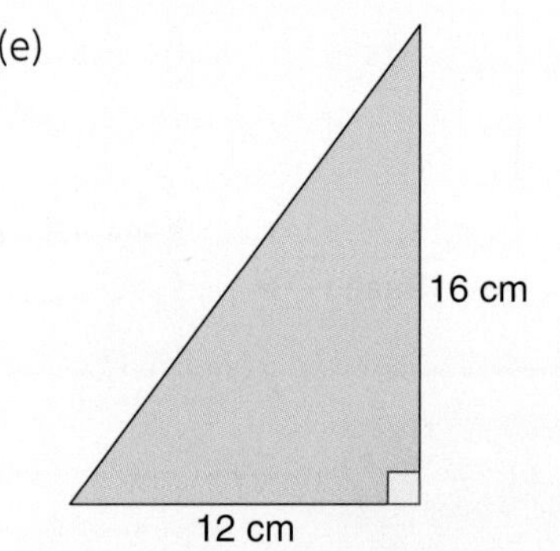

(f)

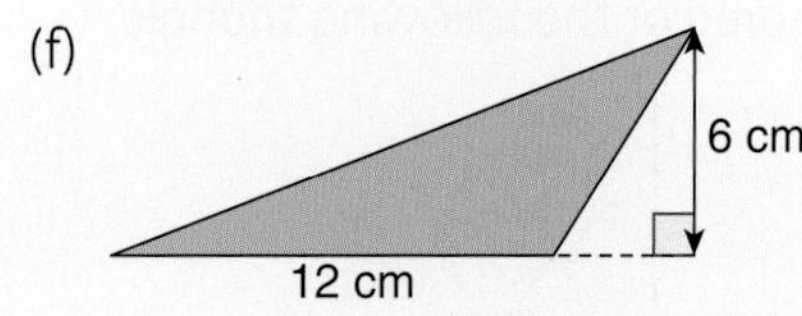

3. Find the missing dimension, given the area of each of the following triangles:

(a) Area = 150 cm²

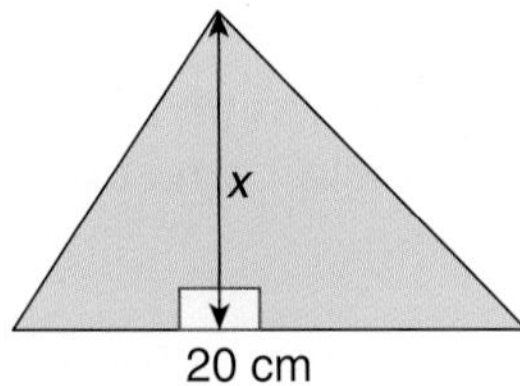

(b) Area = 45 cm²

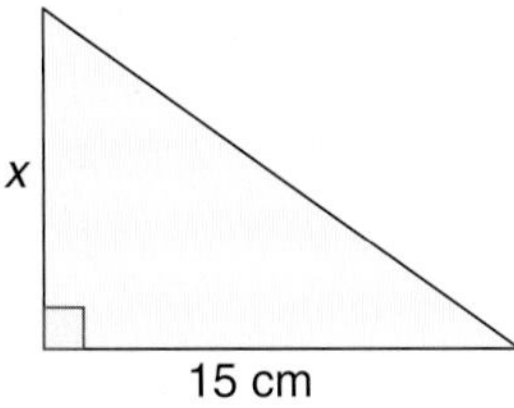

(c) Area = 33.25 cm²

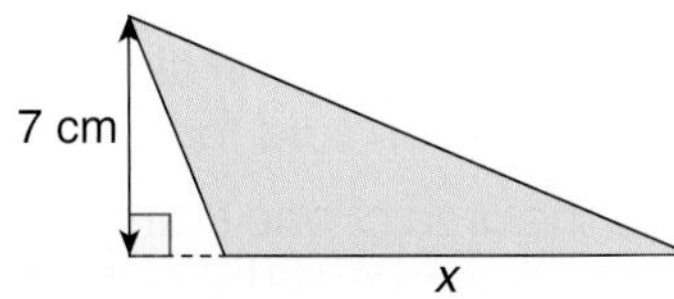

(d) Area = 250 cm²

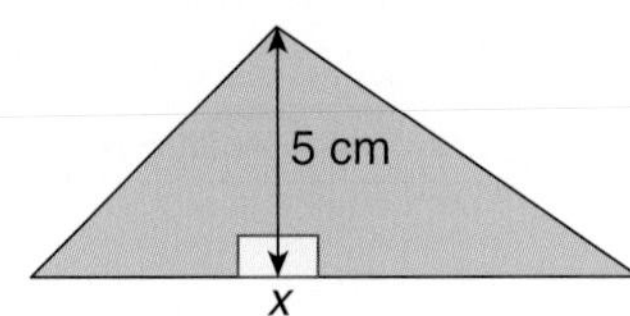

(e) Area = 16 cm²

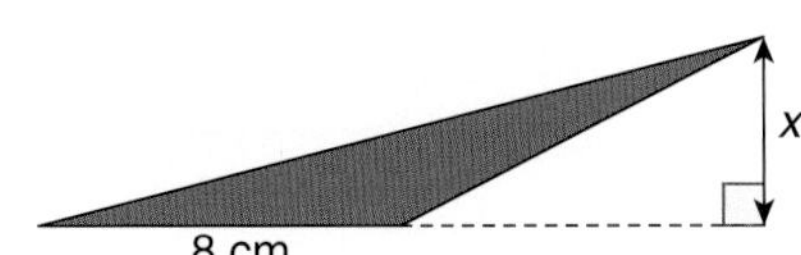

(f) Area = 275 cm²

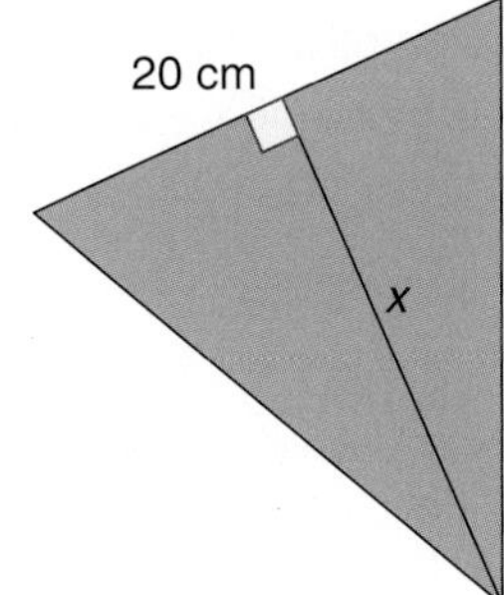

(g) Area = 70 cm²

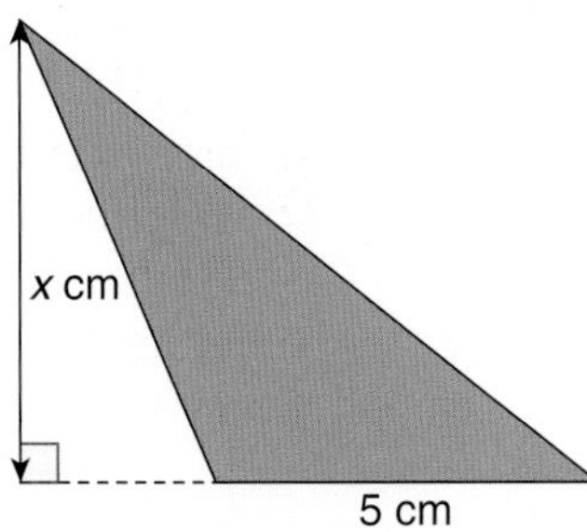

(h) Area = 196 cm²

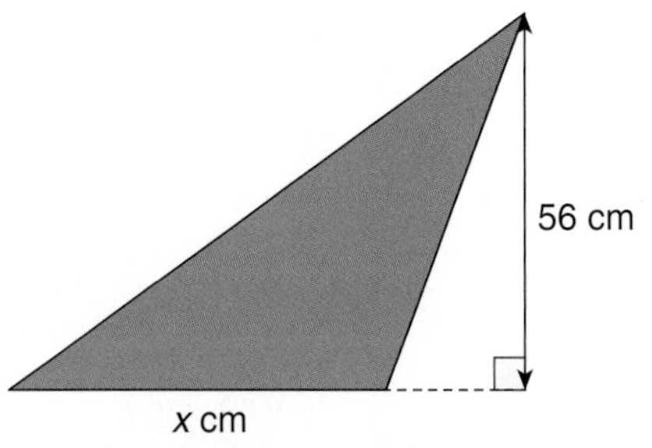

4. Find the area of the shaded parts in each of the following:

(a)

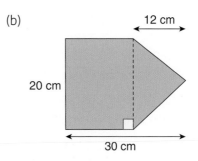

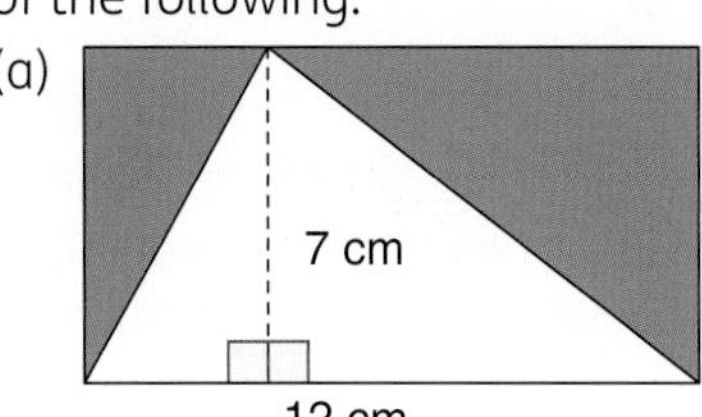

(b)

(c)

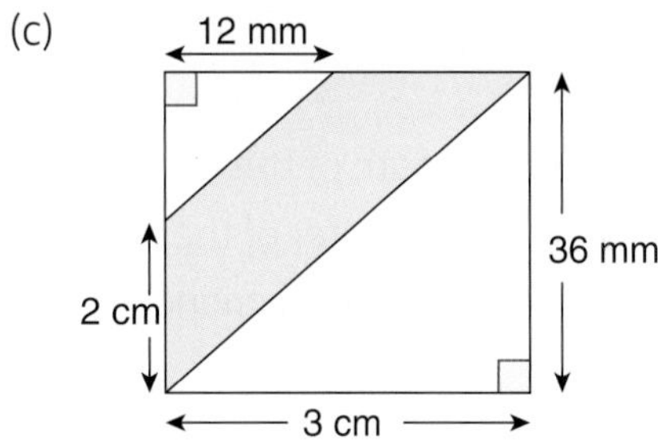

(d)

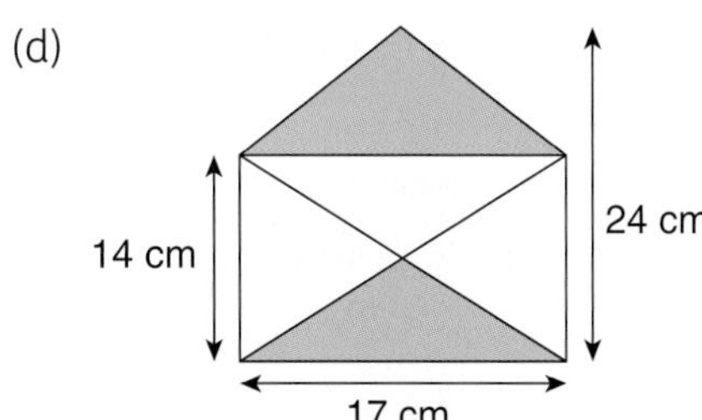

(e)

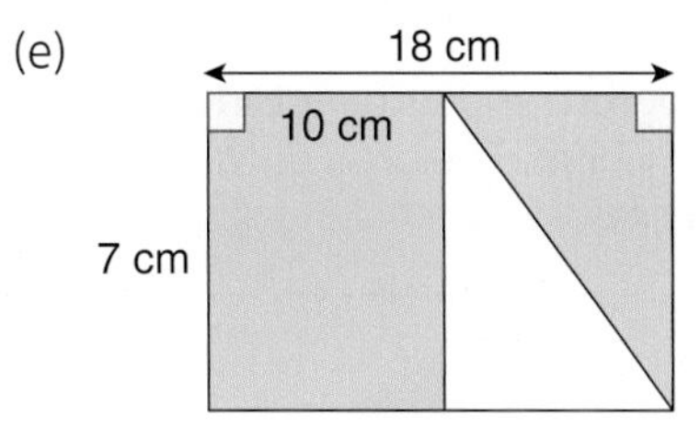

(f)

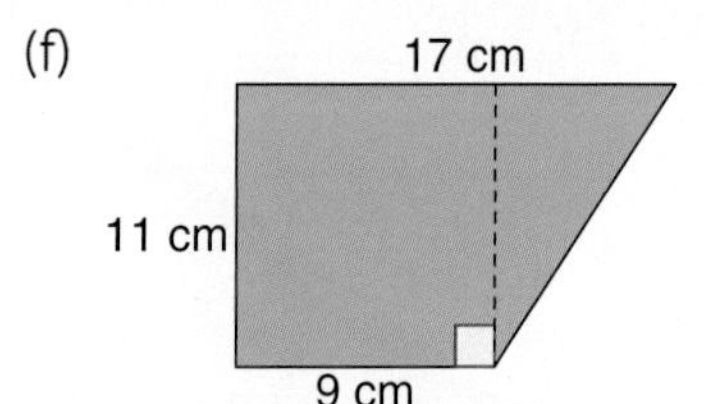

(g)

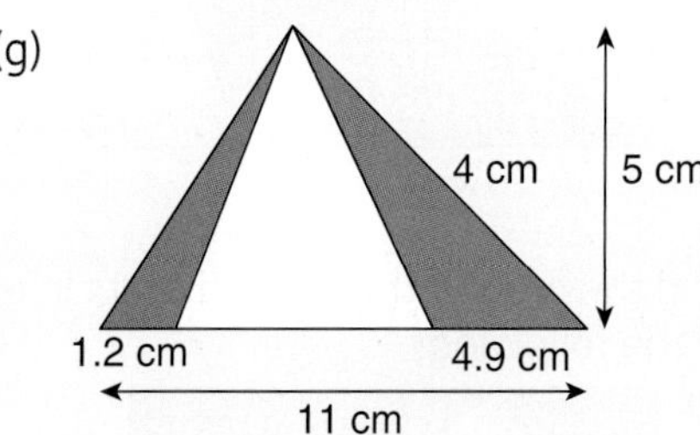

5. In the given triangle, $|AB| = 8$ cm and the perpendicular height of the triangle is 4 cm. Calculate the area of the triangle.

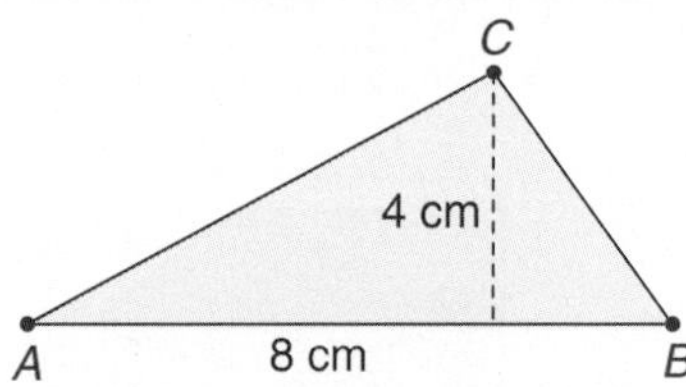

6. The right-angled triangle shown has sides of length 10 cm and 24 cm.

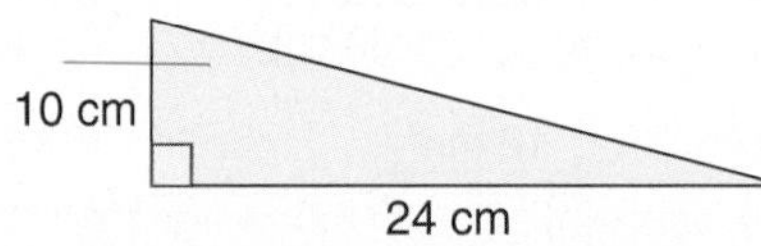

(a) Find the length of the third side.

(b) Find the perimeter of the triangle.

(c) Find the area of the triangle.

7. The area of a triangle is 39 cm². The perpendicular height of the triangle is 6 cm. Find *a*, the length of the base of the triangle.

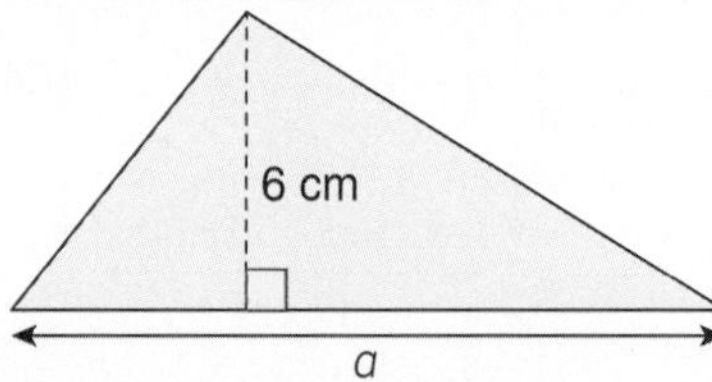

8. The diagram shows a rectangle of length 42 cm. The area of the rectangle is 966 cm².

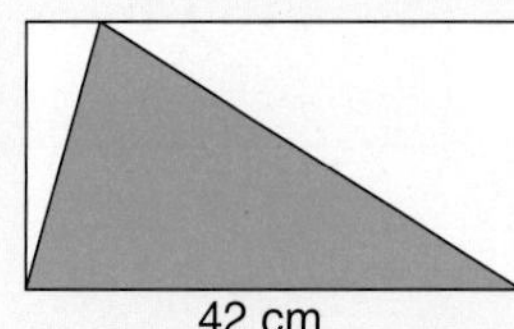

(a) Find the height of the rectangle.

(b) Find the area of the shaded triangle.

(c) What percentage of the rectangle is shaded?

9. A rectangle is twice as long as it is wide. The width of the rectangle is 6 cm.

(a) Find the length of the rectangle.

(b) Find the area of the rectangle.

(c) Find the length of a diagonal of the rectangle, correct to one decimal place.

10. A rectangle has length 21 cm and width 20 cm.

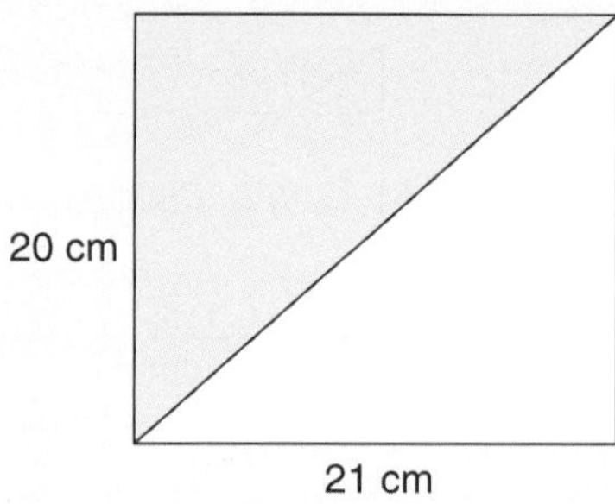

(a) Find the length of the diagonal, giving your answer in surd form.

(b) Find the area of one triangle formed by the diagonal of the rectangle.

11. (a) Calculate the area of the rectangle shown.

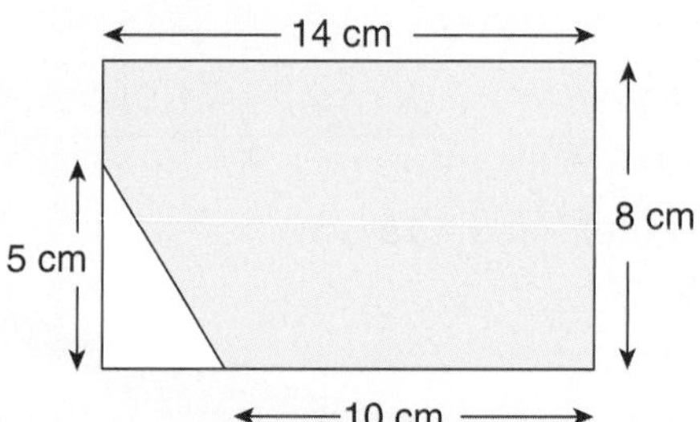

(b) Hence, calculate the area of the shaded region.

12. Each side of an equilateral triangle measures 4 units.

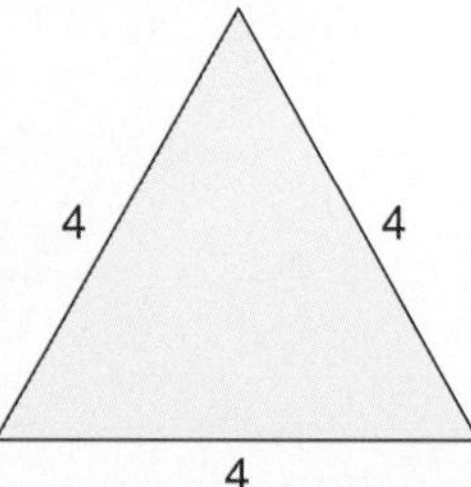

(a) Using the theorem of Pythagoras, calculate the perpendicular height.

(b) Calculate the area of the triangle, giving your answer in surd form.

Section 13.4: Circumference and area of a circle

Student Activity 13D

1. Follow each step carefully.
   (a) Draw a circle of radius 4 cm.
   (b) Get a piece of string and lay the string on top of the circle edge.
   (c) Mark the endpoint of the string where it meets the starting point.
   (d) Measure the length of the string.
   (e) Divide the length of the string by the diameter of the circle and record your answer.
2. A circle of diameter 8 cm is shown. The perimeter of the circle is 25.13 cm.

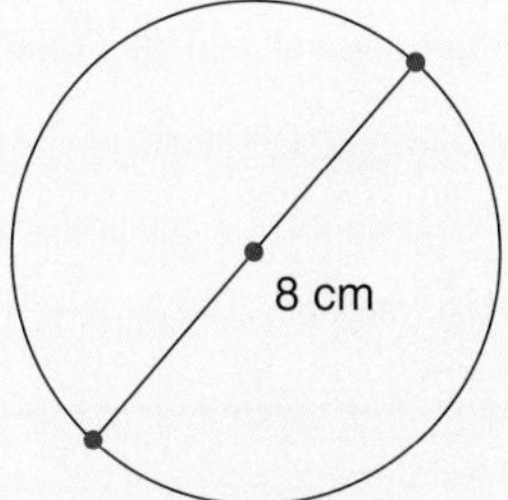

   (a) What is the radius of the circle?
   (b) Find the value of the circumference divided by the diameter, correct to two decimal places.
   (c) Find the value of the circumference divided by twice the radius, correct to two decimal places.
3. A circle has a diameter of 14 cm. The perimeter of the circle is 43.98 cm.

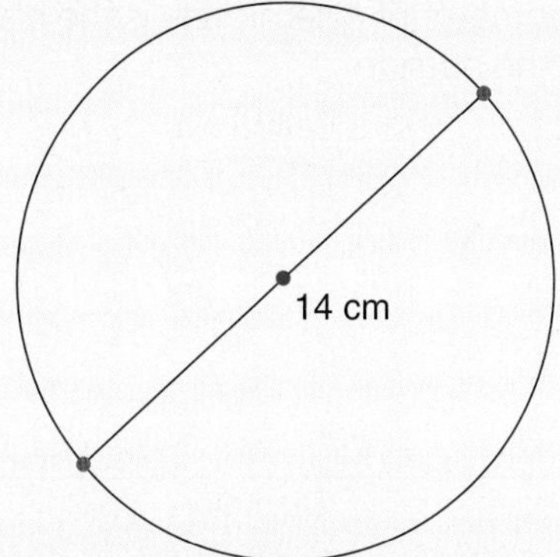

   (a) What is the radius of the circle?
   (b) Find the value of the circumference divided by the diameter, correct to two decimal places.
   (c) Find the value of the circumference divided by twice the radius, correct to two decimal places.
4. Compare your answers from Questions 1, 2 and 3. Explain what you notice.

CIRCUMFERENCE AND AREA OF A CIRCLE EXPLAINED

The perimeter of a circle is called its circumference.

A **circumference** is the perimeter of a circle.

Student Activity 13D examined a very important fact about all circles. The length of any circle divided by its diameter produces a constant value.

This value is called pi and is given the symbol π. In Chapter 1, we learned that π is a non-repeating and non-terminating decimal. This means it is an irrational number. When carrying out a calculation, use the 'π' button on your calculator. Otherwise, the question may ask you to use pi as $\frac{22}{7}$ or 3.14 or to give your answer in terms of π, e.g. 15π.

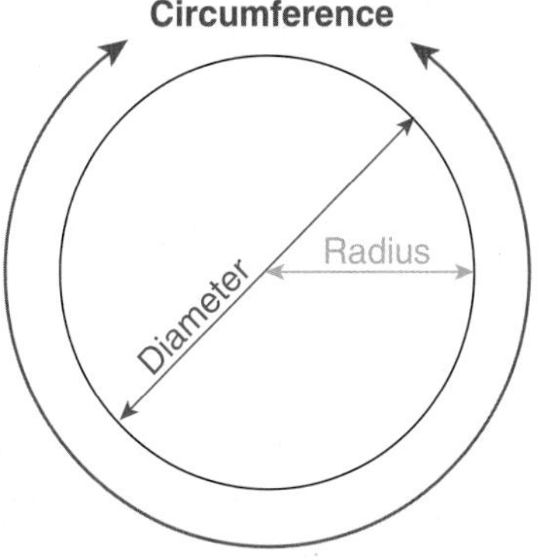

In 1995, Hiroyuki Goto set the world record for memorising the value of pi correct to 42,195 places!

When dealing with circles, you need to be able to use the following formulae:

Area = πr^2

Circumference = $2\pi r$

These are given on page 8 of the *Formulae and Tables*.

Semicircle

A semicircle is exactly half of a circle $\left(\frac{180°}{360°} = \frac{1}{2}\right)$. The perimeter of a semicircle is the distance round the outside.

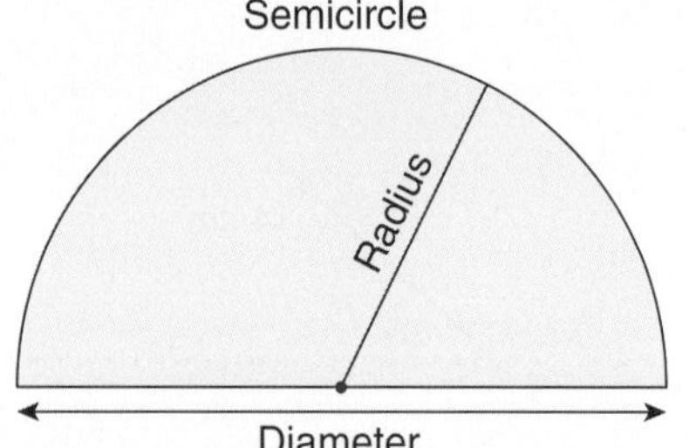

- To find the perimeter of a semicircle, add the diameter to half of the full circle's circumference.
- To find the area of a semicircle, we just halve the area of a full circle.

Sector

To calculate the area and perimeter of a sector of a circle, use the following formulae:

$$\text{Area of a sector} = \frac{\text{Angle in degrees}}{360} \times \pi r^2$$

$$\text{Length of an arc} = \frac{\text{Angle in degrees}}{360} \times 2\pi r$$

Total perimeter of a sector = Length of the Arc + 2 Radii

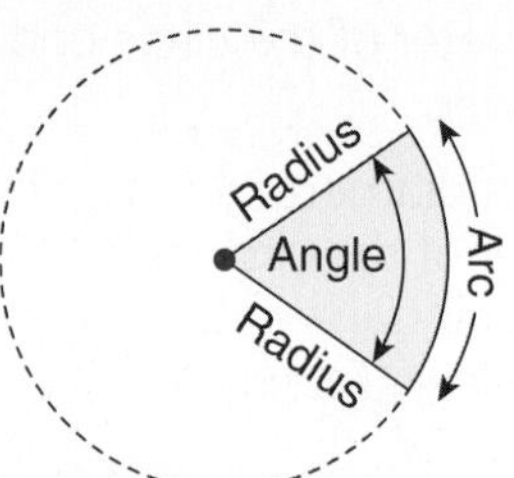

EXAMPLE 7

(a) Find the:

(i) Length of the circumference

(ii) Area of the circle shown. $\left(\text{Take } \pi = \frac{22}{7}.\right)$

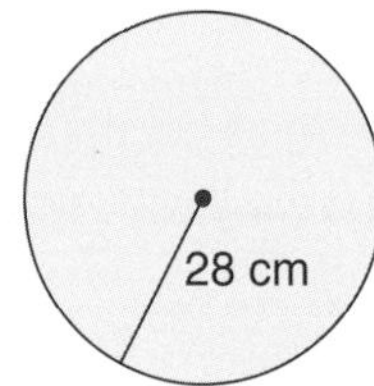

(b) Find the radius of a circle with an area of 154 cm^2. Take $\left(\pi = \frac{22}{7}.\right)$

Solution

(a) (i) Length of the circumference =

$2\pi r = 2\left(\frac{22}{7}\right)(28) = 176$ cm

(ii) Area = $\pi r^2 = \frac{22}{7}(28)^2 = 2{,}464$ cm^2

Solution

(b) Area = πr^2

$154 = \frac{22}{7}(r)^2$

$(154)(7) = (22)(r)^2$

$1{,}078 = 22r^2$

$1{,}078 \div 22 = r^2$

$49 = r^2$

$\sqrt{49} = r$

$7 \text{ cm} = r$

EXAMPLE 8

Find the radius of a circle in which the length of the circumference is 159 cm. Give your answer correct to one decimal place.

Solution

Circumference = $2\pi r$

$159 = 2(\pi)(r)$

$159 \div 2\pi = r$

$25.3056 = r$

$25.3 \text{ cm} = r$

EXAMPLE 9

Calculate (a) the area and (b) the perimeter of the following semicircle. Let $\pi = 3.14$.

Solution

For this semicircle, the radius equals 4 cm.

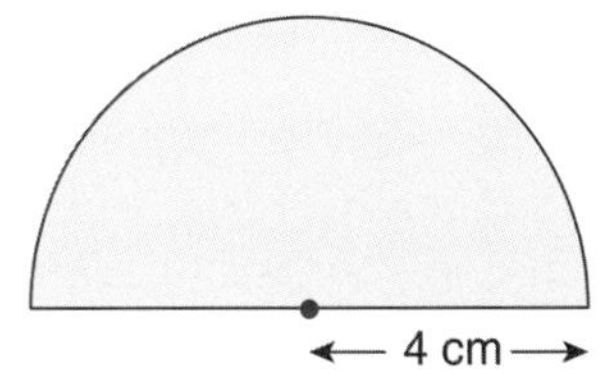

(a) Area $= \frac{180}{360} \times \pi r^2 = \frac{1}{2} \times (3.14)(4)(4)$

$= 25.12 \text{ cm}^2$

(b) Perimeter $= \left(\frac{180}{360} \times \text{Length of the circumference of the entire circle}\right) + \text{Length of the diameter}$

$= \frac{1}{2} \times 2\pi r + d$

$= \frac{1}{2} \times (2)(3.14)(4) + 8$

$= \frac{1}{2} \times 25.12 + 8$

$= 20.56 \text{ cm}$

Exercise 13.4

1. Calculate (i) the area and (ii) the length of the circumference in each of the following circles.
Take $\pi = \frac{22}{7}$.

(a)

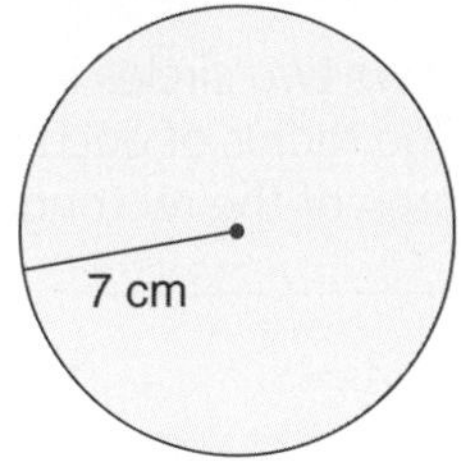

(b)

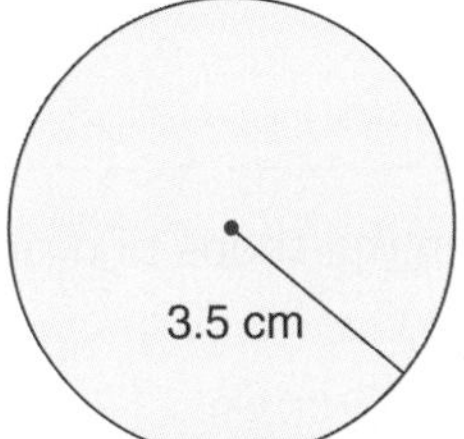

(c)

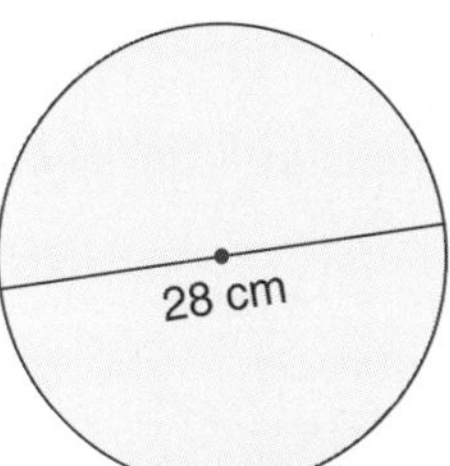

(d)

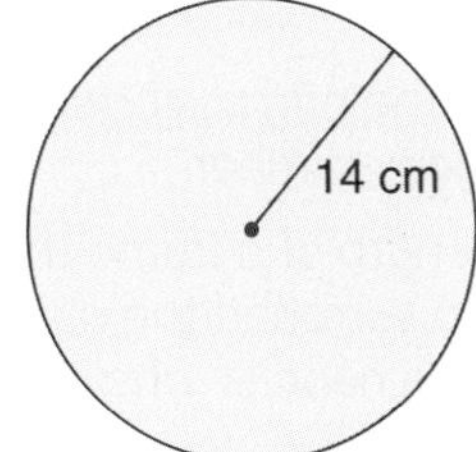

2. Calculate (i) the length of the circumference and (ii) the area of each of the following circles. Give your answer correct to two decimal places:

(a)

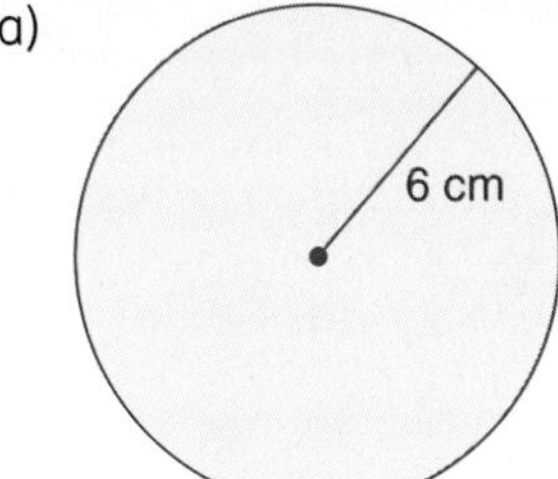

(b)

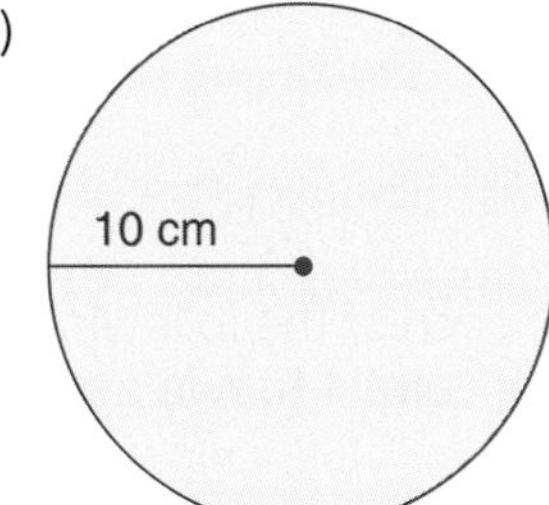

(c)

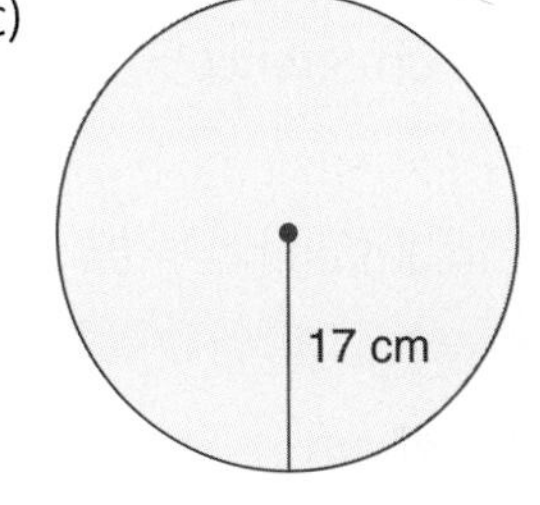

(d)

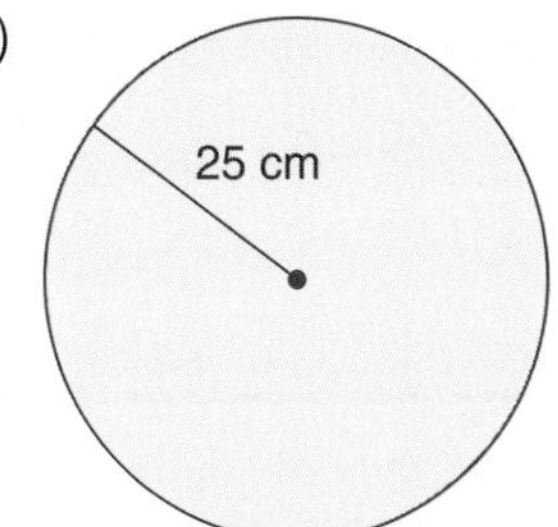

(e)

(f)

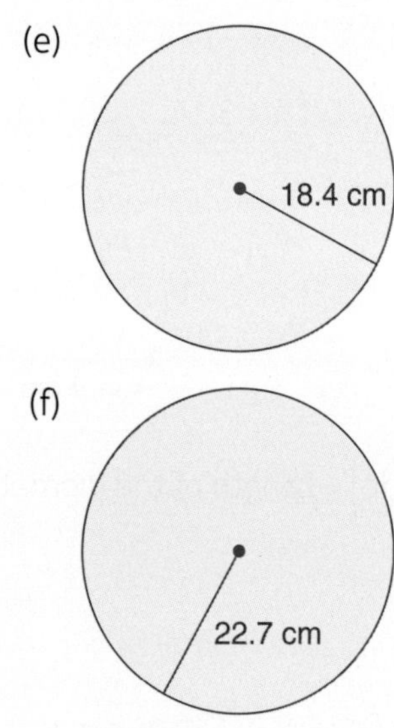

3. Calculate (i) the perimeter and (ii) the area of each of the following sectors, correct to two decimal places:

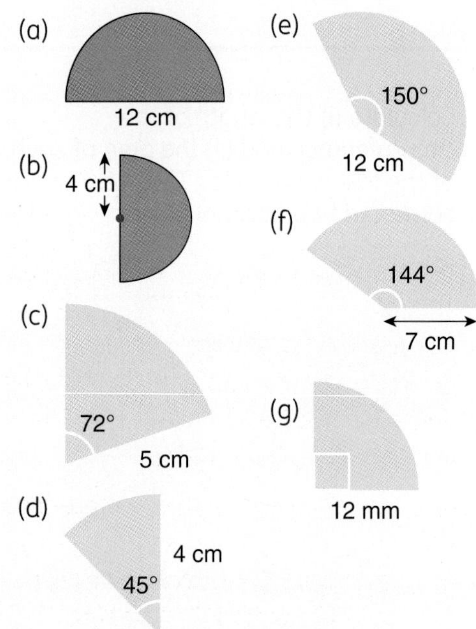

Find the radius of each of the following circles, giving your answer correct to two decimal places:

4. Area = 210 cm^2

5. Length of the circumference = 160 cm

6. Area = 90 cm^2

7. Length of the circumference = 97 cm

8. Area = 37 cm^2

9. Circumference = 37 cm

10. Area = 48 cm^2

11. Circumference = 99 cm

12. A circle is inscribed in a square as shown. Find the area of the shaded region, giving your answer correct to one decimal place. Take $\pi = 3.14$.

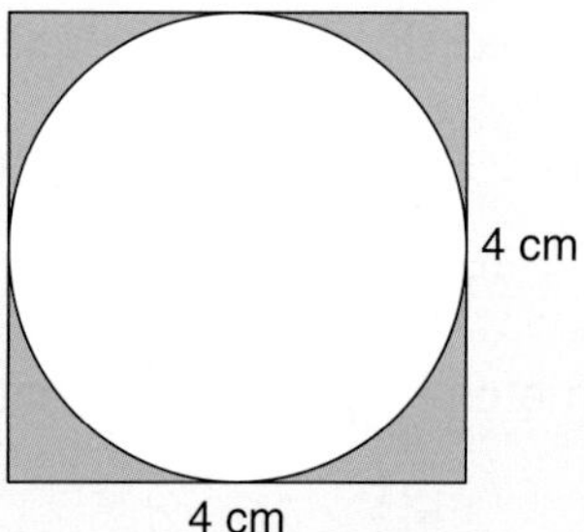

13. The diagram shows a circle inscribed in a square. The area of the square is 36 cm^2.

(a) Find the radius length of the circle.

(b) Find the area of the shaded region in cm^2, correct to one decimal place.

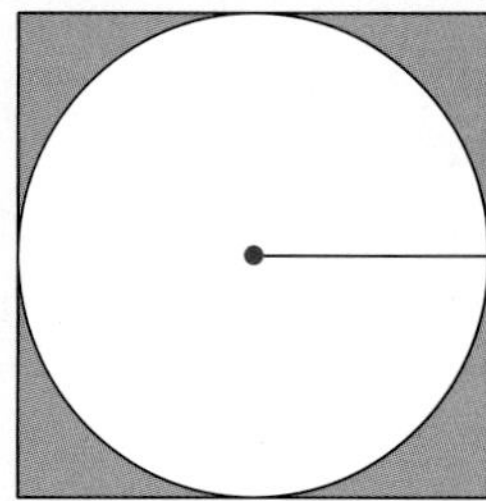

14. The diagram shows two circles inscribed in a rectangle. The radius of each circle is 6 cm. Find the area of the rectangle.

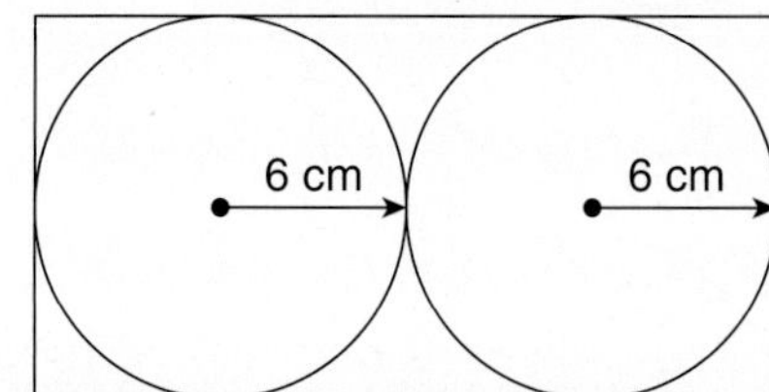

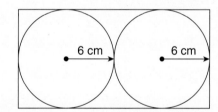

15. A mirror is cut in the shape of a circle as shown.

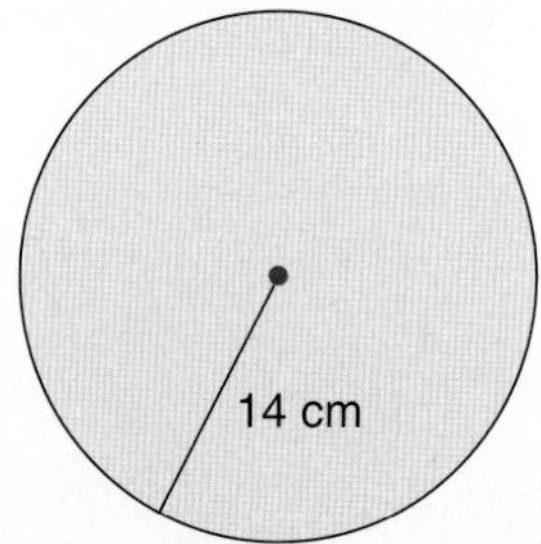

If the radius of the mirror is 14 cm, calculate:

(a) The area of the mirror, correct to the nearest whole number

(b) The inner length of a frame that is needed to surround the mirror, correct to the nearest whole number

16. A farmer used 210 m of wire to fence off a circular pond. Calculate the radius of the pond, correct to the nearest whole number.

17. A race track has dimensions as shown.

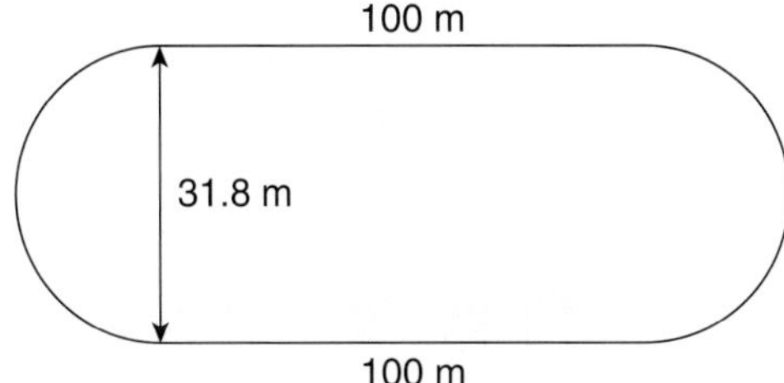

Calculate, correct to the nearest whole number:

(a) The area enclosed by the race track

(b) The total length of the race track

18. Calculate the area of the window shown, giving your answer correct to one decimal place.

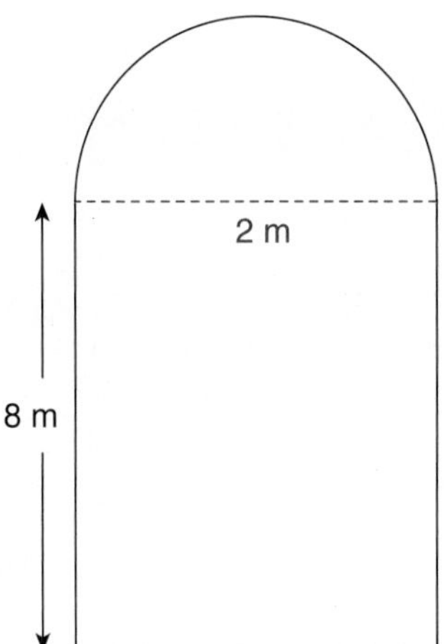

19. An artist creates the following piece from a sheet of metal measuring 5 m by 5 m. What area of the metal sheet was wasted? Give your answer correct to one decimal place.

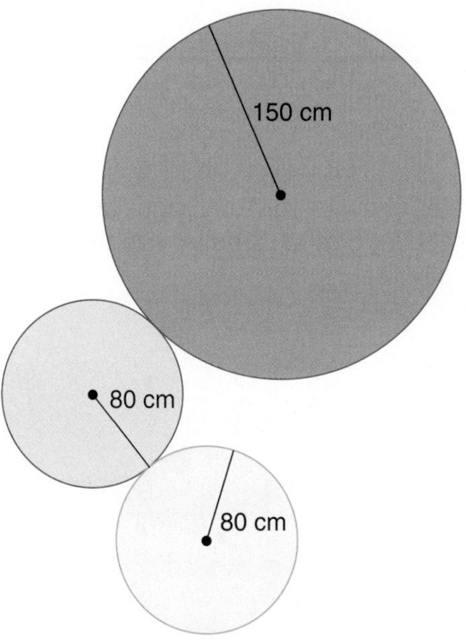

20. Study the following diagrams and write down what this activity tells you.

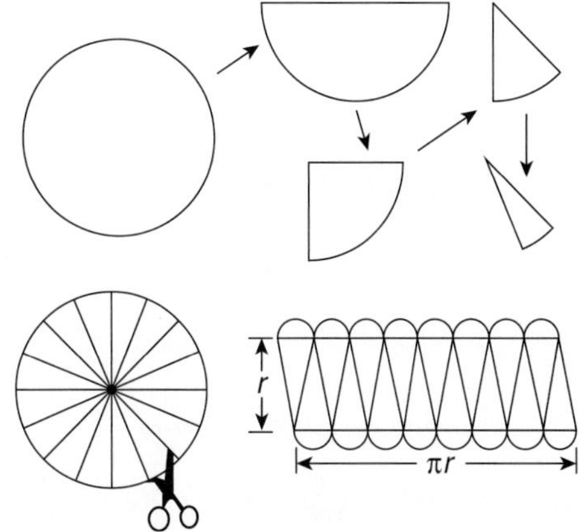

21. The window at the top of a door is in the shape of a semicircle. The door is 0.8 m wide. If the glass in the window is broken, what area of glass is needed to replace it?

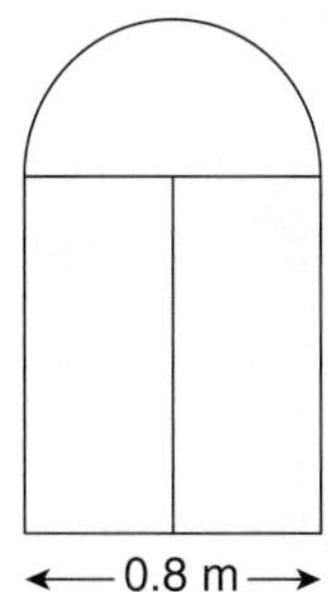

22. A, B and C are points on a circle with centre O. $[AC]$ is a diameter of the circle.

$|AB| = 8$ cm, $|BC| = 6$ cm and $|\angle ABC| = 90°$.

(a) Find the area of ΔABC.

(b) Find the length of the diameter $[AC]$.

(c) Find the area enclosed by the circle, taking $\pi = 3.14$. Give your answer correct to two decimal places

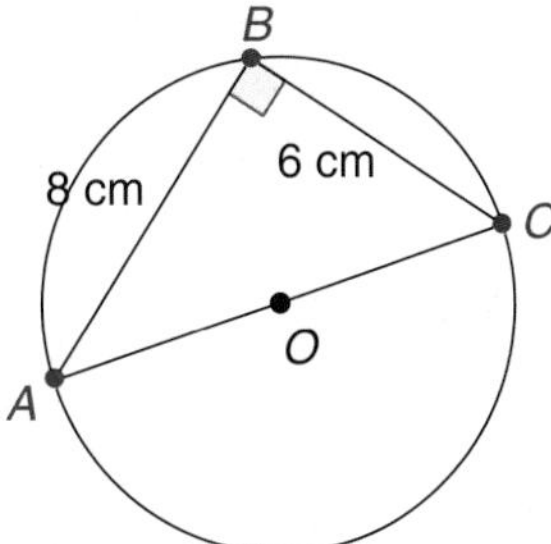

23. The diagram shows two pulley wheels of equal size, connected by a drive belt. The radius of each wheel is 7 cm and the distance between the centres is 28 cm. Calculate the length of the belt. Give your answer correct to the nearest whole number.

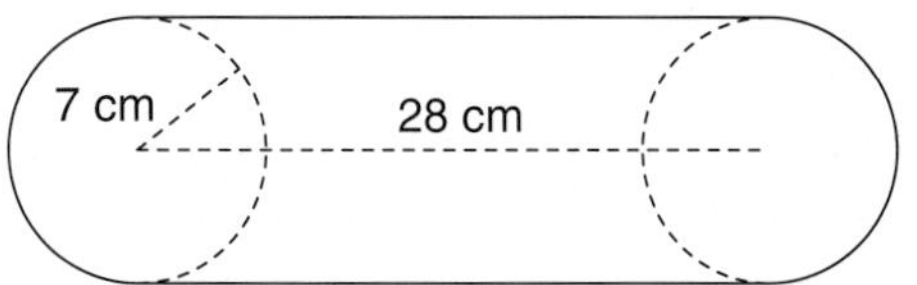

24. At the recent Montessori sports day, a group of toddlers huddled together for a team talk. Given the diameter of the circle created was 2.3 metres, calculate:

(a) The area of the circle created within the huddle, correct to one decimal place

(b) The length of the circumference of the inner circle created

(c) The average width of a toddler, correct to the nearest whole number

25. Calculate, correct to one decimal place, the area of the design shown.

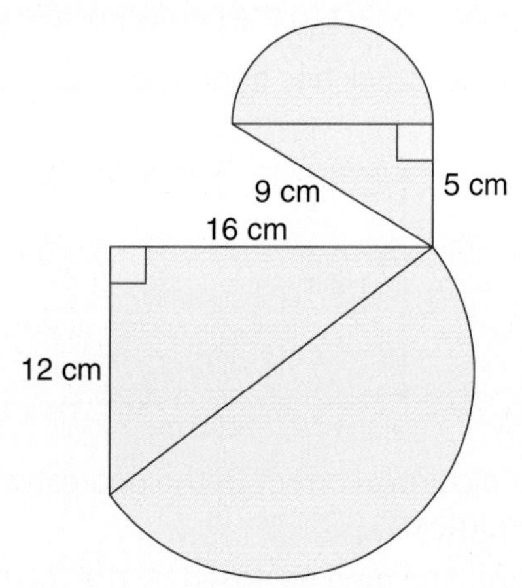

Section 13.5: Measurement scales

Student Activity 13E

1. Can you give three example of where you might see or use a scale?

2. Study the map of Ireland shown and answer the questions that follow.

Use your ruler to measure the distance from:

(a) Dublin to Galway

(b) Cork to Killarney

(c) New Ross to Tullamore

(d) Lifford to Waterford

(e) Convert each of these measurements to distances in km using the scale indicated.

3. Give one advantage and one disadvantage of using a scale on a map.

MEASUREMENT SCALES EXPLAINED

Scales allow us to study maps and other objects at a much smaller size than they really are. For example, a model airplane may be geometrically the same as a real plane but much smaller in size.

By building model planes people can own a scaled down size of the real plane. This is much easier to store!

Scales are important mathematical tools that allow engineers to build and test models before creating a final design.

Scales also allow us to read distances from maps. For example, 10 km could be represented by 1 cm on a map.

The model ship shown has a scale of 1 mm:500 cm.

(a) If the model ship is 400 mm long, what is the length of the real ship?

(b) If the front gun on the real ship is 10 m long, how long is the model gun?

Solution

(a) $400 \times 500 = 200{,}000$ mm

(b) 10 m $= 10 \times 100 = 1{,}000$ cm

$1{,}000 \div 500 = 2$ mm

Exercise 13.5

1. Use the following scale to answer the questions:

(a) A distance of 50 cm on a map would covert to ____.

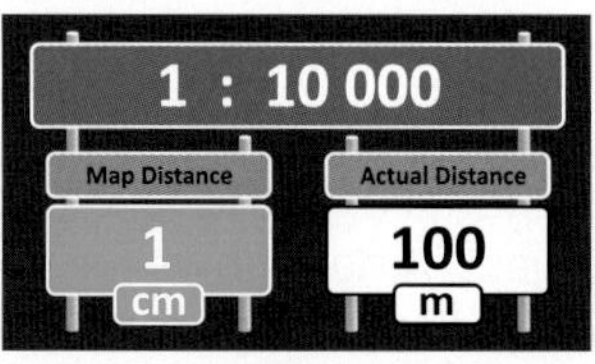

(b) A distance of 120 cm on a map would convert to ____.

(c) An actual distance of 20,000 m would convert to ____.

(d) An actual distance of 10 km would convert to ____.

(e) An actual distance of 500 m would convert to ____.

(f) An actual distance of 20,000 cm would convert to ____.

2. Study the map of Spain and use the scale to find the approximate distances between each of the following:

(a) Madrid and Valencia

(b) Malaga and Lisbon

(c) La Coruña and Alicante

(d) Toledo and Barcelona

(e) Salamanca to Zaragoza

3. The tank shown has a scale of 1 cm:16 cm.

(a) The main gun is 10 cm long. How long is the gun on the real tank?

(b) The actual tank is 6.4 m long and 2.4 m wide. What are the dimensions of the model tank?

4. John hangs two pictures from a horizontal rail. The smaller picture frame is a rectangle measuring 42 cm by 28 cm. The larger picture frame is double the length and width of the smaller picture frame.

(a) Find the measurements of the larger picture.

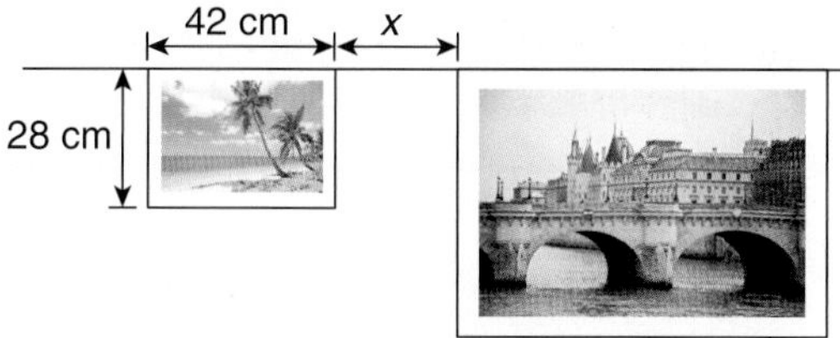

John decides that the picture might look better if he moved the larger one across and up. To arrange them, he drew the triangle shown and noted the measurements, in centimetres.

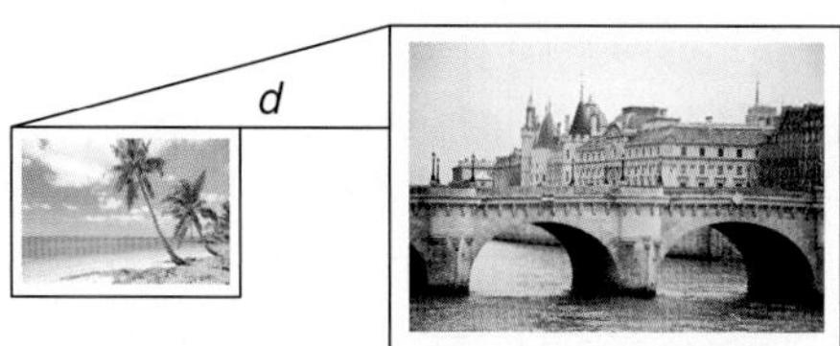

(b) Use the theorem of Pythagoras to calculate the length d, correct to the nearest cm.

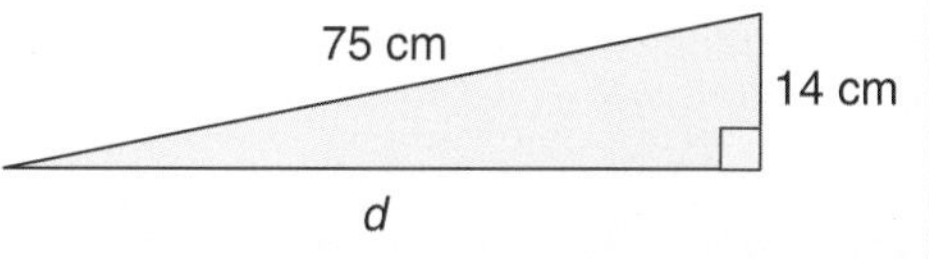

Section 13.6: Nets of rectangular solids

Student Activity 13F

Draw the following diagram on a sheet of paper:

(a) Cut out the diagram.

(b) Fold along the dotted lines.

(c) What shape have you made?

(d) Unfold the object. What shapes can you name?

(e) How would you find the area of each shape?

(f) How would you find the surface area of the entire shape?

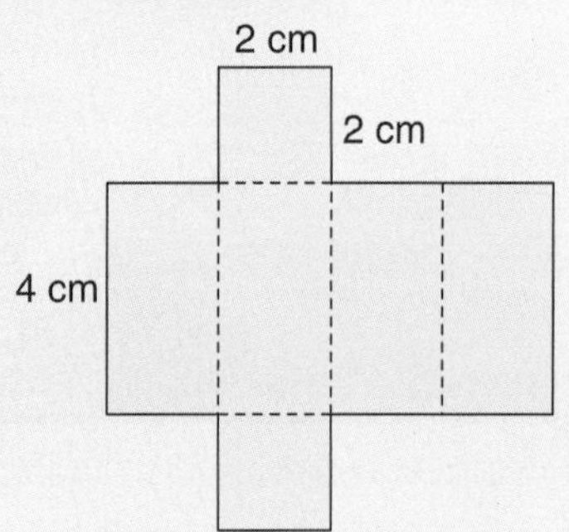

NETS OF RECTANGULAR SOLIDS EXPLAINED

Students who have studied technical graphics will be familiar with the idea of the development of shapes. A **net** is a flattened out version of a 3D object. A net shows each face of the object on one flat surface. Looking at a net of an object, we can calculate the total surface area it takes up. This is very important for businesses that manufacture products.

A **cube** is a 3D solid with six square faces. The Rubik Cube is a famous puzzle.

A **cuboid** is a 3D solid with six quadrilateral faces. Rectangular boxes are examples of rectangular cuboids.

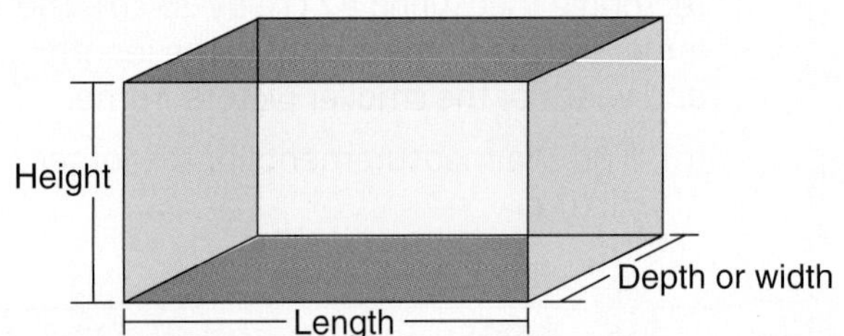

EXAMPLE 11

Examine the cuboid shown.

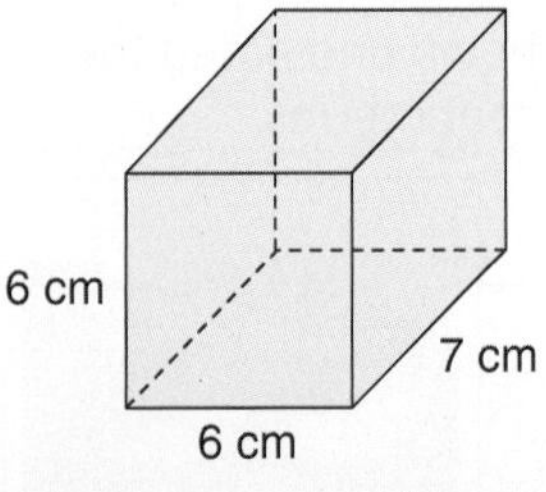

(a) Draw a net of the solid.

(b) Calculate the surface area of the solid.

Solution

(a)

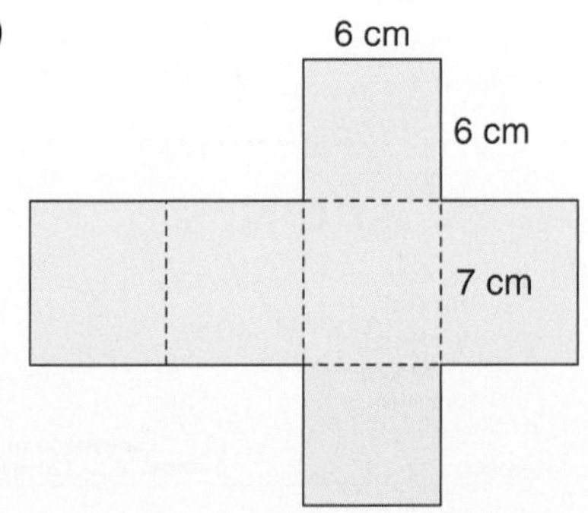

(b) $2(L \times W) + 2(L \times H) + 2(W \times H)$

$= 2(6 \times 6) + 2(6 \times 7) + 2(6 \times 7)$

$= 240 \text{ cm}^2$

Exercise 13.6

1. Draw the following diagram on a sheet of paper.

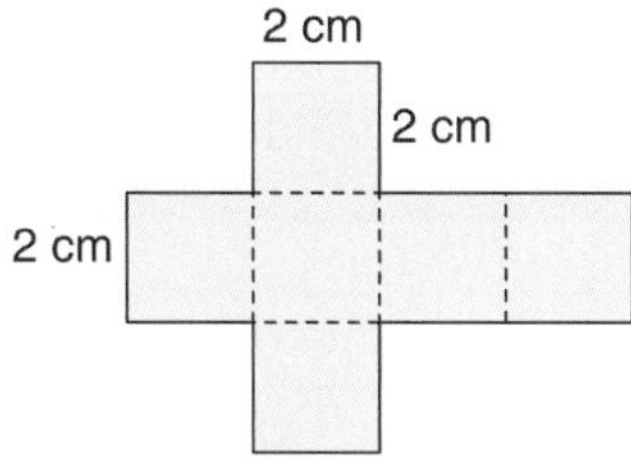

(a) Cut out the diagram.
(b) Fold along the dotted lines.
(c) What shape have you made?
(d) Unfold the object. What shapes can you name?
(e) How would you find the area of each shape?
(f) How would you find the surface area of the entire shape?

For each of the following shapes, draw a net of the shape and calculate the total surface area of the net.

2.

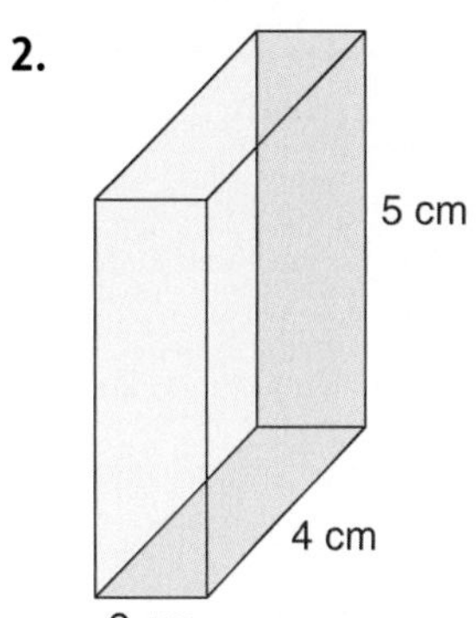

3.

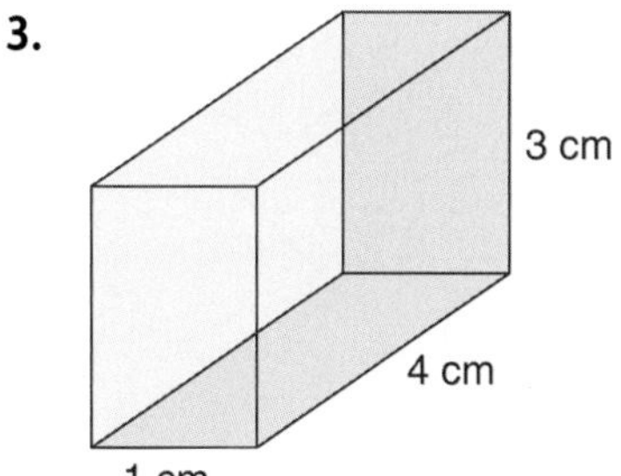

4.

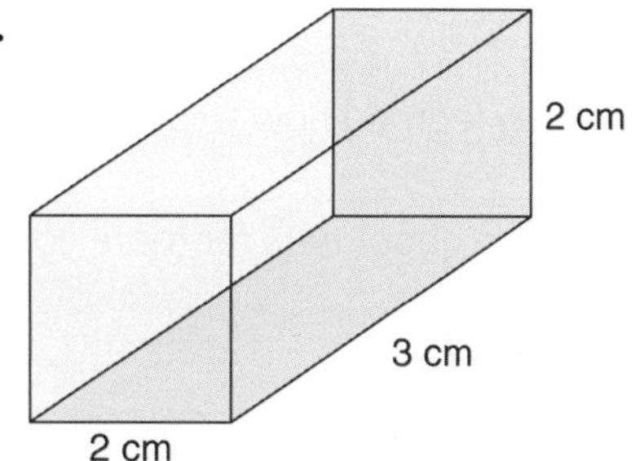

5.

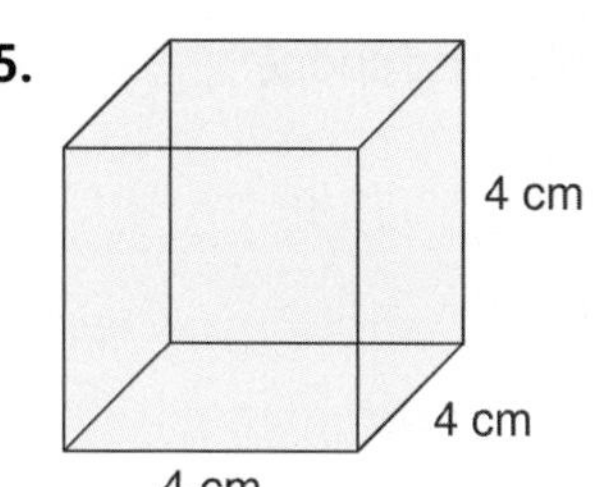

For each of the following, draw the net of the 3D solid using the dimensions given and calculate the total surface area.

6. A cube of side length 3 cm
7. A cuboid: 3 cm, 1 cm and 2 cm
8. A cuboid: 2 cm, 1 cm and 4 cm
9. A cube of side length 2 cm
10. A cuboid: 3 cm, 3 cm and 4 cm
11. A cuboid: 4 cm, 5 cm and 6 cm
12. A cuboid: 5 cm, 2 cm and 5 cm
13. A cuboid: 6 cm, 4 cm and 4 cm
14. A cuboid: 6 cm, 2 cm and 2 cm
15. A cuboid: 2.5 cm, 3 cm and 4 cm
16. A cuboid: 6 cm, 1 cm and 6 cm
17. A cuboid: 1.5 cm, 1.2 cm, 3 cm
18. A cuboid: 7 cm, 2.5 cm, 8 cm
19. A cuboid: 6 cm, 9 cm, 10.5 cm
20. A cuboid: 6.5 cm, 7.2 cm, 8 cm

Section 13.7: More complicated nets

Student Activity 13G

Examine the can shown.

(a) What is this shaped called?
(b) What shape is the top and the bottom of the can?
(c) If the top and bottom are removed and the remainder of the can is flattened what shape would it be?
(d) How would you calculate the total surface area of the flattened shape?

MORE COMPLICATED NETS EXPLAINED

You have already learned how to draw the nets for cubes and cuboids. More complicated shapes also have nets.

You will now learn about nets for more complicated shapes such as cylinders, cones and prisms.

EXAMPLE 12

Draw a net of the following shape:

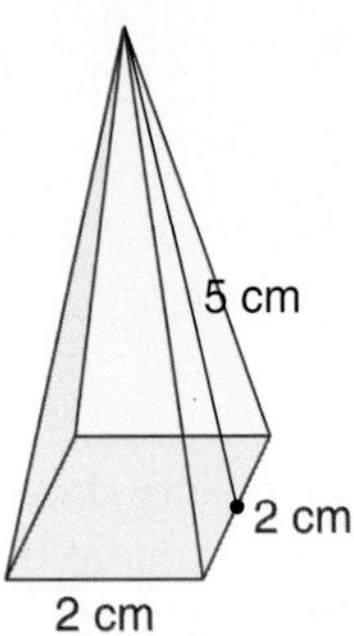

Solution

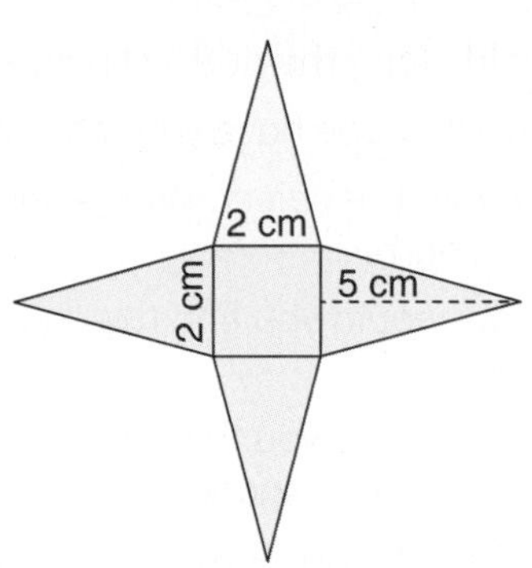

Exercise 13.7

Can you identify the shapes from the following nets? (Hint: copy the shape onto a sheet of paper and cut it out.)

1.

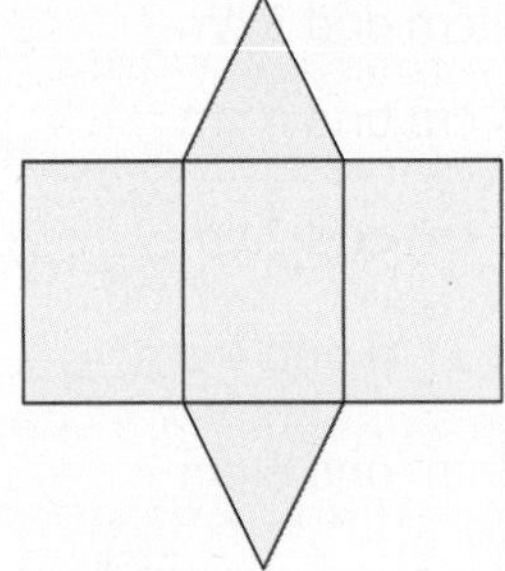

2.

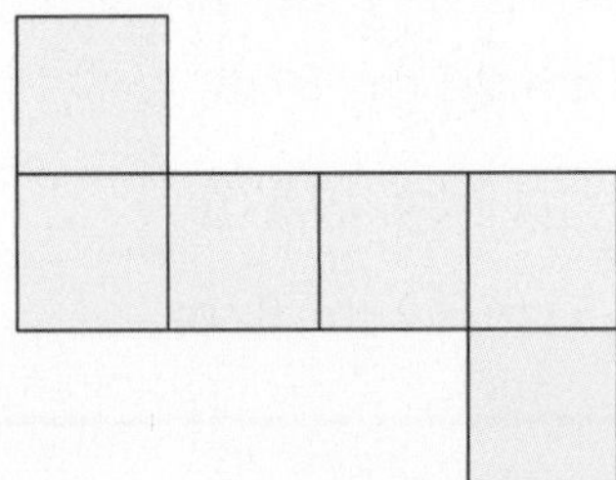

3.

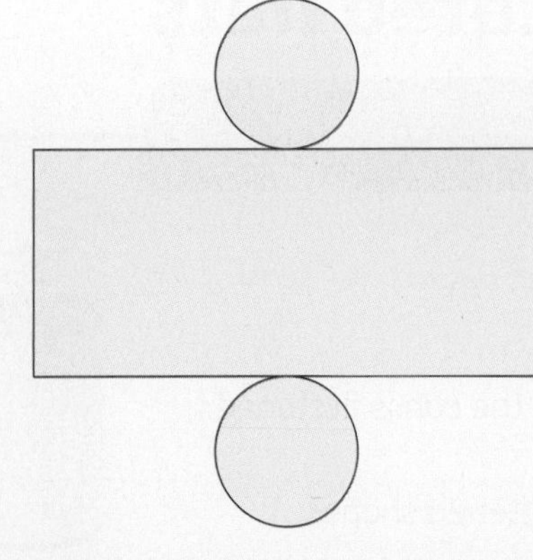

4.

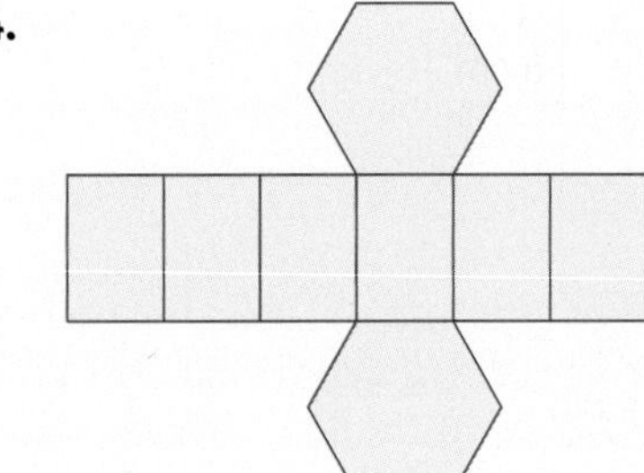

5.

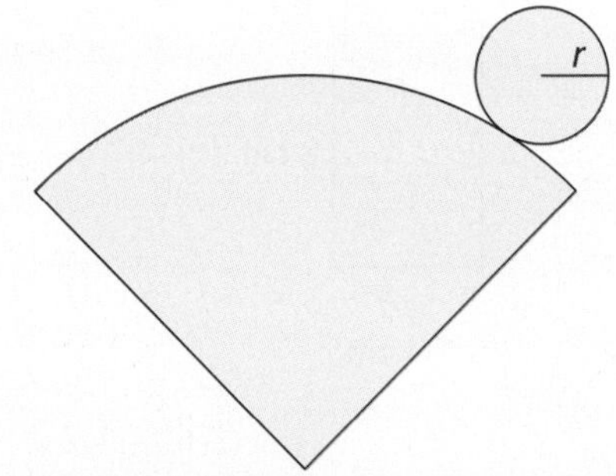

Draw a net for each of the following 3D shapes in questions 6–9:

6.

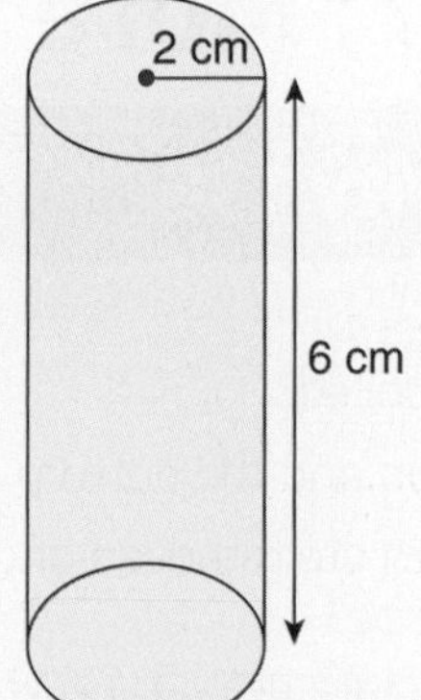

7.

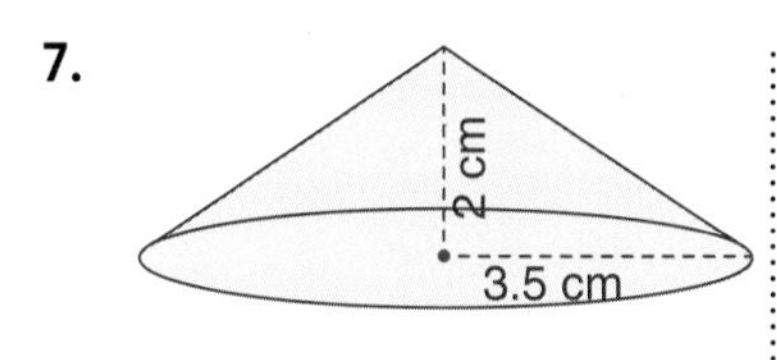

8.

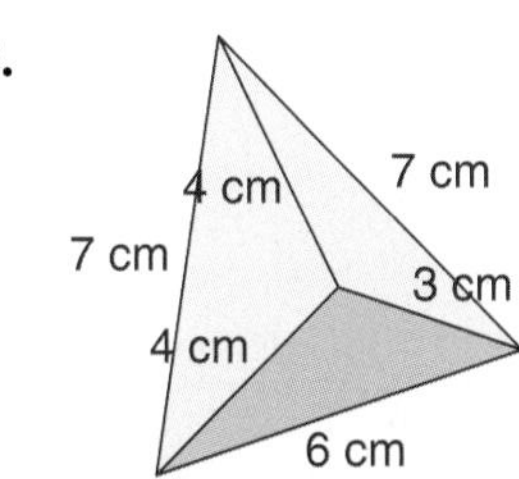

9.

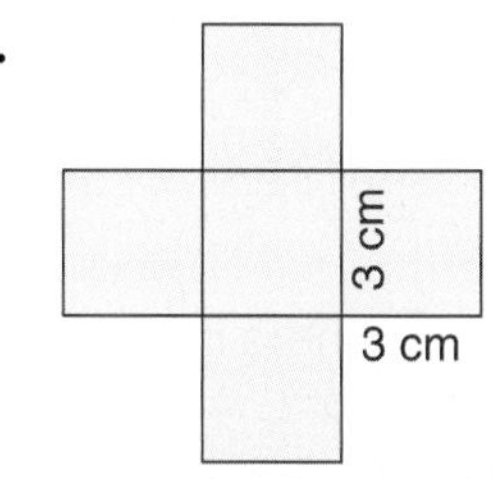

Section 13.8: Further surface area

Student Activity 13H

1. Draw a net of the cylinder shown.
   (a) Describe how you could find the area of each part of the net.
   (b) How might you find the total surface area of the net?

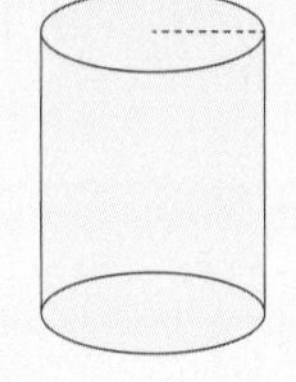

2. Draw a net of the cone shown.
   (a) Describe how you could find the area of each part of the net.
   (b) How might you find the total surface area of the net?

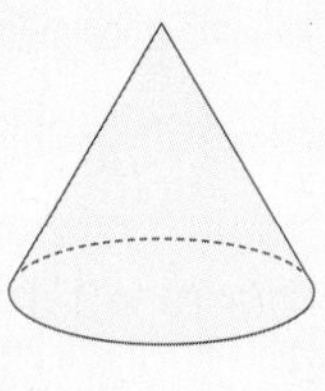

FURTHER SURFACE AREA EXPLAINED

In this section, you will learn how to calculate the surface areas of more complicated shapes such as cylinders, cones, spheres, hemispheres and prisms.

A prism is a 3D shape that has the same cross-section (base) along the length of the shape. The cross-section (base) can be triangular or rectangular in shape.

To find the surface area of any prism, you must first be able to develop the net. This will allow you to find the sum of all the faces to calculate the surface area of the prism.

The formulae for the surface areas of cylinders, cones and spheres are given on page 10 of the *Formulae and Tables*.

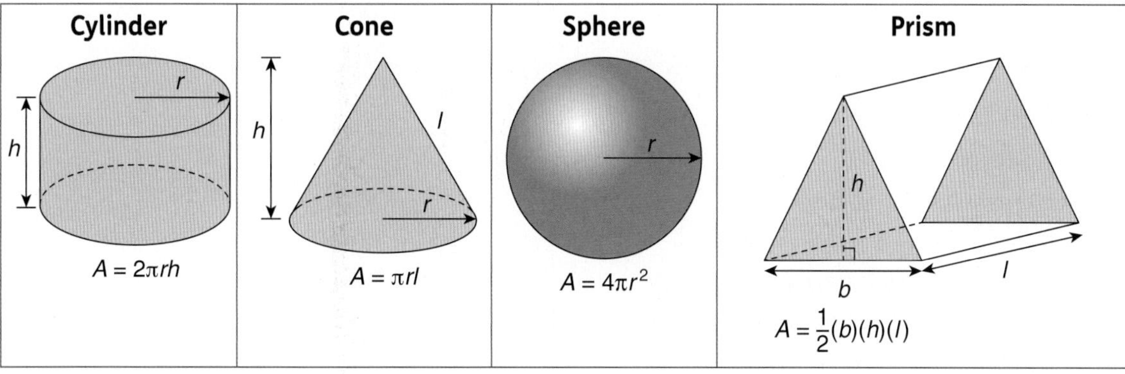

The **curved surface area** of a cylinder opens out into a flat rectangular shape (like the label on a tin of beans). It has length $2\pi r$ (the same as the circumference of the circular lid) and a width of h (the same as the height of the cylinder). So, the formulae for the area of the curved surface area is:

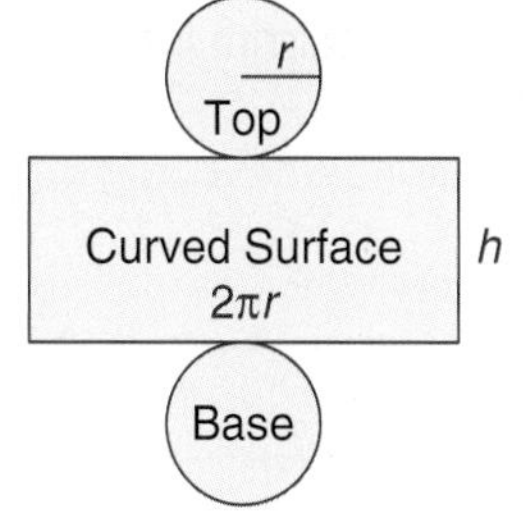

Area of a curved surface $= 2\pi r \times h = 2\pi rh$

To calculate the total surface area of a closed cylinder, we must include the top and bottom lids. Each lid is in the shape of a circle and has an area of πr^2.

Therefore:

> Total surface area of a cylinder = $2\pi rh + 2\pi r^2$

Similarly, a cone is made up of its curved surface area with a circle at the bottom, so:

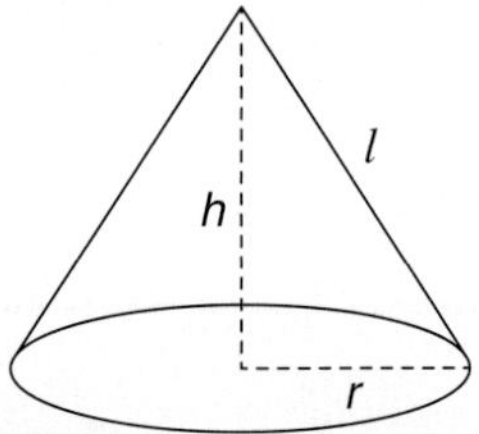

> Total surface area of a cone = $\pi rl + \pi r^2$

The curved surface area of a sphere is $4\pi r^2$. If you cut a sphere in half through the centre, you create two identical hemispheres. For example, the equator cuts planet Earth into the Northern and Southern Hemispheres. The curved surface area of a hemisphere is $2\pi r^2$. The total surface area of a hemisphere includes the circular lid, so:

> Total surface area of a hemisphere = $2\pi r^2 + \pi r^2 = 3\pi r^2$

EXAMPLE 13

In the following cylinder, find:

(a) The curved surface area

(b) The total surface area

$\left(\text{Take } \pi = \frac{22}{7}\right)$

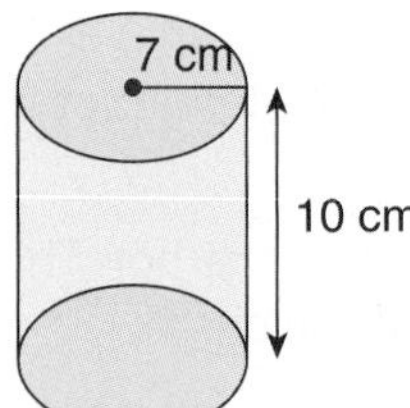

Solution

(a) Curved surface area = $2\pi rh$

$= 2\left(\frac{22}{7}\right)(7)(10)$

$= 440 \text{ cm}^2$

(b) Total surface area = Area of the net of the shape

= Curved surface + Area of the 2 circles

$= 2\pi rh + 2\pi r^2$

$= 2\left(\frac{22}{7}\right)(7)(10) + 2\left(\frac{22}{7}\right)(7)^2$

$= 440 + 308$

$= 748 \text{ cm}^2$

EXAMPLE 14

For the following cone, find:

(a) The slant height of the cone

(b) The curved surface area, giving your answer correct to two decimal places

(c) The total surface area, correct to two decimal places $\left(\text{Take } \pi = \frac{22}{7}\right)$

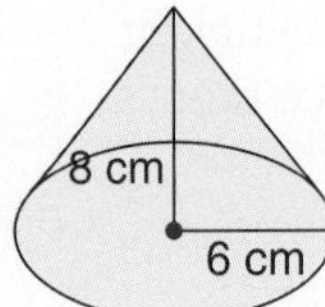

Solution

(a) **Note:** A cone contains a right-angled triangle. This means we can use the theorem of Pythagoras to find one of the missing lengths.

$l^2 = h^2 + r^2$

$l^2 = (8)^2 + (6)^2$

$l^2 = 64 + 36$

$l^2 = 100$

$l = \sqrt{100}$

$l = 10$ cm

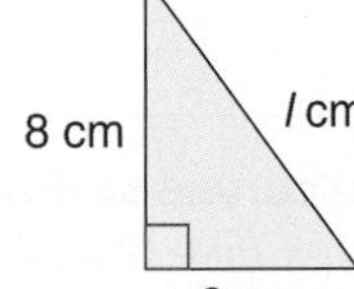

(b) Curved surface area = πrl

Surface area = $\left(\frac{22}{7}\right)(6)(10)$

Surface area = 188.57cm^2

(c) Total surface area = $\pi rl + \pi r^2$

Total surface area = $\left(\frac{22}{7}\right)(6)(10) + \left(\frac{22}{7}\right)(6)^2$

Total surface area = 301.71 cm^2

EXAMPLE 15

Find the surface area of a sphere of radius 8 cm, giving your answer correct to one decimal place.

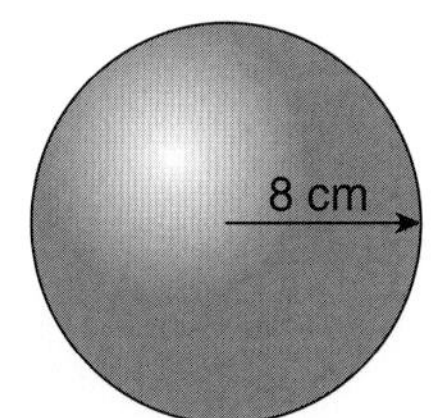

Solution

Surface area = $4\pi r^2$

Surface area = $4\pi(8)^2$

Surface area = 804.2cm^2

Exercise 13.8

Find (a) the curved surface area and (b) the total surface area of each of the following cylinders. Give your answer correct to the nearest whole number.

1. Radius = 6 cm, Height = 8 cm
2. Radius = 5 cm, Height = 14 cm
3. Radius = 7 cm, Height = 13 cm
4. Radius = 9 cm, Height = 4 cm
5. Diameter = 10 cm, Height = 16 cm
6. Radius = 2 cm, Height = 20 cm
7. Radius = 3 cm, Height = 12 cm
8. Diameter = 14 cm, Height = 9 cm
9. Radius = 7 cm, Height = 17 cm
10. Diameter = 14 cm, Height = 13 cm

Find (a) the curved surface area and (b) the total surface area of each of the following cones. Give your answer correct to the nearest whole number.

11. Radius = 3 cm, Height = 4 cm
12. Radius = 6 cm, Height = 8 cm
13. Radius = 5 cm, Height = 12 cm
14. Radius = 5 cm, Height = 18 cm
15. Radius = 13 cm, Height = 14 cm
16. Radius = 3 cm, Height = 6 cm
17. Diameter = 10 cm, Height = 10 cm
18. Radius = 15 cm, Height = 17 cm
19. Radius = 13 cm, Height = 15 cm
20. Diameter = 12 cm, Height = 10 cm

Find the surface area of each of the following spheres. Give your answer correct to the nearest whole number.

21. Radius = 7 cm
22. Diameter = 10 cm
23. Radius = 14 cm
24. Diameter = 21 cm
25. Diameter = 18 cm
26. Radius = 6 cm
27. Radius = 4 cm

Find the surface area of each of the following prisms. Give your answer correct to the nearest whole number.

28.

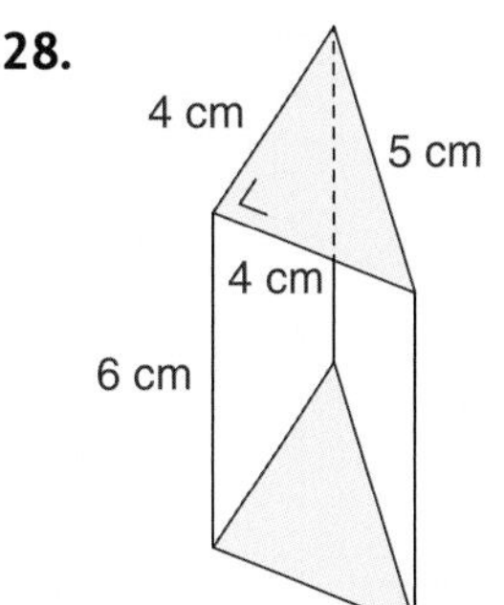

29.

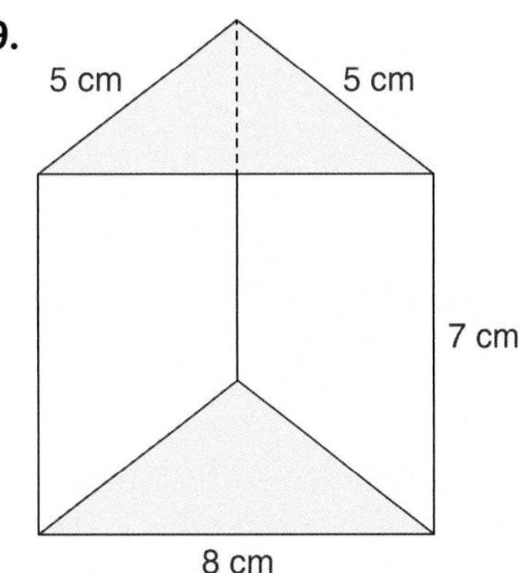

30.

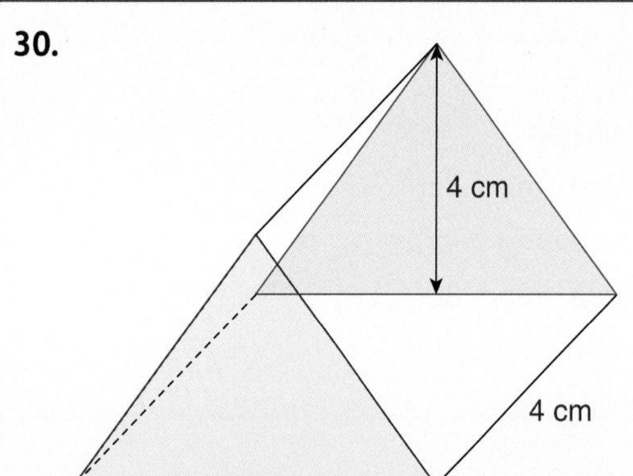

31.

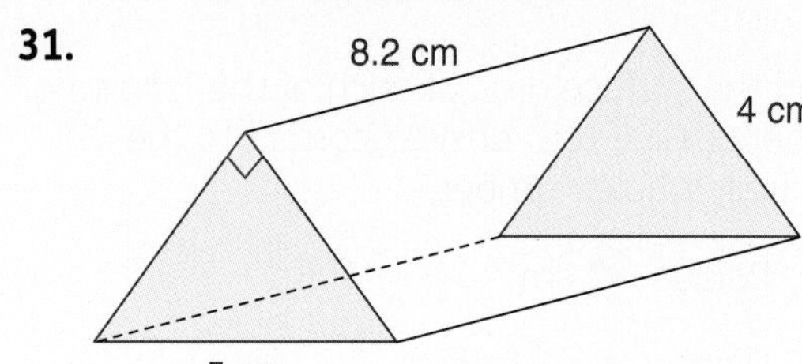

32.

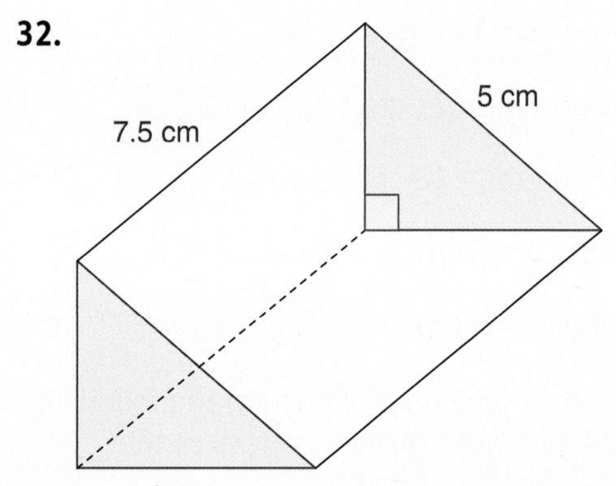

33.

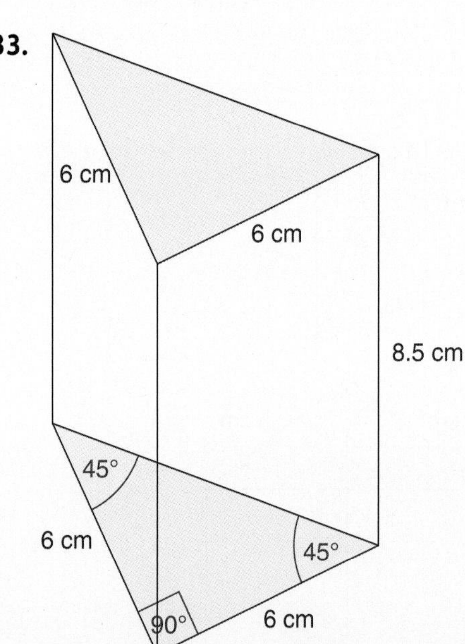

34. A cylinder has a curved surface area of 30π cm² and a height of 5 cm. Calculate the radius and the total surface area of the cylinder.

35. A cylinder has a curved surface area of 40π cm² and a radius of 4 cm. Calculate the height and the total surface area of the cylinder.

36. The surface area of a sphere is 100π cm². Calculate the radius and the total surface area of one of its hemispheres.

37. An open test-tube has a radius of 8 cm and a total height of 21 cm as shown. Calculate the total internal surface area of the test-tube.

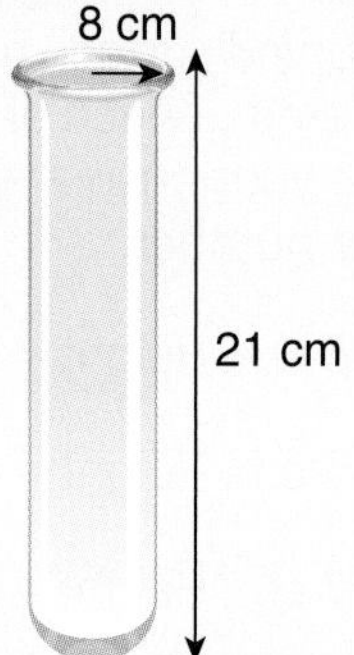

38. A conical shape has a curved surface area of 550 cm². The length of the slant side is 25 cm. Find the length of the diameter of the base.

39. The curved surface area of a conical container is 1,848 cm². The diameter of its base is 42 cm.

(a) Find the length of the slant side, correct to one decimal place.

(b) Find the vertical height of the container.

40. The toy shown consists of a cone on top of a hemisphere. The overall height of the toy is 20 cm and the diameter of the hemisphere is 8 cm.

(a) Calculate the surface area of the toy.

(b) If the height and the diameter of the toy above was increased by 30%, would the surface area of the toy also increase by 30%?

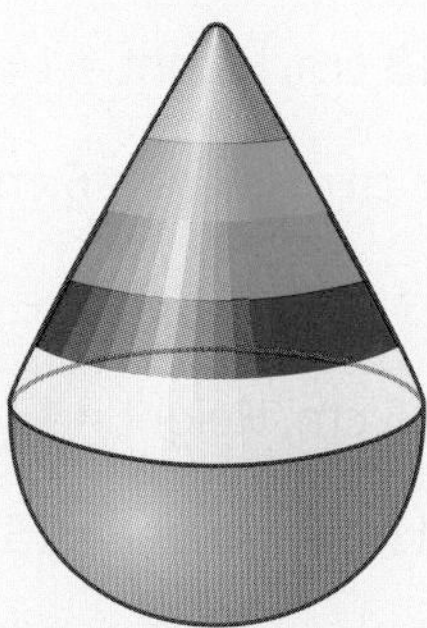

CHAPTER 13 SELF-CHECK TEST

1. The diagram shows three-fifths of a rectangle. Copy and complete the entire rectangle on the grid given.

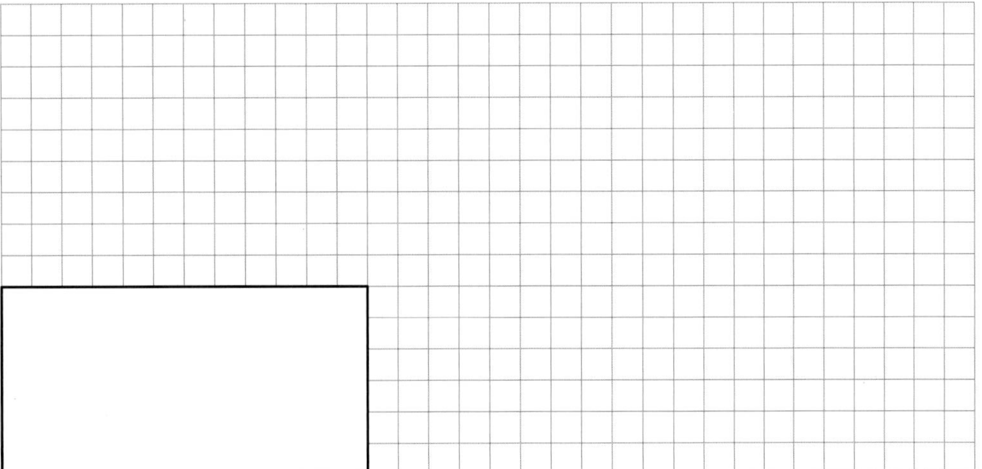

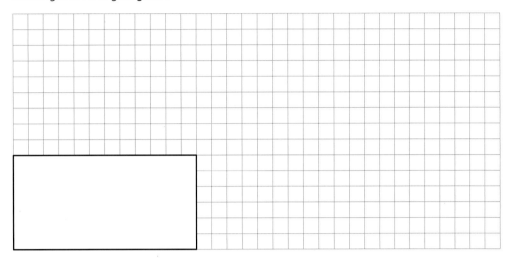

2. Calculate the (i) area and (ii) perimeter of each of the following shapes:

(a)

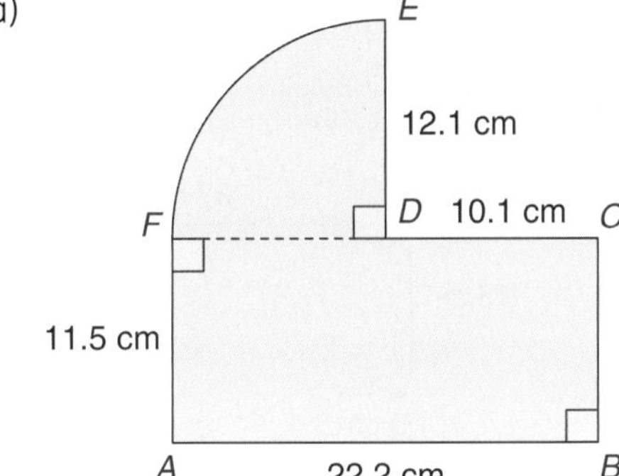

(b)

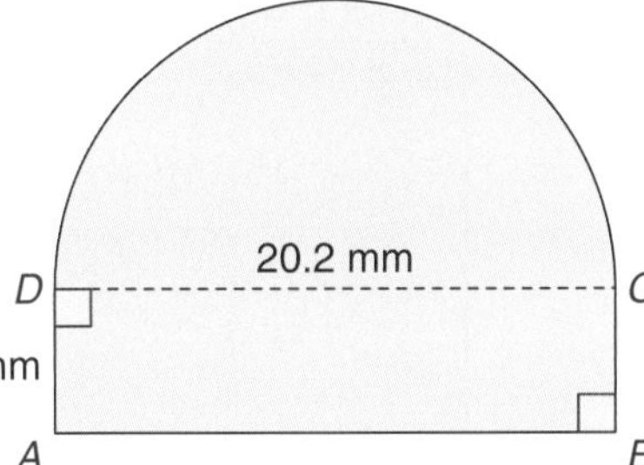

(c)

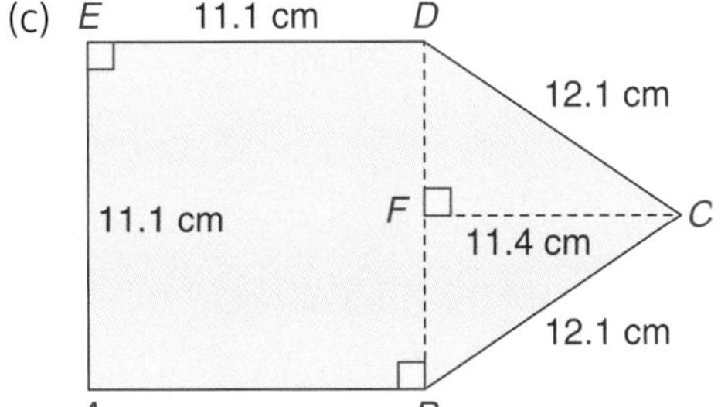

(d)

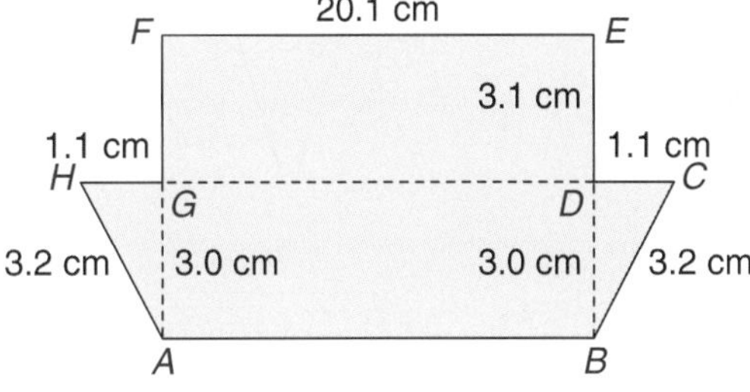

(e)

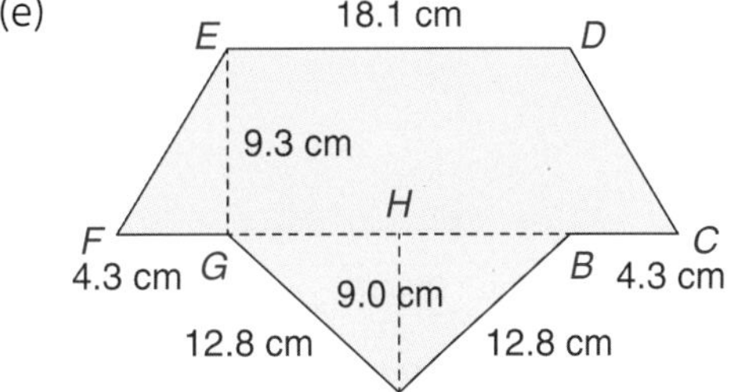

(f)

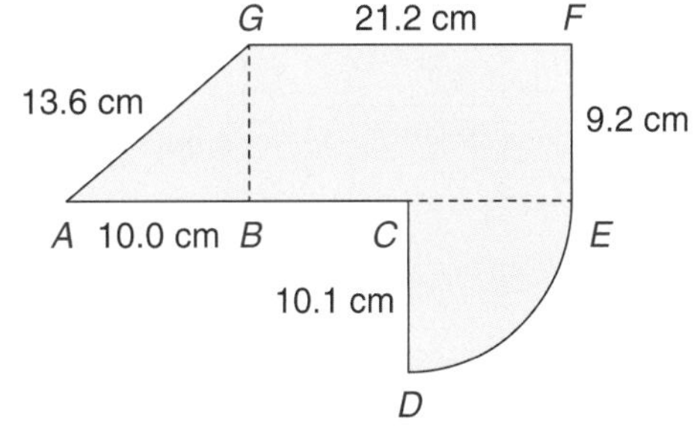

(g)

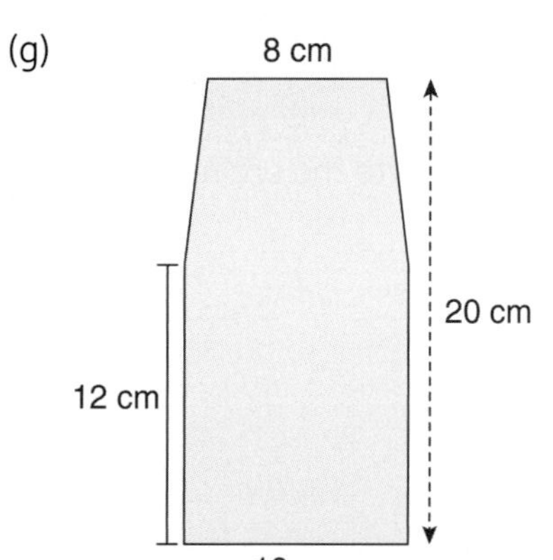

(h)

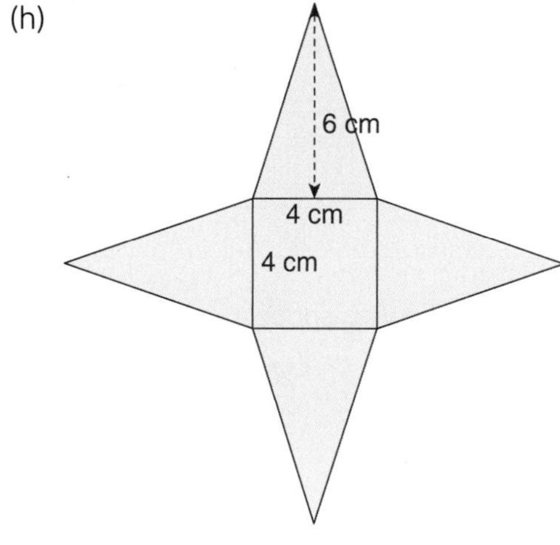

(i)

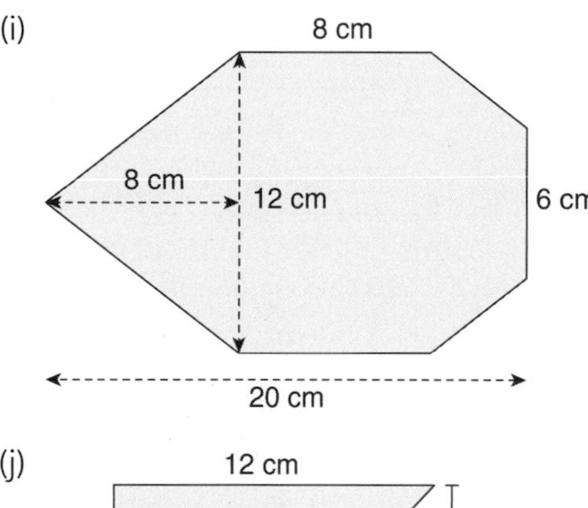

(j)

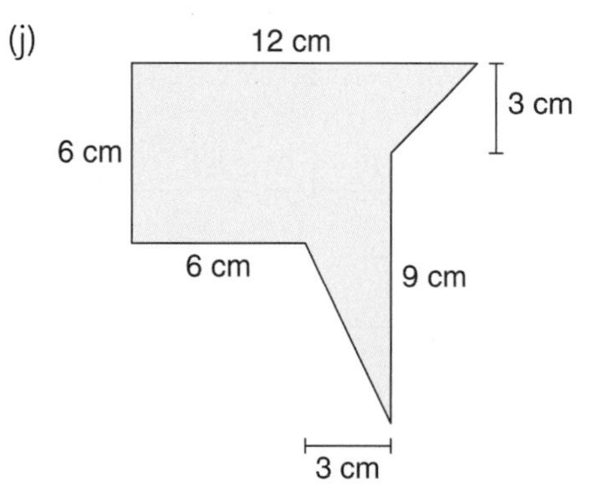

(k)

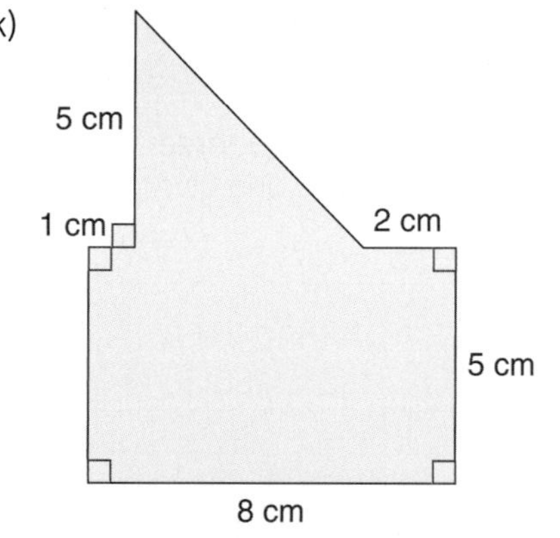

(l)

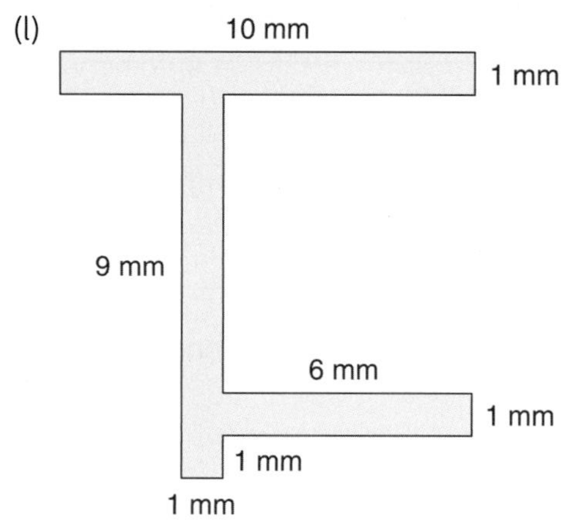

(m)

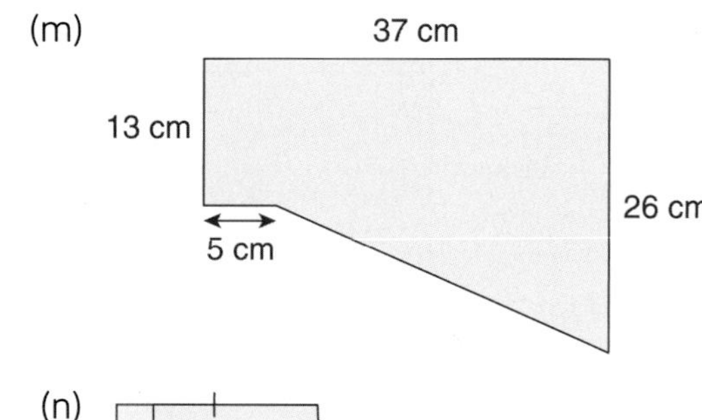

(n)

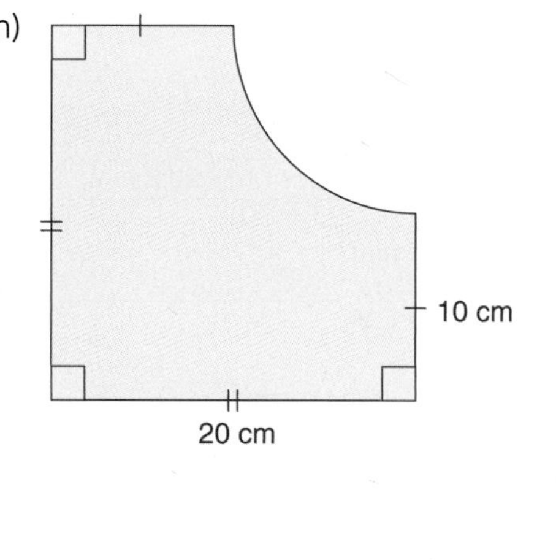

3. The designs of different machine parts are shown. Calculate the area of each machine part.

(a)

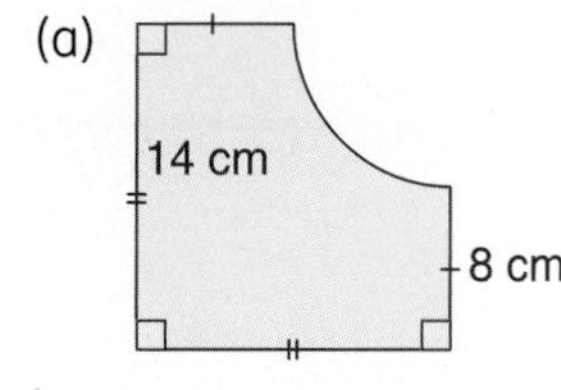

(b)

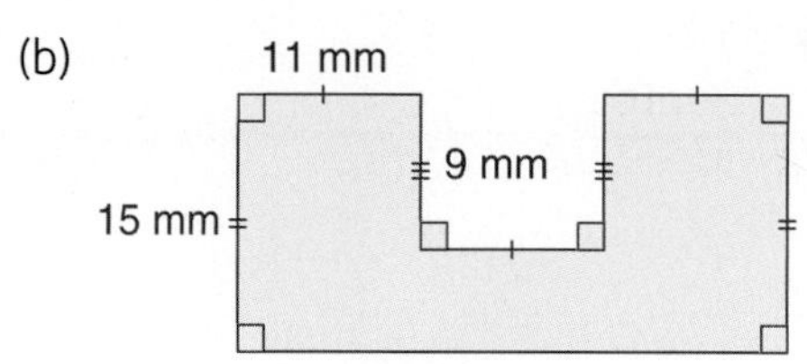

(c)

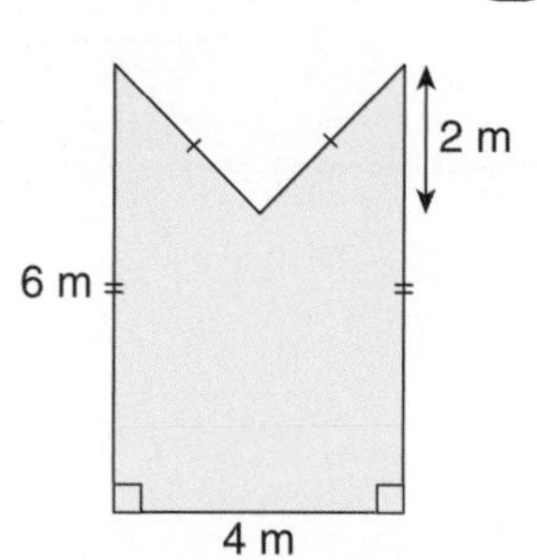

4. The perimeter of a rectangular field is 280 m. The length of the longer side is 100 m.

(a) Find the length of the shorter side.

(b) Find the area of the field.

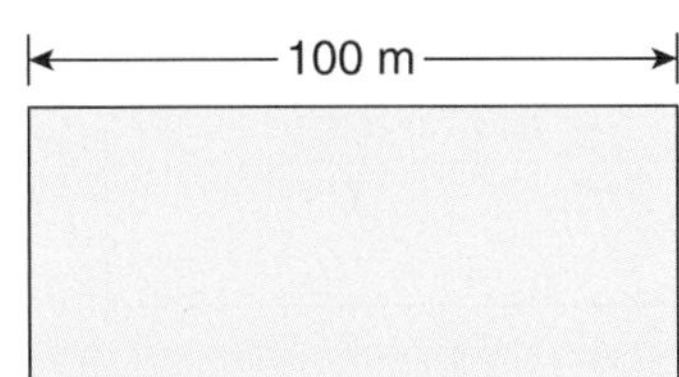

5. The area of a rectangular playing pitch is 9,900 m². The width of the playing pitch is 90 m.

(a) Find the length of the playing pitch.

(b) Find the perimeter of the playing pitch.

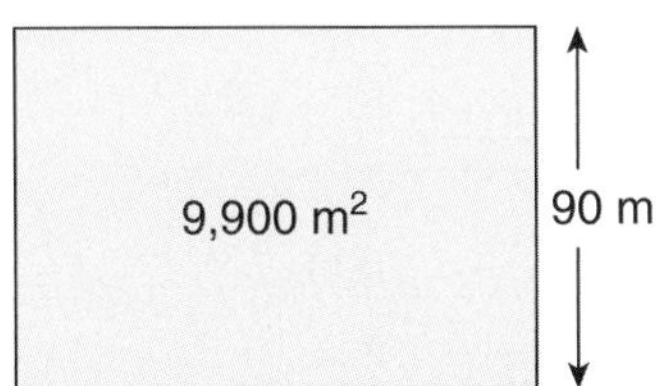

6. Claire owns an apartment. The plans for it are as follows:

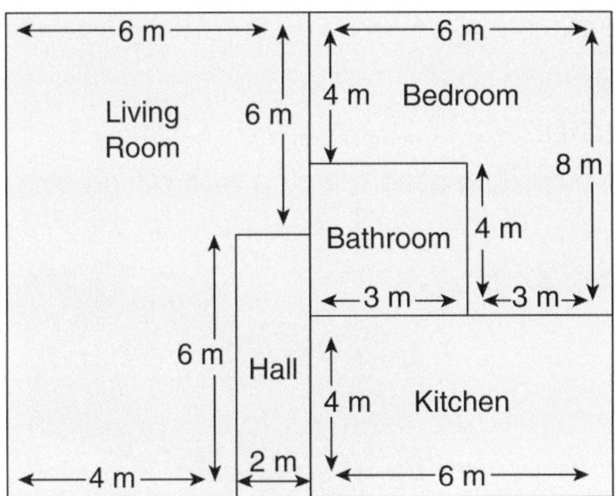

Calculate the area of the:

(a) Living room

(b) Hall

(c) Kitchen

(d) Bathroom

(e) Bedroom

(f) Calculate the total area of the apartment.

(g) What percentage of the apartment does the bathroom occupy?

(h) If a recent property tax charges €15 per 3 m², how much tax must Claire pay?

7. The diagram shows a garden. The dimensions are given in metres. Calculate the area of the garden.

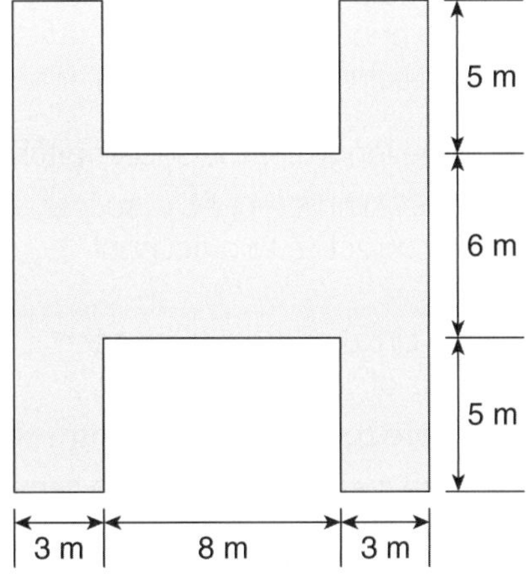

8. The diagram shows a running track at a school. It consists of two parallel line segments with a semicircle at each end. The track is 10 m wide.

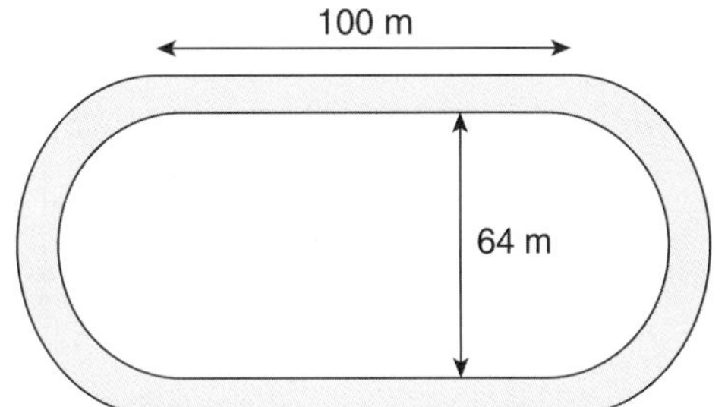

(a) If Fiona runs on the inside of the track. How far does she run in one lap, correct to the nearest metre?

(b) Ciara runs on the outer edge. How far does she run in one lap?

(c) Find the difference between the distances run by Fiona and Ciara.

9. Which of these nets form a cube?

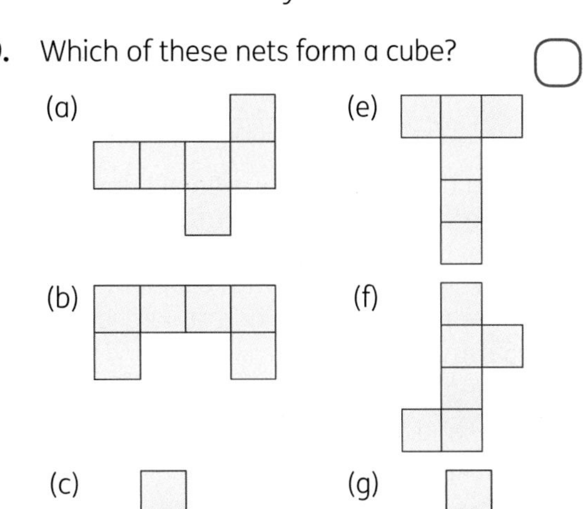

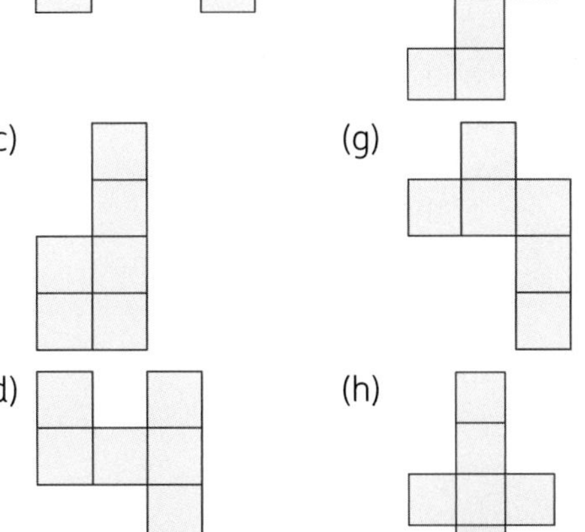

10. Liam wants to draw a diagram of a soccer pitch using a scale of 1 cm = 6.25 m. He begins by drawing a rectangle measuring 16 cm long and 11 cm wide and adds in the centre circle.

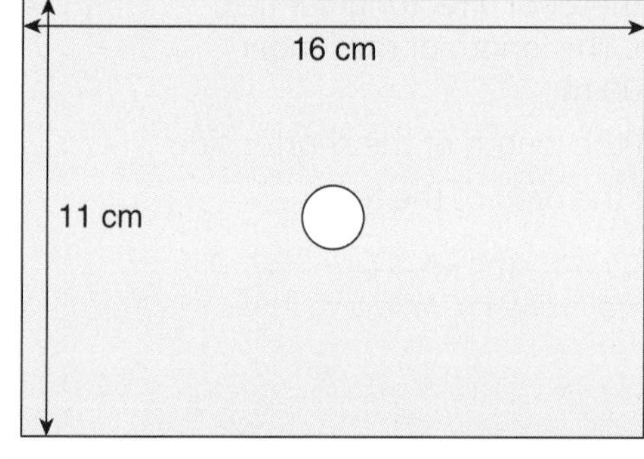

(a) Find the length of the soccer pitch.

(b) Find the perimeter of the soccer pitch, correct to two decimal places.

The centre circle of the soccer pitch has a radius of 19.5 m.

(c) Calculate the area of the centre circle on the soccer pitch, correct to the nearest metre.

(d) Find the correct radius of the centre circle for Liam's scaled diagram, correct to two decimal places.

11. Joe wants to extend his kitchen. He has two plans. The extension is the shaded area in each plan.

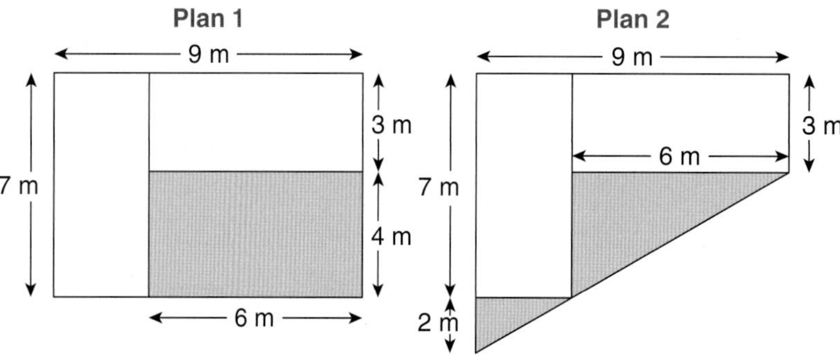

(a) Find the area of the extension for each plan.

(b) Which plan gives the bigger area to the kitchen?

(c) How many extra square metres would Joe have if he used the plan with the greater extension, rather than the other plan?

12. A solid rectangular concrete block has a length of 32 cm and a width of 12 cm and a height of 20 cm.

(a) Draw a sketch of the block's net.

(b) Find the total surface area of the block in cm^2.

(c) How many full blocks are needed to build a wall 1.5 metres long and 1 metre high. Explain how you got your answer.

13. Find the total surface area of a solid hemisphere of diameter 14 cm. Give your answer correct to one decimal place.

14. The net for a figure with a square base is shown. Each grid square is 5 mm in length.

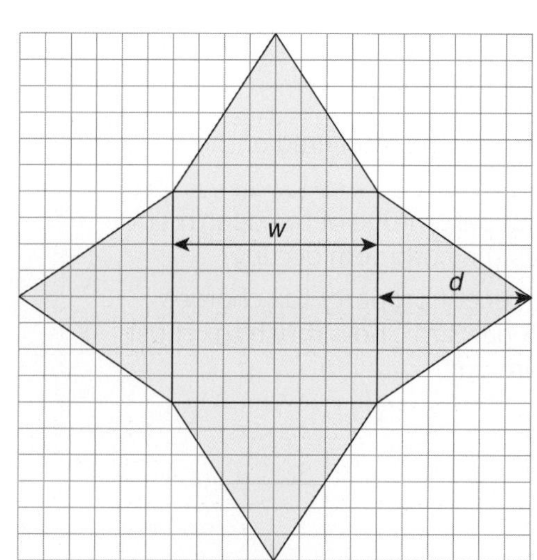

(a) Find w, the length of the base, and d, the height of each triangular side.

(b) Find the area of the base of the figure.

(c) Find the total surface area of the figure.

15. Aidan arranges his collection of five cent coins on the base of his moneybox as shown. Given that the diameter of a single five cent coin is 21.25 mm, calculate the total amount of space in between the coins. Give your answer correct to two decimal places.

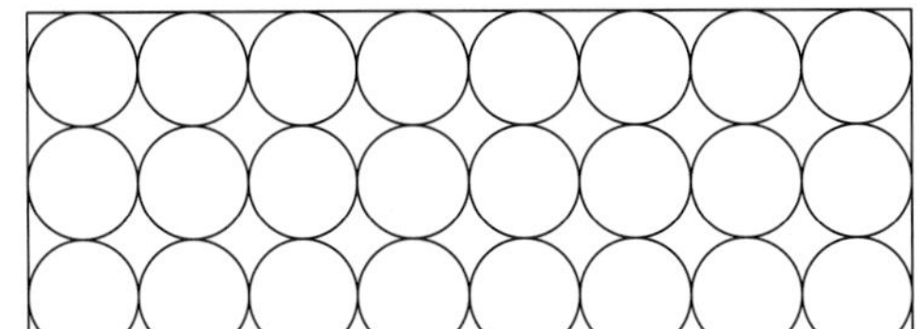

16. The diagram shows a prism-shaped building on a farm. One of the end walls is $ABCD$. AB and CD are perpendicular to BC. The internal length is $|CK|$, where CK is perpendicular to BC. The internal measurements of the building are $|AB| = 3$ m, $|BC| = |DC| = 2$ m and $|CK| = 4$ m. Draw a net of the shape, clearly showing all measurements.

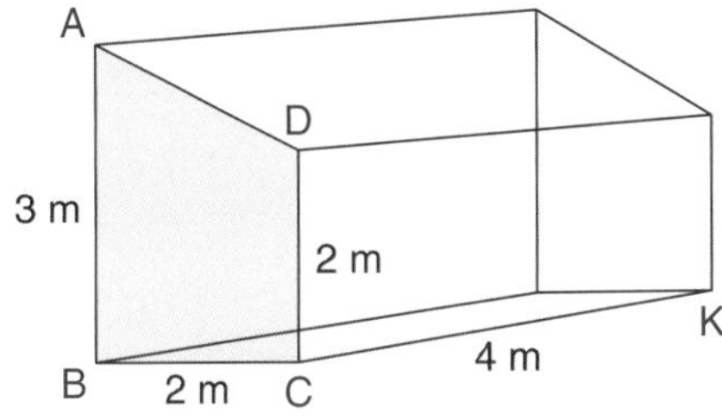

17. A rectangular piece of metal has a width of 16π cm. Two circular pieces, each of radius 7 cm, are cut from the rectangular piece, as shown.

(a) Find the length l of the rectangular piece of metal.

(b) Calculate the area of the metal not used (i.e. the shaded section), giving your answer in terms of π.

(c) Express the area of the metal not used as a percentage of the total area.

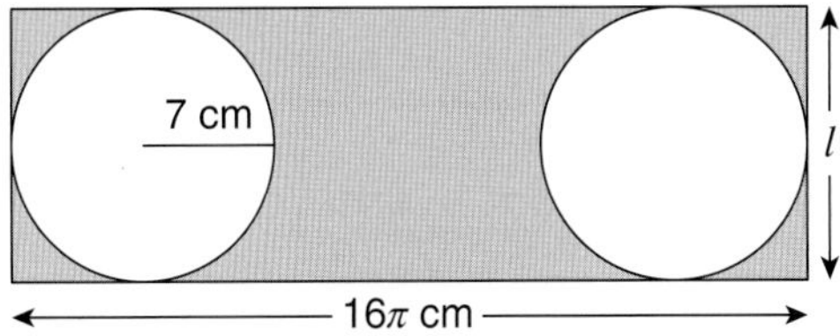

18. The diagram shows the perimeter of a running track, consisting of two straight sections of length l, and two semicircular sections at either end of radius $\frac{100}{\pi}$ m as shown.

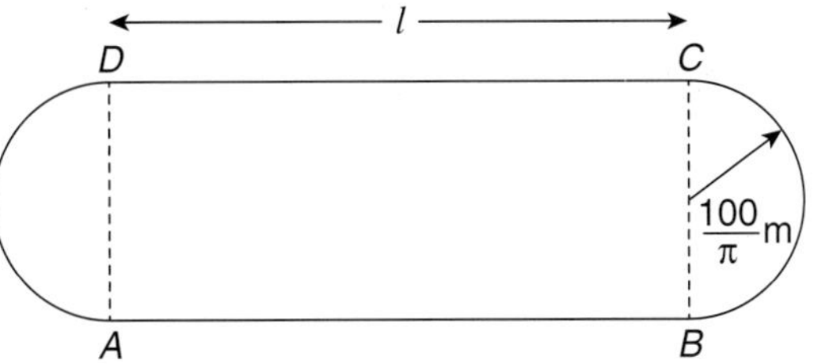

(a) Given that the perimeter of the track measures 400 m, find l.

(b) A 1,500 m race starts at the point A and goes in the direction $ABCD$. At what point does the race finish?

(c) An athlete completes this distance in 3 minutes 26 seconds. Find her average speed in metres per second, correct to one decimal place.

19. The height and the diameter of a solid cylinder are both 8 cm. Find the curved surface area of the cylinder, correct to the nearest whole number.

20. A solid cylinder has a radius of 10 mm and a height of 45 mm. Draw a sketch of the net of the surface of the cylinder and write its dimensions on the sketch.

21. A circle is inscribed in a square as shown. The radius of the circle is 9 cm.

(a) Find the perimeter of the square.

(b) Calculate the area of the square.

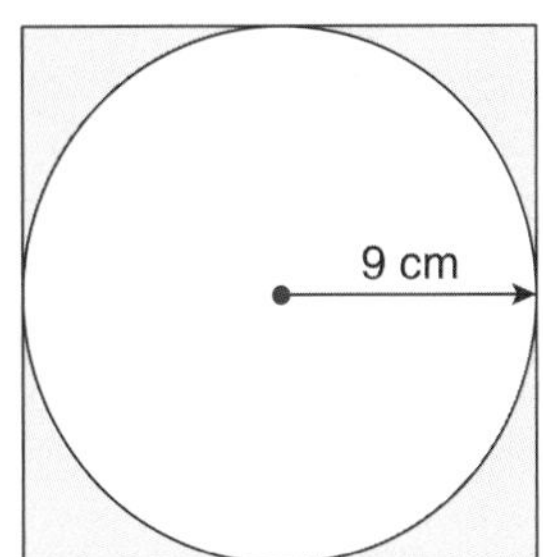

22. A mirror has the shape of a rectangle with a semicircular top as shown. The rectangular section has a width of 0.6 m and a height of 1.2 m. The semicircular part has a radius of 0.2 m.

(a) Find the area of the rectangular section.

(b) Find the area of the semicircular part, taking $\pi = 3.14$.

(c) Find the perimeter of the mirror, taking $\pi = 3.14$.

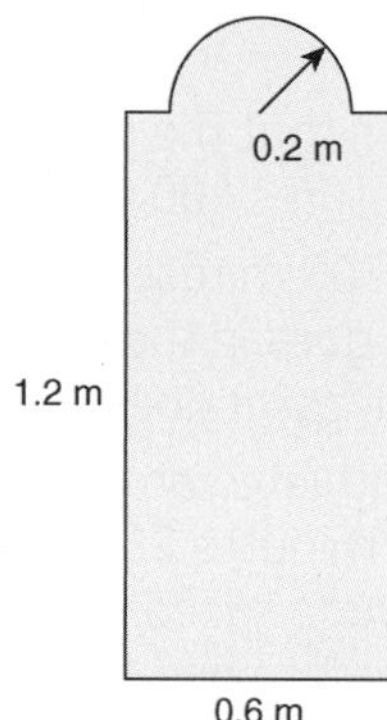

23. Chris is a scout. The scoutmaster has made an equilateral triangle with pegs and a rope, as shown in the diagram. Chris measures one side of the triangle. It is 6 m in length.

(a) Find the perimeter of the triangle.

(b) Construct an accurate scale diagram of the equilateral triangle using a scale of 1 cm to represent 1 m.

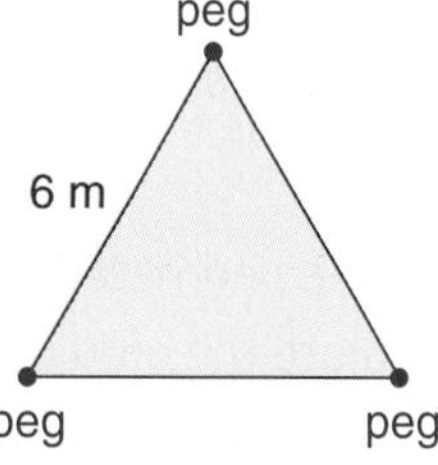

24. The diagram shows an opened-out, flattened envelope. *PQRS* is a rectangle. The opened out parts are triangles. Calculate the surface area of the opened-out envelope.

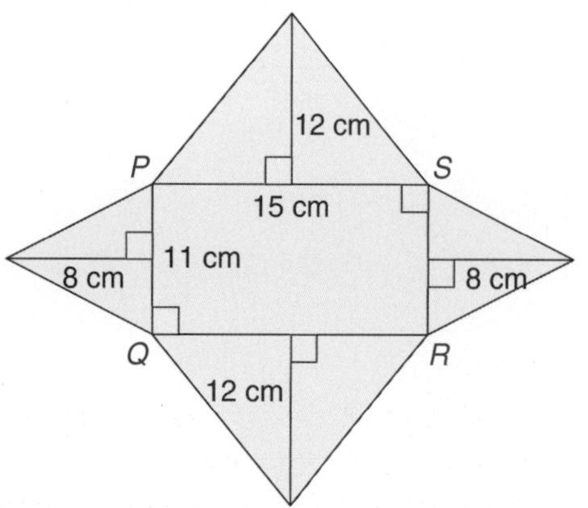

25. (a) The perimeter of a square lawn is 96 m. Calculate the area of the lawn.

(b) A cylindrical-shaped garden roller has a diameter of 75 cm and is 1 m wide, as shown in the diagram. Calculate the curved surface area of the roller in m^2, correct to one decimal place.

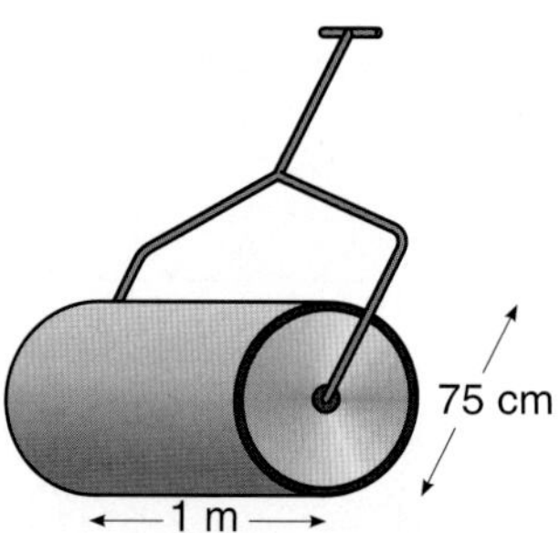

(c) What percentage of the lawn will be rolled when the roller has completed 9 revolutions?

26. A solid metal cylinder has a height of 20 cm and a diameter of 14 cm.

(a) Find its curved surface area in terms of π.

A hemisphere with a diameter of 14 cm is removed from the top of this cylinder as shown.

(b) Find the total surface area of the remaining solid in terms of π.

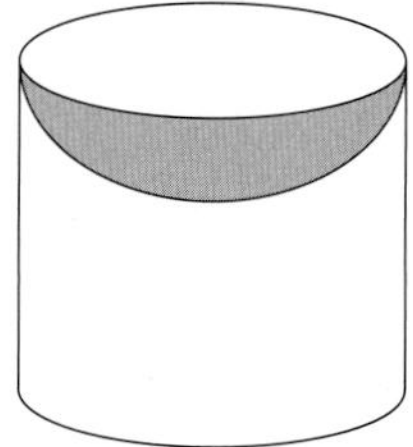

27. *A*, *B* and *C* are points on a circle with centre *O*. [*AC*] is the diameter of the circle. $|AB| = 3$ cm, $|BC| = 4$ cm and $|\angle ACB| = 37°$. Given that $|\angle ABC|$ is a right angle:

(a) Find the measure of $|\angle BAC|$.

(b) Calculate the length of the diameter [*AC*].

(c) Calculate the area of the shaded region, taking $\pi = 3.14$.

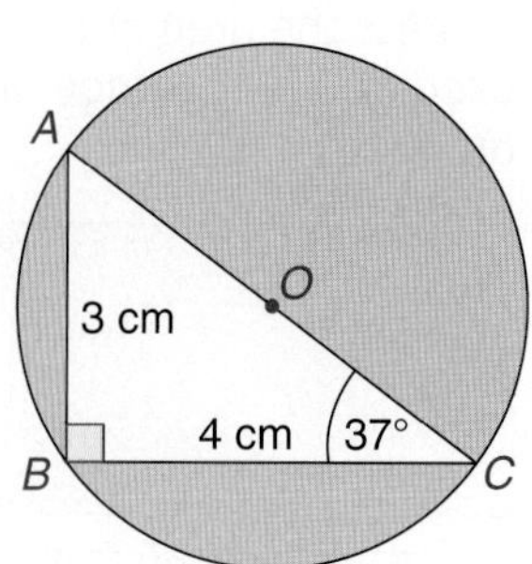

28. Given that each small disc shown has a diameter of 4 cm, calculate the amount of remaining space inside the larger circle. Give your answer in terms of π.

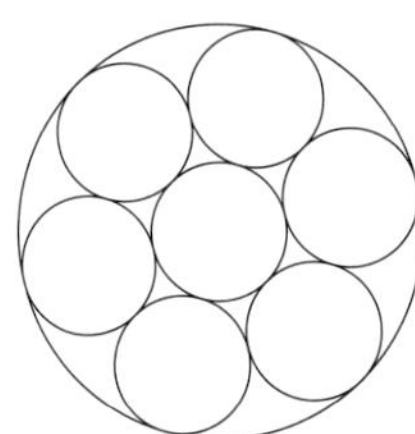

29. A running track is made up of two straight parts and two semicircular parts, as shown in the diagram. The length of each of the straight parts is 90 metres. The diameter of each of the semicircular parts is 70 metres. Calculate the length of the track, correct to the nearest metre.

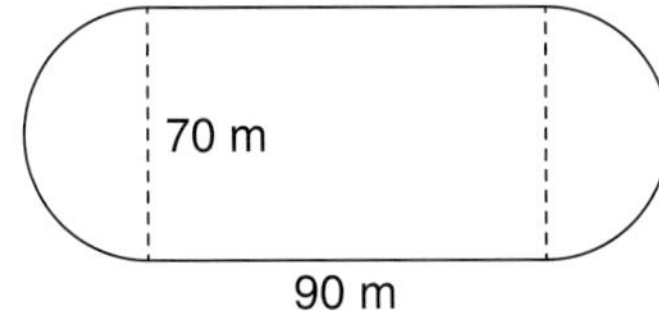

30. The length of wire used to create the side of a square is 8.3 cm. Calculate the total amount of wire used to create the following design. Take π as 3.14. Give your answer correct to one decimal place.

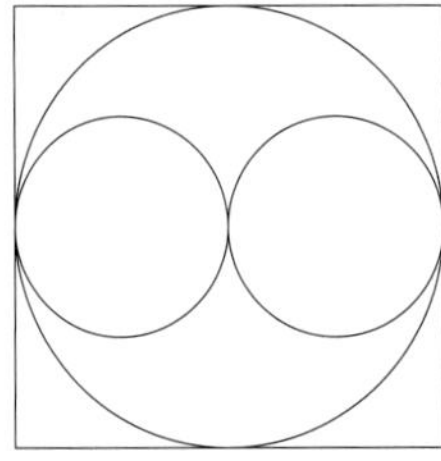

31. Examine the image. Given that the length of the inner circumference created by the photographer is 72 cm, calculate:

(a) The average length of a hand

(b) The approximate area of the circle created in terms of π

(c) Explain why this approximation may be inaccurate.

32. The figure below shows two circles with centres P and Q. $|PQ| = |QR| = |RS| = 3$ m. What is the area of the shaded region? Give your answer in terms of π.

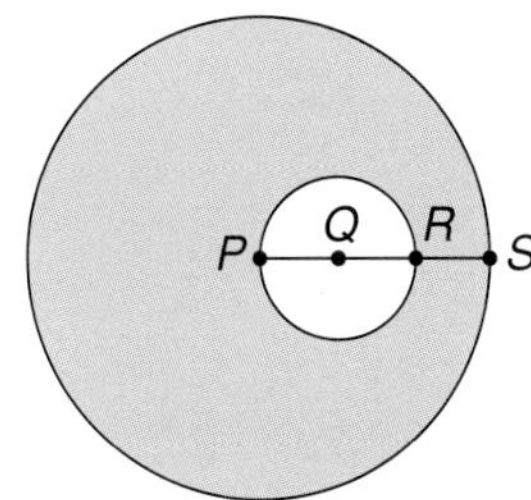

33. Circles A and B have radii of 2 units and 3 units respectively. By how much is the circumference of circle B greater than the circumference of circle A? Give your answer correct to one decimal place.

34. Examine the image below and calculate the length of the green rope in terms of x and π.

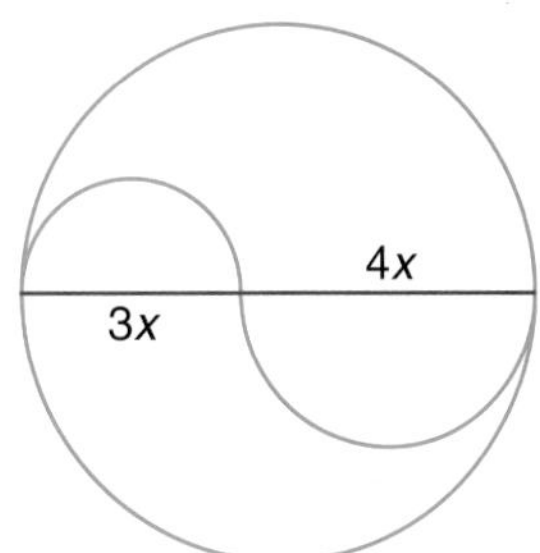

35. In the figure below, the diameters of the five dotted semicircles are equal and lie on the line segment AB. If the length of line segment AB is 20 cm, what is the length of the dotted curve from A to B? Give your answer correct to one decimal place.

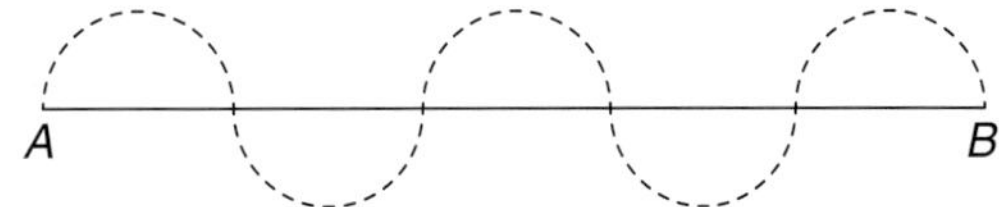

36. A piece of public art shows 18 plastic people exactly 1.5 metres tall, 1.3 metres wide and standing 0.8 metres away from the figure to their left and their right-hand sides.

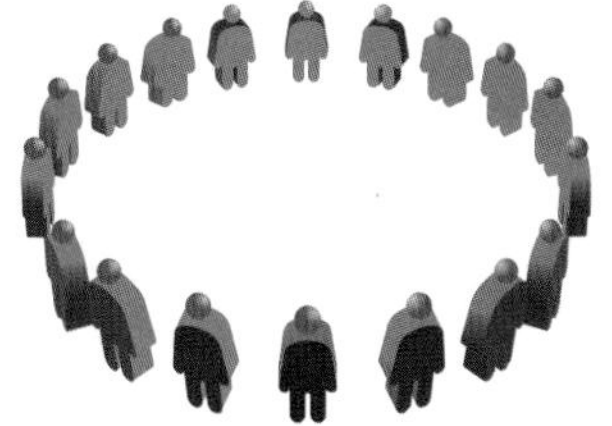

Calculate:

(a) The length of the inner circumference created by the art piece

(b) The approximate area enclosed by the art piece

37. Four spherical bowling balls are lined up beside each other in ascending order. Given that their circumferences are in the ratio 100:300:600:1200, investigate whether:

(a) Their radii are in the same ratio

(b) Their surface areas are in the same ratio

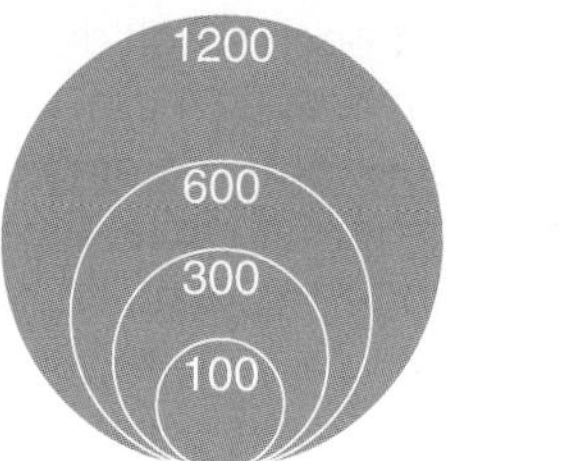

38. Complete the following crossword:

Across

3. A 2D drawing of a 3D shape

4. The amount of space inside a shape

6. The length of a circle divided by its diameter

7. Half a ball

8. The shape of a tin can

9. The shape of a 3D globe

Down

1. The name of any boundary of a shape

2. Another name for the boundary of a circle

5. Distance from the centre of a circle to a point on its circumference

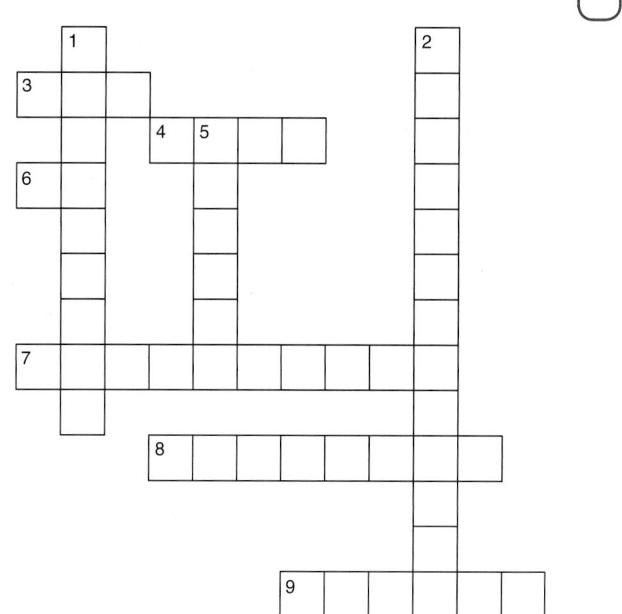

CHAPTER 13 KNOWLEDGE CHECKLIST

After completing this chapter, I now:

- Know how to calculate the circumference of a circle
- Know how to calculate the perimeter of a shape
- Know how to calculate the areas of squares, rectangles parallelograms, triangles, circles, semicircles and sectors
- Know how to draw nets of prisms, cylinders, cones, cubes and cuboids
- Know how to investigate the nets of rectangular solids to find their surface areas
- Know how to draw and interpret scaled models
- Know how to calculate the surface areas for prisms, cylinders, cones, cubes and cuboids
- Know how to calculate the curved surface areas for cylinders, cones and spheres

Challenge

IN THE OLD TOWN OF PERPLEX CITY ARE SEVEN BRIDGES CROSSING THE RIVER MAZY. IN THE PAST, VISITORS WERE OFTEN ASKED WHETHER THEY COULD GO FOR A WALK THAT WOULD CROSS ALL SEVEN BRIDGES ONCE, BUT NOT ANY OF THEM TWICE. CAN YOU?

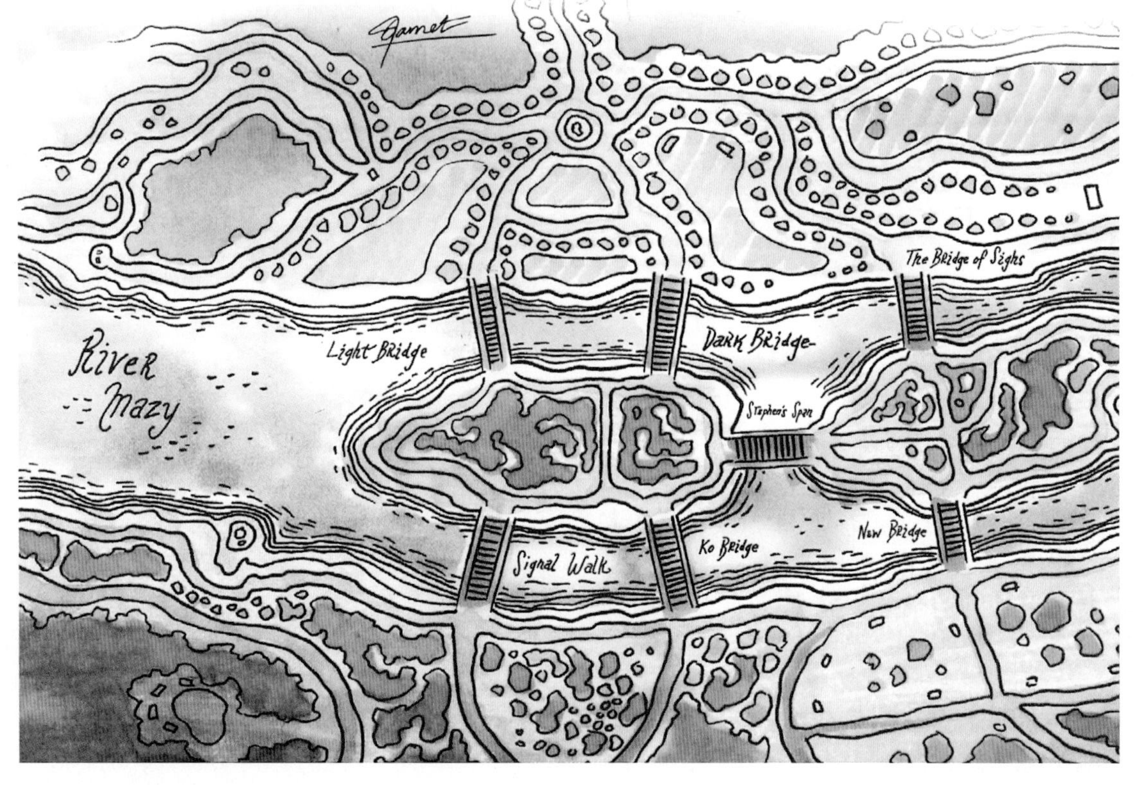

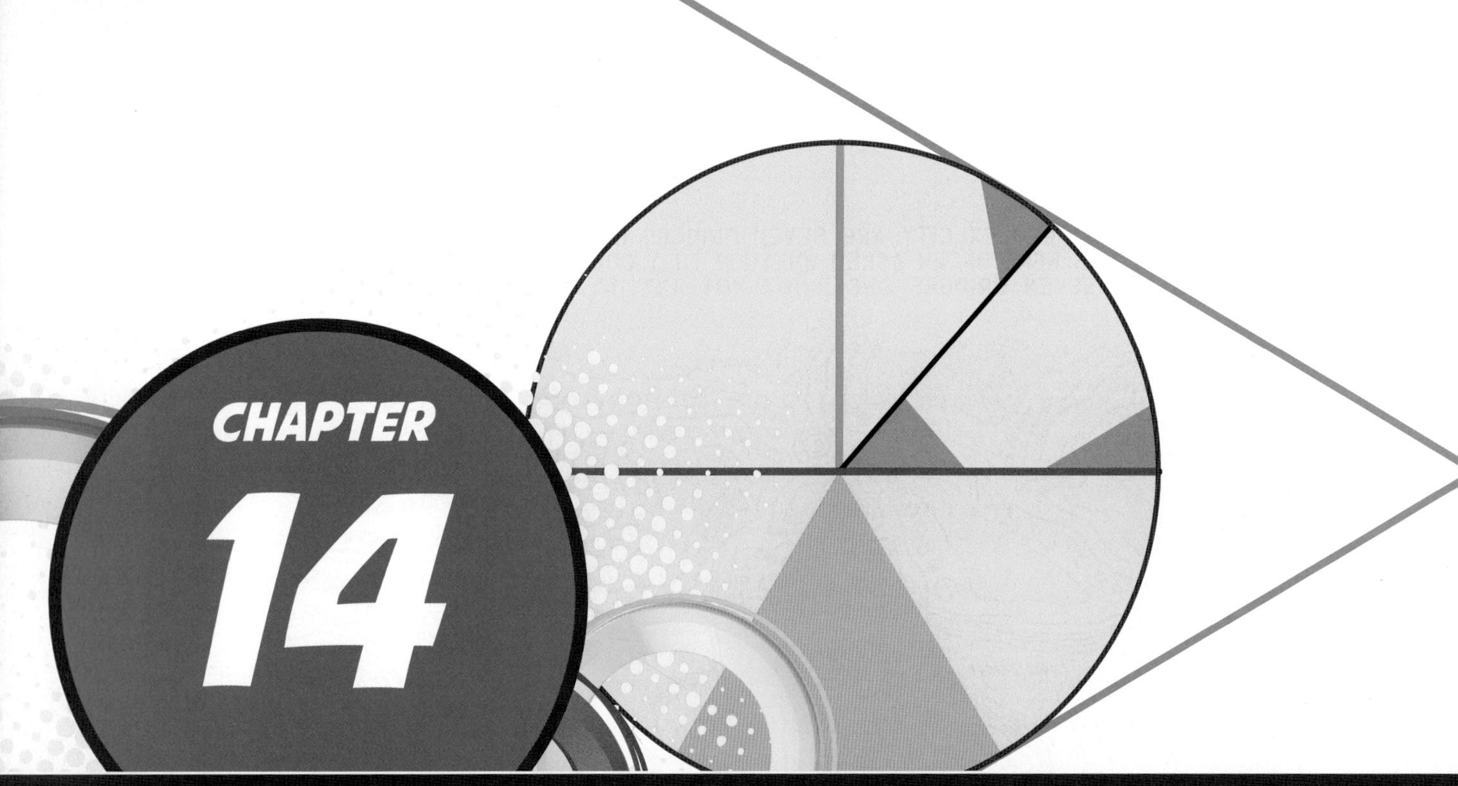

GEOMETRY 3

KEY WORDS

- Arc
- Axiom
- Chord
- Circumference
- Converse
- Corollary
- Cyclic quadrilateral
- Diameter
- Radius
- Sector
- Semicircle
- Tangent
- Theorem

LEARNING OUTCOMES

In this chapter you will learn:

- ✓ **About the terms associated with the circle: diameter, radius, arc, sector, circumference, chord and tangent**
- ✓ **All angles at points on the circumference of a circle, standing on the same arc, are equal (and its converse)**
- ✓ **That if the angle standing on a chord at some point on the circle is 90°, then the chord is a diameter**
- ✓ **That the angle at the centre of a circle is twice the angle at the circumference of the circle, both angles standing on the same arc**
- ✓ **That opposite angles in a cyclic quadrilateral sum to 180° (and its converse)**

INTRODUCTION

From the simple wheel to its use in architecture, the circle is an extremely important geometrical shape. If the wheel was not round, how far could humans have travelled in the past?

In the Bronze Age (3500 BC), cavemen were casting metal alloys (mixing two metals together) and building canals, sailboats and even harps. But in Poland, someone thought of the idea of rolling a cylinder on its edge! The invention of the wheel triggered the invention of water wheels, spinning wheels, propellers and turbines.

Before using circles to solve geometrical problems, it is very important to learn and understand the words we use when talking about circles. You might have met some of these in other subjects.

Section 14.1: Circle terms

Student Activity 14A

1. What do you call the line through the centre O of the circle below?

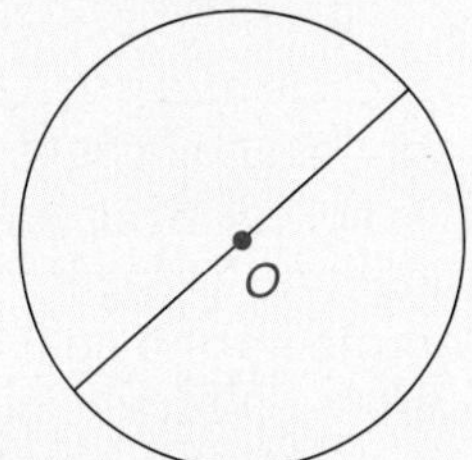

2. What do you call the line from the centre O of the circle to its circumference?

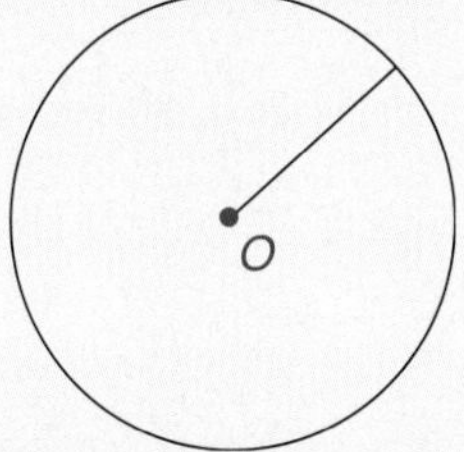

3. Can you explain the word 'circumference'?
4. Can you explain what an arc is? Use the image to help.

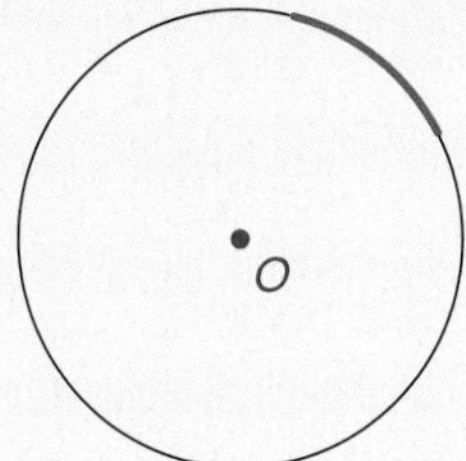

5. Can you explain the word 'sector'? Use the image to help.

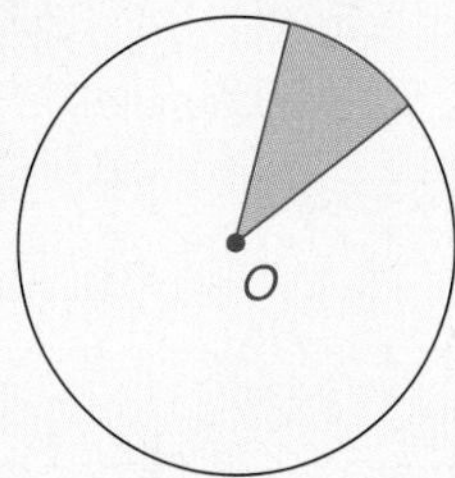

6. Can you explain the word 'chord'? Use the image to help.

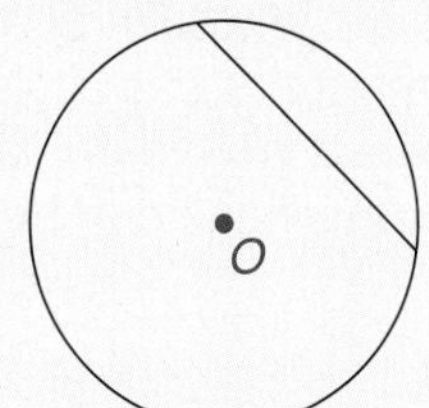

7. What do you understand by the term 'tangent to the circle'? Use the image to help.

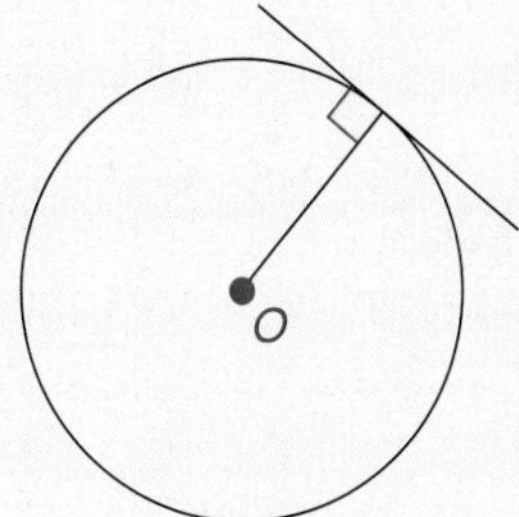

CIRCLE TERMS EXPLAINED

In Student Activity 14A, you met the most common terms that mathematicians use when dealing with circles. You must learn these terms and understand their exact meaning.

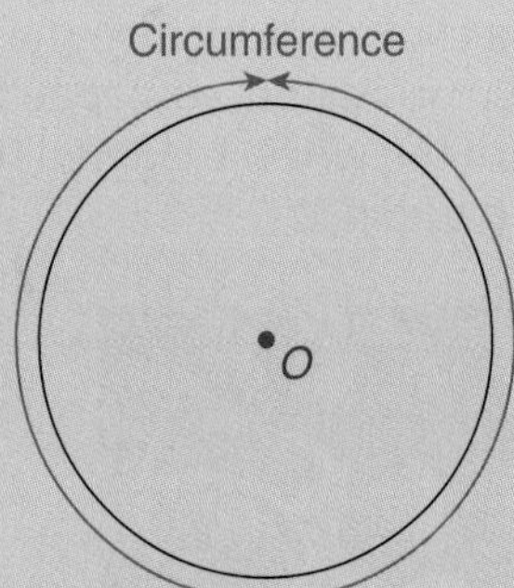

The **circumference** is the distance or length around the outside of a circle. It is the perimeter of the circle.

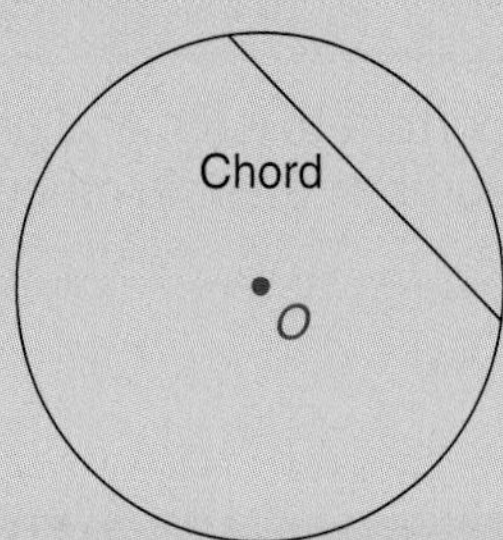

A **chord** of a circle is a line segment whose endpoints both lie on the circumference of a circle.

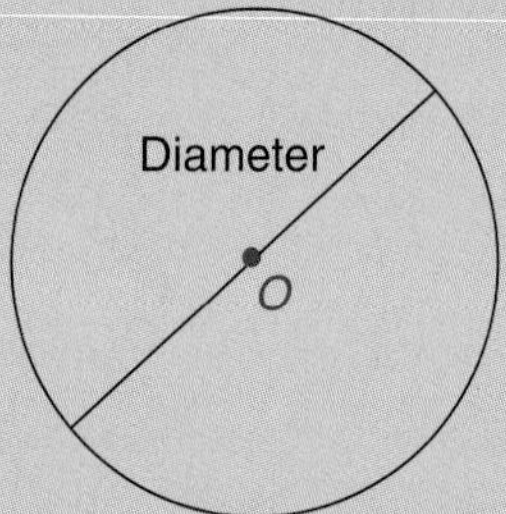

The **diameter** of a circle is any straight line segment that passes through the centre of the circle and whose endpoints also lie on the circumference of a circle. Any diameter is the longest chord of the circle. Every circle has an infinite number of diameters.

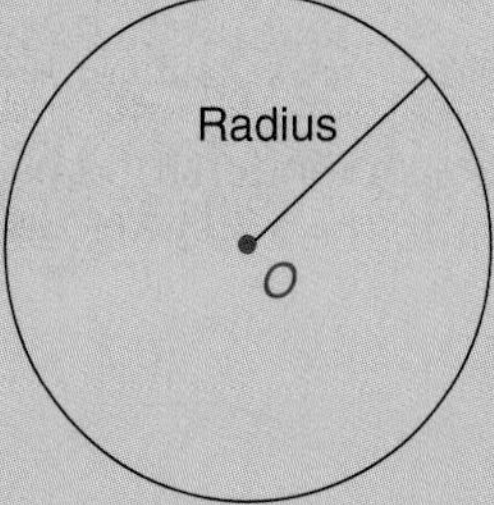

The **radius** of a circle is the length of a line segment from its centre to a point on the circumference. It is exactly half the length of the diameter. Every circle has an infinite number of radii (the plural of radius).

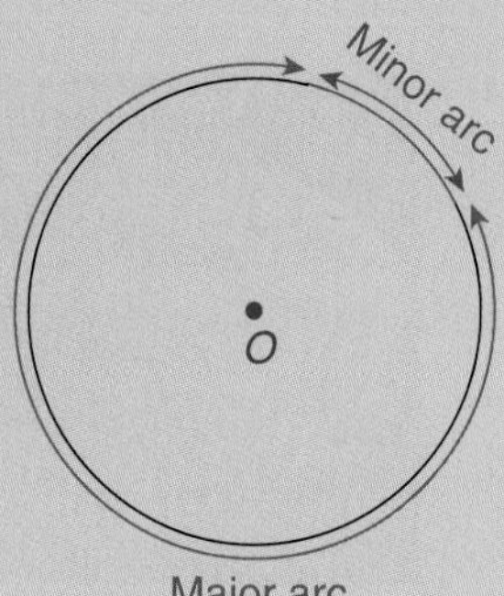

An **arc** is a segment of the circumference of a circle. The smaller arc is called the minor arc and the larger arc is called the major arc.

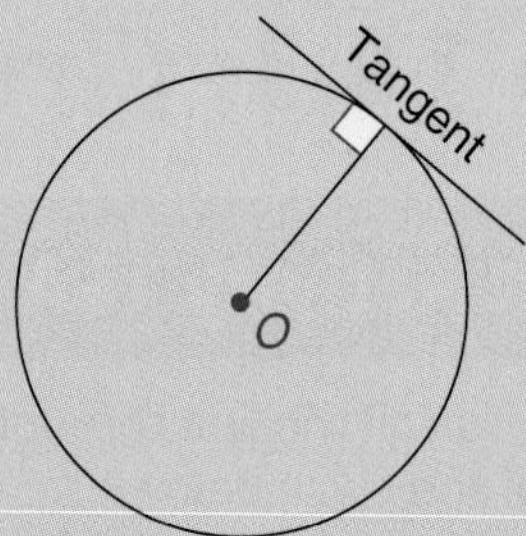

A **tangent** to a circle at a given point is the straight line that only touches the circle at one point. Every circle has an infinite number of tangents. A tangent is always perpendicular (meets at a right angle) to the radius from the centre point to the point of contact of the tangent.

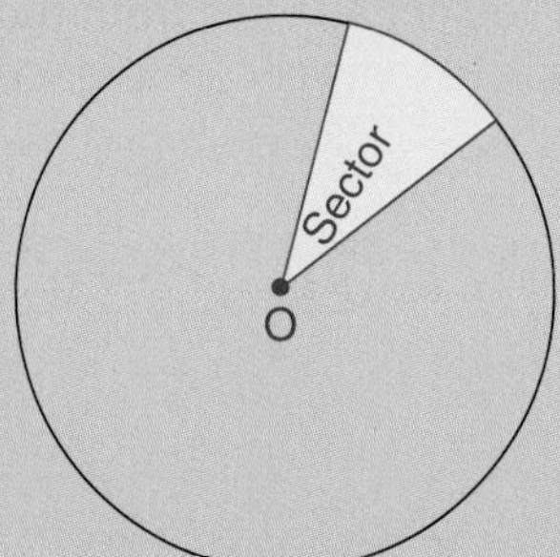

A **circular sector** is the portion of a circle enclosed by two radii and an arc. The smaller area is known as the minor sector and the remaining larger area is called the remaining major sector.

Exercise 14.1

1. Match each word to its corresponding meaning.

(a) Chord	(i) The distance or length around the outside of a circle
(b) Radius	(ii) A portion of a circle enclosed by 2 radii and an arc
(c) Tangent	(iii) A straight line that passes through the centre of a circle and extends from 2 points on the circumference
(d) Arc	(iv) A line that passes through a circle but not through the centre
(e) Circumference	(v) A straight line that only touches a circle at one point
(f) Diameter	(vi) A circular segment of the circumference
(g) Sector	(vii) A line from the centre of a circle to a point on the circumference

2. Identify whether the line segments are diameters, radii or chords.

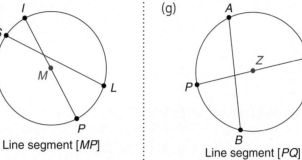

(a)

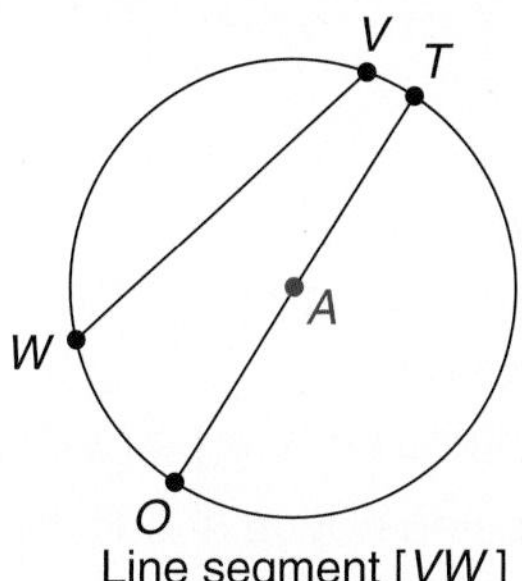

Line segment [*VW*]

(b)

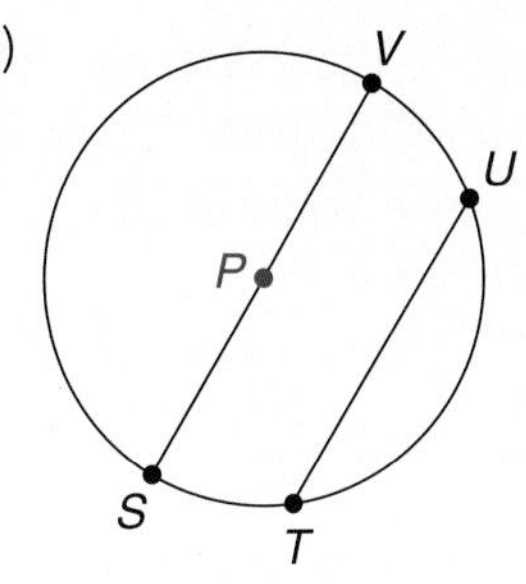

Line segment [*SV*]

(c)

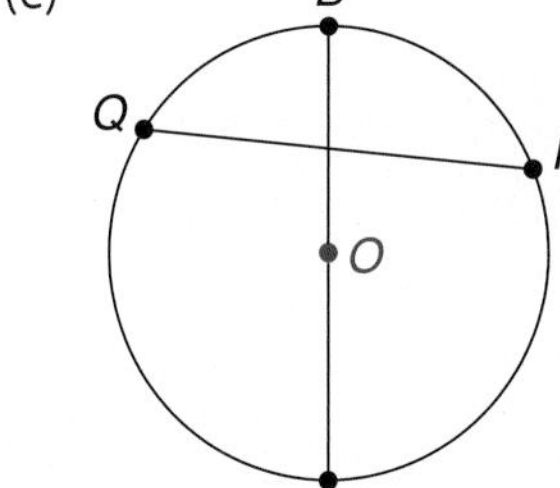

Line segment [*RQ*]

(d)

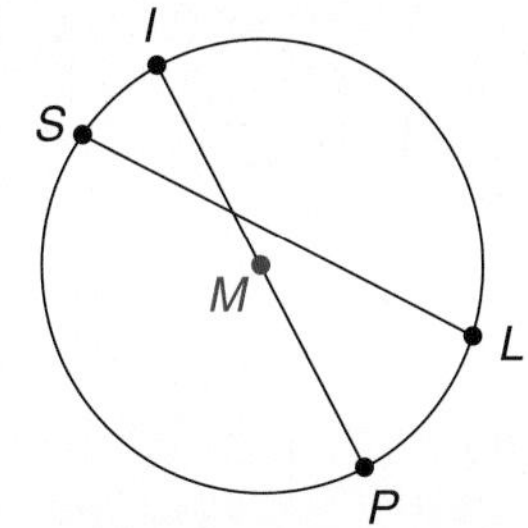

Line segment [*MP*]

(e)

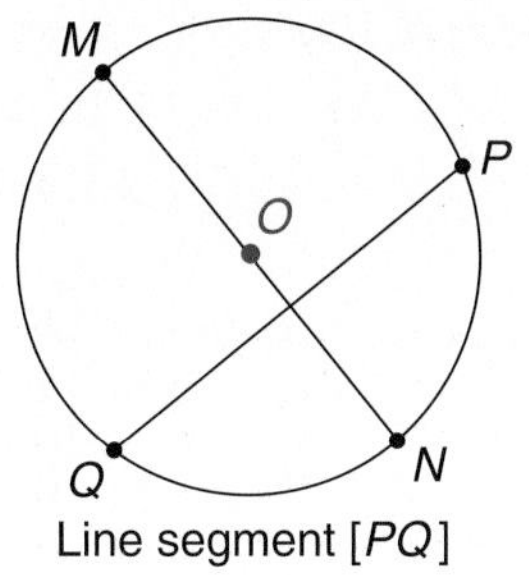

Line segment [*PQ*]

(f)

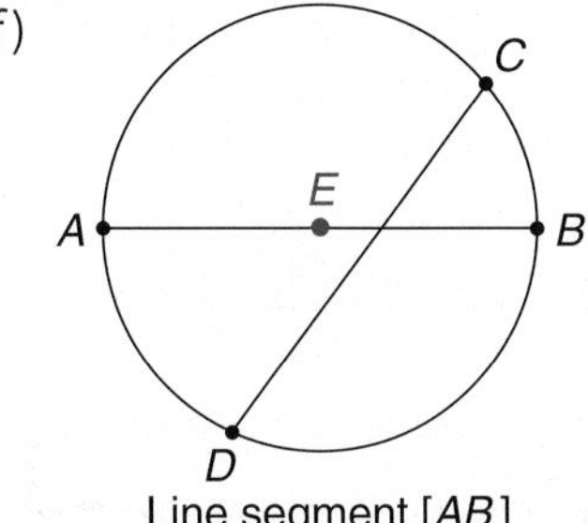

Line segment [*AB*]

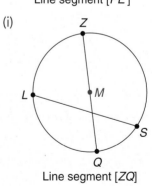

(g)

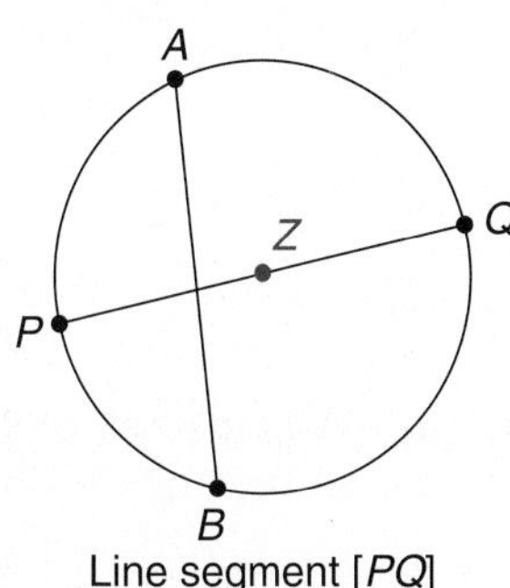

Line segment [*PQ*]

(h)

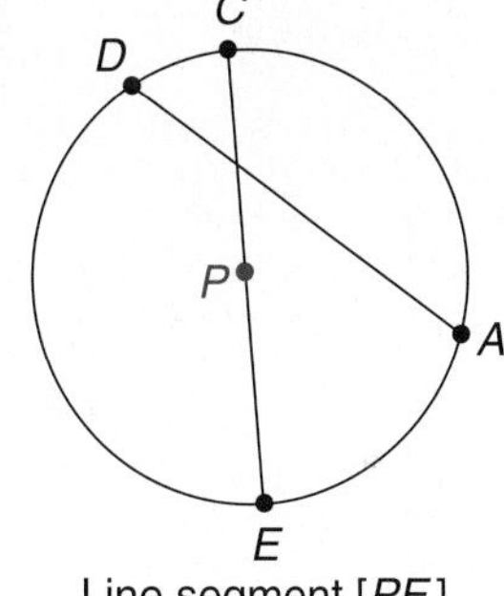

Line segment [*PE*]

(i)

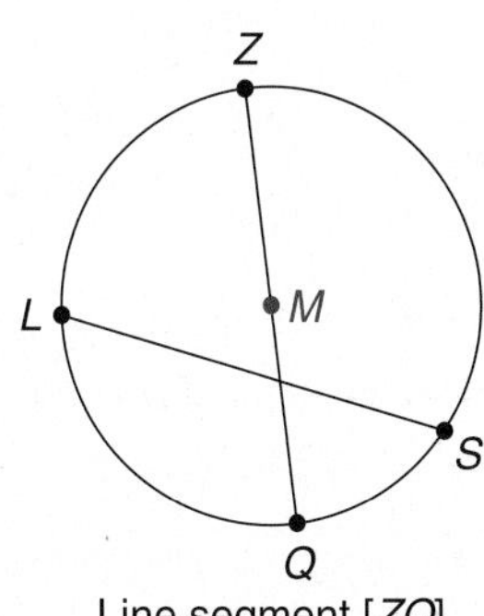

Line segment [*ZQ*]

3. Identify the centre, all radii and the diameter of each of the following circles:

(a)

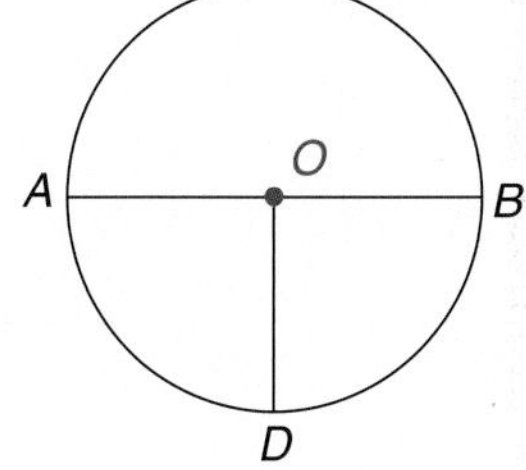

(b)

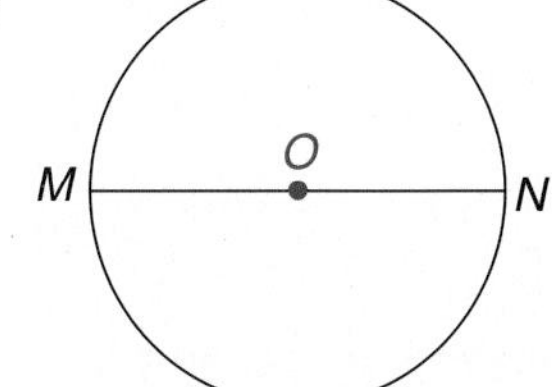

(c)

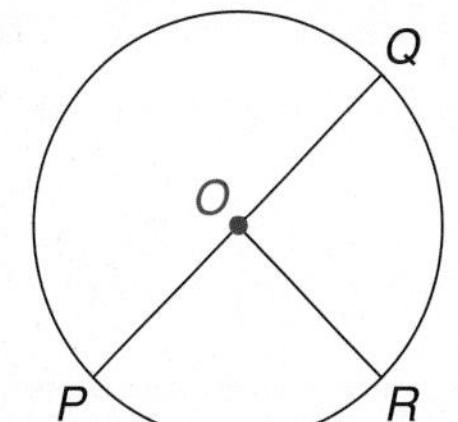

Section 14.2: The angle at the centre of a circle

Student Activity 14B

In each of the following questions, measure the angles indicated using your protractor.

1.

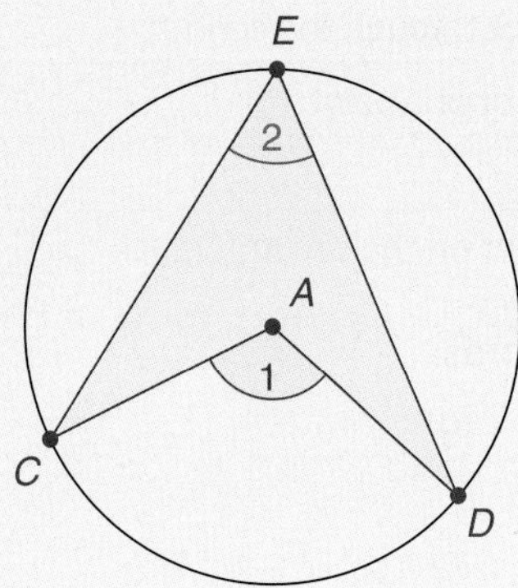

(a) Name the angle which is at the centre of the circle.

(b) Which angle is at the circumference at the point *E*?

(c) Measure the two angles and explain what you notice about the size of the angles.

2.

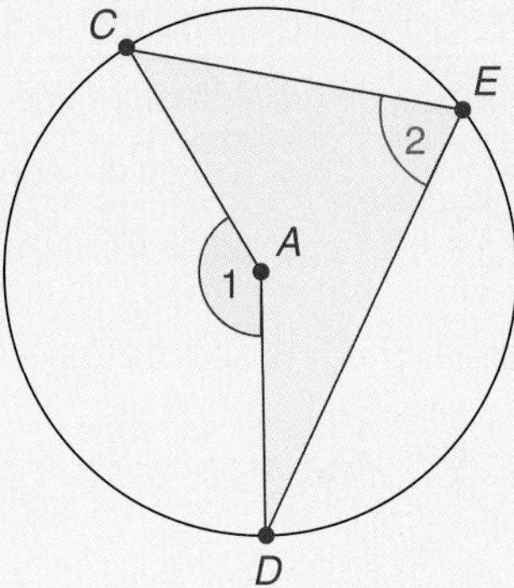

(a) What size is the angle at the centre?

(b) What size is the angle at the circumference at the point *E*?

(c) What do you notice about the size of these two angles?

3. Copy and complete the following sentence based on your findings in Questions 1 and 2:

The measure of the angle at the c _ _ _ _ _ of the circle is t _ _ _ _ the measure of the _ _ _ _ _ at the c _ _ _ _ _ _ _ _ _ _ _, both angles standing on the same arc.

THE ANGLE AT THE CENTRE OF A CIRCLE EXPLAINED

In Student Activity 14B, you examined another theorem on your course.

Theorem 19

The angle at the centre of a circle standing on a given arc is twice the angle at any point of the circle standing on the same arc.

Or, in a diagram we can say $|\angle COD| = 2|\angle CED|$.

The **converse** of this is also true:

Converse

Given two angles standing on the same arc, then the angle at the circumference is half the size of the angle at the centre of the circle.

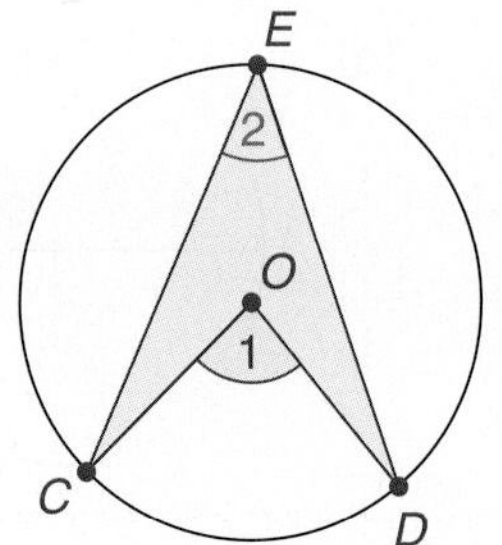

EXAMPLE 1

(a) Find the missing angle X in the circle shown.

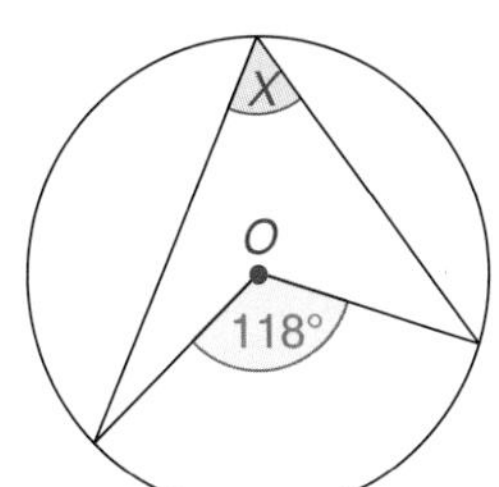

(b) Find the missing angle in X the circle shown.

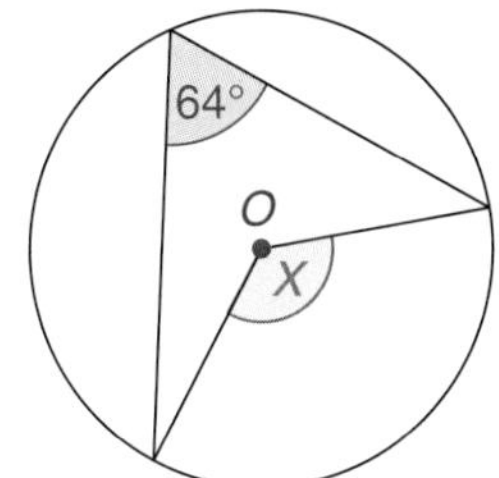

Solution

(a) The angle at the centre is twice the angle at the circumference.

$X = 118° \div 2$

$X = 59°$

(b) The angle at the centre is twice the angle at the circumference.

$X = 64° \times 2$

$X = 128°$

Exercise 14.2

Find the missing angles, marked by the letter X, in each of the following diagrams.

1.

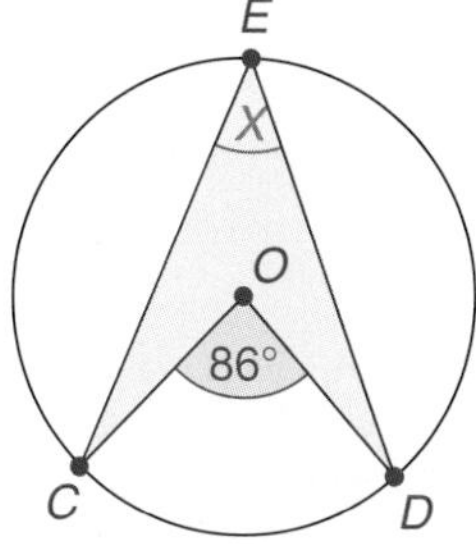

2.

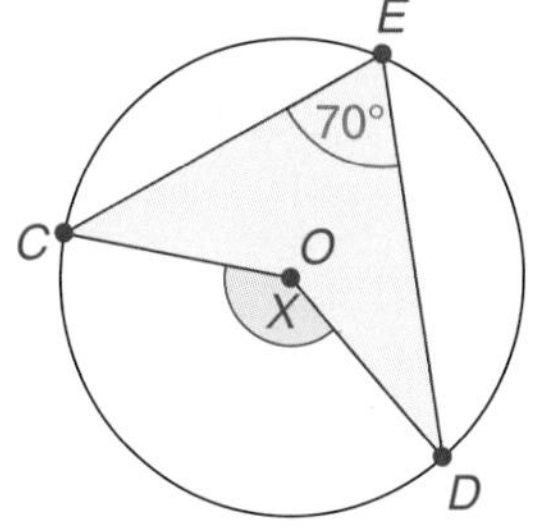

3.

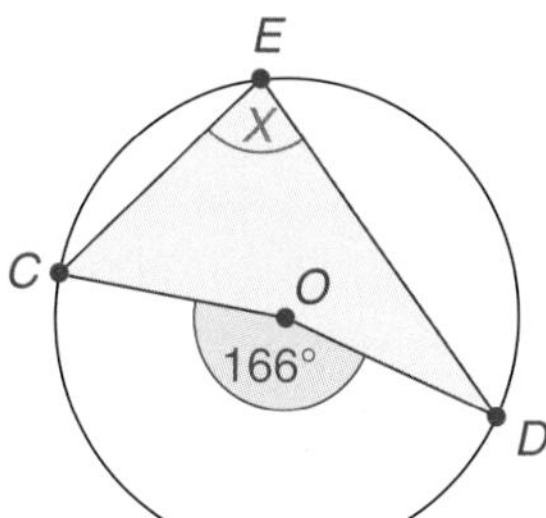

4.

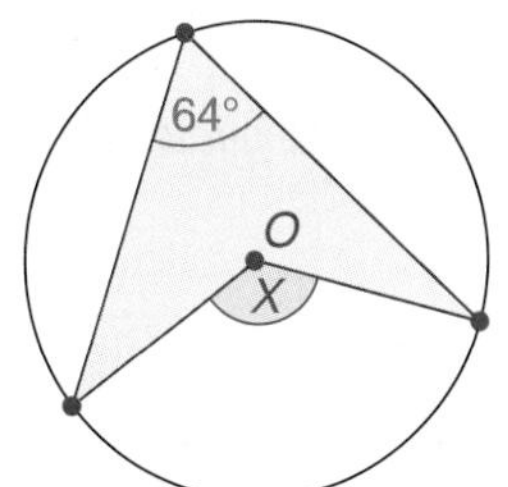

5.

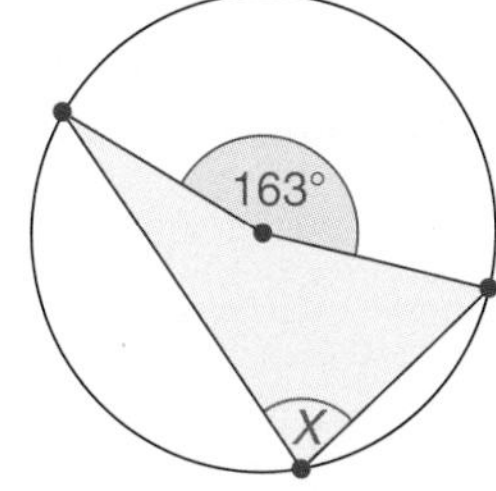

6.

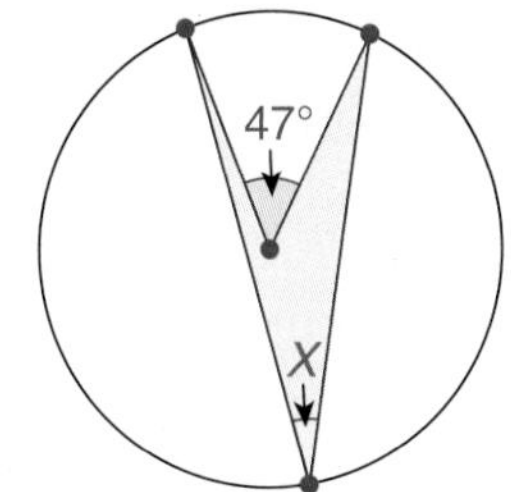

7.

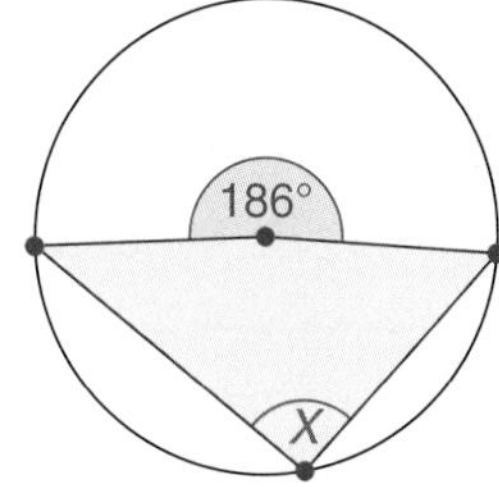

8.

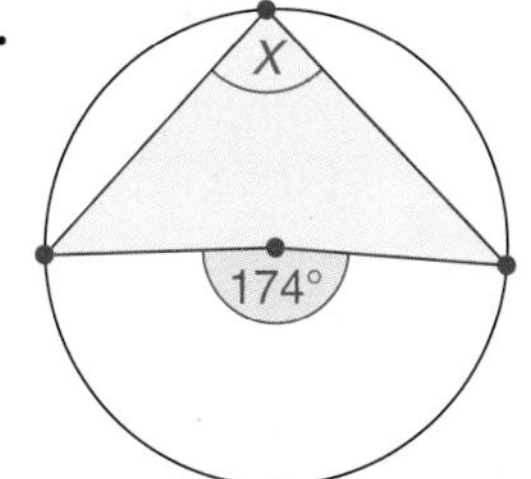

9.

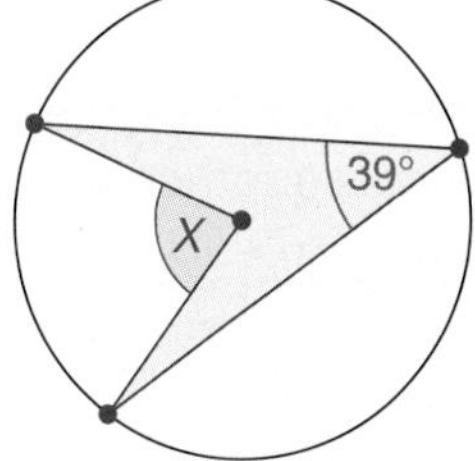

10.

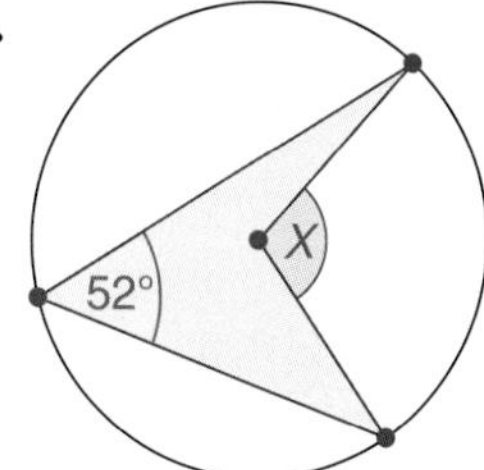

11.

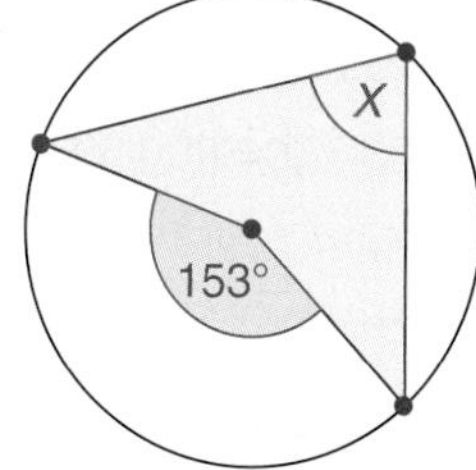

12.

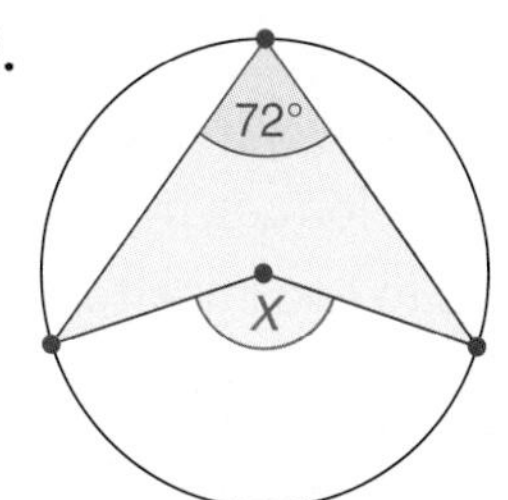

Section 14.3: The angle at the circumference in a semicircle

Student Activity 14C

For each of the questions, measure the angles in each triangle using your protractor.

1. (a) What is the measure of the angle at the point *B*?
   (b) What is another name for [*EC*]?
   (c) Find $|\angle EAC|$.

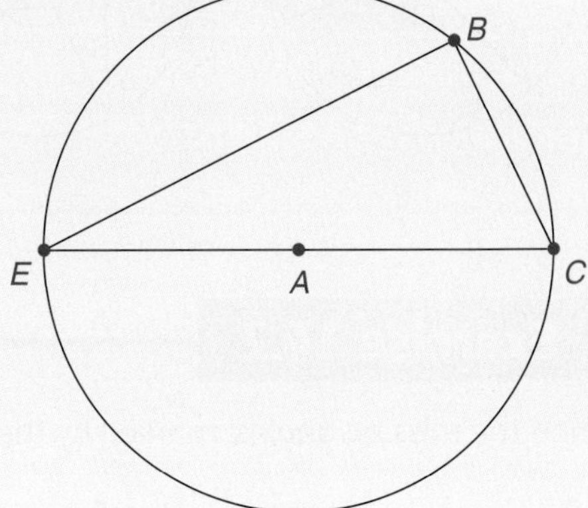

2. (a) What is the measure of the angle at the point *Y*?
   (b) What is another name for [*XZ*]?
   (c) Find $|\angle XOZ|$.

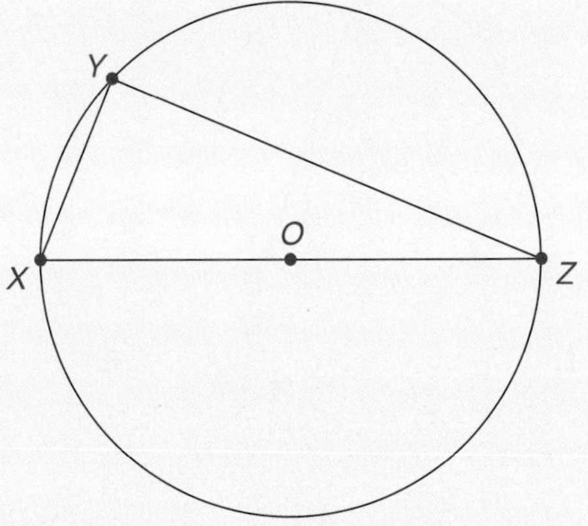

3. Follow these steps:
   (a) Using a compass, draw a circle.
   (b) Draw a diameter using a straight edge.
   (c) Mark the endpoints of the diameter.
   (d) Mark a third point anywhere on your circle and complete the triangle.
   (e) Measure the angle standing on the diameter.
   (f) Compare your result to that of your friends. What do you notice?

THE ANGLE AT THE CIRCUMFERENCE IN A SEMICIRCLE EXPLAINED

In Student Activity 14C, you saw that all of the triangles had the diameter of the circle as one side. The angle formed by the other two sides at the circle always measures 90°.

This leads us to two important corollaries.

A **corollary** is a statement that can be deduced from a theorem and is true based on a previous theorem. No proof is required to show it is true.

These two corollaries state:

Corollary 3

Each angle in a semicircle is a right angle.

Corollary 4

If the angle standing on a chord [BC] is a right angle, then [BC] is a diameter.

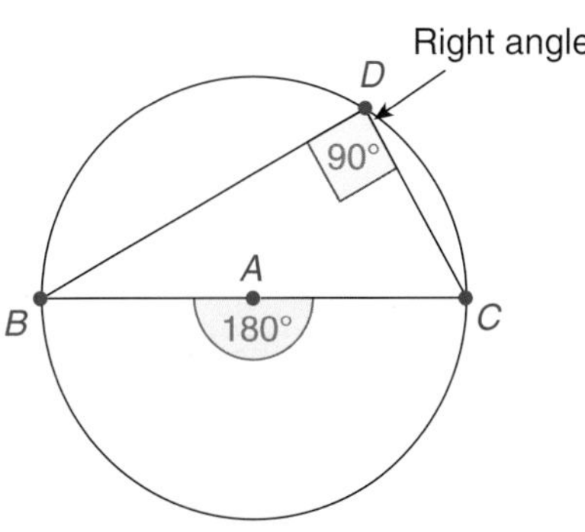

This means that if you draw a circle and create a triangle where one of the sides is the diameter of the circle, then the other two sides will always meet at a 90° angle.

EXAMPLE 2

Find the missing angle X in the circle shown.

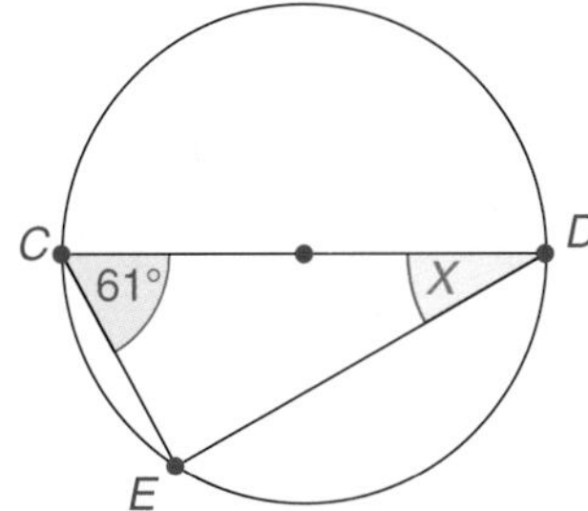

Solution

The angle at point E is 90° as the angle in a semicircle is always a right angle.

$90° + 61° = 151°$

$\therefore 180° - 151° = 29°$ **The three angles in a triangle sum to 180°**

$X = 29°$

Exercise 14.3

In each of the following diagrams, identify the right angle. (Hint: remember to use the three-letter method for naming the angle.)

1.

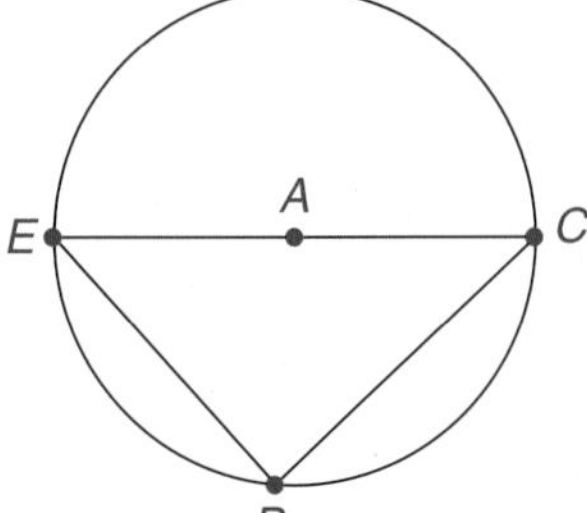

2.

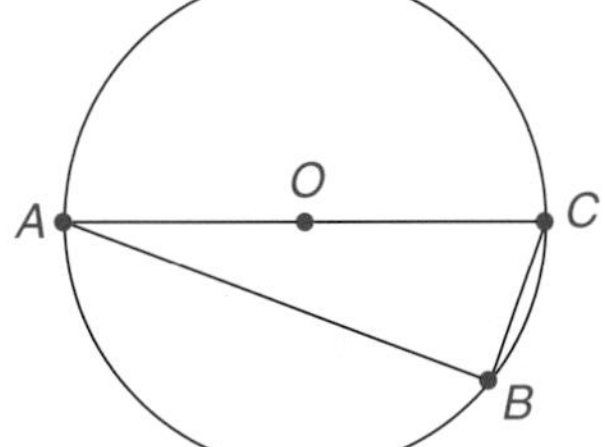

3.

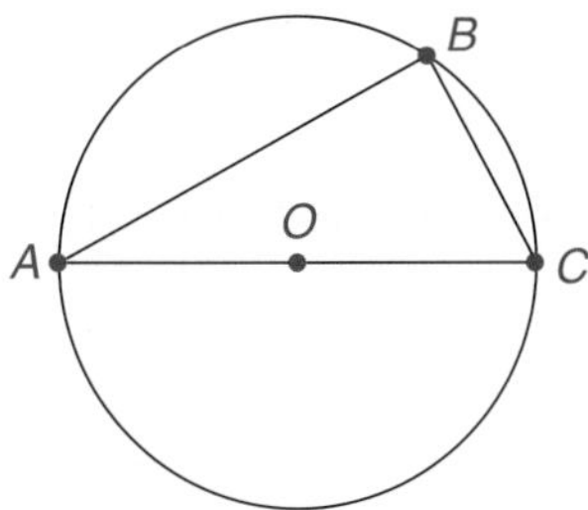

4.

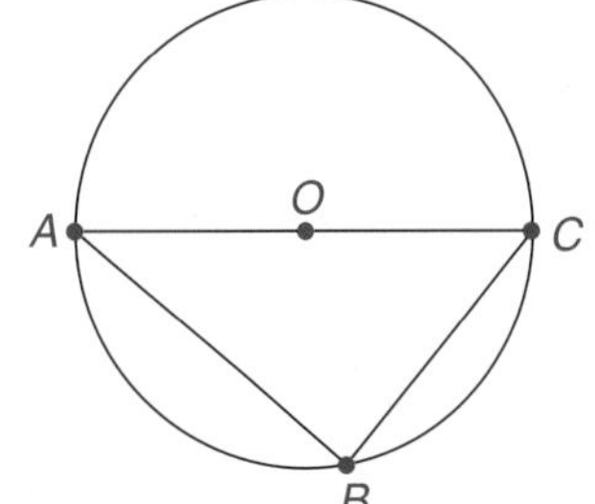

5.

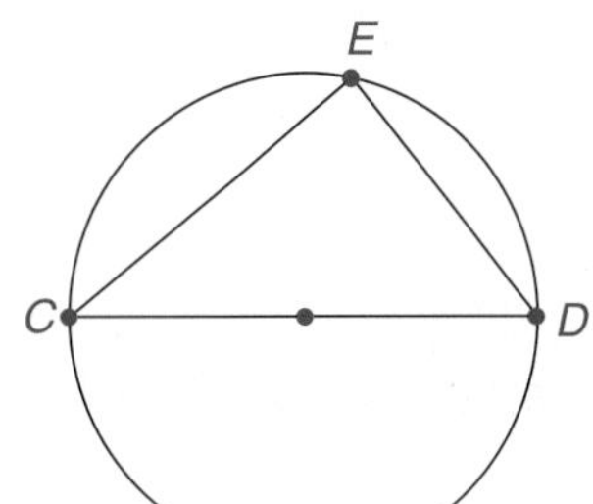

6.

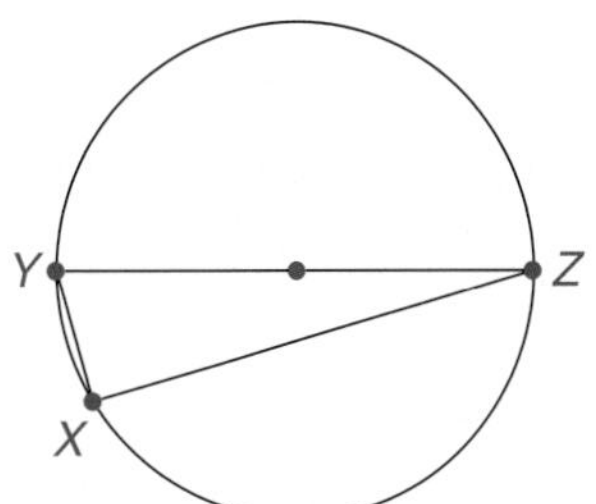

Find the values of the missing angles in each of the following. O is the centre of each circle.

7.

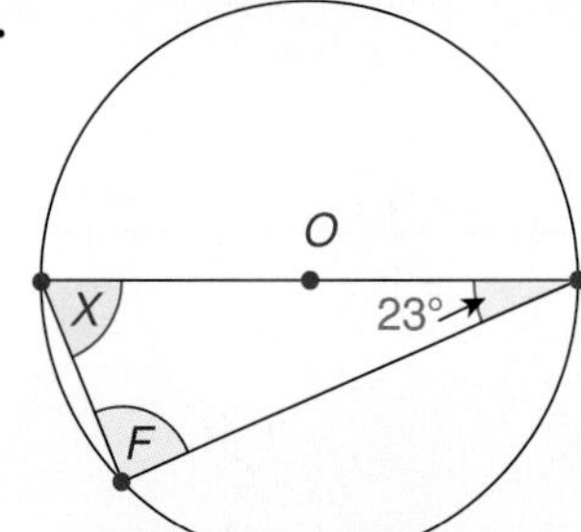

8.

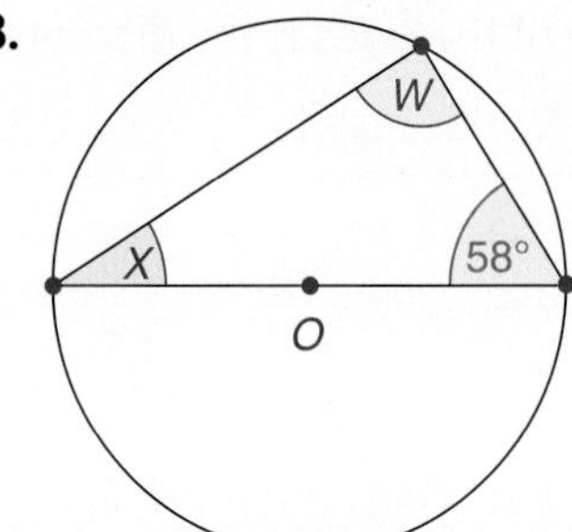

9.

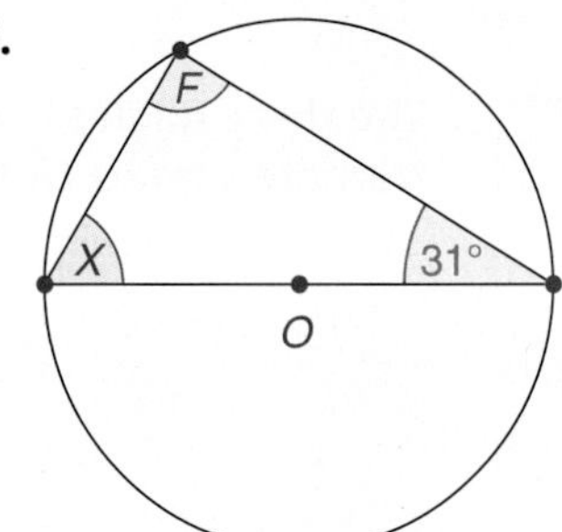

10.

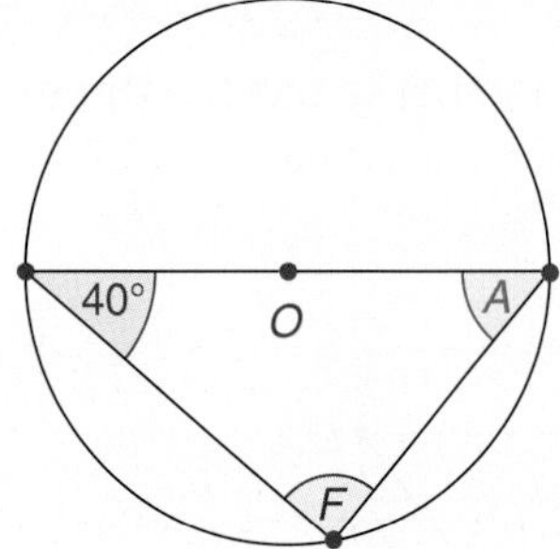

11.

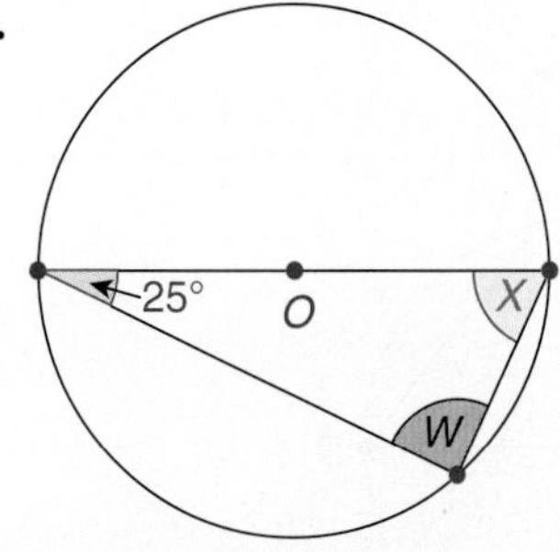

12.

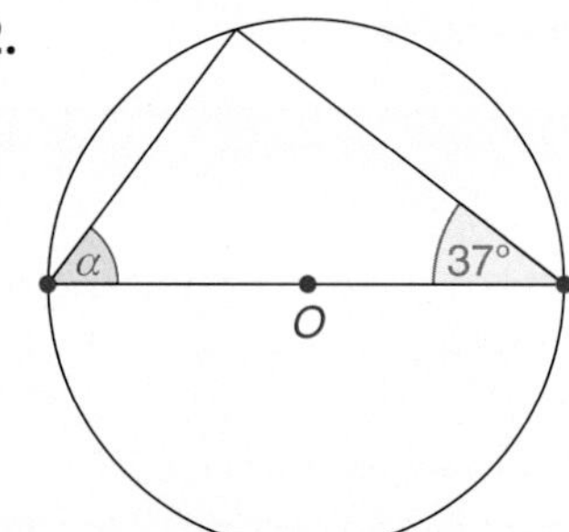

13.

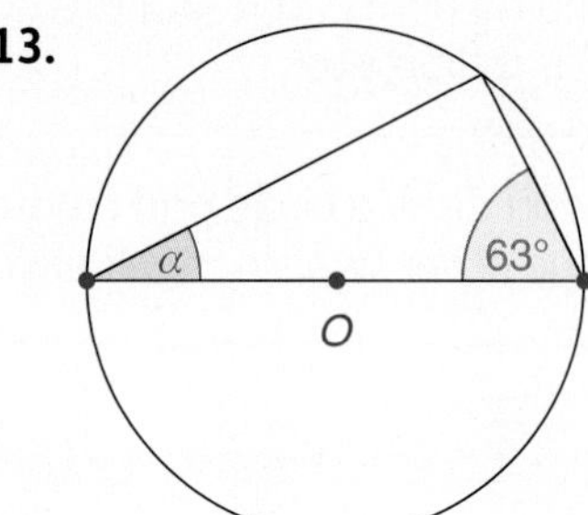

14.

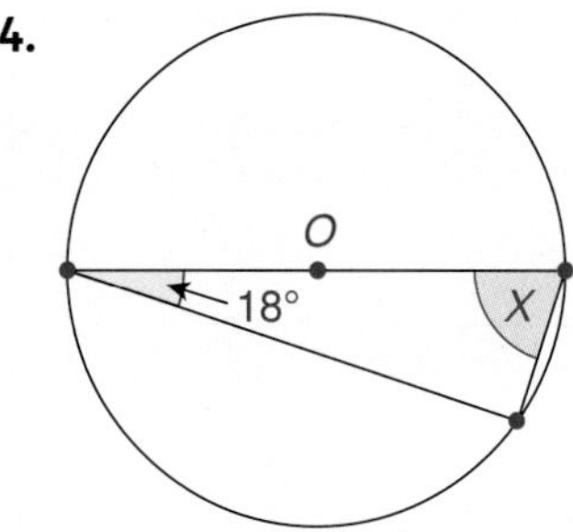

15. Below is a circle with centre O.

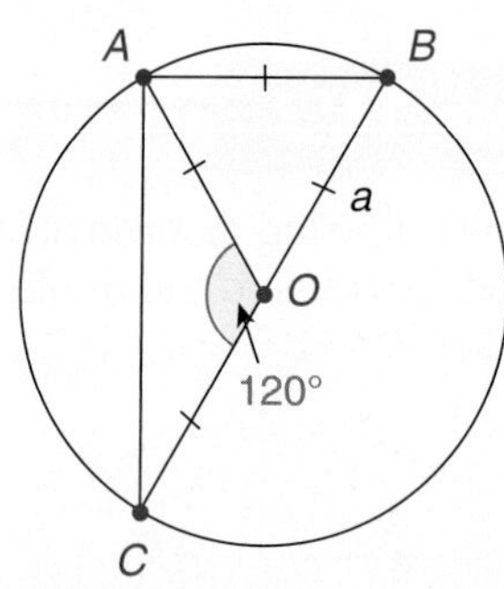

Without using a protractor, find:

(a) $|\angle AOB|$ (c) $|\angle CAB|$

(b) $|\angle OCA|$ (d) $|\angle OAB|$

(e) Why is $|OC| = |OB| = |OA|$?

16. Below is a circle with centre O. Find the missing numbered angles.

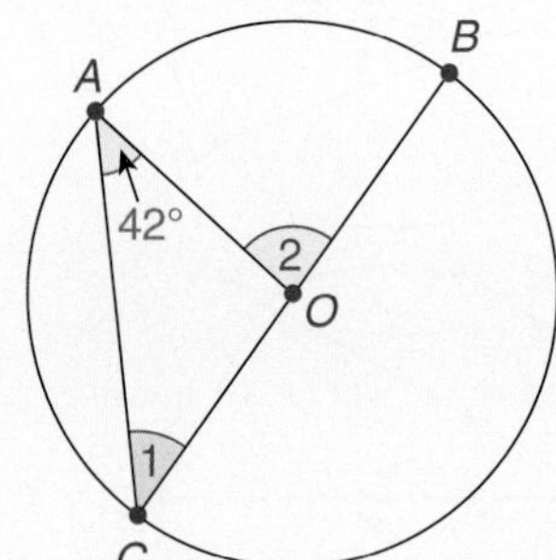

Section 14.4: Angles standing on the same arc

Student Activity 14D

Using what you have already learned, find the missing angles in the following diagrams:

1. Find:

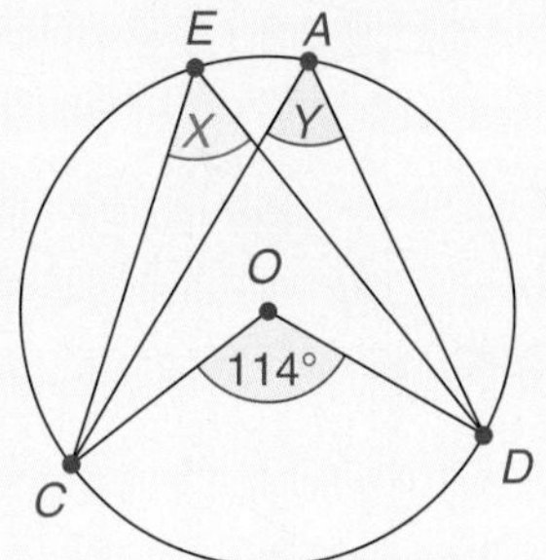

(a) $|\angle CED|$ (b) $|\angle CAD|$

(c) What do you notice about $|\angle CED|$ and $|\angle CAD|$? Explain your answer.

2. Find:

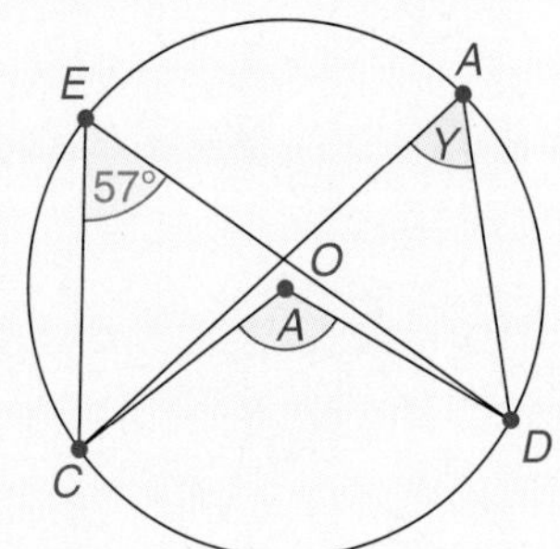

(a) $|\angle CED|$

(b) $|\angle CAD|$

(c) What do you notice about $|\angle CED|$ and $|\angle CAD|$? Explain your answer.

ANGLES STANDING ON THE SAME ARC EXPLAINED

The investigations in Student Activity 14D lead us on to another corollary:

Corollary 2

All angles at points on a circle, standing on the same arc, are equal.

Converse

If points standing at the circle are on the same arc, then the angles made at these points are equal in measure.

EXAMPLE 3

Find the missing angles x and y in the diagram below.

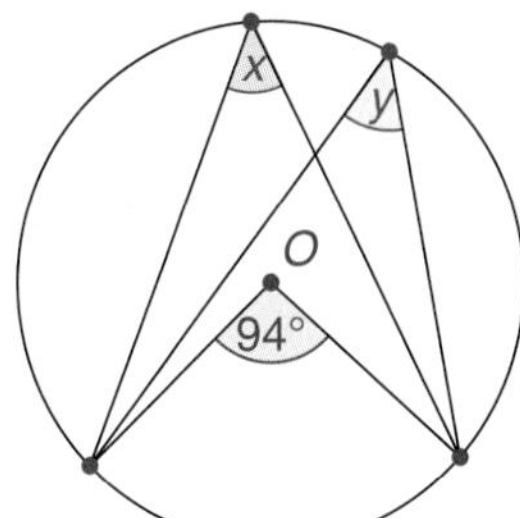

Solution

The angle at the centre is twice the angle at the circumference.

$x = 94° \div 2 = 47°$

We have just learned that angles on the same arc are equal in measure so:

$x = y$

$\therefore y = 47°$ also

Exercise 14.4

Find the missing angles in each of the following diagrams:

1.

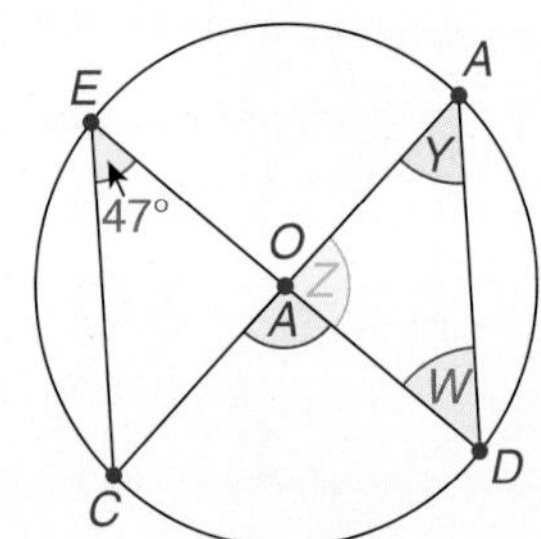

2.

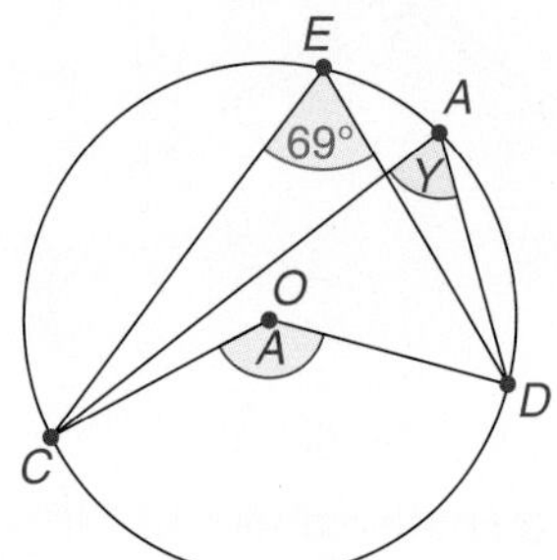

3.

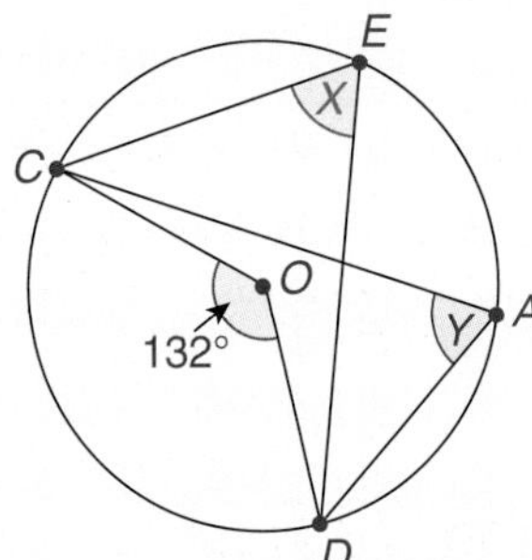

4.

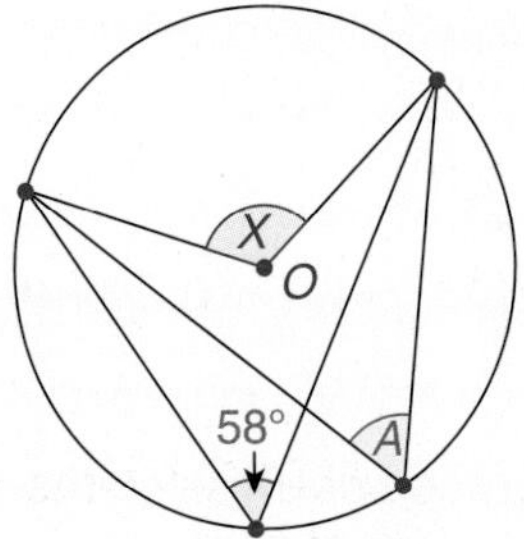

5.

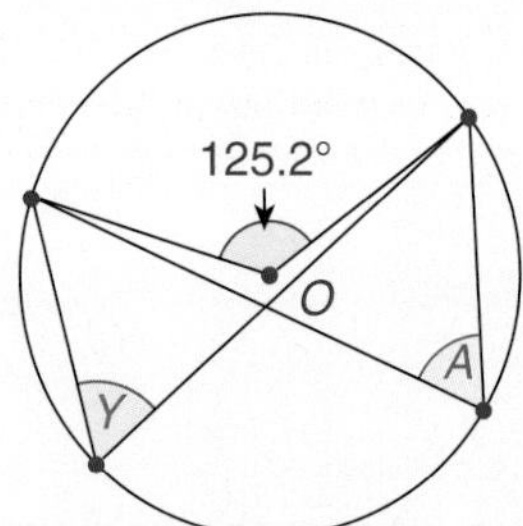

6.

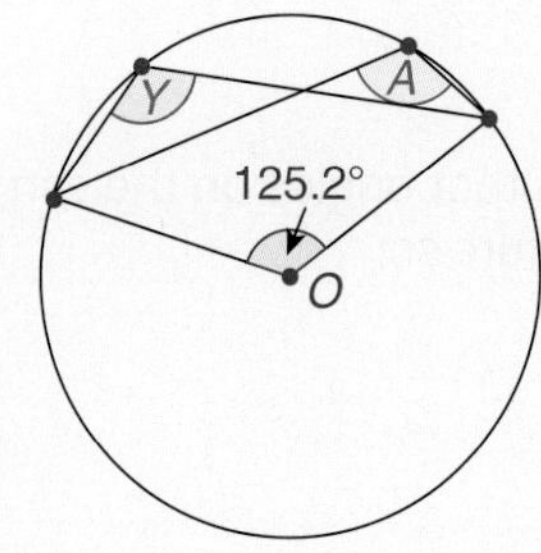

7.

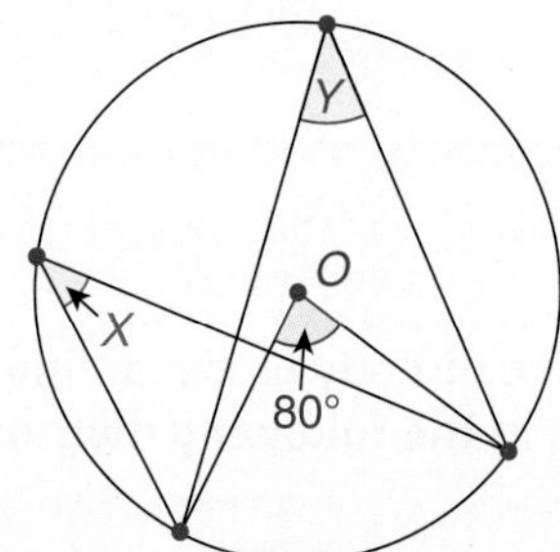

8.

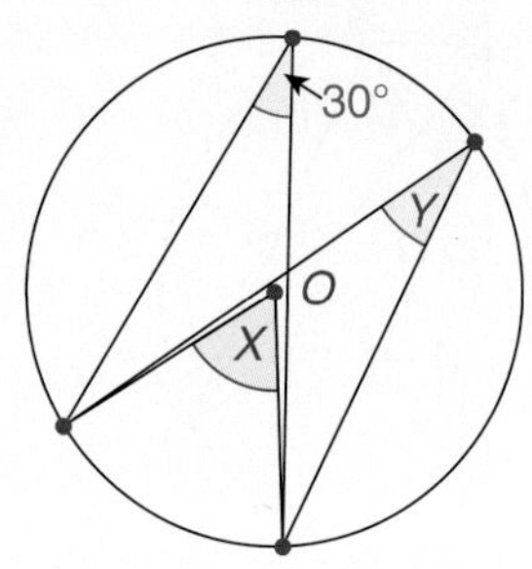

9.

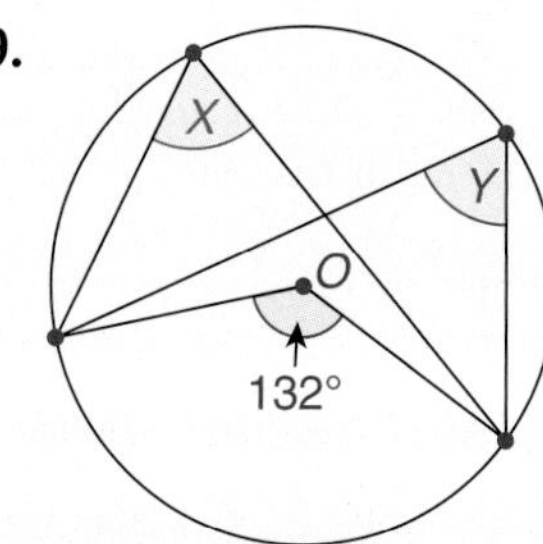

10.

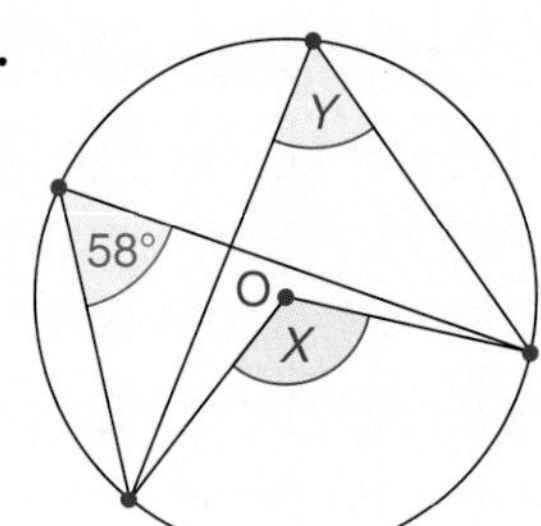

11.

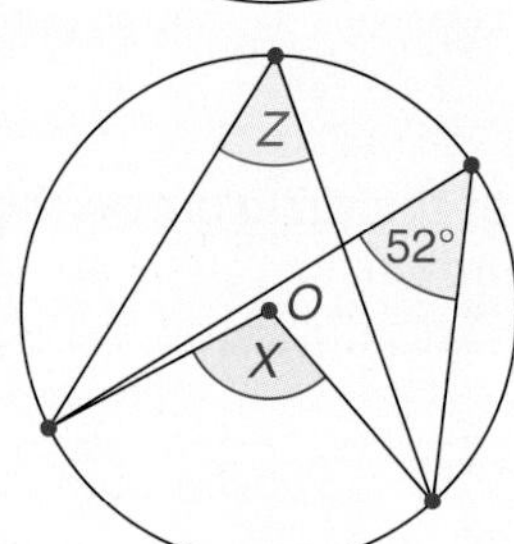

12.

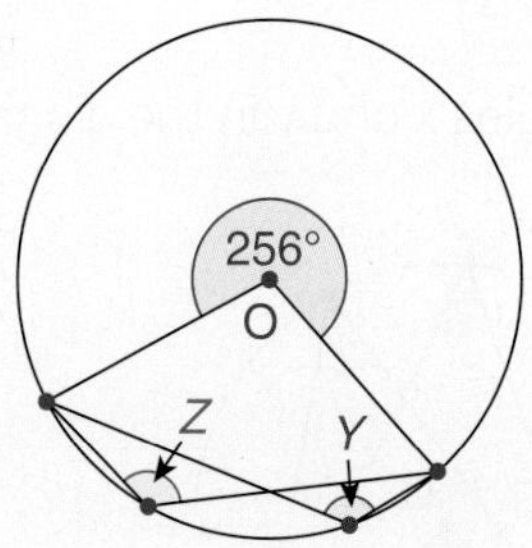

Section 14.5: Cyclic quadrilaterals

Student Activity 14E

1. Explain what a quadrilateral is.
2. The diagram shows a cyclic quadrilateral CDBE inscribed in a circle with centre *O*. Using what you have learned in the previous section, answer the questions that follow.

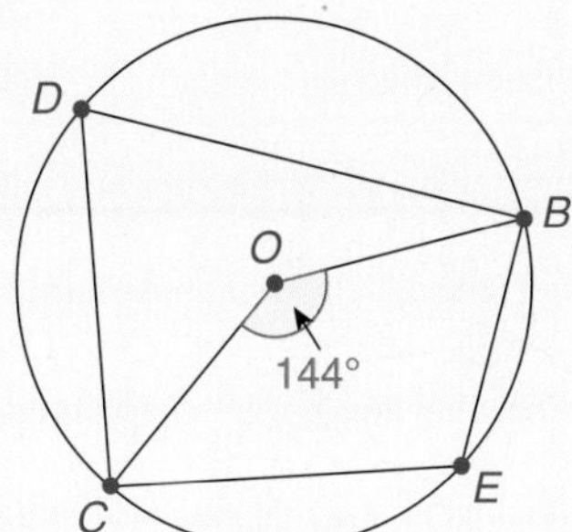

Find:
(a) $|\angle CDB|$
(b) $|\angle COB|$ (reflex angle)
(c) Hence, find $|\angle CEB|$.
(d) $|\angle CDB| + |\angle CEB|$
(e) What would $|\angle ECD| + |\angle EBD|$ equal? Explain your answer.
(f) Measure all of the angles of the quadrilateral *CDBE*. What do you notice?

3. The diagram shows a cyclic quadrilateral *BECD* inscribed in a circle with centre *O*.

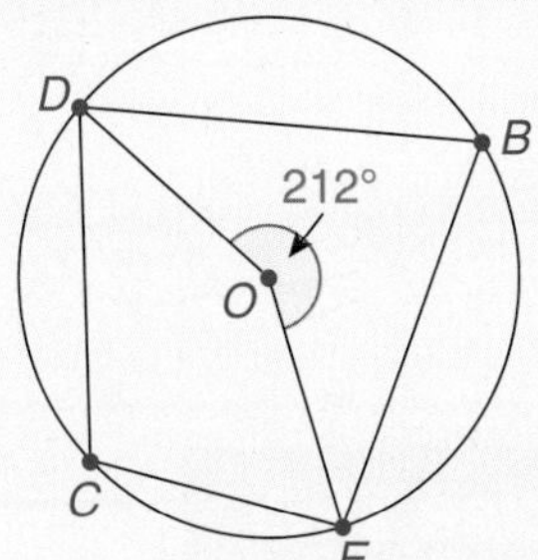

Find:
(a) $|\angle ECD|$
(b) $|\angle DOE|$ (obtuse angle)
(c) Hence, find $|\angle EBD|$.
(d) $|\angle ECD| + |\angle EBD|$
(e) What would $|\angle CDB| + |\angle CEB|$ equal? Explain your answer.
(f) Measure all the angles of the quadrilateral *CEBD*. What do you notice?

4. Copy and complete the following sentence:
In a cyclic ______________,
o ________ angles add up to ___°

CYCLIC QUADRILATERALS EXPLAINED

A quadrilateral is a four-sided figure, where all of the angles add up to a total of 360°. A cyclic quadrilateral is a four-sided figure where all four vertices touch a circle's circumference.

A **cyclic quadrilateral** is a four-sided figure where all four vertices touch a circle's circumference.

In Student Activity 14E, you discovered another corollary .

Corollary 5

If *ABCD* is a cyclic quadrilateral, then its opposite angles sum to 180°.

The converse of this is also true:

Converse

If the opposite angles in a quadrilateral inscribed in a circle sum to 180°, then the quadrilateral is a cyclic quadrilateral.

EXAMPLE 4

Find the missing angles X and Y in the diagram below.

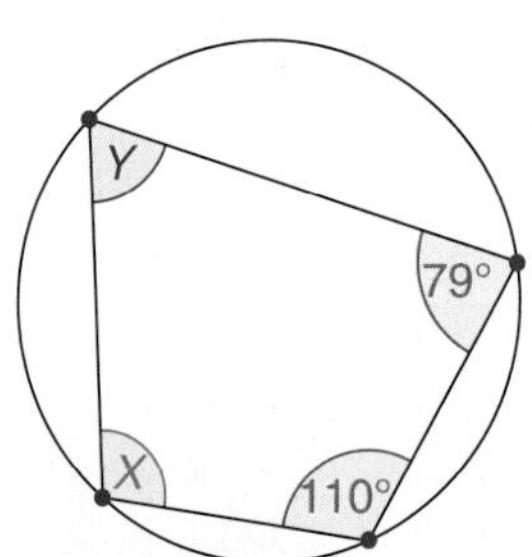

Solution

From corollary 5, we know that opposite angles sum to 180°.

$\therefore Y = 180° - 110° = 70°$

$X = 180° - 79° = 101°$

Exercise 14.5

Find all the missing angles in each of the following diagrams:

1.

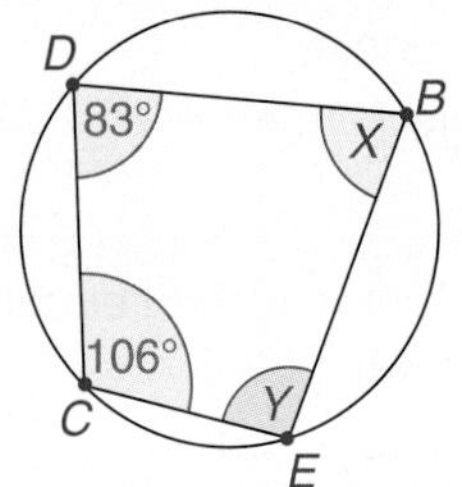

2.

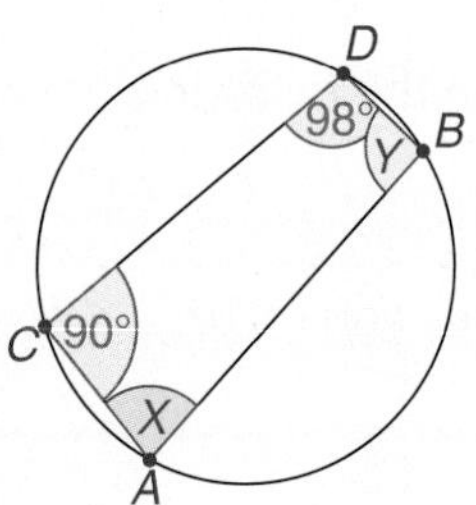

3.

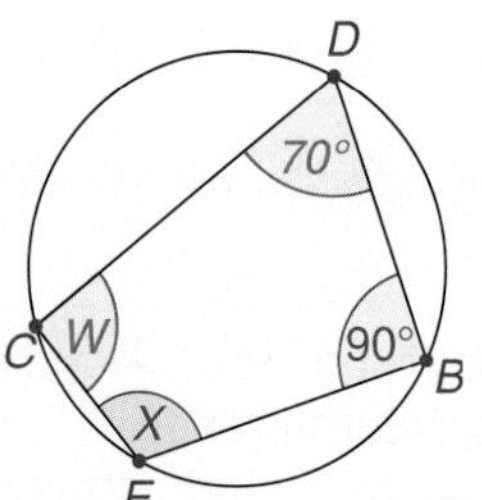

4.

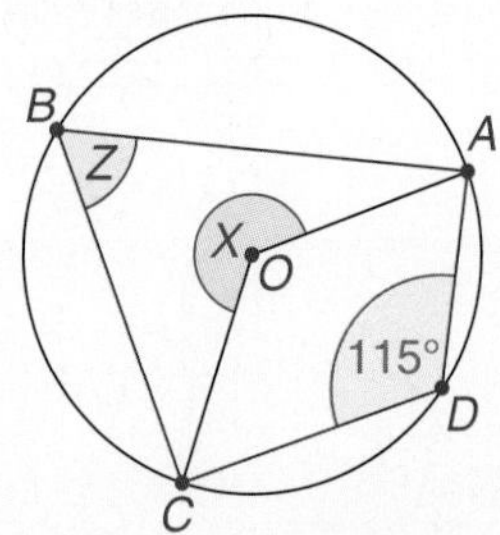

5.

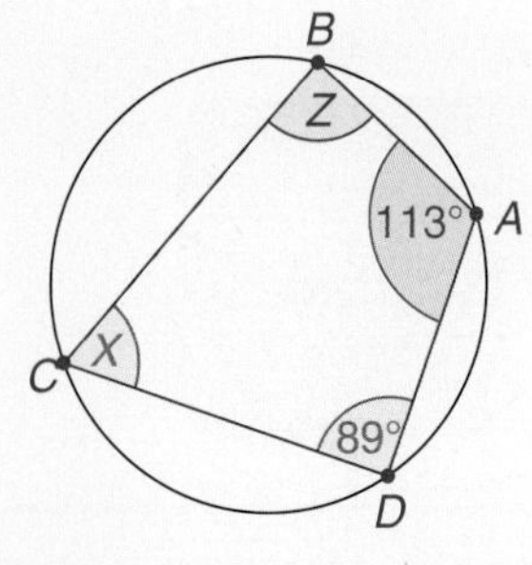

6.

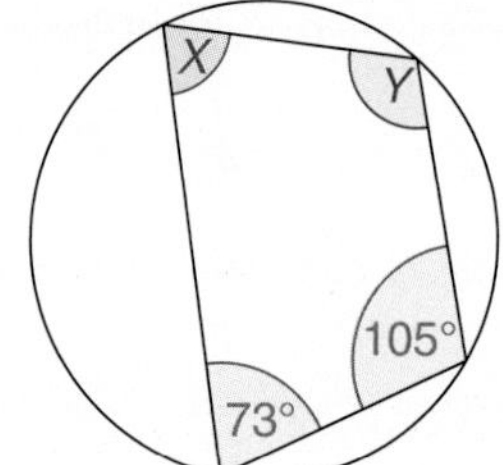

7.

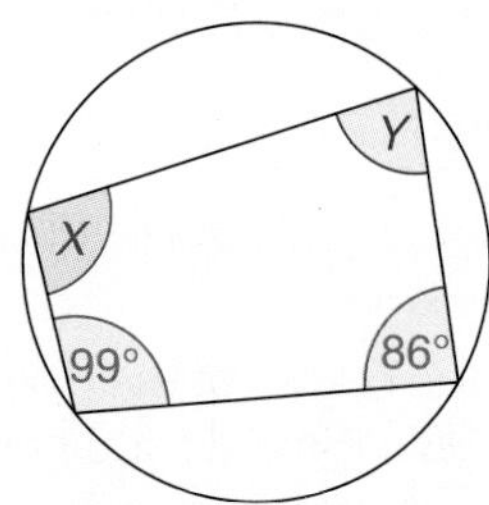

8.

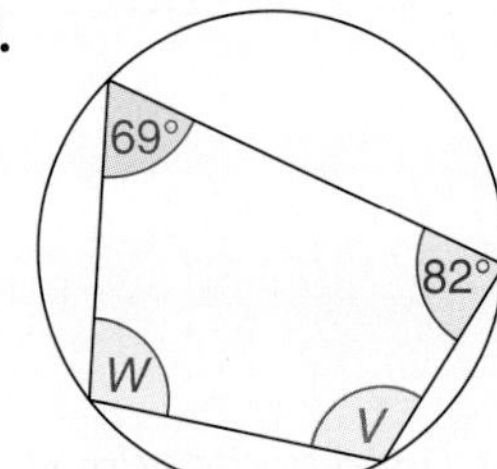

9.

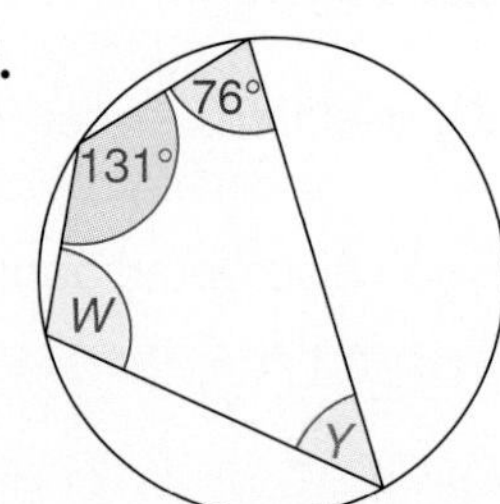

10.

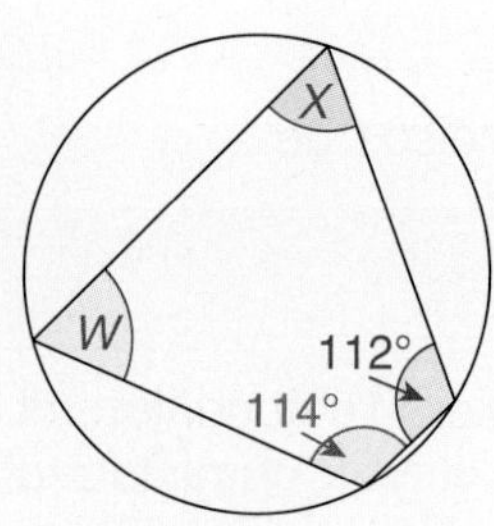

11.

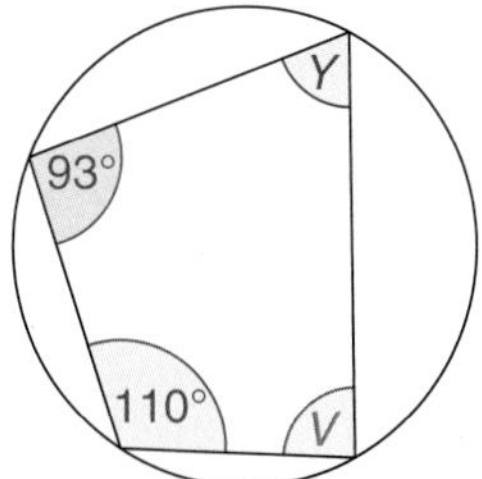

12.

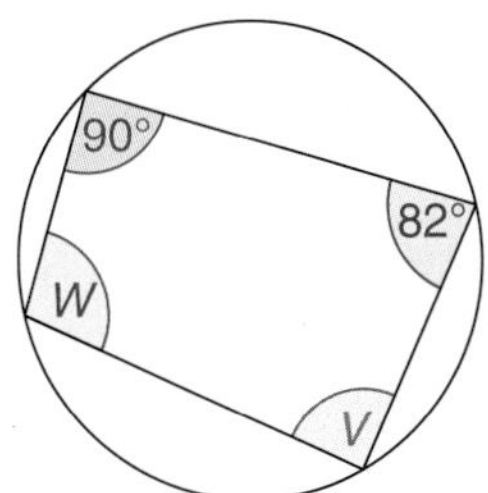

13.

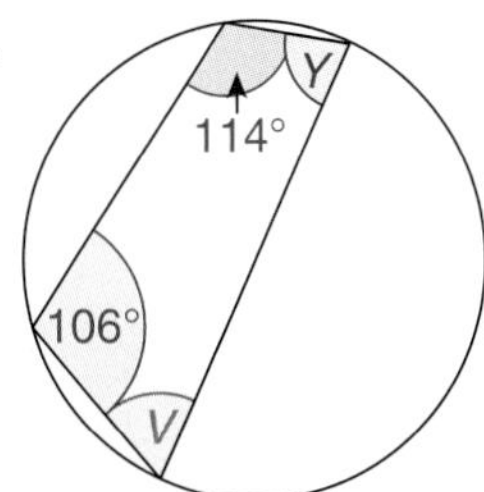

14.

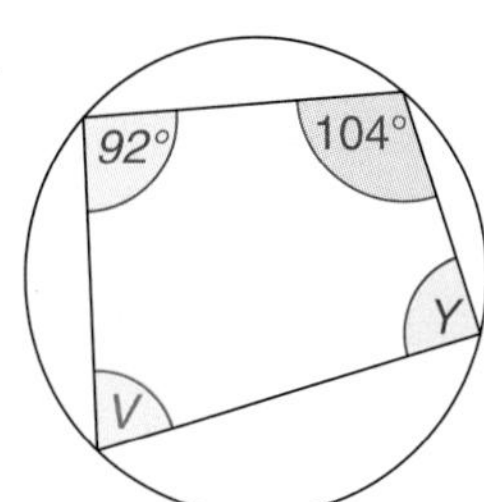

CHAPTER 14 SELF-CHECK TEST

1. Using words and a diagram, explain each of the following terms:

(a) Tangent

(b) Arc

(c) Sector

2. Explain in three sentences three facts about angles in the centre of a circle. Use diagrams to support your answers.

3. (a) What is a corollary?

(b) Give two examples.

4. (a) What is a quadrilateral?

(b) What is a cyclic quadrilateral?

(c) Clearly explain whether or not each of the following are cyclic quadrilaterals.

(i)

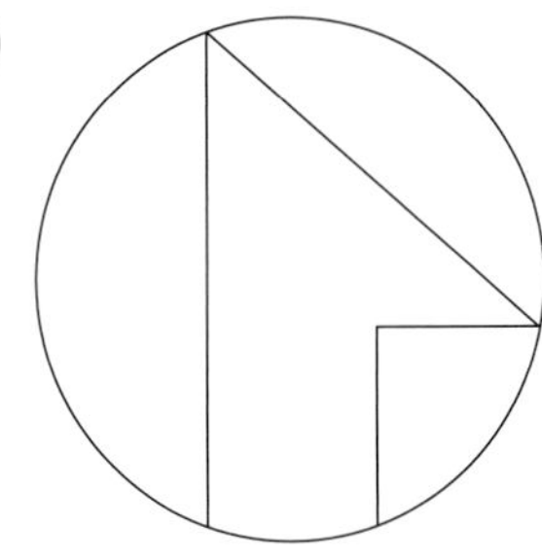

(ii)

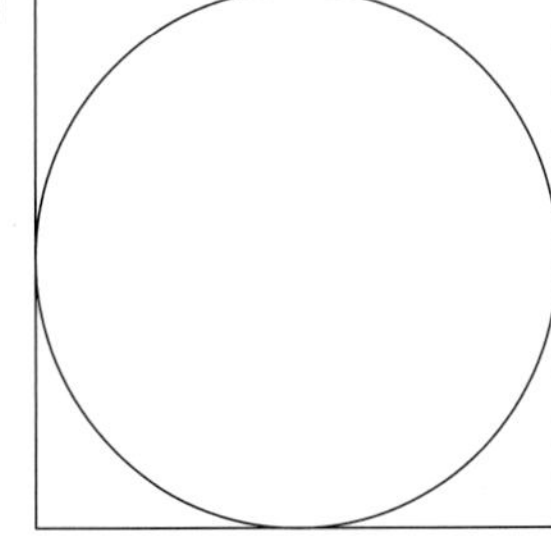

(iii)

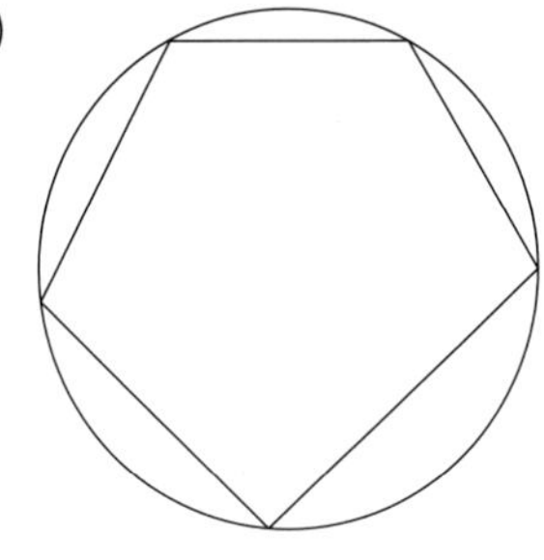

(iv)

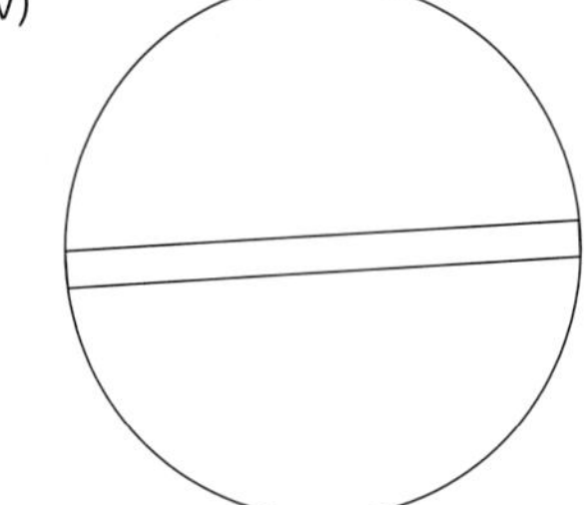

(v)

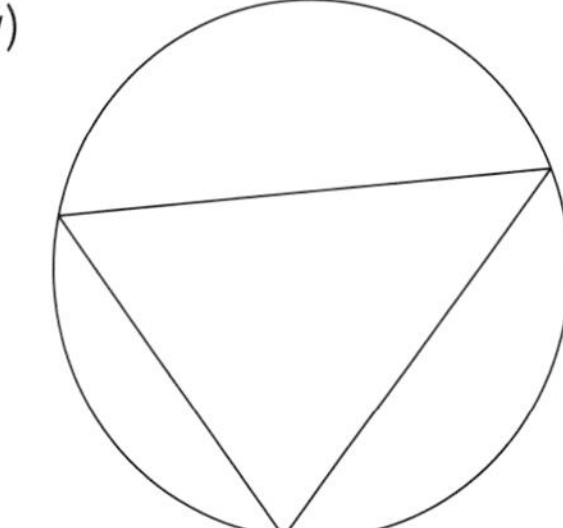

(vi)

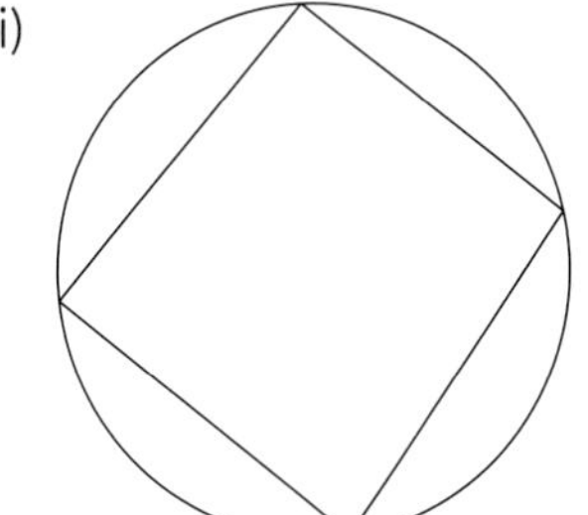

5. Find the value of the letter(s) in each of the following circles:

(a)

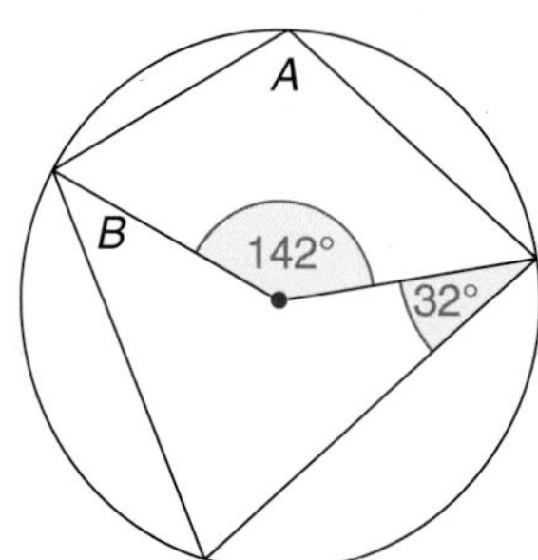

(b)

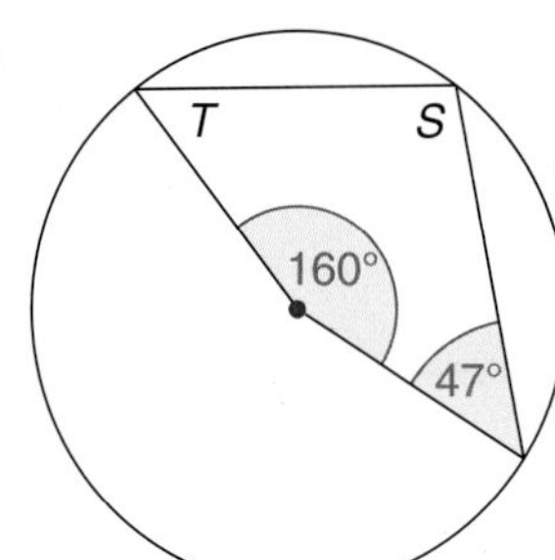

(c)

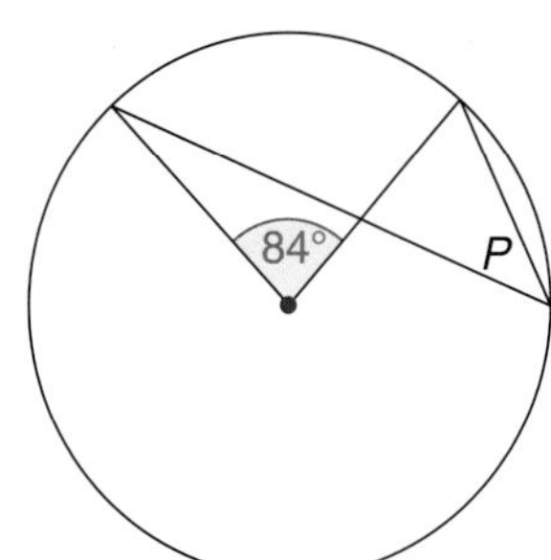

(d)

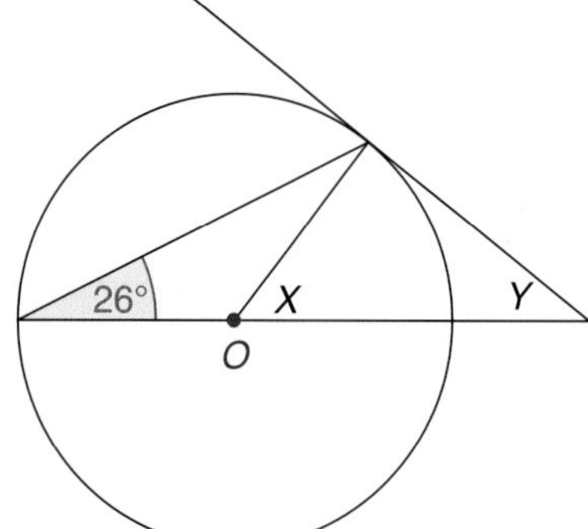

(e)

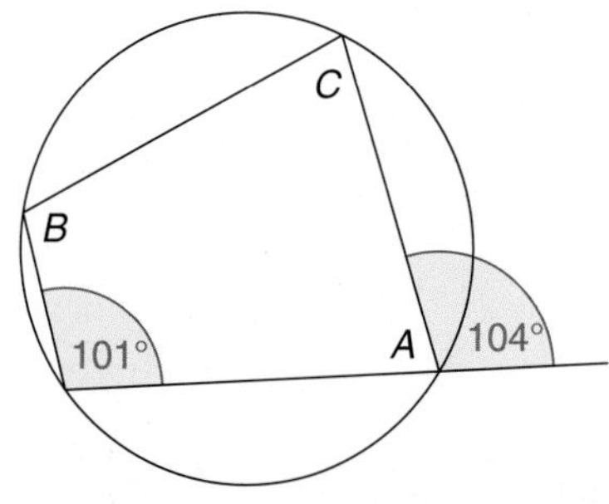

(f)

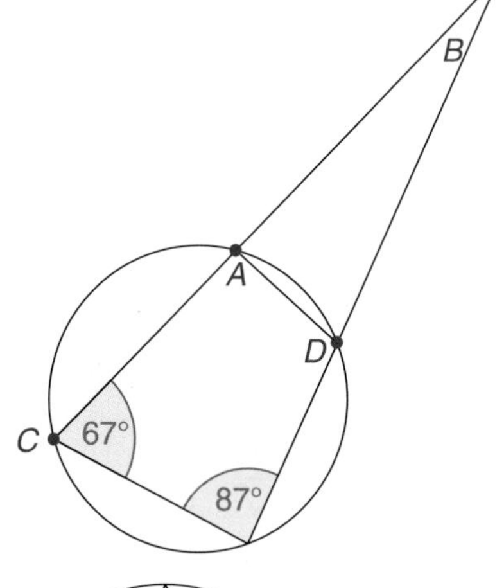

(g)

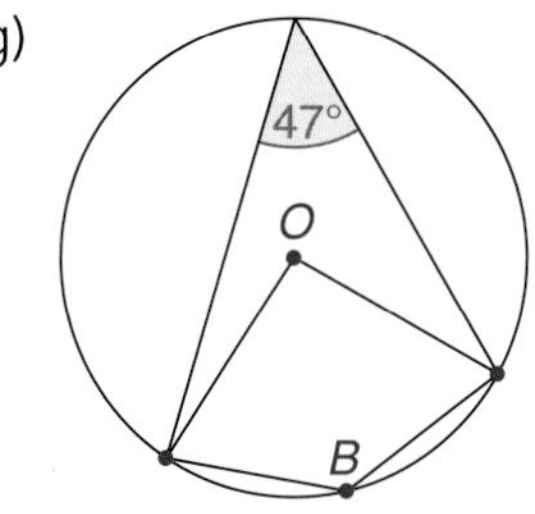

6. A, D, B and C are points on a circle with centre O. Given $|\angle ACB| = 60°$ and $|AD| = |DB|$, find:

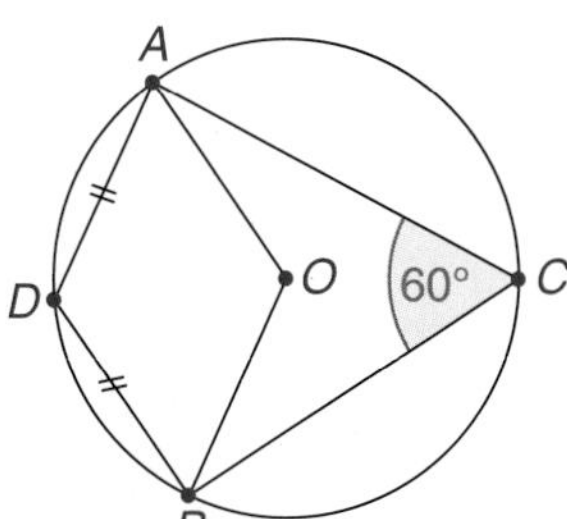

(a) $|\angle AOB|$ (b) $|\angle ADB|$

(c) By joining A to B, find $|\angle OAB|$.

7. Find the value of the angles marked A, B, C, D and E in the diagram below.

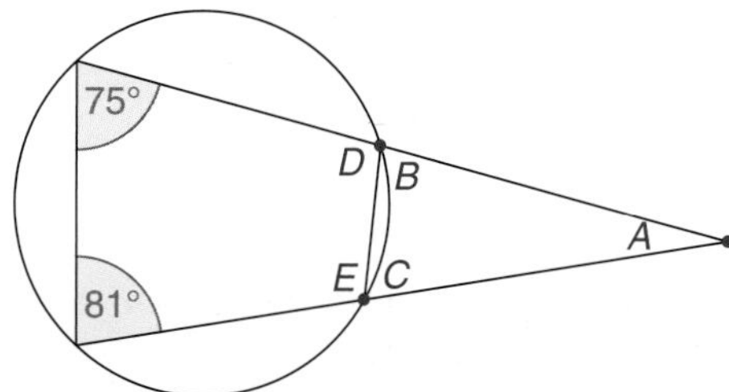

8. The point O is the centre of the circle. Find the values of the angles X and Y in the diagram.

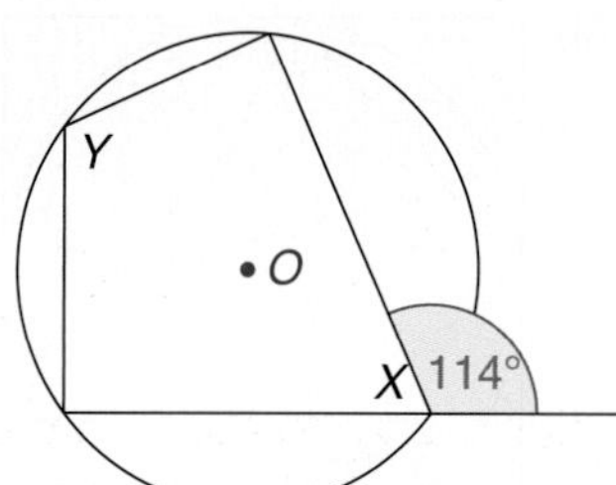

9. *A*, *D*, *B* and *C* are points on a circle as shown. [*AB*] is a diameter of the circle.

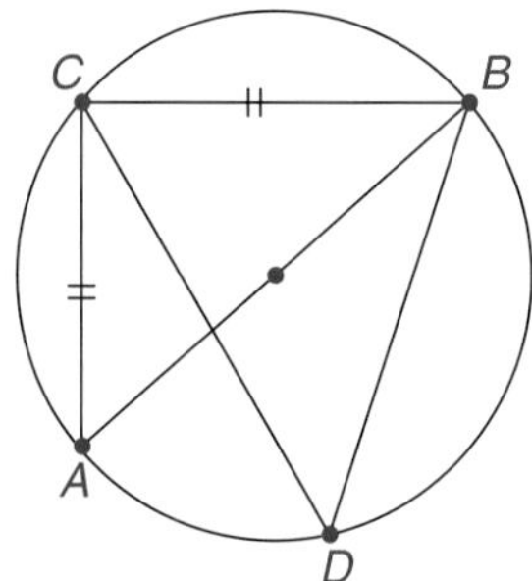

$|AB| = 12$ cm and $|AC| = |CB|$.

(a) Write down $|\angle BCA|$, giving a reason for your answer.

(b) Find $|\angle CDB|$.

(c) Find $|BC|$.

(d) Find the area of the ΔABC.

10. Examine the following diagram and find (a) $|\angle A|$ and (b) $|\angle B|$.

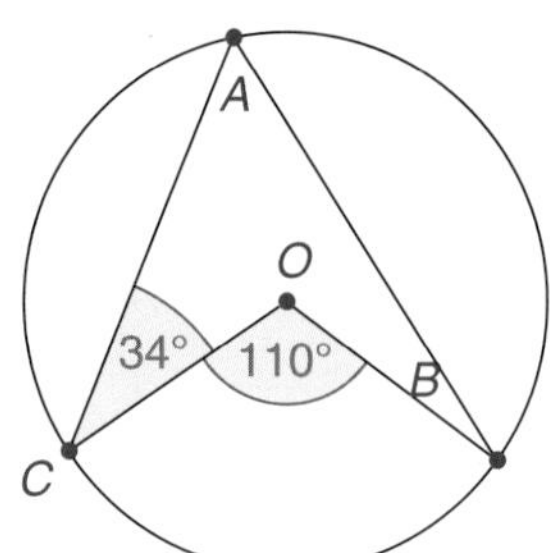

11. If $|\angle ABD| = |\angle DBC|$ and $|\angle ADB| = |\angle BDC|$, show that $|\angle BCD|$ is a right angle.

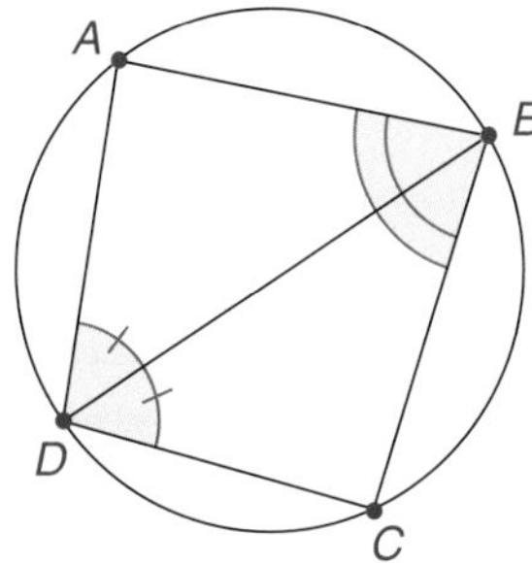

12. The chords [*WY*] and [*XZ*] intersect at the point *O*.

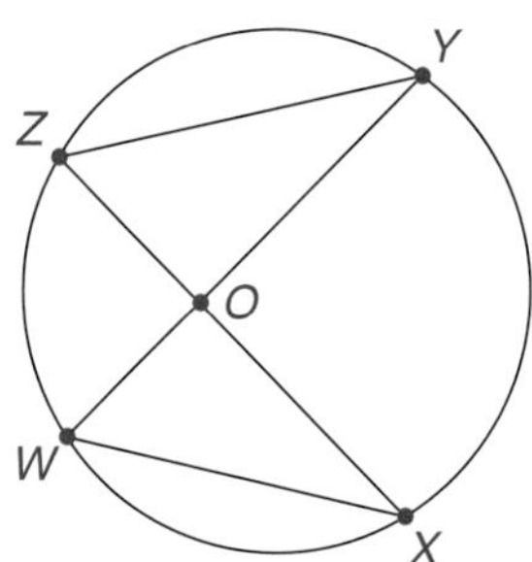

Show that ΔWXO and ΔZOY are similar triangles.

13. *O* is the centre of the given circle. Show that $|\angle ABO| + |\angle OCB| = 90°$.

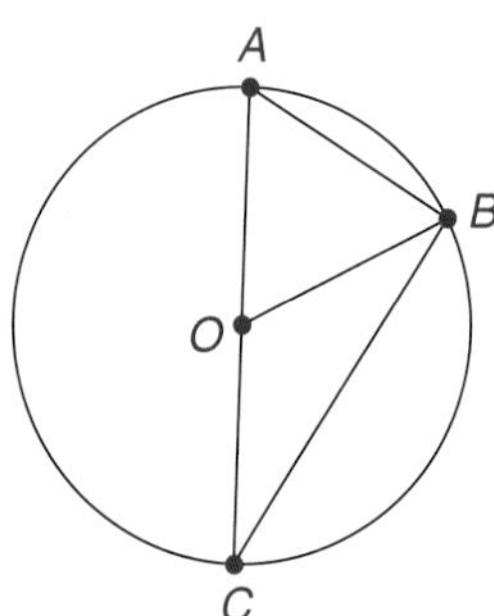

14. *A*, *B*, *C* and *D* are points on the circle as shown. $|\angle ABD| = 37°$ and $|\angle ADB| = 53°$.

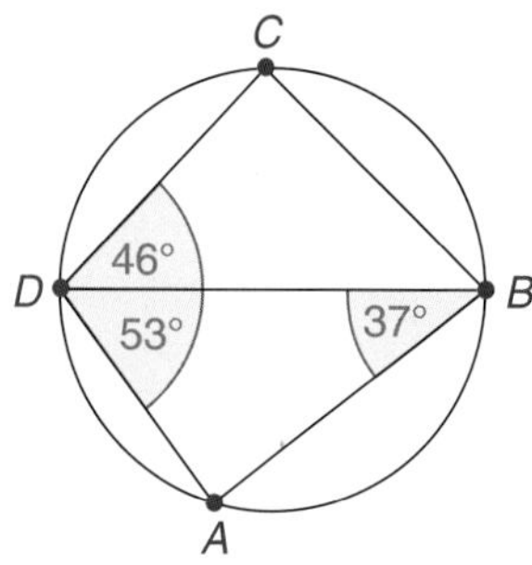

(a) Explain why [*BD*] is a diameter of the circle.

(b) Given that $|\angle BDC| = 46°$, find $|\angle CBD|$.

15. *A*, *B*, *C*, *D* and *E* are points on a circle and $|\angle BDE| = 108°$.

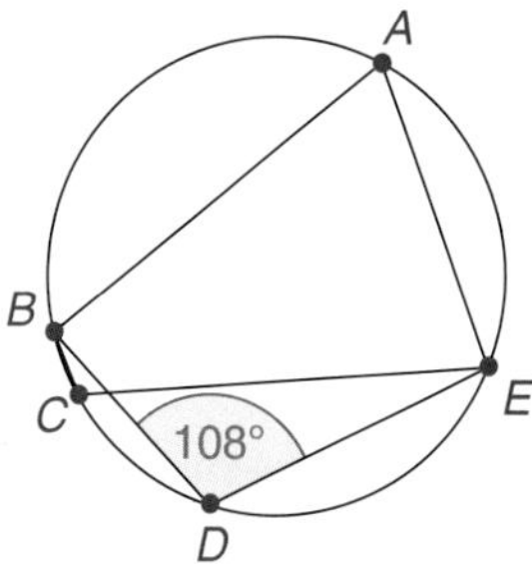

Find, giving a reason for your answer:

(a) $|\angle BAE|$ (b) $|\angle BCE|$

16. [*BD*] is a diameter of the circle. *C* is the centre of the circle and $|BA| = |AD|$.

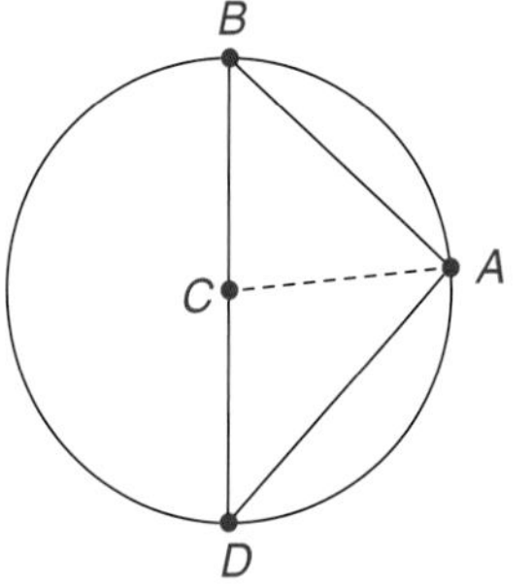

Find, giving reasons for your answer:

(a) $|\angle ADB|$ (b) $|\angle DAC|$

17. [AB] is the diameter of a circle with centre O. $|\angle OCB| = 50°$.

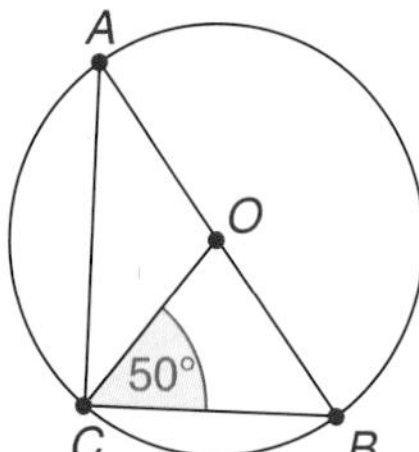

Find:

(a) $|\angle BOC|$ (b) $|\angle BAC|$

18. $ABCD$ is a cyclic quadrilateral. Given that $|\angle DAB| = 73°$ and $|\angle ABC| = 84°$, find:

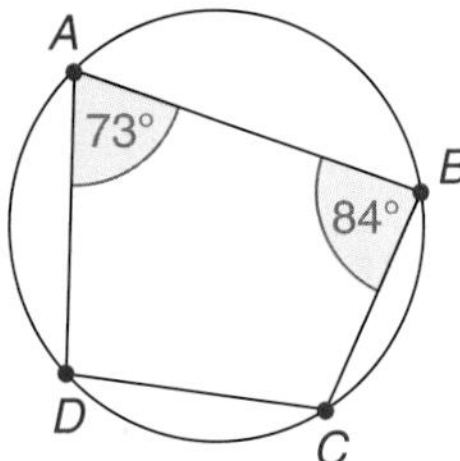

(a) $|\angle ADC|$ (b) $|\angle BCD|$

19. t is a tangent to the circle and O is the centre of the circle. $|\angle XYW| = 40°$.

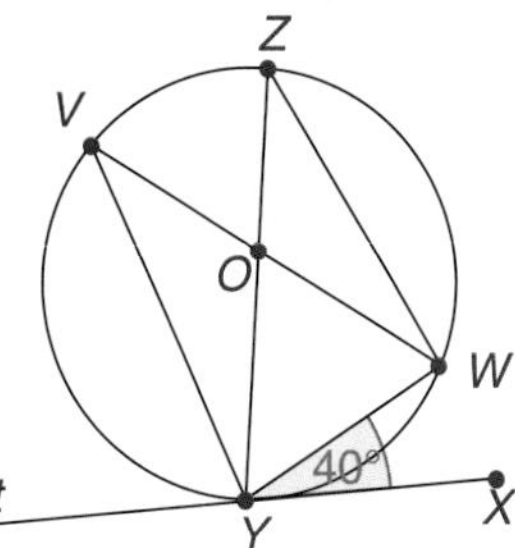

(a) Find $|\angle WVY|$.

(b) Using congruent triangles or otherwise, show $|ZW| = |VY|$.

20. [AB] and [CD] are chords of the circle shown and $|AB| = |CD|$. The chords [AD] and [BC] intersect at the point E.

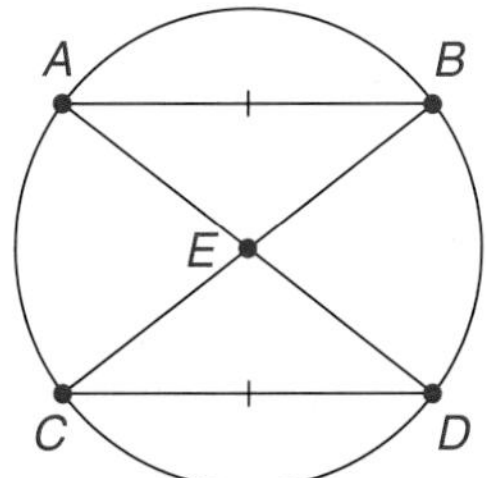

(a) State why $|\angle BAD| = |\angle BCD|$.

(b) Show that the ΔBAE and ΔDCE are congruent.

(c) Show that $|AD| = |BC|$.

21. $ABCD$ is a parallelogram. A, B, Y and D are points on the circle and $|\angle ABY| = 50°$.

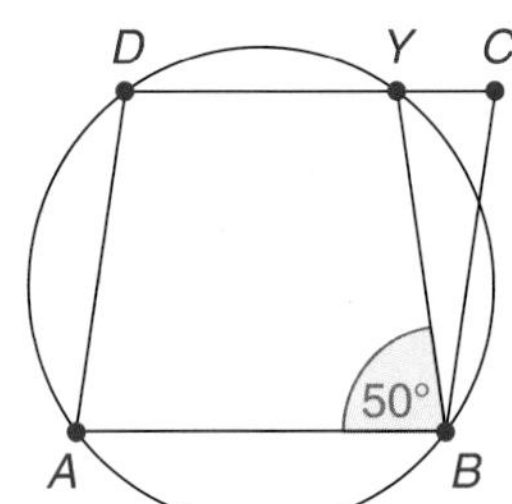

Find:

(a) $|\angle ADY|$

(b) $|\angle ABC|$

(c) $|\angle DYB|$

(d) Show $|BY| = |BC|$.

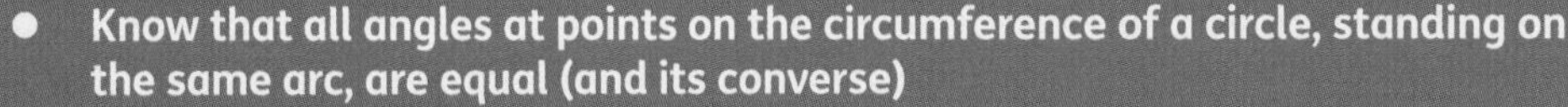

After completing this chapter, I now:

- **Know and understand the terms diameter, radius, arc, sector, circumference, chord and tangent**
- **Know that all angles at points on the circumference of a circle, standing on the same arc, are equal (and its converse)**
- **Know that if the angle standing on a chord at some point on the circle is 90°, then the chord is a diameter**
- **Know that the angle at the centre of a circle is twice the angle at the circumference of the circle, both angles standing on the same arc**
- **Know that opposite angles in a cyclic quadrilateral sum to 180° (and its converse)**

SETS

LEARNING OUTCOMES

In this chapter you will learn:

✓ **To draw Venn diagrams for three sets**

✓ **To carry out intersection, union, set difference and set complement for three sets**

✓ **How to show the associative, distributive and commutative properties of union and intersection**

✓ **How to show that set difference is neither commutative nor associative**

✓ **How to use Venn diagrams to solve for a missing piece of information**

KEY WORDS

- **Associative**
- **Cardinal number**
- **Commutative**
- **Complement**
- **Distributive**
- **Intersection**
- **Set difference**
- **Subset**
- **Union**
- **Universal set**

15 INTRODUCTION

In *Maths in Action 1*, you learned about sets, the symbols used for sets and how to represent two sets on a Venn diagram.

In this chapter, you will look at some of that material again and expand your understanding by using three sets.

First year revision

1. What is a set?
2. Give the meaning of each of the following symbols used in sets:
   (a) $\cup$ (d) $\subset$ (g) $'$
   (b) $\cap$ (e) $\notin$ (h) $\{\}$ or $\emptyset$
   (c) $\in$ (f) #
3. Write out the elements of each of the following sets:
   (a) A = {months of the year beginning with the letter J}
   (b) B = $\{x|x$ is a factor of 12$\}$
   (c) C = {prime numbers between 1 and 20}
4. If A = {the factors of 20} and B = {the factors of 16}:
   (a) Write out the elements of the sets A and B.
   (b) Draw a Venn diagram to represent the sets A and B.
   (c) From your Venn diagram, identify the highest common factor of 16 and 20.
5. For each of the following, draw a Venn diagram of the sets A and B overlapping contained in the universal set U and shade in the area indicated.
   (a) $A \cup B$ (e) A'
   (b) $A \cap B$ (f) B'
   (c) $A \setminus B$ (g) $(A \cup B)'$
   (d) $B \setminus A$ (h) $(A \cap B)'$
6. A is the set of prime numbers less than 13.
   (a) List the elements of the set A.
   B = {1, 3, 5, 7, 9, 11}.
   (b) Write down the elements of the set $B \setminus A$.
7. A leisure centre has 110 members. The weights room (W) is used by 82 members. The swimming pool (S) is used by 57 members. 15 members do not use either facility.
   Draw a suitable Venn diagram to show the above information.
8. 24 students are asked whether they own a cat or a dog. 5 own a dog, 13 own a cat and 7 own neither.
   (a) Represent this information on a Venn diagram.
   How many students:
   (b) Own a cat only?
   (c) Own a dog only?
   (d) Own both a cat and a dog?

Section 15.1: Venn diagrams with three sets

Student Activity 15A

Consider the following objects:

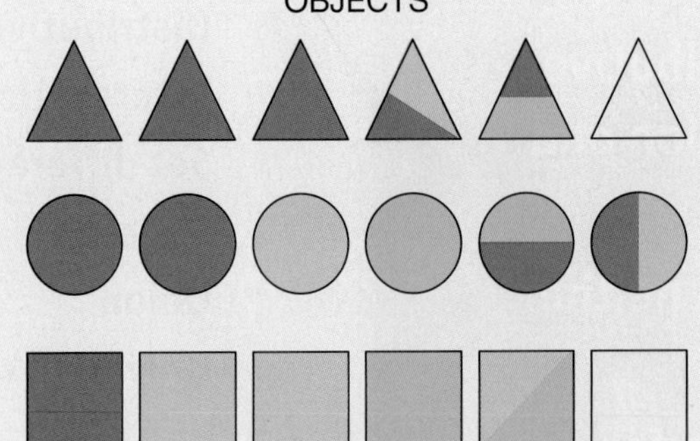

(a) Draw the following Venn diagram.

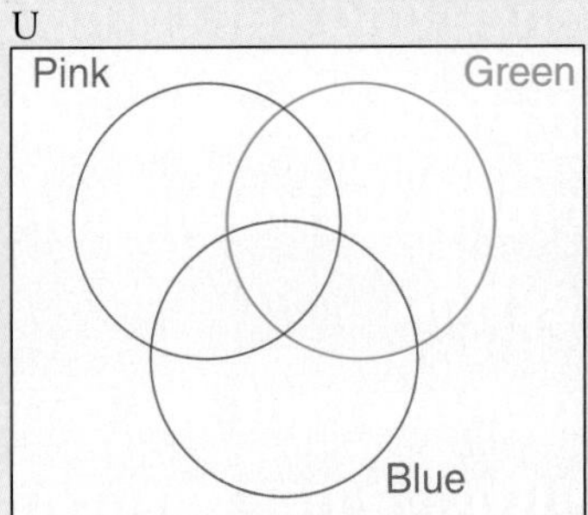

(b) Place each object into the relevant part of the Venn diagram. Explain each of your choices.

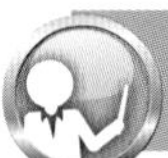

VENN DIAGRAMS WITH THREE SETS EXPLAINED

In *Maths in Action 1*, you learned that a set is a collection of clearly defined objects called **elements.** Any set can be displayed in a Venn diagram and can be written in shorthand notation.

In Higher Level maths, you must also be able to work with three sets. The Venn diagram shows the different areas of a Venn diagram with three sets.

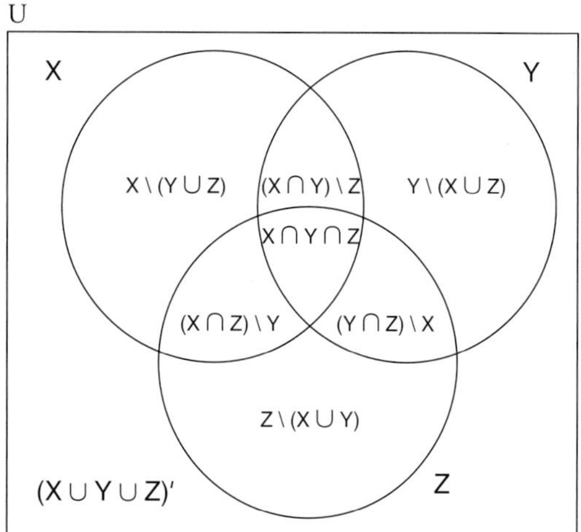

EXAMPLE 1

50 people were asked which sports they played. The results are shown in the Venn diagram.

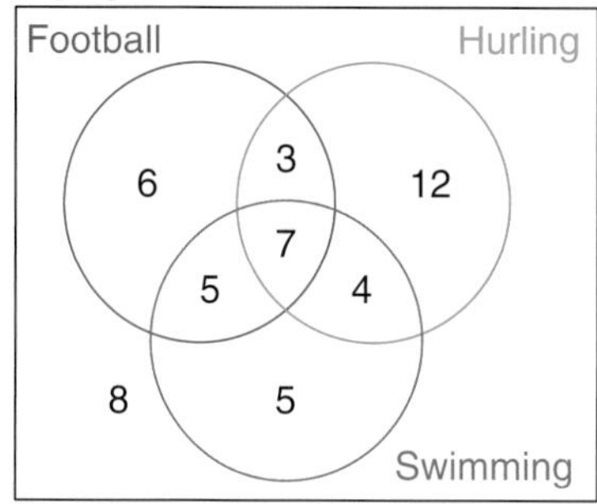

How many people take part in:

(a) Football?
(b) Hurling?
(c) Swimming?
(d) All three sports?
(e) Football and swimming?
(f) Hurling and swimming?
(g) Swimming only?
(h) Exactly two sports?
(i) None of the sports?
(j) Swimming and hurling but not football?

Solution

(a) Football: $6 + 3 + 7 + 5 = 21$
(b) Hurling: $12 + 3 + 7 + 4 = 26$
(c) Swimming: $5 + 5 + 7 + 4 = 21$
(d) 3 sports: 7
(e) Football and swimming: $5 + 7 = 12$
(f) Hurling and swimming: $7 + 4 = 11$
(g) Swimming only: 5
(h) Exactly two sports: $3 + 5 + 4 = 12$
(i) None of the sports: 8
(j) Swimming and hurling but not football: 4

EXAMPLE 2

For each of the following, draw a Venn diagram and shade in the required region:

(a) $A \cap B \cap C$ (c) $(A \cup B) \setminus C$ (e) $(B \cap A) \setminus C$ (g) $(A \cup C) \setminus B$ (i) $(B \cap C) \setminus A$
(b) $A \cup B \cup C$ (d) $(A \cup B \cup C)'$ (f) $(B \cup C) \setminus A$ (h) C' (j) $A \cap C$

Solution

(a)

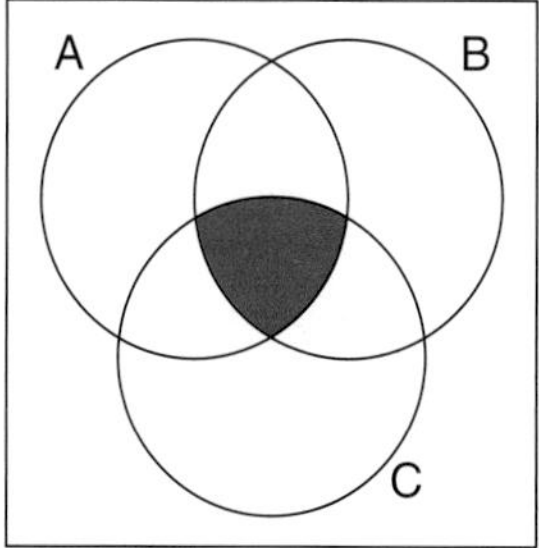

$A \cap B \cap C$

(b)

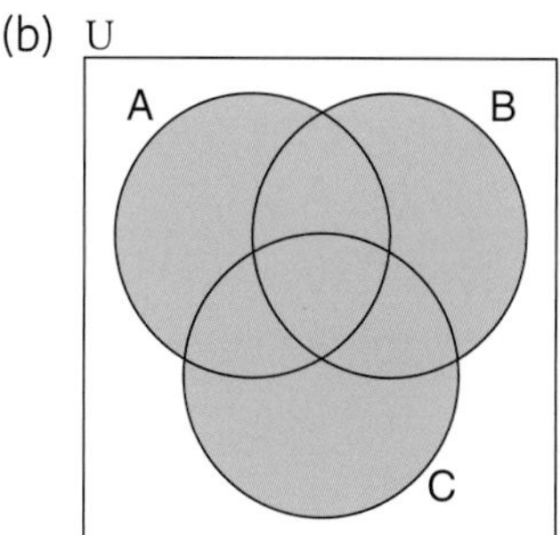

$A \cup B \cup C$

(c) U

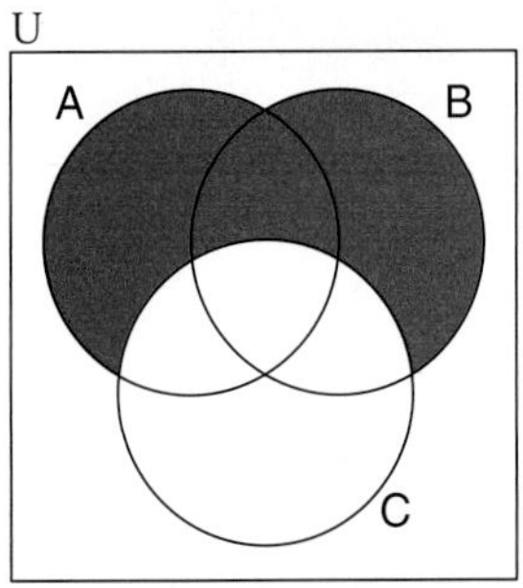

(A ∪ B) \ C

(d) U

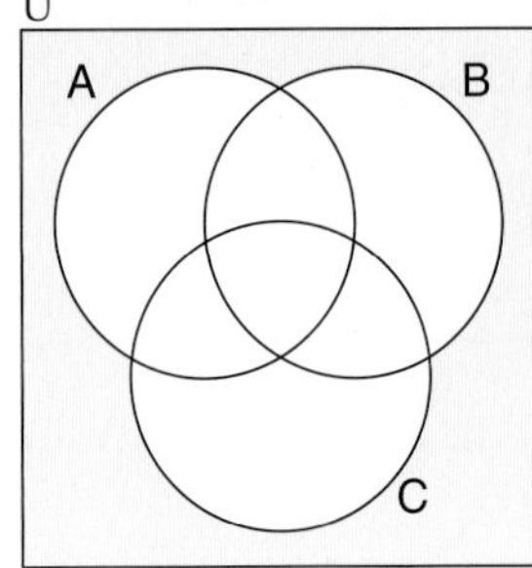

(A ∪ B ∪ C)′

(e) U

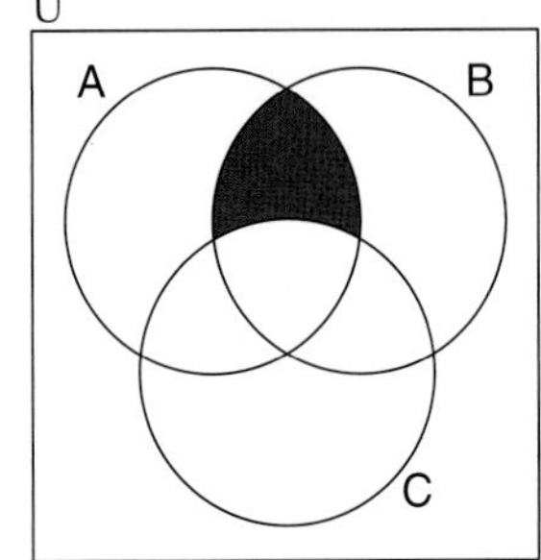

(B ∩ A) \ C

(f) U

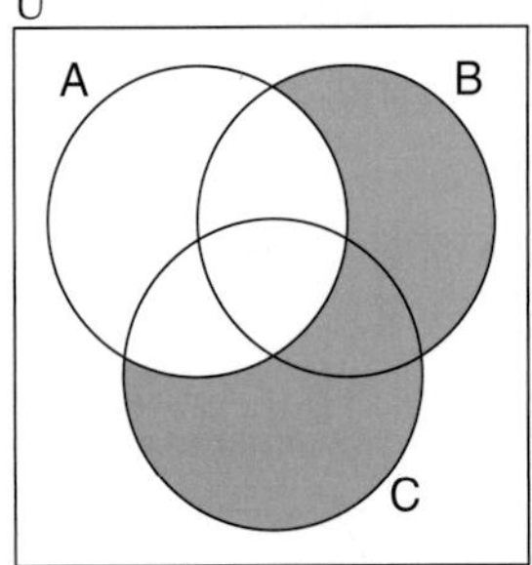

(B ∪ C) \ A

(g) U

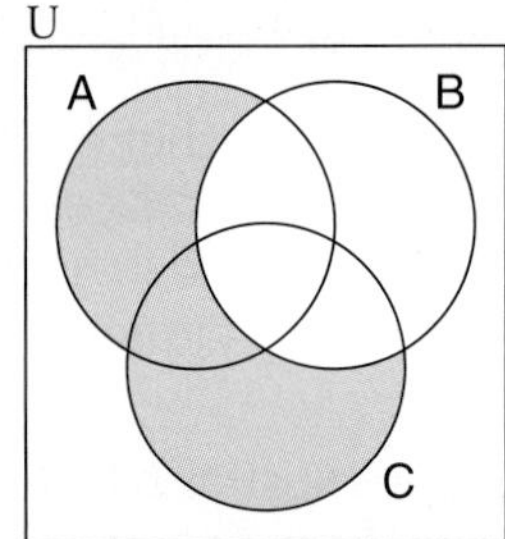

(A ∪ C) \ B

(h) U

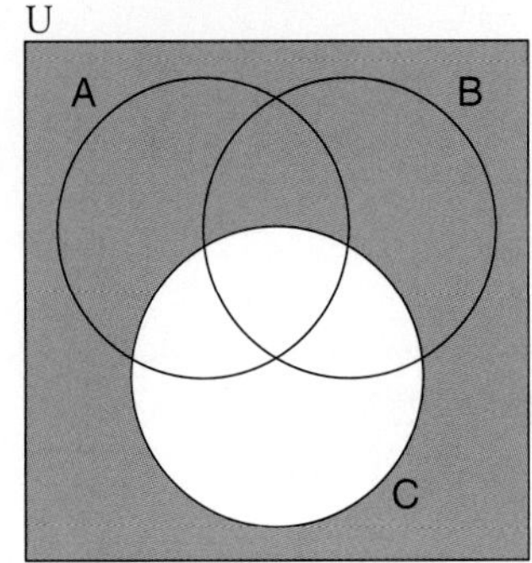

C′

(i) U

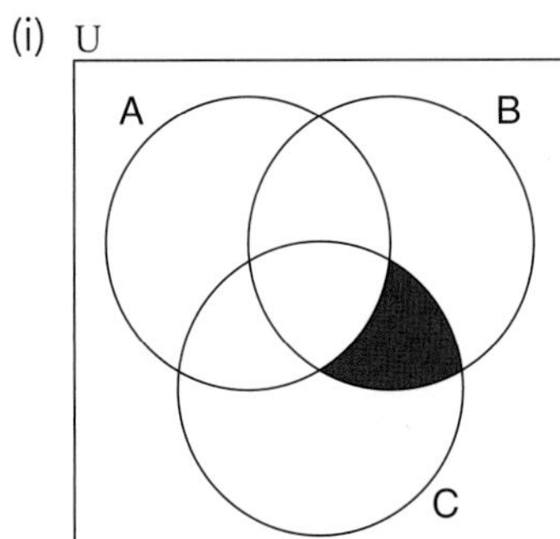

(B ∩ C) \ A

(j) U

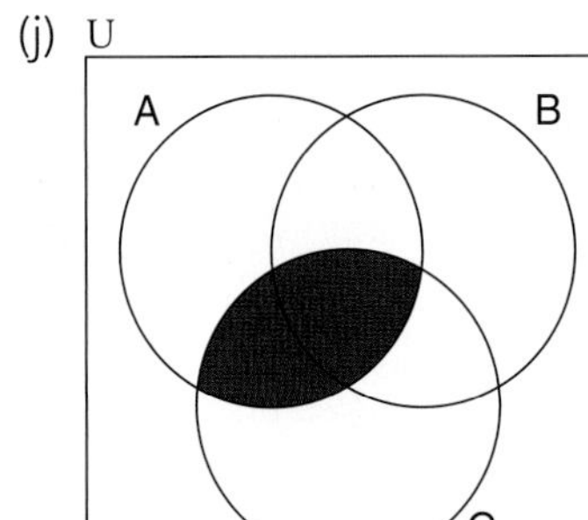

A ∩ C

Exercise 15.1

1. Draw a Venn diagram showing the universal set U and containing three sets A, B and C for each of the following. Shade the area represented:

(a) A ∪ B ∪ C	(e) A ∪ C	(i) A \ (B ∪ C)	(m) (A ∩ B) \ C
(b) A ∪ B	(f) (A ∪ C) \ B	(j) B \ (A ∪ C)	(n) (A ∩ C) \ B
(c) (A ∪ B) \ C	(g) B ∪ C	(k) C \ (A ∪ B)	(o) (B ∩ C) \ A
(d) A ∩ B ∩ C	(h) (B ∪ C) \ A	(l) (A ∪ B ∪ C)′	

2. Name the shaded region in each of the following Venn diagrams:

(a)
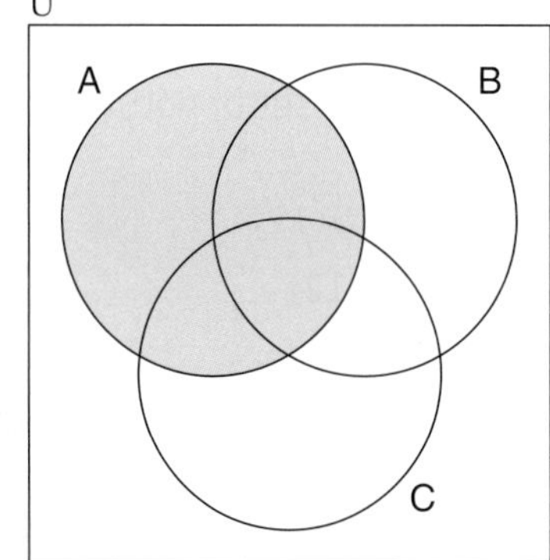

(b)
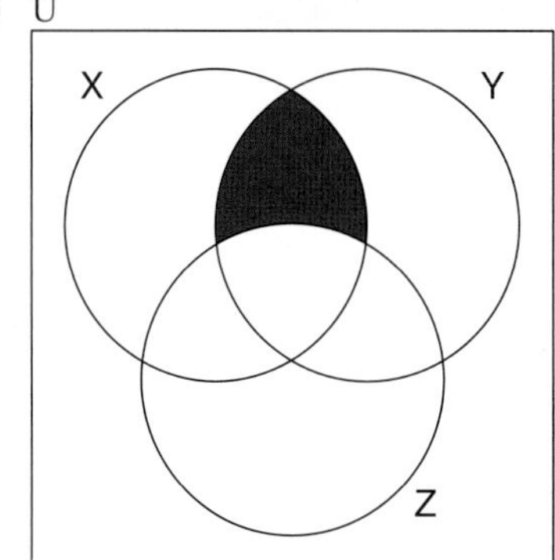

(c)
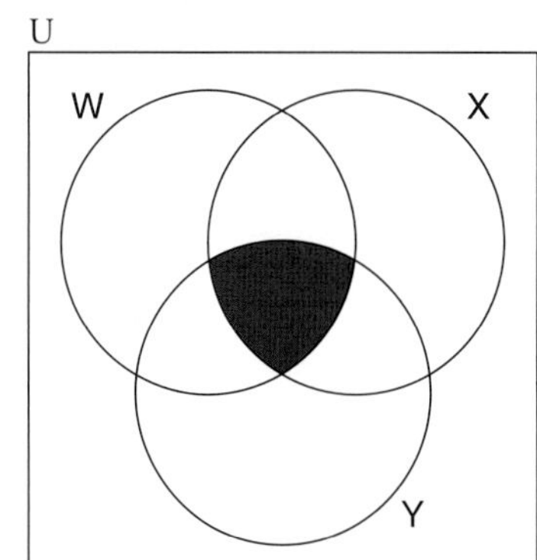

(d)
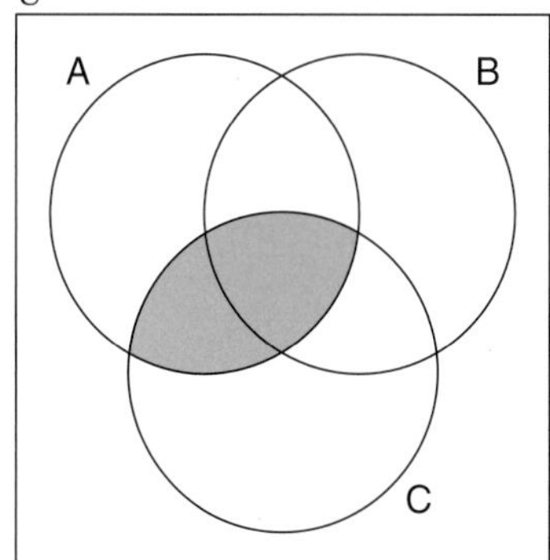

(e)
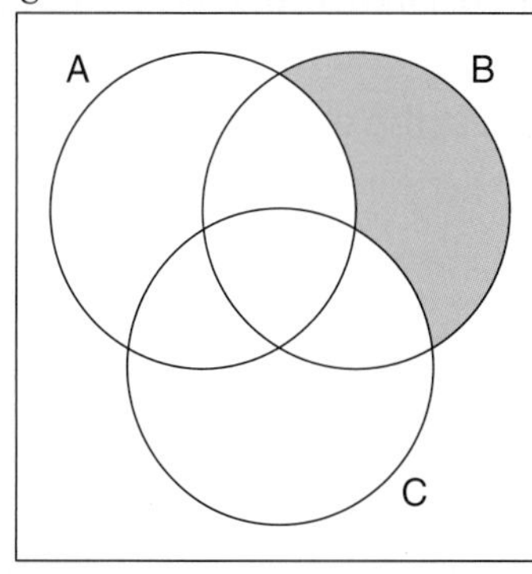

(f)
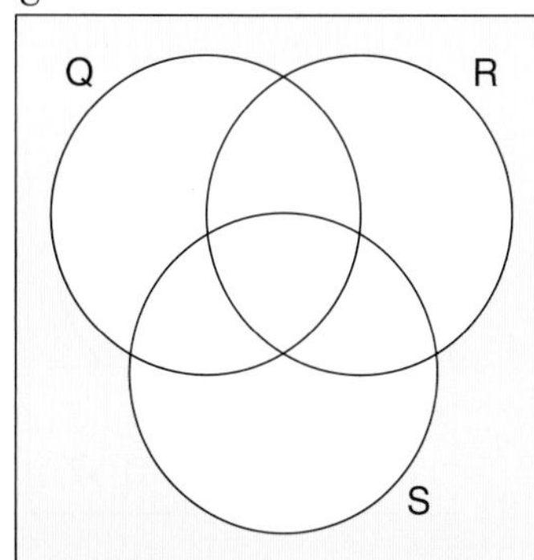

(g)
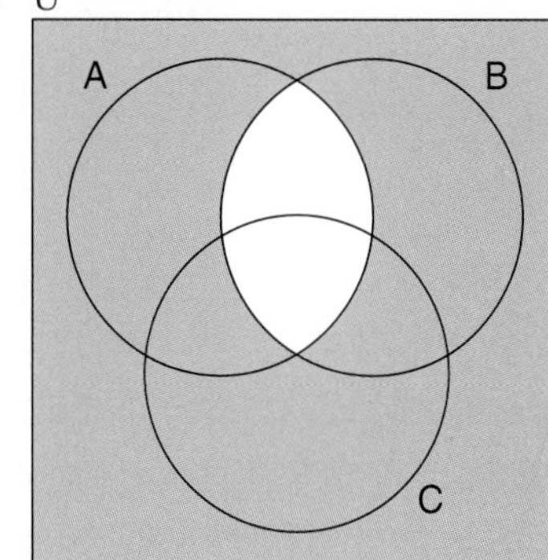

(h)
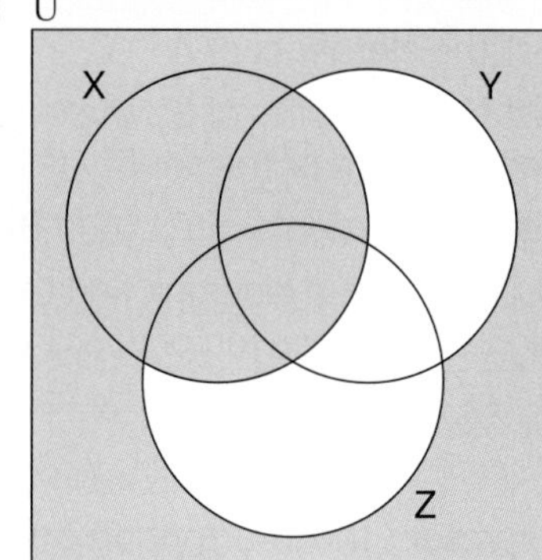

(i)
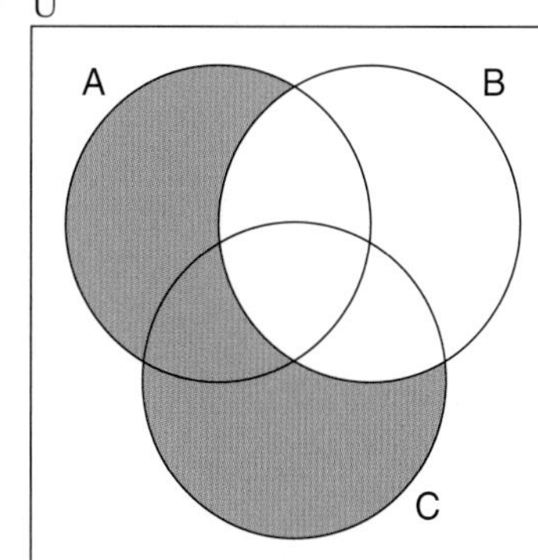

(j)
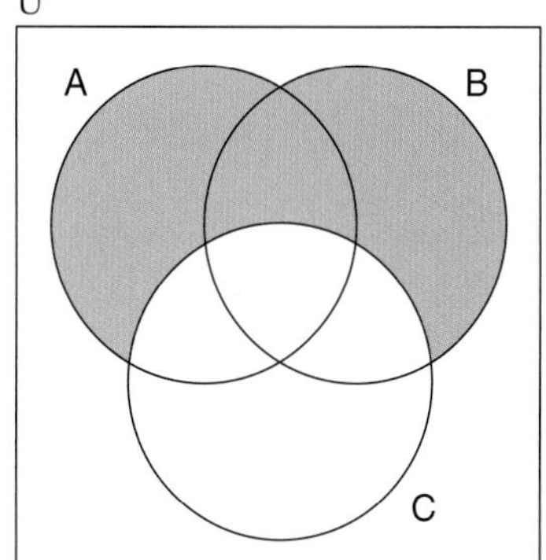

3. U is the universal set, A = {3, 8, 9}, B = {1, 2, 6, 8, 9} and C = {1, 2, 4, 5, 8}.

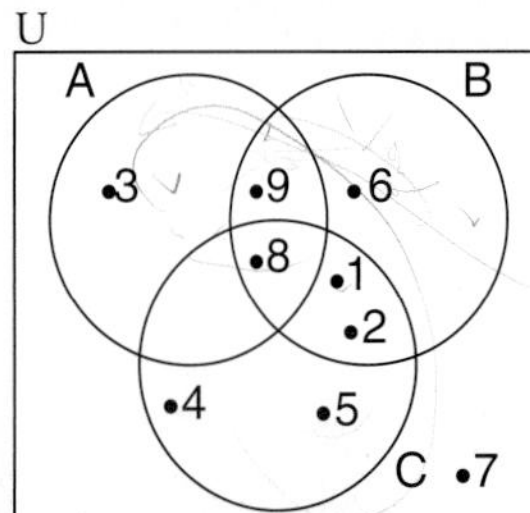

List the elements of:

(a) U
(b) A ∪ B
(c) B \ C
(d) A′
(e) A ∪ (B \ C)

4. U is the universal set, where:
U = {1, 2, 3, 4, 5, 6, 7, 8, 9, 10, 12, 20}
A = {1, 2, 4, 8}, the set of divisors of 8.

B = {1, 2, 3, 4, 6, 12}, the set of divisors of 12.

C = {1, 2, 4, 5, 10, 20}, the set of divisors of 20.

(a) Draw a Venn diagram to represent the sets A, B and C.
(b) List the elements of A ∩ C.
(c) List the elements of B′, the complement of the set B.
(d) List the elements of C \ (A ∩ B).
(e) Using the Venn diagram, find the highest common factor of 8, 12 and 20.

5. U = {1, 2, 3, 4, 5, 6, 7, 8, 9, 10}, P = {1, 4, 5, 7}, Q = {4, 6, 7, 9, 10} and R = {1, 7, 8, 10}.

(a) Represent the information on a Venn diagram.

List the elements of:

(b) Q ∪ R
(c) Q \ (P ∪ R)
(d) P′, the complement of the set P
(e) What is #R?

6. U = {1, 2, 3, 4, 5, 6, 7, 8, 9, 10} is the universal set. P = {4, 7, 8}, Q = {1, 2, 5, 7, 8}, R = {1, 2, 3, 6, 7}.

(a) Represent the information on a Venn diagram.

List the elements of:

(b) P ∪ Q
(c) P \ R
(d) (P ∪ R) ∩ Q
(e) (P ∪ Q)′

7. U = {1, 2, 3, 4, 5, 6, 7, 8, 9, 10}, P = {2, 3, 6, 7, 8}, Q = {1, 6, 8, 10} and R = {2, 4, 6}.

(a) Represent the information on a Venn diagram.

List the elements of:

(b) P ∩ Q
(c) Q \ R
(d) (Q ∪ R)′
(e) (P ∪ Q ∪ R)
(f) (P ∪ R) ∩ Q
(g) Q \ (P ∪ R)
(h) (Q ∪ R) \ (P ∪ R)
(i) (P ∪ Q ∪ R)′
(j) (Q ∪ R)′ ∪ (P \ Q)

8. U is the universal set of natural numbers less than 13.

P = {2, 4, 6, 8, 10, 12}

Q = {3, 6, 9, 11, 12}

R = {4, 8, 11, 12}

(a) Represent the information on a Venn diagram.
(b) List the elements of P ∩ Q ∩ R.
(c) List the elements of R′, the complement of the set R.
(d) List the elements of P \ (Q ∩ R).
(e) List the elements of R \ Q.
(f) List the elements of P′, the complement of set P.
(g) List the elements of Q ∪ (P ∩ R).
(h) List the elements of Q ∩ (R \ P).
(i) List the elements of (Q ∩ R) \ P.
(j) Write down #(Q ∪ R).

9. A is the set of the divisors of 6, B is the set of the divisors of 8 and C is the set of the divisors of 20.

(a) List the elements of set A.
(b) List the elements of set B.
(c) List the elements of set C.
(d) Draw a Venn diagram to represent the three sets.
(e) List the elements of B ∪ C.
(f) List the elements of A \ (B ∪ C) .
(g) List the elements of B ∩ C.
(h) List the elements of the common divisors of 6, 8 and 20.
(i) Find #(C \ (A ∩ B)).
(j) Find #(A ∪ (B \ C)).

10. U = {1, 2, 3, 4, 5, 6, 7, 8, 9, 10, 11, 12} is the universal set. P = {3, 5, 6, 8, 10}, Q = {2, 4, 6, 8, 10, 12} and R = {2, 5, 6, 7, 9, 12}.

(a) Represent the above information on a Venn diagram.

Hence, list the elements of:

(b) (P ∪ Q ∪ R)′
(c) (P ∩ Q) \ R

11. A = {1, 2, 3, 4}, B = {2, 3, 5} and C = {1, 3, 4, 5, 6}. List the elements of (A \ B) ∪ (C ∩ B) and the elements of (A ∪ B) ∩ (C ∩ B).

Section 15.2: Word problems involving three sets

Student Activity 15B

70 teenagers responded to a survey about whether they had visited France, Italy or Spain.

- 30 had travelled to France.
- 26 had travelled to Spain.
- 28 had travelled to Italy.
- 12 had travelled to both France and Spain.
- 8 had travelled to both Spain and Italy.
- x teenagers had travelled to France and Italy only.
- 4 teenagers had travelled to all three countries.
- Twice as many had never travelled to any of these destinations as those who had travelled to France and Italy only.

(a) Represent the information on a Venn diagram.

(b) Find the number of teenagers who had travelled to France only.

WORD PROBLEMS INVOLVING THREE SETS EXPLAINED

Once you understand Venn diagrams for three sets, you can use them to solve real-life problems.

EXAMPLE 3

A group of 100 people were asked which country – England, Spain or America – they would like to visit. 50 chose England, 46 chose Spain and 41 chose America, while 8 said none of the three. 17 said they would like to visit England and Spain, 20 said they would like to visit Spain and America, while 18 said they would like to visit England and America. 10 said they would like to visit all three countries.

Draw a Venn diagram to represent this information.

Solution

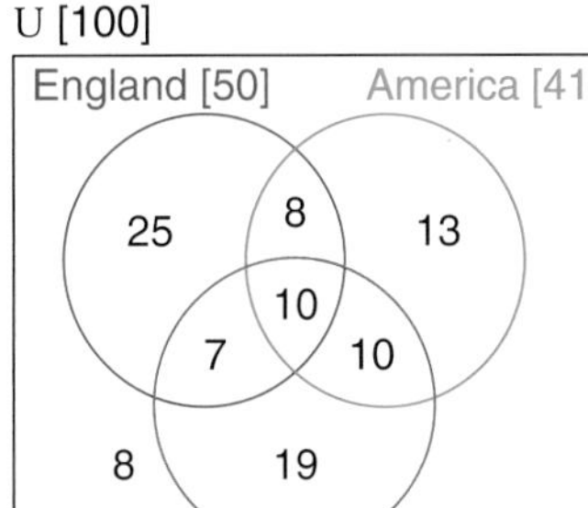

EXAMPLE 4

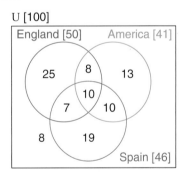

90 students were asked if they travelled to school by bus or by car or walked in a particular week. 30 travelled by bus, 33 by car and 38 walked, 7 travelled by bus and walked, 5 travelled by bus and car, while 6 travelled by car and walked. 5 students used none of the three methods. By letting x be the number who used all three, find the number of students who travelled by:

(a) All three modes of transport

(b) Car only

(c) Bus only

(d) Walking only

(e) Car and bus but not walking

Solution

When tackling a question of this type, draw a Venn diagram and fill in the information you know.

1. Place x in the intersection of the three sets as instructed.
2. The intersection of Bus and Car must total 5 which means (Bus ∩ Car) \ Walk = $5 - x$
3. The remaining intersections are filled in the same manner: $(7 - x)$, $(6 - x)$

You can now deal with each set separately:

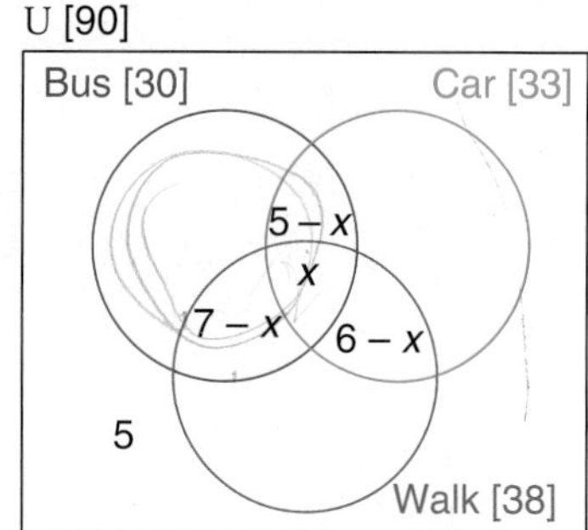

Bus must total 30, so the remainder of the set must hold:

$30 - (5 - x) - (x) - (7 - x)$

$= 30 - 5 + x - x - 7 + x$

$= 18 + x$

Car must total 33, so the remainder of the set must hold:

$33 - (5 - x) - (x) - (6 - x)$

$= 33 - 5 + x - x - 6 + x$

$= 22 + x$

Walking must total 38, so the remainder of the set must hold:

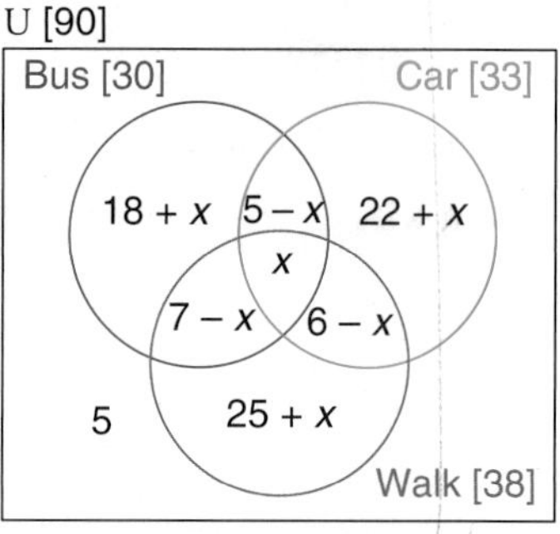

$38 - (7 - x) - (x) - (6 - x)$

$= 38 - 7 + x - x - 6 + x$

$= 25 + x$

Fill in the Venn diagram with this information.

All the sections added together should total 90.

$(18 + x) + (5 - x) + (22 + x) + (7 - x) + (x) + (6 - x) + (25 + x) + 5 = 90$

$88 + x = 90$

$x = 90 - 88$

$x = 2$

Redraw the Venn diagram by substituting $x = 2$.

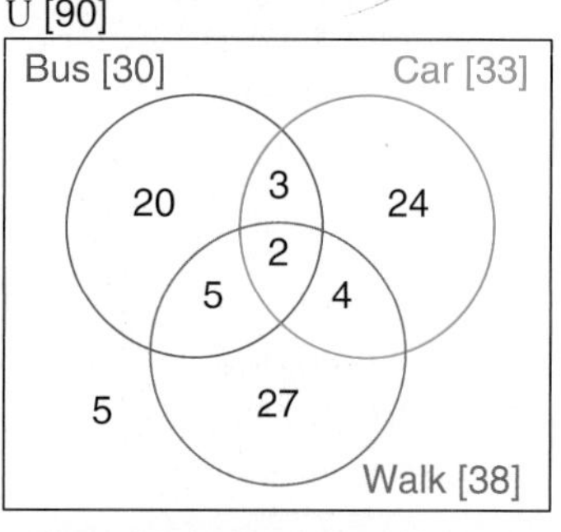

Answering the questions we now find:

(a) All three modes of transport = 2

(b) Car only = 24

(c) Bus only = 20

(d) Walking only = 27

(e) Car and bus but not walking = 3

Exercise 15.2

1. A canteen in a school offers three choices on its lunch menu: soup, drink and a sandwich. 100 pupils were asked which they bought:

   52 bought soup, 55 bought a sandwich and 42 bought a drink. 35 bought soup and a sandwich, 32 bought soup and a drink while 33 bought a sandwich and a drink. 30 people bought all three.

   (a) Draw a Venn diagram to represent this information.

   (b) How many students bought soup only?

   (c) How many students bought a sandwich only?

   (d) How many students bought soup and a drink but not a sandwich?

   (e) How many students bought none of the three items?

2. A group of 120 students were asked if they had considered entering Transition Year (TY), Leaving Certificate Applied (LCA) or the 5th Year programme:
   105 said 5th year, 23 said LCA and 49 said TY. 40 replied they had considered 5th year and TY, 20 had considered LCA and 5th year while 17 had considered TY and LCA. 15 students said they had considered all three.

   (a) Draw a Venn diagram to represent this information.

   (b) How many students considered 5th year only?

(c) How many students considered LCA only?
(d) How many students considered TY only?
(e) How many considered TY and LCA but not 5th year?
(f) How many students considered none of the three?
(g) How many students considered 5th year and TY but not LCA?

3. 60 cinema goers were asked if they liked horror, action or comedy films: 28 liked horror, 25 liked action and 34 liked comedies. 17 liked horrors and action movies, 14 liked horrors and comedies and 15 liked action movies and comedies. 10 liked all three.

(a) Draw a Venn diagram to represent this information.
(b) How many liked horror movies only?
(c) How many liked comedies and action movies but not horrors?
(d) How many liked comedies only?
(e) How many liked only one type of film?
(f) How many liked exactly two of the film types?

4. 100 tourists were asked if they had visited Cork, Dublin or Galway while in Ireland:

39 visited Cork, 53 visited Dublin and 43 visited Galway. 15 visited Cork and Galway, 18 visited Galway and Dublin while 21 visited Cork and Dublin. 12 visited all three.

(a) Draw a Venn diagram to represent this information.
(b) How many visited Dublin only?
(c) How many visited Cork and Dublin but not Galway?
(d) How many visited exactly two of the cities?
(e) How many visited only one of the cities?
(f) How many visited none of the cities?

5. 100 teenagers were asked if they had a personal computer (PC), a games console (GC) or a laptop (L) at home.

45 had a PC, 62 had a games console while 66 had a laptop. 25 had a PC and a games console, 54 had a games console and a laptop and 27 had a PC and a laptop. 13 owned none of the items.

(a) Taking the number who owned all three as x, draw a Venn diagram to represent this information.
(b) Use your Venn diagram to find the value of x.
(c) How many teenagers owned exactly one of the items?
(d) How many teenagers owned exactly two of the items?
(e) How many teenagers owned a PC and a games console but not a laptop?

6. 171 people were asked if they read a broadsheet newspaper (B), a tabloid (T) or a local paper (L).

83 read a broadsheet paper, 87 read a local paper and 82 read a tabloid paper. 25 read a broadsheet and a tabloid, 47 read a tabloid and a local paper, while 40 read a broadsheet and a local paper. 11 read none of these papers.

(a) Taking the number who read all three as x, draw a Venn diagram to represent this information.
(b) Using your Venn diagram, find the value of x.
(c) How many read exactly one of the papers?
(d) How many read a broadsheet and a tabloid but not a local paper?
(e) How many read a local paper only?

7. 60 people were asked if they preferred Chinese, Indian or Thai food.

33 liked Chinese, 31 liked Thai and 27 liked Indian. 15 liked Thai and Indian, 12 liked Chinese and Indian, 8 liked all three and 2 people did not like any of the three.

(a) Taking the number of people who liked Chinese and Thai only as x, draw a Venn diagram to represent the information.
(b) Using your Venn diagram, find the number of people who liked Chinese and Thai but not Indian.
(c) How many people liked exactly one type of food?
(d) How many people liked exactly two types of food?
(e) How many people liked Chinese food only?

8. 85 students were asked if they studied maths, applied maths or physics.

67 studied maths, 17 studied applied maths and 26 studied physics. 15 studied maths and physics and 7 students studied maths and applied maths. 5 students studied all three, while all students studied at least one of the subjects.

(a) Taking the number of people who studied applied maths and physics only as x, draw a Venn diagram to represent the information.
(b) Using your Venn diagram, find the value of x.

(c) How many people studied maths only?

(d) How many people studied exactly two of the subjects?

(e) How many people studied maths and physics but not applied maths?

9. 140 shoppers were asked to sample three different colas: CC, P and DC.

82 liked P, 86 liked DC, while 90 liked CC. 58 liked CC and DC, 57 liked DC and P. 12 liked none of the three while 40 liked all three.

(a) Taking the number of people who liked CC and P only as x, draw a Venn diagram to represent the information.

(b) Using your Venn diagram, find the value of x.

(c) How many people liked CC only?

(d) How many people liked exactly one type of drink?

(e) How many people liked P and DC but not CC?

10. A survey of 40 students was carried out to calculate how many owned an MP3 player, a digital camera or a smart phone. 1 student did not own any of these. x students owned all three, while $2x$ owned an MP3 player and a digital camera but not a smart phone. 10 owned an MP3 player and a smart phone, while 11 owned a digital camera and a smart phone. 22 owned an MP3 player, 22 owned a digital camera and 24 owned a smart phone.

(a) Construct a suitable Venn diagram to represent the information and solve for x.

(b) Hence, calculate the percentage of students who owned one item only.

Section 15.3: Associative, distributive and commutative properties for the intersection, union and difference of sets

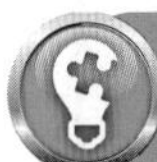

Student Activity 15C

Work in pairs to answer the following questions.

1. What does the word 'associative' mean?

2. What does the word 'distributive' mean?

Draw a Venn diagram with three sets. Use this diagram to answer activities 3–8.

3. Use your Venn diagram to investigate whether the following are true:

(a) $(A \cap B) \cap C = A \cap (B \cap C)$

(b) $(A \cap C) \cap B = A \cap (C \cap B)$

(c) $(C \cap B) \cap A = C \cap (B \cap A)$

(d) What do you notice about your answers?

(e) When examining the **intersection** of sets, does the order of the intersection of the sets matter? Explain your answer.

4. Use your Venn diagram to investigate whether the following are true:

(a) $(A \cup B) \cup C = A \cup (B \cup C)$

(b) $(A \cup C) \cup B = A \cup (C \cup B)$

(c) $(C \cup B) \cup A = C \cup (B \cup A)$

(d) What do you notice about your answers?

(e) When examining the **union** of sets, does the order of the union of the sets matter? Explain your answer.

5. Use your Venn diagram to investigate whether the following are true:

(a) $(A \setminus B) \setminus C = A \setminus (B \setminus C)$

(b) $(A \setminus C) \setminus B = A \setminus (C \setminus B)$

(c) $(C \setminus B) \setminus A = C \setminus (B \setminus A)$

(d) What do you notice about your answers?

(e) When examining **set difference**, does the order of the operation on the sets matter? Explain your answer.

6. Use your Venn diagram to investigate whether the following are true:

(a) $A \cap (B \cap C) = (A \cap B) \cap (A \cap C)$

(b) $B \cap (A \cap C) = (B \cap A) \cap (B \cap C)$

(c) C ∩ (A ∩ B) = (C ∩ A) ∩ (C ∩ B)

(d) What do you notice about your answers?

(e) When examining the **intersection** of sets, can the intersection be distributed across the bracket? Explain your answer.

7. Use your Venn diagram to investigate whether the following are true:

(a) A ∪ (B ∪ C) = (A ∪ B) ∪ (A ∪ C).

(b) B ∪ (A ∪ C) = (B ∪ A) ∪ (B ∪ C).

(c) C ∪ (A ∪ B) = (C ∪ A) ∪ (C ∪ B).

(d) What do you notice about your answers?

(e) When examining the **union** of sets, can the union be distributed across the bracket? Explain your answer.

8. Use your Venn diagram to investigate whether the following are true:

(a) A \ (B \ C) = (A \ B) \ (A \ C)

(b) B \ (A \ C) = (B \ A) \ (B \ C)

(c) C \ (A \ B) = (C \ A) \ (C \ B)

(d) What do you notice about your answers?

(e) When examining **set difference**, can the operation be distributed across the bracket? Explain your answer.

ASSOCIATIVE, DISTRIBUTIVE AND COMMUTATIVE PROPERTIES FOR THE INTERSECTION, UNION AND DIFFERENCE OF SETS EXPLAINED

In *Maths in Action 1*, you learned the following terms:

Mathematical operations are **associative** if the order in which the tasks are carried out does not matter when the sequence of the values remains unchanged.

A mathematical operation is **distributive** if an operation through a bracket gives the same answer as if the operation was performed on each number or set individually.

Mathematical operations are **commutative** if the order of the operations can be interchanged without affecting the answer.

EXAMPLE 5

Examine the Venn diagram and answer the questions that follow.

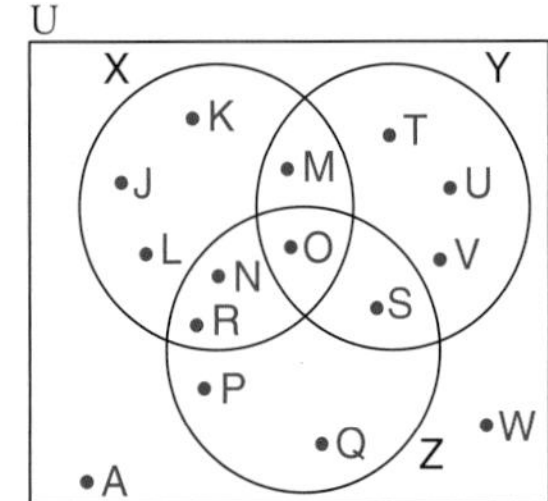

Investigate whether:

(a) X ∪ (Y ∪ Z) = (X ∪ Y) ∪ (X ∪ Z)

(b) Z \ (X \ Y) = (Z \ X) \ (Z \ Y)

Solution

(a) Taking the LHS:

(Y ∪ Z) = {M, N, O, P, Q, R, S, T, U , V}

X ∪ (Y ∪ Z) = {J, K, L, M, N, O, P, Q, R, S, T, U , V}

Taking the RHS:

(X ∪ Y) = {J, K, L, M, N, O, R, S, T, U, V}

(X ∪ Z) = {J, K, L, M, N, O, P, Q, R, S}

(X ∪ Y) ∪ (X ∪ Z) = {J, K, L, M, N, O, P, Q, R, S, T, U , V}

∴ X ∪ (Y ∪ Z) = (X ∪ Y) ∪ (X ∪ Z)

(b) Taking the LHS:

X \ Y = {J, K, L, R, N}

Z \ (X \ Y) = {O, S, P, Q}

Taking the RHS:

(Z \ X) = {P, Q, S}

(Z \ Y) = {R, N, P, Q}

(Z \ X) \ (Z \ Y) = {S}

∴ Z \ (X \ Y) ≠ (Z \ X) \ (Z \ Y)

Exercise 15.3

1. Draw a Venn diagram with three sets and investigate whether each of the following is true:
   (a) A ∩ (B ∪ C) = (A ∩ B) ∪ (A ∩ C)
   (b) B ∩ (A ∪ C) = (B ∩ A) ∪ (B ∩ C)
   (c) C ∩ (A ∪ B) = (C ∩ A) ∪ (C ∩ B)
2. State whether the following statements are true or false:
   (a) The union of sets is not associative.
   (b) The intersection of sets is distributive.
   (c) Set difference is both associative and distributive.
   (d) The union of sets is distributive
3. Draw a Venn diagram to represent the sets P = {factors of 20}, Q = {factors of 25} and R = {factors of 12}. Investigate whether each of the following is true:
   (a) P \ (Q \ R) = (P \ Q) \ (P \ R)
   (b) P ∩ (Q ∩ R) = (P ∩ Q) ∩ (P ∩ R)
   (c) P ∪ (Q ∪ R) = (P ∪ Q) ∪ (P ∪ R)
4. Use the following Venn diagram to investigate whether the following are true:

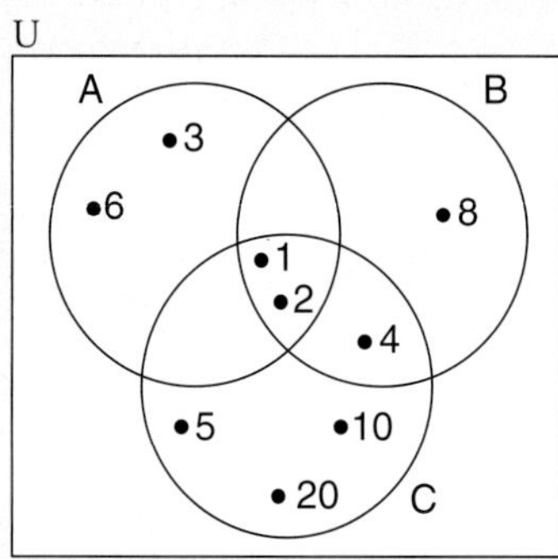

   (a) A ∩ (B ∩ C) = (A ∩ B) ∩ (A ∩ C)
   (b) B ∩ (A ∩ C) = (B ∩ A) ∩ (B ∩ C)
   (c) C ∩ (A ∩ B) = (C ∩ A) ∩ (C ∩ B)
   (d) What do you notice about your answers?
   (e) When examining the **intersection** of sets, can the intersection be distributed across the bracket? Explain your answer.
5. Use the following Venn diagram to investigate whether the following are true:

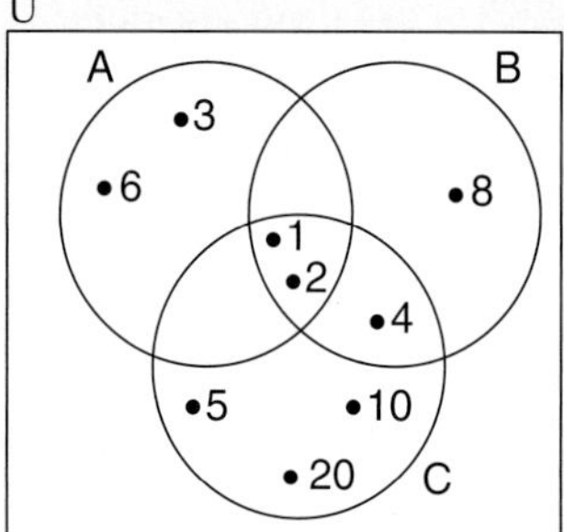

   (a) A ∪ (B ∪ C) = (A ∪ B) ∪ (A ∪ C)
   (b) B ∪ (A ∪ C) = (B ∪ A) ∪ (B ∪ C)
   (c) C ∪ (A ∪ B) = (C ∪ A) ∪ (C ∪ B)
   (d) What do you notice about your answers?
   (e) When examining the **union** of sets, can the union be distributed across the bracket? Explain your answer.
6. Use a Venn diagram to investigate whether the following are true:
   (a) A \ (B \ C) = (A \ B) \ (A \ C)
   (b) B \ (A \ C) = (B \ A) \ (B \ C)
   (c) C \ (A \ B) = (C \ A) \ (C \ B)
   (d) What do you notice about your answers?
   (e) When examining **set difference,** can the operation be distributed across the bracket? Explain your answer.

CHAPTER 15 SELF-CHECK TEST

1. Examine the Venn diagram, and list the elements in each of the sections:

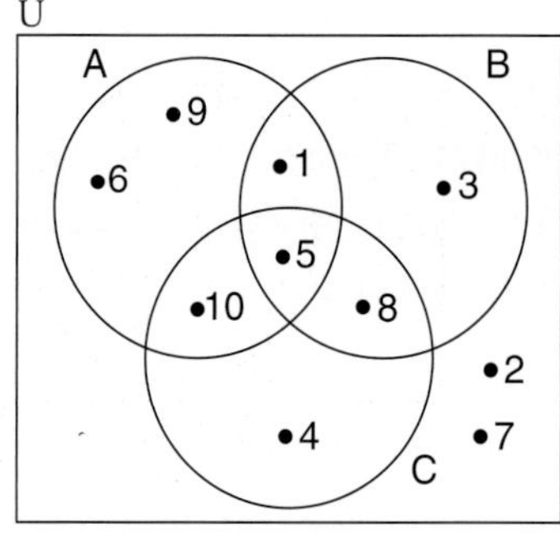

   (a) A ∩ B ∩ C
   (b) A \ B
   (c) (B ∩ C) \ A
   (d) (A ∪ B ∪ C)′
   (e) (A ∪ B ∪ C) \ A
   (f) (A ∪ B ∪ C) \ (A ∩ B)
   (g) (A ∪ B ∪ C)
   (h) (A ∪ B) \ C
   (i) (A ∩ B ∩ C)′
   (j) (B ∩ A) \ C
   (k) (B ∪ C) \ A
   (l) (A ∪ C) \ B
   (m) C′
   (n) (A ∩ C)

2. Study the Venn diagram and investigate whether the following statements are true:

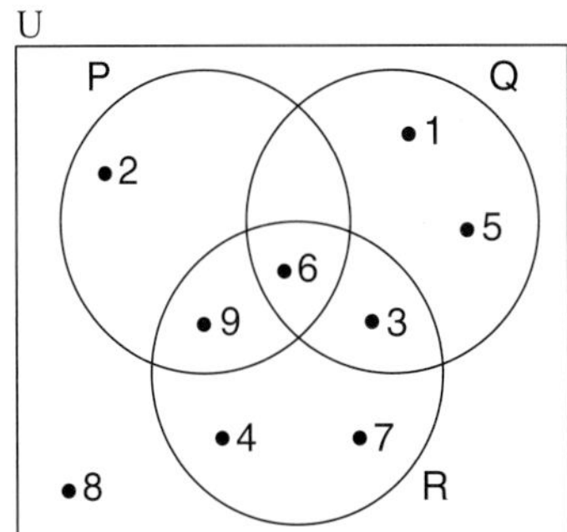

(a) P \ (Q \ R) = (P \ Q) \ (P \ R)
(b) P ∩ (Q ∩ R) = (P ∩ Q) ∩ (P ∩ R)
(c) P ∪ (Q ∪ R) = (P ∪ Q) ∪ (P ∪ R)

3. State whether the following statements are true or false:
(a) The union of sets is not associative.
(b) The intersection of sets is distributive.
(c) Set difference is both associative and distributive.
(d) The union of sets is distributive.

4. A group of 49 students was asked which fruit they liked.
- 28 said they liked apples. 25 said they liked pears, while 26 said they liked oranges.
- 8 said they liked all three types of fruit.
- 17 said they liked pears and oranges.
- 11 said they liked apples and oranges.
- 5 said they did not like any of the three types of fruit.

Let x represent those students who liked apples and pears but not oranges.
(a) Represent the above information on a Venn diagram.
(b) Calculate the value of x.
(c) Calculate the percentage of students who liked one type of fruit only. Give your answer correct to the nearest whole number.

5. A group of 100 students was asked if they used social networking websites A, B and C.
- 50 students used A, 40 used B and 50 used C.
- 14 students had a presence on A and B but not on C.
- 18 students had a presence on A and C but not on B.
- 8 students had a presence on B and C but not on A.
- 12 students stated that they did not have a presence on any of the websites.

(a) Using x to represent the number of students who used all three websites, draw a Venn diagram and solve for x.
(b) Calculate the ratio of students who used B only to the students who used C only.

6. A survey was carried out in a class to find which of the films A, B or C the students had seen. The following data was collected:
- 42% saw film A, 41% saw film B and 45% saw film C.
- 12% saw both A and B, 18% saw both B and C and 15% saw both A and C.
- 15% saw none of these films.

(a) Represent this information on a Venn diagram.
(b) What percentage of the students in the class saw all three films?
(c) What percentage of the students in the class saw two or more of the films?

7. U = {1, 2, 3, ... , 12}. P is the set of prime numbers less than 12. E is the set of even numbers less than 12. Q is the set of odd numbers less than 12.
(a) Represent these sets on the Venn diagram.

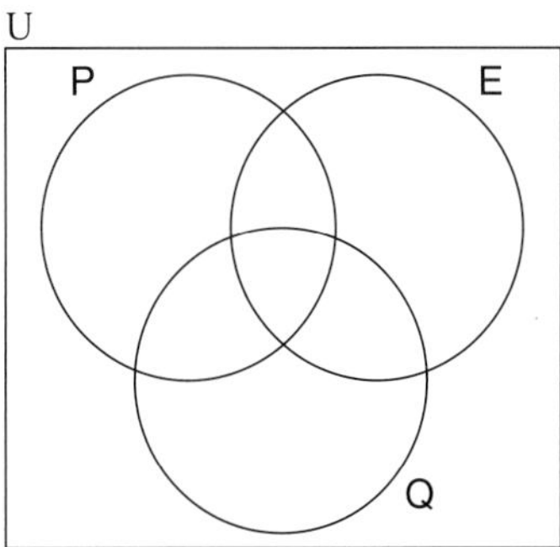

(b) Name any parts on this diagram that is a null set.

8. (a) For diagrams (i) and (ii) shade in the named region.

(i)

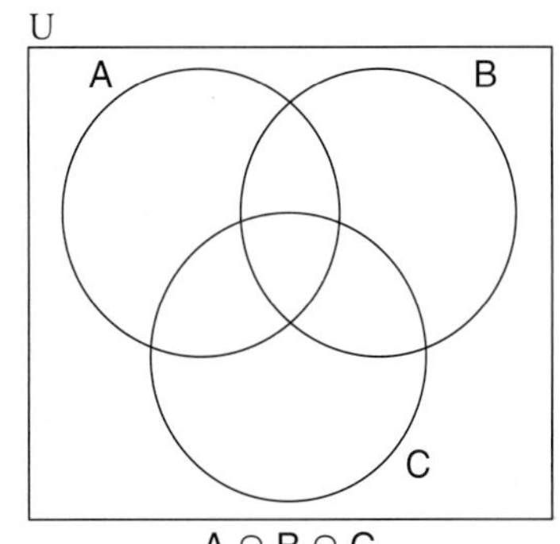

A ∩ B ∩ C

(ii) 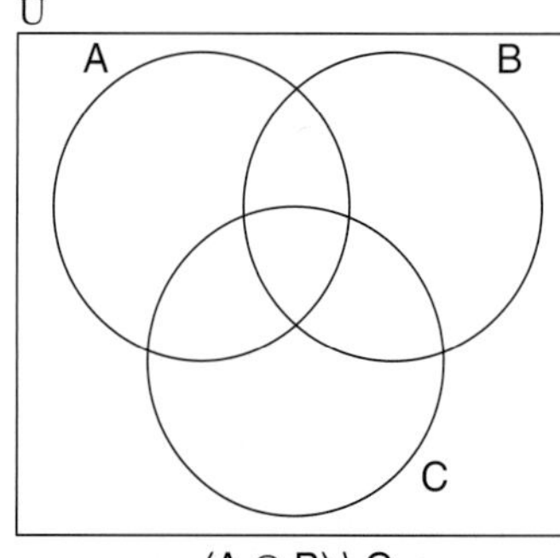

$(A \cap B) \setminus C$

(b) The box contains six statements. A number of the statements are correct. Write down which ones are correct.

Statements

(i) $A \cup B = B \cup A$

(ii) $(A \cup B) \cup C = A \cup (B \cup C)$

(iii) $(A \setminus B) \setminus C = A \setminus (B \setminus C)$

(iv) $(A \cap B)' = A' \cap B'$

(v) $A \setminus B = B \setminus A$

(vi) $B \setminus (A \cup C) = (B \cup C) \setminus A$

(c) Draw a diagram or give an example to explain your choices.

9. A group of 38 students was asked if they had ever been to France or Spain.

- The number who had been to Spain only was 3 more than the number who had been to both countries.
- Twice as many had been to France as Spain.
- 4 students had not been to either country.

Find how many had been to both countries.

10. **U** is the universal set and A and B are two subsets of **U**.

$\#U = 25$, $\#A = 15$ and $\#B = 7$.

(a) Find, with the aid of a Venn diagram, the minimum value of $\#(A \cup B)'$.

(b) Find, with the aid of a Venn diagram, the maximum value of $\#(A \cup B)'$.

11. $\#U = u$, $\#A = a$, $\#B = b$ and $\#(A \cup B)' = y$.

Show, with the aid of a Venn diagram, that if $a > b$ and y is a maximum, then $u = a + y$.

12. **U** is the universal set and X and Y are two subsets of **U**.

$\#U = 29$, $\#(X \cap Y) = a$, $\#(X \setminus Y) = 3a$, $\#((X \cup Y)') = 5$, $\#X = 2(\#Y)$.

(a) Represent this information on a Venn diagram.

(b) Hence, or otherwise, find the value of $\#Y$.

CHAPTER 15 KNOWLEDGE CHECKLIST

After completing this chapter, I now:

- **Am able to draw Venn diagrams for three sets**
- **Am able to carry out intersection, union, set difference and set complement for three sets**
- **Understand and am able to show the associative, distributive and commutative properties of union and intersection**
- **Understand and am able to show that set difference is neither commutative nor associative**
- **Am able to use Venn diagrams to solve for a missing piece of information**

PROBABILITY

LEARNING OUTCOMES

In this chapter you will learn:

- ✓ To calculate relative frequency and expected frequency
- ✓ The composition of a deck of cards
- ✓ To calculate the probability of events involving objects such as spinners, dice, cards and coins
- ✓ To calculate the probability of combined events
- ✓ About set theory and probability

KEY WORDS

- Biased
- Combined event
- Event
- Expected frequency
- Fair
- Frequency
- Outcome
- Probability
- Probability scale
- Relative frequency
- Sample space
- Trial

16 INTRODUCTION

MATHS IN ACTION 3

In *Maths in Action 1*, you learned that probability is a measure of 'how likely' or 'how unlikely' an event is to occur. You also examined how you can associate the probability of an event with a number. This number lies on a **probability scale** from 0 to 1 (or from 0% to 100%).

When writing probabilities, we often use the abbreviation P. 'The probability that Tom threw 2 heads' could be written as P(2 heads).

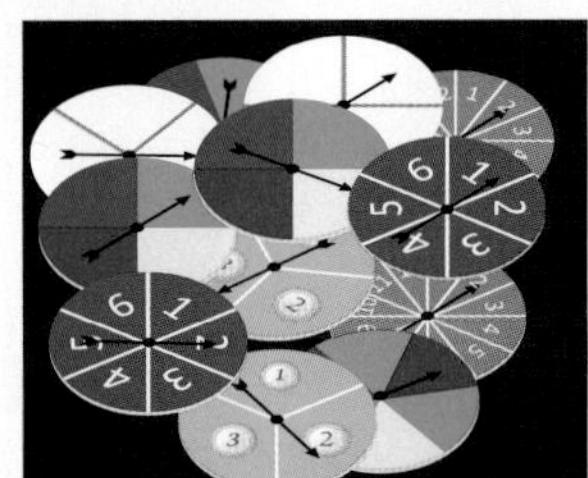

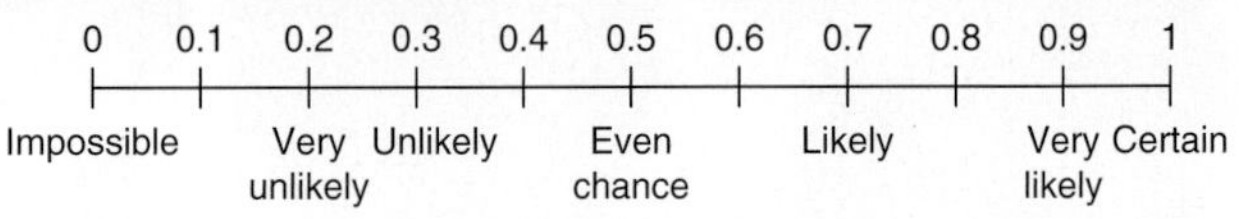

First year revision

1. Decide, on a scale of 0% to 100%, how likely each of the following events is:
   (a) Wayne Rooney managing Liverpool FC.
   (b) Ireland declaring war on the USA.
   (c) You win the lotto in the next draw.
   (d) You will eat your lunch tomorrow.
   (e) Friday will come before Saturday this week.
   (f) You will get an even number on the throw of a die.

2. Explain each of the following terms: event, sample space, trial and outcome.
3. Paul throws a fair coin twice. Copy and complete the following tree diagram to show all of the possible outcomes:
   (a) What is the probability that he will throw two heads?
   (b) What is the probability that he will throw no heads?
   (c) What is the probability that he will throw one head and one tail?
   (d) What is the probability that Paul will throw a head followed by a tail?

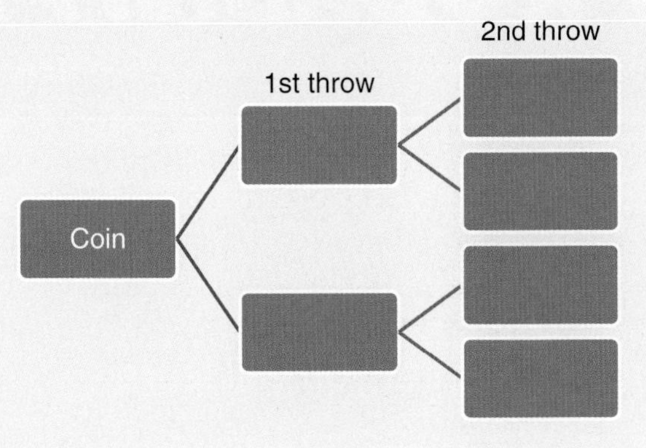

Section 16.1: Relative frequency and expected frequency

Student Activity 16A

1. Working in pairs, toss a fair die a total of 100 times.
2. Record the number of times each number on the die occurs.
3. Copy and fill out the following frequency table to show your results:

Result	1	2	3	4	5	6
Tally						
Frequency						

4. If you tossed the die 5,000 times, how many of each number would you expect to get?

RELATIVE FREQUENCY AND EXPECTED FREQUENCY EXPLAINED

The **frequency** of an event is how often the event occurs. For example, if 12 marbles were picked out of a bag and 9 of them were green, the frequency of green marbles would be 9.

Sometimes the probability of an event occurring is difficult to predict. For example:

- How many ice-creams will a shop sell next month?
- How many goals will a football team score in their next match?
- How much rain will fall next September?

We can use the **relative frequency** of an event to estimate how many times that event would occur over a certain number of trials.

To calculate the relative frequency of the green marbles mentioned above, divide the frequency by the total number of marbles: $\frac{9}{12}$ or $\frac{3}{4}$ or 0.75 or 75%.

$$\text{Relative frequency} = \frac{\text{The number of times the event happens}}{\text{Total number of trials}}$$

The more times an experiment is repeated, the more accurate the estimate of the probability of the event occurring will be. Using relative frequency, we can determine whether an experiment is fair or biased (unfair).

Expected frequency = Relative frequency (Probability) × Number of trials

So if we repeated the above experiment 300 times, we would expect to pick a green marble $0.75 \times 300 = 225$ times. The **expected frequency** = 225.

Relative frequencies are used to calculate expected frequencies (expected values) for a set of results.

EXAMPLE 1

100 people were asked whether they owned or rented a property. 60 people replied that they were homeowners.

(a) Calculate the relative frequency of homeowners.

(b) Estimate how many of the 10,000 population of the town own their own house.

Solution

(a) Relative frequency $= \frac{60}{100} = \frac{3}{5} = 0.6$

(b) Expected frequency of house ownership $= 10{,}000 \times 0.6 = 6{,}000$

Exercise 16.1

1. Six discs were picked out of a bag. If 4 of them were blue, calculate:

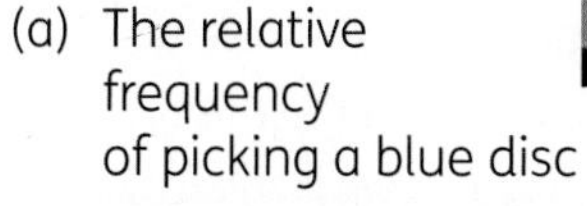

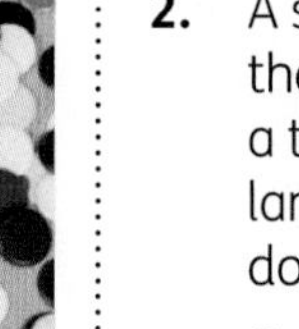

   (a) The relative frequency of picking a blue disc

   (b) The expected frequency of picking blue discs if 300 discs were taken out of the bag

2. A student recorded that, out of 50 throws, a thumbtack landed flat side down 33 times.

   Calculate:

   (a) The relative frequency of the tack landing flat side down

   (b) The expected frequency of the tack landing flat side down if thrown 700 times

3. A survey showed that 42 people out of 50 owned a car less than 2 years old.
   (a) Calculate the relative frequency of owning a car no more than 2 years old.
   (b) Use the relative frequency to estimate how many people out of 4,000 would own a car no more than 2 years old.

4. Statistics show that about 10% of people are left-handed. In a survey of 2,000 people, how many would you expect to be left-handed?

5. About 1 in every 100 people suffer from coeliac disease. In a survey of 10,000 people, how many people would you expect to suffer from this condition?

6. A manufacturing plant produces tyres. For every 1,000 tyres produced, 20 are defective.
   (a) In a week, the factory produces 9,500 tyres. How many of these would you expect to be defective?
   (b) A competitor finds that for every 6,500 tyres produced, 150 tyres are defective. Which producer has the lowest relative frequency of defective tyres?

7. A student carried out a survey of 50 girls and 50 boys in his school to find how many students follow the healthy eating plan in the school. From those surveyed, he found that 38 girls and 30 boys follow the plan.

   (a) Calculate the relative frequency of all those who follow the plan.
   (b) If the school has 650 students (boys and girls) in total, how many would you expect to follow the plan?

8. An unfair (or biased) die is rolled 50 times. It lands on a 6 a total of 28 times.
   (a) Calculate the relative frequency of rolling the number 6.
   (b) How many times would you expect this die to land on a 6 if thrown 700 times?

9. A fair die is rolled 300 times. It lands on the number 5 a total of 58 times.
   (a) Calculate the relative frequency of the number 5.
   (b) How many times would you expect this die to land on the number 5 if it were thrown 1,200 times?

10. A student carries out a survey to find out how many students in a class of 30 exercise for more than 30 minutes daily. The student found that 22 of the students exercise for more than 30 minutes each day.
   (a) Calculate the relative frequency of a student exercising for more than 30 minutes daily.
   (b) If there are 900 students in the school, how many would you expect to exercise for more than 30 minutes daily?

11. An archer hits the target 24 times out of a total of 30 shots.
   (a) Calculate the relative frequency for hitting the target.
   (b) If the archer fires 1,200 arrows, how many arrows would you expect to hit the target?

12. A surveyor finds that 27 out of 35 houses have more than two television sets.
   (a) Calculate the relative frequency of a house having more than two television sets.
   (b) If the surveyor visits 7,000 houses, how many would you expect to have more than two televisions?

13. The table shows the results of a number football matches played by five teams:

Team	Games won	Games drawn	Games lost
Chelsea	7	4	3
Bayern Munich	12	0	8
Porto	18	1	9
Lyon	11	7	0
Real Madrid	13	7	2

   (a) What is the relative frequency of a win for each team?
   (b) Which team is the best in your opinion? Explain your reasons.
   (c) Is this a fair way of picking the best team? Explain your answer.

14 The number of burgers sold by a fast food restaurant in a given week is recorded as follows:

Day	Mon	Tue	Wed	Thurs	Fri	Sat	Sun
Burgers sold	62	57	44	46	119	187	85

(a) How many burgers were sold in total?

(b) Calculate the relative frequency of the number of burgers sold for each day of the week.

(c) What is the relative frequency of a burger being sold on a Monday or a Tuesday?

Section 16.2: Composition of a deck of playing cards

A deck of cards is commonly used in probability questions, so you should be familiar with the contents of a deck. We do not usually include jokers in the deck. The picture shows all the cards in a deck.

Note
A = ace

The contents of a deck of cards can also be shown using the following diagram:

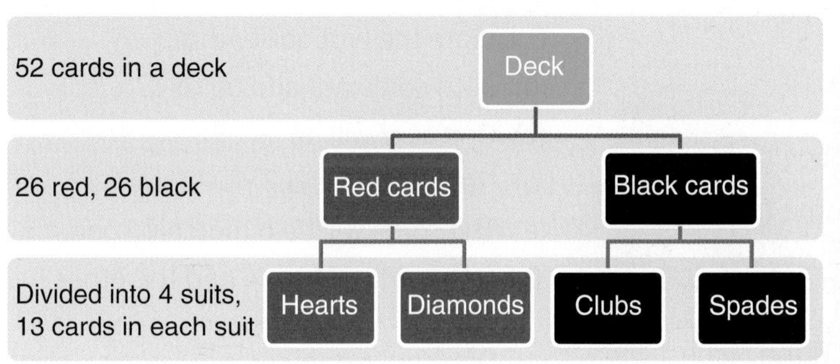

Each suit has an A, 2, 3, 4, 5, 6, 7, 8, 9, 10, Jack, Queen, and King.

The J, Q and K are known as 'picture cards' or 'court cards'.

EXAMPLE 2

A card is drawn at random from a standard pack of cards. Calculate:

(a) P(King) (b) P(Black 7) (c) P(Not getting a red card)

Solution

(a) There are 4 Kings in a deck of 52 cards.

$P(\text{King}) = \frac{4}{52} = \frac{1}{13}$

(b) There are 2 black 7 cards in a deck of 52 cards.

$P(\text{Black } 7) = \frac{2}{52} = \frac{1}{26}$

(c) There are 26 red cards so there are 26 non-red cards (black).

$P(\text{Not getting a red card}) = \frac{26}{52} = \frac{1}{2}$

Exercise 16.2

1. A card is picked at random from a deck of cards. Find the probability that the card will be:
   (a) A red card
   (b) A club
   (c) A heart
   (d) The King of spades
   (e) A black Ace
   (f) A red Queen
   (g) A Jack
   (h) 9 of diamonds
   (i) A black 7
   (j) Not a heart
   (k) A diamond
   (l) Not a picture card
   (m) A Queen
   (n) A spade
   (o) A black even-numbered card
   (p) An even-numbered card
   (q) A black card
   (r) A card with a prime number
2. Paul and Joe are playing a game to see who can pull the highest card from a deck of cards. They list the cards in order as follows: Ace, 2, 3, 4, 5, 6, 7, 8, 9, 10, Jack, Queen, King, where the King is the highest card and the Ace is the lowest card. Find the probability that Joe will win if Paul picks a:
   (a) 6 (c) Jack (e) 5
   (b) 10 (d) Queen (f) King
   (g) The highest possible prime number
3. Amy is trying to figure out if the deck of cards she has is a fair deck. She draws a single card from the deck 50 times and replaces it each time. A spade is drawn 15 times.
   (a) Calculate the relative frequency of her drawing a spade.
   (b) How many spades would she expect to draw if a card was drawn 1,000 times?
   (c) From your calculations, would you say the deck is a fair deck of cards? Explain your answer.
4. One card is taken randomly from two piles. The following playing cards are in each pile:
   - **Pile A:** 2, 3 4 and 5
   - **Pile B:** 6, 7, 8, 9 and 10

   (a) Construct a suitable sample space diagram showing all possible outcomes when a card is removed from each pile.

   Calculate the probability that:
   (b) Both cards will add up to 12.
   (c) One card will be 9.
   (d) Neither card is a 7.
   (e) The cards will be a matching pair.
   (f) One card will be a 4 and the other card will be a 9.
   (g) One card's number is at least twice as big as the other card's number.
   (h) The sum of the cards is greater than ten.
   (i) The difference in the two cards is less than three.
   (j) The product of the two cards is a prime number.

Section 16.3: Probability and combined events

Student Activity 16B

Work in pairs to answer the following questions.

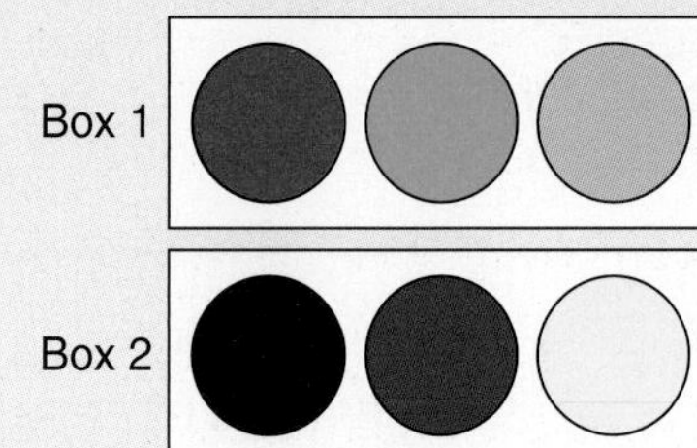

1. (a) How many discs are in box 1?
   (b) How many discs are in box 2?
2. A disk is chosen from box 1 **and** a disc is chosen from box 2.
   (a) Write out the sample space.
   (b) How many outcomes are possible?
   (c) Can you relate the number of discs in the boxes to the number of outcomes using a mathematical operation?

3. (a) If only one disc is chosen from box A **or** box B, how many outcomes are possible?
(b) Can you relate the number of discs in the boxes to the number of outcomes using a mathematical operation?

PROBABILITY AND COMBINED EVENTS EXPLAINED

For probability problems, you must learn two types of combinations. You can be asked to combine the results in two ways:

1. The AND rule

P(Event 1 **AND** Event 2) = P(Event 1) × P(Event 2)

In this case, the two events will occur together, so we **multiply** the individual probabilities.

2. The OR rule

P(Event 1 **OR** Event 2) = P(Event 1) + P(Event 2)

In this case, only one of two events will occur, so we **add** the individual probabilities.

It is often necessary to calculate the probability that an event will not occur.

The probability of an event not occurring

P(Event **NOT** occurring) = 1 **–** P(Event occurring)

EXAMPLE 3

Áine is playing a board game. It involves spinning two spinners. One spinner has three equal segments coloured red, blue and green. The second spinner has four equal segments each numbered 1, 2, 3 and 4.

Áine needs a green and the number 4 to win.

(a) What is the probability she will win on her next turn?

(b) What is the probability that she spins a green or a 4 on her next turn?

(c) What is the probability that Áine will not win the game?

(d) The prize is €10. If Áine must pay €2 per game, do you think it is a good idea for her to play this game? Explain your answer.

Solution

P(Green) = $\frac{1}{3}$ P(Number 4) = $\frac{1}{4}$

(a) Áine needs the green sector **AND** the number 4 to win. In probability, the word AND means we multiply the results.

Combining the results:

P(Green **AND** 4) = $\frac{1}{3} \times \frac{1}{4} = \frac{1}{12}$

(b) In probability the word **OR** means add.

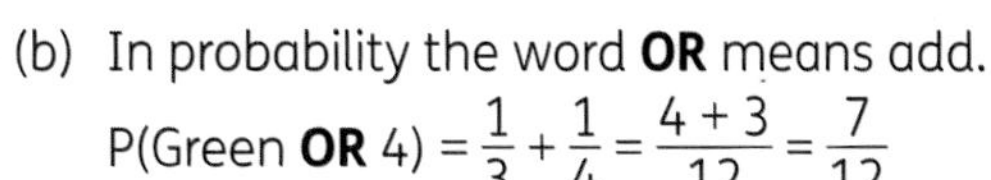

P(Green **OR** 4) = $\frac{1}{3} + \frac{1}{4} = \frac{4+3}{12} = \frac{7}{12}$

(c) P(Not winning) = 1 − P(winning)

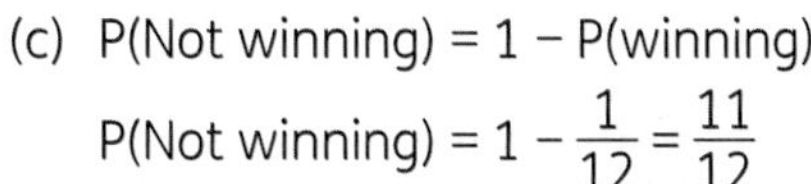

P(Not winning) = $1 - \frac{1}{12} = \frac{11}{12}$

(d) It is not a good idea as she will most likely lose based on her low probability of winning.

Exercise 16.3

1. George is trying to determine if a five-sided spinner is a fair spinner. Each segment is equal in size and labelled A, B, C, D and E. He spins the spinner 30 times and records the results each time. The letter D occurred 3 times.

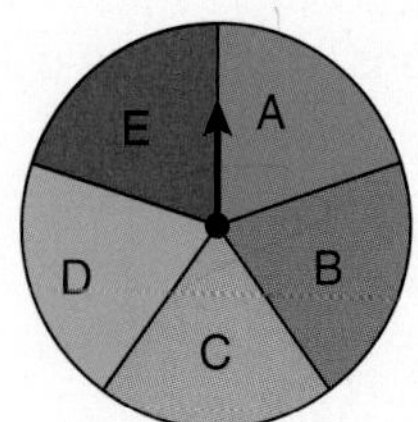

   (a) Calculate the relative frequency of getting the letter D.
   (b) How many letter Ds would you expect if the spinner was spun 1,000 times?
   (c) From your calculations, would you say the spinner is a fair? Explain your answer.

2. A five-sided spinner with the numbers 1, 2, 3, 4 and 5 printed on its five equal sectors is spun. At the same time one card is drawn randomly from a set of three coloured cards (blue, red, and white) which are lying face down on the table.
   (a) Write out the sample space for this experiment.

   Find the probability of each of the following:
   (b) P(2 **AND** white)
   (c) P(Even number **AND** blue)
   (d) P(5 **OR** Red)
   (e) P(Odd number **OR** white)

3. Paul finds a die and is trying to decide if it is biased. He throws the die 30 times and notices it lands on a 6 twelve times. He decides the die is biased.
   (a) Would you agree with Paul? Explain your answer.

   Paul's friend Grace repeats the experiment, but she throws it 6,000 times. She notices it lands on a 6 a total of 998 times. She tells Paul the die is not biased.
   (b) Would you agree with Grace? Explain your answer.
   (c) Why did Grace's figures differ from Paul's?

4. A fruit grower notices that each day one in every two boxes of fruit she picks is bad.
   (a) What is the probability of picking a bad box of fruit on any given day?
   (b) (i) Fill out the following tree diagram for choosing three boxes on a given day:

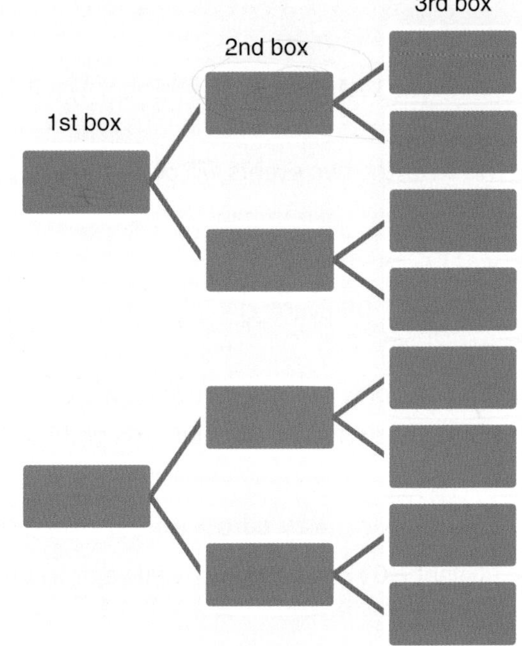

   (ii) Using the tree diagram, list all the possible outcomes.

5. A fair five-sided spinner, with each sector coloured red, green, blue, white and black, is spun twice and the colour is noted after each spin. Find the probability that:
   (a) The spinner will land on green both times.
   (b) The spinner will land on a blue and then a red.
   (c) The spinner will land on white both times.

6. The probability that a letter is delivered on the next working day is 0.9 or $\frac{9}{10}$. Síle posts 200 wedding invitations on a Thursday. How many would Síle expect to be delivered on the following day?

7. A fair six-sided die is rolled and a fair four-sided spinner (with numbers from 1 to 4) is spun. The sum of the scores is noted.

Draw a table to represent the sample space.

(a) What is the probability that the total score is 2?

(b) What is the probability that the total score is less than 5?

(c) What is the probability that the total score is greater than or equal to 7?

8. Two fair dice are rolled together. The scores on both are added together and noted. Draw a table to represent the sample space. Use the table to calculate the probability that:

(a) The total is 8.

(b) The total is a prime number.

(c) The total is at least 8.

(d) The two dice show the same number.

9. A box contains 30 pieces of card, each numbered from 1 to 30. A card is picked at random from the box. Find:

(a) P(Multiple of 3)

(b) P(Multiple of 4)

(c) P(Multiple of 6)

(d) P(Multiple of 3 **OR** multiple of 4)

(e) P(Multiple of 3 **AND** multiple of 5)

(f) P(Multiple of 4 **AND** multiple of 7)

(g) P(Multiple of 4 **OR** multiple of 7)

(h) P(Factor of 18)

10. Three fair coins are tossed. Calculate the probability that:

(a) The outcome will be three heads.

(b) The outcome will be at least one head.

(c) The outcome will have no tail.

(d) The outcome will be two heads and one tail.

(e) The outcome will be two tails and one head.

11. The table shows how 150 students travel to school.

	Bus	Car	Train	Bike	Walk
Girl	16	7	24	20	30
Boy	8	12	15	8	10

Two students are chosen at random. Find the probability that the people chosen are:

(a) A boy who walks and a girl who cycles

(b) A boy who travels by car and a girl who travels by train

(c) A girl who walks to school and a boy who takes the bus

(d) A girl who travels by car and a boy who takes the bus

(e) A girl who walks or a girl who cycles

(f) A boy who cycles or a girl who travels by bus

12. A card is selected at random from a deck of cards. Calculate the probability that the card is:

(a) A heart or a club

(b) A Jack and a black card

(c) A diamond or a black picture card

(d) Not a diamond or an Ace

(e) Not a heart or a picture card

13. Two unbiased die are rolled. Calculate the probability that:

(a) The numbers are the same.

(b) The numbers are the same **OR** the sum of the numbers is 6.

(c) The difference between the two numbers is 2 **AND** the sum is 8.

(d) The sum is greater than 9 **OR** the numbers are the same.

Section 16.4: Set theory and probability

SET THEORY AND PROBABILITY EXPLAINED

In *Maths in Action 1*, you learned how to use sets to find the probability of certain events occurring.

We sometimes need to find some information by completing a Venn diagram that contains two or three intersecting sets.

EXAMPLE 4

50 students were asked if they liked maths (M) or English (E) in school. 28 chose maths, 25 chose English and 4 picked neither.

(a) Draw a Venn diagram to represent this information.

If a person is picked at random, find the probability that the person chose:

(b) Maths
(c) English
(d) Both subjects
(e) Neither subject
(f) Maths only
(g) English only

Solution

The questions states that 50 people were surveyed but adding our figures gives:

28 + 25 + 4 = 57 people.

The extra people are those who liked both subjects. We place them in the intersection of the two sets.

As there are 7 people in the intersection, we only have 21 more in the set of people who liked maths to make 28, and 18 more in the set who liked English to make 25.

(a)

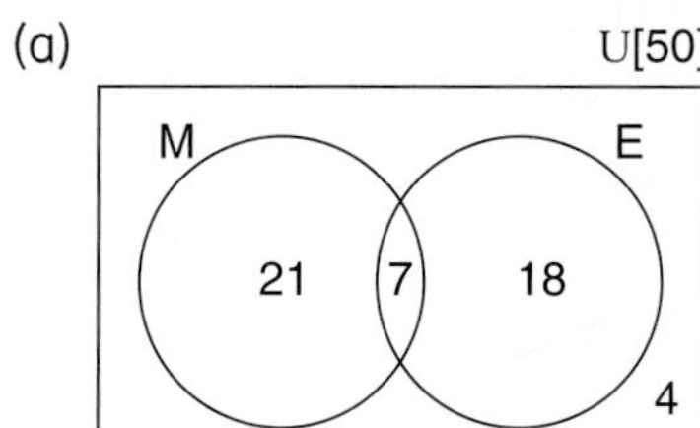

(b) $\frac{28}{50} = \frac{14}{25}$

(c) $\frac{25}{50} = \frac{1}{2}$

(d) $\frac{7}{50}$

(e) $\frac{4}{50} = \frac{2}{25}$

(f) $\frac{21}{50}$

(g) $\frac{18}{50} = \frac{9}{25}$

EXAMPLE 5

65 students were asked which country Spain (S), France (F) or Germany (G) they have visited. The Venn diagram below shows their replies. Study the Venn diagram and answer the questions which follow.

If a person is picked at random, find the probability that they have travelled to:

(a) France
(b) Spain
(c) Germany
(d) All three countries
(e) France and Germany only
(f) Spain and Germany
(g) None of the countries
(h) Germany only
(i) Spain and Germany only
(j) France and Spain but not Germany

Solution

(a) France = 15 + 5 + 7 + 4 = 31 = $\frac{31}{65}$

(b) Spain = 17 + 3 + 7 + 4 = 31 = $\frac{31}{65}$

(c) Germany = 12 + 5 + 7 +3 = 27 = $\frac{27}{65}$

(d) All three countries = $\frac{7}{65}$

(e) France and Germany only = $\frac{5}{65} = \frac{1}{13}$

(f) Spain and Germany = $\frac{10}{65} = \frac{2}{13}$

(g) None of the countries = $\frac{2}{65}$

(h) Germany only = $\frac{12}{65}$

(i) Spain and Germany only = $\frac{3}{65}$

(j) France and Spain but not Germany = $\frac{4}{65}$

Exercise 16.4

1. Twenty students were asked if they liked swimming (S) and running (R). The following Venn diagram shows their replies. Study the Venn diagram and answer the questions that follow.

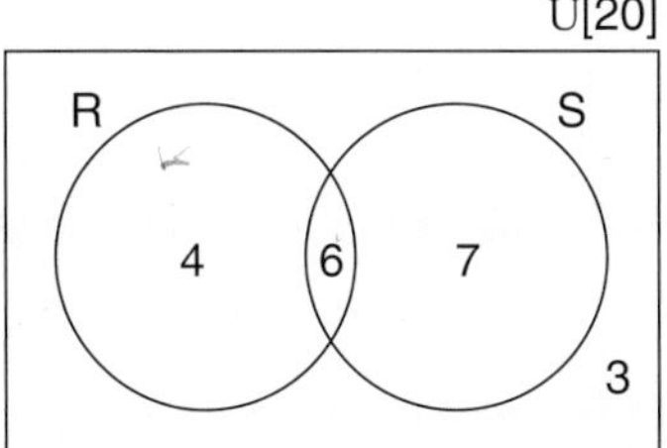

If a student is picked at random, find the probability that he or she likes:

(a) Running
(b) Swimming
(c) Both sports
(d) Running only
(e) Swimming only
(f) Only one sport
(g) Neither sport

2. Thirty people were asked if they liked action movies (A) or comedies (C). The following Venn diagram shows their replies. Study the Venn diagram and answer the questions that follow.

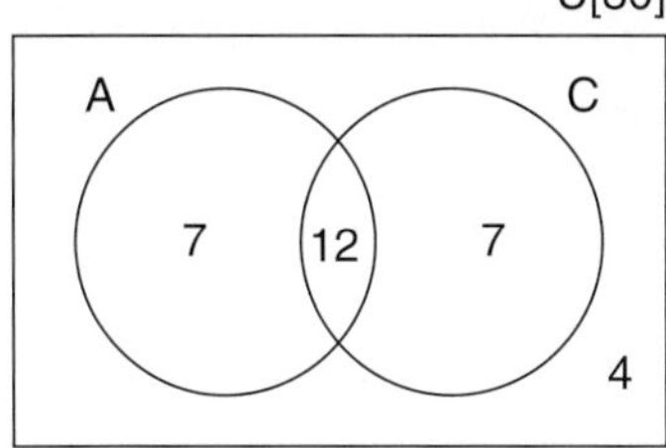

If a person is picked at random, find the probability that he or she likes:

(a) Both types of movie
(b) Action movies only
(c) Comedies
(d) Neither type of movie
(e) Comedies only
(f) Only one type of movie

3. A total of 250 people were asked if they had a dog (D) or a cat (C) as a pet. The following Venn diagram shows their replies.

Study the Venn diagram and answer the questions that follow.

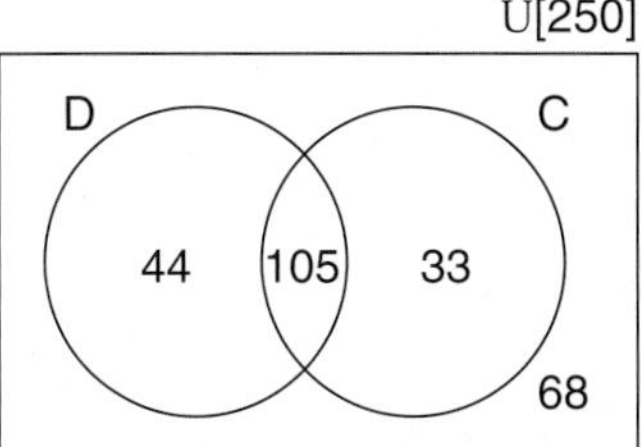

If a person is picked at random, find the probability that he or she:

(a) Has a dog as a pet
(b) Has neither a dog nor a cat as a pet
(c) Has a cat only as a pet
(d) Has a dog and a cat as pets
(e) Has a dog only as a pet

4. Forty girls were asked if they liked dance music (D) or rock music (R). 22 liked dance music, 19 liked rock music, 4 liked both and 3 liked neither.

(a) Draw a Venn diagram to represent this information.

If a girl is picked at random, what is the probability that she will like:

(b) Dance music?
(c) Rock music?
(d) Neither type of music?
(e) Both types of music?

5. Fifty-five people were asked if they liked rice (R), potatoes (P) or spaghetti (S). The Venn diagram shows their answers.

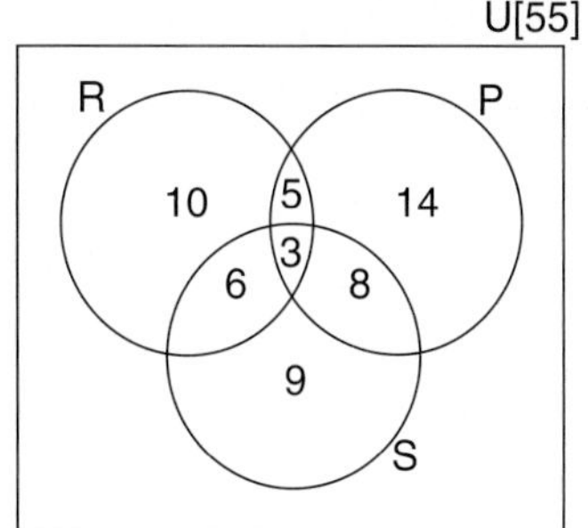

If a person is picked at random, find the probability that he or she likes:

(a) Rice
(b) Potatoes and spaghetti
(c) Potatoes and spaghetti but not rice
(d) None of the three
(e) Spaghetti only
(f) All three
(g) Only one of the three
(h) Exactly two of the three
(i) Rice only
(j) Rice and spaghetti only

6. A total of 100 people were asked if they liked apples (A), oranges (O) or pears (P). The Venn diagram shows their answers. Study the Venn diagram and answer the questions that follow.

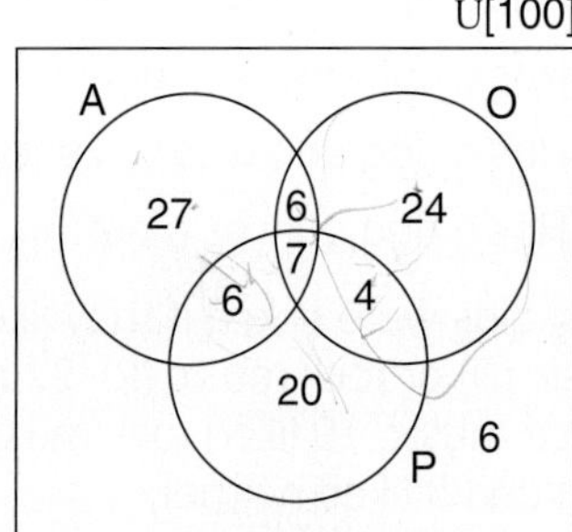

If a person is picked at random, find the probability that he or she likes:

(a) Pears
(b) Apples and oranges
(c) Oranges and pears but not apples
(d) None of the three
(e) Apples only
(f) All three
(g) Only one of the three
(h) Exactly two of the three
(i) Oranges only
(j) Pears only

7. Thirty foreign tourists were asked if they had visited Dublin or Cork during their stay. 18 had visited Dublin, 13 had visited Cork and 6 had visited both.

(a) Draw a Venn diagram to show this information.

If a person is chosen at random, find the probability that he or she visited:

(b) Cork
(c) Dublin
(d) Both cities
(e) Cork only
(f) Neither city
(g) Dublin only
(h) Only one of the two cities

8. A student has a 55% chance of passing their maths exam and a 45% chance of passing their science exam. There is a 75% chance that the student will pass one or both exams.

(a) Draw a Venn diagram to display the information.

What is the probability that the student will:

(b) Pass both exams?
(c) Pass one exam only?
(d) Pass maths only?
(e) Pass neither exam?

9. An archer has a 57% chance of hitting target A on her first shot and a 55% chance of hitting target B. There is an 85% chance he will hit one or both targets.

(a) Draw a Venn diagram to display the information.

What is the probability that the archer will:

(b) Hit both targets?
(c) Hit a target?
(d) Miss both targets?

10. A farmer plants two types of potato crop. There is 0.91 chance that one or both crops will grow. Crop A has a 0.64 chance of growing while crop B has a 0.45 chance of growing.

(a) Draw a Venn diagram to display the information.

What is the probability that:

(b) Both crops will fail?
(c) Both crops will grow?
(d) Only crop B will grow?

CHAPTER 16 SELF-CHECK TEST

1. Explain each of the following terms:
(a) Event
(b) Trial
(c) Outcome
(d) Sample space
(e) Probability

2. A fair die is rolled. Calculate:
(a) P(6)
(b) P(even number)
(c) P(Factor of 12)
(d) P(Prime number)
(e) P(Perfect square)

3. (a) How many cards are in a standard deck of playing cards?
(b) Write down the names of the four suits.

4. A card is chosen at random from a standard deck. Find the probability that the card chosen is:
(a) A red card
(b) A King
(c) The King of hearts
(d) A non-picture card
(e) A prime number

5. A coin is tossed and a fair die is thrown.

(a) Write out the sample space.

Find:

(b) P(Head and a 5)

(c) P(Head or a 4)

(d) P(The outcome not containing a tail)

(e) P(Tail and an odd number).

6. A thumbtack is dropped 60 times. It lands with its pin up 53 times. Calculate:

(a) The relative frequency of the tack landing with its pin up.

(b) If the thumbtack was dropped 12,000 times, how many times would you expect it to land with the pin down?

7. Eighty people were asked if they owned a mobile phone (M), an MP3 player (MP3) or a games console (GC). The Venn diagram shows their answers.

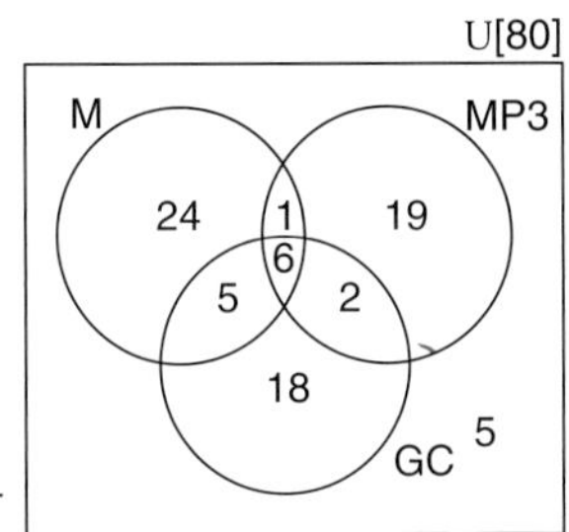

If a person is picked at random, find the probability that he or she owns:

(a) An MP3 player

(b) All three items

(c) None of the items

(d) A games console only

(e) A mobile phone

(f) A mobile phone and a games console

(g) Only one of the three items

(h) Exactly two of the three items

(i) An MP3 player only

(j) A mobile phone only

8. Sixty homeowners were asked whether they used oil (O), gas (G) or solid fuel (S) to heat their homes. The Venn diagram shows their answers.

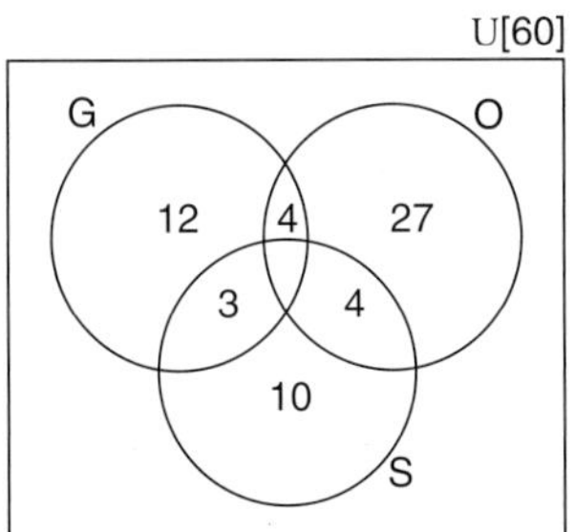

If a person is picked at random, find the probability that he or she uses:

(a) Oil

(b) Gas or oil but not both

(c) Solid fuel only

(d) None of the three

(e) Gas only

(f) All three

(g) Only one of the three

(h) Exactly two of the three

(i) Gas

(j) Oil only

9. A group of 120 students were asked if they have fixed line broadband or wireless broadband at home. 75 people had fixed, 35 had wireless, while 20 had no broadband.

(a) Draw a Venn diagram to show this information.

If a person is chosen at random, find the probability that he or she has:

(b) Wireless broadband

(c) Both types of broadband

(d) Fixed line broadband

(e) No broadband

(f) Wireless broadband only

(g) Only one type of broadband

10. Fifty members of a GAA club were asked if they played football or hurling. 27 played hurling and 30 played football and 2 said they did not play either sport.

(a) Draw a Venn diagram to show this information.

If a person is chosen at random, find the probability that he or she played:

(b) Hurling

(c) Football

(d) Both sports

(e) Neither sport

(f) Football only

(g) Hurling only

11. A machine runs two tests on a manufactured part. There is a 50% chance that each part will pass the first test (Test A) and a 68% chance it will pass the second test (Test B). There is an 80% chance that a part will pass either or both tests.

Draw a Venn diagram to show this information. Find:

(a) P(Passing the first test or the second test)

(b) P(Passing test A and failing test B)

(c) P(Failing both tests)

(d) P(Passing test B only)

12. Paddy, Tommy and Jimmy each roll a different die 120 times. Their results are recorded as follows:

Number	Paddy	Tommy	Jimmy
1	13	1	16
2	17	17	22
3	32	22	19
4	14	45	23
5	26	11	19
6	18	24	21

(a) What is the relative frequency of Paddy throwing a 2?

(b) What is the relative frequency of Tommy throwing a 6?

(c) What is the relative frequency of Jimmy throwing a 4?

(d) Based on the above results, whose die is the fairest? Give reasons for your answer.

(e) Whose die is the most biased? Explain your answer.

(f) If Paddy threw his die 240 times, what is the expected frequency of throwing a 1?

13. The colour of 500 cars that passed a particular set of traffic lights during a two-hour period is recorded by a group of students. Copy the table.

Colour	Frequency	Relative frequency	Daily frequency
Red	70		
Blue	100		
Yellow	45		
White	55		
Black			
Silver	140		
Total	500		

(a) Calculate the number of black cars and write it into the table.

(b) Calculate the relative frequency of each colour and write these into the table.

(c) Suggest a method to check that your relative frequency calculations are correct. Perform this check.

(d) What is the probability that the next car to pass the lights is red?

(e) Use the information to estimate the frequency of each colour if 2,400 cars pass the lights in a full day. Write this information into the table.

(f) The data collected by the students is not a random sample of the cars passing throughout the day. Do you think this makes your estimates in part (e) above unreliable? Give a reason for your answer.

14. A, B, C, D and E represent the probabilities of certain events occurring.
Copy the table and write the probability of each of the events listed, then place each of the letters A, B, C, D and E at its correct position on the probability scale.

Event		Probability
A club is selected in a random draw from a pack of playing cards.	A	
A tossed fair coin shows a tail on landing.	B	
The sun will rise in the east tomorrow.	C	
May will follow directly after June.	D	
A randomly selected person was born on a Thursday.	E	

0 ———————————————— 1

15. A fair circular spinner consists of three equal sectors. Two are coloured blue and one is coloured red. The spinner is spun and a fair coin is tossed.

(a) What is the probability of the spinner landing on a blue sector?

(b) Find the probability of getting a head and landing on a red sector.

(c) Find the probability of getting a tail and landing on a blue sector.

16. (a) What is the probability of getting a 1 when a fair die is tossed?

(b) A fair die is tossed 500 times. The results are partially recorded in the table below. Copy the table and answer the following:

Number on die	1	2	3	4	5	6
Frequency	70	82		90	91	81
Relative frequency						

(c) Calculate the number of times a 3 appeared.

(d) Calculate the relative frequency of each outcome and write it into the table.

(e) Give a possible reason for the difference in value between the relative frequency for 1 in the table and your answer to part (a).

17. In a survey, 54 people were asked which political party they had voted for in the last three elections. The results are as follows:

- 30 had voted for Fine Gael.
- 22 had voted for the Labour Party.
- 22 had voted for Fianna Fáil.
- 12 had voted for Fine Gael and for the Labour Party.
- 9 had voted for the Labour Party and for Fianna Fáil.
- 8 had voted for Fine Gael and for Fianna Fáil.
- 5 had voted for all three parties.

(a) Represent the information on a Venn diagram.

(b) If one person is chosen at random, what is the probability that the person chosen did not vote in any of the three elections?

(c) If one person is chosen at random, what is the probability that the person chosen voted for at least two different parties?

(d) If one person is chosen at random, what is the probability that the person chosen voted for the same party in all three elections?

18. Complete the following crossword:

Across

1. List of all possible outcomes of a trial
3. The result of a trial
5. The act of carrying out an experiment in probability
7. The probability of an event definitely occuring
8. The number of cards in a regular deck

Down

2. The likelihood of an event occurring is called its ______.
4. The occurrence of a favourable outcome
6. The probability of an event never occurring

CHAPTER 16 KNOWLEDGE CHECKLIST

After completing this chapter, I now:

- Am able to calculate the relative frequency of an event
- Understand the composition of a deck of cards
- Am able to calculate the expected frequency for an experiment
- Am able to calculate probabilities of experiments involving spinners, dice, cards and coins
- Am able to calculate the probability of events
- Know about set theory and probability

Challenge

You are a prisoner sentenced to death. Your captor offers you a chance to live by playing a simple game. He gives you 50 black marbles, 50 white marbles and 2 empty bowls. He then says, 'Divide these 100 marbles into these 2 bowls. You can divide them any way you like as long as you use all the marbles. Then I will blindfold you and mix the bowls around. You can then choose one bowl and remove one marble. If the marble is **WHITE** you will live, but if the marble is **BLACK**, you will die.'

How do you divide the marbles up so that you have the greatest probability of choosing a **WHITE** marble?

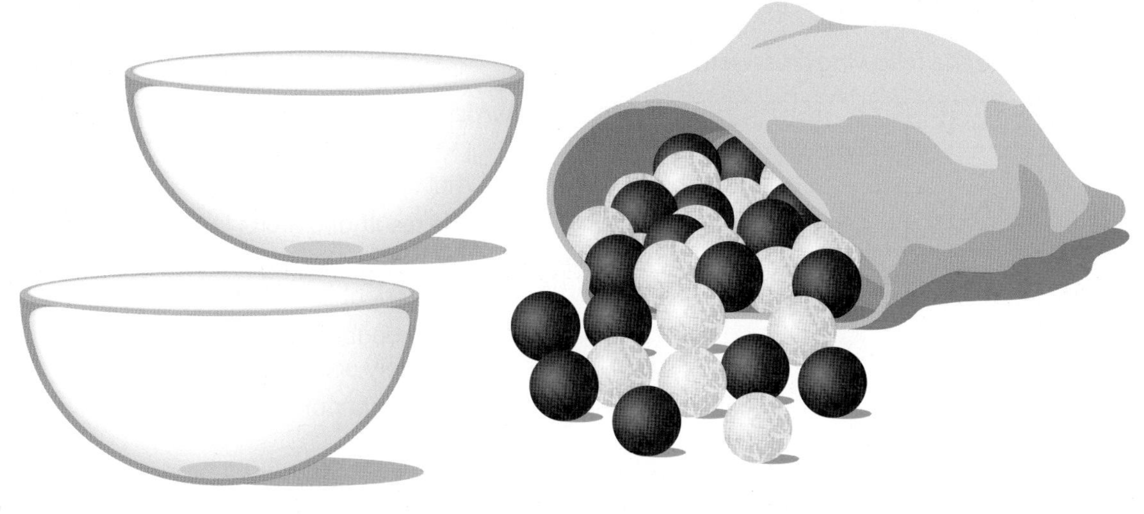

DISTANCE, SPEED AND TIME

LEARNING OUTCOMES

In this chapter you will learn:

- ✓ To change between different types of units
- ✓ To perform calculations involving average speed, distance and time
- ✓ To perform calculations for multi-part journeys
- ✓ To solve distance, time and speed problems involving graphs

KEY WORDS

- 12-hour clock
- 24-hour clock
- Accelerate
- Average speed
- Decelerate
- Distance
- Speed
- Time

17

MATHS IN ACTION 3

INTRODUCTION

The concept of time was first used by the Egyptians. They created a 24-hour day where the night had 12 hours, the day had 10 hours and the rest was the twilight before dawn and sunset. They used the stars at night and a shadow clock during the day to keep track of time.

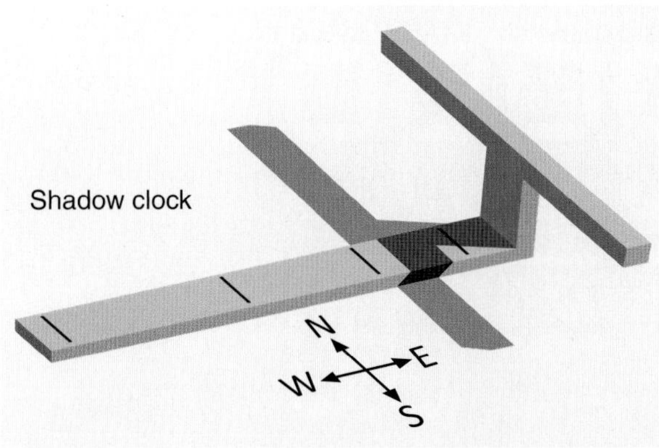

Around the same time, the Chinese, Babylonians, Greeks and the Romans were using instruments called sundials to tell time.

About 4,000 years ago, the Babylonians developed a sexagesimal system of counting. This uses 60 as its base. We still use this system every day whenever we tell the time or refer to the degrees of an angle of a circle.

Section 17.1: Time and distance

Student Activity 17A

1. How many minutes are in an hour?
2. How many seconds are in a minute?
3. Using your answers to Questions 1 and 2, can you calculate how many seconds are in an hour?
4. Change each of the following into minutes only:
   (a) 3 hours 23 minutes
   (b) 2 hours 55 minutes
   (c) 300 seconds
   (d) 7,200 seconds
   (e) 0.5 hours
5. How many metres are in a kilometre?
6. How many centimetres are in a metre?
7. Using your answers to Questions 5 and 6, can you calculate how many centimetres are in a kilometre?
8. Convert each of the following into metres only:
   (a) 2 km
   (b) 1 km 347 m
   (c) 450 cm
   (d) 4 km 23 m
   (e) 10 km 498 m
9. The graph represents the famous race between the tortoise and the hare. Study the graph and answer the questions.

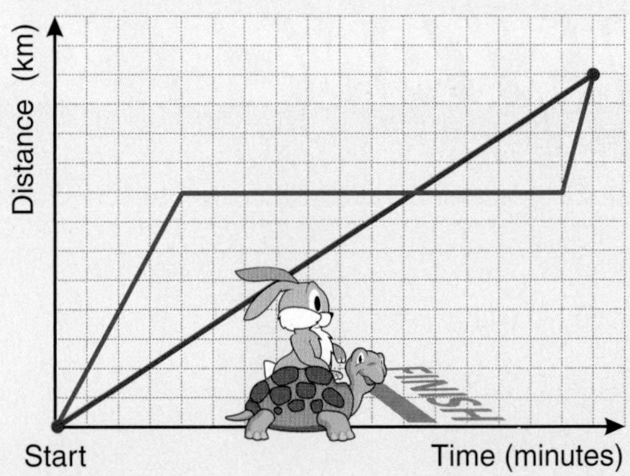

   (a) Which line do you think represents the hare? Explain your answer.
   (b) Why do you think the pink line contains a long flat section?

TIME AND DISTANCE EXPLAINED

When dealing with problems involving speed, distance and time, we need to make sure that all quantities are in the same unit. It is often necessary to convert units, such as changing minutes to hours, or metres to kilometres. It is often easier to change your units before carrying out any calculations.

A button on your calculator can be used to help with calculations involving units of time.

You should only use your calculator once you are able to carry out the calculations yourself.

You should also be familiar with using the 24-hour clock. Remember that 12 a.m. or midnight is 00:00 on the 24-hour clock. If the time is less than 12:00, it is a.m. and if it is greater than 12:00 it is p.m.

- **Casio: °’’’** button ⇒ 1 hour 25 min = 1 [°’’’] 25 [°’’’]
- **Sharp: D°M’S** button ⇒ 1 hour 25 min = 1 [D°M’S] 25 [D°M’S]

EXAMPLE 1

(a) Change each of the following to 12-hour time:

(i) 13:20 (ii) 05:47 (iii) 19:13

(b) A man leaves home at 08:43 and arrives at work 48 minutes later. At what time does he arrive at work?

(c) A taxi driver collects a passenger at Dublin airport at 15:45 and drops her off in Sandyford at 17:13. How long did the journey take?

Solution

(a) (i) 13:20 − 12:00 = 1:20 p.m. **p.m. since 13:30 > 12:00**

(ii) 05:47 = 5:47 a.m. **a.m. since 05:47 < 12:00**

(iii) 19:13 − 12:00 = 7:13 p.m. **p.m. since 19:13 > 12:00**

(b) 08:43 + 00:48 = 09:31 or 9:31 a.m.

(c) 17:13 − 15:45 = 1 hr 28 min

Exercise 17.1

Convert each of the following to 24-hour time:

1. 5:33 a.m. **5.** 11:13 a.m.

2. 4:12 p.m. **6.** 9:45 p.m.

3. 9:57 a.m. **7.** 6:27 p.m.

4. 5:33 p.m.

Convert each of the following to 12-hour time:

8. 11:27 **12.** 15:20

9. 06:32 **13.** 19:00

10. 18:19 **14.** 12:04

11. 23:57

15. Calculate each of the following:

(a) 3 hr 42 min + 5 hr 07 min

(b) 6 hr 11 min + 8 hr 56 min

(c) 4 hr 34 min + 9 hr 45 min

(d) 9 hr 24 min − 6 hr 12 min

(e) 12 hr 13 min − 9 hr 44 min

(f) 7 hr 28 min − 4 hr 57 min

(g) 8 hr 19 min + 5 hr 34 min + 2 hr 56 min

(h) 6 hr 49 min + 4 hr 56 min + 12 hr 17 min

(i) 18 hr 33 min + (11 hr 37 min − 7 hr 06 min)

(j) 9 hr 25 min − (4 hr 37 min + 2 hr 56 min)

16. Convert each of the following to metres:

(a) 2.5 km (c) 10,000 mm (e) 50 cm

(b) 3,000 cm (d) 220 km

17. Convert each of the following to kilometres:

(a) 6,500 m (c) 500,000 mm

(b) 30,000 cm (d) 220,000 m

18. A truck driver drives 50 km between 09:00 and 10:00. After a break, he drives another 75 km. How many metres did the truck driver travel in total?

19. A factory worker starts work at 09:00 every morning and finishes at 17:45 each day from Monday to Saturday. There is a 15-minute break at 11:00 and a 45 minute break at 12:30. How many hours does she work each week?

20. A film started at 19:55 and lasted 2 hours and 40 minutes. At what time did the film finish?

21. The following is a timetable for Bus Éireann between Dublin Airport and Wexford. Study the timetable and answer the questions.

AIRPORT – DUBLIN – ARKLOW – GOREY – ENNISCORTHY – WEXFORD **2**

MONDAY TO SUNDAY (including Public Holidays)

SERVICE NUMBER		*002*	*002*		*002*	*002*	*002*	*002*	*002*	*002*	*002*	*X2*	*002*	*002*		*002*	*002*	*002*
						SuX		**SuX**		**SuX**								
Dublin Airport (Atrium Rd Zone 12)	dep.	0600	0800	....	1000	1100	1200	1300	1400	1500	1600	1700	1800	1900	....	2100	2200	2400
Dublin (Opp The 02 North Wall Quay)		0615	0815	....	1015	1115	1215	1315	1415	1515	1615	1715	1815	1915	....	2115	2215	0015
Custom House Quay (Opp Jurys Inn)		0618	0818	....	1018	1118	1218	1318	1418	1518	1618	1718	1818	1918	....	2118	2218	0018
Dublin (Busáras)		0630	0830	....	1030	1130	1230	1330	1430	1530	1630	1730	1830	1930	....	2130	2230	0020
Merrion Square West (Clare St)		0635	0835	....	1035	1135	1235	1335			1635	1735		1935	....	2135	2235	0025
Dublin (Leeson St (Fitzwilliam Place)		0638	0838	....	1038	1138	1238	1338			1638	1738		1938	....	2138	2238	0028
Donnybrook (Stadium)		0640	0840	....	1040	1140	1240	1340			1640	1740		1940	....	2140	2240	0030
Merrion Square North (Jct Clare St)				....					1435	1535			1835		....			
Dublin (Merrion Rd (Show House Pub)				....					1440	1540			1840		....			
Nutley Lane (St Vincent's Hospital)				....					1443	1543			1843		....			
Dublin UCD (Montrose Hotel)		0645	0845	....	1045	1145	1245	1345	1445	1545	1645	1745	1845	1945	....	2145	2245	0035
Loughlinstown (Opp Hospital)		0655	0855	....	1055	1155	1255	1355	1455	1555	1655	1755	1855	1955	....	2155	2255	0045
Kilmacanogue (Topaz)		0705	0905	....	1105	1205	1305	1405	1505	1605	1705	1805	1905	2005	....	2205	2305	0055
Beehive (Beehive Pub)			0928	....		1228		1428		1633			1933		....	2220		0110
Ballincor (Opp Barrindarrig Station)			0931	....		1231		1431		1636			1936		....	2225		0115
Jack Whites Cross (Pub)			0934	....		1234		1434		1639			1939		....	2227		0117
Arklow (Ferrybank ESB)		0733	0942	....	1142	1242	1342	1442	1542	1647	1747		1947	2042	....	2232	2332	0122
Arklow (Tourist Office)		0735	0945	....	1145	1245	1345	1445	1545	1650	1750		1950	2045	....	2235	2335	0125
Arklow (Opp Lidl)		0738	0948	....	1148	1248	1348	1448	1548	1653	1753		1953	2048	....	2238	2338	0128
Gorey (Main St – Gerry's Supermarket)		0750	1005	....	1205	1305	1405	1505	1605	1710	1810	1855	2010	2105	....	2250	2350	0140
Clough (Service Station)		0800	1015	....	1215	1315	1415	1515	1615	1720	1820	1905	2020	2115	....	2300	2400	0150
Camolin (Mercedes Benz Garage)		0805	1020	....	1220	1320	1420	1520	1620	1725	1825	1910	2025	2120	....	2305	0005	0155
Ferns (Applegreen)		0810	1025	....	1225	1325	1425	1525	1625	1730	1830	1915	2030	2125	....	2310	0010	0200
Enniscorthy (Templeshannon)		0820	1035	....	1235	1335	1435	1535	1635	1740	1840	1925	2040	2135	....	2320	0020	0210
Oylegate (Opposite Mernagh's Pub)		0830	1045	....	1245	1345	1445	1545	1645	1750	1850	1935	2050	2145	....	2330	0030	0220
Wexford (O'Hanrahan Stn)	arr.	0840	1055	....	1255	1355	1455	1555	1655	1800	1900	1945	2100	2155	....	2340	0040	0230

(a) At what time does the first bus depart Dublin Airport?

(b) How long does it take the 08:00 bus departing from Dublin to travel to Ferns?

(c) Which buses departing from Dublin Airport stop at Nutley Lane?

(d) How long does it take the 12:00 bus departing from Dublin to travel to Wexford?

(e) Which bus travels to Wexford in the shortest time?

(f) If Áine lives in Loughlinstown and must be at a meeting in Wexford at 15:15, which bus should she catch?

(g) Paul catches the 11:05 bus from Kilmacanogue to Ferns. How long does the journey take?

(h) Paul's sister arrives at Kilmacanogue bus stop at 12:48 p.m. How long must she wait before the next bus arrives?

22. The train timetable on the next page shows the arrival and departure times between Dundalk and Gorey. Study the timetable shown and answer the questions:

(a) How long does it take the 09:19 train to travel from Lansdowne Road to Dalkey?

(b) How long does it take the 09:00 train to travel from Malahide to Sandymount?

(c) How long does it take the 08:56 train to travel from Kilbarrack to Bray?

(d) Ursula arrives at Raheny station at 08:15 to catch the next train to Killester. How long will she have to wait for the next train to arrive?

(e) Theresa suffers from motion sickness. Which train travels the fastest from Howth Junction to Dublin's Pearse Station?

(f) Theresa decides to travel on the 09:20 train from Howth Junction, get off at Dublin Pearse Station and board the next train to Sandymount. How long was Theresa actually on a train (do not include the time she waited for trains)?

(g) Eddie, who lives on Tara Street, has an exam in Greystones at 10:40. What is the latest train he should board to get to the exam on time?

		MON TO FRI	MON TO FRI	MON TO FRI	MON TO FRI	MON TO FRI	MON TO FRI	MON TO FRI
DUNDALK Clarke	Dep	....	....	....	....	....	....	....
DROGHEDA MacBride	Dep	..	..	..	08.35	..	..	..
Laytown	Dep	....	....	....	08.41	....	....	....
Gormanston	Dep	..	..	..	08.48	..	..	..
BALBRIGGAN	Dep	....	....	....	08.51	....	....	....
Skerries	Dep	..	..	..	08.57	..	..	..
Rush & Lusk	Dep	....	....	....	09.04	....	....	....
Donabate	Dep	..	..	..	09.08	..	..	..
MALAHIDE	Dep	....	....	09.00	09.12	....	....	....
Portmarnock	Dep	..	..	09.04	09.17	..	..	..
Clongriffin	Dep	....	....	09.07	....	....	....	....
HOWTH	Dep	..	08.45	..	..	..	09.15	..
Sutton	Dep	....	08.48	....	....	....	09.18	....
Bayside	Dep	..	08.50	..	..	..	09.20	..
Howth Jctn. & Donaghmede	Dep	From Maynooth	08.54	09.09	09.20	....	09.24	From Maynooth
Kilbarrack	Dep		08.56	09.11	..	..	09.26	
Raheny	Dep		08.58	09.13	....	....	09.28	
Harmonstown	Dep		09.00	09.15	..	..	09.30	
Killester	Dep		09.02	09.17	....	....	09.32	
Clontarf Road	Dep		09.06	09.21	..	..	09.36	
DUBLIN Connolly	Arr	09.04	09.09	09.25	09.30	....	09.42	09.50
DUBLIN Connolly Ⓛ Ⓐ	Dep	09.05	09.10	09.26	09.31	09.40	09.44	09.51
Tara Street	Dep	09.08	09.13	09.29	09.34	09.43	09.48	09.53
DUBLIN Pearse	Arr	09.10	09.14	09.30	09.36	09.45	09.49	09.56
Grand Canal Dock	Dep	....	09.17	09.33	....	....	09.52	....
Lansdowne Road	Dep	..	09.19	09.35	..	..	09.54	..
Sandymount	Dep	....	09.21	09.37	....	....	09.56	....
Sydney Parade	Dep	..	09.23	09.39	..	..	09.58	..
Booterstown	Dep	....	09.25	09.41	....	....	10.00	....
Blackrock	Dep	..	09.27	09.43	..	..	10.02	..
Seapoint	Dep	....	09.29	09.45	....	....	10.04	....
Salthill & Monkstown	Dep	..	09.31	09.47	..	..	10.06	..
DUN LAOGHAIRE Mallin	Arr	....	09.34	09.50	....	09.58	10.09	....
Sandycove & Glasthule	Dep	..	09.37	09.53	..	..	10.12	..
Glenageary	Dep	....	09.39	09.55	....	....	10.14	....
Dalkey	Dep	..	09.41	09.57	..	..	10.16	..
Killiney	Dep	....	09.45	10.01	....	....	10.20	....
Shankill	Dep	..	09.48	10.04	..	..	10.23	..
BRAY Daly	Arr	....	09.54	10.09	....	10.16	10.29	....
BRAY Daly	Dep	..	..	10.11	..	10.17	..	..
GREYSTONES	Arr	....	....	10.20	....	10.26	....	....
Kilcoole	Dep	..	..	..	..	..	..	..
Wicklow	Dep	....	....	....	....	10.40	....	....
Rathdrum	Dep	..	..	..	..	10.53	..	..
Arklow	Dep	....	....	....	....	11.08	....	....
GOREY	Arr	..	..	..	..	11.20	..	..
		....	....	....	....	To Rosslare	....	....

23. The following is a listing of programmes on RTÉ Two. Study the guide and answer the questions:

RTÉ Two
16:00 Kung Fu Panda
16:28 news2day
16:34 The Looney Tunes Show
17:25 Neighbours
18:00 The Simpsons
18:32 Home and Away
19:05 The Curious World of Professor Fun and Dr Dull
19:38 MasterChef: The Professionals
20:35 2 Broke Girls
21:00 Mad Men
22:37 Father Ted
23:03 RTÉ News on Two and World Forecast
23:11 National Lottery EuroMillions
23:23 Teleshopping

(a) How long was *The Looney Tunes Show* cartoon?
(b) How long was *news2day?*
(c) How long was *The Curious World of Professor Fun and Dr Dull* show?
(d) If I watched television from the second half of *The Simpsons* until the end of *The Curious World of Professor Fun and Dr Dull*, for how long was I watching television?
(e) Grace is allowed to watch only one television programme between 5 p.m. and 9 p.m. Which programme lasts the longest?
(f) Liam came in from work and fell asleep ten minutes into *Home and Away*. He awoke to the starting theme tune of *2 Broke Girls*. Approximately how long was he asleep?
(g) A key witness to a robbery gave a Garda the following report: 'I had watched the first ten minutes of MasterChef, when I saw the suspect go around to the back of the house. The show *Mad Men* was just over, when I saw him reappear and be picked up by a strange van.' How long did it take the suspect to burgle the house?

Section 17.2: Average distance, speed and time

Student Activity 17B

1. What units can speed be measured in? (Hint: think of the speedometer in a car.)

2. A car's journey is shown below.

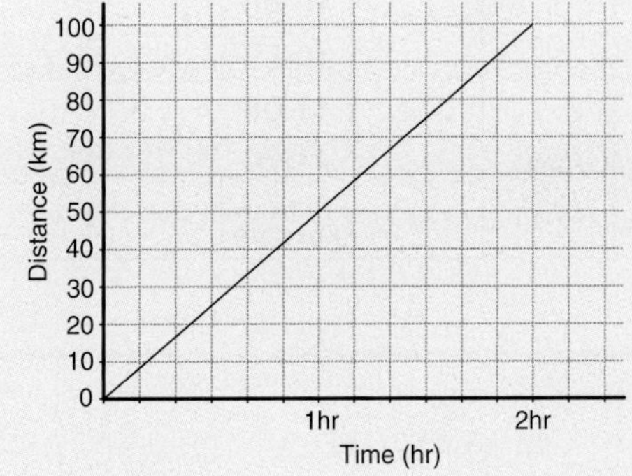

(a) How far did the car travel in 1 hour?
(b) Find the slope $\left(\frac{\text{Rise}}{\text{Run}}\right)$ of the graph.
(c) What is the average speed of the car in km/hr?
(d) What do you notice about your answers in parts (b) and (c)?

3. A person completed a journey of 320 km in 4 hours at a constant speed.

(a) Represent this information on a graph.
(b) How far did the person travel in the first hour?
(c) What average speed did the person travel at over the entire journey?

(d) Find the slope $\left(\frac{\text{Rise}}{\text{Run}}\right)$ of the graph.

(e) What do you notice about your answers in parts (b) and (c)?

4. A train travelled from Limerick Junction to Dublin, a journey of 150 km in two hours.

(a) Represent this information on a graph.

(b) How far did the train travel in the first hour?

(c) What average speed did the train travel at over the journey?

(d) Find the slope $\left(\frac{\text{Rise}}{\text{Run}}\right)$ of the graph.

(e) What do you notice about your answers in parts (c) and (d)?

5. Copy and complete the following sentence:

To find the average s _ _ _ _ of a body, you d _ _ _ _ _ the d _ _ _ _ _ _ _ travelled by the t _ _ _ taken for the journey.

6. A car drives at an average speed of 55 km/hr for 2 hours. What distance did the car travel?

7. A plane flies at an average speed of 500 km/hr for 5 hours. What distance did the plane fly?

8. A boat sets sail from Cork and sails south for 3 hours at an average speed of 20 km/hr. What distance did the boat sail?

9. Copy and complete the following sentence:

To find the d _ _ _ _ _ _ _ a body travels, you m _ _ _ _ _ _ _ the average s _ _ _ _ by the t _ _ _ taken for the journey.

10. A man runs 20 km at an average speed of 8 km/hr. How long did it take the man to complete his run?

11. A plane flies a distance of 3,000 km at an average speed of 500 km/hr. How long did it take the plane to complete its journey?

12. An athlete runs 100 m at an average speed of 10 m/s. How long did it take the athlete to complete the race?

> **Note**
> m/s means metres per second.

13. Copy and complete the following sentence:

To find the t _ _ _ taken for a journey, you d _ _ _ _ _ the d _ _ _ _ _ _ _ by the s _ _ _ _.

14. What word is used to indicate that an object such as a car is increasing its speed? (Hint: think of the three pedals in a car.)

AVERAGE DISTANCE, SPEED AND TIME EXPLAINED

In Student Activity 17B, you calculated the average speed, distance and time for certain problems.

We can use the following to help us remember how to carry out these types of calculations:

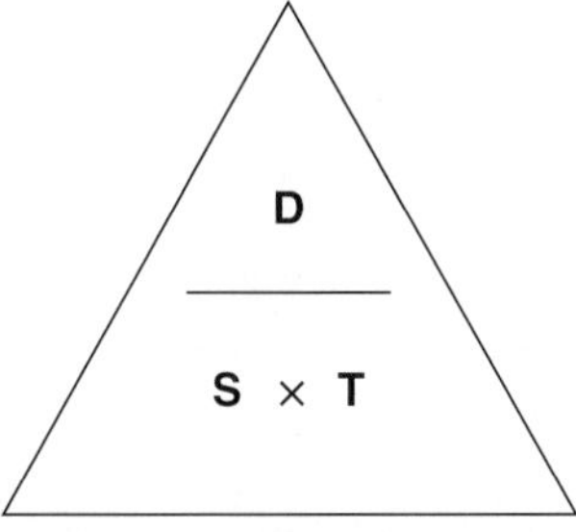

This is referred to as 'Dad's Silly Triangle'. From this we can derive our three formulae:

$$\text{Average speed} = \frac{\text{Distance}}{\text{Time}}$$

$$\text{Time} = \frac{\text{Distance}}{\text{Average speed}}$$

$$\text{Distance} = \text{Average speed} \times \text{Time}$$

When attempting a question, you should identify the information you know. This will help you to understand what you are being asked to find.

It is very important to check your units in each calculation.

The average speed of a body can also be found from a Distance-Time graph as shown in Student Activity 17B. The slope or $\frac{\text{Rise}}{\text{Run}}$ of the graph is equal to the average speed of the travelling body.

> **Accelerate** means to speed up.

> **Decelerate** means to slow down.

EXAMPLE 2

(a) A train travels from Thurles to Dublin, a journey of 120 km in 2 hours. What is the average speed of the train?

(b) A person drives 300 km in 3 hours. Calculate the average speed in m/s, correct to two decimal places.

Solution

(a) Distance = 120 km

Time = 2 hours

Average speed = ?

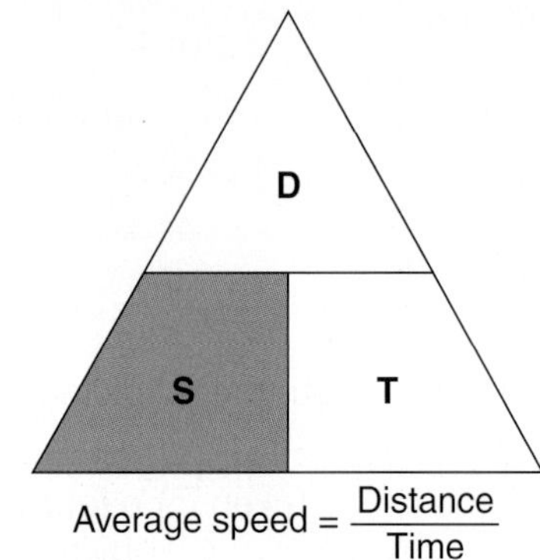

Average speed = $\frac{\text{Distance}}{\text{Time}}$

Average speed = $\frac{\text{Distance}}{\text{Time}}$

Average speed = $\frac{120 \text{ km}}{2 \text{ hrs}}$

Average speed = 60 km/hr

(b) **Note:** The answer is required in units different to the original units.

Distance = 300 km

Time = 3 hrs

Average speed = ?

300 km = $300 \times 1{,}000 = 300{,}000$ m

3 hrs = $3 \times 60 \times 60 = 10{,}800$ sec

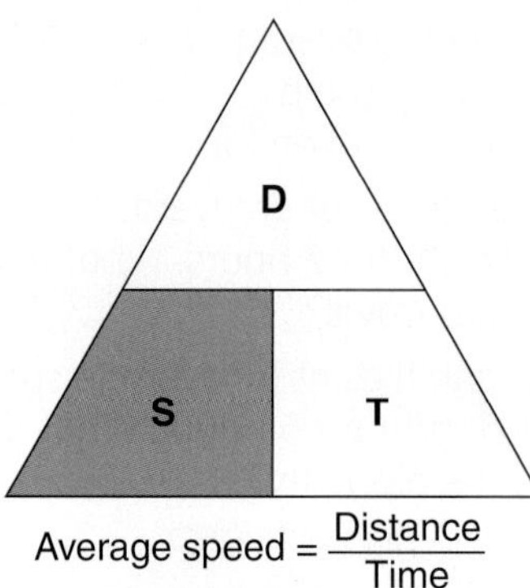

Average speed = $\frac{\text{Distance}}{\text{Time}}$

Average speed = $\frac{\text{Distance}}{\text{Time}}$

Average speed = $\frac{300{,}000 \text{ m}}{10{,}800 \text{ sec}}$

Average speed = 27.78 m/s to 2 decimal places

EXAMPLE 3

A bird flies for 4 hours at an average speed of 10 km/hr. What distance did the bird travel?

Solution

Distance = ?

Time = 4 hrs

Average speed = 10 km/hr

Distance = Average speed × Time

Distance = 10×4

Distance = 40 km

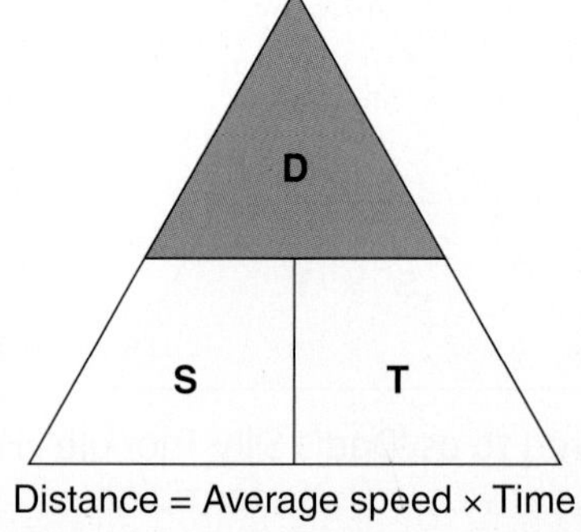

Distance = Average speed × Time

EXAMPLE 4

Bernie cycles at 4 km/hr and covers a distance of 13 km. How long does her journey take?

Solution

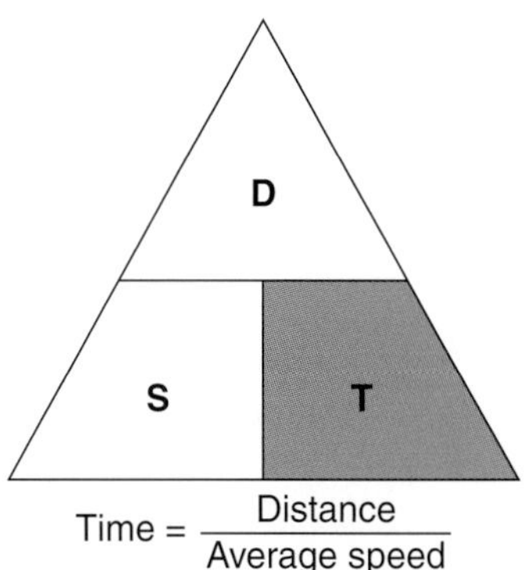

Distance = 13 km

Time = ?

Average speed = 4 km/hr

Time = $\frac{\text{Distance}}{\text{Speed}}$

Time = $\frac{13}{4}$

Time = 3.25 hrs

Time = 3 hrs 15 mins

Remember: $\frac{1}{4}$ of an hour equals 15 minutes

EXAMPLE 5

An athlete runs 1,500 metres in 3 minutes and 12 seconds. Calculate the average speed of the athlete in m/s, correct to one decimal place.

Solution

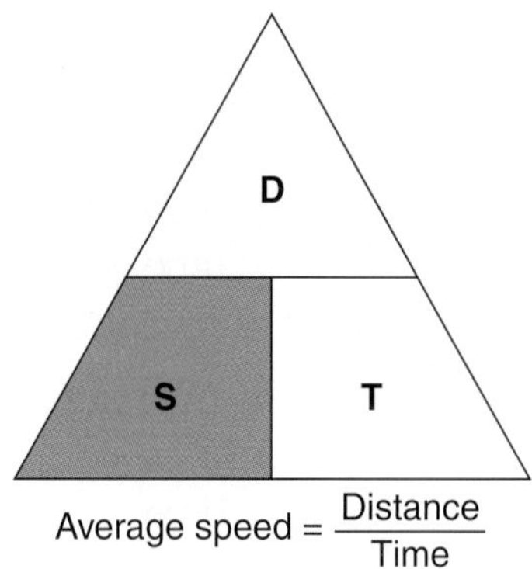

Distance = 1,500 metres

Time = 3 minutes 12 seconds = $3 \times 60 + 12 = 192$ seconds

Average speed = ?

Average speed = $\frac{\text{Distance}}{\text{Time}}$

Average speed = $\frac{1{,}500}{192}$

Average speed = 7.8 m/s to 1 decimal place

Graphs

We can use graphs that show distance against time to describe journeys. The vertical scale (y-axis) shows the distance from the starting point, while the horizontal scale (x-axis) shows the time taken. In science, a Go-motion sensor can track a person's movement towards or away from a sensor or starting point.

Graph A

Travelling away from the starting point at a constant speed

Returning to the starting point at a constant speed

Not moving

Distance from Starting point

Time

Graph A illustrates three parts of a journey.

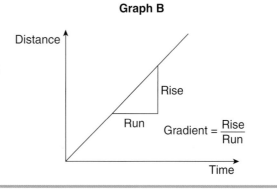

The **gradient** of a straight line (*see* Graph B) gives the speed of a moving object. Gradient is a measure of the speed. It is important to note that a negative gradient indicates that the object is moving towards the starting point rather than away from it.

Graph B

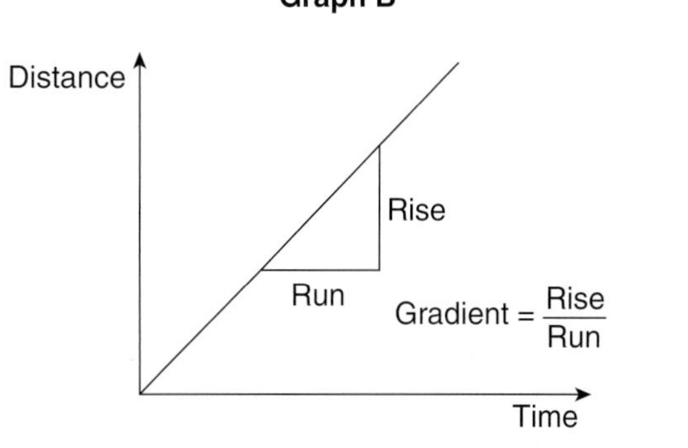

EXAMPLE 6

(a) The graph shows a car's journey.

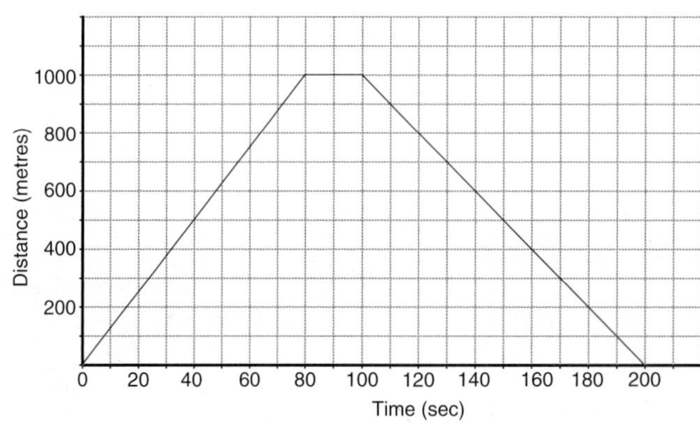

(i) Describe each part of the car's journey.

(ii) Calculate the speed of the car on each part of the journey.

Solution

(a) (i) The first part of the graph shows the car is moving away from home at a constant speed. The second part (horizontal line) of the graph shows that the car remains in the same position. The third part of the graph shows the car returning to the starting point at a steady speed.

(ii) During the first stage, the car travels 1,000 m in 80 seconds.

$$\text{Speed} = \frac{\text{Distance}}{\text{Time}} = \frac{1{,}000}{80} = 12.5 \text{ m/s}$$

During the second stage, the speed of the car is zero.

During the third stage, the car travels 1,000 m in 100 seconds.

$$\text{Speed} = \frac{\text{Distance}}{\text{Time}} = \frac{1{,}000}{100} = 10 \text{ m/s}$$

(b) On a journey, Aidan drives at 50 km per hour for 2 hours, rests for 1 hour and then drives 70 km in $1\frac{1}{2}$ hours. Draw a distance-time graph to illustrate this journey.

Solution

(b)

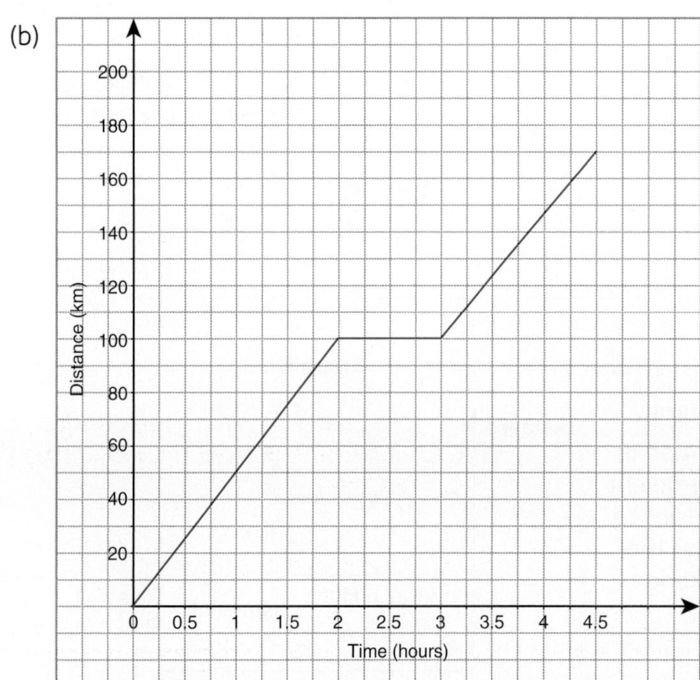

Exercise 17.2

1. A person travels 180 km in 3 hours at a constant speed.
   (a) Represent this information on a graph.
   (b) How far did the person travel in the first hour?
   (c) How far did the person travel in the second hour?
   (d) Calculate the average speed of the car in km/hr.
2. A woman walks 25 km in a time of 5 hours at a constant speed.
   (a) Represent this information on a graph.
   (b) How far did the woman travel in the first hour?
   (c) How far did the woman travel in the second hour?
   (d) Find the average speed of the woman using your graph.
   (e) Calculate the average speed of the woman in km/hr.
   (f) Calculate the average speed the woman walked in metres per minute.
3. An athlete runs a race. The average speed of the athlete was recorded in the following graph:

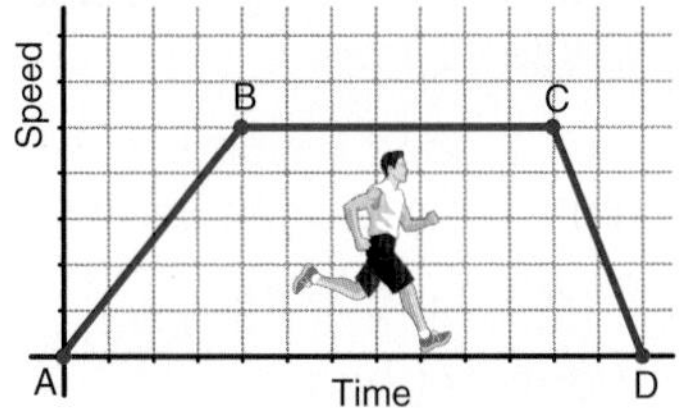

   (a) Describe the athlete's motion between points A and B.
   (b) Describe the athlete's motion between points B and C.
   (c) Explain the athlete's motion between points C and D.
   (d) Which point on the graph would you consider to be the finish line? Explain your answer.
4. The following graph shows the motion of a cheetah chasing a springbok.

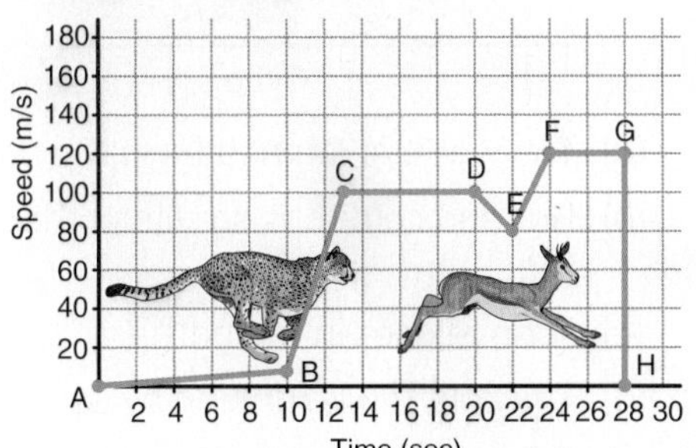

   Match each statement with the relevant section of the graph.
   (a) The cheetah is running at constant speed.
   (b) The cheetah is slowly accelerating.
   (c) The cheetah makes the kill.
   (d) The cheetah is accelerating quickly.
   (e) The cheetah is not moving.
   (f) The cheetah decelerates.
5. A car journey of 60 km takes half an hour. Calculate the average speed in km/hr.
6. An athlete runs 2,000 m in 3 minutes 20 seconds. Calculate the athlete's average speed in m/s.
7. A journey of 210 km began at 09:30 and ended at 10:40. Calculate the average speed in m/min.
8. A racing car completes a course of 240 km at an average speed of 80 km/hr. How long did the race last?
9. After a meal, an earthworm moves a distance of 45 cm in 90 seconds. Find the average speed per hour of the earthworm.
10. A car leaves Athlone at 8.00 a.m. and arrives in Letterkenny at 10.30 a.m. If the distance is 220 km, find the average speed per hour.
11. A killer shark swims at an average speed of 13 m/s for half a minute. How far does it swim in this time?
12. A car leaves London at 8.30 a.m. and arrives in Edinburgh at 5.30 p.m. If the car travels at an average speed of 75 km/hr, how far is it from London to Edinburgh?
13. A car travels at 88 km/hr over a distance of 22 km. Find in minutes the time taken for the car to travel this journey.
14. A car travelling at a constant speed takes 4 hours to travel 244 km. Find the average speed of the car.
15. A car travels at an average speed of 60 km/h for 3 hours. How far does the car travel?
16. An octopus swims 7 km at an average speed of 3 km/hr. How long does it take in hours and minutes?
17. A horse runs for 2 hours 15 minutes at an average speed of 8 km/hr. How far does it run?

18. The distance from Rosslare to Galway by rail is 280 km. At what average speed must a train travel to cover this distance in 4 hours?

19. A bus travels at an average speed of 40 km/hr. Calculate the average speed of the bus in:

(a) Metres per hour

(b) Metres per second

20. A salesperson can travel from town A to town B using either of two roads. If the salesperson drives at an average speed of 50 km/hr, how much quicker is the journey if road 1 is used?

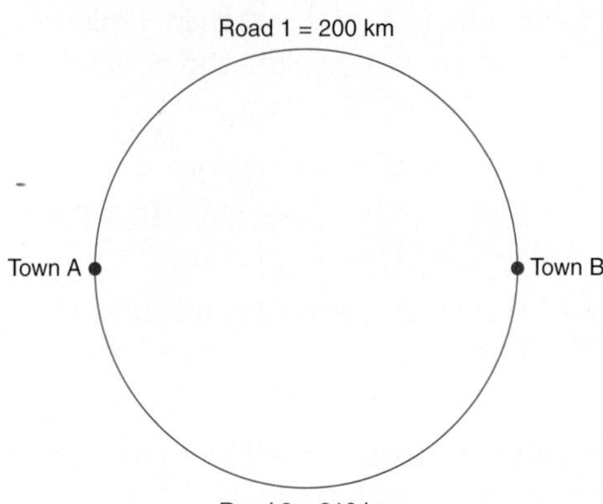

21. A sailor plans to sail from Galway to Dublin. The routes she plans are shown.

(a) What is the total length of each route?

(b) If she sails at an average speed of 25 km/hr, how long will each route take?

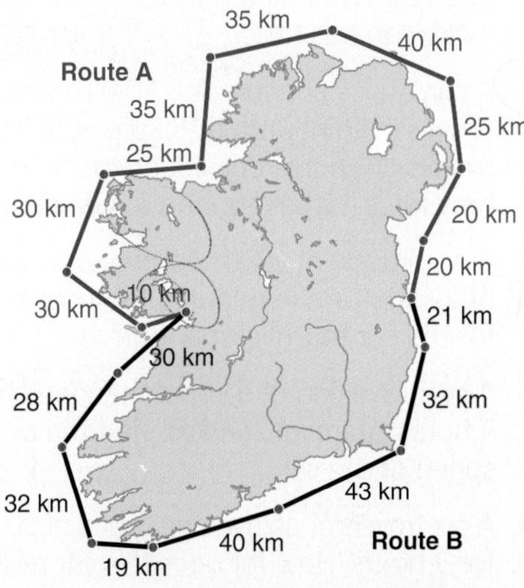

22. A charity race consists of running the course shown. An athlete completes the course in 2 hours 15 minutes.

(a) What is the total length of the course in metres?

(b) What average speed did the athlete run in m/s, correct to 3 decimal places?

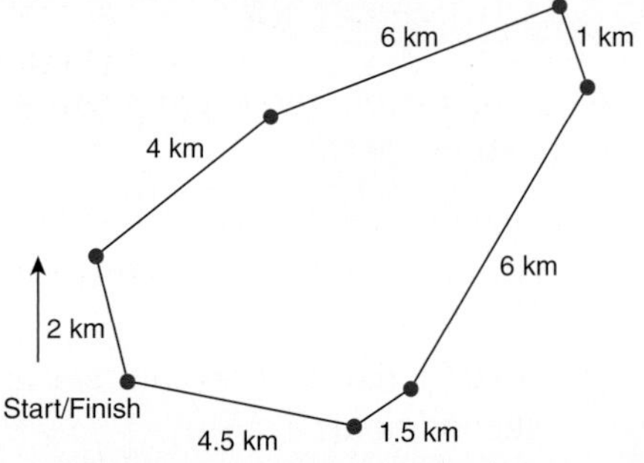

23. A truck driver began a journey at 08:30 and completed the journey at 10:50. If the average speed of the truck was 81 km/hr, how far had the truck travelled?

24. How long does it take to complete a journey of 263.5 km at an average speed of 62 km/h?

25. A plane that was scheduled to leave Shannon Airport at 10:45 was delayed for 36 minutes.

(a) At what time did the plane leave?

(b) The plane flew to London Heathrow and arrived at 12:56. How long did the flight take?

(c) If the distance from Shannon to London Heathrow is 803 km, at what average speed did the plane fly? Give your answer correct to the nearest whole number.

26. Jack can type 960 words in 20 minutes. Calculate his average typing speed in:

(a) Words per minute

(b) Words per hour

27. The following graph shows the water level in a bath as John fills and takes a bath. Examine the graph and match each section with an explanation from the list.

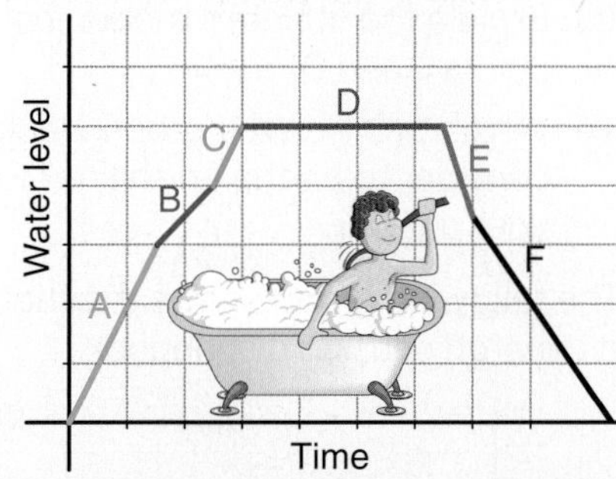

(a) The water is drained from the bath.

(b) Hot and cold taps are filling the bath together.

(c) John relaxes in the bath.

(d) The cold tap is running by itself.

(e) John gets out of the bath.

(f) John gets into the bath.

28. A student carried out an experiment to record the depth changes that take place in a beaker. Study the graph and answer the questions.

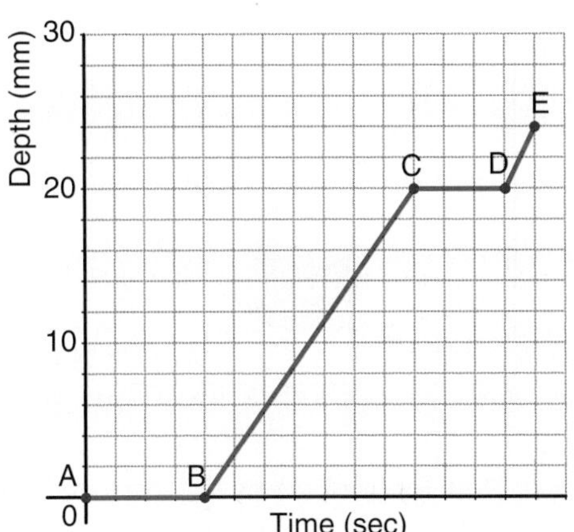

(a) Explain why the depth does not rise between the points A and B.

(b) Explain what you think is happening between the points B and C.

(c) Why does the depth not rise between the points C and D?

(d) Explain what is happening between the points D and E.

29. A student recorded the height of a plant in centimetres as it grew over a period of weeks. Study the graph and answer the questions.

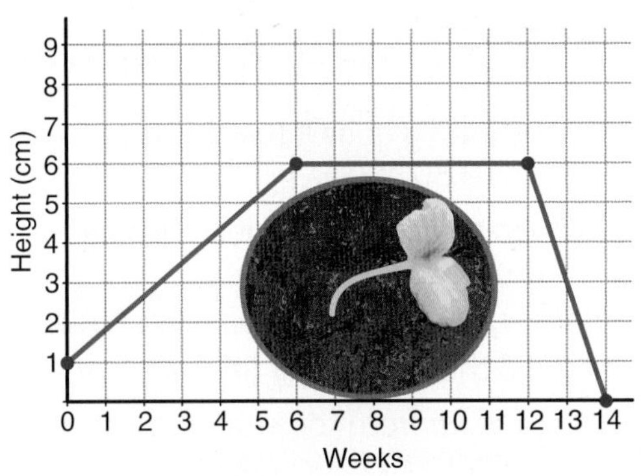

(a) What was the height of the plant after 4 weeks?

(b) What was the maximum recorded height of the plant?

(c) Give two reasons why you think the height of the plant decreased after 12 weeks.

30. The following graph shows the water level in a small stream over the course of 12 months. Study the graph and answer the questions.

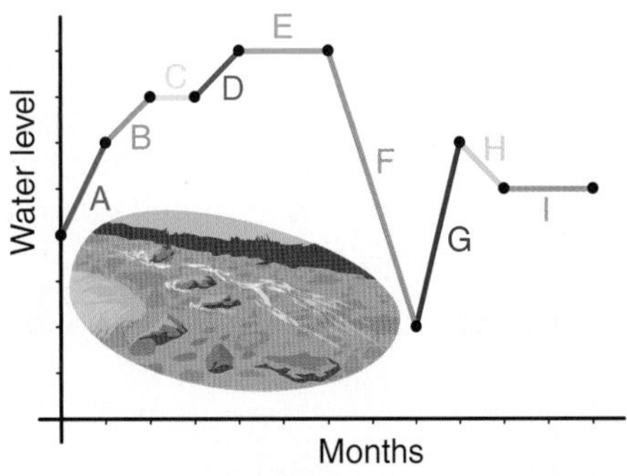

(a) Identify which sections of the graph show an increase in the water level.

(b) Identify which sections of the graph show a decrease in the water level.

(c) Identify which sections of the graph show no change in the water level.

(d) Which sections of the graph do you think represent the summer months? Explain your answer.

(e) Which sections of the graph do you think represent the winter and autumn months? Explain your answer.

31. The graph shows how Tom's distance from home varies with time, when he visits his granny.

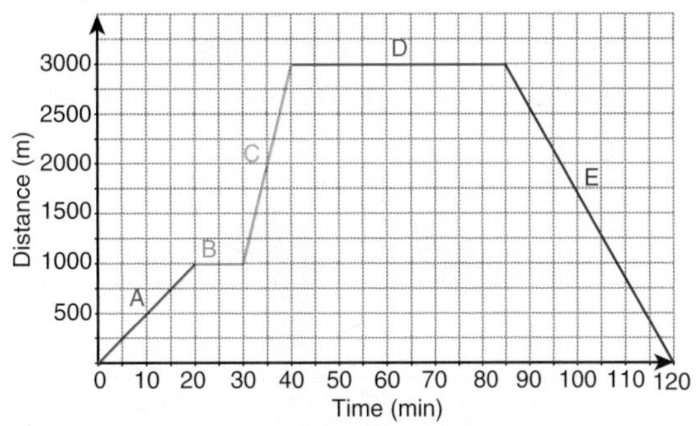

(a) How long does Tom spend at his granny's?

(b) How far does Tom live from his granny's house?

(c) For how long does Tom stop on his way to his granny's?

(d) On which part of the journey does Tom travel the fastest?

(e) How fast does Tom walk on his way back from his granny's?

32. On a journey, Matthew drives 200 kilometres in 4 hours, rests for one hour and then drives another 100 kilometres in two hours. Draw a distance-time graph to represent Matthew's journey.

33. Mary leaves home for school. On the way, Mary remembers that she has forgotten her maths homework. She runs home to get it and then sets off to school again. Study the graph and match each section with its correct explanation.

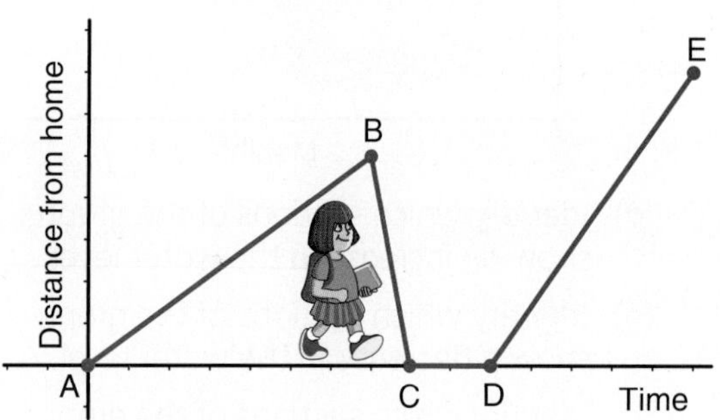

(a) Mary searches for her homework.

(b) Mary runs home.

(c) Mary sets off to school again.

(d) Mary leaves home for school.

34. A student is using a Go-Motion Sensor in science. The sensor tracks the student's movement as he walks away from the sensor. Write down the instructions required to produce the following graph:

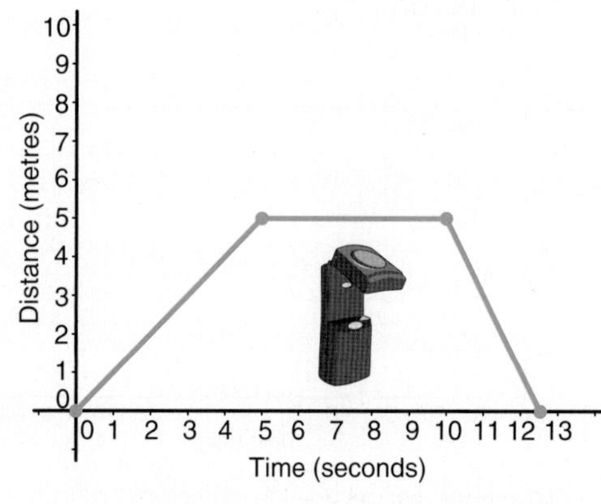

35. A racing pigeon's distance from home is recorded in the following graph:

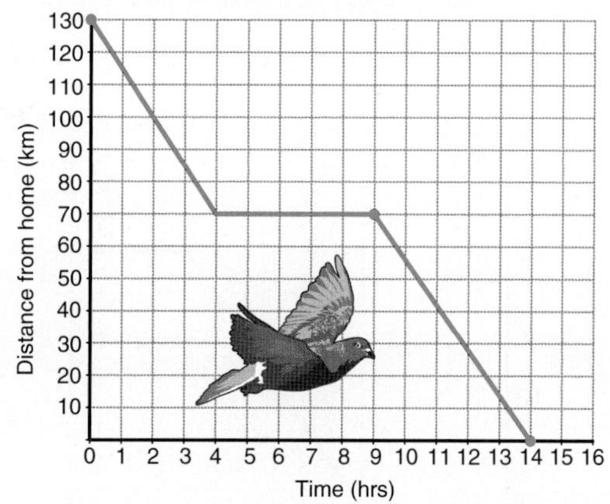

(a) How far from home did the race begin?

(b) Why do you think the distance is unchanged between 4 and 9 hours?

(c) How long did it take the pigeon to complete the race?

36. Two cars begin a 100 m race from rest.

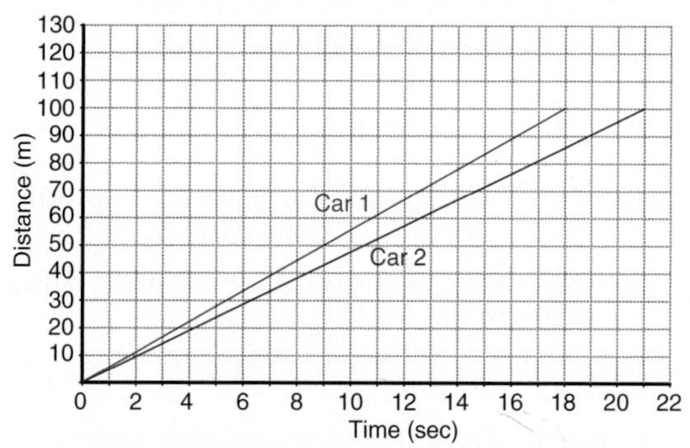

(a) How long does it take both cars to travel 50 m?

(b) Which car won the race? Explain your answer.

(c) How long after the winner finished did the second car finish?

(d) How far from the start line were both cars after 12 seconds?

Section 17.3: Multiple-part journeys

Student Activity 17C

1. A delivery van drives from Tullamore to Portlaoise covering a distance of 35 km. After making a delivery, the van then travels to Clonmel, a distance of 95 km.

(a) If the journey from Tullamore to Portlaoise took 35 minutes, at what average speed was the van travelling?

(b) If the journey from Portlaoise to Clonmel took 1 hour and 10 minutes, at what average speed was the van travelling?

(c) If the van drove straight from Tullamore to Clonmel, what would the total distance of the journey have been?

(d) How long would the journey have taken in total?

(e) What would the average speed of the van have been if it had not stopped?

2. A car travels for 180 km at an average speed of 60 km/hr and then travels for 210 km at an average speed of 70 km/hr.
   (a) How long did the first leg of the journey take?
   (b) How long did the second leg of the journey take?
   (c) What was the total distance travelled by the car?
   (d) What was the total time taken to complete the journey?
   (e) What was the average speed of the car over the entire journey?

MULTIPLE-PART JOURNEYS EXPLAINED

In this section, we will deal with journeys made up of more than one part, with different distances, speeds and times.

By law, truck drivers must take a break after driving for a certain number of hours. In this way, they can take a rest and make sure that they are not overtired while driving. An instrument called a tachometer records how long they have been driving. Gardaí can check the tachometer at any time to make sure they are not driving for longer than they should.

When dealing with a multiple-part problem, it is often necessary to calculate **total distance** and **total time** for the journey. The following formula is useful for this type of problem:

$$\text{Average speed for a journey} = \frac{\text{Total distance travelled}}{\text{Total time taken}}$$

EXAMPLE 7

A ship sails 200 km from port A to port B. It then continues to port C, a further 150 km away from B. If the journey from A to B took 5 hours and the journey from B to C took 3 hours, calculate:

(a) The average speed of the boat from A to B
(b) The average speed of the boat from B to C
(c) The total length of the journey
(d) The average speed of the boat over the entire journey

Solution

(a) $\text{Average speed} = \frac{\text{Distance}}{\text{Time}}$

$\text{Average speed} = \frac{200}{5}$

Average speed = 40 km/hr

(b) $\text{Average speed} = \frac{\text{Distance}}{\text{Time}}$

$\text{Average speed} = \frac{150}{3}$

Average speed = 50 km/hr

(c) Total journey = 200 + 150 = 350 km

(d) $\text{Average speed} = \frac{\text{Total distance travelled}}{\text{Total time taken}}$

$\text{Average speed} = \frac{350}{8}$

Average speed = 43.75 km/hr

Exercise 17.3

1. A flight of 900 km from Dublin to another airport takes 4 hours on the outward journey and 40 minutes less on the return journey. Calculate:
   (a) The average speed of the plane on the outward journey
   (b) The average speed of the plane on the return journey
   (c) The total distance travelled by the plane
   (d) The total time the plane was in flight
   (e) The overall average speed for the entire journey, correct to two decimal places

2. A car travels for 200 km in 4 hours and then continues for 240 km for a further 6 hours. Calculate:
   (a) The average speed of the car for the first stage of the journey
   (b) The average speed of the car for the second stage of the journey
   (c) The total distance travelled by the car
   (d) The total time taken to complete both journeys
   (e) The overall average speed for the complete journey

3. A truck travels 200 km at an average speed of 80 km/hr and a further 280 km at an average speed of 70 km/hr. Calculate:
   (a) The time taken to complete the entire journey
   (b) The total distance travelled by the truck
   (c) The overall average speed for the entire journey, correct to two decimal places

4. A car travels 182 km in 3 hours and 15 minutes. It then travels for 3 hours at an average speed of 65 km/hr.
   (a) How far did the car travel?
   (b) What was the total time for the journey?
   (c) What was the overall average speed for the entire journey, correct to two decimal places?

5. A van travels 260 km at an average speed of 80 km/hr and then travels 300 km at an average speed of 75 km/hr. Calculate:
   (a) The time taken to complete the entire journey
   (b) The total distance travelled
   (c) The overall average speed of the van for the entire journey, correct to the nearest km

6. An athlete competes in a triathlon which consists of a 1 km swim, a 50 km cycle and a 20 km run.

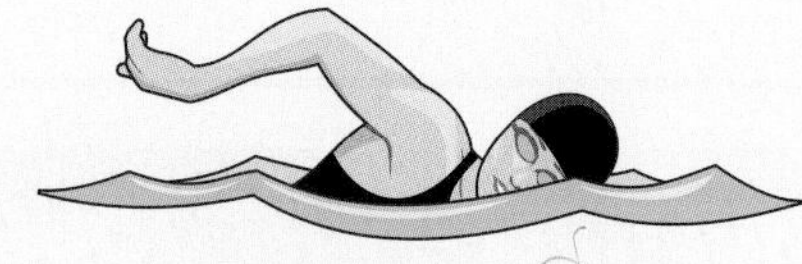

The swim lasted for 30 minutes. The run took the athlete 3 hours and 20 minutes to complete. If the athlete completed the triathlon in 6 hours and 20 minutes, calculate:
   (a) The time taken to complete the cycling stage
   (b) The average speed of the athlete during the swim
   (c) The average speed of the athlete during the cycle
   (d) The average speed of the athlete during the run
   (e) The total distance covered in the triathlon
   (f) The athlete's overall average speed for the complete course, correct to the nearest km/h

CHAPTER 17 SELF-CHECK TEST

1. Paul drives for 3 hours at an average speed of 75 km/hr.
   (a) Represent this information on a suitably labelled graph.
   (b) How far did Paul travel in the first hour?
   (c) What was Paul's average speed over the entire journey?
   (d) Find the slope $\left(\frac{\text{Rise}}{\text{Run}}\right)$ of the graph.

2. Jane runs for one and a half hours at an average speed of 9 km/hr.
   (a) Represent this information on a suitably labelled graph.
   (b) How far did Jane travel in the first hour?

3. Find the distance travelled for each of the following:
   (a) A bird flies for 6 hours at an average speed of 20 km/hr.
   (b) A dog chases a rabbit for 30 seconds at an average speed of 3 m/s.

4. Paul and Jack decide to have a race over 100 metres. The following graph shows the distance from the starting line of the race:

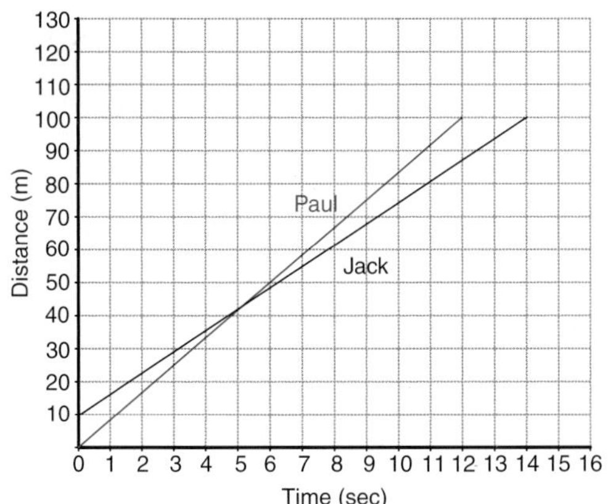

(a) Which runner had a head start? Explain your answer.

(b) Who won the race?

(c) Using slopes, calculate the average speed of each runner.

(d) How long did it take Paul to overtake Jack?

(e) How far had Jack to run when Paul finished the race?

5. Find the time taken to complete each of the following journeys:

(a) Paul drives 200 km at an average speed of 50 km/hr.

(b) Áine runs 1.44 km at an average speed of 6 m/s.

(c) A bus travels 60 km at an average speed of 50 km/hr.

(d) A plane flies 8,500 km at an average speed of 400 km/hr.

(e) An athlete runs a 100 m race in 10 m/s.

6. A bird flies 100 km in 5 hours at a constant speed.

(a) Represent this information on a graph.

(b) How far did the bird fly in the first hour?

(c) What was bird's average speed over the entire journey?

(d) Find the slope $\left(\frac{\text{Rise}}{\text{Run}}\right)$ of the graph.

7. A car travels 240 km in 4 hours at a constant speed.

(a) Represent this information on a graph.

(b) How far did the car travel in the first hour?

(c) What was car's average speed over the entire journey?

(d) Find the slope of the graph.

8. Find the average speed of each of the following:

(a) A train travels 150 km in 2 hours.

(b) A ship sails 400 km in 20 hours.

(c) A cyclist cycles 150 km in 6 hours.

9. A truck driver drives from Athlone to Limerick, a distance of 140 km in 1 hour and 10 minutes. After a short break, the driver continues driving to Killarney a distance of 120 km in 1 hour and 20 minutes. Find:

(a) The total distance driven

(b) The total time taken to complete the journey

(c) The average speed of the journey

10. A cyclist has a choice of two roads to get to her destination as shown.

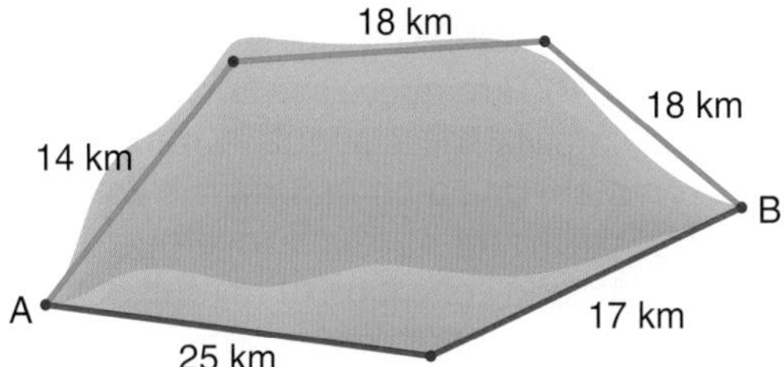

(a) Find the total distance of each route.

(b) If the cyclist travels at an average speed of 15 km/hr, which route will be quickest?

(c) Suggest why the cyclist might decide to take the longer of the two routes?

11. A bus travels 120 km at an average speed of 90 km/hr. It then travels a further 80 km at an average speed of 100 km/hr. Find:

(a) The time taken to travel the first 120 km

(b) The time taken to travel the final 80 km

(c) The total time taken for the entire journey

(d) The total distance travelled by the bus

(e) The average speed for the entire journey

12. The Earth orbits the sun in a circular path. The Earth is 1.496×10^8 km from the sun.

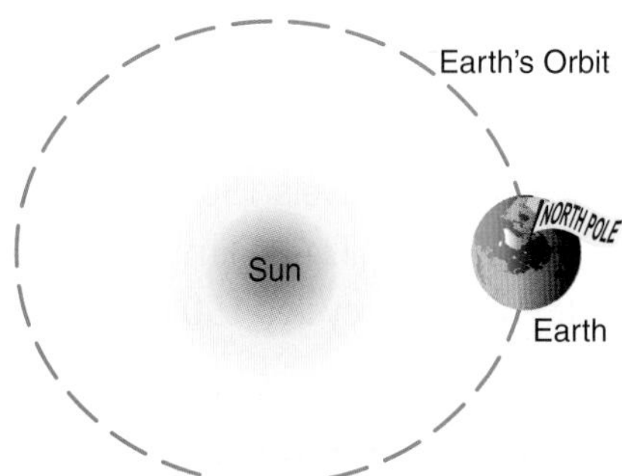

(a) Calculate the length of the Earth's orbit around the sun and give your answer in the form $a \times 10^n$, where $1 \leq a < 10$, $n \in \mathbb{N}$.

(b) How long does it take the Earth to orbit the sun?

(c) How many hours are in 1 year?

(d) Calculate the Earth's average speed per hour as it orbits the Sun, correct to the nearest km/hr.

13. The Tropical Rainfall Measuring Mission (TRMM) satellite is flying about 400 km above the Earth's surface. The satellite takes about 91 minutes to complete one orbit around the Earth. This allows for as much coverage of the Tropics and collection of rainfall data over the 24-hour day as possible.

> **Note**
>
> The diameter of earth is approximately 12,700 km.

(a) How many orbits, to the nearest whole number, does the TRMM satellite complete in 24 hours?

(b) Convert 400 km to metres.

(c) How many seconds are in 91 minutes?

(d) Calculate the average speed of the satellite in m/s.

14. NASA's Aqua satellite studies the water cycle. It orbits Earth about 750 km above the Earth's surface. It completes one orbit every 23 hours 56 minutes and 4 seconds.

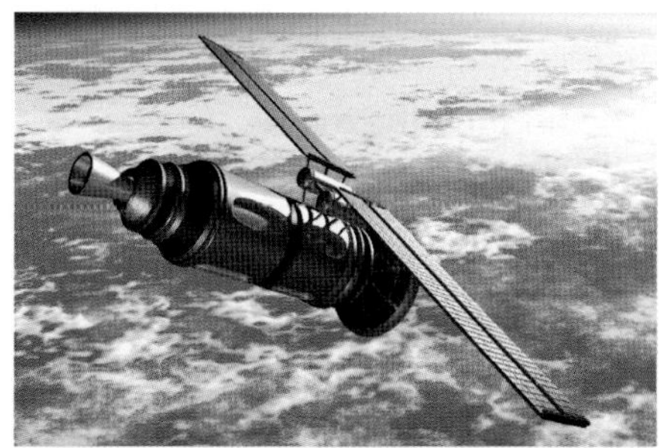

Calculate the average speed of the satellite in m/s.

15. Complete the following word search:

SPEED
DISTANCE
TIME
ACCELERATE
DECELERATE
KILOMETRE
METRE
HOUR
SECOND
SLOPE
RISE
RUN
AVERAGE

A	A	R	A	L	L	M	L	S	L	O	P	E	C	D
C	W	H	A	G	X	E	T	Y	O	U	E	Y	I	E
C	T	X	O	J	L	T	M	E	S	P	E	S	I	R
E	D	T	B	U	C	R	X	E	O	Y	T	Z	A	I
L	G	R	D	H	R	E	P	L	R	A	I	A	O	S
E	O	A	U	Q	Y	D	S	P	N	O	M	B	C	E
R	I	N	I	N	N	E	N	C	H	K	E	F	J	D
A	M	V	R	O	H	V	E	B	O	U	M	H	X	I
T	U	E	C	L	K	I	L	O	M	E	T	R	E	C
E	J	E	Q	I	N	T	R	I	A	S	P	E	E	D
O	S	M	A	M	Q	W	C	A	F	T	P	K	O	L
C	Z	I	E	G	A	R	E	V	A	T	I	O	N	A
E	K	T	K	D	E	C	E	L	E	R	A	T	E	M

CHAPTER 17 KNOWLEDGE CHECKLIST

After completing this chapter, I now:

- Am able to change between different types of units
- Am able to perform calculations involving average speed, distance and time
- Am able to perform calculations for multi-part journeys
- Am able to solve distance, time, speed problems involving graphs

Challenge

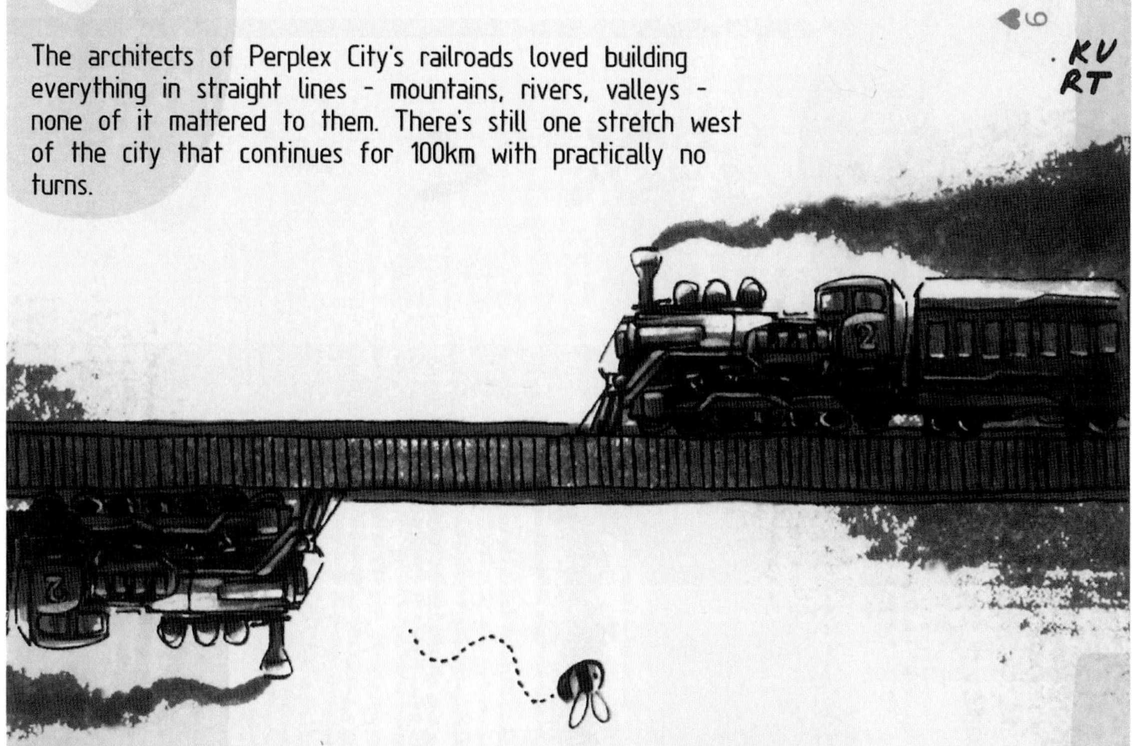

The architects of Perplex City's railroads loved building everything in straight lines - mountains, rivers, valleys - none of it mattered to them. There's still one stretch west of the city that continues for 100km with practically no turns.
KURT
Imagine there are two trains travelling towards each other at either end of the 100km stretch at 50km/h. Flying back and forth directly between the two trains at 75km/h is a bee that starts on the front of one of the trains when they're 100km apart, and immediately turns around to the other train as soon as it reaches it, and so on. How far will the bee have travelled in this zig zag fashion before the two trains meet?

$$3x + 2 < x - 4$$
$$-x \qquad -x$$
$$2x + 2 < -4$$
$$-2 \qquad -2$$
$$2x < -6$$

CHAPTER

18

LINEAR INEQUALITIES

KEY WORDS

- Compound
- Equal to
- Greater than
- Inequality
- Integer
- Less than
- Linear equation
- Linear inequality
- Natural number
- Rational number
- Real number
- Variable

LEARNING OUTCOMES

In this chapter you will learn:

- ✓ To distinguish between the terms 'greater than' and 'less than'
- ✓ To solve linear inequalities
- ✓ To solve compound linear inequalities
- ✓ To plot the solution set of linear inequalities on a number line

INTRODUCTION

In mathematics, both sides of an equation do not always equal each other. Sometimes, one side has a bigger or a smaller value than the other side.

A linear inequality contains a linear expression and an inequality sign. In mathematics, an inequality divides a plane into two half planes.

In the graph, the dotted line shows the equation $6x + 3y = 0$.

The point (2, 1) is to the right of this line. If we substituted this point into the equation, we would see that $6(2) + 3(1) = 15$ which is > 0.
Hence, for the half plane containing (2, 1) we can say that $6x + 3y > 0$.
Similarly, if we tested a point to the left of the line, we would find that $6x + 3y < 0$. Any point on the line will satisfy the equation $6x + 3y = 0$.

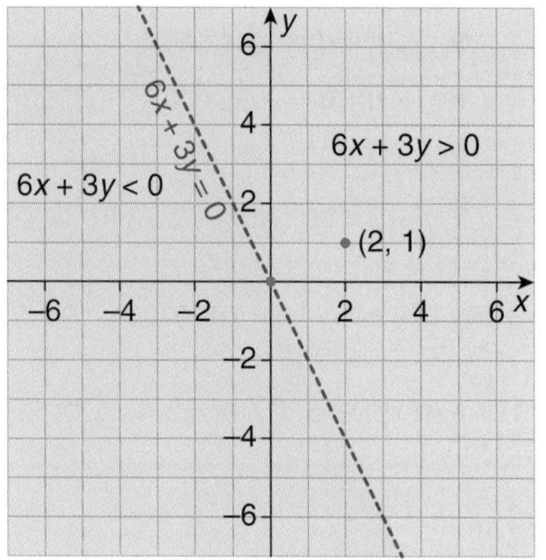

Section 18.1: Inequalities

Student Activity 18A

1. Arrange the people from the smallest to the tallest.

State whether the following are true or false:

(a) King's height is greater than Boomer's height.

(b) Timmy's height is less than Carmello's height.

(c) Larry's height is equal to Julie's height.

(d) What mathematical symbol could you use to show that Carmello's height is greater than Julie's height?

(e) What mathematical symbol could you use to show that Timmy's height is less than Larry's height?

2. Write down all the natural numbers that are less than 6. Show these numbers on a number line.

3. Write down all the natural numbers that are less than 3. Show these numbers on a number line.

4. A student asks a classmate to draw a number line for the following:
All natural numbers x, where $x < 5$.
Can you draw this number line?

INEQUALITIES EXPLAINED

The word **'inequality'** means being unequal. An inequality tells you about the relative size of two values. For example: Patrick beats Laura in a race. So Patrick is faster than Laura.

We can write that as: Laura's time $>$ Patrick's time.

Here '$>$' means **'greater than'**.

The following signs are used when working with inequalities:

- $<$ means less than.
- $\leq$ means less than or equal to.
- $>$ means greater than.
- $\geq$ means greater than or equal to.

They are easy to remember. The 'small' pointed end of the inequality sign always points to the smaller number.

For example: $3 < 7$ or $-5 < -1$ or $10 > 8$ or $6 > -2$.

EXAMPLE 1

Write as an inequality: You must be 18 or older to watch a movie.

Solution

You must be 18 or older to watch a movie.

The 'inequality' is between your age and the age of 18.

Your age must be 'greater than or equal to 18', which is written as:

Age ≥ 18

Exercise 18.1

1. State whether the following statements are true or false:

(a) $2 > -2$
(b) $-3 > -4$
(c) $-2 < -8$
(d) $7 \geq 7$
(e) $10 \geq \sqrt{64}$
(f) $0.5 > 0.25$
(g) $\sqrt{99} < 10$
(h) $-8 \leq -12$
(i) $\frac{7}{22} < \frac{7}{23}$
(j) $(0.8)^2 < (0.8)$

2. To enter a radio competition, you must be under the age of 16. Which of the following statements represents this information?

(a) Age < 16
(b) Age > 16
(c) Age ≥ 16
(d) Age ≤ 16

3. To be a heavyweight boxer, you should weigh more than 130 kg. Which of the following statements represent this information?

(a) Weight $>$ 130 kg
(b) Weight $<$ 130 kg
(c) Weight $\leq$ 130 kg
(d) Weight $\geq$ 130 kg

4. Write the following equations as sentences:

(a) $x > 10$
(b) $x + 3 > 2$
(c) $5 \geq x - 1$
(d) $7x < 28$
(e) $2y + 1 \leq 7$

5. The speed limit on the M6 motorway is 120 km/h. Which inequality represents the legal speed, s, of a motorist?

(a) $s < 120$
(b) $s > 120$
(c) $s \leq 120$
(d) $s \geq 120$

6. Write down a simple inequality for each of the following statements:

(a) To drive a tractor, your must be 16 or over.
(b) The greatest weight that is allowed in an elevator is 500 kg.
(c) The maximum number of passengers a bus can seat is 55.

(d) Primary school is for students under the age of 12.

(e) A standard golf ball has more than 300 dimples.

(f) To go through to the next round of a quiz, you must have a minimum of 26 points.

(g) A hunting cheetah is capable of a speed of up to 100 km/h.

(h) All Leaving Certificate students will achieve 625 points or less.

(i) To drive a car, you must be aged 18 or over.

(j) For health reasons, humans should drink at least 2 litres of water a day.

7. The maximum attendance at a match is 45,230. Which inequality represents the maximum attendance, a, at the match?

(a) $a < 45{,}230$ (c) $a \geq 45{,}230$

(b) $a > 45{,}230$ (d) $a \leq 45{,}230$

8. John's mother promises to teach him to drive once he reaches the age of 17. Which inequality represents the age, x, at which John can start driving lessons?

(a) $x < 17$ (c) $x \geq 17$

(b) $x > 17$ (d) $x \leq 17$

9. On a certain day it is x °C in Galway. The weather forecast predicts it will be at least 3 °C warmer in Dublin. Which inequality represents the temperature, t, in Dublin?

(a) $t < x$ (d) $t \leq x + 3$

(b) $t > x$ (e) $t \geq x$

(c) $t \geq x + 3$

Section 18.2: Linear inequalities

Student Activity 18B

1. Draw a number line from −4 to 4 and mark each natural number that is greater than −4 but less than 4.

2. Draw a number line from −4 to 4 and mark each integer that is greater than −4 but less than 4.

3. Draw a number line from −4 to 4 and mark each real number that is greater than −4 but less than 4.

4. In Chapter 1, you met the different types of numbers represented by the symbols $\mathbb{N}$, $\mathbb{Z}$ and $\mathbb{R}$.

(a) Write a sentence explaining what each symbol means.

(b) Identify six elements that belong to each set.

(c) Complete the following sentence:

On a number line, ________ numbers and _________ are represented by dots but ____ numbers are represented by a continuous line.

LINEAR INEQUALITIES EXPLAINED

Linear inequalities are solved in a similar way to linear equations.

As with an equation, we want a letter on one side of the inequality sign and a number on the other. For example, $x > 5$.

However, we must also pay attention to the direction of the inequality.

We can do the following mathematical operations without affecting the direction of the inequality:

- Add a number to or subtract a number from both sides.
- Multiply or divide both sides by a **positive** number.

Multiplying or dividing both sides of an inequality by a negative number reverses (or flips) the inequality sign.

For example, $-3 < 4$ is true. If we multiply both sides by -1, we get $3 > -4$, which is also true.

Inequalities on the number line

Inequalities can also be represented on a number line. Natural numbers and integers are represented by dots but real numbers are different. We use a continuous line and then dots on either end to show the smallest or largest value that satisfies the inequality.

- We use a hollow dot for < and >.
- We use a solid dot for ≤ and ≥.

The diagram shows that x is greater than or equal to -1, or the inequality $x \geq -1$ for all $x \in \mathbb{R}$, where $\mathbb{R}$ is the set of real numbers.

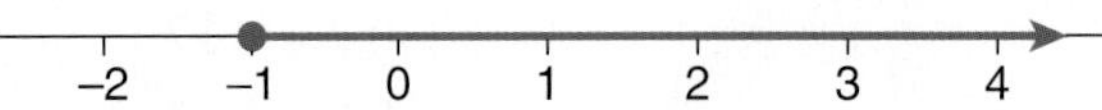

This example shows that x is less than 2, or the equation $x < 2$ for all $x \in \mathbb{R}$, where $\mathbb{R}$ is the set of real numbers.

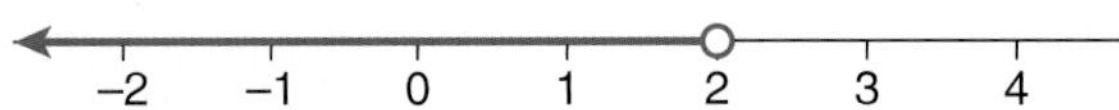

EXAMPLE 2

Solve the inequality $3x - 7 < 14$, where $x \in \mathbb{N}$. Graph the solution set on a number line.

Solution

$3x - 7 < 14$

$3x - 7 + 7 < 14 + 7$ **Add 7 to both sides**

$3x < 14 + 7$

$3x < 21$

$\frac{3x}{3} < \frac{21}{3}$ **Divide both sides by 3**

$x < 7$

{1, 2, 3, 4, 5, 6} is the set of natural numbers less than 7.

Note that a solid dot is on each element of the set.

EXAMPLE 3

Solve the inequality $2x - 1 \leq 4x + 5$, where $x \in \mathbb{Z}$. Graph the solution set on a number line.

Solution

$2x - 1 \leq 4x + 5$

$2x - 4x \leq 1 + 5$ **Letters on one side, numbers on the other side**

$-2x \leq 6$

$\frac{-2x}{2} \leq \frac{6}{2}$ **Divide both sides by 2**

$-x \leq 3$

$x \geq -3$ **Multiply by −1 and reverse the inequality sign**

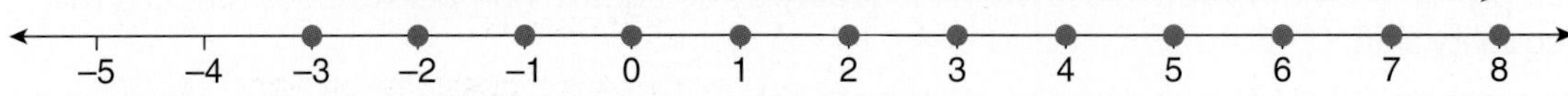

As the solutions to this set go to infinity, we use an arrow to show it continues.

EXAMPLE 4

Solve the inequality $4x + 7 \leq 2x + 5$, where $x \in \mathbb{Z}$. Graph the solution set on a number line.

Solution

$4x + 7 \leq 2x + 5$

$4x - 2x \leq 5 - 7$

$2x \leq -2$

$\frac{2x}{2} \leq \frac{-2}{2}$ **Divide both sides by 2**

$x \leq -1$

−7 −6 −5 −4 −3 −2 −1 0 1

The solutions begin at −1 and continue to **−∞** (minus infinity).

EXAMPLE 5

Solve the inequality $7x + 1 \leq 4x + 10$, where $x \in \mathbb{R}$. Graph the solution set on a number line.

Solution

$7x + 1 \leq 4x + 10$

$7x - 4x \leq 10 - 1$

$3x \leq 9$

$\frac{3x}{3} \leq \frac{9}{3}$ **Divide both sides by 3**

$x \leq 3$

−4 −3 −2 −1 0 1 2 3 4

We draw a heavy line starting at 3 on the number line to show it includes all solutions, as $x \in \mathbb{R}$. The arrow indicates that the set continues to $-\infty$ (minus infinity).

Exercise 18.2

1. Copy the table and write the relevant numbers given below into each of the boxes A, B, C, E, F, G and H. (Note: numbers may be used more than once.)

   $-3, 0.25, 6, 7, 17, -2, 19, -5, 3\frac{1}{2}, -6.2, 1, 11, 2, 3, 9, 5, 5.2, -7, 7.8, 13, 11.4.$

A: A natural number greater than 1	B: A real number greater than 1
C: A natural number less than 8	D: An integer less than 8
E: A real number greater than 6	F: A real number greater than or equal to 10
G: A real number greater than −3 and less than or equal to 6	H: An integer greater than −3

2. Plot each of the following on a number line:
   (a) $x < 5, x \in \mathbb{N}$
   (b) $x > -6, x \in \mathbb{Z}$
   (c) $x > 0, x \in \mathbb{R}$
   (d) $x > -3, x \in \mathbb{R}$
   (e) $x < 2, x \in \mathbb{Z}$

Solve each of the following inequalities and graph the solution set on a number line:

3. $4x < 16, x \in \mathbb{N}$
4. $2x < 10, x \in \mathbb{N}$
5. $6x < 36, x \in \mathbb{N}$
6. $7x < 14, x \in \mathbb{N}$
7. $-5x \geq -20, x \in \mathbb{N}$
8. $-12x > -60, x \in \mathbb{N}$
9. $3x + 7 < 4, x \in \mathbb{Z}$
10. $-6x - 9 \geq 27, x \in \mathbb{Z}$
11. $6x - 12 < 0, x \in \mathbb{N}$
12. $4x + 5 \leq 2x + 13, x \in \mathbb{Z}$
13. $2x + 5 < 5x - 7, x \in \mathbb{N}$
14. $4x \leq 16, x \in \mathbb{R}$
15. $5x \leq 10, x \in \mathbb{R}$
16. If $x \leq 4, x \in \mathbb{N}$, which of the following statements are true? Give a reason for your answer.
    (a) 4 is a possible solution.
    (b) 5.9 is a possible solution.

(c) −3 is a possible solution.

(d) 11 is a possible solution.

(e) The solution set contains 4 elements.

17. If $x \leq 9, x \in \mathbb{Z}$, which of the following statements are true? Give a reason for your answer.

(a) 5 is a possible solution.

(b) 12.6 is a possible solution.

(c) −3 is a possible solution.

(d) 9 is a possible solution.

Solve each of the inequalities in questions 18–30 and graph the solution set on a number line:

18. $7x - 5 \leq 3x + 19, x \in \mathbb{R}$

19. $1 - x > 3x + 9, x \in \mathbb{N}$

20. $2x + 2 < 5x - 16, x \in \mathbb{N}$

21. $5x - 17 < x + 3, x \in \mathbb{Z}$

22. $6x + 7 > 4x + 10, x \in \mathbb{R}$

23. $3x - 5 < x + 7, x \in \mathbb{Z}$

24. $2x - 3 \leq 8x + 21, x \in \mathbb{R}$

25. $2(x - 3) < 3(8 - x), x \in \mathbb{N}$

26. $3(5 - x) + 2 > 4(x - 1), x \in \mathbb{R}$

27. $3 + 5(2x + 1) < 1 - 4x, x \in \mathbb{Z}$

28. $\frac{x - 3}{2} < -5, x \in \mathbb{R}$

29. $\frac{x - 8}{2} > -8, x \in \mathbb{R}$

30. $-1 > \frac{12 + x}{4}, x \in \mathbb{R}$

31. Graph the solution set for $\frac{-11 + x}{15} < -1$, $x \in \mathbb{R}$.

32. Graph the solution set for $\frac{x}{-6} - 8 \leq -12$, $x \in \mathbb{R}$.

Section 18.3: Compound linear inequalities

Student Activity 18C

1. Draw a number line from −3 to 3 and mark each natural number that is greater than −3 but less than 3.
2. Draw a number line from −3 to 3 and mark each integer that is greater than −3 but less than 3.
3. Draw a number line from −3 to 3 and mark each real number that is greater than −3 but less than 3.
4. A student wants to write an inequality to represent all the real numbers greater than or equal to −3 and less than or equal to 3.
   Represent the information above by replacing the shapes below with appropriate symbols:
   −3 ■ x ■ 3
5. A student drew the following number line:

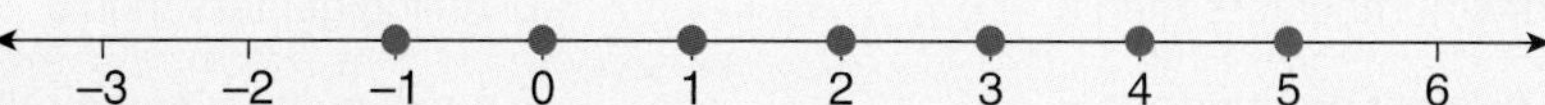

   Replace the shapes with the correct inequality sign:
   −1 ■ x ■ 5, x ∈ ♦
6. A student drew the following number line:

   Replace the shapes with the correct inequality sign:
   −5 ■ x ■ 8, x ∈ ♦
7. What numbers would you include in the set for x, if $-2 < x \leq 4, x \in \mathbb{Z}$. Draw a number line to display your answer.

COMPOUND LINEAR INEQUALITIES EXPLAINED

In Section 18.2, you learned how to solve a linear inequality and to graph the solution set on a number line. In this section, you will have to solve two inequalities side by side. These are called **compound linear inequalities.**

The number lines here will be a closed set as the results will be bound on both sides. The following examples explain how to solve this type of problem.

EXAMPLE 6

What inequality is represented by the following number line?

Solution

This shows that x is greater than or equal to −1 and x is less than 3, or the equation $x \geq -1$ and $x < 3$. We can write this in one single line as $-1 \leq x < 3, x \in \mathbb{R}$.

Notice how we changed around the order of the first part, but it still means the same thing. So $x \geq -1$ is the same as $-1 \leq x$.

EXAMPLE 7

Solve the inequality $3 \leq 2x - 1 \leq 11$ and graph the solution set on a number line, where $x \in \mathbb{N}$.

Solution

$3 \leq 2x - 1 \leq 11$

Method 1: Solve both sides simultaneously

Add +1 to each part of the inequality:

$3 + 1 \leq 2x - 1 + 1 \leq 11 + 1$

$4 \leq 2x \leq 12$

$\frac{4}{2} \leq \frac{2x}{2} \leq \frac{12}{2}$

$2 \leq x \leq 6$

Now draw the required number line:

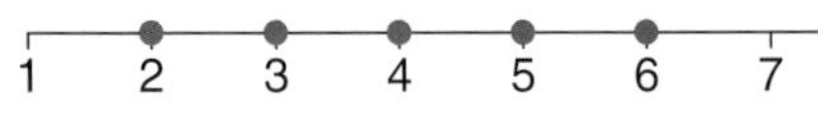

Method 2: Split it up into two linear inequalities

$3 \leq 2x - 1 \leq 11$

On the LHS:

$3 \leq 2x - 1$

$3 + 1 \leq 2x$ **Put numbers on one side, x on the other**

$4 \leq 2x$ **Tidy up**

$\frac{4}{2} \leq \frac{2x}{2}$ **Divide both sides by 2**

$2 \leq x$ **Tidy up**

On the RHS:

$2x - 1 \leq 11$

$2x \leq 11 + 1$ **Put numbers on one side, x on the other**

$2x \leq 12$ **Tidy up**

$\frac{2x}{2} \leq \frac{12}{2}$ **Divide both sides by 2**

$x \leq 6$ **Tidy up**

Putting both answers together: $2 \leq x \leq 6$.

Now draw the required number line:

EXAMPLE 8

Solve the inequality $-5 < 3x + 4 \leq 16$ and graph the solution set on a number line, where $x \in \mathbb{R}$.

Solution

Method 1: Solve both sides simultaneously

$-5 < 3x + 4 \leq 16$

$-5 - 4 < 3x + 4 - 4 \leq 16 - 4$ **Subtract 4 from each part of the inequality**

$-9 < 3x \leq 12$

$-3 < x \leq 4$ **Divide by 3**

Draw the required number line:

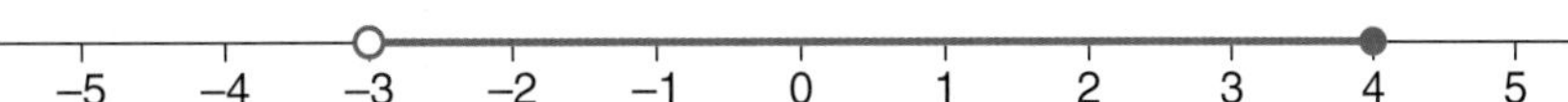

Note the empty circle at −3 indicates that −3 is not included in the solution set.

Method 2: Split it up into two linear inequalities

$-5 < 3x + 4 \leq 16$

On the LHS:

$-5 < 3x + 4$

$-5 - 4 < 3x$ **Put numbers on one side, x on the other**

$-9 < 3x$ **Tidy up**

$\frac{-9}{3} < \frac{3x}{3}$ **Divide both sides by 3**

$-3 < x$ **Tidy up**

On the RHS:

$3x + 4 \leq 16$

$3x \leq 16 - 4$ **Put numbers on one side, x on the other**

$3x \leq 12$ **Tidy up**

$\frac{3x}{3} \leq \frac{12}{3}$ **Divide both sides by 3**

$x \leq 4$ **Tidy up**

Putting both answers together: $-3 < x \leq 4$.

Draw the required number line:

Note the empty circle at –3 indicates that –3 is not included in the solution set.

Exercise 18.3

1. The temperature in Wexford town ranged between 19 °C and 25 °C on a particular day. Represent this as a compound inequality in the form $a < t < b$, where t represents temperature.
2. Aobha wants to spend a minimum of €30 and a maximum of €75 on a coat. If €x is the amount she wishes to spend, represent this using a compound inequality.
3. The number of peas in a bag ranges between 950 and 1,000. Represent this statement as a compound inequality.
4. Seán has €y saved. Last week he had €3 less. Last week he had between €5 and €11. Represent this as a compound inequality and solve it.
5. Show each of the following on a number line:
   (a) $-3 \leq x < 1, x \in \mathbb{Z}$
   (b) $0 < x < 6, x \in \mathbb{N}$
   (c) $-3 \leq x \leq 4, x \in \mathbb{Z}$
   (d) $2 < x < 6, x \in \mathbb{N}$
   (e) $-3 < x < 1, x \in \mathbb{Z}$
   (f) $0.5 \leq x \leq 3.5, x \in \mathbb{Z}$
   (g) $-1 \leq x \leq 4, x \in \mathbb{R}$
   (h) $3 < x \leq 7, x \in \mathbb{N}$
   (i) $-7 < x \leq 4.5, x \in \mathbb{N}$
   (j) $-2 < x < -1, x \in \mathbb{Z}$

Solve each of the following inequalities and plot the solution set on a number line:

6. $-2 \leq 2x \leq 6, x \in \mathbb{Z}$
7. $-6 < 2x + 8 \leq 6, x \in \mathbb{Z}$
8. $-10 \leq 4x + 6 \leq 10, x \in \mathbb{R}$
9. $-13 \leq 5x + 2 \leq 12, x \in \mathbb{Z}$
10. $20 \leq 4x + 4 < 32, x \in \mathbb{Z}$
11. $3 > -3x - 6 \geq -6, x \in \mathbb{R}$
12. $2 > -2x > -8, x \in \mathbb{Z}$
13. $3 \geq 1 - 2x > -5, x \in \mathbb{Z}$
14. $11 < 2x + 7 < 19, x \in \mathbb{N}$
15. $27 < 10x - 3 < 47, x \in \mathbb{R}$
16. $16 < 7x + 2 < 51, x \in \mathbb{N}$
17. $9 > 5x - 1 > -6, x \in \mathbb{Z}$
18. $-3 \leq 6x + 3 < 21, x \in \mathbb{R}$
19. $-7 \leq 2x - 5 \leq 9, x \in \mathbb{R}$
20. $-17 < 6x - 11 < 1, x \in \mathbb{R}$
21. $-1 \leq 4x + 7 \leq 7, x \in \mathbb{R}$
22. $1 < 3x + 7 \leq 10, x \in \mathbb{R}$
23. $-3 \leq 2x + 5 \leq 5, x \in \mathbb{Z}$
24. $43 \leq 4x - 9 \leq 59, x \in \mathbb{R}$
25. John thinks of a natural number and doubles it. He then adds 5 to the number. If the answer lies between 25 and 35, find all possible values for the number John may have thought of.
26. Andrew is 21 years old, Paul is 15 and Eimear is $2n + 3$ years old. Eimear is older than Paul but younger than Andrew. Find the possible ages in years Eimear could be.

CHAPTER 18 SELF-CHECK TEST

1. Put the following values in order of size, starting with the largest, where $x \geq 3, x \in \mathbb{N}$:

(a) $x, 4x, 0.5x, x + 3, x - 1$
(b) $2x, -2x, 7x, x - 3, x + \frac{1}{2}, x^2$
(c) $-x, \frac{x}{2}, x, x + 2, x^3 - 1$

2. Graph each of the following inequalities on a suitable number line:

(a) $x \leq -5, x \in \mathbb{R}$
(b) $x > 2, x \in \mathbb{N}$
(c) $x > 5, x \in \mathbb{R}$
(d) $x \leq -2, x \in \mathbb{Z}$
(e) $x < -5, x \in \mathbb{Z}$
(f) $x \geq 2, x \in \mathbb{N}$
(g) $-5 \geq x, x \in \mathbb{R}$
(h) $-2 \geq x, x \in \mathbb{N}$
(i) $x \leq 5, x \in \mathbb{Z}$
(j) $-2 > x, x \in \mathbb{R}$

3. Solve each of the following inequalities and graph the solution set on a suitable number line:

(a) $12x \geq 84, x \in \mathbb{N}$
(b) $-168 > -12x, x \in \mathbb{N}$
(c) $32 \geq -16x, x \in \mathbb{R}$
(d) $-13x < -156, x \in \mathbb{N}$
(e) $-3x > 3, x \in \mathbb{Z}$
(f) $\frac{x}{3} > 3, x \in \mathbb{Z}$
(g) $\frac{x}{4} < -4, x \in \mathbb{R}$
(h) $-22 > -10 + x, x \in \mathbb{R}$
(i) $\frac{x}{3} > 6, x \in \mathbb{R}$
(j) $8 \geq x - 6, x \in \mathbb{N}$
(k) $-1 + x \geq 4, x \in \mathbb{Z}$
(l) $11 \leq 5 + x, x \in \mathbb{N}$
(m) $25 \geq x + 13, x \in \mathbb{R}$
(n) $-3 \leq x - 4, x \in \mathbb{Z}$
(o) $-22 > -20 + x, x \in \mathbb{R}$
(p) $\frac{x}{3} - 3 \leq -6, x \in \mathbb{R}$
(q) $-3(x + 1) \leq -18, x \in \mathbb{R}$
(r) $-4(-4 + x) > 56, x \in \mathbb{R}$

4. Solve each of the following inequalities and graph the solution set on a suitable number line:

(a) $-90 \geq -5(x - 3), x \in \mathbb{R}$
(b) $4 < 1 + \frac{x}{7}, x \in \mathbb{N}$
(c) $5(6 + 3x) > 7, x \in \mathbb{R}$
(d) $-8x + 2x - 16 < -5x + 7x, x \in \mathbb{R}$
(e) $-3 < 2x + 1 < 5, x \in \mathbb{R}$
(f) $2 > -2x > -8, x \in \mathbb{Z}$
(g) $-13 \leq 4x - 1 \leq 3, x \in \mathbb{R}$
(h) $4 \leq 5x - 6 \leq 14, x \in \mathbb{R}$
(i) $-3 \leq 2x - 1 \leq 7, x \in \mathbb{R}$
(j) $-4(3 + x) > -32, x \in \mathbb{R}$
(k) $4 + \frac{x}{3} < 6, x \in \mathbb{R}$
(l) $84 \geq -7(x - 9), x \in \mathbb{Z}$
(m) $-3(x - 7) \geq 21, x \in \mathbb{R}$
(n) $\frac{-9 + x}{15} > 1x, x \in \mathbb{Z}$
(o) $\frac{x - 3}{2} \leq 5, x \in \mathbb{N}$
(p) $-1 \leq \frac{x - 2}{21}, x \in \mathbb{R}$
(q) $-13 > 12(x + 9), x \in \mathbb{R}$

5. What inequality is represented by each of the following number lines?

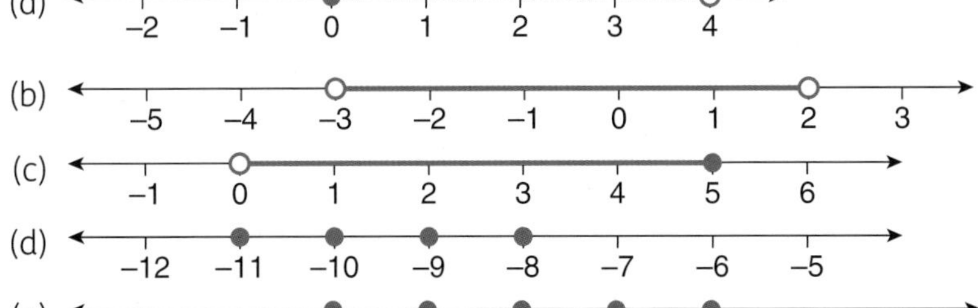

6. (a) Find the solution set A if $11 - 2x \geq 7, x \in \mathbb{N}$.
(b) Find the solution set B if $3x - 13 \leq 5, x \in \mathbb{N}$.
(c) Find A ∩ B and graph your solution on a number line.

7. (a) Find the solution set A of $2 - x \leq 8, x \in \mathbb{R}$.
(b) Find the solution set B of $4x + 1 \leq -3, x \in \mathbb{R}$.
(c) Find A ∩ B and graph your solution on a number line.

8. Given $x < 9.5$, $x \in \mathbb{Z}$, state whether the following are true or false. Explain each of your answers.

(a) x is less than or equal to 10.

(b) x is greater than 9.

(c) x is less than 9.

(d) x is 9.

(e) x can be a decimal.

9. Jason wants to keep the cost of his phone calls between €7 and €15 per week. Calls cost €0.20 each.

(a) Write a compound inequality to represent this information.

(b) Solve the inequality to find the maximum number of calls Jason can make per week.

CHAPTER 18 KNOWLEDGE CHECKLIST

After completing this chapter, I now:

- **Can distinguish between the terms 'greater than' and 'less than'**
- **Am able to solve linear inequalities**
- **Am able to solve compound linear inequalities**
- **Am able to plot the solution set of linear inequalities on a number line**

Challenge

Carl Friedrich Gauss was a legendary German mathematician, astronomer and physicist. His contributions to science have been so great that he is sometimes referred to as the 'Prince of Mathematics'.

Even from an early age his talent was evident. His father guessed he had a child prodigy on his hands when at the tender age of three his son spotted an error while he was calculating his payroll.

Gauss Junior was also making similar waves at school. His class was particularly rowdy and one afternoon his exasperated teacher set them all a problem to try and keep them quiet for as long as possible. The task was to add up all the numbers between 1 and 100. Most of the children had barely put chalk to slate when the five-year-old Gauss announced he had the solution. What answer did Gauss give to his startled teacher?

Now, before you plough headlong into this problem and spend ages summing the numbers one by one, is there an easier way to tackle this problem? You never know when such a shortcut might come in handy.

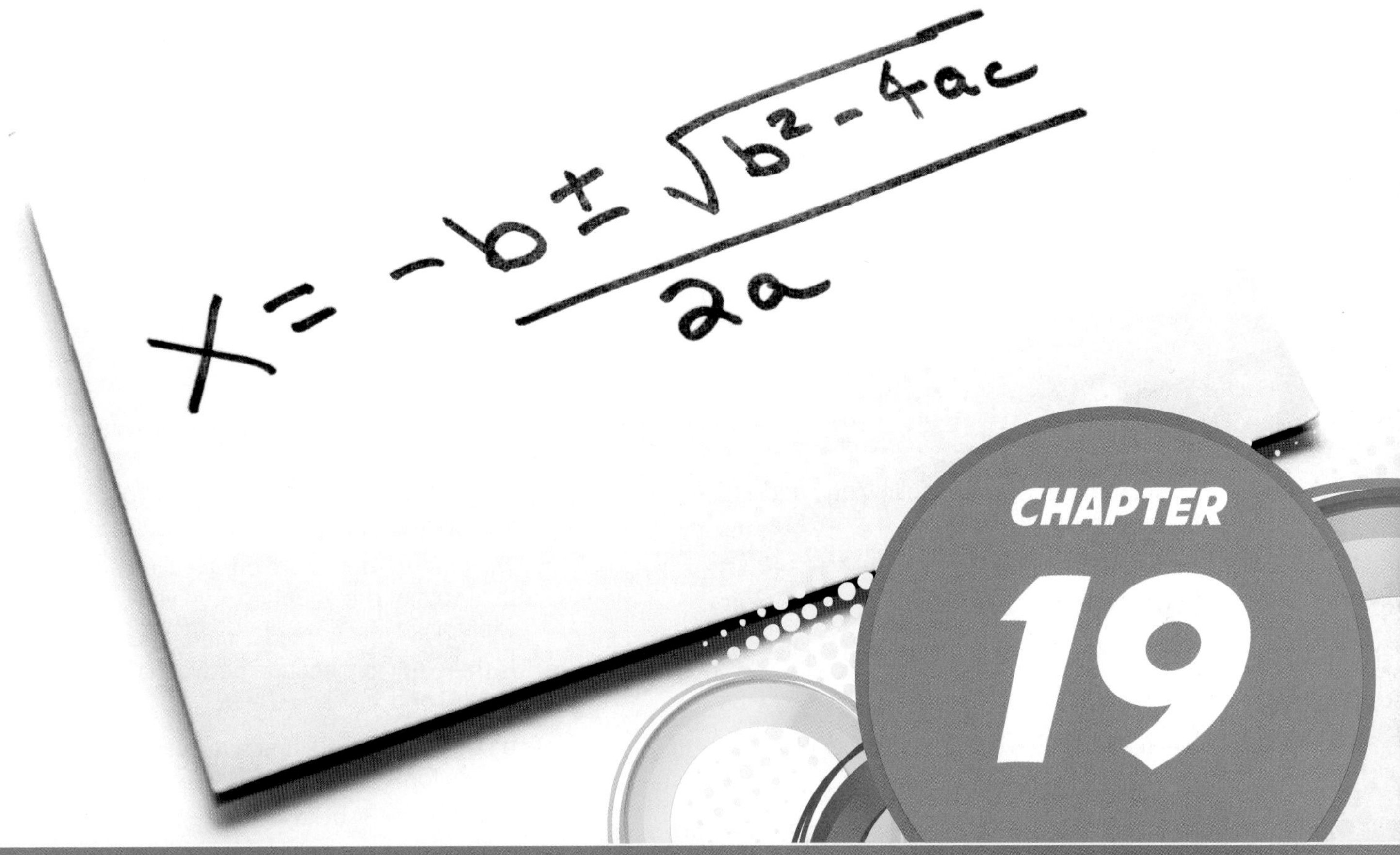

QUADRATIC EQUATIONS

LEARNING OUTCOMES

In this chapter you will learn:

- ✓ **To solve quadratic equations of the form $x^2 + bx + c = 0$, where $b, c \in \mathbb{Z}$**
- ✓ **To solve equations involving algebraic fractions**
- ✓ **To use the quadratic formula to solve quadratic equations**
- ✓ **To form quadratic equations given whole number roots**
- ✓ **To solve quadratic equations of the form $ax^2 + bx + c = 0$, where $a, b, c \in \mathbb{Q}$ and $x \in \mathbb{R}$**
- ✓ **To solve problems using quadratic equations**

KEY WORDS

- **Difference of two squares**
- **Equation**
- **Factors**
- **Polynomial**
- **Quadratic**
- **Roots**
- **Solve**
- **Surd**
- **Trinomials**

19

MATHS IN ACTION 3

INTRODUCTION

As early as 2000 BC, Babylonian mathematicians were using quadratics to solve problems. These can be seen on many clay tablets from that time.

In the word 'polynomial', 'poly' means 'many' and 'nomial' means 'numbers'. A quadratic equation is a **polynomial** of second degree. Second degree means it has an x term to the power of two or an 'x squared' as its highest power.

For example, $x^2 - 5x + 4 = 0$ and $-2x^2 - 5x + 14 = 0$ are polynomials.

Both Euclid and Pythagoras used quadratic equations in their works.

Section 19.1: Quadratic equations 1

Student Activity 19A

Factorise each of the following quadratic trinomials:

1. $x^2 + 7x + 12$

2. $x^2 + 9x + 20$

3. $x^2 - 14x + 48$

4. $x^2 - 12x + 27$

5. $x^2 - 11x + 24$

6. $x^2 + 13x + 40$

7. $x^2 - 4x - 45$

8. $x^2 + 3x - 54$

9. $x^2 - 5x - 84$

10. $x^2 + 7x - 30$

Evaluate each of the following:

11. $(5)(0)$

12. $(-4)(0)$

13. $(20)(0)$

14. $(x)(0)$

15. $(2x)(0)$

16. $(2x + 4)(0)$

17. $(x - 2)(0)$

18. If any two numbers A and B are multiplied and the answer is 0, what can you conclude about A or B?

19. (a) If $(a - 4)(a - 3) = 0$, find two possible values for a.

(b) If $(x + 2)(x - 1) = 0$, find two possible values for x.

20. (a) If $(x - 2)(x - 1) = 0$, find two possible values for x.

(b) Multiply $(x - 2)$ by $(x - 1)$.

(c) Substitute both of your values for x from part (a) into the resulting quadratic expression from part (b). What do you notice about both answers?

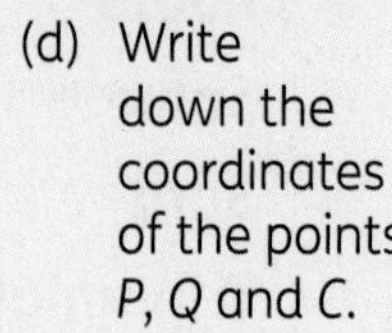

A graph of $x^2 - 3x + 2 = 0$ is shown.

(d) Write down the coordinates of the points P, Q and C.

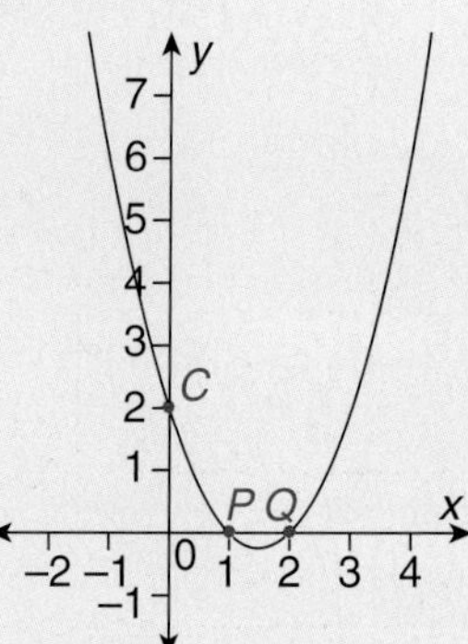

(e) Do you notice any connection to your earlier answers?

(f) The points P and Q are often called the roots of the equation. Can you explain why?

(g) Is there any connection between the point C and $x^2 - 3x + 2 = 0$?

21. (a) If $(x + 3)(x + 2) = 0$, find two possible values for x.

(b) Multiply $(x + 3)$ by $(x + 2)$.

(c) Substitute both of your values for x from part (a) into the resulting quadratic expression from part (b). What do you notice about both answers?

A graph of $x^2 + 5x + 6 = 0$ is shown below.

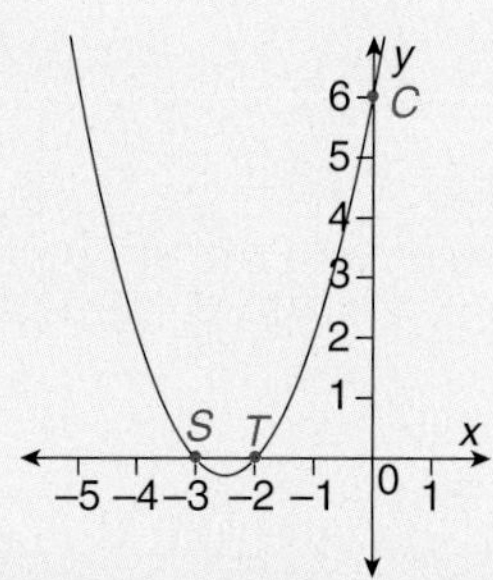

(d) Write down the coordinates of the points S, T and C.

(e) Do you notice any connection to your earlier answers?

(f) Is there any connection between the point C and $x^2 + 5x + 6 = 0$?

22. (a) If $(-x + 1)(x + 2) = 0$, find two possible values for x.

(b) Multiply $(-x + 1)$ by $(x + 2)$.

(c) Substitute both of your values for x from part (a) into the resulting quadratic expression from part (b). What do you notice about both answers?
A graph of $-x^2 - x + 2 = 0$ is shown.

(d) Write down the coordinates of the points P, Q and C.

(e) Do you notice any connection to your earlier answers?

(f) Is there any connection between the point C and $-x^2 - x + 2 = 0$?

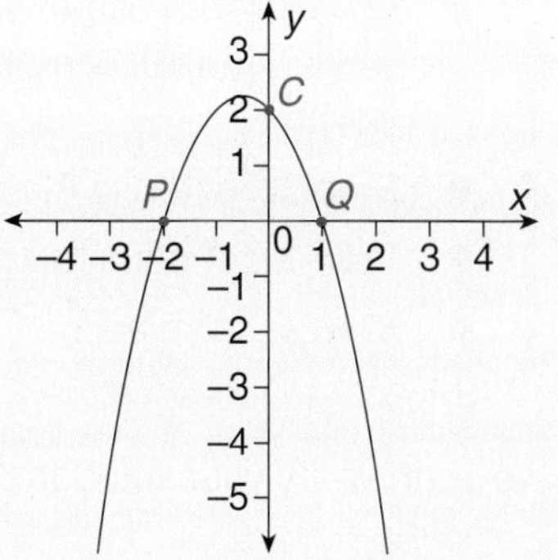

QUADRATIC EQUATIONS EXPLAINED

In Chapter 3, you learned how to factorise quadratic expressions of the form $ax^2 + bx + c$, where $a, b, c \in \mathbb{Z}$. A quadratic equation is a polynomial equation with one variable of the second degree. This means it contains a squared variable as the highest power.

A quadratic equation can be written in the general form $ax^2 + bx + c = 0$. In Chapter 21, you will learn how to graph these equations more accurately.

Here are some important facts about quadratic equations:

- A quadratic function can be written in the form $ax^2 + bx + c = 0$.
- It is a curved graph with exactly one turning point.
- The curve has a ∪ shape if the value of **'a'** is **positive.**
- The curve has an ∩ shape if the value of **'a'** is **negative.**
- The value of **c** tells us where the graph cuts the y-axis, for example $(0, c)$. This is the ***y*-intercept.**
- The equation has two roots or solutions.

In Student Activity 19A, you took your first steps towards solving quadratic equations in this form. It is important to know that, when given an equation equal to zero, the word 'solve' means that, at the end, we want:

A letter = A number

The resulting numbers are called the **roots** or the solutions of the equation. All quadratic equations have two roots. The roots can be identical.

These roots tell us the exact values of x which satisfy the equation. At the roots, the graph cuts the x-axis. The roots help us to draw a more accurate sketch of the function.

Different real roots

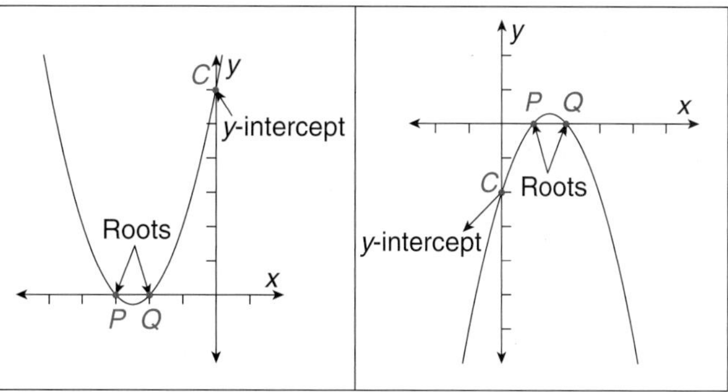

Identical real roots

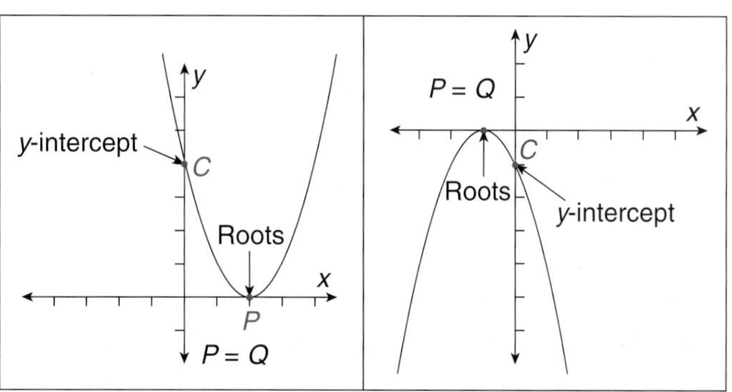

To solve a quadratic equation, use the following steps:

- **Step 1:** Bring all terms to one side of the equals sign. If the coefficient of the squared term is negative, multiply all terms by −1 to make the coefficient of the squared term positive.
- **Step 2:** Factorise the resulting quadratic equation as normal.
- **Step 3:** Let each factor = 0.
- **Step 4:** Solve each of the resulting equations.

You can verify your solutions by substituting these values back into the original equation.

When sketching a graph:

- Write the quadratic equation in the form $ax^2 + bx + c = 0$.
- Decide on the shape of the graph. It will have a ∪ shape if the coefficient of x^2 is positive or an ∩ shape if the coefficient of x^2 is negative.
- Solve the quadratic to find the roots of the equation.
- Plot the roots on a Cartesian plane.
- Plot the y-intercept $(0, c)$.
- Sketch the graph.

EXAMPLE 1

Solve for x in the equation $x^2 + x - 6 = 0$ and sketch the resulting graph.

Solution

1. Write the quadratic equation in the form $ax^2 + bx + c = 0$:
   $$x^2 + x - 6 = 0$$
2. Determine the shape of the graph:
   $$a = 1, b = 1 \text{ and } c = -6$$
   As the 'a' value is positive, the graph will have a ∪ shape.
3. Solve the equation:
   $(x + 3)(x - 2) = 0$ **Factorise the quadratic equation**
   $(x + 3) = 0$ or $(x - 2) = 0$ **Let each factor = 0**
   $x = -3$ or $x = 2$ **Solve each equation**
4. Determine the y-intercept:
   $(0, -6) = (0, c)$
5. Sketch the graph. The graph passes through the points $(-3, 0)$ and $(2, 0)$ on the x-axis and $(0, -6)$ on the y-axis.

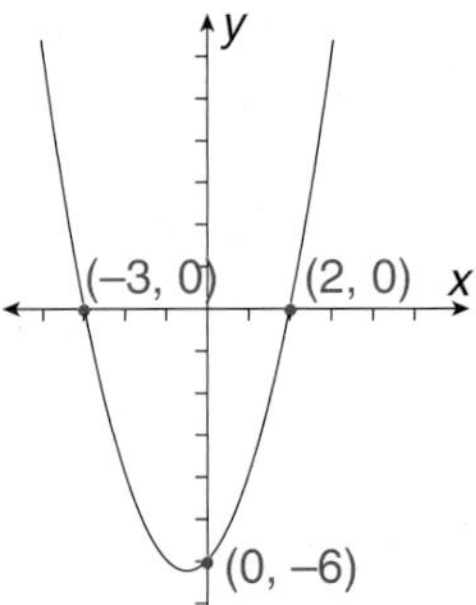

EXAMPLE 2

Solve for x in the equation $x^2 - 9x = -18$ and sketch the resulting graph.

Solution

1. Write the quadratic equation in the form $ax^2 + bx + c = 0$:
   $$x^2 - 9x + 18 = 0$$
2. Determine the shape of the graph:
   $$a = 1, b = -9 \text{ and } c = +18$$
   As the 'a' value is positive, the graph will have a ∪ shape.

3. Solve the equation:

$(x - 3)(x - 6) = 0$	**Factorise the quadratic equation**
$(x - 3) = 0$ or $(x - 6) = 0$	**Let each factor = 0**
$x = 3$ or $x = 6$	**Solve each equation**

4. Determine the y-intercept:
   $(0, +18) = (0, c)$

5. Sketch the graph: The graph passes through the points (3, 0) and (6, 0) on the x-axis and (0, 18) on the y-axis.

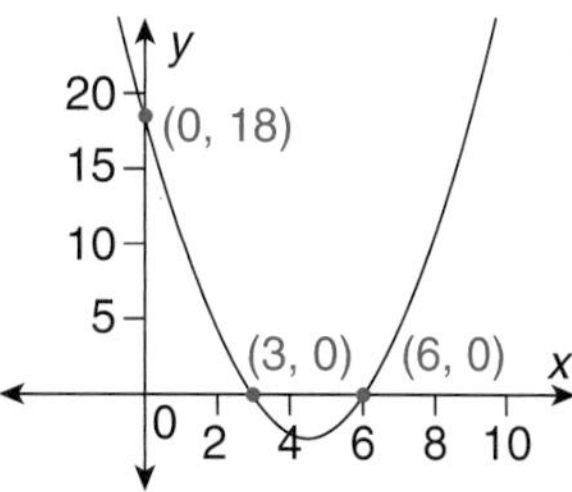

EXAMPLE 3

Solve for x in the equation $x^2 - 4x = 0$ and sketch the resulting graph.

Solution

1. Write the quadratic equation in the form $ax^2 + bx + c = 0$:
   $$x^2 - 4x + 0 = 0$$
2. Determine the shape of the graph:
   $$a = 1, b = -4 \text{ and } c = 0$$
   As the 'a' value is positive, the graph will have a ∪ shape.
3. Solve the equation:

$x(x - 4) = 0$	**Factorise the quadratic equation, taking out the HCF**
$x = 0$ or $x - 4 = 0$	**Let each factor = 0**
$x = 0$ or $x = 4$	**Solve each equation**

4. Determine the y-intercept:
   $$(0, 0) = (0, c)$$
5. Sketch the graph: The graph passes through the points (0, 0) and (4, 0) on the x-axis. The starting equation could be written as $x^2 - 4x + 0 = 0$. Therefore the graph cuts the y-axis at the point (0, 0).

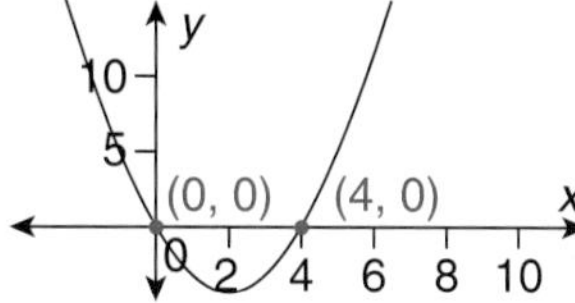

EXAMPLE 4

Solve for x in the equation $6 - x - x^2 = 0$ and sketch the resulting graph.

Solution

1. Write the quadratic equation in the form $ax^2 + bx + c = 0$:
   $$-x^2 - x + 6 = 0$$
2. Determine the shape of the graph:
   $$a = -1, b = -1 \text{ and } c = 6$$
   As the 'a' is negative, the graph will have an ∩ shape.
3. Multiply each term by −1 to make the x^2 term positive. Solve the equation:
   $x^2 + x - 6 = 0$

$(x + 3)(x - 2) = 0$	**Factorise the quadratic equation**
$(x + 3) = 0$ or $(x - 2) = 0$	**Let each factor = 0**
$x = -3$ or $x = 2$	**Solve each equation**

4. Determine the y-intercept from the original equation: $-x^2 - x + 6 = 0$
   $$(0, 6) = (0, c)$$
5. Sketch the graph: The graph passes through the points (−3, 0) and (2, 0) on the x-axis and (0, 6) on the y-axis.

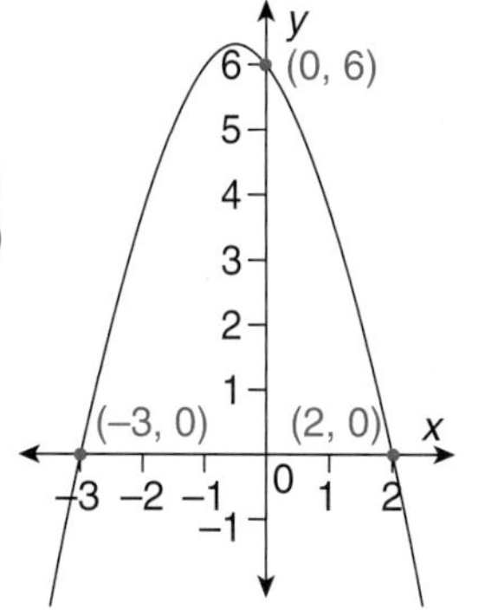

EXAMPLE 5

Solve for x in the equation $x^2 = 4$ and sketch the resulting graph.

Solution

Method 1

$x^2 = 4$

$x^2 - 4 = 0$

$(x)^2 - (2)^2 = 0$ **Difference of two squares**

$(x + 2)(x - 2) = 0$ **Factorise the quadratic equation**

$(x + 2) = 0$ or $(x - 2) = 0$ **Let each factor = 0**

$x = -2$ or $x = 2$ **Solve each equation**

Method 2

$x^2 = 4$

$x = \sqrt{4}$ **Find the square root of both sides**

$x = \pm 2$

$x = -2$ or $x = 2$

Sketch the graph: The graph passes through the points $(-2, 0)$ and $(2, 0)$ on the x-axis. The starting equation could be written as $x^2 + 0x - 4 = 0$. Therefore the graph is ∪ shaped and cuts the y-axis at the point $(0, -4)$.

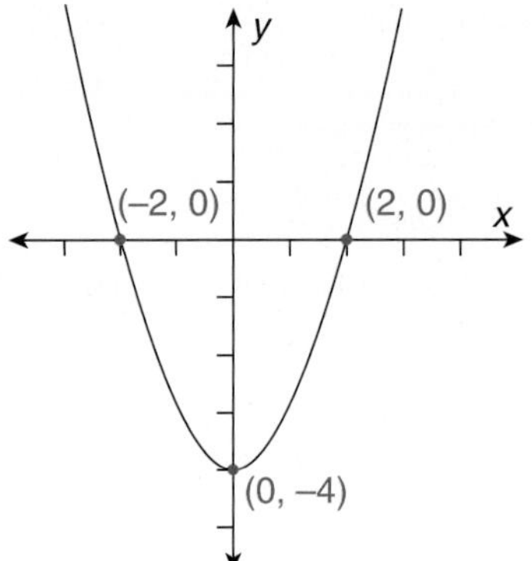

Exercise 19.1

Solve for x in each of the following equations:

1. $(x - 1)(x - 3) = 0$
2. $(x + 2)(x - 3) = 0$
3. $(x + 1)(x - 5) = 0$
4. $(x)(x - 7) = 0$
5. $(x + 2)(x - 5) = 0$
6. $(x - 5)(x + 7) = 0$
7. $(x - 8)(x - 9) = 0$
8. $(x - 16)(x + 16) = 0$
9. $(x - 10)(x + 10) = 0$
10. $(x + 12)(x - 12) = 0$

Solve each of the following equations and sketch the resulting graphs:

11. $x^2 - 7x + 12 = 0$
12. $x^2 + 6x + 5 = 0$
13. $x^2 + 3x - 18 = 0$
14. $x^2 - 3x - 4 = 0$
15. $x^2 + 7x + 6 = 0$
16. $x^2 - 10x + 21 = 0$
17. $x^2 - 2x - 15 = 0$
18. $x^2 + 3x - 28 = 0$
19. $x^2 - 6x + 9 = 0$
20. $x^2 - 5x - 24 = 0$
21. $x^2 + 7x - 18 = 0$
22. $x^2 - 3x - 70 = 0$
23. $x^2 + 8x - 33 = 0$
24. $x^2 - 2x - 3 = 0$
25. $x^2 + 8x + 15 = 0$
26. $x^2 - 12x + 11 = 0$
27. $x^2 + 9x + 14 = 0$
28. $x^2 - 16x + 48 = 0$
29. $x^2 + 14x + 48 = 0$
30. $x^2 - 7x - 60 = 0$
31. $x^2 - 5x = 0$
32. $x^2 + 3x = 0$
33. $x^2 - 12x = 0$
34. $x^2 - 20x = 0$
35. $x^2 = -13x$
36. $x^2 = -10x$
37. $x^2 = 7x$
38. $x^2 - 100 = 0$
39. $x^2 - 64 = 0$
40. $x^2 - 25 = 0$
41. $x^2 = 121$
42. $x^2 = 9$
43. $3x - x^2 = 0$
44. $5 - 4x - x^2 = 0$
45. $4 - 3x - x^2 = 0$
46. $5 - 4x - x^2 = 0$
47. $3 + 2x - x^2 = 0$
48. $2 - x - x^2 = 0$
49. $7x - x^2 + 8 = 0$

Section 19.2: Quadratic equations 2

Student Activity 19B

Factorise each of the following quadratic trinomials:

1. $2x^2 - 11x + 5$
2. $2x^2 - 5x - 3$
3. $7x^2 + 6x - 1$
4. $15x^2 + 7x - 2$
5. $4x^2 + 4x - 8$
6. $6x^2 + 5x - 21$

QUADRATIC EQUATIONS 2 EXPLAINED

In Chapter 3, you learned to factorise quadratic trinomials of the form $ax^2 + bx + c$. In Section 19.1, you learned how solve quadratic equations in which the coefficient of x^2 was 1. You will now look at quadratic equations in which the coefficient of x^2 is not equal to 1.

When factorising, you must also consider the factors of the coefficient of x^2.

You must follow the same four steps:

- **Step 1:** Bring all terms to one side of the equals sign. If the coefficient of the squared term is negative, multiply all terms by −1 to make the squared term positive.
- **Step 2:** Factorise the resulting quadratic equation as normal.
- **Step 3:** Let each factor = 0.
- **Step 4:** Solve each of the resulting equations.

EXAMPLE 6

Solve the equation $6x^2 + 23x + 7 = 0$ and sketch the resulting graph.

Solution

1. Write the quadratic equation in the form $ax^2 + bx + c = 0$:

$$6x^2 + 23x + 7 = 0$$

2. Determine the shape of the graph:

$$a = 6, b = 23 \text{ and } c = 7$$

As the 'a' value is positive, the graph will have a ∪ shape.

3. Solve the equation:

$(2x + 7)(3x + 1) = 0$ **Factors**

$2x + 7 = 0$ or $3x + 1 = 0$

$2x = -7$ or $3x = -1$

$x = -\frac{7}{2}$ or $x = -\frac{1}{3}$ **The roots of the equation**

4. Determine the y-intercept:

$(0, 7) = (0, c)$

5. Sketch the graph: The graph passes through the points $\left(-\frac{7}{2}, 0\right)$ and $\left(-\frac{1}{3}, 0\right)$ on the x-axis and $(0, 7)$ on the y-axis.

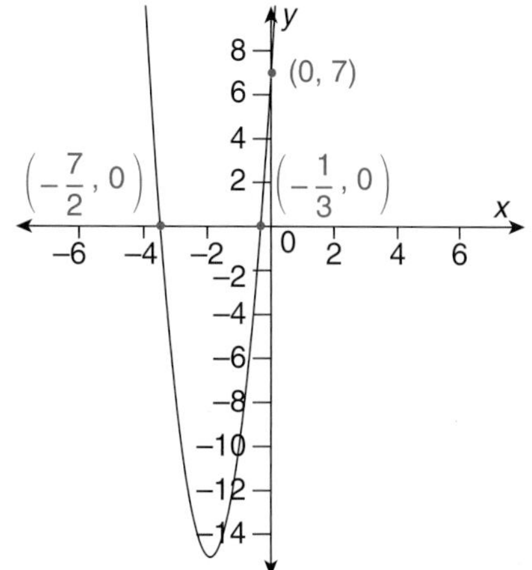

EXAMPLE 7

Solve the equation $12x^2 + 5x = 2$ and sketch the resulting graph.

Solution

1. Write the quadratic in the form $ax^2 + bx + c = 0$:

$$12x^2 + 5x - 2 = 0$$

2. Determine the shape of the graph.

$$a = 12, b = 5 \text{ and } c = -2$$

As the 'a' value is positive, the graph will have a ∪ shape.

3. Solve the equation

$(4x - 1)(3x + 2) = 0$

$4x - 1 = 0$ or $3x + 2 = 0$ **Factors**

$4x = 1$ or $3x = -2$

$x = \frac{1}{4}$ or $x = -\frac{2}{3}$ **Roots**

4. Determine the y-intercept: $(0, -2) = (0, c)$

5. Sketch the graph: The graph passes through the points $\left(\frac{1}{4}, 0\right)$ and $\left(-\frac{2}{3}, 0\right)$ on the x-axis and $(0, -2)$ on the y-axis.

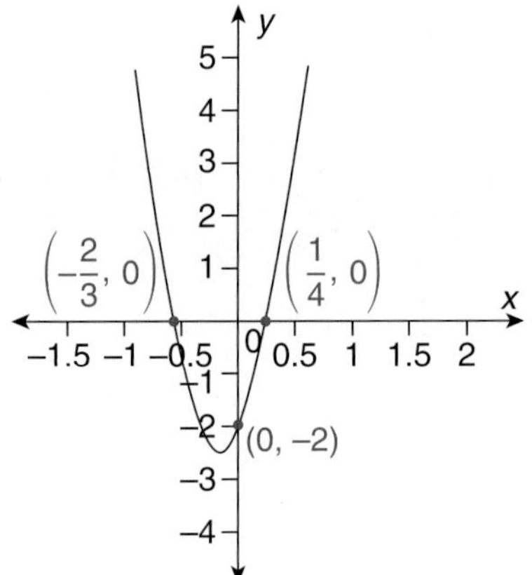

Exercise 19.2

Solve the following equations:

1. $2x^2 + x - 3 = 0$
2. $3x^2 + 2x - 1 = 0$
3. $4x^2 - 6x + 2 = 0$
4. $3x^2 - 19x - 14 = 0$
5. $2x^2 - 17x - 9 = 0$
6. $7x^2 - 23x - 20 = 0$
7. $7x^2 + 41x - 6 = 0$
8. $2x^2 - 25x + 12 = 0$
9. $3x^2 - 28x - 20 = 0$
10. $8x^2 + 14x - 15 = 0$
11. $16x^2 - 24x - 7 = 0$
12. $21x^2 - 7x - 14 = 0$
13. $30x^2 + 29x - 7 = 0$
14. $20x^2 + 32x + 12 = 0$
15. $2x^2 - 3x - 27 = 0$
16. $3x^2 - 4x - 7 = 0$

Solve each of the following equations and sketch the resulting graph:

17. $2x^2 + 4x - 30 = 0$
18. $3x^2 - 3x - 4 = 0$
19. $3x^2 - 4x - 20 = 0$
20. $3x^2 + 7x - 66 = 0$
21. $-3x^2 + 16x + 35 = 0$
22. $3x^2 + 22x - 16 = 0$
23. $-10x^2 + 11x + 6 = 0$
24. $7x^2 - 17x - 12 = 0$
25. $-11x^2 - 32x + 3 = 0$
26. $6x^2 - 7x + 2 = 0$
27. $-8x^2 - 22x + 6 = 0$
28. $4x^2 - 6x - 4 = 0$
29. $20x^2 - 26x - 6 = 0$

Section 19.3: The quadratic formula

Student Activity 19C

1. Try to factorise $x^2 - 4x - 11 = 0$. What problem did you encounter?
2. Try to factorise $x^2 - 5x - 7 = 0$. What problem did you encounter?
3. Write down 5 other quadratic equations that you cannot factorise.

THE QUADRATIC FORMULA EXPLAINED

Student Activity 19C was very short as you found that you could not factorise the given quadratic equations. This is because the factors do not involve whole numbers or simple fractions.

We use the quadratic formula to solve any quadratic equation in the form $\boldsymbol{ax^2 + bx + c = 0}$ which cannot be easily factorised:

$$x = \frac{-b \pm \sqrt{b^2 - 4ac}}{2a}$$

This formula is given on page 20 of the *Formulae and Tables*.

It is worth noting that the **quadratic formula can be used to solve any quadratic equation!**

Remember that every term of the equation must be on the left-hand side of the equation and in the form $ax^2 + bx + c = 0$. Notice the ± in the formula gives us two answers. These answers can be written in either **surd form** or correct to **any decimal place.**

EXAMPLE 8

(a) Solve the equation $2x^2 - 5x - 10 = 0$, giving your answers correct to one decimal place.

Solution

$2x^2 - 5x - 10 = 0$

$a = 2, b = -5, c = -10$

$$x = \frac{-(-5) \pm \sqrt{(-5)^2 - 4(2)(-10)}}{2(2)}$$

$$x = \frac{5 \pm \sqrt{25 + 80}}{4}$$

$$x = \frac{5 \pm \sqrt{105}}{4}$$

$$x = \frac{5 + \sqrt{105}}{4} \text{ or } \frac{5 - \sqrt{105}}{4}$$

$x = 3.8$ or $x = -1.3$

(b) Solve the equation $3x^2 + 15x - 11 = 0$, giving your answers correct to two decimal places.

Solution

$3x^2 + 15x - 11 = 0$

$a = 3, b = +15, c = -11$

$$x = \frac{-(15) \pm \sqrt{(15)^2 - 4(3)(-11)}}{2(3)}$$

$$x = \frac{-15 \pm \sqrt{225 + 132}}{6}$$

$$x = \frac{-15 \pm \sqrt{357}}{6}$$

$$x = \frac{-15 + \sqrt{357}}{6} \text{ or } \frac{-15 - \sqrt{357}}{6}$$

$x = 0.65$ or $x = -5.65$

(c) Solve the equation $2x^2 - 2x - 1 = 0$, giving your answers in surd form.

Solution

$2x^2 - 2x - 1 = 0$

$a = 2, b = -2, c = -1$

$$x = \frac{-(-2) \pm \sqrt{(-2)^2 - 4(2)(-1)}}{2(2)}$$

$$x = \frac{2 \pm \sqrt{4 + 8}}{4}$$

$$x = \frac{2 \pm \sqrt{12}}{4}$$

Remember

$\boldsymbol{\sqrt{12} = \sqrt{4} \times \sqrt{3} = 2\sqrt{3}}$

$$x = \frac{2 + 2\sqrt{3}}{4} \text{ or } \frac{2 - 2\sqrt{3}}{4}$$

Divide across by 2

$$x = \frac{1 + \sqrt{3}}{2} \text{ or } x = \frac{1 - \sqrt{3}}{2}$$

Exercise 19.3

Solve the following quadratic equations, correct to two decimal places:

1. $x^2 - 5x - 10 = 0$

2. $x^2 + 7x - 17 = 0$

3. $x^2 + 3x - 7 = 0$

4. $x^2 + 5x - 13 = 0$

5. $2x^2 + 3x - 13 = 0$

6. $5x^2 - 3x - 1 = 0$

7. $7x^2 + 10x - 20 = 0$

8. $2x^2 - 15x + 7 = 0$

9. $x^2 + 4x + 1 = 0$

10. $9x^2 - 13x + 2 = 0$

Solve the following quadratic equations, giving your answers in surd form where necessary:

11. $2x^2 - 3x - 11 = 0$

12. $3x^2 - x - 7 = 0$

13. $2x^2 - 7x + 3 = 0$

14. $2x^2 + 3x - 17 = 0$

15. $3x^2 - 10x + 1 = 0$

16. $3x^2 - 11x + 3 = 0$

17. $2x^2 - 5x - 10 = 0$

18. $7x^2 - 10x + 1 = 0$

19. $2x^2 + 12x - 4 = 0$

20. $9x^2 - 8 = 0$

Solve the following equations and sketch the graph, showing your solutions:

21. $4x^2 = 29x - 7$

22. $9 - (2x + 1)^2 = (x - 2)^2$

23. $25 = 4x^2$

24. $x(3 - 4x) - 2 = 6x(x - 1)$

25. $(2x - 1)(x - 5) = (3x + 5)(x - 1)$

26. $(x + 2)^2 = (3x - 1)^2$

27. Verify that $1 + \sqrt{3}$ is a solution of the equation $x^2 - 2x - 2 = 0$.

28. Verify that $4 + 2\sqrt{3}$ is a solution of the equation $x^2 - 8x + 4 = 0$.

29. Verify that $3 - 2\sqrt{2}$ is a solution of the equation $x^2 - 6x + 1 = 0$.

Section 19.4: Similar quadratic equations

Student Activity 19D

1. (a) Solve the following equation: $x^2 + 3x + 2 = 0$.

(b) Using your answers from part (a), state the two values of a that will satisfy the equation $a^2 + 3a + 2 = 0$. Explain your answer.

(c) Using your answers from part (a) and (b), solve the equation:

$(y - 1)^2 + 3(y - 1) + 2 = 0$

2. (a) Solve the following equation: $2x^2 - 11x + 5 = 0$.

(b) Using your answers from part (a), state the two values of t that will satisfy the equation $2t^2 - 11t + 5 = 0$. Explain your answer.

(c) Using your answers from part (a) and (b), solve the equation:

$2(5 + a)^2 - 11(5 + a) + 5 = 0$

SIMILAR QUADRATIC EQUATIONS EXPLAINED

Sometimes, we can be given a very difficult equation. To multiply and write it in the form of $ax^2 + bx + c = 0$ may take a lot of time. Therefore, we try to simplify the equation to a more familiar format and use the answers to solve the original problem. This linking of two equations is a form of **substitution.**

EXAMPLE 9

(a) Solve the equation $x^2 - 10x + 24 = 0$. Hence, solve $(y + 2)^2 - 10(y + 2) + 24 = 0$.

(b) Solve the equation $10x^2 - 30x + 20 = 0$. Hence, solve $10\left(p + \frac{1}{2}\right)^2 - 30\left(p + \frac{1}{2}\right) + 20 = 0$.

Solution

(a) $x^2 - 10x + 24 = 0$

$(x - 6)(x - 4) = 0$ **Factorise the quadratic equation**

$(x - 6) = 0$ or $(x - 4) = 0$ **Let each factor = 0**

$x = 6$ or $x = 4$ **Solve each equation**

In the equation $(y + 2)^2 - 10(y + 2) + 24 = 0$.

Let $(y + 2) = x$

Therefore: $y + 2 = 6$ or $y + 2 = 4$:

$y = 6 - 2$ or $y = 4 - 2$ **Solve for *y***

$y = 4$ or $y = 2$ **Tidy up**

(b) $10x^2 - 30x + 20 = 0$

$10(x^2 - 3x + 2) = 0$ **HCF = 10**

$(x - 1)(x - 2) = 0$ **Factorise the quadratic equation**

$x - 1 = 0$ or $x - 2 = 0$ **Let each factor = 0**

$x = 1$ or $x = 2$ **Solve each equation**

In the equation $10\left(p + \frac{1}{2}\right)^2 - 30\left(p + \frac{1}{2}\right) + 20 = 0$,

let $\left(p + \frac{1}{2}\right) = x$.

Therefore: $p + \frac{1}{2} = 1$ or $p + \frac{1}{2} = 2$

$p = 1 - \frac{1}{2}$ or $p = 2 - \frac{1}{2}$ **Solve for *p***

$p = 0.5$ or $p = 1.5$ **Tidy up**

Exercise 19.4

1. Solve the equation $x^2 + 13x + 40 = 0$. Hence, solve for the values of t for which $(t + 1)^2 + 13(t + 1) + 40 = 0$.
2. Solve the equation $x^2 - 4x - 45 = 0$. Hence, solve for the values of k for which $(k + 5)^2 - 4(k + 5) - 45 = 0$.
3. Solve the equation $x^2 + 3x - 54 = 0$. Hence, solve for the values of f for which $(2f - 1)^2 + 3(2f - 1) - 54 = 0$.
4. Solve the equation $x^2 - 5x - 84 = 0$. Hence, solve for the values of g for which $\left(\frac{1}{g}\right)^2 - 5\left(\frac{1}{g}\right) - 84 = 0$.
5. Solve the equation $x^2 + 7x - 30 = 0$. Hence, solve for the values of y in surd form for which $\left(y + \frac{1}{y}\right)^2 + 7\left(y + \frac{1}{y}\right) - 30 = 0$.
6. Solve the equation $6x^2 - 7x + 2 = 0$. Hence, solve for the values of x correct to one decimal place for which $6(2x - 4)^2 - 7(2x - 4) + 2 = 0$.
7. Solve the equation $8x^2 + 14x - 15 = 0$ correct to one decimal place. Hence, solve for the values of t correct to one decimal place for which $8\left(2t - \frac{2}{t}\right)^2 + 14\left(2t - \frac{2}{t}\right) - 15 = 0$.
8. Solve the equation $2x^2 - 17x - 9 = 0$ correct to one decimal place. Hence, solve for the values of h correct to one decimal place for which $2\left(\frac{1}{h} + 4\right)^2 - 17\left(\frac{1}{h} + 4\right) - 9 = 0$.
9. Solve the equation $7x^2 + 41x - 6 = 0$ correct to. Hence, solve for the values of p correct to two decimal places for which $7\left(3 - \frac{1}{p}\right)^2 + 41\left(3 - \frac{1}{p}\right) - 6 = 0$.
10. Solve the equation $20x^2 - 26x + 6 = 0$ correct to one decimal place. Hence, solve for the values of y in surd form for which $20\left(\frac{2}{y^2}\right)^2 - 26\left(\frac{2}{y^2}\right) - 6 = 0$.

Section 19.5: Forming quadratic equations

Student Activity 19E

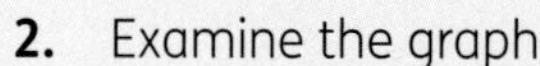

1. Examine the graph:
   (a) At what points does the graph cut the x-axis?
   (b) At what point does the graph cut the y-axis?
   (c) Write the quadratic equation that represents this graph in the form $x^2 + bx + c = 0$.

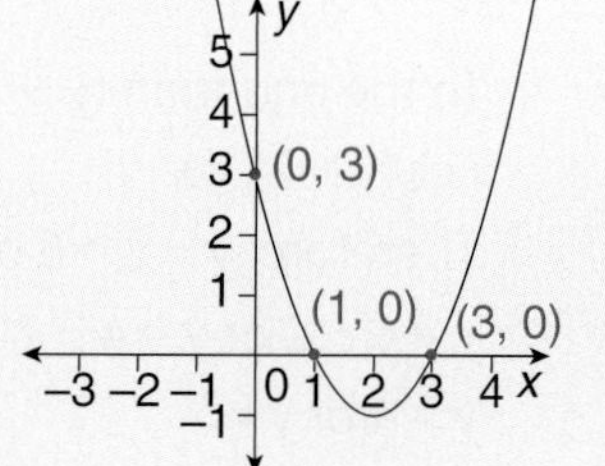

2. Examine the graph:
   (a) At what points does the graph cut the x-axis?
   (b) At what point does the graph cut the y-axis?
   (c) Write the quadratic equation that represents this graph in the form $x^2 + bx + c = 0$.
   (d) Find the sum of the roots.
   (e) Find the product of the roots.
   (f) How do the answers in parts (d) and (e) relate to the quadratic equation in part (c)?

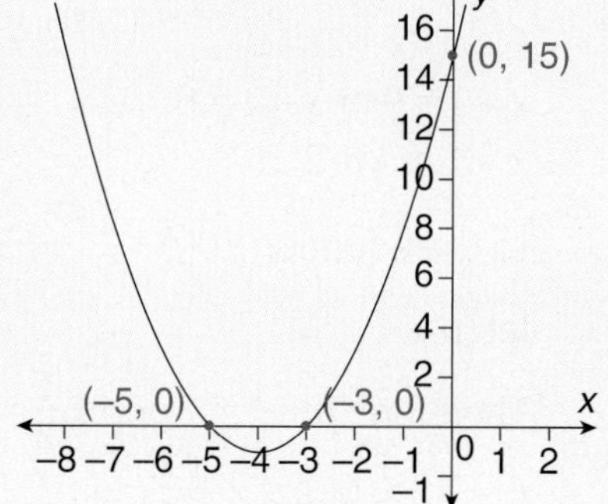

3. Sketch a quadratic graph. Get a classmate to write the quadratic equation which represents your graph.

FORMING QUADRATIC EQUATIONS EXPLAINED

It is sometimes necessary to form a quadratic equation when given its roots. It is the reverse process of solving a quadratic function. The roots of a quadratic equation are given and you must determine the starting equation.

It can be shown that, in a quadratic equation of the form $x^2 + bx + c = 0$, the value of ***b* = the sum of the roots** and the value of ***c* = the product of the roots.**

This means that any quadratic in the form $x^2 + bx + c$ can also be written in the form:

$$x^2 - x(\text{sum of the roots}) + (\text{product of the roots}) = 0$$

EXAMPLE 10

Find the quadratic equation which has roots 3 and 4.

Solution

Method 1

If the roots are 3 and 4:

$x = 3$ and $x = 4$

Form the factors of the quadratic:

$(x - 3) = 0$ and $(x - 4) = 0$

Multiply the factors:

$(x - 3)(x - 4) = 0$

$x(x - 4) - 3(x - 4) = 0$

$x^2 - 4x - 3x + 12 = 0$

$x^2 - 7x + 12 = 0$

Method 2

$x^2 - x(\text{sum of the roots}) + (\text{product of the roots}) = 0$

$x^2 - x(3 + 4) + (3)(4) = 0$

$x^2 - x(7) + 12 = 0$

$x^2 - 7x + 12 = 0$

EXAMPLE 11

Find the quadratic equation which has roots −5 and 2.

Solution

Method 1

If the roots are −5 and 2:

$x = -5$ and $x = 2$

Form the factors of the quadratic:

$(x + 5) = 0$ and $(x - 2) = 0$

Multiply the factors:

$(x + 5)(x - 2) = 0$

$x(x - 2) + 5(x - 2) = 0$

$x^2 - 2x + 5x - 10 = 0$

$x^2 + 3x - 10 = 0$

Method 2

$x^2 - x(\text{sum of the roots}) + (\text{product of the roots}) = 0$

$x^2 - x(-5 + 2) + (-5)(2) = 0$

$x^2 - x(-3) - 10 = 0$

$x^2 + 3x - 10 = 0$

EXAMPLE 12

Find the quadratic equation which is shown in the following graph:

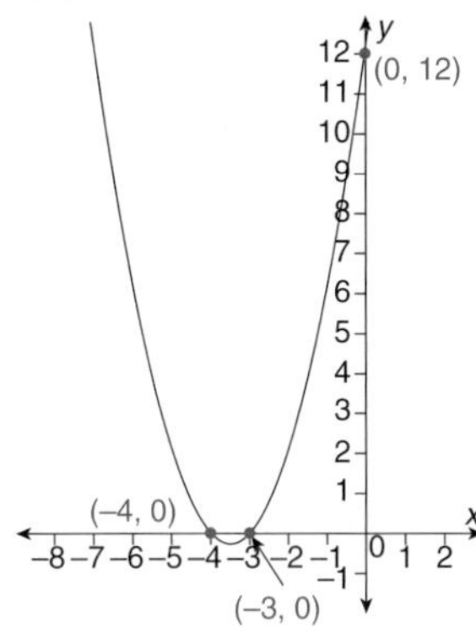

Solution

Method 1

The graph crosses the x-axis at the points (−4, 0) and (−3, 0).

$x = -4$ and $x = -3$

Form the factors of the quadratic:

$(x + 4) = 0$ and $(x + 3) = 0$

Multiply the factors:

$(x + 4)(x + 3) = 0$

$x(x + 3) + 4(x + 3) = 0$

$x^2 + 3x + 4x + 12 = 0$

$x^2 + 7x + 12 = 0$

Method 2

$x^2 - x(\text{sum of the roots}) + (\text{product of the roots}) = 0$

$x^2 - x(-4 - 3) + (-4)(-3) = 0$

$x^2 - x(-7) + 12 = 0$

$x^2 + 7x + 12 = 0$

EXAMPLE 13

Find the quadratic equation which is shown in the following graph:

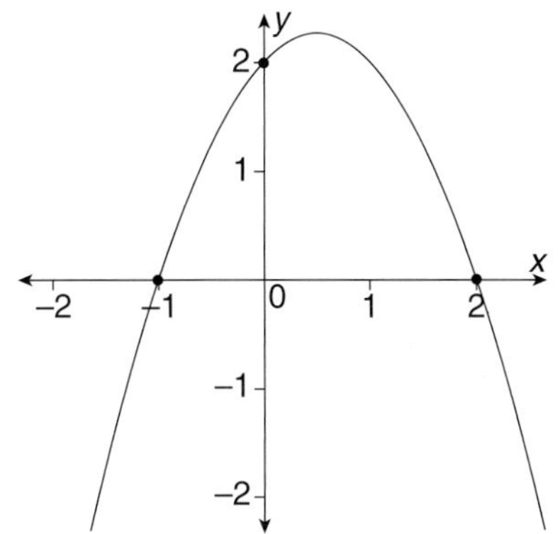

Solution

Method 1

If the roots are −1 and 2:

$x = -1$ and $x = 2$

Form the factors of the quadratic:

$(x + 1) = 0$ and $(x - 2) = 0$

Multiply the factors:

$(x + 1)(x - 2) = 0$

$x(x - 2) + 1(x - 2) = 0$

$x^2 - 2x + 1x - 2 = 0$

$x^2 - x - 2 = 0$

$-x^2 + x + 2 = 0$ **As the graph is an ∩ shaped curve**

Method 2

$x^2 - x(\text{sum of the roots}) + (\text{product of the roots}) = 0$

$x^2 - x(-1 + 2) + (-1)(2) = 0$

$x^2 - x(1) - 2 = 0$

$x^2 - x - 2 = 0$

$-x^2 + x + 2 = 0$ **As the graph is an ∩ shaped curve**

EXAMPLE 14

Find the quadratic equation which is shown in the following graph:

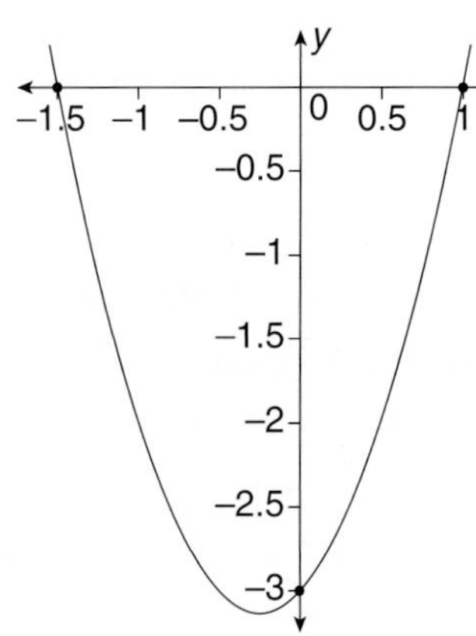

Solution

Method 1

If the roots are $-\frac{3}{2}$ and 1:

$x = -\frac{3}{2}$ and $x = 1$

Form the factors of the quadratic:

$\left(x + \frac{3}{2}\right) = 0$ and $(x - 1) = 0$

Multiply the factors:

$\left(x + \frac{3}{2}\right)(x - 1) = 0$

$x(x - 1) + \frac{3}{2}(x - 1) = 0$

$x^2 - x + \frac{3}{2}x - \frac{3}{2} = 0$

$x^2 + \frac{1}{2}x - \frac{3}{2} = 0$

$2x^2 + x - 3 = 0$ **Multiply by 2 to eliminate fractions**

Method 2

$x^2 - x(\text{sum of the roots}) + (\text{product of the roots}) = 0$

$x^2 - x\left(-\frac{3}{2} + 1\right) + \left(-\frac{3}{2}\right)(1) = 0$

$x^2 - x\left(-\frac{1}{2}\right) - \frac{3}{2} = 0$

$x^2 + \frac{1}{2}x - \frac{3}{2} = 0$

$2x^2 + x - 3 = 0$ **As the graph is a ∪ shaped curve**

Exercise 19.5

Form the quadratic equations with the following roots:

1. 2, 4
2. 1, 6
3. 3, 5
4. 2, 7
5. 4, 5
6. 3, 4
7. 9, 1
8. 1, 8
9. 2, 10
10. −1, 2
11. −2, 5
12. 6, −3
13. 10, −6
14. −2, −5
15. −12, −2
16. $\frac{1}{3}$, 4
17. $\frac{2}{5}$, −1
18. $\frac{2}{3}$, −3
19. $\frac{1}{4}$, −1
20. $\frac{3}{4}$, 1
21. $\frac{3}{5}$, 3
22. $\frac{2}{7}$, −2
23. $\frac{1}{8}$, −3
24. $\frac{2}{9}$, 5
25. $\frac{1}{6}$, −2
26. 4, 4

27. Study the following graphs and determine the quadratic equation for each graph:

(a)

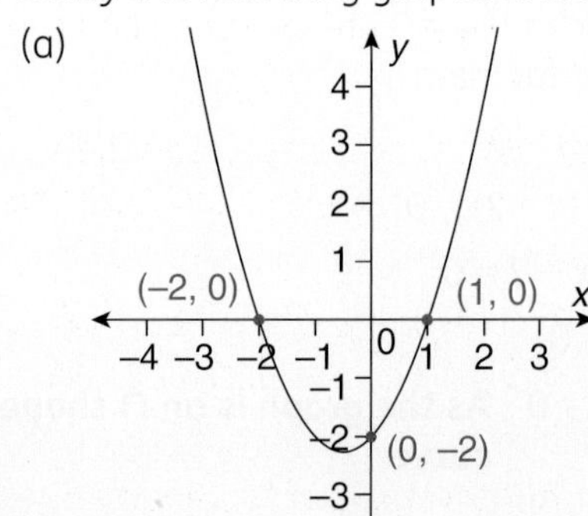

(b)

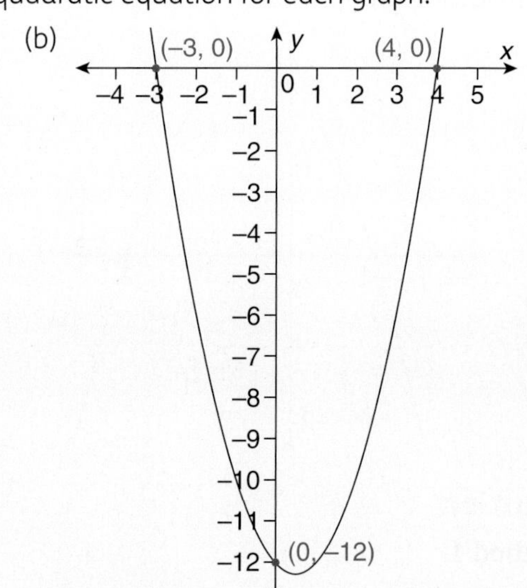

(c)

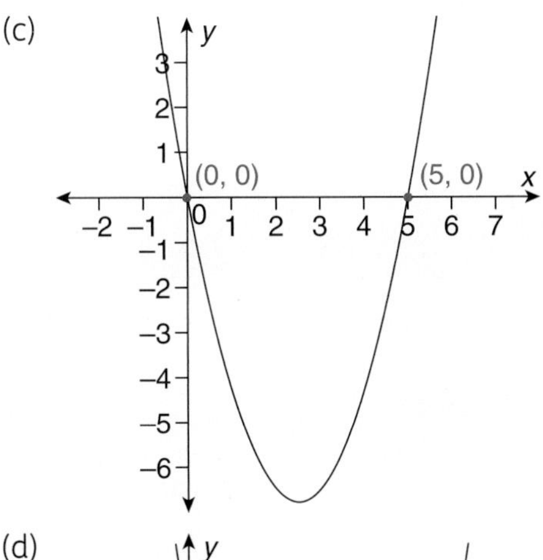

(d)

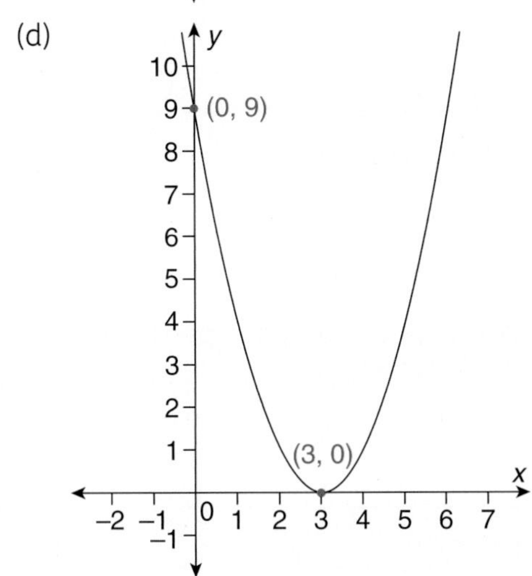

(e)

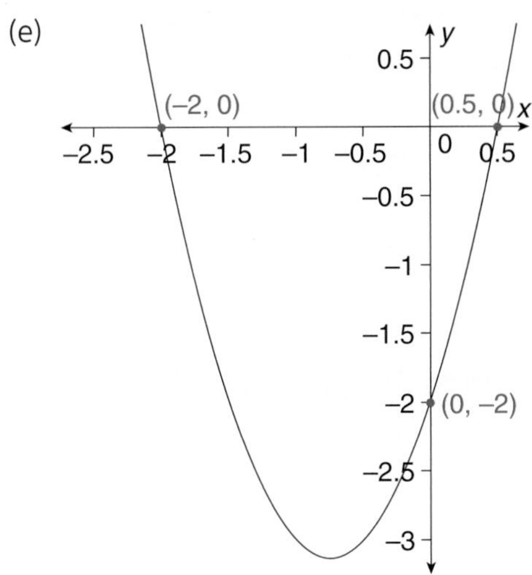

(f)

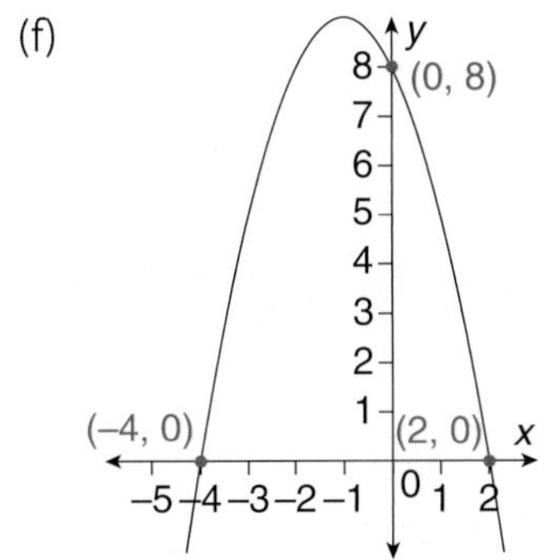

(g)

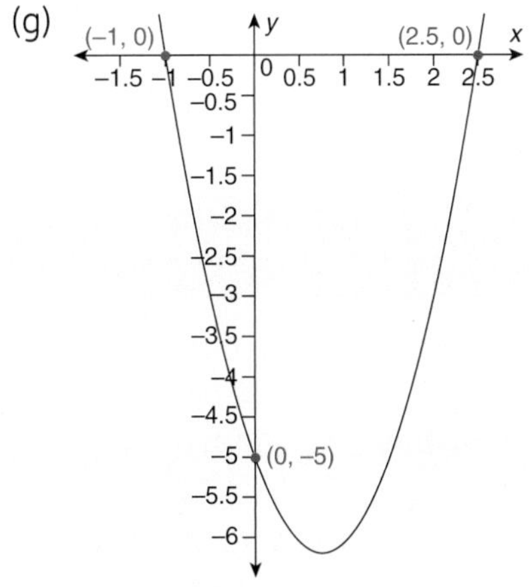

28. If the roots of the equation $ax^2 + bx + c = 0$ are 4 and 5, find the values of *a*, *b* and *c*.

29. If the roots of the equation $ax^2 + bx + c = 0$ are −1 and 7, find the values of *a*, *b* and *c*.

30. If the roots of the equation $ax^2 + bx + c = 0$ are −4 and −5, find the values of *a*, *b* and *c*.

31. If the roots of the equation $ax^2 + bx + c = 0$ are $\frac{1}{3}$ and $-\frac{4}{5}$, find the values of *a*, *b* and *c*.

32. Given that the roots of the equation $x^2 + 10x + c = 0$ are identical, find the value of *c*.

33. Given that the roots of the equation $x^2 - 6x + c = 0$ are identical, find the value of *c*.

34. Given that the roots of the equation $4x^2 + 4x + c = 0$ are identical, find the value of *c*.

35. Given that the roots of the equation $9x^2 + bx + 1 = 0$ are identical, find two possible values for *b*.

36. Given that the roots of the equation $4x^2 + bx + 16 = 0$ are identical, find two possible values for *b*.

37. Given that the roots of the equation $25x^2 + bx + 4 = 0$ are identical, find the value of *b* if $b > 0$.

38. Given that the roots of the equation $9x^2 + 18x + c = 0$ are identical, find the value of *c*.

39. Given that the roots of the equation $x^2 + bx + 9 = 0$ are identical, find two possible values for *b*.

40. Given that the roots of the equation $49x^2 + bx + 1 = 0$ are identical, find two possible values for *b*.

41. Given that the roots of the equation $4x^2 - 36x + c = 0$ are identical, find the value of *c*.

19

Section 19.6: Problems using quadratic equations

Student Activity 19F

1. A farmer is fencing a rectangular field. He has 5,000 m of wire. If the field is 275 m long, how wide is the field? Explain your answer fully.
2. (a) Write down the width of the rectangle shown in terms of x.

   (b) Write down the area of the rectangle in terms of x.

Perimeter = 800 m | x m

PROBLEMS USING QUADRATIC EQUATIONS EXPLAINED

The Babylonians used quadratics to solve problems involving area. Over time, people realised that quadratic equations could be applied to many different problems.

When answering problems, it is often necessary to create an equation using the information supplied. It is also helpful to sketch a picture of the problem.

EXAMPLE 15

A gardener has a 200 m border to put around a rectangular flower-bed of width x metres. Show:

(a) That the length of the flower-bed is $(100 - x)$ metres

(b) That the area of the flower-bed is $(100x - x^2)$ m^2

Solution

(a) The gardener has 200 m of border.

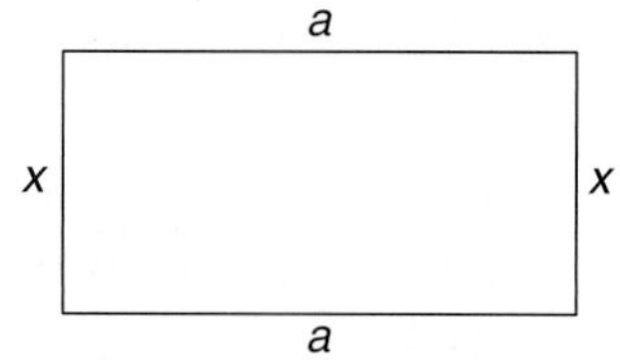

Call the length a.

Perimeter = $2a + 2x$

$200 = 2a + 2x$

$200 - 2x = 2a$

$\frac{(200 - 2x)}{2} = a$

$\therefore$ Length = $100 - x$

$\therefore$ Dimensions are x and $100 - x$

(b) Area = Length × Width

Area = $(x)(100 - x)$

Area = $100x - x^2$ m^2

EXAMPLE 16

Paul thinks of a positive number and calls it x. If he subtracts 6 from the number and then multiplies his answer by the number plus 4, the answer is 39. What is the value of x?

Solution

Original number is x

$(x - 6)$ **Number minus 6**

$(x + 4)$ **Number plus 4**

Multiply these and the answer will be 39.

$(x + 4)(x - 6) = 39$

$x(x - 6) + 4(x - 6) = 39$

$x^2 - 6x + 4x - 24 = 39$

$x^2 - 2x - 63 = 0$

$(x - 9)(x + 7) = 0$

$(x - 9) = 0$ or $(x + 7) = 0$

$x = 9$ or $x = -7$ **Not valid as Paul thought of a positive number**

$\therefore x = 9$

EXAMPLE 17

In a certain week, a prize of €200 is divided equally among a certain number of people.

(a) Taking x as the number of people, write an expression in terms of x to represent the amount won by each person.

(b) In the second week, an extra person shared in the prize. Write an expression in terms of x to represent the amount won by each person.

The amount won by each person in the second week was €10 less than the first week.

(c) Write an equation to represent this information.

(d) Solve the equation and find the value of x.

Solution

(a) $\frac{200}{x}$ (b) $\frac{200}{x+1}$ (c) $\frac{200}{x} - \frac{200}{x+1} = 10$

(d) $\frac{200}{x} - \frac{200}{x+1} = \frac{10}{1}$

$\frac{(x)(x+1)(1)(200)}{x} - \frac{(x)(x+1)(1)(200)}{x+1} = \frac{(x)(x+1)(1)(10)}{1}$ **Multiply by the LCM of the denominators**

$(x+1)(1)(200) - (x)(1)(200) = (x)(x+1)(10)$ **Multiply out the brackets**

$\cancel{200x} + 200 - \cancel{200x} = 10x^2 + 10x$ **Simplify**

$200 = 10x^2 + 10x$

$0 = 10x^2 + 10x - 200$ **Bring all terms to one side**

$0 = x^2 + x - 20$ **Simplify by dividing by 10 and solve**

$(x+5)(x-4) = 0$

$x = -5$ or $x = 4$

$x = -5$ is not a valid answer as you cannot have a negative number of people.

$\therefore x = 4$

Check your solution:

$\frac{200}{x} - \frac{200}{x+1} = 10$

$\frac{200}{4} - \frac{200}{5} = 10$

$50 - 40 = 10$

$10 = 10 \therefore 4$ is the correct answer

Exercise 19.6

1. Jane thinks of a natural number and subtracts three. Peter adds two to the same number. When they multiply the two numbers, the answer is 50. Find the value of the number Jane thought of.
2. A positive number plus 3 multiplied by the same number minus 7 is equal to 75. Find the number.
3. Paul thinks of a natural number and multiplies it by itself. If the answer is 16, what number did Paul think of?
4. Jill thinks of a natural number and subtracts 3. She multiplies her answer by the original number. If her answer is 10 what number did Jill first think of?
5. Jack thinks of a natural number and adds 1. Bríd thinks of the same number and subtracts 6. When they multiply their answers, the result is 18. What number did Jack and Bríd think of?
6. (a) The length of a rectangle is $(x + 4)$ cm. Its width is $(x - 3)$ cm. If its area is known to be 18 cm^2, can you find the value of x.
   (b) What is the perimeter of the rectangle?
7. (a) Find the dimensions of a rectangle which is $(x + 4)$ cm long and $(x - 2)$ cm wide given that its area is 7 cm^2.
   (b) What is the perimeter of the rectangle?

8. The small lawn in front of a house is $(x + 4)$ metres long and $(x - 3)$ metres wide. The area of the lawn is 78 m^2.

(a) Find the dimensions of the lawn.

(b) What is the perimeter of the lawn?

9. In a right-angled triangle, the length of the shortest side is x, the length of the longest side is $(x + 8)$ and the length of the third side is $(x + 4)$.

(a) Using your knowledge of the theorem of Pythagoras, find the value of x.

(b) What is the area of this triangle?

10. The width of a rectangular lawn is 4 m shorter than its length. If the area of the lawn is 60 m^2, calculate the perimeter of the lawn.

11. A picture frame has length x cm. The width is 5 cm less than the length. If the area of the frame is 300 cm^2, calculate the perimeter of the frame.

12. If a natural number minus 7 multiplied by the same number plus 1 gives an answer of 20, find the number.

13. (a) If a square lawn has an area of 100 m^2, find the length of a side of the lawn.

(b) Find the length of the diagonal of the lawn.

14. If a natural number minus 5 multiplied by the same number plus 7 gives an answer of 45, find the number.

15. Harry thinks of a natural number and subtracts 8. Joe thinks of the same number and adds 2. If the product of their answers is 56, what number did they think of?

16. A landscaper measures a rectangular garden. He finds the width is 13 m less than the length. If the area of the garden is 140 m^2, find the dimensions of the garden.

17. A certain number of people shared a prize of €100 equally.

(a) Taking x as the number of people, write an expression in terms of x to represent the amount won by each person.

(b) In the second week, the prize is shared amongst a group with one extra person. Write an expression in terms of x to represent the amount won by each person.

The amount won by each person the second week was €5 less than the first week.

(c) Write an equation to represent the above information.

(d) Solve the equation and find the value of x.

18. 200 seats in a theatre are in rows of x seats per row.

(a) Write an expression to represent the number of rows in the theatre.

(b) The owners are planning to decrease the number of rows by increasing the number of seats per row by 5. If the overall number of seats remains unchanged, write an expression to represent the number of seats per row.

(c) If the number of rows will decrease by 2, write an equation to represent this information.

(d) Solve the equation to find the number of rows in the theatre at present.

19. A packet of toilet rolls cost €12 and contains x number of rolls of toilet paper.

(a) Write an expression to represent the price per roll.

During a promotion two free rolls are added for the same price.

(b) Write an expression to represent the price per roll during the promotion.

During the promotion the price per roll was €0.20 less.

(c) Write an equation to represent the information given.

(d) Solve the equation to find the price per roll during the promotion.

20. A €10-per-month mobile phone package offers x number of minutes talk time per month.

(a) Write an expression to represent the cost per minute.

A second mobile phone company offers double the amount of minutes.

(b) Write an expression to represent the cost per minute for the second company.

(c) If the price per minute is 5 cent cheaper for the second company, write an equation to represent the above information.

(d) Solve the equation to find the cost per minute for each company.

CHAPTER 19 SELF-CHECK TEST

Solve each of the following equations and sketch the graphs:

1. $x^2 - 12x + 35 = 0$
2. $x^2 + 15x + 56 = 0$
3. $x^2 - 3x + 2 = 0$
4. $x^2 + 11x + 18 = 0$
5. $x^2 - 4x - 77 = 0$
6. $x^2 - 5x - 126 = 0$
7. $x^2 - 11x - 60 = 0$
8. $x^2 - 7x - 30 = 0$
9. $x^2 + 5x - 84 = 0$
10. $x^2 + 3x - 88 = 0$
11. $2x^2 - 3x - 5 = 0$
12. $3x^2 - 10x - 13 = 0$
13. $2x^2 + 5x - 7 = 0$
14. $7x^2 + 4x - 3 = 0$
15. $5x^2 + 11x + 2 = 0$

Use the quadratic formula to solve each of the following quadratic equations, correct to two decimal places:

16. $6x^2 + x - 17 = 0$
17. $x^2 - 4x - 7 = 0$
18. $4x^2 + 4x - 21 = 0$
19. $2x^2 + 5x - 11 = 0$
20. $7x^2 - 33x - 10 = 0$
21. $3x^2 + 5x - 1 = 0$
22. $2x^2 - 7x + 2 = 0$
23. $x^2 - 10x + 2 = 0$
24. $4x^2 - 9x + 3 = 0$
25. $5x^2 - 12x + 4 = 0$
26. $3x^2 + 7x - 4 = 0$
27. $2x^2 + 5x - 18 = 0$
28. $3x^2 + 9x - 3 = 0$

Form the quadratic equations whose roots are:

29. $-5, -6$
30. $2, -10$
31. $3, 9$
32. $4, -3$
33. $-1, 5$
34. $10, 8$
35. $-11, 5$
36. $-3, -9$
37. Solve the equation $3x^2 - 28x - 20 = 0$. Hence, find the values of y, correct to one decimal place for which $3\left(\frac{1}{y}\right)^2 - 28\left(\frac{1}{y}\right) - 20 = 0$.
38. Solve the equation $3x^2 - 19x - 14 = 0$. Hence, find the values of t, correct to one decimal place for which $3(t^2 - 2)^2 - 19(t^2 - 2) - 14 = 0$.
39. Solve the equation $4x^2 - 6x - 4 = 0$ giving your answer in surd form. Hence, find the values of p correct to one decimal place for which $4\left(5 - \frac{1}{p^2}\right)^2 - 6\left(5 - \frac{1}{p^2}\right) - 4 = 0$.
40. (a) A square has sides of length $(40 - 3x)$ cm. If its perimeter is 76 cm, calculate the value of x.
    (b) Find the area in terms of x.
41. A rectangle has sides of length $(4a - 3)$ cm and 12 cm. If its area is 252 cm^2, find the value of a.
42. When 4 is added to a certain natural number and the result is squared, the answer is 121. Find the number.
43. A certain number is squared and added to four times the original number, giving a result of −3. Find the two possible values for the original number.

44. A box of tea bags cost €8 and contains x number of tea bags. During a promotion, 100 extra tea bags are added free, reducing the cost per tea bag by 4 cent.

(a) Write an equation to represent the above information.

(b) Solve the equation to find the cost per tea bag.

45. A number of people share a taxi fare of €36 equally.

(a) Taking x as the number of people, write an expression to represent the cost of the fare per person.

If three more people shared the fare, the price per person would have decreased by €2.

(b) Write an equation to represent this new information.

(c) Solve the equation and find the price per person in each case.

46. The cost of a class trip for x amount of students to a showing of *Romeo & Juliet* is €400. If four extra students attend, the price per student will fall by €5.

(a) Write an equation to represent the above information.

(b) Solve the equation to find the cost per student in both cases.

CHAPTER 19 KNOWLEDGE CHECKLIST

After completing in this chapter, I now:

- **Am able to solve quadratic equations of the form $x^2 + bx + c = 0$, where $b, c \in \mathbb{Z}$**
- **Am able to solve equations involving algebraic fractions**
- **Am able to solve problems using quadratic equations**
- **Am able to solve quadratic equations of the form $ax^2 + bx + c = 0$, where $a, b, c \in \mathbb{Q}$ and $x \in \mathbb{R}$**
- **Am able to form quadratic equations given whole number roots**

QUADRATIC PATTERNS, RELATIONSHIPS AND FUNCTIONS

LEARNING OUTCOMES

In this chapter you will learn:

- ✓ To identify, name and draw quadratic patterns
- ✓ To describe a quadratic pattern using a general formula
- ✓ To graph quadratic functions
- ✓ To understand the terms associated with graphs and functions, such as domain, codomain, range and *y*-intercept
- ✓ To use function notation and to interpret quadratic graphs
- ✓ To find solutions to problems of the form $f(x) = g(x)$ and to interpret these results
- ✓ About transformation of quadratic graphs
- ✓ To apply all the above to real-life situations

KEY WORDS

- Codomain
- Couples
- Difference
- Domain
- Function
- General formula
- Intercept
- Intersection
- Mapping diagram
- Maximum
- Minimum
- Parabola
- Range
- Term

INTRODUCTION

In Chapter 5, you examined linear patterns. Not all patterns form straight-line graphs. Have you ever watched the flight path of a golf ball or a sliotar in hurling? Or maybe a ball of scrap paper aimed at the dustbin? These missiles travel a curved flight path similar to that of a rollercoaster ride. In this chapter, we will examine another type of pattern called the **quadratic pattern.**

Section 20.1: Quadratic patterns

Student Activity 20A

1. Investigate whether the following are linear or non-linear patterns. Explain your answers.
   (a) 7, 15, 23, 31, 39, ...
   (b) 99, 93, 87, 81, 75, ...
   (c) 2, 6, 12, 20, 30, ...
   (d) 3, 6, 11, 18, 27, ...
   (e) −11, −14, −17, −20, −23, ...
2. Can you predict the next three terms in the following non-linear patterns?
   (a) 1, 4, 9, 16, 25, ..., ..., ...
   (b) 0, 3, 8, 15, 24, ..., ..., ...
   (c) 2, 8, 18, 32, ..., ..., ...
3. Seán has been setting out some flower-beds, planting the flowers in such a way that each group forms a rectangle.

   (a) In your own words, explain the pattern you notice.
   (b) What will the length and width of the next two patterns be?
   (c) Copy and complete the following table:

Pattern	1st	2nd	3rd	4th	5th	6th	7th	8th
Length	2	3	4					
Width	1	2	3					
No. of flower plants	2	6	12					

   (d) Can you be sure what the dimensions will be for **any** pattern?
   (e) What would the length be for the 50th rectangle?
   (f) What would the width be for the 50th rectangle?
   (g) How many flower plants would be needed for the 50th rectangle?
   (h) Michael says that the formula $n^2 + n$ can also be used to calculate the number of flowering plants required, where n represents the pattern. Is he correct?

4. Study the following sequence of growing squares:

(a) Draw the next three patterns of the growing square.

(b) Copy and complete the following table:

Side length of each square	Number of tiles to complete each square
1	$1 \times 1 = 1^2 = 1$
2	$2 \times 2 = 2^2 = 4$
3	
4	
5	
6	
7	

(c) In one sentence, explain how the number of tiles in each pattern is related to the side length of each square.

(d) Using suitable symbols, write a general formula for the number of tiles needed to make a larger square of side length n units.

(e) Looking at the table in part (b), explain with reasons, whether the number of tiles required is a linear pattern.

(f) What do you think the graph would look like?

(g) Plot and join on graph paper the points in the table to check your prediction.

(h) What do you notice about the **first difference**?

(i) Complete the following table by calculating the first and second differences:

Side length	No. of tiles	1st difference	2nd difference
1	1		
2	4	3	
3	9	5	2
4			
5			
6			
7			

(j) Explain what you notice about all the second differences?

QUADRATIC PATTERNS EXPLAINED

A sequence is a set of numbers that follow a certain pattern. We call each number in any sequence a **term.** The starting number of any pattern is called the first term (T_1). The next number is the second term (T_2), which is followed by the third term (T_3) and so on. The general term in the sequence is called T_n, the nth term.

In Student Activity 20A, you examined a special type of sequence called a **quadratic pattern.** When the **first difference, *d*,** is calculated in a quadratic pattern, the value between one term and the next is never constant as in a linear pattern. However, the **second difference** is constant. The second difference is found by adding (or subtracting) the same value from each of the first differences.

> A **quadratic pattern** is an increasing or decreasing sequence of numbers in which the second difference between any two consecutive terms is constant.

The following is an increasing quadratic pattern: 1, 2, 5, 10, 17, 26, ...

Looking carefully, you can see each term has a common second difference of 2.

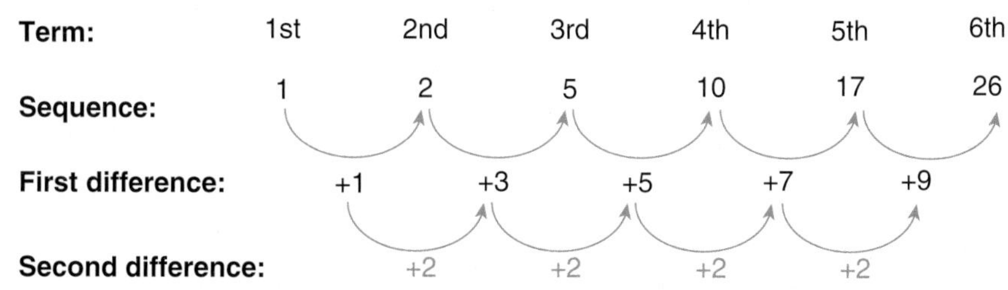

The following is a decreasing quadratic pattern: −2, −3, −6, −11, −18, −27, ... This time, each term has a common second difference of −2.

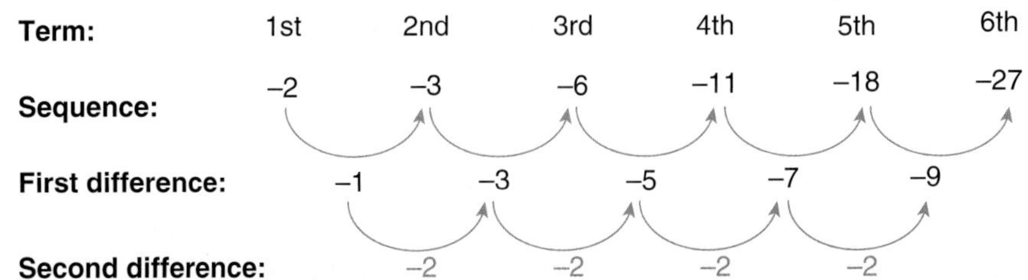

Every quadratic pattern is based on an algebraic polynomial expression of degree two. 'Of degree two' means there is always a squared value in the expression.

The **general formula** for any quadratic expression is of the form: $ax^2 + bx + c$, where a, b and c are real numbers.

Therefore, we can say the general formula for any term in a quadratic pattern is: $T_n = an^2 + bn + c$, where n is the number of the term and a, b and $c \in \mathbb{R}$.

There is also another noticeable pattern: The value of a in the quadratic expression $ax^2 + bx + c$ is exactly half the value of the second difference. Therefore:

- If the second difference is **2,** start with **1**n^2. Hence $T_n = n^2 + bn + c$.
- If the second difference is **4,** start with **2**n^2. Hence $T_n = 2n^2 + bn + c$.
- If the second difference is **6,** start with **3**n^2. Hence $T_n = 3n^2 + bn + c$

To find the general rule for any quadratic pattern:

- **Step 1:** Find the value of the common second difference in the sequence.
- **Step 2:** Half the value of the second difference to get the value of a.
- **Step 3:** Substitute this value for a into the general equation $T_n = an^2 + bn + c$, which represents any term in the sequence.
- **Step 4:** Use any two terms to form two equations.
- **Step 5:** Solve these two equations simultaneously to find the value of b and c.
- **Step 6:** Fill in the values to complete the equation $T_n = an^2 + bn + c$.

EXAMPLE 1

Study the following quadratic pattern: 5, 12, 25, 44, 69, 100, ...

(a) Find the general term (T_n) of the sequence.

(b) Find the value of the 15th term.

Solution

(a)

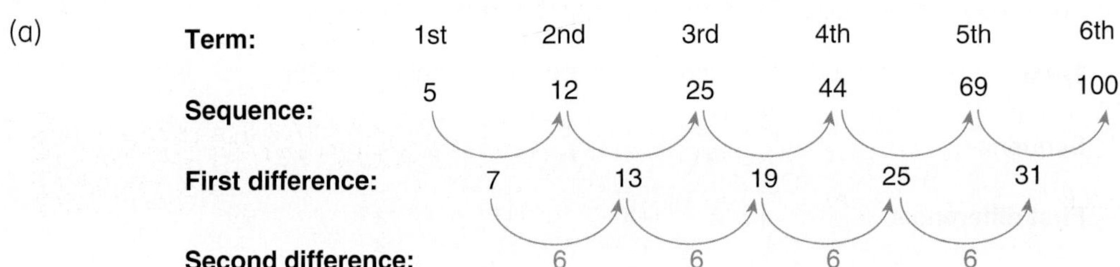

The second difference is the constant 6, therefore the value of a is 3.

Hence $T_n = 3n^2 + bn + c$.

To find the value of b and c, use the first two terms to form two equations and then solve the simultaneous equations.

Term 1: $(T_1) = 5$

$T_n = 3n^2 + bn + c$

$T_1 = 3(1)^2 + b(1) + c = 5$ **Substitute $n = 1$**

$3 + b + c = 5$

$\mathbf{b + c = 2}$ **The 1st simultaneous equation**

Term 2: $(T_2) = 12$

$T_n = 3n^2 + bn + c$

$T_2 = 3(2)^2 + b(2) + c = 12$ **Substitute $n = 2$**

$2b + c = 12 - 12$

$\mathbf{2b + c = 0}$ **The 2nd simultaneous equation**

Now solve the two simultaneous equations:

$b + c = 2$

$\underline{2b + c = 0}$

$-b - c = -2$ **Multiply across by −1**

$\underline{2b + c = 0}$

$\mathbf{b \quad = -2}$

Substitute into either the 1st or 2nd simultaneous equation:

$-2 + c = 2$

$c = 2 + 2$

$\mathbf{c = 4}$

Now we know $a = 3$, $b = -2$ and $c = 4$ and $T_n = an^2 + bn + c$.

Therefore, the formula for the general term is $\mathbf{T_n = 3n^2 - 2n + 4}$.

(b) To find the value of the fifteenth term, substitute 15 for n into the general term:

$T_n = 3n^2 - 2n + 4$

$T_{15} = 3(15)^2 - 2(15) + 4$

$T_{15} = 675 - 30 + 4$

$T_{15} = 649$

The fifteenth term is 649.

EXAMPLE 2

Investigate whether the following sequence is a quadratic pattern: 2, 6, 12, 20, ...

Solution

Method 1

	1st		2nd		3rd		4th
Term:	1st		2nd		3rd		4th
Sequence:	2		6		12		20
First difference:		+4		+6		+8	
Second difference:			+2		+2		

It is a quadratic pattern since the second difference is a constant (+2).

Method 2

Sequence	First difference	Second difference
2		
6	+4	
12	+6	+2
20	+8	+2

It is a quadratic pattern since the second difference is a constant (+2).

EXAMPLE 3

Write down the next two terms of the following quadratic pattern 5, 12, 23, 38, ...

Solution

Method 1

- **Step 1:** Find the first difference between the terms.
- **Step 2:** Find the common second difference between the terms.
- **Step 3:** Complete the next missing first differences.
- **Step 4:** Now find the next missing terms in the sequence.

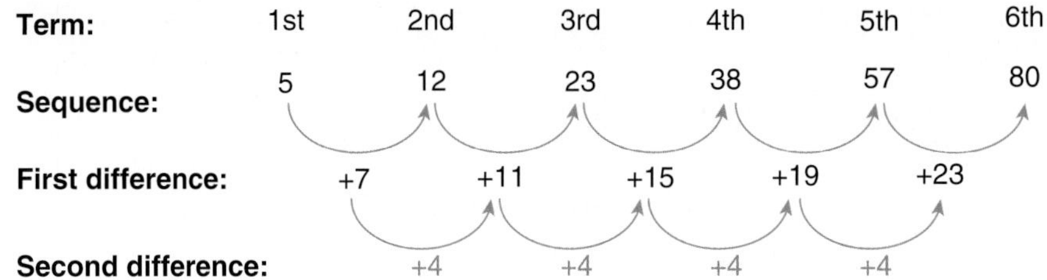

The next two terms are 57 and 80.

Method 2

Using the following table, we know that since it is a quadratic pattern we have the same second difference (+4).

Remember the first difference is found by adding the 2nd difference to the previous 1st difference.

Then we calculate the missing terms in the sequence by adding the previous term in the sequence to the first difference.

Sequence	First difference	Second difference
5		
12	7	
23	11	+4
38	15	+4
38 + 19 = 57	15 + 4 = 19	+4
57 + 23 = 80	19 + 4 = 23	+4

The next two terms are 57 and 80.

Exercise 20.1

1. Investigate whether the following are quadratic patterns, giving your reasons:
   (a) 1, 10, 100, 1000, ...
   (b) 3, 12, 21, 30, ...
   (c) 13, 38, 77, 130, ...
   (d) 2, 4, 6, 8, ...
   (e) 3, 4, 9, 18, ...
   (f) 90, 79, 68, 57, ...
   (g) 12, 20, 34, 54, ...
   (h) −30, −15, −7.5, −3.75, ...
   (i) 89, 92, 95, 98, ...
   (j) 100, 81, 64, 49, ...
2. Write down the first five terms in the following sequences, if the general term is:
   (a) $T_n = n^2 - 7n$
   (b) $T_n = n^2 + 13n$
   (c) $T_n = n^2 + 5n - 50$
   (d) $T_n = n^2 + n - 9$
   (e) $T_n = n^2 + 20n + 36$
   (f) $T_n = 7n^2 - 11n - 45$
   (g) $T_n = 5n^2 + n - 9$
   (h) $T_n = 3n^2 - 2n - 15$
   (i) $T_n = 5n^2 - 7n - 60$
   (j) $T_n = 4n - n^2$

3. For each of the quadratic patterns (i)–(x):

(a) Identify the first term.

(b) Find the second difference.

(c) Write as an algebraic expression the formulae for the general term in the form $ax^2 + bx + c$, where a, b and $c \in \mathbb{Z}$.

(d) Evaluate the 21st term in each:

(i) −3, 4, 13, 24, 27, ...
(ii) 1, 3, 7, 13, 21, ...
(iii) 5, 14, 25, 38, 53, ...
(iv) 16, 24, 34, 46, 60, ...
(v) 5, 0, −3, −4, −3, ...
(vi) −1, − 5, −7, −7, −5, ...
(vii) −14, −16, −16, −14, −10, ...
(viii) 4, 3, 4, 7, 12, ...
(ix) 1, 7, 15, 25, 37, ...
(x) −17, −23, −27, −29, −29, ...

4. For each of the quadratic patterns (i)–(ix):

(a) Identify the first term.

(b) Find the second difference.

(c) Write as an algebraic expression the formulae for the general term in the $ax^2 + bx + c$, where a, b and $c \in \mathbb{Z}$.

(d) Evaluate the hundredth term in each:

(i) 3, 12, 29, 54, 87, ...
(ii) 6, 13, 28, 51, 82, ...
(iii) 7, 26, 49, 76, 107, ...
(iv) 5, 21, 47, 83, 129, ...
(v) 12, 36, 74, 126, 192, ...
(vi) 2, 16, 46, 92, 154, ...
(vii) 25, 50, 85, 130, 185, ...
(viii) −6, −1, 14, 39, 74, ...
(ix) −9, −1, 13, 33, 59, ...

5. Study the following sequence of growing rectangles:

(a) Draw the next two patterns of the growing rectangle.

(b) Copy and complete the following table:

Height of the rectangle	Width of the rectangle	Area of the rectangle	Number of tiles needed to make each rectangle
1	2	1 × 2	2
2	3		
3			
4			
5			
6			
7			
8			

(c) Using the previous table, explain how the number of tiles in each pattern is related to the size of each rectangle.

(d) Copy and complete the following table:

Height of rectangle	Number of tiles	1st difference	2nd difference
1	2		
2	6	4	
3			
4			
5			
6			
7			

(e) Using suitable symbols, write a general formula for the number of tiles needed to make a larger rectangle of height n units.

(f) Predict what the graph would look like.

(g) Ita notices that each rectangle in the pattern below can be broken down into a square and a smaller rectangle as follows:

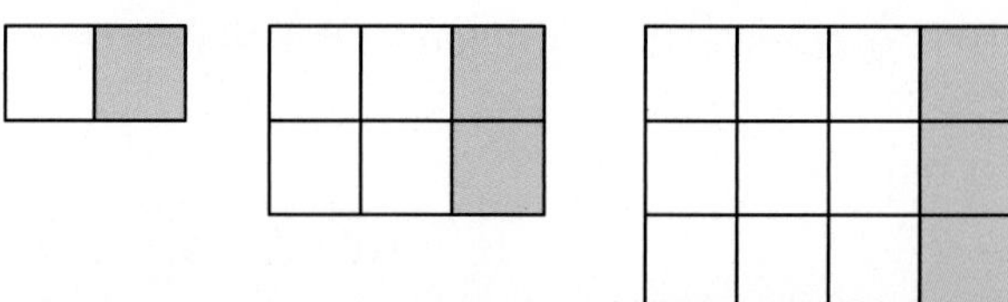

(h) Copy and complete the following table for the number of tiles in each rectangle in terms of the height of each rectangle.

Height	Number of tiles	Area of the rectangle = Area of square + Area of a rectangle
1	2	$1^2 + 1$
2	6	
3	12	
4		
5		
6		
7		
8		

(i) Using the previous table, write a general formula for the number of tiles in a rectangle of height n in the above sequence.

(j) Show that the two formulae from parts (e) and (i) representing the number of tiles needed in each rectangle are equivalent using both substitution and the distributive law.

6. Study the following sequence of growing staircases:

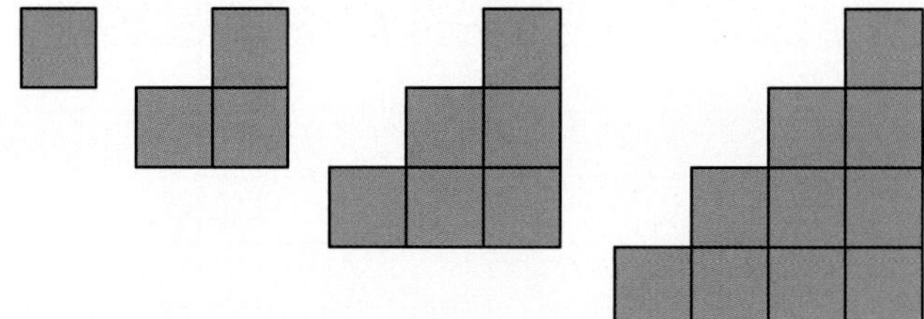

(a) Draw the next two patterns of the growing staircase.

(b) Copy and complete the following table:

Number of towers	Number of tiles	1st difference	2nd difference
1	1		
2	3	2	
3	6	3	1
4			
5			
6			
7			

(c) Are the second differences constant?

(d) What does that tell us about the pattern?

Now compare the following pattern of growing rectangles with that of the previous staircase towers:

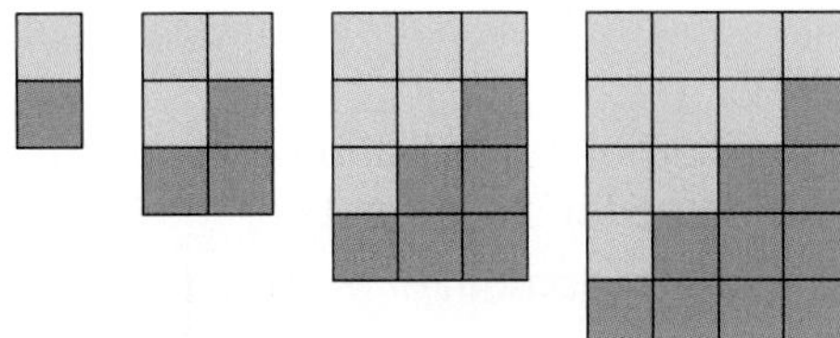

(e) Copy and complete the following table for the growing rectangles:

Side of length	Number of tiles	1st difference	2nd difference
1	2		
2	6	4	
3	12	6	2
4			
5			
6			
7			

(f) Write a general formula for the number of tiles in the *n*th rectangle in terms of *n*.

(g) Compare both tables, focusing on the first two columns. Record all of your observations.

(h) Now write a formula for the number of tiles in the *n*th staircase in terms of *n*.

7. Investigate whether the pattern in the table below is linear, quadratic or neither. Explain your conclusion.

Term 1	Term 2	Term 3	Term 4	Term 5
$2a - b + 2c$	$8a - 2b + 2c$	$18a - 3b + 2c$	$32a - 4b + 2c$	$50a - 5b + 2c$

Section 20.2: The quadratic function machine

Student Activity 20B

1. A machine's output is found by squaring and then subtracting 1 from any input it is given. What will the outputs be for the following inputs?

(a) 2 (b) 3 (c) 12 (d) 0 (e) –8 (f) $\frac{1}{2}$

2. Another machine subtracts 10 from any input it is given and then squares the answer. What will the outputs be for the following inputs?

(a) 10 (b) 90 (c) 38 (d) 74 (e) –10 (f) –3

3. A third machine squares any input. It then adds the answer to five times the input minus 2. Calculate what inputs would give the following outputs as answers:

(a) 2 (b) 16 (c) 8 (d) –2 (e) 38 (f) 4

THE QUADRATIC FUNCTION MACHINE EXPLAINED

In Chapter 5, we compared a function to a machine.

- We put in the inputs (**domain**).
- Each input underwent the mathematical operation outlined in the function to produce an output. The **range** is another name for the outputs of the function.
- All possible outputs are called the **codomain** of the function.

When performing a function, you are simply using a rule. Suppose you have a function, *f*, which takes the input *x*, squares it and then adds double the input plus 7 to the answer. You could write this in a mathematical form as follows:

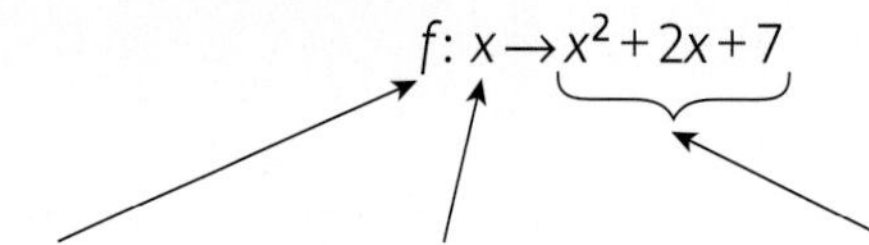

The *x* is just a place-holder. It is there to show you where the input goes and what happens to it. It could be any value! For example:

Input (domain) *x*	Relationship (function) $x^2 + 2x + 7$	Output (range) *y*
1	$(1)^2 + 2(1) + 7$	10
2	$(2)^2 + 2(2) + 7$	15
3	$(3)^2 + 2(3) + 7$	22
4	$(4)^2 + 2(4) + 7$	31

Every input of a function can only have **one** output. In mathematics, we say that each input is **mapped to one output** only. A **mapping diagram** can be used to represent the above function:

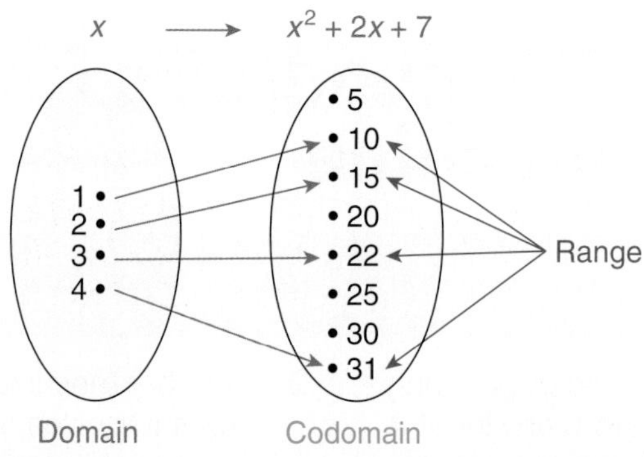

- The **domain** is {1, 2, 3, 4}.
- The **range** produced by the function $x^2 + 2x + 7$ is {10, 15, 22, 31}.
- The set of used and unused *y*-values in the **codomain** is {5, 10, 15, 20, 22, 25, 30, 31}.

As with linear patterns, we normally write our answers as ordered pairs or **couples** in the form of (domain, range), (*x*-value, *y*-value) or (input, output). For the example above, the couples of the function are {(1, 10), (2, 15), (3, 22), (4, 31)}.

Remember that in any relation, no two elements in the domain can be the same since:

A **function** is a relation in which no two couples have the same first component and which works for every possible input value.

Therefore as in a linear function, the domain of any quadratic function is all of the possible inputs to the function and the range is all of the outputs. Each term in the domain corresponds to a specific term in the range. However, any term in the range may correspond to multiple terms in the domain.

The following is a function (one-to-one):

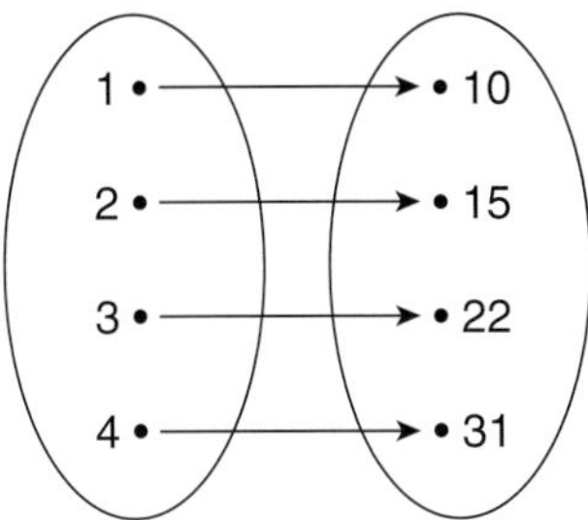

The following is a function (many-to-one):

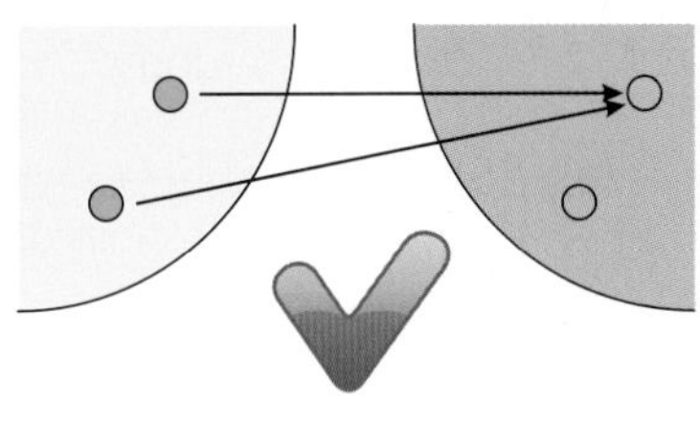

The following is **not** a function (one-to-many):

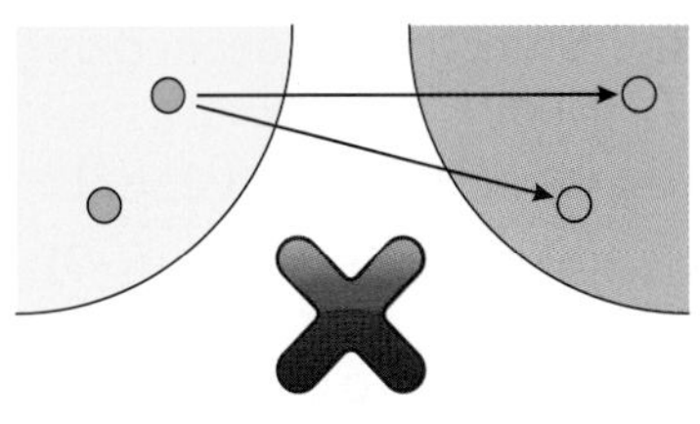

EXAMPLE 4

A function g is defined as $g: x \to 3x^2 + 4x - 2$. Find:

(a) $g(1)$ (b) $g(-2)$ (c) $g\left(\frac{2}{3}\right)$ (d) $g(k)$

Solution

(a) $g(1) = 3(1)^2 + 4(1) - 2 = 3 + 4 - 2 = 5$

(b) $g(-2) = 3(-2)^2 + 4(-2) - 2 = 12 - 8 - 2 = 2$

(c) $g\left(\frac{2}{3}\right) = 3\left(\frac{2}{3}\right)^2 + 4\left(\frac{2}{3}\right) - 2 = 1\frac{1}{3} + 2\frac{2}{3} - 2 = 2$

(d) $g(k) = 3(k)^2 + 4(k) - 2 = 3k^2 + 4k - 2$

EXAMPLE 5

Given that $y = 5x^2 - 2x + 11$, complete the table below, showing all your work:

x	1	2	3	4
y				

Solution

Turn the table sideways and add an extra column for your workings:

x	$5x^2 - 2x + 11$	y
1	$5(1)^2 - 2(1) + 11$	14
2	$5(2)^2 - 2(2) + 11$	27
3	$5(3)^2 - 2(3) + 11$	50
4	$5(4)^2 - 2(4) + 11$	83

So the answer is (1, 14), (2, 27), (3, 50), (4, 83).

EXAMPLE 6

A function f is defined as $f: x \to 2x^2 - 8x + 10$. Given that $f(t) = 20$ find the value of t.

Solution

$f(t) = 2(t)^2 - 8(t) + 10 = 2t^2 - 8t + 10$

We are given that $f(t) = 20$.

$\therefore 2t^2 - 8t + 10 = 20$

$2t^2 - 8t + 10 - 20 = 0$

$2t^2 - 8t - 10 = 0$

$t^2 - 4t - 5 = 0$ **Divide across by 2 before factorising**

$(t - 5)(t + 1) = 0$

$(t - 5) = 0$ or $(t + 1) = 0$

$t = 5$ or $t = -1$

Exercise 20.2

1. A function f is defined as $f: x \to x^2$. Find:
   (a) $f(0)$ (c) $f(-2)$ (e) $f(-4)$
   (b) $f(3)$ (d) $f(5)$ (f) $f(2)$

2. A function f is defined as $f: x \to x^2 + 2x$. Find:
   (a) $f(0)$ (c) $f(2)$ (e) $f(4)$
   (b) $f(1)$ (d) $f(3)$ (f) $f(-3)$

3. A function f is defined as $f: x \to x^2 + x - 4$. Find:
   (a) $f(1)$ (c) $f(2)$ (e) $f(5)$
   (b) $f(-1)$ (d) $f(-3)$ (f) $f(10)$

4. A function g is defined as $g: x \to x^2 + 3x - 1$. Find:
   (a) $g\left(\frac{1}{3}\right)$ (c) $g(t)$ (e) $g(-k)$
   (b) $g\left(\frac{5}{6}\right)$ (d) $g(2k)$ (f) $g(k + 2)$

5. A function f is defined as $f: x \to 4x^2 - 2x - 3$. Find:
   (a) $f(-1)$ (c) $f(4)$ (e) $f(7)$
   (b) $f(-3)$ (d) $f(5)$ (f) $f(k)$

6. $f: x \to x^2 - 4$ is a function. If the domain of f is {1, 3, 5, 7}, find the range.

7. $g: x \to x^2 + 5x - 1$ is a function. If the domain of g is {−1, 0, 3, −5, 11}, find the range.

8. $f: x \to x^2 + 8x + 7$ is a function. If the domain of f is {−4, −2, 1, 6, 9}, find the range.

9. $f: x \to 8x^2 - 6x - 4$ is a function. If the domain of f is {2, 4, 6, 8}, find the range.

10. $f: x \to 3x^2 - 2$ is a function. If $f(t) = 25$, find the value of t.

Section 20.3: Graphing quadratic functions

Student Activity 20C

1. Study the following images and describe what they have in common:

2. (a) Copy the following Cartesian plane:
   (b) Plot each of the following series of points and join the points without using a ruler. Use the coloured pen indicated.
      (i) (−2, 4), (−1, 1), (0, 0), (1, 1), (2, 4) in blue
      (ii) (−2, 5), (−1, 2), (0, 1), (1, 2), (2, 5) in black
      (iii) (−2, −7), (−1, −4), (0, 3), (1, −4), (2, −7) in red
      (iv) (−2, −7), (−1, −4), (0, −2), (1, −4), (2, −7) in green
   (c) Describe what shape each of these series of points have formed.

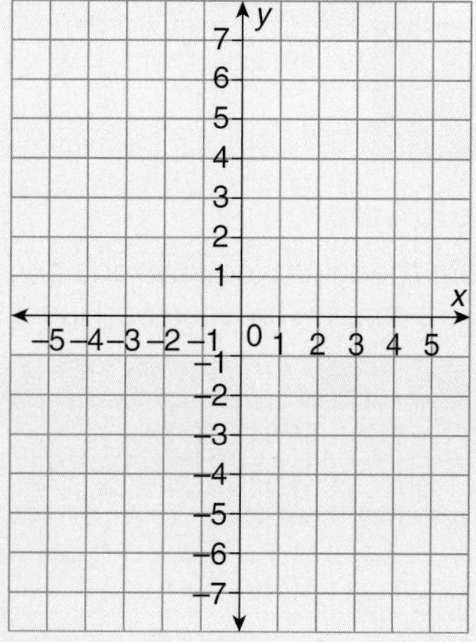

GRAPHING QUADRATIC FUNCTIONS EXPLAINED

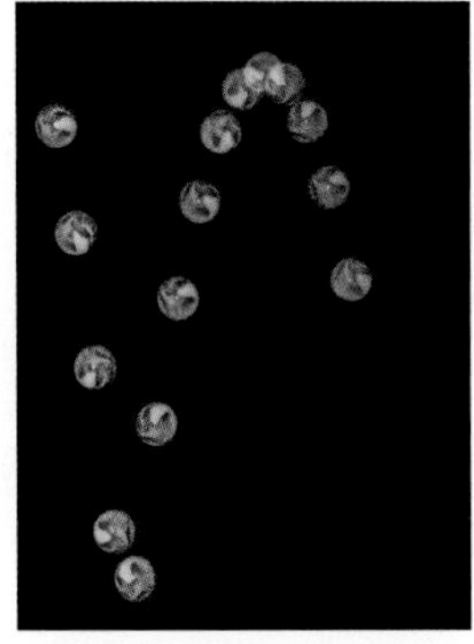

Functions can be used in mathematics to draw graphs.

- The input into the function f is the **x-coordinate.**
- The output or the $f(x)$ value is more commonly known as the ***y*-coordinate** of the point that satisfies the function.

Therefore we can write any couple belonging to a function as a point on the Cartesian plane:

> (input, output) = (domain, range) = $(x, f(x)) = (x, y)$

These points plotted and joined together produce a graph. This graph gives us a diagram, clearly showing us how a certain mathematical pattern behaves.

When plotted on a graph, quadratic functions in the form $ax^2 + bx + c = 0$ always have similar-shaped paths.

If the coefficient of x^2 is positive ($a > 0$), such as in $f(x) = 3x^2 - 7x - 8$ or $g(x) = 7x^2 + 4x - 8$ or $y = 5x^2 + 6x + 11$, then the graph will have a concave up or a U-shape as shown:

$+ ax^2$

If the coefficient of x^2 is negative ($a < 0$), such as in $f(x) = -3x^2 + 7x + 8$ or $g(x) = -7x^2 + 4x - 8$ or $y = -5x^2 + 6x + 11$, then the graph will have a concave down or an ∩-shape as shown:

$- ax^2$

An easy way to remember the shape of a quadratic function is to think of:

- A **positive** answer to extra money from your parents results in you **smiling.**
- A **negative** answer to money from your parents results in you **sulking.**

> When graphing any quadratic function, follow these steps:
>
> - **Step 1:** Determine all the points that satisfy the function within the given domain.
> - **Step 2:** On graph paper, draw a horizontal (x-axis) and a vertical (y-axis) line.
> - **Step 3:** On these axes, insert an appropriate scale and clearly label what each axis represents.
> - **Step 4:** Draw the graph of the function by plotting the points and drawing a freehand line through the points. Do not use a straight-edged ruler as the function is a curve.

It is useful to know as much information as we can about a function before we graph it. You should note the following:

- The overall shape of the function
- The output when the input of the function is 0
- Any other special behaviours of the function

The point or points where the graph crosses the x-axis is called the **x-intercept.** The coordinates are always (real number, 0). The point where the graph crosses the y-axis is called the **y-intercept.** Its coordinates are always (0, **real number**).

For any function of the form $f(x) = ax^2 + bx + c$, **the value of c is where the graph cuts the y-axis.** Hence, $f(x) = -2x^2 - 5x - 10$ cuts the y-axis at $(0, -10)$. $f(x) = x^2$ is the same as $f(x) = x^2 + 0x + 0$ as it cuts the y-axis at the origin.

EXAMPLE 7

(a) Draw the graph of the function: $f: x \rightarrow 2x^2 - x - 1$ in the domain $-2 \leq x \leq 3$.

(b) Write down the coordinates of the x-intercepts.

(c) Write down the coordinate of the point of the y-intercept.

Solution

(a)

Input (domain) x	Relationship (function) $2x^2 - x - 1$	Output (range) y
−2	$2(-2)^2 - (-2) - 1 = 8 + 2 - 1$	9
−1	$2(-1)^2 - (-1) - 1 = 2 + 1 - 1$	2
0	$2(0)^2 - (0) - 1 = 0 - 0 - 1$	−1
1	$2(1)^2 - (1) - 1 = 2 - 1 - 1$	0
2	$2(2)^2 - (2) - 1 = 8 - 2 - 1$	5
3	$2(3)^2 - (3) - 1 = 18 - 3 - 1$	14

So the points on the graphed function are: (**−2**, 9), (**−1**, 2), (**0**, −1), (**1**, 0), (**2**, 5), (**3**, 14).

Note that the x values go from **−2** to **3** and the corresponding y-values go from **−1** to **14.** So, this should be the scale on the graph.

Plotting the points and joining them together we get the following graph:

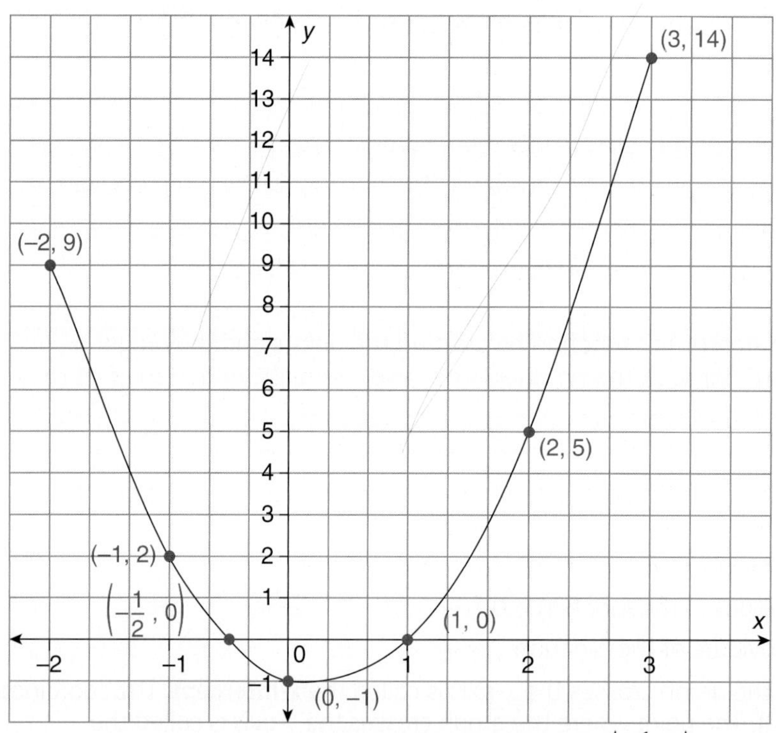

(b) The coordinates of the x-intercepts on the graph are $\left(-\frac{1}{2}, 0\right)$ and (1, 0).

(c) The coordinate of the y-intercept on the graph is (0, −1).

EXAMPLE 8

(a) Draw the graph of the function: $f: x \to -2x^2 + x + 3$ in the domain $-2 \leq x \leq 3$.

(b) Write down the coordinates of the x-intercepts.

(c) Write down the coordinates of the point of the y-intercept.

Solution

(a)

Input (domain) x	Relationship (function) $-2x^2 + x + 3$	Output (range) y
−2	$-2(-2)^2 + (-2) + 3 = -8 - 2 + 3$	−7
−1	$-2(-1)^2 + (-1) + 3 = -2 - 1 + 3$	0
0	$-2(0)^2 + (0) + 3 = 0 + 0 + 3$	3
1	$-2(1)^2 + (1) + 3 = -2 + 1 + 3$	2
2	$-2(2)^2 + (2) + 3 = -8 + 2 + 3$	−3
3	$-2(3)^2 + (3) + 3 = -18 + 3 + 3$	−12

So the points on the graphed function are: (**−2**, −7), (**−1**, 0), (**0**, 3), (**1**, 2), (**2**, −3), (**3**, −12).

Note that the x-values go from −2 to 3 and the corresponding y-values go from −12 to 3. So this should be the scale on the graph.

Plotting the points and joining them together we get the following graph:

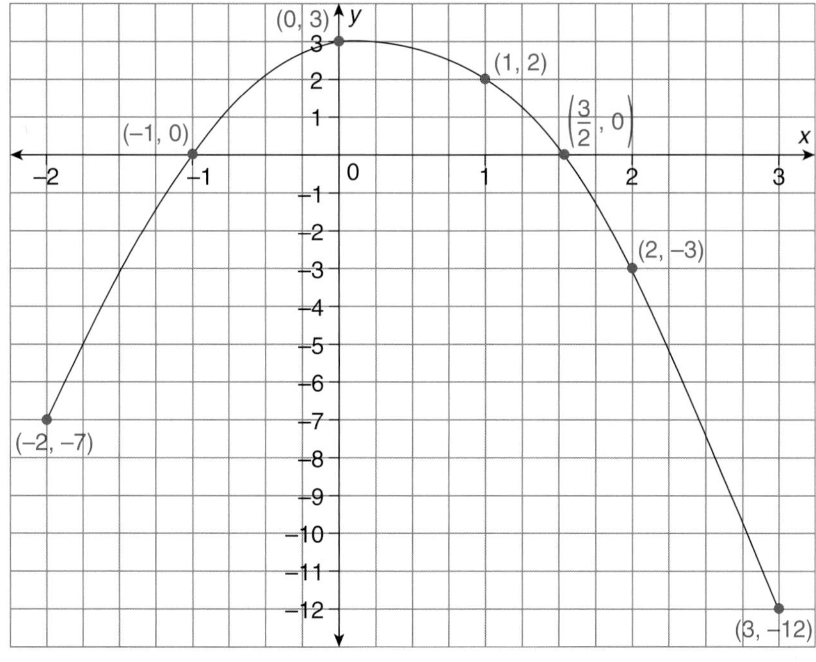

(b) The coordinates of the x-intercepts on the graph are (−1, 0) and (1.5, 0).

(c) The coordinate of the y-intercept on the graph is (0, 3).

Exercise 20.3

Draw the graph of each of the following functions in the given domain:

1. $f: x \to x^2 - x$ in the domain $-3 \leq x \leq 3$
2. $f: x \to x^2 - 2x$ in the domain $-3 \leq x \leq 3$
3. $f: x \to x^2 + x - 2$ in the domain $-3 \leq x \leq 3$
4. $f: x \to 5x^2 - 4x + 3$ in the domain $-1 \leq x \leq 2$
5. $g: x \to x^2 - 3x + 2$ in the domain $-1 \leq x \leq 4$
6. $h: x \to 2x^2 - 6x + 5$ in the domain $-1 \leq x \leq 4$
7. $f: x \to 5x^2 + 3x + 2$ in the domain $-2 \leq x \leq 1$
8. $f: x \to 2x^2 - x - 6$ in the domain $-3 \leq x \leq 3$

9. $f: x \to 7x^2 - 6x - 4$ in the domain $-1 \le x \le 2$
10. $f: x \to 2x^2 + 5x + 3$ in the domain $-3 \le x \le 1$
11. $f: x \to -x^2 - 3x + 4$ in the domain $-4 \le x \le 1$
12. $f: x \to -x^2 + x + 2$ in the domain $-3 \le x \le 3$
13. $f: x \to -x^2 + x + 6$ in the domain $-3 \le x \le 5$
14. $f: x \to -2x^2 - x + 1$ in the domain $-2 \le x \le 2$
15. $f: x \to -2x^2 + 2$ in the domain $-2 \le x \le 2$
16. $f: x \to -3x^2 + 8x + 3$ in the domain $0 \le x \le 3$

Section 20.4: Interpreting quadratic graphs

Student Activity 20D

1. Superman loses his power when he is close to a source of Kryptonite. Lois Lane notices that the percentage of reduction in Superman's strength is related to how far he is from the Kryptonite. She made several measurements and recorded the data in the table below:

   (a) Copy and complete the table.

   (b) List the couples of the function.

   (c) How far away should Superman stay to be at full strength?

   (d) Graph the data on graph paper to support your previous answer.

   (e) Write a general formula to represent the function.

Distance in metres	Percentage reduction in Superman's strength
10	99
20	96
30	91
40	84
50	
60	

2. When we eat a meal, we digest many different food types such as carbohydrates, protein and fats. The quadratic graph shows the rate at which a typical human body can break down starch at different pH levels. Examine the diagram and answer the questions:

   (a) At what pH level is the breakdown of starch at a maximum?

   (b) At what pH level is the breakdown of starch at (i) 8? (ii) 2? (iii) 0?

   (c) What is the breakdown of starch at a pH of 9?

   (d) Suggest why the pH levels shown are only between 5 and 10.

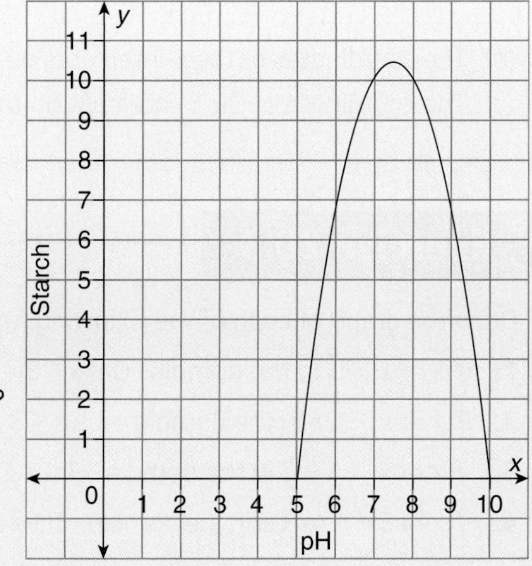

INTERPRETING QUADRATIC GRAPHS EXPLAINED

Using the completed graph of a function, we can find important information about a certain mathematical problem. Here are some of the more common questions asked:

1. **What are the roots of a quadratic function?**

   This question is asking you to find the point or points where the graph of the quadratic function crosses the x-axis. Because the points are on the x-axis, this implies that the y-value of the point is 0. So an alternative way of asking this question is to find the values of x for which $f(x) = 0$. This information can be found by examining the graph of the function.

   We can clearly see this function crosses the x-axis at the points (−2, 0) and (1, 0).

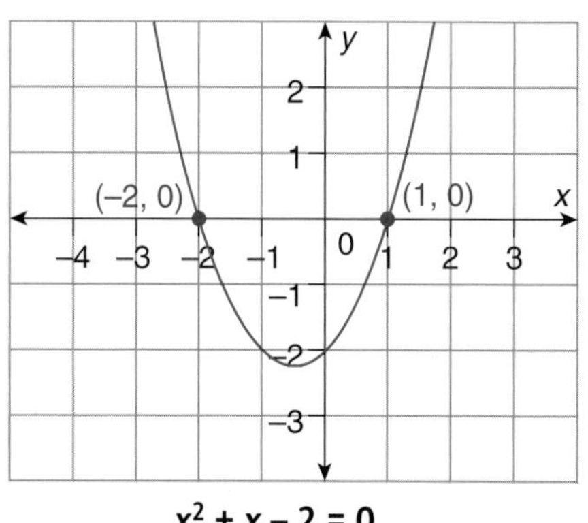

$x^2 + x - 2 = 0$

   In Chapter 19, we used an alternative method of finding these points. When we factorise a quadratic equation algebraically, we are also calculating the roots of the function. For example: $f(x) = 0$ *means* $x^2 + x - 2 = 0$.

   $(x + 2)(x - 1) = 0$ **Factorise**

   $(x + 2) = 0$ or $(x - 1) = 0$ **Let each bracket equal to zero**

   $x = -2$ or $x = 1$

   This also implies that the function crosses the x-axis at (−2, 0) and (1, 0).

2. **Find the minimum point of the graph.**

   This question applies only to quadratic functions where the coefficient of x^2 is positive. It is asking you to find the **lowest point** on your graph, which in this case is (−0.5, −2.3). However, if you are asked for the **minimum value,** then you give the function's minimum y value of −2.3.

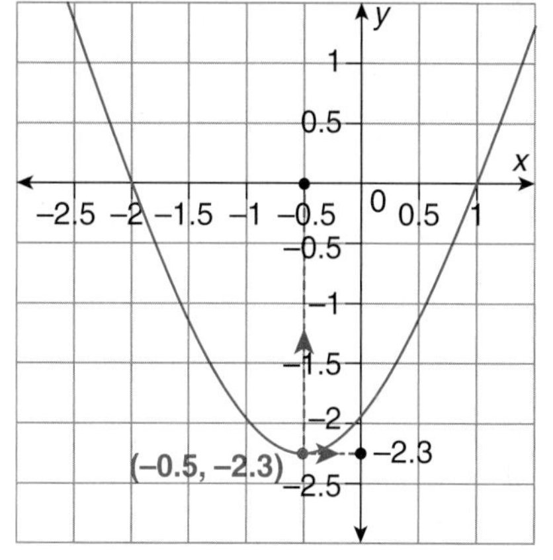

3. **Find the maximum point of the graph.**

   This question applies only to quadratic functions where the coefficient of x^2 is negative. It is asking you to find the highest point on your graph. In this case, the maximum point is (1.5, 0.3). However, if you are asked for the maximum value, then you only give the maximum y value of 0.3.

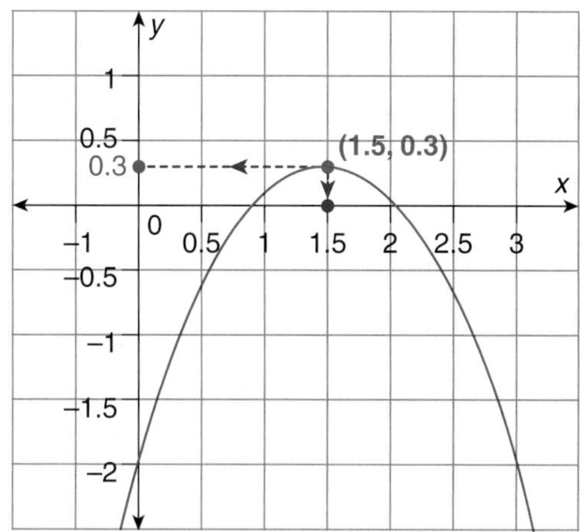

QUADRATIC PATTERNS, RELATIONSHIPS AND FUNCTIONS

4. **Find the increasing and decreasing parts of a function.**

When examining a graph, we read it from left to right in the same way that you read the text on a page. A function is said to be increasing if it is rising, and decreasing if it is falling. The **turning point** of the function (the maximum or minimum point) is where the graph stops rising or falling and changes direction.

For example, in the graph below, we can say the function is increasing for all values of x less than 1.5 ($x < 1.5$) and the function is decreasing for all values of x greater than 1.5 ($x > 1.5$).

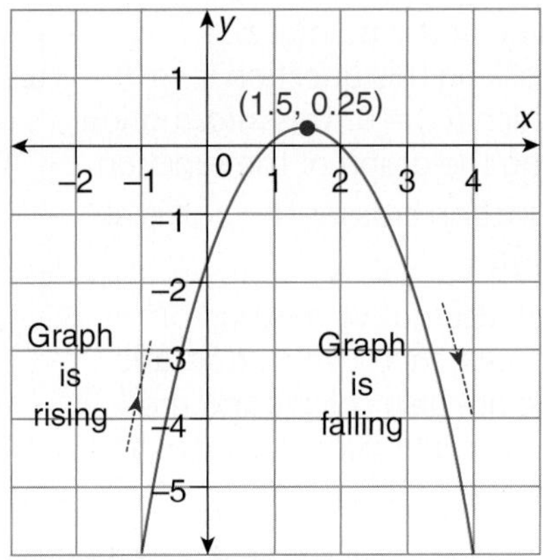

5. **Find the values of x for which $f(x)$ = any number.**

Remember $f(x)$ also means the y value. This question is asking you to find the values of x when $f(x)$ or y is a certain value. For example, if you are asked to find the values of x for which $f(x) = 1$, then draw a horizontal line through $y = 1$. Where this horizontal line intersects the graph, drop two vertical lines to the x-axis. From the diagram we can see $f(x) = 1$ at x approximately equal to -2.3 and 1.3.

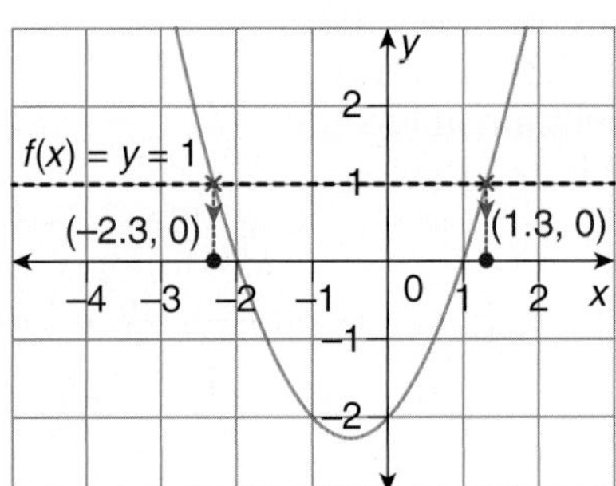

There is an alternative method of finding these points. When you factorise a quadratic equation algebraically and let it equal any number, you are also calculating the x-values that satisfy this function. For example:

Find the values of x for which $x^2 + x - 2 = 1$.

When we tidy up the quadratic equation you get: $x^2 + x - 3 = 0$.

To factorise, we must use the formula:

$x = \dfrac{-b \pm \sqrt{b^2 - 4ac}}{2a}$ on page 20 of the *Formulae and Tables*.

$a = 1, b = 1, c = -3$

$$x = \frac{-(1) \pm \sqrt{(1)^2 - (4)(1)(-3)}}{2(1)}$$

$$x = \frac{-1 \pm \sqrt{1 + 12}}{2}$$

$$x = \frac{-1 \pm \sqrt{13}}{2}$$

$$x = \frac{-1 + \sqrt{13}}{2} \text{ or } \frac{-1 - \sqrt{13}}{2}$$

$x = 1.3$ or $x = -2.3$ **Correct to one decimal point**

Note that these are the same values we got from reading the graphed function.

6. **Find the values of *f*(*any number*).**

This question is asking when x is equal to any number on the function, what is the value of y in the coordinate? For example: Find the value of $f(1.5)$ on the graphed quadratic function. First draw a vertical line through $x = 1.5$. Where it intersects the graph, draw a horizontal line towards the y-axis and read the exact y value.

In this case, $f(1.5)$ gives an answer of 1.75.

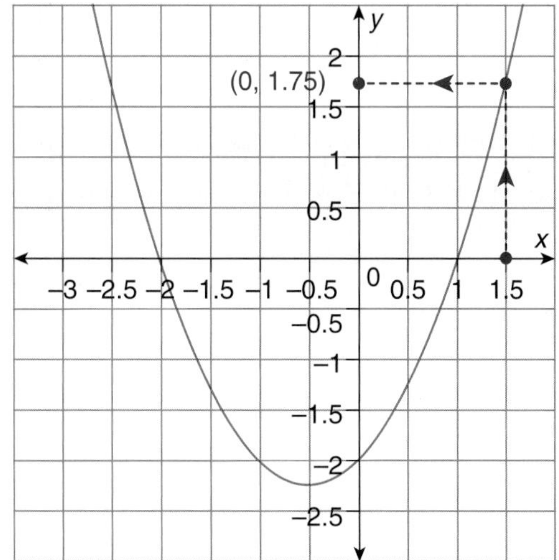

There is an alternative method of finding this value. When we substitute any number for x into a given function, we are calculating algebraically the value of $f(x)$ or y. For example: Given the function, $f(x) = x^2 + x - 2$ evaluate $f(1.5)$.

$f(x) = x^2 + x - 2$

$f(1.5) = (1.5)^2 + (1.5) - 2$

$f(1.5) = 1.75$

7. **Find the positive and negative values of the function $f(x)$.**

When finding the roots of a function, we are determining the point or points where the graph crosses the x-axis. At this point or these points we say $f(x) = 0$.

All of the points on a graph drawn above the x-axis represent where $f(x) > 0$.

All of the points on a graph drawn below the x-axis represents where $f(x) < 0$.

For example, in the graphed function $f(x) = x^2 + x - 2$:

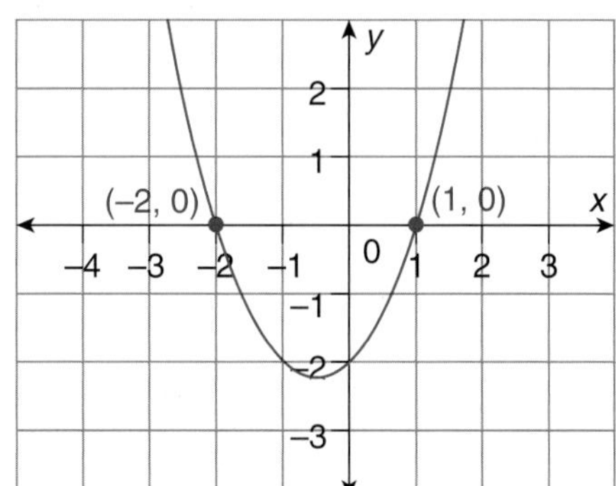

$f(x) = 0$ at the points $x = -2$ and $x = 1$.

$f(x) < 0$ for all values of x greater than -2 and less than 1, which we write as the inequality $-2 < x < 1$.

$f(x) > 0$ for all values of x greater than 1 and/or less than -2. This must be written as two separate inequalities: $x > 1$ and $x < -2$ or $1 > x > 1 \cup x < -2$.

EXAMPLE 9

(a) Draw the graph of the function: $f: x \to x^2 + x - 2$ in the domain $-3 \leq x \leq 3$.
(b) Write down the coordinates of the point where the graph cuts the y-axis.
(c) Write down the coordinates of the points where the graph cuts the x-axis.
(d) Solve algebraically $f(x) = 0$ and by examining your graph comment on the solutions.
(e) Find the minimum value of $f(x)$.

Solution

(a)

Input (domain) x	Relationship (function) $x^2 + x - 2$	Output (range) y
−3	$(-3)^2 + (-3) - 2 = 9 - 3 - 2$	4
−2	$(-2)^2 + (-2) - 2 = 4 - 2 - 2$	0
−1	$(-1)^2 + (-1) - 2 = 1 - 1 - 2$	−2
0	$(0)^2 + (0) - 2 = 0 - 0 - 2$	−2
1	$(1)^2 + (1) - 2 = 1 + 1 - 2$	0
2	$(2)^2 + (2) - 2 = 4 + 2 - 2$	4
3	$(3)^2 + (3) - 2 = 9 + 3 - 2$	10

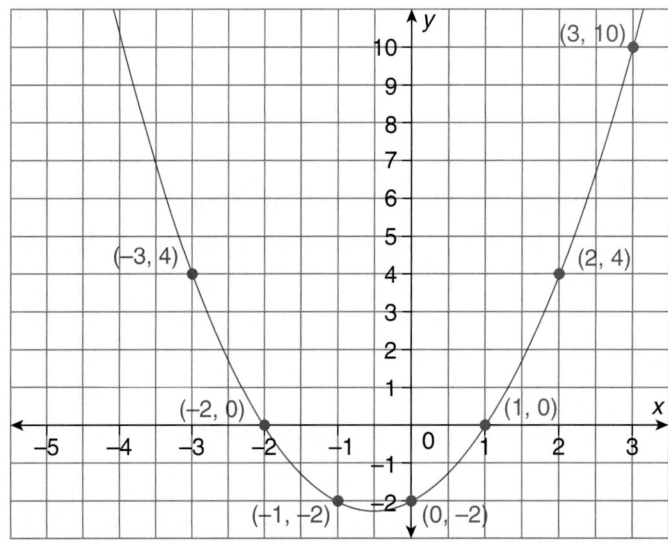

(b) The point where the graph cuts the y-axis is $(0, -2)$.

(c) The function cuts the x-axis at -2 and 1 so the points are $(-2, 0)$ and $(1, 0)$.

(d) Solving algebraically $f(x) = 0$ to get $x^2 + x - 2 = 0$:

$(x - 1)(x + 2) = 0$
$x - 1 = 0$ and $x + 2 = 0$
$\therefore x = 1$ and $x = -2$

The solutions to $f(x) = 0$ are the two x-coordinates where the graph cuts the x-axis.

(e) The minimum value of $f(x)$ is -2.3.

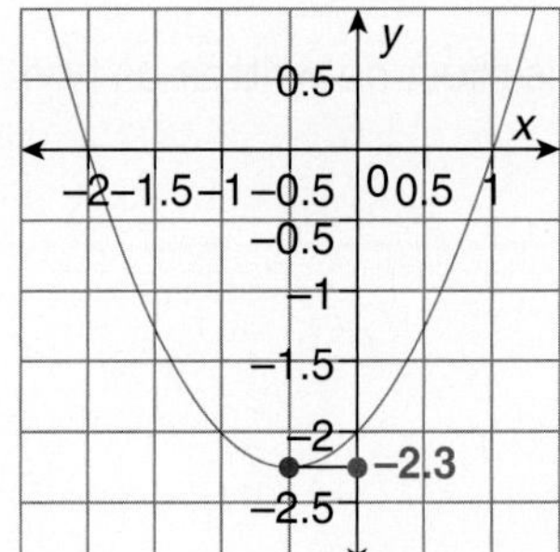

EXAMPLE 10

(a) Draw the graph of the function: $f: x \to -x^2 + x + 2$ in the domain $-2 \leq x \leq 3$.

(b) The graph cuts the y-axis at the point C. Use your graph to find the coordinates of the point C.

(c) The graph cuts the x-axis at the points D and E. Use your graph to find the coordinates of the points D and E.

(d) Find the maximum value of $f(x)$.

(e) Find the values of x when $f(x) = -2$.

Solution

(a)

Input (domain) x	Relationship (function) $-x^2 + x + 2$	Output (range) y
−2	$-(-2)^2 + (-2) + 2 = -4 - 2 + 2$	−4
−1	$-(-1)^2 + (-1) + 2 = -1 - 1 + 2$	0
0	$-(0)^2 + (0) + 2 = 0 - 0 + 2$	2
1	$-(1)^2 + (1) + 2 = -1 + 1 + 2$	2
2	$-(2)^2 + (2) + 2 = -4 + 2 + 2$	0
3	$-(3)^2 + (3) + 2 = -9 + 3 + 2$	−4

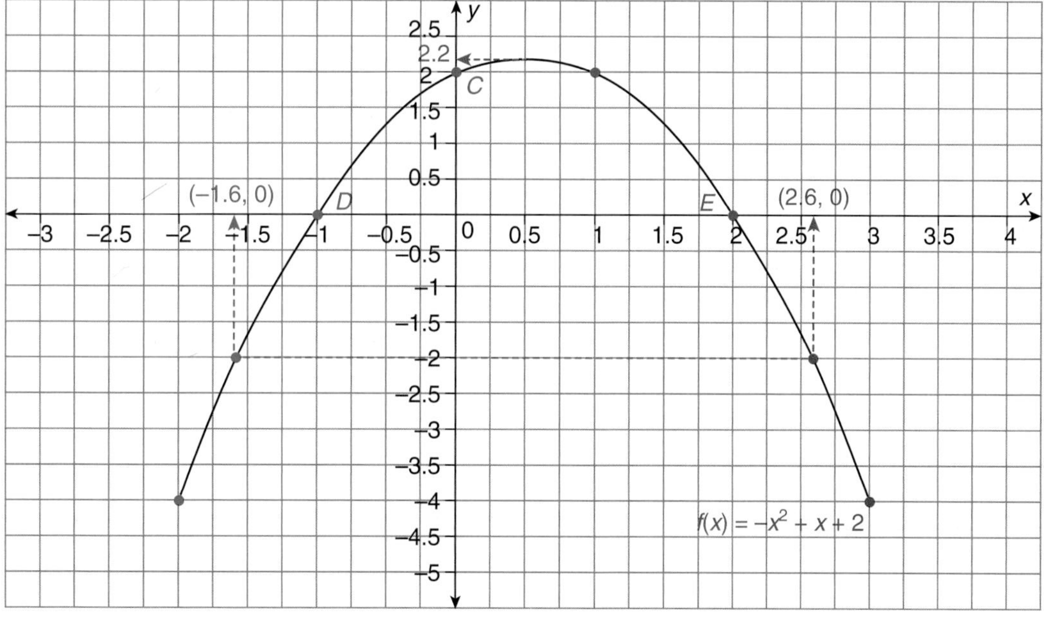

(b) The graph cuts the y-axis at the point C with coordinates (0, 2).

(c) The graph cuts the x-axis at the points $D(-1, 0)$ and E(2, 0).

(d) The maximum value of $f(x)$ is 2.2.

(e) The values of x when $f(x) = -2$ when $x = -1.6$ and $x = 2.6$.

EXAMPLE 11

A rectangle has dimensions in metres as shown:

7 − x

x

(a) Write down an expression in terms of x representing the area of the rectangle.

(b) Draw a graph of the function $f: x \to 7x - x^2$ in the domain $0 \le x \le 7$.

(c) Using your graph, find the maximum area of the rectangle.

(d) Calculate the side length of the rectangle when its area is at its maximum.

(e) Calculate the width of the rectangle when the area is 8 m^2.

Solution

(a) Area = Length × Width

Area = $(x)(7 - x)$

Area = $7x - x^2$

(b)

Input (domain) x	Relationship (function) $7x - x^2$	Output (range) y
0	$7(0) - (0)^2$	0
1	$7(1) - (1)^2$	6
2	$7(2) - (2)^2$	10
3	$7(3) - (3)^2$	12
4	$7(4) - (4)^2$	12
5	$7(5) - (5)^2$	10
6	$7(6) - (6)^2$	6
7	$7(7) - (7)^2$	0

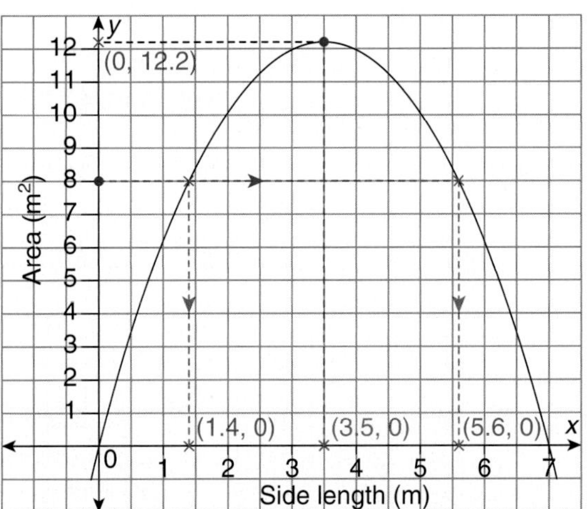

(c) The maximum area of the rectangle from the diagram above is approximately 12.2 m^2.

(d) The side length of the rectangle when its area is at its maximum is found as follows:

Algebraically: Length = $\frac{\text{Area}}{\text{Width}} = \frac{12.2}{3.5} = 3.49$

Graphically: The maximum point is approximately (3.5, 12.2). The length corresponds to the x value. $x = 3.5$

(e) When the area is 8 m^2, the width of the rectangle is approximately 1.4 m or 5.6 m.

Exercise 20.4

1. (a) Draw the graph of the function $f: x \to x^2$ in the domain $-3 \le x \le 3$.

(b) The graph cuts the y-axis at the point A. Use your graph to find the coordinates of the point A.

(c) Find the values of x when $f(x) = 4$.

(d) Find the minimum value of $f(x)$.

2. (a) Draw the graph of the function $f: x \to x^2 - 2$ in the domain $-3 \le x \le 3$.

(b) The graph cuts the y-axis at the point D. Use your graph to find the coordinates of the point D.

(c) Find the minimum point of $f(x)$.

(d) Evaluate $f(1.5)$.

3. (a) Draw the graph of the function $f: x \to x^2 + 3$ in the domain $-3 \le x \le 3$.

(b) The graph cuts the y-axis at the point T. Use your graph to find the coordinates of the point T.

(c) Evaluate $f(-1.5)$.

(d) Use your graph to find the values of x when $f(x) = 5$.

4. (a) Draw the graph of the function function $f: x \to x^2 + x - 2$ in the domain $-3 \leq x \leq 3$.

(b) The graph cuts the y-axis at the point C. Use your graph to find the coordinates of the point C.

(c) The graph cuts the x-axis at the points D and E. Use your graph to find the coordinates of the points D and E.

(d) Find the minimum value of $f(x)$.

5. (a) Draw the graph of the function $f: x \to x^2 - 4x + 3$ in the domain $-1 \leq x \leq 5$.

(b) The graph cuts the y-axis at the point A. Use your graph to find the coordinates of the point A.

(c) The graph cuts the x-axis at the points W and V. Use your graph to find the coordinates of the points W and V.

(d) Find the minimum value of $f(x)$.

6. (a) Draw the graph of the function $g: x \to x^2 - 3x + 2$ in the domain $-1 \leq x \leq 4$.

(b) The graph cuts the y-axis at the point C. Use your graph to find the coordinates of the point C.

(c) The graph cuts the x-axis at the points D and E. Use your graph to find the coordinates of the points D and E.

(d) Find the minimum value of $g(x)$.

7. (a) Draw the graph of the function $f: x \to 3x^2 + x - 2$ in the domain $-2 \leq x \leq 1$.

(b) Find the coordinates of the minimum point of $f(x)$.

(c) Use your graph to find the values of x when $f(x) = 1$.

(d) Find the value of $f(2.5)$.

8. (a) Draw the graph of the function $f: x \to 2x^2 + x - 3$ in the domain $-2 \leq x \leq 2$.

(b) Find the coordinates of the minimum point of $f(x)$.

(c) Find the values of x when $f(x) = 1.5$.

(d) Find the value of $f(1.5)$.

9. (a) Draw the graph of the function $f: x \to -x^2 + 6x - 5$ in the domain $0 \leq x \leq 6$.

(b) Find the values of x when $f(x) = 3$.

(c) Find the maximum point on the curve.

(d) Find the value of $f(3.5)$.

10. (a) Draw the graph of the function $h: x \to x^2 - 6x + 5$ in the domain $0 \leq x \leq 6$.

(b) The graph cuts the y-axis at the point Q. Use your graph to find the coordinates of the point Q.

(c) The graph cuts the x-axis at the points R and S. Use your graph to find the coordinates of the points R and S.

(d) Find the minimum value of $h(x)$.

11. (a) Draw the graph of the function $f: x \to x^2 + 3x + 2$ in the domain $-4 \leq x \leq 1$.

(b) The graph cuts the y-axis at the point C. Use your graph to find the coordinates of the point C.

(c) The graph cuts the x-axis at the points D and E. Use your graph to find the coordinates of the points D and E.

(d) Evaluate $f(1.5)$.

12. (a) Draw graphs of the functions $f: x \to x^2 - x - 12$ in the domain $-3 \leq x \leq 4$.

(b) From your graph, write down the values of x where $f(x) = 0$.

(c) Find the minimum value of $f(x)$.

(d) Calculate the values of x for which the function is increasing.

13. (a) Draw the graph of the function $f: x \to x^2 - x - 6$ in the domain $-3 \leq x \leq 4$.

(b) The graph cuts the y-axis at the point C. Use your graph to find the coordinates of the point C.

(c) The graph cuts the x-axis at the points D and E. Use your graph to find the coordinates of the points D and E.

(d) Find the values of x where $f(x) \leq -2$.

14. (a) Draw the graph of the function $f: x \to -x^2 + x + 6$ in the domain $-3 \leq x \leq 4$.

(b) Find the values of x when $f(x) = 0$.

(c) Find the values of x when $f(x) = -3$.

(d) Find the value of $f(2.5)$.

15. (a) Draw the graph of the function $f: x \to -3x^2 + 10x - 3$ in the domain $0 \leq x \leq 3$.

(b) Find the values of x when $f(x) = 0$.

(c) Find the values of x when $f(x) = -2.5$.

(d) Find the value of $f(1.5)$.

16. (a) Draw the graph of the function $f: x \to -2x^2 + x + 10$ in the domain $-2 \leq x \leq 1$.

(b) Find the values of x when $f(x) = 1$.

(c) Find the maximum point on the curve.

(d) Find the value of $f(-2.5)$.

17. Study the following steel structure and answer the following questions:

(a) Find the maximum height of the arch.

(b) Find the height when the width is 4 m.

(c) Find the height when the width is 8 m.

(d) Find the two widths when the height is 5 m.

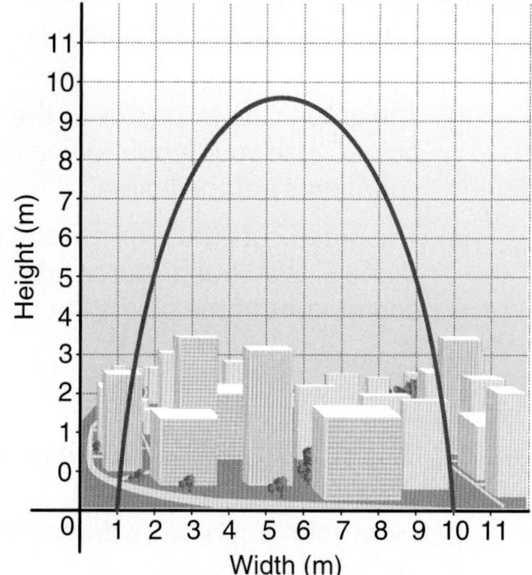

18. Study the following basketball shot showing the height in metres against time and answer the following questions:

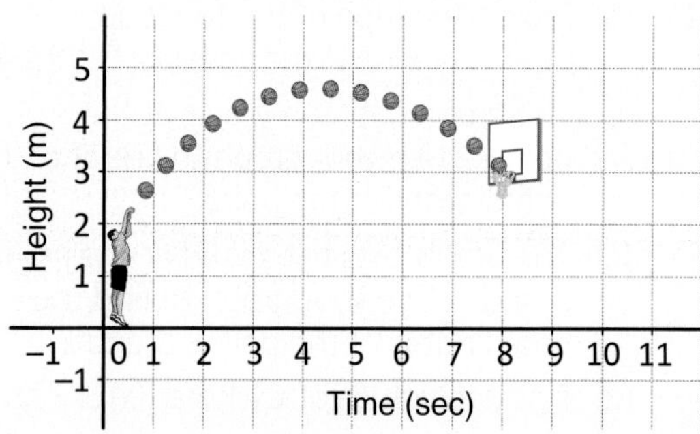

(a) Find the maximum height reached in this basketball shot.

(b) Find the height of the rim of the basket from the ground.

(c) Find the two times when the height of the parabola is 3 m.

19. A rectangular piece of cardboard has dimensions as shown in metres.

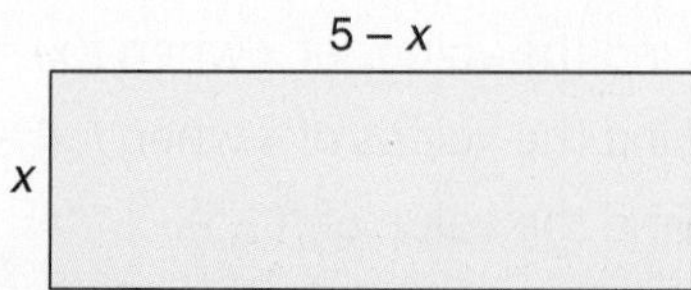

(a) Show that the area of the field can be written as $5x - x^2$.

(b) Draw the graph of the function $f: x \to 5x - x^2$ in the domain $0 \leq x \leq 5$.

From your graph find:

(c) The maximum area of the cardboard

(d) The width of the cardboard when the area is 3 m^2

(e) The length of the cardboard when the area is at its maximum

20. A garden has dimensions in metres as shown:

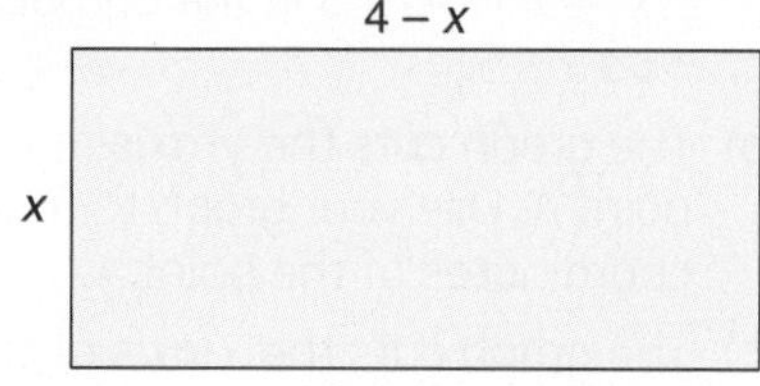

(a) Show that the area of the garden is $4x - x^2$.

(b) Draw the graph of the function $f: x \to 4x - x^2$ in the domain $0 \leq x \leq 4$.

From your graph find:

(c) The maximum area of the garden

(d) The width of the garden when the area is 3 m^2

(e) The length of the garden when the area is at its maximum

21. A farmer has 14 m of wire to fence a rectangular piece of lawn that requires reseeding of width x metres.

(a) Express the length of one side of the lawn in terms of x.

(b) Show that the area of the lawn is given by $7x - x^2$.

(c) Draw the graph of the function $f: x \to 7x - x^2$ in the domain $0 \leq x \leq 7$.

From your graph find:

(d) The maximum area of the lawn

(e) The length of the lawn when the area is 5 m^2

(f) The length of the lawn when the area is at its maximum

22. A garden has a perimeter of 24 m. The garden has length x metres. A path 1 m wide surrounds a lawn in the centre of the garden.

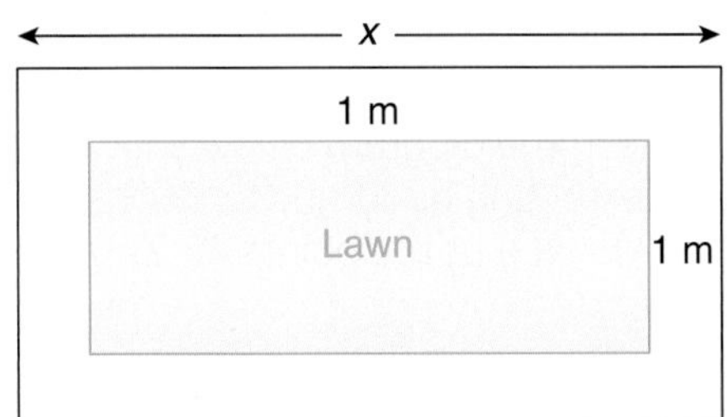

(a) Write an expression in x for the width of the garden.

(b) Write an expression in x for the length of the lawn.

(c) Show that the area of the lawn is $-x^2 + 12x - 20$.

(d) Draw a graph of the function $f: x \rightarrow -x^2 + 12x - 20$ in the domain $2 \leq x \leq 10$.

From your graph find:

(e) The maximum area of the lawn

(f) The length of the lawn when the area is $4\ m^2$

23. The formula for the height of a kite, y metres above ground level, can be represented by the function $y = 35x - 5x^2$.

(a) Draw the graph of y for $0 \leq x \leq 7$ minutes.

Use your graph to estimate:

(b) The maximum height reached by the kite

(c) The height of the kite after 5.5 minutes

(d) The two times when the kite is exactly 20 m above the ground

Section 20.5: Intersecting graphs

Student Activity 20E

1. Explain what the word 'intersection' means. Give an example of where you have met the word before.

2. (a) Draw the graph of the function $g: x \rightarrow 2x + 1$ in the domain $-2 \leq x \leq 5$.

(b) On the same graph draw the function $h: x \rightarrow x^2 - 3x$ in the domain $-2 \leq x \leq 5$.

(c) Find the coordinates of the points where the functions $g(x)$ and $h(x)$ intersect.

(d) Will both graphs intersect at another point? Explain the reason for your answer.

3. In a laboratory, a scientist is examining the rates of growth by different harmful food bacteria as the temperature increases. Specimen X7841 grows in the form of the linear function $h(x) = x + 1$, while the more harmful strain of the bacteria specimen X7999 grows in the form of a quadratic function $f(x) = -2x^2 + x + 3$ when the room temperature is between $-2°$ and $2°$.

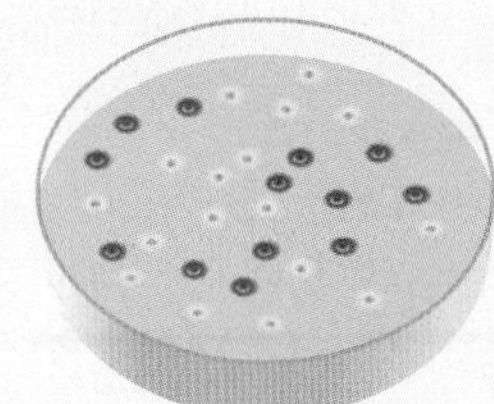

(a) Represent specimen X7841's growth on a suitable graph.

(b) Represent specimen X7999's growth on the same graph.

(c) By studying both graphs, find the points of intersection.

(d) Explain what the points of intersection mean with respect to both bacteria.

INTERSECTING GRAPHS EXPLAINED

Sometimes when two different functions are drawn on the one graph, they criss-cross or intersect each other. The point or points where the two graphs meet are called the **points of intersection.** The points of intersection are the only x and y values common to both functions.

When both functions are drawn on the same axes and to the same scale, they are easily identified on a graph. At these points, we say that the functions f and g are equal or $f(x) = g(x)$. These two functions will not meet again on the Cartesian plane.

For example, in the diagram, we see a graph showing both a quadratic and a linear function. In this diagram, $f(x) = g(x)$ at the points $(-1, 0)$ and $(3, 4)$.

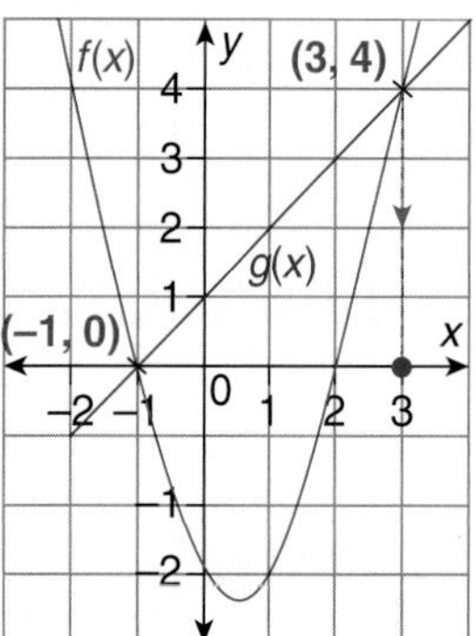

An exam question might ask: 'For what values of x is $f(x) = g(x)$?'. This is asking for the x values of the intersecting functions. Hence, we give the answers: $x = -1$ and $x = 3$.

Likewise in the diagram below showing the two intersecting quadratic functions, we say that $h(x) = k(x)$ at the points $A(-2, -4)$ and $B(2, -4)$.

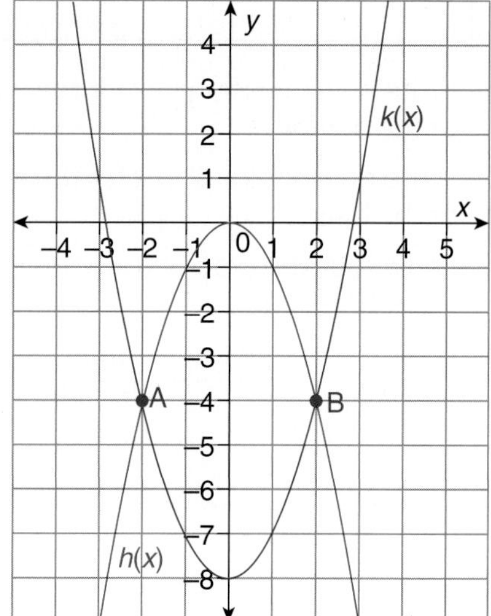

EXAMPLE 12

(a) On the same axes and scales, graph the functions $f:x \to 2x^2 - 3x - 8$ and $g:x \to 3x - 2$ in the domain $-2 \leq x \leq 4$, for all $x \in \mathbb{R}$.

Use your graph to find:

(b) For what values of x is $f(x) = g(x)$

(c) The points where $f(x) = g(x)$

(d) For what values of x is $f(x) > g(x)$

(e) For what values of x is $f(x) < g(x)$

Solution

(a) First, you must determine the points on each of the functions.
In $f:x \to 2x^2 - 3x - 8$:

x	$2x^2 - 3x - 8$	y
−2	$2(-2)^2 - 3(-2) - 8$	6
−1	$2(-1)^2 - 3(-1) - 8$	−3
0	$2(0)^2 - 3(0) - 8$	−8
1	$2(1)^2 - 3(1) - 8$	−9
2	$2(2)^2 - 3(2) - 8$	−6
3	$2(3)^2 - 3(3) - 8$	1
4	$2(4)^2 - 3(4) - 8$	12

The points on the function f are $(-2, 6)$, $(-1, -3)$, $(0, -8)$, $(1, -9)$, $(2, -6)$, $(3, 1)$, $(4, 12)$.

In $g:x \to 3x - 2$:

x	$3x - 2$	y
−2	$3(-2) - 2$	−8
−1	$3(-1) - 2$	−5
0	$3(0) - 2$	−2
1	$3(1) - 2$	1
2	$3(2) - 2$	4
3	$3(3) - 2$	7
4	$3(4) - 2$	10

The points on the function g are $(-2, -8)$, $(-1, -5)$, $(0, -2)$, $(1, 1)$, $(2, 4)$, $(3, 7)$, $(4, 10)$.

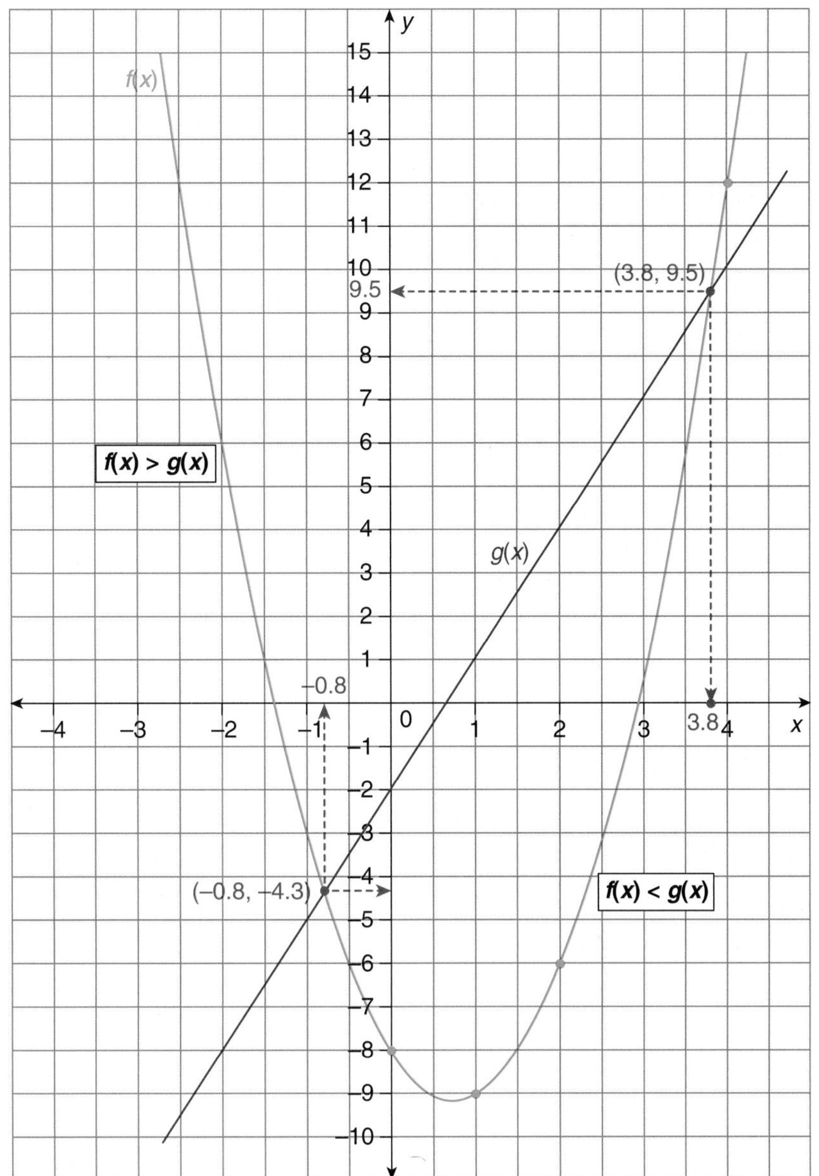

(b) The values of x where $f(x) = g(x)$ are −0.8 and 3.8.

(c) The points where $f(x) = g(x)$ are (−0.8, −4.3) and (3.8, 9.5).

(d) From the graph we can see that $f(x)$ is above $g(x)$ or $f(x) > g(x)$ when $x < -0.8$ and $x > 3.8$.

(e) From the graph we can see that $f(x)$ is below $g(x)$ or $f(x) < g(x)$ when $-0.8 < x < 3.8$.

EXAMPLE 13

(a) On the same axes and scales, graph the functions $f: x \rightarrow 2x^2 - 3x - 5$ in the domain $-2 \leq x \leq 4$ and $g: x \rightarrow 9 + x - x^2$ in the domain $-3 \leq x \leq 4$, for all $x \in \mathbb{R}$.

Use your graph to find:

(b) For what values of x is $f(x) = g(x)$

(c) The points where $f(x) = g(x)$

(d) For what values of x is $f(x) > g(x)$

(e) For what values of x is $f(x) < g(x)$

Solution

(a) First we must determine the points on each of the functions.
In $f: x \to 2x^2 - 3x - 5$:

x	$2x^2 - 3x - 5$	y
−2	$2(-2)^2 - 3(-2) - 5$	9
−1	$2(-1)^2 - 3(-1) - 5$	0
0	$2(0)^2 - 3(0) - 5$	−5
1	$2(1)^2 - 3(1) - 5$	−6
2	$2(2)^2 - 3(2) - 5$	−3
3	$2(3)^2 - 3(3) - 5$	4
4	$2(4)^2 - 3(4) - 5$	15

The points on the function f are (−2, 9), (−1, 0), (0, −5), (1, −6), (2, −3), (3, 4), (4, 15).

In $g: x \to 9 + x - x^2$:

x	$9 + x - x^2$	y
−3	$9 + (-3) - (-3)^2$	−3
−2	$9 + (-2) - (-2)^2$	3
−1	$9 + (-1) - (-1)^2$	7
0	$9 + (0) - (0)^2$	9
1	$9 + (1) - (1)^2$	9
2	$9 + (2) - (2)^2$	7
3	$9 + (3) - (3)^2$	3
4	$9 + (4) - (4)^2$	−3

The points on the function g are (−3, −3), (−2, 3), (−1, 7), (0, 9), (1, 9), (2, 7), (3, 3), (4, −3).

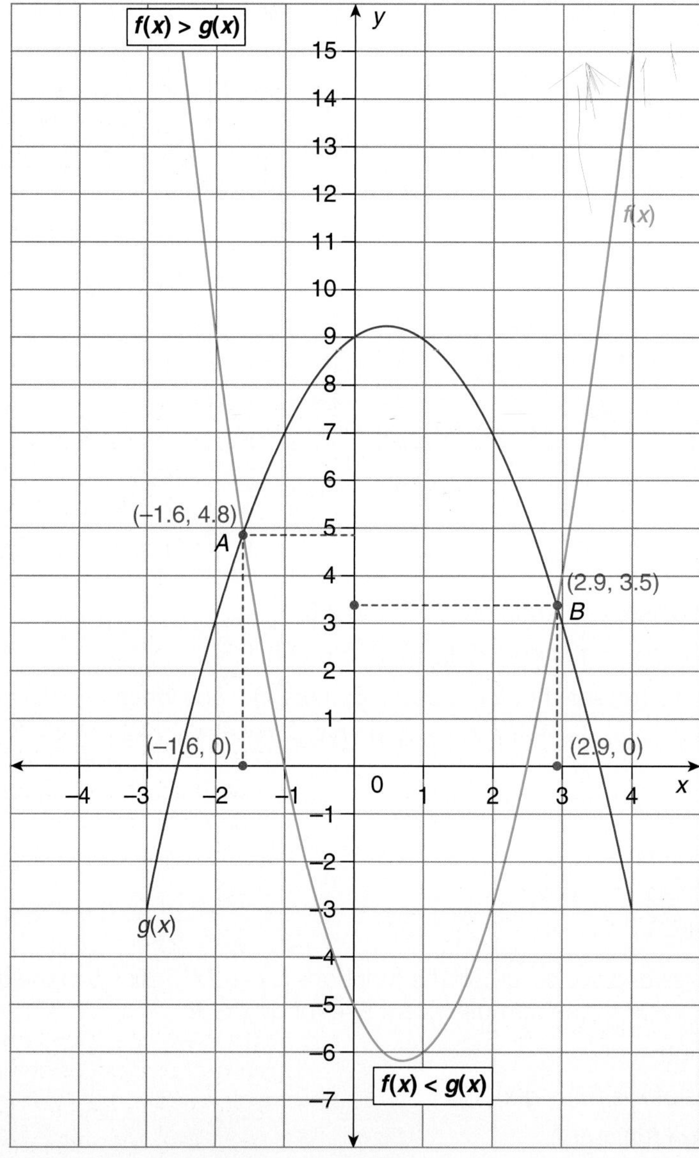

(b) The values of x where $f(x) = g(x)$ are −1.6 and 2.9.

(c) The points where $f(x) = g(x)$ are $A(-1.6, 4.8)$ and $B(2.9, 3.5)$.

(d) From the graph we can see that $f(x)$ is above $g(x)$ or $f(x) > g(x)$ when $x < -1.6$ and $x > 2.9$.

(e) From the graph we can see that $f(x)$ is below $g(x)$ or $f(x) < g(x)$ when $-1.6 < x < 2.9$.

Exercise 20.5

1. Using the same scales and axes, draw graphs of the functions $f: x \to -x^2 - 2x + 3$ and $g: x \to \frac{1}{2}x + 2$ in the domain $-4 \le x \le 2$.
   From your graph, write down where:
   (a) $f(x) = g(x)$
   (b) $f(x) < g(x)$
   (c) $f(x) > g(x)$
2. Using the same scales and axes, draw graphs of the functions $f: x \to x^2 + 4x + 4$ and $g: x \to 3x + 6$ in the domain $-5 \le x \le 1$.
   From your graph write down where:
   (a) $f(x) = g(x)$
   (b) $f(x) < g(x)$
   (c) $f(x) > g(x)$
3. Using the same scales and axes, draw graphs of the functions $f: x \to x^2 + x - 6$ and $g: x \to x + 3$ in the domain $-4 \le x \le 3$.
   From your graph write down where:
   (a) $f(x) < g(x)$
   (b) $f(x) > g(x)$
   (c) $f(x) = g(x)$
4. Using the same scales and axes, draw graphs of the functions $f: x \to x^2 + x - 6$ and $g: x \to 2 - x$ in the domain $-4 \le x \le 3$.
   From your graph write down where:
   (a) $f(x) < g(x)$
   (b) $f(x) > g(x)$
   (c) $f(x) = g(x)$
5. Using the same scales and axes, draw graphs of the functions $f: x \to -2x^2 - 3x + 1$ and $g: x \to x + 2$ in the domain $-3 \le x \le 1$.
   From your graph write down where:
   (a) $f(x) = g(x)$
   (b) $f(x) < g(x)$
   (c) $f(x) > g(x)$
6. Using the same scales and axes, draw graphs of the functions $f: x \to x^2 + 7x + 3$ and $g: x \to -x^2 - 7x - 4$ in the domain $-7 \le x \le 0$.
   From your graph write down where:
   (a) $f(x) = g(x)$
   (b) $f(x) < g(x)$
   (c) $f(x) > g(x)$
7. Using the same scales and axes, draw graphs of the functions $f: x \to -x^2 + 6x - 5$ and $g: x \to x^2 - 6x + 8$ in the domain $0 \le x \le 6$.
   From your graph write down where:
   (a) $f(x) = g(x)$
   (b) $f(x) < g(x)$
   (c) $f(x) > g(x)$
8. Using the same scales and axes, draw graphs of the functions $f: x = -x^2 + 5x + 14$ in the domain $-2 \le x \le 7$ and $g: x = x^2 - 8x + 15$ in the domain $0 \le x \le 7$.
   From your graph write down where:
   (a) $f(x) = g(x)$
   (b) $f(x) < g(x)$
   (c) $f(x) > g(x)$
9. Using the same scales and axes, draw graphs of the functions $f: x = x^2 - 4x + 4$ in the domain $-1 \le x \le 5$ and $g: x = -x^2 + 3x$ $0 \le x \le 3$.
   From your graph write down where:
   (a) $f(x) = g(x)$
   (b) $f(x) < g(x)$
   (c) $f(x) > g(x)$
10. Using the same scales and axes, draw graphs of the functions $f: x \to x^2 + 3x + 2$ in the domain $-4 \le x \le 1$ and $g: x \to x + 2$ in the domain $-4 \le x \le 1$.
    From your graph write down where:
    (a) $f(x) = g(x)$
    (b) $f(x) < g(x)$
    (c) $f(x) > g(x)$
11. Using the same scales and axes, draw graphs of the functions $f: x \to x^2 - 2x + 1$ in the domain $-1 \le x \le 3$ and $g: x \to x$ in the domain $-2 \le x \le 4$.
    From your graph write down where:
    (a) $f(x) = g(x)$
    (b) $f(x) < g(x)$
    (c) $f(x) > g(x)$
12. Using the same scales and axes, draw graphs of the functions $f: x = x^2 + x - 2$ in the domain $-3 \le x \le 2$ and the line $g(x) = 2$.
    From your graph write down where:
    (a) $f(x) = g(x)$
    (b) $f(x) < g(x)$
    (c) $f(x) > g(x)$

13. Using the same scales and axes, draw graphs of the functions $f(x) = 8x^2 - 10x - 3$ in the domain $-1 \leq x \leq 2$ and the line $g(x) = 2$.

From your graph write down where:

(a) $f(x) = g(x)$

(b) $f(x) < g(x)$

(c) $f(x) > g(x)$

14. Study each of the following graphs and then answer the questions.

(a) Write down the values of x such that $f(x) = g(x)$.

(b) Write down where $f(x) < g(x)$.

(c) Write down where $f(x) > g(x)$.

(i)

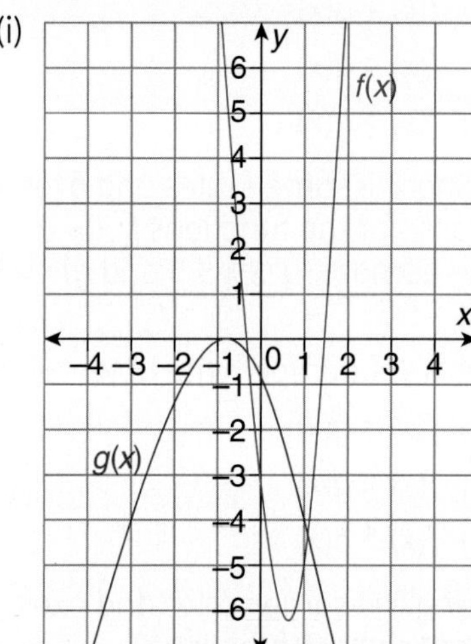

(ii)

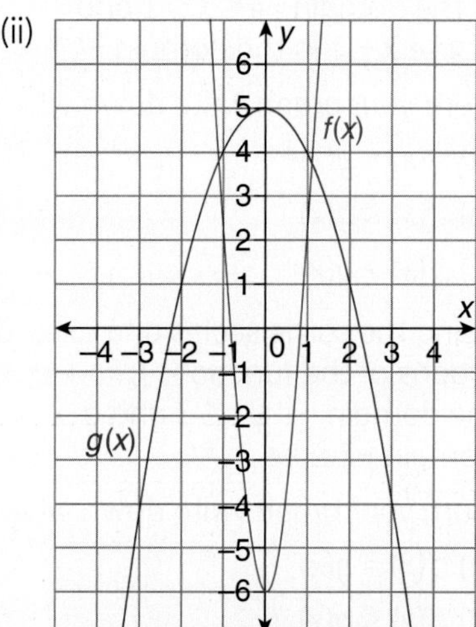

(iii)

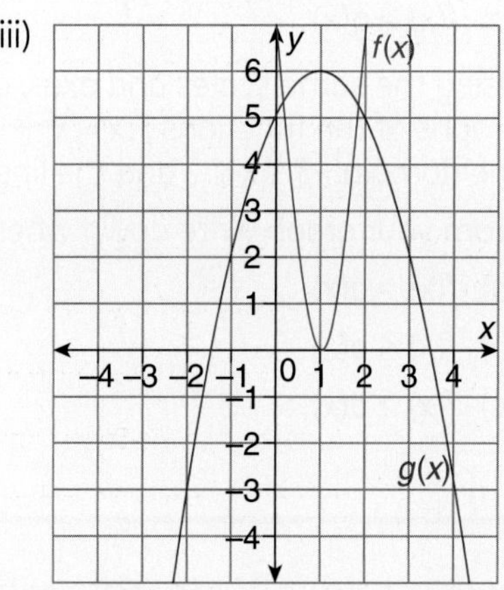

(iv)

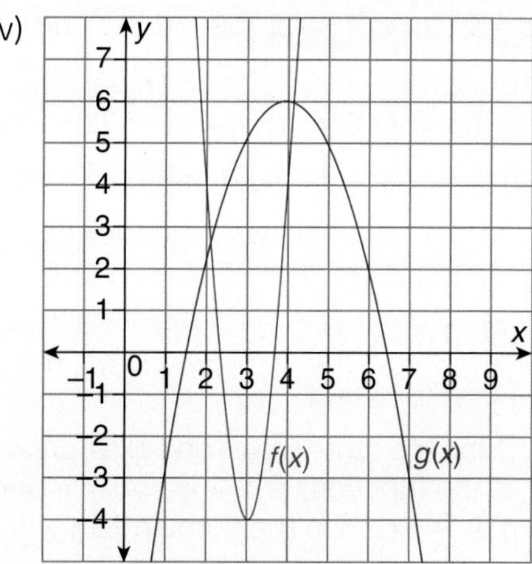

15. Given that $f: x \rightarrow 3x + 1$ and $g: x \rightarrow 1 + x^2$, solve for x where $f(x) = g(x)$ for all $x \in \mathbb{N}$.

16. Let f be the function $f: x \rightarrow 1 - 3x$ and g be the function $g: x \rightarrow 1 - x^2$.

(a) Find $f(-2)$.

(b) Find $g(5)$.

(c) Express $f(x + 1)$ in the form $ax + b$, a and $b \in \mathbb{Z}$.

(d) Solve for x: $f(x + 1) = f(-2) + g(5)$.

17. (a) Let f be the function $f: x \rightarrow x^2 + 5x$ and g be the function $g: x \rightarrow x + 2$. Using the same axes and scales, draw the graph of f and the graph of g for $-6 \leq x \leq 1$, $x \in \mathbb{R}$.

(b) Estimate the minimum value of $f(x)$.

(c) Calculate the values of x for which $f(x) = g(x)$.

(d) Find the range of values of x for which $f(x) \leq g(x)$.

18. The diagram shows part of the graph of the function $f: x \rightarrow x^2 - 2x - 8$, $x \in \mathbb{R}$.

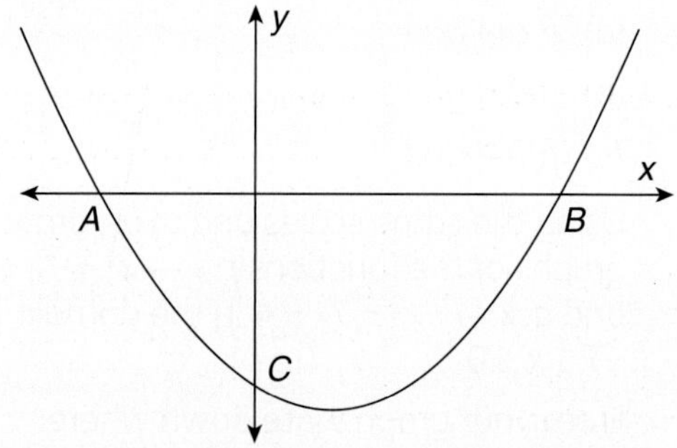

(a) The graph intersects the x-axis at A and B and the y-axis at C. Find the coordinates of A, B and C.

(b) Find the range of values of x for which $x^2 - 2x - 8 \leq 0$.

19. The following image from the game Furious Fowls shows a missile travelling in a line crossing the flight path of a bird. The flight of the bird forms a quadratic function.

(a) What is the maximum height attained by the bird in metres?

(b) Write down the equation of the line representing the trajectory of the missile.

(c) Write down the point of intersection of the missile and the bird.

(d) Explain what the x- and y-coordinate of the point of intersection represent.

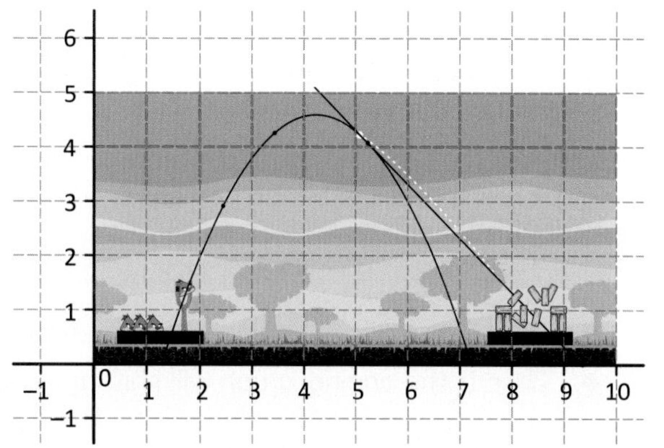

Section 20.6: Transformation of quadratic graphs

Student Activity 20F

1. Sketch the function $y = x^2$.
2. Now sketch the function $y = 4x^2$.
3. Describe how this function differs from the original function $y = x^2$.
4. Next sketch the function $y = x^2 - 4$.
5. Describe how the given function differs from the original function $y = x^2$.
6. Predict how the function $y = x^2 + 4$ differs from the function $y = x^2$.
7. Sketch the function $y = x^2 + 4$ and investigate whether your previous answer was correct.

TRANSFORMATION OF QUADRATIC GRAPHS EXPLAINED

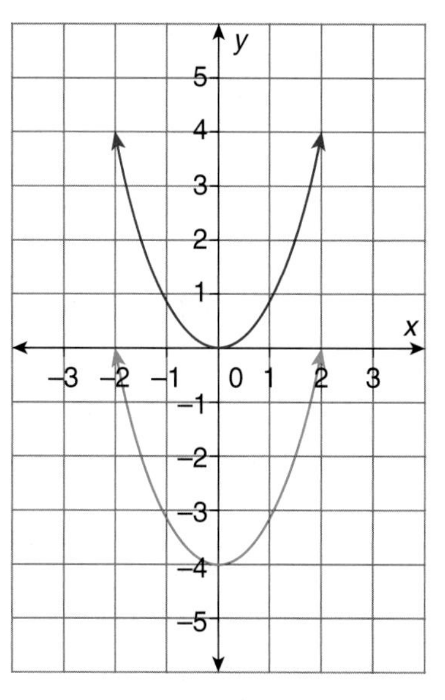

In *Maths in Action 1*, you learned that the word 'transformation' means to change the position of a shape. By now, you have probably noticed some relationships between the different functions' equations and graphs. All quadratic functions make a smooth curved shape called a **parabola.** So what happens mathematically to cause a parabola to open wider or become narrower? Or what causes a parabola to shift upwards or downwards?

Moving a graph up or down

Let's examine a picture of the function $f(x) = x^2$. In the diagram of this function, we can see its minimum point is located at the origin (0, 0).

Suppose we subtract 4 from the original function and graph the new function $f(x) = x^2 - 4$. We can see that this function (in green) is 4 units beneath the original function $f(x) = x^2$ (in blue). The minimum point of new parabola is (0, −4).

Similarly, we can increase the original function by 25 and graph the new function $f(x) = x^2 + 25$. We can see that the new function (in green) is now 25 units above the original function (in blue). The minimum point of the new parabola is (0, 25).

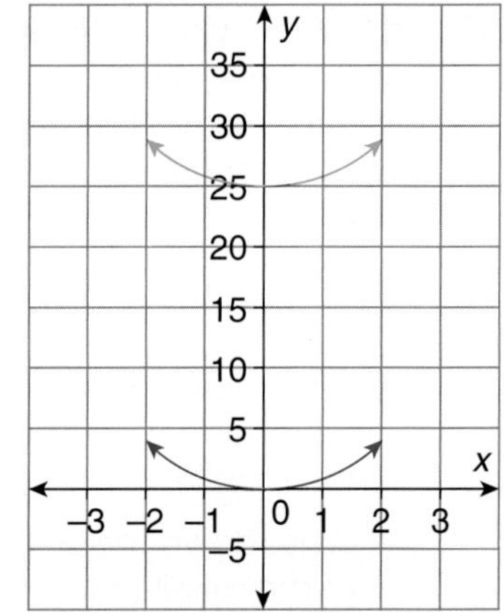

This implies that any change in a quadratic function to form $y = f(x) + k$, will cause either an upward or a downward vertical translation.

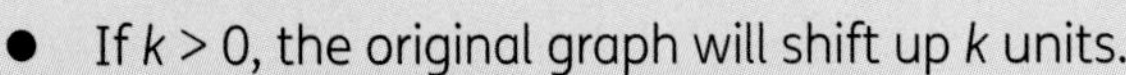

- If $k > 0$, the original graph will shift up k units.
- If $k < 0$, the original graph will shift down k units.

The new quadratic function's graph is still a parabola. It has one line of symmetry, and the greatest exponent of the function is 2 but its turning point has moved either upwards or downwards.

Sliding a graph to the left or the right

What happens when we change $f(x) = x^2$ to $f(x) = (x + 3)^2$? By examining the diagram on the right, we can see the new function $f(x) = (x + 3)^2$ has moved three units to the left.

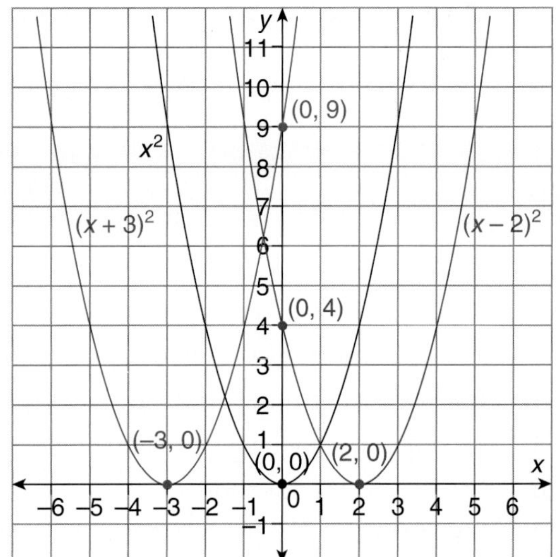

Likewise, the function $f(x) = (x - 2)^2$ causes the original parabola of the function $f(x) = x^2$ to move two units to the right.

This translation, or sliding horizontally to the left or right, of a quadratic function is given by the function $y = (x - h)^2$.

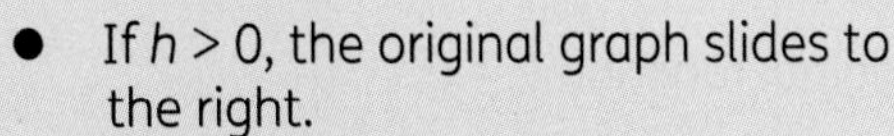

- If $h > 0$, the original graph slides to the right.
- If $h < 0$, the original graph slides to the left.

The y-intercept will occur at $(0, h^2)$.

> **Note**
>
> Many students mistakenly think that $f(x + 3)$ moves $f(x)$ to the right by three. But the left–right shifting is the opposite of what you might have expected since $f(x + 3) = (x -(-3))$. Adding moves a function to the left, whereas subtracting moves a function to the right.

Making a graph wider or narrower

Lastly, we will examine another transformation which causes a parabola to become narrower or wider. The parabola of $f(x) = 2x^2$ grows twice as fast as $f(x) = x^2$, so its graph is tall and skinny.

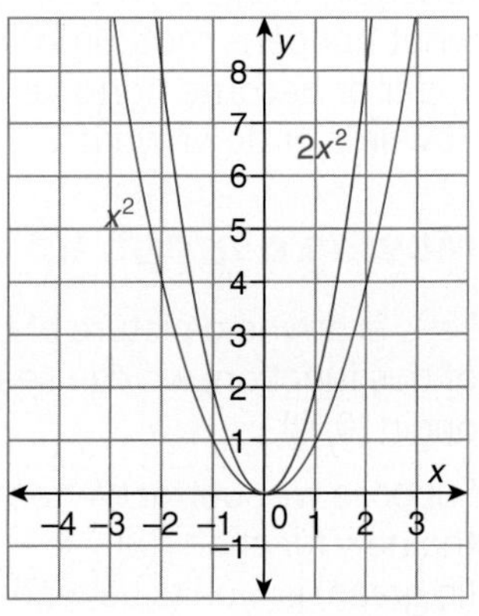

On the other hand, the parabola of the function $f(x) = \frac{1}{2}x^2$ grows only half as fast as $f(x) = x^2$, so its graph is more open and wider.

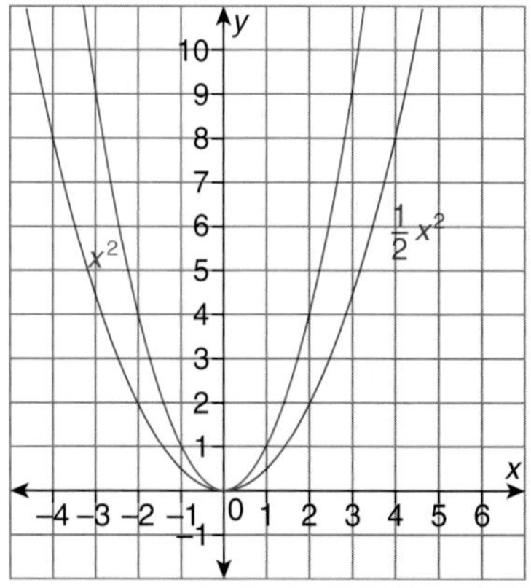

Therefore, we can conclude that a function **widens** or **compresses** when of the form $y = ax^2$.

- If $0 < a < 1$ (a proper fraction), the graph is made **wider.**
- If $a > 1$, the graph is made **narrower** by a factor of a units.

We can generalise all the above information for a function of the form:

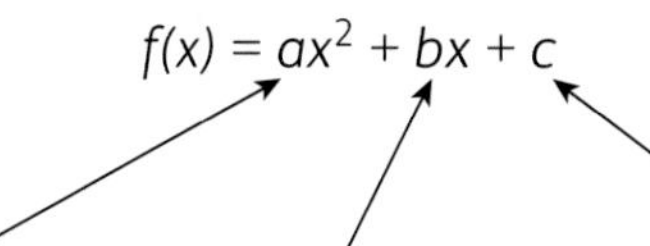

a indicates a narrowing or widening of the graph.

b indicates a horizontal sliding to the left or right of the graph.

c indicates a vertical sliding up or down of the graph.

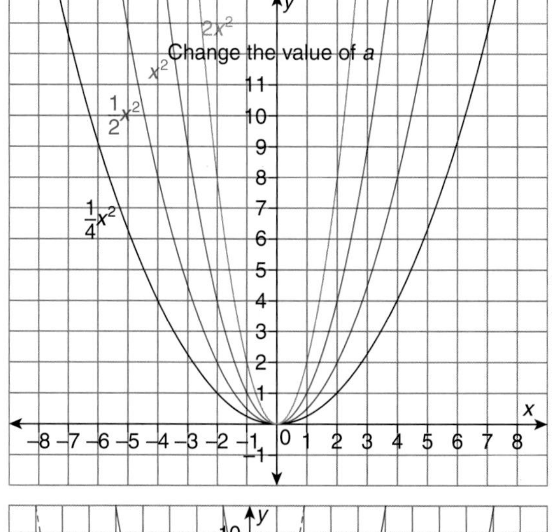

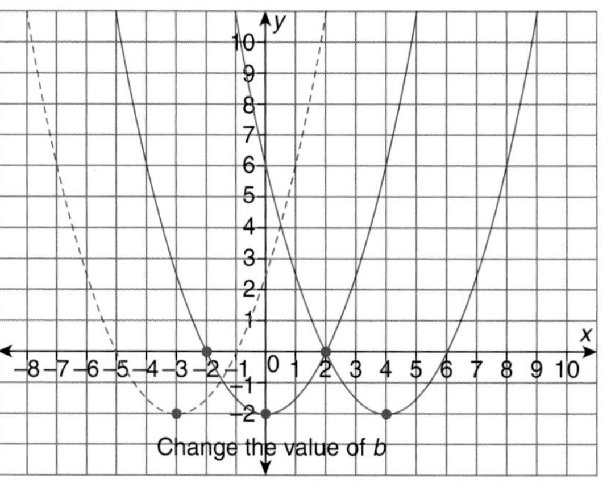

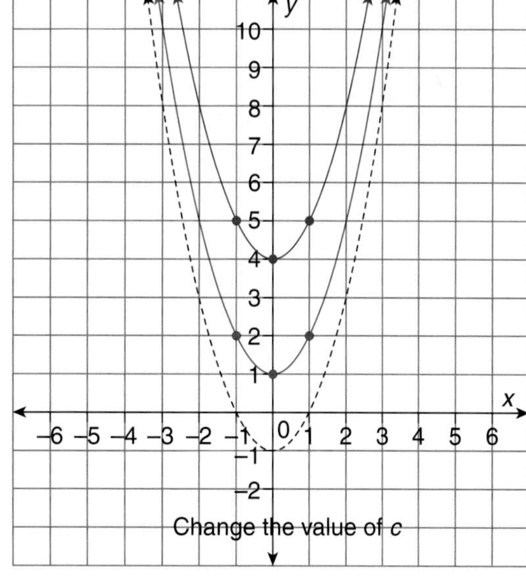

EXAMPLE 14

Match each of the following functions with its graphed image, clearly explaining the reasons for your answer.

Functions

(i) $f(x) = -x^2 - 4x + 5$

(ii) $f(x) = x^2 - 3x - 4$

(iii) $f(x) = (x + 4)^2$

Images

A
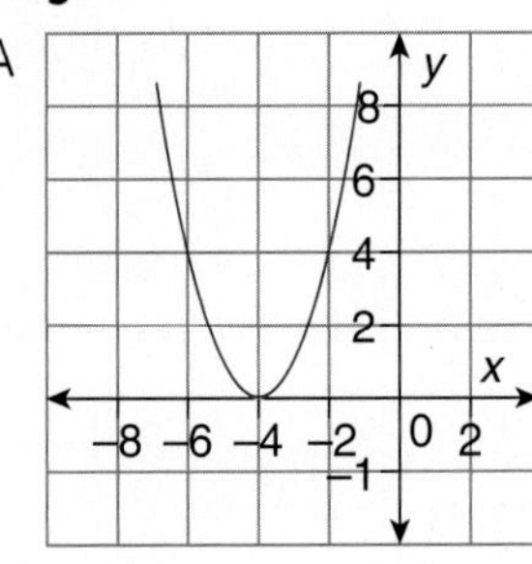

B
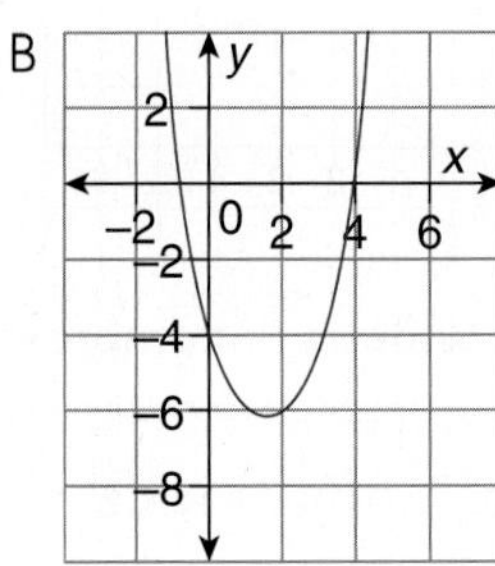

C
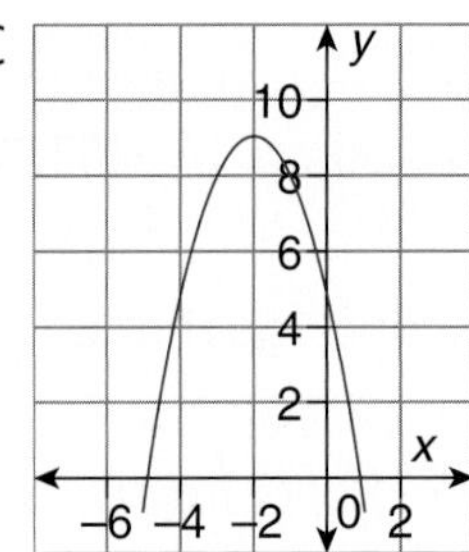

Solution

$f(x) = -x^2 - 4x + 5$ = Image C. Reason: The function is negative, therefore it has an ∩-shape. The constant at the end of the function is +5, which means the function cuts the y-axis at the point (0, 5).

$f(x) = x^2 - 3x - 4$ = Image B. Reason: The function is positive, therefore it has a U-shape. The constant at the end of the function is −4, which means the function cuts the y-axis at the point (0, −4).

$f(x) = (x + 4)^2$ = Image A. Reason: The function is positive therefore it has a U-shape. Since it is of the form $f(x + h)^2$ and slides 4 units to the right.

Exercise 20.6

1. Draw the graphs of all the following functions on the same axes in the indicated colours and in the domain $-3 \leq x \leq 3$.
   (a) In **red**, $f: x \rightarrow x^2$
   (b) In **blue**, $f: x \rightarrow x^2 + 1$
   (c) In **green**, $f: x \rightarrow x^2 + 2$
   (d) In **black**, $f: x \rightarrow x^2 + 3$
   (e) In **brown**, $f: x \rightarrow x^2 + 4$
   (f) In **purple**, $f: x \rightarrow x^2 + 5$
   (g) Explain what happens when any function of the form $x^2 + c$, has an increase in the value of the constant term.

2. Draw the graphs of all the following functions on the same axes in the indicated colours and in the domain $-3 \leq x \leq 3$.
   (a) In **red**, $f: x \rightarrow x^2$
   (b) In **blue**, $f: x \rightarrow x^2 - 1$
   (c) In **green**, $f: x \rightarrow x^2 - 2$
   (d) In **black**, $f: x \rightarrow x^2 - 3$
   (e) In **brown**, $f: x \rightarrow x^2 - 4$
   (f) In **purple**, $f: x \rightarrow x^2 - 5$
   (g) Explain what happens when any function of the form $x^2 + c$, has a decrease in the value of the constant term.

3. Draw the graphs of all the following functions on the same axes in the indicated colours and in the domain $-3 \leq x \leq 3$.
   (a) In **red**, $f: x \rightarrow x^2$
   (b) In **blue**, $f: x \rightarrow 2x^2$
   (c) In **green**, $f: x \rightarrow 3x^2$
   (d) In **black**, $f: x \rightarrow 4x^2$
   (e) In **brown**, $f: x \rightarrow 5x^2$
   (f) In **purple**, $f: x \rightarrow 6x^2$
   (g) Explain what happens when any function of the form ax^2, has an increase in the coefficient of x^2.

4. Draw the graphs of all the following functions on the same axes in the indicated colours and in the domain $-3 \leq x \leq 3$.

(a) In **red**, $f: x \to -x^2$

(b) In **blue**, $f: x \to -2x^2$

(c) In **green**, $f: x \to -3x^2$

(d) In **black**, $f: x \to -4x^2$

(e) In **brown**, $f: x \to -5x^2$

(f) In **purple**, $f: x \to -6x^2$

(g) Explain what happens when any function of the form ax^2, has a decrease in the coefficient of x^2.

5. Draw the graphs of all the following functions on the same axes in the indicated colours and in the domain $-3 \leq x \leq 3$.

(a) In **red**, $f: x \to -x^2 + x$

(b) In **blue**, $f: x \to -x^2 + x + 1$

(c) In **green**, $f: x \to -x^2 + x + 3$

(d) In **black**, $f: x \to -x^2 + x + 5$

(e) In **brown**, $f: x \to -x^2 + x + 7$

(f) Explain what happens when any function of the form $-x^2 + x + c$, has an increase in the value of the constant term.

6. Draw the graphs of the following functions on the same axes in the indicated colours and in the domain $-3 \leq x \leq 3$:

(a) In **red**, $f: x \to 5x^2 + 3x + 0$

(b) In **blue**, $f: x \to 5x^2 + 3x + 3$

(c) In **green**, $f: x \to 5x^2 + 3x + 5$

(d) In **black**, $f: x \to 5x^2 + 3x - 2$

(e) Explain what happens when any function of the form $ax^2 + bx + c$ has a change in the value of the constant term.

7. Draw the graphs of the following functions on the same axes in the indicated colours and in the domain $-3 \leq x \leq 3$:

(a) In **red**, $f: x \to x^2 + 2x - 4$

(b) In **blue**, $f: x \to 2x^2 + 2x - 4$

(c) In **green**, $f: x \to -2x^2 + 2x - 4$

(d) In **black**, $f: x \to 5x^2 + 2x - 4$

(e) In **brown**, $f: x \to -5x^2 + 2x - 4$

(f) Explain what happens when any function of the form $ax^2 + bx + c$, has a change in the coefficient of x^2.

8. (a) Write an equation of a quadratic function in the form $f(x) = ax^2 + bx + c$.

(b) Using a suitable function and graph, explain what must be changed to move a function's maximum (or minimum) point higher up the graph.

(c) Using a suitable function and graph, explain what variable must be changed to move a function's maximum (or minimum) point lower down the graph.

(d) Using a suitable function and graph, explain what variable must be changed to cause the function to expand (get wider).

(e) Using a suitable function and graph, explain what must be changed to cause the function to contract (become narrower).

9. Match each diagram showing a green parabola to its correct function, explaining your reasons.

(i) $y = x^2 + 1$

(ii) $y = x^2 - 1$

(iii) $y = x^2 + 5$

(iv) $y = x^2 - 3$

(a)

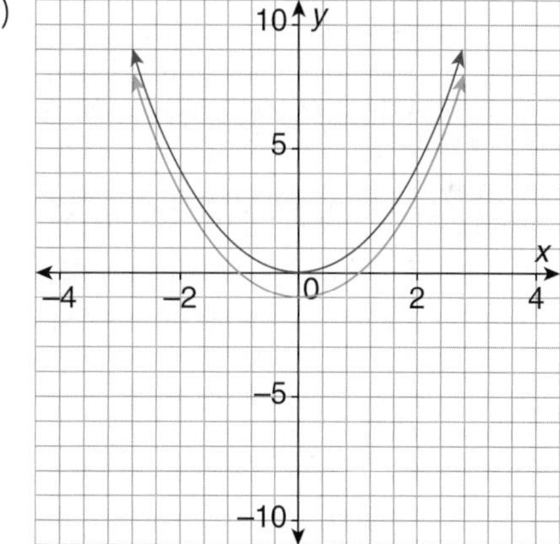

(b)

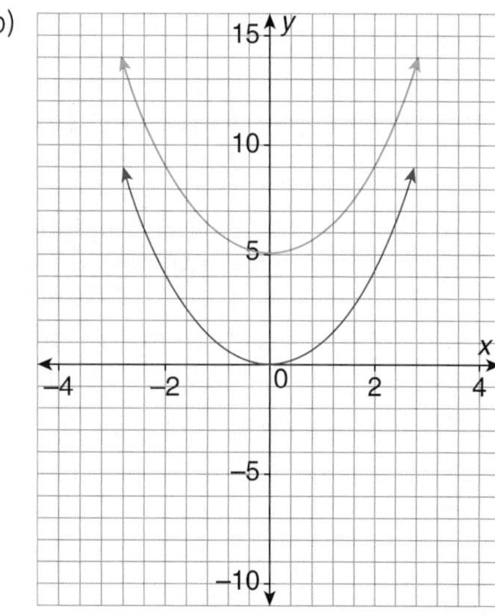

(c)

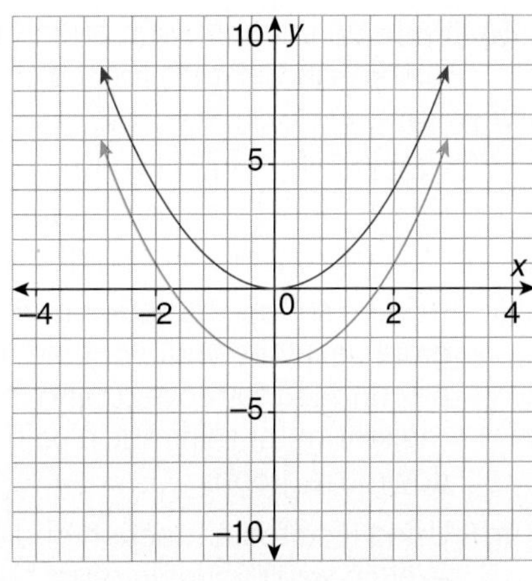

(d)

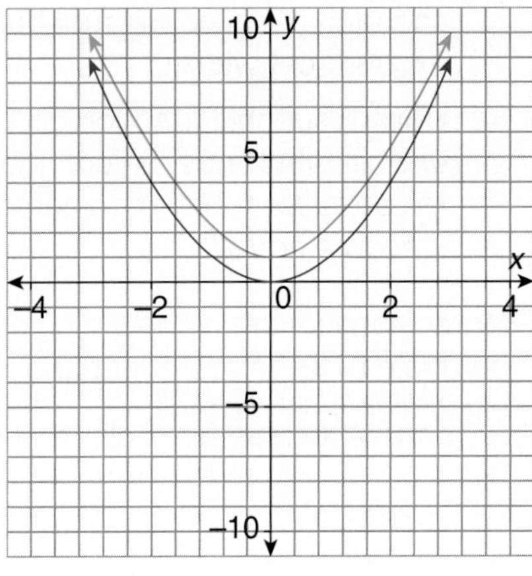

10. Which function matches with each graph: $f(x) = (2x)^2 - 4$ or $f(x) = x^2 - 4$? Give reasons for your answers.

A

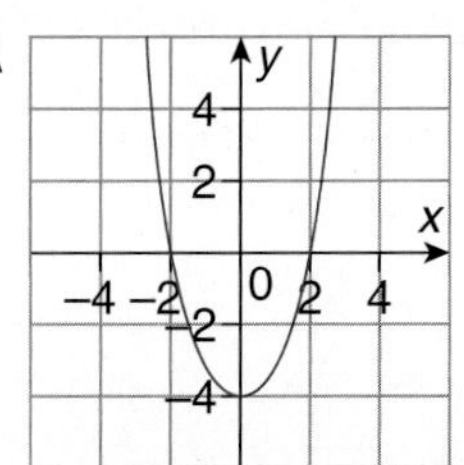

B

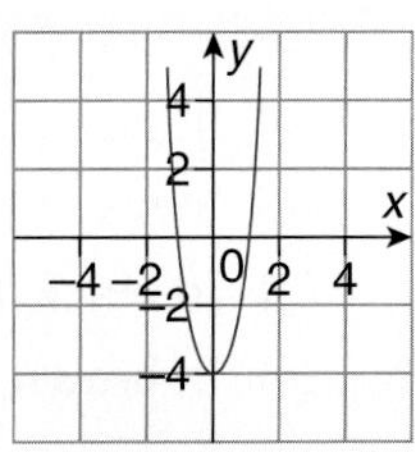

11. Given $f(x) = x^2$, explain what the following functions would look like:

(a) $f(x - 2)^2 + 1$

(b) $f(x + 6)^2$

(c) $f(x + 8)^2 - 3$

(d) $f(x - 3)^2$

(e) $f(x - 1)^2 - 3$

12. Describe the effect of h on the equation $f(x) = (x - h)^2$.

CHAPTER 20 SELF-CHECK TEST

1. Determine the second difference between the terms for the following sequences:

(a) 5, 20, 45, 80, ...

(b) 6, 11, 18, 27, ...

(c) 1, 4, 9, 16, ...

(d) 3, 0, –5, –12, ...

(e) 1, 3, 7, 13, ...

(f) 0, –6, –16, –30, ...

(g) –1, 2, 9, 20, ...

(h) 1, –3, –9, –17, ...

(i) $3a + 1$, $12a + 1$, $27a + 1$, $48a + 1$, ...

(j) $t - 2$, $4t - 1$, $9t$, $16t + 1$, ...

2. Find the missing terms in each of the following quadratic patterns:

(a) 11, 21, 35, ..., 75

(b) 20, ..., 42, 56, 72

(c) ..., 37, 65, 101

(d) 3, ..., –13, –27, –45

(e) 24, 35, 48, ..., 80

(f) ..., 11, 26, 47

3. Use the general term to generate the first four terms in each quadratic sequence:

(a) $T_n = n^2 + 3n - 1$

(b) $T_n = -n^2 - 5$

(c) $T_n = 3n^2 - 2n$

(d) $T_n = -2n^2 + n + 1$

(e) $T_n = 5n^2 + 3n + 4$

4. Given $T_n = 4n^2 + 5n + 10$, find T_8.

5. Given $T_n = 2n^2$, for which value of n does $T_n = 32$?

6. (a) Write down the next two terms of the quadratic sequence: 16, 27, 42, 61, ...

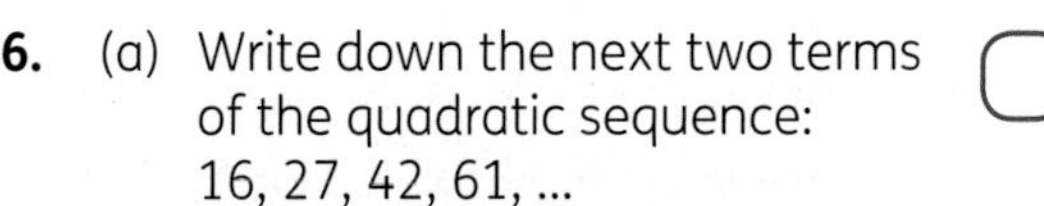

(b) Write the general formula for the quadratic sequence above.

7. The curvature on a banana can be represented by the function: $f: x \to 2x^2 - 4x + 5$ in the domain $-2 \le x \le 4, x \in \mathbb{R}$.

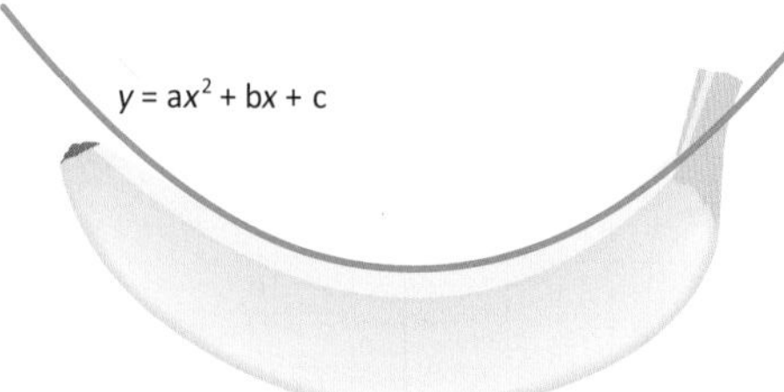

(a) Draw a graph of the function.

(b) Use your graph to find the values of x for which $f(x) = 7$.

8. The diagram shows part of the graph of the function $f: x \to x^2 + bx + c$ where $x \in \mathbb{R}$ and $b, c \in \mathbb{Z}$.

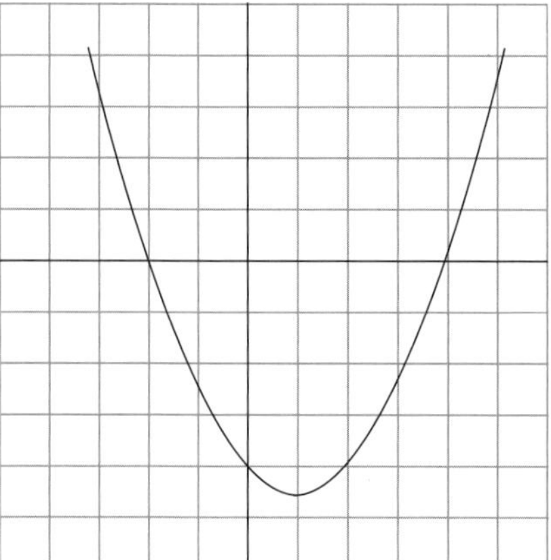

The graph intersects the x-axis at $(-1, 0)$ and $(2, 0)$.

(a) Given that the graph intersects the x-axis at $(-1, 0)$ and $(2, 0)$, calculate the value of b and the value of c for the function.

(b) $(k, -k + 14)$ is a point on the graph, where $k \in \mathbb{Z}$. Find the values of k.

9. Dara has planted heads of lettuce in his garden.

(a) Can you explain how his rectangles are 'growing'?

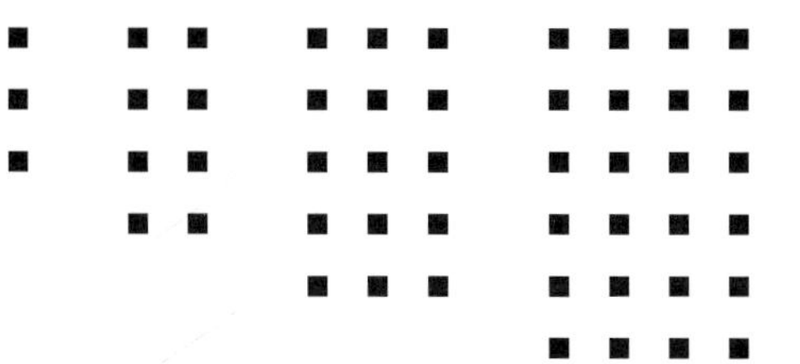

(b) Can you describe the pattern?

(c) Construct a rule so we can determine the dimensions of any rectangle. Explain all letters used.

(d) Using the rule, work out the dimensions of the 10th rectangle.

10. (a) Describe any four features of each parabola by examining its equation. (Hint: describe the x- and y-intercepts, the vertex, its concavity and so on.)

(i) $f(x) = (x - 5)^2$

(ii) $g(x) = (x - 2)^2 + 5$

(iii) $h(x) = (-4x)^2$

(b) Sketch each of the functions.

11. The formula for the height, y metres, of a golf ball above ground level x seconds after it is hit, is given by $7x - x^2$.

(a) Draw a graph of the function in the domain {0, 1, 2, 3, 4, 5, 6, 7}.

(b) Find the maximum height reached by the golf ball.

(c) Estimate the number of seconds the golf ball was more than 2 m above the ground.

(d) The graph below represents the flight path of another golf ball. The flight path of the golf ball is given by the formula $y = ax - x^2$. Find the value of a.

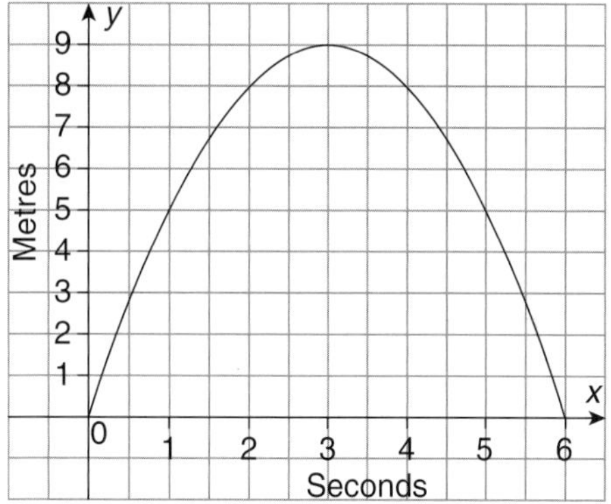

12. When designing a bend on a motorway, the engineers used the function $f(x) = x^2 - 7x - 7$.

(a) Draw a graph of the function f for $0 \le x \le 7, x \in \mathbb{R}$.

(b) Use your graph to find the minimum value of $f(x)$.

(c) Use your graph to find the range of values of x for which $f(x) \ge 0$.

13. Examine the following functions and determine the y-intercept of each:

(a) $f(x) = x^2 - 3x - 2$

(b) $f(x) = x^2 + 3x - 8$

(c) $f(x) = x^2 + 1$

(d) $f(x) = x^2 + x - 1$

(e) $f(x) = x^2 + 10$

(f) Explain how you can determine the y-intercept for any function of the form $f(x) = ax^2 + bx + c$.

14. Draw a graph for each of the functions (a) to (e) on the same axes using a different colour for each graph. The domain for each is $-3 \le x \le 3$.

(a) $f(x) = x^2$

(b) $f(x) = 2x^2$

(c) $f(x) = 4x^2$

(d) $f(x) = x^2 + 1$

(e) $f(x) = x^2 - 1$

(f) By examining the graphs in parts (a), (b) and (c), explain the effect of a change in the value of a to any function of the form $f(x) = ax^2$.

(g) By examining the graphs in parts (a), (d) and (e), explain the effect of a change in the value of b to any function of the form $f(x) = x^2 + b$.

15. (a) Draw the graph of the function $g: x \to x^2 - 3x + 2$ in the domain $-1 \le x \le 4$.

(b) The graph cuts the y-axis at the point C. Use your graph to find the coordinates of the point C.

(c) The graph cuts the x-axis at the points D and E. Use your graph to find the coordinates of the points D and E.

(d) Find the minimum value of $g: x$.

(e) Hence, find the minimum point.

(f) Calculate $g(4.5)$.

(g) Given $g(x) = 6$, evaluate algebraically the values of x.

16. (a) Draw the graph of the function $f: x \to 2x^2 + 5x - 3$ in the domain $-3 \le x \le 3$.

(b) Find the minimum value of x on the function.

(c) Find the y-intercept.

(d) Find the minimum point on the function.

(e) For what values of x is the function decreasing?

(f) For what values of x is $f(x) = 3$?

17. A group of four students were studying the graphs of functions of the form $f: x \to x^2 + 2x + k$, $x \in \mathbb{R}$. Each takes an integer value of k and draws the graph of their function in a suitable domain.

(a) Maria chose $k = -8$ and drew the following graph:

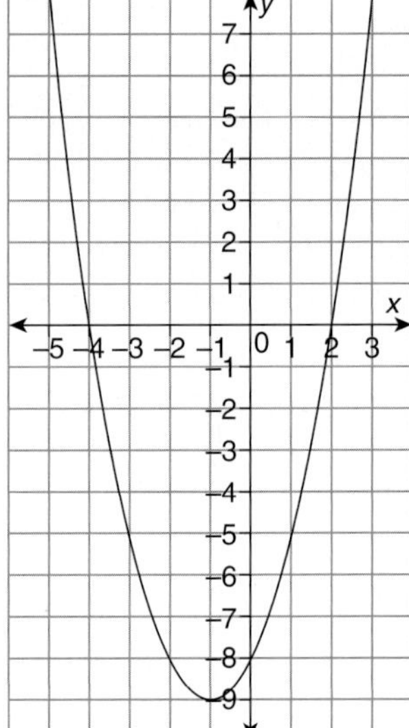

Use the graph to write down the roots of the equation $x^2 + 2x - 8 = 0$.

(b) Keith's graph passes through the point (3, 2). Find the value of k that Keith used.

(c) On Alice's graph, the two roots of the function are the same. Find the value of k that Alice used.

(d) Draw a sketch of Alice's function on the diagram shown in part (a).

(e) Emma's graph shows that the roots of her function are –5 *and* 3. Find the value of k that she used.

18. The height in metres of the BMX biker in seconds is found using the following function $h(x) = -x^2 - 4x + 5$.

(a) Find the coordinates of the points where the graph of $h: x$ cuts the x-axis?

(b) Solve $h(x) = h(x + 1)$.

19. A parabola is created when a ball is thrown between two players. It is represented by the function $g(x) = -x^2 + 7x$.

(a) Draw the graph of the function g for $0 \leq x \leq 6, x \in \mathbb{R}$.

(b) Use your graph to estimate the maximum height attained in the throw.

(c) Estimate the times in seconds when the ball was exactly 6 m in the air.

20. Let f be the function $f(x) = x^2 - 3x$.

(a) Express $f(t)$ and $f(2t + 1)$ in terms of t.

(b) Find the values of t for which $f(t) = f(2t + 1)$.

21. A rectangular site with one side facing a road is to be fenced off. The side facing the road which does not require fencing is l m in length. The sides perpendicular to the road are x m in length. The length of fencing that will be used to enclose the rest of the site is 140 m.

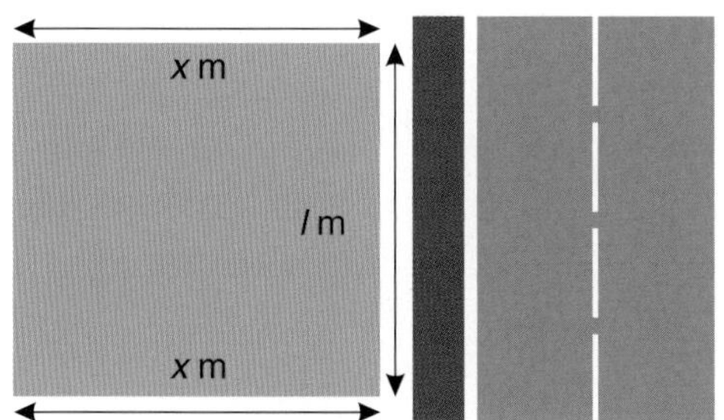

(a) Write an expression, in terms of x, for the length (l) of the side facing the road.

(b) Show that the area of the site, in m^2, is $-2x^2 + 140x$.

(c) Let f be the function $f: x \rightarrow -2x^2 + 140x$. Evaluate $f(x)$ when $x = 0, 10, 20, 30, 40, 50, 60$ and 70 m.

(d) Hence, draw a graph of f for $0 \leq x \leq 70, x \in \mathbb{R}$.

(e) Use your graph to estimate the maximum possible area of the site.

(f) Use your graph to estimate the area of the site when the road frontage (l) is 30 m long.

22. Deduce as much information as possible from the following table!

x	0	1	2	3	4	5
y	1	2	5	10	17	

23. A bomb is dropped from a plane at a distance of 100 km from a target on ground level and follows a path, p, where $p(x) = 2x$. At the same instance, an intercepting rocket is fired 70 km from the target and follows a course, c, where $c(x) = -x^2 + 50x$.

(a) Using the same scales and axes, draw graphs to represent both functions.

(b) Find the point at which the rocket intercepts the bomb.

(c) How far from the target is the bomb when it is intercepted?

24. A clay pigeon is fired from a trap. Its distance from the trap, s, in metres is given by the function $s(x) = -x^2 + 5x$. A marksman fires a shot that follows a path, p, given by the function $p(x) = 2x$.

(a) Using the same scales and axes, draw graphs to represent both functions.

(b) From your graph find the maximum height reached by the clay pigeon.

(c) Find the point at which the shot hits the clay pigeon.

CHAPTER 20 KNOWLEDGE CHECKLIST

After completing this chapter, I now:

- Am able to identify, name and draw quadratic patterns
- Am able to describe a quadratic pattern using a general formula
- Am able to graph quadratic functions
- Understand the terms associated with graphs and functions such as domain, codomain, range and y-intercept
- Am able to use function notation and to interpret quadratic graphs
- Am able to find solutions to problems of the form $f(x) = g(x)$ and to interpret these results
- Understand transformation of quadratic graphs
- Am able to apply all the above to real-life situations

Challenge

Once upon a time, a particularly cruel dictator with an overactive imagination devised a punishment for four of his prisoners. He buried the four in a line up to their heads in the ground, with a wall separating them. They were all buried facing the wall so they could only see what was in front of them, so Dave can see Bella and Charlie, and Charlie can see Bella but not Dave.
The dictator then placed hats on top of the prisoners' heads as in this picture. The prisoners knew that there were two black hats and two white hats, but they didn't know the colour of their own hat. If one of the prisoners could correctly say what colour their hat was, they'd all be freed.
Which prisoner ended up saving the day?
Andrea
Bella
Charlie
Dave

STATISTICS 2

LEARNING OUTCOMES

In this chapter you will learn:

- ✓ To draw and interpret line plots
- ✓ To draw and interpret bar charts
- ✓ To draw and interpret pie charts
- ✓ To draw and interpret histograms
- ✓ To draw and interpret back-to-back stem and leaf plots
- ✓ To calculate the median, mode, quartiles and interquartile range from back-to-back stem and leaf plots
- ✓ To interpret shapes of distribution
- ✓ About the misuses of statistics

KEY WORDS

- Bar chart
- Histogram
- Interquartile range
- Line plot
- Negative skew
- Normal distribution
- Pie chart
- Positive skew
- Quartiles
- Sector
- Stem and leaf plot
- Symmetrical

INTRODUCTION

In Chapter 6, you looked at how and why statisticians gather information. You examined the different types of data that can be collected and the ways it can be collected. In this chapter, you will learn about how this information can be presented and interpreted. You will look at the representation of statistical information in real life.

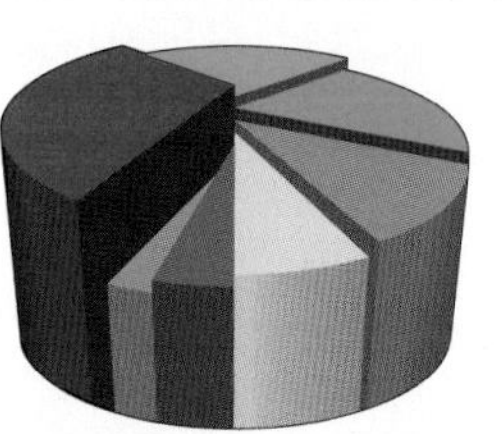

First year revision

1. The following line plot shows the number of matches per box.

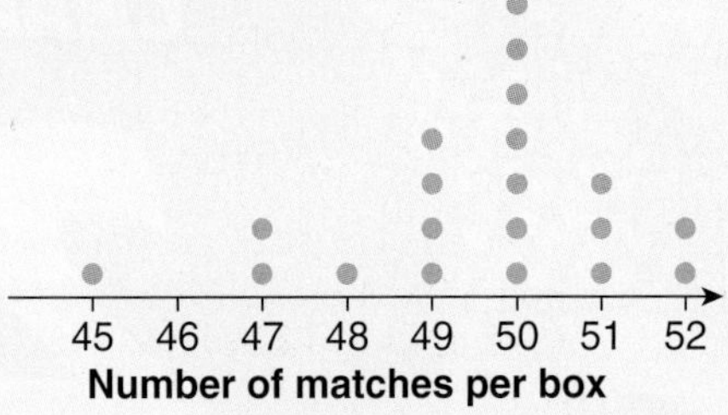

(a) What does each dot represent?
(b) How many boxes of matches were sampled?
(c) How many boxes had 50 matches?
(d) How many boxes had 47 matches or more?
(e) What was the greatest number of matches in a box?
(f) What was the least amount of matches in a box?

2. Examine the following results of a survey on favourite fruits and answer the questions:

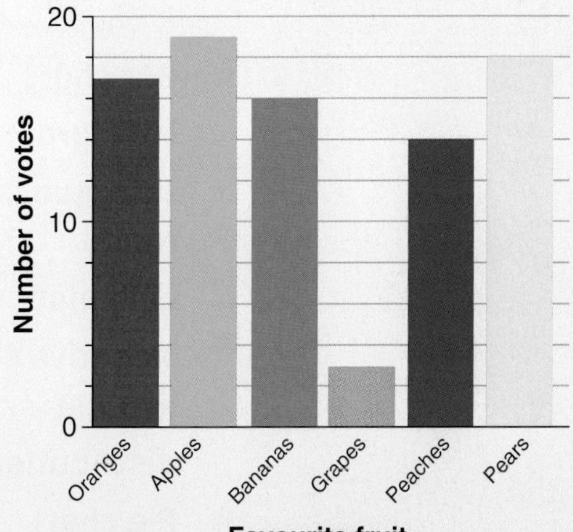

(a) What do you call this type of diagram?
(b) What type of data is represented in the diagram?
(c) List the ways this diagram differs from a line plot.
(d) What type of fruit is the most popular? Explain clearly how you calculated your answer.
(e) What is the second most popular fruit?

3. The following pie chart shows the number of students in a school who own a PlayStation, an Xbox or a Wii.

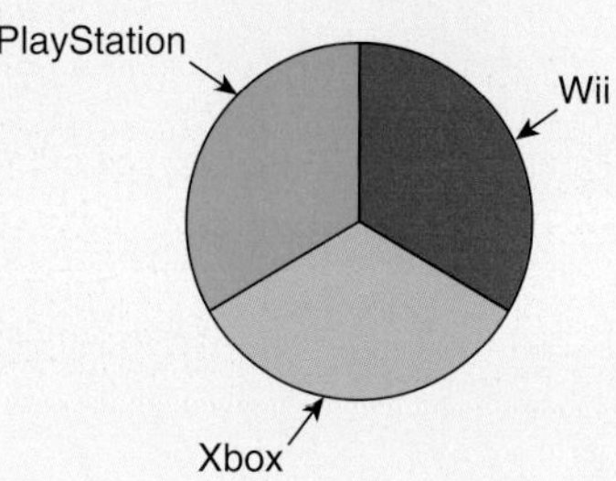

(a) How many different angles are there in this diagram? Name each type of angle.
(b) What instrument do you need to measure the size of the angles in the diagram?
(c) Measure the angles for each sector and complete the table below:

Games console	Angles in degrees
Xbox	
PlayStation	
Wii	

(d) What do all the angles add up to?
(e) If 1° represents one person, how many people in total took part in the survey?

4. A teacher records the mark each student scored out of a maximum of 20 in a test. The results are shown below.

13	17	11	8	13	12	17	18	18	14
11	10	11	17	14	6	9	8	12	11
11	11	13	14	10	7	11	20	15	11

(a) Draw a stem and leaf plot to display the data.

(b) What was the highest mark in the test?

(c) What was the lowest mark in the test?

(d) What mark occurred most frequently?

(e) What was the range of marks for the test?

5. Thirty people were asked which flavour of crisp they most preferred. Examine the results below and then enter the data in the table:

Salt & Vinegar, Cheese & Onion, Smoky Bacon, Cheese & Onion, Cheese & Onion, Smoky Bacon, Cheese & Onion, Cheese & Onion, Cheese & Onion, Cheese & Onion, Smoky Bacon, Cheese & Onion, Salt and Vinegar, Cheese & Onion, Cheese & Onion, Salt and Vinegar, Salt and Vinegar, Smoky Bacon, Prawn Cocktail, Prawn Cocktail, Smoky Bacon, Cheese & Onion, Cheese & Onion, Salt and Vinegar, Salt and Vinegar, Prawn Cocktail, Cheese & Onion, Smoky Bacon, Smoky Bacon, Prawn Cocktail.

Flavour	Tally	No. of people
Salt & Vinegar		
Prawn Cocktail		
Cheese & Onion		
Smoky Bacon		

(a) Which flavour was the least popular among the 30 people surveyed?

(b) Which was the modal flavour?

(c) Draw a bar chart to display this information.

(d) Draw a line plot to display this information.

(e) Can a stem and leaf plot be used to display this information? Explain your answer.

Section 21.1: Line plots

Student Activity 21A

Sinéad records the number of hours she studies each day for one week as follows:

Monday	Tuesday	Wednesday	Thursday	Friday	Saturday	Sunday
4	3	4	3	2	8	6

She records these figures on a line plot:

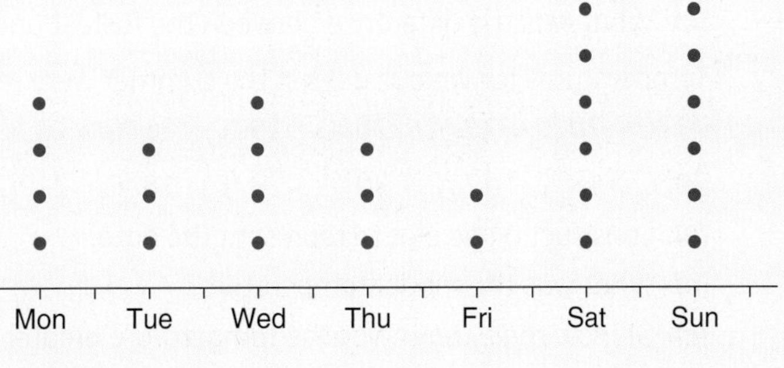

(a) Examine the line plot and discuss how Sinéad drew the plot.

(b) On which day was the most amount of study done?

(c) On which day was the least amount of study done?

(d) On which days were equal amounts of study done?

(e) How many hours of study were completed in the week?

(f) Calculate the mean amount of study hours per day.

LINE PLOTS EXPLAINED

In *Maths in Action 1*, you learned that a line plot or a dot plot is a way of representing data visually. A line plot consists of a series of columns of dots. No key is needed for a line plot. Line plots are very useful for displaying small amounts of data as it is collected. It is a very quick and simple way to organise data. Line plots can display numerical discrete data or categorical data only.

EXAMPLE 1

A student carried out an investigation to determine the number of people in each car passing through the school gate in a 15-minute interval. He recorded the following results:

1	2	4	1	1	1	2	1	2	2	1
4	1	3	3	4	2	1	2	1	1	2
3	1	2	2	3	1	1	3	3	2	1

(a) Construct a suitable line plot to display the data.

(b) What was the modal number of people per car?

(c) How many cars contained 3 or more people?

(d) What was the total number of cars that passed through the school gate?

Solution

(a)

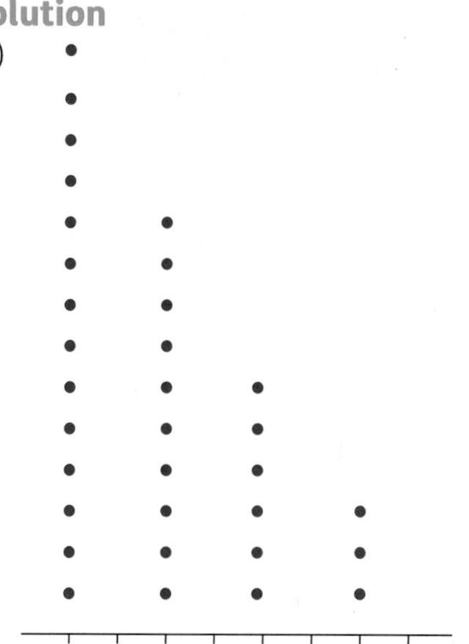

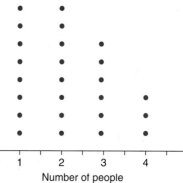

(b) The modal number of people per car is 1 person.

(c) $6 + 3 = 9$ cars contained three or more people.

(d) $14 + 10 + 6 + 3 = 33$ cars passed through the school gate.

Exercise 21.1

1. The following table shows the length of time, in minutes, it took 15 students to finish a race:
   12, 13, 12, 14, 15, 11, 12, 12, 14, 12, 10, 11, 13, 14, 15.
   (a) Display the data on a line plot.
   (b) Is the data numerical or categorical data?
   (c) What was the difference between the fastest and slowest times?
2. Temperatures for various days in the summer were recorded as follows:
   23 °C, 20 °C, 18 °C, 20 °C, 19 °C, 21 °C, 23 °C,
   20 °C, 18 °C, 17 °C, 20 °C, 23 °C, 18 °C, 21 °C, 23 °C.
   (a) Construct a line plot to represent the data.
   (b) What was the modal temperature?
   (c) On how many days was the temperature greater than 20 °C?
   (d) Write as a fraction the number of days with temperatures less than 21 °C.
   (e) What was the mean temperature?
   (f) What is the range in temperatures?

3. A number of students were asked to name their favourite sport. The results were recorded as follows:

Rugby	Soccer	Football	Hurling	Camogie
Hurling	Camogie	Soccer	Golf	Soccer
Football	Hurling	Football	Golf	Hurling
Rugby	Football	Camogie	Hurling	Camogie

(a) How many students were surveyed?

(b) Draw a line plot to display the data.

(c) What was the modal sport?

Section 21.2: Bar charts

Student Activity 21B

1. The chart below shows a group of students' favourite type of movie. Examine the chart and answer the following questions:

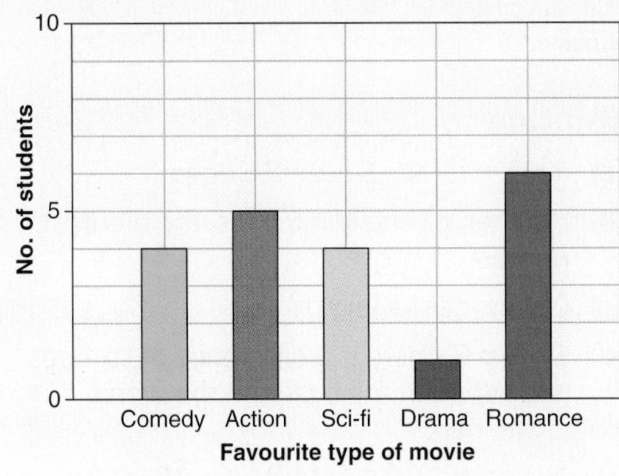

(a) What is the name for this type of chart?

(b) Which type of movie is most popular?

(c) Which type of movie is the second most popular?

(d) Which type of movie is the least popular?

(e) How many students were surveyed?

(f) What fraction of the entire class preferred comedies?

(g) What percentage of the students chose action movies?

2. The following table shows the favourite make of car of 20 people:

Car	Toyota	Ford	Nissan	Honda	Skoda
Frequency	9	3	4	2	2

(a) Draw a bar chart to represent the data.

(b) Write a brief summary of your findings.

BAR CHARTS EXPLAINED

Bar charts are one of the most popular ways of presenting data because we can see the information by looking at the heights of the bars. A bar chart is very similar to a line plot but it uses columns instead of dots.

To draw a bar chart, put one element of the information on the horizontal axis and the other on the vertical axis. Bar charts can be either vertical or horizontal. A different bar is drawn for each category or quantity. The length or height of each bar shows the frequency of each category or quantity. It is important to note that each bar should be of equal width.

Bar charts are used to display categorical and numerical discrete data. The bars in a bar chart are usually separated by a space but they do not have to be.

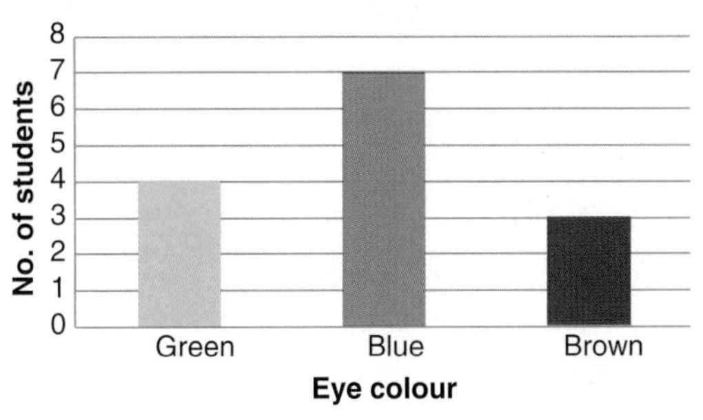

Some bar charts do not have spaces between the bars as shown here.

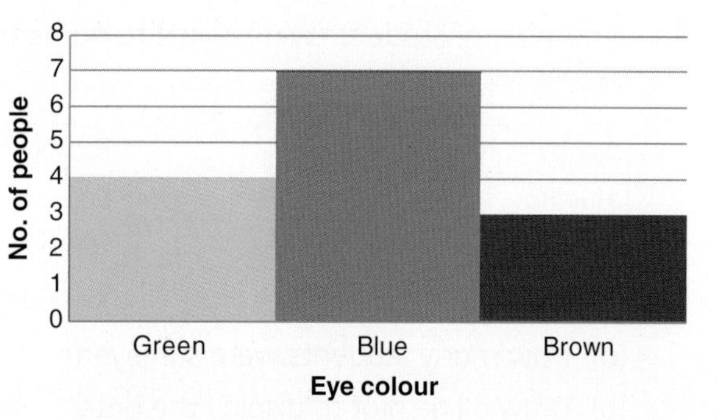

EXAMPLE 2

The bar chart shows the number of eggs which were laid in one week by six different hens.

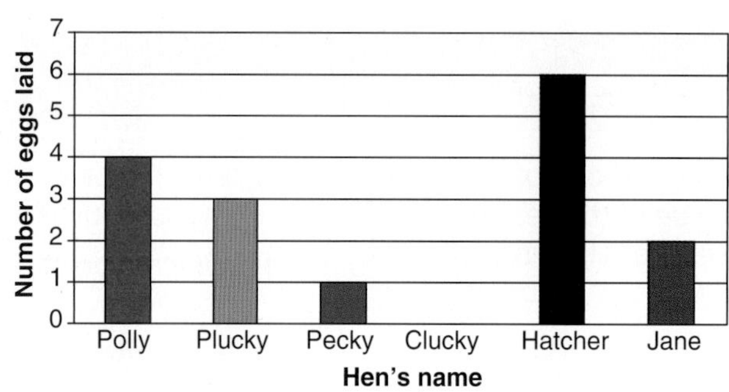

(a) What was the total number of eggs laid in the week?

(b) Which hen do you think is the most valuable? Explain your answer.

(c) Which hen do you think is the least valuable? Explain your answer.

(d) What is the range of eggs laid?

(e) What is the mean number of eggs laid per day?

Solution

(a) $4 + 3 + 1 + 0 + 6 + 2 = 16$ eggs

(b) Hatcher, as she laid 6 eggs, the greatest number of eggs.

(c) Clucky, as she laid 0 eggs.

(d) $6 - 0 = 6$. There is a difference of six eggs laid between the best and the worst laying hen.

(e) Mean $= \frac{4 + 3 + 1 + 0 + 6 + 2}{6} = \frac{16}{6} = 2.67$ eggs

Exercise 21.2

1. After sitting her pre-Junior Certificate exams, Emily wanted to compare all her results using a bar chart. Study the chart and answer the questions which follow:

(a) Which do you think is Emily's best subject?

(b) Which is Emily's worst subject?

(c) In how many subjects did Emily score more than 60%?

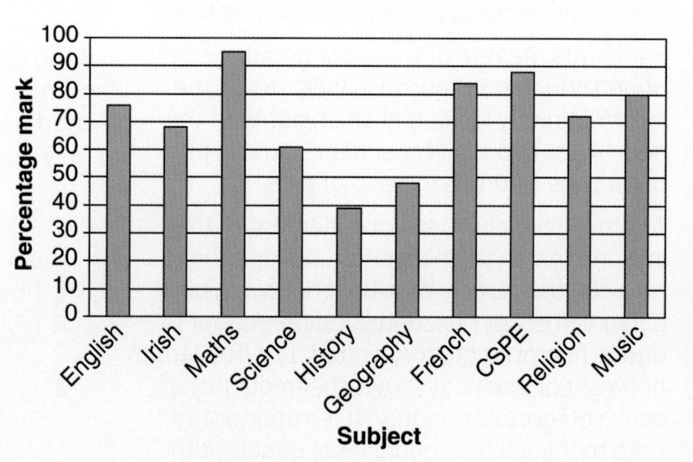

2. The table shows the recorded score on a die after it was rolled several times:

Score	1	2	3	4	5	6
Frequency	2	12	9	3	6	9

(a) Draw a bar chart to represent this data.
(b) What number is the modal score?
(c) What number appeared the least amount of times?
(d) How many times was the die thrown?

3. Twenty people were asked to name their favourite sport. The results were as follows:
Table tennis, Snooker, Rugby, Swimming, Table tennis, Swimming, Rugby, Snooker, Snooker, Rugby, Table tennis, Rugby, Snooker, Snooker, Rugby, Snooker, Snooker, Swimming, Rugby, Snooker.
(a) Draw a bar chart to display the data.
(b) What is the most popular sport?
(c) What is the least popular sport?

4. A number of students were asked to choose their favourite science subject. The results are recorded as follows:

Biology	Chemistry	Physics	Biology	Physics	Physics	Physics	Biology
Chemistry	Biology	Physics	Chemistry	Biology	Chemistry	Biology	Biology

(a) Construct a frequency table showing the above information.
(b) Draw a bar chart to represent the data.
(c) What is the modal subject?

Section 21.3: Pie charts

Student Activity 21C

1. The following pie chart shows the country a certain number of students in a school would most like to visit.

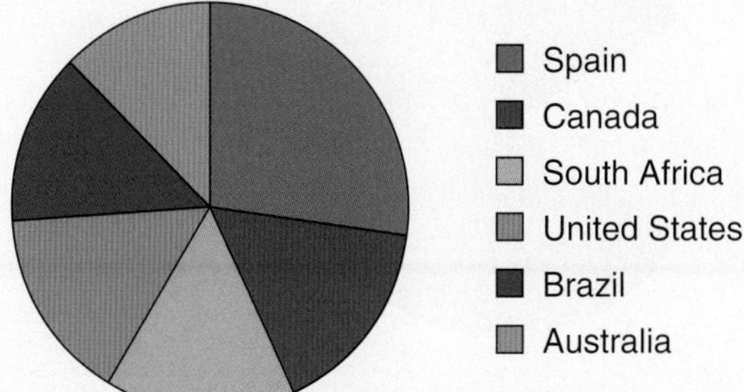

(a) How many different angles are there in this diagram?
(b) Using your protractor, measure the angles for each sector. Write the angles in your copy and beside each angle state what country it represents.
(c) What do all the angles add up to?
(d) If 2° were used to represent each person in the survey, how many would like to visit each country?
(e) How many in total took part in this survey?

2. A survey was carried out to determine which TV channel students preferred. The results are shown in the following table:

Channel	No. of students	Angle
MTV	4	
RTÉ Two	28	
Sky One	10	40°
Setanta		72°
BBC1		120°

(a) Copy and complete the table.
(b) Draw a pie chart to display the information.

PIE CHARTS EXPLAINED

In *Maths in Action 1*, you learned how to measure the angles in a pie chart and how to interpret a pie chart. You learned that a pie chart is a whole circle divided up into **sectors.** The area of each sector is proportional to the frequency. The largest sector represents the mode. Pie charts can display categorical and numerical discrete data.

In *Maths in Action 1*, you learned how to draw a pie chart given some data.

Drawing a pie chart

- **Step 1:** Calculate the size of each sector in the circle in degrees.
- **Step 2:** Mark a centre point on the page of your exercise copy. Using a compass, draw a large circle. Finally draw a line from the centre point of your circle to the edge of the circle (a radius).
- **Step 3:** Use your protractor to mark in the angles for each sector.
- **Step 4:** Label your pie chart.

Or alternatively, to find the angle of any sector, use:

$$\frac{\text{The number in the sector}}{\text{The total in the survey}} \times 360°$$

EXAMPLE 3

John kept a record of his free time over a week and how he used it. He recorded the following information:

- Hurling: 3 hours
- Studying: 9 hours
- Swimming: 1 hour
- Watching TV: 2 hours
- Xbox: 3 hours

Draw a pie chart to represent this information.

Solution

$3 + 9 + 1 + 2 + 3 = 18$ hrs

$360° \div 18 = 20°$

This means we will use 20° for each hour in the pie chart.

- Hurling: $3 \times 20 = 60°$
- Studying: $9 \times 20 = 180°$
- Swimming: $1 \times 20 = 20°$
- Watching TV: $2 \times 20 = 40°$
- Xbox: $3 \times 20 = 60°$

Check these angles all add up to 360° to verify the calculations are correct. Use a protractor, compass and a straight edge to draw the relevant pie chart.

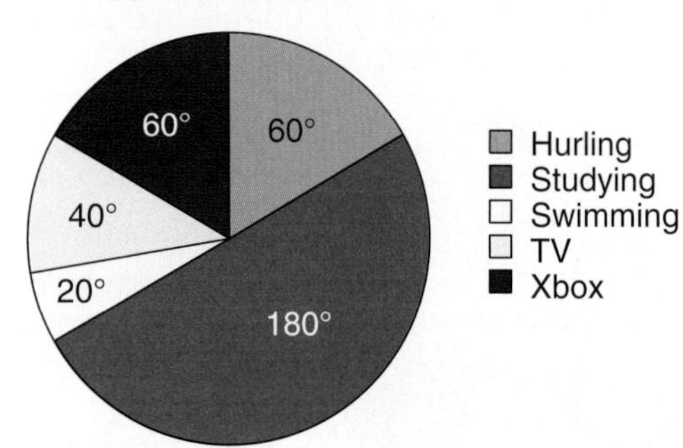

Exercise 21.3

1. If you wanted to draw a pie chart to represent the following numbers of people, how many degrees would each person be? Explain how you arrived at your answers.

(a) 360 (b) 180 (c) 90 (d) 36 (e) 45 (f) 60 (g) 20 (h) 30 (i) 720 (j) 24

2. The following pie chart shows the ingredients needed to bake a cake weighing 720 g. The degree measure of each ingredient is shown in the pie chart.

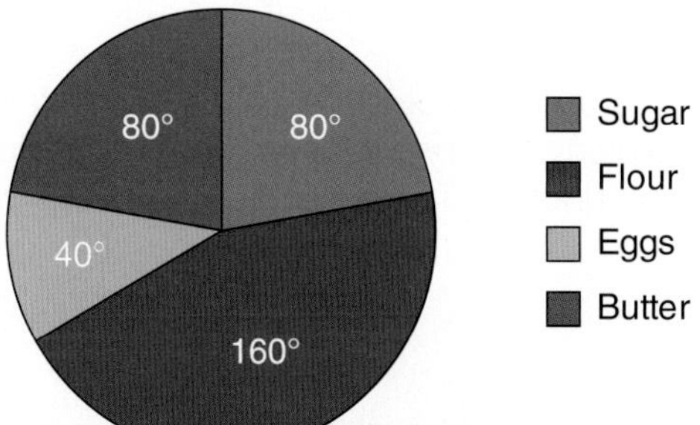

Use the pie chart to calculate the weight of each ingredient. Copy and complete the following table.

Ingredient	Weight (g)
Sugar	
Flour	
Butter	
Eggs	

3. This pie chart shows the causes of road accidents in a county in a certain year. Study the pie chart and answer the questions that follow:

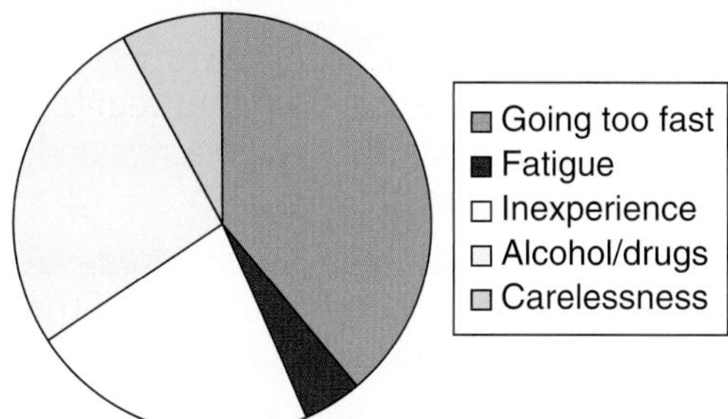

(a) Using your protractor, measure the angles for each sector and make a list of the angles and the causes they represent.

(b) What was the most common cause of accidents in that county for that particular year?

(c) What was the second most common cause of accidents in that county?

(d) If there were 90 accidents in the county in that year, can you calculate how many accidents were caused by each of the listed causes?

4. The following pie chart shows the amount of electricity used in US households in 2001. Study the pie chart and answer the questions that follow:

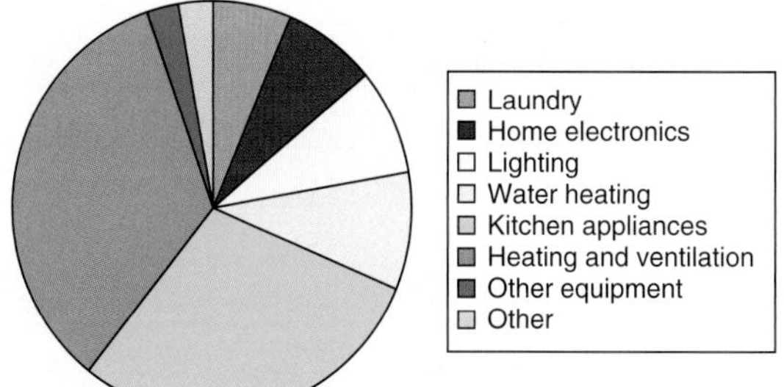

(a) What activity uses the most electricity in US households?

(b) What activity uses the second-greatest amount of electricity in US households?

(c) What activity uses the least amount of electricity in US households?

(d) In what way do you think the pie chart for Irish households might be different from the one for US households? Explain your answer.

5. A survey was conducted in a capital city to discover how most office workers commuted into the city each day. The table shows how the commuters responded.

Method	No. of people
Walk	9
Car	6
Bus	14
Train	10
Tram	13
Cycle	8

(a) How many people were surveyed?

(b) Draw a suitable pie chart to represent this data.

(c) What was the modal type of transport?

(d) In a short paragraph, explain the results of your findings.

6. In Clare last year, there were 4,000 small cars, 3,000 medium cars and 1,000 large cars sold. Illustrate this information on a pie chart.

7. Tom did a survey in his school car park. He noted the colour of all the cars in the park. Copy and complete the table for the number of cars and the angle they would represent on a pie chart.

Colour of car	No. of cars	Angle
Black		18°
Blue	12	
Red	7	
Gold	9	
Green	10	90°

(a) What is the modal colour in this survey?

(b) What colour of car is the least popular?

(c) How many cars were involved in this survey?

(d) Draw a pie chart to display the information.

(e) In a short paragraph, explain the results of Tom's findings.

8. In a survey, 20 second year students were asked what their favourite food was. The results are shown in the following table:

Meal	No. of students	Angle
Pizza	7	
Chicken and chips	4	
Steak	5	
Curry	3	
Undecided	1	
		360°

(a) Copy and complete the table.

(b) Show how you calculated each angle.

(c) Draw a pie chart to represent this information.

9. Draw a pie chart to indicate how a lottery prize could be divided in the ratio 3:2:1.

10. A group of people were surveyed to find out which province each came from. The pie chart represents the results of that survey.

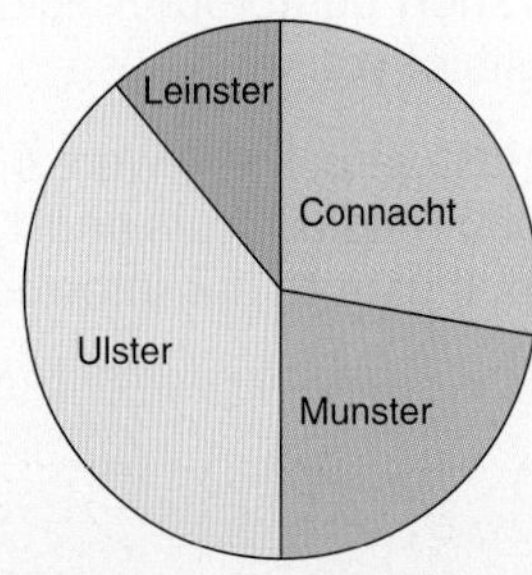

(a) What is the measure of the angle for Leinster?

(b) 35 people said they came from Connacht. How many people in total were in the group that was surveyed?

(c) How many people gave Ulster as their reply?

(d) What is the mode?

(e) How many people gave Munster as their reply?

(f) How many people gave Leinster as their reply?

11. A group of people were surveyed to find which country was their preferred holiday destination. The pie chart represents the results of that survey.

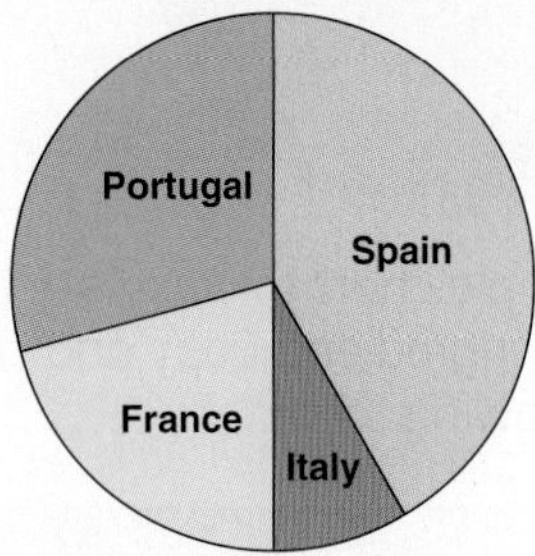

(a) What is the measure of the angle for Portugal?

(b) Ten people replied that Italy was their favourite holiday destination. How many people were surveyed in total?

How many people gave:

(c) Spain as their reply?

(d) Portugal as their reply?

(e) France as their reply?

(f) What is the modal country?

12. During a particular month, a family spent €66 on meat, €23 on fruit and vegetables, €9 on soft drinks, €12 on toiletries and €10 on DVD rentals.

(a) Calculate, to the nearest degree, the angle corresponding to each of the above classifications.

(b) Represent this data on a pie chart.

(c) The following month, the family spent 20% more on each item of shopping. If the information was represented on a new pie chart, would it differ from the original pie chart? Explain your answer fully.

13. Using your CensusAtSchool data for your class, draw pie charts to represent the following pieces of data:

(a) Which would you prefer to be?

Rich, Happy, Famous, Healthy

(b) What superpowers would you most like to have?

(c) What mobile phone network are you on?

(d) Do you believe you have too many exams in school?

14. In a US survey, 1,000 people were asked to name their favourite hero. The results are shown in the pie chart below:

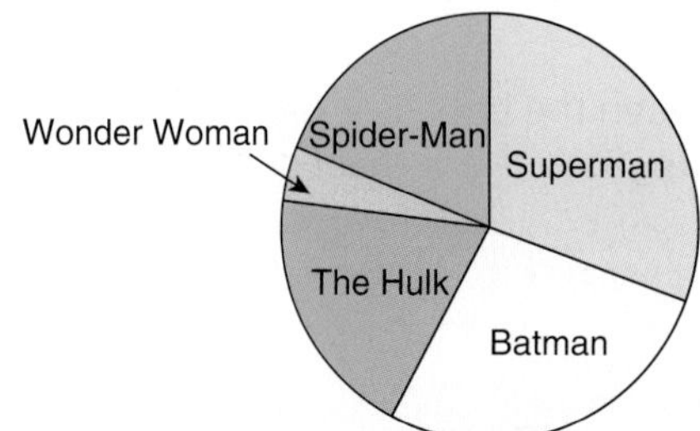

Later in Ireland, when 120 people were asked the same question, the results were as follows:

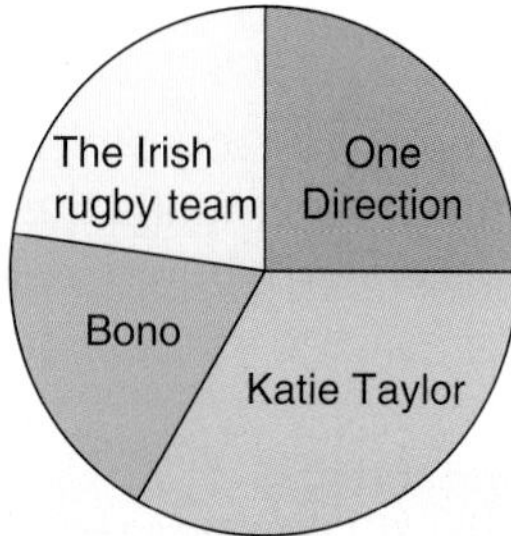

Looking at both pie charts, the surveyor concluded, 'The same number of people liked Spider-Man as Bono'. Is this correct? Explain your answer.

Section 21.4: Histograms

Student Activity 21D

A survey is carried out to find the ages of the residents of a small housing estate. The results are recorded as follows.

45	43	13	3	1	6	35	37	50	56
70	3	29	26	2	41	46	35	12	13
9	28	35	41	23	17	15	12	5	7
2	29	36	68	21	33	14	29	33	45

(a) Copy and complete the following grouped frequency table.

Age	0–10	10–20	20–30	30–40	40–50	50–60	60–70	70–80
No. of people								

(Note: 10–20 means 10 years or more but less than 20 years.)

(b) What is the modal age group?

(c) Is this data discrete or continuous? Explain your answer.

(d) Eamonn and Gráinne decide to draw a chart to display the data. Their charts are shown below.

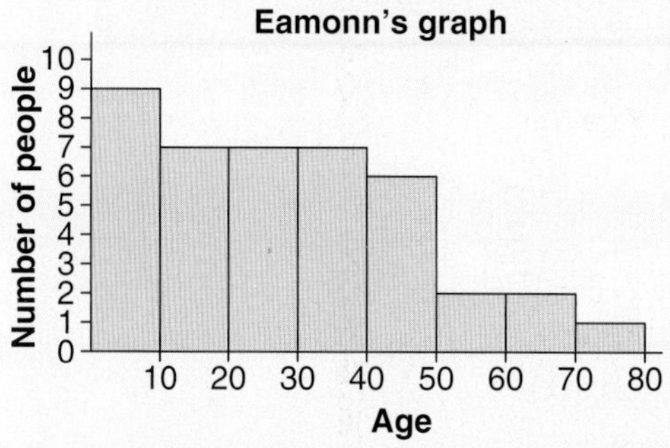

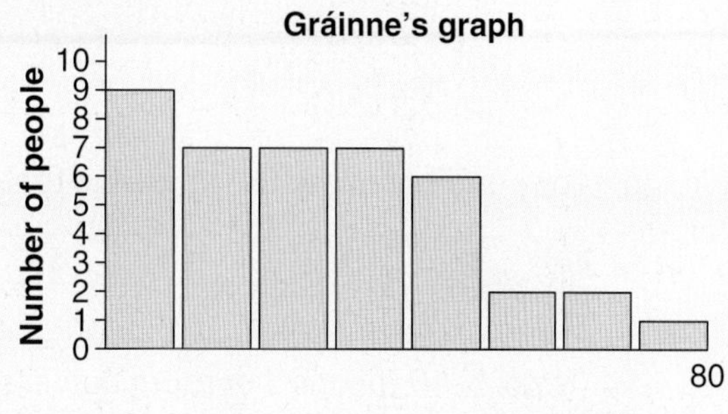

Their teacher states that one of the graphs is incorrect. Which graph do you think is incorrect? Explain your answer fully. (Hint: think about the type of data represented.)

HISTOGRAMS EXPLAINED

In *Maths in Action 1*, you learned how to draw and read data from bar charts. You will now learn another type of chart that is used to represent **continuous data.** This type of chart is called a **histogram.**

Unlike a bar chart, a histogram cannot have gaps in between the bars as it represents **continuous data.** This means there is no break in the data. Both the vertical and horizontal axes should be labelled and drawn to scale.

EXAMPLE 4

The distance a taxi driver travelled on a number of calls was recorded in the following grouped frequency table:

No. of kilometres	0–5	5–10	10–15	15–20
No. of journeys	6	13	7	4

(Note: 5–10 means 5 km or more but less than 10 km.)

(a) How many fares did the taxi driver collect?

(b) What was the modal distance travelled?

(c) Draw a histogram to display the information.

Solution

(a) 6 + 13 + 7 + 4 = 30 fares

(b) 5 − 10 km

(c)

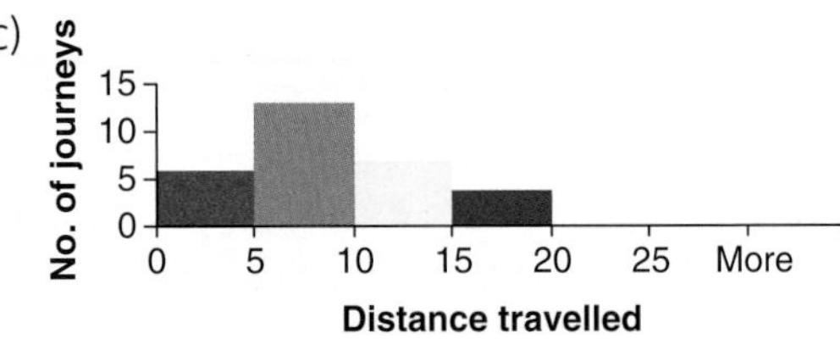

Exercise 21.4

1. The following histogram shows the ages of members of a club:

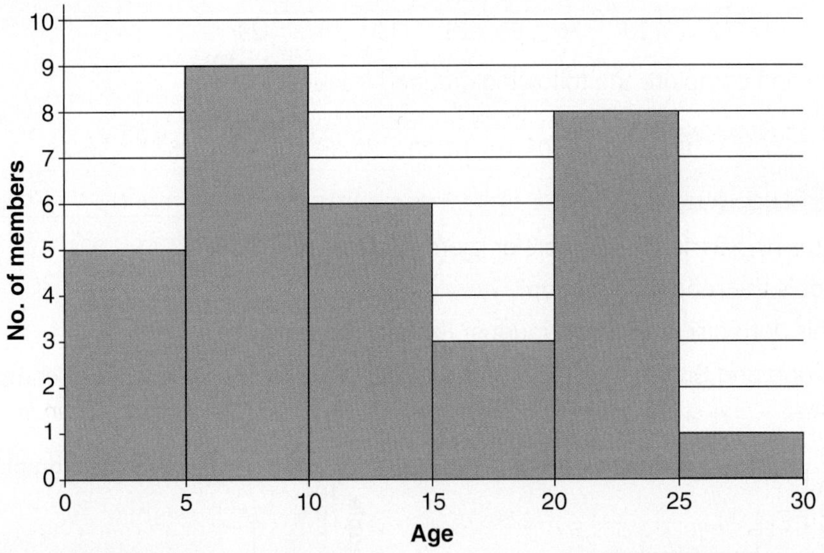

(a) Copy and complete the following table.

Age	0–5	5–10	10–15	15–20	20–25	25–30
No. of members						

(Note: 5–10 means 5 or more but less than 10.)

(b) How many people took part in the survey?

(c) What was the modal age group in this survey?

(d) In which interval does the median person lie?

(e) Calculate the mean age of the club members, correct to the nearest year.

2. The following histogram shows the time in hours spent studying by a number of students over a weekend:

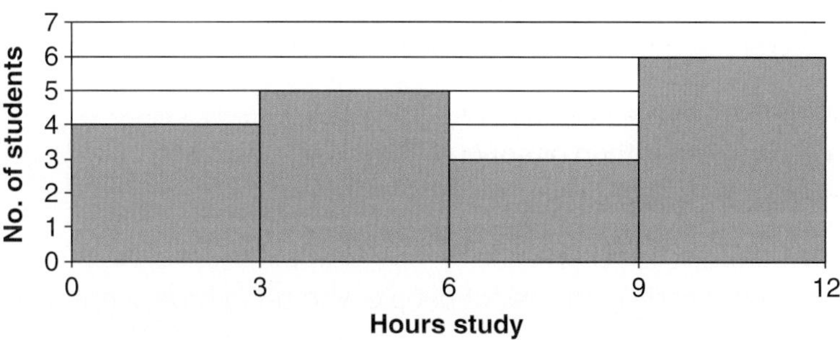

(a) Copy and complete the following table.

Hours' study	0–3	3–6	6–9	9–12
No. of pupils				

(Note: 3–6 means greater than or equal to 3 hours but less than 6 hours.)

(b) How many pupils were in the class?

(c) What percentage of students spent between 3 and 6 hours studying, correct to the nearest whole number?

(d) What was the maximum number of people who could have spent at least 7 hours studying?

(e) What was the minimum number of people who could have spent at least 7 hours studying?

3. The following histogram shows the time taken for 30 customers to be served at a supermarket checkout:

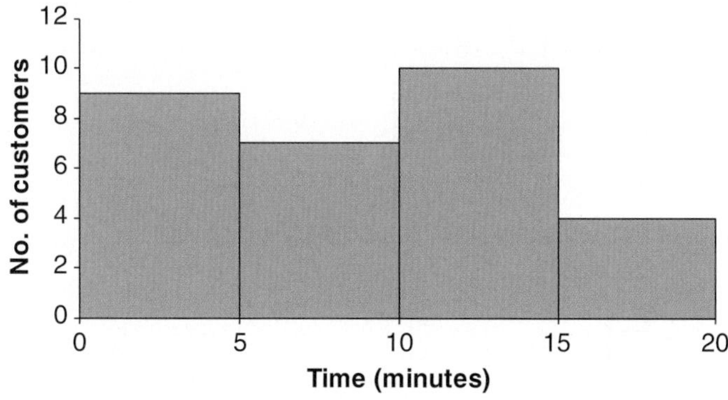

(a) Copy and complete the following grouped frequency table:

Time (minutes)	0–5	5–10	10–15	15–20
No. of customers				

(Note: 5–10 means greater than or equal to 5 mins but less than 10 mins.)

(b) What percentage of customers was served in less than 10 minutes, correct to one decimal place?

(c) In which interval does the median person lie?

(d) Calculate the mean time it takes to be served?

4. The amount of money spent by 50 shoppers in one shop on a Saturday afternoon was recorded as follows:

Amount spent (€)	0–10	10–20	20–30	30–40	40–50
No. of shoppers	8	12	10	9	11

(Note: 0–10 means greater than or equal to €0 but less than €10.)

(a) Draw a histogram to represent the data.

(b) What is the least possible number of people who could have spent less than €35?

(c) What is the greatest possible number of people who could have spent more than €35?

5. Twenty-five students were asked how many minutes they spent online on a particular day. The results were recorded in the following grouped frequency table:

Time (minutes)	0–20	20–40	40–60	60–80
No. of students	4	9	7	5

(Note: 0–20 means greater than or equal to 0 mins but less than 20 mins.)

(a) Draw a histogram to represent this data.

(b) What percentage of students spent no more than one hour online?

(c) What is the least possible number of people who could have spent no more than 30 minutes online?

(d) What is the greatest possible number of people who could have spent more than 43 minutes online?

6. The following table shows the amount of time 25 students spent playing sport on a Saturday:

Time (minutes)	0–20	20–40	40–60	60–80	80–100	100–120
No. of students	1	8	6	3	2	5

(Note: 20–40 means greater than or equal to 20 mins but less than 40 mins.)

(a) Draw a histogram to represent the data.

(b) What is the least possible number of pupils who could have spent no more than 45 minutes playing sport?

(c) What percentage of students spent 60 minutes or more playing sport?

7. The heights of 40 rose bushes in cm was recorded as follows:

9	14	13	16	21	26	15	8
16	13	15	9	23	19	17	19
31	14	13	8	15	17	19	21
21	23	18	19	16	10	12	16

(a) Copy and complete the following grouped frequency table:

Height (cm)	0–10	10–20	20–30	30–40
Number of bushes				

(Note: 0–10 means greater than or equal to 0 cm but less than 10 cm.)

(b) Draw a histogram to display the information.

(c) Calculate the mean height of the bushes.

8. Thirty students were asked how long in minutes it takes to travel to school each morning. They recorded their results as follows:

7	18	29	40	8	32
28	33	4	2	18	15
14	13	21	25	35	21
27	29	14	9	8	21
21	18	13	11	3	21

(a) Draw a histogram to display the results.

(b) Calculate the mean time to travel to school.

9. Twenty-five students were asked to stand on one leg for as long as possible. Their times in seconds are shown below:

45	79	41	56	112
47	69	78	110	97
85	47	76	111	85
34	45	78	97	34
76	89	95	98	120

(a) Draw a histogram to display the results.

(b) Calculate the mean time achieved.

10. The following frequency table shows the times in minutes a number of students took to solve a puzzle:

Time (min)	0–4	4–8	8–12	12–16	16–20
No. of students	2	5	8	4	3

(Note: 4–8 means greater than or equal to 4 mins but less than 8 mins.)

(a) Draw a histogram to display the results.

(b) Calculate the mean time to complete the puzzle, correct to one decimal place.

(c) What was the modal time for completing the puzzle?

11. A car park opens at 07:30. The number of cars entering the car park during 15-minute intervals on a particular morning is recorded in the following table:

Time	07:30–07:45	07:45–08:00	08:00–08:15	08:15–08:30	08:30–08:45	08:45–09:00
Number of cars	20	40	100	165	105	50

(Note: 07:30–07:45 means 07:30 or later, but before 07:45.)

(a) How many cars entered the car park between 07:45 and 08:30?

(b) What was the maximum number of cars that could have entered the car park by 08:20?

(c) Draw a histogram to represent the data.

(d) Write a short report, summarising your findings. (Hint: refer to the different measures of central tendency and spread.)

12. The following table shows the time in minutes spent by customers in a cafeteria:

Time in mins	0–10	10–20	20–30	30–40
No. of customers	80	100	160	60

(Note: 10–20 means at least 10 mins but less than 20 mins.)

(a) Calculate the total number of customers.

(b) Draw a histogram to represent the data.

(c) By taking the data at the mid-interval values, calculate the mean number of minutes per customer.

(d) What is the greatest number of customers who could have spent more than 25 minutes in the cafeteria?

(e) What is the least number of customers who could have spent more than 25 minutes in the cafeteria?

(f) Write a short report, summarising your findings. (Hint: refer to the different measures of central tendency and spread.)

Section 21.5: Back-to-back stem and leaf plots

Student Activity 21E

A study was carried out to examine whether boys or girls need more driving lessons before passing their driving test. A number of driving instructors were asked to keep a record of the number of lessons given to teenage boys and girls for a month. The following table shows the results of their findings:

(a) Draw an ordered stem and leaf plot for the boys.

(b) Draw an ordered stem and leaf plot for the girls.

(c) A student decides to try to make a single plot so that the boys and girls can be compared. Can you suggest any way this could be carried out?

No. of lessons for boys	No. of lessons for girls
5, 8, 12, 15, 9, 7, 10, 12, 22, 14, 16, 10, 7, 10, 12, 8, 9, 15.	12, 10, 7, 19, 18, 24, 28, 16, 15, 18, 16, 12, 12, 6, 8, 24, 30, 26.

BACK-TO-BACK STEM AND LEAF PLOTS EXPLAINED

In *Maths in Action 1,* you learned how to construct a stem and leaf plot for a data set. Stem and leaf plots are a very useful way of comparing two sets of numerical data.

When two sets of data are compared in this way, we use a **back-to-back stem and leaf plot.** A back-to-back stem and leaf plot allows us to quickly compare two sets of figures because it shows us all the numerical data on the same stem. To distinguish between the two sets of data, we put one set of leaves on the left and the other set of leaves on the right of the stem.

When drawing a stem and leaf plot or a back-to-back stem and leaf plot, always check the following three properties of the plot:

1. Does the plot have the correct number of entries?
2. Are the leaves ordered correctly?
3. Does the plot have a key?

EXAMPLE 5

A number of students were surveyed in order to establish whether girls or boys spend more time in a month listening to music. Each student was asked to record the number of hours per month they listened to music. The results were recorded in the following back-to-back stem and leaf plot:

Girls		Boys
5 4 4 2	0	1 2 3 3
7 5 1 1	1	1 1 3 5 6 7
8 8 7 5 3 3	2	5 5 6 7 9 9 9
6 6 6 3 2 2	3	3 4 4

Key: 2|3 = 23 hours

(a) How many girls listened to music for more than 15 hours?

(b) How many boys listened to music for more than 15 hours?

(c) What is total number of hours spent listening to music by all the girls?

(d) What is total number of hours spent listening to music by all the boys?

(e) What is the mean amount of time spent listening to music by the girls?

(f) What is the mean amount of time spent listening to music by the boys?

Solution

(a) 13 girls

(b) 12 boys

(c) Total time for girls = 2 + 4 + 4 + 5 + 11 + 11 + 15 + 17 + 23 + 23 + 25 + 27 + 28 + 28 + 32 + 32 + 33 + 36 + 36 + 36 = 428 hours

(d) Total time for boys = 1 + 2 + 3 + 3 + 11 + 11 + 13 + 15 + 16 + 17 + 25 + 25 + 26 + 27 + 29 + 29 + 29 + 33 + 34 + 34 = 383 hours

(e) Mean for girls = 428 ÷ 20 = 21.4 hours or 21 hours and 24 minutes

(f) Mean for boys = 383 ÷ 20 = 19.15 hours or 19 hours and 9 minutes

Exercise 21.5

1. Construct back-to-back stem and leaf plots to compare the following sets of data.
   (a) Group A: 27, 36, 45, 54, 63, 28, 44, 52, 37, 19, 12, 28
   Group B: 12, 22, 49, 24, 28, 17, 31, 33, 67, 52, 51, 58
   (b) Class A: 137, 171, 160, 145, 183, 139, 140, 152, 133, 147, 159, 155
   Class B: 131, 175, 190, 147, 175, 180, 144, 189, 159, 140, 153, 157
   (c) Team 1: 4.5, 9.2, 6.6, 5.7, 5.3, 7.1, 9.3, 8.5, 8.1, 4.8, 7.2, 8.1
   Team 2: 7.4, 9.5, 8.8, 5.9, 4.2, 9.6, 6.4, 5.0, 4.0, 8.9, 5.8, 6.0

2. A number of students were surveyed in order to establish if girls study more than boys. Each student was asked to record the number of hours per week they spent studying. The results were recorded in the following back-to-back stem and leaf plot:

Girls		Boys
5 3 1	0	2 2 3 4
6 3 2 1	1	1 1 4 5 6 7
9 9 8 8 5 4 4	2	5 5 6 7 9 9 9
4 4 4 3 2 1	3	3 4 4

Key: 2|5 = 25 hours

(a) How many girls were surveyed?

(b) How many boys were surveyed?

(c) How many girls studied for more than 20 hours?

(d) How many boys studied for more than 20 hours?

(e) Did more boys or girls study for at least 30 hours?

(f) What is the total number of hours spent studying by all of the girls?

(g) What is the total number of hours spent studying by all of the boys?

(h) What is the mean amount of time spent studying by the girls?

(i) What is the mean amount of time spent studying by the boys?

(j) On a visual examination of the stem and leaf plot, would you think the boys or girls studied more during the month? Explain your answer.

(k) Do your calculations of the mean support your answer? Explain your answer.

3. To determine if boys are taller than girls, a number of second year students had their heights recorded to the nearest cm. The results were recorded in the following back-to-back stem and leaf plot:

Girls		Boys
3 3 2 1	14	1
9 8 8 8 6 3 2 1	15	5 5 6
6 5 5 5 4 4	16	4 5 8 9
2 1	17	3 3 4 6 7 7 8 9 9
	18	4 4 7

Key: 14|1 = 141 cm

(a) How many girls were surveyed?

(b) How many boys were surveyed?

(c) On a visual examination of this plot, what conclusion can you draw about the heights of boys and girls?

(d) How many boys are over 170 cm in height?

(e) How many girls are over 170 cm in height?

(f) Calculate the mean height of the boys.

(g) Calculate the mean height of the girls.

(h) Do your calculations of the mean support your answer to part (c)? Explain your answer.

4. This table shows the average number of hours worked per week by full-time employees, by gender, in some countries in 1999.

Country	Hrs by males	Hrs by females
UK	45.2	40.7
Greece	41.7	39.3
Portugal	41.5	39.4
R. of Ireland	41.3	38.0
Spain	41.1	39.6
Germany	40.5	39.4
France	40.2	38.6
Italy	39.7	36.3

[Labour Force Surveys, Eurostat]

(a) Draw an ordered back-to-back stem and leaf diagram to compare the hours worked on average by males and by females. (Remember to only include the decimal point in your key.)

(b) Can you draw any conclusions from your plot?

5. A class of 20 second year students took an online test of 20 random general knowledge questions. They were disappointed with their scores so they retook the test the following week with 20 different general knowledge questions. Both sets of results are as follows:

1st test scores: 9, 13, 8, 10, 11, 6, 7, 12, 10, 11, 14, 12, 7, 9, 6, 14, 7, 9, 15, 4.

2nd test scores: 11, 14, 12, 17, 8, 9, 7, 10, 11, 15, 13, 20, 10, 16, 9, 15, 13, 9, 6, 15.

(a) Draw an ordered back-to-back stem and leaf plot to represent this information. (Hint: place the score for the first test on the left of the plot.)

(b) By examining the stem and leaf plot, do you think the class did better the first or the second time? Explain your answer.

(c) Calculate the mean mark of the class for both tests.

6. Áine claims that boys spend more time surfing the web each day than girls. She randomly selects 20 boys and 20 girls and asks each person how many minutes per day they spend online. She displays the results in the following back-to-back stem and leaf plot.

Girls		Boys
4 3 2	1	1 5
6 3 2 1	2	5 6 7
6 5 5 5 4 4 2 2	3	4 5 5 6 6 8 9
6 5 2 1	4	4 5 7 8 9 9
8	5	4 8
		Key: 4|5 = 45 mins

(a) Following a visual examination, what conclusion can you draw from the plot about the amount of time spent on the internet by boys and girls?

(b) How many boys spent more than 35 minutes on the internet?

(c) How many girls spent more than 35 minutes on the internet?

7. The following stem and leaf plot shows the number of text messages sent by a number of students over a three-day period:

Girls		Boys
8 7 7	1	3 4 5
9 7 7 7 2 2 1	2	2 2 2 5 6 7 7 8
6 6 6 6 4 4 4 3	3	4 4 4 4 7 7 8 9
5 5 4 3	4	4 5 7 8
1 1 1	5	2 4
		Key: 1|5 = 15 texts

(a) On visual examination, do you think the boys or girls sent more text messages?

(b) How many girls sent more that 30 text messages?

(c) How many boys sent more that 30 text messages?

(d) Calculate the mean number of text messages sent by the boys, correct to the nearest whole number.

(e) Calculate the mean number of text messages sent by the girls, correct to the nearest whole number.

(f) Do the calculations for the mean number of texts for both boys and girls support your answer in part (a)? Explain your answer.

8. The length of time taken (in seconds) by a group of students to complete a short obstacle course was recorded in the following back-to-back stem and leaf plot.

Girls		Boys
9 3 3 2 1	14	1 2 2
8 8 8 6 3 2 1	15	0 0 0 1 5 5 6
6 5 5 5 4 4	16	4 5 8 8 8 8 9
7 6 5 2 1	17	3 4 6 7 7 7 8 9
7 7 3 3 3 1 1	18	0 1 4 4 7
		Key: 14|1 = 141 seconds

(a) How many boys and girls completed the obstacle course?

(b) Calculate the mean time for the boys to complete the course, correct to the nearest whole second.

(c) Calculate the mean time for the girls to complete the course, correct to the nearest whole second.

(d) What was the median time for the (i) boys and (ii) girls?

9. The following stem and leaf plot shows the distance in kilometres town and country students live from their local school:

Town school		Country school
3 3 3 2 2 2 1 1 1	0	1 1 3 4
9 9 9 8 8 8 7 7 6 6 5 5 5 5 5	0	5 7 7
4 4 4 4 3 3	1	1 1 1 2 2 2 2 2 2 2 2 3 3 3 3 4 4
6 6 6 6 5 5	1	7 7 8 9
3 2 2 1	2	2 2 2 2 3 3 3 3 4
		5 7 8
		Key: 1|2 = 12 km

(a) What is the modal distance for students in the town school?

(b) What is the modal distance for students in the country school?

(c) By examining the stem and leaf diagram, what conclusion can you reach about the distance students live from their respective schools?

(d) Calculate the mean distance the students live from the country school.

(e) Calculate the mean distance the students live from the town school.

10. A number of teenagers were asked to record the number of albums they owned. The results were as follows:

Boys	Girls
12, 8, 22, 14, 20, 6, 13, 21, 30, 10, 9, 13, 14, 10, 15, 10, 17, 5, 14, 7	19, 14, 11, 16, 8, 12, 9, 15, 14, 14 16, 15, 15, 14, 14, 12, 10, 10, 11, 11

(a) Draw a back-to-back stem and leaf plot to display the information.

(b) What was the modal number of albums owned by the (i) girls and (ii) boys?

(c) What was the median number of albums owned by the (i) girls and (ii) boys?

(d) Calculate the mean number of albums owned by the (i) girls and (ii) boys.

(e) What was the range of albums owned by the (i) girls and (ii) boys?

11. The length of time in minutes a number of teenagers spend on a social networking site each day was recorded as follows:

Girls		Boys
9 9 8 5 5 5 4 3 2	1	0 0 5 5 6 6 6 9
7 6 5 5 5 3 1 1 0 0 0 0 0	2	2 2 2 4 4 6 8 9
8 8 7 7 6 5 3 3 2 2	3	0 0 0 0 5 5 5 7 8 8 8 9 9
9 5 5 5 5 5 5 5 0 0	4	4 4 4 4 4 4 4 6 8 8 9
5 5 5 0 0 0 0 0	5	3 3 6 7 7 7 8 8 8 9

Key: 1|5 = 15 mins

(a) By inspecting the stem and leaf, do you think that the boys or the girls spend more time on the social networking site? Explain your answer.

(b) Calculate the mean length of time spent on the sites by (i) the boys and (ii) the girls.

(c) What was the modal time for (i) the boys and (ii) the girls?

(d) What was the median time for (i) the boys and (ii) the girls?

(e) Write a brief report commenting on your findings.

Section 21.6: The median, mode, quartiles and interquartile range of a stem and leaf plot

Student Activity 21F

A delicatessen owner records the amount of money (€) that a number of customers spent during lunchtime. The stem and leaf plot shows the data:

Tens	Units
0	1 2 4
0	5 6 6 8 9
1	1 1 2 2 2 3 4 4
1	5 5 6 7 8 8
2	2 3 3 4
2	5 5 8
3	2

Key: 2|2 = €22

(a) What was the least amount of money spent?

(b) What was the most amount of money spent?

(c) What was the range of spending?

(d) How many customers entered the shop?

(e) What was the most common amount of money spent?

(f) Explain how we might calculate the median of a set of data.

(g) What is the median amount of money spent by the customers?

THE MEDIAN, MODE, QUARTILES AND INTERQUARTILE RANGE OF A STEM AND LEAF PLOT EXPLAINED

In Chapter 6, you learned how to calculate the mean, median and mode for a set of numbers. In this section, you will learn how to identify the mean, median and the mode on a stem and leaf plot.

You will also learn to calculate the **interquartile range** by finding the **lower quartile** and the **upper quartile.** From their names, you may have guessed that **quartiles** are based on **quarters.** In order to find the quartiles, we must first rank the data in ascending order.

- The lower quartile (Q_1) is the value that is one-quarter of the way along the distribution. This quarter mark is the halfway piece of data between the start to the median on a stem and leaf plot.
- The upper quartile (Q_3) is the value that is three-quarters of the way along the distribution. This three-quarter mark is the halfway piece of data between the median on a stem and leaf plot and the last piece of data.

Lower quartile (Q_1)	First quarter: one-quarter of the ranked data is less than or equal to this value.
Median (Q_2)	Second quarter: half of the ranked data is less than or equal to this value.
Upper quartile (Q_3)	Third quarter: three-quarters of the ranked data is less than or equal to this value.
Interquartile range	$Q_3 - Q_1$ This tells us about the spread of the data.

Interquartile range = Upper quartile – Lower quartile

The interquartile range tells us about the spread of the data. Since neither the smallest nor the greatest numerical data values are used, it cannot be distorted by outliers. It examines the range of the middle 50% of the data.

EXAMPLE 6

Use the following stem and leaf plot to calculate:

(a) The median
(b) The mode
(c) The lower quartile
(d) The upper quartile
(e) The interquartile range

Tens	Units
0	5 5 8
1	2 7 8 9 9 9
2	0 0 1 1 2 3 4 5 6 7
3	0 3 5
4	0

Key: 2|0 = 20

Solution

First, count all the leaves in the table to obtain the total number pieces of data.

Total = 23

(a) The median is the central entry.

$\therefore 23 \div 2 = 11.5$

This is not a whole number, and we always round **up** to the nearest whole number.

So the median is the 12th value of the ordered plot = 21.

(b) The mode is the most frequent figure in the plot. 19 appears three times, so it is the mode.

(c) The lower quartile is one-quarter of the total.

$\therefore 23 \div 4 = 5.75$

This is not a whole number, and we always round **up** to the nearest whole number.

The lower quartile is the 6th value of the ordered plot = 18.

(d) The upper quartile is three-quarters of the total.

$\therefore (23 \div 4) \times 3 = 17.25$

This is not a whole number, and we always round **up** to the nearest whole number. The lower quartile is the 18th value of the ordered plot = 26.

(e) The interquartile range = $Q_3 - Q_1$

$= 26 - 18 = 8$

Exercise 21.6

Where you are asked to comment on your findings in this exercise, use the following headings:

(i) Measures of central tendency
(ii) Measures of spread

1. Study the following distribution of numbers. Then identify (i) the median, (ii) the lower quartile and (iii) the upper quartile.

(a) 2, 2, 3, 5, 7, 8, 9, 10, 11, 13, 14
(b) 7, 8, 11, 15, 16, 17, 21, 30, 31, 35, 37
(c) 3, 5, 9, 13, 14, 17, 19, 21, 25, 29, 33, 36, 44, 48, 49
(d) 17, 21, 25, 29, 35, 42, 51
(e) 4, 8, 10, 11, 17, 18, 22, 28

2. Study the following stem and leaf plot showing the number of press-ups a group of people did and answer the questions:

Tens	Units
1	1 5
2	5 6 7
3	4 5 5 6 6 8 9
4	4 5 7 8 9 9
5	4 8

Key: 4|5 = 45 press-ups

Calculate the:
(a) Mean
(b) Median
(c) Lower quartile
(d) Upper quartile
(e) Interquartile range
(f) Range
(g) Comment on your findings.

3. Study the following stem and leaf plot on spending pocket money and answer the questions:

Tens	Units
1	2 3 4
2	1 2 3 6
3	2 2 4 4 5 5 5 6
4	1 2 5 6
5	8

Key: 5|8 = €58

Calculate the:
(a) Mean, correct to one decimal place
(b) Mode
(c) Median
(d) Lower quartile
(e) Upper quartile
(f) Interquartile range
(g) Range
(h) Comment on your findings.

4. Study the following back-to-back stem and leaf plot on girls' and boys' heights and answer the questions:

Girls		Boys
9 8 8 3 3 2 1	14	1
8 6 3 2 1	15	5 5 6
6 5 5 5 4 4	16	4 5 8 9
2 1	17	3 3 4 6 7 7 8 9 9
	18	4 4 7

Key: 16|9 = 169 cm

Calculate separately for the boys and girls the:
(a) Mean, correct to one decimal place
(b) Median
(c) Lower quartile
(d) Upper quartile
(e) Interquartile range
(f) Range
(g) Comment on your findings.

5. Study the ages in the following back-to-back stem and leaf plot and answer the questions:

Girls		Boys
5 3 1	0	2 2 3 4
6 3 2 1	1	1 1 4 5 6 7
9 9 8 8 5 4 4	2	5 5 6 7 9 9 9
4 4 4 3 2 1	3	3 4 4

Key: 2|5 = 25 years

Calculate separately for the boys and girls the:
(a) Mean, correct to one decimal place
(b) Mode
(c) Median
(d) Lower quartile
(e) Upper quartile
(f) Interquartile range
(g) Range
(h) Comment on your findings.

6. Study the heights in cm in the following back-to-back stem and leaf plot and answer the questions:

Girls		Boys
9 8 8 4 4 3 3 2 1	14	1 2 2
8 6 3 2 1	15	0 0 0 1 5 5 6
6 5 5 5 4 4	16	4 5 8 8 8 8 9
7 6 5 2 1	17	3 4 6 7 7 7 8 9

Key: 14|1 = 141 cm

Find the:

(a) Lower quartile
(b) Upper quartile
(c) Interquartile range
(d) Mean, correct to the nearest cm
(e) Mode
(f) Median
(g) Range
(h) Comment on your findings.

7. Study the following back-to-back stem and leaf plot on the number of sit-ups a group of girls and boys did and answer the questions:

Girls		Boys
9 4 4 3 3 2 1	14	1 2 2
8 8 8 6 3 2 1	15	0 0 0 1 5 5 6
6 5 5 5 4 4	16	4 5 8 8 8 8 9
7 6 5 2 1	17	3 4 6 7 7 7 8 9

Key: 15|1 = 151 sit-ups

Find the:

(a) Lower quartile
(b) Upper quartile
(c) Interquartile range
(d) Mean, correct to nearest whole number
(e) Mode
(f) Median
(g) Range
(h) Comment on your findings.

8. Study the savings in the following back-to-back stem and leaf plot and answer the questions:

Girls		Boys
9 9 7 7 6 6 4 2 0	1	0 0 0 0 4 4 5 7 8 9
7 6 5 3 0	2	5 7 7 8 9 9
7 4 4 4 4 4	3	3 3 3 3 3 3
7 6 6 1 1	4	1 5 7

Key: 2|5 = €25

Find the:

(a) Lower quartile
(b) Upper quartile
(c) Interquartile range
(d) Mean, correct to the nearest €
(e) Mode
(f) Median
(g) Range
(h) Comment on your findings.

9. Study the test scores in the following back-to-back stem and leaf plot and answer the questions:

Girls		Boys
7 7 6 5 5 5 5 4 2 0 0	0	0 0 2 2 3 3 3 8 9
8 8 7 6 5 4 4 3 3 2 1 1	1	0 1 1 1 2 4 4 4 5 5 5 6 6
7 7 7 7 3 3 3 2 2 2 0 0	2	1 2 2 2 2 2 7 7 8 8 8 9 9 9
4 4 3 3 3 2 1 0 0 0	3	3 3 5 7 7 8 8 9 9

Key: 2|1 = 21 marks

Find the:

(a) Lower quartile
(b) Upper quartile
(c) Interquartile range
(d) Mean, correct to the nearest whole number
(e) Mode
(f) Median
(g) Range
(h) Comment on your findings.

10. The ages of the Academy Award winners for best male actor and best female actor (at the time they won the award) from 1992 to 2011 are as follows:

Male actor: 54, 52, 37, 38, 32, 45, 60, 46, 40, 36, 47, 29, 43, 37, 38, 45, 50, 48, 60, 50

Female actor: 42, 29, 33, 36, 45, 49, 39, 26, 25, 33, 35, 35, 28, 30, 29, 61, 32, 33, 45, 29

(a) Represent the data on a back-to-back stem and leaf diagram.

(b) State one similarity and one difference that can be observed between the ages of the male and female winners.

(c) Mary says, 'The female winners were younger than the male winners.' Investigate this statement in relation to:

(i) The mean age of the male winners and the mean age of the female winners
(ii) The median age of the male winners and the median age of the female winners
(iii) The interquartile ranges of the ages of the male winners and the female winners

Section 21.7: Interpreting distribution shape

Statisticians often use the shape of distributions to draw conclusions from a data set. The diagram shows a **normal distribution curve** drawn on a histogram. Notice that the curve is symmetrical. Much statistical analyses are based on the shape of the distribution.

You will look at three different types of distribution.

1. Right-skewed distributions

As you can see in the diagram, in a right-skewed distribution, the majority of the distribution is concentrated on the left of the figure. The tail on the right is longer than on the left. The distribution is said to be **right-skewed** or **skewed to the right.** This is also called a **positive skew.**

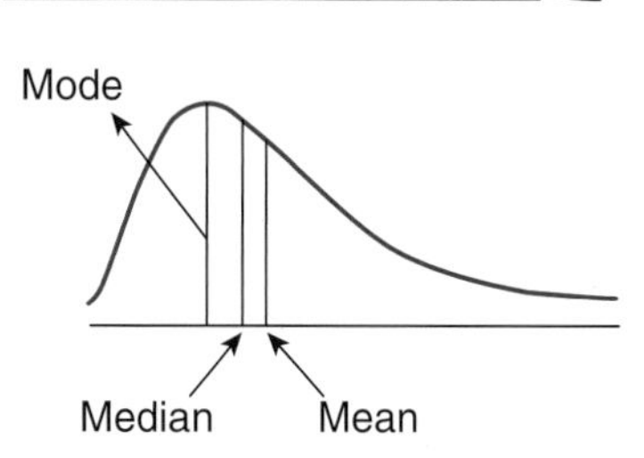

As you can see from the diagram, the mean is greater than the median and the median is greater than the mode.

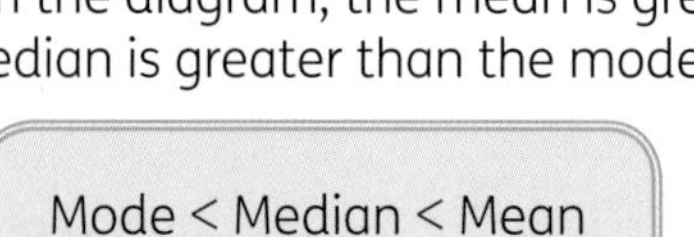

2. Symmetric distributions

In a symmetric distribution, both tails are of equal length. The majority of the data is in the centre of the curve. This curve is called the **normal distribution curve.**

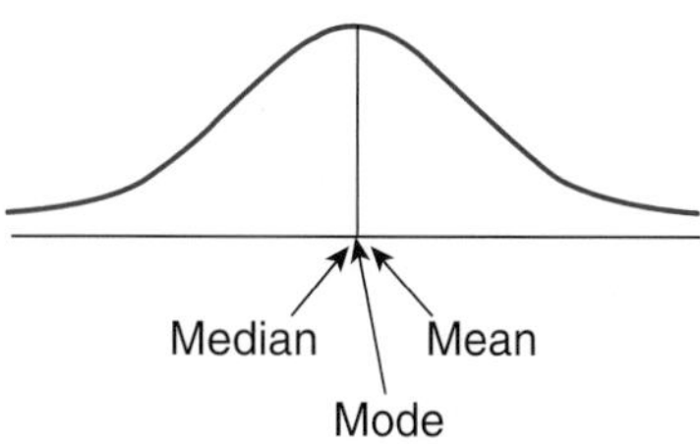

The mean, mode and the median are equal in a perfectly symmetric distribution.

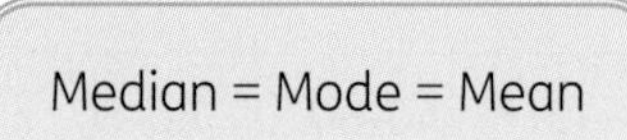

3. Left-skewed distributions

As you can see, in a left-skewed distribution the majority of the distribution is concentrated on the right of the figure. The tail is longer on the left than on the right. The distribution is said to be **left-skewed** or **skewed to the left.** This is also called a **negative skew.**

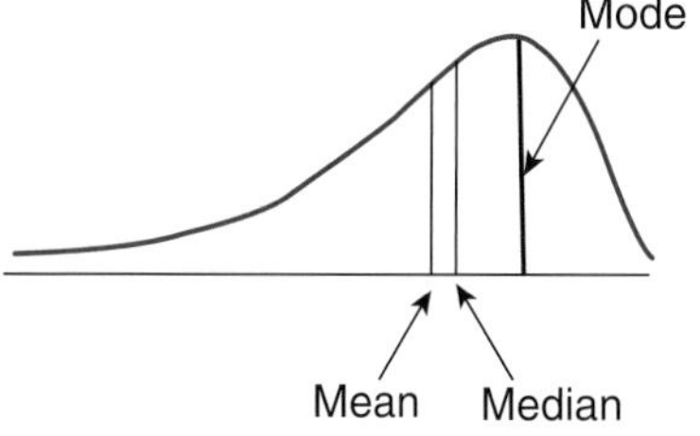

As you can see from the diagram, the mode is greater than the median and the median is greater than the mean.

Mode > Median > Mean

When describing how skewed a set of data is, we generally use histograms. Stem and leaf plots can also be used to examine the shape of a distribution.

By turning a stem and leaf plot on its side, you can draw a curve to outline the figures. This curve will tell you the shape of the distribution. The plot shown here is skewed to the left.

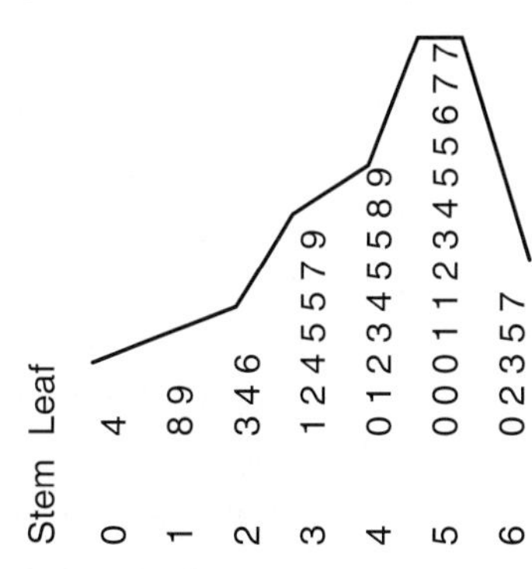

By careful examination, it is also possible to predict the shape of a distribution from a frequency table.

x	0	1	2	3	4	5	6
Frequency	3	5	9	9	6	3	1

You can see that the frequency starts low and increases to a maximum in the centre. It then begins to decrease again. The distribution is reasonably symmetrical. This table will **approximate** to a normal distribution curve.

Exercise 21.7

1. State the type of distribution curve each of the following stem and leaf plots will produce:

(a)

Leaf	Stem
4 3 2	1
6 3 2 1	2
6 5 5 5 4 4 2 2	3
6 5 2 1	4
8	5

Key: 5|8 = 58

(b)

Stem	Leaf
1	1 5
2	5 6 7
3	4 5 5 6 6 8 9
4	4 5 7 8 9 9
5	4 8

Key: 4|7 = 47

(c)

Stem	Leaf
0	2 2 3 4
1	1 1 4 5 6 7
2	5 5 6 7 9 9 9
3	3 4 4

Key: 2|5 = 25

(d)

Leaf	Stem
5 3 1	0
6 3 2 1	1
9 9 8 8 5 4 4	2
4 4 4 3 2 1	3

Key: 1|3 = 13

(e)

Stem	Leaf
14	1
15	5 5 6
16	4 5 8 9
17	3 3 4 6 7 7 8 9 9
18	4 4 7

Key: 14|1 = 141

(f)

Leaf	Stem
3 3 2 1	14
9 8 8 8 6 3 2 1	15
6 5 5 5 4 4	16
2 1	17
	18

Key: 14|3 = 143

2. (a) State the type of distribution curve each of the following frequency tables will produce.
   (b) Then draw a suitable histogram with a distribution curve to verify your answer.

(i)

Percentage in exam	0–20	20–40	40–60	60–80	80–100
No. of students	1	2	5	9	5

(Note: 0–20 means including 0% and less than 20%.)

(ii)

Age	0–5	5–10	10–15	15–20	20–25	25–30
No. of people	1	2	3	5	8	7

(Note: 0–5 means including 0 years and less than 5 years.)

(iii)

Body temp. (°C)	36.0–36.2	36.2–36.4	36.4–36.6	36.6–36.8	36.8–37.0	37.0–37.2
No. of people	1	6	4	1	1	0

(Note: 36.0–36.2 means including 36 °C and less than 36.2 °C.)

(iv)

No. of hours	0–4	4–8	8–12	12–16	16–20
No. of students	2	7	11	5	1

(Note: 0–4 means including 0 hours and less than 4 hours.)

(v)

Speed in km/h	20–30	30–40	40–50	50–60	60–70
No. of cars	0	12	48	25	15

(Note: 20–30 means including 20 km and less than 30 km.)

3. For each of the following graphs state whether they are skewed to the left, symmetrical or skewed to the right:

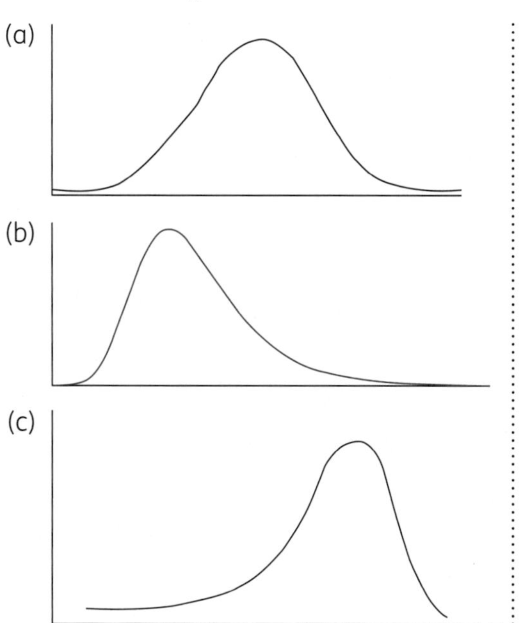

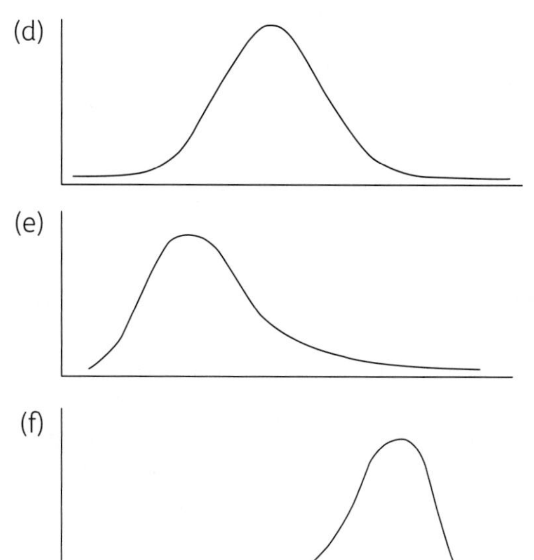

Section 21.8: The misuses of statistics

Student Activity 21G

The owner of a factory records the wages of all the employees, including himself and other senior management in the table:

€26,000	€32,000	€250,000	€22,000	€33,000
€35,000	€30,000	€500,000	€21,000	€450,000

The owner states that the average salary of his workforce is €139,900. He argues that his workforce is among the best paid in the country.

A workers' representative states the average annual wage of the workforce is roughly €28,400 and the workers are entitled to a pay rise.

(a) Discuss the validity of both statements.

(b) Which statement do you think is a better reflection of the workers' wages? Explain your answer fully.

THE MISUSES OF STATISTICS EXPLAINED

In Student Activity 21G, you saw how statistics can be used to misrepresent the truth or mislead the public. **Outliers** or **extreme values** distort the mean of a data set. Graphs and charts can also be misleading. It is important to examine them carefully to make sure they are accurate. In the famous words of Benjamin Disraeli, 'There are three kinds of lies: lies, damned lies and statistics.'

Statistical diagrams can be misleading in a number of ways:

1. The scales might not start at zero and can give a misleading representation.
2. Lines can be drawn too thick on graphs.
3. Scales might not be uniform, which could distort the shape of the graph.
4. Axes might not be labelled.
5. 3D diagrams can distort the proportions of a diagram.

6. Bright colours can make parts of a chart stand out more than others.
7. Non-uniform size of bars or images can distort the graph.
8. Data may be excluded from the plot or diagram.
9. Separating parts of diagrams can make them harder to compare.

Even signs in front of us can be misleading!

EXAMPLE 7

The following bar chart shows that the average amount of money spent by students in a shop has increased dramatically between 2010 and 2011. Examine the graph and discuss how it may be misleading.

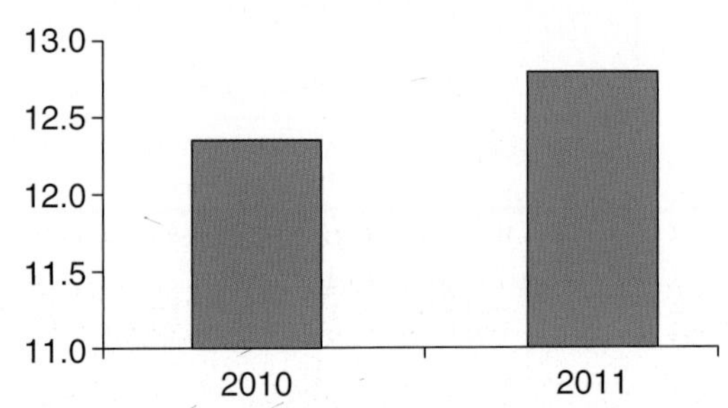

Solution

The vertical axis is not labelled.

The graph does not start at zero.

If the graph was drawn properly it is easy to see there is not a dramatic rise in spending.

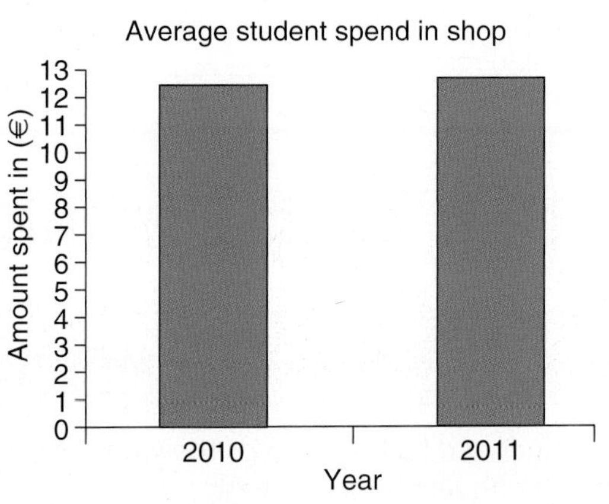

Exercise 21.8

1. The following pie chart shows the popularity among 360 people of 4 soft drinks:

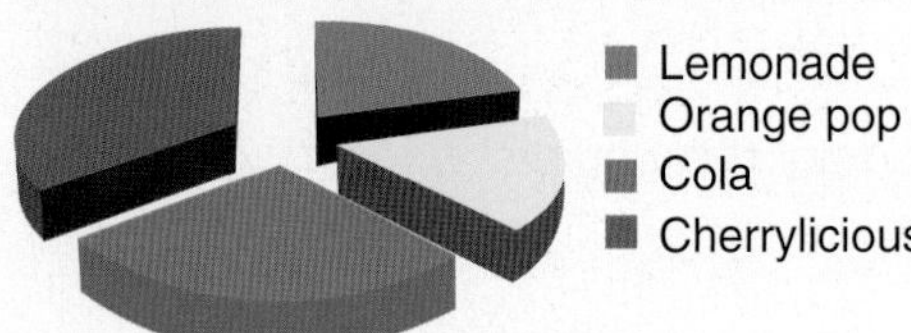

Discuss how the pie chart may be misleading.

2. The following bar chart shows the change in sales of online films over the past few years:

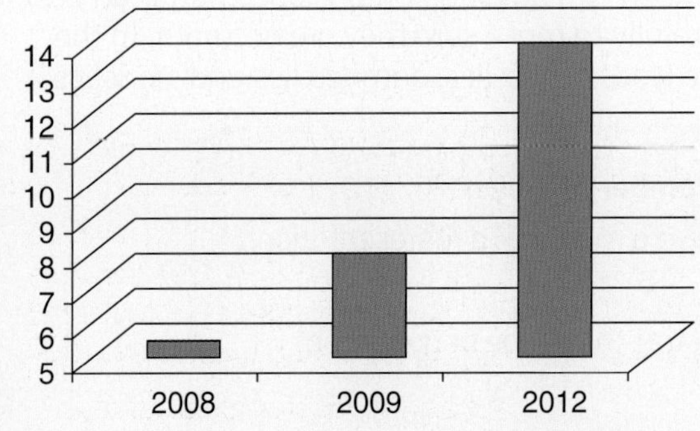

Discuss any issues with the graph that may cause it to be misleading.

3. The following graph shows the rise in the price of product:

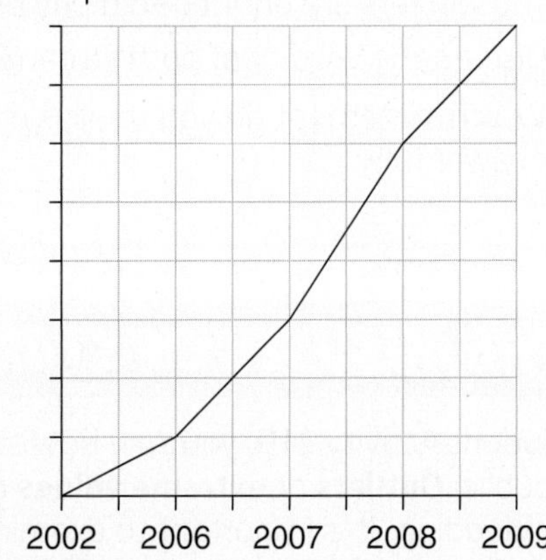

How might this graph be misleading?

4. The following graph was shown on Fox Business channel. It examined how the number of people in the top tax rate in America would change if tax cuts made by President Bush ended.

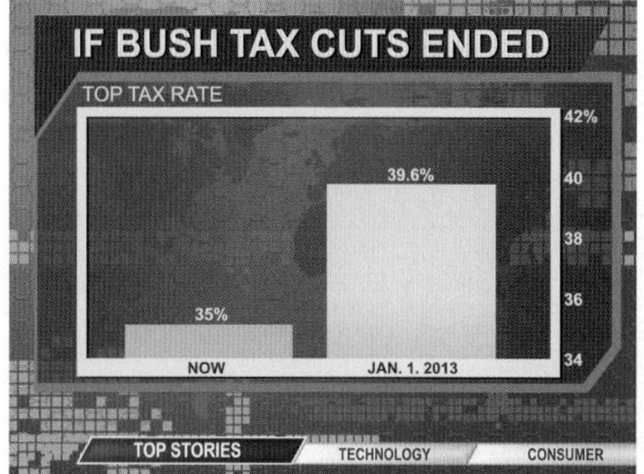

Examine the graph and state how it is misleading.

5. The following chart shows the amount of sweets collected by Daithí and Siobhán on Hallowe'en night.

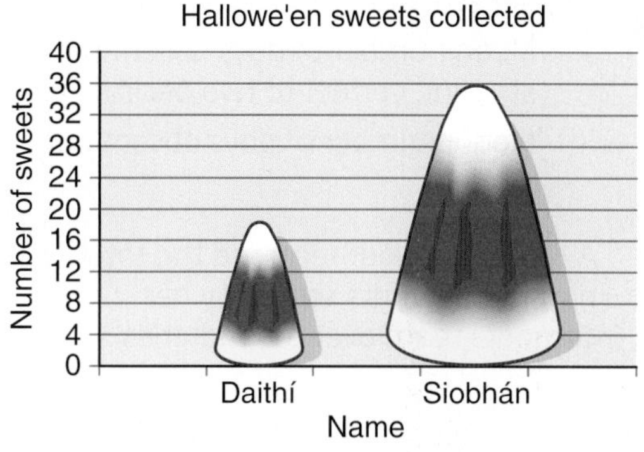

Is this graph misleading? Explain your answer fully.

6. List two things that may be considered misleading in the following graphs:

(a) Makes of cars

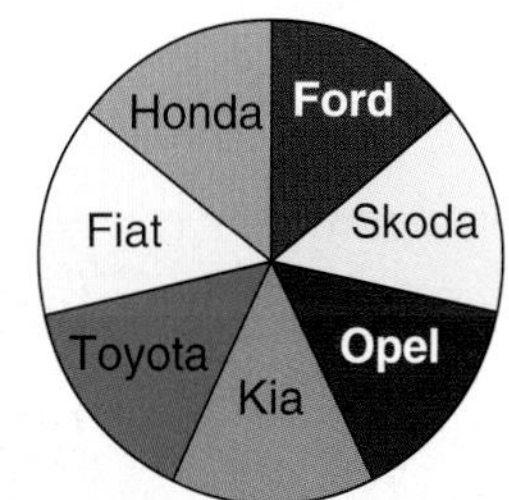

(b) House prices

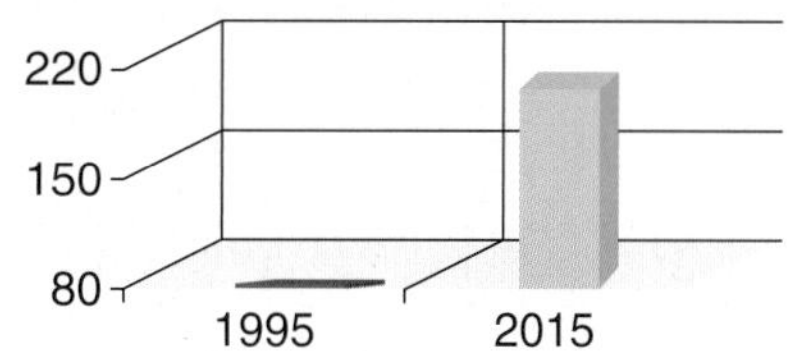

(c) Increase in employment

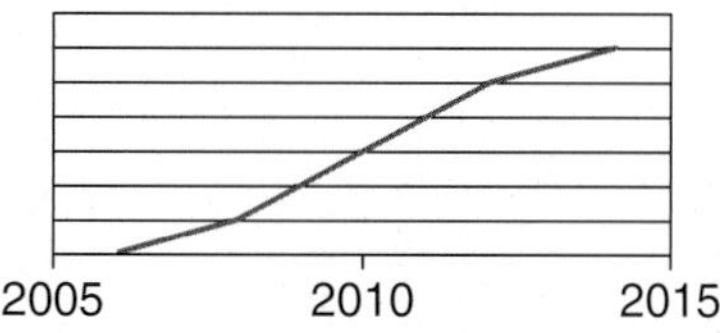

(d) Exports of beef cattle

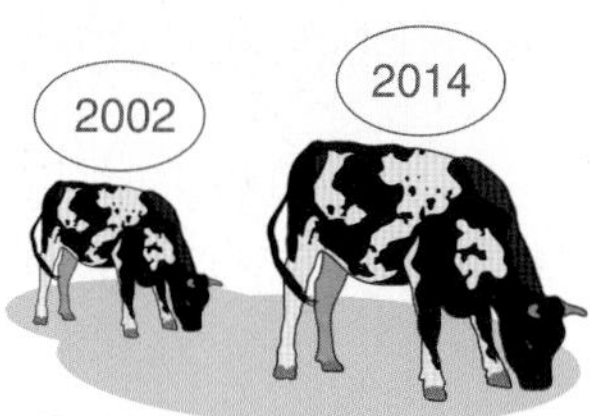

CHAPTER 21 SELF-CHECK TEST

1. The data shows the heights of a group of men and women:

Name	Height (cm)	Name	Height (cm)
Jane	120	Lorraine	144
Seán	148	John	152
Susan	152	Frank	163
Patrick	131	George	157
James	158	Donna	133
Mary	165	Debra	147
Michael	172	Bernie	164
Tom	170	Jack	169
Ita	158	Deirdre	135
Laura	155	Eimear	127
Liam	143	Ellie	134

(a) Display the results in a way that will allow you to compare the two sets of data.

(b) Compare the two sets of data in relation to:

(i) The mean height of the males surveyed and the mean height of the females surveyed

(ii) The median height of the males surveyed and the median heights of the females surveyed

(iii) The interquartile ranges of the heights of the males and the females surveyed

(iv) The range of the heights of the males and the females surveyed

(c) What do you conclude about all the above data?

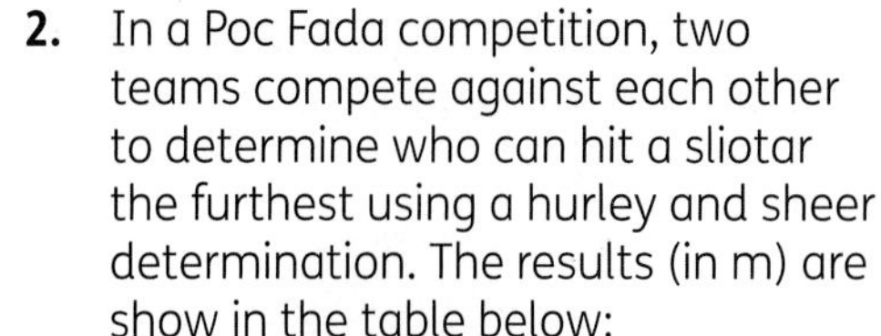

2. In a Poc Fada competition, two teams compete against each other to determine who can hit a sliotar the furthest using a hurley and sheer determination. The results (in m) are show in the table below:

Team Glas			Team Buí		
40.3	40.3	40.3	37.1	39.0	41.4
44.5	41.0	41.2	42.8	45.1	38.8
42.1	37.2	42.2	38.8	40.1	40.2
39.4	43.1	39.7	41.7	39.7	41.5
45.4	42.2	41.6	42.9	43.3	38.9
41.7	45.2	46.0	39.5	38.7	39.1
43.2	40.1	43.6	40.3	40.2	37.3

(a) Draw a back-to-back stem and leaf diagram that compares the puck outs for the two teams.

(b) Does your diagram indicate a winner? Explain.

(c) Support your claim using measures of central tendency.

3. The following shows the number of mobile phones in 20 families:

3	2	4	1	4
2	4	3	2	5
4	3	3	2	2
2	1	4	3	5

(a) Copy and complete the following frequency table:

No. of mobiles	1	2	3	4	5
Frequency					

(b) Draw a bar chart to display the information.

(c) Draw a line plot to display the information.

(d) Draw a pie chart to display the information.

Find the:

(e) Mean number of phones owned

(f) Modal number of phones owned

(g) Range in the number of phones owned

4. A teacher recorded how many days students were absent in a month as follows:

0	0	3	0	1	1
1	2	3	1	5	0
0	2	1	2	1	1
0	0	0	1	2	3
1	2	3	0	1	0

(a) How many students were in the class?

(b) Copy and complete the following frequency table:

No. of days absent	0	1	2	3	4	5
Frequency						

(c) Display the data on a suitable graph.

Find the:

(d) Range in the number of days absent per student

(e) Mean number of days absent per student, correct to two decimal places

(f) Modal number of days absent per student

5. A team manager recorded the total number of points scored by her camogie team over ten matches.

11	14	12	13	15
12	13	14	15	19
11	15	11	14	17

(a) How many points in total were scored?

(b) Calculate the mean number of points scored per match.

(c) If the full forward on the team scored 20% of the total number of points, how many did she score, correct to the nearest whole number?

(d) Copy and complete the following frequency table:

Number of points	11	12	13	14	15	16	17	18	19
Frequency									

(e) Display the data on a suitable graph.

6. A student threw a die 30 times and recorded the result of each throw as follows:
   (a) Record the results in a frequency table.
   (b) Display the data on a suitable graph.
   (c) Write a short report on what you notice, making reference to measures of central tendency.

6	3	5	1	3	6
2	5	2	1	3	4
6	5	3	1	1	3
1	4	1	5	1	3
4	5	2	3	1	1

7. The length of time in minutes for a number of people to complete a fundraising swim was recorded in the stem and leaf diagram below:

Stem	Leaf
1	7 7 8 9 9
2	2 2 4 5 5 5 7 8 9
3	1 1 1 4 4 6 7 7 8 8 8 9 9
4	3 3 3 3 3 3 4 6 7 7
5	1 1 1

Key: 1|4 = 14 minutes

   (a) Copy and complete the following grouped frequency table:

Time (mins)	0–10	10–20	20–30	30–40	40–50	50–60
No. of people						

(Note: 0–10 means more than or equal to 0 but less than 10 mins.)

   (b) Calculate the mean time to complete the swim.
   (c) What was the modal time to complete the swim?
   (d) Calculate the interquartile range.

8. The following grouped frequency table shows the length of time in minutes spent exercising in a certain week:

No. of minutes	0–20	20–40	40–60	60–80	80–100	100–120
No. of people	3	11	17	22	14	5

(Note: 0–20 means more than or equal to 0 but less than 20 mins.)

   (a) How many people took part in the survey?
   (b) What was the modal length of time spent exercising?
   (c) Display the data on a suitable graph.
   (d) Describe the shape of the distribution.
   (e) What does this shape tell you about its measures of central tendency?

9. The following grouped frequency table shows the time, in minutes, taken by 30 students in English class to solve a crossword puzzle:

Minutes	0–5	5–10	10–15	15–20	20–25	25–30	30–35
No. of students	0	1	3	5	6	7	8

(Note: 0–5 means more than or equal to 0 but less than 5 mins.)

   (a) What was the modal length of time spent solving the puzzle?
   (b) Display the data on a suitable graph.
   (c) Describe the shape of the distribution.
   (d) What does this shape tell you about the measures of central tendency?
   (e) Verify your answer to part (d).

10. The following grouped frequency table shows the number of customers in a shop between 10 a.m. and 11 a.m. on one particular morning.

Time	10:00–10:10	10:10–10:20	10:20–10:30	10:30–10:40	10:40–10:50	10:50–11:00
No. of customers	7	9	11	14	17	22

(Note: 10:10–10:20 means later than or at 10:10 but before 10:20.)

(a) How many customers entered the shop in total?

(b) What is the greatest number of customers that could have been in the shop at 10:32?

(c) What is the least number of customers that could have been in the shop at 10:32?

(d) Draw a histogram to display the information.

(e) Could a bar chart be used to display the information? Explain your answer.

11. The ages of the 30 people who took part in an aerobics class are as follows:

18, 24, 32, 37, 19, 13, 22, 41, 51, 49, 15, 42, 37, 58, 48, 53, 27, 54, 42, 24, 33, 48, 56, 17, 61, 37, 63, 45, 20, 39

The ages of the 30 people who took part in a swimming class are as follows:

16, 22, 29, 17, 36, 45, 12, 38, 52, 13, 33, 41, 24, 35, 51, 18, 47, 22, 14, 24, 42, 62, 15, 24, 23, 31, 53, 36, 48, 18

(a) Represent this data on a back-to-back stem and leaf plot.

(b) Use your diagram to identify the median in each case.

(c) What other measure of central tendency could have been used when examining this data?

(d) Based on the data, make one observation about the ages of the two groups.

Aerobics class								Swimming class						
							0							
							1							
							2							
							3							
							4							
							5							
							6							
								Key:						

12. In total 7,150 second level school students from 216 schools completed the 2011/2012 phase 11 CensusAtSchool questionnaire. The questionnaire contained a question relating to where students keep their mobile phones while sleeping.

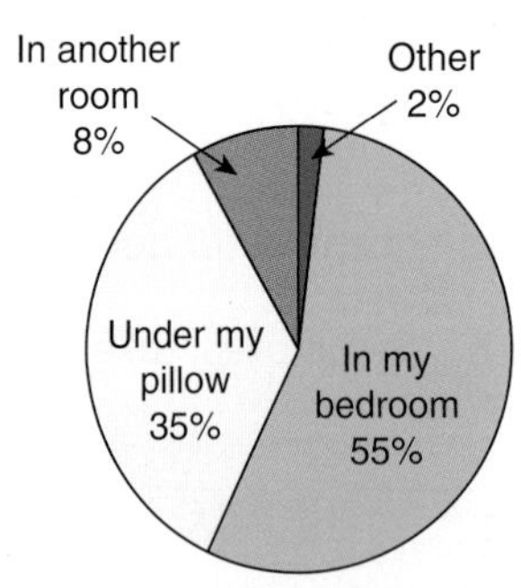

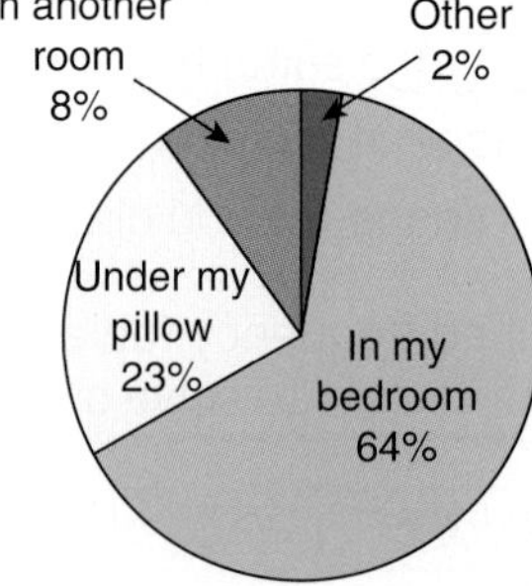

(a) Given that this question was answered by 4,171 girls and 2,979 boys, calculate how many female students kept their mobile phones under their pillows, correct to two decimal places.

(b) Calculate the overall percentage of students who kept their mobile phones under their pillows, correct to the nearest whole number.

(c) A new pie chart is to be drawn showing where all students kept their mobile phone. Calculate the measure of the angle that would represent the students who kept their mobile phones under their pillows.

13. The salaries, in €, of the different employees working in a call centre are listed below.

22, 000	16,500	38,000	26,500	15,000	21,000	15,500	46,000
42,000	9,500	32,000	27,000	33,000	36,000	24,000	37,000
65,000	37,000	24,500	23,500	28,000	52,000	33,000	25,000
23,000	16,500	35,500	25,000	33,000	20,000	19,500	16,000

(a) Use this data to complete the grouped frequency table below.

Salary (€1,000s)	0–10	10–20	20–30	30–40	40–50	50–60	60–70
No. of employees							

(Note: 10–20 means €10,000 or more but less than €20,000.)

(b) Using mid-interval values, find the mean salary of the employees.

(c) Outline another method which could have been used to calculate the mean salary.

(d) Which method is more accurate? Explain your answer.

(e) Represent this data on a suitable graph.

14. A garage recorded the different makes of cars it serviced in the past week for different travelling salespersons as follows:

Opel	Toyota	Opel	Toyota	Toyota	Toyota	Honda	Skoda	Skoda
Opel	Skoda	Volvo	Toyota	Opel	Honda	Honda	Skoda	Skoda
Honda	Toyota	Toyota	Opel	Toyota	Skoda	Volvo		

(a) What types of graphs can be used to graphically represent the above data.

(b) What types of graphs cannot be used to visually display the above data.

(c) In your opinion, is the graphical display or visual display better to display the above data. Clearly explain your reasons.

(d) Draw a suitable graph showing your previous answer.

(e) Write a summary of your findings from the drawn graph.

15. The ages of the local factory employees were recorded as follows:

25	30	27	31	28	32	39	35	40	37	41	42
42	38	34	45	34	46	40	47	21	21	46	44
44	44	49	50	54	57	22	23	23	43	49	50
55	58	50	57	59	60	64	63	59	60	63	42

(a) What types of graphs can be used to graphically represent the above data?

(b) What types of graphs cannot be used to visually display the above data?

(c) In your opinion, which is the better one? Clearly explain your reasons.

(d) Draw a graph verifying your previous answer.

(e) Write a summary of your findings from the drawn graph.

16. Examine the following graphic:

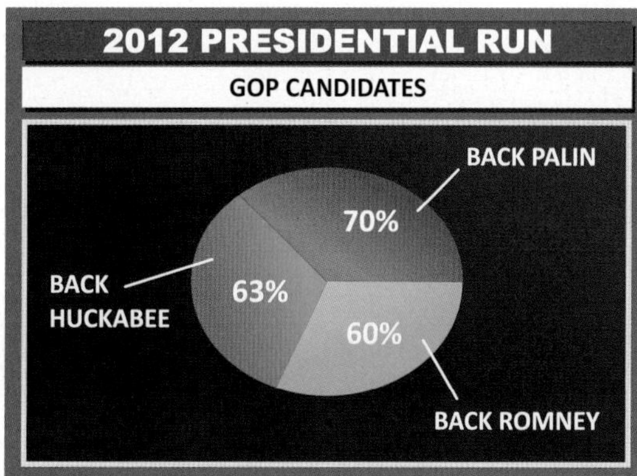

Write down two ways in which the graph is misleading.

17. The following graph was used by Fox News to show job losses in America.

Write down two ways in which the graphic is misleading.

18. Examine the following graphic and discuss how it may be misleading.

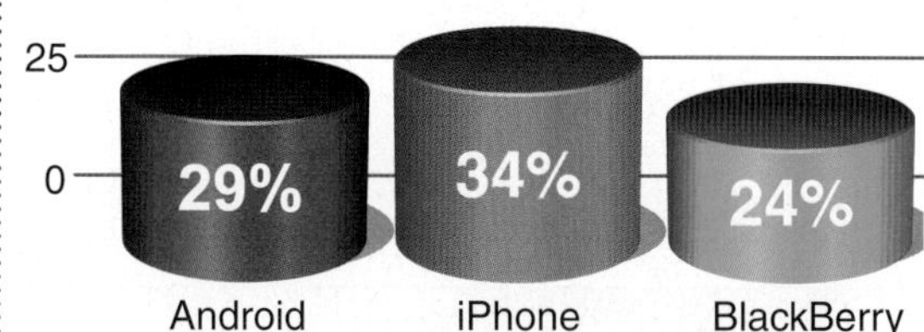

19. Complete the following word search:

STATISTICS
FREQUENCY
HISTOGRAM
BAR CHART
PIE CHART
OUTLIER
MISLEADING
MEAN
MODE
ORDINAL
NUMERICAL
CATEGORICAL
CONTINUOUS
DISCRETE
QUARTILE
RANGE
MEDIAN

N	N	N	T	E	E	C	N	C	H	U	D	O	C
L	S	C	T	R	A	H	C	E	I	P	I	E	R
S	E	N	C	R	L	O	I	L	S	T	S	U	L
U	R	A	S	T	A	T	I	S	T	I	C	S	M
E	I	B	U	M	C	H	S	Q	O	H	R	L	D
M	E	R	O	F	I	O	C	O	G	M	E	A	N
E	R	C	U	S	R	S	D	R	R	R	T	C	C
D	L	E	N	D	O	E	L	D	A	I	E	I	C
I	M	I	I	I	G	L	Q	E	M	B	R	R	R
A	E	N	T	L	E	P	G	U	A	U	N	E	R
N	A	A	N	R	T	N	C	T	E	D	O	M	P
L	O	R	O	D	A	U	D	T	P	N	I	U	O
G	G	N	C	R	C	U	O	D	I	E	C	N	A
I	E	T	O	I	D	A	Q	M	H	D	C	Y	G

CHAPTER 21 KNOWLEDGE CHECKLIST

After completing this chapter, I now:

- Am able to draw and interpret line plots, bar charts, pie charts, histograms and back-to-back stem and leaf plots ☐
- Am able to calculate the mean, mode, median, quartiles and interquartile range from a stem and leaf plot ☐
- Am able to interpret shapes of a distribution ☐
- Am able to recognise misuses of statistics ☐

Challenge

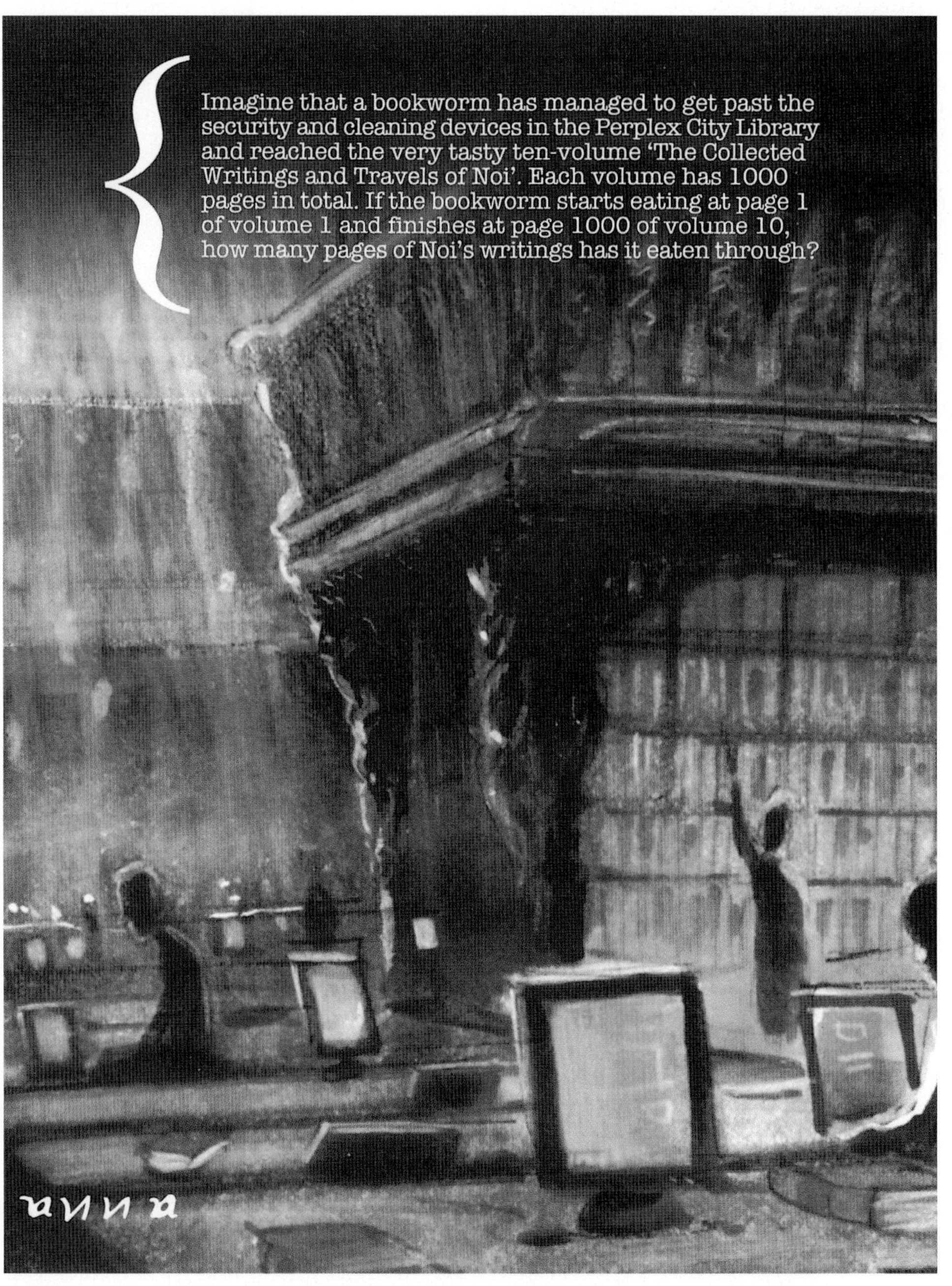

Imagine that a bookworm has managed to get past the security and cleaning devices in the Perplex City Library and reached the very tasty ten-volume 'The Collected Writings and Travels of Noi'. Each volume has 1000 pages in total. If the bookworm starts eating at page 1 of volume 1 and finishes at page 1000 of volume 10, how many pages of Noi's writings has it eaten through?

CHAPTER 22

ARITHMETIC 2

KEY WORDS

- Gross pay
- Gross tax
- Higher rate of tax
- Income tax
- Net pay
- PAYE
- PRSI
- Standard rate cut-off point
- Standard rate of tax
- Tax credit
- Tax payable
- Universal Social Charge (USC)

LEARNING OUTCOMES

In this chapter you will learn:

- ✓ **The terms associated with income tax and the Irish tax system**
- ✓ **To calculate income tax at the standard rate of tax and net pay**
- ✓ **To calculate income tax to include two tax rates and calculate net pay**
- ✓ **To calculate tax rates based on net income**

INTRODUCTION

Income tax is a tax that every individual pays on their income (the money they earn from work). This tax is paid to the government. The government uses the money to build infrastructure such as roads, hospitals and schools. It is also used to pay the wages of the country's civil servants, who include nurses, gardaí and politicians.

The Revenue Commissioners are responsible for collecting all tax. Income tax is deducted from a person's wages weekly, bimonthly or monthly. Any self-employed person must pay their own tax directly to the Revenue Commissioners.

Section 22.1: Income tax terms

Student Activity 22A

Working in pairs, find the meaning for the following terms:

Term	Explanation
Gross pay	
Tax	
Standard rate of tax	
Tax credit	
Deductions	
Net pay	
USC	
PRSI	

INCOME TAX TERMS EXPLAINED

It is very important to understand the terms used to calculate income tax.

Term	Explanation
Gross pay or gross income	The money you earn before any deductions are made from your income
Tax	The percentage deduction from your gross pay that is paid to the government
Standard rate cut-off point	The amount of your income that is taxed at the standard tax rate (the lower tax rate)

Standard rate of tax	The percentage tax rate that is applied to all income up to the standard rate cut-off point
Higher rate of tax	The percentage tax rate that is applied to all income over the standard rate cut-off point
Gross tax	The total tax bill to be paid to the Revenue Commissioners
Tax credit	An amount that is deducted from your gross tax bill
Tax payable or net tax	Gross tax minus your tax credit. This is the actual tax that will finally be paid.
Universal Social Charge (USC)	A percentage charge calculated on your gross income
Pay-Related Social Insurance (PRSI)	Normally payable by both the employer and the employee. It is a percentage of the employee's gross income.
Pay As You Earn (PAYE)	For PAYE workers, all income above the standard rate cut-off point is taxed at the higher rate of tax. This means that more that you earn, the more tax you pay.
Deductions	This covers any other monies that are paid out of a person's income such as health insurance, pension and loans.
Net pay or net income	The amount of income you earn after all deductions have been made.

The PRSI contribution goes to the Social Insurance Fund (SIF). This helps to pay for social welfare, medical cards and pensions.

PRSI rates can change each year. For this chapter, we will use the rates in the table below.

PRSI contribution rates

Persons in industrial, commercial and service type employment under a contract of service:

Non-cumulative weekly earnings band (including if appropriate shared-based remuneration)	PRSI subclasses	How much of weekly earnings (including if appropriate shared-based remuneration)	Employee's % (including if appropriate shared-based remuneration)	Employer's % (including if appropriate shared-based remuneration)	Employee + Employer %
Up to €37.99	J0	ALL	0	0.50	0.50
€38–€352	AO	ALL	0	4.25	4.25
€352.01–€356	AX	ALL	4.00	4.25	8.25
€356.01–€500	AL	ALL	4.00	10.75	14.75
More than €500	A1	ALL	4.00	10.75	14.75

The Universal Social Charge came into effect on 1 January 2011. It is a tax payable on gross income before any pension contributions are deducted. Currently all individuals must pay the Universal Social Charge on their gross income.

For this chapter, we will use the following USC rates:

2% on the first €10,036
4% on the next €5,980
7% on the balance

EXAMPLE 1

A person earns €28,000 per annum. Tax is paid at the rate of 21% on all the income and a tax credit of €2,500 applies. Loans amounting to €1,555 per annum and health insurance amounting to €1,000 per annum are also deducted from the income.

(a) Which figure above represents the person's gross income?

(b) Which figure above represents the standard rate of tax?

(c) How much tax credit has the person?

(d) What figures would you consider to be other deductions?

Solution

(a) €28,000 represents the person's gross income.

(b) The standard rate of tax is 21%.

(c) €2,500

(d) Loans and health insurance amounting to €2,555 in total are the other deductions.

Exercise 22.1

1. Jack earns €36,000 per annum. Tax is paid at the rate of 22% on all income and a tax credit of €2,450 applies. A pension plan monthly payment of €276 is also deducted from Jack's income.

(a) Which figure above represents Jack's gross income?

(b) What is the standard rate of tax?

(c) Has Jack any other deduction from his income?

2. Claire earns €29,000 per annum. Tax is paid at the rate of 19% on all her income. PRSI amounting to €3,000 per annum is deducted from her income. Claire has tax credits amounting to €750 per annum.

(a) Which figure above represents Claire's gross income?

(b) Which figure above represents the standard rate of tax?

(c) What figures would you consider to be a deduction?

3. Paul has a gross income of €55,000 and has a standard rate cut-off point of €28,000. He pays tax at the rate of 21% on all income up to the standard rate cut-off point and 41% on all other income. He has tax credits of €3,500 and pays health insurance, pension and loans which amount to €600 monthly.

(a) Which figure represents Paul's gross income?

(b) Which figure represents the standard rate of tax?

(c) How much income will be taxed at the rate of 41%?

(d) What are Paul's other deductions?

(e) How much has Paul in tax credits?

4. Janet earns €45,000 per annum and has a standard rate cut-off point of €30,000. Her income is taxed at 20% up to the standard rate cut-off point and all remaining income is taxed at 40%. PRSI and the USC are applied at the rates shown in the tables earlier.

(a) Which figure above represents Janet's gross income?

(b) Which figure above represents the standard rate of tax?

(c) How much income will be taxed at 40%?

(d) What PRSI rates will apply to Janet?

(e) What USC rates will apply to Janet?

Section 22.2: Income Tax 1

Student Activity 22B

Seán earns €27,500 per annum. He pays tax at the standard rate of 22.5% and has tax credits of €1,650. A deduction of €50 per month is made for a car loan. He pays €480 per annum for his pension contribution and €1,100 PRSI per annum.

(a) How much is Seán's gross income?

(b) What is the standard rate of tax?

(c) Calculate Seán's tax at the standard rate.

(d) How much does Seán pay for his car loan per annum?

(e) Calculate Seán's other deductions for a year.

(f) Calculate Seán's yearly take-home pay.

(g) Copy and complete the following. Fill in the relevant figures as you work through the boxes:

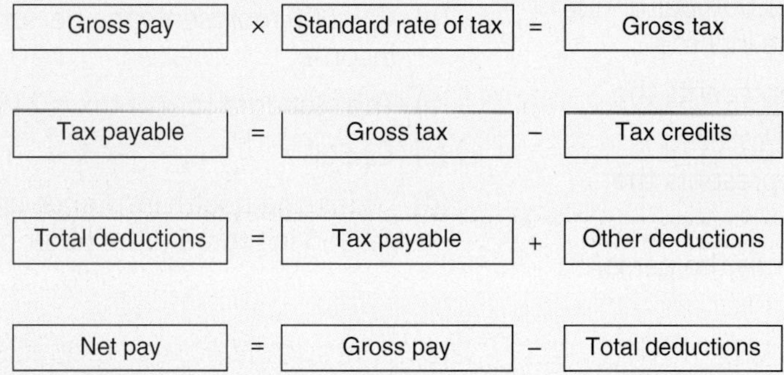

INCOME TAX 1 EXPLAINED

In Student Activity 22B, you began deducting taxes and charges from a gross income. In this section, we will deal with calculating net income involving the standard rate of tax only. We will also apply the USC and PRSI rates to gross incomes.

EXAMPLE 2

Keith earns €25,000 per annum. He pays tax at the standard rate of 21% and has tax credits of €1,250. A deduction of €50 per month for a loan is paid at source and he pays €1,100 PRSI per annum. Calculate his:

(a) Gross tax

(b) Tax payable

(c) Total deductions

(d) Net pay

Solution

(a) Gross tax = 25,000 × 21%
= €5,250

(b) Tax payable = 5,250 − 1,250 **Gross tax – Tax credit**
= €4,000

(c) Total deductions = (50 × 12) + 1,100 + 4,000
= €5,700

(d) Net pay = 25,000 − 5,700 **Gross income – Total deductions**
= €19,300

EXAMPLE 3

Calculate the amount that will be deducted from the following staff's annual pay if the USC is applied:

(a) Secretary Jim earns €15,000 per annum.

(b) Accountant Deirdre earns €45,000 per annum.

Use the USC rates given on page 469.

Solution

(a) €10,036 × 2% = €200.72 **2% of the first €10,036 of Jim's gross income**

€15,000 − €10,036 = €4,964

€4,964 × 4% = €198.56 **Jim must pay 4% on the remainder**

Total USC = €200.72 + €198.56

Total USC = €399.28

(b) €10,036 × 2% = €200.72 **2% of the first €10,036 of Deirdre's gross income**

€5,980 × 4% = €239.20 **4% on the next €5,980**

€10,036 + €5,980 = €16,016

€45,000 − €16,016 = €28,984

€28,984 × 7% = €2,028.88 **7% on the remainder**

Total USC = €200.72 + €239.20 + €2,028.88

Total USC = €2,468.80

EXAMPLE 4

If Eimear is an employee and earns €354 per week, calculate:

(a) Eimear's PRSI contribution

(b) Her employer's PRSI contribution

(c) The total PRSI contribution, correct to the nearest cent

Use the PRSI rates given on page 468.

Solution

(a) Eimear must pay 4% on all her income as she earns over €352.01.

€354 × 4% = €14.16

(b) As Eimear earns between €352.01 and €356, her employer must pay 4.25% PRSI.

€354 × 4.25% = €15.05

(c) €14.16 + €15.05 = €29.21

Exercise 22.2

1. Calculate the tax payable and the net pay for each of the following. **Note:** questions are based on a 52-week year.

	Gross pay	Tax credits	Standard rate of tax
(a)	€25,000	€1,250	20%
(b)	€28,500	€2,400	15%
(c)	€21,490	€1,400	19%
(d)	€28,000	€2,350	18%
(e)	€20,400	€1,100	19.5%
(f)	€23,500	€1,200	16%
(g)	€27,000	€2,300	21%
(h)	€25,600	€2,250	22%
(i)	€24,700	€2,350	20%
(j)	€29,090	€2,500	21%

2. Joan earns €29,500 per annum. She pays tax at the standard rate of tax of 24% and has tax credits of €1,350. Her pension contribution is €1,140 per annum and she also pays €1,340 PRSI per annum. Calculate Joan's net pay.

Copy the following table and fill in the relevant figures as you work through the boxes:

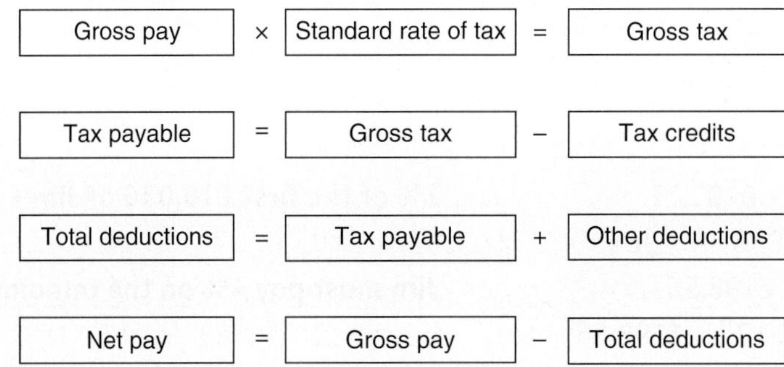

3. Paul earns €23,000 per annum. He pays tax at the standard rate of tax of 18.5% and has tax credits of €1,700. A deduction of €67 per month is made for a personal loan, €60 per month for his pension contribution and he pays €1,600 PRSI per annum. Calculate Paul's yearly take-home pay.

Copy the following table and fill in the relevant figures as you work through the boxes:

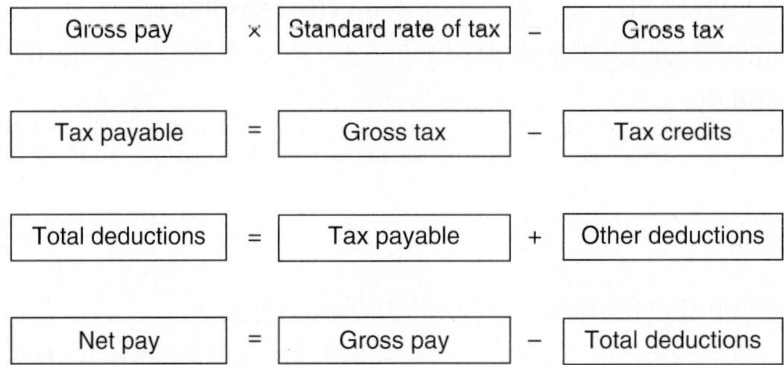

4. Vicky pays tax at the standard rate of 17.5%. Deductions of €20 per month for savings and €30 per month for insurance are taken from her wages at source. She pays €1,000 in PRSI per annum and has tax credits of €1,100 per annum. If Vicky's gross pay is €24,600, calculate her take-home pay.

Copy the following table and fill in the relevant figures as you work through the boxes:

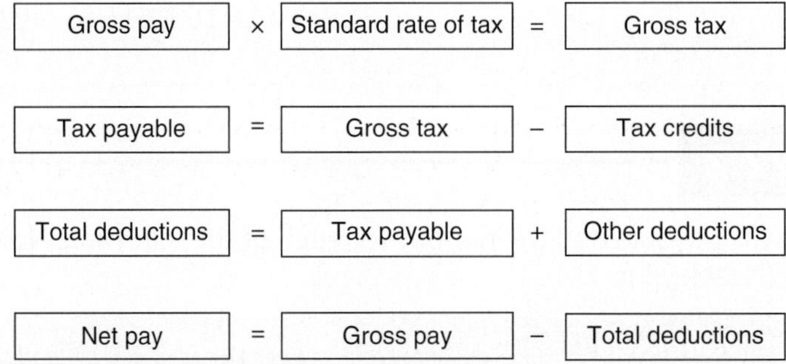

5. Bob earns €29,500 per annum. He pays tax at the standard rate of 21% and has tax credits of €1,500. A deduction of €100 per month is made for a personal loan and he pays €1,100 PRSI per annum. Calculate:

(a) The gross tax due

(b) The tax payable

(c) The amount of money deducted for his loan per annum

(d) The total deductions from Bob's monthly income

(e) Bob's net yearly pay

6. Síle earns €25,000 per annum. She pays tax at the standard rate of 19% and has tax credits of €1,250. A deduction of €66 per month is made towards her pension and she pays €900 PRSI per annum. Calculate:
   (a) The gross tax due
   (b) The tax payable
   (c) The amount of money deducted for her pension per annum
   (d) The total deductions from Síle's monthly pay
   (e) Sile's net monthly pay, correct to the nearest euro
7. Mary earns €21,900 per annum. She pays tax at the standard rate of 19% and has tax credits of €1,900. She pays €1,548 PRSI per annum. Calculate Mary's yearly take-home pay.
8. Daithí has a yearly income of €25,600. He pays tax at the standard rate of 19.5% and has tax credits of €1,800. A deduction of €79 per month is made for a car loan and he pays €1,700 PRSI per annum. Calculate Daithí's yearly take-home pay.
9. Calculate the USC for each of the following people:
   (a) John earns €590 per week working as a butcher.
   (b) Marie earns €450 per week working in a hair salon.
   (c) Patrick, a computer technician, earns €18,500 per annum.
   (d) Liam, a sales representative, earns €31,200 per annum.
   (e) Theresa, a managing director, earns €61,750 per annum.
10. Use the PRSI rates given on page 468 to answer the following questions:
    (a) Deirdre, an accountant, earns €480 per week.
        (i) How much PRSI does Deirdre pay?
        (ii) How much PRSI does Deirdre's employer pay?
    (b) Patrick, a computer technician, earns €660 per week.
        (i) How much PRSI does Patrick pay?
        (ii) How much PRSI does Patrick's employer pay?
    (c) Liam, a sales representative, earns €312 per week.
        (i) How much PRSI does Liam pay?
        (ii) How much PRSI does Liam's employer pay?
    (d) Theresa, a managing director, earns €918 per week.
        (i) How much PRSI does Theresa pay?
        (ii) How much PRSI does Theresa's employer pay?
11. Mark earns €27,000 per annum. He pays PRSI and the USC at the specified rates. He has tax credits of €2,500 and all his income is taxed at 21%. He pays a monthly personal loan of €75 and pays €200 every month towards his pension.
    (a) Calculate Mark's monthly pay, correct to the nearest euro.
    (b) Calculate Mark's PRSI payment.
    (c) Calculate Mark's UCS payment.
    (d) Calculate his gross tax due.
    (e) Calculate the total tax payable by Mark.
    (f) Calculate Mark's net annual income.
12. Peter earns €26,500 per annum. He pays PRSI and the USC at the specified rates. He has tax credits amounting to €1,950 and pays tax at the standard rate of 21%. Calculate Peter's yearly net pay.
13. Mary earns €18,000 per annum. She pays PRSI and the USC at the specified rates. She has tax credits amounting to €1,500 and pays tax at the standard rate of 20%. She has a weekly personal loan of €40. Calculate Mary's weekly net pay, correct to the nearest euro.
14. Keith earns €22,000 per annum. He has tax credits amounting to €1,950 and pays tax at the standard rate of 21%. He has a monthly loan repayment of €110 and saves €50 per month. If he pays PRSI and the USC at the specified rates, calculate his yearly net pay.

Section 22.3: Income tax 2

Student Activity 22C

Siobhán earns €55,000 per annum. The standard rate cut-off point is €29,000 and the standard rate of tax is 21%. The remainder of her income is taxed at 40%. Siobhán has tax credits of €3,500. A deduction of €120 per month is made for a loan from her wages.

(a) Copy the following template:

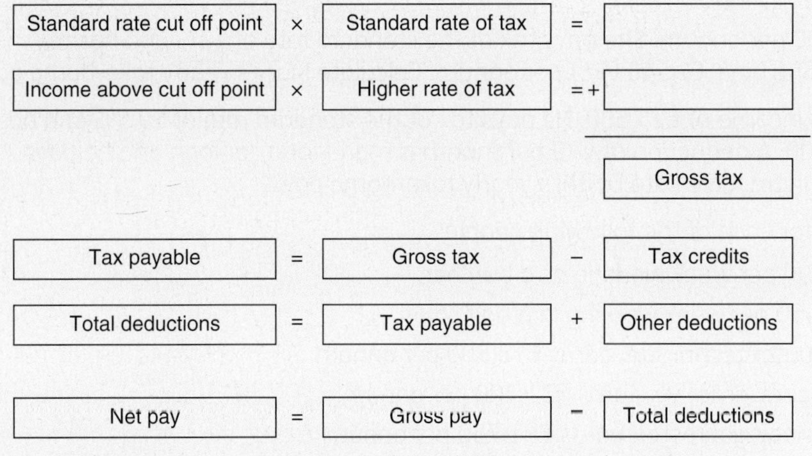

Standard rate cut off point × Standard rate of tax =
Income above cut off point × Higher rate of tax = +
Gross tax
Tax payable = Gross tax − Tax credits
Total deductions = Tax payable + Other deductions
Net pay = Gross pay − Total deductions

(b) Use the boxes as a guide to calculate Siobhán's net income.

INCOME TAX 2 EXPLAINED

In Ireland, income tax is charged at two different rates. The **standard rate cut-off point** is the upper limit on earnings taxed at the standard rate of tax.

All income above the **standard rate cut-off point** is taxed at the higher rate of tax. This means that the more you earn, the more tax you pay. This is called **PAYE (Pay As You Earn)**.

EXAMPLE 5

Keith earns €52,000 per annum. The standard rate cut-off point is €32,000 and the standard rate of tax is 21%. The remainder of the income is taxed at 41%. Keith has tax credits of €2,425. Calculate his net annual income.

Solution

32,000	×	21%	=	6,720		
20,000	×	41%	= +	8,200		
				14,920	← Gross tax	
Tax payable	=	14,920	−	2,425	=	12,495
Total deductions	=	12,495	+	0		
Net pay	=	52,000	−	12,945	=	€39,505

EXAMPLE 6

Síle earns €49,000 per annum. The standard rate cut-off point is €29,000 and the standard rate of tax is 19%. Síle has tax credits of €1,750. If her net income is €37,240, calculate the higher rate of tax.

Solution

A question like this can be very simple if you start at the end and work your way back:

Net pay = Gross pay − Total deductions

€37,240 = €49,000 – Total deductions

Total deductions = €11,760

As no extra deductions are to be made, we get:

Tax payable = €11,760

Tax payable = Gross tax – Tax credit

€11,760 = Gross tax – €1,750

Gross tax = €13,510

	×		=		
	×		= +		
				€13,510	← Gross tax
			−	€1,750	↑ + Going backwards add the tax credit
				€11,760	

Tax at 19% on €29,000 = €5,510

€29,000	×	19%	=	€5,510	
	×		= +		
				€13,510	← Gross tax
			−	€1,750	↑ + Going backwards add the tax credit
				€11,760	

Tax at the higher rate = €13,510 − €5,510
= €8,000

€29,000	×	19%	=	€5,510	
	×		= +	€8,000	
				€13,510	← Gross tax
			−	€1,750	↑ + Going backwards add the tax credit
				€11,760	

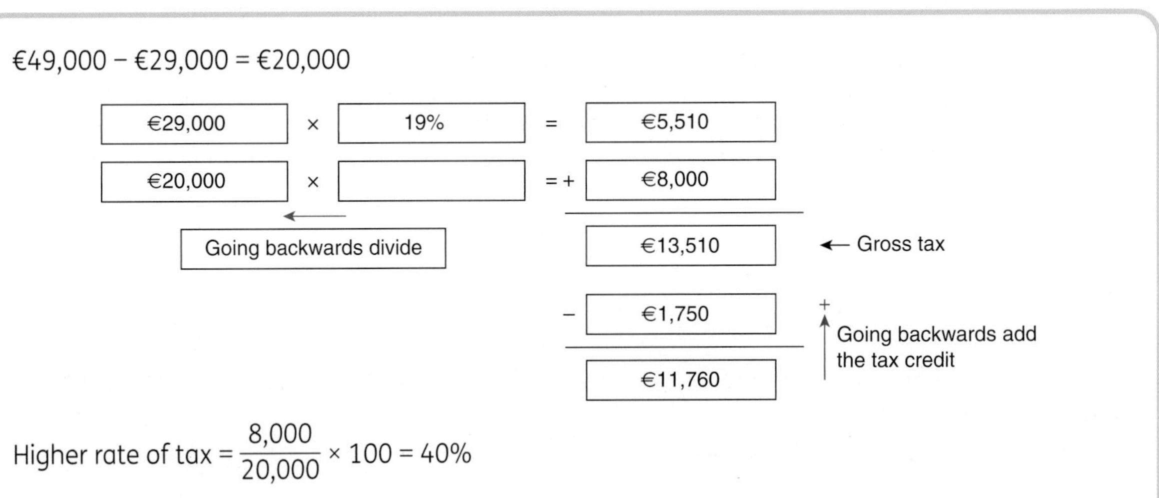

Exercise 22.3

1. Paul earns €45,000 per annum. The standard rate cut-off point is €30,000 and the standard rate of tax is 20%. The remainder of his income is taxed at 42%. Paul has tax credits of €3,500.
   - (a) Calculate the amount of tax paid on the first €30,000.
   - (b) Calculate how much Paul earns in excess of €30,000.
   - (c) Calculate the tax at 42% on the remainder of the income.
   - (d) Calculate the gross tax owed by Paul.
   - (e) Calculate the net tax due.
   - (f) Calculate Paul's net income.

2. Michael earns €47,000 per annum. The standard rate cut-off point is €28,000 and the standard rate of tax is 22%. The remainder of the income is taxed at 42%. Michael has tax credits of €2,400. Calculate Michael's net income using the following template as a guide:

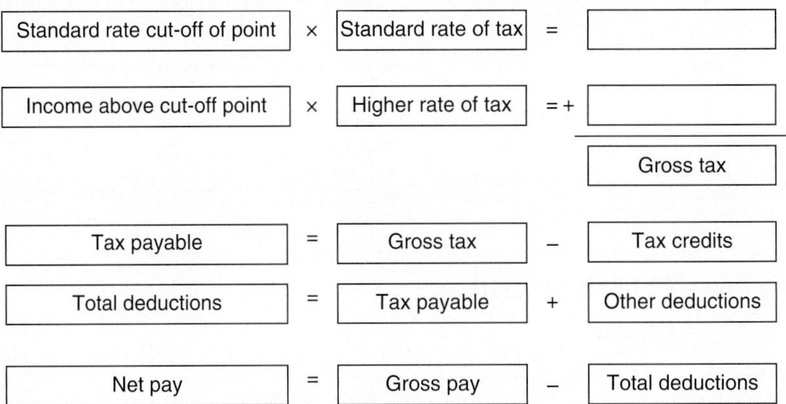

3. John earns €68,000 per annum. The standard rate cut-off point is €25,000 and the standard rate of tax is 21%. The remainder of the income is taxed at 39%. If John has tax credits of €2,400, calculate his net yearly income.

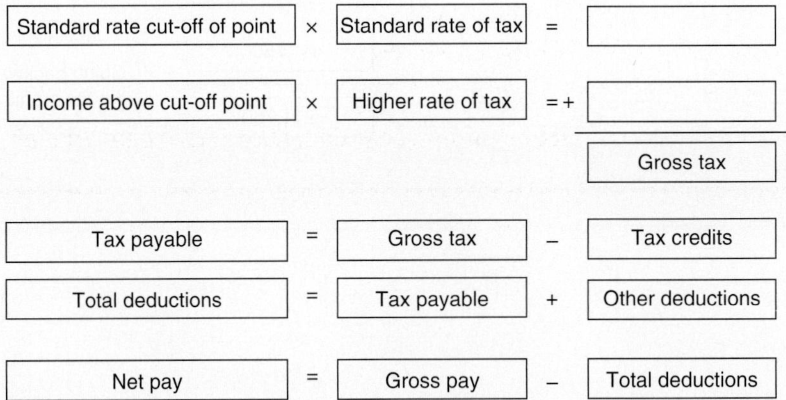

4. Deirdre earns €75,000 per annum. The standard rate cut-off point is €32,000 and the standard rate of tax is 24%. The remainder of the income is taxed at 45% and tax credits of €1,850 apply. If Deirdre has a monthly loan repayment of €100 deducted from her earnings, calculate her net yearly income.

5. Catherine earns €29,000 per annum. The standard rate cut-off point is €28,000 and the standard rate of tax is 20%. The remainder of the income is taxed at 42%. If Catherine has tax credits of €1,200, calculate her net yearly income.

6. Joan earns €38,000 per annum. The standard rate cut-off point is €25,000 and the standard rate of tax is 23%. The remainder of the income is taxed at 39%. PRSI of €90 per month is deducted from Joan's income. Calculate Joan's net income if her tax credits amount to €1,720 per annum.

7. Gavin earns €94,000 per annum. The standard rate cut-off point is €29,000 and the standard rate of tax is 21%. The remainder of the income is taxed at 42%. A car loan of €250 per month and PRSI of €150 per month are deducted from Gavin's income. If Gavin has tax credits of €1,800, calculate his monthly net income, correct to the nearest euro.

8. John earns €52,000 per annum. The standard rate cut-off point is €29,000 and the standard rate of tax is 21%. The remainder of the income is taxed at 41%. PRSI of €110 is deducted from John's income on a monthly basis. If John's tax credits amount to €1,950 per annum, calculate:
   (a) John's take-home pay per annum.
   (b) John gets a pay rise of 12%. Calculate John's new yearly net income.

9. Mary earns €72,500 per annum. The standard rate cut-off point is €32,000 and the standard rate of tax is 18%. PRSI of €120 per month is deducted from Mary's income. She also has a direct debit for her health insurance of €130 per month. The remainder of the income is taxed at 39%. Mary's tax credits amount to €2,100 per annum. Calculate Mary's monthly income, correct to the nearest cent.

10. A farmer earns €92,000 per annum by selling milk. The standard rate cut-off point is €30,000 and the standard rate of tax is 20%. The higher rate of tax is 40%. The farmer has tax credits of €2,700. A payment of €150 per month is paid into his pension account and he has a direct debit of €260 per month for a farm loan. The farmer receives non-taxable grants which total €3,400 per annum. Calculate the farmer's yearly income.

11. James earns €48,000 per annum. The standard rate cut-off point is €28,500 and the standard rate of tax is 19%. The higher rate of tax is 43%. James pays €1,200 per annum in PRSI and has a monthly loan repayment of €90. If James has tax credits of €3,200, calculate his take-home pay per month.

Note

For the following questions involving USC and PRSI, use the rates given on pages 468 and 469.

12. Ita has a gross income of €65,000 per annum. Her standard rate cut-off point is €24,000. The standard rate of tax is 21% and the higher rate is 42%. She has an annual tax credit of €2,830. She is in Class A1 for PRSI (assuming a 52-week year).
   (a) What is her PRSI contribution per week?
   (b) What is her employer's PRSI contribution per week?
   (c) Calculate her annual USC payment.
   (d) What is her weekly net income after all her deductions have been made?

13. Laura has a gross income of €57,000 per annum. Her standard rate cut-off point is €22,500. The standard rate of tax is 22% and the higher rate is 41%. She has an annual tax credit of €2,600. She is in Class A1 for PRSI (assuming a 52-week year).

(a) What is her PRSI contribution per annum?

(b) What is her employer's PRSI contribution per annum?

(c) Calculate her annual USC payment.

(d) What is her weekly net income after all the deductions, correct to the nearest euro?

14. Aidan has a gross income of €82,000 per annum. His standard rate cut-off point is €27,500. The standard rate of tax is 23% and the higher rate is 44%. He has an annual tax credit of €3,200. He is in Class A1 for PRSI (assuming a 52-week year).

(a) What is his PRSI contribution per week, correct to the nearest euro?

(b) What is his employer's PRSI contribution per week, correct to the nearest euro?

(c) Calculate his annual USC payment.

(d) What is his weekly net income after all the deductions, correct to the nearest euro?

15. Edward has a gross income of €74,700 per annum. His standard rate cut-off point is €27,800. The standard rate of tax is 21.5% and the higher rate is 45%. He has an annual tax credit of €2,830. He is in Class A1 for PRSI (assuming a 52-week year).

(a) What is his PRSI contribution per week, correct to the nearest euro?

(b) What is his employer's PRSI contribution per week?

(c) Calculate his annual USC payment.

(d) What is his weekly net income after all the deductions?

16. Michael and Donna have a combined annual income of €147,000. They pay tax at 21% on the first €55,000 they earn and 42% on the remainder. They have an annual tax credit of €7,200. They both pay PRSI at class A1 rates. Their total pension contributions amount to €4,700, Union fees amount to €848 and loans amount to €2,450 per annum.

(a) What is their total combined PRSI payment for a 52-week year?

(b) What is their total combined USC payment for a 52-week year?

(c) Calculate the total tax payable annually.

(d) What is their total annual net income?

17. Patrick and Pauline have a combined annual income of €113,000. They pay tax at 20% on the first €47,000 they earn and 41% on the remainder. They have an annual tax credit of €7,000. They both pay PRSI at class A1 rates. Their total pension contributions amount to €3,500, Union fees amount to €550 and loans amount to €1,245 per annum.

(a) What is their total combined PRSI payment for a 52-week year?

(b) What is their total combined USC payment for a 52-week year?

(c) Calculate the total tax payable annually.

(d) What is their annual net income?

18. Jim and Maire have a combined annual income of €210,000. They pay tax at 23% on the first €67,000 they earn and 44% on the remainder. They have an annual tax credit of €8,000. They both pay PRSI at class A1 rates. Their total pension contributions amount to €7,100, Union fees amount to €988 and loans amount to €6,123 per annum.

(a) What is their total combined PRSI payment for a 52-week year?

(b) What is their total combined USC payment for a 52-week year?

(c) Calculate the total tax payable annually.

(d) What is their annual net income?

19. Brad and Angelina have a combined annual income of €980,000. They pay tax at 27% on the first €78,200 they earn and 42% on the remainder. They have an annual tax credit of €9,000. They both pay PRSI at class A1 rates. Their total pension contributions amounts to €14,300, Union fees amount to €248 and loans amount to €178,550 per annum.

(a) What is their total combined PRSI payment for a 52-week year?

(b) What is their total combined USC payment for a 52-week year?

(c) Calculate the total tax payable annually.

(d) What is their annual net income?

CHAPTER 22 SELF-CHECK TEST

1. Mary earns €84,500 per annum. The standard rate cut-off point is €30,000 and the standard rate of tax is 20%. PRSI of €150 per month is deducted from Mary's income. She also has a direct debit for her health insurance of €160 per month. The remainder of the income is taxed at 40%. Mary's tax credits amount to €2,100 per annum. Calculate Mary's monthly income correct to the nearest cent.

2. A worker earns €110,000 per annum. The standard rate cut-off point is €25,000 and the standard rate of tax is 22%. The remainder of the income is taxed at 45%. A personal loan of €150 per month and PRSI of €190 per month are deducted from the income. If the person has tax credits of €2,400, calculate their monthly net income, correct to the nearest euro.

Note

For the following questions involving USC and PRSI, use the rates given on pages 468 and 469.

3. Lorraine has a gross income of €45,000 per annum. Her standard rate cut-off point is €18,000. The standard rate of tax is 21% and the higher rate is 42%. She has an annual tax credit of €3,500. She is in Class A1 for PRSI (assuming a 52-week year).
   (a) What is her PRSI contribution per week?
   (b) What is her employer's PRSI contribution per week?
   (c) Calculate her annual USC payment.
   (d) What is her weekly net income after all the deductions?

4. David has a gross income of €72,000 per annum. His standard rate cut-off point is €23,070. The standard rate of tax is 24% and the higher rate is 45%. His annual tax credit is €5,200. He is in Class A1 for PRSI (assuming a 52-week year).
   (a) What is his PRSI contribution per week?
   (b) What is his employer's PRSI contribution per week?
   (c) Calculate his annual USC payment.
   (d) What is his weekly net income after all the deductions?

5. Ursula has a gross income of €63,000 per annum. Her standard rate cut-off point is €32,200. The standard rate of tax is 23% and the higher rate is 44%. She has an annual tax credit of €4,620. She is in Class A1 for PRSI (assuming a 52-week year).
   (a) What is her PRSI contribution per week?
   (b) What is her employer's PRSI contribution per week?
   (c) Calculate her annual USC payment.
   (d) What is her weekly net income after all the deductions, correct to the nearest euro?

6. Gary has a gross income of €97,700 per annum. His standard rate cut-off point is €37,800. The standard rate of tax is 23.5% and the higher rate is 45%. He has an annual tax credit of €4,880. He is in Class A1 for PRSI (assuming a 52-week year).
   (a) What is his PRSI contribution per week?
   (b) What is his employer's PRSI contribution per week?
   (c) Calculate his annual USC payment.
   (d) What is his weekly net income after all the deductions?

7. Pat and Deirdre have a combined annual income of €450,000. They pay tax at 23% on the first €37,820 they earn and 40% on the remainder. They have an annual tax credit of €9,200. They both pay PRSI at Class A1 rates. Their total pension contributions amount to €11,200, Union fees amount to €648 and loans amount to €48,550 per annum.
   (a) What is their total combined PRSI payment for a 52-week year?
   (b) What is their total combined USC payment for a 52-week year?
   (c) Calculate the total tax payable annually.
   (d) What is their annual net income?

8. Seán and Stella have a combined annual income of €180,000. They pay tax at 25% on the first €38,500 they earn and 42% on the remainder. They have an annual tax credit of €3,300. They both pay PRSI at Class A1 rates. Their total pension contributions amounts to €4,200, Union fees amount to €826 and loans amount to €33,200 per annum.
   (a) What is their total combined PRSI payment for a 52-week year?
   (b) What is their total combined USC payment for a 52-week year?

(c) Calculate the total tax payable annually.

(d) What is their annual net income?

9. (a) The standard rate of income tax is 20% and the higher rate is 41%. The standard rate cut-off point is €36,500. Aisling has a gross income of €47,000 and total tax credits of €1,830. Calculate Aisling's net income.

(b) The following year Aisling's gross income increases. The tax rates, cut-off point and tax credits remain unchanged. Her net tax now amounts to €15,105. What is her new gross income?

10. Theresa has a gross income of €50,000. Her total income tax payable amounts to €10,460. The standard rate cut-off point is €32,000. The standard rate of tax is 20% and the higher rate is 42%. What are Theresa's tax credits for the year?

11. Síle pays tax of €18,000 per annum. The standard rate cut-off point is €25,000 and the standard rate of tax is 20%. The higher rate of tax is 40%. If Síle has tax credits of €3,000 per annum, calculate her gross yearly income.

12. Paul pays €26,290 in tax per annum. The standard rate cut-off point is €29,000 and the standard rate of tax is 21%. The higher rate of tax is 40%. If Paul has tax credits of €2,900 per annum, calculate his gross yearly income.

13. Mary has a gross yearly income of €75,000 and pays €19,000 in tax per annum. The standard rate cut-off point is €30,000 and the standard rate of tax is 20%. If Mary has tax credits of €5,000 per annum, calculate the higher rate of tax.

14. The standard rate of income tax is 20% and the higher rate is 42%. For a single person, the annual personal tax credit is €1,520 and the standard rate cut-off point is €28,000. Tom earns €22,000 per annum and Mairéad earns €36,000 per annum. Both of them are single and have no tax credits other than their personal tax credit.

(a) Calculate the tax payable by Tom for the year.

(b) Calculate the tax payable by Mairéad for the year.

(c) If Tom and Mairéad were married to each other, their joint personal tax credit would be €3,040 and their joint standard rate cut-off point would be €56,000. How much less tax would they have to pay between them in this case?

15. (a) The standard rate of income tax is 20% and the higher rate is 42%. Sheila has tax credits of €2,700 for the year and a standard rate cut-off point of €22,000. Sheila has a gross income of €45,000 for the year. Calculate the tax payable by Sheila for the year.

(b) Jack pays tax at the same rates as Sheila. Jack has tax credits of €2,900 for the year and has the same standard rate cut-off point as Sheila. His total tax payable amounts to €13,680 for the year. Calculate Jack's gross income for the year.

CHAPTER 22 KNOWLEDGE CHECKLIST

After completing this chapter, I now:

- **Understand the terms associated with income tax and the Irish tax system**
- **Am able to calculate income tax at the standard rate of tax and net pay**
- **Am able to calculate income tax to include two tax rates and calculate net pay**
- **Am able to calculate tax rates based on net income**

Equation of Circle

CHAPTER 23

TRIGONOMETRY 2

LEARNING OUTCOMES

In this chapter you will learn:

- ✓ To name the sides of a right-angled triangle
- ✓ How to measure angles using a clinometer
- ✓ To understand angles of elevation and depression and to use them to solve problems
- ✓ About special trigonometric ratios
- ✓ To find the sine, cosine and tangent of an angle
- ✓ To find the inverse of sin, cos and tan of an angle
- ✓ About the four quadrants in the unit circle
- ✓ To use trigonometric ratios to solve problems involving right-angled triangles
- ✓ To express trigonometric ratios in surd form

KEY WORDS

- Adjacent
- Angle of elevation
- Angle of depression
- Clinometer
- Cosine
- Hypotenuse
- Opposite
- Right-angled triangle
- Sine
- Surd form
- Tangent
- Theorem of Pythagoras
- Trigonometric ratios

INTRODUCTION

It is thought that the reason there are 360 degrees in a rotation is related to the approximate number of days in a year. Thousands of years ago, astronomers noticed that the sun followed a circular path over the course of the year, moving around 1° each day. Archimedes was the first Greek known to have divided a degree into 60 parts called minutes, something he learned from mathematicians in ancient India!

We have previously looked at the theorem of Pythagoras and how we can use it to find a missing side in a right-angled triangle.

As we learned in Chapter 10, trigonometry is a branch of mathematics which deals with triangles. We use trigonometry to solve problems such as finding the heights of buildings by measuring angles and distances.

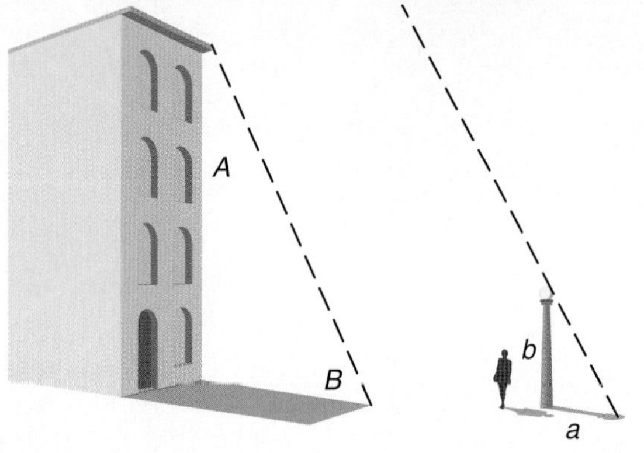

Section 23.1: Right-angled triangles

Student Activity 23A

1. Examine the triangle and answer the questions that follow.
   (a) What type of triangle is shown?
   (b) Which side is the longest in the triangle shown? Explain your answer.
   (c) What name is given to the longest side in a triangle?
   (d) If a fly landed in the angle marked 1, what side would be across from it?
   (e) If a fly landed in the angle marked 1, what side other than [AC] would be beside it?
   (f) Write down as many words as you can that mean the same as 'across from'.
   (g) Write down as many words as you can that mean the same as 'beside'.
2. Examine the triangle and answer the questions that follow.
   (a) Without measuring the sides, can you say which side is the longest? Explain your answer.
   (b) What do we call the longest side in a right-angled triangle?
   (c) If you were standing at the angle marked 1, can you think of an appropriate name for the side [BC]?
   (d) If you were standing at the angle marked 1, can you think of an appropriate name for the side [AB]?

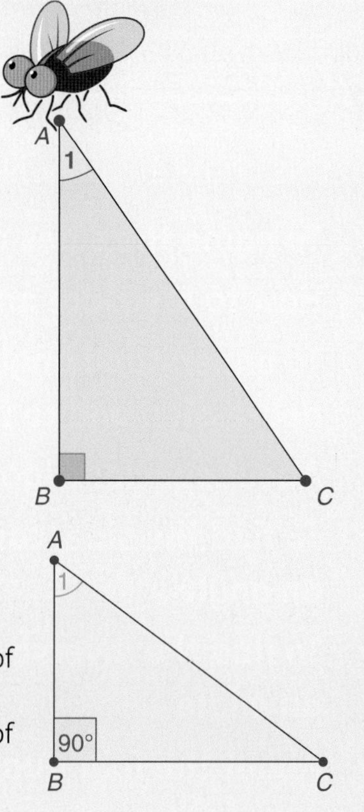

RIGHT-ANGLED TRIANGLES EXPLAINED

You have already learned that the longest side in a right-angled triangle is always opposite the right angle. This side is called the **hypotenuse.**

The other two sides are called the **opposite** and the **adjacent.** Which side is which will depend on the angle you are basing your calculations on.

For example, the following images show how the name of the side changes depending on the angle you are using. However, note that the hypotenuse is always the side opposite the right angle and does not change.

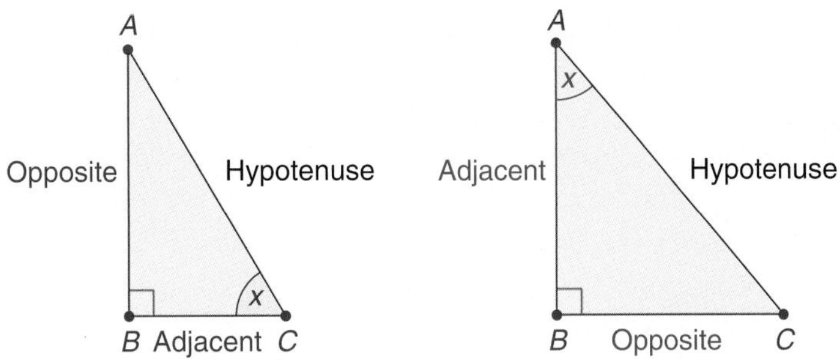

When naming the sides of a triangle:

- **Step 1:** Identify the hypotenuse, the longest side, which is directly in front of the right angle.
- **Step 2:** Identify the opposite side, which is directly in front of the angle you are working on.
- **Step 3:** Name the remaining side of the triangle, the adjacent.

EXAMPLE 1

Name the hypotenuse and the sides that are opposite and adjacent to the angle indicated.

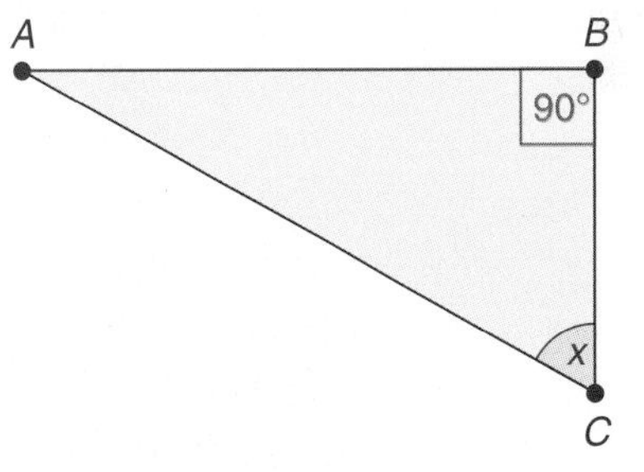

Solution

[AC] is the hypotenuse.

[AB] is opposite to the angle.

[BC] is adjacent to the angle.

Exercise 23.1

In each of the following triangles, name the (a) hypotenuse and the sides that are (b) opposite and (c) adjacent to the angle indicated.

1. 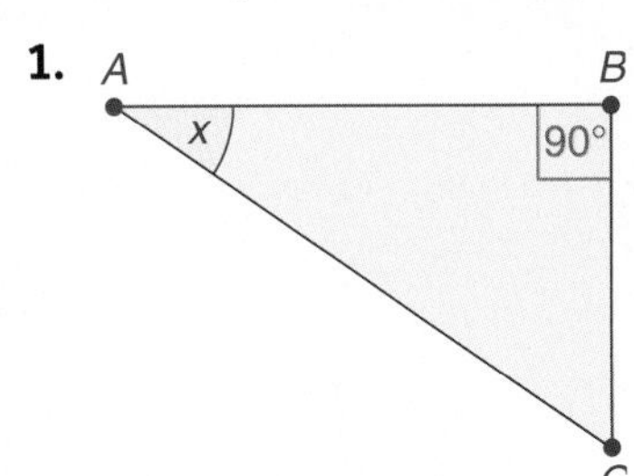

2. 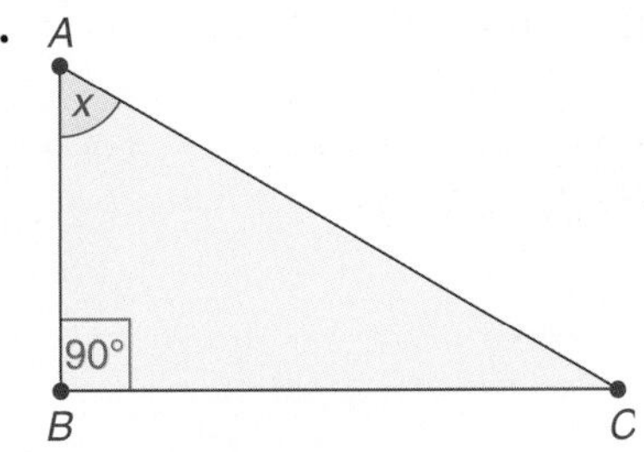

3. 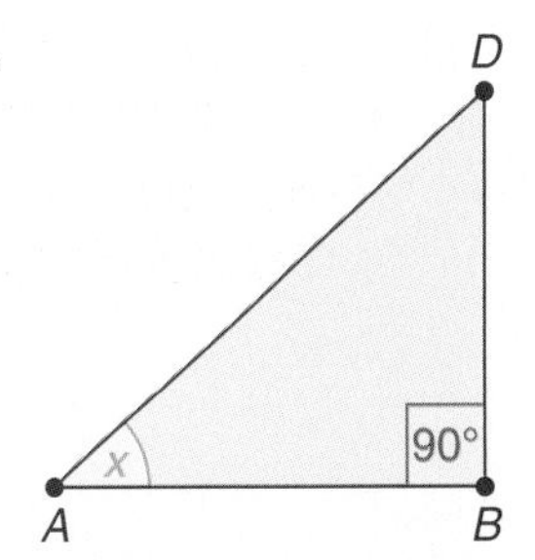

4. 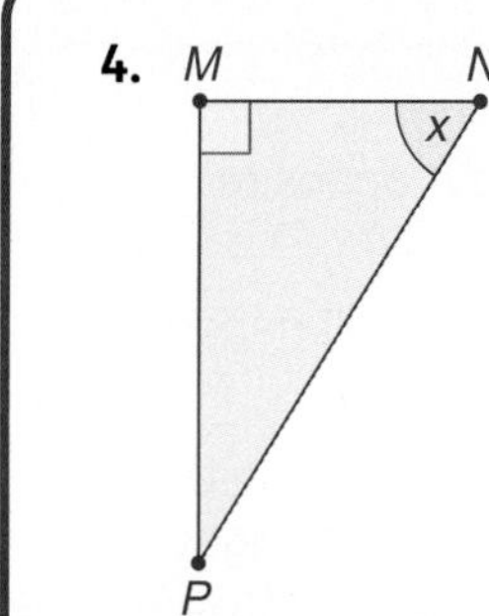

5. 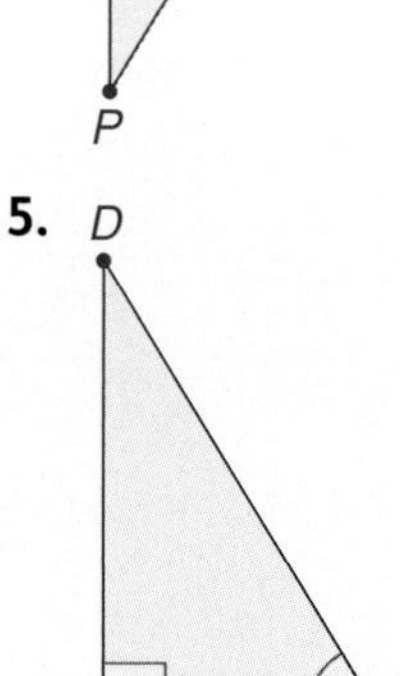

6. 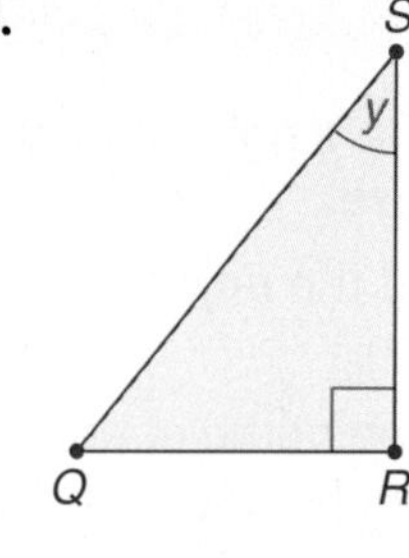

7. 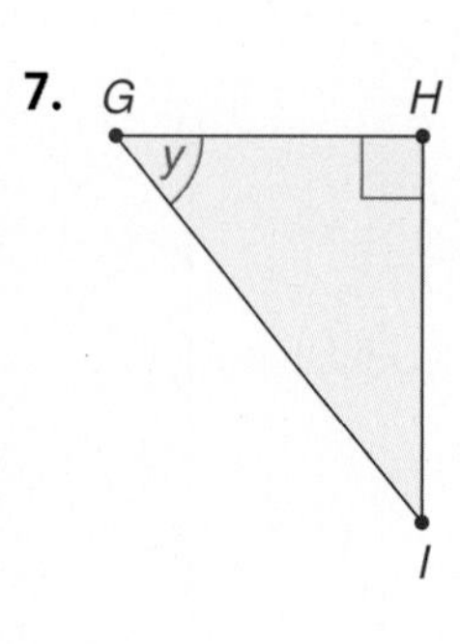

8. 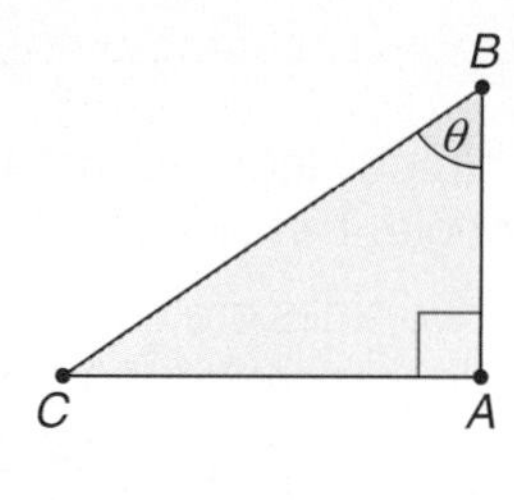

9. 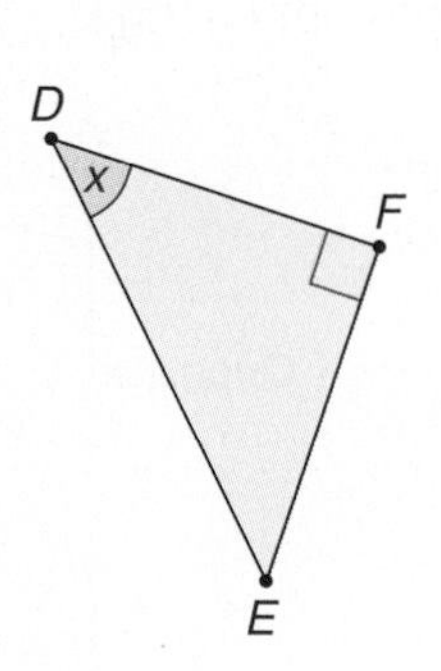

Section 23.2: Measuring angles

Student Activity 23B

Constructing a clinometer

Materials required: Straw, tape, thread, a weight (e.g. a key, 5c coin or a fishing weight). You will also need a 180° protractor. Alternatively photocopy the protractor template below. Glue the template to a sheet of cardboard. Then cut out the semicircular protractor.

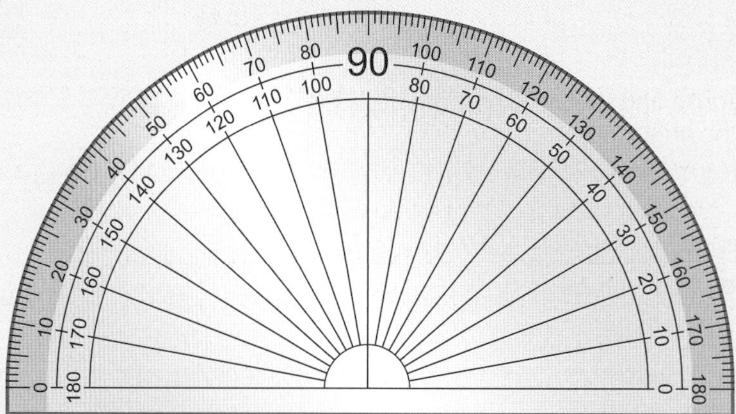

- **Step 1:** Tape a drinking straw to the base of the protractor as shown. Make sure you can peep through the taped straw.

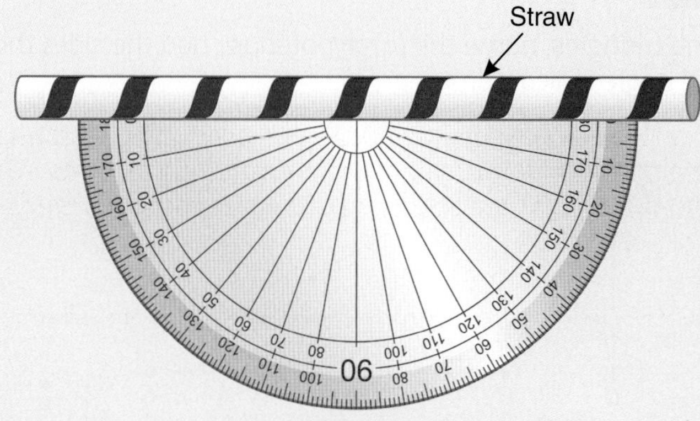

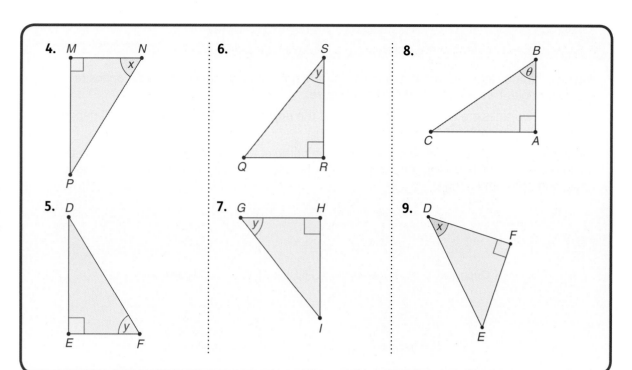

- **Step 2:** Tape one end of the thread to the centre of the protractor. Tie a weight to the free end of the thread.

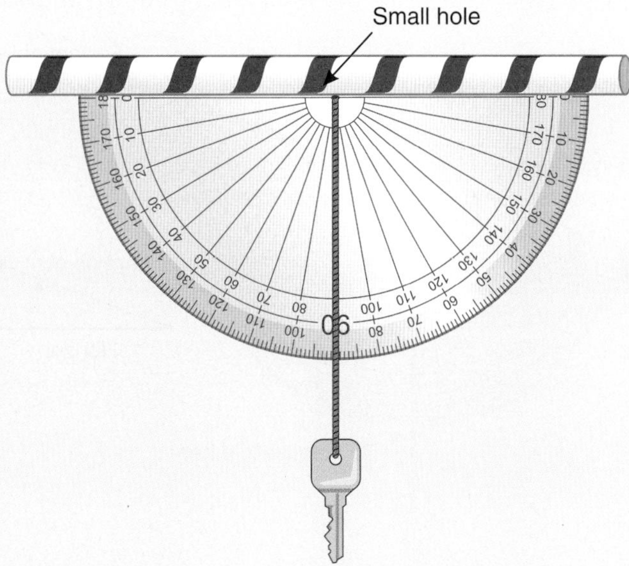

- **Step 3:** Let the weight swing free. When the straw is horizontal, the thread should lie along the 90° line and extend about 10 centimetres, as shown in the diagram above.

MEASURING ANGLES EXPLAINED

In Chapter 17, we learned that an hour can be broken down into smaller parts called minutes and seconds. In a full circle, there are 360 degrees.

- Each degree can also be split up into 60 parts called **minutes.** Each part is $\frac{1}{60}$ of a degree. The symbol for minutes is **’.**
- A minute can then also be split up into 60 parts called **seconds.** Each part is $\frac{1}{60}$ of a minute. The symbol for seconds is **”.**

An angle of 40 degrees, 20 minutes, 50 seconds is usually written as follows: 40°20′50″

You can use your calculator to change this angle to decimal form as follows:

- **Casio: °’’’** button ⇒ 40 [°’’’] 20 [°’’’] 50. Press the equals sign and then s↔d.
- **Sharp: D˚M’S** button ⇒ 40 [D°M'S] 20 [D°M'S] 50. Press the equals sign, the “shift button” followed by [D°M'S].

So 40°20′50″ = 40.3472 degrees (correct to four decimal places).

- 1 rotation = 360 degrees
- 1 degree = 60 minutes
- 1 minute = 60 seconds

You have already learned how to measure an angle on a page using a protractor. As we saw in Student Activity 23B, we need an instrument called a clinometer to measure the angle between the ground and a taller object such as a tree or a building. Clinometers are frequently used in astronomy, surveying and engineering.

You will now use the clinometer you made for Student Activity 23B. Working with a partner, one person looks through the straw at the higher object. The other person should be able to read the angle from the scale on the protractor when the weight hangs down and is motionless.

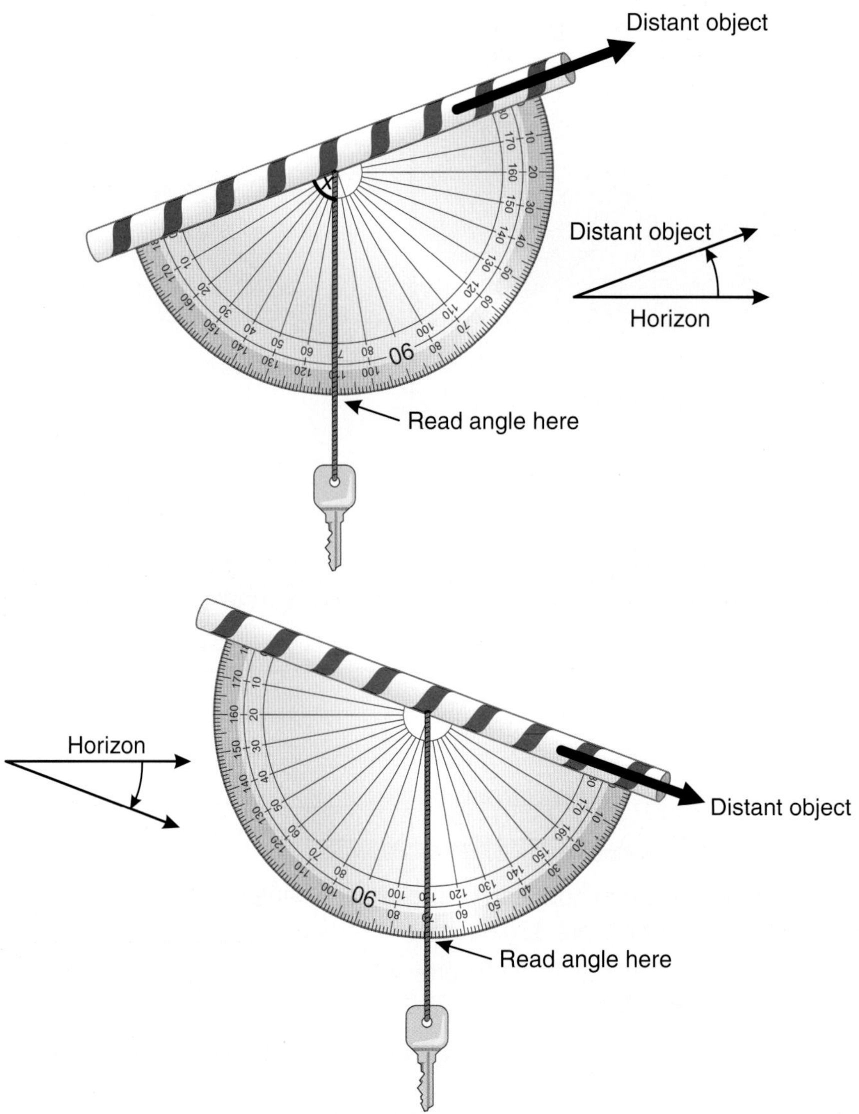

- An **angle of elevation** is the acute angle a line segment (the straw) makes with a horizontal line when measured above the horizon. For example, a person looking up at a flying kite soaring towards the sun makes an angle of elevation. The angle is measured from the person's eye level.
- An **angle of depression** is the acute angle a line segment (the straw) makes with a horizontal line when measured below the horizon. For example, a pilot in a flying airplane looking down at the runway makes an angle of depression. Again, the angle is measured from the person's eye level.

An **angle of elevation** is the acute angle a line makes with a horizontal line when measured above the horizon.
An **angle of depression** is the acute angle a line makes with a horizontal line when measured below the horizon.

Angles of elevation and depression are **alternate angles.**

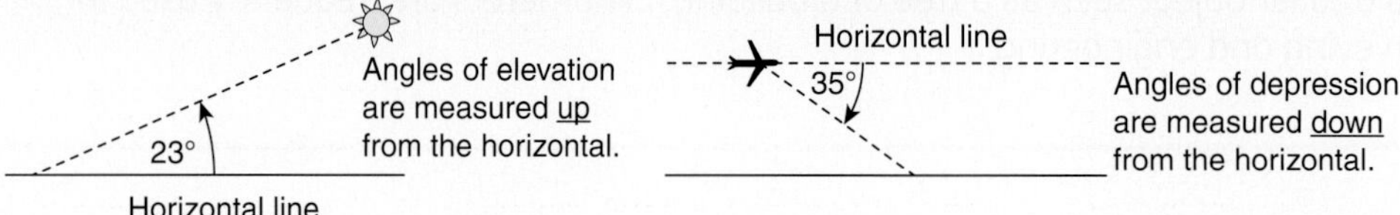

Later we will look at real-life trigonometry problems and see that it is easier to work with angles in relation to horizontal lines.

Exercise 23.2

1. Add the following angles:
   (a) 42°16′41″ + 36°45′15″
   (b) 19°21′52″ + 67°53′17″
   (c) 123°45′7″ + 71°39′18″
   (d) 45°56′16″ + 78°47′23″ + 38°48′56″
   (e) 101°57′34″ + 18°56′28″ + 87°41′41″

2. Subtract the following angles:
   (a) 142°16′41″ − 136°45′32″
   (b) 48°56′52″ − 17°33′11″
   (c) 123°59′46″ − 81°48′25″
   (d) 245°56′16″ − (78°47′23″ + 38°48′56″)
   (e) 211°57′34″ − (18°56′28″ + 7°41′41″)

3. Explain what an angle of depression is. Draw a diagram to illustrate your explanation.
4. Explain what an angle of elevation is. Draw a diagram to illustrate your explanation.
5. Sketch the triangles in the following images and identify the angles of elevation and depression:

(a)

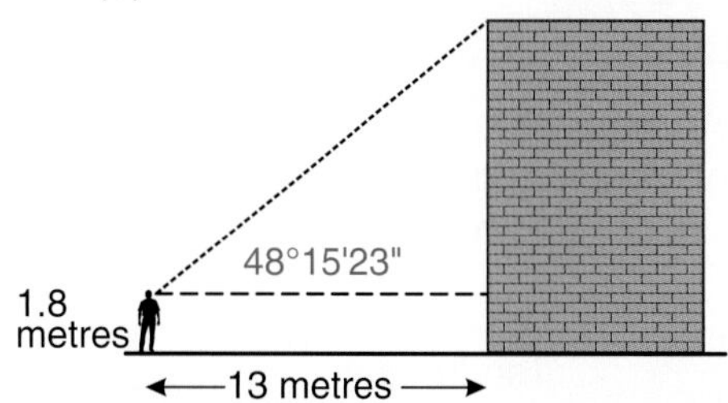

(b)

(c)

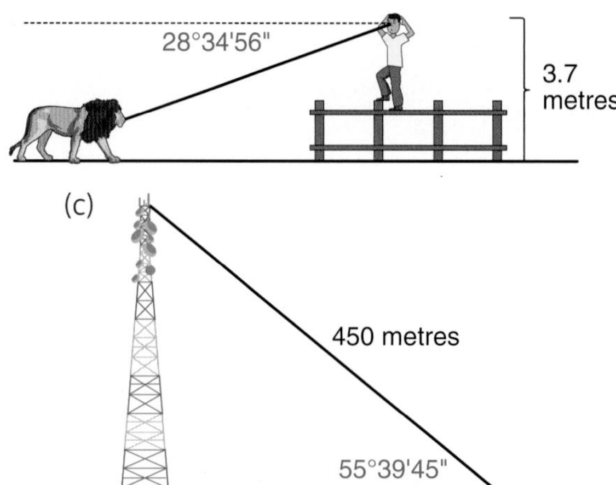

(d)

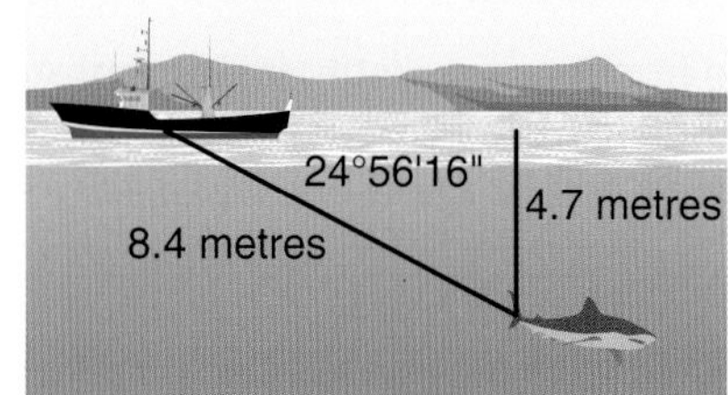

(e)

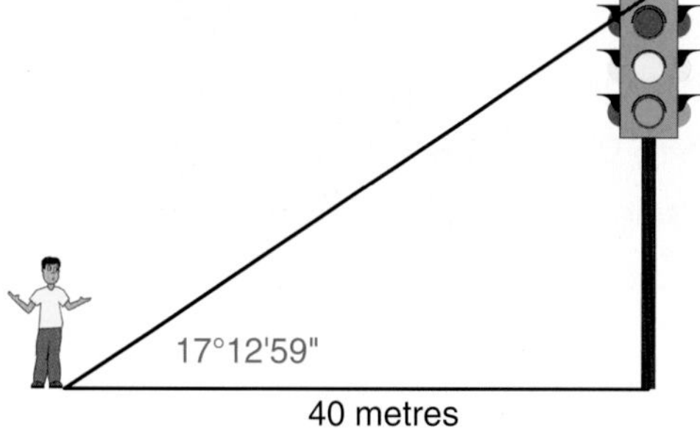

6. (a) What is a clinometer?
   (b) What is the largest angle of elevation you can measure on a clinometer?
   (c) What is the largest angle of depression you can measure on a clinometer?
7. (a) Working in pairs, use the clinometers you made in Student Activity 23A to measure the angle of elevation made with five tall objects around your school (e.g. a lamppost, a tree).
   (b) Calculate your distance from the object in metres using a trundle wheel.
   (c) Measure your height in metres.
   (d) Copy the table and record your results.

Name	Angle of elevation	Distance from object (metres)	Your own height (metres)
1.			
2.			
3.			
4.			
5.			

Section 23.3: Trigonometric ratios

Student Activity 23C

Examine the triangle and answer the questions that follow.

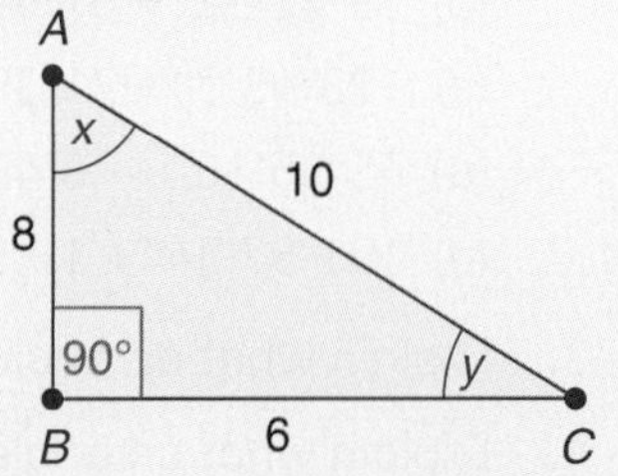

1. Can you write down six fractions using the lengths of the sides of the triangle shown?
2. For each of the fractions you have written down, write in words the sides involved. For example: $\frac{\text{Opposite}}{\text{Adjacent}}$.

TRIGONOMETRIC RATIOS EXPLAINED

All of the fractions you listed in Student Activity 23C are very important. They are known as **trigonometric ratios.** We use them when working with right-angled triangles. They are called **sine, cosine** and **tangent** but we usually shorten them to **sin, cos** and **tan.**

$\text{Sin (angle)} = \frac{\text{Opposite}}{\text{Hypotenuse}}$ $\text{Cos (angle)} = \frac{\text{Adjacent}}{\text{Hypotenuse}}$ $\text{Tan (angle)} = \frac{\text{Opposite}}{\text{Adjacent}}$

You will find these ratios on page 16 of the *Formulae and Tables.*

We can use the following rhyme to help us remember the fractions:

'**S**illy **O**ld **H**arry **C**aught **A** **H**erring **T**rawling **O**ff **A**merica'.

Using the first letter from each word, we can write: SOH CAH TOA.

EXAMPLE 2

Write down the (a) sin, (b) cos and (c) tan (as a common fraction) of the angle indicated in the triangle.

Solution

(a) $\sin (A) = \frac{3}{5}$

(b) $\cos (A) = \frac{4}{5}$

(c) $\tan (A) = \frac{3}{4}$

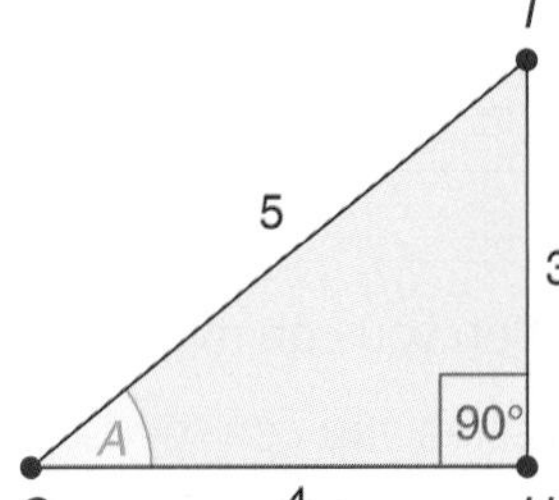

Exercise 23.3

Write down the sin, cos and tan (as a common fraction) of the angle indicated in each of the following questions:

1.

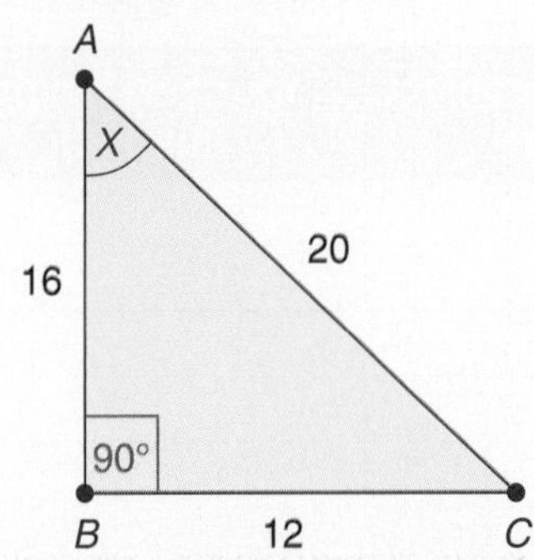

2.

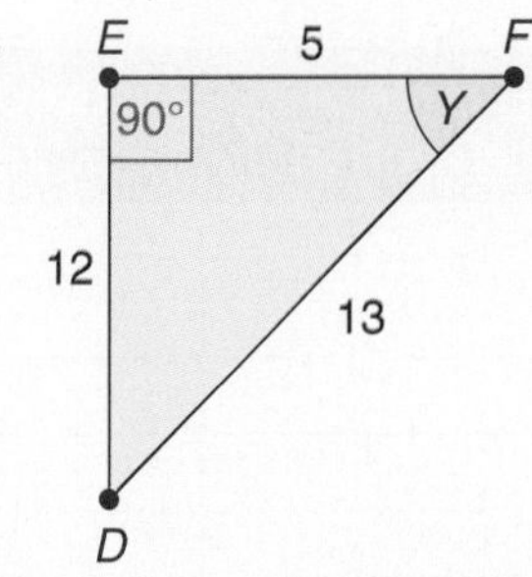

3.

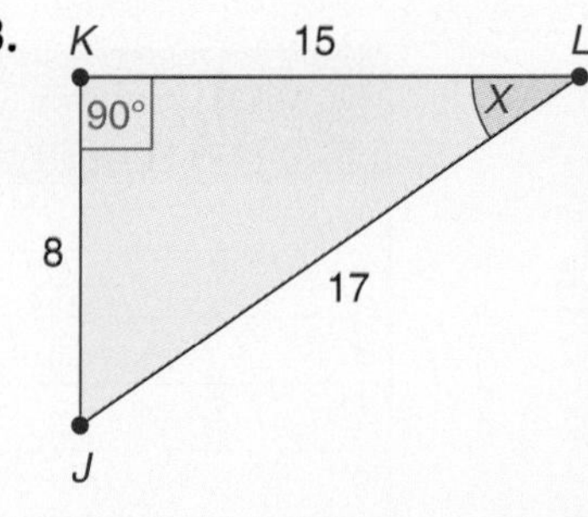

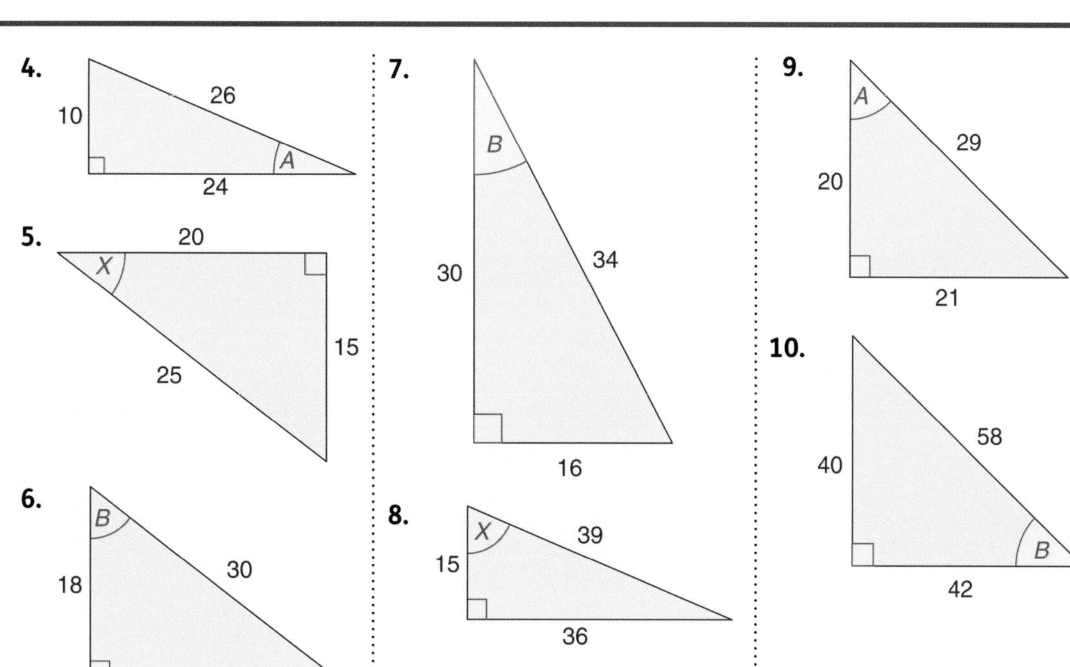

11. Examine the following triangles.

(a) Use the theorem of Pythagoras to calculate the length of the missing side.

(b) Then write down the sin, cos and tan of the angle indicated in fraction or surd form, where necessary.

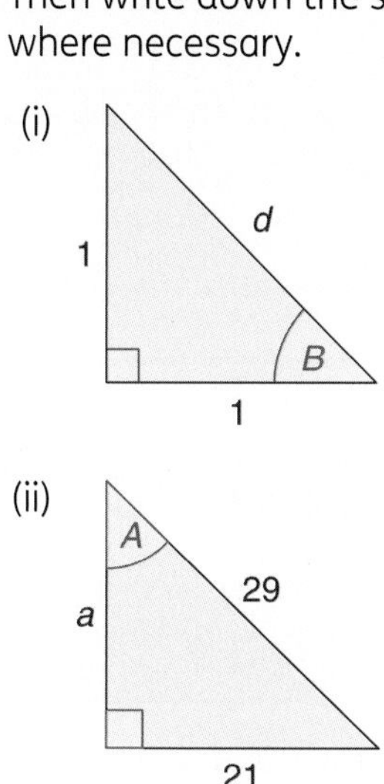

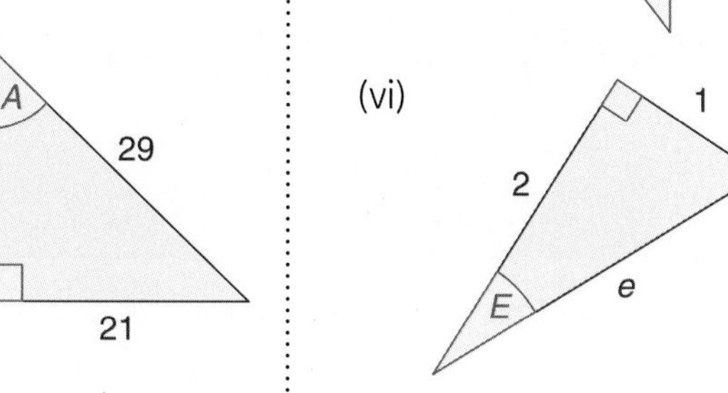

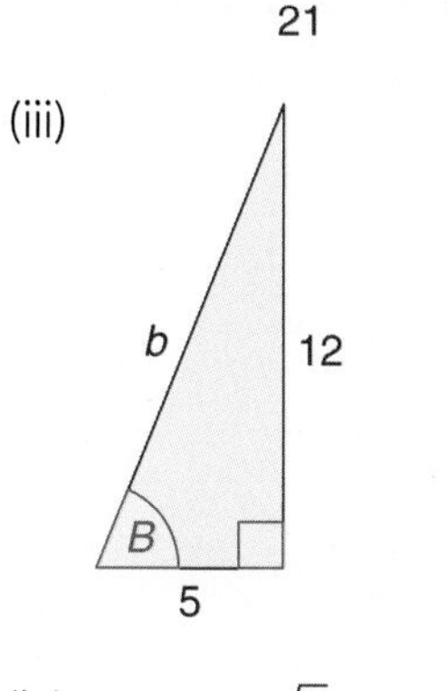

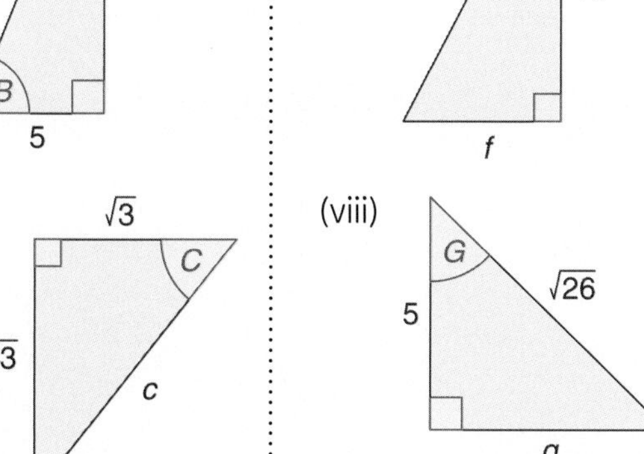

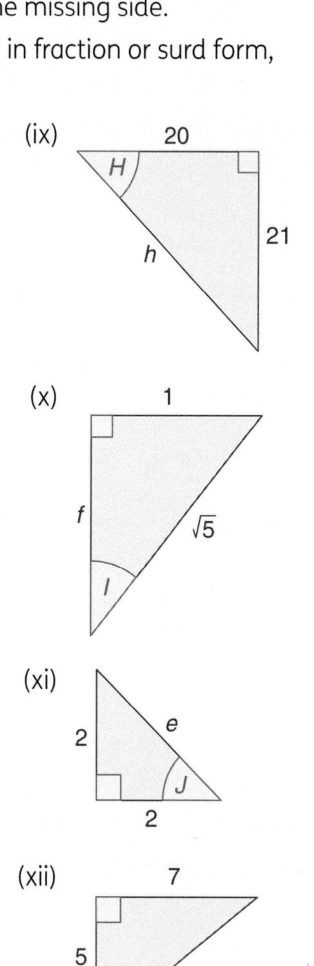

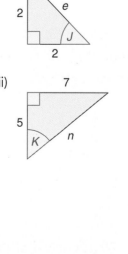

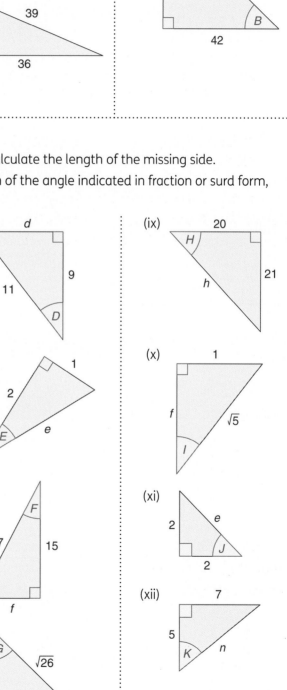

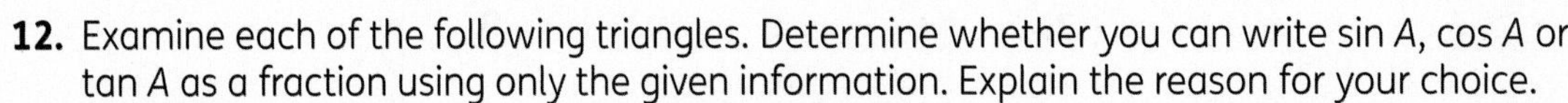

12. Examine each of the following triangles. Determine whether you can write sin A, cos A or tan A as a fraction using only the given information. Explain the reason for your choice.

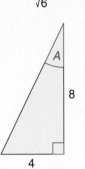

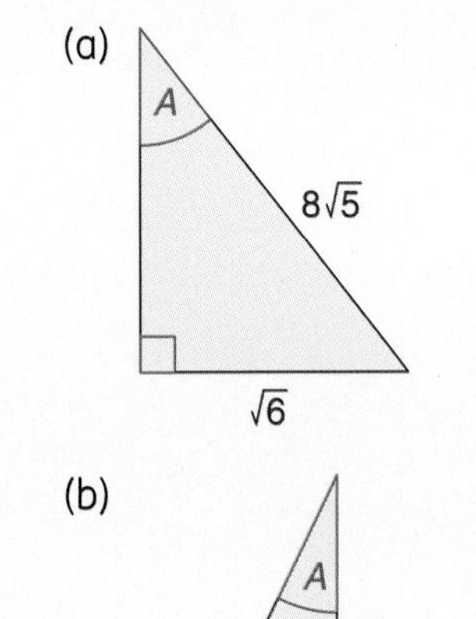

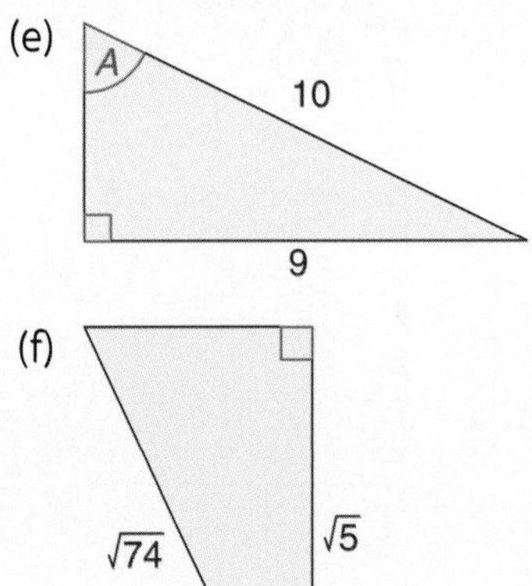

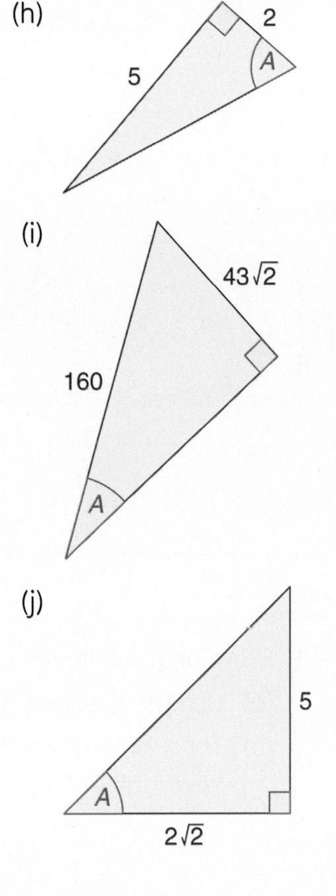

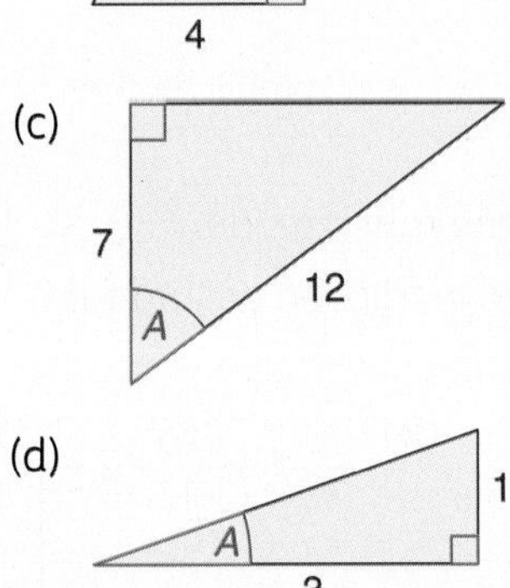

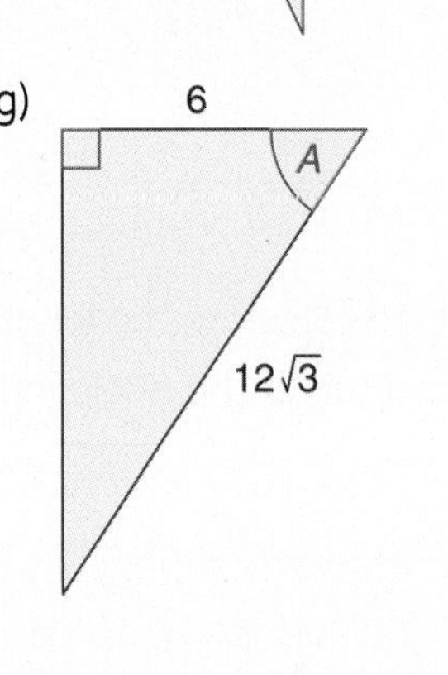

(c) 7, 12, A

(d) 1, A, 3

(g) 6, A, $12\sqrt{3}$

Section 23.4: Special trigonometric ratios

Student Activity 23D

1. (a) Measure the angles in the following triangles and indicate the 90° and 30° angles:

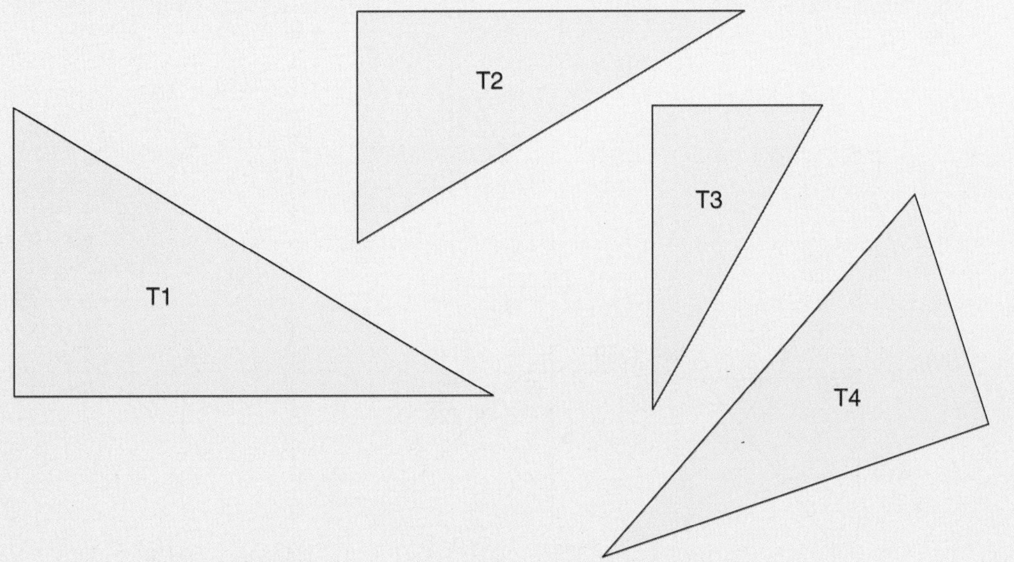

(b) Measure the lengths of the sides of the triangles in millimetres.

(c) Task A: Let A be the angle of size 30°.

(i) Copy and complete the following table:

30°	Hyp	Opp	Adj	$\frac{\text{Opp}}{\text{Hyp}}$		$\frac{\text{Adj}}{\text{Hyp}}$		$\frac{\text{Opp}}{\text{Adj}}$	
				Fraction	**Decimal**	**Fraction**	**Decimal**	**Fraction**	**Decimal**
T1									
T2									
T3									
T4									
Average (2 dec. pl.)									

(ii) Using your calculator, calculate the value of cos 30°, sin 30° and tan 30°. (Hint: make sure your calculator is in degree mode.)

(iii) Compare your results with this table.

(iv) Calculate $\frac{\sin 30°}{\cos 30°}$. Is this result like any other result you have just calculated?

2. (a) Measure the angles in the following triangles and indicate the 90° and 60° angles:

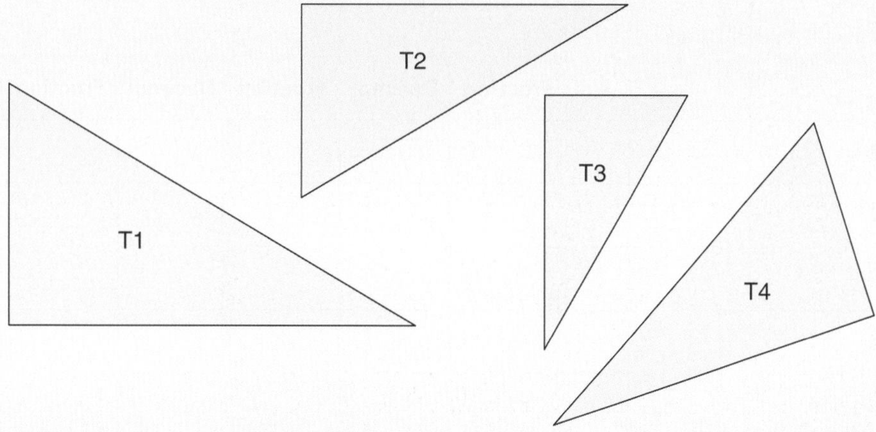

(b) Task B: Let A be the angle of size 60°.

(i) Copy and complete the following table:

60°	Hyp	Opp	Adj	$\frac{\text{Opp}}{\text{Hyp}}$		$\frac{\text{Adj}}{\text{Hyp}}$		$\frac{\text{Opp}}{\text{Adj}}$	
				Fraction	**Decimal**	**Fraction**	**Decimal**	**Fraction**	**Decimal**
T1									
T2									
T3									
T4									
Average (2 dec. pl.)									

(ii) Using your calculator, calculate the value of cos 60°, sin 60° and tan 60°.

(iii) Compare your results with this table.

(iv) Calculate $\frac{\sin 60°}{\cos 60°}$. Is this result like any other result you have just calculated?

3. (a) Measure the angles in the following triangles and indicate the 90° and 45° angles:

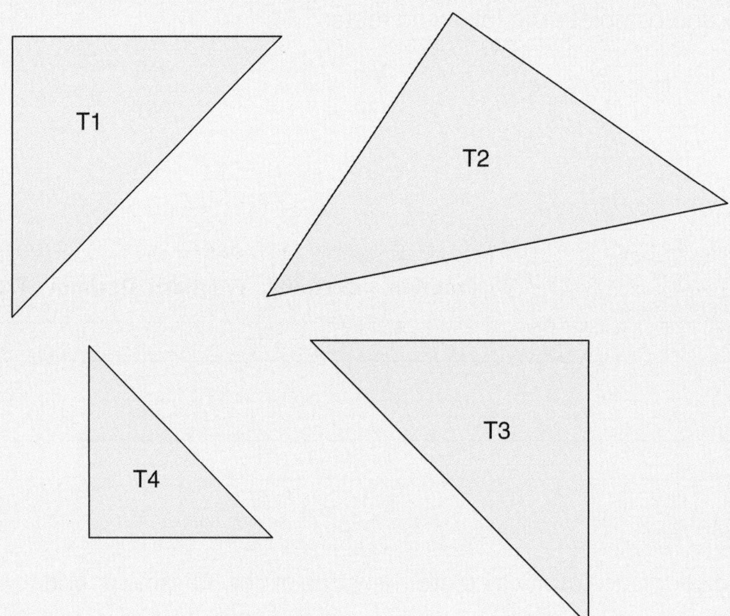

(b) Task C: Let A be the angle of size 45°.

(i) Copy and complete the following table:

45°	Hyp	Opp	Adj	$\frac{\text{Opp}}{\text{Hyp}}$		$\frac{\text{Adj}}{\text{Hyp}}$		$\frac{\text{Opp}}{\text{Adj}}$	
				Fraction	**Decimal**	**Fraction**	**Decimal**	**Fraction**	**Decimal**
T1									
T2									
T3									
T4									
Average (2 dec. pl.)									

(ii) Using your calculator, calculate the value of cos 45°, sin 45° and tan 45°.

(c) Compare your results with this table.

(d) Calculate $\frac{\sin 45°}{\cos 45°}$. Is this result like any other result you have just calculated?

4. Examine the triangles below.

(a) Calculate the missing sides in both triangles, giving your answer in surd form.

(b) Copy and complete the following table:

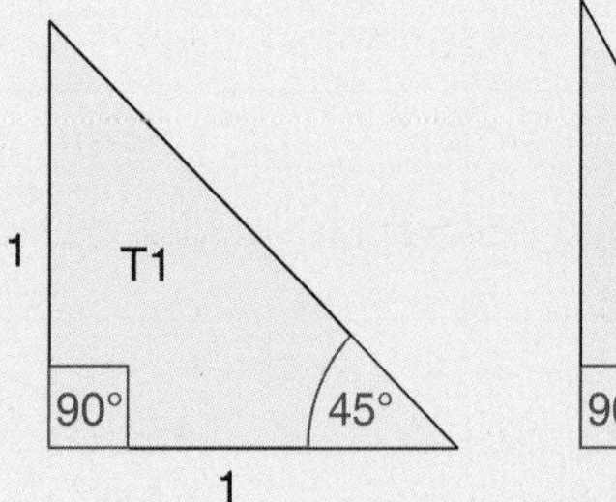

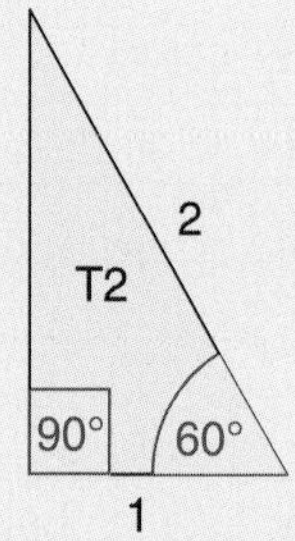

Angle A	30°	45°	60°	90°
Cos A				
Sin A				
Tan A				

SPECIAL TRIGONOMETRIC RATIOS EXPLAINED

In Student Activity 23D, you examined the fact that:

$$\text{Tan (angle)} = \frac{\text{Sin (angle)}}{\text{Cos (angle)}}$$

You can also use your calculator to find the sin, cos or tan of any angle.

In this activity, you expressed a trigonometric ratio in **surd form.** The angles you filled in the table on the previous page are normally expressed as these fractions. They are given on page 13 of the *Formulae and Tables.*

Make sure you understand how to read the table before practising using these ratios.

EXAMPLE 3

Calculate:

(a) sin 45° (b) cos 90° (c) tan 60° (d) $\cos^2 45°$

Solution

(a) $\sin 45° = \frac{1}{\sqrt{2}}$ (in surd form) or 0.707 (correct to 3 decimal places)

(b) $\cos 90° = 0$

(c) $\tan 60° = \sqrt{3}$ (in surd form) or 0.577 (correct to 3 decimal places)

(d) $\cos^2 45° = (\cos 45°)^2 = (\cos 45°)(\cos 45°) = \left(\frac{1}{\sqrt{2}}\right)\left(\frac{1}{\sqrt{2}}\right) = \frac{1}{2}$

EXAMPLE 4

Without using a calculator, find the value of each of the following, giving your answer in surd form.

(a) 1 + tan 45° (b) (sin 60°)(tan 30°)

Solution

(a) $1 + \tan 45° = 1 + 1 = 2$

(b) $(\sin 60°)(\tan 30°) = \left(\frac{\sqrt{3}}{2}\right)\left(\frac{\sqrt{3}}{3}\right) = \frac{3}{6} = \frac{1}{2}$

Exercise 23.4

Use the calculator to evaluate each of the following, correct to two decimal places:

1. sin 46° **3.** tan 46° **5.** tan 87° **7.** sin 47° **9.** sin 35°

2. cos 27° **4.** sin 27° **6.** sin 33° **8.** cos 54° **10.** tan 42°

Use the *Formula and Tables* to write the following in surd form:

11. tan 30° **13.** cos 90° **15.** cos 0° **17.** tan 60° **19.** cos 60°

12. sin 60° **14.** tan 45° **16.** sin 30° **18.** sin 45° **20.** sin 90°

21. Examine the following triangle and, without using your calculator, evaluate:

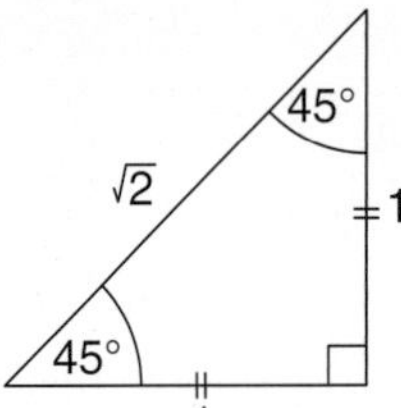

(a) $\sin 45°$

(b) $\cos 45°$

(c) $\dfrac{\sin 45°}{\cos 45°}$

(d) $\tan 45°$

(e) What can you conclude from your answers to parts (c) and (d)?

22. Examine the following triangle and, without using your calculator, evaluate:

(a) $\sin 30°$

(b) $\cos 30°$

(c) $\tan 30°$

(d) $\sin 60°$

(e) $\cos 60°$

(f) $\tan 60°$

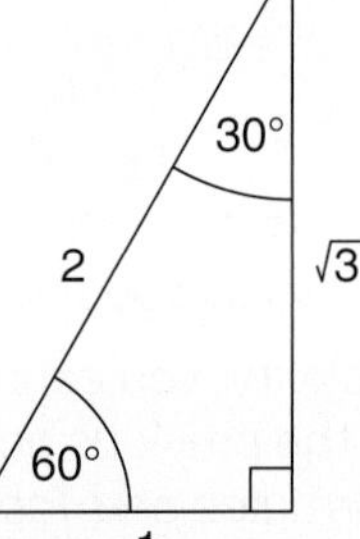

23. Without using a calculator, calculate the value for each of the following. Give your answer in surd form.

(a) $\tan^2 60°$ (b) $\cos^2 30°$ (c) $\sin^2 30°$ (d) $(\sin 60°)(\sin 30°)$ (e) $(\tan 45°)(\cos 45°)$

24. Show that $\sin 30° + \cos 60° = 1$.

25. Show that $\cos 60° = \cos^2 30° - \sin^2 30°$.

26. If $A = 30°$ and $B = 60°$, find the value of $\cos A \sin B$.

27. (a) Investigate if $\cos^2 60° + \sin^2 60° = \cos^2 30° + \sin^2 30°$.

(b) Investigate if $\cos^2 45° + \sin^2 45° = \cos^2 25° + \sin^2 25°$.

(c) Investigate if $\cos^2 (22°52') + \sin^2 (22°52') = \cos^2 (54.5°) + \sin^2 (54.5°)$.

(d) Investigate if $\cos^2 (26°) + \sin^2 (26°) = \cos^2 \left(78\tfrac{1}{2}°\right) + \sin^2 \left(78\tfrac{1}{2}°\right)$.

(e) Based on the above results, what can you conclude?

Section 23.5: Inverse trigonometric ratios

As with all other mathematical operations, sin, cos and tan have an **inverse,** or opposite operation.

- The inverse operation of + is −.
- The inverse operation of × is ÷.

The inverse operations for sin, cos and tan are a little more complicated. We use our calculators to do the work for us.

The $\sin^{-1}$, $\cos^{-1}$ and $\tan^{-1}$ buttons are located above the sin, cos and tan buttons on your calculator.

To use the inverse button you must press '2ndF' or 'Shift' first.

x=y EXAMPLE 5

If $\sin A = 0.787$, find the angle A correct to the nearest degree.

Solution

$\sin A = 0.787$

$A = \sin^{-1}(0.787)$

Press the SHIFT or 2ndF button.

Press Sin key.

Type in 0.787.

Press the '=' button to get $A = 52°$.

EXAMPLE 6

If $\cos X = 0.4487$, find the angle X correct to the nearest minute.

Solution

$\cos X = 0.4487$

$X = \cos^{-1}(0.4487)$

Press SHIFT or 2ndF button.

Press Cos key.

Type in 0.4487.

Press '='.

$X = 63.33969°$

Then press Shift/2ndF and °′″ to convert to degrees and minutes.

$X = 63°20'$

Exercise 23.5

Calculate each of the following angles, correct to three decimal places:

1. $\sin^{-1}(0.654)$ **3.** $\tan^{-1}(1.32)$ **5.** $\tan^{-1}(0.698)$ **7.** $\sin^{-1}(0.6293)$ **9.** $\tan^{-1}(-1.732)$

2. $\cos^{-1}(0.435)$ **4.** $\sin^{-1}(0.79)$ **6.** $\cos^{-1}(0.287)$ **8.** $\cos^{-1}(0.848)$ **10.** $\cos^{-1}(0.8434)$

Calculate each of the following and give your answer correct to the nearest degree:

11. $\sin^{-1}(0.342)$ **13.** $\cos^{-1}(0.5)$ **15.** $\tan^{-1}(0.4663)$ **17.** $\sin^{-1}(0.7071)$ **19.** $\tan^{-1}(0.1763)$

12. $\tan^{-1}(-0.7)$ **14.** $\tan^{-1}(1.02)$ **16.** $\sin^{-1}(0.5)$ **18.** $\cos^{-1}(0.7071)$ **20.** $\sin^{-1}(-0.866)$

Find to the nearest degree, the measure of the named angle.

21. $\cos A = 0.407$ **23.** $\tan C = 7.916$ **25.** $\sin E = 0.6173$ **27.** $\cos G = 0.4868$ **29.** $\tan J = 3.2107$

22. $\sin B = 0.1346$ **24.** $\cos D = 0.0578$ **26.** $\tan F = 0.4621$ **28.** $\sin H = 0.7541$ **30.** $\cos K = 0.4773$

Section 23.6: Using trigonometric ratios to solve right-angled triangles

We can also use sin, cos and tan to find a missing angle in a right-angled triangle. This is where we now apply our trigonometric knowledge to help us solve some practical problems.

When approaching a question of this type, use the following steps:

- **Step 1:** Label the sides given as hypotenuse, opposite or adjacent in relation to the required angle.
- **Step 2:** Choose which ratio (sin, cos or tan) to use based on the information you know.
- **Step 3:** Use $\sin^{-1}$, $\cos^{-1}$, $\tan^{-1}$ to find the unknown angle.

EXAMPLE 7

A building is 50 m high and casts a shadow 24 m long on the horizontal ground as shown. Calculate the angle of elevation to the top of the building, correct to the nearest degree.

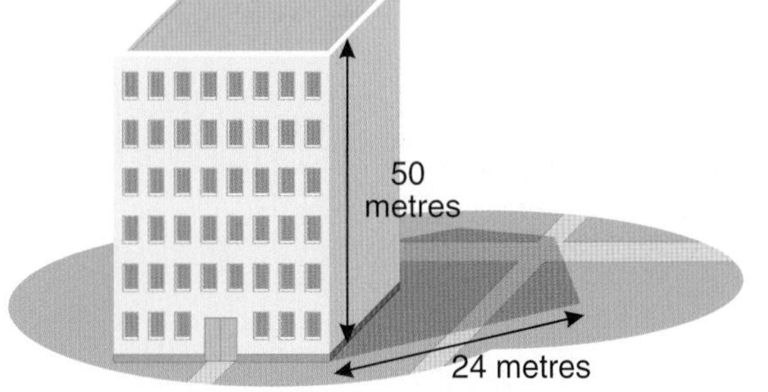

Solution

First, convert the given information into a more suitable diagram so we can easily identify the relevant information.

We have the opposite side = 50 m and adjacent side = 24 m so we use tan of the angle.

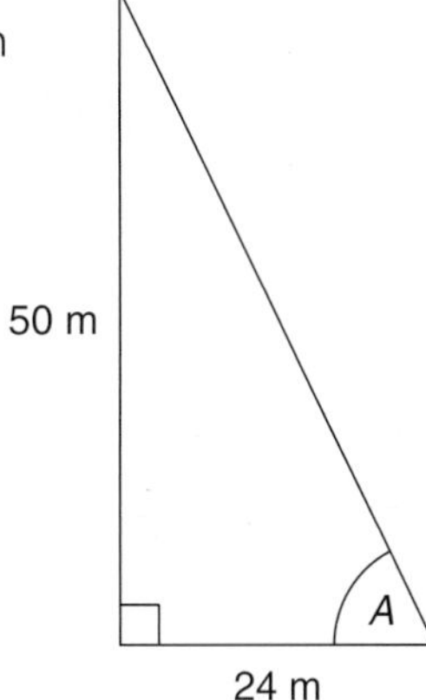

$\tan A = \frac{\text{Opp}}{\text{Adj}}$

$\tan A = \frac{50}{24}$

$A = \tan^{-1}\frac{50}{24}$

$A = 64.358°$

$A = 64°21'$

$A = 64°$

EXAMPLE 8

Find the angle indicated in the given triangle, correct to the nearest degree:

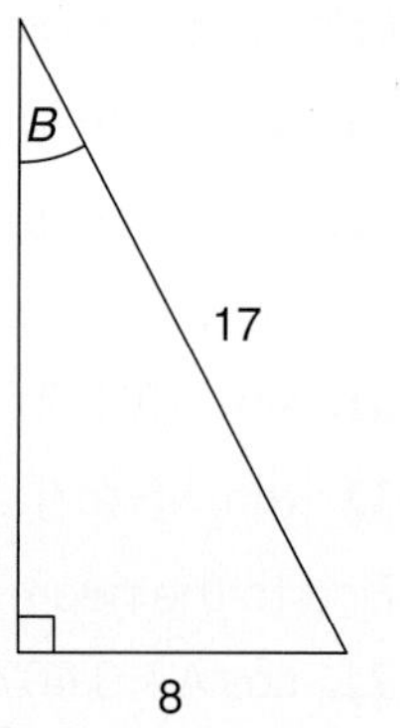

Solution

From the given triangle we can see that:

Hypotenuse = 17

Opposite = 8

We are not given the adjacent, so ignore all formulae involving the 'adjacent'.

Use sine.

$\sin B = \frac{\text{Opp}}{\text{Hyp}}$

$\sin B = \frac{8}{17}$

$B = \sin^{-1} \frac{8}{17}$

$B = \sin^{-1} (0.470588235)$

$B = 28°$

Exercise 23.6

1. Find the angle indicated in the given triangles, correct to the nearest degree:

(a)

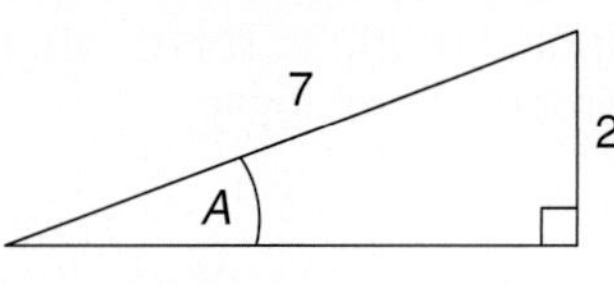

(b)

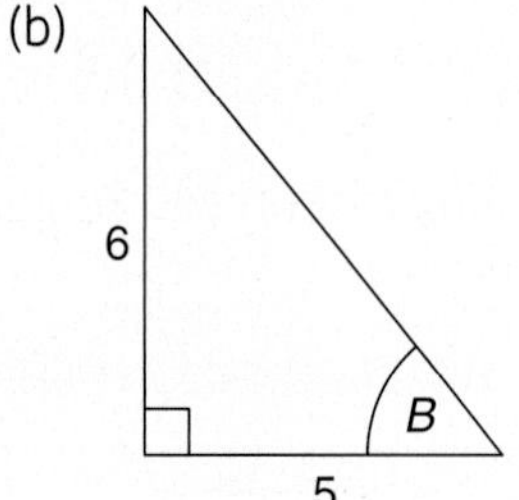

(c)

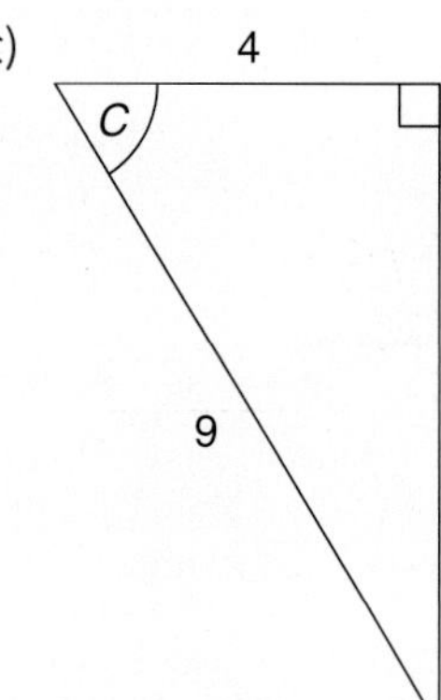

(d)

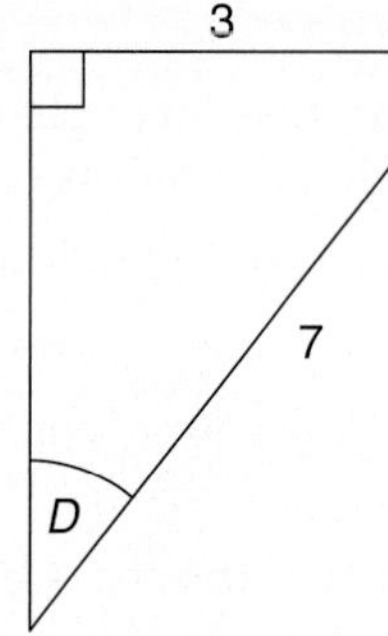

(e)

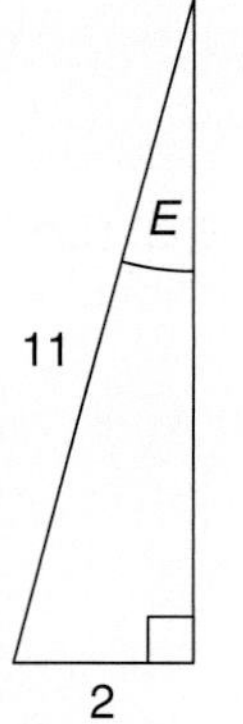

(f)

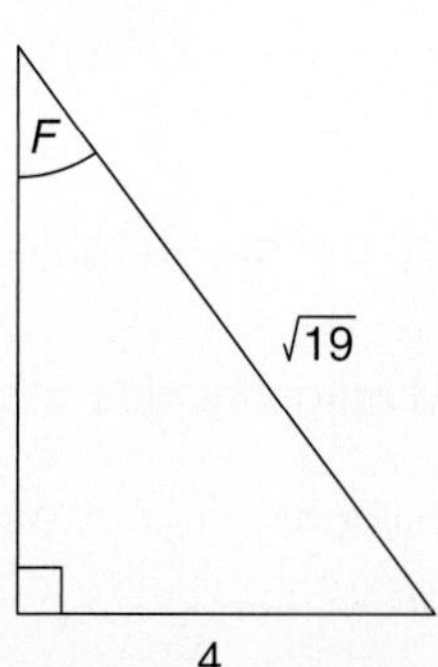

(g)

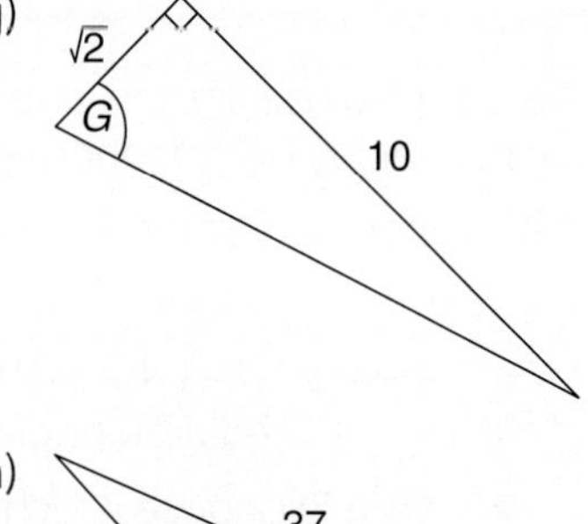

(h)

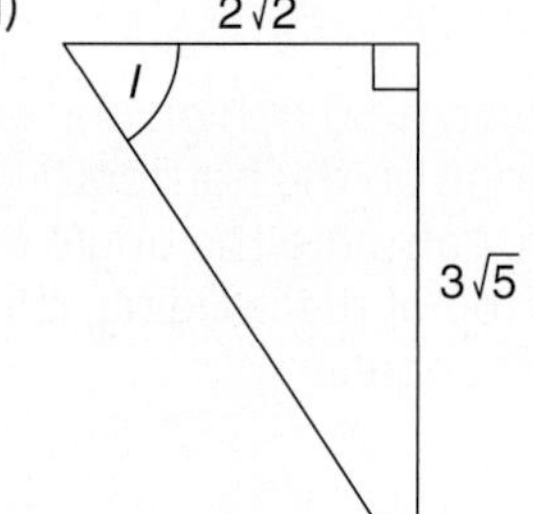

(i)

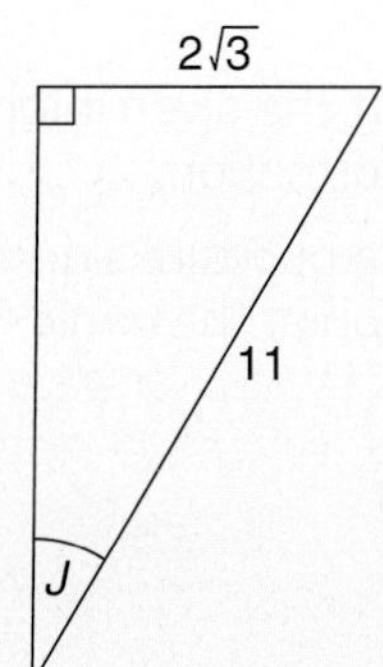

(j) $2\sqrt{3}$, 11, J

2. Find the missing side indicated in the given triangles, correct to one decimal place:

(a)
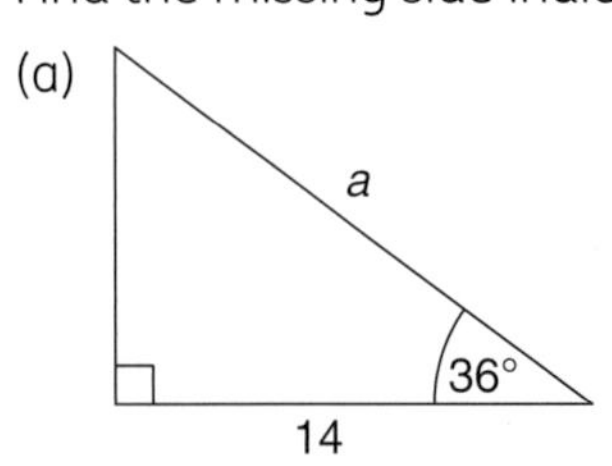

(b)
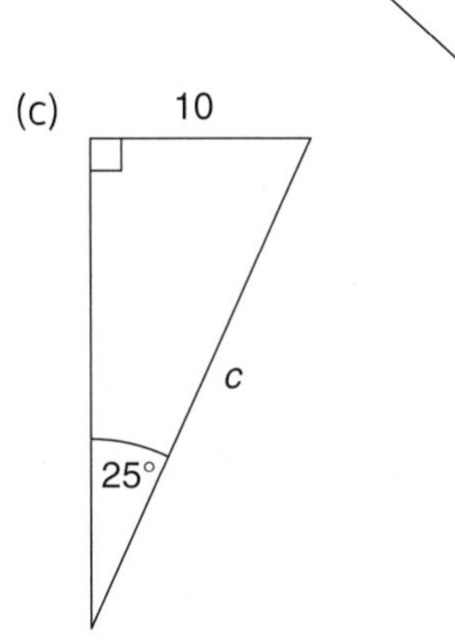

(c)

(d)
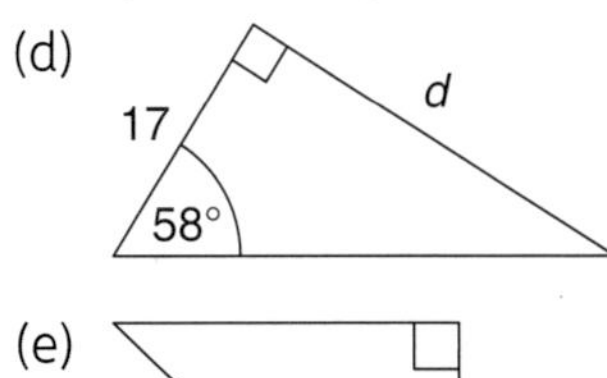

(e)
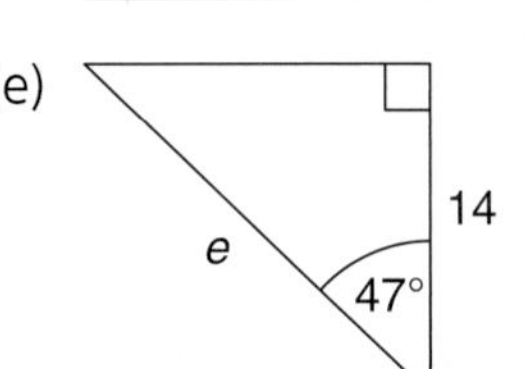

(f)
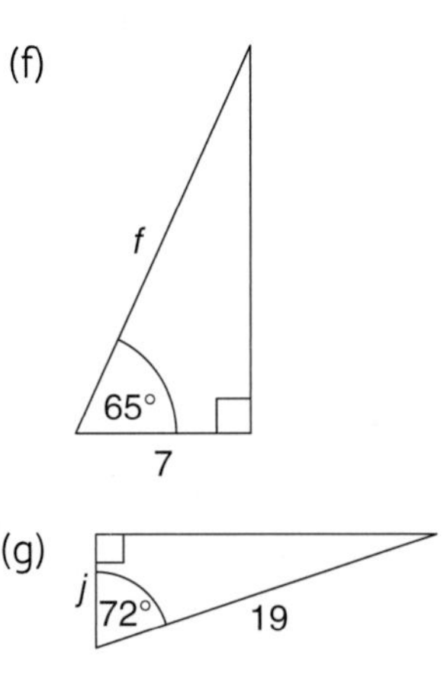

(g)

(h)
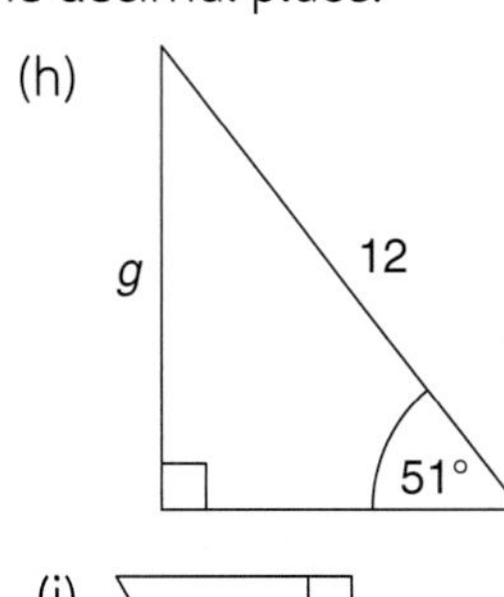

(i)
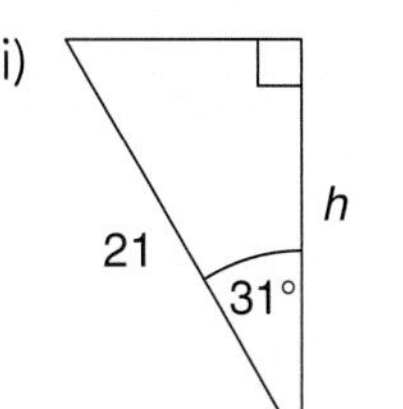

(j)
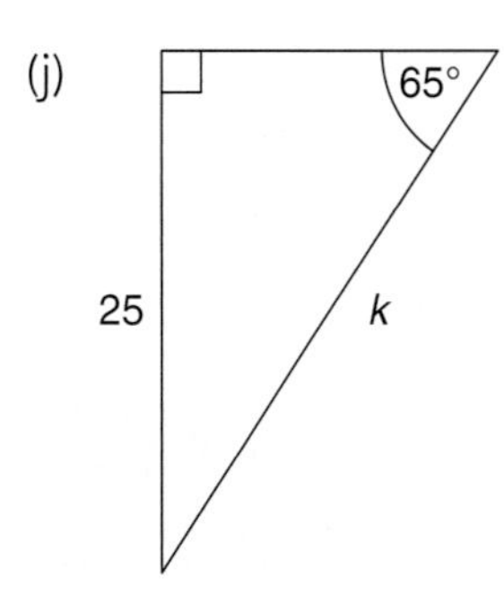

3. John is making a zip line for his friends. He secures a rope from a tree 25 m above ground and needs to connect it to a secure post in the ground, 40 m away from the foot of the tree as shown.

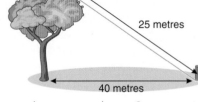

(a) What length of rope will John need? Give your answer correct to one decimal place.

(b) What angle will the rope make with the ground correct to the nearest degree?

4. After take-off, a plane is 20 km from a beacon and is at an angle of 37° to the beacon. What height above the ground is the plane correct to one decimal place?

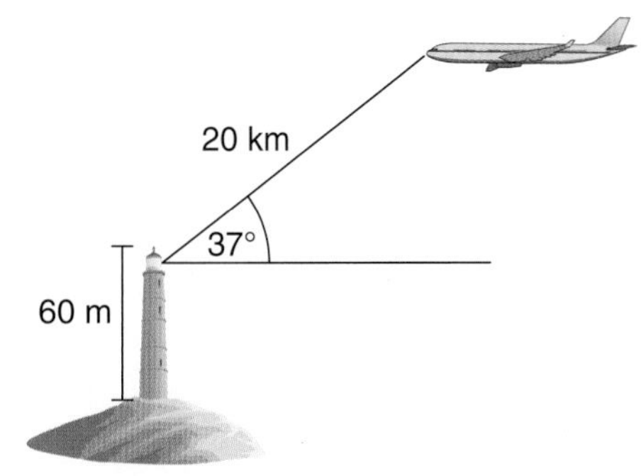

5. A carpenter is measuring a new house before he builds the roof. The roof will span 12 m and must be 5 m high at its centre. What pitch (the degree of slope) is the roof, correct to the nearest degree?

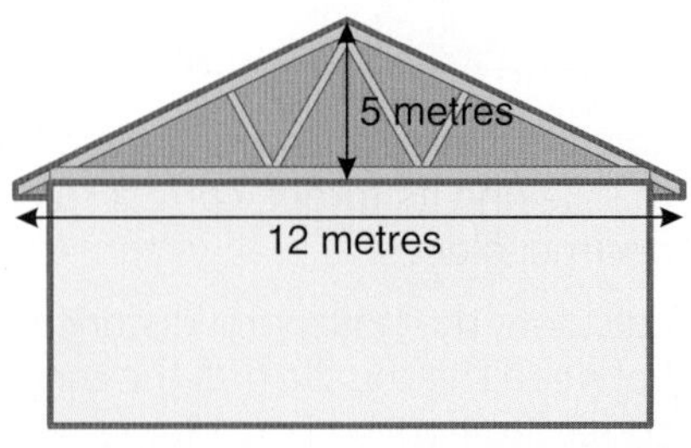

6. A gardener is building a prism-shaped polytunnel as shown. If the tunnel is 1.5 m high at its centre and 6 m wide, what angle will the side poles be to the ground, correct to the nearest degree?

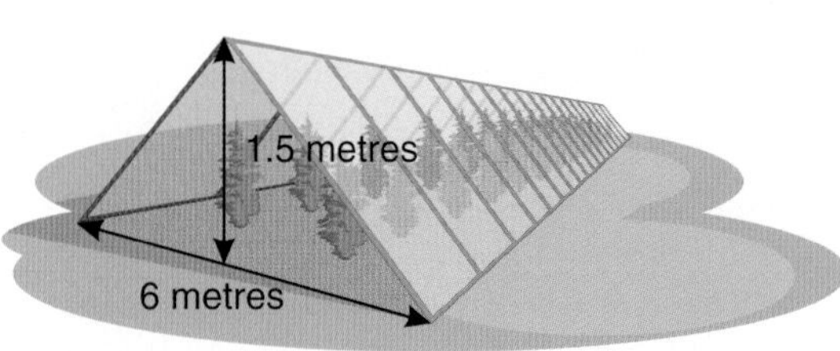

7. A flag pole is supported by a cable which is attached to a peg in the ground 24 m away. If the angle of elevation of the cable is 20°, find:

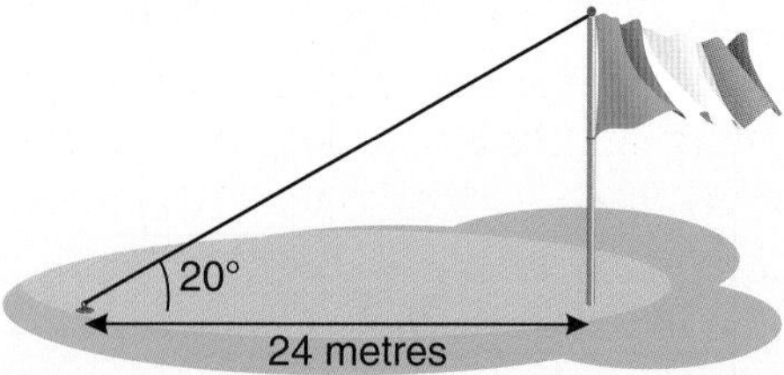

(a) The length of the cable, correct to two decimal places

(b) The height of the flag pole, correct to two decimal places

8. A man walking along a river bank spots his friend on the other side at an angle of 48° to the side of the bank. If his friend is 45 m downstream, how wide is the river, correct to the nearest metre?

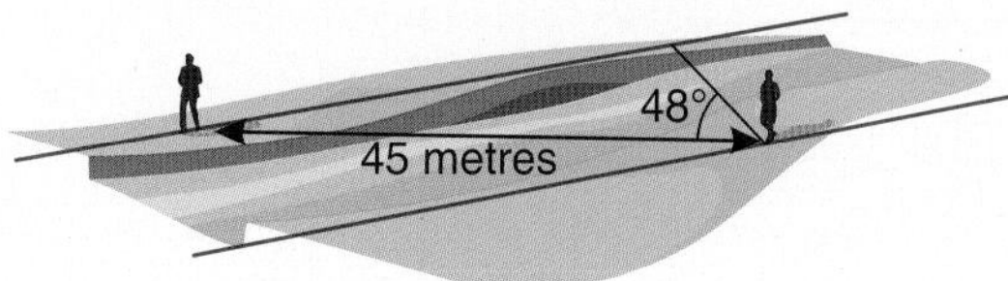

9. A boy 1.6 m tall is flying his kite as shown. The string attached to the kite is 45 m long and the string makes an angle of 73° with the boy's arm. Find the perpendicular height of the kite above the ground, correct to the nearest metre.

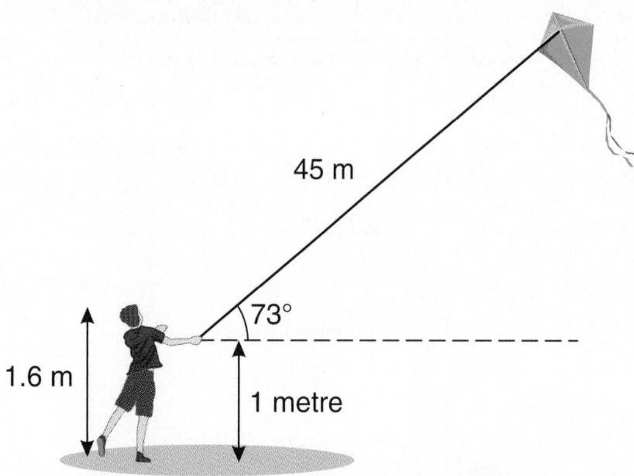

10. A woman standing on a vertical cliff 85 m high sees a fishing boat 150 m from the base of the cliff.

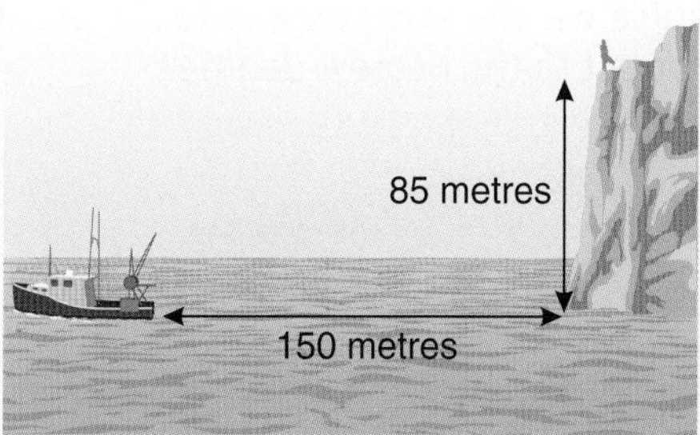

Find:

(a) The angle of elevation from the boat to the top of the cliff, correct to the nearest degree

(b) The distance from the top of the cliff to the top of the boat, correct to two decimal places

(c) The angle of depression from the top of the cliff to the boat, correct to the nearest degree

11. Two cars leave town A. One drives north towards town B for 3 hours at a speed of 54 km per hour, while the other car travels east towards town C for 45 minutes at a speed of 120 km per hour. Calculate the distance between the cars, correct to the nearest km.

12. In the diagram shown, find:

(a) The perpendicular height of the plane above the ground, correct to the nearest metre

(b) The angle of elevation of the plane, correct to the nearest degree

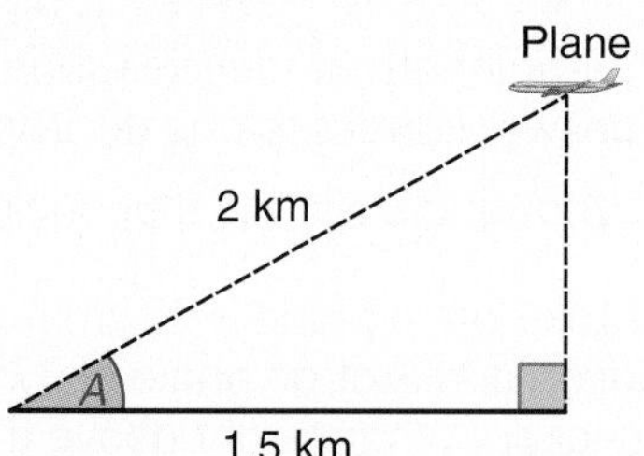

13. A missile is fired from a plane heading for target A as shown.

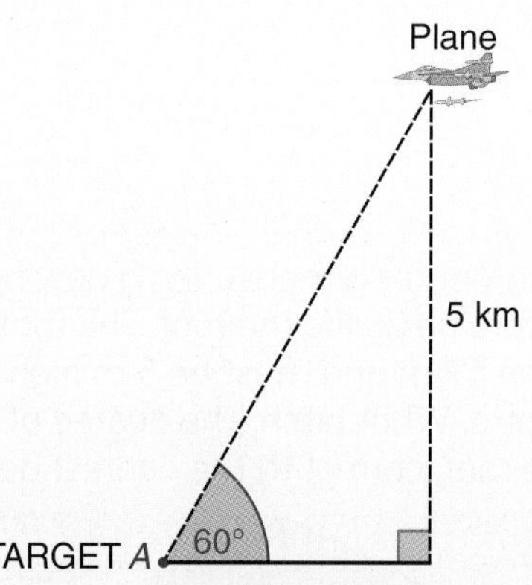

(a) Calculate the distance between the missile and its target, correct to two decimal places.

(b) Calculate the horizontal distance between the missile and the target, correct to two decimal places.

14. A quantity surveyor is measuring the distance from a point on a road to a tree top of height 20 m as shown.

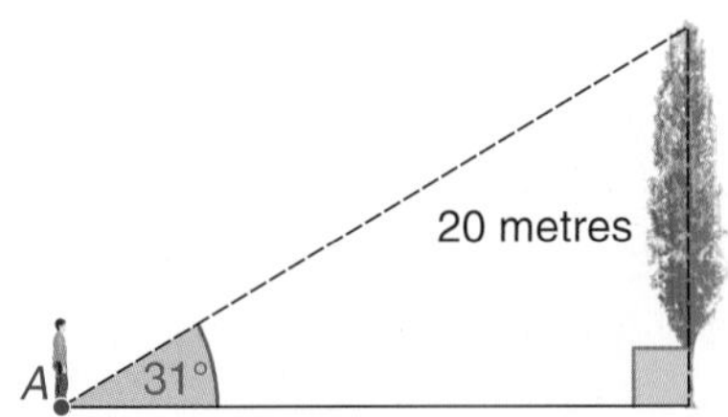

(a) Calculate the horizontal distance between the surveyor and the base of the tree, correct to two decimal places.

(b) Calculate the distance between the surveyor and the top of the tree, correct to two decimal places.

15. A flag pole [*BC*] is suspended from a vertical wall of height 4 m as shown and is supported by a metal bar [*AC*].

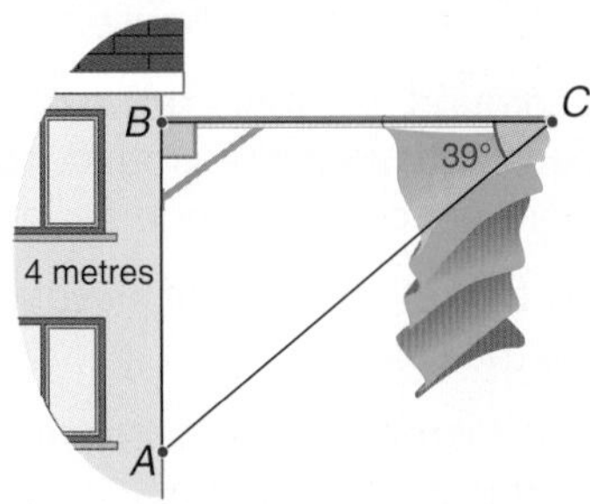

(a) Calculate the length of the metal bar, correct to two decimal places.

(b) Calculate the length of the flag pole, correct to two decimal places.

16. A welder is soldering two pieces of metal to make a decorative piece for her house.

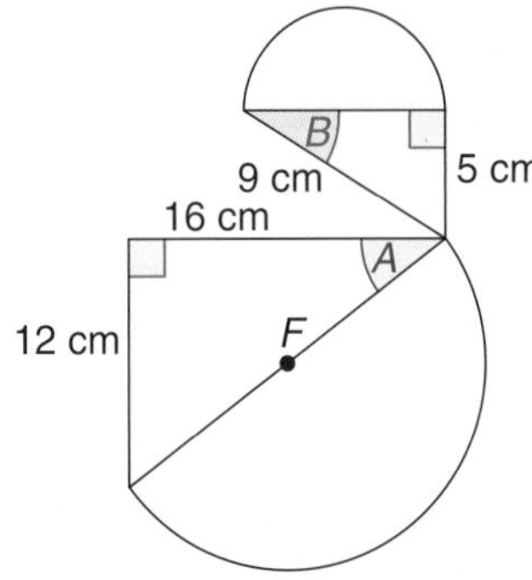

(a) Calculate the angles indicated.

The point *F* is the centre of the larger semicircle and the midpoint of the side of shown.

(b) Calculate the length of the arc in the larger semicircle, correct to two decimal places.

(c) Calculate the length of the arc in the smaller semicircle, correct to two decimal places.

(d) Calculate the total length of metal needed to make the piece, correct to the nearest cm.

17. A bracket for a shelf is fixed to a wall with two screws. The shelf is 3 cm wider than the bracket from the wall.

(a) Calculate the width of the shelf, correct to the nearest cm.

A carpenter decides to support the shelf by inserting a timber support indicated by the dotted line in the diagram.

(b) Calculate the length of the timber support, correct to the nearest cm.

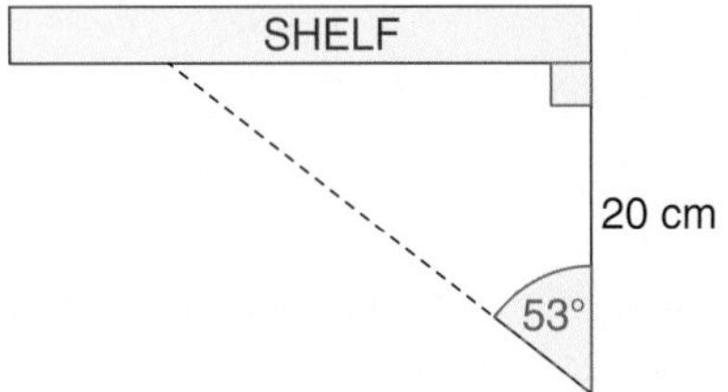

18. Find the angles indicated in the given triangles, correct to the nearest degree.

(a)

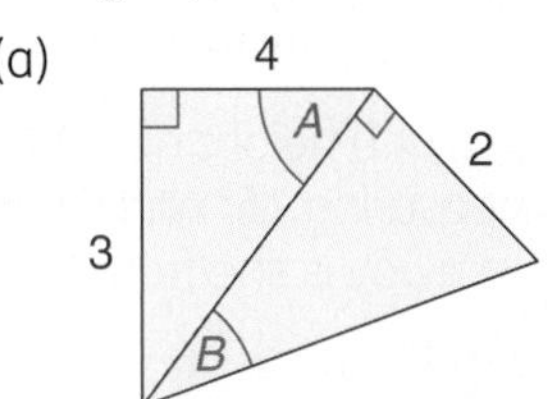

(b)

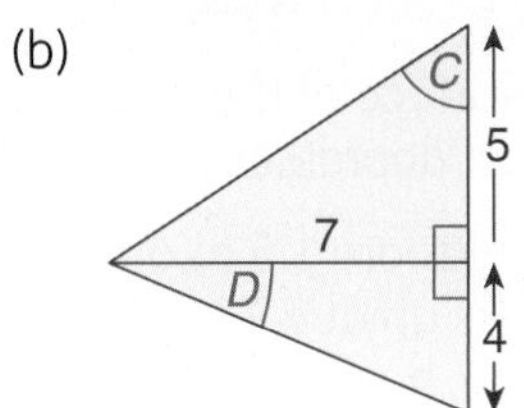

(c)

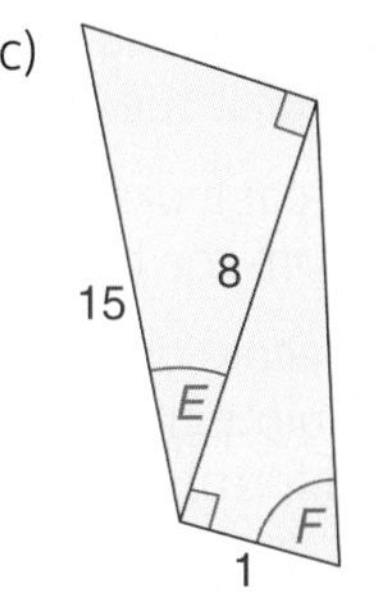

(d)

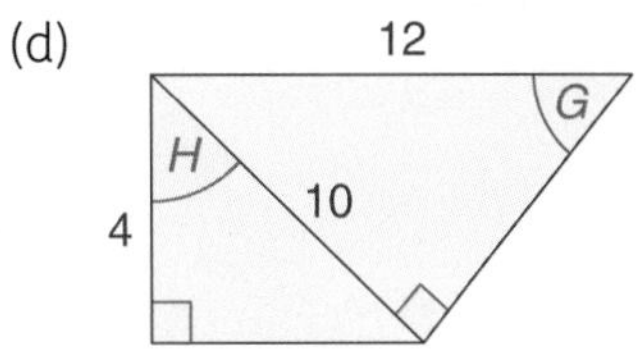

(e)

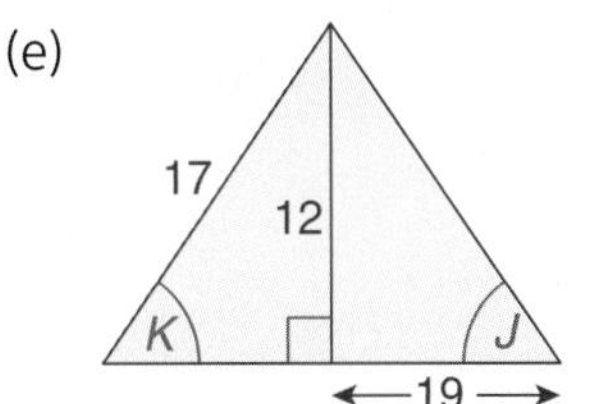

(f)

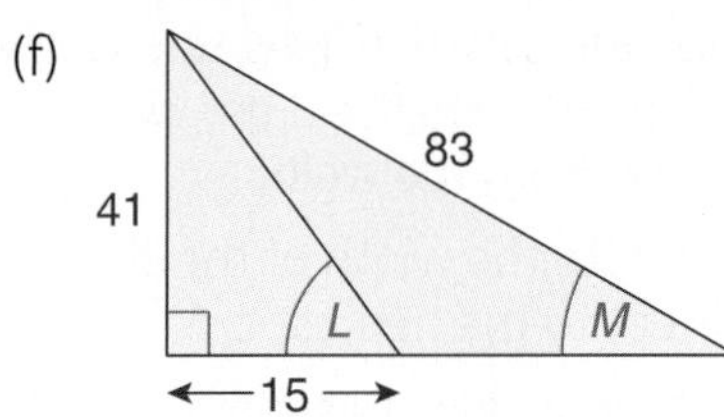

(h)

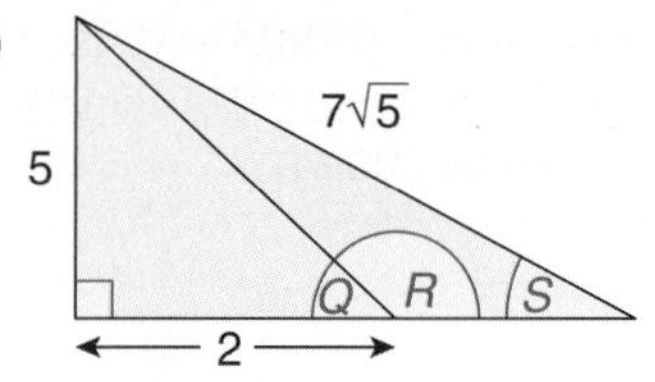

(g)

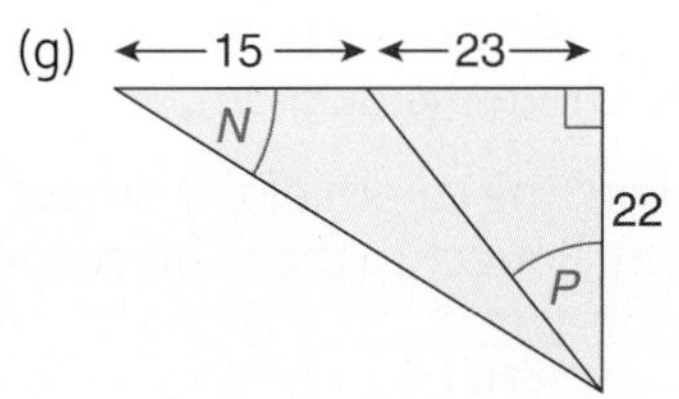

(i)

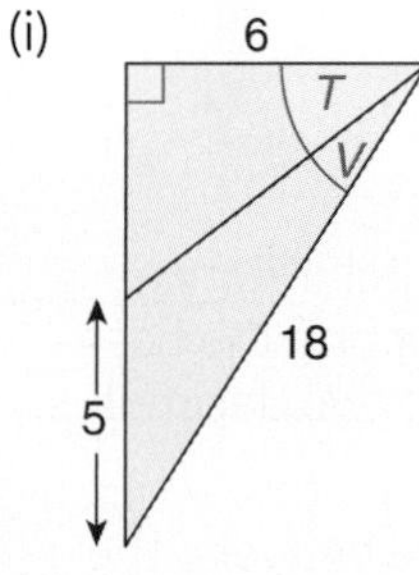

(j)

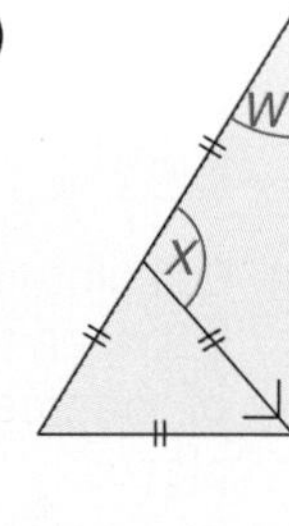

19. Jade wants to find the height of her house. She measures the angle of elevation to the top of the roof using a clinometer and gets an angle of 35°.

(a) What other information is needed to find the height of her house?

(b) Draw a suitable diagram and estimate the necessary measurements needed.

(c) Using these measurements, calculate the perpendicular height of her house.

20. A pilot is travelling at a height of 3,000 metres above level ground. She looks down at an angle of depression measuring 16° and spots the runway. As measured along the ground, how many kilometres away is she from the runway? Give your answer correct to one decimal place.

21. A dog is 8 m from the base of a tree. He spots a cat in the tree at an angle of elevation of 40°. What is the direct line distance between the dog and the cat?

22. A ship is on the surface of the water and its radar detects a submarine at a distance of 238 m and at an angle of depression of 23°. How deep underwater is the submarine?

23. Pauline, whose eyes are 1.6 m off the ground, is standing 50 m away from the base of a building. She looks up at a 73° angle of elevation to a point on the edge of building's roof. To the nearest metre, how tall is the building?

24. A tree casts a shadow 20 m long on the ground. The angle of elevation of the sun to the top of the tree is 58°. How tall is the tree, correct to the nearest metre?

25. After climbing a tree, a cat looks down and sees a mouse at a 28° angle of depression. If the mouse is 34 m from the base of the tree, how high up in the tree is the cat?

26. An architect needs to record all the angles and wall lengths in the plan shown before building can start. Calculate the missing angles and lengths indicated (angles to the nearest degree, lengths in surd form).

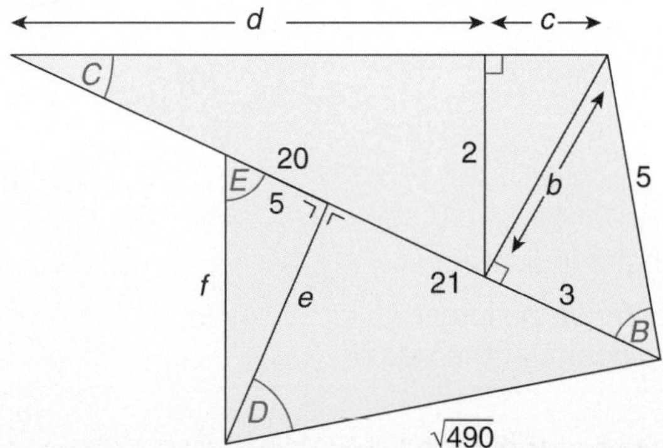

27. An observer on the ground looks up to the top of a building at a 30° angle of elevation. When he moves 50 m closer, the angle of elevation is 40°. Consider the diagram below:

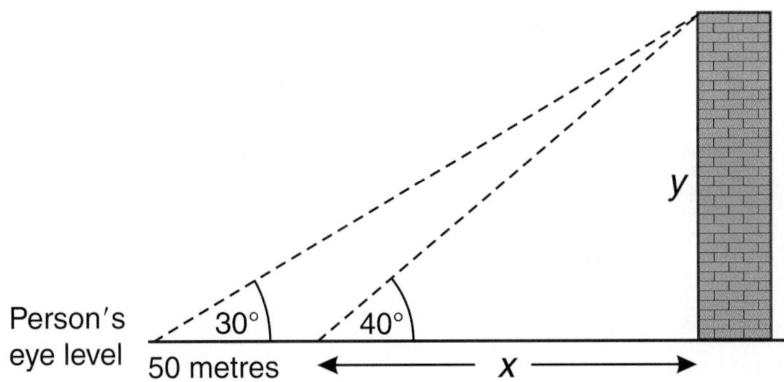

(a) Write an equation representing the situation from the first vantage point. Your equation will incorporate the 30° angle, x, y, and the 50 m.

(b) Write an equation representing the situation from the second vantage point. Your equation will incorporate the 40°, x and y.

(c) You now have two equations in two variables. Solve them simultaneously to determine the value of x, the distance from the second vantage point to the base of the building.

(d) Solve for y, the height of the building.

Section 23.7: The four quadrants

Student Activity 23E

Examine the four diagrams below.

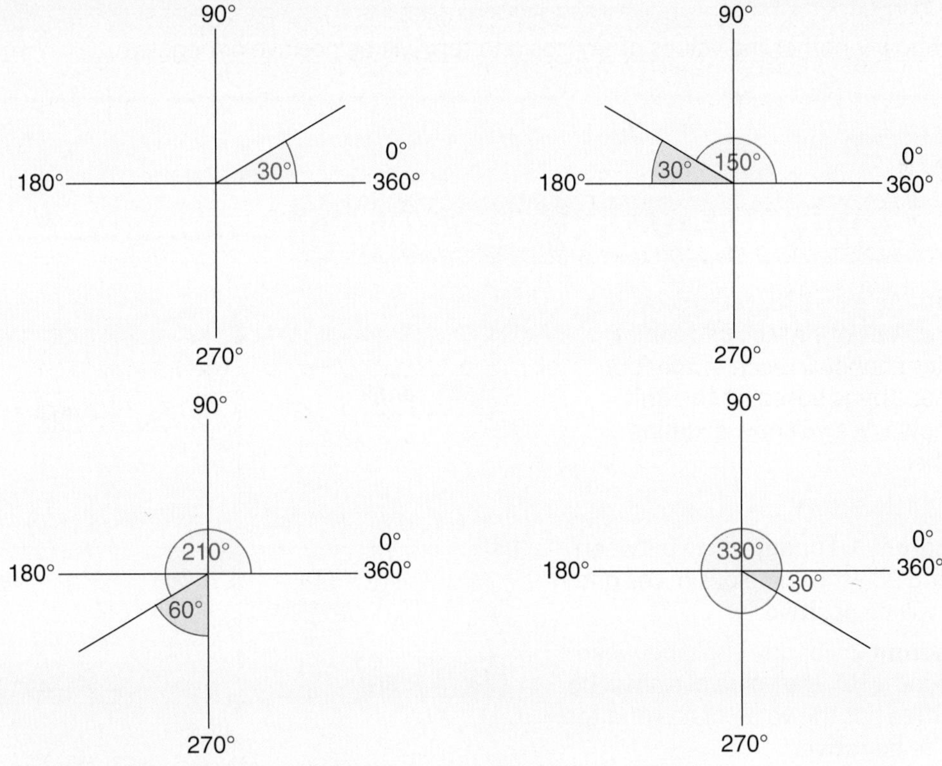

1. (a) Copy and complete the table. Give your answers correct to three decimal places.

Angle A	30°	150°	210°	330°
Cos A				
Sin A				
Tan A				

(b) Examine the values in the table. Can you draw any conclusions from the values you have calculated?

(c) Copy the following table. Try to work out the next three angles. (Hint: look at the diagrams above, and part (a) just completed.) Complete the table, giving your answers correct to three decimal places where necessary.

Angle A	60°	?°	?°	?°
Cos A				
Sin A				
Tan A				

(d) Explain why you chose these three specific missing angles.

2. Copy the following table. Try to work out the next three angles. (Hint: look at the previous diagrams.) Complete the table, giving your answers correct to three decimal places where necessary.

Angle A	50°	?°	?°	?°
Cos A				
Sin A				
Tan A				

(a) Explain why you chose these three specific missing angles.

(b) Using the answers from the questions above, copy and complete the following table:

	$0° < A < 90°$	$90° < A < 180°$	$180° < A < 270°$	$270° < A < 360°$
Sin A				
Cos A				
Tan A				

(c) Show whether the values of sin, cos and tan, will be positive or negative.

THE FOUR QUADRANTS EXPLAINED

In Student Activity 23E, you discovered that the values of sin, cos and tan of the angles change in each of the four quadrants. This is based on the **unit circle** shown. We will now examine this further.

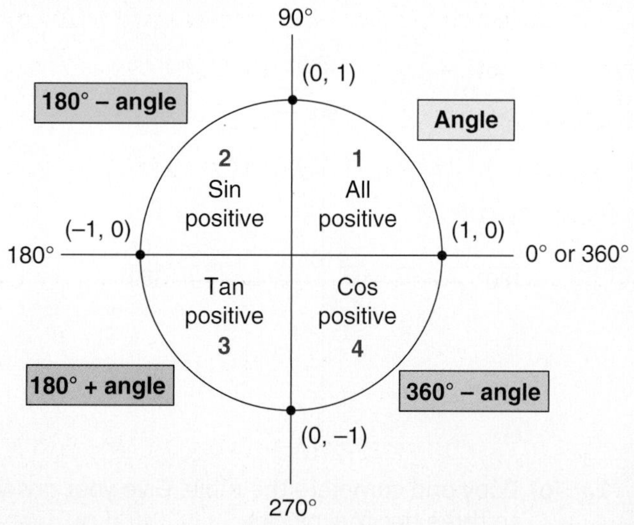

The unit circle shows:

- **Quadrant 1:** For any angle between 0° and 90°, the value of sin, cos and tan will be **positive.**
- **Quadrant 2:** For any angle between 90° and 180°, the value of sin will be **positive** but the value of cos and tan will be **negative.**
- **Quadrant 3:** For any angle between 180° and 270°, the value of tan will be **positive** but the value of cos and sin will be **negative.**
- **Quadrant 4:** For any angle between 270° and 360°, the value of cos will be **positive** but the value of sin and tan will be **negative.**

EXAMPLE 9

Solve for A if $\cos A = \frac{1}{2}$, and $0° \le A \le 360°$.

Solution

As $\cos A$ has a positive value, $+\frac{1}{2}$, we need only consider Quadrants 1 and 4.

Page 16 of the *Formulae and Tables* shows that $\cos 60°$ will give us an answer of $+\frac{1}{2}$.

The other angle is in the 4th quadrant: $360° - 60° = 300°$

$\therefore A = 60°$ and $300°$

EXAMPLE 10

Solve for A if $\sin A = -\frac{1}{\sqrt{2}}$, and $0° \le A \le 360°$.

Solution

As $\sin A$ has a negative value, $-\frac{1}{\sqrt{2}}$, we need only consider Quadrants 3 and 4.

Looking in the *Formulae and Tables*, we see that $\sin 45°$ will give us $\frac{1}{\sqrt{2}}$.

In the 3rd quadrant, we see $180° + 45° = 225°$.

In the 4th quadrant, we see $360° - 45° = 315°$.

$\therefore A = 225°$ and $315°$

Exercise 23.7

Without using tables or a calculator, state whether the values for the following will be positive or negative:

1. $\cos 46°$
2. $\tan 123°$
3. $\sin 123°$
4. $\tan 246°$
5. $\cos 345°$
6. $\sin 300°$
7. $\cos 180°$
8. $\cos 65°$
9. $\tan 89°$
10. $\tan 195°$
11. $\tan 223°$
12. $\cos 321°$
13. $\tan 47°$
14. $\sin 168°$
15. $\tan 320°$

Solve each of the following for two values of A or B, where $0° \le A$ or $B \le 360°$:

16. $\cos A = \frac{\sqrt{3}}{2}$
17. $\sin A = -\frac{\sqrt{3}}{2}$
18. $\cos B = -\frac{1}{2}$
19. $\tan B = -\frac{1}{\sqrt{3}}$
20. $\sin A = \frac{1}{\sqrt{2}}$
21. $\cos A = -\frac{1}{\sqrt{2}}$
22. $\tan A = 1$
23. $\cos B = 0$
24. $\sin B = \frac{1}{2}$
25. $\tan A = \sqrt{3}$

Find, correct to the nearest degree, the two solutions for the angle A, given $0° \le A \le 360°$:

26. $\sin A = 0.4321$
27. $\cos A = 0.8049$
28. $\tan A = -0.0244$
29. $\sin A = -0.9832$
30. $\cos A = 0.6428$
31. $\tan A = -0.7188$
32. $\sin A = -0.4321$
33. $\cos A = 0.6777$
34. $\tan A = 0.6745$
35. $\sin A = 0.8192$
36. $\cos A = -0.8211$
37. $\tan A = -4.9594$
38. $\sin A = -0.7046$
39. $\cos A = -0.8141$
40. $\tan A = 0.6249$

CHAPTER 23 SELF-CHECK TEST

1. Use your calculator to evaluate each of the following, correct to four decimal places: 

(a) $\cos 11°$
(b) $\sin 82°$
(c) $\tan 59°$
(d) $\cos 5°$
(e) $4 \sin 43°$
(f) $10 \tan 53°$
(g) $\frac{1}{4} \cos 38°$
(h) $\frac{1}{2} \tan 26°$
(i) $\frac{3}{4} \sin 72°$
(j) $\frac{1}{4} \tan 66°$

2. Use your calculator to find each of the following angles, correct to the nearest degree:

(a) $\tan \theta = 0.25$ (f) $\tan \theta = 2$

(b) $\sin \theta = 0.5436$ (g) $\cos \theta = 0.25$

(c) $\cos \theta = 0.843$ (h) $\tan \theta = \frac{2}{5}$

(d) $\sin \theta = 1$ (i) $\cos \theta = \frac{5}{10}$

(e) $\sin \theta = 0.4$ (j) $\sin \theta = \frac{35}{100}$

3. In this triangle:

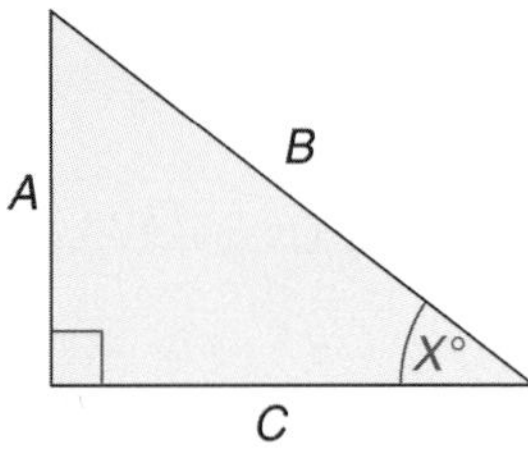

(a) Which side is the hypotenuse?
(b) Which side is adjacent to angle *X*?
(c) Which side is opposite to angle *X*?

4. Which option is the correct ratio for sin *X*?

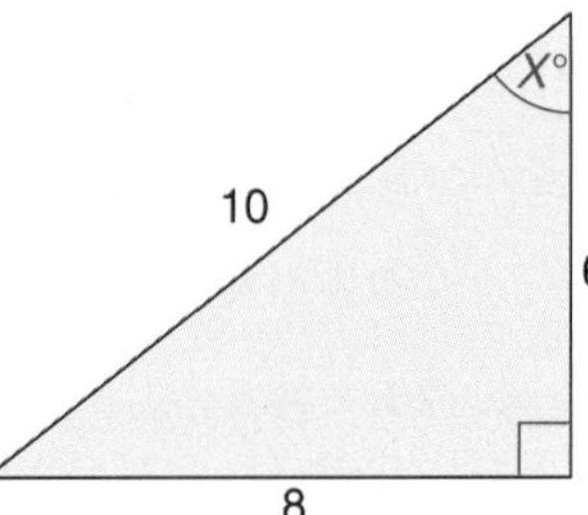

5. Which option is the correct ratio for tan *X*?

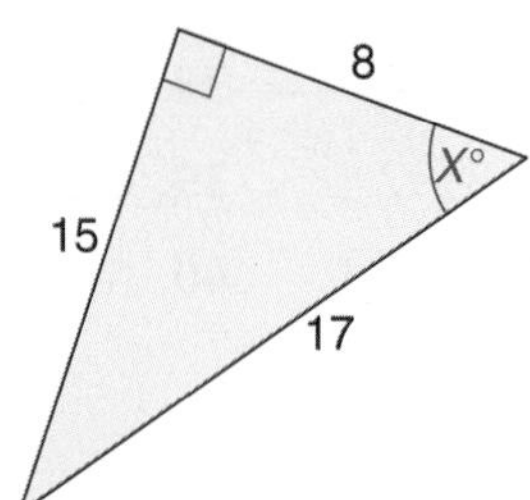

6. Calculate the size of the angle *A*. Give your answer in degrees, minutes and seconds.

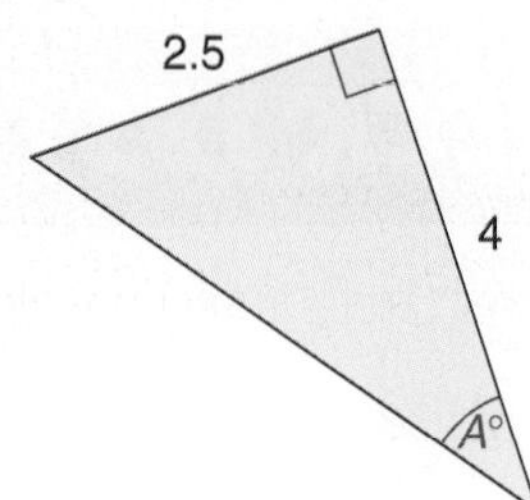

7. Calculate the side b. Give your answer correct to one decimal place.

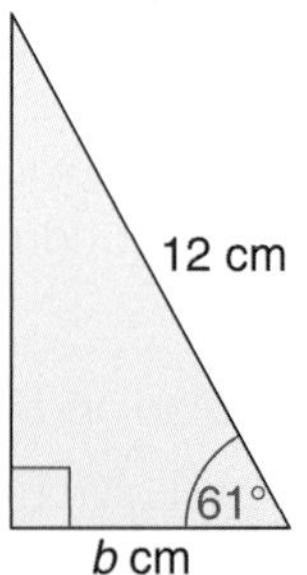

8. Without using a calculator, evaluate each of the following. Give your answer in surd form.

(a) $\sin 30° + \cos 60°$
(b) $\cos 30° \sin 60°$
(c) $\tan 30° \sin 60°$
(d) $\cos 60° \sin 30°$
(e) $\tan 45° + \cos^2 45°$
(f) $\sin 30° \sin 60°$
(g) $\cos 30° \cos 60°$
(h) $(\cos 60°)^2 + (\sin 60°)^2$
(i) $\tan 30° \tan 60°$

9. A 15 m ladder leans against a wall so that the base of the ladder is 5 m from the base of the building. What is the ladder's angle of elevation?

10. A 55 m vertical tower is braced with a cable secured at the top of the tower and tied 27 m from the base. What is the angle of depression from the top of the tower to the point on the ground where the cable is tied?

11. At a point on the ground 18 m from the foot of the tree, the angle of elevation to the top of the tree is 53°. Find the height of the tree.

12. From the top of a lighthouse 47.8 metres high, the angle of depression to a boat is 42°. Find the horizontal distance from the boat to the lighthouse. Assume the lighthouse was built at sea level.

13. A person at one end of a 165 m bridge spots the river's edge directly below the opposite end of the bridge. The angle of depression is 54°. How far below the bridge is the river?

14. The angle of elevation from a car to the top of a tower is 29°. If the tower is 18.6 m tall, how far is the car from the base of the tower?

15. A radio tower 123 m high casts a shadow 47 m long. What is the angle of elevation of the sun?

16. An escalator from the ground floor to the second floor of a department store is 22 m long and rises 13 m vertically.

(a) What is the escalator's angle of elevation?

(b) What is the escalator's angle of depression?

17. A rescue team 314 m away from the base of a vertical cliff measures the angle of elevation to the top of the cliff (*y* metres high) to be 72°. A climber is stranded on a ledge, *w* metres above sea level. The angle of elevation from the rescue team to the ledge is 51°. How far is the stranded climber from the top of the cliff?

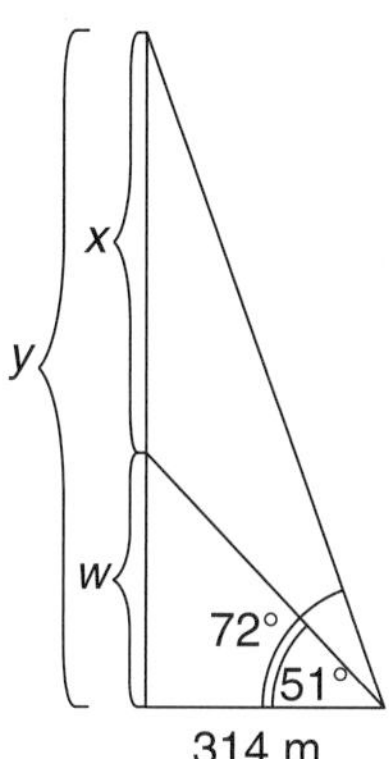

18. A ladder on a fire truck has its base 2.7 m above the ground. The length of the ladder is 28 m.

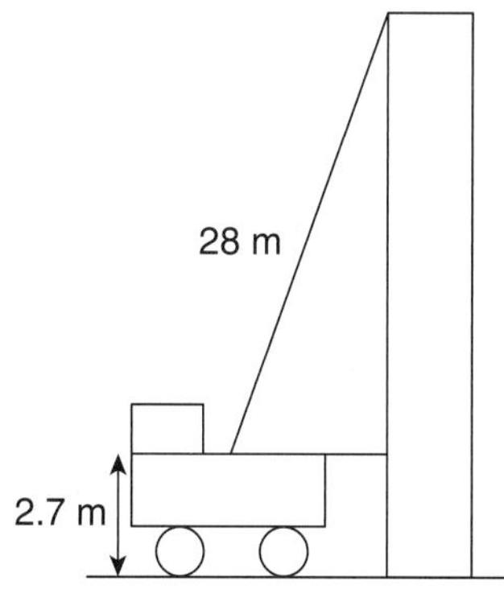

(a) If the ladder's angle of elevation is 55°, what is the greatest possible height above the ground that the ladder can reach?

(b) If the ladder's greatest angle of elevation is 70°, what is the greatest perpendicular height from the ground that the ladder can reach?

19. A person in an apartment building sights the top and bottom of an office building 350 m away. The angle of elevation to the top of the office building is 30° and the angle of depression to the base of the building is 45°. How tall is the office building, correct to the nearest metre?

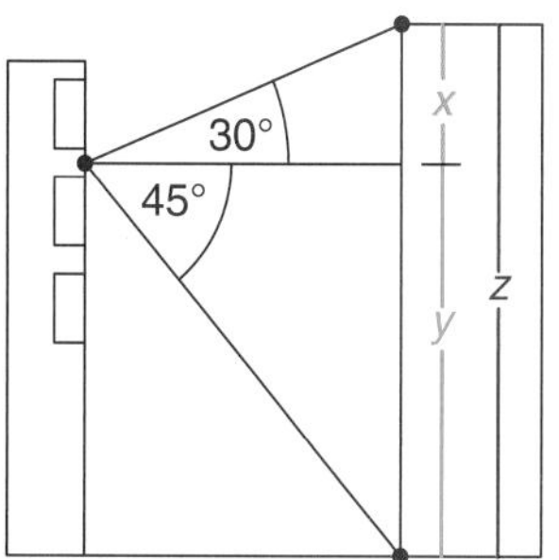

20. An electronic instrument on a treasure hunting ship detects the sunken *Titanic* resting on the sea floor. The angle of depression is 29°. The instrument indicates that the direct line distance between the ship and the object is 480 m.

(a) How far below the surface of the water is the *Titanic*, correct to the nearest metre?

(b) How far must the ship travel to be directly over the *Titanic*?

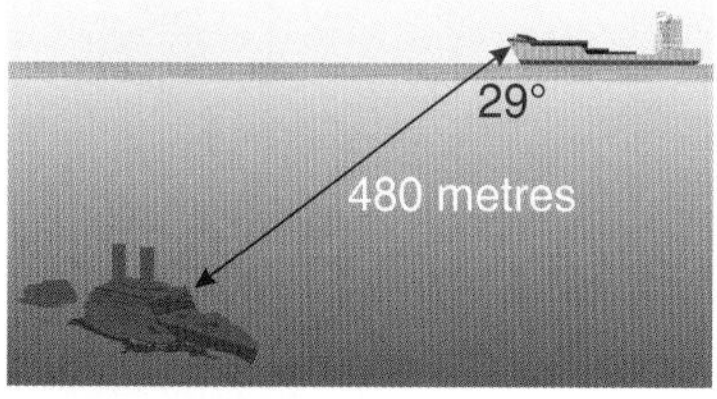

21. A man on the deck of a ship is 15 metres above sea level. He observes that the angle of elevation to the top of a cliff is 70° and the angle of depression to its base at sea level is 50°. Find the height of the cliff and its distance from the ship, correct to one decimal place.

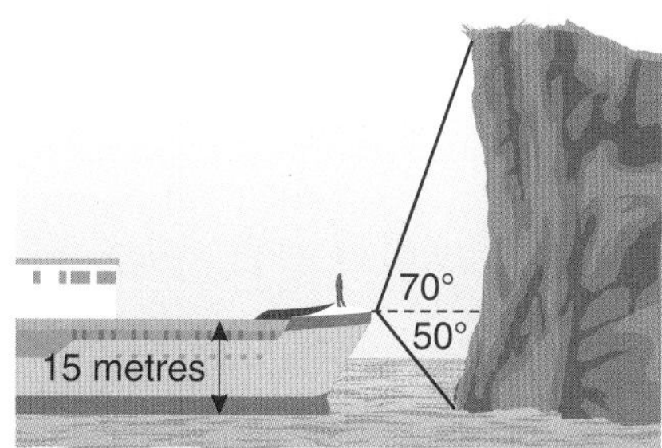

22. The angle of elevation of an unfinished tower from a distance 120 m away from its base is 20°. How much higher must the tower be raised so that its angle of elevation from the same point will be 37°?

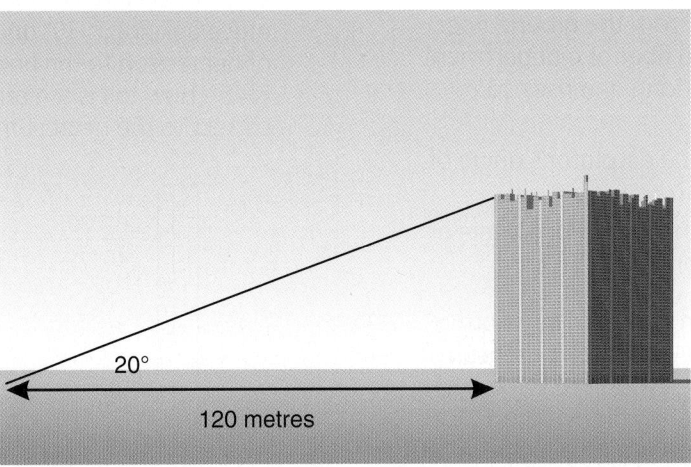

23. From the top of a spire of height 17 m, the angles of depression to two cars on a straight road at the same level as the base of the spire and on the same side of it are 25° and 40°. Calculate the distance between the two cars, correct to the nearest metre.

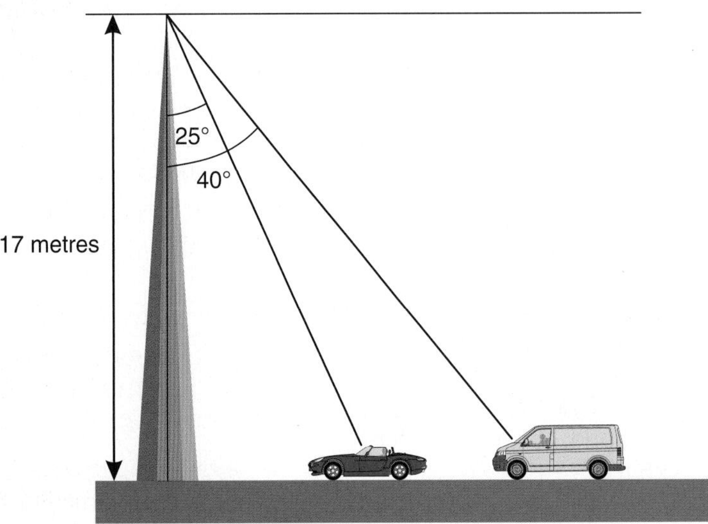

24. The angles of elevation of 30° and 60° are taken from a building 60 m away. What is the height of the tower?

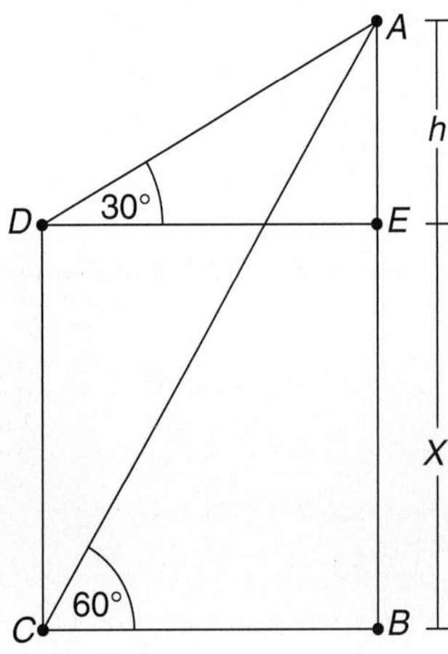

25. From the top of a house, 50 metres high, the angle of elevation to a tower is found to be equal to the angle of depression to the foot of the tower. Find the height of the tower.

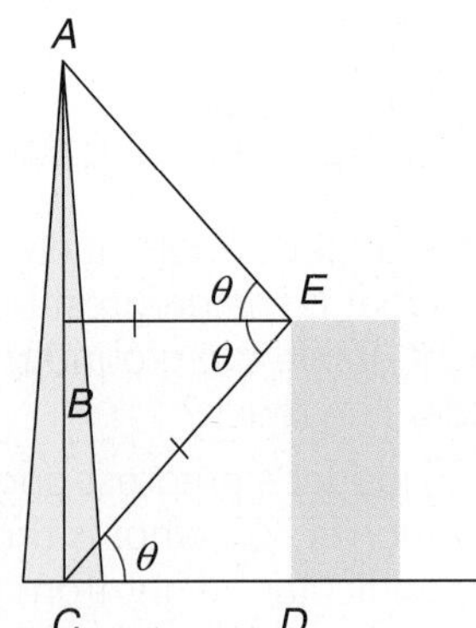

26. Mary is thinking of buying a new television. The television is advertised as having a 40 inch screen. This refers to the diagonal measurement of the screen. The aspect ratio of a television screen is the ratio of its width to its height. For this television, the aspect ratio is 16:9 (sixteen units wide for every nine units high).

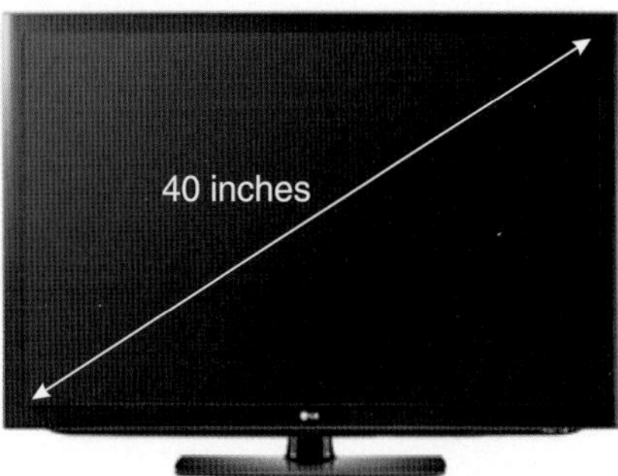

(a) Convert 40 inches to centimetres if 1 inch = 2.54 cm.

(b) Find the width and the height of the screen in centimetres. Give your answers correct to the nearest cm.

(c) A different 40 inch television screen has an aspect ratio of 4:3. Which of the two television screens has the greatest area, and by how much?

27. A group of students wish to calculate the height of the Millennium Spire in Dublin. The Spire stands on flat level ground. Ita, who is 1.84 m tall, looks up at the top of the Spire using a clinometer and records an angle of elevation of 65°. Her feet are 74 m from the base of the Spire. Meanwhile Laura measures the circumference of the base of the Spire as 7.14 m.

(a) Explain how Laura's measurement will be used in the calculation of the height of the Spire.

(b) Using the measurements from part (a), draw a suitable diagram and calculate the height of the Spire, correct to the nearest metre.

28. A cable-stayed bridge AE is supported by a tower BX on only one side of a bank. This type of bridge is convenient to build if conditions are not suitable on the far bank. In the bridge shown below $|AB| = 13$ m, the cable tie AX is 37 m long and $|\angle BCX| = 65°$.

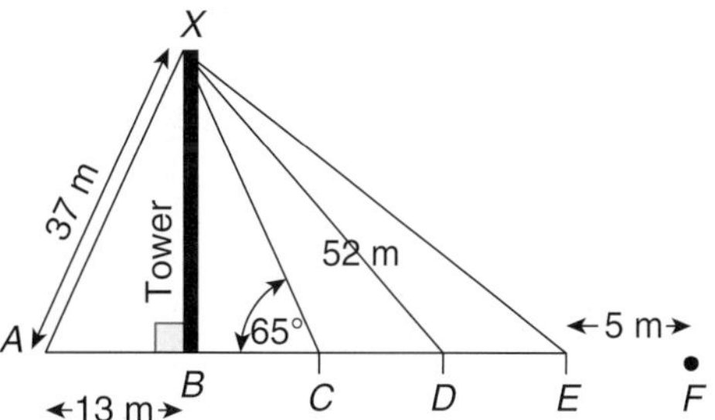

(a) Calculate the height of the tower, correct to one decimal place.

(b) Calculate $|\angle BAX|$, correct to the nearest degree.

Given that the cables lengths of XC, XD and XE are in the ratio of 2:5:11 and $|XD|$ is 52 m long:

(c) Calculate the angle of elevation from the point D on the bridge to point X on the top of the tower, correct to the nearest degree.

(d) Calculate the length of the entire bridge AE, correct to the nearest metre.

(e) The bridge is extended by another 5 m to a point F. What length is the extra cable XF, correct to one decimal place?

29. Roofs of buildings are often supported by frameworks of timber called roof trusses. A quantity surveyor needs to find the total amount of timber needed in order to make the triangular truss shown below.

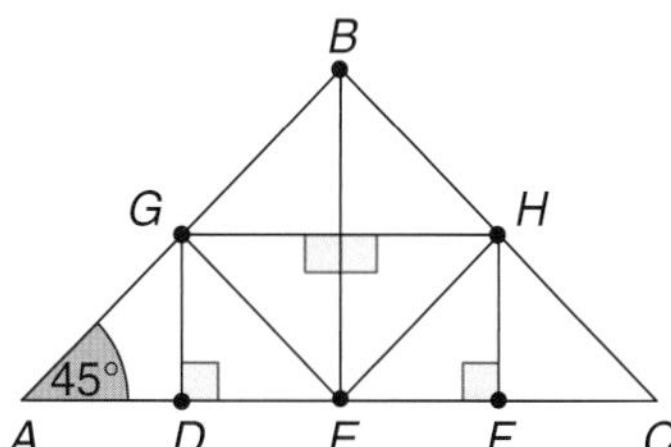

The length of $[AC]$ is 6 m and the pitch of the roof is 45°, as shown.

$|AD| = |DE| = |EF| = |FC|$ and $|AG| = |GB| = |BH| = |CH|$.

(a) Calculate the length of $|AB|$ in metres, correct to two decimal places.

(b) Calculate the total length of timber required to make the truss.

CHAPTER 23 KNOWLEDGE CHECKLIST

After completing this chapter, I now:

- Am able to name the sides in a right-angled triangle
- Know how to measure angles using a clinometer
- Understand angles of elevation and depression and how to use them to solve problems
- Know about special trigonometric ratios
- Am able to find sin, cos and tan of an angle
- Am able to find the inverse of sin, cos and tan of an angle
- About the four quadrants in the unit circle
- Am able to use trigonometric ratios to solve right-angled triangles
- Am able to express trigonometric ratios in surd form

Challenge

Imagine you're a mapmaker.

One of the more enjoyable parts of your job is when you get to colour in a brand new map. All sorts of weird and wonderful maps cross your desk and you have to decide how different areas are coloured, ensuring that no bordering segments share the same colour.

You only ever use four colours (red, green, blue and yellow), knowing that it would be impossible with just three and a waste of ink to use five.*

This imaginary country is divided into nineteen different regions. While it can be coloured in in many different ways, all of them require the area marked ? to be one particular colour.

What colour must it be?

*Discovering why 4 colours is always sufficient managed to perplex mathematicians for decades

VOLUME

LEARNING OUTCOMES

In this chapter you will learn:

- ✓ **To calculate the volume of cubes and cuboids**
- ✓ **To calculate the volume of prisms**
- ✓ **To calculate the volumes of cylinders, cones, spheres and hemispheres**
- ✓ **To solve problems involving volumes of shapes and compound shapes**
- ✓ **To calculate rates of flow**
- ✓ **To understand flow graphs**

KEY WORDS

- **Capacity**
- **Compound**
- **Cone**
- **Cubed units**
- **Cuboid**
- **Cylinder**
- **Flow graph**
- **Hemisphere**
- **Prism**
- **Rate of flow**
- **Sphere**
- **Volume**

INTRODUCTION

As you have probably learned in science, the **volume** of an object is the amount of three-dimensional (3D) space enclosed by some boundary.

All 3D shapes have a volume – a space that contains a liquid, a gas or a solid. Volume is measured in **cubed units** such as cm^3 or m^3. **Capacity** is another word for volume.

The volume of a liquid is usually measured in litres. It is important to remember that:

1 litre = 1,000 cm^3

Health experts now have proof that laughter is a good medicine. A good laugh can increase the volume of blood flowing through your body by 20%. This increased blood flow is the perfect antidote to stress. So have a good giggle. Your heart will thank you!

Section 24.1: Volume of rectangular solids

Student Activity 24A

1. Use a jug and graduated cylinder to measure out the following fun volume equivalents:
50 cm^3 = 1 million grains of sugar
100 cm^3 = volume of a T. rex's brain
140 cm^3 = volume of salt in a human body
200 ml = 500 drops of water
450 cm^3 = volume of body cells that die in a day
600 cm^3 = volume of a human brain
630 cm^3 = as many grains of flour as people in the planet (over 6.8 billion)

2. The diagram shows a box.
(a) In what units might its length, width and height be measured?
(b) How would you calculate the volume of the box?

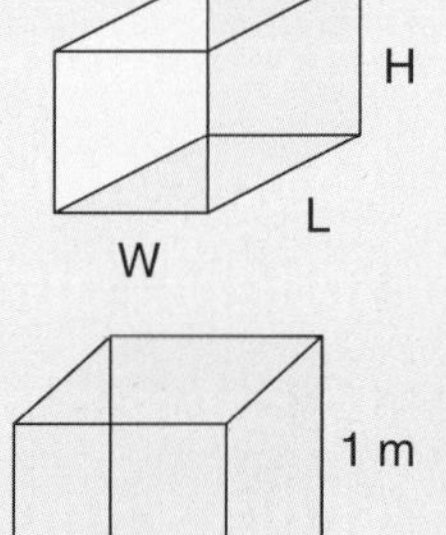

3. Examine the cube:
(a) How many centimetres are in 1 m?
(b) Sketch the diagram of the cube and convert the lengths of the sides to centimetres.
(c) Calculate the volume of the cube in m^3.
(d) Calculate the volume of the cube in cm^3.

VOLUME OF RECTANGULAR SOLIDS EXPLAINED

You have already learned that:

Area = L × W

The volume of a cuboid can be found by:

Volume = L × W × H

Putting these formulae together we can show that:

Volume = Area of the cross-section × H

In Student Activity 24A, you converted from m^3 to cm^3.

$1\ m^3 = 100\ cm \times 100\ cm \times 100\ cm$

$1\ m^3 = 1{,}000{,}000\ cm^3$

It is important to know how to change between the different units. It is often easier to convert to the required units before carrying out any calculations.

EXAMPLE 1

(a) Find the volume of a cuboid with the dimensions L = 3 cm, W = 40 cm and H = 12 cm.

(b) Find the volume of a cuboid with the dimensions L = 30 cm, W = 4 m, H = 2 m. Give your answer in m^3.

(c) The volume of a box with height 8 cm and width 12 cm is 480 cm^3. Find the length of the box.

Solution

(a) Volume = L × W × H

Volume = 3 × 40 × 12

Volume = 1,440 cm^3

(b) Note: The dimensions are not all in the same units. As the answer is required in m^3, change the 30 cm to metres first before calculating the volume.

30 cm ÷ 100 = 0.3 m

Volume = L × W × H

Volume = 0.3 × 4 × 2

Volume = 2.4 m^3

(c) Volume = L × W × H

480 = 8 × 12 × L

480 = 96L

L = 480 ÷ 96

L = 5 cm

Exercise 24.1

Find the volume of the cuboids with the following dimensions in cm^3:

1. W = 10 cm, L = 15 cm, H = 30 cm
2. W = 12 cm, L = 7 cm, H = 9 cm
3. W = 5 cm, L = 14 cm, H = 13 cm
4. W = 11 cm, L = 10 cm, H = 10 cm
5. W = 9 cm, L = 7 cm, H = 11 cm

Find the volume of the cuboids with the following dimensions in m^3:

6. W = 3 m, L = 3 m, H = 4 m
7. W = 2 m, L = 4 m, H = 5 m
8. W = 10 cm, L = 2 m, H = 30 cm
9. W = 1 m, L = 1 m, H = 25 cm
10. W = 2 m, L = 15 cm, H = 3 m
11. W = 2 cm, L = 2 m, H = 12 cm
12. A box has a height of 40 cm and a width of 20 cm. If the volume of the box is 1,600 cm^3, what is the length of the box?
13. A cuboid has a height of 20 cm and a length of 15 cm. If the volume of the box is 900 cm^3, what is the height of the box?

14. A box has a length of 1.25 m and a height of 40 cm. If the volume of the box is 10,000 litres, calculate the width of the box.

15. A box has a length of 2.4 m and a width of 1.3 m. If the volume of the box is 15.6 m^3, calculate the height of the box.

16. Find the length of a side of each cube given the following volumes:

(a) 125 mm^3

(b) 216 cm^3

(c) 1,771.561 m^3

(d) 3.375 litres

(e) 2.744 litres

Section 24.2: Volume of prisms

Student Activity 24B

Work in pairs to answer the following questions:

1. Calculate the area of the shaded triangular face.

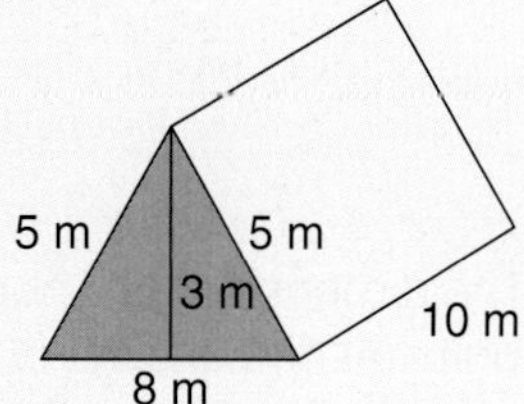

Suggest how you could find the volume of the prism.

2. (a) Suggest how you could find the volume of the given shape.

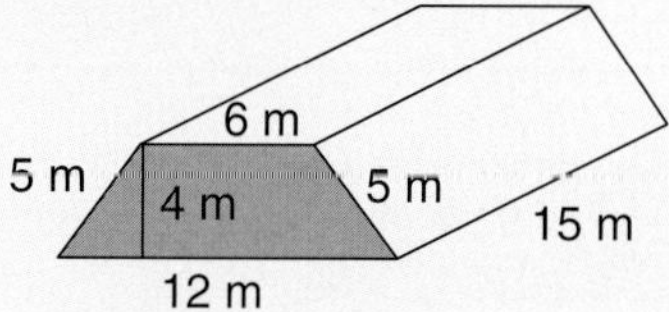

(b) Calculate the volume of the prism.

VOLUME OF PRISMS EXPLAINED

As you learned in Chapter 13, a **prism** is a solid shape which has the same cross-section all the way through. Earlier you learned to calculate the area of a triangle using the formula:

$$\text{Area} = \frac{1}{2} \times \text{Base} \times \perp \text{Height}$$

To calculate the volume of a triangular-based prism, you simply multiply the area of the triangular face by the depth or length of the prism.

$$\text{Volume} = \text{Area of the cross-section} \times \text{Length}$$

For a triangular prism:

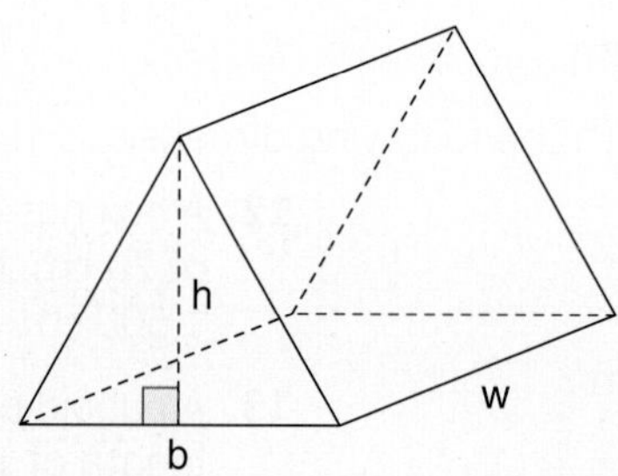

$$\text{Volume of a prism} = \frac{1}{2} \times \text{Base} \times \perp \text{Height} \times \text{Width}$$

EXAMPLE 2

Calculate the volume of the prism shown.

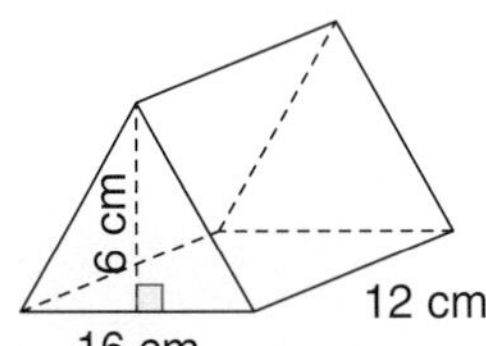

Solution

Volume = $\frac{1}{2}$ × Base × ⊥ Height × Width

Volume = $\frac{1}{2} \times 16 \times 6 \times 12$

Volume = 576 cm^3

Exercise 24.2

1. Find the volume of each of the following prisms:

(a)

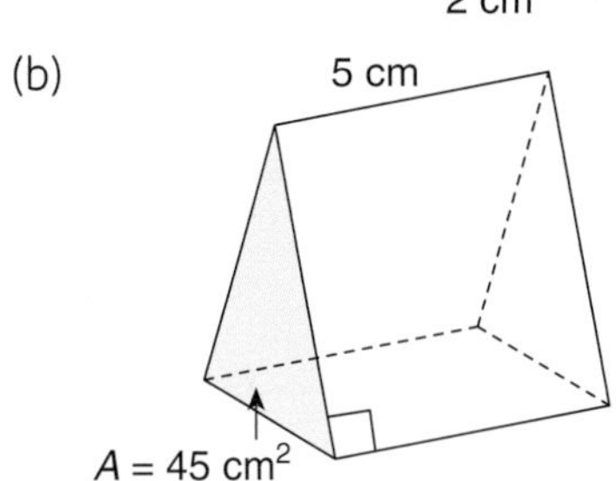

(b)

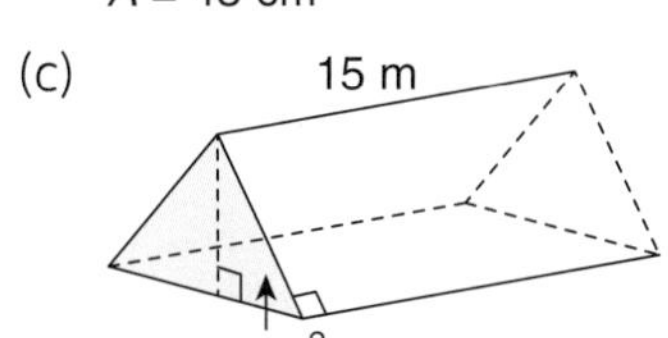

(c)

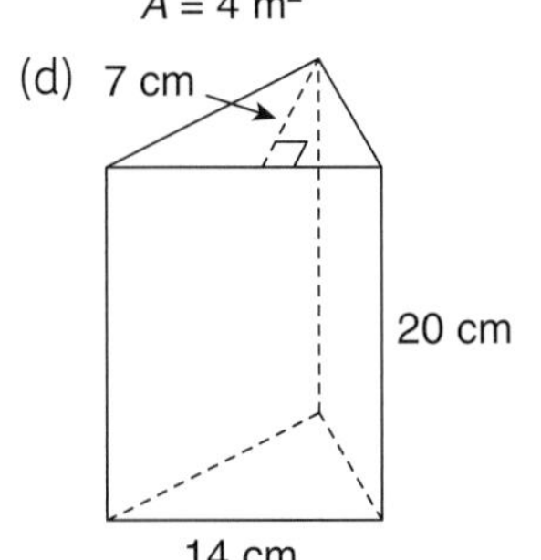

(d)

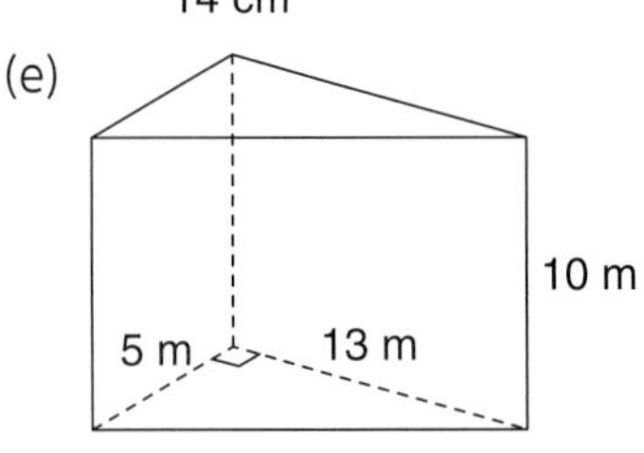

(e)

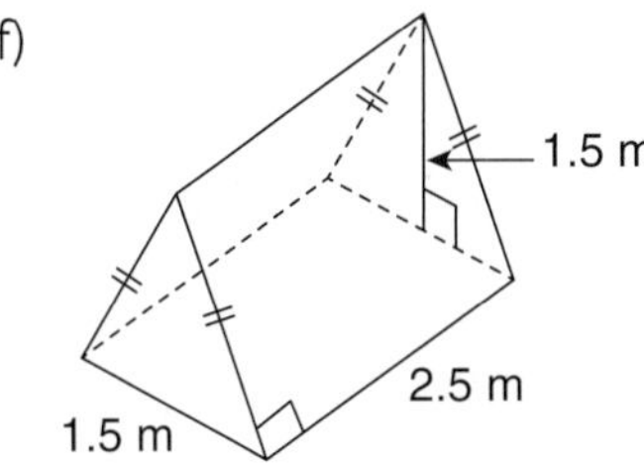

(f)

2. Calculate the total volume of water (in litres) the trough can hold.

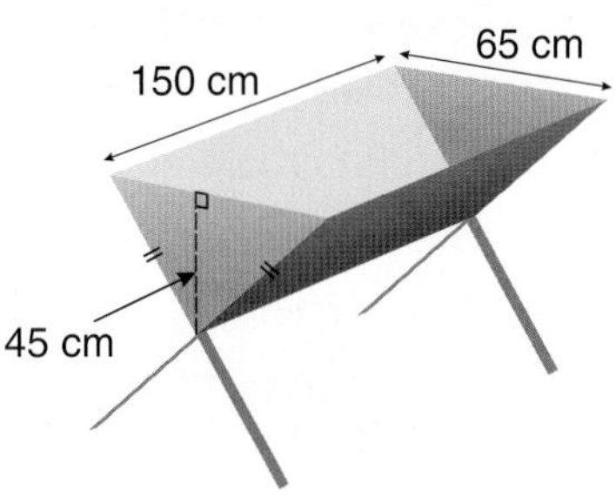

3. A 400 g triangular chocolate bar has length of 48 cm, base width of 4.5 cm and perpendicular height of 2.5 cm.

Calculate the volume of chocolate in the bar if 14% of the overall volume is air.

4. Which fish tank will hold the greatest volume of water?

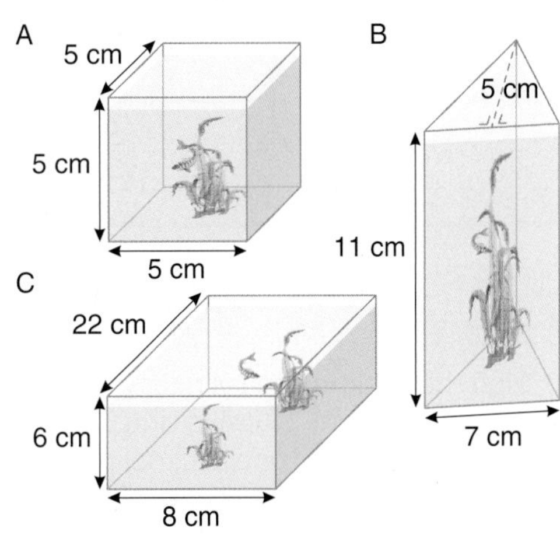

5. A triangular prism has a volume of 3,000 cm^3. If the area of the triangular face is 100 cm^2, calculate the length of the prism.

6. A wedge of cheese has an equilateral triangular face of side length 12 cm and is 6 cm thick.

Calculate the volume of the cheese if the holes occupy 12% of the overall volume, correct to the nearest whole number.

Section 24.3: Volume of a cylinder

Student Activity 24C

A head chief is trying to determine if he has enough meat in his restaurant for the salad menu being served later that day. In the cold meat section, he notices that he has only one open roll of luncheon meat to serve. He is trying to determine its volume.

(a) Can you suggest any way of determining the volume of meat he has left?

He measures the diameter of the open circular disc as 12 cm.

(b) Can you calculate the area of the circular disc?

He measures the length of the roll as 25 cm.

(c) Suggest how he might use this measurement to calculate the total volume.

He knows that the volume of any item is normally found using the formula:

Area of the cross-section × height.

(d) Using this formula, can you write a general formula to calculate the volume of a cylinder?

VOLUME OF A CYLINDER EXPLAINED

In Student Activity 24C, you discovered that a cylinder is a 3D shape based on a circle.

You previously learned that:

Area of a circle = πr^2

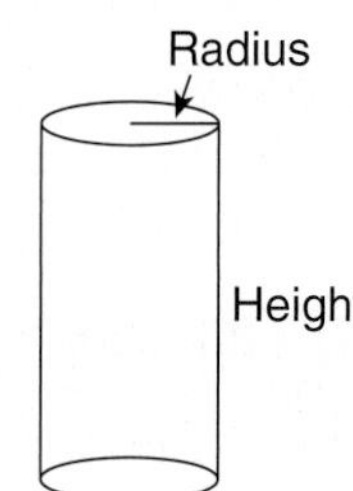

If you multiply the area of the circle by a third dimension (the height), you get:

Volume of a cylinder = $\pi r^2 h$

EXAMPLE 3

(a) Find the volume of a cylinder with radius 6 cm and height 14 cm, giving your answer correct to one decimal place.

Solution

(a) Volume = $\pi r^2 h$

Volume = $(\pi)(6)^2(14)$

Volume = 1,583.36

Volume = 1,583.4 cm^3

(b) Find the volume of a cylinder with radius 7 cm and height 12 cm in terms of π.

Solution

(b) Volume = $\pi r^2 h$

Volume = $(\pi)(7)^2(12)$

Volume = 588π cm^3

Note

In terms of π means you leave in the symbol π in your answer.

(a) Find the height of a cylinder with radius 14 cm and volume 1,848 cm^3. Take $\pi = \frac{22}{7}$.

Solution

(a) Volume = $\pi r^2 h$

$\left(\frac{22}{7}\right)(14)^2(h) = 1,848$

$616h = 1,848$

$h = 1,848 \div 616$

$h = 3$ cm

(b) Find the radius of a cylinder with height 7 cm and volume 550 cm^3. Take $\pi = \frac{22}{7}$.

Solution

(b) Volume = $\pi r^2 h$

$\left(\frac{22}{7}\right)(r)^2(7) = 550$

$22r^2 = 550$

$r^2 = 550 \div 22 = 25$

$r = \sqrt{25}$

$r = 5$ cm

Exercise 24.3

Find the volume of each cylinder with the following dimensions, giving your answer correct to the nearest whole number. (Take $\pi = 3.14$.)

1. Radius = 3 cm, Height = 14 cm
2. Radius = 7 cm, Height = 12 cm
3. Radius = 14 cm, Height = 11 cm
4. Diameter = 21 cm, Height = 8 cm
5. Diameter = 14 cm, Height = 9 cm
6. Diameter = 35 cm, Height = 7 cm
7. Diameter = 11 cm, Height = 12 cm

Find the volume of each of the cylinders in terms of π.

8. Radius = 3 cm, Height = 12 cm
9. Radius = 5 cm, Height = 10 cm
10. Radius = 7 cm, Height = 4 cm
11. Radius = 6 cm, Height = 5 cm
12. Diameter = 2 cm, Height = 24 cm
13. Diameter = 1 cm, Height = 14 cm

Find the height of each of the following cylinders, correct to the nearest whole number:

14. Radius = 3 cm, Volume = 396 cm^3
15. Radius = 7 cm, Volume = 616 cm^3
16. Radius = 15 cm, Volume = 4,948 cm^3
17. Radius = 12 cm, Volume = 905 cm^3
18. Radius = 6 cm, Volume = 339 cm^3
19. Radius = 9 cm, Volume = 255 cm^3
20. Diameter = 14 cm, Volume = 616 cm^3
21. Diameter = 21 cm, Volume = 3,464 cm^3
22. Diameter = 17 cm, Volume = 2,724 cm^3
23. Diameter = 18 cm, Volume = 3,054 cm^3

Find the radius of each of the following cylinders. $\left(\text{Take } \pi = \frac{22}{7}.\right)$

24. Height = 6 cm, Volume = 924 cm^3
25. Height = 14 cm, Volume = 704 cm^3
26. Height = 21 cm, Volume = 1,650 cm^3
27. Height = 7 cm, Volume = 198 cm^3
28. Height = 35 cm, Volume = 440 cm^3
29. Height = 6 cm, Volume = 3,696 cm^3
30. Height = 9 cm, Volume = 346.5 cm^3
31. Height = 8 cm, Volume = 1,10.88 cm^3
32. Height = 11 cm, Volume = 6,776 cm^3
33. A cylinder of radius 10 cm and height 60 cm contains liquid. (Take $\pi = 3.14$.)
    (a) Find the volume of liquid in the container.
    (b) A leak in the container allows water to drip from it. If after 4 hours 1,300π cm^3 of water has leaked, what depth of water is left in the container?

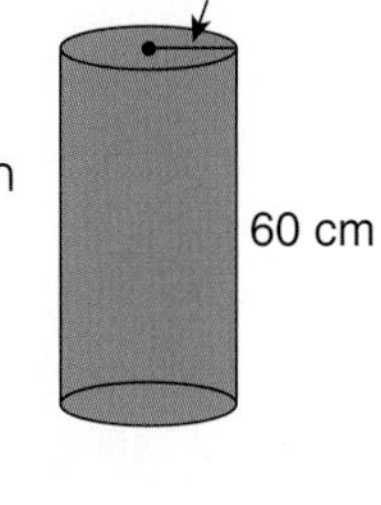

34. A cylindrical candle with diameter 50 cm and a height of 120 cm is melted down and recast as smaller cylindrical candles with a radius of 5 cm and a height of 6 cm.
    (a) Calculate the volume of the larger candle.
    (b) Calculate the volume of the smaller candle.
    (c) During the recasting, 10% of the wax is lost to spillages. How many complete smaller candles can be manufactured?

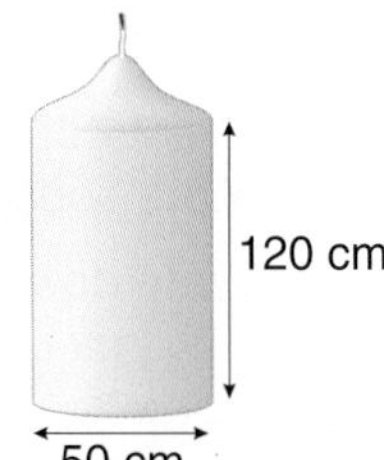

35. A cylindrical jug of height 30 cm and diameter 16 cm is filled with diluted orange up to 10 cm from the top of the jug.

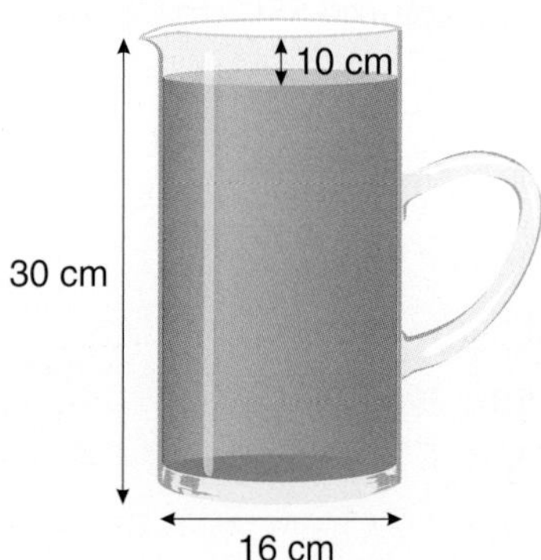

(a) Find the volume of diluted orange in the jug.

(b) The orange is poured into cylindrical glasses of height 10 cm and radius 2.5 cm. How many glasses can be filled to within 1 cm from the top of the glass?

36. A cylindrical solid steel rod has length 1.5 m and diameter 90 cm. A hole is bored through the length of the rod with radius 5 cm and recycled.

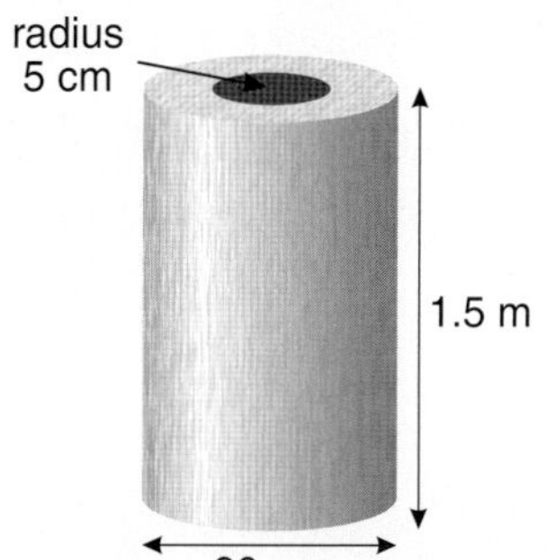

Calculate the percentage of metal removed from the solid rod, correct to two decimal places.

37. A cylindrical block of cheese has diameter 90 cm and height 90 cm. Smaller barrels of cheese with radius 1.5 cm and height 30 cm are cut from the block.

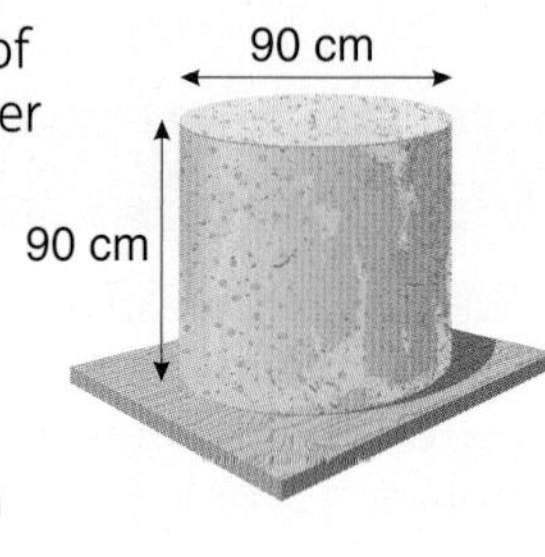

How many complete barrels can be cut from the block?

Section 24.4: Volume of a cone

Student Activity 24D

The diagram shows two popcorn containers: a cylindrical bucket and conical funnel. The radii of both circular bases and the heights of both shapes are equal to each other.

(a) In your opinion, which shape contains more popcorn?

(b) Write down the formula for the volume of a cylinder.

(c) Using your tables, write down the formula for the volume of a cone.

(d) Describe any similarities that you may notice about both formulae.

(e) If all the popcorn in the larger container is to be transferred into the smaller container, how many smaller containers are needed to hold all the popcorn? Explain your answer.

(f) One of the pictures **A–E** shows how the cone-shaped containers will be filled up after all the popcorn from the cylindrical container is transferred. Select the correct picture and justify your answer.

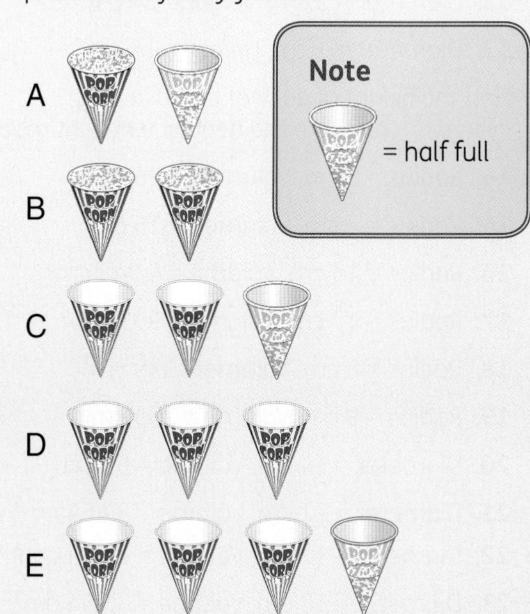

VOLUME OF A CONE EXPLAINED

A cone has a circular base and contains a right-angled triangle.

We can use the theorem of Pythagoras to calculate the radius (r), perpendicular height (h) or the slant height (l), since $l^2 = h^2 + r^2$

The volume of a cone is given by:

$$\text{Volume} = \frac{1}{3}\pi r^2 h$$

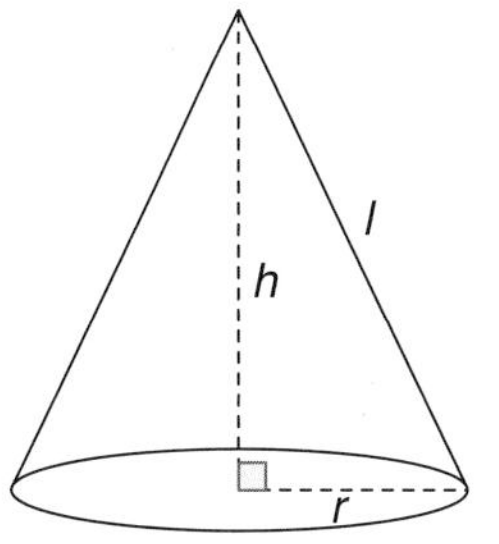

This formula can be found on page 10 of the *Formulae and Tables*.

EXAMPLE 5

Find the volume of a cone of vertical height 10 cm and radius 6 cm, correct to nearest whole number.

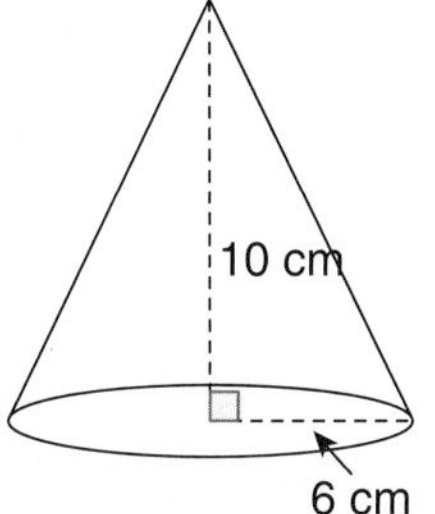

Solution

Volume $= \frac{1}{3}\pi r^2 h$

Volume $= \frac{1}{3}(\pi)(6^2)(10)$

Volume $= 377$ cm^3

EXAMPLE 6

A cone has radius 8 cm and perpendicular height 6 cm.

(a) Find the slant height of the cone.

(b) Hence, find its volume, correct to one decimal place.

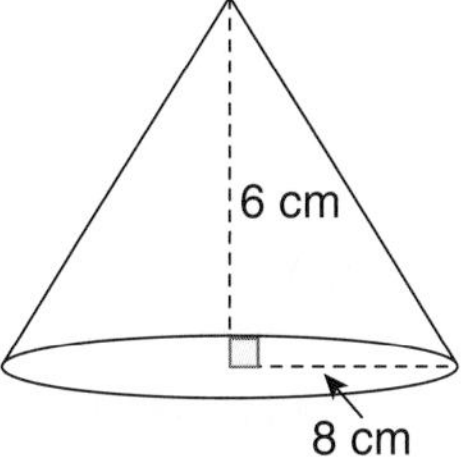

Solution

(a) $l^2 = (8)^2 + (6)^2$

$l^2 = 100$

$l = \sqrt{100}$

$l = 10$ cm

(b) Volume $= \frac{1}{3}\pi r^2 h$

Volume $= \frac{1}{3}(\pi)(8)^2(6)$

Volume $= 128\pi$ cm^3

Volume $= 402.1$ cm^3

Exercise 24.4

Find the (a) slant height and (b) the volume of each of the following cones. Give your answer correct to one decimal place. Take $\pi = 3.14$.

1. Radius = 3 cm, Perpendicular height = 4 cm
2. Radius = 2 cm, Perpendicular height = 5 cm
3. Radius = 10 cm, Perpendicular height = 13 cm
4. Radius = 13 cm, Perpendicular height = 7 cm

Find the (a) radius and (b) the volume of each of the following cones. Give your answer correct to one decimal place. Take $\pi = \frac{22}{7}$.

5. Slant height = 10 cm, Perpendicular height = 8 cm
6. Slant height = 5 cm, Perpendicular height = 3 cm
7. Slant height = 17 cm, Perpendicular height = 15 cm
8. Slant height = 29 cm, Perpendicular height = 20 cm

9. A plastic mould in the shape of a cone has a base radius of 6 cm and a perpendicular height of 20 cm.

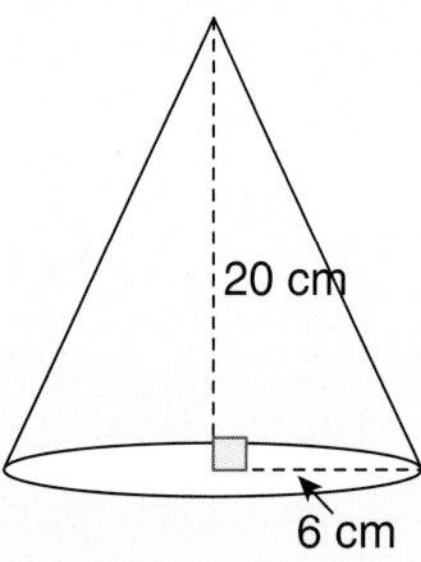

(a) Calculate the volume of the mould.

The contents of the conical mould are then poured into smaller cylindrical moulds of radius 1 cm and height 2 cm.

(b) How many cylindrical moulds can be filled completely?

10. A cylindrical container full of salt with height 90 cm and diameter 10 cm is poured into conical salt cellars with base radius 3.5 cm and height 6 cm.

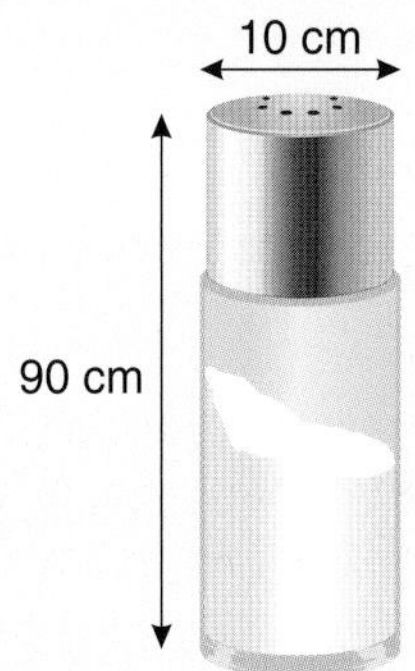

(a) Calculate the volume of salt in the cylindrical container.

(b) Each conical salt cellar is filled to $\frac{2}{3}$ of its capacity. Calculate the volume of salt in each salt cellar.

(c) How many conical salt cellars can be filled?

11. A solid metal cone of radius 3 cm and height 14 cm is dropped into a cylindrical container of radius 10 cm and height 50 cm which is half full of water.

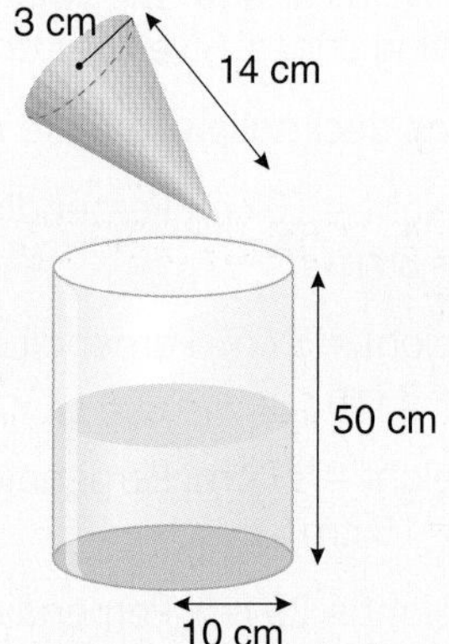

Calculate the rise in the depth of the water.

12. Three conical candles are packed into a rectangular box as shown. Calculate the volume of free space in the box.

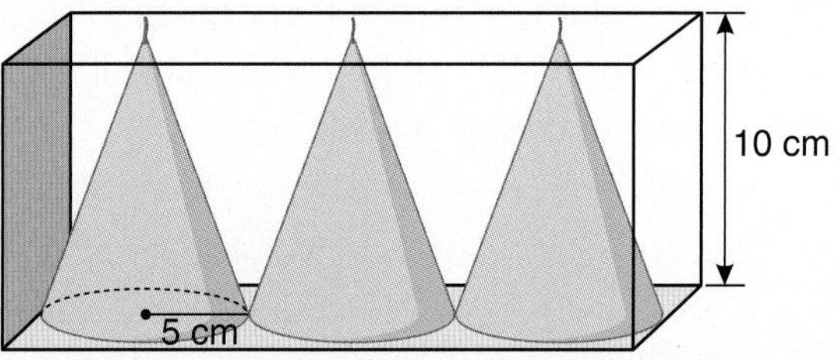

13. A cattle feeder is in the shape of an inverted cone with radius 1 m and height 1.2 m.

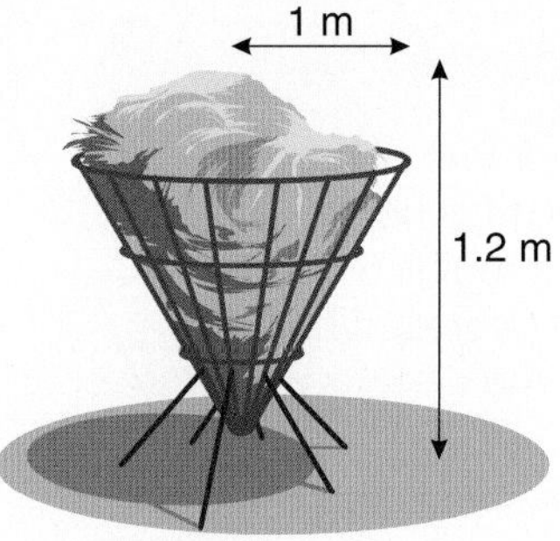

(a) How much feed is needed to fill the container?

(b) If each cow consumes 1,629 cm^3 of feed, how many cattle will be fed?

14. A sculptor wants to remove wood from a cylindrical block 3 m high and turn it into a cone. The diameter of the base of the cone and cylinder is 2 m. What is the volume of the wood that the sculptor must remove? (Let $\pi = 3.14$.)

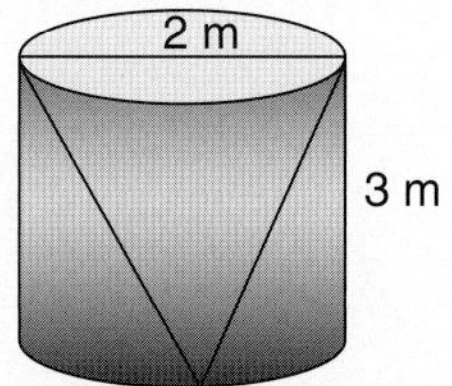

15. The part of a dish designed for holding ice-cream is shaped like an inverted cone. The base of the cone has a radius of 6 cm and the perpendicular height is 10 cm.

Calculate the volume of the cone, giving your answer correct to one decimal place.

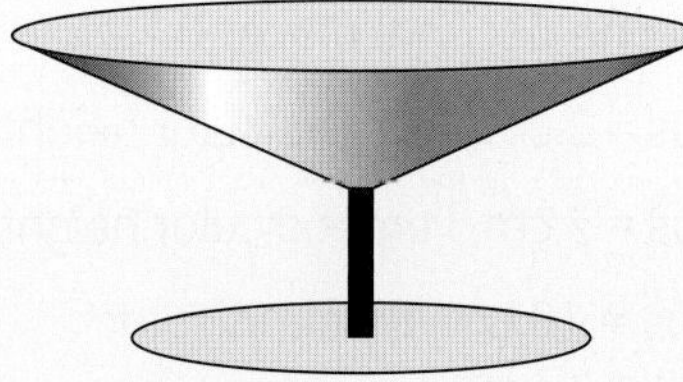

16. Calculate the radius of each of the following conical containers of height 10 cm, given their volume is (a) 360π cm^3, (b) 250π cm^3, (c) $705{\cdot}6\pi$ cm^3, (d) $562{\cdot}5\pi$ cm^3.

Section 24.5: Volume of a sphere and a hemisphere

Student Activity 24E

1. Give three examples of spheres in everyday life.
2. The Earth is divided into two hemispheres, the Northern hemisphere and the Southern hemisphere. What is a hemisphere?
3. Draw a sphere and a hemisphere into your copy.
4. What dimensions do a sphere and a hemisphere have in common?

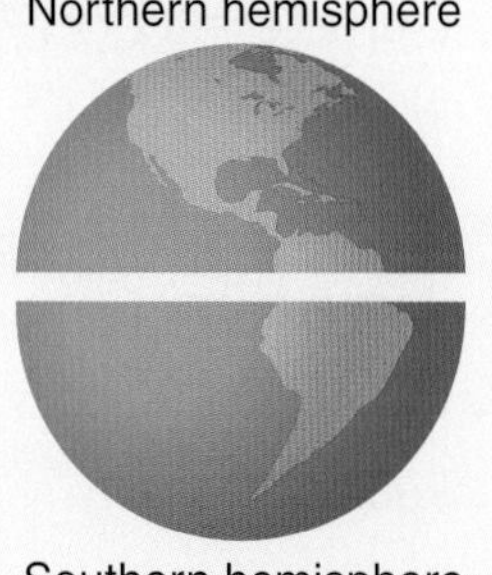

VOLUME OF A SPHERE AND A HEMISPHERE EXPLAINED

A sphere and a hemisphere are both 3D circular-based objects. As with a circle, they both have a diameter and a radius.

The formula for the volume of a sphere is:

$$\text{Volume} = \frac{4}{3}\pi r^3$$

This formula can be found on page 10 of the *Formulae and Tables.*

- In a sphere, all points on the surface are the same distance from the centre. Of all the shapes, a sphere has the smallest surface area for its volume. For example, if you blow up a balloon it naturally forms a sphere because it is trying to hold as much air within as small a surface area as possible.
- A hemisphere is half a sphere. To calculate the volume of a hemisphere, you can use the formula for the volume of a sphere and divide your answer by 2. Or you can use the formula:

$$\text{Volume} = \frac{2}{3}\pi r^3$$

EXAMPLE 7

Find, in terms of π, the volume of a sphere of radius 4 cm.

Solution

$\text{Volume} = \frac{4}{3}\pi r^3$

$\text{Volume} = \frac{4}{3}(\pi)(4)^3$

$\text{Volume} = \frac{256}{3}\pi \text{ cm}^3$

$\text{Volume} = 85\frac{1}{3}\pi \text{ cm}^3$

EXAMPLE 8

The volume of a hemisphere is 486π cm^3. Calculate its radius.

Solution

$\frac{2}{3}\pi r^3 = 486\pi$

$r^3 = \dfrac{486\pi}{\frac{2}{3}\pi}$ **Divide both sides by $\frac{2}{3}\pi$**

$r^3 = \sqrt[3]{729}$ **Get the cube root of both sides**

$r^3 = 729$

$r = 9$ cm

The radius is 9 cm.

Exercise 24.5

Find the volume of each of the following spheres, correct to one decimal place.
Take $\pi = \frac{22}{7}$.

1. Radius = 3 cm
2. Diameter = 12 cm
3. Radius = 8 cm
4. Diameter = 8 cm
5. Radius = 9 cm
6. Diameter = 20 cm
7. Radius = 14 cm
8. Radius = 21 cm

Find the volume of each of the following hemispheres, correct to one decimal place. Take $\pi = 3.14$.

9. Radius = 5 cm
10. Diameter = 22 cm
11. Radius = 18 cm
12. Diameter = 30 cm
13. Radius = 1.3 cm
14. Diameter = 2.5 cm
15. A rectangular block of chocolate measuring 55 mm × 50 mm × 40 mm is melted down and recast as small spherical balls of chocolate of radius 1 cm.

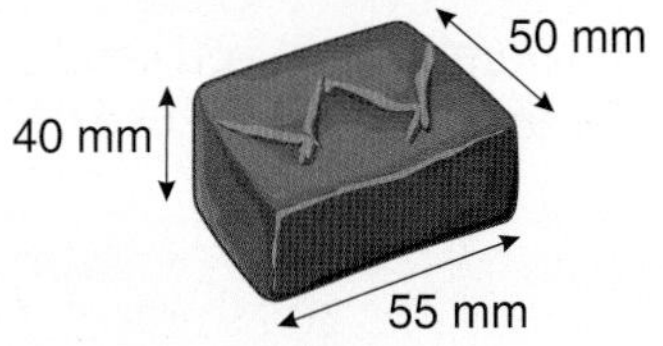

(a) Calculate the volume of the bar of chocolate.

(b) Calculate the volume of a chocolate ball.

(c) How many balls can be produced from four bars of the chocolate?

16. A solid cylindrical rod of length 2 m and radius 50 cm is melted down and recast as hemispheres of radius 10 cm. How many hemispheres can be made?
17. A soup ladle is in the shape of a hemisphere of radius 3 cm. Calculate the volume that the ladle can hold.
18. A spherical mould of radius 5 cm is used to manufacture a hemispherical wax candle. Calculate the volume of a candle.
19. A basketball has a diameter of 24 cm. Calculate the volume of a basketball.
20. A sphere of radius 4 cm is submerged in an overflow can and the water is collected in a graduated cylinder.

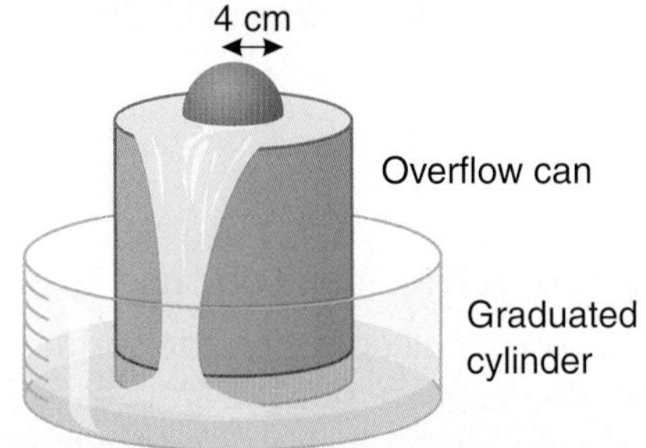

Calculate the volume of water collected.

21. To pump his beach ball, Neil needs 288π cm^3 of air.

(a) Calculate the radius of the beach ball.

(b) Calculate the length of the circumference of the beach ball, where the two hemispheres are joined.

Section 24.6: Compound shapes

In the previous sections, you learned to calculate the volume of various 3D shapes. In the following exercise, you will have to combine all these skills to solve surface area and volume problems.

When tackling any problem of this type:

- **Step 1:** Identify the shapes in the question.
- **Step 2:** Write down the formulae you will need for each shape.
- **Step 3:** Identify the variables you know.
- **Step 4:** Substitute the variables you know into the formulae.
- **Step 5:** Solve for any missing variables.

EXAMPLE 9

A new sweet container is designed in the shape of a cylinder as shown.

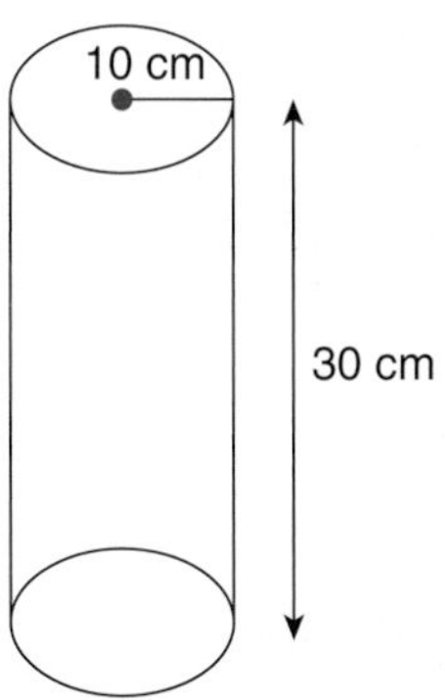

(a) What surface area of cardboard is required to create the box?

(b) How many complete containers can be made from a sheet measuring 20 m × 40 m?

(c) What is the volume of the container?

(d) If each spherical sweet has a radius of 2 cm, how many sweets can the cylindrical tube hold?

Solution

(a) Surface area = $2\pi rh + 2\pi r^2$

Surface area = $2(\pi)(10)(30) + 2(\pi)(10)^2$

Surface area = 2,513.27 cm^2

(b) $20\text{ m} \times 40\text{ m} = 2{,}000 \times 4{,}000 = 8{,}000{,}000\text{ cm}^2$

Number of containers = $\dfrac{8{,}000{,}000}{2{,}513.27}$

Number of containers = 3,183

(c) Volume = $\pi r^2 h$

Volume = $(\pi)(10)^2(30)$

Volume = 9,424.78 cm^3

(d) Volume of a sweet = $\frac{4}{3}\pi r^3$

Volume of a sweet = $\frac{4}{3}(\pi)(2)^3$

Volume of a sweet = 33.51 cm^3

Number of sweets = $\dfrac{9{,}424.78}{33.51}$

Number of sweets = 281 sweets per box.

Exercise 24.6

1. A child's toy is made from a cone sitting on a hemisphere.

(a) Calculate the volume of the cone.

(b) Calculate the volume of the hemisphere.

(c) Calculate the volume of the toy, correct to the nearest whole number.

(d) If a plastic cube of side length 4 m is melted down to make the toys, how many complete toys can be made?

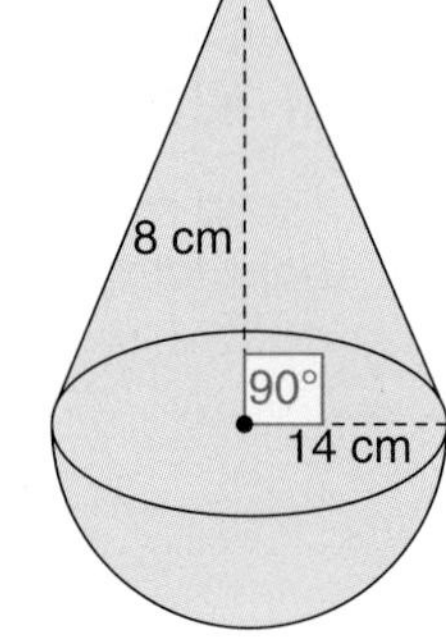

2. A crayon is in the shape of a cone sitting on a cylinder as shown.

(a) Calculate the vertical height of the cone.

(b) Calculate the volume of the cone in terms of π.

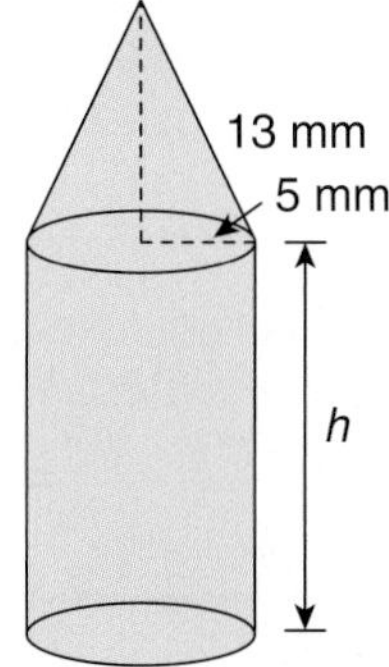

(c) If the volume of the cylinder is 20 times the volume of the cone, find the perpendicular height of the cylinder.

(d) Calculate the total volume of the crayon, correct to two decimal places.

(e) If 16 crayons fit upright into a square base box, find the volume of the box.

3. A cylindrical jug with dimensions as shown is filled with water.

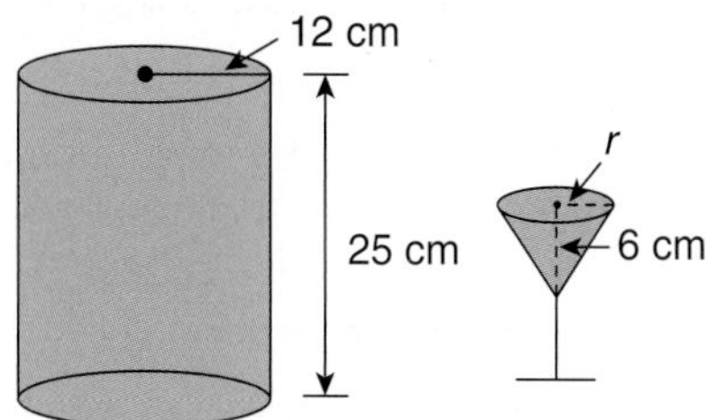

(a) Calculate the volume of the jug in terms of π.

(b) If the jug fills 100 glasses as shown, calculate the volume of each glass in terms of π.

(c) Calculate the radius of each glass.

4. A candle is in the shape of a cone as shown.

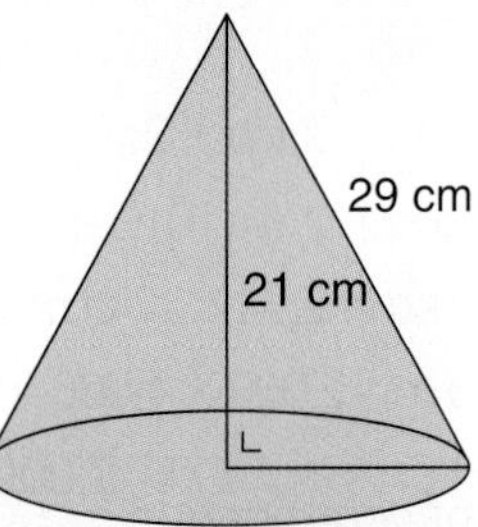

(a) Calculate the radius of the cone.
(b) Calculate the volume of the cone.
(c) If the cones are made from a block of wax measuring 2 m × 2 m × 3 m, how many complete candles can be made?

5. Tennis balls are sold in a cylindrical tube as shown.

Calculate:

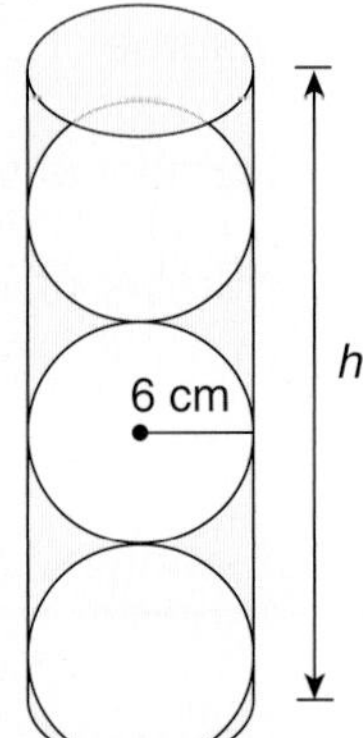

(a) The total volume of the 3 tennis balls
(b) The height of the cylinder
(c) The volume of the cylinder
(d) The percentage volume of the tube that is filled by the tennis balls

6. A cylindrical glass has dimensions as shown. $\left(\text{Take } \pi = \frac{22}{7}.\right)$

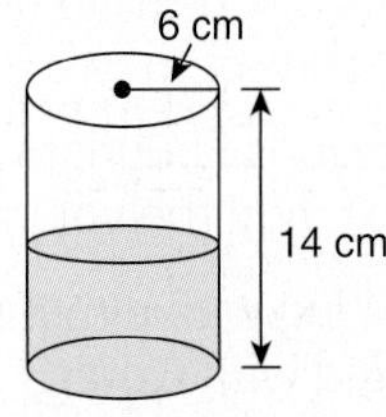

(a) Calculate the volume of the liquid in the glass if the glass is half full.
(b) Ten ice cubes of side length 2 cm are dropped into the glass. Find the volume of the ten ice cubes.

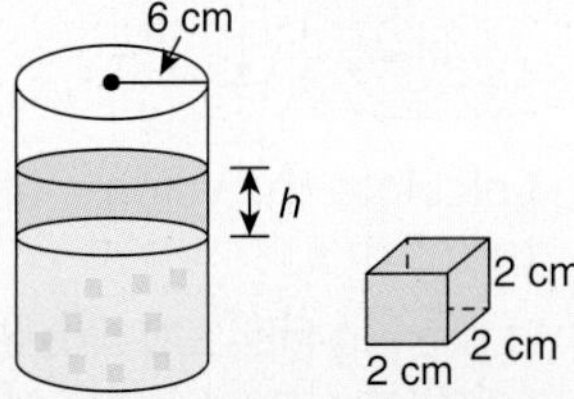

(c) Find the rise in the height of the liquid in the glass, correct to one decimal place.

7. A manufacturer makes two types of ball bearings as shown from a block of metal measuring 1 m × 1 m × 2 m.

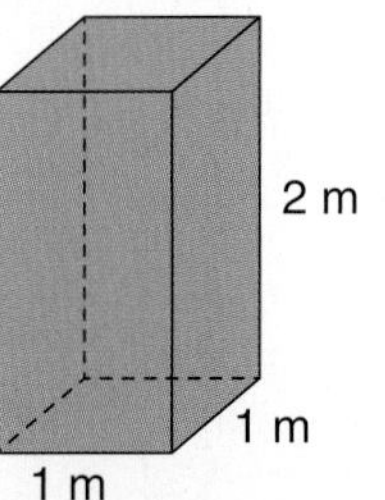

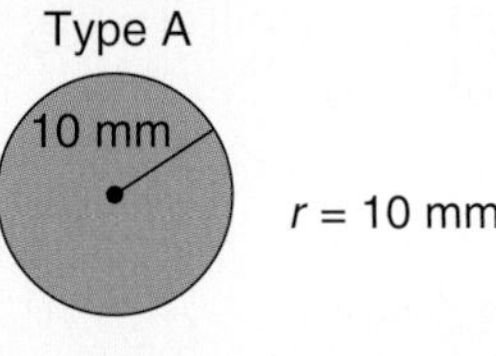

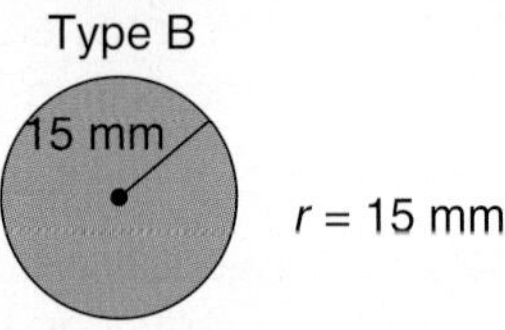

(a) Find the volume of the block of metal.
(b) If half the block is used to make type A ball bearings, how many complete ball bearings can be made?
(c) How many type B ball bearings are made from the remainder of the block?
(d) If 0.3% of the total number of ball bearings are faulty, how many complete ball bearings are of a sellable quality.

8. A solid metal cylinder is used to manufacture a length of pipe.

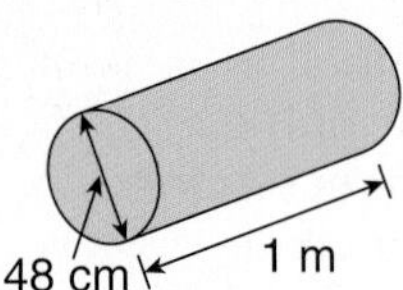

(a) Taking $\pi = \frac{22}{7}$, calculate the volume of the solid metal pipe in m^3.
(b) A smaller cylinder is hollowed through the centre to make a pipe as shown. Find the volume of metal used to make the pipe.

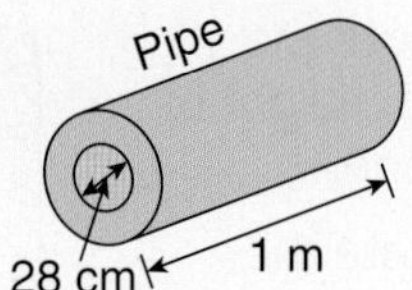

9. A salt shaker is in the shape of a cylinder with a hemisphere on top as shown.

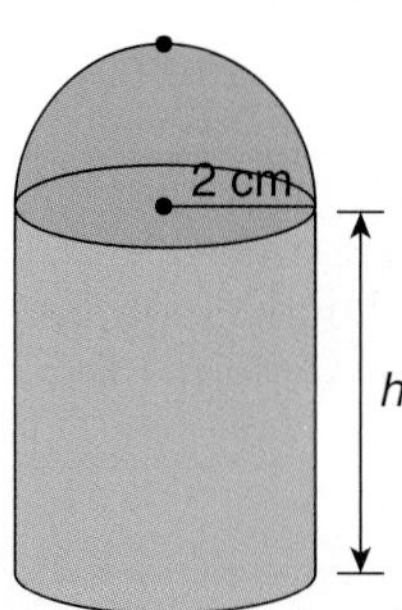

(a) Find the volume of the hemisphere in terms of π.

(b) If the volume of the cylinder is nine times the volume of the hemisphere, calculate the volume of the cylinder.

(c) Find the height of the cylinder.

10. Pellets of sodium metal in the shape of spheres are stored under oil in a cylindrical container as shown.

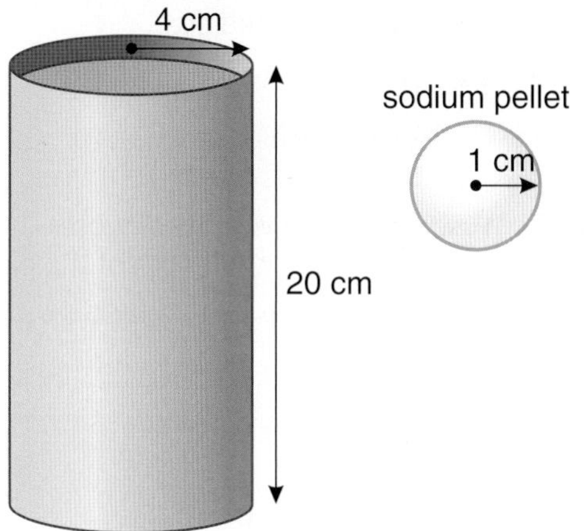

(a) Calculate the volume of the container.

(b) Find the volume of one pellet of sodium.

(c) The container is one-quarter full of oil. 15 pellets are placed in the container. Find the depth of oil in the container after the pellets are added.

11. A gun shell in the shape of a cylinder is filled with spherical lead shot.

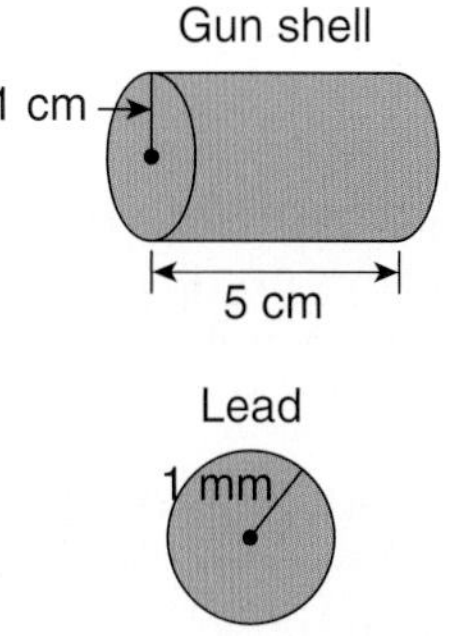

(a) Find the volume of the shell in cm^3.

(b) How many spherical pellets are required to fill the casing?

12. Coffee is sold in cylindrical tins as shown.

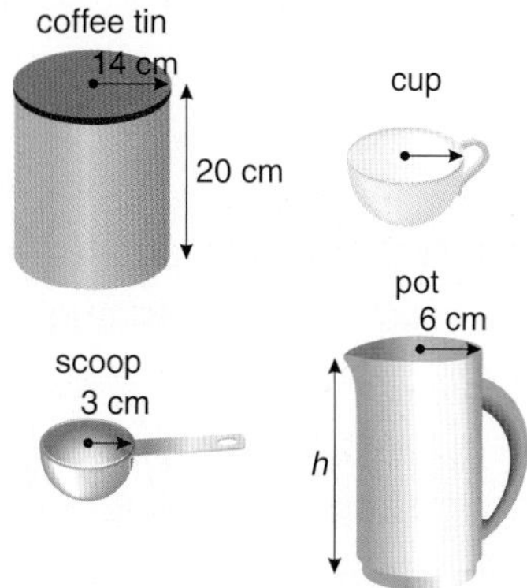

(a) Find the volume of coffee in a tin in terms of π.

(b) A scoop in the shape of a hemisphere is used to place the coffee in a coffee pot. Find the volume of the scoop in terms of π.

(c) How many full scoops of coffee are in one tin?

(d) One scoop, when used in the machine, makes a pot of coffee in the shape of a cylinder of radius 6 cm. The pot is 60 times the volume of one scoop. Find the height of the coffee pot.

(e) The pot fills 10 hemispherical cups of radius r cm. Find the radius of each cup, correct to one decimal place.

Section 24.7: Rates of flow

Student Activity 24F

A cylindrical container 10 cm in length and of radius 5 cm is full of water.

(a) Calculate the volume of water in the cylinder.

(b) A small leak in the container allows water to drip at a rate of 2 cm^3 per second. How long will it take to completely empty the container?

RATES OF FLOW EXPLAINED

Many questions on volume involve liquids flowing in pipes or from one container to another. It is often necessary to calculate the length of time it will take for a container to fill or empty.

> Blood travels around the entire body in 20 seconds. The average heart pumps 2,000 litres of blood every day. An adult body contains about 5 litres of blood, whereas a baby's body contains about 1 litre.

When dealing with rates of flow questions, there are three variables that must be considered: volume, time and the rate of flow. These can be linked in a triangle:

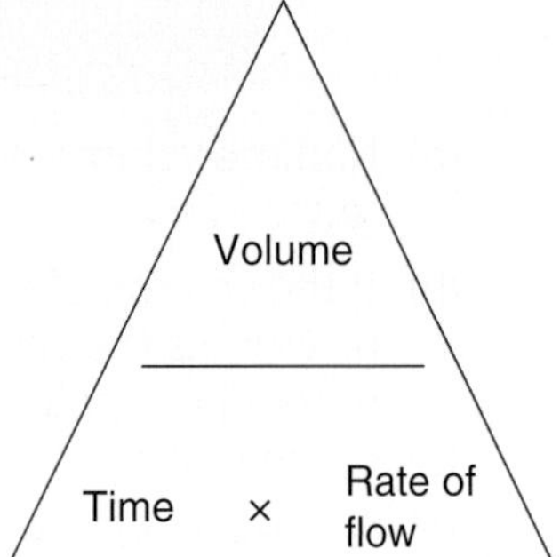

This gives us three formulae:

1. Volume = Time × Rate of flow
2. $\text{Time} = \dfrac{\text{Volume}}{\text{Rate of flow}}$
3. $\text{Rate of flow} = \dfrac{\text{Volume}}{\text{Time}}$

The rate of flow is always measured in cubic units per second, for example, cm^3/sec.

The volume of liquid flowing through a pipe at any time can also be calculated by:

> Volume = Speed of flow × Cross-sectional area of the pipe

If water is flowing through a cylindrical pipe at a rate of 5 cm^3/sec, then the volume of water leaving the pipe (called the discharge) is equal to the volume of water in a 5 cm length of the pipe.

EXAMPLE 10

Water flows through a cylindrical pipe of internal radius 5 cm at a speed of 10 cm/sec.

(a) Calculate, in terms of π, the rate of flow of water from the pipe.

(b) How long will it take to fill a spherical tank of radius 30 cm?

Solution

(a) Rate of flow = Volume of water in 10 cm of the pipe, with radius of 5 cm

Rate of flow = $\pi r^2 h$ **Volume of a cylinder**

Rate of flow = $\pi(5^2)(10)$

Rate of flow = 250π cm^3/sec

(b) Volume of sphere = $\frac{4}{3}\pi r^3$

Volume of sphere = $\frac{4}{3}\pi(30)^3$

Volume of sphere = $36{,}000\pi$ cm^3

$\text{Time} = \dfrac{\text{Volume}}{\text{Rate of flow}}$

$\text{Time} = \dfrac{36{,}000\pi}{250\pi}$

Time = 144 seconds or 2 minutes and 24 seconds

> Did you ever notice that when filling some bottles, the water all of a sudden spurts out of the top? Why does this happen? It occurs because the bottle is narrower at the top so holds less liquid. This means this section fills more quickly. We will now examine sketches of flow graphs of height versus volume in 3D shapes.

EXAMPLE 11

Imagine filling each of the six bottles below, pouring water in at a constant rate.

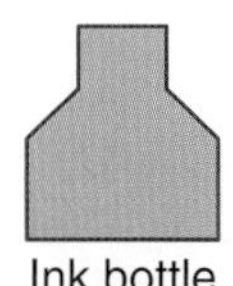
Ink bottle

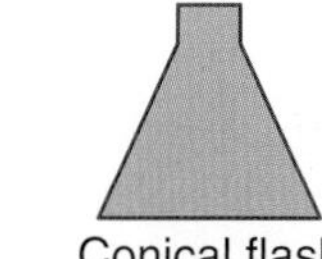
Conical flask

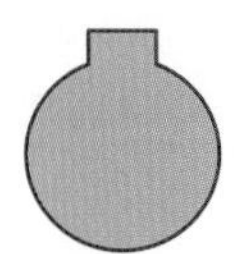
Boiling flask

Bucket

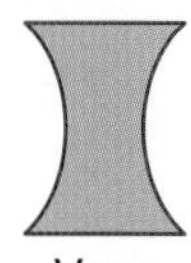
Vase

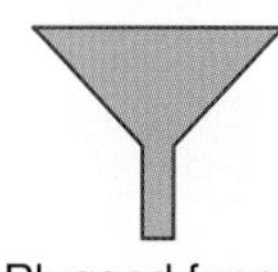
Plugged funnel

(a) For each bottle, choose the correct flow graph, relating the height of the water to the volume of water that's been poured in. (Hint: when will the graph of a bottle's height increase most slowly and most rapidly?)

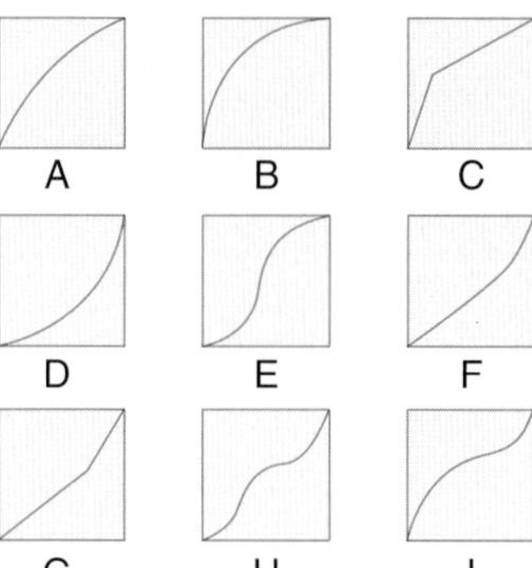

(b) For the remaining three graphs, sketch what the bottles should look like.

Solution

(a) Ink bottle = F

Conical flask = D

Boiling flask = I

Bucket = A

Vase = E

Plugged funnel = B

(b) Graphs C and G require quick changes to a constant width. Graph C would go from a small width to a large width, whereas G is the opposite.

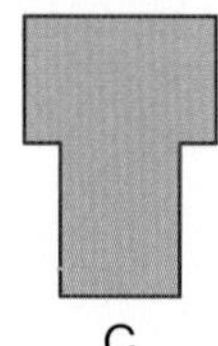
C

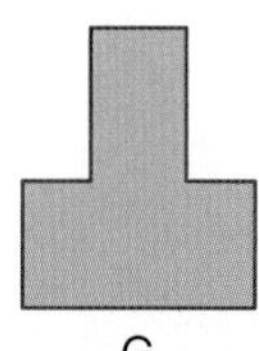
G

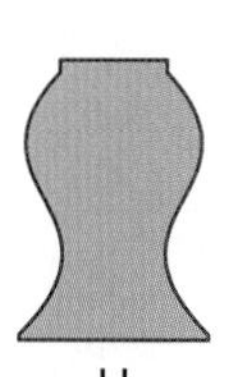
H

Exercise 24.7

1. Water flows through a cylindrical pipe of internal radius 7 cm at a rate of 28 cm/sec.

(a) Calculate, in terms of π, the rate of flow of water from the pipe per second.

(b) How long will it take to fill a cylindrical tank of height 70 cm and radius 14 cm?

2. Water flows through a cylindrical pipe of internal radius 10 cm at a rate of 45 cm/sec.

(a) Calculate, in terms of π, the rate of flow of water from the pipe.

(b) How long will it take to fill a cylindrical tank of height 1 m and radius 20 cm?

3. Oil flows through a pipe of radius 10 cm at a rate of 50 cm/s.

(a) Calculate, in terms of π, the rate of flow of oil from the pipe.

(b) How long will it take to fill a 50 litre cylindrical drum?

4. $2{,}450\pi$ cm^3 of cola flows through a cylindrical pipe of radius r cm at a rate of 50 cm/s.

(a) Calculate the radius of the pipe.

(b) How long will it take to fill a 5,000 litre storage container?

5. Water flows through a cylindrical pipe of internal radius 8 cm at a rate of 32 cm/sec.

(a) Calculate, in terms of π, the rate of flow of water from the pipe.

(b) How long will it take to fill a rectangular tank with dimensions 1.5 m × 2 m × 1 m?

6. An inverted conical container of diameter 10 cm and height 15 cm is filled with water. If water drips from the vertex of the container at a rate of 1.25 cm^3/sec, how long will it take to empty the container?

7. Oil flows through a pipe of internal diameter 1 m at 25 cm/sec. How many litres of oil flows through the pipe in one hour?

8. Water flows through a pipe of internal diameter 50 cm into a swimming pool with dimensions 15 m × 8 m × 3 m. If it takes 3 hours to raise the water level by 2 m, what is the speed of the flow through the pipe in cm/sec, correct to one decimal place?

9. Molten gold flows through a cylindrical pipe of radius 3 cm at a rate of 9 cm per second. It flows into rectangular moulds of dimensions 3 cm × 10 cm × 2 cm. How long will it take to fill one mould?

10. Two cylindrical containers, A and B, are being filled with water.

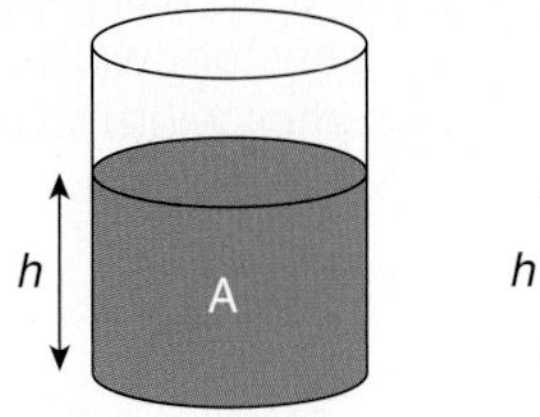

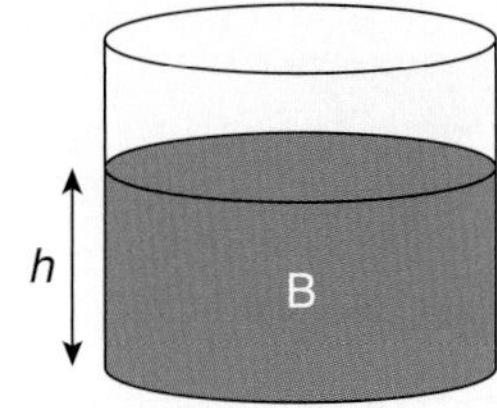

The volume of water increases at the same rate in both. The height of both containers is 12 cm.

(a) On one flow graph, copy and sketch the rate at which the height of the water level changes with time for both containers, given container A is full after 6 seconds and container B is full after 24 seconds.

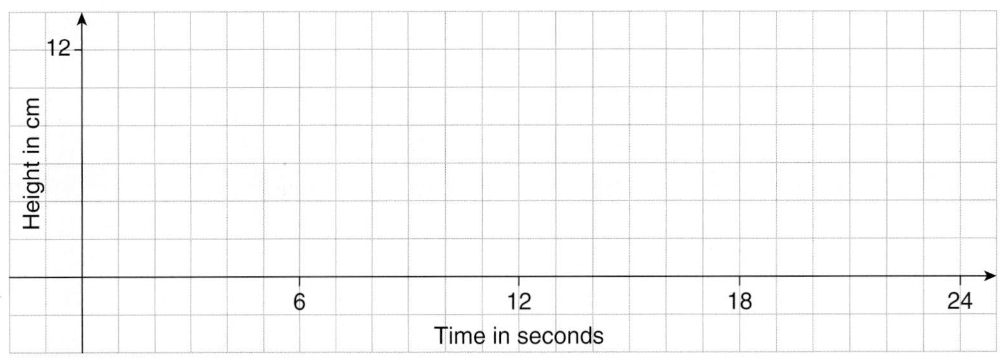

(b) Why does it take container B longer to fill?

11. These graphs represent the volume of liquid in a container versus the height of the liquid.

(i)

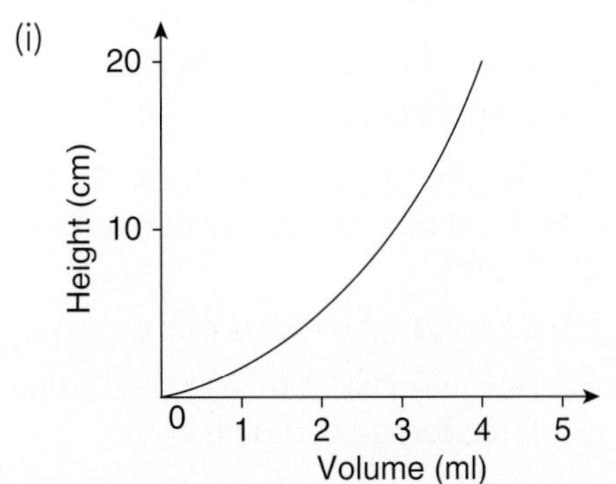

(ii)

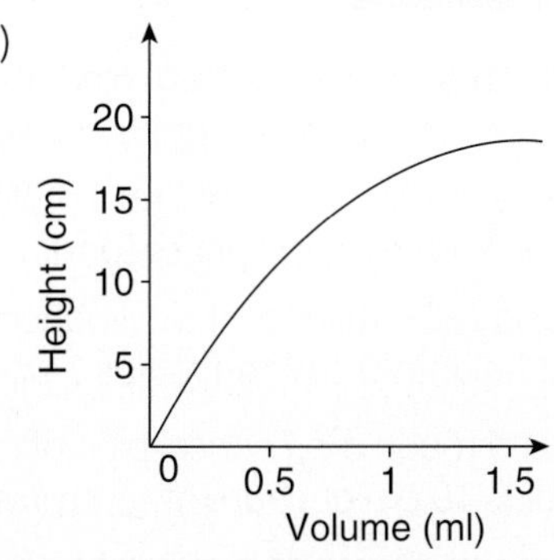

The diagrams are two-dimensional representations of possible containers.

(a) Which of the containers could each graph represent?

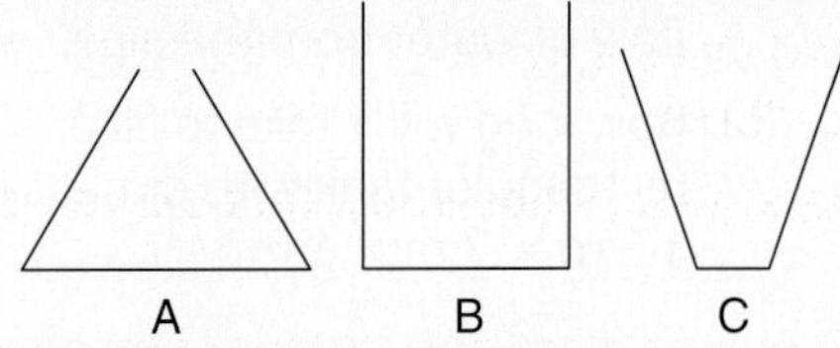

(b) Draw a graph to represent the remaining shape.

12. Water flows into a vessel in the shape of an inverted cone as shown.

Sketch a rough graph to show how the height of the water level changes with time as water is poured into the vessel. (Hint: put time on the horizontal axis and height on the vertical axis.)

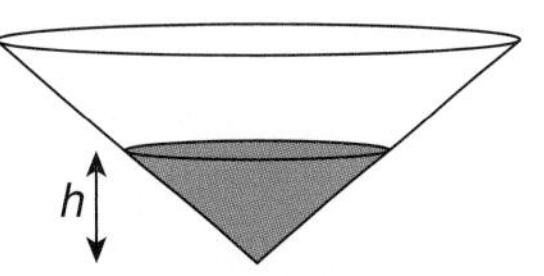

13. Draw a rough sketch of the shape of the container represented by the following graph as water is being poured into it.

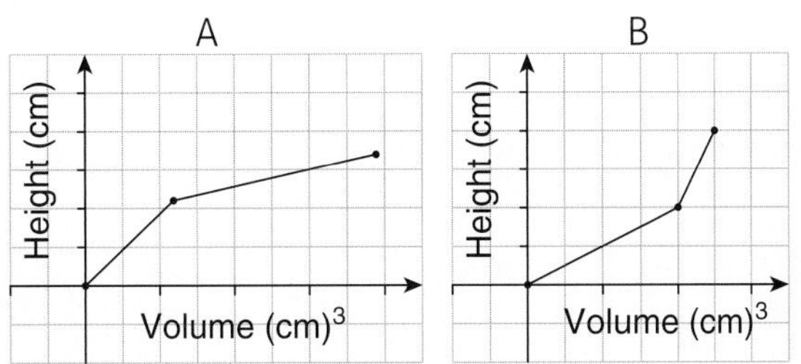

14. The picture shows five different shapes. For the drinking glass, the bottom section shown in black is solid glass.

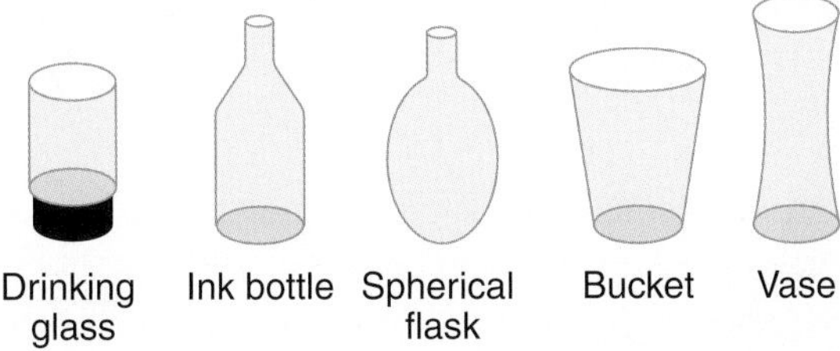

(a) Match the graph of height versus volume to the correct shape.

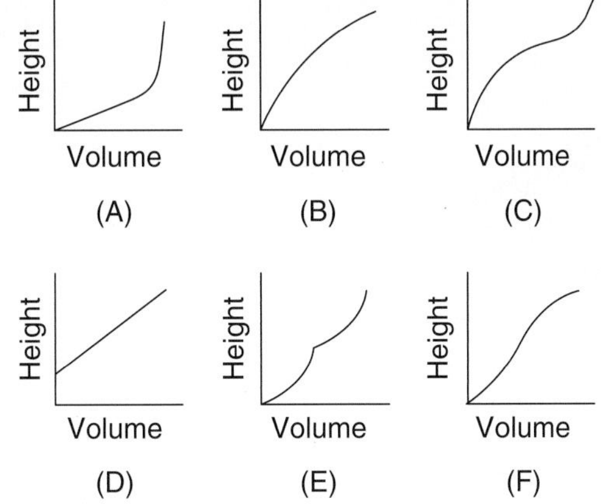

(b) For the remaining graph, sketch what you think it would look like.

15. Sketch graphs for the following sequence of bottles:

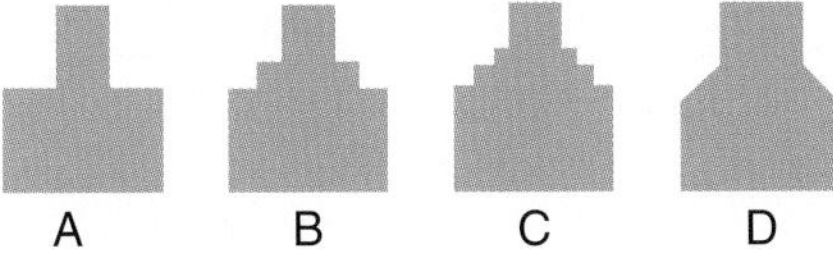

16. On the basis of your understanding of the way that height changes with volume, consider the following questions:

(a) What does it mean if the graph is a straight line?

(b) What does it mean if the first point is on the vertical axis?

(c) What does it mean if the first point on the graph was on the horizontal axis, as shown in the diagram?

First point of graph here

(d) If the slope of the graph is getting steeper and steeper, what would that tell you about the shape of the container?

(e) If the slope of the graph becomes less and less steep, what would that tell you about the shape of the container?

(f) What is the meaning of a single point on the graph? What does that tell you about the shape of the container?

CHAPTER 24 SELF-CHECK TEST

1. Find the volume of each of the following:

(a)

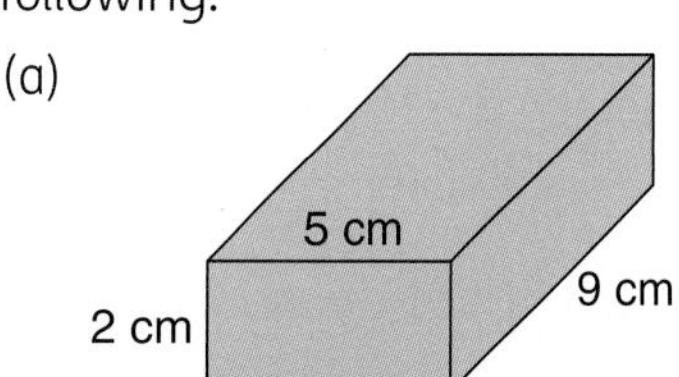

(b)

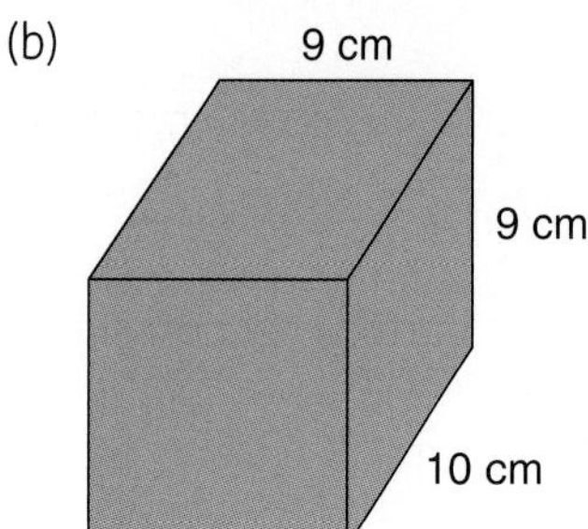

(c)

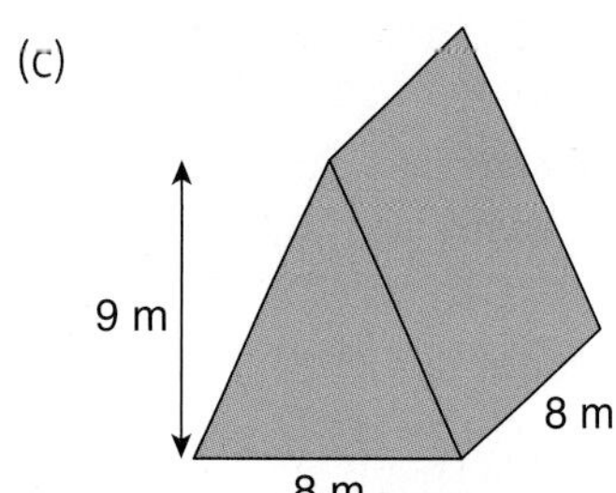

(d)

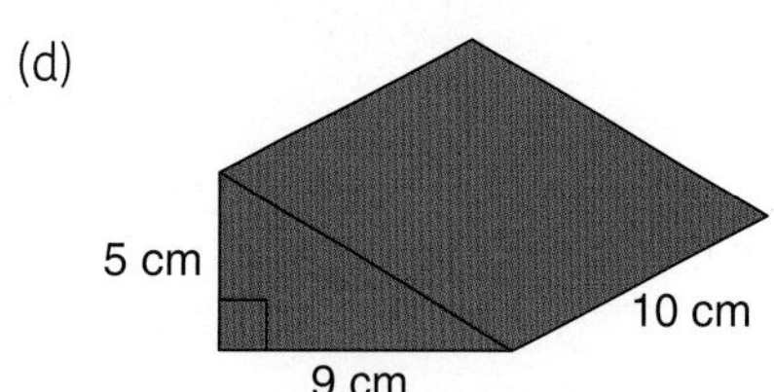

(e)

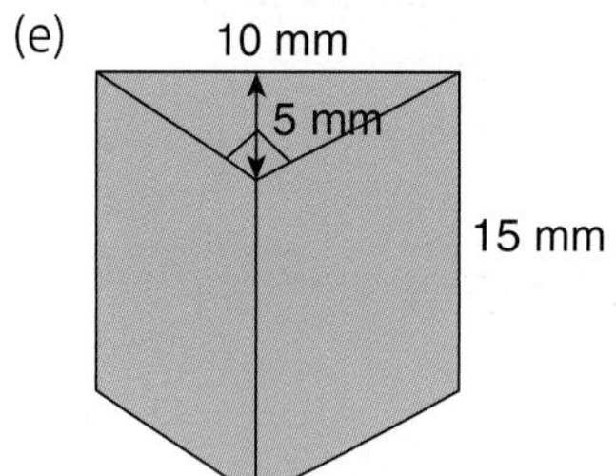

(f)

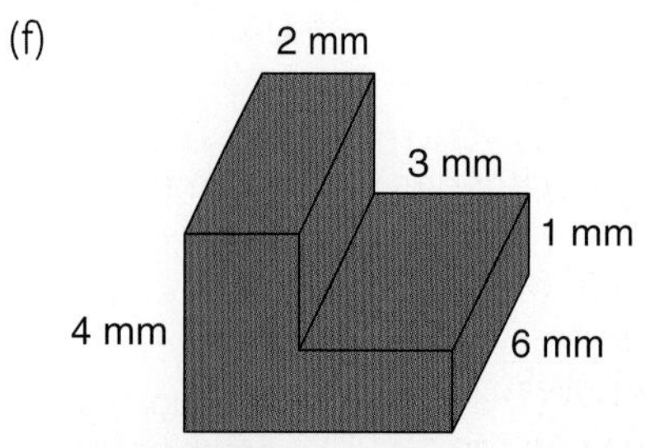

(g)

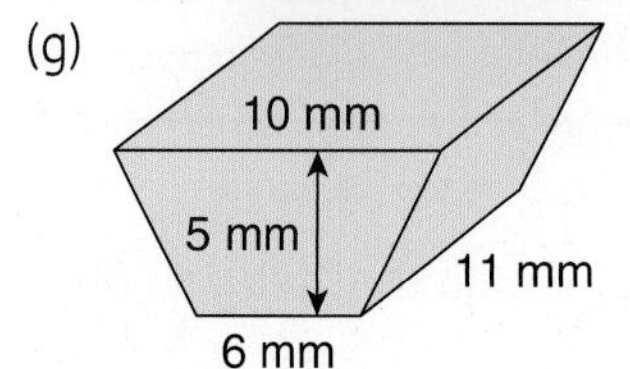

(h)

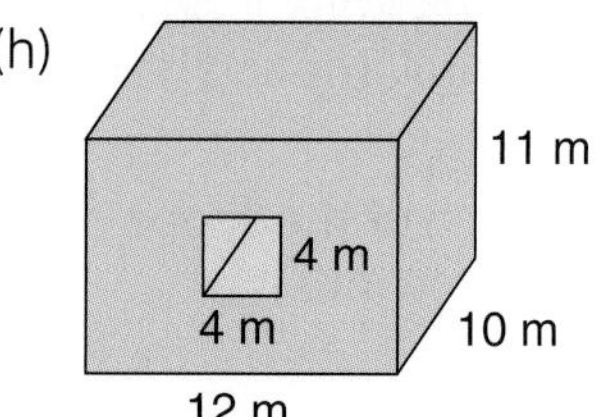

(i)

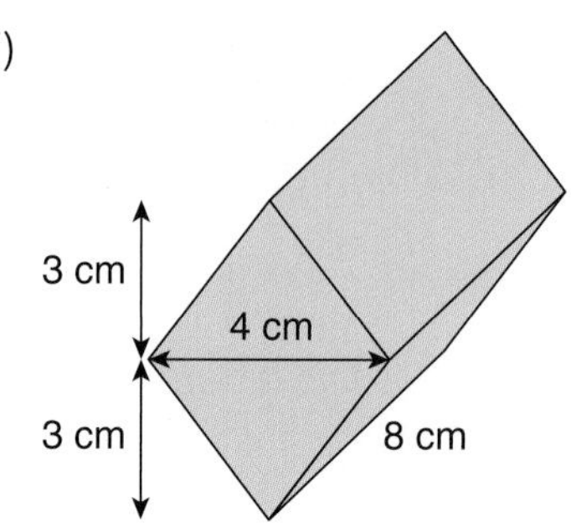

(j)

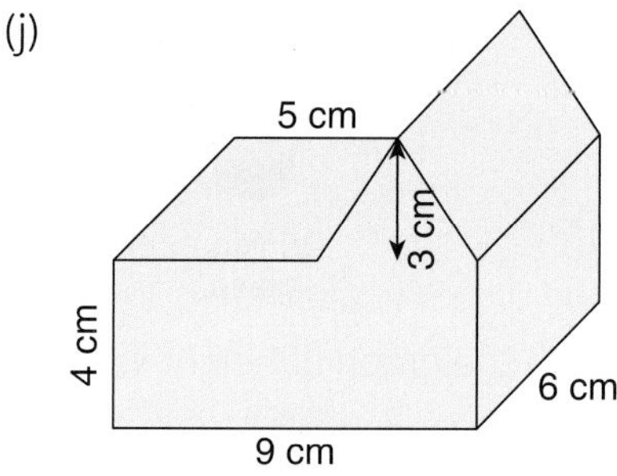

(k)

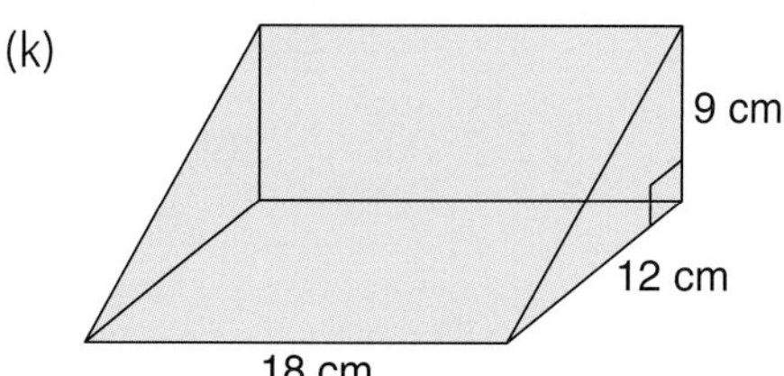

(l)

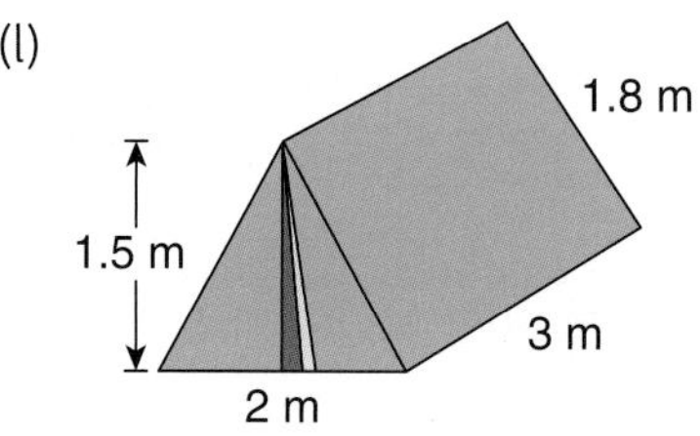

(m)

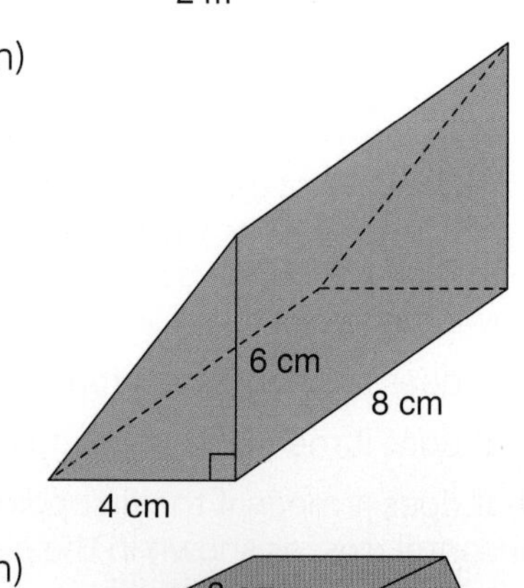

(n)

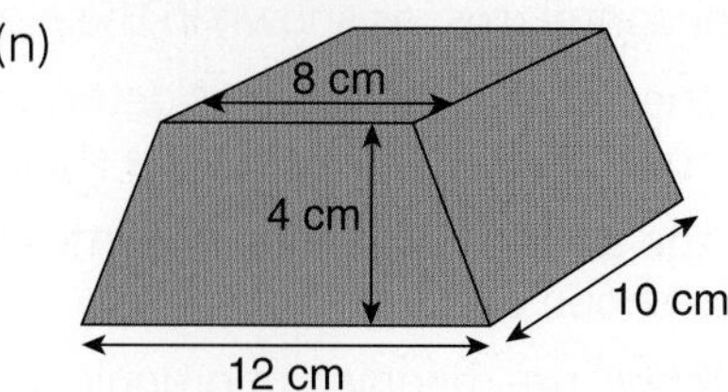

(o)

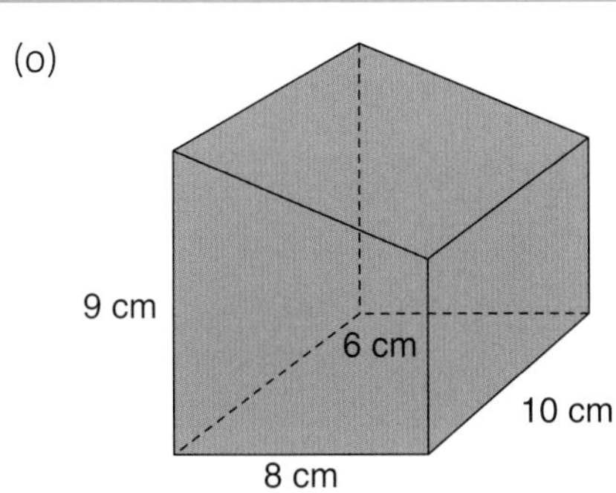

2. A company manufactures diving boards with dimensions 240 cm long × 50 cm wide × 20 cm high.

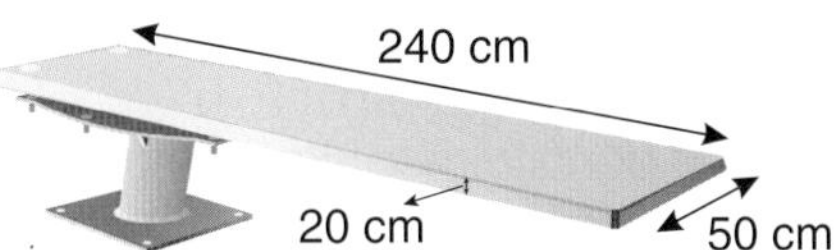

(a) Calculate the volume of a diving board.

A shipping company packs the diving boards into a truck with dimensions 8 m long × 3 m wide × 4 m high.

(b) Calculate the maximum number of diving boards that can be packed into the truck.

3. The dimensions of a swimming pool are shown:

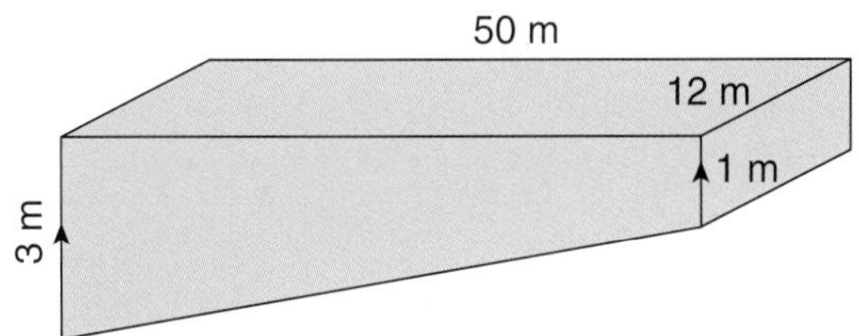

Calculate the volume of water in the pool when it is full.

4. This solid shape is made from cubes of side 1 cm. Work out the volume of the solid shape.

5. A 20 cm × 20 cm piece of cardboard is used to make a box. What are the dimensions of the box with the maximum volume?

6. A cuboid consists of a number of cubes of side length 1 cm.

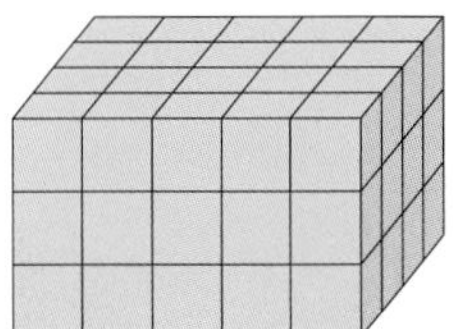

(a) Calculate the volume of the cuboid.

(b) The cuboid is broken down and all the blocks are used to form a new cuboid as shown.

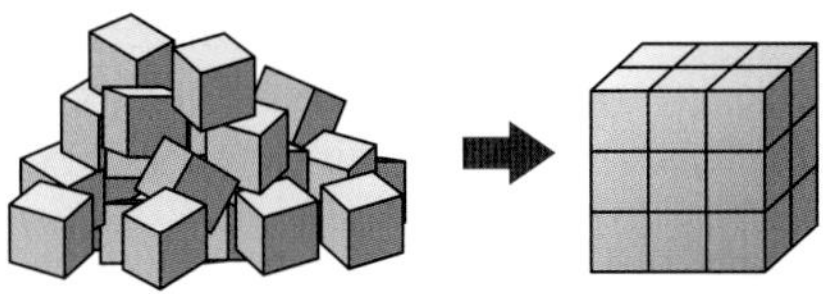

If all the blocks are used, how many new cuboids are formed?

7. A cuboid with dimensions 6 cm × 4 cm × 3 cm is made up of a number of cubes of side length 1 cm.

If the cuboid is broken down to form a new cuboid of height 9 cm and length 4 cm, find the width of the new cuboid.

8. Find the volume of each of the following cylinders, giving your answer correct to one decimal place. (Take $\pi = 3.14$.)

(a) Radius = 3 cm, Perpendicular height = 7 cm

(b) Radius = 5 cm, Perpendicular height = 10 cm

(c) Diameter = 12 cm, Perpendicular height = 14 cm

(d) Diameter = 8 cm, Perpendicular height = 13 cm

(e) Radius = 9 cm, Perpendicular height = 8 cm

(f) Diameter = 6 cm, Perpendicular height = 6 cm

(g) Radius = 4 cm, Perpendicular height = 14 cm

(h) Radius = 7 cm, Perpendicular height = 7 cm

9. A can of orange is in the shape of a cylinder with a radius of 4 cm and a height of 15 cm.

Calculate the volume of the cylinder, giving your answer correct to 3 significant figures.

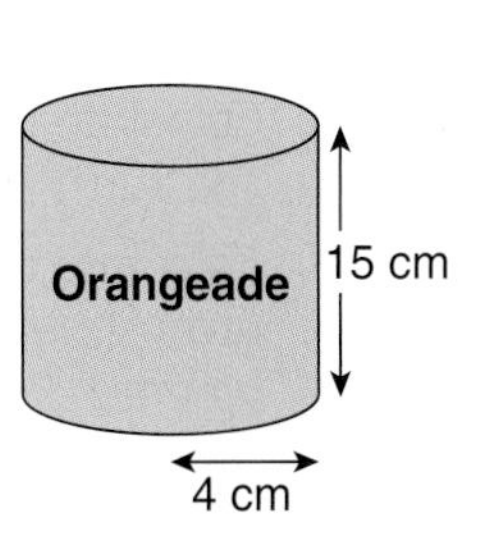

10. Swim tubes are cylindrical in shape. They come in three different sizes. Which one has the greatest volume?

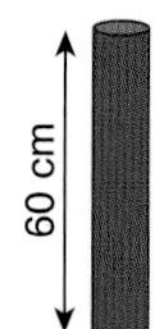

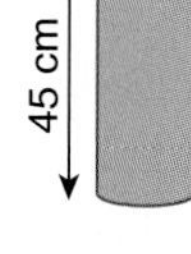

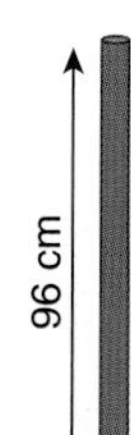

Tube A
Radius = 4 cm

Tube B
Radius = 7 cm

Tube C
Diameter = 4 cm

11. A 20 cm × 20 cm piece of cardboard is used it to make a cylindrical box. What are the dimensions of the box with the maximum volume?

12. A spherical metal ball of radius 70 cm is melted down and recast as solid cylindrical rods of radius 3 cm and height 10 cm. If 5% of the metal is lost in the process, how many rods can be manufactured?

13. Which formula can be used to find the volume of the composite solid figure represented in the drawing?

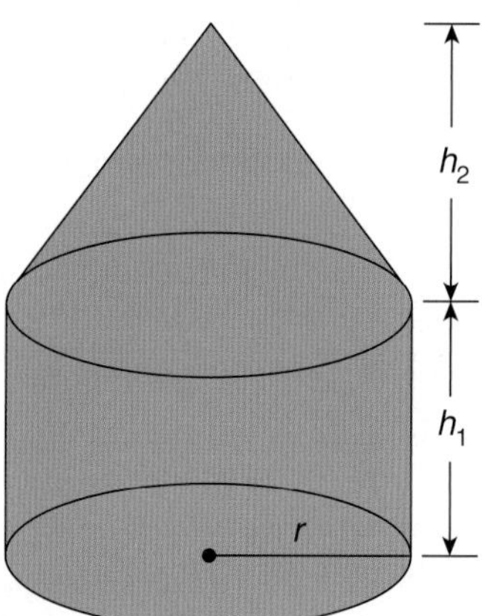

(a) $V = \frac{1}{3}\pi r^2(h_1 + h_2)$

(b) $V = \pi r^2(h_1 + h_2)$

(c) $V = \frac{1}{3}\pi r^2 h_1 + h_2$

(d) $V = \frac{1}{3}\pi r^2 h_2 + r^2 h_2$

(e) $V = \pi r^2\left(\frac{1}{3}h_2 + h_1\right)$

14. The Earth is almost a sphere with a radius of 6,378 kilometres. About 99% of Earth's atmosphere is contained in a 31 kilometre thick layer that circles the planet.

(a) Calculate the approximate volume of the Earth (taking Earth as a sphere).

(b) Calculate the volume of gas in the atmosphere, in the form of $a \times 10^n$, where $1 \leq a < 10$, $n \in \mathbb{N}$.

15. A catering company is purchasing new glasses.

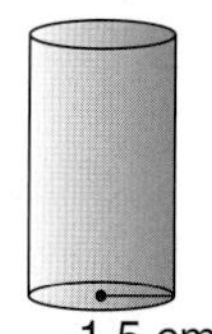

If the cylindrical glass can hold $2\frac{1}{2}$ times as much as the hemispherical glass, calculate the height of the cylindrical glass, correct to one decimal place.

16. Water flows through a pipe of internal diameter 25 cm into a cylindrical pond with radius 5 m and depth 5 m. If it takes 2 hours to raise the water level by 3 m, what is the speed of the flow of water through the pipe in cm/sec?

17. A saucepan in the shape of a cylinder has a base of diameter 28 cm. The saucepan is filled to a height of 20 cm with soup.

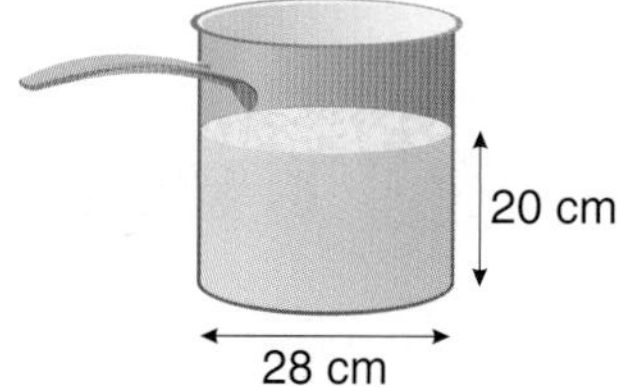

(a) Calculate the volume of the soup in the saucepan.

(b) If 5 litres of soup are removed from the saucepan, calculate the new level of the soup in the saucepan, correct to the nearest cm.

(c) If the 5 litres of soup are poured into five hemispherical bowls, find the radius of the cans correct to one decimal place.

(d) Find the number of bowls that could be filled to the top with the remaining soup in the saucepan.

18. A large building has a flat roof of length 50 m and of width 40 m. On average 5 mm of rain falls on the roof in a week.

(a) Calculate the average volume of rain that will fall on the roof in a week. Give your answer in m^3.

(b) The rain is collected in a cylindrical tank of diameter 7 m. Calculate the average rise in the level of the water in the tank in a week. Give your answer in metres, correct to two decimal places.

(c) The tank is emptied when the water reaches a height of 3.38 m. How many times a year on average will the tank be emptied?

19. A jeweller buys a rectangular block of gold of length 4 cm, width 3 cm and height 2 cm. 1 cm^3 of gold costs €400.

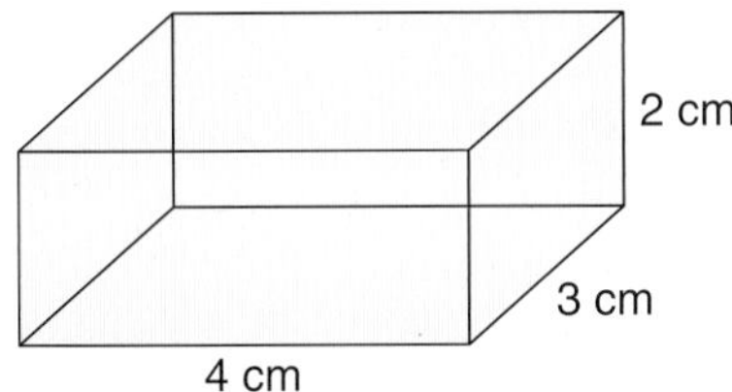

(a) Calculate the cost of the block of gold.

(b) The jeweller needs 250 mm^3 of gold to make a gold ring. How many rings can be made from the block?

(c) Each ring is sold for €120. Calculate the amount of profit the jeweller makes on each ring.

20. A float in the shape of a cone on top of a hemisphere is made from solid rubber.

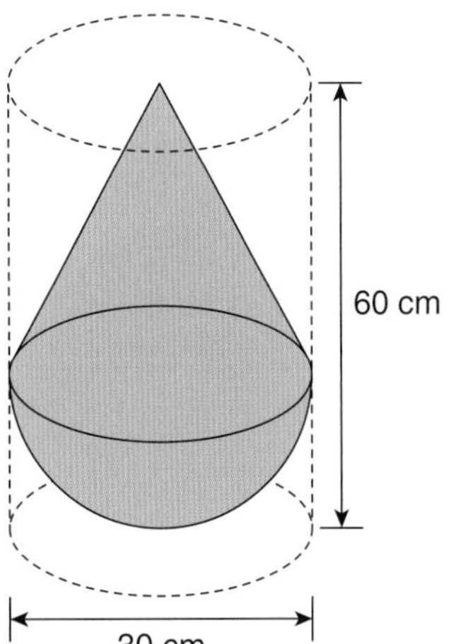

(a) The diameter of the hemisphere is 30 cm and the height of the float is 60 cm. Find the volume of the float in terms of π.

(b) The float is cut from a solid rubber cylinder of diameter 30 cm and height 60 cm. Express the volume of rubber used in the float as a percentage of the volume of the cylinder. Give your answer correct to the nearest whole number.

CHAPTER 24 KNOWLEDGE CHECKLIST

After completing this chapter, I now:

- **Am able to calculate the volume of cubes and cuboids**
- **Am able to calculate the volume of prisms**
- **Am able to calculate the volumes of cylinders, cones, spheres and hemispheres**
- **Am able to solve problems involving volumes of shapes and compound shapes**
- **Am able to calculate rates of flow**
- **Understand flow graphs**

Challenge

You have a 3 litre and a 5 litre water container. Each container has no markings except for that which gives you its total volume. You also have a running tap. You must use the containers and the tap in such a way as to exactly measure out 4 litres of water. How is this done?

CHAPTER

25

ALGEBRAIC LONG DIVISION

KEY WORDS

- Cubic expression
- Linear factor
- Quadratic expression

LEARNING OUTCOMES

In this chapter you will learn:

- ✓ To divide a linear expression by a linear factor
- ✓ To divide a quadratic expression by a linear factor
- ✓ To divide a cubic expression by a linear factor

INTRODUCTION

In primary school, you learned how to carry out long division using numbers. It is often necessary to carry out long division in algebra in order to show that one algebraic expression is a factor of another.

$$\begin{array}{r} 193 \\ 5\overline{)965} \\ -5 \\ \hline 46 \\ -45 \\ \hline 15 \\ 15 \\ \hline 0 \end{array}$$

Since 5 divides into 965 a total of 193 times with a remainder of zero, then we say 5 is a factor of 965.

Section 25.1: Dividing a linear expression and a quadratic expression by a linear factor

Student Activity 25A

1. Is 5 a factor of 20? Explain your answer fully.
2. Is 4 a factor of 16? Explain your answer fully.
3. Is 4 a factor of 15? Explain your answer fully.
4. Explain in your own words how you would show that one number is a factor of another number, for example, that 10 is a factor of 100.
5. Given that $4 \times 5 = 20$, can you say that both 4 and 5 are factors of 20? Explain your answer fully.
6. Given that $(5)(x + 2) = 5x + 10$, can you say that both (5) and $(x + 2)$ are factors of $5x + 10$? What mathematical method could you use to prove this?
7. Given that $(x + 1)(x + 2) = x^2 + 3x + 2$, can you say that both $(x + 1)$ and $(x + 2)$ are factors of $x^2 + 3x + 2$? What mathematical method could you use to prove this?
8. Simplify fully each of the following:

   (a) $\dfrac{8x + 12}{4}$ (d) $\dfrac{x^2 - 11x + 30}{x - 5}$

   (b) $\dfrac{3x + 6}{x + 2}$ (e) $\dfrac{x^2 - x - 6}{x + 2}$

   (c) $\dfrac{x^2 + 9x + 20}{x + 4}$
9. How many factors has any quadratic expression?

DIVIDING A LINEAR EXPRESSION AND A QUADRATIC EXPRESSION BY A LINEAR FACTOR EXPLAINED

As with the division of numbers, the division of algebraic expressions can be used to show that an expression is a factor of another expression.

If a number divides into a second number with a remainder of zero, we can say it is a factor of that number. For example, 5 divides into 35 with a remainder of zero, so we can say that 5 is a factor of 35.

This concept can also be applied to algebraic expressions. If an expression divides into another expression with no remainder, we then say that it is factor of that expression.

EXAMPLE 1

Divide $6x - 18$ by $(x - 3)$.

Solution

Method 1

$$\begin{array}{r|l} & \ \ 6 \\ x-3 & 6x - 18 \\ & \ominus 6x \oplus 18 \\ \hline & \quad\ 0 \end{array}$$

Method 2

Rewrite as $\frac{6x - 18}{x - 3}$.

Factorise the numerator: $\frac{6\cancel{(x-3)}}{\cancel{x-3}} = 6$

Note how we cancelled the common factors $(x - 3)$ to get an answer of 6.

Therefore $6x - 18$ can also be rewritten as $6(x - 3)$ so 6 and $(x - 3)$ are its factors.

EXAMPLE 2

Divide $x^2 - 5x + 6$ by $(x - 3)$.

Solution

Method 1

$$\begin{array}{r|l} & x \\ x-3 & x^2 - 5x + 6 \end{array}$$

1. Divide the **x term** on the outside into the first term on the inside. Write the answer on top.
$$\frac{x^2}{x} = \frac{(x)(x)}{x} = x$$

2. Multiply 'around the corner'.
$$\begin{array}{r|l} & x \\ x-3 & x^2 - 5x + 6 \\ & x^2 - 3x \end{array}$$

3. Change signs on the bottom line.
$$\begin{array}{r|l} & x \\ x-3 & \cancel{x^2} - 5x + 6 \\ & -\cancel{x^2} + 3x \\ \hline & \quad -2x + 6 \end{array}$$
x^2 terms cancel

4. Start at step ① again.
$$\frac{-2x}{x} = -2$$
$\therefore$
$$\begin{array}{r|l} & x - 2 \\ x-3 & \cancel{x^2} - 5x + 6 \\ & -\cancel{x^2} + 3x \\ \hline & \quad -2x + \cancel{6} \\ & \quad \oplus\cancel{2x} \ominus 6 \\ \hline & \qquad 0 \end{array}$$
Change sign

$\Rightarrow$ zero remainder

Method 2

Rewrite as $\frac{x^2 - 5x + 6}{(x - 3)}$.

Factorise the numerator: $\frac{\cancel{(x-3)}(x-2)}{\cancel{(x-3)}}$

Cancel any common factors in both the numerator and denominator to get the answer $(x - 2)$.

EXAMPLE 3

Divide $2x^2 - 5x - 12$ by $(x - 4)$.

Solution

Method 1

$$\begin{array}{r} 2x \\ x-4 \overline{\big)\, 2x^2 - 5x - 12} \\ -2x^2 + 8x \\ \hline 3x - 12 \end{array}$$

1. Divide $\frac{2x^2}{x} = 2x$. Write the answer on top.
2. Multiply 'around the corner'.
3. Change signs and add. Bring down the next term.

$$\begin{array}{r} 2x + 3 \\ x-4 \overline{\big)\, 2x^2 - 5x - 12} \\ -2x^2 + 8x \\ \hline 3x - 12 \\ -3x + 12 \\ \hline 0 \end{array}$$

4. Start again:
   1. $\frac{3x}{x} = 3$
   2. Multiply 'around the corner'.
   3. Change signs and add.

Method 2

Rewrite as $\frac{2x^2 - 5x - 12}{x - 4}$.

Factorise the numerator: $\frac{(2x + 3)\cancel{(x - 4)}}{\cancel{(x - 4)}}$

Cancel any common factors in both the numerator and denominator to get the answer $(2x + 3)$.

Exercise 25.1

1. Simplify each of the following:
   (a) $\frac{x^2}{x}$
   (b) $\frac{6x}{x}$
   (c) $\frac{13x}{13x}$
   (d) $\frac{-6x}{x}$
   (e) $\frac{-8x}{-4}$
   (f) $\frac{-8x}{-4x}$
   (g) $\frac{9x^2}{3x}$
   (h) $\frac{-24x^2}{8x^2}$
   (i) $\frac{40x^2}{-5x^2}$
   (j) $\frac{56x^2}{28x^2}$
2. Simplify each of the following. In one sentence explain your answer for each.
   (a) $\frac{11x - 11}{11}$
   (b) $\frac{15 - 25x}{5}$
   (c) $\frac{14x - 35}{7}$
   (d) $\frac{90 - 60x}{15}$
   (e) $\frac{5x^2 - 35}{5}$
   (f) $\frac{12 + 15x - 18x^2}{3}$
   (g) $\frac{4x^2 - 6x}{2x}$
   (h) $\frac{9x^2 - 21x + 3}{3}$
   (i) $\frac{44x - 66x^2}{22x}$
   (j) $\frac{16x - 56x^2}{-8x}$
3. Divide $x^2 + 6x + 5$ by $(x + 1)$.
4. Divide $x^2 + 8x + 15$ by $(x + 3)$.
5. Divide $x^2 + 8x + 16$ by $(x + 4)$.
6. Divide $x^2 + 11x + 18$ by $(x + 2)$.
7. Divide $x^2 - 3x - 4$ by $(x - 4)$.
8. Divide $x^2 - 10x + 21$ by $(x - 3)$.
9. Divide $x^2 - 10x + 16$ by $(x - 2)$.
10. Divide $x^2 - 9x - 10$ by $(x - 10)$.
11. Divide $x^2 - 13x + 40$ by $(x - 5)$.
12. Divide $x^2 + 6x - 27$ by $(x - 3)$.
13. Divide $a^2 - 12a + 36$ by $(a - 6)$.
14. Divide $d^2 - 11d + 24$ by $(d - 8)$.
15. Divide $b^2 - 11b + 10$ by $(b - 1)$.
16. Divide $x^2 - 9x + 20$ by $(x - 4)$.
17. Divide $x^2 - 2x - 35$ by $(x - 7)$.
18. Divide $6n^2 + 5n - 6$ by $(2n + 3)$.
19. Divide $2n^2 + n - 10$ by $(n - 2)$.
20. Divide $5n^2 - 27n + 10$ by $(n - 5)$.
21. Divide $3n^2 + 2n - 5$ by $(n - 1)$.
22. Divide $6n^2 - 7n - 3$ by $(3n + 1)$.
23. Verify that $x + 6$ is a factor of $x^2 + 3x - 18$ and find the other factor.
24. (a) Verify that $2n + 1$ is a factor of the quadratic expression $2n^2 + 15n + 7$.
    (b) Write down the second factor of $2n^2 + 15n + 7$.
    (c) Multiply both factors to verify your solution.
25. If $x - 3$ is a factor of $x^2 - 8x + 15$:
    (a) Find the other factor.
    (b) Multiply both factors to verify your solution.

26. (a) Verify that $c + 3$ is a factor of the quadratic expression $c^2 + 10c + 21$.
(b) Write down another factor of $c^2 + 10c + 21$.

For each of the following fractions:

(a) Divide the given fraction using long division.

(b) Simplify the fraction by factorising the numerator.

27. $\dfrac{x^2 + 5x + 6}{x + 2}$

28. $\dfrac{2x^2 + 3x + 1}{2x + 1}$

29. $\dfrac{x^2 - 4x + 4}{x - 2}$

30. $\dfrac{3x^2 + 7x + 2}{3x + 1}$

31. $\dfrac{2x^2 + 13x + 11}{x + 1}$

32. $\dfrac{8x^2 + 14x - 15}{4x - 3}$

33. $\dfrac{2x^2 + 11x + 15}{2x + 5}$

In each of the following, there is no x term. Simplify each of the following using long division by inserting $0x$ into the numerator. Then verify your answer by factorising the numerator and doing the relevant cancelling.

34. Divide $x^2 - 36$ by $x + 6$.

35. Divide $x^2 - 49$ by $x - 7$.

36. Divide $2x^2 - 50$ by $x + 5$.

37. Divide $9x^2 - 36$ by $x - 2$.

38. Divide $100x^2 - 100$ by $5x - 5$.

39. $f(x) = 5x^2 + 35x - 90$ and $g(x) = x - 9$.
Given $\dfrac{f(x)}{g(x)} = ax + b$, write down the values of a and b and evaluate $\sqrt{4a^2 + 6b}$.

40. Show that $3x - 1$ is not a factor of $15x^2 + 7x - 5$. Give a reason for your answer.

Section 25.2: Dividing a cubic expression by a linear factor

Student Activity 25B

1. Write out the factors of each of the following:
(a) x^3
(b) d^3
(c) y^3
(d) $125w^3$
(e) $8a^3$

2. What name is given to a term with a power (index) of 3 (such as x^3)?

3. How many factors has a cubed term?

DIVIDING A CUBIC EXPRESSION BY A LINEAR FACTOR EXPLAINED

A **cubic expression** is an algebraic expression where the highest power on x is 3.

In this section, you will learn how to divide a cubic expression by a linear expression. The method for doing this is the same as for a quadratic expression. However, it is slightly longer as a further line of division is required.

EXAMPLE 4

(a) Divide $x^3 + 4x^2 + x - 6$ by $(x + 2)$.

(b) Divide $2x^3 - 3x^2 - 8x - 3$ by $(2x + 1)$

Solution

(a)

$$\begin{array}{rl} & x^2 + 2x - 3 \\ x + 2 \,\big) & x^3 + 4x^2 + x - 6 \\ & \ominus x^3 \ominus 2x^2 \\ \hline & 2x^2 + x \\ & \ominus 2x^2 \ominus 4x \\ \hline & -3x - 6 \\ & \oplus 3x \oplus 6 \\ \hline & 0 \end{array}$$

$\dfrac{x^3}{x} = x^2$

$\dfrac{2x^2}{x} = 2x$

$\dfrac{-3x}{x} = -3$

Solution

(b)

$$\begin{array}{rl} & x^2 - 2x - 3 \\ 2x + 1 \,\big) & 2x^3 - 3x^2 - 8x - 3 \\ & \ominus 2x^3 \ominus x^2 \\ \hline & -4x^2 - 8x \\ & \oplus 4x^2 \oplus 2x \\ \hline & -6x - 3 \\ & \oplus 6x \oplus 3 \\ \hline & 0 \end{array}$$

$\dfrac{2x^3}{2x} = x^2$

$\dfrac{-4x^2}{2x} = -2x$

$\dfrac{-6x}{2x} = -3$

Exercise 25.2

1. Divide $x^3 - x^2 - x + 10$ by $(x + 2)$.
2. Divide $x^3 - 5x^2 + 10x - 12$ by $(x - 3)$.
3. Divide $2x^3 + x^2 - 3x + 1$ by $(2x - 1)$.
4. Divide $12x^3 + 11x^2 - 7x - 6$ by $(3x + 2)$.
5. Divide $4x^3 + 4x^2 - 37x + 5$ by $(2x - 5)$.
6. Divide $9x^3 + 12x^2 - 15x - 20$ by $(3x + 4)$.
7. Divide $x^3 - 3x^2 - x + 3$ by $(x - 3)$.
8. Divide $x^3 - 3x^2 - 13x + 15$ by $(x + 3)$.
9. Divide $x^3 - 3x^2 - 9x - 5$ by $(x - 5)$.
10. Divide $x^3 + 3x^2 - 4x - 12$ by $(x + 3)$.
11. Divide $3x^3 + 4x^2 + 5x - 12$ by $(x - 1)$.
12. Divide $2x^3 - 5x^2 - 4x + 3$ by $(x - 3)$.
13. Divide $x^3 + 6x^2 + 11x + 6$ by $(x + 1)$.
14. Divide $6x^3 + 11x^2 + x - 4$ by $(3x + 4)$.
15. Divide $-6x^3 + x^2 + 4x + 1$ by $(3x + 1)$.
16. Verify that $2a + 3$ is a factor of $2a^3 - 5a^2 - 4a + 12$.
    (a) Write down a quadratic factor of $2a^3 - 5a^2 - 4a + 12$.
    (b) Write down the three linear factors of $2a^3 - 5a^2 - 4a + 12$.
17. Verify that $(3b + 1)$ is a factor $3b^3 - 14b^2 + 13b + 6$.
    (a) Write down a quadratic factor of $3b^3 - 14b^2 + 13b + 6$.
    (b) Write down the three linear factors of $3b^3 - 14b^2 + 13b + 6$.
18. Verify that $(2c + 3)$ is a factor of $2c^3 - 11c^2 + 3c + 36$.
19. Investigate whether $(4x - 2)$ is a factor of $8x^3 - 6x + 2$
20. Show that $(-5x + 2)$ is a factor of $-15x^3 - 29x^2 + 4x + 4$.
21. Verify that $(3x - 5)$ is a factor of $-6x^3 + 7x^2 + 8x - 5$.

In each of the following, there is no x^2 term or x term. Simplify each of the following using long division by inserting $0x^2$ and $0x$ into the numerator.

22. Divide $x^3 + 1$ by $(x + 1)$.
23. Divide $x^3 - 8$ by $(x - 2)$.
24. Divide $x^3 - 27$ by $(x - 3)$.
25. Divide $64x^3 - 125$ by $(4x - 5)$.
26. Divide $1{,}000x^3 - 1$ by $(10x - 1)$.
27. $f(x) = 8x^3 - 84x^2 + 294x - 343$ and $g(x) = 2x - 7$.
    (a) Given that $\frac{f(x)}{g(x)} = ax^2 + bx + c$, write down the values of a, b and c.
    (b) Factorise $ax^2 + bx + c$.
    (c) Is $f(x) = [g(x)][ax^2 + bx + c]$? Explain your answer.
28. Show that $3x - 1$ is not a factor of $3x^3 - x^2 - 3x + 2$. Give a reason for your answer.

CHAPTER 25 SELF-CHECK TEST

1. Simplify each of the following by factorising the numerator: ◯
    (a) $\frac{x^2 - 5x + 6}{3 - x}$
    (b) $\frac{x^2 - 6x - 40}{x - 10}$
    (c) $\frac{x^2 + x - 132}{x - 11}$
    (d) $\frac{12 - x - x^2}{3 - x}$
    (e) $\frac{5 + 4x - x^2}{x + 1}$
    (f) $\frac{x^2 + 2x - 63}{x - 7}$
    (g) $\frac{11x - 10 - x^2}{1 - x}$
    (h) $\frac{7 + 6x - x^2}{7 - x}$
2. Divide $x^2 - 2x - 35$ by $(x - 7)$. ◯
3. Divide $3x^2 + 10x - 8$ by $(x + 4)$. ◯
4. Divide $5x^2 + 27x + 10$ by $(x + 5)$. ◯
5. Divide $2x^2 + x - 6$ by $(2x - 3)$. ◯
6. Divide $5x^2 - 11x + 6$ by $(x - 1)$. ◯
7. Divide $5x^2 - 17x + 6$ by $(5x - 2)$. ◯
8. Divide $2n^2 + n - 15$ by $(2n - 5)$. ◯
9. Divide $5n^2 - 16n + 3$ by $(n - 3)$. ◯
10. Divide $9x^2 - 1$ by $(3x - 1)$. ◯
11. Divide $2x^2 + 7x + 3$ by $(x + 3)$. ◯
    (a) Write down another factor of $2x^2 + 7x + 3$.
    (b) Multiply both factors to verify your solution.

12. (a) Divide $2x^3 + 7x^2 - 5x - 4$ by $(x + 4)$.
(b) Multiply both factors to verify your solution.

13. (a) Divide $3x^3 - x^2 - 12x + 4$ by $(x - 2)$.
(b) Multiply both factors to verify your solution.

14. (a) Divide $6x^3 + 7x^2 - x - 2$ by $(x + 1)$.
(b) Multiply both factors to verify your solution.

15. (a) Divide $x^3 + 2x^2 - 4x + 1$ by $(x - 1)$.
(b) Multiply both factors to verify your solution.

16. (a) Divide $2x^3 - x^2 - 5x - 2$ by $(x - 2)$.
(b) Multiply both factors to verify your solution.

17. (a) Divide $x^3 + 7x^2 + 16x + 12$ by $(x + 2)$.
(b) Multiply both factors to verify your solution.

18. (a) Divide $x^3 + 7x^2 - 12x - 12$ by $(x - 2)$.
(b) Multiply both factors to verify your solution.

19. (a) Divide $4x^3 + 0x^2 - 7x - 3$ by $(2x - 3)$.
(b) Multiply both factors to verify your solution.

20. (a) Divide $6x^3 - x^2 - 31x - 10$ by $(2x - 5)$.
(b) Multiply both factors to verify your solution.

21. Divide $2x^3 - 3x^2 - 12x + 20$ by $x - 2$ and verify your answer by letting $x = 2$.

22. Divide $3x^3 + 7x^2 + 5x + 1$ by $3x + 1$ and verify your answer by letting $x = -\frac{1}{3}$.

23. Divide $8x^3 - 125$ by $2x - 5$ and verify your answer by letting $x = \frac{5}{2}$.

24. Divide $27x^3 - 64$ by $3x - 4$ and verify your answer by letting $x = \frac{4}{3}$.

25. $f(x) = 8x^3 + 2x^2 - 5x + 1$ and $g(x) = 2x - 1$.
(a) Given that $\frac{f(x)}{g(x)} = ax^2 + bx + c$, write down the values of a, b and c.
(b) Hence, evaluate $a^2 + 5b - 3c$.

26. $g(x) = 2x^3 - 5x^2 + 1$ and $h(x) = 2x - 1$.
(a) Given that $\frac{g(x)}{h(x)} = ax^2 + bx + c$, write down the values of a, b and c.
(b) Hence, evaluate $5a^2 - 3b + 9$.

27. Investigate whether $g(x) = 4x - 2$ and $h(x) = 2x + 5$ are factors of the function $f(x) = 24x^3 + 32x^2 - 62x + 20$.

28. The length of one side of a rectangle is $x + 4$. The area of the rectangle is $x^2 + 16x + 48$.

Find an expression for the length of the other side in terms of x.

29. For each of the following cubes, calculate:
(a) The volume
(b) The area of one face of the cube
(c) The total surface area of the cube

(i)
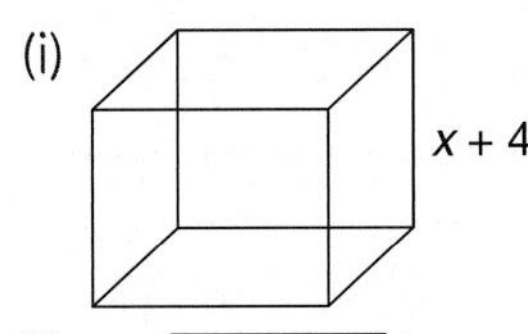

(ii)
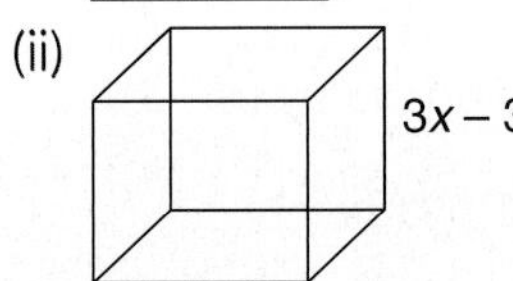

(iii)
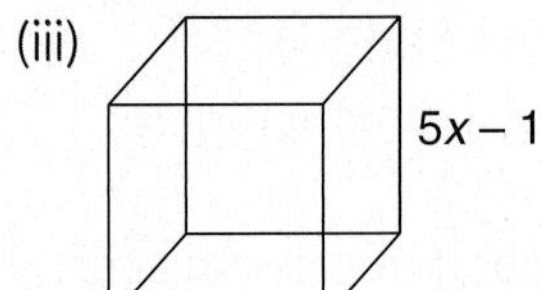

(iv)
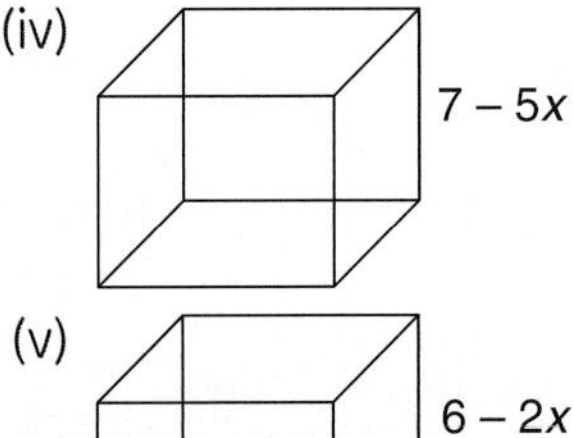

(v)

(vi)
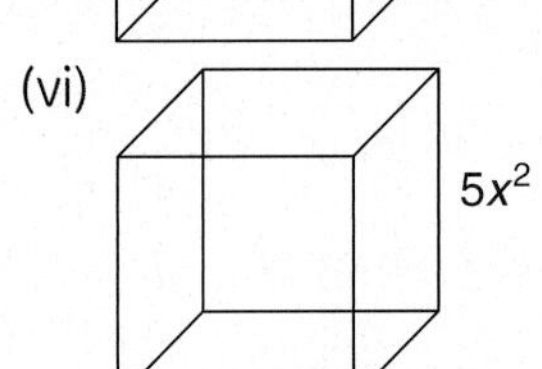

30. (a) For each of the cuboids listed in the table below, one piece of information is missing. Fill in the blank spaces.

	Length	Width	Height	Volume
(i)	$x - 3$	$2x - 4$	$5x + 7$	
(ii)	$3x - 1$		$x - 5$	$6x^3 - 38x^2 + 42x - 10$
(iii)	$5x$	$8 - 2x$		$-20x^3 + 120x^2 - 160x$
(iv)		$6x + 7$	$3 - 4x$	$192x^3 - 40x^2 - 218x + 105$
(v)	$4x + 5$	$4x - 5$	$3x - 9$	

(b) Hence, find the total surface area of each of the cuboids.

31. The diagram shows a rectangular garden of perimeter 24 metres. The length of the garden is x metres.

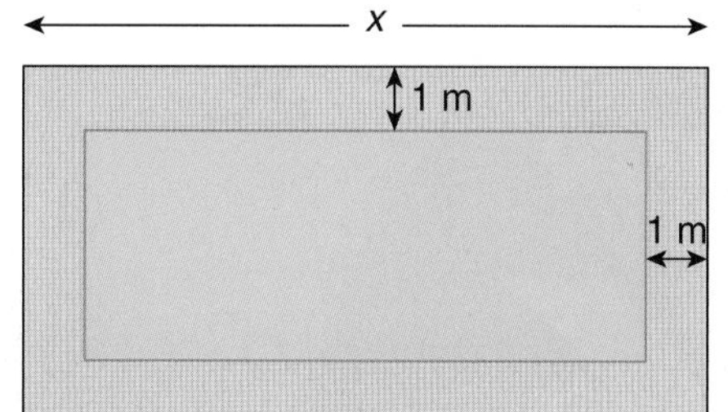

(a) Write down an expression in x for the width of the garden.

(b) Paving of width 1 metre was placed around the garden as shown. Given the area of the inner section is $-x^2 + 12x - 20$, calculate the length and width of the inner section.

32. A square sheet of cardboard measures 6 cm by 6 cm. A square of side x cm is removed from each corner. The remaining piece of cardboard is folded to form an open box as shown.

(a) Show that the area in cm^2 of each side of the box is $6x - 2x^2$.

(b) Let f be the function $f: x \rightarrow 6x - 2x^2$. Evaluate $f(x)$ when $x = 0, 1, 2, 3, 4$. Hence, draw the graph of $f(x)$ for $0 \leq x \leq 4$.

Use your graph to estimate:

(c) The area of a side when $x = 0.5$

(d) The maximum possible area

(e) The value of x that gives sides of maximum area

(f) The length and height of a side of maximum area

(g) Calculate the volume of the box.

(h) Laura claims she can make another box with the same volume as the one above. Its height will be $4x$ and it will have the same length and width. Find in terms of x the length of this new box.

CHAPTER 25 KNOWLEDGE CHECKLIST

After completing this chapter, I now:

- **Am able to divide a linear expression by a linear factor**
- **Am able to divide a quadratic expression by a linear factor**
- **Am able to divide a cubic expression by a linear factor**

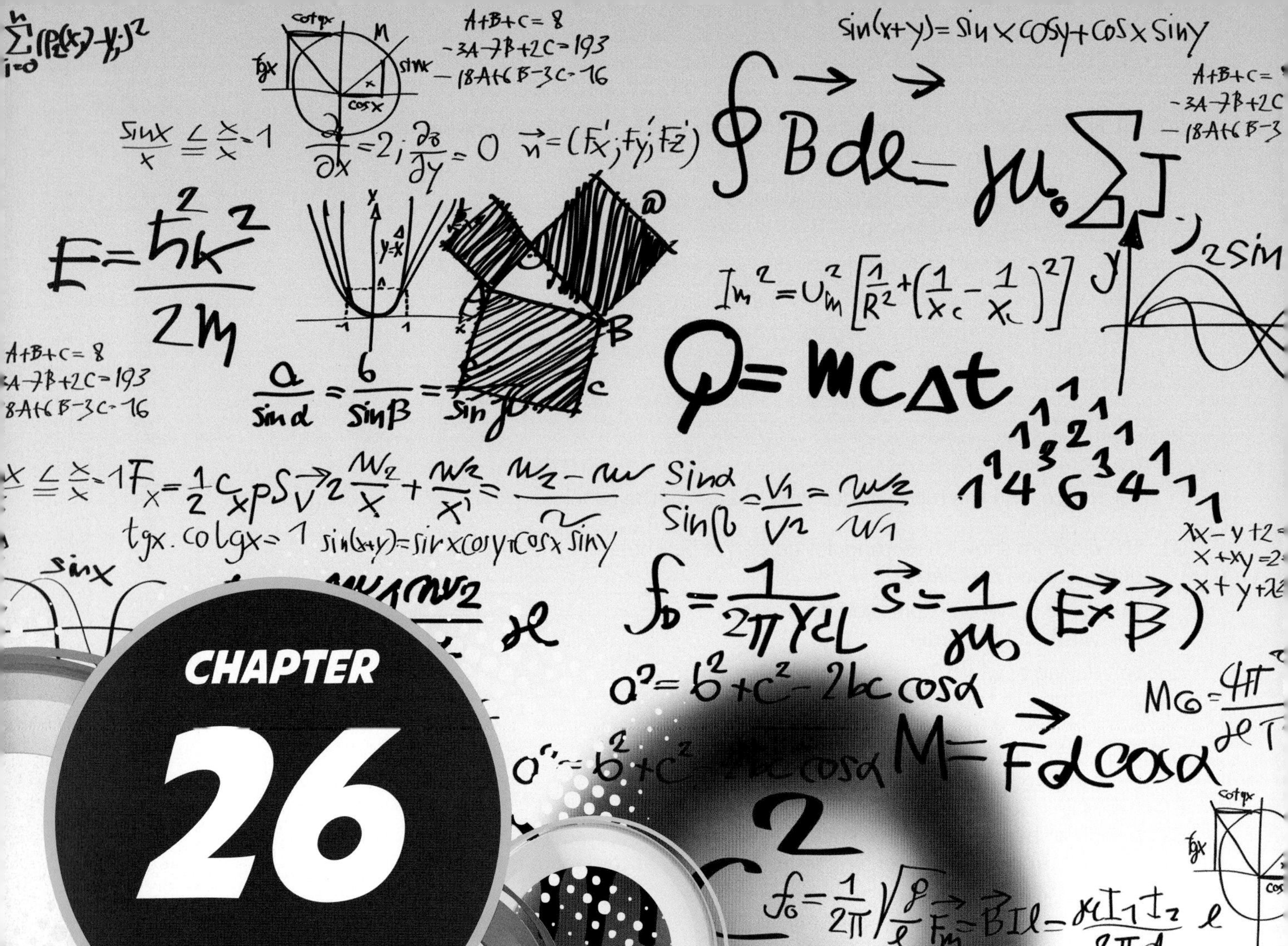

CHAPTER 26

MANIPULATION OF FORMULAE

KEY WORDS

- Manipulation
- Subject of a formula
- Transpose

LEARNING OUTCOMES

In this chapter you will learn:

✓ To rearrange a formula in terms of a given variable

✓ To manipulate a formula to solve real-life problems

INTRODUCTION

To solve problems in subjects such as mathematics, science and business, you often need to reorganise a given formula. You must rearrange the **subject of the formula.**

For example, in Chapter 17 you met the formula: Distance = Speed × Time.

By rearranging the subject of this formula, you were able to determine that:

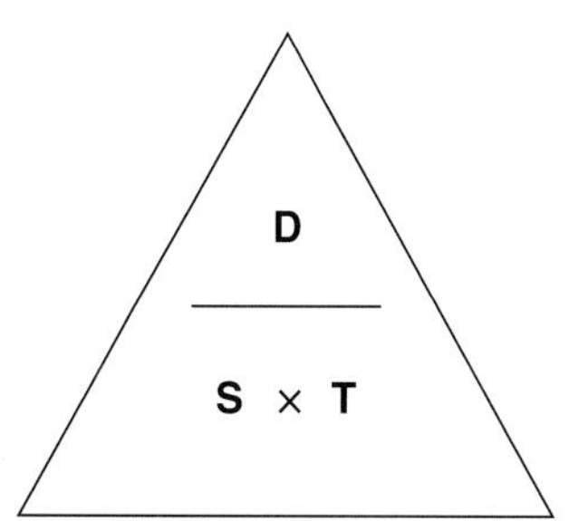

$$\text{Speed} = \frac{\text{Distance}}{\text{Time}} \text{ and Time} = \frac{\text{Distance}}{\text{Speed}}$$

Rewriting a formula in terms of one specific variable is better known as **transposing the formula.**

To **transpose** means to change the position or order of something.

Section 26.1: Rearranging linear equations

Student Activity 26A

If $x + y = 5$, state whether each of the following is true or false. Give reasons for each of your answers.

(a) $x = 5 + y$ (b) $x = y - 5$ (c) $y = 5 - x$ (d) $y = x + 5$ (e) $x = 5 - y$

REARRANGING LINEAR EQUATIONS EXPLAINED

In Student Activity 26A, you began looking at a linear transposition. Both *x* and *y* were made the **subject** of the formula. The subject of the formula is isolated on one side of the equals sign and all other terms are moved to the other side. When you rearrange a formula in terms of one variable, you are simply rewriting the equation and obeying all the rules of balancing an equation.

To ensure the equation is balanced, you must remember to do the same task to both sides of the equals sign.

EXAMPLE 1

(a) Express u as the subject of the formula $v = u + at$.

(b) If $f = bc - am$, express m in terms of a, b, c and f.

Solution

(a) $v = u + at$ — **We need u = every other term**

$v - at = u + at - at$ — **Subtract at from each side of the equation**

$v - at = u$

(b) $f = bc - am$ — **We need m = every other term**

$f - bc = bc - bc - am$ — **Subtract bc from both sides of the equation**

$f - bc = -am$

$am = bc - f$ — **Rearrange to make m positive**

$\frac{am}{a} = \frac{bc - f}{a}$ — **Divide both sides by a**

$m = \frac{bc - f}{a}$

EXAMPLE 2

(a) Given $\frac{1}{x} + \frac{1}{y} = \frac{1}{w}$ express x in terms of y and w.

(b) Make m the subject of the equation $f = ma$.

Solution

(a) $\frac{1}{x} + \frac{1}{y} = \frac{1}{w}$ — **We need x = every other term**

$(xyw)\frac{1}{x} + (xyw)\frac{1}{y} = (xyw)\frac{1}{w}$ — **Multiply each term by the common denominator xyw**

$yw + xw = xy$

$xw - xy = -yw$ — **Bring all the terms with an x to one side**

$x(w - y) = -yw$ — **Take out x as a common factor**

$x = \frac{-yw}{w - y}$

(b) $f = ma$ — **We need m = every other factor**

$\frac{f}{a} = \frac{ma}{a}$ — **Divide both sides by a**

$\frac{f}{a} = m$

Exercise 26.1

Make the letter in square brackets the subject of the formula for each of the following:

1. $x + y = 7$ [x]
2. $2x + y = 0$ [x]
3. $V = IR$ [R]
4. $W = mg$ [g]
5. $F = ma$ [a]
6. $P = \frac{F}{A}$ [F]
7. $D = ST$ [S]
8. $\rho = \frac{m}{V}$ [v]
9. $A = 2\pi rh$ [h]
10. $E = \frac{F}{q}$ [q]
11. $m = \frac{v}{u}$ [u]
12. $V = \frac{w}{q}$ [w]
13. $F = LB$ [B]
14. $C = \frac{q}{V}$ [v]
15. $c = f\lambda$ [λ]
16. $T = Fd$ [d]
17. $F = -ks$ [s]
18. $A = 2\pi rh$ [r]
19. $A = \pi(r + R)l$ [R]
20. $l = 2\pi r$ [r]
21. (a) Rearrange each of the following equations in the form $y = mx + c$, where m and c are constants.
    (b) Explain the significance of the value of m and c for each of the answers above.
    (c) Using the information above, sketch each of the following lines:
    (i) $x + y = 7$
    (ii) $3x + y = -6$
    (iii) $5x + y = 7$
    (iv) $4x - y = 10$
    (v) $2x - 7y = 14$
    (vi) $5x - 10y = -20$
    (vii) $-6x - 8y = 4$
    (viii) $-7x - 10y = -18$
    (ix) $18 - 3y = 15x$
    (x) $25 - 5y = 50x$
    (xi) $\frac{x}{2} + 3y = 5$
    (xii) $\frac{2x}{5} - 7y = \frac{2}{3}$
    (xiii) $5x - \frac{1}{6}y = -1$
    (xiv) $\frac{3x}{5} + \frac{9y}{2} = 8$
    (xv) $\frac{-4x}{2} - \frac{3y}{7} = \frac{5}{-1}$

22. Express each of the following equations in terms of x:

(a) $d = \frac{x}{g} + h$
(b) $\frac{c}{2} = \frac{x}{5} + k$
(c) $\frac{x}{8} - d = \frac{p}{3}$
(d) $\frac{z}{2} = \frac{x}{3} - \frac{2}{y}$
(e) $\frac{1}{x} = \frac{5}{t} + \frac{3}{d}$
(f) $\frac{p}{2} + \frac{4}{x} = \frac{2r}{p}$
(g) $\frac{7t}{3n} - \frac{5}{x} = \frac{3w}{4m}$
(h) $\frac{3y}{2d} = c - \frac{9x}{s}$
(i) $\frac{5c}{h} = km - \frac{2l}{x}$
(j) $x + \frac{x}{5} = \frac{p}{t}$

23. Express the variable in the square brackets in terms of the other variables:

(a) $g = k + hg$ [g]
(b) $fg = h(2f - 3g)$ [f]
(c) $6g - c = d(c + 5f)$ [c]
(d) $b(7a - g) = g(4f - 2h)$ [g]
(e) $t = \frac{hp - k}{5p}$ [p]
(f) $g = \frac{c}{a + c}$ [c]
(g) $k = \frac{5ht}{h + t}$ [t]
(h) $e = \frac{a + b}{a - b}$ [a]
(i) $c = \frac{2f - de}{f - d}$ [d]
(j) $\frac{bn - 4k}{b - k} = p$ [b]

24. Express the variable in the square brackets in terms of the other variables:

(a) $\frac{2}{a} = \frac{5}{b} - \frac{3}{c}$ [b]
(b) $\frac{1}{w} + \frac{1}{y} = \frac{1}{z}$ [w]
(c) $\frac{1}{e} - \frac{3}{c} = \frac{4}{d}$ [c]
(d) $\frac{1}{h} + \frac{3c}{w} = \frac{h}{w} + 4$ [w]
(e) $\frac{5c}{f} = \frac{3f}{2} - 5c$ [c]

25. (a) Given that $\frac{1}{x} - \frac{y}{2} = \frac{3}{z}$, express y in terms of x and z. Hence find the value of y, given $z = 4$ and $x = z$.

(b) Given that $\frac{5}{a} = \frac{2}{b} - \frac{3}{c}$, express b in terms of a and c. Hence find the value of b, given $a = -1$ and $c = 2$.

Section 26.2: Rearranging formulae containing powers and roots

Student Activity 26B

1. If $x^2 = 25$, find the value of x. Explain your answer.
2. If $x^3 = 8$, find the value of x. Explain your answer.
3. If $\sqrt{x} = 3$, find the value of x. Explain your answer.
4. If $\sqrt[3]{x} = 4$, find the value of x. Explain your answer.

REARRANGING FORMULAE CONTAINING POWERS AND ROOTS EXPLAINED

Many formulae contain surds or powers. It is important to remember that finding the square root is the inverse (opposite) operation of squaring a term (and vice versa).

For example, in Chapter 13 you learned that the area of a circle is $A = \pi r^2$, where A is the subject of the formula. A question might require you to make r the subject in order to find the radius of the circle in question.

EXAMPLE 3

(a) Make r the subject of the formula $V = \pi r^2 h$.

(b) Given that $p^2 = 2\sqrt{q - 3r}$, express q in terms of p and r.

Solution

(a) $V = \pi r^2 h$ — **We need r = every other term**

$\frac{V}{\pi h} = \frac{\pi r^2 h}{\pi h}$ — **Divide both sides by πh**

$\frac{V}{\pi h} = r^2$ — **Tidy up**

$\sqrt{\frac{V}{\pi h}} = \sqrt{r^2}$ — **Get the square root of both sides of the equation**

The square root and square cancel each other to leave:

$\sqrt{\frac{V}{\pi h}} = r$

(b) $p^2 = 2\sqrt{q - 3r}$ — **We need q = every other term**

$\frac{p^2}{2} = \frac{2\sqrt{q - 3r}}{2}$ — **Divide both sides by 2**

$\frac{p^2}{2} = \sqrt{q - 3r}$ — **Tidy up**

$\left(\frac{p^2}{2}\right)^2 = \left(\sqrt{q - 3r}\right)^2$ — **Square both sides. Note: $\frac{(p^2)^2}{(2)^2} = \frac{(p)^2(p)^2}{(2)(2)} = \frac{p^4}{4}$**

$\frac{p^4}{4} = q - 3r$ — **Tidy up**

$\frac{p^4}{4} + 3r = q$ — **Rearrange in terms of q**

Exercise 26.2

Make the letter in square brackets the subject of each of the following formulae:

1. $W = \frac{1}{2}CV^2$ [V]
2. $E = mc^2$ [c]
3. $a = -\omega^2 s$ [ω]
4. $a^2 + b^2 = c^2$ [a]
5. $V = \frac{1}{3}\pi r^2 h$ [r]
6. $\sigma = \sqrt{npq}$ [p]
7. $r = \sqrt{g^2 + f^2 - c}$ [f]
8. $a = \frac{v^2}{r}$ [v]
9. $V = \frac{4}{3}\pi r^3$ [r]
10. $g = \frac{GM}{d^2}$ [d]
11. $z = \sqrt{a^2 + b^2}$ [b]
12. $f = \frac{1}{2L}\sqrt{\frac{T}{\mu}}$ [μ]
13. $F = \frac{GM}{r^2}$ [r]
14. $P = I^2 R$ [I]
15. $A = 4\pi r^2$ [r]
16. $d = \sqrt{\frac{3h}{2}}$ [h]
17. $v = \pi h^2\left(r - \frac{h}{3}\right)$ [r]
18. $e = \sqrt{\frac{t - k}{k(1 + kt)}}$ [t]
19. $a = 1 - \frac{2b}{ct - b}$ [t]
20. $v = w\sqrt{a^2 - x^2}$ [x]
21. Given that $t = \sqrt{\frac{fg - t^2}{g}}$, show that $g = \frac{-t^2}{t^2 - f}$.
22. Given that $x = \frac{5w^2 - y^2}{y}$, express w in terms of x and y.
23. (a) Write $s = \frac{n}{2}[2a + (n - 1)d]$ in terms of d.
    (b) Find the value of s given $n = 6$, $a = 8$ and $d = -4$.
24. If $x = 5 - 3p$ and $y = -2x - 4p$:
    (a) Express y in terms of p.
    (b) Find the value of y when $p = 31$.
25. If $y = x + a$ and $x = 2a + 3$:
    (a) Express a in terms of y.
    (b) If $w = 3a - 2y$, find the value of w when $y = 0.5$.

26. If $a = 2x - w$, $b = x - 3w - 7$ and $c = a^2 - 2ab$:
(a) Write c in terms of x and w.
(b) Find the value of c when $x = 3$ and $w = 2$.

27. If $x = 4 - 3a - 5b$ and $y = a - 2b - 4$:
(a) Write $(3x - 7y)$ in terms of a and b.
(b) Find the value of $(3x - 7y)$ when $a = 4$ and $b = -5$.

28. If $x = a - 2b$, $y = a - b - 5$ and $z = x^2 - 3y$:
(a) Write $(x - 2y)$ in terms of a and b.
(b) Find the value of z when $a = 2$ and $b = 5$.

29. Given $a = bc + \frac{1}{2}dc^2$ and $e = b + dc$:
(a) Show that $a = ec - \frac{1}{2}dc^2$.
(b) Express e in terms of a, c and d.

30. The formula for the volume of a hemisphere is $V = \frac{2}{3}\pi r^3$.
(a) Express r in terms of V and π.
(b) Hence, find the value of r if $V = 36$ and $\pi = 3$.
(c) What is the volume of the hemisphere when $r = 4.5$ cm?

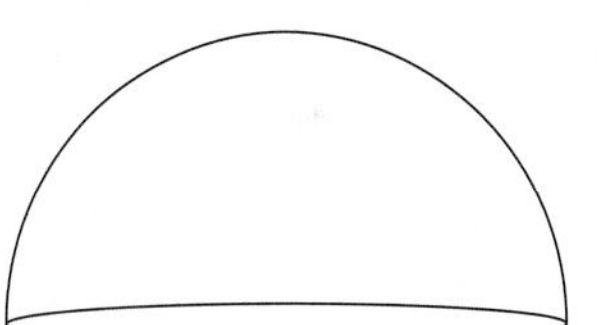

CHAPTER 26 SELF-CHECK TEST

Make the letter in square brackets the subject of each of the following formulae:

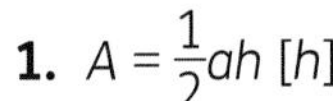

1. $A = \frac{1}{2}ah$ [h]

2. $T = a + (n - 1)d$ [n]

3. $A = \frac{P - S}{t}$ [S]

4. $\frac{1}{u} + \frac{1}{v} = \frac{1}{f}$ [u]

5. $z = \frac{x - \mu}{\sigma}$ [x]

6. $A = \pi rl$ [l]

7. $V = IR$ [R]

8. $Q = IT$ [T]

9. $4x + 3y = 7z$ [x]

10. $y = mx + c$ [m]

11. $x^2 + y^2 = r^2$ [y]

12. $E = mc^2$ [c]

13. $W = \frac{1}{2}CV^2$ [V]

14. $F = mrw^2$ [w]

15. $F = \frac{mv^2}{r}$ [v]

16. $T = 2\pi\sqrt{\frac{L}{g}}$ [g]

17. $s = ut + \frac{1}{2}at^2$ [a]

18. $v^2 = u^2 + 2as$ [u]

19. $v^2 = w^2(A^2 - s^2)$ [A]

20. $T^2 = \frac{4\pi^2R^3}{GM}$ [R]

21. Given $r = \frac{e^2k + k}{1 - e^2k^2}$, express e in terms of r and k.

22. If $3x(2p - 1) = 3p + 2$, express p in terms of x.

23. Write $\theta = \sqrt{g^2 - \frac{p^2}{h^2}}$ in terms of g.

24. Given $y = ax - 2a^2$ and $x = 3 - 2a^2$:
(a) Express y in terms of a.
(b) Express a in terms of x.

25. Given $a^2b = c + 2a^2$:
(a) Express b in terms of a and c.
(b) If $d = a(b - 4)$, show that $d = \frac{c - 2a^2}{a}$.

26. Given $gh - p = c - fh$, express h in terms of c, f, g and p.

27. Farmers store animal feed in a closed cylindrical shaped grain silo. The silo's total surface area is given by the formula $A = 2\pi r^2 + 2\pi rh$.

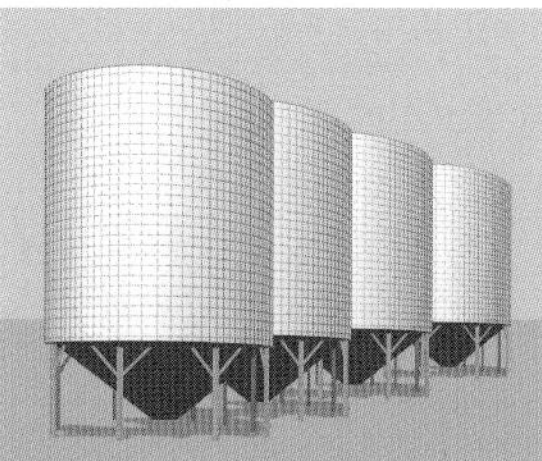

(a) Calculate the total surface area of a silo whose radius is 5.2 m and height is 8 m.

(b) Express h in terms of A and r.

(c) Find the height of the grain silo where the radius is 4.2 m, $\pi = \frac{22}{7}$ and the surface area is 122.64 m^2.

(d) If the radius of the silo was increased by 1 m, what would the percentage increase be in the total surface area when compared to the silo from part (a)?

28. Temperature can be measured in degree Celsius (°C) or in degrees Fahrenheit (°F). The following formula is used to convert temperatures from degrees Fahrenheit to degrees Celsius:

$C = \frac{5}{9}(F - 32)$.

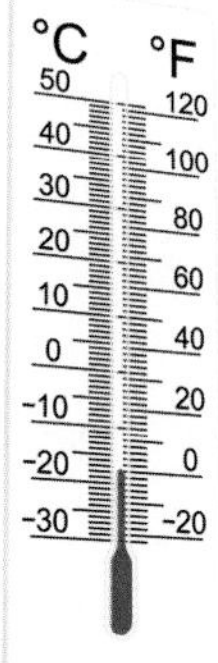

(a) Derive the conversion formula for degrees Celsius to degrees Fahrenheit.

(b) If the temperature on Bondi Beach in Australia is 39 °C, what is the temperature in degrees Fahrenheit?

(c) If the temperature in a meteorological station in Greenland is −42 °C, what is the temperature in degrees Fahrenheit?

(d) If the ocean temperature in Banna Beach in County Kerry was recorded as 38.3 °F, what was the water temperature in degrees Celsius?

(e) The boiling point of water is 100 °C. What is the boiling point in degrees Fahrenheit?

(f) The freezing point of water is 0 °C. What is the freezing point in degrees Fahrenheit?

29. In a science experiment, biologists are examining the rates at which an enzyme breaks down food proteins. The amount of energy (E) released is dependent on the amount of protein (P) and the amount of a catalyst (C).
It is found using the formula:

$$E^2 = \frac{9}{4P^3} + 12C$$

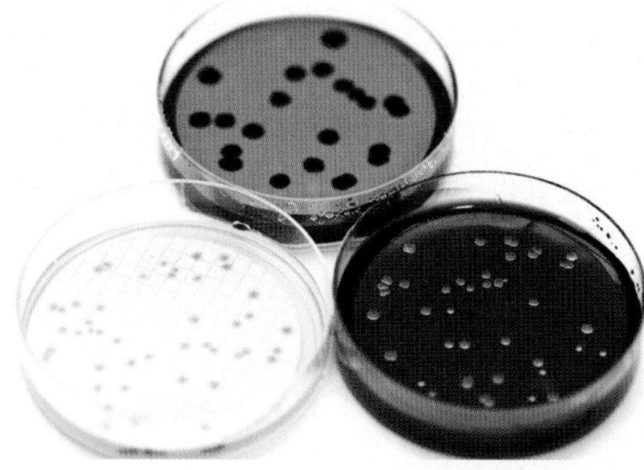

(a) Express the amount of energy (E) in terms of P and C.

(b) Hence, find the value of E correct to one decimal place, when $P = 1$ and $C = 36$.

(c) Express the amount of catalyst (C) in terms of E and P.

(d) Hence, find the value of C, correct to one decimal place when $E = 7.8$ and $P = 10$.

(e) Express the amount of protein (P) in terms of E and C.

30. When trying to decide which bank they should save their money with, savers must study the percentage rate of interest (i), the length of time they must invest their money in years (t) and the original amount or principal invested (P).

The final or future amount is given by the formula:

$$F = P\left(1 + \frac{i}{100}\right)^t$$

(a) Using the formula, express i in terms of F, P and t.

(b) Using the formula, express P in terms of F, T and i.

(c) Sam invested €3,000 at r% per annum compound interest. After two years, he closed the account by withdrawing €3,499.20. Calculate r, the annual rate of interest.

(d) Nora invested €5,000 at 12% compound interest per annum. After a certain number of years, she has €7,024.64 in her account. For how many years did she invest her money?

CHAPTER 26 KNOWLEDGE CHECKLIST

After completing this chapter, I now:

- **Am able to rearrange a formula in terms of a given variable**
- **Am able to use a manipulated formula to solve real-life problems**

Challenge

There aren't many things that are guaranteed to strike fear into the heart of Bill Gates, but Petals Around The Rose is one of them. Unlike normal puzzles, it's said that the smarter you are, the longer it takes you to work out the rules behind this fiendish game, because you start coming up with outlandishly complex formulas to explain it. It's said that Bill took rather a long time on this one, and almost fooled people into thinking he'd solved it when he hadn't, by memorising dozens of dice rolls. Of course, he did get it in the end - eventually.

Here's how it works: You roll five dice, and from them, you have to work out the number of 'petals around the rose'. There is only a single correct answer for each roll. We've included a number of rolls and answers below.

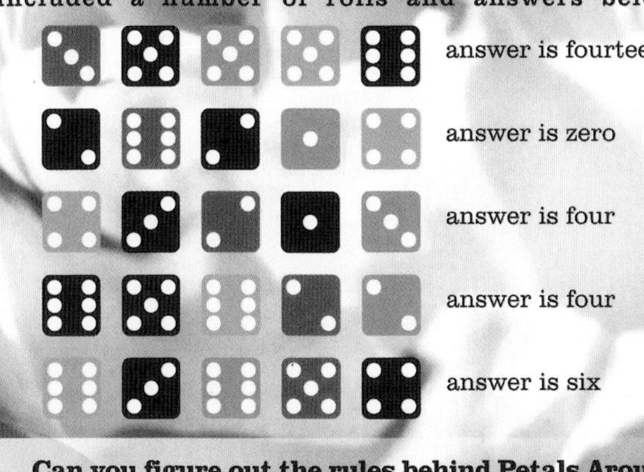

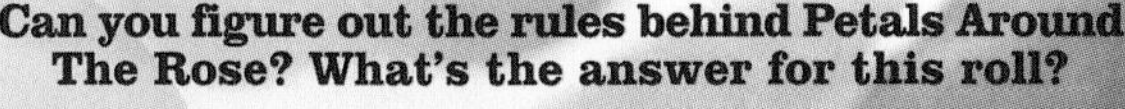

answer is fourteen
answer is zero
answer is four
answer is four
answer is six

Can you figure out the rules behind Petals Around The Rose? What's the answer for this roll?

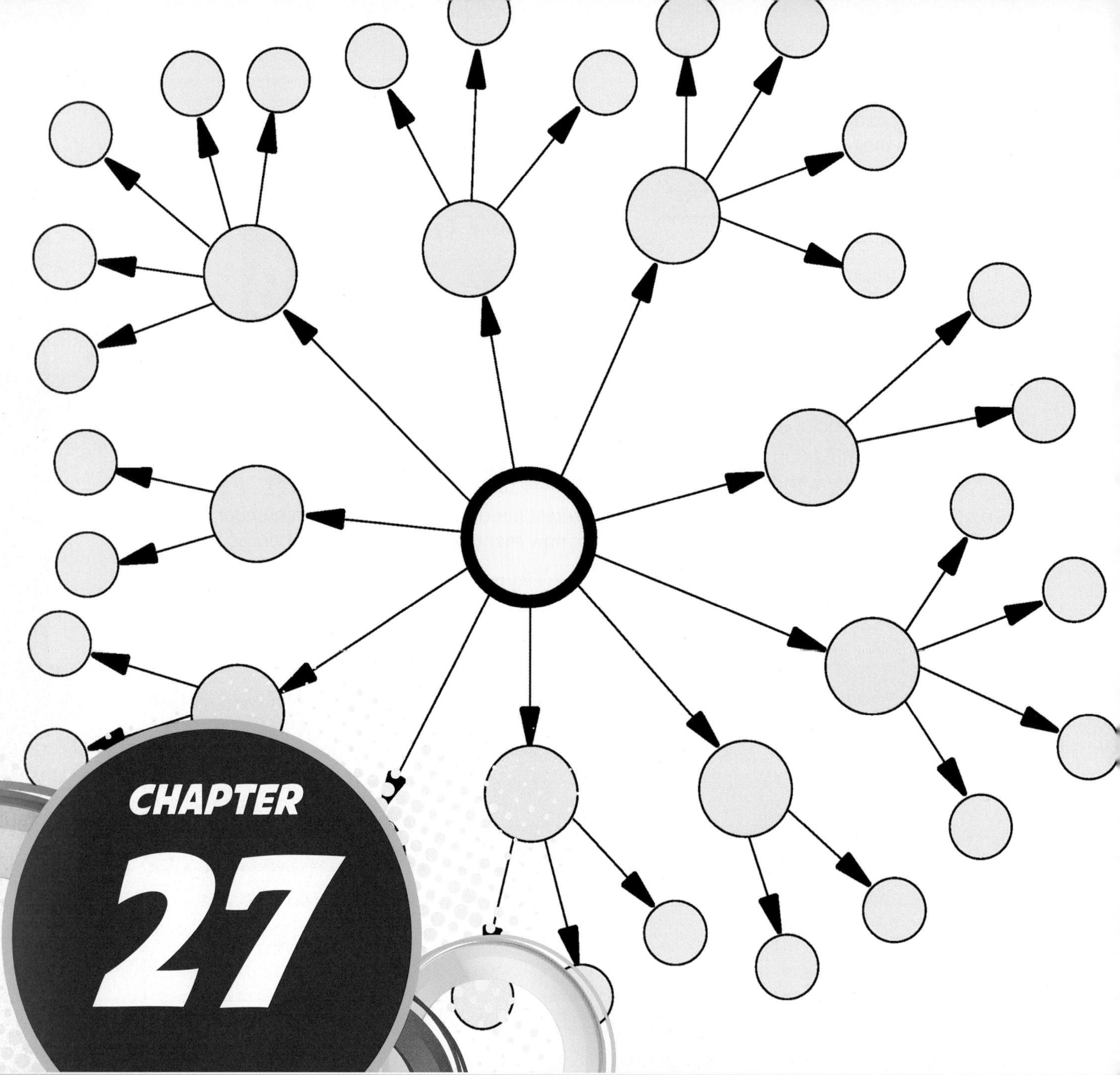

CHAPTER 27

EXPONENTIAL PATTERNS, RELATIONSHIPS AND FUNCTIONS

KEY WORDS

- Exponent
- Exponential
- Doubling
- Tripling

LEARNING OUTCOMES

In this chapter you will learn:

- ✓ About exponential patterns
- ✓ To draw graphs of the form $f(x) = a.2^x$ where $a \in \mathbb{N}; x \in \mathbb{R}$
- ✓ To draw graphs of the form $f(x) = a.3^x$ where $a \in \mathbb{N}; x \in \mathbb{R}$

INTRODUCTION

Hermann Ebbinghaus was a German psychologist. When Ebbinghaus published his findings on how a person's memory retains or forgets information, he used the following curved graph:

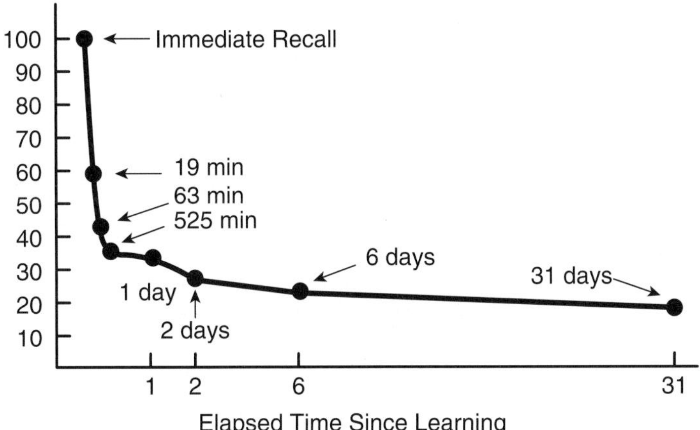

This curve is better known as the **forgetting curve.** It shows how a person's memory of newly learned things halves over the course of a few days unless the material is revised. But what kind of mathematical curve did he use to present his data?

Section 27.1 Exponential patterns

Student Activity 27A

1. Let's make and study a famous fractal called the Sierpinski triangle. Then answer questions as we go through the series of steps:

- **Step 1:** Draw an equilateral triangle with sides of length 12 cm each. Find the halfway point of each side. Then connect the midpoints of each side as shown.

Shade the triangle in the centre.

Think of this as a cut-out hole in the triangle, which we can no longer change in this exercise.

(a) How many equilateral triangles do you now have in total?

- **Step 2:** Repeat step one on each of the small triangles, the one on top, the one on the far left and the one on the far right. For each triangle, connect the midpoints of each of the sides and shade the triangle in the centre as before.

Notice the three small shaded triangles can be considered as three more holes and will no longer be changed in this exercise.

(b) How many equilateral triangles do you now have?

- **Step 3:** Repeat the first step once again on each of the unshaded equilateral triangles. For each little triangle, connect the midpoints of each of the sides and shade the triangle in the centre as before. You should end up with 1 large, 3 medium, and 9 small triangles shaded.

(c) How many equilateral triangles do you now have in total?

- **Step 4:** Keep following step 1 above on each of the unshaded equilateral triangles and complete the Sierpinski triangle.

(d) Keep recording the total number of equilateral triangles.

(e) What kind of numerical pattern is being created?

2. Use your calculator to evaluate each of the following:
   (a) 25^0 (b) 3^0 (c) 49^0 (d) 10.45^0
   (e) What can you conclude about any number to the power of zero?
3. Use your calculator to evaluate each of the following:
   (a) 2^5 (b) 3^4 (c) $49^{0.5}$ (d) 6^3 (e) $36^{\frac{1}{2}}$ (f) $5(3^2)$
   (g) Explain what an exponent is.

EXPONENTIAL PATTERNS EXPLAINED

In Chapters 5 and 20, you examined two special types of number sequences: linear and quadratic patterns. In a linear pattern, each term increases or decreases by a constant value called the first difference. In a quadratic pattern the first difference is never constant. This is why it is called a **non-linear** pattern. When the second difference is constant, we know the sequence is a quadratic pattern. The second difference is found by adding (or subtracting) the same value from each of the first differences.

So what type of sequence is the following: 1, 2, 4, 8, 16, 32, 64, 128, 256, 512, 1024, ...?

Number	First difference	Second difference	Third difference	Fourth difference	Fifth difference	Sixth difference
1						
2	1					
4	2	1				
8	4	2	1			
16	8	4	2	1		
32	16	8	4	2	1	
64	32	16	8	4	2	1
128	64	32	16	8	4	2
256	128	64	32	16	8	4
512	256	128	64	32	16	8
1,024	512	256	128	64	32	16

Looking at the table, it is clear that this pattern is non-linear. But it does not have a common difference. The differences are repeating themselves. Therefore, we call this type of pattern an **exponential pattern.**

An **exponential pattern** is a function that can be written in the form: $f : x \to b^x$.

$f : x \to b^x$

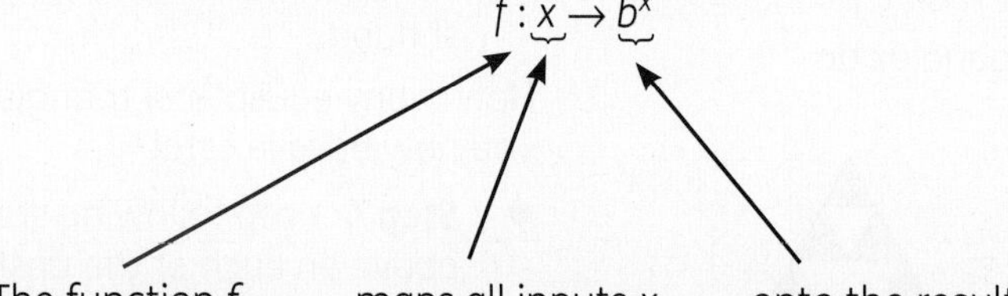

The function f maps all inputs x onto the result from this.

In an exponential function of the form $f : x \to b^x$:

- x is called the **exponent** or **power.** It represents any real number.
- b is called the **base.** On the Junior Certificate Higher Level course, the base is always either **2** or **3.**

The only exponential functions we will examine on our Junior Certificate course are of the form $f(x) = a.\mathbf{2^x}$ or $f(x) = a.\mathbf{3^x}$ where a represents any natural number.

This allows us to summarise that any sequence which involves doubling, halving, tripling or dividing by three can be referred to as an exponential function.

Examining the previous sequence again, we can now clearly see the exponential pattern:

Number	1	2	4	8	16	32	64	128	256
Pattern	2^0	2^1	2^2	2^3	2^4	2^5	2^6	2^7	2^8

Each term in the pattern is derived from the formula 2^x:

EXAMPLE 1

A circus rat called Jinxy is trained to jump through hoops. The hoops are positioned so that the distance between any two hoops is half the distance of that between the previous two hoops. The first two hoops are exactly 4 m apart.

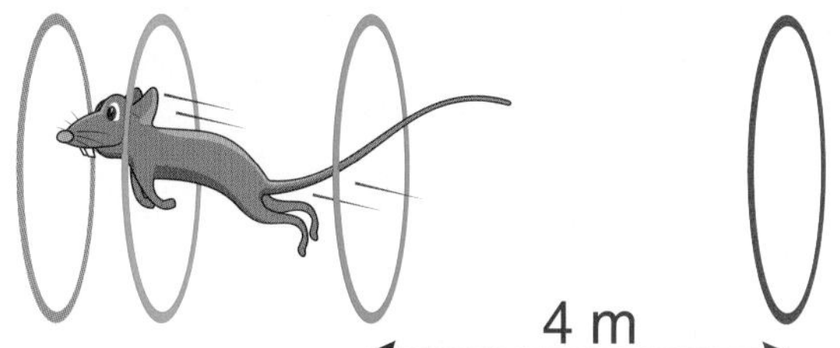

(a) Calculate the distance between the second and the third hoops.

(b) Calculate the distance between the next three sets of hoops.

Solution

(a) 2nd and 3rd hoops $= 4 \text{ m} \times \frac{1}{2} = 2 \text{ m}$

(b) 3rd and 4th hoops $= 4 \text{ m} \times \frac{1}{2} \times \frac{1}{2} = 1 \text{ m}$

4th and 5th hoop $= 4 \text{ m} \times \frac{1}{2} \times \frac{1}{2} \times \frac{1}{2} = 0.5 \text{ m}$

5th and 6th hoop $= 4 \text{ m} \times \frac{1}{2} \times \frac{1}{2} \times \frac{1}{2} \times \frac{1}{2} = 0.25 \text{ m}$

EXAMPLE 2

(a) List the first five terms in the sequence if the general term is $T_n = 2(2^n)$.

(b) Find the value of the 20th term in the pattern.

Solution

(a)

Term	Pattern
1	$2(2^1) = 2(2) = 4$
2	$2(2^2) = 2(4) = 8$
3	$2(2^3) = 2(8) = 16$
4	$2(2^4) = 2(16) = 32$
5	$2(2^5) = 2(32) = 64$

The sequence is 4, 8, 16, 32, 64, ... Each term is double the previous term.

This can be represented using the following mapping diagram:

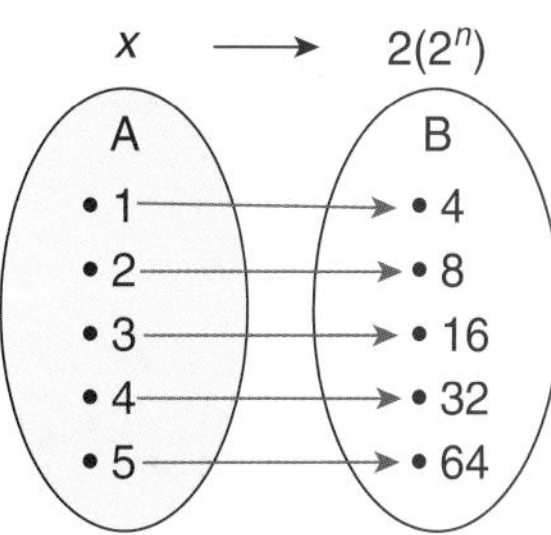

(b) $T_n = 2(2^n)$

$T_{20} = 2(2^{20})$

$T_{20} = 2(1{,}048{,}576)$

$T_{20} = 2{,}097{,}152$

Exercise 27.1

1. Identify whether the following functions are linear, quadratic or exponential, stating the reasons for your choice:
   (a) −2, 2, 8, 16, 26, ...
   (b) 5, 10, 20, 40, 80, ...
   (c) 5, 10, 15, 20, 25, ...
   (d) 9, 16, 23, 30, 37, ...
   (e) 3, 6, 12, 24,48, ...
   (f) 5, 17, 35, 59, 89, ...
   (g) 11, 5, −1, −7, −13, ...
   (h) 12, 6, 3, 1.5, 0.75, ...
   (i) 63, 52, 41, 30, 19, ...
   (j) −5, 25, −125, 625, −3125, ...
   (k) −1, −7, −49, -343, -2401, ...
   (l) 100, 50, 25, 12.5, 6.25, ...
   (m) 3, 9, 27, 81, 243, ..
   (n) $\frac{1}{2}, \frac{1}{4}, \frac{1}{8}, \frac{1}{16}, \frac{1}{32}, ...$
   (o) −1, 9, 27, 53, 87, ...

2. Use your calculator to evaluate each of the following:
   (a) 5^4 (e) $10(5^4)$ (h) $8(3^{-1})$
   (b) $9^{\frac{1}{2}}$ (f) $-3\left(\frac{1}{9}\right)^3$ (i) $2(3^{-4})$
   (c) $3(4^5)$ (g) $5(8^{-2})^2$ (j) $7(2^{-4})$
   (d) $2(3^7)$

3. List the first five terms in the sequence if the general term is:
   (a) $5(2^n)$ (c) $10(2^n)$ (e) $3(2^n)$
   (b) $2(2^n)$ (d) $7(2^n)$

4. List the first five terms in the sequence if the general term is:
   (a) $7(3^n)$ (c) $9(3^n)$ (e) $8(3^n)$
   (b) $2(3^n)$ (d) $6(3^n)$

5. A function f is defined as $f : x \rightarrow 4(2^x)$. Find:
   (a) $f(-1)$ (c) $f(4)$ (e) $f(7)$
   (b) $f(-3)$ (d) $f(5)$

6. A function f is defined as $f : x \rightarrow 3(2^x)$. Find:
   (a) $f(3)$ (c) $f(2)$ (e) $f(0)$
   (b) $f(-4)$ (d) $f(-2)$

7. A function g is defined as $g : x \rightarrow 2(3^x)$. Find:
   (a) $g(-3)$ (c) $g(0)$ (e) $g(-5)$
   (b) $g(5)$ (d) $g\left(\frac{1}{2}\right)$

8. Find the value of the 10th term in the pattern, if the general term is:
   (a) $7(3^n)$ (c) $9(3^n)$ (e) $8(3^n)$
   (b) $2(3^n)$ (d) $6(3^n)$

9. Find the value of the 18th term in the pattern, if the general term is:
   (a) $5(2^n)$ (c) $10(2^n)$ (e) $3(2^n)$
   (b) $2(2^n)$ (d) $7(2^n)$

10. In a charity fundraising event, to qualify for the next round of the competition a person must eat triple the amount of oysters eaten by the previous contestant. The first contestant ate 11 oysters before he felt unwell.

   (a) Calculate the number of oysters to be eaten by the next three contestants.
   (b) Write a general formula for the number of oysters eaten.
   (c) Using this formula, calculate the number of oysters the ninth contestant will have to eat.

11. While holidaying in the West of Ireland, a hillwalker decides that each day she will travel exactly half the distance she travelled on the previous day.

   If she travelled 0.7 km on her last day, calculate:
   (a) How far she walked 3 days earlier
   (b) How far she walked 5 days earlier
   (c) How many days she was walking for if she travelled a total distance of 88.9 km
   (d) If her friend Laura completed the same journey in double the time, how many kilometres did Laura walk on average per day? (Hint: assume Laura walked the same distance every day.)

Section 27.2 Exponential functions and graphs of the form $f(x) = a.2^x$, where $a \in \mathbb{N}$; $x \in \mathbb{R}$

Student Activity 27B

DAILY NEWS FLASH

Friday 25 July 2015

The Incredible Bulk Fails Drug Test

The Incredible Bulk is once again under investigation by the League of Super Heroes for the alleged use of a banned super-hero supplement (SGH). Insider sources have reported that his most recent blood test came back at 0.09 parts per super unit. This is more than 20 times the acceptable level of 0.004 parts per unit of blood.

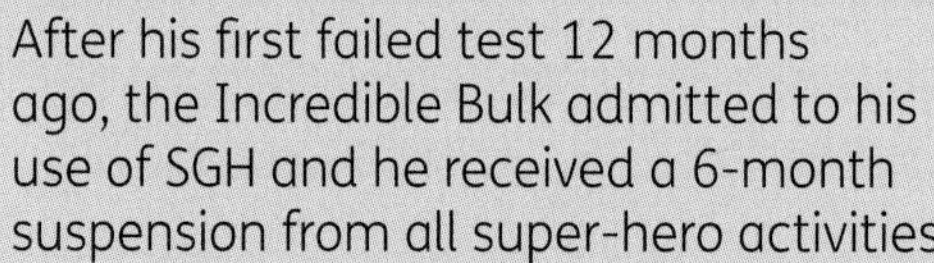

After his first failed test 12 months ago, the Incredible Bulk admitted to his use of SGH and he received a 6-month suspension from all super-hero activities.

In order to be reinstated, Bulk was required to stop using SGH. He also had to enrol in the Super Hero substance abuse rehabilitation programme and to undergo regular testing.

Bulk, of course, denies all use of any banned substances in the past 12 months. He claims that he has followed the League's rule for reinstatement.

A leaked partial copy of Bulk's medical reports shows the following:

Months after first failed test	Banned substance per unit of blood
1	368.64
2	184.32
3	92.16
4	46.08
5	23.04
6	11.52
7	5.76
8	?
9	?
10	?
11	?
12	?

(a) Is the Incredible Bulk telling the truth? Has he taken SGH since his first failed test 12 months ago? Explain your answer, giving reasons.

(b) When will the Bulk's test be again below the acceptable level of 0.004?

(c) Copy, complete and extend the table as necessary to devise a formula to support your answers.

(d) Roughly sketch a graph to represent the data.

EXPONENTIAL FUNCTIONS AND GRAPHS OF THE FORM $f(x) = a.2^x$, WHERE $a \in \mathbb{N}$; $x \in \mathbb{R}$ EXPLAINED

According to an Indian legend, the game of chess was invented around 1,500 years ago. King Shirham was always bored. He told his subjects that he would grant any reward to the person who developed a new game that kept him entertained. A mathematician Sissa Ben Dahir presented the king with the game of chess. He made what seemed like a humble request for his reward:

'Majesty, place one grain of rice on the 1st square of the chess board, place 2 grains on the 2nd square, 4 grains on the 3rd square, 8 on the 4th square and so on until all 64 squares on the board are covered.'

The astonished king replied, 'If that is all you request, poor fool, you may have your wish.' And so they started counting ...

Square	Rice on each square	Total grains of rice on the board
1	1	1
2	2	$1 + 2 = 3$
3	4	$1 + 2 + 4 = 7$
4	8	$1 + 2 + 4 + 8 = 15$
5	16	$1 + 2 + 4 + 8 + 16 = 31$
And so on	And so on	And so on
64	9.2×10^{18}	$1 + 2 + 4 + 8 + 16 + ... + 9.2 \times 10^{18} = 1.844786997 \times 10^{19}$

Sissa's request required more than 18,447,869,970,000,000,000 grains of rice!

To help get this gigantic number in perspective, it was more rice than was produced in all of India. In fact, the amount of rice was worth more than the king's entire country. Today, it is enough rice to feed the entire world's population for the next 140 years! Oh the foolish king!

If we examine the amount of grains of rice on each square we will notice a very distinct pattern:

Square	Rice on each square	Pattern for rice on each square
1	1	2^0
2	2	2^1
3	4	2^2
4	8	2^3
5	16	2^4
64	9.2×10^{18}	2^{63}
n		2^{n-1}

From the table above, we can see the nth square contains 2^{n-1} grains of rice. What would a graph of this function look like?

All graphs associated with the exponential functions of the form $f(x) = a.b^x$ have a very distinctive shape. They can be compared to either side of the Eiffel Tower in Paris.

- When $a \in \mathbb{N}$ and when x is a **positive** real number, the graph of the function makes a smooth **increasing** curve rapidly going upwards.
- When $a \in \mathbb{N}$ and when x is a **negative** real number, the graph of the function makes a smooth **decreasing** curve rapidly going downwards.

All exponential functions of the form $f(x) = a.b^x$ will:

- Never touch or cross the x-axis
- Always pass through the point (0, $\boldsymbol{a}$)

EXAMPLE 3

Draw a graph of the function $f(x) = 2^x$ in the domain $-3 \leq x \leq 3$.

Solution

Input or domain x	Function equation 2^x	Output or range y
−3	$2^{-3} = \frac{1}{8}$	0.125
−2	$2^{-2} = \frac{1}{4}$	0.25
−1	$2^{-1} = \frac{1}{2}$	0.5
0	2^0	1
1	2^1	2
2	2^2	4
3	2^3	8

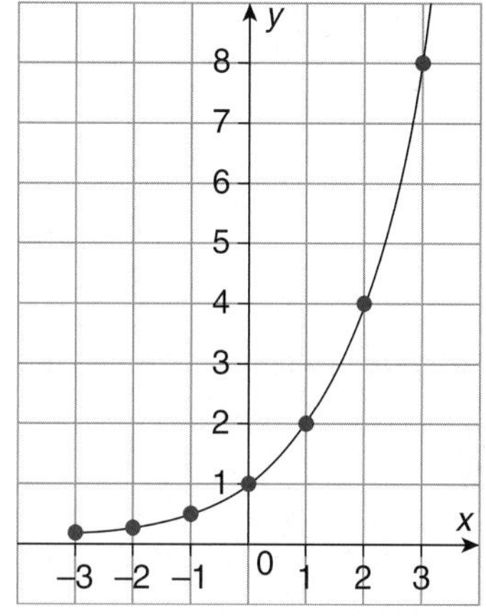

The points on the function are (−3, 0.125), (−2, 0.25), (−1, 0.5), (0, 1), (1, 2), (2, 4), (3, 8). Graphing and joining together these points we get the increasing smooth curve shown on the right.

Notice how the above function can also be written in the form $f(x) = 1(2^x)$.

The curve never touches or crosses the x-axis. However, it crosses the y-axis at the point (0,1).

EXAMPLE 4

(a) Calculate the value of the function $f(x) = 3(2^x)$ given:

(i) $x = 4$ (iii) $x = 2.7$

(ii) $x = \frac{1}{2}$ (iv) $x = -3.5$

(b) When $f(x) = 3(2^x)$, find the value of x for which $f(x) = 384$.

Solution

(a) (i) When $x = 4$, $f(x) = 3(2^4) = 48$

(ii) When $x = \frac{1}{2}$, $f(x) = 3\left(2^{\frac{1}{2}}\right) = 3\sqrt{2} = 4.24$

(iii) When $x = 2.7$, $f(x) = 3(2^{2.7}) = 19.5$

(iv) When $x = -3.5$, $f(x) = 3(2^{-3.5}) = 0.27$

(b) $3(2^x) = 384$

$(2^x) = 384 \div 3$ **Divide both sides by 3**

$(2^x) = 128$

$2^x = 2^7$ **Write both sides in terms of the common base of 2**

$x = 7$ **Cancel the common base on both sides**

Note: if we drew the graph of $f(x) = 3(2^x)$ and then drew a horizontal line from 384 on the y-axis and read the corresponding x value, we would get the identical answer of $x = 7$.

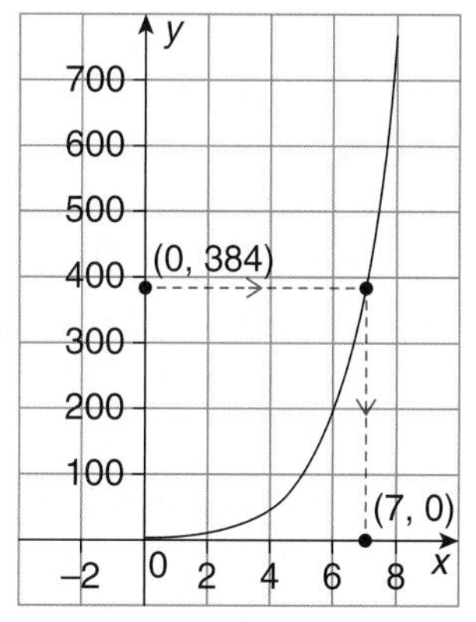

Exercise 27.2

Draw the graphs for Questions 1–4 on the same scale and axes. Use a different colour for each graph.

1. Draw a graph of the function $f(x) = 2^x$ in the domain $-3 \le x \le 3$.
2. Draw a graph of the function $f(x) = 2(2^x)$ in the domain $-3 \le x \le 3$.
3. Draw a graph of the function $f(x) = 3(2^x)$ in the domain $-3 \le x \le 3$.
4. Draw a graph of the function $f(x) = 4(2^x)$ in the domain $-3 \le x \le 3$.
5. If $f(x) = a(2^x)$, explain how changing the value of a affects the graphs you have drawn.
6. Calculate the value of the function $f(x) = 3(2^x)$ given:
   (a) $x = 3$ (b) $x - \frac{1}{4}$ (c) $x = 4.2$ (d) $x = -5$
7. Calculate the value of the function $f(x) = 5(2^x)$ given:
   (a) $x = 2$ (b) $x = \frac{3}{4}$ (c) $x = 3.2$ (d) $x = -6$
8. Calculate the value of the function $f(x) = 10(2^x)$ given:
   (a) $x = 4$ (b) $x = \frac{1}{2}$ (c) $x = 2.7$ (d) $x = -3.5$
9. Calculate the value of the function $f(x) = 4(2^x)$ given:
   (a) $x = 8$ (b) $x = \frac{7}{8}$ (c) $x = 2.4$ (d) $x = -4$
10. Calculate the value of the function $f(x) = 7(2^x)$ given:
    (a) $x = 3$ (b) $x = \frac{3}{8}$ (c) $x = 6.4$ (d) $x = -8$
11. Given $f(x) = 9(2^x)$, find the value of x for which $f(x) = 144$.
12. Given $f(x) = 3(2^x)$, find the value of x for which $f(x) = 0.75$.
13. Given $f(x) = 3(2^x)$, find the value of x for which $f(x) = 3{,}072$.
14. Given $f(x) = 5(2^x)$, find the value of x for which $f(x) = 2{,}560$.
15. Given $f(x) = 7(2^x)$, find the value of x for which $f(x) = 234{,}881{,}024$.
16. The growth of a population in a town was studied over a 5-year period and is shown in the graph:

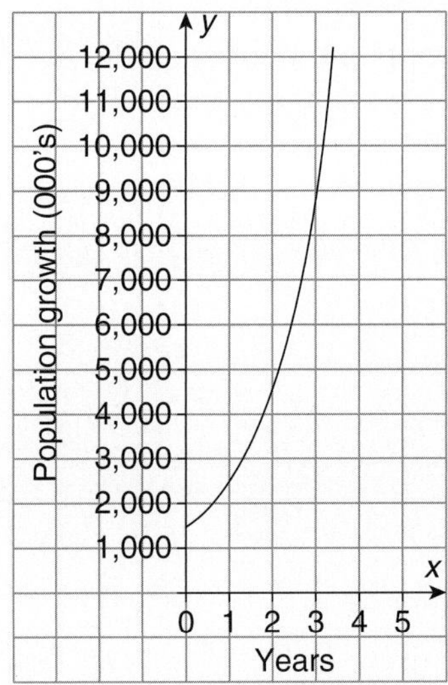

    (a) What was the population at the beginning of the study?
    (b) What was the population after 1 year?
    (c) By how much has the population increased in 2 years?
17. The population growth of a species of rabbits increases by 100% each year. If there are 60 rabbits in the population now, draw a graph to show the growth of the population over the next 6 years.
18. In total, 100,000 bacteria are placed in a Petri dish and an anti-bacterial agent is added. The population halves every 20 minutes. Draw a graph to show the rate of decay in the number of bacteria in the dish over a 3-hour period.
19. Uranium-235, an isotope of uranium, has a half-life of approximately 704 million years. This means half of the sample will decay after 704 million years.

    Draw a graph to model the rate of decay of a 100 kg sample of uranium-235.
20. The growth in the profits of two companies, in € thousands, can be modelled using the functions $f(x): \rightarrow 2x + 5$ and $g(x): \rightarrow 2^x$, where $x \in \mathbb{N}$.
    (a) Using the same scale and axis, draw both functions in the domain $0 \le x \le 5$.
    (b) Describe the growth in the profits of each company.
    (c) After how many years will the profits of both companies be the same?
    (d) After how many years will the profit of each company be €20,000?
    (e) What was the profit of each company after 2.5 years?

Section 27.3 Exponential functions and graphs of the form $f(x) = a.3^x$, where $a \in \mathbb{N}$; $x \in \mathbb{R}$

Student Activity 27C

1. *The Attack of the Mutant Killer Worms!*

(a) Given several sequences of the 'mutant killer worm' patterns, construct the next few worms in the sequence.

Stage 1 □

Stage 2 □□□

Stage 3 □□□□□□□□□

Stage 4

Stage 5

Stage 6

Stage 7

Stage 8

Stage n

(b) Represent the growth pattern of the worm on a suitable graph.

(c) Develop a formula to describe the growth pattern of the worm.

2. The number of germs in a colony triples every 2 hours.

(a) If there are 1,000 in the colony at time $t = 0$, draw a graph to represent the growth in the colony over the first 14 hours.

(b) Discuss the shape of curve.

(c) After how many hours are there 20,000 germs in the colony?

(d) How many germs are in the colony after 9 hours?

EXPONENTIAL FUNCTIONS AND GRAPHS OF THE FORM $f(x)$ $a.3^x$, WHERE $a \in \mathbb{N}$; $x \in \mathbb{R}$ EXPLAINED

In Section 27.2, you learned that any graph of an exponential function of the form $f(x) = a.b^x$ can be compared to either side of the Eiffel Tower. All exponential functions of the form $f(x) = a.b^x$ will never touch or cross the x-axis and they pass through the point $(0, a)$.

- When $a \in \mathbb{N}$ and when x is a **positive** real number, the graph of the function is an **increasing** curve rapidly going upwards.
- When $a \in \mathbb{N}$ and x is a **negative** real number, the graph of the function is a **decreasing** curve rapidly going downwards.

EXAMPLE 5

Draw a graph of the function $f(x) = 1(3^x)$ in the domain $-1 \leq x \leq 2$.

Solution

Input x	Function equation $1(3^x)$	Output y
-1	$1(3^{-1})$	$\frac{1}{3}$
0	$1(3^0)$	1
1	$1(3^1)$	3
2	$1(3^2)$	9

The points on the function are $\left(-1, \frac{1}{3}\right)$, (0, 1), (1, 3) and (2, 9). Graphing and joining together these points we get the following increasing smooth curve:

Notice how the function can also be written in the form $f(x) = 1(3^x)$. The graph never touches or crosses the x-axis. However, it crosses the y-axis at the point (0, 1).

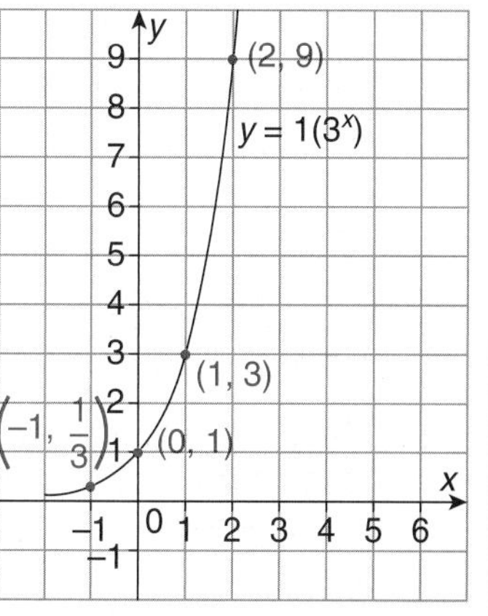

EXAMPLE 6

(a) Calculate the value of the function $f(x) = 5(3^x)$ given:

(i) $x = 4$ (iii) $x = 2.7$

(ii) $x = \frac{1}{2}$ (iv) $x = -3.5$

(b) Given $f(x) = 4(3^x)$, find the value of x for which $f(x) = 972$.

Solution

(a) (i) When $x = 4$, $f(x) = 5(3^4) = 405$

(ii) When $x = \frac{1}{2}$, $f(x) = 5\left(3^{\frac{1}{2}}\right) = 5\sqrt{3} = 8.66$

(iii) When $x = 2.7$, $f(x) = 5(3^{2.7}) = 97.1$

(iv) When $x = -3.5$, $f(x) = 5(3^{-3.5}) = 0.1$

(b) $4(3^x) = 972$

$3^x = 972 \div 4$ **Divide both sides by 4**

$3^x = 243$

$3^x = 3^5$ **Write both sides in terms of the common base of 3**

$x = 5$ **Cancel the common base on both sides**

Note: if we drew the graph of $f(x) = 4(3^x)$ and then drew a horizontal line from 972 on the y-axis and read the corresponding x value, we would get the identical answer of $x = 5$.

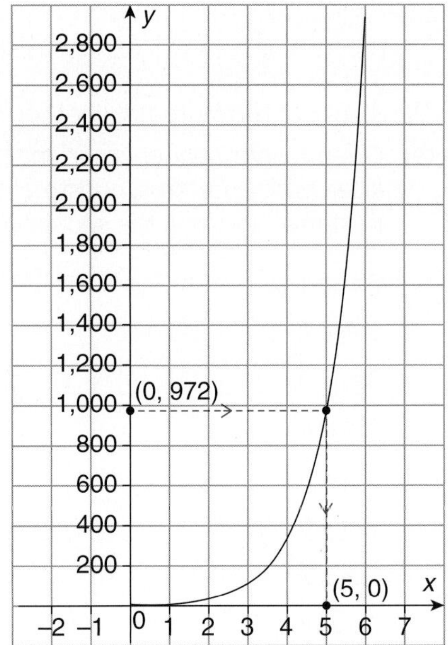

Exercise 27.3

Draw the graphs for Questions 1–4 on the same scale and axes. Use a different colour for each graph.

1. Draw a graph of the function $f(x) = 3^x$ in the domain $-3 \leq x \leq 3$.
2. Draw a graph of the function $f(x) = 2(3^x)$ in the domain $-3 \leq x \leq 3$.
3. Draw a graph of the function $f(x) = 3(3^x)$ in the domain $-3 \leq x \leq 3$.
4. Draw a graph of the function $f(x) = 4(3^x)$ in the domain $-3 \leq x \leq 3$.
5. If $f(x) = a(3^x)$, explain how changing the value of a affects the graphs you have drawn.
6. Calculate the value of the function $f(x) = 2(3^x)$, given:
   (a) $x = 4$ (c) $x = 2.7$
   (b) $x = \frac{1}{2}$ (d) $x = -3.5$
7. Calculate the value of the function $f(x) = 4(3^x)$, given:
   (a) $x = 6$ (c) $x = -8$
   (b) $x = \frac{3}{4}$ (d) $x = -4.5$
8. Calculate the value of the function $f(x) = 5(3^x)$, given:
   (a) $x = 0$ (c) $x = 2$
   (b) $x = -\frac{1}{2}$ (d) $x = 6$
9. Calculate the value of the function $f(x) = 7(3^x)$, given:
   (a) $x = -4$ (c) $x = 2.2$
   (b) $x = -1\frac{1}{2}$ (d) $x = 7$
10. Calculate the value of the function $f(x) = 8(3^x)$, given:
   (a) $x = 4$ (c) $x = 2.7$
   (b) $x = \frac{1}{2}$ (d) $x = -3.5$
11. Given $g(x) = 2(3^x)$, find the value of x for which $g(x) = 486$.
12. Given $h(x) = 4(3^x)$, find the value of x for which $h(x) = 236,196$.
13. Given $f(x) = 5(3^x)$, find the value of x for which $f(x) = 405$.
14. Given $k(x) = 10(3^x)$, find the value of x for which $k(x) = 65,610$.
15. Given $f(x) = 7(3^x)$, find the value of x for which $f(x) = 5,103$.

16. A candle of height 243 cm reduces in size at a rate of 3^x each hour (one third each hour), where x represents every hour as it burns.

(a) Draw a graph to show the decrease in the candle's height over an 8-hour period.

(b) After how many hours will the candle be 50 cm tall?

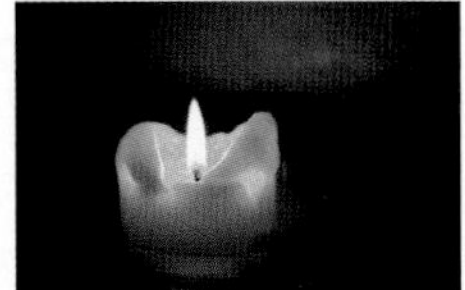

(c) What was the height of the candle after 5 hours?

17. A certain type of building material is tested to find the compression strength it can withstand.

A force of 10 kN (kilonewtons) is applied and is tripled every 15 minutes.

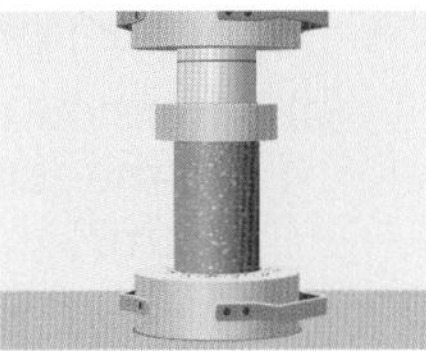

(a) Draw a graph to show the change in the force being applied to the material during the first hour.

(b) After how many minutes was a force of 50 kN being applied?

18. The number of tadpoles in a river is recorded as 200. As the rest hatch, this amount increases by $200(3^x)$, where x represents every hour for a period of 5 hours.

(a) Draw a graph to show the increase in the number of tadpoles in the river.

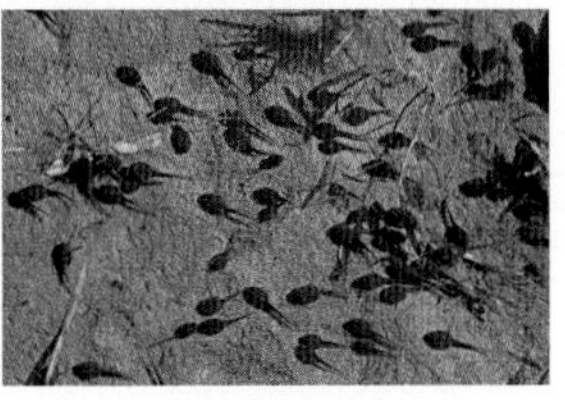

(b) After how many hours were there 4,000 tadpoles?

(c) What was the population after 5 hours?

19. After the summer, the depth of water in a jungle river-bed is 50 cm. During the wet season, the river triples in depth every 12 hours over a 2-day period.

(a) Draw a graph to show the change in the depth of the river over a 2-day period.

(b) What was the depth of the river after 48 hours during the wet season?

(c) After approximately how many hours was the depth of the river 10 metres?

20. As a result of recent pollution, the number of algae per litre of water in a river increases by 100% every day for 5 days.

(a) If there were originally 20,000 algae per litre of water in the river, draw a graph to show the increase in numbers over the 5 days.

(b) After approximately how many hours are there 100,000 algae per litre of water in the river?

(c) How many algae were in a litre of water after 2.5 days?

CHAPTER 27 SELF-CHECK TEST

1. 2,000 fish were recorded in a certain river. 100 non-native fish are introduced into the river in the hope of boosting the fish numbers.

After a number of years, it is found that the numbers of native fish are declining by 50% each year and the non-native fish numbers are increasing by 100% yearly.

(a) Using the same scale and axes, draw a graph to show the change in number of both fish species in the river.

(b) After how many years are the population of both species the same?

(c) How many of both species are in the river after 4 years?

2. The spores from a certain type of fungus increase weekly in a population. This increase can be modelled by the function $f:x \rightarrow 50(2^x)$.

(a) Draw a graph to represent the growth in the population over 3 weeks.

(b) What is the population after 2 weeks?

(c) The habitat can sustain a population of 25,600 only. How long will it take the spores to reach this limit?

3. Plutonium-238 has a half-life of 88 years. This means half of the sample will decay after 88 years.

(a) Draw a graph to represent the decay of a sample mass 500 kg.

(b) After how long has the sample decayed to 150 kg?

(c) What mass of the sample remains after 200 years?

4. In 1990, there were 20 mobile phone subscribers in the small town of Currans. The number of subscribers increased by 100% per annum for a period of 5 years.

(a) Draw a graph to show the growth in subscribers over this time.

(b) How many mobile phone subscribers were in Currans in 1993?

(c) After how many years have 250 people subscribed?

5. A snowball of radius 4 cm is allowed to roll down a steep hill. Its radius increases by 100% every 15 seconds.

(a) Draw a suitable graph to show the change in the radius of the snowball over a 2-minute period.

(b) How long does it take for the radius to be 20 cm?

(c) What is the radius of the snowball after 110 seconds?

6. A sunflower seed is planted. After 1 week a shoot of 1.5 cm appears and doubles in height every week.

(a) Draw a graph to show the height of the sunflower against time.

(b) After how many weeks will the sunflower be 24 cm?

(c) What will be the height of the sunflower after 10 weeks?

7. When Aidan wandered into a strange classroom, he saw the following poster with graphs on the wall:

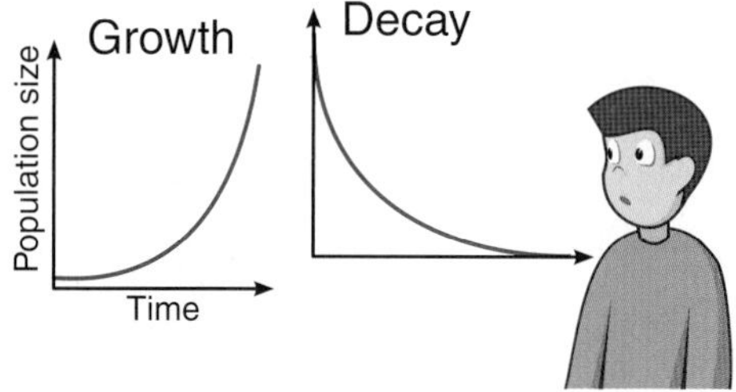

(a) Explain what the graph showing Growth means, giving three real-life examples.

(b) Explain what the graph showing Decay means, giving three real-life examples.

8. You win an amount of money in a draw. The prize is offered in two ways:

- Option A: You can accept €1,000 every year for 20 years.
- Option B: You can accept €1 in the first year, €2 in the second, €4 in the third year and so on, with the amount doubling every year for the next 20 years.

(a) Which option would you choose? Give a reason for your answer.

(b) Copy the following axes into your copy and graph both options.

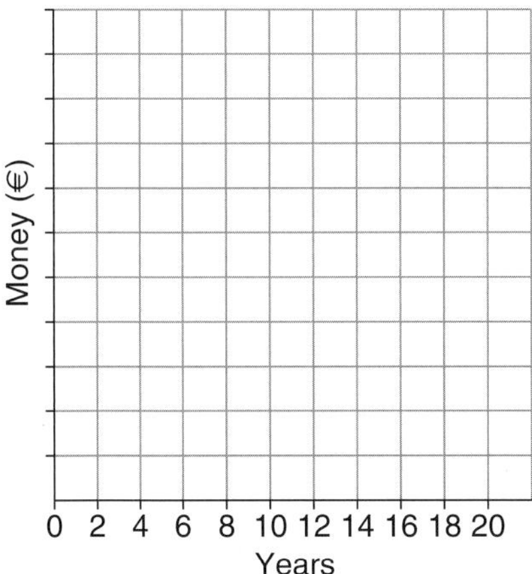

(c) Comment on the pattern formed by option 1.

(d) Comment on the pattern formed by option 2. Have you encountered a pattern like this before?

9. A radioactive material has a half-life of 5 years. This means half of the sample will decay after 5 years. A sample of the material has a mass of 45 kg.

(a) Draw a graph to show the decay of the material over time.

(b) After how many years will the sample be completely decayed?

(c) What will be the mass of the sample after 15 years?

10. During a recent storm, an oil tanker sank. Environmentalists estimate that the circular oil spill will spread as shown in the exponential graph.

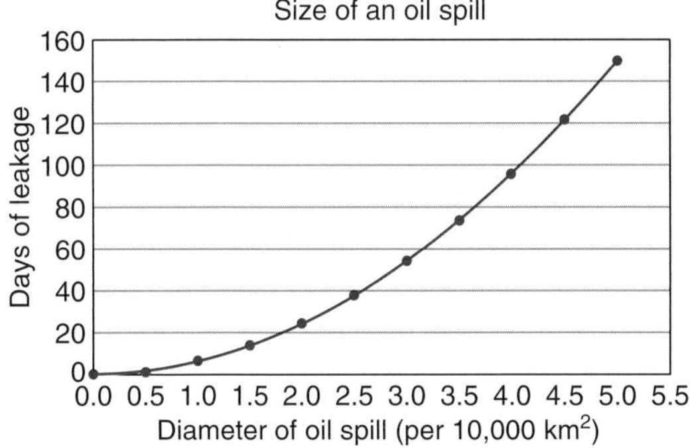

(a) After 40 days, how far will the oil have spread north of the sunken oil tanker?

(b) If the environmentalists have only enough people to clean up 15,000 square kilometres, within how many days must they have gathered up all of the spillage?

11. The national Road Safety Authority recently carried out a series of tests examining the relationship between a car's speed and its breaking distance. The breaking distance is the distance a car travels after the breaks are applied until the car stops.

The report states:

- A car travelling 30 km per hour has a breaking distance of 45 m.
- A car travelling 60 km per hour has a breaking distance of 180 m.
- A car travelling 90 km per hour has a breaking distance of 405 m.

(a) The breaking distance of a car travelling 60 km per hour is 180 m. Does that imply the breaking distance of a car travelling 120 km per hour is 360 metres? Explain your answer.

(b) In words, explain the relationship between the different speeds of the car.

(c) Explain the relationship between the different breaking distances of the car.

(d) Write the relationship between the various breaking distances as a mathematical equation using exponents.

(e) Using a measuring tape, measure the respective distances in the school yard.

(f) Draw a graph representing the above information.

12. €650 is deposited in a fixed-interest bank account. The final value of the money in the account at the end of each year is shown in the following table:

End of year	1	2	3	4	5
Final value (€)	676	703.04	731.16	760.41	790.82

(a) Explain how you can tell from the table whether the above relationship is linear, quadratic or exponential.
(b) If you plot a graph of the final value against time, what does the graph look like for this limited range of times?
(c) How might plotting more points help?
(d) What would be the effect of increasing the interest rate?
(e) Make a table showing the final values for the first 5 years, using a rate of 10% per annum compound interest.
(f) Plot a graph of the data.
(g) Compare this graph to the earlier graph produced with the lower interest rate.
(h) If the initial investment is €650, what is the final value after n years if it earns 10% compound interest?

13. Gary is 4 m away from a wall. He jumps towards the wall. With each jump, he halves the distance between himself and the wall.
(a) Will his distance from the wall ever be zero?
(b) Construct a table of the varying distances Gary is from the wall for the first six jumps.
(c) Looking at successive output values, explain whether the relationship is linear, quadratic or exponential.
(d) Plot a graph of Gary's distance from the wall against the different jumps towards the wall.
(e) How is the graph different to the graph obtained for compound interest in Question 12?
(f) How is the graph similar to the graph obtained for compound interest?
(g) Examine the graph to find when Gary's distance from the wall will be zero.

14. During a visit to the hospital, Patricia receives a dose of radioactive medication which decays or loses its effectiveness at a rate of 20% per hour.
(a) Construct a table showing the amount of radioactive material in her body for each hour, for the first six hours.
(b) If she receives 150 mg of the medication initially, approximately how many milligrams of the medication will remain in her body after the first six hours?
(c) Plot a graph showing mg of medication left in her body against hours elapsed.
(d) Is it possible to reduce the amount of radioactive material in Patricia's body to 0? Explain your answer.
(e) What are the implications of this for the decay of radioactive waste material?

CHAPTER 27 KNOWLEDGE CHECKLIST

After completing this chapter, I now:

- **Am able to explain and recognise exponential patterns**
- **Am able to draw graphs of the form $f(x) = a.2^x$, where $a \in \mathbb{N}$; $x \in \mathbb{R}$**
- **Am able to draw graphs of the form $f(x) = a.3^x$, where $a \in \mathbb{N}$; $x \in \mathbb{R}$**

CHAPTER 28

TRANSFORMATION GEOMETRY

LEARNING OUTCOMES

In this chapter you will learn:

- ✓ **To perform axial symmetry**
- ✓ **To perform central symmetry in a point**
- ✓ **To carry out a translation**
- ✓ **To carry out a rotation**

KEY WORDS

- Axial symmetry
- Central symmetry
- Centre of rotation
- Image
- Object
- Point of symmetry
- Reflection
- Rotation
- Translation

INTRODUCTION

In *Maths in Action 1*, you examined the effect of performing a transformation on an object to create an image.

First year revision

1. Which of the following objects are symmetrical and which are asymmetrical?

(a) 

(b) 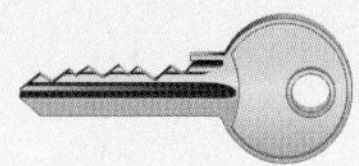

(c) 

(d) 

(e) 

(f) 

(g) 

(h) 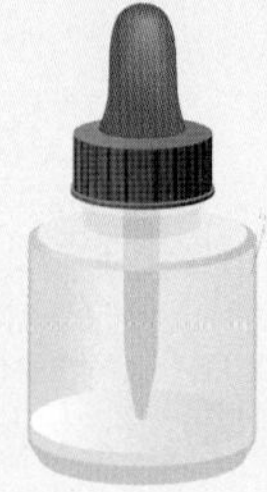

2. Examine the object and the images shown. Then answer the following questions.

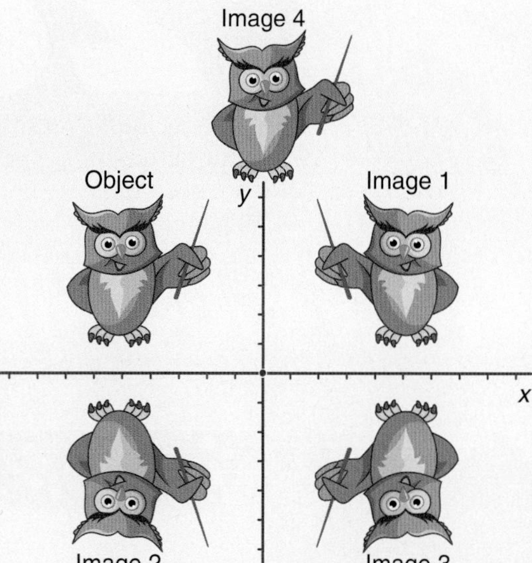

(a) Which image could be described as symmetry in the x-axis? Explain the reason for your answer.

(b) Which image could be described as symmetry in y-axis? Explain the reason for your answer.

(c) Which image could be described as symmetry through the origin? Explain the reason for your answer.

(d) Which image could be described as a translation? Explain the reason for your answer.

3. In your own words, describe how each of the following transformations affects the image of an object:

(a) A translation

(b) Central symmetry in a point

(c) Symmetry in the x-axis

(d) Symmetry in the y-axis

4. Can you work out how many lines of symmetry each flag has?

Albania

Algeria

USA

Australia

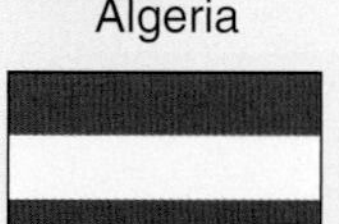
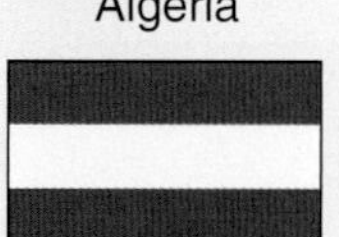
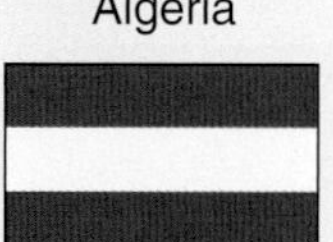
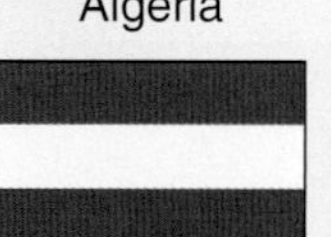
Austria

Belgium

Canada

China

Ireland

Ethiopia

France

Germany

Ghana

Great Britain

Hungary

Section 28.1: Axial symmetry

Student Activity 28A

The following object has been reflected through the y-axis to produce the image as shown.

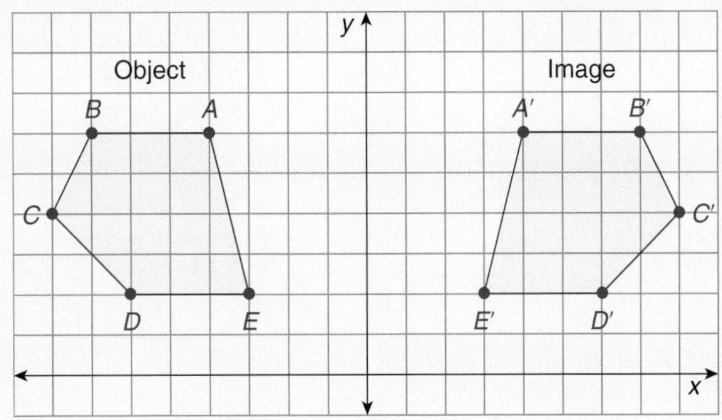

(a) Describe how this image differs from the object.

(b) Describe what properties of the image are the same as in the object.

(c) Measure the distance from each point on the object to the y-axis. Measure the distance from the y-axis to each point on the image. Compare your measurements. What do you notice?

AXIAL SYMMETRY EXPLAINED

The word **'axial'** comes from the Latin word **'axis'.** Axial symmetry means to reflect an object (point, line or shape) perpendicularly through a line. Every point on the object is reflected through the axis of symmetry. Both the original point and the image point are equidistant (the same distance) from the axis of symmetry.

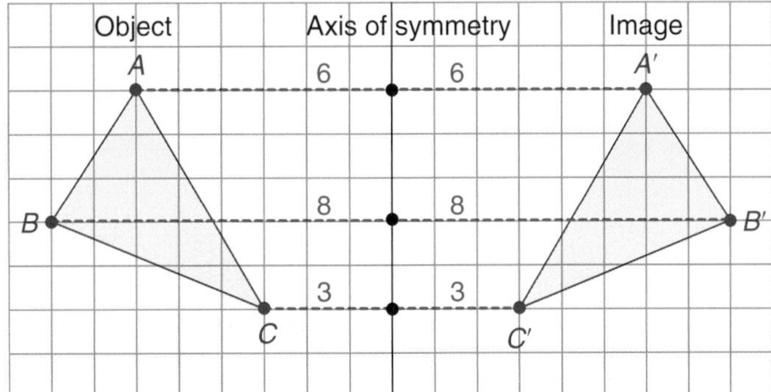

The dimensions and area of the image remain unchanged. The image is the mirror reflection of the object and makes the object appear back to front. In the picture below, both hats are located equal distances from the axis.

Axis of symmetry

An object undergoes **axial symmetry** if the geometric configuration of the object remains unchanged when it is reflected through a given line.

EXAMPLE 1

Reflect the image through the line $x = 3$.

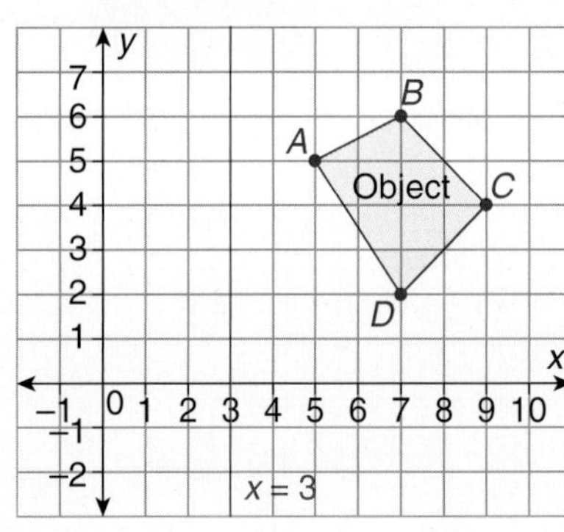

Solution

Using a ruler, draw a line perpendicular from each vertex on the object through the axis of symmetry $x = 3$.

Measure the distance from each point to the axis.

Plot the image point the same distance from the axis of symmetry.

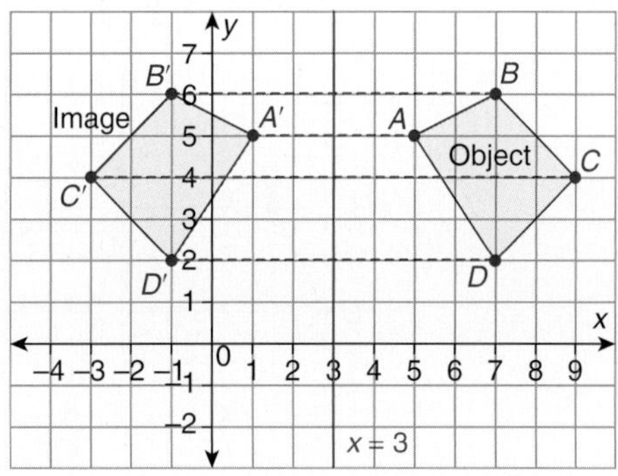

Exercise 28.1

1. Copy the following diagrams and reflect each object through the y-axis:

(a)

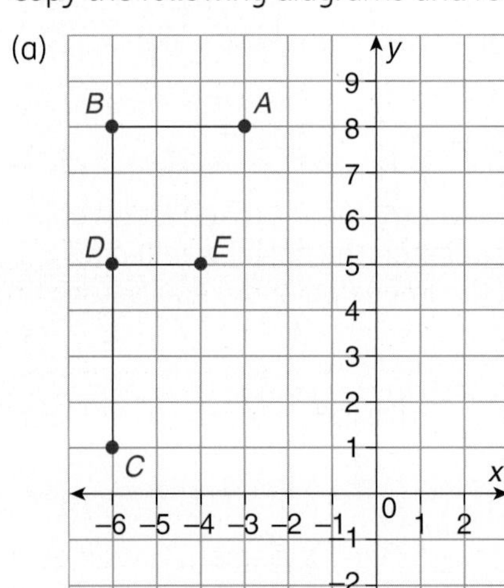

(b)

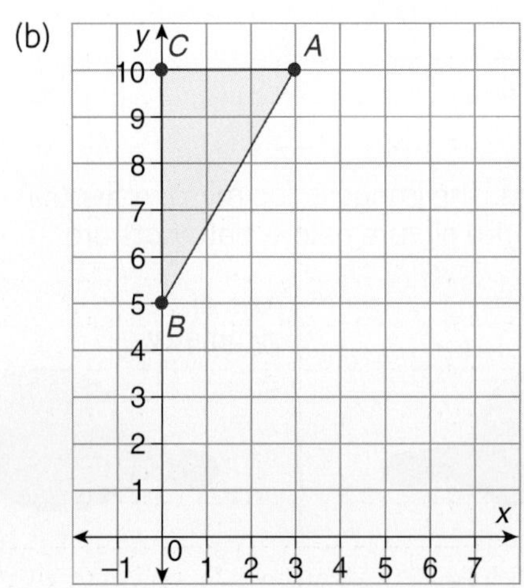

(c)

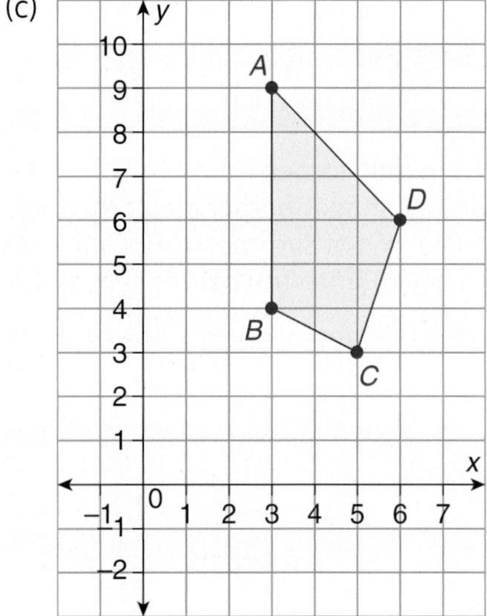

(d)

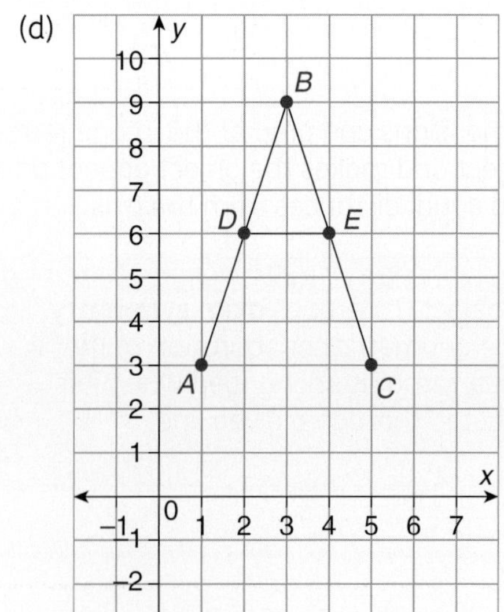

(e)

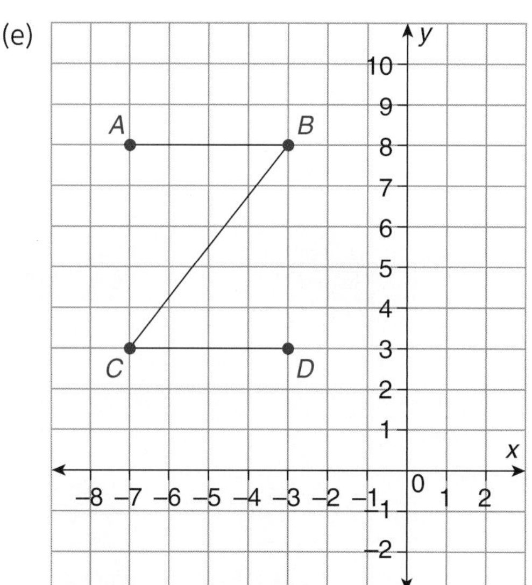

2. Copy the following diagrams and reflect each object through the *x*-axis:

(a)

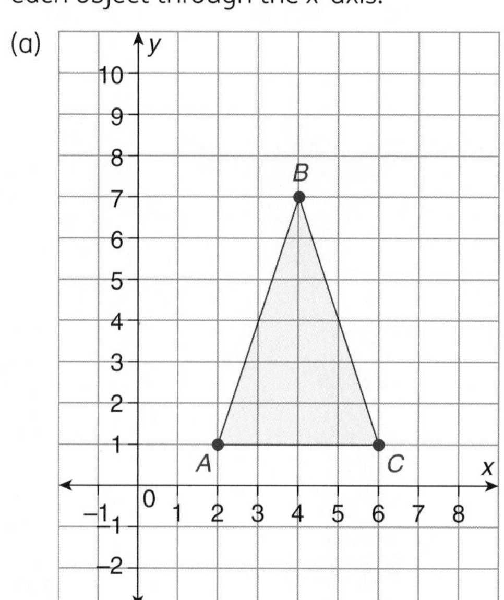

(b)

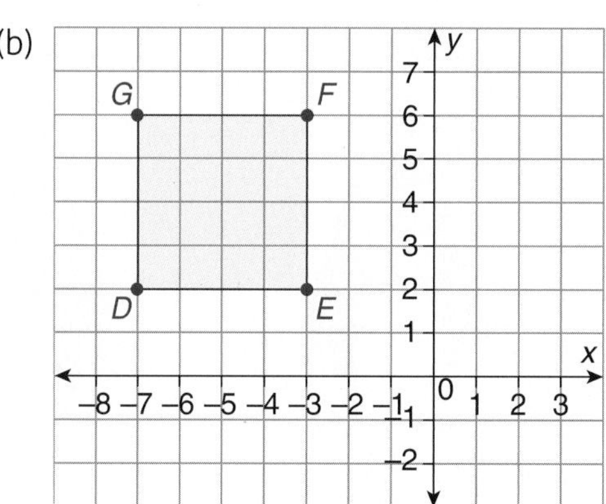

(c)

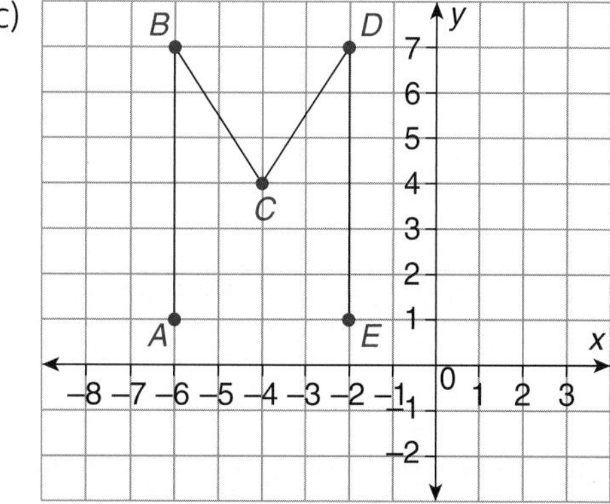

(d)

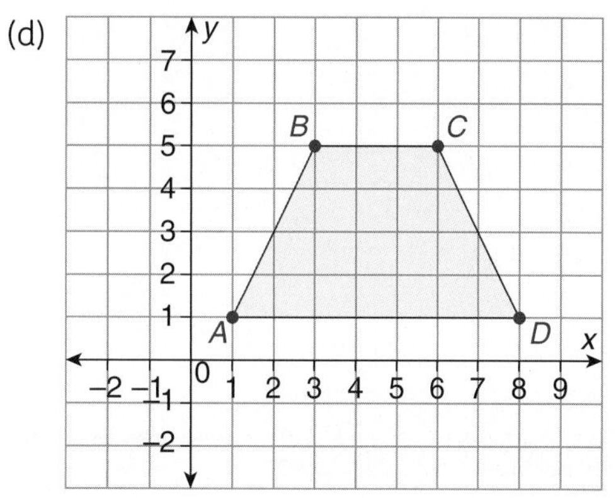

(e)

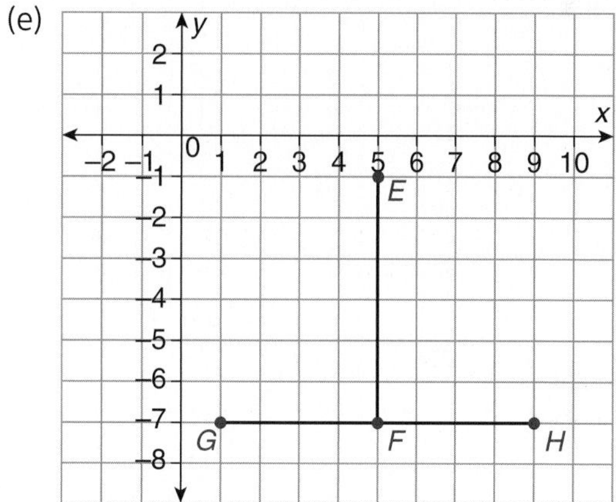

3. Copy the following diagrams and create the image of each object through the given axis of symmetry:

(a)

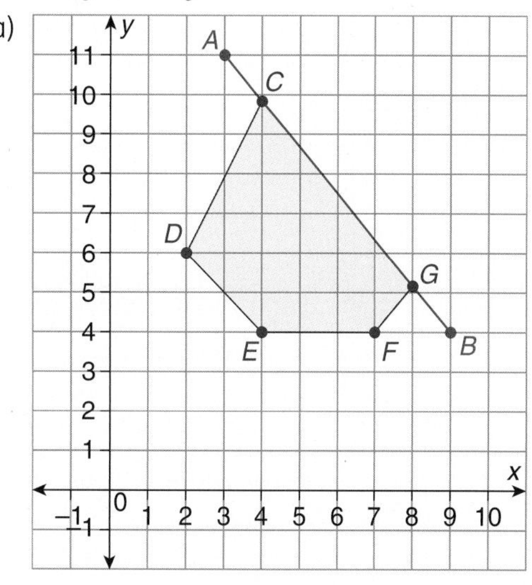

(b)

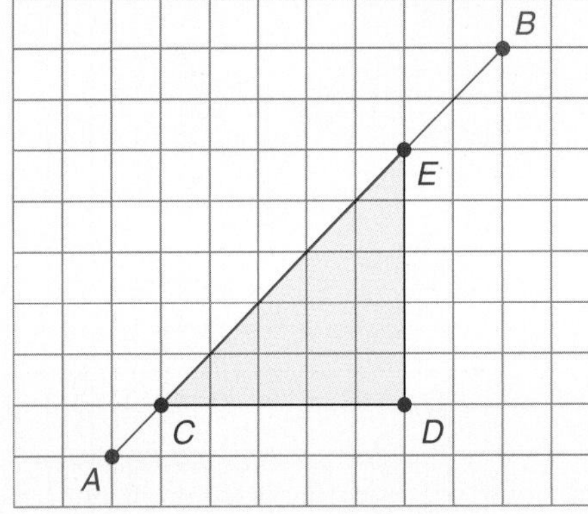

(c)

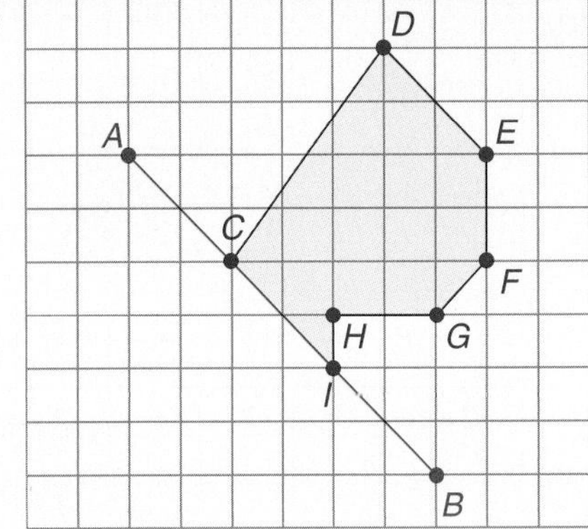

(d)

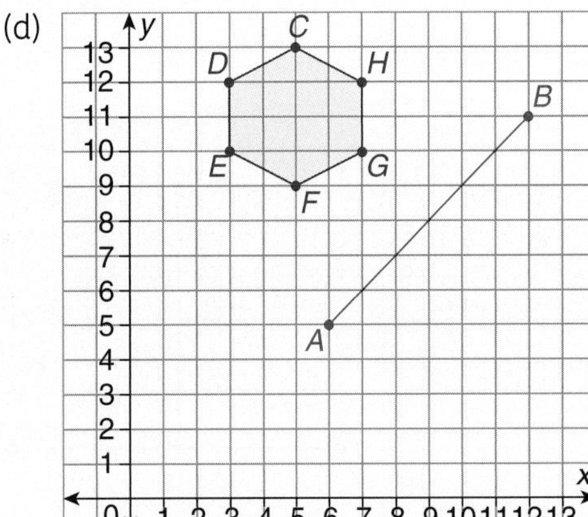

(e)

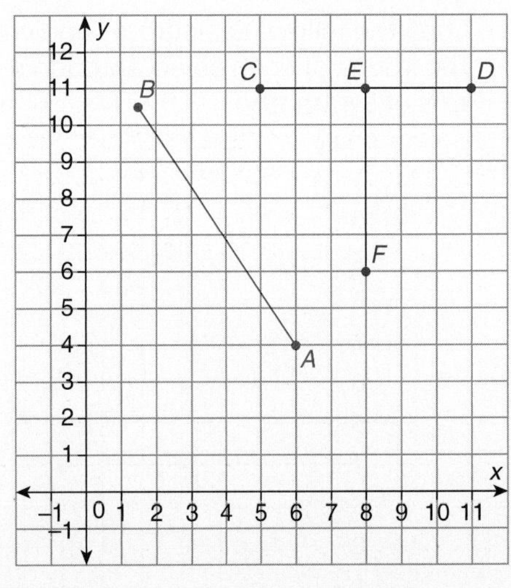

4. State whether the following images have undergone axial symmetry. Explain your answers fully.

(a) Image Object

(b) Object Image

(c) Object Image

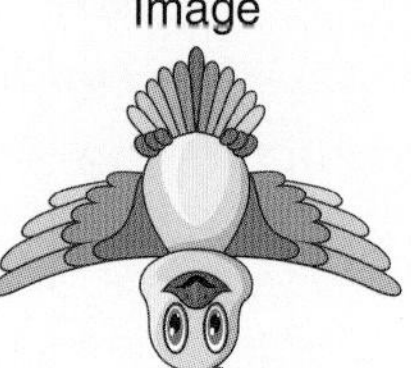

(d) Object Image

(e) Object Image

Section 28.2: Central symmetry in a point

Student Activity 28B

The following object has been reflected through the point X as shown:

(a) Describe how the image has changed.

(b) Describe some properties of the image that have not changed.

(c) Measure the distance from each point on the object to the point X. Then measure the distance from the point X to each point on the image. Compare your measurements. What do you notice?

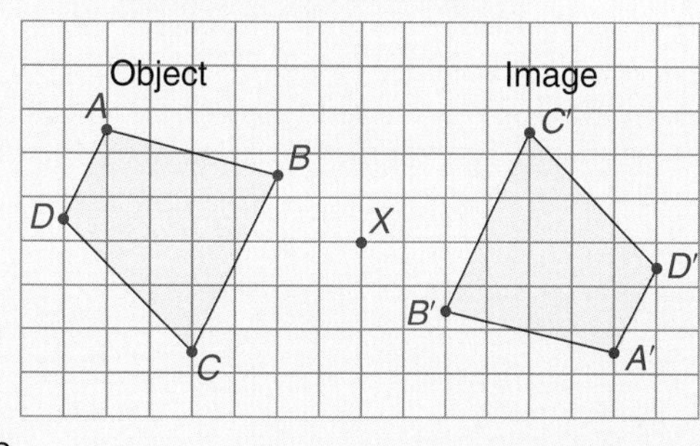

CENTRAL SYMMETRY IN A POINT EXPLAINED

Central symmetry through a point or **point symmetry** can also be called an **inversion.** Every point on the object is reflected through the point of symmetry. The image is identical to the object in dimensions and area but is inverted. This means the shape is upside-down.

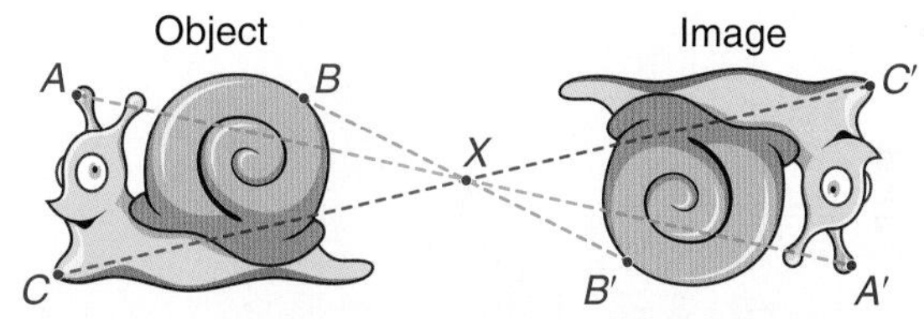

Central symmetry is the reflection of an object through a point and out the same distance beyond the point. The image looks identical to its original. The point around which the image is rotated is called the **point of symmetry.**

Central symmetry gives the same result as the rotation of an object 180° clockwise or anticlockwise about a point.

EXAMPLE 2

Reflect the following object through the point X:

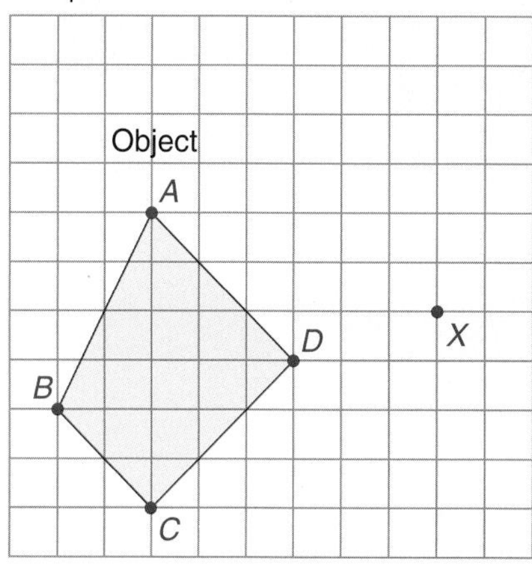

Solution

Every point on the object is reflected through the point of symmetry. The distance from each point on the object to the point of symmetry is equal to the distance from the point of symmetry to the corresponding point on the image.

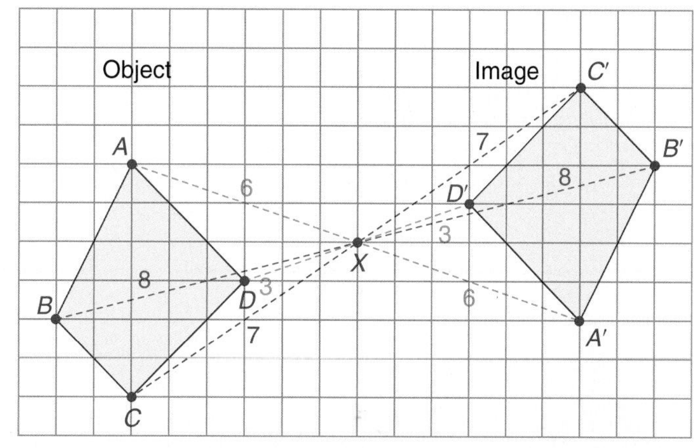

Exercise 28.2

Copy each object and reflect it through the point X (given in red):

1. 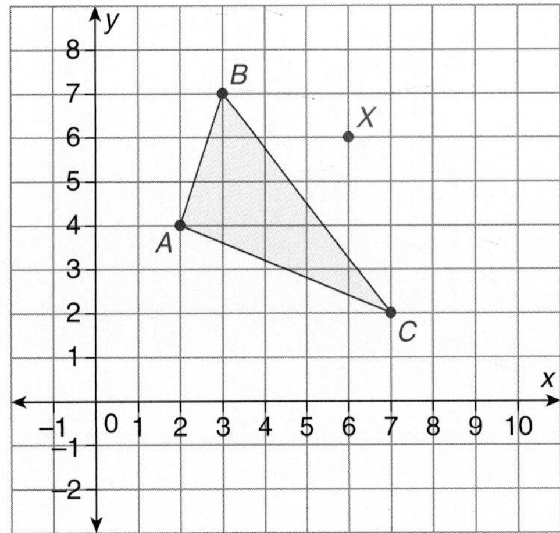

2. 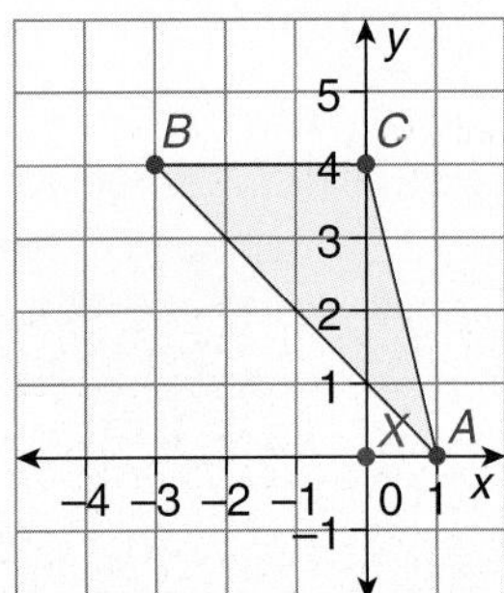

3. 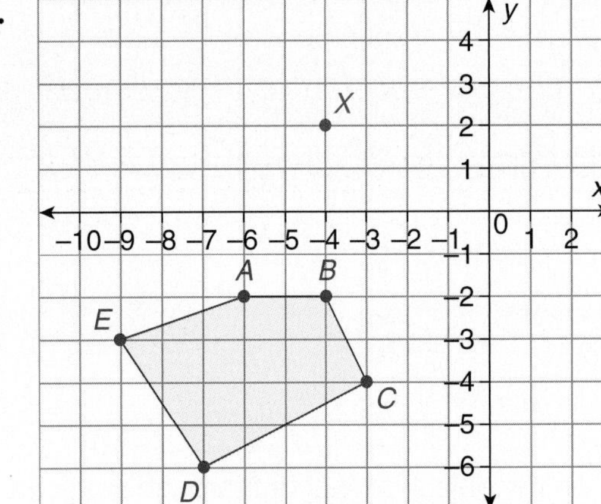

4. 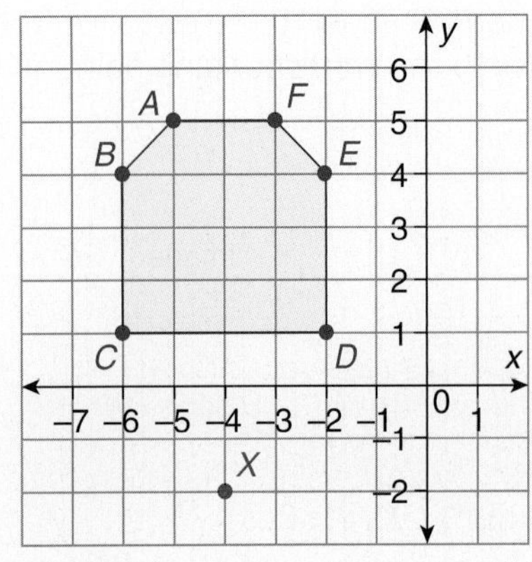

5. 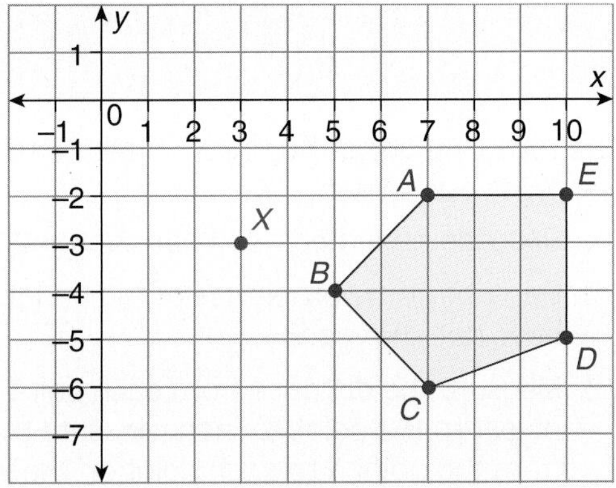

6. State whether the following pairs of images have undergone central symmetry in a point. Explain the reasons for your answers.

(a) 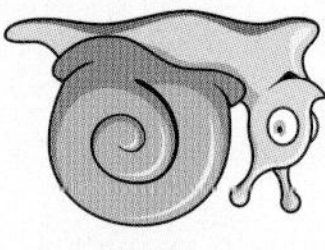 

(b)  

(c)  

(d)  

(e)  

Section 28.3: Translations

Student Activity 28C

The following object has been translated 5 units to the right:

(a) Describe what changes have occurred to the image.

(b) Describe what properties of the image have not changed.

(c) In your own words, describe the effect of a translation upon an object.

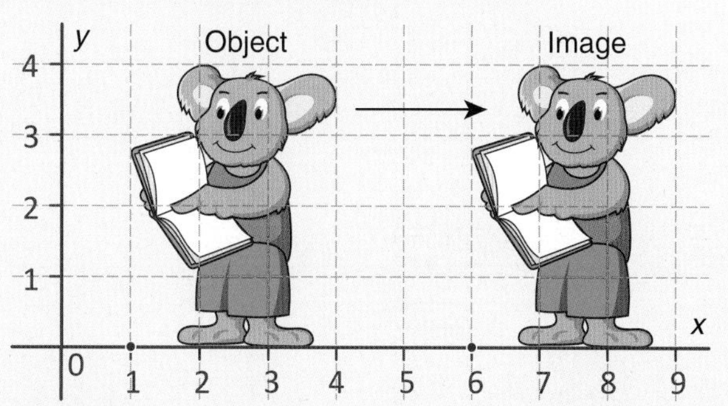

TRANSLATIONS EXPLAINED

A **translation** is a geometrical transformation of the plane that slides every point of an object the same distance in one specific direction.

The original object and its image have the same shape and size. They also face in the same direction. This means a translation creates an image that is **congruent** to the original object.

For example, translating a triangle creates an identical image or a congruent triangle in a new position.

A **translation** moves every point on a figure by the same amount in a given direction.

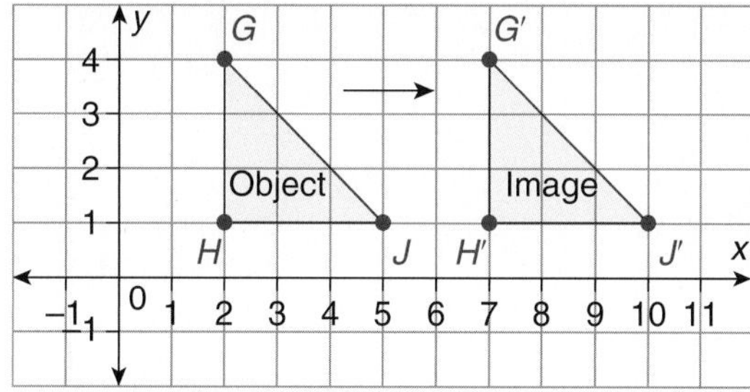

This shows a translation of 5 units to the right, parallel to the x-axis.

EXAMPLE 3

Translate the given object 5 units parallel to the *y*-axis:

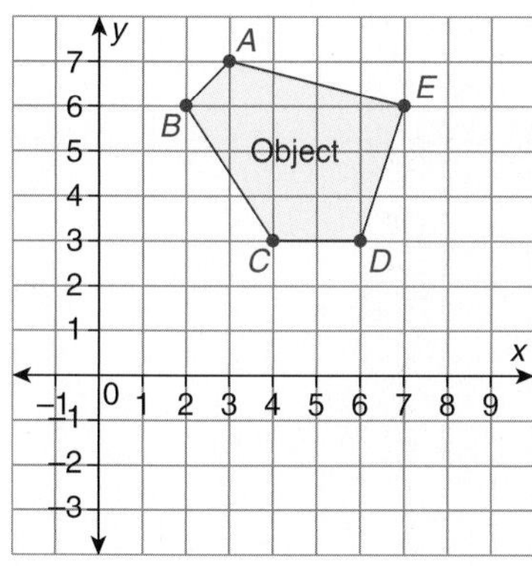

Solution

Each point on the object is moved downwards by 5 units parallel to the *y*-axis.

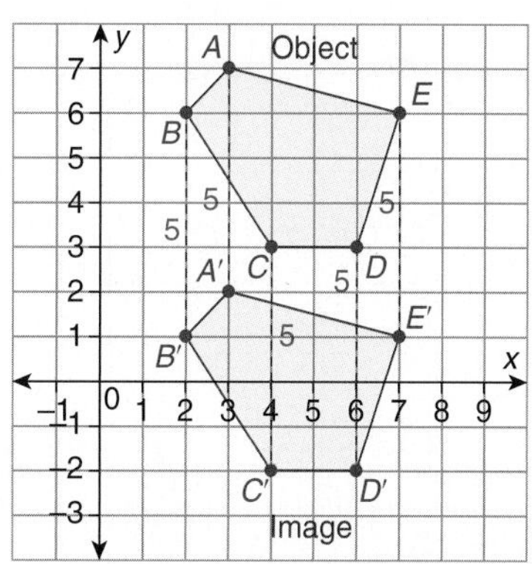

EXAMPLE 4

Translate the given object by the same translation that maps E onto F:

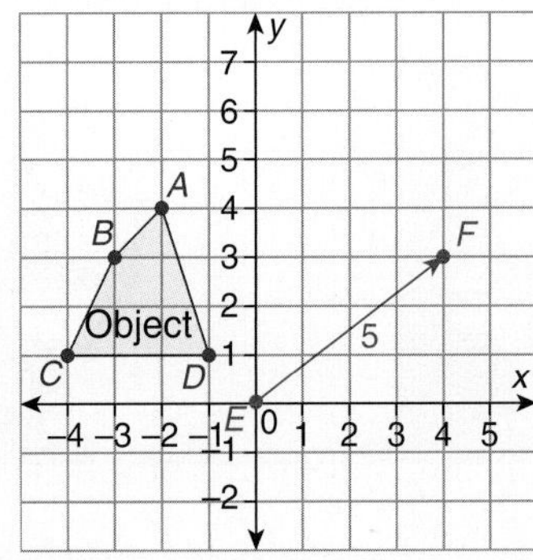

Solution

Draw rays parallel to EF from each point on the object.

Using a ruler, set your compass to 5 units.

Mark off a 5 units distance on each ray and draw the image.

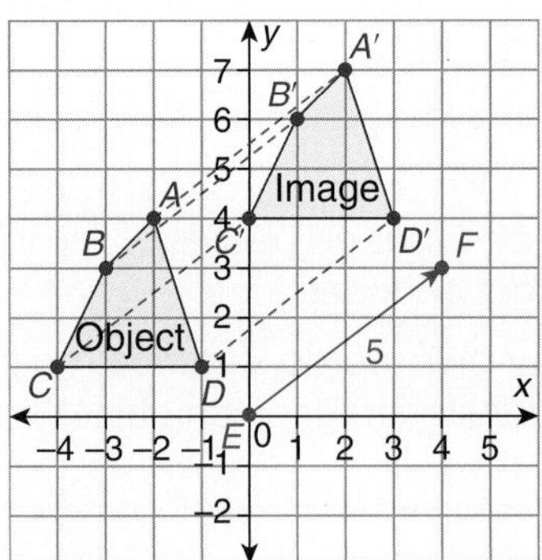

Exercise 28.3

Translate each object under the translation given:

1. 2 units north

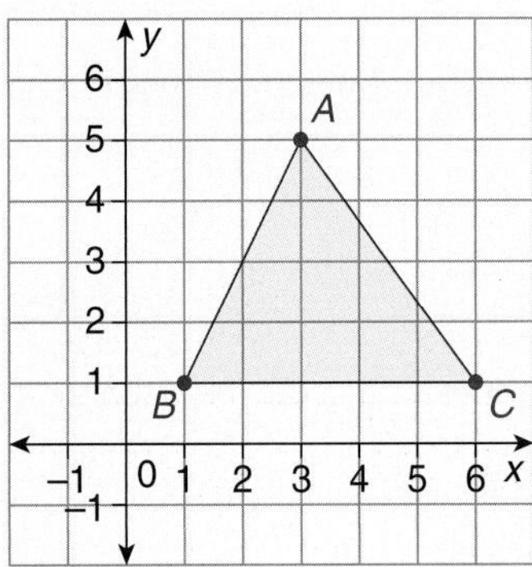

2. 2 units south

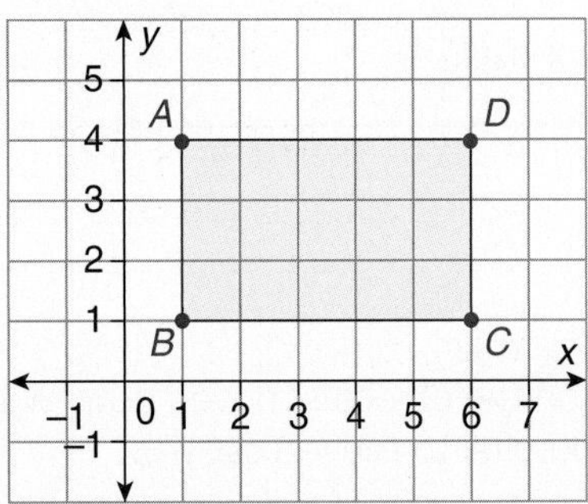

3. 4 units south

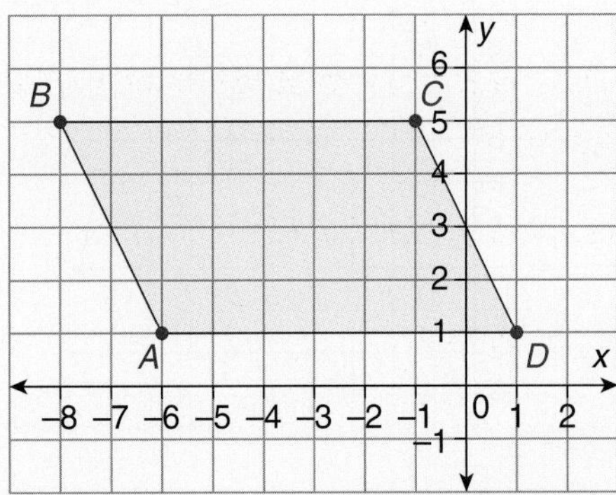

4. 3 units west

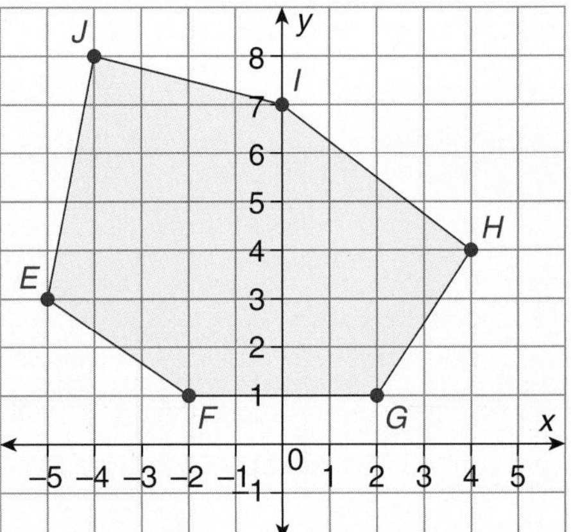

5. 4 units north

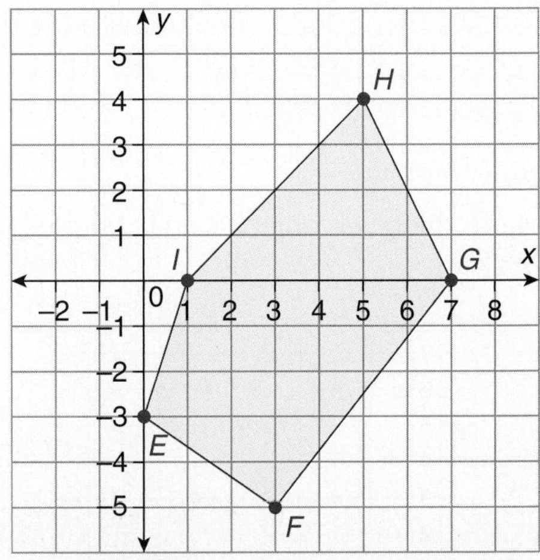

6. State whether the following images have undergone a translation. Explain your answers fully.

(a)

(b)

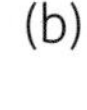

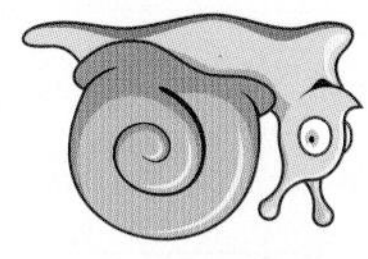

(c)

(d)

(e)

Section 28.4 Rotations

Student Activity 28D

1. The triangle *ABC* and its image *A'B'C'* are both shown. Examine the triangles and answer the questions that follow.
   (a) Measure and compare the lengths of the sides of the triangles. What do you notice?
   (b) In your opinion is the image *A'B'C'* created by central symmetry, axial symmetry or a translation? Give a reason for your answer.

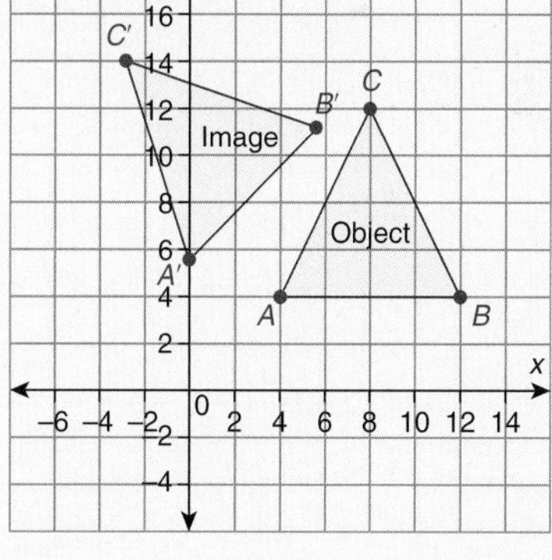

2. (a) Using a straight-edged ruler draw [A'O] and [OA].
   (b) Use a protractor to measure $|\angle A'OA|$.
   (c) Repeat steps (a) and (b) to measure the angles $|\angle C'OC|$ and $|\angle B'OB|$. What do you notice about your answers?
   (d) Place the point of the compass on the point *O* and swing an arc from each vertex on the triangle *ABC*. What do you notice?

ROTATIONS EXPLAINED

A **rotation** is a geometrical transformation in a plane where the object is rotated around a given point by a certain number of degrees. A rotation does not change the dimensions or area of the object.

When working with rotations, it is important to always state the direction of the rotation: whether it is clockwise or anticlockwise.

In Student Activity 28D, the angle of rotation was 45° anticlockwise.

A positive rotation is always anticlockwise.

The image of an object under rotation is found by using a compass, a protractor and a straight edge. As in Student Activity 28D, each vertex on the image lies on the arc from the vertex on the object. The **centre of rotation** is the centre of each arc.

A **rotation** is a transformation where a figure is turned about a given point.

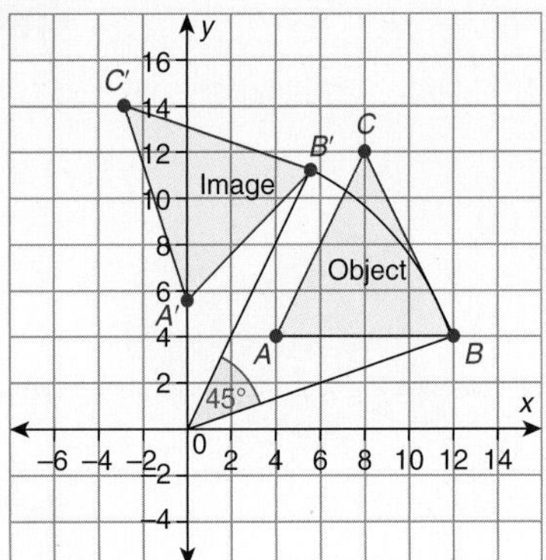

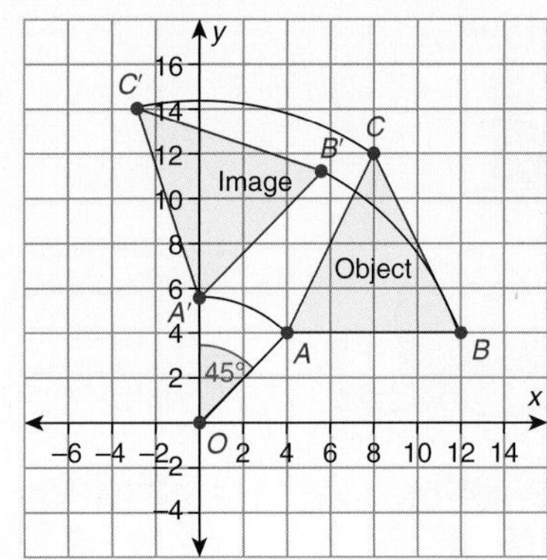

EXAMPLE 5

Find the angle of rotation for the image shown about the point *A*.

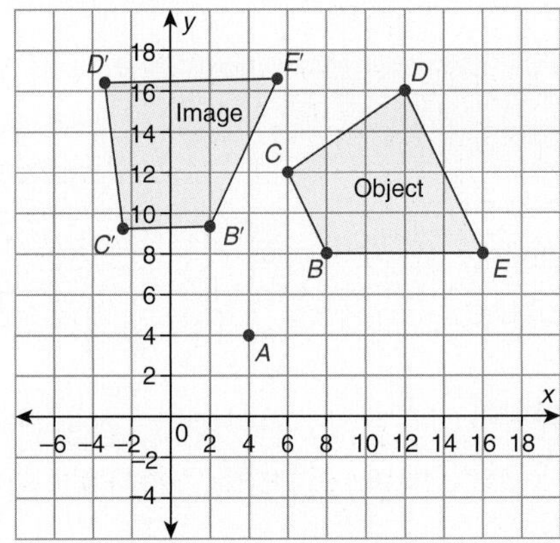

Solution

Join one point on the object to the centre of rotation. Join the centre of rotation to the corresponding point on the image.

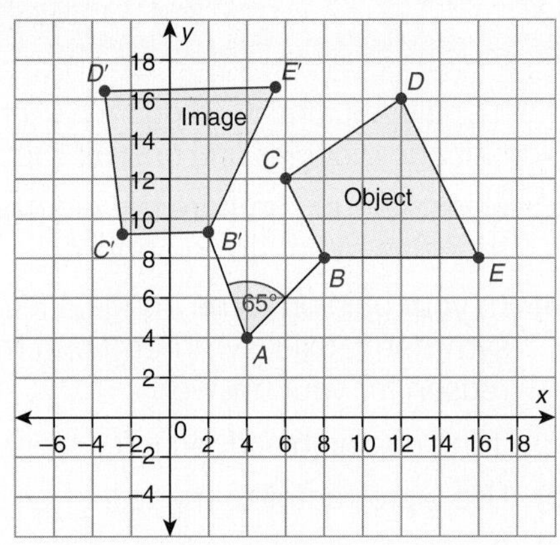

Use a protractor to measure the angle created.

EXAMPLE 6

Rotate the figure shown by 60° clockwise about the point *Z*.

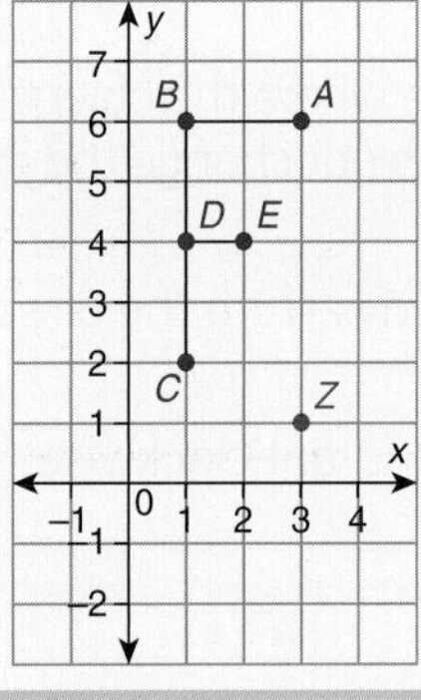

Solution

Use a compass to draw an arc from the point *C* on the object with *Z* as the centre.

Join *C* to *Z* and use your protractor to measure a 60° angle clockwise. Mark the intersection point of the arc and the arm of the angle.

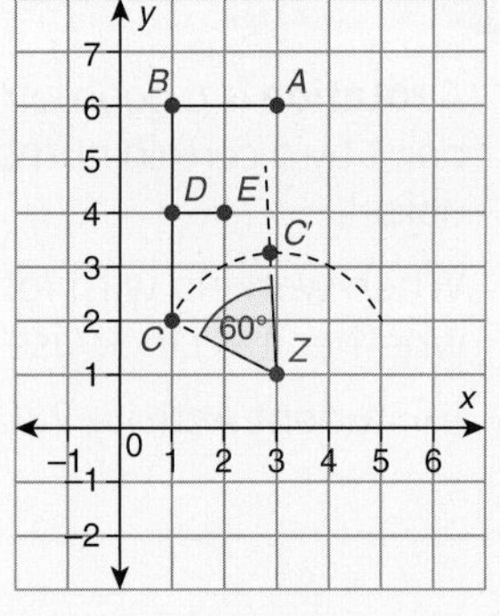

Repeat this for the point *A* on the object as shown.

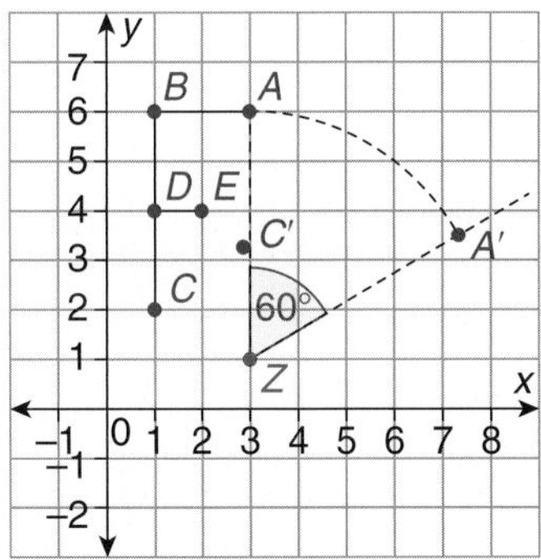

Repeat for each vertex on the object. Then join all of the new points together to form the image.

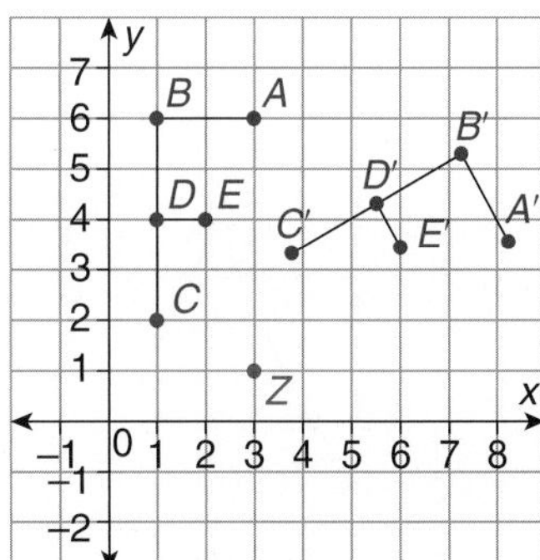

Exercise 28.4

1. The following diagram shows the triangles *A*, *B*, *C* and *D*:

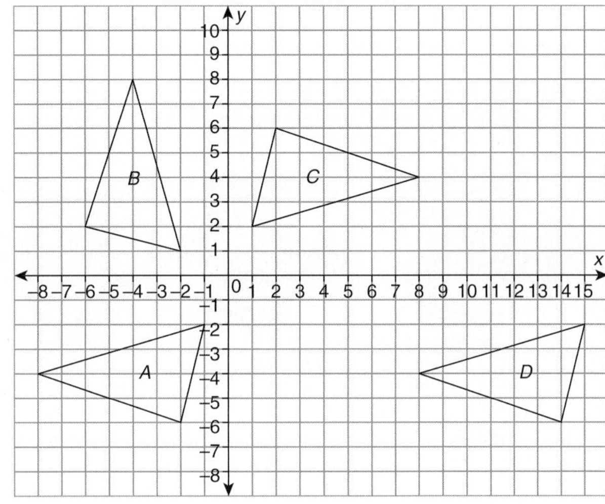

Calculate the angle of rotation that takes you from:

(a) *A* to *B* (b) *A* to *C* (c) *C* to *B* (d) *C* to *D*

2. Find the angle of rotation for each image shown:

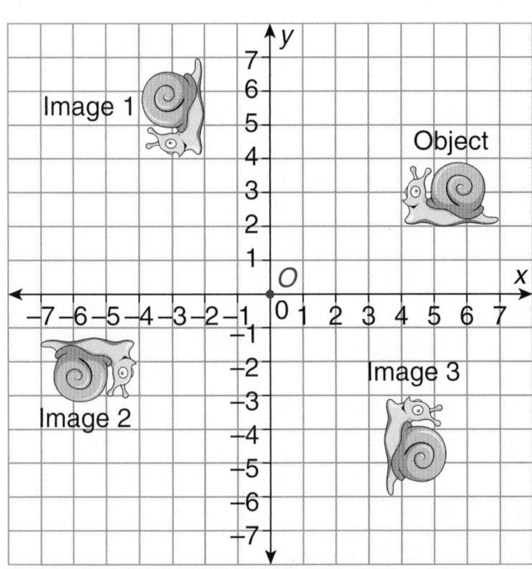

3. Find the angle of rotation for each image shown:

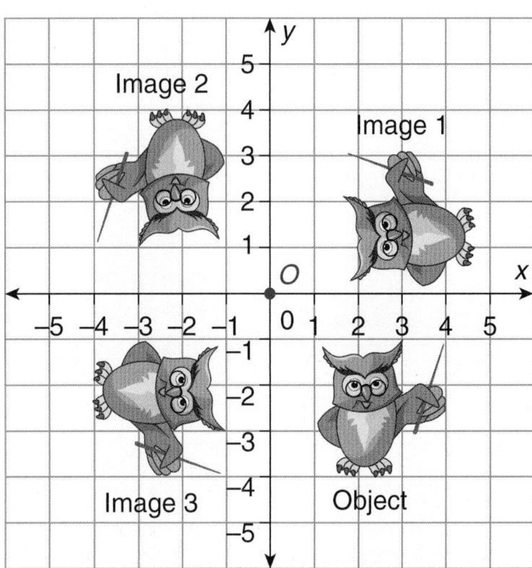

4. Copy the following diagram and rotate the letter **50°** anticlockwise about the point *X*:

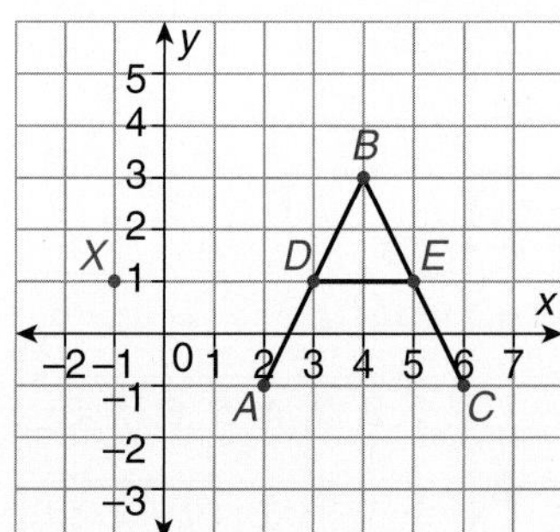

5. Copy the following diagram and rotate the letter **70°** clockwise about the point *W*:

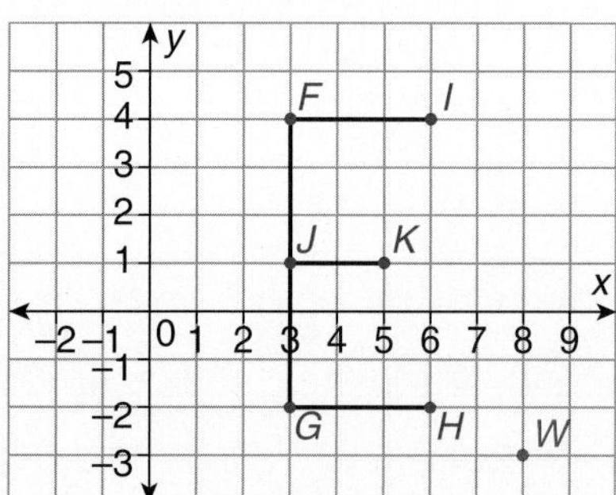

CHAPTER 28 SELF-CHECK TEST

For each image, state whether it is a result of axial symmetry through the *x*-axis or through the *y*-axis, central symmetry through a point, a rotation or a translation.

1.

Object	Image A	Image B	Image C

2.

Object	Image A	Image B	Image C

3.

Object	Image A	Image B	Image C

4.

Object	Image A	Image B	Image C
$y = 2x + 1$	$y = -2x - 1$	$y = -2x + 1$	$y = 2x + 4$

5.

Object	Image A	Image B
$x^2 - 2$	$-x^2 + 2$	$y = x^2 - 4x + 2$

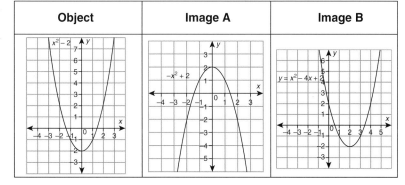

6. (a) Draw the image of the triangle in the diagram under axial symmetry in the line k.

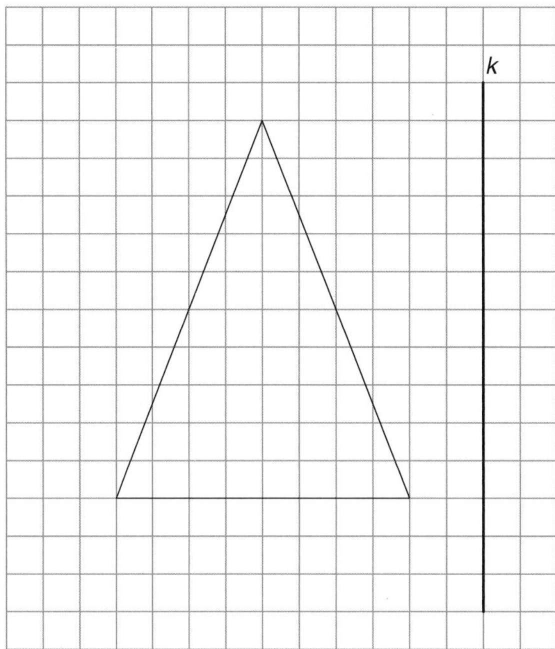

(b) Does axial symmetry change the area of an object? Explain your answer, giving a reason.

7. (a) Construct the image of the letter L in the diagram under central symmetry in the point O.

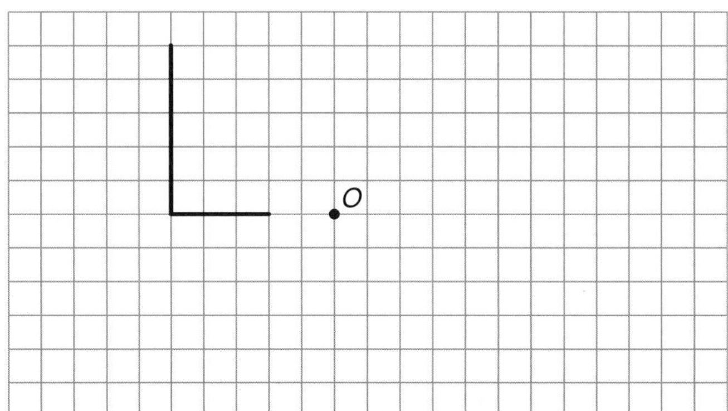

(b) Explain what changes, if any, occurred under central symmetry in the point O.

(c) Name another transformation that would give a similar result.

8. The diagram below shows the letter Z on the coordinate plane and its image under a number of transformations. Write down the coordinates of the images of the vertices of Z under each of the transformations listed below.

Transformation	Coordinates of vertices
Axial symmetry in the *y*-axis	(,), (,), (,), (,)
Central symmetry in the point (0, 0)	(,), (,), (,), (,)
Axial symmetry in the *x*-axis	(,), (,), (,), (,)

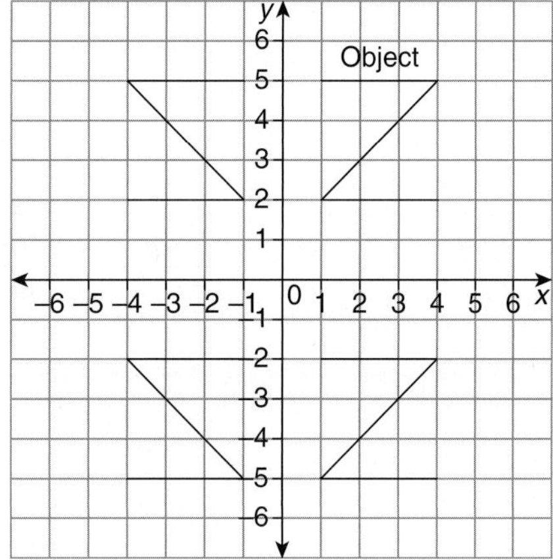

9. (a) Construct the image of the triangle under central symmetry in the point *O*.

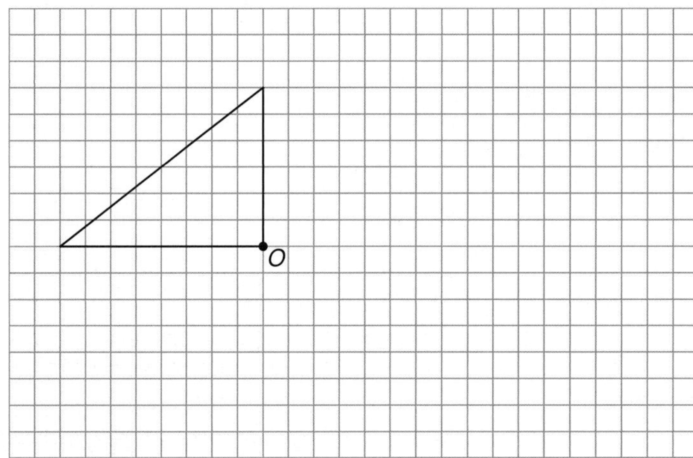

(b) Central symmetry does not change certain properties of an object. Is this true? Explain your answer, giving reasons.

10. Find the angle of rotation for each image shown:

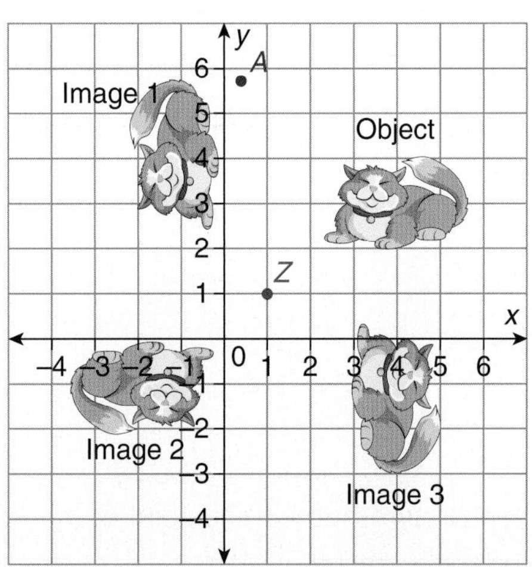

11. Copy the following diagram:

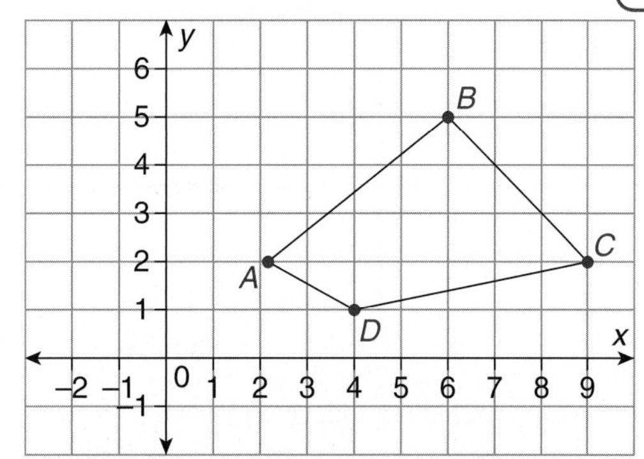

(a) Rotate the letters 70° clockwise about the point (1, 1).

(b) Rotate the letters 60° anticlockwise about the point (0, 4).

(c) Rotate the letters 180° clockwise about the point (0, 0).

12. Each of the three figures labelled A, B and C shown is the image of the object shown on the left under a transformation. For each of A, B and C, state what the transformation is (translation, central symmetry, axial symmetry or rotation). In the case of a rotation, state the angle.

Object

A

B

C

13. Each of the three figures labelled A, B and C shown is the image of the object shown on the left under a transformation. For each of A, B and C, state what the transformation is (translation, central symmetry, axial symmetry or rotation). In the case of a rotation, state the angle.

Object

A

B

C

14. The diagram shows a regular hexagon. (A regular hexagon has six equal sides and six equal angles.)
    (a) How many axes of symmetry has the hexagon?
    (b) Copy the diagram and draw in the axes of symmetry.
    (c) [*ad*] and [*cf*] intersect at *o*. What is the measure of the angle of rotation about *o*, which maps *a* onto *c*?
    (d) Describe one transformation which maps [*af*] to [*cd*].

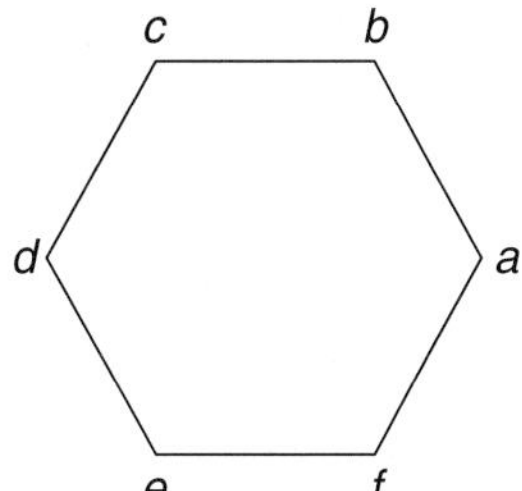

15. The diagram shows a regular octagon.

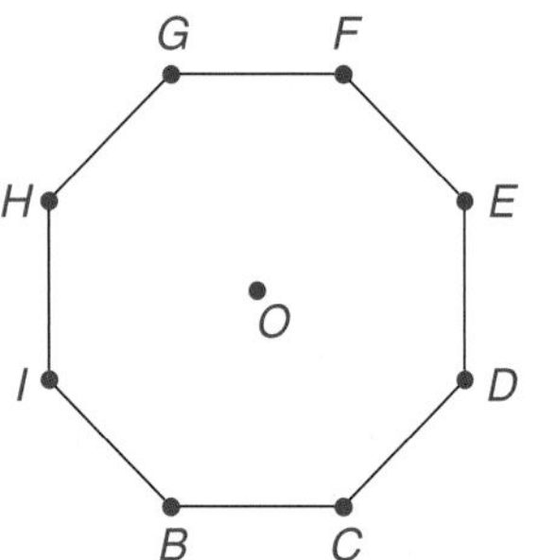

    (a) How many axes of symmetry has an octagon?
    (b) What is the measure of the angle of rotation that maps *G* onto *C*?
    (c) [*GC*] and [*FB*] intersect at the point *O*. Find the image of [*GH*] under a central symmetry in *O*.

CHAPTER 28 KNOWLEDGE CHECKLIST

After completing this chapter, I now:

- **Am able to perform axial symmetry**
- **Am able to perform central symmetry in a point**
- **Am able to perform a translation**
- **Am able to carry out a rotation**

CHAPTER 29

GEOMETRY 4 : PROOF OF THEOREMS

KEY WORDS

- Axiom
- Converse
- Corollary
- Implies
- Proof
- Theorem

LEARNING OUTCOMES

In this chapter you will learn:

- ✓ The terms theorem, proof, axiom, converse, corollary and implies
- ✓ To prove the theorems required for the Junior Certificate Higher Level course
- ✓ The converse of the required theorems and corollaries
- ✓ To solve problems using these theorems

INTRODUCTION

As you learned in *Maths in Action 1*, Euclid was a famous mathematician who wrote the book *The Elements.*

In this chapter, you will examine the formal geometrical proofs required for the Higher Level course. These are largely based on parts of Euclid's book. You have already examined these theorems through practical investigations. The formal proofs of theorems 4, 6, 9, 14 and 19 and the relevant converses are examinable at Higher Level.

Student Activity 29A

1. Patrick and Michael are driving past Thomond Park. The floodlights are on.
   (a) Is that enough proof that the Munster rugby team are playing tonight?
   (b) Suggest other ways they could prove whether a game was on without having to enter the grounds.

2. Julie left her house at 9:00 p.m. and arrived at her aunt's house 90 km away at 10:00 p.m. Prove that Julie exceeded the 60 km per hour speed limit.
3. If Peter buys two PlayStation games for just over €90, can you prove that at least one of the games cost more than €45?

Section 29.1: Terms used in proofs

It is important to remember the terms we have met earlier when studying any theorem. We will also look at the new word **'implies'.**

Theorem	A theorem is a statement which has been proven to be true by following a number of logical steps or by using other theorems or axioms.
Corollary	A corollary follows after a theorem and is a proposition which must be true because of that theorem. It is a given result which follows from a previous result.
Converse	The converse of a theorem is the reverse of a theorem formed by taking the conclusion as the starting point and having the starting point as the conclusion. For example, theorem 2 states: In an isosceles triangle the angles opposite the equal sides are equal in measure. The converse of theorem 2 states: If two angles are equal in measure in a triangle, then the triangle is isosceles.
Implies	Implies indicates a logical relationship between two statements, such that if the first is true, then the second must be true. We use '⇒' as the symbol for implies.
Proof	A proof is a sequence of statements made up of axioms, assumptions and arguments leading to the establishment of the truth of one final statement.
Axiom	An axiom is a statement which is accepted to be true without any proof. It is used as a basis for developing a system. For example: There is exactly one line through any two given points.

Section 29.2: Steps in proving a theorem

As you will see in each of the following proofs, you must follow a certain number of steps to prove a theorem. You must learn to write these under the following headings:

1. **Theorem:** State the title of the theorem to be proved.
2. **Given:** Draw a rough sketch of the theorem in question and insert the relevant information.
3. **Construction:** Draw any additional construction lines you will need to add to the given diagram in order to prove the theorem.
4. **To prove:** State exactly what you are setting out to prove. For example: 'Angle 1 is equal to angle 2.'
5. **Proof:** State step by step the series of statements that will prove what is required.

Section 29.3: Proofs

THEOREM 4: THE ANGLES IN ANY TRIANGLE ADD TO 180°

Given: Triangle *ABC* with angles marked 2, 4 and 5

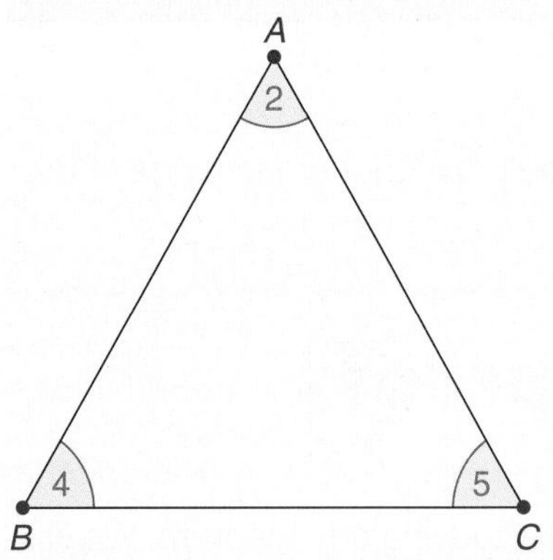

Construction: Draw a line through *A* parallel to [*BC*].

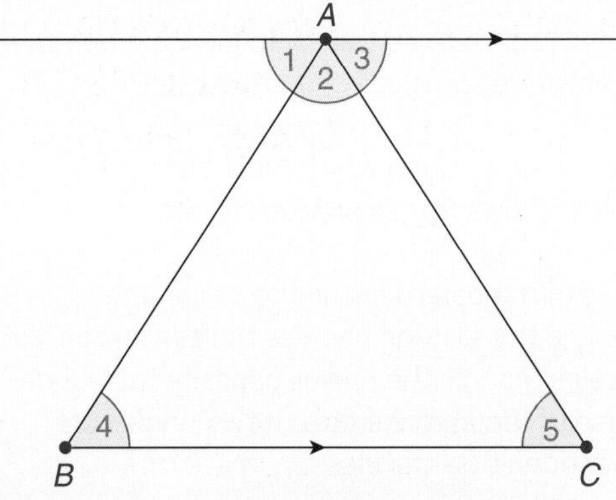

To prove: $|\angle 2| + |\angle 4| + |\angle 5| = 180°$

Proof:

$|\angle 1| + |\angle 2| + |\angle 3| = 180°$ **Straight line**

$|\angle 1| = |\angle 4|$ **Alternate angles**

$|\angle 3| = |\angle 5|$ **Alternate angles**

Substitute $|\angle 4|$ for $|\angle 1|$ and $|\angle 5|$ for $|\angle 3|$.

$\therefore |\angle 2| + |\angle 4| + |\angle 5| = 180°$

THEOREM 6: EACH EXTERIOR ANGLE OF A TRIANGLE IS EQUAL TO THE SUM OF THE TWO INTERIOR OPPOSITE ANGLES

Given: Triangle *ABC* with angles marked 1, 2 and 3

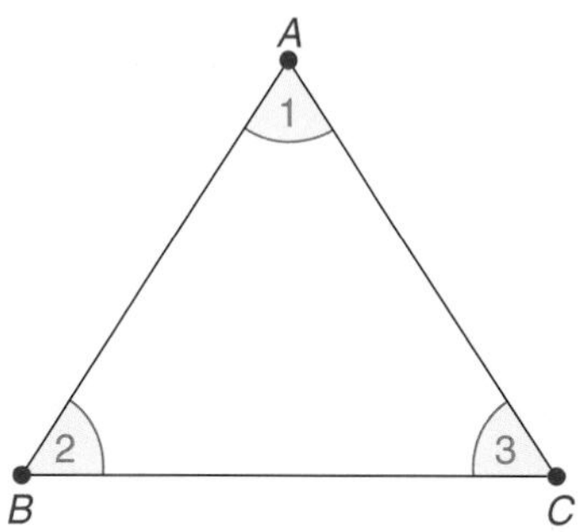

Construction: Extend [*BC*] to point *D* as shown and mark in angle 4.

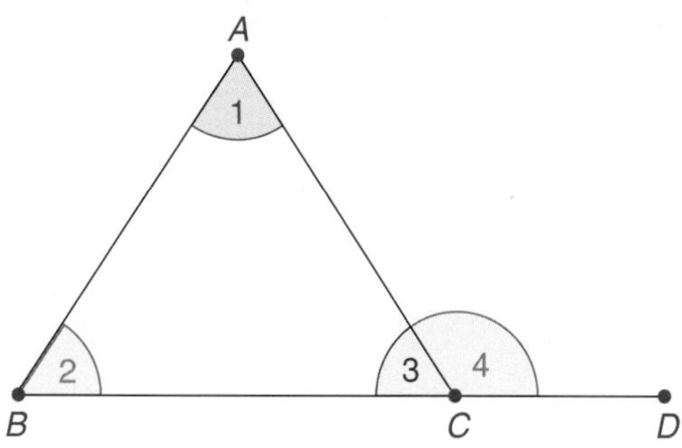

To prove: $|\angle 1| + |\angle 2| = |\angle 4|$

Proof:

$\lvert\angle 1\rvert + \lvert\angle 2\rvert + \lvert\angle 3\rvert = 180°$	**By theorem 4**
$\lvert\angle 3\rvert + \lvert\angle 4\rvert = 180°$	**Straight line**
$\lvert\angle 1\rvert + \lvert\angle 2\rvert + \lvert\angle 3\rvert - \lvert\angle 3\rvert = \lvert\angle 4\rvert + \lvert\angle 3\rvert - \lvert\angle 3\rvert$	**Subtract $\lvert\angle 3\rvert$ from both sides**
$\therefore \lvert\angle 1\rvert + \lvert\angle 2\rvert = \lvert\angle 4\rvert$	

THEOREM 9: IN A PARALLELOGRAM, OPPOSITE SIDES ARE EQUAL AND OPPOSITE ANGLES ARE EQUAL (AND ITS CONVERSE)

Given: Parallelogram *ABCD*

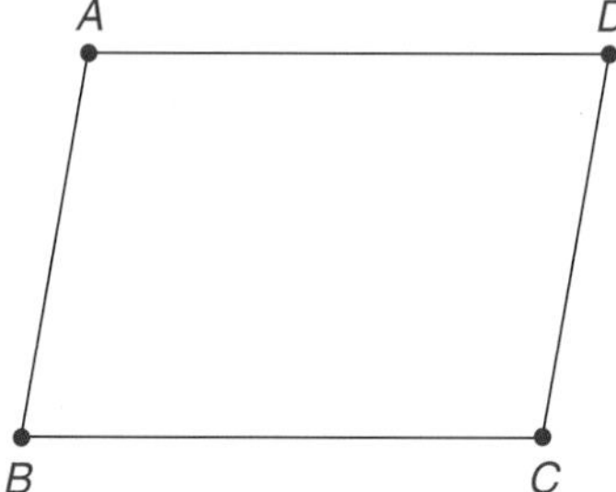

Construction: Draw diagonal [*DB*] and mark in angles 1, 2, 3 and 4.

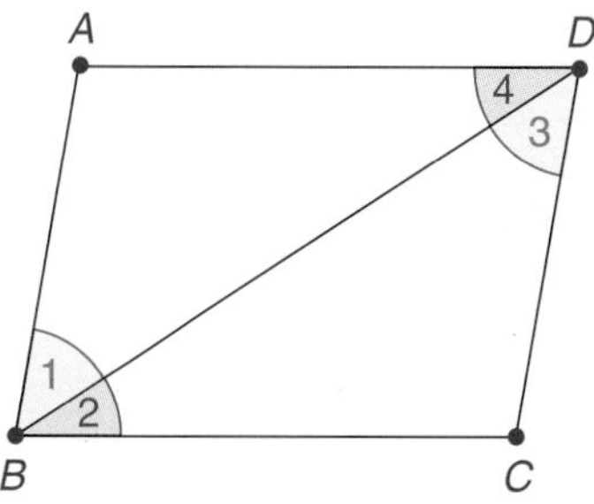

To prove: $|AB| = |DC|$, $|AD| = |BC|$, $|\angle ABC| = |\angle ADC|$ and $|\angle BAD| = |\angle BCD|$

Proof:

Consider the two triangles ΔABD and ΔBCD.

$\lvert\angle 1\rvert = \lvert\angle 3\rvert$	**Alternate angles (A)**
$\lvert DB\rvert = \lvert DB\rvert$	**Common side (S)**
$\lvert\angle 2\rvert = \lvert\angle 4\rvert$	**Alternate angles (A)**
$\therefore \Delta ABD \equiv \Delta BCD$	**By Angle Side Angle (ASA)**

$\therefore |AB| = |CD|$, $|AD| = |BC|$ and $|\angle ABC| = |\angle ADC|$, $|\angle BAD| = |\angle BCD|$

Converse

The converse of this theorem is also true: If the opposite angles and opposite sides of a quadrilateral are equal, then it is a parallelogram.

Corollary 1

A diagonal divides a parallelogram into two congruent triangles.

THEOREM 14: IN A RIGHT-ANGLED TRIANGLE, THE SQUARE OF THE HYPOTENUSE IS THE SUM OF THE SQUARES OF THE OTHER TWO SIDES

Given: Triangle ABC with $|\angle ABC| = 90°$

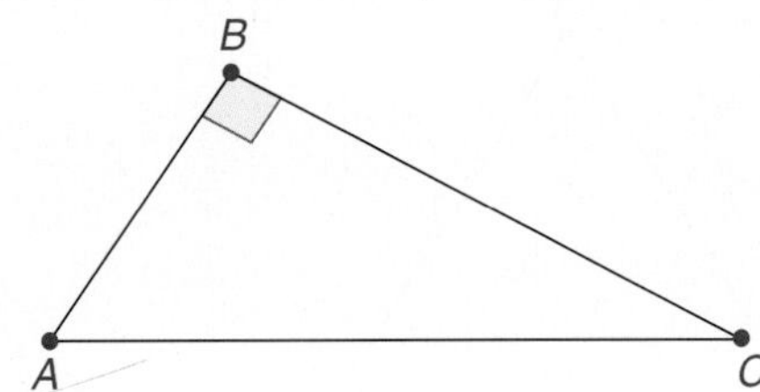

Construction: Draw $BD \perp AC$.

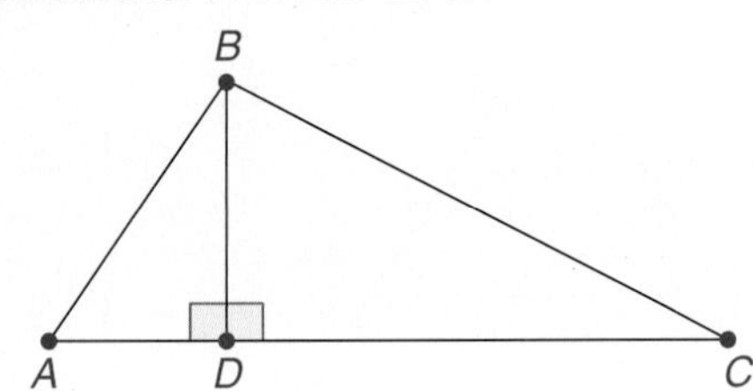

To prove: $|AC|^2 = |AB|^2 + |BC|^2$

Proof:

Step 1: Consider the two triangles ΔABD and ΔABC.

$|\angle ADB| = |\angle ABC|$ **Both 90°**

$|\angle BAD| = |\angle CAB|$ **Common to both triangles**

$\therefore \Delta ABD$ and ΔABC are similar.

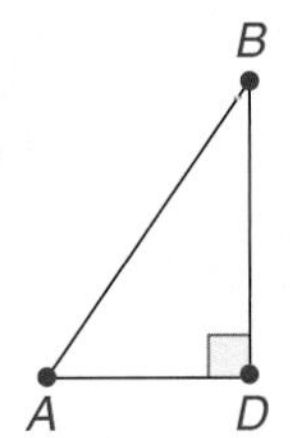

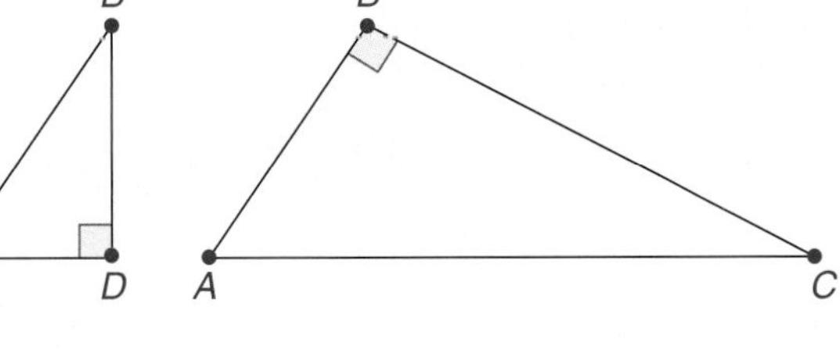

$\Rightarrow \dfrac{|AC|}{|AB|} = \dfrac{|AB|}{|AD|}$

$\Rightarrow |AB| \,.\, |AB| = |AC| \,.\, |AD|$

$\Rightarrow |AB|^2 = |AC| \,.\, |AD|$

Step 2: Consider the two triangles

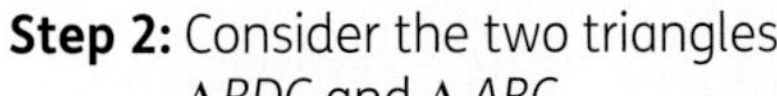

ΔBDC and $\Delta\, ABC$.

$|\angle CDB| = |\angle ABC|$ **Both 90°**

$|\angle BCD| = |\angle BCA|$ **Common to both triangles**

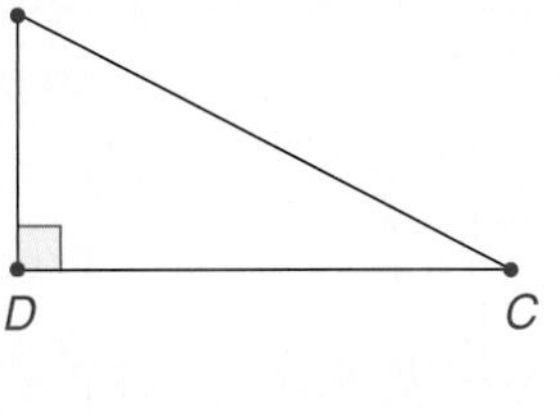

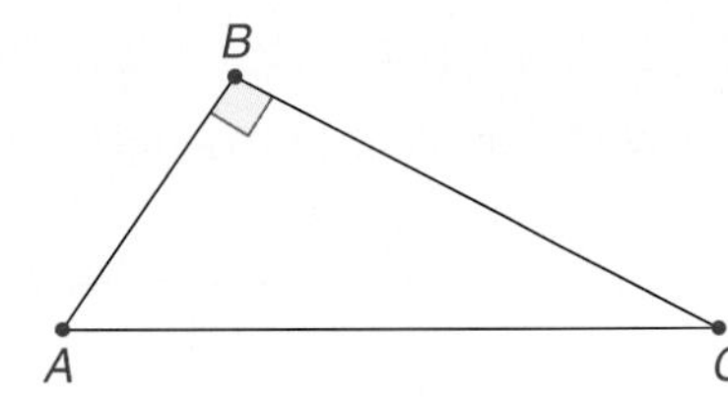

$\therefore \Delta BDC$ and ΔABC are similar.

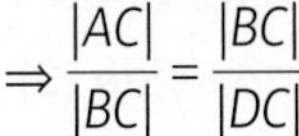

$\Rightarrow \dfrac{|AC|}{|BC|} = \dfrac{|BC|}{|DC|}$

$\Rightarrow |BC| \,.\, |BC| = |AC| \,.\, |DC|$

$\Rightarrow |BC|^2 = |AC| \,.\, |DC|$

Step 3: Combining these results:

$|AB|^2 + |BC|^2 = |AC| \,.\, |AD| + |AC| \,.\, |DC|$

$|AB|^2 + |BC|^2 = |AC|(|AD| + |DC|)$

Since:

$|AD| + |DC| = |AC|$

$|AB|^2 + |BC|^2 = |AC|\,|AC|$

$|AB|^2 + |BC|^2 = |AC|^2$

Converse

The converse of this theorem is also true: If the square on the longest side of the triangle is equal to the sum of the squares of the other two sides, then the triangle is a right-angled triangle.

THEOREM 19: THE ANGLE AT THE CENTRE OF A CIRCLE STANDING ON A GIVEN ARC IS TWICE THE ANGLE AT ANY POINT OF THE CIRCLE STANDING ON THE SAME ARC

Given: Circle with centre at point *A* where the points *B*, *C* and *D* are on the circumference

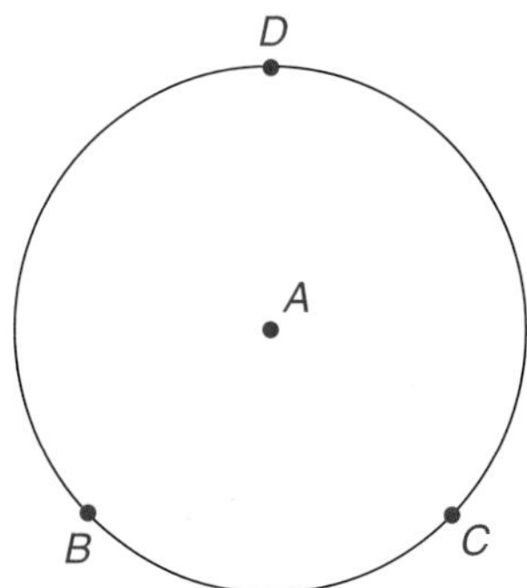

Construction: Join *D* to *B* and *D* to *C*. Join *D* to *A* and extend to point *E*. Label the angles.

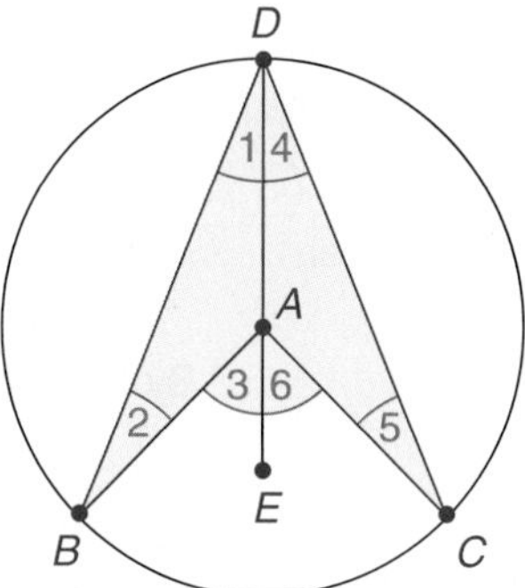

To prove: $|\angle BAC| = 2|\angle BDC|$

Proof:

Consider ΔABD:

$|AB| = |AD|$ **Both radii**

$\therefore \Delta ABD$ is isosceles.

$\therefore |\angle 1| = |\angle 2|$

Also:

$|\angle 1| + |\angle 2| = |\angle 3|$ **Exterior angle**

Hence, $|\angle 3| = 2|\angle 1|$

Similarly

$|AC| = |AD|$ **Both radii**

$\therefore \Delta ACD$ is isosceles.

$\therefore |\angle 4| = |\angle 5|$

Also:

$|\angle 4| + |\angle 5| = |\angle 6|$ **Exterior angle**

$\therefore |\angle 6| = 2|\angle 4|$

$\therefore |\angle 3| + |\angle 6| = 2|\angle 1| + 2|\angle 4|$

$\therefore |\angle 3| + |\angle 6| = 2(|\angle 1| + |\angle 4|)$

$\therefore |\angle BAC| = 2|\angle BDC|$

COROLLARY 2: ALL ANGLES AT POINTS OF A CIRCLE, STANDING ON THE SAME ARC, ARE EQUAL

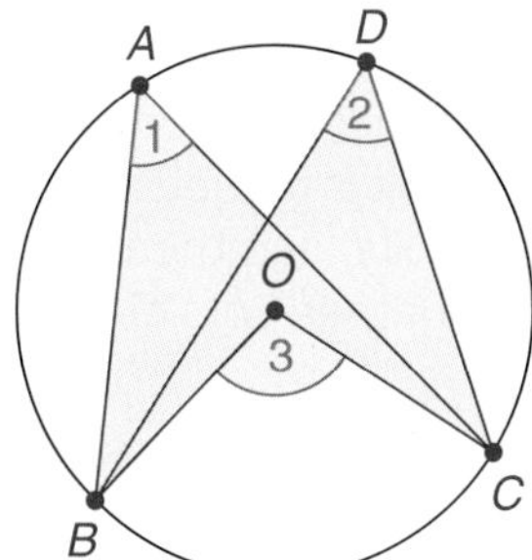

To prove: $|\angle 1| = |\angle 2|$

Proof:

$|\angle 3| = 2|\angle 1|$ **By theorem**

Also:

$|\angle 3| = 2|\angle 2|$ **By theorem**

$\therefore 2|\angle 1| = 2|\angle 2|$ **Since both equal $\angle 3$**

$\therefore |\angle 1| = |\angle 2|$ **Divide by 2**

Converse

If points standing at the circle are on the same arc, then the angles made at these points are equal in measure.

COROLLARY 3: EACH ANGLE IN A SEMICIRCLE IS A RIGHT ANGLE

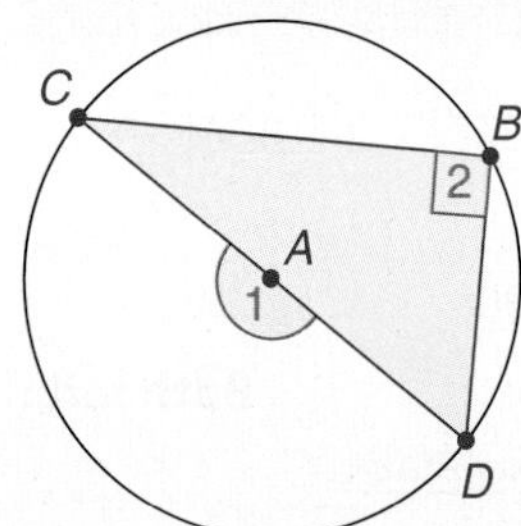

To prove: $|\angle 2| = 90°$

Proof:

$|\angle 1| = 180°$	**Straight line**
But	
$|\angle 1| = 2|\angle 2|$	**By theorem**
$\therefore 2|\angle 2| = 180°$	**Since both equal ∠1**
$\therefore |\angle 2| = 90°$	

Corollary 4

If the angle standing on a chord [*CD*] at some point of the circle is a right angle, then [*CD*] is a diameter.

COROLLARY 5: IF ABCD IS A CYCLIC QUADRILATERAL, THEN OPPOSITE ANGLES SUM TO 180°

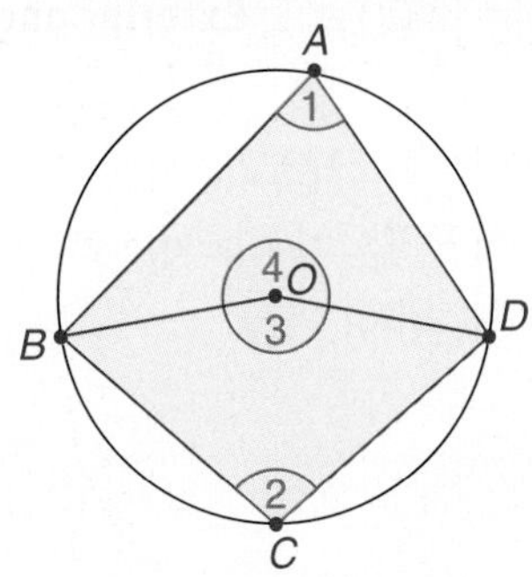

To prove: $|\angle 1| + |\angle 2| = 180°$

Proof:

$|\angle 3| = 2|\angle 1|$	**By theorem**
Also:	
$|\angle 4| = 2|\angle 2|$	**By theorem**
$|\angle 3| + |\angle 4| = 360°$	**Full rotation**
$\therefore 2|\angle 1| + 2|\angle 2| = 360°$	**Divide by 2**
$\therefore |\angle 1| + |\angle 2| = 180°$	

Section 29.4: Solving problems using proofs

Now we will look at how to apply the theorems to solve more complicated problems. In these kinds of problems, the diagram often consists of several shapes. So it is a good idea to examine each shape separately. Read the information in the question carefully, and then look for similar or congruent triangles or common sides. Piece the information together. Lots of practice gives you the best chance of doing well in the exam.

EXAMPLE 1

ABC is an equilateral triangle. *BCDE* is a square.

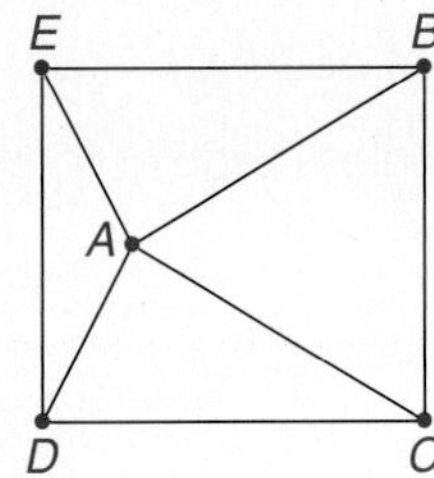

Prove that $|DA| = |EA|$.

Solution

To prove: $|\angle DCA| = |\angle EBA|$

We must first prove that ΔADC is congruent to ΔAEB.

$|AC| = |AB|$ since they are the sides of an equilateral triangle **(Side).**

$|\angle ACD| = |\angle ABE|$, since both equal to $90° - 60° = 30°$ **(Angle).**

$|DC| = |BE|$, since they are the sides of a square **(Side).**

Therefore, ΔADC is congruent to ΔAEB by **SAS.**

Hence, $|DA| = |EA|$.

EXAMPLE 2

The points A, B, C, D and E are on a circle with centre O. $|\angle AOE| = \frac{1}{3}|\angle DOE|$. Prove that $|\angle DBA| = 4|\angle ACE|$.

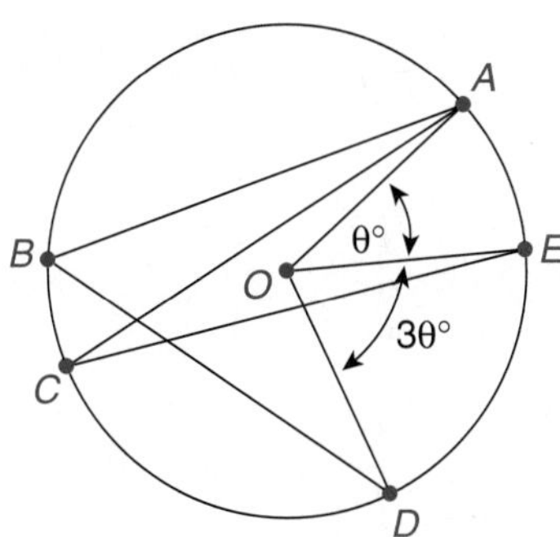

Solution

Since $|\angle AOE| = \theta°$, then $|\angle ACE| = \frac{1}{2}\theta°$.

(By theorem 19: the angle at the centre of the circle is twice the size of the angle at the circle standing on the same arc AE.)

$|\angle AOD| = |\angle DOE| + |\angle EOA|$

$|\angle AOD| = 3\theta° + \theta°$

$|\angle AOD| = 4\theta°$

So by theorem 19: $|\angle ABD| = 2\theta°$.

$2\theta : \frac{1}{2}\theta$ is in the ratio of 4:1

Therefore $|\angle ABD| = 4|\angle ACE|$.

CHAPTER 29 SELF-CHECK TEST

1. $ABCD$ is a cyclic quadrilateral.

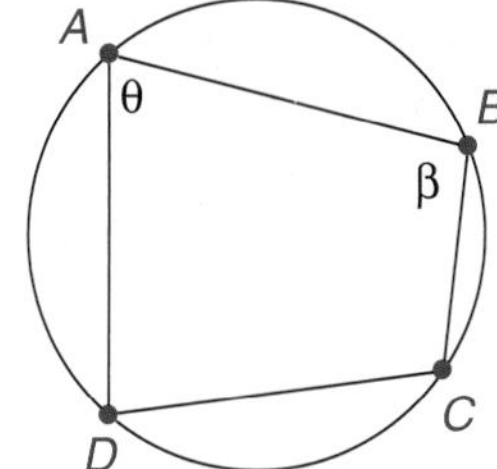

Given that $|\angle DAB| = \theta°$ and $|\angle ABC| = \beta°$, evaluate:

(a) $|\angle ADC|$ (b) $|\angle BCD|$

2. $[BD]$ is the diameter of the circle, C is the centre of the circle and $|BA| = |AD|$.

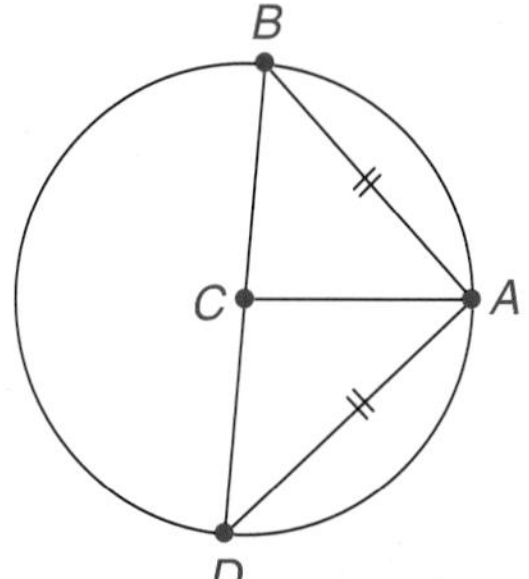

(a) Find $|\angle ADB|$, giving a reason for your answer.

(b) Find $|\angle DAC|$, giving a reason for your answer.

3. In the diagram, $[AB]$ and $[CD]$ are diameters of the circle with centre O.

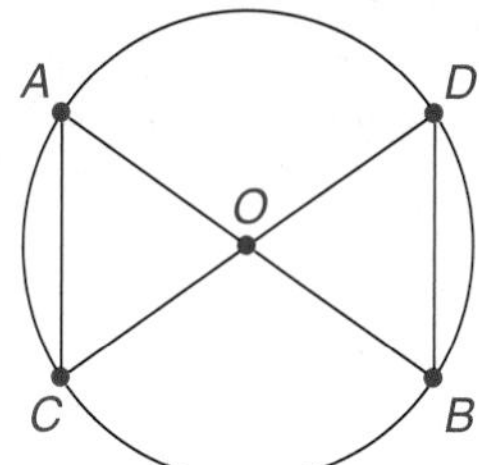

Prove that the triangles AOC and DBO are congruent.

4. O is the centre of the circle and t is a tangent to the circle. $|\angle XYW| = 40°$ and $|\angle ZYW| = 50°$.

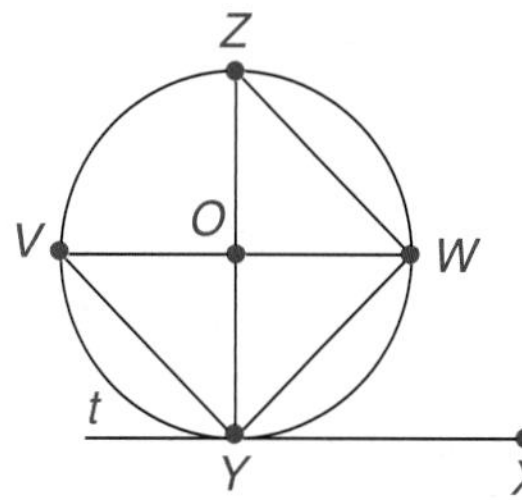

(a) Find $|\angle WVY|$.

(b) Prove $|ZW| = |VY|$.

5. $[AB]$ is the diameter of a circle with centre O. $|\angle OCB| = 50°$.

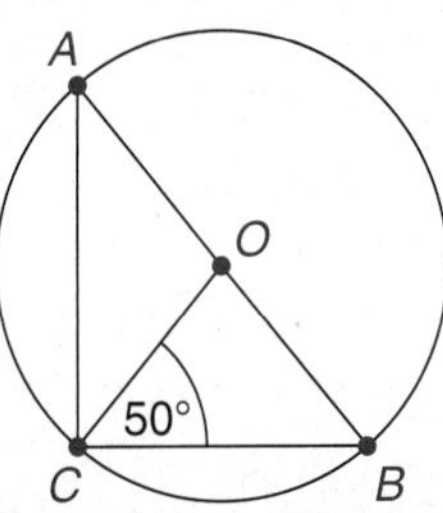

(a) Find $|\angle BOC|$. (b) Find $|\angle BAC|$.

In a different diagram, $[AB]$ and $[CD]$ are chords of the circle as shown and $|AB| = |CD|$. The chords $[AD]$ and $[BC]$ intersect at the point E.

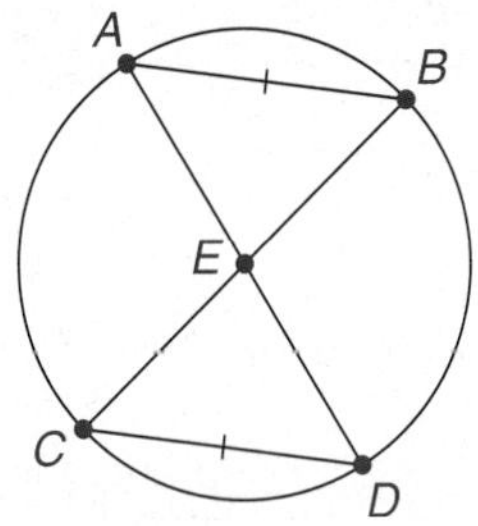

(c) State why $|\angle BAD| = |\angle BCD|$.

(d) Prove that the triangles BAE and DEC are congruent.

6. A, B, C and D are four points on a circle as shown. $[AD]$ bisects $|\angle BAC|$. P is the point of intersection of AD and BC.

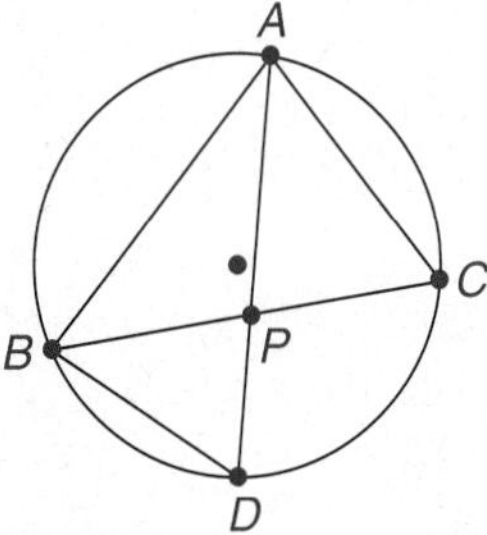

(a) Show that ΔADB and ΔAPC are similar.

(b) Show that $|AC|.|BD| = |AD|.|PC|$.

7. The triangle ABC has $|AB| = |AC|$. The line MN is parallel to BC and $|\angle NMB| = 115°$.

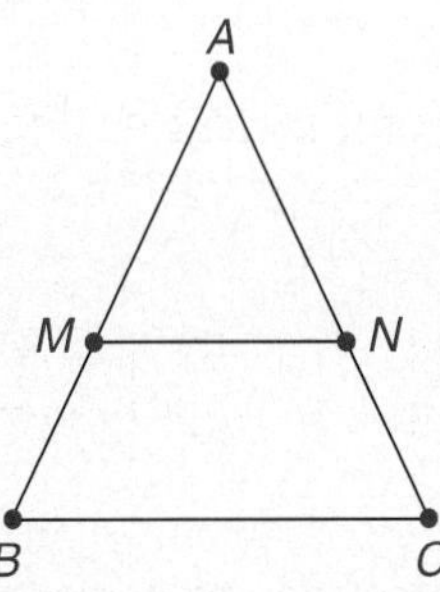

(a) Find $|\angle ABC|$, explaining your reasons.

(b) Find $|\angle BAC|$, explaining your reasons.

8. Prove that $x + y + z = 360°$.

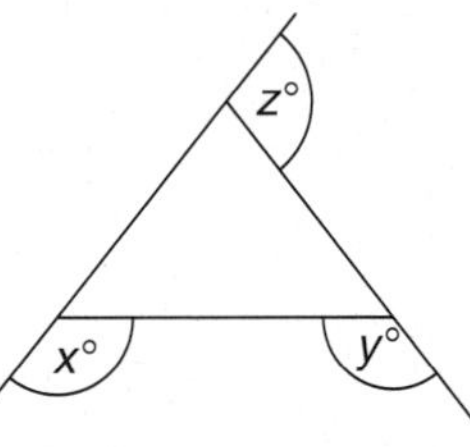

9. In the ΔABC, $|\angle BAC| = 90°$ and D is a point on $[AC]$.

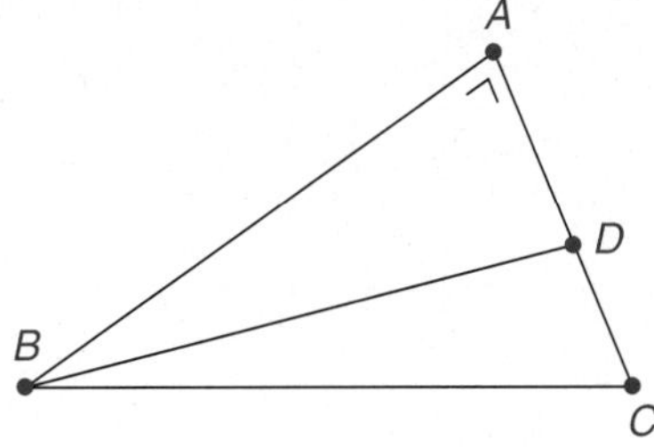

Prove that $|AC|^2 + |BD|^2 = |BC|^2 + |AD|^2$.

10. ABC is an isosceles triangle with $|AB| = |AC|$. $[BA]$ extends to the point D. AE is parallel to BC.

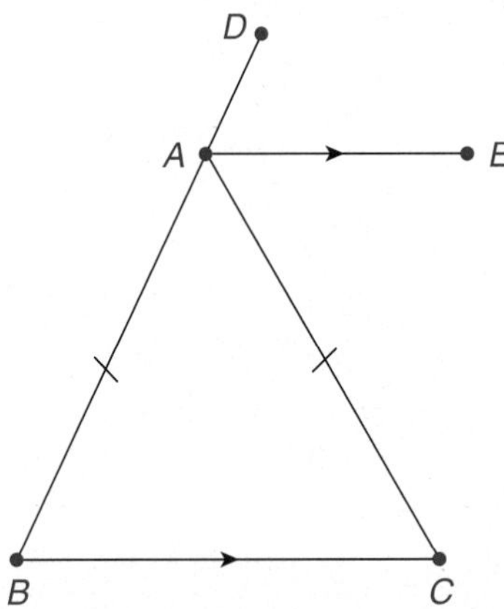

(a) Prove that $[AE]$ bisects $|\angle DAC|$.

(b) Would the previous result still apply if $|AB|$ and $|AC|$ were not equal? Give a reason for your answer.

11. The lines KD and KR are tangents to a circle at the points D and R, respectively. S is a point on the circle as shown.

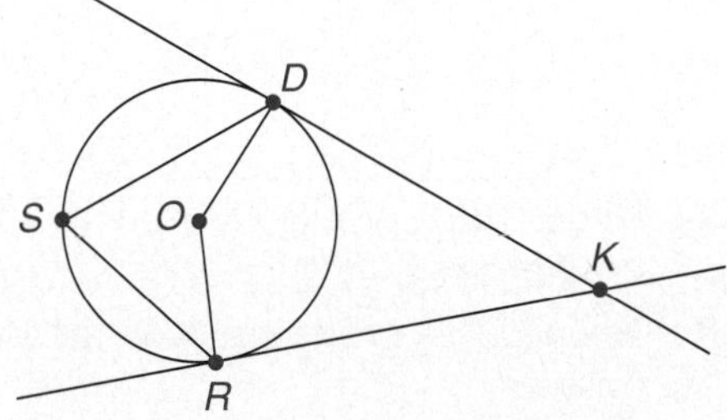

(a) Name two angles in the diagram equal in measure to $|\angle DSR|$.

(b) Find $|\angle RKD|$, given that $|\angle DSR| = 65°$.

(c) Is $|DK| = |RK|$? Give a reason for your answer.

12. *ABCD* is a square whose diagonals meet at the point *E*.

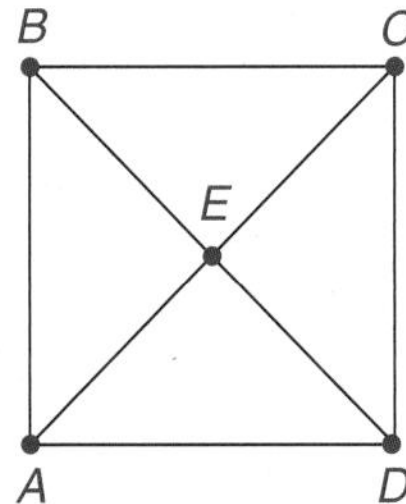

Prove that $|AD|^2 = 2|EC|^2 - |CD|^2$.

13. Study the following diagram:

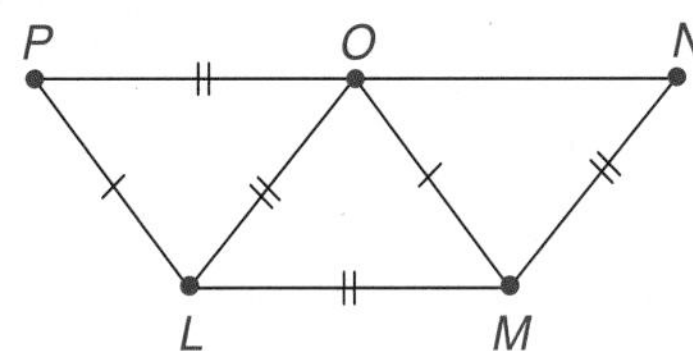

(a) What type of triangle is *MON*?

(b) Explain why $|\angle LPO| = |\angle LMO|$.

(c) Investigate whether ΔLPO is congruent with ΔMON.

(d) Show that *POML* is a rhombus, clearly stating your reasons.

14. Study the following diagram:

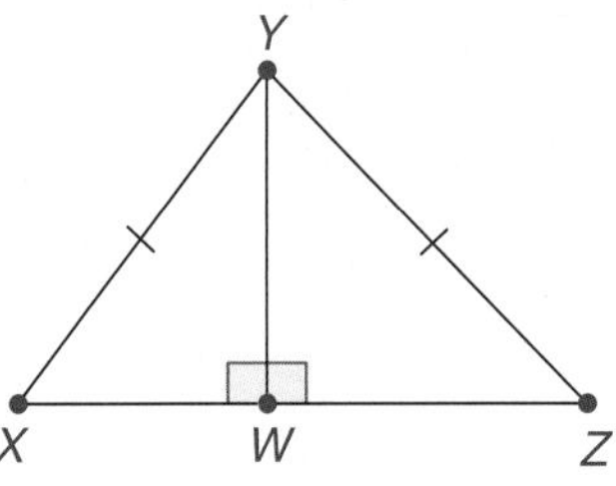

(a) What type of triangle is ΔXYZ?

(b) Investigate if ΔYWZ is congruent to ΔXYW?

(c) Explain in your own words what congruency means.

15. In the ΔABC, $|AB|^2 = |AD|^2 + |CD|^2$ and *BD* is perpendicular to *AC*.

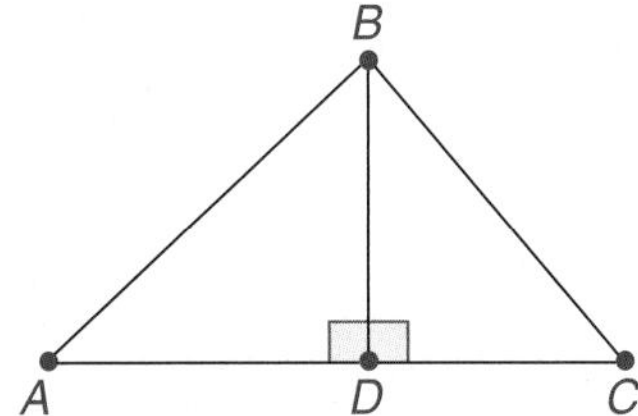

Prove that $|\angle BCA| = 45°$.

16. In the following diagram *ABCD* is a parallelogram.

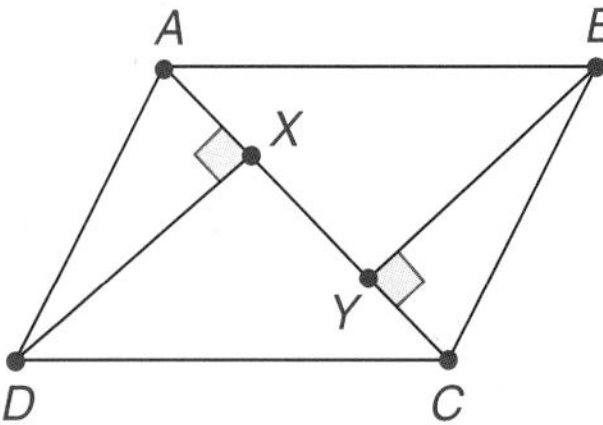

(a) Show that ΔDAC is congruent to ΔABC.

(b) Show that ΔDAX is congruent to ΔBYC.

17. Consider the following parallelogram *ABCD*:

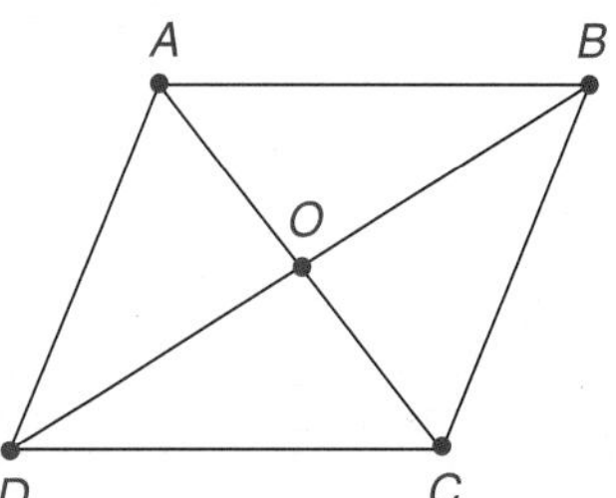

State, giving a reason, whether each of the following is true or false:

(a) $|AB| = |CD|$

(b) $|\angle CDO| = |\angle BAO|$

(c) $|DO| = |OC|$

(d) $|\angle COD| = |\angle AOB|$

(e) $|CO| = |BO|$

18. *YT* and *YK* are tangents to the circle at the points *Z* and *X*, respectively.

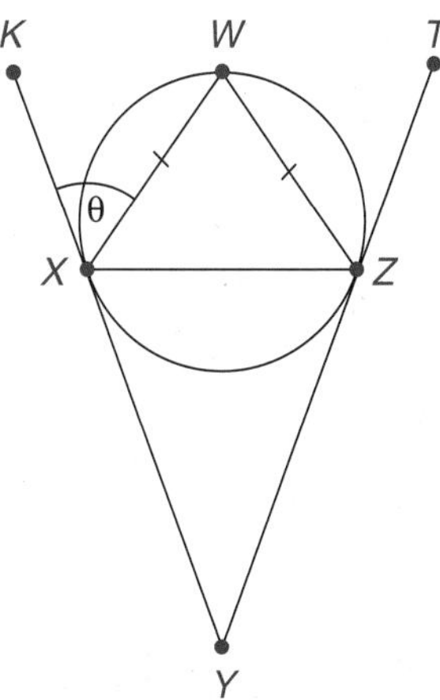

W is a point on the circle such that $|WX| = |WZ|$ and $|\angle WXK| = \theta$.

Find in terms of θ:

(a) $|\angle XZW|$

(b) $|\angle WXZ|$

(c) $|\angle ZWX|$

(d) $|\angle XYZ|$

19. The diagram shows two squares, $ABCD$ and $AODE$.

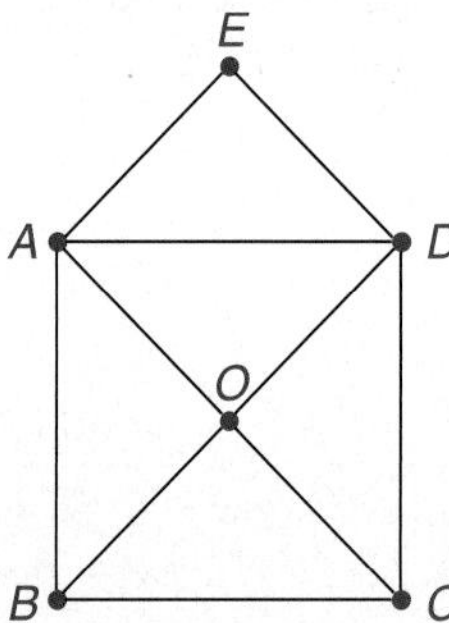

Prove that 2(Area of the square $AODE$) = (Area of the square $ABCD$).

20. The points A, B, C and D lie on a circle. $|AB| = |BC| = |AC|$ and $[BD]$ bisects $|\angle ABC|$.

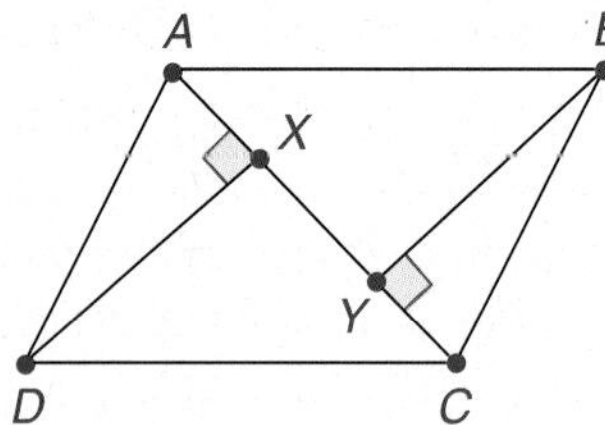

Find, giving a reason for your answer:

(a) $|\angle CAB|$

(b) $|\angle CDB|$

(c) $|\angle BCD|$

(d) Is $[BD]$ a diameter of the circle? Explain.

21. The points A, B and C lie on a circle. The line t passing through the point A is a tangent to the circle. $|AB| = |AC|$ and $|\angle CAB| = \theta°$.

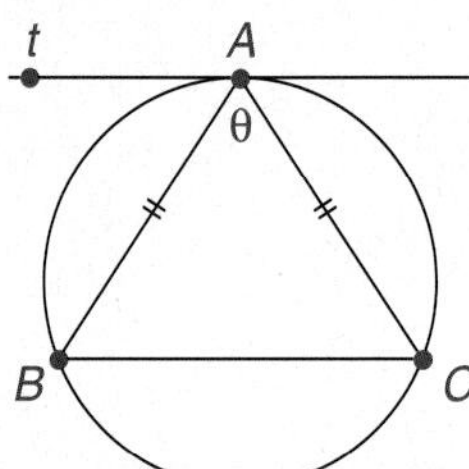

Find in terms of θ:

(a) $|\angle ABC|$ (b) $|\angle TAC|$

22. (a) In your own words, explain what a parallelogram is.

(b) In the quadrilateral below, $FE \parallel GH$ and $|FE| = |GH|$.

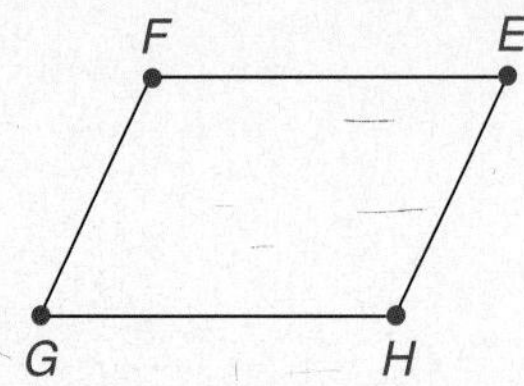

Prove that $FEHG$ is a parallelogram.

(c) Given a quadrilateral $ABCD$, describe two other ways to determine whether it is a parallelogram, other than the method in part (b) above.

23. Find the value of $X + Y + Z + W$ in this diagram.

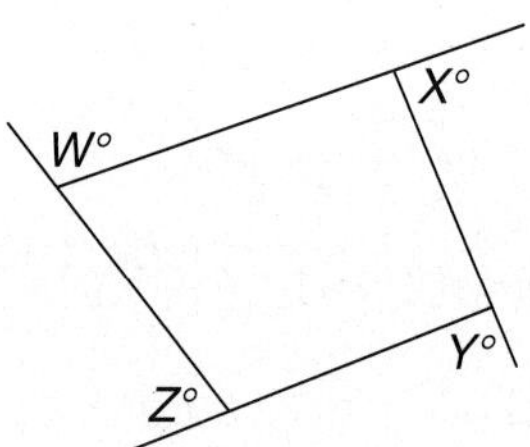

24. (a) What is meant by the word 'axiom'? Explain why axioms are needed to prove theorems.

(b) State a theorem which outlines a property of an isosceles triangle.

(c) State the converse of the theorem in part (b).

Triangle ABC is an isosceles triangle with $|AB| = |AC|$. DE is parallel to AB.

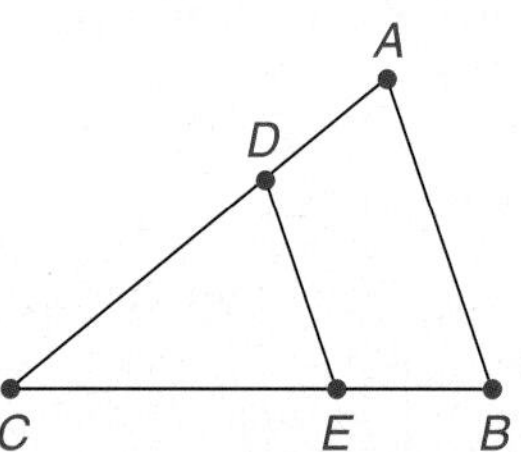

(d) Prove that DEC is also isosceles.

25. A, B, C and D are points on a circle. $|\angle ACB| = |\angle DCA|$. Also $|\angle CAB| = |\angle DAC|$.

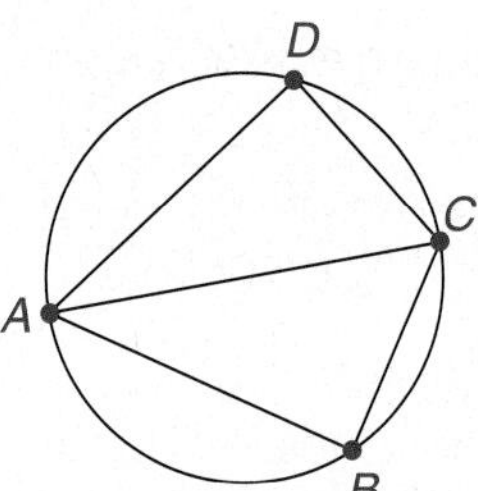

Prove that the diameter of the circle is AC.

26. X, Y and Z are points on a circle with centre O.

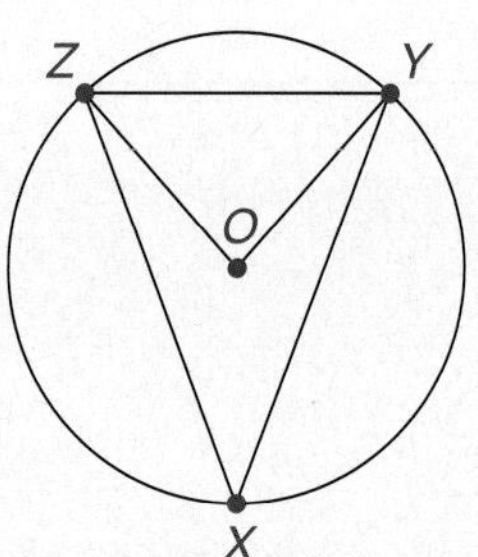

The points X, Y and Z also form an equilateral triangle. Prove that $|\angle OYZ| = 30°$.

27. The points A, B, C and D are on a circle whose centre is O.

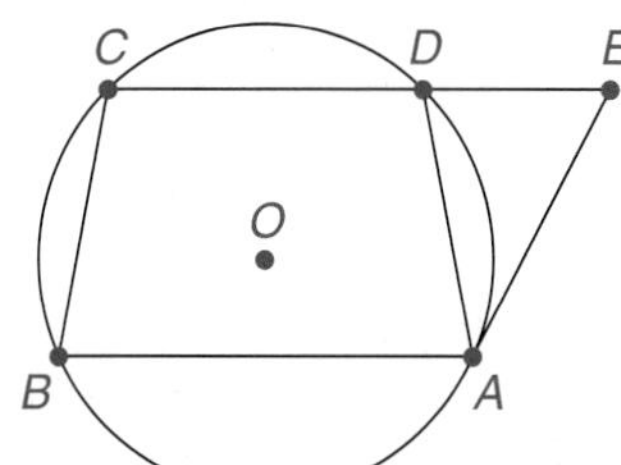

The points $ABCE$ form a parallelogram. Prove that ΔADE is an isosceles triangle.

28. A, B, D and E are points on the circles C1 and C2 with centres X and Y.

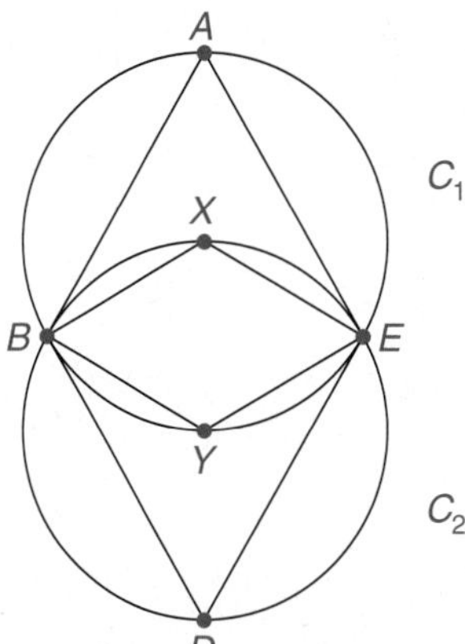

(a) Prove that $XEYB$ is a parallelogram.

(b) Prove that $|\angle BAE| = |\angle BDE|$.

29. O is a point within the triangle ABC.

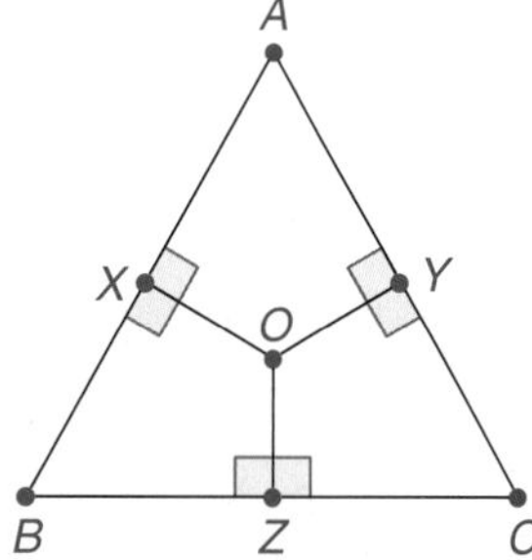

OX is perpendicular to AB. OY is perpendicular to AC and OZ is perpendicular to BC.

Show that $|BZ|^2 + |CY|^2 + |AX|^2 = |XB|^2 + |CZ|^2 + |AY|^2$.

30. Explain, giving your reasons, whether each of the following statements are always true, sometimes true or never true.

(a) Adjacent angles in a parallelogram add to 180°.

(b) If a quadrilateral is divided into two congruent triangles by a diagonal, then it is a parallelogram.

(c) A diagonal divides a parallelogram into two congruent triangles.

(d) Two triangles are congruent if one has two sides and an angle that are equal to two sides and an angle of the other.

(e) If $WXYZ$ is a cyclic quadrilateral, then opposite angles sum to 180°.

(f) A parallelogram has a centre of symmetry.

31. Which one of the director's chairs is the most stable? Explain your answer.

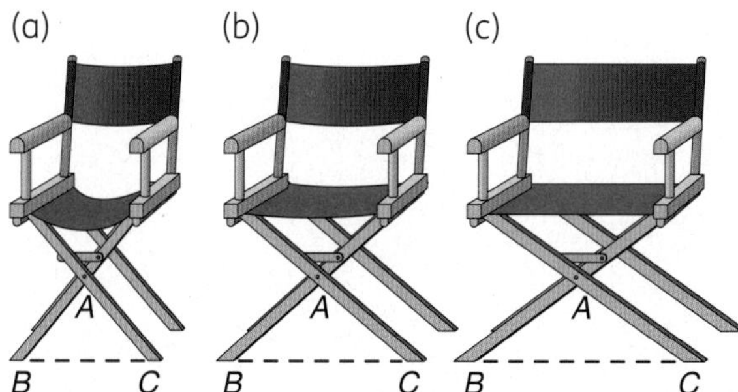

CHAPTER 29 KNOWLEDGE CHECKLIST

After completing this chapter, I now:

- **Understand the terms theorem, proof, axiom, converse, corollary and implies**
- **Am able to prove the required theorems**
- **Understand the converse of the required theorems and corollaries**
- **Am able to solve problems using these theorems**

Challenge

Four people must cross a rickety old bridge at night. They need a torch to get across but only have one torch which has 17 minutes of battery life left. The bridge will support only two people at any one time. Each group of two must walk at the same pace, so at the pace of the slowest person. Jack can get across in 1 minute, Jane in 2 minutes, Ciara in 5 minutes and Bob in 10 minutes. How can they get across before the torch runs out?

Answers

Chapter 1

Exercise 1.1

1. (a) $\mathbb{N}, \mathbb{Z}, \mathbb{R}$ (b) $\mathbb{Z}, \mathbb{R}$ (c) $\mathbb{R}$ (d) $\mathbb{R}$ (e) $\mathbb{R}$ (f) $\mathbb{N}, \mathbb{Z}, \mathbb{R}$ (g) $\mathbb{R}$ **2.** (a) $A = \{0, 1, 2, 3, 4, 5, 6, 7, 8, 9, 10\}$ $B = \{1, 4, 9, 16, 25, 36, 49, 64, 81, 100\}$ **3.** (a) $G = \{-3, -2, -1, 0, 1, 2, 3, 4, 5, 6\}$ (b) $H = \{1, 2, 3, 4, 5, 6\}$ (c) $G \cap H = \{1, 2, 3, 4, 5, 6\}$ (d) $G \cup H = \{-3, -2, -1, 0, 1, 2, 3, 4, 5, 6\}$ (c) $G' = \{\ \}$ or ϕ (f) $H' = \{-3, -2, -1, 0\}$ **4.** (a) $D = \{1, 2, 4, 8\}$ (b) $M = \{1, 2, 3, 4, 6, 12\}$ (d) $D \cap M = \{1, 2, 4\}$ (e) $D \cup M = \{1, 2, 3, 4, 6, 8, 12\}$ (f) HCF = 4

Exercise 1.2

1. $\{\mathbb{R}\}$ **2.** $\{\mathbb{R}\}$ **3.** $\{\mathbb{R}\}$ **4.** $\{\mathbb{R}\backslash\mathbb{Q}\}$ **5.** $\{\mathbb{R}\}$ **6.** $\{\mathbb{R}\backslash\mathbb{Q}\}$ **7.** $\{\mathbb{R}\backslash\mathbb{Q}\}$ **8.** $\{\mathbb{R}\backslash\mathbb{Q}\}$ **9.** $\{\mathbb{R}\}$ **10.** $\{\mathbb{R}\backslash\mathbb{Q}\}$ **11.** $\{\mathbb{R}\backslash\mathbb{Q}\}$ **12.** $\{\mathbb{R}\}$ **13.** $\{\mathbb{R}\backslash\mathbb{Q}\}$ **14.** $\{\mathbb{R}\backslash\mathbb{Q}\}$ **15.** $\{\mathbb{R}\}$ **16.** $\{\mathbb{R}\}$ **17.** $\{\mathbb{R}\backslash\mathbb{Q}\}$ **18.** $\{\mathbb{R}\}$ **19.** (a) $0.\dot{6}$ (b) $0.\dot{5}7142\dot{8}$ (c) $0.1\dot{6}$ (d) $0.\dot{8}\dot{1}$ (e) $0.71428\dot{5}$ (f) $0.\dot{6}1538\dot{4}$ (g) $0.8\dot{3}$ (h) $0.\dot{0}\dot{9}$ (i) $0.\dot{8}0952\dot{3}$ (j) $0.\dot{3}5\dot{1}$ **20.** (a) True (b) False (c) True (d) False (e) True (f) True (g) False (h) True (i) False (j) False (k) True (l) True **22.** (a) and (d) **23.** (b) and (g)

Exercise 1.3

1. 4^8 **2.** 3^{13} **3.** 5^{10} **4.** 8^{11} **5.** 9^6 **6.** 10^9 **7.** 2^{22} **8.** 6^{20} **9.** 5^{21} **10.** 3^{18} **11.** a^5 **12.** m^{10} **13.** p^{16} **14.** c^{14} **15.** t^{10} **16.** p^6

Exercise 1.4

1. 5^4 **2.** 2 **3.** 3^3 **4.** 7^2 **5.** 6^3 **6.** 8 **7.** 5^3 **8.** 4^3 **9.** 7^5 **10.** 9^3 **11.** 3^5 **12.** 2^2 **13.** 4^3 **14.** 2 **15.** 3^3 **16.** 5^4 **17.** 7^3 **18.** 9 **19.** a **20.** w^2 **21.** v^{10} **22.** y^7 **23.** q^5 **24.** 1

Exercise 1.5

1. 3^{10} **2.** 2^{20} **3.** 4^8 **4.** 7^6 **5.** 2^{25} **6.** 9^6 **7.** 6^{24} **8.** 4^{10} **9.** 3^9 **10.** 8^{10} **11.** a^{15} **12.** h^{12} **13.** n^{16} **14.** x^{16} **15.** y^{72} **16.** $a^2 \times b^2$ **17.** $x^4 \times y^4$ **18.** $a^3 \times c^3$ **19.** $z^4 \times w^4$ **20.** $u^7 \times v^7$ **21.** $8b^3c^3$ **22.** $32a^{10}x^5$ **23.** $625x^4y^8$ **24.** $144a^6b^2$ **25.** $16z^8w^{12}$

Exercise 1.6

1. 9 **2.** 5 **3.** 25 **4.** 30 **5.** 90 **6.** 20 **7.** 13 **8.** 15 **9.** 17 **10.** 33

Exercise 1.7

1. 10 **2.** 6 **3.** 8 **4.** 5 **5.** 6 **6.** 8 **7.** 6 **8.** 10 **9.** 7 **10.** 2 **11.** 11 **12.** 2·5 **13.** 8 **14.** 1·3 **15.** 5 **16.** $\frac{1}{2}$ **17.** 9 **18.** 12 **19.** 1 **20.** 13

Exercise 1.8

1. 8 **2.** 125 **3.** 81 **4.** 16 **5.** 81 **6.** 27 **7.** 25 **8.** 100 **9.** 1,000 **10.** 243 **11.** 16 **12.** 8 **13.** 32 **14.** 81 **15.** $\frac{27}{8}$ **16.** 8 **17.** 9,765,625 **18.** 10,000 **19.** 125 **20.** 64 **21.** $\frac{4}{9}$ **22.** $\frac{5}{9}$ **23.** $\frac{9}{16}$ **24.** $\frac{4}{25}$ **25.** $\frac{2}{3}$

Exercise 1.9

1. $\frac{1}{4}$ **2.** $\frac{1}{27}$ **3.** $\frac{1}{49}$ **4.** $\frac{1}{729}$ **5.** $\frac{1}{216}$ **6.** 16 **7.** 125 **8.** 32 **9.** 10,000 **10.** 36 **11.** 2^{-6} or 4^{-3} **12.** 10^{-2} **13.** 6^{-2} **14.** 3^{-4} **15.** 30^{-2} **16.** 3^{-2} **17.** 2^{-2} **18.** 50^{-2} **19.** 5^{-3} **20.** 2^{-5}

Exercise 1.10

1. 36 **2.** 144 **3.** 225 **4.** 144 **5.** 81 **6.** 64 **7.** 900 **8.** $\frac{16}{81}$ **9.** $\frac{27}{125}$ **10.** $\frac{16}{49}$ **11.** $\frac{125}{216}$

Exercise 1.11

1. 2^7 **2.** 4^5 **3.** 5^2 **4.** 3^4 **5.** 7^5 **6.** $g^{7\frac{1}{6}}$ **7.** $\sqrt{x}$ **8.** $\frac{1}{c^{\frac{59}{60}}}$ **9.** $\sqrt{p^8}$ **10.** (a) 3^2 (b) 3^4 (c) 3^5 (d) 3^7 (e) 3^4 **11.** (a) 5^4 (b) 5^5 (c) 5^6 (d) 5^7 (e) $\frac{1}{5}$ **12.** 25 **13.** $\frac{1}{27}$ **14.** $\frac{1}{125}$ **15.** 1

Exercise 1.12

1. $5\sqrt{2}$ **2.** $5\sqrt{11}$ **3.** $7\sqrt{3}$ **4.** $6\sqrt{7}$ **5.** $10\sqrt{2}$ **6.** $13\sqrt{5}$ **7.** $6\sqrt{2}$ **8.** $20\sqrt{7}$ **9.** $6\sqrt{13}$ **10.** $15\sqrt{21}$ **11.** $25 + 6\sqrt{2}$ **12.** $4 + 18\sqrt{3}$ **13.** $-3 + 4\sqrt{11}$ **14.** 0 **15.** $11 + 3\sqrt{7}$ **16.** $10 + 3\sqrt{2}$ **17.** $4 + 5\sqrt{3}$ **18.** $4(1 + \sqrt{7})$ **19.** $2(4\sqrt{3} + \sqrt{2} + 6)$ **20.** $7\sqrt{5} + 10\sqrt{2}$ **21.** $4\sqrt{2}$ **22.** $8\sqrt{2}$ **23.** $14\sqrt{2}$ **24.** $6\sqrt{3}$ **25.** $5\sqrt{2}$ **26.** $\sqrt{3}$ **27.** $\sqrt{11}(8 - \sqrt{3})$ **28.** $3\sqrt{2}$ **29.** $k = 4$ **30.** $k = 3$ **31.** $9\sqrt{3} - 12\sqrt{7}$ **32.** $a = 2, b = -2$ **33.** $-2\sqrt{2} + 5\sqrt{5}$

Execise 1.13

1. $11 + 6\sqrt{3}$ **2.** $13 + 2\sqrt{2}$ **3.** $17 - 2\sqrt{7}$ **4.** $7(1 - \sqrt{3})$ **5.** $20 + 3\sqrt{11}$ **6.** $10(3 + \sqrt{5})$ **7.** $67 + 3\sqrt{3}$ **8.** $11 + 6\sqrt{5}$ **9.** $2(7 - 6\sqrt{13})$ **10.** $11 - 9\sqrt{7}$ **11.** 12 **12.** −1 **13.** 1 **14.** 11 **15.** −6 **16.** $1 + 2\sqrt{3}$ **17.** $3 + 6\sqrt{5}$ **18.** $4 + 2\sqrt{5}$ **19.** $9 + 5\sqrt{7}$ **20.** 6 **21.** $215 + 14\sqrt{10}$ **22.** 8 **23.** 2 **24.** $2(26 - 7\sqrt{3})$ **25.** $69 + 16\sqrt{5}$ **26.** $223 + 40\sqrt{21}$ **27.** $77 - 24\sqrt{10}$ **28.** 28 **29.** 20 **30.** $p = 28$ **31.** 2 **32.** $\frac{3}{2}$ **33.** $\frac{3}{2}$ **34.** $\frac{2}{3}$ **35.** $\frac{1}{2}$ **36.** $\frac{4\sqrt{2}}{3}$ **37.** $\frac{12}{5}$ **38.** $\frac{2}{3}$ **39.** $k = \frac{11}{2}$ or $5\frac{1}{2}$ **40.** $m = \frac{74}{25}$ or $2\frac{24}{25}$

Execise 1.14

1. 4.5×10^6 **2.** 2.13×10^6 **3.** 6.78×10^6 **4.** 6.87×10^2 **5.** 1.42×10^3 **6.** 3.7×10^7 **7.** 5.41×10^7 **8.** 2.1×10^4 **9.** 3.1×10^3 **10.** 4.5×10^2 **11.** 1.09×10^6 **12.** 4.09×10^5 **13.** 3.4×10^{-5} **14.** 9.8×10^{-3} **15.** 5.6×10^{-3} **16.** 1.5×10^{-5} **17.** 7.8×10^{-3} **18.** 6.7×10^{-7} **19.** 5.7×10^{-5} **20.** 9.6×10^{-3} **21.** 1.817×10^7 **22.** 5.928×10^4 **23.** 6×10^5 **24.** 4.99×10^3 **25.** 6.345×10^7 **26.** 5.96×10^4 **27.** 4.461×10^5 **28.** 3.54×10^4 **29.** 5.24×10^4 **30.** 2.448×10^6 **31.** 4.275×10^6 **32.** 9×10^{-3} **33.** 2.94×10^{-4} **34.** 2.4×10^4 **35.** 5.4×10^2 **36.** 6.4009×10^6 **37.** 3.1684×10^{-4} **38.** 1.5625×10^{-6} **39.** 1.7×10^{-2} **40.** 8×10^{12} **41.** 8.5×10^3 **42.** 4×10^4 **43.** 1.9875×10^1 **44.** 1×10^3 **45.** 3.24×10^3 **46.** 2.99792458×10^8 **47.** 9.10938×10^{-31} **48.** 7.3×10^{22} **49.** 3.2×10^{-19} **50.** 8.2×10^{-5} m **51.** $3.\dot{3} \times 10^3$ **52.** 5.3×10^{-9} **53.** 1×10^{-8}

Self-check Test

1. 2^{10} **2.** 3^{10} **3.** 7^{10} **4.** 5^7 **5.** 9^7 **6.** 6^8 **7.** 8^7 **8.** a^9 **9.** x^{15} **10.** v^{13} **11.** 3^2 **12.** 4^2 **13.** 5^3 **14.** 9^3 **15.** 2^2 **16.** a^2 **17.** x **18.** w^4 **19.** t^2 **20.** 2^3 **21.** 3^7 **22.** 5^3 **23.** a^8 **24.** 1 **25.** w^2 **26.** $x = \frac{-15}{4}$ **27.** (a) $\frac{1}{8}$ (b) $\frac{1}{9}$ (c) $\frac{1}{64}$ (d) $\frac{1}{125}$ (e) $\frac{1}{243}$ (f) $\frac{1}{16}$ (g) $\frac{1}{b^5}$ (h) $\frac{1}{a^2}$ (i) $\frac{1}{t^3}$ (j) $\frac{1}{v^9}$ (k) $\frac{1}{s}$ (l) $\frac{1}{h^6}$ **28.** (a) 125 (b) 16 (c) 25 (d) 1,000 (e) 243 (f) 216 (g) 9 (h) 36 (i) 25 (j) 15 **29.** (a) $\frac{1}{216}$ (b) $\frac{1}{81}$ (c) 16 (d) 25 (e) $\frac{-1}{243}$ (f) −32 (g) $\frac{1}{51}$ (h) 1 (i) $\frac{4}{15}$ (j) 1 **30.** (a) $3\sqrt{7} + 11$ (b) $3\sqrt{2} + 10$ (c) $5\sqrt{3} + 4$ (d) $7\sqrt{2}$ (e) $9\sqrt{5}$ (f) $6\sqrt{2} - 2\sqrt{3}$ (g) $4\sqrt{5}$ **31.** $4 = k$ **32.** $4\sqrt{2} + 6\sqrt{3}$ where $a = 4$ and $b = 6$ **33.** $1\sqrt{5} + 4\sqrt{7}$ **34.** $10\sqrt{10} - 34$ **35.** $\frac{195}{14}$ **36.** $2\sqrt{3} - 21$ **37.** $-\sqrt{6} - 9$ **38.** (a) 125 (b) 16 **39.** Answer (c) **40.** 356,000,000,000 **41.** 0.00002345 **42.** 4.3×10^9 **43.** 3.51×10^6 **44.** 2.05×10^7 **45.** 3.64×10^{14} **46.** Width = 2.56×10^{-6} m Length = 1.4×10^{-7} m Height = 2.75×10^{-4} m **47.** (b) Option B **49.** (b) Rectangle C

Chapter 2

Exercise 2.1

1. $n - 3$ **2.** $2x$ **3.** $3t$ **4.** €$\frac{1}{2}r$ **5.** $2x - 3$ **6.** $b - 6$
7. $(2x + 5)°$ **8.** $\frac{1}{3}(2z + 5)$ **9.** $3y - 10$ **10.** $(10x - 16)$°C
11. $5n + 4$ **12.** $7b - 3$ **13.** $3w - 4$ **14.** $16r$ **15.** $5q + 5$
16. $11 - 11k$ **17.** $4t - 4$ **18.** 4 **19.** $7x - y$ **20.** $4r - 4w + 8$
21. $3x + 7y + 10$ **22.** $9a + 10b$ **23.** $4t - 2s - 3$
24. $-x^2 + 9x + 18$ **25.** 7 **26.** $-2x^2 + 9x + 3$
27. $10a^2b - ab + 9$ **28.** $2x^2 + 4$ **29.** $5xyz - 7$
30. $8t^3m + t^2s + 5ts - 3$ **31.** $5xyz - 16mp$
32. $3x^2 - 6cdx - 3dcy$ **33.** $4cdm + 2 + 6a^3b - 3a^2b$
34. $10 - 4x^2wz + 2px$ **35.** $7x + 14y + 1$ **36.** $9w^2 - 2w + 13$
37. $x^2 - 2x - 23$ **38.** $11x^2 + x - 13$ **39.** $40v^2 - 16v + 37$
40. $23m^2 + 46m - 42$ **41.** 15 **42.** −75 **43.** −184 **44.** −10
45. $9\frac{7}{12}$ **46.** $12\frac{3}{20}$ **47.** −3 **48.** 127 **49.** −52 **50.** −2
51. −12 **52.** $10\frac{3}{4}$ **53.** −4 **54.** $-4\frac{2}{9}$ **55.** Jill and Jemma for $t \le 2$, Jemma for $t > 2$ **56.** Jackie **57.** $y - 1, y, y + 1$

Exercise 2.2

1. $11a - 7b$ **2.** $10a - 7b$ **3.** $5b - 3a$ **4.** $4a + 7b$ **5.** $6a - 8b$
6. $13a$ **7.** $6q - 6p^2$ **8.** $4p$ **9.** $-4x + 11y^2$ **10.** $-17a^3 + 4b$
11. $11a - 18b$ **12.** $5c - 5d$ **13.** $11w - 1 + 2z$ **14.** $-a + 18b$
15. $-5x + 9$ **16.** $10a - 19c + 16$ **17.** $12x - 15y + 20$
18. $-19t + 14s + 10$ **19.** $3x^2 + 10x + 5$ **20.** $-5x + 12y + 22$
21. $11a - 17$ **22.** $6w - 1$ **23.** $9p + 20q$ **24.** $34x - y - 8$
25. $-11x - 7$ **26.** $2a + 13b + 7$ **27.** $20x + 3$
28. $5y^2x + 3xy - 3x^2y + 4$ **29.** $25xy - 3x - 9$ **30.** $4q + 12p + q$
31. $11x + 30y - 59$ **32.** $18x - 31y - 44$ **33.** $-8x - 28y - 36$
34. $-9x + 10y - 44$ **35.** $27v^2 + 44v - 12$
36. $-20x^3 + 44x^2 + 14x - 32$ **37.** $f^2 - 84f + 16$
38. $103x^2 - 53x + 95$ **39.** $182c^3 + 78c^2 + 236c + 17$
40. $-189b^3 - 181b^2 + 117b - 60$ **41.** 55 **42.** 102 **43.** 248
44. 69 **45.** 1,323 **46.** 260 **47.** −8 **48.** $9\frac{1}{2}$ **49.** $26\frac{1}{4}$
50. $401\frac{23}{27}$ **51.** No **52.** Yes

Exercise 2.3

1. $6x^2$ **2.** $-6d^3$ **3.** $-15e^3$ **4.** $16f^3$ **5.** $-10x^4$ **6.** $-6y^6$
7. $-6a^5$ **8.** $-24y^5$ **9.** $24x^4$ **10.** $-72w^4$ **11.** $-12x^2y$
12. $-12r^2s^2$ **13.** $3r^4t^5$ **14.** $12x^4y^4$ **15.** $-6x^7y^4$ **16.** $6a^6b^2$
17. $18p^3q^2$ **18.** $36x^4y^4$ **19.** $-12c^2d^2$ **20.** $-36a^2b^2c^2$
21. $-24a^2b^5c^2$ **22.** $12x^5y^5$ **23.** $-12r^4ts^4$ **24.** $-24x^4y^6$
25. $-24x^4y^5$ **26.** $-12a^4b^5c^2$ **27.** $15ab^3c^3$ **28.** $120x^2y^2z^3$
29. $24p^4q^4r^2$ **30.** $9a^6b^2c^2$

Exercise 2.4

1. $a^2 + 4a + 1$ **2.** $b^2 + 5b + 6$ **3.** $x^2 + 9x + 20$ **4.** $c^2 + 5c + 6$
5. $-c^2 - e + 12$ **6.** $y^2 + 7y + 12$ **7.** $x^2 + 11x + 30$ **8.** $x^2 + x - 2$
9. $w^2 - 2w - 15$ **10.** $2t^2 - 11t + 12$ **11.** $5k^2 + 24k - 5$
12. $6c^2 + 10c - 4$ **13.** $20d^2 + 5d - 25$ **14.** $-6d^2 + d + 1$
15. $3x^2 + 4x - 4$ **16.** $3y^2 + y - 6$ **17.** $-x^2 + 4x - 5$
18. $-2x^2 + x - 2$ **19.** $-2y^2 + 12y - 26$ **20.** $x^3 + 3x^2 + x - 1$
21. $-x^3 + 9x - 3$ **22.** $2x^3 - 2x^2 + 2x - 2$ **23.** $2x^3 + 3x^2 - 2x - 3$
24. $-3x^2 + 7x + 6$ **25.** $-8x^2 + 12x + 8$ **26.** $x^2 + 6x + 9$
27. $x^2 - 8x + 16$ **28.** $4a^2 + 8a + 4$ **29.** $4x^2 - 20x + 25$
30. $4x^2 + 4xy + y^2$ **31.** $x^2 - 12xy + 36y^2$ **32.** $x^2 - y^2$
33. $x^2 - 2xy + y^2$ **34.** $t^2 - 2pt + p^2$ **35.** $-x^2 + 2xy - y^2$
36. $p^2 - 2pg + g^2$ **37.** $k^2 - 14k + 48$ **38.** $x^3 + 2x^2 - x - 2$
39. $-w^2 + 2w + 2$ **40.** $6r^2 + 12r + 3$ **41.** $-3x + 27$
42. $6a + 19$ **43.** $6x^2 + 3x$ **44.** $11x - 3$ **45.** $7a - 13$
46. $-54c^3 - 39c^2 + 54c$ **47.** $15x^3 + 53x^2 + 21x - 49$
48. $-54x^3 + 66x^2 - 2x - 12$ **49.** $20g^3 - 57g^2 - 10g + 80$
50. $10u^3 + 18u^2 - 24 - 10$ **51.** $-32p^3 + 128p^2 - 158p + 60$
52. $-35e^3 + 22e^2 - 18e + 3$
53. $5a^2x^3 + 53a^2x^2 + 42a^2x - 21ax - 49a$
54. $27h^2x^3 + 6h^2x^2 - 9hx - 5h^2x - 5h$
55. $40x^3 - 52x^2y - 8xy^2 + 12y^2$ **56.** Yes **57.** Yes **58.** Yes
59. Yes **60.** Yes

Exercise 2.5

1. $\frac{17}{6}$ **2.** $\frac{1}{6}$ **3.** $\frac{26}{21}$ **4.** $\frac{x}{6}$ **5.** $\frac{7x}{6}$ **6.** $\frac{4x}{21}$ **7.** $\frac{7x + 9}{10}$
8. $\frac{27 - x}{6}$ **9.** $\frac{7x - 9}{12}$ **10.** $\frac{-16x + 2}{24}$ **11.** $\frac{9x + 9}{6}$ **12.** $\frac{7x + 10}{6}$
13. $\frac{14x - 16}{12}$ **14.** $\frac{23x + 5}{20}$ **15.** $\frac{25x + 15}{28}$ **16.** $\frac{1 - 7x}{6}$
17. $\frac{10x + 24}{28}$ **18.** $\frac{13x - 9}{10}$ **19.** $\frac{-2x - 28}{12}$ **20.** $\frac{-14x - 9}{6}$
21. $\frac{4x - 6}{15}$ **22.** $\frac{4x - 7}{12}$ **23.** $x - 2$ **24.** $\frac{-18x - 66}{12}$
25. $\frac{17x - 21}{21}$ **26.** $\frac{62 - 5x}{15}$ **27.** $\frac{10x - 64}{12}$ **28.** $\frac{-4p - 20}{6}$
29. $\frac{5h + 28}{10}$ **30.** $\frac{-7y - 54}{12}$ **31.** $\frac{6x + 2}{(x - 2)(x + 5)}$
32. $\frac{26x + 25}{(3x + 5)(x - 2)}$ **33.** $\frac{-x + 25}{(x + 8)(x - 3)}$ **34.** $\frac{3x - 1}{(x + 2)(x + 1)}$
35. $\frac{6x - 32}{(x + 4)(x - 3)}$ **36.** $\frac{-3x - 24}{(x + 5)(x + 2)}$ **37.** $\frac{4x - 72}{(x + 7)(x - 3)}$
38. $\frac{5x + 1}{(2x + 1)(x - 1)}$ **39.** $\frac{8x + 2}{(2x - 1)(x + 1)}$ **40.** $\frac{21x - 26}{(3x + 2)(x - 6)}$
41. $\frac{12x + 24}{(x + 7)(4x - 2)}$ **42.** $\frac{9x - 9}{(2x - 1)(x - 2)}$ **43.** $\frac{10x - 35}{(6x - 5)(2x + 5)}$
44. $\frac{16x - 9}{(6x + 1)(2x + 2)}$ **45.** $\frac{-21x + 4}{(3x + 1)(5x - 2)}$ **46.** $\frac{26x - 13}{(2 - 4x)(3 - 6x)}$
47. $\frac{29 - 3x}{(5 - x)(3 - 2x)}$ **48.** (a) $\frac{18x - 4}{(3x + 1)(4x - 2)}$ (b) $\frac{34}{91}$
49. (a) $\frac{21x - 23}{20}$ (b) $-\frac{13}{4}$ **50.** (a) $\frac{5x + 109}{(3 - 4x)(3x + 8)}$ (b) $\frac{104}{35}$

Exercise 2.6

1. 2 **2.** $\frac{35}{6}$ **3.** $\frac{8}{21}$ **4.** $\frac{x^2}{6}$ **5.** $\frac{x^2}{3}$ **6.** $\frac{x^2}{21}$ **7.** $\frac{x^2 + 3x + 2}{10}$
8. $\frac{x^2 - 4x - 21}{6}$ **9.** $\frac{x^2 - 2x - 3}{12}$ **10.** $\frac{2x^2 - x - 2}{24}$
11. $\frac{4x^2 + 12x - 18}{18}$ **12.** $\frac{2x^2 + 6x - 8}{6}$ **13.** $\frac{4x^2 - 10x + 4}{6}$
14. $\frac{6x^2 + 2x}{20}$ **15.** $\frac{3x^2 + 7x + 2}{28}$ **16.** $\frac{2x^2 - x - 1}{6}$
17. $\frac{2x^2 + 6x + 4}{28}$ **18.** $\frac{3x^2 + 5x - 2}{10}$ **19.** $\frac{2y^2 - 4y - 16}{12}$
20. $\frac{8x^2 + 14x - 15}{6}$ **21.** $\frac{3x^2 + 12x + 9}{15}$ **22.** $\frac{2x^3 + 5x^2 + 2x}{24}$
23. $\frac{-4x^4 + 2x^2 + 6x}{100}$ **24.** $\frac{-36p^3 + 108p^2 - 80p}{36}$ **25.** $\frac{10}{147}$
26. $\frac{-24}{5}$ **27.** −6 **28.** $\frac{-13}{6}$ **29.** 13 **30.** −19

Self-check Test

1. 40 **2.** 32 **3.** −31 **4.** −6 **5.** 21 **6.** 39 **7.** 10
8. −277 **9.** $44\frac{1}{2}$ **10.** 26 **11.** −54 **12.** 10 **13.** $-\frac{2}{5}$
14. $\frac{25}{8}$ **15.** 7 **16.** 69 **17.** $-\frac{8}{3}$ **18.** $-\frac{41}{6}$ **19.** $\frac{20}{19}$ **20.** 0
21. $3p - 10q + 8$ **22.** $n - 8m$ **23.** $12n - 27$
24. $-15n^2 + 50n + 20$ **25.** $23a^2 - 11a + 13$
26. $2x - 10y + 13$ **27.** (a) $10x^2 + 11xy + 3y^2$
(b) $a^3b + ab^2 + a^2b^2 + b^3$ (c) $10a^3 + 41a^2 + 25a^2b + 15ab + 21a$
(d) $3x^4 + 3x^3 + 5x^2y + 5y^3y$ **28.** (a) $-6x^5$ (b) $4x^6$ (c) $6x^3y^4$
(d) $-24x^2y^2z^3$ (e) $a^3b^3c^4$ **29.** (a) $2x^3 - 8x^2 + 18x - 12$
(b) $-16x^3 - 20x^2 + 6x + 6$ (c) $36x^4 - 57x^3 + 69x^2 - 18x$
(d) $63x^4 - 35x^3 + 11x^2 - 10x - 2$ (e) $540x^2 - 1044x + 306$
(f) $28x - 40$ **30.** (a) $\frac{11x}{12}$ (b) $\frac{8x + 5}{6}$ (c) $\frac{62x + 3}{20}$
(d) $\frac{-33x + 90}{55}$ (e) $\frac{33 - 14x}{(7 - 2x)(2x - 3)}$ (f) $\frac{6x + 6}{(3x - 1)(3x + 1)}$
(g) $\frac{19x - 32}{(4 - 3x)(6 - 2x)}$ (h) $\frac{11x + 10}{12}$ (i) $\frac{-4x - 1}{15}$
(j) $\frac{6x^2 - 3x - 30}{(4)(2x - 1)(x + 2)}$ (k) $\frac{8}{28x^2 - 43x + 9}$ (l) $\frac{-54}{2x^2 + x - 1}$
(m) $\frac{14x^2 - 11x - 15}{15}$ (n) $\frac{-12x^2 + 9x + 21}{60}$ **31.** (a) $\frac{132}{25}$
(b) $-15\frac{1}{2}$ (c) $\frac{-191}{25}$ (d) 37 (e) 16 (f) $11\frac{3}{10}$
32. $y = 2a$ **33.** $\frac{16t}{3} - 3$

Chapter 3

Exercise 3.1

1. $p(a+b)$ **2.** $s(r-3t)$ **3.** $3(m-4n)$ **4.** $2y(a-2b)$
5. $x(1+7y)$ **6.** $2(w+4a)$ **7.** $p(5q-3)$ **8.** $4x(1-4y)$
9. $3r(s+5t)$ **10.** $z(5z+7w)$ **11.** $5(a+b)$ **12.** $3(g-3m)$
13. $2(2x^2-3y)$ **14.** $2(p^2+4p+3)$ **15.** $5p(q+2t)$
16. $n(8m+7p)$ **17.** $3x(x-1)$ **18.** $5ab(a+3b-2)$
19. $7pq(pq^2-2pq-3)$ **20.** $x(y+z-1)$ **21.** $5(a+3b)$
22. $7(2p-3q)$ **23.** $2(6c+7d)$ **24.** $q(p-3)$ **25.** $c(17+a)$
26. $x(1-a)$ **27.** $2(7-2q)$ **28.** $p(13-a)$ **29.** $10p(p+3)$
30. $a(a+bc)$ **31.** $5xy(1+4y)$ **32.** $bc(a+d)$ **33.** $\frac{1}{2}(e-f)$
34. $3y(xy+3+2y)$ **35.** $5g(3g^2-5+g)$ **36.** $a(3+b)$
37. $3t(s-2p)$ **38.** $7(x^2+2)$ **39.** $g(g-8)$ **40.** $mp(p+1)$
41. $4ab(2b+a)$ **42.** $3g(g+5m)$ **43.** $m(5m+1)$
44. $5(m^2-1)$ **45.** $xy(1+3y-2x)$ **46.** $b(d+c+1)$
47. $p(4t^2-7g+6n+2ps)$ **48.** $7ax(2ax-4a^2+3x^2)$
49. $x^3(10x^2+5x-1)$ **50.** $3y(9y^4+3-y)$

Exercise 3.2

1. $4(x+2)$ **2.** $3(y-5)$ **3.** $3(2x+3)$ **4.** $5x(x+4)$
5. $2b(2a+9b)$ **6.** $4xy(3+5x)$ **7.** $2a^2b(4b^2-7a)$
8. $7xy(z+5y)$ **9.** $(y+2)(x+3)$ **10.** $(b+d)(a+c)$
11. $(y+z)(w+x)$ **12.** $(a+b)(c+d)$ **13.** $(x+z)(a+2)$
14. $(a+b)(x+2y)$ **15.** $(3-x)(y+z)$ **16.** $(r+3)(a+b)$
17. $(t+3)(s+2)$ **18.** $(y+4)(z-2)$ **19.** $(a+3)(d-g)$
20. $(r+s)(w-t)$ **21.** $(m-n)(b-3)$ **22.** $(2-x)(a-c)$
23. $(3-s)(t-2)$ **24.** $(b-3)(x+y)$ **25.** $(n+m)(p-r)$
26. $(y-4)(z+2)$ **27.** $(b-4)(p-q)$ **28.** $(2-3x)(a-c)$
29. $(a-3)(d+g)$ **30.** $(a-b)(s-t)$ **31.** $(a+d)(b-a)$
32. $(2p-q)(2r-3)$ **33.** $(a-w)(a+d)$ **34.** $(w+3b)(w-2a)$
35. $(y-b)(b-2x)$ **36.** $(x-b)(x-c)$ **37.** $(3p-t)(5s+p)$
38. $(m-n)(m-2)$ **39.** $(a-b)(3t-s)$ **40.** $(c-2s)(c+2)$
41. $(m+n)(a-b)$ **42.** $(4d+2c)(3f-5g)$
43. $(2c-4d)(7m+3h)$ **44.** $(10k+8h)(2b-5e)$
45. $(15h-35j)(l-2m)$ **46.** $(2d+5f)(3g+c)$
47. $(7m-5n)(3c-1)$ **48.** $(pt+4n)(ps-7m)$
49. $(7a^2b-5a^2c)(2b-5g)$ **50.** $(2pt+9gs)(3st-4gp)$
51. $(g+f)(3g-h)$ **52.** $(5a+b)(2b-c)$ **53.** $(b-2)(b-2d)$
54. $(4p-m)(-3m+n)$ **55.** $(t+2s)(t+1)$ **56.** $(7m-n)(m+3p)$
57. $(x-z)(y-z)$ **58.** $(-2k+j)(h+j)$ **59.** $(x-y)(-3+x)$
60. $(6pth-p^2t)(2h-t)$

Exercise 3.3

1. $(n+1)(n+3)$ **2.** $(n+2)(n+3)$ **3.** $(n+3)(n+3)$
4. $(n+9)(n+2)$ **5.** $(n+5)(n+5)$ **6.** $(n-2)(n+6)$
7. $(x+8)(x-1)$ **8.** $(x-3)(x-8)$ **9.** $(x-7)(x-7)$
10. $(a+1)(a-12)$ **11.** (a) $(a+3)(a+4)$ (b) $(a+8)(a+5)$
(c) $(a+7)(a-1)$ (d) $(a+6)(a-2)$ (e) $(a-5)(a-3)$
12. $(x+1)(x+3)$ **13.** $(x+1)(x+2)$ **14.** $(x+1)(x+4)$
15. $(x+2)(x+3)$ **16.** $(x+3)(x+4)$ **17.** $(x+2)(x+5)$
18. $(x+4)(x+7)$ **19.** $(x+4)(x+9)$ **20.** $(x+1)(x+10)$
21. $(x-2)(x-3)$ **22.** $(x-1)(x-7)$ **23.** $(x-4)(x-2)$
24. $(x-5)(x-5)$ **25.** $(x-6)(x-4)$ **26.** $(x-7)(x-4)$
27. $(x+3)(x-2)$ **28.** $(x-6)(x+4)$ **29.** $(x+4)(x-1)$
30. $(x-3)(x+5)$ **31.** $(x-4)(x+2)$ **32.** $(x-6)(x+2)$
33. $(x+6)(x-3)$ **34.** $(x-8)(x+5)$ **35.** $(x-9)(x+7)$
36. $(x+10)(x-6)$ **37.** $(x-10)(x+4)$ **38.** $(x-7)(x+8)$
39. $(x-12)(x+8)$ **40.** $(x-11)(x+4)$ **41.** $(p+2)(p+9)$
42. $(l-8)(l+3)$ **43.** $(w-3)(w+1)$ **44.** $(b-7)(b-3)$
45. $(a+2)(a+15)$ **46.** $(j-5)(j+1)$ **47.** $(t-2)(t+11)$
48. $(d-2)(d-1)$ **49.** $(e-5)(e+3)$ **50.** $(c+6)(c+2)$

Exercise 3.4

1. $(2x+1)(x-3)$ **2.** $(2x-8)(x+2)$ **3.** $(3x-1)(x+3)$
4. $(5x-6)(x+4)$ **5.** $(3x+2)(x+3)$ **6.** $(2x+2)(x-3)$
7. $(7x-2)(x-4)$ **8.** $(3x-2)(x+3)$ **9.** $(5x-7)(x-3)$
10. $(3x-2)(x-2)$ **11.** $(2x+7)(x+2)$ **12.** $(7x-2)(x-3)$
13. $(11x+2)(x-3)$ **14.** $(7x-7)(x-3)$ **15.** $(3x+10)(x-5)$
16. $(13x-1)(x+7)$ **17.** $(3x-5)(x+4)$ **18.** $(7x+5)(x+5)$
19. $(3x+6)(x-3)$ **20.** $(5x-7)(x+7)$ **21.** $(3x-1)(x+9)$
22. $(5x-2)(x-4)$ **23.** $(2x+6)(x+2)$ **24.** $(7x-3)(x-2)$
25. $(3x+8)(x+1)$ **26.** $(3x+4)(2x+2)$ **27.** $(6x-2)(2x+1)$
28. $(5x+1)(2x+4)$ **29.** $(7x-5)(3x-3)$ **30.** $(4c+1)(c+3)$
31. $(3d+2)(d-1)$ **32.** $(5e-1)(e+2)$ **33.** $(2f+3)(f+2)$
34. $(11g+3)(g-2)$ **35.** $(3h+2)(h+3)$ **36.** $(5j+3)(j-2)$
37. $(3k-2)(2k+1)$ **38.** $(2l+7)(l+2)$ **39.** $(6m-1)(m-2)$

Exercise 3.5

1. $(a)^2$ **2.** $(x)^2$ **3.** $(1)^2$ **4.** $(2x)^2$ **5.** $(4)^2$ **6.** $(5y)^2$
7. $(r+t)(r-t)$ **8.** $(s+w)(s-w)$ **9.** $(a+y)(a-y)$
10. $(x+h)(x-h)$ **11.** $(k+v)(k-v)$ **12.** $(m+n)(m-n)$
13. $(d+b)(d-b)$ **14.** $(e+c)(e-c)$ **15.** $(x+5)(x-5)$
16. $(y+1)(y-1)$ **17.** $(t+10)(t-10)$ **18.** $(a+8)(a-8)$
19. $(w+11)(w-11)$ **20.** $(r+9)(r-9)$ **21.** $(12+g)(12-g)$
22. $(7+m)(7-m)$ **23.** $(13+a)(13-a)$ **24.** $(2x+4y)(2x-4y)$
25. $(9a+6d)(9a-6d)$ **26.** $(5c+8s)(5c-8s)$
27. $(s+5t)(s-5t)$ **28.** $(11y+7x)(11y-7x)$
29. $(10p+q)(10p-q)$ **30.** $5(s+t)(s-t)$ **31.** $2(w+r)(w-r)$
32. $7(d+b)(d-b)$ **33.** $11(q+p)(q-p)$ **34.** $13(x+v)(x-v)$
35. $15(y+t)(y-t)$ **36.** $3(1+b)(1-b)$ **37.** $9p(u+1)(u-1)$
38. $14(g+1)(g-1)$ **39.** $c^2e(2g+5d)(2g-5d)$
40. $t(3+8w^3)(3-8w^3)$ **41.** $c(14p^2+7)(14p^2-7)$
42. $3(2q+5p)(2q-5p)$ **43.** $2xy(2z+w)(2z-w)$
44. $2d(7e+5d)(7e-5d)$ **45.** $(3a+4)(a-2)$
46. $(5c-1)(3c-3)$ **47.** $(7h+2)(3h+4)$ **48.** $(8x+5)(-2x+9)$
49. $8(m+d)(-m+d)$

Exercise 3.6

1. 5 **2.** 7 **3.** $\frac{3}{2}$ **4.** $\frac{8}{9}$ **5.** 6 **6.** -3 **7.** $c+d$ **8.** $\frac{p-q}{q+p}$
9. $-x$ **10.** $-7x$ **11.** $\frac{x-5}{x+5}$ **12.** $-x+3$ **13.** $\frac{x-7}{x-3}$ **14.** $\frac{-x+4}{x-1}$
15. $-x+5$ **16.** $\frac{x}{2}$ **17.** $\frac{2x+3}{x+4}$ **18.** $\frac{3x-2}{x-7}$ **19.** $\frac{-x+2}{x-1}$
20. $\frac{-2x+3}{3x+1}$

Self-check Test

1. $a(b+c)$ **2.** $b(a-1)$ **3.** $a(a+1)(a-1)$ **4.** $pq(q+1)$
5. $5p(2q-3r)$ **6.** $10d(2c+3)$ **7.** $x^2(1+x)$ **8.** $5p(q-2)$
9. $5x(x^2+2)$ **10.** $4x^3(2x-1)$ **11.** $(2p+3)(q-2)$
12. $(a+2b)(c-d)$ **13.** $(r+2p)(s+3t)$ **14.** $(x+y)(a+b)$
15. $2(x-z)(x+w)$ **16.** $(3p-4r)(2r+s)$
17. $(2w-3z)(x-y)$ **18.** $(x+4)(x+4)$ **19.** $(x+3)(x+10)$
20. $(x-4)(x-2)$ **21.** $(x-5)(x+9)$ **22.** $(x-11)(x-7)$
23. $(x-8)(x-9)$ **24.** $(x+6)(x+6)$ **25.** $(x+20)(x-3)$
26. $3(x+1)(x-6)$ **27.** $2(5x+1)(1x-1)$ **28.** $(4x-3)(5x-1)$
29. $(7x-1)(3x+5)$ **30.** $(2x+3)(3x-1)$ **31.** (a) $(a+1)(a+3)$
(b) $(a+5)(a+8)$ (c) $(a+4)(a+6)$ (d) $(a+2)(a+10)$
32. (a) $(n+4)(n+3)$ (b) $(n-1)(n-1)$ (c) $(n-2)(n-6)$
(d) $(n-1)(n+7)$ (e) $(n-3)(n-6)$ (f) $(n+3)(n-6)$
(g) $(n+5)(n-2)$ (h) $(n+3)(n-1)$ (i) $(n+4)(n+4)$
(j) $(n-6)(n-6)$ **33.** $(x+a)(x-a)$ **34.** $(d+5b)(d-5b)$
35. $(w+r)(w-r)$ **36.** $(3w+4y)(3w-4y)$ **37.** $(c+1)(c-1)$
38. $(x-1)(x-11)$ **39.** $6ab(1+2b)$ **40.** $9x(2x^3+3)$
41. $5xy(x-2y)$ **42.** $2xyz(4x^2y^2-5z)$ **43.** $(x-2y)(2t+3s)$
44. $2a^2(b+3)$ **45.** $4w(3w-5t^2)$ **46.** $2(5x-2)(x-1)$
47. $2(3x-1)(x+4)$ **48.** $7(m+3g)(m-3g)$
49. $(x-3)(x+13)$ **50.** $(x+4)(b-3a)$ **51.** $(7x+4)(5x-6)$
52. $4(3y+2v)(3y-2v)$ **53.** $3(3w^2-h)(3w^2-h)$
54. $20t(s+2p)(s-2p)$ **55.** $2vw(2w+v)(2w-v)$
56. $2(5+7a)(5-7a)$ **57.** $3f(g-2)(g-12)$ **58.** $\frac{5}{3}$
59. $\frac{1}{3}$ **60.** $\frac{1}{2}$ **61.** $\frac{x}{7}$ **62.** $\frac{x+9}{x}$ **63.** $\frac{x-3}{x}$ **64.** $\frac{x+4}{x+7}$
65. $\frac{5x+2}{2x+3}$ **66.** $\frac{-3(x-1)}{7x+1}$ **67.** $\frac{4x+3}{x-1}$

Chapter 4

Exercise 4.1

1. 1 turkey = 4 kg **2.** 4 kg = 1 gold bar **3.** 1 dog = 11 kg
4. 1 sheep = 60 kg **5.** 1 bag = 4 kg **6.** 1 tin = 3 kg
7. 2 kg = 1 tin

Exercise 4.2

1. (a) $3x+6$ (b) $2n-5$ (c) $x+17$ (d) $4a-18$ (e) $11b+14$
(f) $11(x+14)$ (g) $5x-10$ **2.** (a) A number minus four
(b) Two times a number plus five (c) A number minus 8
and the answer is multiplied by 4 (d) Four minus a number.

The answer is multiplied by 5 and then ten is added (e) A number plus nine and the answer is multiplied by minus one. (f) A number divided by three and eight is added to it. Then three is added to the answer **3.** (a) $x = 2$ (b) $x = 27$ (c) $x = 10$ (d) $x = 14$ (e) $x = 2$ (f) $x = -5$ (g) $x = 35$ (h) $x = -44$ (i) $x = 18$ (j) $x = 46$ (k) $x = 27$ (l) $x = 11$ **4.** (a) $x = 6$ (b) $a = 6$ (c) $c = -18$ (d) $x = 21$ (e) $b = 6$ (f) $22 = f$ (g) $d = 10$ (h) $g = -6$ (i) $x = 30$ (j) $x = -24$ **5.** (a) $x = 11$ (b) $w = 6$ (c) $7 = c$ (d) $0 = k$ (e) $p = 10$ (f) $x = -14$ (g) $q = -1$ (h) $y = -12$ (i) $x = -21$ (j) $t = 0$ (k) $s = 22$ (l) $x = -9$ (m) $f = 2$ (n) $e = 19$ (o) $r = 30$ (p) $f = 6$ **6.** (a) $x = 20$ (b) $a = 5$ (c) $x = 12$ (d) $b = 2$ (e) $c = -3$ (f) $7 = p$ (g) $x = -5$ (h) $f = -7$ (i) $x = -3$ (j) $g = -7$ (k) $x = -11$ (l) $k = 6$ (m) $x = -6$ (n) $p = 9$ (o) $z = 3$ (p) $t = -4$ (q) $e = 6$ (r) $a = -3$ (s) $h = -51$ (t) $k = -8$ **7.** (a) $a = 3$ (b) $a = 7$ (c) $a = 3$ (d) $x = 4$ (e) $x = 10$ (f) $a = -5$ (g) $x = 12$ (h) $x = 20$ (i) $x = 12$ (j) $x = 3$ (k) $y = -6$ (l) $x = -50$ (m) $x = 2$ (n) $y = -20$ (o) $a = 2$ (p) $-3 = a$ (q) $a = -1$ (r) $x = -15$ (s) $x = 42$ (t) $x = 7$ **8.** (a) $n = 7$ (b) $n = 11$ (c) $n = 7$ (d) $n = 7$ (e) $n = 3$ (f) $x = 2$ (g) $a = 4$ (h) $a = 3$ (i) $a = 5$ (j) $a = 2$ (k) $c = 7$ (l) $n = 3$ (m) $x = -22$ (n) $a = -4$ (o) $a = 3$ (p) $n = 2$ (q) $n = -3$ (r) $x = 5$ (s) $n = 1$ (t) $p = 1$ **9.** 70 boys, 80 girls **10.** Angles 90°, 55°, 35° **11.** $x = 33$ **12.** Robert is 14 yrs old, Courtney is 16 yrs old **13.** Sides = 7 m, 45 m, 57 m, 91 m **14.** (a) $a = 80°, 20°, 80°$ **15.** (a) $y + 6$ (b) $y + 30$ (c) $4(y + 6) = y + 30, y = 2$; Aine is 2 yrs old, her mother is 26 yrs old. **16.** $x = 7$ **17.** (a) $x - 8$ (b) $2x - 8$ (c) $2x - 8 = 100$ (d) $x = 54$ **18.** (a) $a + 0.10$ (b) $2a + (a + 0.10)$ (c) $2a + (a + 0.10) = 4$ (d) $a = €1.30$

Exercise 4.3

1. $5 = a$ **2.** $7 = a$ **3.** $x = 11$ **4.** $x = 13$ **5.** $x = -5$ **6.** $4 = x$ **7.** $18 = x$ **8.** $30 = x$ **9.** $x = \frac{1}{5}$ **10.** $10 = x$ **11.** $-6 = x$ **12.** $-8 = x$ **13.** $x = 15$ **14.** $x = 20$ **15.** $x = 6$ **16.** $x = 12$ **17.** $10 = x$ **18.** $x = 9$ **19.** $x = 5$ **20.** $2 = x$ **21.** $x = 10$ **22.** $x = 1$ **23.** $x = 2$ **24.** $n = 4$ **25.** $x = -3$ **26.** $n = 4$ **27.** $x = 4$ **28.** $x = 11$ **29.** $a = 14$ **30.** $x = 3$ **31.** $x = 3$ **32.** $x = 0$ **33.** $x = -3$ **34.** $x = -1$ **35.** $n = 6$

Self-check Test

1. (a) $3x + 10$ (b) $2x - 6$ (c) $5x + 17$ (d) $10x - 8$ (e) $6x + 14$ (f) $3(x + 14)$ **2.** (a) A number minus five (b) Three times a number plus one (c) A number minus five and the answer is multiplied by two (d) Seven minus a number. The answer is multiplied by three and the eighteen is added (e) A number plus four. The answer is multiplied by negative two (f) A number divided by three and one is added to the answer. Then two is added to the answer **3.** $a = 7$ **4.** $x = -6$ **5.** $x = -4$ **6.** $a = 13$ **7.** $2 = a$ **8.** $4 = b$ **9.** $b = \frac{10}{4}$ **10.** $n = 6$ **11.** $n = 8$ **12.** $n = -\frac{6}{8}$ **13.** $n = 5$ **14.** $a = \frac{42}{28}$ **15.** $a = \frac{13}{7}$ **16.** $a = \frac{56}{20}$ **17.** $a = 2$ **18.** $2 = x$ **19.** $x = -53$ **20.** $b = 5$ **21.** $a = \frac{35}{25}$ **22.** $n = -3$ **23.** $x = \frac{30}{12}$ **24.** $a = \frac{48}{42}$ **25.** $x = 8$ **26.** $b = \frac{5}{10}$ **27.** $d = \frac{-3}{6}$ **28.** $a = \frac{1}{4}$ **29.** $n = -3$ **30.** $n = -6$ **31.** $5 = x$ **32.** $x = 4$ **33.** $x = 1$ **34.** $x = \frac{1}{4}$ **35.** $6 = x$ **36.** $x = -11$ **37.** $x = 3$ **38.** $x = 5$ **39.** $x = 4$ **40.** $x = 7$ **41.** $x = -5$ **42.** (a) $w + 30$ (b) $w + 5$ (c) $w + 35$ (d) $w = 2\frac{1}{2}$ yrs old **43.** (a) $x + 30$ (b) $x + 34$ (c) $x + 4$ (d) $x = 11$ **44.** $a = 40$ **45.** $x = 33$ **46.** $x = 60$ **47.** (a) $y + 4y + 6 = 61$ (b) $y = 11$ **48.** $(x - 6)°C$ **49.** $x = 18$ km **50.** (a) $x - 3$ (b) $x + x - 3 = 47$ (c) $x = 25$ (d) $58 + 55 = 113$ yrs

Chapter 5

Exercise 5.1

1. (a) Orange, Pink (b) Blue, Red, Yellow, Orange, Brown (c) Yellow, Yellow, Purple, Blue, Red (d) Pink, Yellow, Blue, Yellow, Blue (e) Yellow, Purple, Blue, Purple, Pink (f) Dark Purple, Purple, Red, Purple, Purple (g) Orange, Red, Pink, Red, Orange (h) Red, Yellow, Brown, Pink (i) 6 balls in each pattern ⇒ Colours. **2.** (a) 6 in each pattern (b) 6 in each pattern (c) 5 in each pattern (d) 7 in each pattern (e) 7 in each pattern **3.** (i) (a) 5 in each pattern (b) 19th (c) ★ 45th (d) ★ 100th (ii) (a) 7 in each pattern (b) ■ (c) ★ (d) (iii) (a) 6 in each pattern (b) (c) (d) ■ (iv) (a) 7 in each pattern (b) ■ (c) (d) (v) (a) 5 in each pattern (b) 19th (c) 45th (d) 100th (vi) (b) 100th (c) ⬟ 45th (d) ▲ 19th (vii) (b) 19th (c) ● 45th (d) ⬟ 100th (viii) (b) ● 19th (c) ⬟ 45th (d) ⬟ 100th (ix) (b) ▲ 19th (c) ■ 45th (d) ■ 100th (x) (b) ▲ 100th (c) ■ 45th (d) ⬟ 19th **4.** (i) (a) 7, 1, 7, 5, 8 (b) 5 (c) 5 (d) 7 (ii) (a) 7, 6, 6, 6, 0 (b) 6 (c) 6 (d) 6 (iii) (a) 0, 8, 0, 2, 2 (b) 2 (c) 2 (d) 2 (iv) (a) 8, 8, 8, 8, 8 (b) 8 (c) 8 (d) 8 (v) (a) 7, 6, 3, 1, 8 (b) 7 (c) 7 (d) 8 (vi) (a) 4, 5, 6, 3, 6 (b) 4 (c) 4 (d) 2 (vii) (a) 8, 4, 4, 1, 7 (b) 8 (c) 8 (d) 0 (viii) (a) 0, 8, 1, 1, 1 (b) 6 (c) 6 (d) 1 **6.** (i) Group of 3 [8, 8, 11] add 6 to each to get next group [14, 14, 17] (ii) Add 3 ⇒ 34, 37, 40 (iii) 145, 160, 175 (Add 15) (iv) [−7, −7, −5] Add 4 to each [5, 5, 7] (v) Subtract 2 ⇒ 15, 13, 11 (vi) [10, 10, 7] minus 6 from each ⇒ [−8, −8, −11] (vii) Add 1 ⇒ 20, 21, 22 (viii) Add 2 ⇒ 24, 26, 28 (ix) [−3, −3, −2] Add 2 to each [3, 3, 4] (x) −1 from each ⇒ −6, −7, −8 (xi) 29, 35, 7 divide by 5, next term add 6. (xii) [2, 7] Add 6 to 2, Add 5 to 7 to get [8, 13] = 31, 32, 37 (xiii) $9 \times 5 = 45 - 7 = 38 \times 5 = 190 - 7 = 183$ = 22,665, 22,658, 113,290 (xiv) Add 1 ⇒ 18, 19, 20 (xv) $7 \times 3 = 21, 21 - 7 = 14, 14 \times 3 = 42$ etc. = 861, 854, 2,562 (xvi) Subtract 5 = 70, 65, 60 (xvii) Subtract 2 = 7, 5, 3 (xviii) Subtract 3 = 10, 7, 4 (xix) [13, 13] − 2 ⇒ [11, 11] therefore 5, 3, 3 (xx) [−2, 10] Add 3 ⇒ [1, 13] therefore 22, 13, 25

Exercise 5.2

1. (a) No. No common difference (b) Yes. Increases by 23 each time (c) No. No common difference (d) No. No common difference (e) Yes. Increases by 3 each time (f) Yes. Decreases by 13 each time (g) Yes. Decreases by 5.8 (h) Yes. Decreases by 5.6 (i) No. No common difference (j) Yes. Decreases by 12 **2.** (i) (a) 11 (b) 11 (c) 66, 77, 88 (ii) (a) 4 (b) 5 (c) 29, 34, 39 (iii) (a) 19 (b) −7 (c) −16, −23, −30 (iv) (a) 63 (b) −6 (c) 33, 27, 21 (v) (a) 51 (b) −13 (c) −14, −27, −40 (vi) (a) 27 (b) 15 (c) 102, 117, 132 (vii) (a) 112 (b) 63 (c) 427, 490, 553 (viii) (a) −71 (b) −22 (c) −181, −203, −225 (ix) (a) −56 (b) 22 (c) 54, 76, 98 (x) (a) 18 (b) −29 (c) −127, −156, −185 **3.** (a) −18, −60, −102, −144, −186, −228 (b) 0, 17, 34, 51, 68, 85 (c) 4, 17, 30, 43, 56, 69 (d) 138, 111, 84, 57, 30, 3 (e) 11, 19, 27, 35, 43, 51 **4.** (a) 3, 9, 15, 21, 27 (b) 9, 29, 49, 69, 89 (c) −6, 3, 12, 21, 30 (d) −13, 1, 15, 29, 43 (e) 56, 49, 42, 35, 28 (f) 24, 13, 2, −9, −20 (g) −29, −52, −75, −98, −121 (h) −16, −22, −28, −34, −40 (i) 22, −88, −198, −308, −418 (j) −51, −59, −67, −75, −83 **5.** (a) 4 (b) 3 (c) 4 (d) 2 (e) 5 (f) −2 (g) −4 (h) 4 (i) 3 (j) 5 **6.** (a) 8 (b) 1 (c) 3 (d) 13 (e) 0 (f) 4 **8.** (b) 46 tiles (c) 106 tiles (d) 2 blue tiles added each time **9.** 50, 53, 56, 59, 62, 65, 68, 71, 74, 77, 80 **10.** (a) 8:23, 8:38, 8:53, 9:08 (b) 15 minutes between commercials

Exercise 5.3

1. (i) (a) 5 (b) 5 (c) $5n$ (d) 105 (ii) (a) 2 (b) 2 (c) $2n$ (d) 42 (iii) (a) 1 (b) 2 (c) $2n - 1$ (d) 41 (iv) (a) 100 (b) −10 (c) $110 - 10n$ (d) −100 (v) (a) 88 (b) −11 (c) $99 - 11n$ (d) −132 (vi) (a) 55 (b) −14 (c) $69 - 14n$ (d) −225 (vii) (a) 95 (b) −15 (c) $110 - 15n$ (d) −205 (viii) (a) 14 (b) 12 (c) $12n + 2$ (d) 254 (ix) (a) −27 (b) −15 (c) $-12 - 15n$ (d) −327 (x) (a) −33 (b) 26 (c) $26n - 59$

(d) 487 (xi) (a) 75 (b) −18 (c) $93 - 18n$ (d) −285 (xii) (a) 3.7 (b) 6.2 (c) $6.2n - 2.5$ (d) 127.7 (xiii) (a) −108 (b) −9.9 (c) $-98.1 - 9.9n$ (d) −306 (xiv) (a) $\frac{1}{2}$ (b) $\frac{3}{4}$ (c) $\frac{3}{4}n - \frac{1}{4}$ (d) $\frac{31}{2}$ (xv) (a) $\frac{42}{5}$ (b) $\frac{-6}{5}$ (c) $\frac{48}{5} - \frac{6}{5}n$ (d) $\frac{-78}{5}$
2. (a) 55 (b) −29 (c) −61, −90, −119 (d) Decreasing by 29 (e) 55, 26, −3, −32, −61, −90, −119, −148, −177, −206, −235, −264 (f) $84 - 29n$ (g) −583 **3.** (a) 73 (b) 19 (c) 149, 168, 187 (d) Increasing by 19 (e) 73, 92, 111, 130, 149, 168, 187, 206, 225, 244, 263, 282 (f) $19n + 54$ (g) 947 **4.** (a) 67 (b) −25.5 (c) −35, −60.5, −86 (d) Decreasing by 25.5 (e) 67, 41.5, 16, −9.5, −35, −60.5, −86, −111.5, −137, −162.5, −188, −213.5 (f) $92.5 - 25.5n$ (g) −2457.5 **5.** 8 **6.** 11 **7.** 18 **8.** 23 **9.** 52 **10.** (a) 9, 11, 13 (b) 3, 5, 7, 9, 11, 13 (c) Increasing by 2 (d) $2n + 1$ **11.** (a) $3n$ (b) €84 **12.** (a) $2n + 21$ (b) 41 points (c) 22 **13.** Will form a line if drawn on graph paper.

Exercise 5.4

1. (a) 21 (b) 17 (c) 31 (d) 10 (e) 29 **2.** (a) 6 (b) −11 (c) 4 (d) −3 (e) −36 **3.** (a) −21 (b) 24 (c) 0 (d) 69 (e) 52 **4.** (a) −5 (b) 15 (c) $\frac{3}{5}$ (d) 11 (e) −24 **5.** (a) −13 (b) 8 (c) 35 (d) 77 (e) −205 **6.** (a) −25 (b) 14 (c) 58 (d) −8 (e) 65 **7.** (a) −8 (b) −17 (c) −6 (d) −211 (e) 597 **8.** −7, −2, 3, 8, 13, 18 **9.** 44, 26, 8, −10, −28, −46 **10.** (a) 2 (b) −4 (c) 14 (d) 20 (e) 26 **11.** (a) −5 (b) −9 (c) −13 (d) −17 (e) −21 **12.** (a) 2 (b) 10 (c) −10 (d) −14 (e) 4 **13.** (a) 4 (b) 12 (c) −8 (d) 20 (e) −16 **14.** (i) (a) {2, 3, 4, 5} (b) {3, 5, 7, 9} (c) {3, 5, 7, 9, 11} (d) {(2,3), (3,5), (4,7), (5,9)} (ii) (a) {0, 2, 7, 8} (b) {−2, 19, 4, 22} (c) {−2, 2, 19, 4, 22} (d) {(0,−2), (2,4), (7,19), (8,22)} (iii) (a) {2, 4, 6, 8, 10} (b) {6, 12, 18, 24, 30} (c) {6, 12, 18, 24, 30} (d) {(2,6), (4,12), (6,18), (8,24), (10,30)} (iv) (a) {1, 2, 3, 4} (b) {2, 4, 6, 8} (c) {1, 2, 3, 4, 5, 6, 7, 8} (d) {(1,2), (2,4), (3,6), (4,8)} (v) (a) {1, 2, 3, 4, 5} (b) {2, 3, 4, 5, 6} (c) {1, 2, 3, 4, 5, 6, 7} (d) {(1,2), (2,3), (3,4), (4,5), (5,6)} **17.** (a), (b), (d), (e) Yes. Each element in the domain has a unique output in range (c) No. 9 is mapped to 2 outputs (f) No. "d" has 2 outputs **18.** (b) {(1,3), (3,7), (4,9), (6,13), (8,17)} **19.** (b) {4, 3, 18, 7, 9} (c) {4, 3, 18, 7, 9} (d) {(12,4), (21,7), (54,18), (27,9), (9,3)} **20.** $\frac{-5}{3}$ **21.** 3 **22.** 5 **23.** $w = 0, x = 6, y = 12$ **24.** $5 = r, -7 = s, -11 = t$ **25.** $w = -12, x = -28, y = 24$ **26.** $s = 1$ **27.** $k = 11$ **28.** $t = 7$ **29.** $h = -7$

Exercise 5.5

1. (i) (a) 6, 9, 12, 15, 18 (b) {(1,6), (2,9), (3,12), (4,15), (5,18)} (ii) (a) 5, 9, 13, 17, 21 (b) {(1,5), (2,9), (3,13), (4,17), (5,21)} (iii) (a) −1, 3, 7, 11, 15 (b) {(1,−1), (2,3), (3,7), (4,11), (5,15)} (iv) (a) 7, 9, 11, 13, 15 (b) {(1,7), (2,9), (3,11), (4,13), (5,15)} (v) (a) 4, 7, 10, 13, 16 (b) {1,4), (2,7), (3,10), (4,13), (5,16)} (vi) (a) 8, 13, 18, 23, 28 (b) {(1,8), (2,13), (3,18), (4,23), (5,28)} **14.** (b) $P(0,-7)$ **15.** (b) $W(0,-12)$ **16.** (b) $S(0,1)$ **17.** (b) 5 hours (c) €265 **18.** (b) 11.25 weeks (c) 13.25 cm **19.** (b) 75 days (c) 78 litres (d) 37.5 days **20.** (b) 7 hours (c) 55 cm **21.** (b) 66 cm (c) 50 cm (d) 4 tonnes **22.** (b) 40 cm (c) 16 days **23.** (b) 24 kPa (c) 18 days **24.** (b) 2.5 (d) Above 40 °F (e) 90 °F

Exercise 5.6

1. (2,4) **2.** (a) (3,4) (b) (2,6) (c) 5,−11) (d) (1,−3) (e) (−5,−2.5) (f) (−1,−1) (g) (1.6,4.8) (h) (−4,−8) (i) (2,−1) (j) (2,1) **3.** (a) (−4,−2) (b) $A(0,6)$ (c) $B(0,2)$ **4.** (a) (1,5) (b) $A(0,6)$ (c) $B(0,2)$ **5.** (a) (−0.2, −0.6) (b) (0, 0) (c) (0, −1) **6.** (a) $A = 5 + 3x, B = 11 + 2x$ (b) 6 days (d) 23 cm **7.** (a) $25 + 17x, 40 + 12x$ (c) 3 mins (d) 76 metres (e) They won't as the Balloon from Knock is released from a greater height and rises faster than the other two balloons. **8.** (b) Saucepan *B* (c) 44 mins (d) 49.4°C **9.** (b) 6.5 mins **10.** (a) $y = -25x - 300, y = -45x$ (c) (15,−675) (d) 15 days (e) 750 m deep

Self-check Test

1. (a) 5 (b) 4 (c) $\frac{1}{3}$ (d) −6 (e) 8 **2.** (a) 8, 13, 18, 23, 5 (b) 5, 8, 11, 14, 3 (c) 7, −4, −11, −18, −7 (d) 2, 0, −2, −4, −2 (e) 4, 8, 12, 16, 4 **3.** (a) 2 (b) 4 (c) 6 (d) 8 (e) 10 **4.** (a) −3 (b) −7 (c) −11 (d) −15 (e) −19 **5.** (a) 17 (b) 11 (c) 19 (d) 23 (e) 7 **6.** (a) −5 (b) $-\frac{7}{2}$ (c) $3t - 6$ (d) $6k - 6$ (e) $-3k - 6$ **7.** 4, 9, 14, 19 **8.** −21, 21, −33, 33 **9.** 0, 3, 12, 21, 30 **10.** −17, 39, −33, 55 **11.** $w = -8, x = 9, y = -11$ **12.** $w = 6, x = -55, y = 8$ **13.** (a) 3 (b) 9 (c) 48, 57, 66 (d) Increasing by 9 (e) 3, 12, 21, 30, 39, 48, 57, 66, 75, 84, 93, 102 (f) $9n + 3$ (g) 651 **14.** (a) $5n + 7$ (b) €32 **15.** (a) Each arm of the *x* is gaining a dot (b) Number of dots in the shape (c) 5, 9, 13, 17, 21, 25 (e) 81 dots **16.** (b) Number of green tiles is double the number of red tiles. **17.** (b) 14 reds **19.** $Q(0,4)$ **20.** $F(0,-9)$ **21.** $f: x \rightarrow 2x$, Graph A, Statement (d); $f(x): \rightarrow -3x$, Graph B, Statement (a); $f(x): \rightarrow -x$, Graph D, Statement (c); $f(x): \rightarrow x$, Graph C, Statement (b). **22.** 5 has 2 possible outputs **23.** (i) Not linear (ii) Not linear (iii) Not linear (iv) Linear $3n - 2$ (v) Linear $-25n + 31$ (vi) Linear $5n + 3$ (vii) Linear $10n - 24$ (viii) Not linear **24.** (a) 120 logs (b) *n* **25.** $T_n = 75n + 25$ (a) €14.50 (b) €22.75 **26.** (a) €37,750 (b) €40,250 **27.** $T_n = 8n + 52$ (a) 212 seats (b) 156 seats (c) €7,197.12 **28.** 55 blocks, 10 in bottom row **29.** $T_n = 1{,}750n + 20{,}000$ (a) €34,000 (b) €4,000 **30.** (a) $T_n = -15{,}000n + 365{,}000$ (b) €275,000 **31.** $T_n = 180n$, 2,160° **32.** (b) €150 (d) Straight line (f) €120 (i) 9 weeks

Chapter 6

Exercise 6.1

1. Name: Categorical nominal
D.O.B: Numerical discrete
Address: Categorical nominal
Weight: Numerical continuous
Height: Numerical continuous
Blood Type: Categorical nominal
Next of kin: Categorical nominal
Allergies: Categorical nominal
Phone: Numerical discrete
Occupation: Categorical nominal
2. General: Categorical nominal
Preference: Numerical ordinal
Calories: Numerical discrete
Sodium: Numerical discrete
3. Boat name: Categorical nominal
Flag: Categorical nominal
Built: Numerical discrete
Length: Numerical discrete
4. (a) Categorical (b) Numerical/discrete (c) Numerical/discrete (d) Continuous

Exercise 6.2

1. (a) Yes as they are sending to *all* houses in the locality. (b) People might not respond to it (c) Cheap. Everyone is asked. **2.** (a) No. The survey is for national house prices. She has only looked at prices in Dublin which are usually more expensive. (b) Take a random sample from each county.

Exercise 6.3

1. 4 **2.** 19.7 **3.** 2 **4.** €2.34 **5.** 3 min 7 sec **6.** 1.361 kg **7.** 3.8535 m **8.** 19 hr 8 min **9.** 16.58 **10.** 20.1 **11.** 30 **12.** 21 **13.** 20 **14.** 30 **15.** 32 **16.** 12 **17.** 9 **18.** 14 **19.** 16 **20.** 10 **21.** 15 **22.** 25 **23.** 25 **24.** 21 **25.** 13 **26.** 23 **27.** 35 **28.** 45 **29.** 3 **30.** −16 **31.** 46 **32.** €5.62 **33.** €3.11 **34.** €9.50 **35.** (a) €184.35 (b) €31 **36.** (a) 20 (b) 34 (c) 6 scoreless games

Exercise 6.4

1. (a) 2 (b) 1 (c) No mode (d) 3 (e) No mode (f) 22 (g) 106 **2.** (a) Pizza (b) Fish (c) Categorical **3.** (a) Reading (b) Going to the cinema (c) Categorical **4.** (a) Bus (b) Cycling (c) Categorical **5.** (a) 200 (b) Grand Canyon

(c) Eiffel Tower (d) Categorical **6.** (a) 33 (b) Hurling (c) Swimming (d) Categorical (e) No. Can't calculate mean for categories **7.** (a) BMW (b) Kia (c) Categorical **8.** (a) Tue, Wed, Sat, Sun (b) 12 (c) Sunday (d) Increases from Mon to Wed, Decreases Thur and Fri, Increases Sat and Sun **9.** (a) Tench (b) Carp (c) No, this is categorical data **10.** (a) 90 (b) Comedy (c) Horror **11.** (a) $x = 2$ (b) $x = 5$ (c) $x = 11$ (d) $x = 13$ (e) $x = 15$ (f) $x = 18$ (g) $x = 19$ (h) $x = 21$ **12.** 1, 2, 3, 7, 7 **13.** 5, 10, 10, 10, 10 **14.** 2, 3, 4, 5, 5, 5 **15.** 3, 6, 6

Exercise 6.5

1. (a) 4 (b) 4.7 (c) 8 **2.** (a) 1.2 (b) 1.77625 (c) 3.96 **3.** (a) 2 (b) 3 (c) 5 **4.** (a) 2 (b) 9 **5.** (a) 3 (b) 8 (c) 20 **6.** (a) No mode (b) 1.009 kg (c) 1.791 kg **7.** (a) 10 m (b) 37 m (c) 95 m **8.** (a) 29 m, 37 m, 44 m, 45 m, 47 m, 51 m, 53 m, 59 m (b) 30 m **9.** 3 min 1 sec, 2 min 10 sec, 2 min 9 sec, 1 min 50 sec, 1 min 46 sec **10.** 1 min 11 sec, 1 min 12 sec, 1 min 13 sec, 1 min 17 sec, 1 min 19 sec, 1 min 22 sec **12.** 2, 4, 7, 7, 10

Exercise 6.6

1. (a) 98 (b) 11.5 (c) €10.80 (d) 5.5 (e) 51% (f) 1.025 m **2.** (a) 1, 1, 1, 1, 1, 1, 1, 1, 1, 2, 2, 2, 2, 2, 2, 2, 3, 4, 5, 5 (b) 2 people (c) 1 person (d) 2 people **3.** (a) 30.2 yrs (b) 18 (c) 24 yrs (d) 38 yrs (e) 150 yrs. Unlikely anyone will be 150. **4.** (a) €0.69, €0.79, €0.99, €1.00, €1.04, €1.18, €1.28, €1.35, €1.39, €3.99 (b) €1.11 (c) €1.37 (d) No mode **5.** (a) 7.5 (b) 8 (c) 7.5 (d) 6 (e) Modal. Most common size so will need to stock more size 8s. (f) Median **6.** (a) 1.8 goals (b) 1 goal (c) 1 goal (d) 6 goals **7.** 3, 3, 7, 10, 21 **8.** 7, 10, 11, 11, 11 **9.** 1, 3, 6, 6, 8, 12 **10.** (a) 8 (b) 8 (c) $7.\dot{3}$ (d) 10 **11.** (a) 2.16 mins (b) 2 mins (c) 2 mins (d) 3 mins **12.** (a) 1.0925 m (b) 1 m (c) 1.05 m (d) 0.4 m **13.** (a) €3.50 (b) €4 (c) €3.75 (d) €9.60 **14.** (a) 133.11c (b) 133.9c (c) 132.9c (d) 130.9c (e) 3c

Exercise 6.7

1. (b) 1 goal (c) 3 goals (d) 9 matches (e) 2 goals (f) 2 goals **2.** (c) Silver (d) Categorical (e) Can only calculate for numerical data **3.** (a) 25 (b) 12 (c) 9 (d) 15 (e) 6 (f) 12 **4.** (a) 15 people (b) $5.2\dot{6}$ (c) 7 games **5.** (a) 0.5° (b) $k = 2$ (c) 36.8°C **6.** (b) 10–15 years **7.** (a) 30 people (b) 8–12 hours (c) 33.3% (d) 10 (e) 5 (f) 8–12 hours **8.** (a) 30 (b) 10–15 minutes (c) 66.6% (d) 20 (e) 9 (f) 10–15 minutes (g) 12.5 minutes **9.** (a) 100 cars (b) 40–50 km/h (c) 40% (d) 88 cars (e) 40 cars (f) 40–50 km/hr (g) 49.3 km/hr **10.** (a) 20 (b) €4–6 (c) 5 people (d) 1, 3, 5, 7, 9 (e) 14 people (f) 7 **11.** (a) 2.75 (b) 2 children (c) 22.5% **12.** (a) 3.57 skittles (b) 4 skittles (c) 9 (d) 28.57% (e) 14.29% (f) 4 **13.** (a) 25 (b) 40–60 minutes (c) 54 minutes (d) 40–60 minutes (e) 20% (f) 10 (g) 4 **14.** (a) 100 (b) 60–120 (c) €144 (d) 60–120 (e) 21% (f) 47 (g) 26 **15.** (a) 30 (b) 3 hours **16.** (b) 2–4 minutes (c) 4.8 minutes (d) 4–6 minutes **17.** (a) $x = 8$ (b) 40–60 **18.** (a) $x = 5$ (b) 12–16 mins **19.** (a) $4 = x$ (b) 20 (c) 25–35 minutes **20.** (a) $x = 3$ (b) 12–18

Exercise 6.8

1. (a) €30.50 (b) €30 (c) €35.40 (d) Mean. Extreme values of €5 and €90 will distort it. **2.** Mode - categorical data **3.** (a) Jam (b) No. Can't order the data (c) No. Categorical data **4.** (a) Mode. Used with categorical data (b) No. Categorical data

Self-check Test

1. (a) 3 (b) 3.5 (c) 2.4 (d) 0 (e) $2x$ (f) $3x + 5$ **2.** $y = 10$ **3.** (a) $a = 3$ (b) Mode = 0 **4.** 7 yrs 3 months **8.** (a) 40 (b) 60–80 (c) 23.40 minutes (d) 60–80 **9.** (a) 130 (b) 20–30 (c) 22.31 years (d) 40 people **10.** (a) 20 (b) 40–60% (c) 54 (d) 16 people **11.** (a) 60 plants (b) 31.3 cm (c) 30–40 cm **12.** (a) €36,300 (b) €25,000 (c) €27,500 (d) Mean as it will be distorted by the €110,000 salary (e) Remove €110,000

Chapter 8

Exercise 8.1

1. D **2.** (a) $\frac{|AB|}{|XY|} = \frac{|AC|}{|XZ|} = \frac{|BC|}{|YZ|}$ (b) $\frac{|EF|}{|MN|} = \frac{|DE|}{|LM|} = \frac{|DF|}{|LN|}$ (c) $\frac{|QS|}{|GJ|} = \frac{|RQ|}{|HJ|} = \frac{|RS|}{|GH|}$ (d) $\frac{|TV|}{|PN|} = \frac{|TU|}{|PM|} = \frac{|UV|}{|MN|}$ (e) $\frac{|WY|}{|AB|} = \frac{|XY|}{|AC|} = \frac{|WX|}{|BC|}$ (f) $\frac{|DE|}{|YZ|} = \frac{|EF|}{|XZ|} = \frac{|DF|}{|XY|}$ **3.** (a) $x = 20$ (b) $x = 14$ (c) $x = 12.5$ (d) $x = 3.6$ (e) $x = 12.5$ (f) $x = 47.36$ (g) $x = 52.5$ (h) $x = 19.2$ (i) $x = 14$ (j) $x = 14.8$

4. (a) (i) $|DE| = 7$, $|EF| = 3$, (ii) ΔABC has a scale factor of 3 or ΔDEF has a scale factor of $\frac{1}{3}$ (b) (i) $|KL| = 3.33$, $|KM| = 6$, (ii) ΔGHJ is 3 times ΔKML or ΔKML is $\frac{1}{3}$ of ΔGHJ (c) (i) $|PQ| = 25$, $|NQ| = 20$, (ii) ΔNPQ has a scale factor of 5, ΔRST has a scale factor of $\frac{1}{5}$ (d) (i) $|YZ| = 5.25$, $|XZ| = 4.5$, (ii) ΔUVW has a scale factor of $\frac{4}{3}$, ΔXYZ has a scale factor of $\frac{3}{4}$ (e) (i) $|EF| = 5\sqrt{8}$, $|DF| = 10$, (ii) ΔABC has a scale factor of $\frac{1}{5}$, ΔDEF has a scale factor of 5 (f) (i) $|KM| = 3.8$, $|KL| = 4.2$, (ii) ΔGHJ has a scale factor of 1.5, ΔKML has a scale factor of $\frac{2}{3}$ (g) (i) $|PQ| = 4.2$, $|NQ| = 2.1$, (ii) ΔNPQ has a scale factor of $\frac{3}{4}$, ΔRST has a scale factor of $\frac{4}{3}$ (h) (i) $|VW| = 8\frac{1}{3}$, $|UW| = 10.8\dot{3}$, (ii) ΔUVW has a scale factor of $\frac{5}{3}$, ΔXYZ has a scale factor of $\frac{3}{5}$ **5.** $|AB| = 3.75$, $|BE| = 7.5$ **6.** $|CE| = 3$, $|BC| = 6$

Exercise 8.2

1. (a) *ASA* (b) *SAS* (c) *RHS* (d) *SAS* (e) *SSS* (f) *RHS* (g) *ASA* (h) *SAS* (i) *SAS* (j) *SSS* **2.** $|AC| = |CE|$ told (S), $|\angle ACB| = |\angle DCE|$ vertically opposite (A), $|BC| = |CD|$ told (S), Congruent by SAS **3.** $|AC| = |AD|$ told (S), $|BC| = |BD|$ told (S), $|AB| = |AB|$ common (S), Congruent by *SSS* **4.** By since *SAS*, $|BC| = |CD|$ told (S), $|\angle BCA| = |\angle ACD|$ both 90° (A), $|AC| = |AC|$ common (S) **5.** $|CD| = |CF|$ told (S), $|\angle DCE| = |\angle ECF|$ since $\angle DCF$ is bisected (A), $|CE| = |CE|$ common side (S), Congruent by *SAS*. **6.** $\Delta ABE \equiv \Delta CDF$ by *RHS* since $|\angle AEB| = |\angle DFC|$ ... told 90° (A), $|AB| = |CD|$ opposite sides of a parallelogram (S), $|\angle ABE| = |\angle FDC|$ alternate angles **7.** $|AB| = |BD|$ told (S), $|\angle ACB| = |\angle DCB|$ both 90° (Angle), $|BC| = |BC|$ Common side, Congruent by *RHS* **8.** (a) 2 triangles (b) $\Delta ABC \equiv \Delta CDA$, by *SSS*, Since, $\left.\begin{matrix}|BC| = |AD|\\|AB| = |CD|\end{matrix}\right\}$ opposite sides of a parallelogram, $|AC| = |AC|$ common side **9.** Congruent by *SAS* **10.** $\Delta PQA \equiv \Delta RBS$ since $|\angle AQP| = |\angle BSR|$ (alternate angle), $|PQ| = |RS|$ (opposite sides of a parallelogram), $|\angle QPA| = |\angle SRB|$ told, hence $|PA| = |BR|$ **11.** $|\angle ACF| = |\angle BDF|$ by theorem, $|CF| = |FD|$ told, $|\angle AFC| = |\angle BFD|$ vertically opposite, therefore $\Delta ACF \equiv FBD$, hence $|AC| = |BD|$

Self-check Test

1. Two shapes are similar if one is a replica or a scale model of the other, e.g. different sizes of football jerseys. Dissimiliar shapes are 2 shapes that have no resemblence, e.g. a triangle and a square. **2.** The first picture shows similiarity; the second image is an enlarged version of the first. In Picture B the triangles are dissimilar because the first has a 90° angle but the second triangle has none **3.** B **4.** If their corresponding angles are equal and the lengths of their corresponding sides have been scaled down or up by the same scale factor **5.** (a) Yes they are similiar since both have the same sized angles of 42°, 42° and 96° (b) They are similiar since ABC has a scale factor of 2

(c) $\frac{10}{8} \neq \frac{8}{6} \neq \frac{6}{4}$ They are not similiar since they do not have a common scale factor **6.** $x = 3$ **7.** (a) $x = 30.29$ (b) $x = 13.6$, $y = 8.15$ (c) $x = 12, y = 9$ (d) $x = 5, y = 5$, angles = 30° **8.** $c = 8, d = 3$ **9.** Similar triangles mean that one is a replica of the other, albeit on a larger or smaller scale. *AAA* only guarantees identical angles, not identical side lengths or areas, therefore, it cannot show congruency. **10.** Tree = 9.6 m **11.** 12 **12.** (a) Both triangles are similar by *AAA*, $|\angle BAC| = |\angle CED|$, $|\angle ACB| = |\angle DEC|$, $|\angle ABC| = |\angle CDE|$ (b) $|DE| = 10$ **13.** Scale factor 2: 16 cm, 20 cm, 16 cm, 20 cm, Scale factor of $\frac{1}{2}$: 4 cm, 5 cm, 4 cm, 5 cm **14.** *EFGH* is $\frac{3}{4}$ the size of *ABCD*

15. (a) *RHS* (b) *ASA* (c) *SAS* (d) *ASA* (e) *RHS* **16.** $\Delta ADB \equiv \Delta BCD$, Congruent by *SSS* ⇒ Area *ADB* equals Area *BCD* **17.** $\Delta ABC \equiv \Delta ADC$, since $|AC| = |AC|$ common side, $|AB| = |AD|$ told, $|BC| = |CD|$ told, Congruent by *SSS* **18.** $|\angle AXW| = |\angle AZY|$ alternate (A), $|XW| = |YZ|$ opposite sides (S), $|\angle AWX| = |\angle AYZ|$ alternate (A), Since ΔXWA $\angle\Delta YAZ$ then $|XA| = |AZ|$ **19.** Since by RHS, hence $|AE| = |EC|$, $\Delta ADE \equiv \Delta DEC$, $|AD| = |CD|$ bisected, $|DE| = |DE|$ common, $|\angle EDA| = |\angle EDC| = 90°$ angle **20.** $|BF| = |EF|$ since F is midpoint of diagonal in a parallelogram (S), $|FC| = |DF|$ told (S), $|\angle BFC| = |\angle DFE|$ vertically opposite (A), Congruent by *SAS* **21.** $|AB| = |CD|$ opposite sides (S), $|\angle BAE| = |\angle FCD|$ vertically opposite angles (A), $|AE| = |FC|$ told (S), Congruent by *SAS*

Chapter 9

Exercise 9.1

1. $d = 5, h = 3, W = 46°, X = 48°, V = 94°, Y = 132°$ **2.** $h = 3$, $X = 114°, W = 66°, Z = 56°$ **3.** $Y = 4, X = 5$ **4.** $y = 3$ cm, $x = 2.9$ cm, $P = 103°, \theta = 64°, \alpha = 116°$ **5.** $y = 5$ cm, $\alpha = 131°$, $\beta = 49°, \varepsilon = 63°, \theta = 63°$ **6.** $w = 2.3$, $z = 3.1$ **7.** $y = 3$ cm, $x = 4$ cm, $P = 122°, \theta = 107°, \alpha = 73°$ **8.** $y = 4.5$ cm, $x = 3.2$ cm, $\varepsilon = 94°, \theta = 94°, \beta = 73°, \alpha = 107°$ **9.** $A = 4, B = 2.5$ **10.** $y = 4.2$ cm, $\alpha = 82°$, $x = 2.5$ cm, $\theta = 50°$ **11.** $y = 4.2$ cm, $\alpha = 109°$, $x = 2.5$ cm, $\theta = 91°$

Exercise 9.2

1. $y = 6$ **2.** $y = 7$ **3.** $y = 7.2$ **4.** $y = 10.5$ **5.** $y = 20$ **6.** $y = 15$ **7.** (a) 2 : 3 (b) 2 : 5 (c) 3 : 5 (d) 2 : 5 **8.** *DE* is not parallel with *AC*. **9.** (a) $x = 5.7$ (b) $|AD| = 4.7$, $|AC| = 12$ (c) $|AD| = 4.7$ **10.** (a) $|BE| = 3.3$ (b) $|CE| = 5.2$ (c) $|DE| = 4.7$ (d) $|CD| = 7.1$ **11.** (a) $|XY| = 7.5$ (b) $|XZ| = 10$ (c) $|PY| = 4.5$ **12.** (a) $|CE| = 7.5$ (b) $|CB| = 27.5$ (c) $|AC| = 16.5$

Self-check Test

1. (a) $C = 74°, W = 74°, Y = 106°$ (b) $X = 58°, Y = 122°$, $Q = 58°, R = 58°, P = 122°, S = 122°$ (c) $Z = 110°, X = 110°$, $W = 70°, Y = 70°$ (d) $A = 65°, B = 115°, C = 65°, Y = 115°$, $X = 115°, W = 65°, Z = 65°$ (e) $A = 61°, B = 119°, C = 61°$, $W = 61°, X = 119°$ (f) $A = 58°, C = 58°, Y = 58°, W = 58°$, $X = 122°, Z = 122°$ **2.** (a) $y = 13$ cm (b) $y = 15$ m (c) $y = 12.625$ m (d) $y = 10$ m (e) $y = 3$ m **3.** (a) $|AD| = 6$ cm (b) $|GH| = 9$ cm (c) $|EF| = 9$ cm (d) $|EH| = 27$ cm **4.** (a) $a = 8, b = 16$ (b) $b = 16, a = 26$ (c) $a = 11, b = 7$ **5.** (a) Not parallel (b) Not parallel (c) Parallel (d) Parallel **6.** (a) $|BC| = 20$ cm (b) $|CD| = 22.5$ cm **7.** (a) $|RY| = 37.5$ mm (b) $|XS| = 12$ mm **8.** (a) $|MN| = 20.4$ m (b) $|OP| = 3.75$ m (c) 71.85 m **9.** Tree = 710 cm **10.** (a) $\frac{\text{Small building}}{\text{Big building}} = \frac{\text{Small Shadow}}{\text{Big Shadow}}$ (b) 50 m **11.** (a) 111 cm (b) 123 cm (c) 118 cm (d) 125 cm **12.** (a) $[AG] = \frac{|AB|}{|AF|} = \frac{|AC|}{|AG|}$, $[FG] = \frac{|AB|}{|AF|} = \frac{|BC|}{|FG|}$ (b) 16 cm (c) $5\frac{1}{3}$ cm (d) 20 cm **13.** (a) Use similar triangles (b) 480 m **14.** (a) Create two triangles: a smaller one *ABE* and a larger one *ACD* (b) 31.2 m (c) 55.46 m (d) Multiple possible answers. E.g. They might have ensured a rope from *B* was perpendicular to [*CD*] and was the same length when lined up from *E* to the perpendicular line [*CD*]

Chapter 10

Exercise 10.1

5. (a) Yes (b) Yes (c) Yes (d) Yes (e) Yes **6.** 29 **7.** 13 **8.** 22.67 OR $\sqrt{514}$ **9.** 6 **10.** $\sqrt{85}$ OR 9.22 **11.** $2\sqrt{13}$ **12.** $\sqrt{7}$ **13.** 20 **14.** $\sqrt{15}$ **15.** (a) Yes (b) No (c) No (d) Yes **16.** (a) (i) Yes (ii) Yes (iii) Yes (iv) No (v) Yes (vi) No (vii) No (viii) Yes (ix) Yes (x) No

Exercise 10.2

1. 8 m **2.** 17 cm **3.** 6 m **4.** 5 m **5.** 66 cm **6.** 8 m **7.** 7 m, 14 cm **8.** 123.4 mm **9.** 192 mm **10.** 934 m

Self-Check Test

2. (a) $\sqrt{2}$ m (b) $2\sqrt{2}$ cm (f) (c) $4\sqrt{2}$ (d) $5\sqrt{2}$ cm (e) $8\sqrt{2}$ mm (f) $11\sqrt{2}$ km (g) $\sqrt{14}$ m (h) $2\sqrt{5}$ km (i) $2\sqrt{6}$ cm (j) $7\sqrt{10}$ mm **3.** (a) $\sqrt{13}$ cm (b) $\sqrt{353}$ cm (c) $\sqrt{40{,}169}$ cm (d) 6.08 m (e) $\sqrt{7}$ m (f) $\sqrt{10}$ m (g) $\sqrt{107}$ m (h) $\sqrt{670}$ m (i) $\sqrt{485}$ mm (j) $\frac{\sqrt{739}}{10\sqrt{2}}$ km **4.** (a) No (b) Yes (c) No (d) Yes (e) No **5.** (a) No (b) Yes (c) Yes (d) Yes (e) No (f) True, yes (g) No (h) No **6.** (a) True (b) Not true (c) True (d) True (e) True (f) True **7.** (a) $x = 3$ (b) $x = 8$ **8.** (a) 30 m (b) $16\sqrt{5}$ m **9.** 3.5 m **10.** (a) 498 cm (b) 4.21 m **11.** (a) $30\sqrt{6}$ m (b) $25\sqrt{19}$ m **12.** $|AO| = 6$ units $|OC| = 15$ units, $|AC| = 21$ units **13.** 25 km **14.** $2\sqrt{11}$ units **15.** Rope = 3 m 54 cm **16.** 183 m **17.** 116 m **18.** (a) 830 m (b) 294 m (c) 56.46 laps **19.** (a) 8 m 8 cm (b) 4 m 79 cm (c) 9 m 34 cm **20.** (a) $a = \sqrt{2}$

Chapter 11

Exercise 11.1

1. (a) 14 (b) 1,400 (c) 13% **2.** (a) 12 (b) 1,200 **3.** 900 **4.** 600 **5.** 900 **6.** 12,200 **7.** 1,200 **8.** 1,350 **9.** 2,600 **10.** 500 **11.** 8,500 **12.** 5,800 **13.** €140.25 **14.** €141,87.50 **15.** €1,175 + 23.50 = €1,198.50 **16.** €5,600 **17.** €1,230 **18.** €540 **19.** €258.75 **20.** €851.25 **21.** €287.70 **22.** €271.04

Exercise 11.2

1. (a) 20% Profit (b) 18.2% Profit (c) 16.7% Loss (d) 10% Profit (e) 20% Loss (f) 66.7% Profit (g) 20% Profit (h) 46.3% Profit (i) 111% Profit (j) 19.2% Loss **2.** 316.6% Profit **3.** 13.3% Loss **4.** €120 **5.** €96 **6.** €3,400 **7.** €933.33 **8.** €21,000 **9.** €320,000 **10.** €128,000

Exercise 11.3

1. €123 **2.** €67.83 **3.** €410.13 **4.** €36.55 **5.** €117 **6.** €200 **7.** €65.45 **8.** €299 **9.** €1,093.75 **10.** €5,604 **11.** €282.03 **12.** €599.03 **13.** €2,130.10 **14.** €9,333 **15.** €11,597.25 **16.** €26.79 **17.** €222,250 **18.** €66,150 **19.** €205,590 **20.** €753.30 **21.** 2.04% **22.** 26.5% **23.** 131% **24.** 64%

Exercise 11.4

1. (a) €15 = 10% (b) €13 = 10.8% (c) €13 = 13.7% (d) €6 = 10.9% (e) €10 = 25% (f) €20 = 10% (g) €99.99 = 10% (h) €125 = $8\frac{1}{3}$% (i) €7.50 = 15.8% (j) €4.99 = 25% **2.** (a) €306.25 (b) €87.50 (c) €393.75 (d) €866.25 (e) €599.38 **3.** (a) $8\frac{1}{3}$% (b) 25% (c) 4% (d) 20.8% (e) 9.1% (f) 2.1% (g) 2.5% **4.** (a) €14,040 (b) €11,934 **5.** (a) €15,799 (b) €11,558.07 **6.** €18,839.28 **7.** €103,973.12 **8.** €241,918 **9.** €15,407.33

Exercise 11.5

1. (a) €6.30; €36.30 (c) €100.80; €940.80 (d) €16.17; €163.17 (e) €65; €315 (f) €3.24; €27.24 (g) €5.25; €30.25

(h) €1.26; €15.26 (i) €15.01; €94.01 (j) €227.50; €1,527.50 **2.** (a) €150 (b) €200 (c) €321 (d) €175 (e) €90 (f) €45 (g) €2400 (h) €15,540 (i) €4,300 (j) €165 **3.** €2,610.50 **4.** €133.10 **5.** €184.80 **6.** (a) €29.70 (b) €220 **7.** €199 **8.** €1,200; €102; €13.77; €115.75 **9.** (a) €4 (b) €2 (c) €46 (d) €52.44 **10.** €28,500 **11.** €392 **12.** €250 **13.** €16.67 **14.** (a) €148 (b) €183.52 **15.** (a) €51 (b) €306 (c) €12.75 **16.** (a) €78.80 (b) €89.44 **17.** (a) €170 (b) €192.95

Exercise 11.6

1. Thailand = Baht New Zealand = NZ $ Vietnam = Dong USA = US $ Japan = Yen ¥ Cuba = Peso South Africa = Rand Latvia = Euro **2.** (a) £205.40 (b) £395 (c) €750 (d) €1,200 (e) £195.13; £375.25; €712.50; €1,140 **3.** (a) ¥12,852,000 (b) $390 (c) €750 (d) €600 (e) $780 (f) €420 (g) ¥10,584,000 (h) £200 (i) ¥8,190,000 (j) $585 **4.** £206.63; 19,950 baht **5.** (a) 8190 Rand (b) They would have got an extra 682.5 Rand **6.** (a) The car is cheaper in England by €799 (b) The car is no longer cheaper, it is €3,205 dearer. **7.** (a) £267.92 (b) Yes Belfast offers better value by £14.32 **8.** €1,250 **9.** €878 **10.** New York

Exercise 11.7

1. 4.5% **2.** 21% **3.** 2% **4.** 21% **5.** (a) 20% (b) €268.40 **6.** 25% **7.** 21% **8.** (a) 24% (b) €38.40

Exercise 11.8

1. €256.25 **2.** €9,834.54 **3.** (a) €15,918.12 (b) €918.12 **4.** €489.60 **5.** (a) €27,318.18 (b) €2,318.18 **6.** €31,827 **7.** €146,232.32 **8.** (a) €53,707 (b) €130,560.30 **9.** (a) €11,451.54; €1,451.51 (b) €5,788.13; €788.13 (c) 23,370.88; €3,370.88 (d) €11,140.48; €1,140.48 (e) €11,140.48; €1,140.48 (f) €43,254.75; €8,254.75 (g) €113,374.08; €23,374.08 (h) €27,052.31; €2052.31 (i) €53,628.54; €3,628.54 (j) €157,459.68; €7,459.68

10. €7155 **11.** €50,000 **12.** 5% **13.** Withdrew €788 **14.** €16,320 **15.** €707,14 **16.** €2,479 **17.** €674.67 **18.** €5,531.97 **19.** €5,031.40 **20.** €20,000 **21.** (a) €52,787.50 (b) 4% **22.** €50,000 **23.** (a) €86,131.03 (b) €200,000 **24.** (a) €287,370 (b) 0.8%

Exercise 11.9

1. (a) €0.75 (b) 100% (c) 50% **2.** (a) €2,775 (b) $\frac{3}{17}$ (c) 17.6% **3.** (a) €23,000 (b) $\frac{46}{517}$ (c) 8.9% **4.** (a) 20%; 16.7% (b) 50%; $33\frac{1}{3}$% (c) 125%; 55.6% (d) 66.7%; 40% (e) 62.5%; 38.5% (f) 37%; 27% (g) 45%; 31% (h) $36\frac{1}{2}$%; 26.7% (i) 47%; 32% (j) 34%; 25.4% **5.** (a) €160 (b) €128.6% (c) €56.25% **6.** (a) €190 (b) €166.25 **7.** (a) €19,230.77 (b) €3,269.23 **8.** (a) €210,000 (b) €48,000 (c) 19% **19.** (a) €34,300 (b) 145.3% (c) 59% **10.** (a) €7 (b) 70% (c) 41% (d) €3 (e) 30% (f) 23% **11.** (a) €80 (b) 40% (c) 29% (d) €52 (e) 26% (f) 21% **12.** (a) 16.7% (b) 20% **13.** (a) 12.5% (b) 14.3% **14.** 37% **15.** (a) 239% (b) 71%

Self-check Test

1. 13.5 **2.** 30 **3.** 100 **4.** 295 **5.** 1,875 **6.** 90 **7.** 110 **8.** 592.2 **9.** 5.07 **10.** 582.8 **11.** 261 **12.** 300 **13.** 40% **14.** 25% **15.** 10% **16.** 16.7% **17.** 50% **18.** 16.7 **19.** $8\frac{1}{3}$% **20.** 14.3% **21.** (a) €600 (b) 71% **22.** €127.50 **23.** €24,725 **24.** €120 **25.** €1,500 **26.** €2,731.82 **27.** €678.13 **28.** €208 **29.** (a) ¥30,870,000 (b) €2,156 (c) ¥15,435,000 **30.** (a) €150 (b) 75% (c) 43% **31.** 19% **32.** (a) 59% (b) 142% (c) 49% **33.** (a) €24 (b) 73% (c) 42% **34.** (a) €27,758.45 (b) €17,241.55 (c) €52,000 **35.** (a) €13,879 (b) €12,409.18 **36.** €1,478

Chapter 12

Exercise 12.1

1. 5 **2.** 10 **3.** 1 **4.** $4\sqrt{2}$ **5.** $\sqrt{97}$ **6.** $\sqrt{122}$ **7.** $\sqrt{269}$ **8.** 10 **9.** $\sqrt{185}$ **10.** $2\sqrt{13}$ **11.** $3\sqrt{10}$ **12.** $2\sqrt{65}$ **13.** $\sqrt{41}$ **14.** 7.1 **15.** (a) No collinear (b) $|AC| = |CA|$ **16.** (a) Collinear (b) $\sqrt{13}$ **17.** $10 \neq \sqrt{13} + \sqrt{41}$ **18.** Station 1 is closer **19.** $\sqrt{26}$ **20.** Δ is isosceles **21.** Δ*XYZ* is right angled **22.** *ABCD* is a parallelogram **23.** Scalene **24.** Rhombus **25.** (a) $\sqrt{58}$ (b) $\sqrt{41}$ (c) $\sqrt{52}$ (d) $\sqrt{50}$ (e) 13 (f) $\sqrt{113}$ (g) $\sqrt{34}$ **26.** (a) $\sqrt{37}$ (b) $3\sqrt{2}$ (c) 34.8 **27.** $2\sqrt{10}$ **28.** (a) 2.86 (b) 0.94 (c) 2.9 (d) (i) 4.038566×10^{15} (ii) 2.298294×10^{15}

Exercise 12.2

1. (3, 4) **2.** (2, 7) **3.** (4, 5) **4.** $\left(\frac{3}{2}, -4\right)$ **5.** $\left(2, \frac{17}{2}\right)$ **6.** (5, 8) **7.** $\left(-\frac{9}{2}, 0\right)$ **8.** $\left(\frac{3}{2}, \frac{3}{2}\right)$ **9.** $\left(\frac{7}{2}, -\frac{7}{2}\right)$ **10.** (3, 6) **11.** (a) (8, −2) (b) (11, 2) (c) (15, 5) **12.** (6, 0) on *x*-axis **13.** (0, 3) on *y*-axis **14.** *P*(3, −1) **15.** *R*(3, 2) **16.** *E*(1, −1) **17.** (b) $\left(\frac{15}{2}, 2\right)$ (c) $\left(\frac{15}{2}, 2\right)$ **18.** (a) $\left(\frac{5}{2}, \frac{1}{2}\right)$ (b) (5, 1) (c) (6, −2) **19.** (a) (8, 8) **20.** (b) *W*(2, 7) (c) *X*(6, 3) (d) *Y*(6, 7) (e) (6, 5), (4, 7), (4, 5)

Exercise 12.3

1. $\frac{4}{9}$ **2.** 5 **3.** 4 **4.** $-\frac{1}{2}$ **5.** $-\frac{8}{5}$ **6.** $-\frac{1}{4}$ **7.** $\frac{4}{7}$ **8.** $\frac{7}{3}$ **9.** 3 **10.** 2 **11.** −3 **12.** 2 **13.** −2 **14.** −1 **15.** −1 **16.** $\frac{7}{5}$ **17.** −3 **18.** $f = 0; e = 0.5; h = 2; k = 7; i = -\frac{2}{5}; g = -1; j = -4$ **19.** (a) $2, -\frac{4}{5}$ (b) $2, -\frac{4}{3}$ (c) $\frac{3}{4}, -\frac{1}{2}$ (d) $\frac{5}{2}, -\frac{7}{4}$ (e) $-\frac{2}{5}, -\frac{1}{5}$ (f) $-\frac{5}{3}, 0$ **20.** (a) $\frac{3}{4}$ (b) 1 (c) $\frac{4}{3}$ **21.** $\frac{8}{7}$ **22.** $h = 5$ **23.** $t = -40$ **24.** $k = 10$ **25.** $S = -16$ **26.** $\frac{4}{5}$ **27.** (a) $M[AB] = 4; M[DC] = \frac{1}{2}; M[EF] = \frac{3}{4}$ (b) [*DC*] is Beginner, [*EF*] is Intermediate, [*AB*] is Advanced

Exercise 12.4

1. Parallel **2.** Parallel **3.** Parallel **4.** Not parallel **5.** Not parallel **6.** Not parallel **7.** Parallel **8.** Not parallel **9.** (a) Parallel (b) Parallel (c) Parallel (d) Parallel **10.** Yes, Slope = $\frac{5}{4}$ of both roads. **11.** (a) $\frac{7}{3}$ (b) $\frac{7}{3}$ (c) Parallel **12.** Yes **13.** (a) $-\frac{3}{4}$ (b) $-\frac{2}{3}$ (c) $-\frac{7}{5}$ (d) $+\frac{9}{4}$ (e) $+\frac{11}{5}$ (f) $+\frac{3}{2}$ (g) $-\frac{1}{2}$ (h) $+\frac{1}{3}$ (i) $-\frac{1}{4}$ (j) −7 (k) −9 (l) −13 (m) $+\frac{13}{4}$ (n) $-\frac{3}{11}$ (o) $+\frac{7}{10}$ **14.** Perpendicular **15.** $-\frac{7}{4}$ **16.** Not right angled **17.** Right angled **18.** Not right angled **19.** Not perpendicular **20.** No **21.** *WXYZ* is a parallelogram **22.** Not a parallelogram **23.** (a) Rhombus (b) *GHIJ* is a square (c) Perpendicular to each other

Exercise 12.5

1. $3x - 4y - 11 = 0$ **2.** $x + 2y - 4 = 0$ **3.** $x + 4y - 24 = 0$ **4.** $4x - y - 2 = 0$ **5.** $4x + 3y - 12 = 0$ **6.** $y = 3$ **7.** $2x - y = 0$ **8.** $3x - 4y + 3 = 0$ **9.** $x + y - 15 = 0$ **10.** $x + 8y + 3 = 0$ **11.** $x + 3y - 6 = 0$ **12.** $10x + 3y + 2 = 0$ **13.** $4x - 3y - 5 = 0$ **14.** $2x - 5y + 3 = 0$ **15.** $3x + y + 5 = 0$ **16.** (a) $3x - 4y - 32 = 0$ (b) $x - y - 9 = 0$ (c) $4x - 3y - 45 = 0$ **17.** (a) $4x - y - 6 = 0$ (b) $2x - y + 7 = 0$ (c) $x + y - 3 = 0$ (d) $2x + y - 4 = 0$ (e) $3x - 7y - 3 = 0$ (f) $4x + 7y - 2 = 0$ (g) $3x - 4y - 2 = 0$ (h) $3x + 5y + 9 = 0$ **18.** (a) $y = 5$ (c) (0, 5) **19.** (a) $y = 1$ (c) (0, 1) **20.** (a) $y = 4$ (b) $y = -2$ (c) $y = -2$ (d) $y = -4$ (e) $y = 6$ **21.** (a) $x = 4$ (b) $x = -2$ (c) $x = 1$ (d) $x = -1$ (e) $x = 0$ **22.** Parallel **23.** Parallel **24.** (a) $x - 6y + 45 = 0$ (b) $y = 3$ (c) $3x - y - 18 = 0$ **25.** $3x + 7y - 6 = 0$

Exercise 12.6

1. $y = 1x + 4$ **2.** $y = -\frac{2}{3}x + 6$ **3.** $y = -2$ **4.** $y = \frac{2}{4}x - 2$ **5.** $y = \frac{2}{4}x - 6$ **6.** $y = -\frac{2}{3}x + 8$ **7.** $y = -\frac{7}{3}x - 4$ **8.** $y = -1x$ **9.** $y = \frac{2}{3}x + 1$ **10.** $y = -\frac{8}{5}x + 5$ **11.** $y = \frac{2}{3}x - 5$ **12.** $y = -\frac{1}{2}x$ **13.** $y = -\frac{5}{2}x + 4$ **14.** $y = 3x + 12$ **15.** $y = \frac{5}{2}x + \frac{7}{2}$

16. $y = \frac{7}{5}x + \frac{12}{5}$ **17.** $y = \frac{2}{3}x + \frac{7}{3}$ **18.** $y = -\frac{1}{12}x + 2$
19. $y = -5x + 9$ **20.** $y = \frac{1}{3}x - \frac{8}{3}$ **21.** (a) $y = 3x + 2$
(b) $y = -4x - 1$ (c) $y = \frac{2}{3}x + 5$ (d) $y = -\frac{3}{5}x - 3$ (e) $y = 2.5x + 4$
22. (a) $y = -\frac{1}{5}x + 5$ (c) (5, 4) **23.** (a) $y = -\frac{1}{2}x + 4$, $y = \frac{2}{3}x - 3$
(c) (6, −1) **24.** (a) $y = \frac{1}{4}x + 2$, $y = -\frac{3}{2} - 5$ (c) (−4, 1)

Exercise 12.7

1. (a) $\frac{1}{2}$, (0, 5) (b) $y = \frac{1}{2}x + 5$ **2.** (a) $\frac{5}{2}$, (0, −4) (b) $y = \frac{5}{2}x - 4$
3. (a) $-\frac{3}{4}$, (0, 0) (b) $y = -\frac{3}{4}x + 0$ **4.** (a) $-\frac{4}{3}$, (0, −4)
(b) $y = -\frac{4}{3}x - 4$ **5.** (a) $\frac{2}{3}$, (0, −6), (b) $y = \frac{2}{3}x - 6$
6. (a) $\frac{1}{2}$, (0, 4) (b) $y = \frac{1}{2}x + 4$ **7.** (a) $\frac{2}{5}$, 3 (b) $y = \frac{2}{5}x + 3$
8. (a) −1, −4 (b) $y = -x - 4$ **9.** (a) $-\frac{3}{7}, \frac{5}{7}$ (b) $y = -\frac{3}{7}y + \frac{5}{7}$
10. Perpendicular (b) Perpendicular (c) Perpendicular (d) Perpendicular (e) Perpendicular (f) Parallel (g) Not parallel or perpendicular (h) Not parallel or perpendicular

Exercise 12.8

1. (a) $\frac{3}{4}$ (b) $\frac{4}{3}$ (c) $3x - 4y - 7 = 0$ (d) l: $y = \frac{3}{4}x + 3$;
m: $y = \frac{3}{4}x - \frac{7}{4}$; y-intercept is different. **2.** (a) $\frac{2}{7}$ (b) $-\frac{7}{2}$
(c) $7x + 2y - 20 = 0$ **3.** $3x + 2y - 23 = 0$ **4.** $2x - 3y = 0$
5. $x + y - 6 = 0$ **6.** $x + y - 8 = 0$ **7.** $4x - 3y - 8 = 0$
8. $4x + 3y - 37 = 0$ **9.** $2x + 3y - 21 = 0$ **10.** $3x - 4y - 12 = 0$
11. $4x + 3y + 8 = 0$ **12.** $2x - 5y - 14 = 0$ **13.** $5x + 6y - 39 = 0$
14. $3x - 5y - 19 = 0$ **15.** $2x - 3y + 8 = 0$ **16.** $x - 5y + 4 = 0$
17. $4x - 3y - 5 = 0$ **18.** $x - 6y + 21 = 0$ **19.** $2x - 3y - 20 = 0$
20. $x + 2y + 2 = 0$ **22.** Wall is not perpendicular to beam

Exercise 12.9

5. $t = 2$ **6.** $k = 5$ **7.** $s = 2$ **8.** $k = -1$ **9.** $s = -1$ **10.** $g = -2$

Exercise 12.10

1. (−6, 0) (0, 4) **2.** (−3, 0) (0, −3) **3.** (7, 0) (0, 7) **4.** (4, 0) (0, −2) **5.** (−6, 0) (0, 5) **6.** (2, 0) (0, 7) **7.** (−5, 0) (0, −3) **8.** (4, 0) (0, −4) **9.** (a) (0, 6) (3, 0) (b) (0, −3) (2, 0) (c) (0, 5) (−2, 0) (d) (0, 4) (−2, 0) (e) (0, 2) (5, 0) (f) (0, 7) (2, 0)
10. Negative **11.** Positive **12.** Positive **13.** Positive
14. Negative **15.** Undefined **16.** Undefined **17.** Slope = 0
18. Slope = 0 **19.** Undefined **20.** Positive **21.** Positive

Exercise 12.11

1. (−2, 4) **2.** (3, 0) **3.** (3, 2) **4.** (4, 6) **5.** (3, 8) **6.** (3, −5)
7. $\left(-\frac{5}{3}, -3\right)$ **8.** (3, −3) **9.** $\left(\frac{5}{4}, 3\right)$ **10.** (4, 5) **11.** (3, −2)
12. (12, 6) **13.** (2, 2) **14.** (9, 4) **15.** (3, 2) **16.** (a) (10, 4)
(b) (4, −3) (c) $\left(\frac{3}{2}, 1\right)$ (d) (4, 1) (e) (6, 1)
17. Standard = 7 grams, Superior = 8 grams **18.** $x = 15, y = 30$
19. Abelia = €12, Camellia = €15 **20.** Adult = €18, Child = €10
21. 15 geese, 6 sheep **22.** $x = 45, y = 36$

Exercise 12.12

1. (2, −4) **2.** (3, −5) **3.** (−1, −4) **4.** (−2, 3) **5.** (3, 2)
6. (−3, 5) **7.** (0, −3) **8.** (0, 0) **9.** (−2, 9) **10.** (−3, 0)
11. (0, 4) **12.** (−4, 5) **13.** (0, −3) **14.** (3, 0) **15.** (−1, 3)
16. (1, −2) **17.** (−2, −3) **18.** (−1, 2) **19.** (−5, 4) **20.** (6, 1)
21. (1, 1) **22.** (−2, 9) **23.** (−3, 1) **24.** (0, 5)

Self-check Test

1. (a) 5 (b) $\left(\frac{9}{2}, 6\right)$ (c) $-\frac{4}{3}$ (d) $y = -\frac{4}{3}x + 12$ **2.** (a) 6
(b) (5, 3) (c) Undefined (d) $x = 5$ **3.** (a) 7
(b) $\left(-4, \frac{17}{2}\right)$ (c) Undefined (d) $x = -4$ **4.** (a) $\sqrt{13}$
(b) $\left(\frac{7}{2}, 7\right)$ (c) $\frac{2}{3}$ (d) $y = \frac{2}{3}x + \frac{14}{3}$ **5.** (a) $\sqrt{226}$ (b) $\frac{-9}{2}, \frac{-1}{2}$
(c) 15 (d) $y = 15x + 67$ **6.** (a) $\sqrt{164}$ (b) (1, 1) (c) $-\frac{5}{4}$
(d) $y = -\frac{5}{4}x + \frac{9}{4}$ **7.** (a) $4\sqrt{10}$ (b) (1, −2) (c) −3
(d) $y = -3x + 1$ **8.** (a) $\sqrt{730}$ (b) $\left(\frac{9}{2}, -\frac{27}{2}\right)$ (c) 7
(d) $y = 7x - 45$ **9.** (a) (6, 0) (b) (0, 4) (c) $-\frac{2}{3}$ (d) $y = \frac{2}{3}x + 4$
10. (a) l: $y = x + 2$ (b) k: $y = -\frac{4}{3}x + 2$ (c) (0, 2) (d) (0, 2)
11. (a) $m = -\frac{5}{3}$ (b) $m = \frac{3}{5}$ (c) Perpendicular **13.** $2x - y = 0$
14. (a) $p = 5, q = 8$ (b) $a = 4, b = -1$ (c) $m = 1, n = 5$
(d) $h = 3, k = 2$ (e) $m = 2, n = \frac{1}{2}$ (f) $x = 3, y = 2$
15. (a) $6x - 5y - 22 = 0$ (b) $5x + 6y - 34 = 0$
(c) $6x - 5y + 8 = 0$ **16.** Not parallel **17.** Perpendicular
18. Parallelogram. **19.** (10, 7) **20.** (5, 4) **21.** (−3, 3)

Chapter 13

Exercise 13.1

1. 44 m **2.** 44 mm **3.** 33.5 m **4.** 57 m **5.** 56 cm
6. 68 m **7.** 44 cm **8.** 92 mm **9.** 92 cm **10.** 104 m
11. 112 km **12.** 105 cm **13.** 12 cm **14.** 14.5 m
15. $\sqrt{200}$ **16.** 39.8 cm **17.** 35 m **18.** 35.5 m, 106.5 m
19. 5 cm **20.** 57 cm **21.** Scalene triangle

Exercise 13.2

1. (b) 160 m (c) 1,500 m^2 **2.** (b) 24 m (c) 36 m^2
3. (a) Perimeter = 20 m, Area = 24 m^2
(b) Perimeter = 140 cm, Area = 1,200 cm^2
(c) Perimeter = 420 mm, Area = 2,000 mm^2
(d) Perimeter = 70 mm, Area = 300 mm^2
(e) Perimeter = 440 cm, Area = 4,000 cm^2
(f) Perimeter = 2,040 mm, Area = 20,000 mm^2
(g) Perimeter = 10,012 m, Area = 30,000 m^2
(h) Perimeter = 100 cm, Area = 600 cm^2
(i) Perimeter = 12.4 m, Area = 9.6 m^2
(j) Perimeter = 92 m, Area = 522.75 m **4.** (a) Area = 13.8 m^2
(b) Area = 60 cm^2 (c) Area = 70 m^2 (d) Area = 99.22 m^2
(e) Area = 184.92 m^2 (f) Area = 240 mm^2
(g) Area = 42.35 m^2 (h) Area = 38.22 m^2
5. (a) Perimeter = 83 mm, Area = 227 mm^2
(b) Perimeter = 108 cm, Area = 538 cm^2 (c) Perimeter = 68 m, Area = 111 m^2 (d) Perimeter = 1,180 cm, Area = 47,300 cm^2
6. (a) Inner Shape = 12 cm^2, Shaded = 60 cm^2
(b) Inner Area = 9.75 cm^2, Shaded Area = 26.97 cm^2
(c) Inner Area = 24 cm^2, Shaded = 24 cm^2 **7.** 6 cm
8. (a) 44 m (b) 112 m^2 (c) 3.5 bags **9.** (a) 400 cm^2
(b) 560,000 cm^2 (c) 1,400 tiles **10.** (a) 75 m^2 (b) 15 packs
(c) €239.85 (d) €41.40 **11.** (a) 892.5 m^2 (b) 10.5 packs
(c) €341 **12.** (a) 272 m^2 (b) 0.25 m^2 (c) 1,088 stones
(d) €816 (e) €850 **13.** (a) 135 m (b) 11,475 m^2
(c) €212,287.50 **14.** (a) 50.5 m^2 (b) 4.25 m
15. (a) 13,500 m^2 (b) 480 m (c) €4,257

Exercise 13.3

1. (a) 10.5 cm^2 (b) 11 cm^2 (c) 8 cm^2 **2.** (a) 24 cm^2
(b) 35 cm^2 (c) 20 cm^2 (d) 18 cm^2 (e) 96 cm^2 (f) 36 cm^2
3. (a) $h = 15$ cm (b) $x = 6$ cm (c) $x = 9.5$ cm (d) $x = 100$ cm
(e) $x = 4$ cm (f) $x = 27.5$ cm (g) $x = 28$ cm (h) $x = 7$ cm
4. (a) 42 cm^2 (b) 180 cm^2 (c) 3.48 cm^2 (d) 144.5 cm^2
(e) 98 cm^2 (f) 143 cm^2 (g) 15.25 cm^2 **5.** 16 cm^2
6. (a) $x = 26$ cm (b) 60 cm (c) 120 cm^2 **7.** $a = 13$ cm
8. (a) 23 cm (b) 483 cm^2 (c) 50% **9.** (a) 12 cm
(b) 72 cm^2 (c) $x = 13.4$ cm **10.** (a) $x = 29$ cm (b) 210 cm^2
11. (a) 112 cm^2 (b) 102 cm^2 **12.** $h = 2\sqrt{3}$ cm (b) $4\sqrt{3}$ cm^2

Exercise 13.4

1. (a) Area = 154 cm^2, Circumference = 44 cm
(b) Area = 38.5 cm^2, Circumference = 22 cm
(c) Area = 616 cm^2, Circumference = 88 cm
(d) Area = 1,386 cm^2, Circumference = 132 cm
2. (a) Area = 113.10 cm^2, L = 37.70 cm (b) A = 314.16 cm^2, L = 62.83 cm (c) A = 907.92 cm^2, L = 108.81 cm
(d) A = 1,963.49 cm^2, L = 157.08 cm (e) A = 1,063.62 cm^2, L = 115.61 cm (f) Area = 1,618.83 cm^2, L = 142.63 cm
3. (a) (i) L = 30.85 cm (ii) A = 56.55 cm^2 (b) (i) L = 20.57 cm

(ii) A = 25.13 cm^2 (c) (i) L = 6.28 cm (ii) A = 15.71 cm^2 (d) (i) L = 6.28 cm (ii) A = 6.28 cm^2 (e) (i) L = 31.42 cm (ii) A = 188.50 cm^2 (f) (i) L = 17.59 cm (ii) A = 61.58 cm^2 (g) (i) L = 18.85 mm (ii) A = 113.10 cm^2 **4.** r = 8.18 cm **5.** r = 25.46 cm **6.** r = 5.35 cm **7.** r = 15.44 cm **8.** r = 3.43 cm **9.** r = 5.89 cm **10.** r = 3.91 cm **11.** r = 15.76 cm **12.** Circle = 12.56; Shaded = 3.44 cm^2 **13.** (a) 3 cm (b) 7.7 cm^2 **14.** 288 cm^2 **15.** (a) 616 cm^2 (b) 88 cm **16.** r = 33 m **17.** (a) 3,944 m^2 (b) 300 m **18.** 19.1 m^2 **19.** 13.9 m^2 **21.** 0.5 m^2 **22.** (a) 24 cm^2 (b) x = 10 cm (c) 78.5 cm^2 **23.** 100 cm **24.** (a) 4.2 m^2 (b) 7 m (c) 0.38 m **25.** 440.6 cm^2

Exercise 13.5

1. (a) 5 km (b) 12 km (c) 200 cm (d) 100 cm (e) 5 cm (f) 2,000 km **3.** (a) 1.6 m (b) 40 cm, 15 cm **4.** (a) 84 cm, 56 cm (b) d = 74 cm

Exercise 13.7

1. Prism **2.** Cube **3.** Cylinder **4.** Hexagon **5.** Cone

Exercise 13.8

1. (a) 302 cm^2 (b) 528 cm^2 **2.** (a) 440 cm^2 (b) 597 cm^2 **3.** (a) 572 cm^2 (b) 880 cm^2 **4.** (a) 226 cm^2 (b) 735 cm^2 **5.** (a) 503 cm^2 (b) 660 cm^2 **6.** (a) 251 cm^2 (b) 276 cm^2 **7.** (a) 226 cm^2 (b) 283 cm^2 **8.** (a) 396 cm^2 (b) 704 cm^2 **9.** (a) 748 cm^2 (b) 1,056 cm^2 **10.** (a) 572 cm^2 (b) 880 cm^2 **11.** (a) 47 cm^2 (b) 75 cm^2 **12.** (a) 188 cm^2 (b) 301 cm^2 **13.** (a) 204 cm^2 (b) 283 cm^2 **14.** (a) 293 cm^2 (b) 372 cm^2 **15.** (a) 780 cm^2 (b) 1,311 cm^2 **16.** (a) 63 cm^2 (b) 91 cm^2 **17.** (a) 176 cm^2 (b) 255 cm^2 **18.** (a) 1,068 cm^2 (b) 1,775 cm^2 **19.** (a) 811 cm^2 (b) 1,342 cm^2 **20.** (a) 220 cm^2 (b) 333 cm^2 **21.** 616 cm^2 **22.** 314 cm^2 **23.** 2,463 cm^2 **24.** 1,385 cm^2 **25.** 1,018 cm^2 **26.** 452 cm^2 **27.** 201 cm^2 **28.** 84 cm^2 **29.** 158 cm^2 **30.** 88 cm^2 **31.** 128 cm^2 **32.** 102 cm^2 **33.** 210 cm^2 **34.** r = 3 cm **35.** h = 5 cm **36.** 5 cm **37.** 527.8 cm^2 **38.** r = 7 cm **39.** l = 24.5 cm **40.** (a) 307.78 cm^2 (b) No

Self-check Test

2. (a) Area = 370.29 cm^2, Perimeter = 86.4 cm (b) Area = 222.86 cm^2, Perimeter = 58.13 cm (c) Area = 186.48 cm^2, Perimeter = 57.5 cm (d) Area = 125.91 cm^2, Perimeter = 56.8 cm (e) Area = 289.77 cm^2, Perimeter = 72.7 cm (f) Area = 298.07 cm^2, Perimeter = 88.47 cm (g) Area = 192 cm^2, Perimeter = 58.12 cm (h) Area = 64 cm^2, Perimeter = 50.6 cm (i) Area = 180 cm^2, Perimeter = 52 cm (j) Area = 67.5 cm^2, Perimeter = 43.95 cm (k) Area = 52.5 cm^2, Perimeter = 33.07 cm (l) Area = 25 mm^2, Perimeter = 52 mm (m) Area = 689 cm^2, Perimeter = 115.54 cm (n) Area = 321.46 cm^2, Perimeter = 75.71 cm **3.** (a) Area = 167.73 cm^2, Perimeter = 53.42 cm (b) Area = 396 mm^2, Perimeter = 114 mm (c) Area = 20 m^2, Perimeter = 21.66 m **4.** (a) 40 m (b) Area = 4,000 m^2 **5.** (a) L = 110 m (b) Perimeter = 400 m **6.** (a) 60 m^2 (b) 12 m^2 (c) 24 m^2 (d) 12 m^2 (e) 36 m^2 (f) 144 m^2 (g) 8.3% (h) €720 **7.** 144 m^2 **8.** (a) 401 m (b) 432 m (c) 31 m **9.** (a) Yes (b) No (c) No (d) No (e) Yes (f) Yes (g) Yes (h) Yes **10.** (a) 100 m (b) 337.5 m (c) 299 m^2 (d) 1.56 cm **11.** (a) 24 m^2 OR 15 m^2 (b) Plan A (c) 9 m^2 **12.** (b) 2,528 cm^2 (c) 25 blocks **13.** 197.9 cm^2 **14.** (a) W = 40 mm, d = 30 mm (b) 1,600 mm^2 (c) 4,000 mm^2 **15.** 2,325.66 mm^2 **17.** (a) 14 cm (b) 126π cm^2 (c) 56.25% **18.** (a) L = 100 m (b) D (c) 7.3 m/s **19.** 402 cm^2 **21.** (a) 72 cm (b) 324 cm^2 **22.** (a) 0.72 m^2 (b) 0.0628 m^2 (c) 3.628 m **23.** (a) 18 m **24.** 433 cm^2 **25.** (a) 576 m^2 (b) 2.4 m^2 (c) 3.75% **26.** (a) 280π cm^2 (b) 427π cm^2 **27.** (a) 53° (b) 5 cm (c) 13.625 cm^2 **28.** 8π cm^2 **29.** 400 m **30.** 85.3 m **31.** (a) 14.4 cm (b) 412.5 cm^2 **32.** 72π cm^2 **33.** 6.3 cm **34.** $10.5\pi x$ cm **35.** r = 2 cm **36.** (a) 37.8 m (b) r = 6 m, A = 113 m^2 **37.** (a) Yes (b) No

Chapter 14

Exercise 14.1

1. (a) = (iv) (b) = (vii) (c) = (v) (d) = (vi) (e) = (i) (f) = (iii) (g) = (ii) **2.** (a) Chord = VW, diameter = OT (b) Diameter = SV, Chord = UV (c) Diameter = BP, Chord = RQ (d) Chord = SL, Diameter = IP, Radius = MP (e) Chord = PQ, Diameter = MN (f) Diameter = AB, Chord = CD (g) Chord = AB, Diameter = PQ (h) Radius = PE, Chord = AD (i) Diameter = ZQ, Chord = LS **3.** (a) Centre = O; Radii = [AO], [OB] and [OD]; Diameter = [AB] (b) Centre = O; Radii = [MO] and [ON]; Diameter = [MN] (c) Centre = O; Radii = [OP] and [OQ] and [OR]; Diameter = [PQ]

Exercise 14.2

1. 43° = X **2.** 140° = X **3.** 83° = X **4.** 128° = X **5.** 81.5° = X **6.** 23.5° = X **7.** 93° = X **8.** 87° = X **9.** 78° = X **10.** 104° = X **11.** 76.5° **12.** 144°

Exercise 14.3

1. $\angle EBC$ **2.** $\angle ABC$ **3.** $\angle ABC$ **4.** $\angle ABC$ **5.** $\angle CED$ **6.** $\angle YXZ$ **7.** F = 90°; X = 67° **8.** W = 90°; X = 32° **9.** F = 90°; X = 59° **10.** F = 90°; A = 50° **11.** W = 90°; X = 65° **12.** 53° **13.** 27° **14.** 72° **15.** (a) 60° (b) 30° (c) 90° (d) 60° (e) All are radii **16.** $\angle 1$ = 42° $\angle 2$ = 84°

Exercise 14.4

1. Y = 47° A = 94° Z = 86° W = 47° **2.** Y = 69° A = 138° **3.** X = 66° Y = 66° **4.** A = 58° X = 116° **5.** A = 62.6° Y = 62.6° **6.** A = 117.4°; Y = 117.4° **7.** X = 40°; Y = 40° **8.** X = 60°; Y = 30° **9.** X = 66°; Y = 66° **10.** Y = 58°; X = 116° **11.** Z = 52° X = 104° **12.** Z = 128° Y = 128°

Exercise 14.5

1. X = 74° Y = 97° **2.** Y = 90° X = 82° **3.** X = 110° W = 90° **4.** X = 230° Z = 65° **5.** X = 67° Z = 91° **6.** X = 75° Y = 107° **7.** X = 94° Y = 81° **8.** V = 111° W = 98° **9.** Y = 49° W = 104° **10.** X = 66° W = 68° **11.** V = 87° Y = 70° **12.** V = 90° W = 98° **13.** Y = 74° V = 66° **14.** Y = 88° V = 76°

Self-check Test

4. (c) (i) No (ii) No (iii) No (iv) No (v) No (vi) Yes **5.** (a) A = 109° B = 39° (b) S = 20° T = 133° (c) P = 84° (d) X = 52° Y = 38° (e) A = 76° B = 104° C = 79° (f) $\angle B$ = 26°; $\angle D$ = 113°; $\angle A$ = 93° (g) 133° **6.** (a) 120° (obtuse) or 240° (reflex) (b) 120° (c) 30° **7.** A = 24°; B = 81°; E = 105°; D = 99°; C = 75° **8.** X = 66°; Y = 114° **9.** (a) 90° (b) 45° (c) $6\sqrt{2}$ cm (d) 36 cm^2 **10.** (a) A = 55° (b) B = 21° **11.** $\angle DBC + \angle BDC + \angle DCB = 180°$; $90° + \angle DCB = 180°$; $\angle DCB = 90°$; $\angle BCD$ = 90 **12.** $|\angle WOX| = |\angle ZOY|$ vertically opposite angles; $|\angle XWO| = |\angle YZO|$ by theorem; $|\angle OXW| = |\angle ZYO|$ by theorem **13.** By theorem $\angle ABC = 90°$; $\angle ABC = \angle ABO + \angle OBC = \angle ABO + \angle OCB$ **14.** (a) In ΔADB $\angle A = 180 - 53 - 37$ $\angle A = 90°$ hence BD = Diameter (b) 44° **15.** (a) 72° (b) 108° **16.** (a) 45° (b) 45° **17.** (a) 80° (b) 40° **18.** (a) 96° (b) 107° **19.** (a) 40° (b) $\Delta YVW \equiv \Delta YZW$, $|\angle YVW| = |\angle YZW|$ both 40°, $|VW| = |YZ|$ both diameters, $|\angle VWY| = |\angle ZYW|$ both 50°, Congruent by ASA **20.** (a) By theorem on the same arc BD. (b) $\angle BAE = \angle ECD$ $|AB| = |CD|$ $\angle ABE = \angle EDC$ by ASA (c) Since $\Delta BAE \equiv \Delta DCE$, $|AE| = |EC|$, $\frac{|ED|}{|AD|} = \frac{|EB|}{|BC|}$

21. (a) 130° cyclic quadrilateral (b) 130° opposite angles of a parallelogram is equal in size (c) 130° since $\angle CYB$ = 50° (alternate) (d) $\angle YBC$ = 80°, $\angle BYC$ = 50°, hence $\angle YCB$ = 50°, Isosceles triangle so $|BY| = |BC|$

Chapter 15

Exercise 15.1

2. (a) A (b) $(X \cap Y) \setminus Z$ (c) $(W \cap X \cap Y)$ (d) $(A \cap C)$ (e) $B \setminus (A \cup C)$ (f) $(Q \cup R \cup S)$ (g) $U \setminus (A \cap B)$ (h) $U \setminus [(Y \cup Z) \setminus X]$ (i) $(A \cup C) \setminus B$ (j) $(A \cup B) \setminus C$
3. (a) {1, 2, 3, 4, 5, 6, 7, 8, 9} (b) {3, 8, 9, 1, 2, 6} (c) {6, 9} (d) {6, 1, 2, 4, 5, 7} (e) {3, 6, 9} **4.** (b) {1, 2, 4} (c) {8, 5, 20, 10, 7, 9} (d) {5, 10, 20} (e) {4}
5. (b) {4, 6, 9, 7, 10, 1, 8} (c) {6, 9} (d) {6, 9, 10, 8, 2, 3} (e) 4 **6.** (b) {4, 7, 8, 1, 2, 5} (c) {4, 8} (d) {1, 2, 7, 8} (e) {3, 6, 9, 10} **7.** (b) {6, 8} (c) {1, 8, 10} (d) {3, 7, 5, 9} (e) {1, 2, 3, 4, 6, 7, 8, 10} (f) {6, 8} (g) {1, 10} (h) {1, 10} (i) {5, 9} (j) {2, 3, 5, 7, 9} **8.** (b) {12} (c) {2, 10, 6, 3, 9, 1, 5, 7} (d) {2, 10, 6, 4, 8} (e) {4, 8} (f) {3, 9, 11, 1, 5, 7} (g) {8, 4, 12, 6, 3, 9, 11} (h) {11} (i) {11} (j) 7
9. (a) {2, 6, 1, 3} (b) {1, 2, 4, 8} (c) {1, 2, 4, 5, 10, 20} (e) {8, 1, 2, 4, 5, 10, 20} (f) {3, 6} (g) {1, 2, 4} (h) {1, 2} (i) 4 (j) 5 **10.** (b) {1, 11} (c) {6, 8, 10}
11. {1, 3, 4, 5} and {5}

Exercise 15.2

1. (b) 15 (c) 17 (d) 2 (e) 18 **2.** (b) 60 (c) 1 (d) 7 (e) 2 (f) 5 (g) 25 **3.** (b) 7 (c) 5 (d) 15 (e) 25 (f) 16 **4.** (b) 26 (c) 9 (d) 18 (e) 63 (f) 7 **5.** (b) 20 (c) 21 (d) 46 (e) 5 **6.** (b) 20 (c) 88 (d) 5 (e) 20 **7.** (b) 6 (c) 33 (d) 17 (e) 15 **8.** (b) 3 (c) 50 (d) 15 (e) 10 **9.** (b) 15 (c) 17 (d) 38 (e) 17 **10.** (a) 4 (b) 35%

Exercise 15.3

1. (a) False (b) True (c) True **2.** (a) True (b) True (c) True (d) True **3.** (a) No (b) True (c) True **4.** (a) True (b) True (c) True **5.** (a) True (b) True (c) True (d) Represents the elements in all 3 sets. (e) Yes, distribution works for union. **6.** (a) Not equal (b) Not equal (c) not equal (d) None (e) Set difference does not obey the laws of distribution.

Self-check Test

1. (a) {5} (b) {6, 9, 10} (c) {8} (d) {2, 7} (e) {3, 4, 8} (f) {6, 9, 10, 3, 8, 4} (g) {6, 9, 1, 5, 10, 3, 8, 4} (h) {6, 9, 1, 3} (i) {6, 9, 1, 3, 10, 8, 4, 2, 7} (j) {1} (k) {3, 4, 8} (l) {6, 9, 4, 10} (m) {6, 9, 1, 3, 2, 7} (n) {5, 10} **2.** (a) False (b) True (c) True **3.** (a) True (b) True (c) True (d) True **4.** (b) 7 (c) 35% **5.** (a) 6 (b) 2 : 3 **6.** (b) 2 2% saw all 3 films (c) 41% **7.** (b) $P / (E \cup Q)$; $P \cap E \cap Q$; $(E \cap Q) / P$
8. (b) (i) True (ii) True (iii) False (iv) False (v) False (vi) False (c) (i) $A \cup B = B \cup A$ (ii) $(A \cup B) \cup C = A \cup (B \cup C)$
9. $x = 5$ **10.** (a) 3 (b) 10 **12.** (b) 12

Chapter 16

Exercise 16.1

1. (a) $\frac{2}{3}$ (b) 200 **2.** (a) $\frac{33}{50}$ (b) 462 **3.** (a) $\frac{21}{25}$ (b) 3,360
4. 200 **5.** 100 **6.** (a) 190 (b) First producer **7.** (a) $\frac{17}{25}$ (b) 442 **8.** (a) $\frac{14}{25}$ (b) 392 **9.** (a) $\frac{29}{150}$ (b) 232 **10.** (a) $\frac{11}{15}$ (b) 660 **11.** (a) $\frac{4}{5}$ (b) 960 **12.** (a) $\frac{27}{35}$ (b) 5,400

13. (a) Chelsea: 0.5, Bayern: 0.6, Porto: 0.64, Lyon: 0.61, Real Madrid: 0.59 (b) Porto (c) No. All play in different Leagues. Different number of games played.

14. (a) 600 (b) Mon: $\frac{31}{300}$, Tues: $\frac{19}{200}$, Wed: $\frac{11}{150}$, Thurs: $\frac{23}{300}$, Fri: $\frac{119}{600}$, Sat: $\frac{187}{600}$, Sun: $\frac{17}{120}$ (c) $\frac{119}{600}$

Exercise 16.2

1. (a) $\frac{1}{2}$ (b) $\frac{1}{4}$ (c) $\frac{1}{4}$ (d) $\frac{1}{52}$ (e) $\frac{1}{26}$ (f) $\frac{1}{26}$ (g) $\frac{1}{13}$ (h) $\frac{1}{52}$ (i) $\frac{1}{26}$ (j) $\frac{3}{4}$ (k) $\frac{1}{4}$ (l) $\frac{10}{13}$ (m) $\frac{1}{13}$ (n) $\frac{1}{4}$ (o) $\frac{5}{26}$ (p) $\frac{5}{13}$ (q) $\frac{1}{2}$ (r) $\frac{3}{13}$ **2.** (a) $\frac{7}{13}$ (b) $\frac{3}{13}$ (c) $\frac{2}{13}$ (d) $\frac{1}{13}$ (e) $\frac{8}{13}$ (f) 0 (g) $\frac{6}{13}$ **3.** (a) $\frac{15}{50}$ (b) 300 (c) Yes as you would expect roughly $\frac{1}{4}$ of 1,000 = 250 **4.** (b) $\frac{1}{5}$ (c) $\frac{1}{5}$ (d) $\frac{4}{5}$ (e) 0 (f) $\frac{1}{20}$ (g) $\frac{7}{10}$ (h) $\frac{7}{10}$ (i) $\frac{3}{20}$ (j) 0

Exercise 16.3

1. (a) $\frac{1}{10}$ (b) 100 (c) No. Would expect $200\left(\frac{1}{5}\right)$ of spins to be 0 **2.** (b) $\frac{1}{15}$ (c) $\frac{2}{15}$ (d) $\frac{7}{15}$ (e) $\frac{11}{15}$ **4.** (a) $\frac{1}{2}$ (b) (ii) GGG; GGB; GBG; GBB; BGG; BGB; BBG; BBB
5. (a) $\frac{1}{25}$ (b) $\frac{1}{25}$ (c) $\frac{1}{25}$ **6.** 180 **7.** (a) $\frac{1}{24}$ (b) $\frac{1}{4}$ (c) $\frac{5}{12}$ **8.** (a) $\frac{5}{36}$ (b) $\frac{13}{36}$ (c) $\frac{5}{12}$ (d) $\frac{1}{6}$ **9.** (a) $\frac{1}{3}$ (b) $\frac{7}{30}$ (c) $\frac{1}{6}$ (d) $\frac{17}{30}$ (e) $\frac{1}{15}$ (f) $\frac{7}{225}$ (g) $\frac{11}{30}$ (h) $\frac{1}{5}$
10. HHH; HHT; HTH; HTT; THH; THT; TTH; TTT (a) $\frac{1}{8}$ (b) $\frac{7}{8}$ (c) $\frac{1}{8}$ (d) $\frac{3}{8}$ (e) $\frac{3}{8}$ **11.** (a) $\frac{200}{5141}$ (b) $\frac{288}{5141}$ (c) $\frac{300}{5141}$ (d) $\frac{56}{5141}$ (e) $\frac{50}{97}$ (f) $\frac{4}{25}$ **12.** (a) $\frac{1}{2}$ (b) $\frac{2}{52}$ (c) $\frac{19}{52}$ (d) $\frac{9}{13}$ (e) $\frac{15}{26}$ **13.** (a) $\frac{1}{6}$ (b) $\frac{11}{36}$ (c) $\frac{1}{18}$ (d) $\frac{1}{3}$

Exercise 16.4

1. (a) $\frac{1}{2}$ (b) $\frac{13}{20}$ (c) $\frac{3}{10}$ (d) $\frac{1}{5}$ (e) $\frac{7}{20}$ (f) $\frac{11}{20}$ (g) $\frac{3}{20}$
2. (a) $\frac{2}{5}$ (b) $\frac{7}{30}$ (c) $\frac{19}{30}$ (d) $\frac{2}{15}$ (e) $\frac{7}{30}$ (f) $\frac{7}{15}$
3. (a) $\frac{149}{250}$ (b) $\frac{34}{125}$ (c) $\frac{33}{250}$ (d) $\frac{21}{50}$ (e) $\frac{22}{125}$ **4.** (b) $\frac{11}{20}$ (c) $\frac{19}{40}$ (d) $\frac{3}{40}$ (e) $\frac{1}{10}$ **5.** (a) $\frac{24}{55}$ (b) $\frac{1}{5}$ (c) $\frac{8}{55}$ (d) 0 (e) $\frac{9}{55}$ (f) $\frac{3}{55}$ (g) $\frac{3}{5}$ (h) $\frac{19}{55}$ (i) $\frac{2}{11}$ (j) $\frac{6}{55}$
6. (a) $\frac{37}{100}$ (b) $\frac{37}{50}$ (c) $\frac{1}{25}$ (d) $\frac{3}{50}$ (e) $\frac{27}{100}$ (f) $\frac{7}{100}$ (g) $\frac{71}{100}$ (h) $\frac{4}{25}$ (i) $\frac{6}{25}$ (j) $\frac{1}{5}$ **7.** (b) $\frac{13}{30}$ (c) $\frac{3}{5}$ (d) $\frac{1}{5}$ (e) $\frac{7}{30}$ (f) $\frac{1}{6}$ (g) $\frac{2}{5}$ (h) $\frac{19}{30}$ **8.** (b) 25% (c) 50% (d) 30% (e) 25% **9.** (b) 27% (c) 85% (d) 15% **10.** (b) 9% (c) 18% (d) 27%

Self-check Test

2. (a) $\frac{1}{6}$ (b) $\frac{1}{2}$ (c) $\frac{5}{6}$ (d) $\frac{1}{2}$ (e) $\frac{1}{3}$ **3.** (a) 52 (b) Hearts, Diamonds, Spades, Clubs **4.** (a) $\frac{1}{2}$ (b) $\frac{1}{13}$ (c) $\frac{1}{52}$ (d) $\frac{10}{13}$ (e) $\frac{3}{13}$ **5.** (a) 1H, 2H, 3H, 4H, 5H, 6H; 1T, 2T, 3T, 4T, 5T, 6T (b) $\frac{1}{12}$ (c) $\frac{1}{12}$ (d) $\frac{1}{2}$ (e) $\frac{1}{4}$ **6.** (a) $\frac{53}{60}$ (b) 10,600 **7.** (a) $\frac{7}{20}$ (b) $\frac{3}{40}$ (c) $\frac{1}{16}$ (d) $\frac{31}{80}$ (e) $\frac{9}{20}$ (f) $\frac{11}{80}$ (g) $\frac{61}{80}$ (h) $\frac{1}{10}$ (i) $\frac{19}{80}$ (j) $\frac{3}{10}$ **8.** (a) $\frac{7}{12}$ (b) $\frac{13}{20}$ (c) $\frac{1}{6}$ (d) 0 (e) $\frac{1}{5}$ (f) 0 (g) $\frac{49}{60}$ (h) $\frac{11}{60}$ (i) $\frac{19}{60}$ (j) $\frac{9}{20}$ **9.** (b) $\frac{7}{24}$ (c) $\frac{1}{12}$ (d) $\frac{5}{8}$ (e) $\frac{1}{6}$ (f) $\frac{5}{24}$ (g) $\frac{3}{4}$ **10.** (b) $\frac{27}{50}$ (c) $\frac{3}{5}$ (d) $\frac{9}{50}$ (e) $\frac{1}{25}$ (f) $\frac{21}{50}$ (g) $\frac{9}{25}$
11. (a) 0.42 (b) 0.12 (c) 0.2 (d) 0.3 **12.** (a) $\frac{17}{120}$ (b) $\frac{1}{5}$ (c) $\frac{23}{120}$ (d) Jimmy (e) Tommy (f) 26 **13.** (d) $\frac{7}{50}$
15. (a) $\frac{2}{3}$ (b) $\frac{1}{6}$ (c) $\frac{1}{3}$ **16.** (a) $\frac{1}{6}$ **17.** (b) $\frac{2}{27}$ (c) $\frac{19}{54}$ (d) $\frac{31}{54}$

Chapter 17

Exercise 17.1

1. 05:33 **2.** 16:12 **3.** 09:57 **4.** 17:33 **5.** 11:13 **6.** 21:45 **7.** 18:27 **8.** 11:27 am **9.** 6:32 am **10.** 6:19 pm **11.** 11:57 pm **12.** 3:20 pm **13.** 7:00 pm **14.** 12:04 pm **15.** (a) 8 hr 49 m (b) 15 hr 07 min (c) 14 hr 19 min (d) 3 hr 12 min (e) 2 hr 29 min (f) 2 hr 31 min (g) 16 hr 49 min (h) 24 hr 02 min (i) 23 hr 04 min (j) 1 hr 52 min **16.** (a) 2,500 m (b) 30 meters (c) 10 m (d) 220,000 m (e) 0.5 m **17.** (a) 6.5 km (b) 0.3 km (c) 0.5 km (d) 220 km **18.** 125,000 m **19.** 7 hrs 45 mins **20.** 22:35 **21.** (a) 06:00 (b) 2 hrs 25 mins (c) 14:43, 15:43 and 18:43 (d) 2 hrs 55 mins (e) 24:00 (f) 12:55 (g) 1 hr 20 mins (h) 00:17 = 17 minutes **22.** (a) 22 minutes (b) 39 minutes (c) 58 minutes (d) 43 minutes (e) 09:20 (f) 23 minutes (g) 09:29 **23.** (a) 51 minutes (b) 6 minutes (c) 33 minutes (d) 1 hr 22 minutes (f) 1 hr 53 mins (g) 2 hrs 49 mins

Exercise 17.2

1. (b) 60 km (c) 60 km (d) 60 km/hr **2.** (b) 5 km (c) 5 km (e) 5 km/hr (f) 83.3 m/min **3.** (a) Accelerating (b) Steady/Constant speed (c) Decelerating (d) D **4.** (a) C → D and F → G (b) A → B (c) G → H (d) B → C (e) G (f) D → E **5.** 120 km/hr **6.** 10 m/s **7.** 3 m/min **8.** 3 hrs **9.** 1,800 cm/hr **10.** 88 km/hr **11.** 390 m **12.** 675 km **13.** 15 mins **14.** 61 km/hr **15.** 180 km **16.** 2 hrs 20 mins **17.** 18 km **18.** 70 km/hr **19.** (a) 40,000 m/hr (b) 11·1 m/sec **20.** 12 mins **21.** (a) Route A: 270 km; Route B: 245 km (b) Route A : 10 hrs, 48 mins; Route B : 9 hrs, 48 mins **22.** (a) 25 km (b) 3·086 m/sec **23.** 189 km **24.** 4 hrs 15 mins **25.** (a) 11:21 (b) 1:35 (c) 507 km/hr **26.** (a) 48 words/min (b) 2,880 words/hr **27.** (a) → F (b) → A (c) → D (d) → B (e) → E (f) → C **28.** (a) Beaker is empty (b) Liquid poured in (c) Stopped pouring liquid in (d) Pouring more liquid in **29.** (a) $4\frac{1}{2}$ cm (b) 6 cm **30.** (a) A, B, D, G (b) F, H (c) C, E, I (d) F and H, water level falling due to less/no rain (e) Any part of graph where water level is rising. eg: A **31.** (a) 45 mins (b) 3 km (c) 10 mins (d) Part C (e) 4.5 km/hr **33.** (a) C → D (b) B → C (c) D → E (d) A → B **35.** (a) 130 km (c) 14 hrs **36.** (a) Car 1 : 9 secs Car 2 : $10\frac{1}{2}$ secs (b) Car 1 (c) 3 seconds (d) Car 1 : 67 m approx; Car 2 : 58 m approx

Exercise 17.3

1. (a) 225 km/hr (b) 270 km/hr (c) 1,800 km (d) 7 hrs 20 mins (e) 245.45 km/hr **2.** (a) 50 km/hr (b) 40 km/hr (c) 440 km (d) 10 hrs (e) 44 km/hr **3.** (a) $6\frac{1}{2}$ hrs (b) 480 km (c) 73.85 km/hr **4.** (a) 377 km (b) $6\frac{1}{4}$ hrs (c) 60.32 km/hr **5.** (a) 7.25 hrs (b) 560 km (c) 77 km/hr **6.** (a) $2\frac{1}{2}$ hrs (b) 2 km/hr (c) 20 km/hr (d) 6 km/hr (e) 71 km (f) 11 km/hr

Self-check Test

1. (b) 75 km (c) 75 km/hr (d) 75 **2.** (b) 9 km **3.** (a) 120 km (b) 90 metres **4.** (a) Jack (b) Paul (c) Paul, $8.3\dot{3}$ m/s; Jack, 7.14 m/s (d) After 5.5 seconds (e) Approx 13 metres **5.** (a) 4 hrs (b) 4 mins (c) 1 hr 12 mins (d) 21.25 hrs (e) 10 seconds **6.** (b) 20 km (c) 20 km/hr (d) 20 **7.** (b) 60 km (c) 60 km (d) 60 **8.** (a) 75 km/hr (b) 20 km/hr (c) 25 km/hr **9.** (a) 260 km (b) $2\frac{1}{2}$ hrs (c) 104 km/hr **10.** (a) Blue : 50 km Red : 42 km (b) Red Route **11.** (a) 1 hr 20 mins (b) 48 minutes (c) 2 hrs 8 mins (d) 200 km (e) 93.75 km/hr **12.** (a) 9.39488×10^8 (b) 1 day (c) 8,760 hours (d) 107,247 km per hour **13.** (a) 15 complete orbits (b) 400,000 m (c) 5,460 seconds (d) 7767.67 m/s **14.** 81.88 m/s

Chapter 18

Exercise 18.1

1. (a) True (b) True (c) False (d) False (e) False (f) True (g) True (h) False (i) False (j) True **2.** (a) Age < 16 **3.** (a) Weight > 130 kg **5.** (c) s ≤ 120 **6.** (a) Age ≥ 16 years (b) Weight ≤ 500 kg (c) Seats ≤ 55 (d) Age < 12 (e) Dimples > 300 (f) Points ≥ 26 (g) Speed ≤ 100 km/h (h) Points ≤ 625 (i) Age ≥ 18 (j) Litres ≥ 2 **7.** (d) $a \le 45, 230$ **8.** (c) $x \ge 17$ **9.** (c) $t \ge x + 3$

Execise 18.2

3. {1, 2, 3} **4.** {1, 2, 3, 4} **5.** {1, 2, 3, 4, 5} **6.** {1} **7.** {1, 2, 3, 4} **8.** {1, 2, 3, 4} **9.** {..., –4, –3, –2} **11.** {1} **13.** {5, 6, 7, 8 ...} **14.** $x \le 4$ **15.** $x \le 2$ **16.** (a) True (b) False (c) False (d) False (e) True **17.** (a) True (b) False (c) True (d) True **18.** $x \le 6$ **19.** {1, 2} **20.** {7, 8, 9, ...} **21.** {..., –1, 0, 1, 2, 3, 4} **22.** $x > \frac{3}{2}$ **23.** {..., 3, 4, 5} **24.** $x \ge 4$ **25.** {1, 2, 3, 4} **26.** $x < 3$ **27.** {..., –3, –2, –1} **28.** $x < -7$ **29.** $x > -8$ **30.** $-16 > x$ **31.** $x < -4$ **32.** $x \ge 24$

Execise 18.3

1. $19 < t < 25$ **2.** €30 ≤ x ≤ €75 **3.** $950 < p < 1{,}000$ **4.** $2 < y < 14$ **6.** $-1 \le x \le 3$ **7.** $-7 < x < -1$ **8.** $-4 \le x \le 1$ **9.** $-3 \le x \le 2$ **10.** $4 \le x < 7$ **11.** $-3 < x \le 0$ **12.** {0, 1, 2, 3} **13.** {–1, 0, 1} **14.** {3, 4, 5} **15.** $3 < x < 5$ **16.** $2 < x < 7$ **17.** $-1 < x < 2$ {0, 1} **18.** $-1 \le x < 3$ **19.** $-1 \le x \le 7$ **20.** $-1 < x < 2$ **21.** $-2 \le x \le 0$ **22.** $-2 < x \le 1$ **23.** {–4, –3, –2, –1, 0} **24.** $13 \le x \le 4\frac{1}{2}$ **25.** $10 < x < 15$ **26.** {7, 8}

Self-check Test

1. (a) $4x, x + 3, x, x - 1, 0.5x$ (b) $7x, x^2, 2x, x + \frac{1}{2}, x - 3, -2x$ (c) $-x, \frac{x}{2}, x, x + 2, x^3, -1$ **3.** (a) $x \ge 7$ (b) $14 < x$ (c) $-2 \le x$ (d) {12, 13, 14,...} (e) {..., –4, –3, –2} (f) {10, 11, 12,...} (g) $x < -16$ (h) $-12 > x$ (i) $x > 18$ (j) $14 \ge x$ (k) $x \ge 5$ (l) $6 \le x$ (m) $12 \ge x$ (n) $1 \le x$ (o) $-2 > x$ (p) $x \le -9$ (q) $x \ge 5$ (r) $x < 10$ **4.** (a) $21 \le x$ (b) $21 < x$ (c) $x > \frac{-23}{15}$ (d) $x > -2$ (e) $-2 < x < 2$ (f) {0, 1, 2, 3} (g) $-3 \le x \le 1$ (h) $2 \le x \le 4$ (i) $-1 \le x \le 4$ (j) $x < 5$ (k) $x < 6$ (l) $-3 \le x$ (m) $x \ge 0$ (n) $x < \frac{-9}{14}$ (o) $x \le 13$ (p) $x \ge -19$ (q) $-10\frac{1}{12} > x$ **5.** (a) $0 \le x < 4, x \in \mathbb{R}$ (b) $-3 < x < 2, x \in \mathbb{R}$ (c) $0 < x \le 5, x \in \mathbb{R}$ (d) $-11 \le x \le -8, x \in \mathbb{Z}$ (e) $4 \le x \le 8, x \in \mathbb{N}$ **6.** (a) A = {1,2} (b) B = {1, 2, 3, 4, 5, 6} **7.** (a) $x \ge -6$ (b) $x \le -1$ (c) $-6 \le x \le -1$ **8.** (a) False (b) False (c) True (d) True (e) True **9.** $35 < x < 105$

Chapter 19

Exercise 19.1

1. 1, 3 **2.** –2, 3 **3.** –1, 5 **4.** 0, 7 **5.** –2, 5 **6.** 5, –7 **7.** 8, 9 **8.** 16, –16 **9.** 10, –10 **10.** –12, 12 **11.** 3, 4 **12.** –1, –5 **13.** –6, 3 **14.** 4, –1 **15.** –6, –1 **16.** 3, 7 **17.** 5, –3 **18.** 4, –7 **19.** 3 **20.** 8, –3 **21.** –9, 2 **22.** 10, –7 **23.** –11, 3 **24.** 3, –1 **25.** –5, –3 **26.** 1, 11 **27.** –7, –2 **29.** –8, –6 **30.** 12, –5 **31.** 0, 5 **32.** –3, 0 **33.** 12, 0 **34.** 20, 0 **35.** –13, 0 **36.** –10, 0 **37.** 7, 0 **38.** 10, –10 **39.** –8, 8 **40.** –5, 5 **41.** 11, –11 **42.** 3, –3 **43.** 3, 0 **44.** –1, 5 **45.** –4, 1 **46.** –5, 1 **47.** 3, –1 **48.** –2, 1 **49.** 8, –1

Exercise 19.2

1. $-\frac{3}{2}, 1$ **2.** $\frac{1}{3}, -1$ **3.** $\frac{1}{2}, 1$ **4.** $-\frac{2}{3}, 7$ **5.** $-\frac{1}{2}, 9$ **6.** $-\frac{5}{7}, 4$ **7.** $\frac{1}{7}, -6$ **8.** $\frac{1}{2}, 12$ **9.** $-\frac{2}{3}, 10$ **10.** $\frac{3}{4}, -\frac{5}{2}$ **11.** $-\frac{1}{4}, \frac{7}{4}$

12. $-\frac{2}{3}, 1$ **13.** $-\frac{7}{6}, \frac{1}{5}$ **14.** $-\frac{3}{5}, -1$ **15.** $\frac{9}{2}, -3$ **16.** $\frac{7}{3}, -1$
17. 3, −5 **18.** $4, -\frac{1}{3}$ **19.** $\frac{10}{3}, -2$ **20.** $\frac{11}{3}, -6$ **21.** $7, -\frac{5}{3}$
22. $-8, \frac{2}{3}$ **23.** $-\frac{2}{5}, \frac{3}{2}$ **24.** $-\frac{4}{3}, 3$ **25.** $-3, \frac{1}{11}$ **26.** $\frac{2}{3}, \frac{1}{2}$
27. $\frac{1}{4}, -3$ **28.** $-\frac{1}{2}, 2$ **29.** $-\frac{1}{5}, \frac{3}{2}$

Exercise 19.3

1. 6.53, −1.53 **2.** 1.91, −8.91 **3.** 1.54, −4.54
4. 1.89, −6.89 **5.** 3.82, −6.82 **6.** 0.84, −0.24
7. 1.12, −2.55 **8.** 7.94, −0.44 **9.** −0.27, −3.73
10. 1.27, 0.18 **11.** $\frac{3 \pm \sqrt{97}}{4}$ **12.** $\frac{1 \pm \sqrt{85}}{6}$ **13.** $3, \frac{1}{2}$
14. $\frac{-3 \pm \sqrt{145}}{4}$ **15.** $\frac{5 \pm \sqrt{22}}{3}$ **16.** $\frac{11 \pm \sqrt{85}}{6}$ **17.** $\frac{5 \pm \sqrt{105}}{4}$
18. $\frac{5 \pm 3\sqrt{2}}{7}$ **19.** $-3 \pm \sqrt{11}$ **20.** $\pm\frac{2\sqrt{2}}{3}$ **21.** $\frac{1}{4}, 7$ **22.** $\pm\frac{2}{\sqrt{5}}$
23. $\pm\frac{5}{2}$ **24.** $\frac{1}{2}, \frac{4}{5}$ **25.** 0.73, −13.73 **26.** $-\frac{1}{4}, \frac{3}{2}$

Exercise 19.4

1. $t = -6, -9$ **2.** $k = -10, 4$ **3.** $f = \frac{7}{2}, -4$ **4.** $g = \frac{1}{12}, -\frac{1}{7}$
5. $\frac{3 \pm \sqrt{5}}{2}, -5 \pm 2\sqrt{6}$ **6.** −1.7, 2.3 **7.** $t = 1.2, -0.8, 0.55, -1.8$
8. $h = \pm 0.2$ **9.** $p = 0.36, 0.11$ **10.** $y = \pm\sqrt{2}, \pm\frac{2\sqrt{5}}{\sqrt{3}}$

Exercise 19.5

1. $x^2 - 6x + 8 = 0$ **2.** $x^2 - 7x + 6 = 0$ **3.** $x^2 - 8x + 15 = 0$
4. $x^2 - 9x + 14 = 0$ **5.** $x^2 - 9x + 20 = 0$ **6.** $x^2 - 7x + 12 = 0$
7. $x^2 - 10x + 9 = 0$ **8.** $x^2 - 9x + 8 = 0$ **9.** $x^2 - 12x + 20 = 0$
10. $x^2 - x - 2 = 0$ **11.** $x^2 - 3x - 10 = 0$ **12.** $x^2 - 3x - 18 = 0$
13. $x^2 - 4x - 60 = 0$ **14.** $x^2 + 7x + 10 = 0$
15. $x^2 + 14x + 24 = 0$ **16.** $3x^2 - 13x + 4 = 0$
17. $5x^2 + 3x - 2 = 0$ **18.** $3x^2 + 7x - 6 = 0$
19. $4x^2 + 3x - 1 = 0$ **20.** $4x^2 - 7x + 3 = 0$
21. $5x^2 - 18x + 9 = 0$ **22.** $7x^2 + 12x - 4 = 0$
23. $8x^2 + 23x - 3 = 0$ **24.** $9x^2 - 47x + 10 = 0$
25. $6x^2 + 11x - 2 = 0$ **26.** $x^2 - 8x + 16 = 0$
27. (a) $x^2 + x - 2 = 0$ (b) $x^2 - x - 12 = 0$ (c) $x^2 - 5x = 0$
(d) $x^2 - 6x + 9 = 0$ (e) $2x^2 + 3x - 2 = 0$ (f) $-x^2 - 2x + 8 = 0$
(g) $2x^2 - 3x - 5 = 0$ **28.** $a = 1, b = -9, c = 20$
29. $a = 1, b = -6, c = -7$ **30.** $a = 1, b = 9, c = 20$
31. $a = 15, b = 7, c = -4$ **32.** $c = 25$ **33.** $c = 9$ **34.** $c = 1$
35. $b = \pm 6$ **36.** $b = \pm 16$ **37.** $b = \pm 20$ **38.** $c = 9$ **39.** $b = \pm 6$
40. $b = \pm 14$ **41.** $c = 81$

Exercise 19.6

1. 8 **2.** 12 **3.** 4 **4.** 5 **5.** 8 **6.** (a) $x = 5$ cm (b) 22 cm
7. (a) 1 cm, 7 cm (b) 16 cm **8.** (a) 13 m, 6 m (b) 38 m
9. (a) $x = 12$ (b) 96 sq. units **10.** 32 m **11.** 70 cm **12.** 9
13. (a) 10 m (b) $10\sqrt{2}$ m **14.** 8 **15.** 12 **16.** 7 m, 20 m
17. (a) $\frac{100}{x}$ (b) $\frac{100}{x+1}$ (c) $\frac{100}{x} - 5 = \frac{100}{x+1}$ (d) $x = 4$
18. (a) $\frac{200}{x}$ (b) $\frac{200}{x+5}$ (c) $\frac{200}{x} - 2 = \frac{200}{x+5}$ (d) 20 rows
19. (a) $\frac{12}{x}$ (b) $\frac{12}{x+2}$ (c) $\frac{12}{x} - \frac{1}{5} = \frac{12}{x+2}$ (d) €1 per roll
20. (a) $\frac{10}{x}$ (b) $\frac{10}{2x}$ (c) $\frac{10}{x} - \frac{1}{20} = \frac{10}{2x}$ (d) 10c, 5c

Self-check Test

1. 5, 7 **2.** −7, −8 **3.** 1, 2 **4.** −2, −9 **5.** −7, 11 **6.** 14, −9
7. −4, 15 **8.** −3, 10 **9.** −12, 7 **10.** −11, 8 **11.** $-1, \frac{5}{2}$
12. $-1, \frac{13}{3}$ **13.** $-\frac{7}{2}, 1$ **14.** $-1, \frac{3}{7}$ **15.** $-2, -\frac{1}{5}$
16. 1.60, −1.77 **17.** 13.27, −1.32 **18.** 1.85, −2.85
19. 1.41, −3.91 **20.** 5, −0.29 **21.** 0.18, −1.85
22. 2.78, 0.72 **23.** 9.80, 0.20 **24.** 1.84, 0.41 **25.** 10, 0.40
26. 0.47, −2.81 **27.** 2, −4.5 **28.** 0.30 OR −3.30
29. $x^2 + 11x + 30 = 0$ **30.** $x^2 + 8x - 20 = 0$
31. $x^2 - 12x + 27 = 0$ **32.** $x^2 - x - 12 = 0$ **33.** $x^2 - 4x - 5 = 0$
34. $x^2 - 18x + 80 = 0$ **35.** $x^2 + 6x - 55 = 0$
36. $x^2 + 12x + 27 = 0$ **37.** $10, \frac{-2}{3}$ $y = 0.1, -1.5$
38. $x = 7, \frac{-2}{3}$ $t = \pm 3, \pm\frac{2}{\sqrt{3}}$ **39.** $p = \pm\sqrt{\frac{2}{11}}, \pm\frac{1}{\sqrt{3}}$
40. (a) $x = 7$ (b) $9x^2 - 240x + 1600$ **41.** $a = 6$ **42.** $x = 7$
43. −1 or −3 **44.** (a) $\frac{8}{x} - \frac{4}{100} = \frac{8}{x+100}$ (b) 8 cent per teabag
45. (a) $\frac{36}{x}$ (b) $\frac{36}{x} - 2 = \frac{36}{x+3}$ (c) €4
46. (a) $\left(\frac{400}{x}\right) - 5 = \left(\frac{400}{x+4}\right)$ (b) 16 students €25 each,
20 students €20 each

Chapter 20

Exercise 20.1

1. (a) No (b) No (c) Yes (d) No (e) Yes (f) No (g) Yes
(h) No (i) No (j) Yes **2.** (a) −6, −10, −12, −12, −10
(b) 14, 80, 48, 68, 90 (c) −44, −36, −26, −14, 0
(d) −7, −3, 3, 11, 21 (e) 57, 80, 105, 132, 161
(f) −49, −39, −15, 23, 75 (g) −3, 13, 39, 75, 121
(h) −14, −7, 6, 25, 50 (i) −62, −54, −36, −8, 30 (j) 3, 4, 3, 0, −5
3. (i) (a) −3 (b) 2 (c) $T_n = n^2 + 4n - 8$ (d) 517 (ii) (a) 1 (b) 2
(c) $T_n = n^2 - n + 1$ (d) 421 (iii) (a) 5 (b) 2 (c) $T_n = n^2 + 6n - 2$
(d) 565 (iv) (a) 16 (b) 2 (c) $T_n = n^2 + 5n + 10$ (d) 556
(v) (a) 5 (b) 2 (c) $T_n = n^2 - 8n + 12$ (d) 285 (vi) (a) −1
(b) 2 (c) $T_n = n^2 - 7n + 5$ (d) 299 (vii) (a) −14 (b) 2
(c) $T_n = n^2 - 5n - 10$ (d) 326 (viii) (a) 4 (b) 2
(e) $T_n = n^2 - 4n + 7$ (d) 364 (ix) (a) 1 (b) 2
(c) $T_n = n^2 + 3n - 3$ (d) 501 (x) (a) −17 (b) 2
(c) $T_n = n^2 - 9n - 9$ (d) 243 **4.** (i) (a) 3 (b) 8
(c) $T_n = 4n^2 - 3n + 2$ (d) 39,702 (ii) (a) 6 (b) 8
(c) $T_n = 4n^2 - 5n + 7$ (d) 39,507 (iii) (a) 7 (b) 4
(c) $T_n = 2n^2 + 13n - 8$ (d) 21,292 (iv) (a) 5 (b) 10
(c) $T_n = 5n^2 + n - 1$ (d) 50,999 (v) (a) 12 (b) 14
(c) $T_n = 7n^2 + 3n + 2$ (d) 70,302 (vi) (a) 2 (b) 16
(c) $T_n = 8n^2 - 10n + 4$ (d) 79,004 (vii) (a) 25 (b) 10
(c) $T_n = 5n^2 + 10n + 10$ (d) 51,010 (viii) (a) 6 (b) 10
(c) $T_n = 5n^2 - 10n - 1$ (d) 48,999 (ix) (a) −9 (b) 6
(c) $T_n = 3n^2 - n - 11$ (d) 29,889 **5.** (c) Quadratic
(e) $T_n = n^2 + n$ (f) U shaped graph **6.** (c) Yes (d) Quadratic
(f) $T_n = n^2 + n$ (h) $T_n = \frac{n^2 + n}{2}$ **7.** Quadratic

Exercise 20.2

1. (a) 0 (b) 9 (c) 4 (d) 25 (e) −16 (f) 4 **2.** (a) 0 (b) 3
(c) 8 (d) 25 (e) 24 (f) 3 **3.** (a) −2 (b) −4 (c) 2 (d) 2
(e) 26 (f) 106 **4.** (a) $\frac{1}{9}$ (b) $\frac{79}{36}$ (c) $g(t) = t^2 + 3t - 1$
(d) $4k^2 + 6k - 1$ (e) $k^2 - 3k - 1$ (f) $k^2 + 7k + 9$ **5.** (a) 3 (b) 39
(c) 53 (d) 87 (e) 179 (f) $4k^2 - 2k - 3$ **6.** −3, 5, 21, 45
7. −5, −1, 23, −1, 175 **8.** −9, −5, 16, 91, 160
9. 16, 100, 248, 460 **10.** $t = 3$

Exercise 20.4

1. (b) $A = (0, 0)$ (c) $x = 2, x = -2$ (d) $x = 0$
2. (b) $D(0, -2)$ (c) $(0, -2)$ (d) 0.25 **3.** (b) $T(0, 3)$ (c) 5.25
(d) $x = -1.4, x = 1.4$ **4.** (b) $C(0, -2)$ (c) $D(-2, 0)$; $E(1, 0)$
(d) $(-0.5, -2.3)$ **5.** (b) $(0, 3)$ (c) $W(1, 0), V(3, 0)$ (d) −1
6. (b) $C(0, 2)$ (c) $D(1, 0), E(2, 0)$ (d) −0.3 **7.** (b) −2.1
(c) $x = -1.2$ or $x = 0.8$ (d) 19.25 **8.** (b) $(-0.3, -3.1)$
(c) $x = -1.2, x = 0.7$ (d) 3 **9.** (b) $x = 2, x = 4$ (c) $(3, 4)$
(d) 3.75 **10.** (b) $Q(0, 5)$ (c) $R(1, 0)$ $S(5, 0)$ (d) $(3, -4)$
11. (b) $C(0, 2)$ (c) $D(-2, 0)$ $E(-1, 0)$
(d) $f(1.5)$: $(1.5)^2 + 3(1.5) + 2 = 8.75$ **12.** (b) $x = -3$ and $x = 4$
(c) $(0.5, -12.25)$ (d) Graph is increasing when $x > 0.5$
13. (b) $C(0, -6)$ (c) $D(-2, 0)$ $E(3, 0)$ (d) $-1.56 \leq x \leq 2.6$
14. (b) $x = -2$ and $x = 3$ (c) $x = -2.5$ and $x = 3.5$
(d) $f(2.5)$: $-(2.5)^2 + (2.5) + 6 = 2.25$ **15.** (b) $x = 0.3, x = 3$
(c) $x = 0.7, x = 2.6$ (d) 5.25 **16.** (b) $x = -1.4, x = 1.9$
(c) $(0.3, 10.1)$ (d) −5 **17.** (a) 9.6 m (b) 9 m (c) 7.5 m
(d) 2 m and 9 m **18.** (a) 4.8 m (b) 3 m (c) 1.2 sec, 8 sec
19. (a) $5x - x^2$ (c) 6.3 m² (d) $w = 0.7$ m, $w = 4.3$ m
(e) $l = 2.52$ m **20.** (a) $4x - x^2$ (c) 4 m² (d) $x = 1$ m, $x = 3$ m
(e) 2 m **21.** (a) $7 - x$ (b) $7x - x^2$ (d) 12.3 m²
(e) $l = 0.8$ m or $l = 6.2$ m (f) 3.51 m **22.** (a) $12 - x$ (b) $x - 2$
(c) $-x^2 + 12x - 20$ (e) 16 m² (f) $l = 0.42$ m **23.** (b) 61.3 m
(c) 41.3 m (d) 6.4 m

Exercise 20.5

1. (a) (−2.9, 0.6) (0.4, 2.2) (b) $x < -2.9, x > 0.4$ (c) $2.9 < x < 0.4$
2. (a) (−2.7, 0.5) (0.7, 7.5) (b) $-2.7 < x < 0.7$ (c) $x < -2.7$ $x > 0.7$
3. (a) $-3 < x < 3$ (b) $x < -3, x > 3$ (c) $x = 3, x = -3$
4. (a) $-4 < x < z$ (b) $x < -4, x > 2$ (c) $x = -4, x = 2$
5. (a) $x = -1.7, x = -0.3$ (b) $x < -1.7, x > -0.3$ (c) $-1.7 < x < -0.3$
6. (a) $x = -6.5, x = -0.5$ (b) $-6.5 < x < -0.5$ (c) $x < -6.5, x > -0.5$
7. (a) $x = 1.4, x = 4.6$ (b) $x < 1.4, x > 4.6$ (c) $1.4 < x < 4.6$
8. (a) $x = 0.1, x = 6.4$ (b) $x < 0.1, x > 6.4$ (c) $0.1 < x < 6.4$
9. (a) $x = 0.7, x = 2.8$ (b) $0.7 < x < 2.8$ (c) $x < 0.7, x > 2.8$
10. (a) $x = -2$ $x = 0$ (b) $-2 < x < 0$ (c) $x < -2, x > 0$
11. (a) $x = 0.4, x = 2.6$ (b) $0.4 < x < 2.6$ (c) $x < 0.4, x > 2.6$
12. (a) $x = -2.6, x = 1.6$ (b) $-2.6 < x < 1.6$ (c) $x < -2.6, x > 1.6$
13. (a) $x = -0.4, x = 1.6$ (b) $-0.4 < x < 1.6$ (c) $x < -0.4, x > 1.6$
14. (i) (a) $x = -0.4, x = 1.1$ (b) $-0.4 < x < 1.1$ (c) $x < -0.4, x > 1.1$
(ii) (a) $x = -1.1, x = 1.1$ (b) $-1.1 < x < 1.1$ (c) $x < -1.1, x > 1.1$
(iii) (a) $x = 0.2, x = 1.8$ (b) $0.2 < x < 1.8$ (c) $x < 0.2, x > 1.8$
(iv) (a) $x = 2.2, x = 4.1$ (b) $2.2 < x < 4.1$ (c) $x < 2.2, x > 4.1$
15. $x = 0, x = 3$ **16.** (a) 7 (b) −24 (c) $-3x - 2$ (d) $x = 5$
17. (b) −6.3 (c) $x = -4.4, x = 0.4$ (d) $-4.4 < x < 0.4$
18. (a) $A(-2,0)$, $B(4,0)$, $C(0,-8)$ (b) $-2 \le x < 4$ **19.** (a) 4.5 m
(b) (5.2, 4.1) (d) Where the missile hits the bird.

Exercise 20.6

9. (i) and (d) (ii) and (a) (iii) and (b) (iv) and (c)

Self-check Test

1. (a) 10 (b) 2 (c) 2 (d) −2 (e) 2 (f) −4 (g) 4 (h) −2
(i) $6a$ (j) $2t$ **2.** (a) 53 (b) 30 (c) 17 (d) −3 (e) 63 (f) 2
3. (a) 3, 9, 17, 27 (b) −6, −9, −14, −21 (c) 1, 8, 21, 40
(d) 0, −5, −14, −27 (e) 12, 30, 58, 96 **4.** 306 **5.** $n = 4$
6. (a) 4 (b) $T_n = 2n^2 + 5n + 9$ **7.** (b) (−0.41, 0) and (2.41, 0)
8. (a) $b = -1, c = -2$ (b) $k = \pm 4$ **9.** (a) 2 (b) Quadratic Growth
(c) $T_n = n^2 + 2n$ (d) 120 **11.** (b) 12.3 m (c) 6.4 sec (d) $a = 6$
12. (b) −5.3 (c) $x \le 1.2, x \ge 5.8$ **13.** (a) (0, −2) (b) (0, −8)
(c) (0, 1) (d) (0, −1) (e) (0, 10) **15.** (b) $C(0, 2)$
(c) $D(1, 0)$, $E(2, 0)$ (d) −0.3 (e) (1.5, −0.3) (f) 8.75
(g) $x = -1, x = 4$ **16.** (b) −6.1 (c) (0, −3) (d) (−1.3, −6.1)
(e) $x < -1.3$ (f) $x = -3.4, x = 0.9$ **17.** (a) $x = -4, x = 2$
(b) $k = -13$ (c) $k = 1$ (e) $k = -15$ **18.** (b) (−5, 0) and (1, 0)
(c) $\frac{-5}{2}$ **19.** (b) 12.12 m (c) 1 sec, 6 sec
20. (a) $t^2 - 3t, 4t^2 - 2t - 2$ (b) $t = \frac{2}{3}, t = -1$ **21.** (a) $l = 140 - 2x$
(b) $140x - 2x^2$ (c) 0, 1,200, 2,000, 2,400, 2,400, 2,000, 1,200, 0
21. (e) 2,460 m^2 (f) 80 m **23.** (b) (8, 16) (c) 80 km
24. (b) (2.5, 6.3) (c) (3, 6)

Chapter 21

Exercise 21.1

1. (b) Numerical (c) 5 minutes **2.** (b) 23° (c) 7 Days
(d) $\frac{9}{16}$ (e) 21.5° (f) 6° **3.** (a) 20 (c) Hurling

Exercise 21.2

1. (a) Maths (b) History (c) 8 **2.** (b) 2 (c) 1 (d) 41 times
3. (b) Snooker (c) Table tennis and swimming **4.** (c) Biology

Exercise 21.3

1. (a) 1° (b) 2° (c) 4° (d) 10° (e) 8° (f) 6° (g) 18°
(h) 12° (i) 0.5° (j) 15° **2.** 0.5°, 160 g, 80 g, 320 g
3. (a) 140°, 20°, 80°, 90°, 30° (b) Fatigue (c) Alcohol/drugs
(d) 35, 5, 20, 22.5, 7.5 **4.** (a) Heating and ventilation
(b) Kitchen appliances (c) Other equipment **5.** (a) 60 people
(c) Bus **7.** (a) Blue (b) Black (c) 40 **10.** (a) 40°
(b) 126 people (c) 49 people (d) Ulster (e) 28 (f) 14
11. (a) 105° (b) 120 people (c) 50 people (d) 35 people
(e) 25 people (f) Spain **12.** (a) 198°, 69°, 27°, 36°, 30°

Exercise 21.4

1. (b) 33 (c) 5–10 years (d) 10–15 years (e) 13 years
2. (b) 18 (c) 28% (d) 9 (e) 6 **3.** (b) 53.3% (c) 5–10
(d) 9 minutes **4.** (b) 30 people (c) 20 people **5.** (b) 80%
(c) 4 (d) 12 **6.** (b) 9 (c) 40% **7.** (c) 16.25 cm
10. (b) 10.2 min (c) 8–12 minutes **8.** (b) 19 min or 18.53 min
9. (b) 74.8 sec **11.** (a) 305 cars (b) 325 cars **12.** (a) 400
(c) 20 min (d) 220 (e) 60

Exercise 21.5

2. (a) 20 (b) 20 (c) 13 (d) 10 (e) Girls (f) 446 hours
(g) 386 hours (h) 22.3 hours (i) 19.3 hours **3.** (a) 20 (b) 20
(c) Boys are taller (d) 12 (e) 2 (f) 170.7 m (g) 157.3 m
5. (c) Mean Test 1: 9.7; Mean Test 2: 12 **6.** (b) 12 (c) 6
7. (b) 15 (c) 14 (d) 33 text messages (e) 33 text messages
8. (a) Boys = 30, Girls = 30 (b) Mean = 166 sec.
(c) Mean = 165 sec. (d) Boys = 168 sec., Girls = 165 sec.
9. (a) 5 km (b) 12 km (d) Mean = 14.8 km
(e) Mean = 9.35 km **10.** (b) (i) 14 (ii) No mode (c) (i) 14
(ii) 13 (d) (i) 11 (ii) 25 **11.** (b) (i) 44 min (ii) 45 min
(c) (i) 38 min (ii) 35 min (d) (i) 38 min (ii) 33 min

Exercise 21.6

1. (a) (i) 8 (ii) 3 (iii) 11 (b) (i) 17 (ii) 11 (iii) 31
(c) (i) 21 (ii) 13 (iii) 36 (d) (i) 29 (ii) 21 (iii) 42
(e) (i) 14 (ii) 8 (iii) 22 **2.** (a) 37.55 (b) 37 (c) 27 (d) 47
(e) 20 (f) 47 **3.** (b) 35 (c) 34 (d) 22 (e) 36 (f) 14
(g) 46 **4.** (a) 170.7, 155.8 (b) Girls = 153, Boys = 173
(c) Girls = 148, Boys = 164 (d) Girls = 165, Boys = 178
(e) Girls = 17, Boys = 14 (f) Girls = 29, Boys = 46
5. (a) Boys = 19.3, Girls = 22.3 (b) Girls = 34, Boys = 29
(c) Girls = 25, Boys = 17 (d) Girls = 12, Boys 11 (e) Girls = 31,
Boys = 29 (f) Girls = 19, Boys = 18 (g) Girls = 33, Boys = 32
6. (a) Girls = 148, Boys = 151 (b) Girls = 165, Boys = 174
(c) Girls = 17, Boys = 23 (d) Boys = 164 cm, Girls = 157 cm
(e) Girls = No mode, Boys = 168 (f) Girls = 156, Boys = 168
(g) Girls = 36, Boys = 38 **7.** (a) Girls = 149, Boys = 151
(b) Girls = 165, Boys = 174 (c) Girls = 16, Boys = 23
(d) Girls = 158, Boys = 163 (e) Girls = No mode, Boys = 168
(f) Girls = 158, Boys = 168 (g) Girls = 36, Boys = 38
8. (a) Girls = 17, Boys = 15 (b) Girls = 34, Boys = 33
(c) Girls = 17, Boys = 18 (d) Girls = €28, Boys = €25
(e) Girls = 34, Boys = 33 (f) Girls = 26, Boys = 27 (g) Girls = 37,
Boys = 37 **9.** (a) Girls = 11, Boys = 11 (b) Girls = 27, Boys = 29
(c) Girls = 16, Boys = 18 (d) Girls = 18, Boys = 20 (e) Girls = 27,
Boys = 22 (f) Girls = 18, Boys = 21 (g) Girls = 34, Boys = 39.

Exercise 21.7

1. (a) Left skewed (b) Symmetric (c) Right skewed
(d) Right skewed (e) Left skewed (f) Symmetric
2. (i) Left skewed (ii) Left skewed (iii) Right skewed
(iv) Symmetric (v) Left skewed **3.** (a) Symmetric
(b) Right skewed (c) Left skewed (d) Symmetric
(e) Right skewed (f) Left skewed

Exercise 21.8

1. 3D hard to read and compare; Gaps in pie chart **2.** Vertical scale starts at 5; Years not evenly spaced (no 2010, 2011)
3. No vertical scale; Years 2002–2006 gap inconsistent
4. Scale starts at 34 not O; Bar on right brighter colour
5. Area of shapes can't be used; Difference looks a lot bigger
6. (a) Bright colour stands out; No info on what is being compared (b) 3D; Vertical scale starts at 80; Inconsistent vertical scales (c) No vertical scale; No info on graph
(d) Perspective; Area of shape being used.

Self-check Test

1. (b) (i) Male: 157 cm, Female: 118.18 cm
(ii) Boys median = 157 cm, Girls median = 135 cm
(iii) Boys IQR = 21 cm, Girls IQR = 22 cm (iv) Boys range = 41 cm,
Girls range = 45 cm **3.** (e) Mean = 2.95 (f) Mode = 2 phones
(g) 4 phones **4.** (a) 30 students (c) Bar chart, or pie chart,
or line plot acceptable (d) 5 (e) 1.23 days (f) No mode. exists
5. (a) 206 (b) 13.73 (c) 41 (e) Any suitable display
6. (b) Line plot or bar chart or pie chart **7.** (b) 20–30 minutes
(c) 34 minutes (d) 18 minutes **8.** (a) 72 people
(b) 60–80 minutes (d) Symmetric **9.** (a) 30–35 minutes
(c) Left skewed **10.** (a) 80 (b) 41 (c) 27
(e) No, continous data. **11.** (b) Swimming = 29, Aerobics = 37

12. (a) 1,459.85 (b) 30% (c) 108° **13.** (b) €28,750 (c) Add up figures given and divide by 32 **14.** (a) Pie chart, Line plot, Bar Chart (b) Stem and leaf; Histogram **16.** Not circular, so sectors are distorted; Blue sector fades into background. **17.** No, vertical scale/inconsistent; Horizontal axis is inconsistent. **18.** Vertical axis is not detailed enough; 3D distorts image.

Chapter 22

Exercise 22.1

1. (a) €36,000 (b) 22% (c) Pension plan **2.** (a) €29,000 (b) 19% (c) PRSI **3.** (a) €55,000 (b) 21% (c) 55,000 − 28,000 = €27,000 (d) Health insurance, pension and loans (e) €3,500 **4.** (a) €45,000 (b) 20% (c) 45,000 − 30,000 = €15,000 (d) A1 (e) All three: 2%, 4% and 7%

Exercise 22.2

1. (a) €3,750, €21,250 (b) €1,875, €26,625 (c) €2,683.10, €18,806.90 (d) €2,690, €25,310 (e) €2,878, €17,522 (f) €2,560, €20,940 (g) €3,370, €23,630 (h) €3,382, €22,218 (i) €2,590, €22,110 (j) €3,608.90, €25,481.10 **2.** Net Pay = €22,354 **3.** Net Pay = €18,125 **4.** Net Pay = €19,795 **5.** (a) €6,195 (b) €4,695 (c) €1,200 (d) €6,995 (e) €22,505 **6.** (a) €4,750 (b) €3,500 (c) €1,692 (d) €5,192 (e) €1,651 **7.** €18,091 **8.** €19,760 **9.** (a) €1,466.40 (b) €956.80 (c) €613.80 (d) €1,502.80 (e) €3,641.30 **10.** (a) (i) €19.20 (ii) €51.60 (b) (i) €26.40 (ii) €70.95 (c) (i) €0 (ii) €13.26 (d) (i) €36.72 (ii) €98.69 **11.** (a) €519 (b) €20.76 (c) €1,208.80 (d) €5,670 (e) €3,170 (f) €21,700.44 **12.** €20,650.40 **13.** €255 **14.** €15,671.20

Exercise 22.3

1. (a) €6,000 (b) €15,000 (c) €6,300 (d) €12,300 (e) €8,800 (f) €36,200 **2.** €35,260 **3.** €48,380 **4.** €48,620 **5.** €4,820 **6.** €27,820 **7.** €57,610 **8.** (a) €36,880 (b) €40,499.20 **9.** €50,645 **10.** €62,380 **11.** €36,320 **12.** (a) €2,600 (b) €6,987.50 (c) €3,868.80 (d) €39,101.20 ÷ 52 = €751.95 **13.** (a) €2,280 (b) €6,127.50 (c) €3,308.80 (d) €671 **14.** (a) €3,280 ÷ 52 = €63.08 (b) €170 (c) €5,058.80 (d) €27,105, €895 **15.** (a) €57 (b) €154 (c) €4,547.80 (d) €42,912.20 ÷ 52 = €825.23 **16.** (a) €5,880 (b) €9,608.80 (c) €42,990 (d) €80,513.20 **17.** (a) €4,520 (b) €7,228.80 (c) €29,460 (d) €66,496.20 **18.** (a) €8,400 (b) €14,018.80 (c) €70,330 (d) €103,040.20 **19.** (a) €39,200 (b) €67,918.80 (c) €390,870 (d) €288,913.20

Self-check Test

1. €55,080 **2.** €64,570 **3.** (a) €1,800 (b) €4,837.50 (c) €2,468.80 (d) €29,111.20 **4.** (a) €2,880 (b) €7,740 (c) €4,358.80 (d) €42,405.90 ÷ 52 = €815.50 **5.** (a) €2,520 (b) €6,772.50 (c) €3,728.80 (d) €777 **6.** (a) €3,908 (b) €10,502.75 (c) €6,157.80 (d) €56,676.20 ÷ 52 = €1,089.93 **7.** (a) €18,000 (b) €30,818.80 (c) €164,370.60 (d) €176,412.60 **8.** (a) €7,200 (b) €11,918.80 (c) €65,755 (d) €95,126.20 **9.** (a) €37,225 (b) €60,000 **10.** €3,500 **11.** €18,000 **12.** €84,000 **13.** 40% **14.** (a) €2,880 (b) €7,440 (c) €1,320 **15.** (a) €11,360 (b) €51,000

Chapter 23

Exercise 23.1

1. (a) $[AC] = H$ (b) $[BC] = O$ (c) $[AB] = A$ **2.** (a) $[AC] = H$ (b) $[BC] = O$ (c) $[AB] = A$ **3.** (a) $[AD] = H$ (b) $[BD] = O$ (c) $[AB] = A$ **4.** (a) $[AP] = H$ (b) $[MP] = O$ (c) $[MN] = A$ **5.** (a) $[DF] = H$ (b) $[DE] = O$ (c) $[EF] = A$ **6.** (a) $[SQ] = H$ (b) $[QR] = O$ (c) $[SR] = A$ **7.** (a) $[GI] = H$ (b) $[HI] = O$ (c) $[GH] = A$ **8.** (a) $[BC] = H$ (b) $[AC] = O$ (c) $[AB] = A$ **9.** (a) $[DE] = H$ (b) $[FE] = O$ (c) $[DF] = A$

Exercise 23.2

1. (a) 79°09′58″ (b) 87°15′9″ (c) 195°24′25″ (d) 163°32′35″ (e) 208°35′43″ **2.** (a) 5°31′09″ (b) 31°23′41″ (c) 42°11′21″ (d) 128°19′57″ (e) 185°19′25″

Exercise 23.3

1. $\frac{3}{5}$ $\frac{4}{5}$ $\frac{3}{4}$ **2.** $\frac{12}{13}$ $\frac{5}{13}$ $\frac{12}{5}$ **3.** $\frac{8}{17}$ $\frac{15}{17}$ $\frac{8}{15}$ **4.** $\frac{5}{13}$ $\frac{12}{13}$ $\frac{5}{12}$ **5.** $\frac{3}{5}$ $\frac{4}{5}$ $\frac{3}{4}$ **6.** $\frac{4}{5}$ $\frac{3}{5}$ $\frac{4}{3}$ **7.** $\frac{8}{17}$ $\frac{15}{17}$ $\frac{8}{15}$ **8.** $\frac{12}{13}$ $\frac{5}{13}$ $\frac{12}{5}$ **9.** $\frac{21}{29}$ $\frac{20}{29}$ $\frac{21}{20}$ **10.** $\frac{20}{29}$ $\frac{21}{29}$ $\frac{20}{21}$

11. (i) (a) $\sqrt{2}$ units (b) $\sin B = \frac{1}{\sqrt{2}}$ $\cos B = \frac{1}{\sqrt{2}}$ $\tan B = \frac{1}{1} = 1$ (ii) (a) 20 units (b) $\sin A = \frac{21}{29}$ $\cos A = \frac{20}{29}$ $\tan A = \frac{21}{20}$ (iii) (a) 13 units (b) $\sin B = \frac{12}{13}$ $\cos B = \frac{5}{13}$ $\tan B = \frac{12}{5}$ (iv) (a) $\sqrt{15}$ units (b) $\sin C = \frac{2\sqrt{3}}{\sqrt{15}}$ $\cos C = \frac{\sqrt{3}}{\sqrt{15}}$ $\tan C = \frac{2\sqrt{3}}{\sqrt{3}} = 2$ (v) (a) $2\sqrt{10}$ units (b) $\sin D = \frac{2\sqrt{10}}{11}$ $\cos D = \frac{9}{2\sqrt{10}}$ $\tan D = \frac{2\sqrt{10}}{9}$ (vi) (a) $\sqrt{5}$ units (b) $\sin E = \frac{1}{\sqrt{5}}$ $\cos E = \frac{2}{\sqrt{5}}$ $\tan E = \frac{1}{2}$ (vii) (a) 8 units (b) $\sin F = \frac{8}{17}$ $\cos F = \frac{15}{17}$ $\tan F = \frac{8}{15}$ (viii) (a) 1 unit (b) $\sin G = \frac{1}{\sqrt{26}}$ $\cos G = \frac{5}{\sqrt{26}}$ $\tan G = \frac{1}{5}$ (ix) (a) 29 units (b) $\sin H = \frac{21}{29}$ $\cos H = \frac{20}{29}$ $\tan H = \frac{21}{20}$ (x) (a) 2 units (b) $\sin I = \frac{1}{\sqrt{5}}$ $\cos I = \frac{2}{\sqrt{5}}$ $\tan I = \frac{1}{2}$ (xi) (a) $e = 2\sqrt{2}$ units (b) $\sin J = \frac{2}{2\sqrt{2}} = \frac{1}{\sqrt{2}}$; $\cos J = \frac{2}{2\sqrt{2}} = \frac{1}{\sqrt{2}}$; $\tan J = \frac{2}{2} = 1$ (xii) (a) $n = \sqrt{74}$ units (b) $\sin K = \frac{7}{\sqrt{74}}$; $\cos K = \frac{5}{\sqrt{74}}$; $\tan K = \frac{7}{5}$

12. (a) $\sin A$ (b) $\tan A$ (c) $\cos A$ (d) $\tan A$ (e) $\sin A$ (f) $\cos A$ (g) $\cos A$ (h) $\tan A$ (i) $\sin A$ (j) $\tan A$

Exercise 23.4

1. 0.72 **2.** 0.89 **3.** 1.04 **4.** 0.45 **5.** 19.08 **6.** 0.54 **7.** 0.73 **8.** 0.59 **9.** 0.57 **10.** 0.90 **11.** $\frac{1}{\sqrt{3}}$ **12.** $\frac{\sqrt{3}}{2}$ **13.** 0 **14.** 1 **15.** 1 **16.** $\frac{1}{2}$ **17.** $\sqrt{3}$ **18.** $\frac{1}{\sqrt{2}}$ **19.** $\frac{1}{2}$ **20.** 1 **21.** (a) $\frac{1}{\sqrt{2}}$ (b) $\frac{1}{\sqrt{2}}$ (c) 1 (d) 1 (e) $\tan 45° = \frac{\sin 45°}{\cos 45°}$ **22.** (a) $\frac{1}{2}$ (b) $\frac{\sqrt{3}}{2}$ (c) $\frac{1}{\sqrt{3}}$ (d) $\frac{\sqrt{3}}{2}$ (e) $\frac{1}{2}$ (f) $\sqrt{3}$ **23.** (a) 3 (b) $\frac{3}{4}$ (c) $\frac{1}{4}$ (d) $\frac{\sqrt{3}}{4}$ (e) $\frac{1}{\sqrt{2}}$ **26.** $\frac{3}{4}$ **27.** (a) yes (b) yes (c) yes (d) yes

Exercise 23.5

1. 40.844° **2.** 64.215° **3.** 52.853° **4.** 52.186° **5.** 34.915° **6.** 73.322° **7.** 38.998° **8.** 32.005° **9.** −59.999° **10.** 32.499° **11.** 20° **12.** −35° or 325° **13.** 60° **14.** 46° **15.** 25° **16.** 30° **17.** 45° **18.** 45° **19.** 10° **20.** −60° or 300° **21.** 66° **22.** 8° **23.** 83° **24.** 87° **25.** 38° **26.** 25° **27.** 61° **28.** 49° **29.** 73° **30.** 61°

Exercise 23.6

1. (a) $A = 17°$ (b) $B = 50°$ (c) $C = 64°$ (d) $D = 25°$ (e) $E = 10°$ (f) $F = 67°$ (g) $G = 82°$ (h) $H = 66°$ (i) $I = 67°$ (j) $J = 18°$ **2.** (a) $A = 17.3$ units (b) $B = 34.5$ units (c) $C = 24°$ (d) $D = 27.2$ units (e) $E = 20.5$ units (f) $F = 16.6$ units (g) $J = 5.9$ units (h) $H = 9.3$ units (i) $J = 18$ units (j) $K = 27.6$ units **3.** (a) $x = 47.2$ m (b) $A = 32°$ **4.** 12.1 km **5.** $A = 40°$ **6.** $A = 27°$ **7.** (a) $x = 25.54$ m (b) 8.73 m $= y$ **8.** 30 m **9.** 44 m **10.** (a) $A = 30°$ (b) 172.41 m (c) 60°

11. 185 km **12.** (a) 1323 m (b) $A = 41°$ **13.** (a) 5.77 km (b) 2.88 km **14.** (a) 33.29 m (b) 38.84 m **15.** (a) 6.36 m (b) 4.74 m **16.** (a) A = 36.87°; B = 33.75° (b) Length = $\frac{220}{7}$ (c) $y = 2\sqrt{14}$ so arc = $\frac{22\sqrt{14}}{7}$ (d) 113 cm **17.** (a) 30 cm (b) 33 cm **18.** (a) $A = 37°$ $B = 22°$ (b) $C = 36°$ $D = 30°$ (c) $E = 58°$ $F = 83°$ (d) $G = 56°$ $H = 66°$ (e) $K = 45°$ $J = 32°$ (f) $M = 30°$ (g) $P = 46°$ $N = 30°$ (h) $Q = 68°$ $R = 112°$ $S = 19°$ (i) $T = 63°$ $V = 8°$ (j) $X = 120°$ $W = 30°$ **20.** 10,462.2 m **21.** 10.44 m **22.** 92.99 m **23.** 16 m **24.** 32 m **25.** 18 m **26.** $b = 4$ units $c = 2\sqrt{3}$ units $d = 6\sqrt{11}$ units $e = 7$ units $f = \sqrt{74}$ units $B = 53°$ $C = 6°$ $D = 72°$ $E = 54°$ **27.** (c) $x = 110.287$ m (d) $y = 92.542$ m

Exercise 23.7

1. Positive **2.** Negative **3.** Positive **4.** Positive **5.** Positive **6.** Negative **7.** (−1) **8.** Positive **9.** Positive **10.** Positive **11.** Positive **12.** Positive **13.** Positive **14.** Positive **15.** Negative **16.** 30°, 330° **17.** 240°, 300° **18.** 120°, 240° **19.** 150°, 330° **20.** 45°, 135° **21.** 135°, 225° **22.** 45°, 225° **23.** 90°, 270° **24.** 30°, 150° **25.** 60°, 240° **26.** 26°, 206° **27.** 36°, 324° **28.** 179°, 359° **29.** 259°, 281° **30.** 50°, 310° **31.** 216°, 324° **32.** 206°, 334° **33.** 47°, 313° **34.** 34°, 214° **35.** 55°, 125° **36.** 145°, 215° **37.** 101°, 281° **38.** 225°, 315° **39.** 144°, 216° **40.** 32°, 212°

Self-check Test

1. (a) 0.9816 (b) 0.9903 (c) 1.6643 (d) 0.9962 (e) 2.7280 (f) 13.2704 (g) 0.1970 (h) 0.2439 (i) 0.7133 (j) 0.5615 **2.** (a) $\theta = 14°$ (b) $\theta = 33°$ (c) $\theta = 33°$ (d) $\theta = 90°$ (e) $\theta = 24°$ (f) $\theta = 63°$ (g) $\theta = 76°$ (h) $\theta = 22°$ (i) $\theta = 60°$ (j) $\theta = 20°$ **3.** (a) C (b) B (c) A **4.** $\frac{8}{10}$ **5.** $\frac{15}{8}$ **6.** 32° 0′ 20″ **7.** 5.8 units **8.** (a) 1 (b) $\frac{3}{4}$ (c) $\frac{1}{2}$ (d) $\frac{1}{4}$ (e) $\frac{3}{2}$ (f) $\frac{\sqrt{3}}{4}$ (g) $\frac{\sqrt{3}}{4}$ (h) 1 (i) 1 **9.** 71° **10.** $A = 64°$ **11.** 23.9 units **12.** 53.1 m **13.** 227.1 m **14.** 33.6 m **15.** 69° **16.** (a) $A = 30.58°$ (b) $B = 59.42°$ **17.** 578.6 m **18.** (a) 25.6 m (b) 29 m **19.** 552 m **20.** (a) 420 m (b) 265 m **21.** Height of Cliff: 49.6 m Distance from Ship: 12.6 m **22.** 46.75 m **23.** 29 m **24.** 104 m **25.** 100 m **26.** (a) 101.6 cm (b) Width: 88.55 cm Height: 49.81 cm (c) TV2 by ≈ 272 cm^2 **27.** (b) 161 m **28.** (a) 34.6 m (b) 70° (c) 42° (d) $|AE| = 122$ m (e) $|XF| = 119$ m **29.** (a) $|AB| = 3\sqrt{2}$ m = 4.24 m (b) 27.73 m

Chapter 24

Exercise 24.1

1. 4,500 cm^3 **2.** 756 cm^3 **3.** 910 cm^3 **4.** 1,100 cm^3 **5.** 693 cm^3 **6.** 36 m^3 **7.** 40 m^3 **8.** 0.06 m^3 **9.** 0.25 m^3 **10.** 0.9 m^3 **11.** 0.0048 m^3 **12.** 2 cm **13.** 3 cm **14.** 2,000 cm **15.** 5 m **16.** (a) 5 mm (b) 6 cm (c) 12.1 m (d) 15 cm (e) 14 cm

Exercise 24.2

1. (a) 18 cm^3 (b) 225 cm^3 (c) 60 m^3 (d) 980 cm^3 (e) 325 m^3 (f) 2.8125 m^3 **2.** $219\frac{3}{8}$ Litres **3.** 232.2 g **4.** C **5.** 30 cm **6.** 329 cm^3

Exercise 24.3

1. 396 cm^3 **2.** 1,846 cm^3 **3.** 6,770 cm^3 **4.** 2,769 cm^3 **5.** 1,385 cm^3 **6.** 6,731 cm^3 **7.** 1,140 cm^3 **8.** 108π cm^3 **9.** 250π cm^3 **10.** 196π cm^3 **11.** 180π cm^3 **12.** 24π cm^3 **13.** 3.5π cm^3 **14.** 14 cm **15.** 4 cm **16.** 7 cm **17.** 2 cm **18.** 3 cm **19.** 1 cm **20.** 4 cm **21.** 10 cm **22.** 12 cm **23.** 12 cm **24.** 7 cm **25.** 4 cm **26.** 5 cm **27.** 3 cm **28.** 2 cm **29.** 14 cm **30.** 3.5 cm **31.** 2.1 cm **32.** 14 cm **33.** (a) 18,840 cm^3 (b) $h = 47$ cm **34.** (a) 47,100 cm^3 (b) 471 cm^3 (c) 90 candles **35.** (a) 4,019.2 cm^3 (b) 176.625 cm^3; 22 glasses **36.** 1.23% **37.** 2,700

Exercise 24.4

1. (a) 5 cm (b) 37.7 cm^3 **2.** (a) 5.4 cm = L (b) 20.9 cm^3 **3.** (a) 16.4 cm = L (b) 1,360.7 cm^3 **4.** (a) 14.8 cm (b) 1,238.2 cm^3 **5.** (a) $r = 6$ cm (b) 301.7 cm^3 **6.** (a) $r = 4$ cm (b) 50.3 cm^3 **7.** (a) $r = 8$ cm (b) 1,005.7 cm^3 **8.** (a) 21 cm (b) 9,240.0 cm^3 **9.** (a) 753.6 cm^3 (b) 358 **10.** (a) 7,065 cm^3 (b) 51.3 cm^3 (c) 137 **11.** 0.42 cm **12.** 73.8% **13.** (a) 1.256 m^3 (b) 77.1 **14.** 3.14 m^3 **15.** 376.8 cm^3 **16.** (a) 10.4 cm (b) 8.7 cm (c) 14.5 cm (d) 13 cm

Exercise 24.5

1. 113.1 cm^3 **2.** 905.1 cm^3 **3.** 2,145.5 cm^3 **4.** 268.2 cm^3 **5.** 3,054.9 cm^3 **6.** 4,190.5 cm^3 **7.** 11,498.7 cm^3 **8.** 38,808.0 cm^3 **9.** 261.7 cm^3 **10.** 2,786.2 cm^3 **11.** 5,425.9 cm^3 **12.** 7,065.0 cm^3 **13.** 4.6 cm^3 **14.** 4.1 cm^3 **15.** (a) 110,000 mm^3 (b) 4,186.7 mm^3 (c) 105 sweets **16.** 750 **17.** 56.52 cm^3 **18.** $523\frac{1}{3}$ cm^3 **19.** 7,234.56 cm^3 **20.** 267.9 cm^3 **21.** (a) 6 cm (b) 37.68 cm

Exercise 24.6

1. (a) 1,641.2 cm^3 (b) 5,744.1 cm^3 (c) 7,385 cm^3 (d) 8,666 toys **2.** (a) 12 mm (b) 100π mm^3 (c) 80 mm (d) 6,594 mm^3 (e) 147,200 mm^3 **3.** (a) $3{,}600\pi$ cm^3 (b) 36π cm^3 (c) $r = 4.24$ cm **4.** (a) 20 cm (b) 8,792 cm^3 (c) 1,364 **5.** (a) 2,712.96 cm^3 (b) 36 cm (c) 4,069.44 cm^3 (d) $66\frac{2}{3}$% **6.** (a) 792 cm^3 (b) 80 cm^3 (c) 0.7 cm **7.** (a) 2 m^3 (b) 238,851 (c) 70,771 (d) 308,693 **8.** (a) 0.18 m^3 (b) 0.1184 m^3 **9.** (a) $5\frac{1}{3}\pi$ cm^3 (b) 48π cm^3 (c) 12 cm **10.** (a) 1,004.8 cm^3 (b) 4.19 cm^3 (c) 1.25 cm **11.** (a) 15.7 cm^3 (b) 3,747 **12.** (a) $3{,}920\pi$ cm^3 (b) 18π cm^3 (c) 217 (d) 30 cm (e) 5.5 cm

Exercise 24.7

1. (a) $1{,}372\pi$ cm^3/sec (b) 10 seconds **2.** (a) $4{,}500\pi$ cm^3/sec (b) 8.9 seconds **3.** (a) $5{,}000\pi$ cm^3/sec (b) 3.2 seconds **4.** (a) 7 cm (b) 10 mins 50 sec's **5.** (a) $2{,}048\pi$ cm^3/sec (b) 466.5 seconds **6.** 314 seconds **7.** 706,500 Litres **8.** 11.3 cm/sec **9.** 23.6 seconds **10.** (b) B is wider **11.** (a) (i) A (ii) C **14.** (a) D, A, C, B, F **16.** (a) Constant rate of flow ⇒ straight side (b) It already has liquid within (c) Nothing changes the volume i.e. volume = zero (d) Wider (e) Narrower (f) It shows the volume with respect to the height

Self-check Test

1. (a) 90 cm^3 (b) 810 cm^3 (c) 288 m^3 (d) 225 cm^3 (e) 375 mm^3 (f) 66 mm^3 (g) 440 mm^3 (h) 1,160 m^3 (i) 96 cm^3 (j) 252 cm^3 (k) 972 cm^3 (l) 4.5 m^3 (m) 96 cm^3 (n) 400 cm^3 (o) 600 cm^3 **2.** (a) 240,000 cm^3 (b) 400 **3.** 1,200 m^3 **4.** 15 cm^3 **5.** A cube of side 7.36 cm **6.** (a) 60 cm^3 (b) $3\frac{1}{3}$ **7.** 2 cm **8.** (a) 197.8 cm^3 (b) 785.0 cm^3 (c) 1,582.6 cm^3 (d) 653.1 cm^3 (e) 2,034.7 cm^3 (f) 169.6 cm^3 (g) 703.4 cm^3 (h) 1,077.0 cm^3 **9.** 754 cm^3 **10.** B **12.** 4,827 rods **13.** (e) **14.** (a) 1,086,230,341,000 km^3 (b) 1.59×10^{10} km^3 **15.** $h = 5.9$ cm **16.** $66\frac{2}{3}$ cm/sec **17.** (a) 12,308.8 cm^3 (b) 12 cm (c) 7.8 cm (d) 7 **18.** (a) 10 m^3 (b) 0.26 m (c) 4 **19.** (a) €9,600 (b) 96 (c) €20 **20.** (a) $5{,}625\pi$ cm^3 (b) 42%

Chapter 25

Exercise 25.1

1. (a) x (b) 6 (c) 1 (d) −6 (e) $2x$ (f) 2 (g) $3x$ (h) −3 (i) −8 (j) 2 **2.** (a) $x - 1$ (b) $3 - 5x$ (c) $2x - 5$ (d) $6 - 4x$ (e) $x^2 - 7$ (f) $4 + 5x - 6x^2$ (g) $2x - 3$ (h) $3x^2 - 7x + 1$ (i) $2 - 3x$ (j) $7x - 2$ **3.** $x + 5$ **4.** $x + 5$ **5.** $x + 4$ **6.** $x + 9$ **7.** $x + 1$ **8.** $x - 7$ **9.** $x - 8$ **10.** $x + 1$ **11.** $x - 8$ **12.** $x + 9$ **13.** $a - 6$ **14.** $d - 3$ **15.** $b - 10$ **16.** $x - 5$ **17.** $x + 5$ **18.** $2n + 3$ **19.** $2n + 5$ **20.** $5n - 2$ **21.** $3n + 5$

22. $2n - 3$ **23.** $x - 3$ **24.** (a) $n + 7$ (b) $n + 7$ (c) $2n^2 + 15n + 7$ **25.** (a) $x - 5$ (b) $x^2 - 8x + 15$ **26.** (a) $c + 7$ (b) $c + 7$ **27.** $x + 3$ **28.** $x + 1$ **29.** $x - 2$ **30.** $x + 2$ **31.** $2x + 11$ **32.** $2x + 5$ **33.** $x + 3$ **34.** $x - 6$ **35.** $x + 7$ **36.** $2x - 10$ **37.** $9x + 18$ **38.** $20x + 20$ **39.** $a = 5, b = 10, 4\sqrt{10}$ **40.** Remainder is 1 hence $(3x - 1)$ is not a factor of $15x^2 + 7x - 5$

Exercise 25.2

1. $x^2 - 3x + 5$ **2.** $x^2 - 2x + 4$ **3.** $x^2 + x - 1$ **4.** $4x^2 + x - 3$ **5.** $2x^2 + 7x - 1$ **6.** $3x^2 - 5$ **7.** $x^2 - 1$ **8.** $x^2 - 6x + 5$ **9.** $x^2 + 2x + 1$ **10.** $x^2 - 4$ **11.** $3x^2 + 7x + 12$ **12.** $2x^2 + x - 1$ **13.** $x^2 + 5x + 6$ **14.** $2x^2 + x - 1$ **15.** $-2x^2 + x + 1$ **16.** (a) $a^2 - 4a + 4$ (b) $(2a + 3)(a - 2)(a - 2)$ **17.** (a) $b^2 - 5b + 6$ (b) $(3b + 1)(b - 3)(b - 2)$ **18.** $c^2 - 7c + 12$ **19.** $2x^2 + x - 1$ **20.** $3x^2 + 7x + 2$ **21.** $-2x^2 - x + 1$ **22.** $x^2 - x + 1$ **23.** $x^2 + 2x + 4$ **24.** $x^2 + 3x + 9$ **25.** $16x^2 + 20x + 25$ **26.** $100x^2 + 10x + 1$ **27.** (a) $a = 4, b = -28, c = 49$ (b) $(2x - 7)^2$ (c) $(2x - 7)^3$, yes **28.** It is not a factor because there is a remainder of 1.

Self-check Test

1. (a) $2 - x$ (b) $x + 4$ (c) $x + 12$ (d) $4 + x$ (e) $5 - x$ (f) $x + 9$ (g) $x - 10$ (h) $1 + x$ **2.** $x + 5$ **3.** $3x - 2$ **4.** $5x + 2$ **5.** $x + 2$ **6.** $5x - 6$ **7.** $x - 3$ **8.** $n + 3$ **9.** $5n - 1$ **10.** $3x + 1$ **11.** (a) $2x + 1$ (b) Multiply out $(x + 3)$ by $(2x + 1)$ to get $2x^2 + 7x + 3$ **12.** (a) $2x^2 - x - 1$ (b) Multiply $(x + 4)$ by $(2x^2 - x - 1)$ to get $2x^3 + 7x^2 - 5x - 4$ **13.** (a) $3x^2 + 5x - 2$ (b) Multiply $(x - 2)$ by $(3x^2 + 5x - 2)$ to get $3x^3 - x^2 - 12x + 4$ **14.** (a) $6x^2 + x - 2$ (b) Multiply $(x + 1)$ by $(6x^2 + x - 2)$ to get $6x^3 + 7x^2 - x - 2$ **15.** (a) $x^2 + 3x - 1$ (b) Multiply $(x - 1)$ by $(x^2 + 3x - 1)$ to get $x^3 + 2x^2 - 4x + 1$ **16.** (a) $2x^2 + 3x + 1$ (b) Multiply $(x - 2)$ by $(2x^2 + 3x + 1)$ to get $2x^3 - x^2 - 5x - 2$ **17.** (a) $x^2 + 5x + 6$ (b) Multiply $(x + 2)$ by $(x^2 + 5x + 6)$ to get $x^3 + 7x^2 + 16x + 12$ **18.** (a) $x^2 + 9x + 6$ (b) Multiply $(x - 2)$ by $(x^2 + 9x + 6)$ by $x^3 + 7x^2 - 12x - 12$ **19.** (a) $2x^2 + 3x + 1$ (b) Multiply $(2x - 3)$ by $(2x^2 + 3x + 1)$ to get $4x^3 + 0x^2 - 7x - 3$ **20.** (a) $3x^2 + 7x + 2$ (b) Multiply $(2x - 5)$ by $(3x^2 + 7x + 2)$ to get $6x^3 - x^2 - 31x - 10$ **21.** $2x^2 + x - 10$ **22.** $x^2 + 2x + 1$ **23.** $4x^2 + 10x + 25$ **24.** $9x^2 + 12x + 16$ **25.** (a) $4x^2 + 3x - 1$, $a = 4, b = 3, c = -1$ (b) 34 **26.** (i) $a = 1, b = -2, c = -1$ (ii) 20 **27.** Since remainder is zero then $(4x - 2)$ and $(2x + 5)$ are factors **28.** $x + 12$ **29.** (i) (a) $x^3 + 12x^2 + 48x + 64$ (b) $x^2 + 8x + 16$ (c) $6x^2 + 48x + 96$ (ii) (a) $27x^3 - 81x^2 + 81x - 27$ (b) $9x^2 - 18x + 9$ (c) $54x^2 - 108x + 54$ (iii) (a) $125x^3 - 75x^2 + 15x - 1$ (b) $25x^2 - 10x + 1$ (c) $150x^2 - 60x + 6$ (iv) (a) $-125x^3 + 525x^2 - 490x + 98$ (b) $25x^2 - 70x + 49$ (c) $150x^2 - 420x + 294$ (v) (a) $-8x^3 + 72x^2 - 216x + 216$ (b) $4x^2 - 24x + 36$ (c) $24x^2 - 144x + 216$ (vi) (a) $125x^6$ (b) $25x^4$ (c) $150x^4$ **30.** (i) $10x^3 - 36x^2 - 10x + 84$ (ii) $2x - 2$ (iii) $2x - 4$ (iv) $5 - 8x$ (v) $48x^3 - 144x^2 - 75x + 225$ (b) Finding the total surface areas (i) $36x^2 - 48x - 74$ (ii) $22x^2 - 72x + 34$ (iii) $-8x^2 + 88x - 64$ (iv) $-80x^2 - 160x + 142$ (v) $80x^2 - 144x - 50$ **31.** (a) $12 - x$ m (b) length $= x - 2$ m, width $= 10 - x$ m **32.** (a) Length $= 6 - 2x$, Width $= x$, Area $= x(6 - 2x) = 6x - 2x^2$ cm^2 (b) Points (0, 0) (1, 4) (2, 4) (3, 0) (4, −8) (c) 2.5 cm^2 (d) 4.1 cm^2 (e) 1.5 cm (f) length = 2.73 cm, width = 1.5 cm (g) 11.2 cm^3 (h) 1.4 cm = x

Chapter 26

Exercise 26.1

1. $7 - y$ **2.** $-\frac{y}{2}$ **3.** $\frac{V}{I}$ **4.** $\frac{W}{m}$ **5.** $\frac{F}{m}$ **6.** PA **7.** $\frac{D}{T}$ **8.** $\frac{m}{\rho}$ **9.** $\frac{A}{2\pi r}$ **10.** $\frac{F}{E}$ **11.** $\frac{v}{m}$ **12.** vq **13.** $\frac{F}{L}$ **14.** $\frac{q}{C}$ **15.** $\frac{c}{f}$ **16.** $\frac{T}{F}$ **17.** $\frac{F}{-k}$ **18.** $\frac{A}{2\pi h}$ **19.** $\frac{A}{\pi l} - r$ **20.** $\frac{l}{2\pi}$

21. (i) (a) $y = -x + 7$ (b) m = slope = −1, c = where it cuts y-axis = 7 (ii) (a) $y = -3x - 6$ (b) m = slope = −3, c = cuts y-axis at −6. (iii) (a) $y = -5x + 7$ (b) $m = -5$ = slope, $c = 7$ cuts y-axis at (0, 7) (iv) (a) $y = 4x - 10$ (b) $m = 4$ = slope, $c = -10$ cuts y-axis at (0, −10) (v) (a) $y = \frac{2}{7}x - 2$ (b) $m = \frac{2}{7}$ = slope, $c = -2$ cuts y-axis at (0, −2) (vi) (a) $y = \frac{1}{2}x + 2$ (b) $m = \frac{1}{2}$ = slope, $c = 2$ cuts y-axis at (0, 2) (vii) (a) $y = -\frac{3}{4}x - \frac{1}{2}$ (b) $m = -\frac{3}{4}$ = slope, $c = -\frac{1}{2}$ cuts y-axis at $(0, -\frac{1}{2})$ (viii) (a) $y = -0.7x + 1.8$ (b) $m = -0.7$ or $-\frac{7}{10}$ slope, $c = 1.8$ cuts y-axis at (0, 1.8) (ix) (a) $y = -5x + 6$ (b) $m = -5$ slope, $c = 6$ cuts y-axis at (0, 6) (x) (a) $y = -10x + 5$ (b) $m = -10$ slope, $c = 5$ cuts y-axis at (0, 5) (xi) (a) $y = -\frac{1}{6}x + \frac{5}{3}$ (b) slope $= m = -\frac{1}{6}$, c = cuts y-axis at $\frac{5}{3}\left(0, 1\frac{2}{3}\right)$ (xii) (a) $y = \frac{2}{35}x - \frac{2}{21}$ (b) slope $= \frac{2}{35} = m$, cuts y-axis at $\left(0, -\frac{2}{21}\right)$ where $c = -\frac{2}{21}$ (xiii) (a) $y = 30x + 6$ (b) slope $= m = 30$, cuts y-axis at $c = 6$ (xiv) (a) $y = -\frac{2}{15}x + \frac{16}{9}$ (b) slope $= m = -\frac{2}{15}$, cuts y-axis at $c = \frac{16}{9}$ or $1\frac{7}{9}$ (xv) (a) $y = -\frac{14}{3}x + \frac{35}{3}$ (b) slope $= -\frac{14}{3} = -4\frac{2}{3} = m$, cuts y-axis at $c = \frac{35}{3}$ or $11\frac{2}{3}$ **22.** (a) $dg - hg$ (b) $\frac{5c - 10k}{2}$ (c) $\frac{8}{3}p + 8d$ (d) $\frac{3yz + 12}{2y}$ (e) $\frac{td}{5d + 3t}$ (f) $\frac{-8p}{p^2 - 4r}$ (g) $\frac{60mn}{28mt - 9nw}$ (h) $\frac{35y - 2cds}{-18d}$ (i) $\frac{hkm - 2lh}{5c}$ (j) $\frac{5p}{5pt + t}$ **23.** (a) $\frac{k}{1 - h}$ (b) $-\frac{3hg}{g - 2h}$ (c) $\frac{6g - 5df}{d + 1}$ (d) $\frac{7ab}{4f - 2h + b}$ (e) $\frac{-k}{5t - h}$ (f) $\frac{ag}{1 - g}$ (g) $\frac{-hk}{k - 5h}$ (h) $\frac{b + be}{e - 1}$ (i) $\frac{cf - 2f}{c - e}$ (j) $\frac{4k - pk}{n - p}$ **24.** (a) $\frac{5ac}{2c + 3a}$ (b) $\frac{-yz}{z - y}$ (c) $\frac{3de}{d - 4e}$ (d) $\frac{h^2 - 3ch}{1 - 4h}$ (e) $\frac{3f^2}{10 + 10f}$ **25.** (a) $\frac{2z - 6x}{xz}$, $-1 = y$ (b) $\frac{2ac}{5c + 3a}$, -4

Exercise 26.2

1. $\sqrt{\frac{2W}{C}}$ **2.** $\sqrt{\frac{E}{m}}$ **3.** $\sqrt{\frac{-a}{s}}$ **4.** $a = \sqrt{c^2 - b^2}$ **5.** $\sqrt{\frac{3V}{\pi h}}$ **6.** $\frac{\sigma^2}{nq}$ **7.** $\sqrt{r^2 - g^2 + c}$ **8.** $\sqrt{ar}$ **9.** $\sqrt[3]{\frac{3V}{4\pi}}$ **10.** $\sqrt{\frac{GM}{g}}$ **11.** $\sqrt{z^2 - a^2}$ **12.** $\frac{T}{4L^2f^2}$ **13.** $\sqrt{\frac{GM}{F}}$ **14.** $\sqrt{\frac{P}{R}}$ **15.** $\sqrt{\frac{A}{4\pi}}$ **16.** $\frac{2d^2}{3}$ **17.** $\frac{3v + \pi h^2}{3\pi h^2}$ **18.** $\frac{-k - e^2k}{e^2k^2 - 1}$ **19.** $\frac{ab - 3b}{ac - c}$ **20.** $\sqrt{\frac{a^2w^2 - v^2}{w^2}}$ **21.** $\frac{-t^2}{t^2 - f}$ **22.** $\sqrt{\frac{xy + y^2}{5}}$ **23.** (a) $\frac{2s - 2an}{n^2 - n}$ (b) −12 **24.** (a) $2p - 10$ (b) 52 **25.** (a) $\frac{y - 3}{3}$ (b) −3 − 5 **26.** (a) $-5w^2 + 10wx - 14w + 12x$ (b) 48 **27.** (a) $-16a - b + 40$ (b) −19 **28.** (a) $-a + 10$ (b) 88 **29.** (b) $\frac{a + \frac{1}{2}dc^2}{c}$ **30.** (a) $\sqrt[3]{\frac{3V}{2\pi}}$ (b) $\sqrt[3]{18} \approx 2.62$ (c) 182.25 cm^3

Self-check Test

1. $\frac{2A}{a}$ **2.** $\frac{T - a + d}{d}$ **3.** $P - At$ **4.** $\frac{-vf}{f - v}$ **5.** $z\sigma + \mu$ **6.** $\frac{A}{\pi r}$ **7.** $\frac{V}{I}$ **8** $\frac{Q}{I}$ **9.** $\frac{7z - 3y}{4}$ **10.** $\frac{y - c}{x}$ **11.** $\sqrt{r^2 - x^2}$ **12.** $\sqrt{\frac{E}{m}}$ **13.** $\sqrt{\frac{2W}{C}}$ **14.** $\sqrt{\frac{F}{mr}}$ **15.** $\sqrt{\frac{Fr}{m}}$ **16.** $\frac{4\pi^2L}{T^2}$ **17.** $\frac{s - ut}{\frac{1}{2}t^2}$ **18.** $\sqrt{v^2 - 2as}$ **19.** $\sqrt{\frac{v^2 + w^2s^2}{w^2}}$ **20.** $\sqrt[3]{\frac{T^2GM}{4\pi^2}}$ **21.** $\sqrt{\frac{r - k}{k + k^2r}}$ **22.** $\frac{2 + 3x}{6x - 3}$ **23.** $\sqrt{\frac{\theta^2h^2 + p^2}{h^2}}$ **24.** (a) $3a - 2a^3 - 2a^2$ (b) $\sqrt{\frac{3 - x}{2}}$ **25.** (a) $\frac{c + 2a^2}{a^2}$ **26.** $\frac{c + p}{g + f}$ **27.** (a) 431 m^2 (b) $\frac{A - 2\pi r^2}{2\pi r}$ (c) 0.45 m (d) 50.6% **28.** (a) $\frac{9C + 160}{5}$ (b) 102.2°

(c) −43.6°F (d) 3.5°C (e) 212°F (f) 32° **29.** (a) $\sqrt{\frac{9}{4p^3} + 12c}$ (b) 20.8 (c) $\frac{E^2 - \frac{9}{4p^3}}{12}$ (d) 5.1 (e) $\sqrt[3]{\frac{9}{4E^2 - 48C}}$

30. (a) $\frac{100\sqrt[t]{F} - 100P}{P} = i$ (b) $\frac{F}{\left(1 + \frac{i}{100}\right)^t} = P$ (c) 8% (d) 3 yrs

Chapter 27

Exercise 27.1

1. (a) Quadratic (b) Exponential (c) Linear (d) Linear (e) Exponential (f) Quadratic (g) Linear (h) Exponential (i) Linear (j) Exponential (k) Exponential (l) Exponential (m) Exponential (n) Exponential (o) Quadratic **2.** (a) 625 (b) 3 (c) 3,072 (d) 4,374 (e) 6,250 (f) $-\frac{1}{243}$ (g) $\frac{5}{4{,}096}$ (h) $\frac{8}{3}$ (i) $\frac{2}{81}$ (j) $\frac{7}{16}$ **3.** (a) 10, 20, 40, 80, 160 (b) 4, 8, 16, 32, 64 (c) 20, 40, 80, 160, 320 (d) 14, 28, 56, 112, 224 (e) 6, 12, 24, 48, 96 **4.** (a) 21, 63, 189, 567, 1,701 (b) 6, 18, 54, 162, 486 (c) 27, 81, 243, 729, 2,187 (d) 18, 54, 162, 486, 1,458 (e) 24, 72, 216, 648, 1944 **5.** (a) 2 (b) $\frac{1}{2}$ (c) 64 (d) 128 (e) 512 **6.** (a) 24 (b) $\frac{3}{16}$ (c) 12 (d) $\frac{3}{4}$ (e) 3 **7.** (a) $\frac{2}{27}$ (b) 486 (c) 2 (d) $2\sqrt{3}$ (e) $\frac{2}{243}$ **8.** (a) 413,343 (b) 118,098 (c) 531,441 (d) 354,294 (e) 472,392 **9.** (a) 1,310,720 (b) 524,288 (c) 2,621,440 (d) 1,835,008 (e) 786,432 **10.** (a) 33, 99, 297 (b) $T_n = 11\,(3^n)$ (c) 216,513 **11.** (a) 5.6 km (b) 22.4 km (c) 7 days (d) 25.4 km per day

Exercise 27.2

6. (a) 24 (b) 3.57 (c) 55.14 (d) 0.09 **7.** (a) 20 (b) 8.41 (c) 45.95 (d) 0.08 **8.** (a) 160 (b) 14.14 (c) 64.98 (d) 0.88 **9.** (a) 1,024 (b) 7.34 (c) 21.11 (d) 0.25 **10.** (a) 56 (b) 9.08 (c) 591.14 (d) 0.03 **11.** $x = 4$ **12.** $x = -2$ **13.** $x = 10$ **14.** $x = 9$ **15.** $x = 25$ **16.** (a) Approx. 1,500,000 (b) Approx. 2,500,000 (c) 2,000,000 **20.** (b) Linear; Exponential (c) 3.6/3.7 years (d) 7.5 years; 4 years 3 months (e) 6 years; 10 years

Exercise 27.3

6. (a) 162 (b) $2\sqrt{3}$ (c) 38.84 (d) 0.0428 **7.** (a) 2,916 (b) 9.12 (c) $\frac{4}{6{,}561}$ (d) 0.029 **8.** (a) 5 (b) $\frac{5}{\sqrt{3}}$ (c) 45 (d) 3,645 **9.** (a) 0.086 (b) 1.347 (c) 78.48 (d) 15,309 **10.** (a) 648 (b) $8\sqrt{3}$ (c) 155.35 (d) 0.171 **11.** $x = 5$ **12.** $x = 10$ **13.** $x = 4$ **14.** $x = 8$ **15.** $x = 6$ **16.** (b) $1\frac{1}{2}$ hours (c) 1 cm **17.** (b) Approx. 23 mins **18.** (b) Approx. $2\frac{3}{4}$ hours (c) 48,600 **19.** (b) 40.5 m (c) Approx. 32 hours **20.** (b) 54 hours (c) Approx. 113,000

Self-check Test

1. (b) Approx. 2 years 3 months (c) Native fish = 125, non-native fish = 1,600 **2.** (b) 200 (c) 9 weeks **3.** (b) 154 years (c) 90 years **4.** (b) 160 (c) $3\frac{3}{4}$ years approx. **5.** (b) Approx. 35 seconds (c) Approx. 275 cm **6.** (b) 5 weeks (c) 786 cm or 7.86 m **8.** (a) Option A **9.** (b) Never (c) 5.625 kg **10.** (a) Approx 2.5 km (b) Approx. 18 days **11.** (a) No (d) Speed = $30n$, Breaking Distance = $45n^2$ **12.** (a) Exponential (h) $650\,(1.1)^n$ **13.** (a) No (c) Exponential **14.** (b) 39.32 mg

Chapter 28

Exercise 28.1

4. (a) Yes (b) No (c) No (d) Yes (e) Yes

Exercise 28.2

6. (a) Yes (b) No (c) No (d) Yes (e) No

Exercise 28.3

6. (a) Yes (b) No (c) Yes (d) No (e) Yes

Exercise 28.4

1. (a) 270° (b) 180° (c) 90° (d) 310° **2.** Image 1: 90°; Image 2: 180°; Image 3: 295° **3.** Image 1: 60°; Image 2: 180°; Image 3: 270°

Self-check Test

1. Image A: S_y; Image B: S_o; Image C: Translation **2.** Image A: S_y; Image B: S_x; Image C: S_o **3.** Image A: S_o Image B: Translation; Image C: S_y **4.** Image A: S_o Image B: S_y; Image C: Translation **5.** Image A: Rotation 180° Image B: Translation **6.** (b) No **7.** (b) Upside down, Back to front. (c) Rotation 180° **8.** Axial symmetry in the y-axis (−1, 2), (−1, 5), (−4, 2), (−4, 5); Central symmetry in the point (0, 0) (−1, −2), (−1, −5), (−4, −2), (−4, −5); Axial symmetry in the x-axis (1, −2), (1, −5), (4, −2), (4, −5) **10.** Image 1: 90°; Image 2: 180°; Image 3: 280° **12.** A: Rotation 90°; B: Rotation 180° or So; C: Sy –axial symmetry in the y-axis **13.** A: So or Rotation 180°; B: Sy; C: Translation **14.** (a) 6 (b) 120° (c) Rotation 180° **15.** (a) 8 (b) 180° (c) [CD]

Chapter 29

Self-check Test

1. (a) $(180 - \beta)°$ (b) $(180 - \theta)°$ **2.** (a) $|\angle ADB| = 45°$ (b) $|\angle DAC| = 45°$ **3.** *SAS* **4.** (a) $|\angle WVY| = 40°$ (b) Congruent by *SAS* **5.** (a) $|\angle BOC| = 80°$ (b) $|\angle BAC| = 40°$ (c) Equal by theorem (d) ASA **6.** (a) ΔADB and ΔAPC are similar triangles by AAA **7.** (a) $|\angle ABC| = 65°$ (b) $|\angle BAC| = 50°$ **10.** (b) No **11.** (a) $|\angle DOK|$ and $|\angle ROK|$ (b) 180 − 65° = 115° (c) Yes, since the lengths of two tangents from a point to a circle are equal. **13.** (a) Isosceles (b) Opposite angles in a parallelogram *POML* are equal in measure. (c) Congruent (d) Opposite angles are equal in measure. **14.** (a) Isosceles (b) Congruent (c) The three side lengths and angles are equal in both triangles and the areas are equal also. **16.** (a) Congruent by SSS (b) Congruent by RHS **17.** (a) True (b) False (c) False (d) True (e) False **18.** (a) $(90 - \theta)°$ (b) $(90 - \theta)°$ (c) 20° (d) $(180 - 2\theta)°$ **20.** (a) 60° (b) 60° (c) $|\angle BCD| = 90°$ (d) Yes **21.** (a) $90° - \frac{1}{2}\theta$ (b) $90° + \frac{1}{2}\theta$ **23.** 360° **25.** $\angle ADC = 90°$ **30.** (a) Always true (b) Sometimes true (c) Always true (d) Sometimes true (e) Always true (f) Not true **31.** Seat (a)